Blai‑ P9-EES-210 ‑ry
‑‑‑‑ ‑‑ ‑‑‑‑‑, Pa.

THE
HOME BOOK OF VERSE

THE HOME BOOK OF VERSE

AMERICAN AND ENGLISH

With an Appendix Containing a Few Well-Known Poems
in Other Languages

Selected and Arranged

By

BURTON EGBERT STEVENSON

Editor of "The Home Book of Modern Verse"
"The Home Book of Verse for Young Folks"
"The Home Book of Quotations"

NINTH EDITION
(Extended in The Home Book of Modern Verse)

3636

NEW YORK
HENRY HOLT AND COMPANY

Blairsville Joint School Library
Blairsville, Pa.

Copyright, 1912, 1918,
BY
HENRY HOLT AND COMPANY
Copyright, 1940,
BY
HENRY HOLT AND COMPANY, Inc.
Copyright, 1945, 1949, 1953,
BY
HENRY HOLT AND COMPANY, Inc.

Ninth Edition
Published, June, 1953
Second Printing, October, 1955

88141-0312

PRINTED IN THE UNITED STATES OF AMERICA

COPYRIGHT NOTICE

For the use of the copyrighted material included in this volume. permission has been secured either from the author or from his authorized publisher, and special arrangements have also been made with the authorized publishers of the older American poets whose works, in whole or in part, have lapsed from copyright. All rights in these poems are reserved by the holders of the copyright, or the authorized publishers, as named below:

D. Appleton & Company: The poems by William Cullen Bryant and Henry Newbolt.

Barse & Hopkins: "The Law of the Yukon," by Robert W. Service, from "The Spell of the Yukon and Other Verses," and "Carry On," from "Rhymes of a Red Cross Man."

The Bobbs-Merrill Company: The poems by James Whitcomb Riley, from the Biographical Edition of his complete works, copyright 1913.

Brentano's: "The Good Inn," by Herman Knickerbocker Vielé, from "The Inn of the Silver Moon."

Edmund D. Brooks: The poems by Arthur Upson.

The Century Company: The poems by Richard Watson Gilder, Robert Underwood Johnson and Aubrey de Vere; S. Weir Mitchell, James Oppenheim, and L. Frank Tooker; "Nebuchadnezzah," by Irwin Russell; "The Secret," by G. E. Woodberry; "High Tide at Gettysburg," by Will Henry Thompson; "Farragut," by William Tucker Meredith.

Henry T. Coates & Company: "The Picket Guard," by Ethel Lynn Beers, and "Monterey" by Charles Fenno Hoffman.

W. B. Conkey Co.: The poems by Ella Wheeler Wilcox, by special permission of the W. B. Conkey Co., who are the exclusive American publishers of her works.

Copeland & Day: The poems by Alice Brown, from "The Road to Castaly."

Dana Estes & Company: The poems by Mrs. Laura E. Richards; "July" by Susan H. Swett.

Dodd, Mead & Company: The poems by Austin Dobson, Paul Laurence Dunbar, William Henry Venable and Carolyn Wells.

George H. Doran Company: The poems by May Byron, Amelia Josephine Burr and Joyce Kilmer.

Doubleday, Page & Co.: The poems by Rudyard Kipling and Don Marquis. (With A. P. Watt & Son for "If —.")

Duffield & Company: The poems by Elsa Barker, Eugene Lee-Hamilton, George Santayana, William Sharp, and Helen Hay Whitney.

E. P. Dutton & Company: "The Spires of Oxford," by Winifred Letts.

Forbes & Company: The poems by Ben King and Nixon Waterman.

The Four Seas Company: The poems by Richard Aldington.

Laurence J. Gomme: The poems by Hilaire Belloc.

The Grafton Press: The poems by John S. McGroarty.

Harper & Brothers: The poems by Guy Wetmore Carryl, Charles Graham Halpine, Edna St. Vincent Millay, Ada Foster Murray, and Justin Huntly McCarthy; "An Omar for Ladies," by Josephine Daskam Bacon; "Driving Home the Cows," by Kate Putnam Osgood.

Henry Holt & Company. The poems by Susan N. Cleghorn, Arthur Colton, Walter de la Mare, Robert Frost, Charles Leonard Moore, Herbert Trench, Louis Untermeyer and Margaret Widdemer.

Houghton, Mifflin & Company: The poems by Thomas Bailey Aldrich, H. H. Bashford, Abbie Farwell Brown, John Burroughs, Alice Cary, Phoebe Cary, John Vance Cheney, Christopher Pearse Cranch, Ralph

Waldo Emerson, James Thomas Fields, Richard Watson Gilder, Louise Imogen Guiney, Bret Harte, John Hay, Oliver Wendell Holmes, Lucy Larcom, Emma Lazarus, Henry Wadsworth Longfellow, James Russell Lowell, William Vaughn Moody, Alice Freeman Palmer, Thomas William Parsons, Josephine Preston Peabody, Nora Perry, Lizette Woodworth Reese, John Godfrey Saxe, Robert Haven Schauffler, Paul Shivell, Edward Rowland Sill, Harriet Prescott Spofford, Ernest Clarence Stedman, William Wetmore Story, Harriet Beecher Stowe, Bayard Taylor, Celia Thaxter, Edith M. Thomas, Maurice Thompson, Henry David Thoreau, John Townsend Trowbridge, Elizabeth Stuart Phelps Ward, John Greenleaf Whittier.

The Howard University Print: "The Babie," by Jeremiah Eames Rankin.

B. W. Huebsch: The poems by Irene Rutherford McLeod.

P. J. Kenedy: The poems by Abram J. Ryan.

Mitchell Kennerley: The poems by Arthur Davison Ficke, William Samuel Johnson, Harry Kemp, Vachel Lindsay, Richard Middleton and Marjorie L. C. Pickthall.

Alfred A. Knopf: The poems by William H. Davies.

John Lane Company: The poems by Laurence Binyon, Rupert Brooke, G. K. Chesterton, T. A. Daly, John Davidson, Ernest Dowson, A. E. Housman, Laurence Hope, Benjamin R. C. Low, Alice Meynell, Henry Newbolt, Marjorie L. C. Pickthall, and Francis Thompson.

J. B. Lippincott Company: The poems by George Henry Boker, Harrison S. Morris, Thomas Buchanan Read and Mary Ashley Townsend.

Little, Brown & Company: The poems by Richard Burton, Susan Coolidge, Emily Dickinson, Helen Hunt Jackson, Louise Chandler Moulton.

Lothrop, Lee & Shepard Company: The poems by Charles Follen Adams, Mary Emily Bradley, Alfred Domett, Paul Hamilton Hayne, William Morris, Emilie Poulsson, Horatio Nelson Powers, David Atwood Wasson.

The Macmillan Company: The poems by Matthew Arnold, Alfred Austin, Wilfrid Wilson Gibson, Thomas Hardy, Ella Higginson, Ralph Hodgson, Charles Kingsley, Amy Lowell, John Masefield, Harriet Monroe, John G. Neihardt, George William Russell, John Addington Symonds, Sara Teasdale, Ridgely Torrence, William Watson, George E. Woodberry and William Butler Yeats.

The Manas Press: The poems by Adelaide Crapsey.

Thomas B. Mosher: The poems by Cecily Fox-Smith, Lucy Lyttleton and Edith M. Thomas.

L. C. Page & Company: The poems by Bliss Carman and Charles G. D. Roberts.

G. P. Putnam's Sons: The poems by William Henry Drummond and Norman Gale; "The Rosary," by Robert Cameron Rogers.

Norman Remington Company: The poems by Patrick R. Chalmers, from "Green Days and Blue Days."

Charles Scribner's Sons: The poems by Josephine Daskam Bacon, H. C. Bunner, George W. Cable, Mary Mapes Dodge, Eugene Field, John Galsworthy, Josiah Gilbert Holland, Sidney Lanier, George Meredith, A. T. Quiller-Couch, Corinne Roosevelt Robinson, George Santayana, Alan Seeger, Robert Louis Stevenson, Charles Warren Stoddard, Benjamin F. Taylor and Henry Van Dyke.

Sherman, French & Company: "The Lonely Road," by Kenneth Rand; "Sunday Evening in the Common," by John Hall Wheelock.

Small, Maynard & Company: The poems by Charlotte Perkins Stetson Gilman, Richard Hovey, Clinton Scollard, John B. Tabb and Walt Whitman.

Stewart & Kidd Co.: The poem by Wm. Haynes Lytle.

F. A. Stokes Company: The poems by Gelett Burgess, Alfred Noyes.

Whitaker & Ray-Wiggin Company: The poems by Joaquin Miller, from his copyrighted and complete poetical works.

Express personal permission has been received by the editor from the following authors for the use of such of their poems as appear in this collection, all rights to which are reserved by them:

Henry Abbey, Zoë Akins, John Albee, Elizabeth Akers Allen, Henry Mills Alden, Margaret Steele Anderson, Everard Jack Appleton, Walter C. Arensberg.

Josephine Daskam Bacon, **Karle Wilson Baker**. John Kendrick Bangs, Kendall Banning, Elsa Barker, H. H. Bashford, Herbert Bashford, Arlo Bates, Katherine Lee Bates, Hilaire Belloc (by Joyce Kilmer), William Rose Benét, Henry Holcomb Bennett, John Bennett, Charles G.Blanden, Augustus Wight Bomberger, Robert Adger Bowen, William Stanley Braithwaite, Anna Hempstead Branch, Mary Bolles Branch, Albert Fletcher Bridges, Abbie Farwell Brown, Alice Brown, William Laird Brown, Alice Learned Bunner (for H. C. Bunner), Gelett Burgess, Dana Burnett, Amelia Josephine Burr, Richard Burton, Samuel H. M. Byers, Witter Bynner (by Mrs. A. L. Wellington).

Bliss Carman, W. H. Carruth, Charles E. Carryl, Willa Sibert Cather, Madison Cawein, Robert W. Chambers, Arthur Chapman, John Vance Cheney, G. K. Chesterton, Joseph I. C. Clarke, Virginia Woodward Cloud, Florence Earle Coates, Zitella Cocke, Robert Collyer, Helen Gray Cone, Grace Hazard Conkling, Ellen Mackay Hutchinson Cortissoz.

T. A. Daly, Mary Carolyn Davies, William H. Davies, Margaret Deland, Charles M. Dickinson, Austin Dobson, Digby Mackworth Dolben (by Gerald Dolben Paul), Julia C. R. Dorr, Walter G. Doty, Arthur Conan Doyle.

Elaine Goodale Eastman, Florence Wilkinson Evans.

Arthur Davison Ficke (by C. A. Ficke), Sara Teasdale Filsinger, A. Hugh Fisher, Mahlon Leonard Fisher, Sam Walter Foss.

Hamlin Garland, Theodosia Garrison, Ellen M. Huntington Gates, Helena de Kay Gilder (for Richard Watson Gilder), Joseph B. Gilder, Strickland W. Gillilan, Charlotte Perkins Gilman, J. Scott Glasgow, Charles Buxton Going, Dora Read Goodale, Homer Greene, Sarah P. McLean Greene, William Griffith.

Hermann Hagedorn, Ruth Guthrie Harding, Virginia Bioren Harrison, Jerome A. Hart, Hildegarde Hawthorne, Frederick Henry Hedge, Theresa Helburn, Barbara Henderson, Daniel Henderson, Oliver Herford, Ella Higginson, Katherine Tynan Hinkson, William Dean Howells, Helen Huntington.

Wallace Irwin.

Margaret Janvier, Orrick Johns, Robert Underwood Johnson, William Samuel Johnson, Amanda T. Jones, Thomas S. Jones, Jr.

Reginald Wright Kauffman, James B. Kenyon, Joyce Kilmer, Harriet McEwen Kimball, Georgiana Goddard King, Rudyard Kipling, D. C. Knowles (for Frederic Lawrence Knowles), George M. W. Kobbé (for Gustave Kobbé).

Andrew Lang, Walter Learned, Louis V. Le Doux, Richard Le Gallienne, Nicholas Vachel Lindsay, Grace Denio Litchfield, Robert Loveman, Benjamin R. C. Low, Amy Lowell, George B. Logan, Jr.

John S. McGroarty, Isabel E. Mackay, Frederick Manning, Edwin Markham, Josephine Peabody Marks, Don Marquis, Edward Sandford Martin, Caroline Atwater Mason, Alice Meynell, Lloyd Mifflin, Edna St. Vincent Millay, Emily Huntington Miller, Harriet Monroe, David Morton, Ada Foster Murray, Kenton Foster Murray, Harold Monro.

John G. Neihardt, Henry Newbolt, Grace Fallow Norton, Alfred Noyes.

Oliver Opdyke, James Oppenheim, Shaemas O Sheel.

Albert Bigelow Paine, Alice Freeman Palmer (by G. H. Palmer), Randall Parrish, Harry Thurston Peck, Samuel Minturn Peck, William Alexander Percy, Frederick Peterson,Sarah M. B. Piatt, Emilie Poulsson, Harriet Waters Preston, Edna Dean Proctor.

Kenneth Rand, Lizette Woodworth Reese, Cale Young Rice, Wallace Rice, Laura E. Richards, James Whitcomb Riley (by E. H. Eitel), Harrison Robertson, Corinne Roosevelt Robinson, Edwin Arlington Robinson, Robert Cameron Rogers. John Jerome Rooney, George William Russell.

Copyright Notice

Margaret E. Sangster, Joseph Sargent (for the poems by Guy Wetmore Carryl), Robert Haven Schauffler, Edmund H. Sears, Paul Shivell, David Banks Sickels, Harriet Prescott Spofford, Victor Starbuck, William Force Stead, Laura Stedman (for Edmund Clarence Stedman), George Sterling, Mildred McNeal Sweeney.

Joseph Russell Taylor, William Roscoe Thayer, Edith M. Thomas, Rose Hartwick Thorpe, L. Frank Tooker, Ridgely Torrence, Charles Hanson Towne, Amélie Rives Troubetzkoy, John Townsend Trowbridge.

Louis Untermeyer.

Henry Van Dyke, William Henry Venable.

Elizabeth Stuart Phelps Ward, Lydia Avery Coonley Ward, William Hayes Ward, Nixon Waterman, Carolyn Wells, Robert Gilbert Welsh, Carl Werner, Edward J. Wheeler, John Hall Wheelock, Margaret Widdemer, Ella Wheeler Wilcox, Francis Howard Williams, William Winter, George Edward Woodberry, William Hervey Woods, Willard Huntington Wright.

Ruth Comfort Mitchell Young.

The compiler is indebted to the editors of the following magazines for permission to use the poems mentioned:

The Atlantic: "Aller Seelen," Mabel Earle; "Birthright," John Drinkwater; "Emilia," Ellen Angus French (Sarah N. Cleghorn); "The Valley of Vain Verses," Henry Van Dyke; "To Daisies," Francis Thompson.

The Bellman: "Immortalis," David Morton.

The Catholic Standard and Times: The poems by T. A. Daly.

The Century: "The Year's End," Timothy Cole; "Kinchinjunga," Cale Young Rice; "Nested," Habberton Lulham; "To Her—Unspoken," Amelia Josephine Burr; "A Lover's Envy," Henry Van Dyke; "Her Pathway," Cornelia Kane Rathbone; "Love is a Terrible Thing," Grace Fallow Norton; "Chavez," Mildred McNeal Sweeney; "Spacially Jim," by Bessie Morgan.

Contemporary Verse: "Tropical Town," Solomon de la Selva; "A Little Page's Song," William Alexander Percy.

Harper's Magazine: "I Shall not Cry Return," Ellen M. H. Gates; "Wise," Lizette Woodworth Reese; "Wild Wishes," Ethel M. Hewitt.

House and Garden: "Gates and Doors," Joyce Kilmer.

Life: "Finnigin to Flannigan," S. W. Gillilan.

The Outlook: "A Poet Enlists," Amelia Josephine Burr.

Poetry: "Sunrise on Rydal Water," John Drinkwater; "Night for Adventures," Victor Starbuck: "An Immorality," Ezra Pound; "A Very Old Song," William Laird Brown.

Reedy's Mirror: "Nora," Zoë Akins.

Scribner's Magazine: "Comrades," George Edward Woodberry; "Constancy," Minor Watson; "Turn of the Road," Alice Rollett Coe; "Where Love Is," Amelia Josephine Burr; "Azrael," Robert Gilbert Welsh.

The White-Smith Music Publishing Company: "Kentucky Babe," by Richard Henry Buck.

TO
HENRY HOLT
WITH SINCERE REGARD

INTRODUCTION

I

THE attempt is made in this collection to bring together the best short poems in the English language from the time of Spenser to the present day, together with a body of verse which, if not great poetry, has at least the distinction of wide popularity. In what degree this attempt has been successful the book itself must show; but it may be worth while to state briefly certain purposes which the compiler had in mind when he undertook the task, and which he has carried out as faithfully as he could.

These purposes were to include nothing which did not seem to him to ring true, but, at the same time, to recognize the validity of popular taste as well as of classical taste; to preserve in authentic form certain fugitive poems which everyone admires but which few know where to find; to lay emphasis upon the lighter forms of verse; and to pay especial attention to the work of living English and American poets, particularly of the younger generation.

It would be idle to suppose that everything included here will appeal to everyone as good poetry. Tastes in poetry differ even more inevitably than tastes in food; but the compiler has tried to spread his table in such a manner that every healthy taste may be abundantly satisfied without having to eat of any dish it does not care for. In one respect, he is free to confess that, in arranging the banquet, he has not relied upon his own taste alone. There is a note of pensive sentiment—the note which Longfellow knew how to strike so successfully—which, according to Professor Trent, "finds an echo in the universal human heart," and this note the compiler did not feel justified in disregarding, or even regarding lightly, simply because his own heart happens to be indifferent to it. Nor has he been deterred from using a poem because it was the common property of anthologists, or tempted to include any because it was little known. For this is a collection, not of curious or unusual, but of favorite verse.

There will be much difference of opinion as to the merit of the selections from the work of living writers included here. Where the test of time is not available, and the stamp of wide approval is withheld, there remains only the test of individual preference, and here the compiler has consulted no judgment but his own. He has been hampered by human limitations as applied to a mass of material so overwhelming in bulk; but he hopes that the selection will be found fairly representative, and that no really great poem of recent years has been overlooked. And while the restrictions of copyright have somewhat limited the representation given certain American poets, he believes that American verse, as a whole, receives far more attention here than in any other general anthology.

II

Practically the first decision the compiler made with regard to this work was that it should be a collection, not of fragments, but of complete poems; and this, while it did not, of course, preclude the use of poems within poems—of lyrics from the dramatists, of songs from Scott's metrical romances, or of such parentheses as Byron's stanzas on Waterloo—while it did not prevent the excision of such obvious digressions as the final stanzas of Timrod's "Spring," and while it was not construed to mean that a sequence such as "Sonnets from the Portuguese" must be given entire, has, nevertheless, resulted in some deprivations. No passages will be found here from any of Shakespeare's plays, no stanzas from the "Fairy Queen," no lines from "Paradise Lost." But the compiler feels that such loss, if it be a loss, is more than counterbalanced by the satisfaction of knowing that, throughout the book, one gets complete the poet's thought, as he embodied it in his verse.

The decision to give every poem entire has resulted in a few exclusions from another cause than that of length; for in some lyrics, especially of Restoration days, there is oc-

casionally a line or stanza too free for modern taste. It is
for this reason that Suckling's inimitable "Ballad of a
Wedding" will not be found between these covers, since it
contains one stanza certainly, and perhaps three or four,
not fitted for a "Home Book of Verse." A few other poems
which had got through the winnowing as far as the first
proofs, were finally cut out for the same reason, rather than
presented in a mangled or Bowdlerized version.

And, as already mentioned, the enforcement of copyright
restrictions has prevented the use of a small number of
poems which the compiler wished to include. There are a
few publishers who seem to regard with pronounced dis-
favor any collection such as this, and who will permit the
use of poems which they control either not at all, or only
upon conditions which are, in effect, prohibitive. Because
of this, the admirers of Henry Cuyler Bunner will look in
vain through these pages for any example of his delicate
art; and for the same reason a few other American poets
are either absent altogether or only meagerly represented.
But the losses from this cause are unimportant when compared with the great body of the work, and the compiler
feels that he has little reason to complain. For the most
part, his requests for copyright permissions have been
granted with a most gratifying courtesy and generosity.

III

Great care has been taken to secure accuracy of text, a
task whose difficulty only the anthologist can appreciate.
In so far as possible, the copy used was taken from the
standard editions of the various poets; and where there
was any question of authenticity, as in the case of fugitive
poems, the poem, if the author was living and could be
found, was submitted to him for correction. In the older
poems, where there were varied readings of equal authority,
the editor has used that which seemed to him the best; and
where there have been repeated revisions of a poem, that
has been chosen which seemed the better version. This has
not been, in every case, the final version; for, as in the case
of Coates Kinney's "Rain on the Roof," over-refinement

has sometimes destroyed the spontaneity of the earlier work.

The spelling has been modernized throughout, as there seemed no reason to preserve an archaism not intended by the poet; and such eccentricities of spelling as various writers affected have been made to conform to the accepted American usage. The numbering of stanzas has been omitted as unnecessary and cumbersome. In every case where a short poem has been taken from a longer one, a line has been added to indicate its source, and where the author himself did not supply a title for his poem, the present editor has usually preferred to quote the first line as the title, rather than use a title invented by someone else. In the old ballads, a modern version has been used in preference to the earliest one, which would be unintelligible to many readers; and the use of the apostrophe to indicate an imaginary shortening of a syllable has been done away with. As a matter of fact, there is, for example, no real difference between the pronunciation of "kiss'd," "kist" and "kissed," and so no reason why the regular spelling should not be used.

IV

The classification used in this volume has been made to fit the poems, and not the poems the classification. In other words, with the exception of some of the children's verse, the work of selection was completed before that of classification was begun. The compiler can claim for it no fundamental originality, since most poetry falls into certain well-recognized classes; but he has tried to make it more searching and exhaustive than is usually attempted. He has tried, for instance, to group the poems dealing with the emotions not only by meaning, but by shades of meaning, so that one poem would seem naturally to suggest the next. This has, of course, been a task too fine for accomplishment with anything like complete success; but, as he has looked through the final proofs, he has been conscious of at least a few happy juxtapositions.

Classification is a nerve-racking task, and, even at the best, must sometimes be purely arbitrary; as, for example, where the present compiler has placed his selection from Meredith's "Modern Love" under "Love Sonnets." For Meredith's stanzas are not sonnets at all, since they consist of sixteen lines each; and yet they have essentially a sonnet effect, and their place seemed to be with the other famous sequences. Then, too, there are many poems which may equally well be placed under various headings, so that it was, more or less, an arbitrary decision which placed "The Courtin'" under "The Comedy of Love" rather than with the humorous poems, and "Kathleen Mavourneen" under "The Parted Lovers" rather than "At Her Window."

And, however complete the classification may be, the anthologist must inevitably, at the end, find himself with a number of poems on his hands which belong distinctly nowhere, and which must yet go somewhere. It has been rather the fashion to solve the difficulty by putting them anywhere; but the present compiler has chosen, rather than break the continuity of arrangement, to set up, in one section of Part VI, a sort of scrap-bag in which these odds and ends are assembled.

V

Where every collection such as this must fail of complete success, as representing the whole field of English poetry, is that it exalts the writers of brief lyrics at the expense of the writers of long odes and epics and narrative poems. Such poets as Milton, Pope and Collins do not loom as large in these pages as their stature merits; to attempt to represent Shakespeare by a few of his songs and sonnets, or Swift by an epigram, is manifestly absurd; so that this collection can claim to be adequate only as a representation of English lyric poetry. That, it is hoped, it will be found to be— something more than that, indeed, since many of the more famous longer poems are also included; and it should be valuable, too, as bringing together in one index a wide range of verse not to be found in the average private library.

In closing this resumé of a task which has occupied some three years in the doing, the compiler wishes to acknowledge his deep indebtedness for many kindnesses to the living writers whose work is represented here. They have been uniformly helpful and obliging; not only have they cordially assented to this use of their poems, but they have made suggestions, have revised copy and have read proofs. Their sympathy and interest have been never-failing, and it was very largely their enthusiasm and encouragement which enabled the compiler to carry through to completion a task before which he faltered more than once. To them and to their predecessors in the field of English song belong whatever honor and glory it may bring; for, to paraphrase Montaigne, the compiler has contributed to this nosegay nothing but the thread which binds it; theirs is its perfume and its beauty.

B. E. S.

CHILLICOTHE, OHIO,
    May 10, 1912

INTRODUCTION TO THE THIRD EDITION

WHEN the first edition of this book was published in 1912, there was a tentative agreement between publisher and compiler that, if it was still alive at the end of ten years, it should be revised in an effort to keep it abreast of the times, and so for every decade thereafter. On neither side was there any real expectation that the agreement would ever need to be carried out; certainly there was no reason to suppose that such a revision would be possible, or in any way necessary, at the end of five years; and yet this third edition represents a far more complete revision than was then contemplated —the addition of five hundred and ninety poems, and the deletion of one hundred and sixty-nine; entire repagination, and innumerable minor changes.

It is, of course, primarily because the book has been commercially successful that the publisher is able to spend still more upon it, but that alone would not have warranted a revision such as this. What really warranted it—almost compelled it—was the astonishing renaissance in English and American poetry which the present century has witnessed. "The Home Book of Verse" was launched, by a fortunate chance, just when this renaissance was gathering volume, and its success was due largely, no doubt, to the new interest in poetry thus evoked. But this also had the effect of putting the book more quickly out of date, and anyone in touch with modern verse could not but be disappointed to look through a volume such as this and find nothing by such poets as Lascelles Abercrombie, and John Masefield, and G. K. Chesterton, and Walter de la Mare, and Robert Frost, and Vachel Lindsay, and Richard Middleton, and Ralph Hodgson, and Rupert Brooke.

It is from the work of this younger choir that the additions have very largely been made, and among them will be found some lyrics as fresh and lovely as any in the volume—and as true to the great traditions of English poetry. The deletions are partly of verses whose inclusion was originally determined—as the compiler now realizes—by quotability rather than by merit, and partly of those which failed to stand the test of repeated re-reading—the deadliest test there is. The revision is based upon a careful examination of every significant book of poetry published in this country since 1912, and of many published in England, as well as of a number of older books to which the compiler had not previously had access.

He has also had the assistance of the many columns of critical comment evoked by the appearance of the original edition, and he is not ashamed to say that his attention was called in this way to many notable poems with which he was entirely unfamiliar. Second in value only to the printed criticism was the great mass of correspondence which came and is still coming from all over the country— delightful letters which prove how widespread and genuine is the love of poetry.

The one general criticism—as against specific complaints of certain omissions—which seemed best founded was that no adequate representation was given to the great odes of English poetry. The compiler's first thought had been that they were too long to be included in a book which is essentially a collection of lyrics; but reflection convinced him that these odes did have a place here, and some six or seven of them have been added.

The well-grounded specific criticisms were too numerous to be enumerated; but a particularly striking one was that, while the "Rubáiyát," the great skeptical poem of the nineteenth century, was given entire, there was nothing, or practically nothing, from the century's great poem of faith, "In Memoriam." A careful selection from "In Memoriam" will be found in this edition, preceded by two sections from another great poem, which also in a way counters the "Rubáiyát," though from a vastly different angle—Sir Richard Burton's "Kasîdah."

Then, too, the prestige which the book had gained made it possible to secure permission to use certain poems which were denied to an unknown adventure. Lovers of H. C. Bunner will find nine of his poems here, and a number of other poets are represented more adequately than was possible five years ago. When the compiler says that he believes this third edition to be a far finer achievement than was the first one, he will be pardoned, since the merit is so largely that of others.

Not least that of other anthologists. Every general collection such as this must have its foundations in other collections, from the very first ones which preserved the "Reliques" and "Pastorals," to the very latest which preserves the magazine verse of the year. The debt varies, of course, but it is nevertheless a debt which the compiler has often felt should have been acknowledged in his original introduction, and which is most heartily acknowledged here.

The general plan of the book has remained unchanged, except in one or two very minor details. The compiler found that, in spite of his best efforts, a few incomplete poems had crept into the first edition. These have either been completed or labelled as extracts; and two or three other incomplete ones have been added—notably Suckling's "Ballad Upon a Wedding," minus five stanzas. It simply had to come in! Several questions of uncertain authorship have been solved. There is no longer any doubt in the compiler's mind as to who wrote "Hoch! der Kaiser," and "There is no Death," and "Little Drops of Water," and "At a Cowboy Dance." And a number of disputed readings have been settled—to his satisfaction, at least. For example, after examining forty-three editions of the "New England Primer," he has found the weight of authority to lie on the side of

> "Now I lay me down to sleep,
>   I pray the Lord my soul to keep,

rather than

> "I pray Thee, Lord, my soul to keep."

He has taken a real joy, by discovering a misplaced comma, in changing the mediocre line,

> "Her hand seemed milk, in milk it was so white,"

to the far more striking

> "Her hand seemed milk in milk, it was so white."

He has corrected all the typographical errors he had himself discovered or which had been pointed out by many correspondents; he has labored to make the biographical data as complete as possible; he has checked up the poems in the book with such definitive or revised or collected editions as have appeared since 1912; and he feels that the text may be relied upon as accurate and authoritative.

Finally, he must again express his deep sense of obligation to those living poets, both English and American, who have been so unstinted in appreciation, and so generous in permitting the use of their work. Without their help, this new edition would have been impossible.

B. E. S.

CHILLICOTHE, OHIO,
   December 1, 1917.

NOTE TO THE SIXTH EDITION

FOR some time past, the publisher and the compiler of THE HOME BOOK OF VERSE have been faced by the necessity of deciding what its future was to be. Its announced mission was "to bring together the best short poems of the English language from the time of Spenser to the present day," but since those words were written, the "present day" had moved up from 1912 to 1925, and those thirteen years had witnessed an astonishing renaissance of poetic production. There was a wealth of material pressing to be used, but, on the other hand, it was evident that the book had reached its utmost limit of size.

One suggested solution was to cut out the less important work of the minor poets of the past century, and so make room for the work of later ones. It sounded practicable enough, but when the compiler looked through the book with this idea in mind, he saw at once that it could not be done — not, at least, without entirely changing the character of the volume. It is true that some of the old verse is extremely mediocre, but nevertheless it has won for itself a niche in public remembrance, sometimes by mere accident, as in the case of "Kaiser & Co.," sometimes because of a notoriety which had nothing to do with literature, as in the case of "'Ostler Joe," sometimes because of the passions of the moment, as in the case of the marching songs of the Civil War. Moreover, an important function of the anthology is to keep alive the meritorious work of obscure poets which would otherwise drop from sight, and to preserve those fatherless fugitive poems, for which there is no other haven. There must be some place where all these can be found, and THE HOME BOOK OF VERSE has had the good fortune to be generally recognized as that place.

Furthermore, as the book stands it forms a more or less well-rounded whole. It has a sort of entity. The idea around which it was built has given it a character of its own — perhaps even a soul! To cut it down might improve the average poetic quality of its contents, but it would no longer be THE HOME BOOK OF VERSE.

So it was finally decided that the only thing to do was to give the book a final revision, and at the same time begin the publication of an extension to be known as THE HOME BOOK OF MODERN VERSE. That is what is now being done; the first edition of the new book appeared a few months ago, and this is the final revision of the present one.

The changes consist of the correction of such errors as have been discovered since the last printing, the bringing up to date of the biographical data, and the addition of perhaps a dozen poems which it was felt should be in the book. Among them are those famous doggerels, "Lasca," "'Ostler Joe," and "The Face Upon the Floor." Two others are Langdon Smith's "Evolution" and Walter Malone's "Agnostic's Creed."

As to errors, these have been pretty well weeded out, thanks largely to the many friends of the book who have been scanning it critically for more than a decade. But one still crops up occasionally, and a very subtle and interesting one was recently brought to light. The famous ninth stanza of Gray's "Elegy in a Country Churchyard" is almost invariably printed as follows:

> The boast of heraldry, the pomp of power,
>   And all that beauty, all that wealth e'er gave,
>   Await alike the inevitable hour:
>   The paths of glory lead but to the grave.

But this is evidently not in the least what Gray wished to say: which is that death awaits alike wealth, position, birth and beauty. "Await," then, should be "awaits," and this was found, upon investigation, to be the reading in the principal manuscript of the poem.

As THE HOME BOOK OF VERSE stands now it will continue to stand to the inevitable hour which no doubt awaits it also, and the compiler can only express anew his indebtedness to the many persons who have helped make it what it is.

B. E. S.

CHILLICOTHE, OHIO,
  December 6, 1925.

TABLE OF CONTENTS

PART I

POEMS OF YOUTH AND AGE

THE ROAD TO SLUMBERLAND

Table of Contents   XXV

PART II

POEMS OF LOVE

Table of Contents

MY LADY'S LIPS

AT HER WINDOW

THE COMEDY OF LOVE

THE HUMOR OF LOVE

THE IRONY OF LOVE

Table of Contents

THE PARTED LOVERS

Table of Contents

THE TRAGEDY OF LOVE

Table of Contents

LOVE'S FULFILLMENT

PAGE

LOVE SONNETS

PART III

POEMS OF NATURE

MOTHER NATURE

DAWN AND DARK

Table of Contents xlix

WOOD AND FIELD AND RUNNING BROOK

Table of Contents

GOD'S CREATURES

lii   Table of Contents

Table of Contents

THE SIMPLE LIFE

WANDERLUST

PART IV

FAMILIAR VERSE, AND POEMS HUMOROUS AND SATIRIC

THE KINDLY MUSE

Table of Contents

Table of Contents

THE BARB OF SATIRE

THE MIMICS

SONS OF THE EMERALD ISLE

PIPE AND CAN

PART V

POEMS OF PATRIOTISM, HISTORY, AND LEGEND

MY COUNTRY

SOLDIER SONGS

Table of Contents

PAGE

POEMS OF PLACES

BALLADS OLD AND NEW

Table of Contents

PAGE

PART VI

POEMS OF SENTIMENT AND REFLECTION

THE MUSIC-MAKERS

FLOWER O' THE MIND

PART VII

POEMS OF SORROW, DEATH, AND IMMORTALITY

"Death be not Proud"............ *John Donne* 3348

IN THE SHADOW

Table of Contents

PAGE

SENTINEL SONGS

Table of Contents

Table of Contents lxxxi

SONGS OF PRAISE

APPENDIX

CONTAINING A FEW OF THE MORE FAMOUS POEMS IN
OTHER LANGUAGES, OF WHICH TRANSLATIONS OR
PARAPHRASES OCCUR IN THE FOREGOING PAGES

PART I

POEMS OF YOUTH AND AGE

THE HUMAN SEASONS

FOUR Seasons fill the measure of the year;
There are four seasons in the mind of man:
He has his lusty Spring, when fancy clear
Takes in all beauty with an easy span:

He has his Summer, when luxuriously
Spring's honeyed cud of youthful thought he loves
To ruminate, and by such dreaming high
Is nearest unto Heaven: quiet coves

His soul has in its Autumn, when his wings
He furleth close; contented so to look
On mists in idleness—to let fair things
Pass by unheeded as a threshold brook:—

He has his Winter too of pale misfeature,
Or else he would forego his mortal nature.

John Keats [1795–1821]

THE BABY

'ONLY A BABY SMALL'

Only a baby small,
  Dropped from the skies,
Only a laughing face,
  Two sunny eyes;
Only two cherry lips,
  One chubby nose;
Only two little hands,
  Ten little toes.

Only a golden head,
  Curly and soft;
Only a tongue that wags
  Loudly and oft;
Only a little brain,
  Empty of thought;
Only a little heart,
  Troubled with naught.

Only a tender flower
  Sent us to rear;
Only a life to love
  While we are here;
Only a baby small,
  Never at rest;
Small, but how dear to us,
  God knoweth best.
                    Matthias Barr [1831–?]

ONLY

Something to live for came to the place,
  Something to die for maybe,
Something to give even sorrow a grace,
  And yet it was only a baby!

3

Cooing, and laughter, and gurgles, and cries,
    Dimples for tenderest kisses,
Chaos of hopes, and of raptures, and sighs,
    Chaos of fears and of blisses.

Last year, like all years, the rose and the thorn;
    This year a wilderness maybe;
But heaven stooped under the roof on the morn
    That it brought them only a baby.

          Harriet Prescott Spofford [1835–1921]

INFANT JOY

"I HAVE no name;
I am but two days old."
What shall I call thee?
"I happy am,
Joy is my name."
Sweet joy befall thee!

Pretty joy!
Sweet joy, but two days old.
Sweet joy I call thee;
Thou dost smile,
I sing the while;
Sweet joy befall thee!

          William Blake [1757–1827]

BABY

From "At the Back of the North Wind"

WHERE did you come from, baby dear?
Out of the everywhere into the here.

Where did you get those eyes so blue?
Out of the sky as I came through.

What makes the light in them sparkle and spin?
Some of the starry spikes left in.

Where did you get that little tear?
I found it waiting when I got here.

What makes your forehead so smooth and high?
A soft hand stroked it as I went by.

What makes your cheek like a warm white rose?
I saw something better than any one knows.

Whence that three-cornered smile of bliss?
Three angels gave me at once a kiss.

Where did you get this pearly ear?
God spoke, and it came out to hear.

Where did you get those arms and hands?
Love made itself into bonds and bands.

Feet, where did you come, you darling things?
From the same box as the cherubs' wings.

How did they all just come to be you?
God thought about me, and so I grew.

But how did you come to us, you dear?
God thought about you, and so I am here.

George Macdonald [1824–1905]

TO A NEW-BORN BABY GIRL

AND did thy sapphire shallop slip
Its moorings suddenly, to dip
Adown the clear, ethereal sea
From star to star, all silently?
What tenderness of archangels
In silver thrilling syllables
Pursued thee, or what dulcet hymn
Low-chanted by the cherubim?
And thou departing must have heard
The holy Mary's farewell word,
Who with deep eyes and wistful smile
Remembered Earth a little while.

Now from the coasts of morning pale
Comes safe to port thy tiny sail.
Now have we seen by early sun,
Thy miracle of life begun.
All breathing and aware thou art,
With beauty templed in thy heart

To let thee recognize the thrill
Of wings along far azure hill,
And hear within the hollow sky
Thy friends the angels rushing by.
These shall recall that thou hast known
Their distant country as thine own,
To spare thee word of vales and streams,
And publish heaven through thy dreams.
The human accents of the breeze
Through swaying star-acquainted trees
Shall seem a voice heard earlier,
Her voice, the adoring sigh of her,
When thou amid rosy cherub-play
Didst hear her call thee, far away,
And dream in very Paradise
The worship of thy mother's eyes.

Grace Hazard Conkling [1878–

TO LITTLE RENÉE ON FIRST SEEING HER LYING IN HER CRADLE

WHO is she here that now I see,
This dainty new divinity,
Love's sister, Venus' child?   She shows
Her hues, white lily and pink rose,
And in her laughing eyes the snares
That hearts entangle unawares.
Ah, woe to men if Love should yield
His arrows to this girl to wield
Even in play, for she would give
Sore wounds that none might take and live.
Yet no such wanton strain is hers,
Nor Leda's child and Jupiter's
Is she, though swans no softer are
Than whom she fairer is by far.
For she was born beside the rill
That gushes from Parnassus' hill,
And by the bright Pierian spring
She shall receive an offering
From every youth who pipes a strain
Beside his flocks upon the plain.

But I, the first, this very day,
Will tune for her my humble lay,
Invoking this new Muse to render
My oaten reed more sweet and tender,
Within its vibrant hollows wake
Such dulcet voices for her sake
As, curvèd hand at straining ear,
I long have stood and sought to hear
Borne with the warm midsummer breeze
With scent of hay and hum of bees
Faintly from far-off Sicily. . . .

Ah, well I know that not for us
Are Virgil and Theocritus,
And that the golden age is past
Whereof they sang, and thou, the last,
Sweet Spenser, of their god-like line,
Soar far too swift for verse of mine
One strain to compass of your song.
Yet there are poets that prolong
Of your rare voice the ravishment
In silver cadences; content
Were I if I could but rehearse
One stave of Wither's starry verse,
Weave such wrought richness as recalls
Britannia's lovely Pastorals,
Or in some garden-spot suspire
One breath of Marvell's magic fire
When in the green and leafy shade
He sees dissolving all that's made.
Ah, little Muse, still far too high
On weak, clipped wings my wishes fly.
Transform them then and make them doves,
Soft-moaning birds that Venus loves,
That they may circle ever low
Above the abode where you shall grow
Into your gracious womanhood.
And you shall feed the gentle brood
From out your hand—content they'll be
Only to coo their songs to thee.

       William Aspenwall Bradley [1878–1939]

A RHYME OF ONE

You sleep upon your mother's breast,
    Your race begun,
A welcome, long a wished-for Guest,
    Whose age is One.

A Baby-Boy, you wonder why
    You cannot run;
You try to talk—how hard you try!—
    You're only One.

Ere long you won't be such a dunce:
    You'll eat your bun,
And fly your kite, like folk who once
    Were only One.

You'll rhyme and woo, and fight and joke,
    Perhaps you'll pun!
Such feats are never done by folk
    Before they're One.

Some day, too, you may have your joy,
    And envy none;
Yes, you, yourself, may own a Boy,
    Who isn't One.

He'll dance, and laugh, and crow; he'll do
    As you have done:
(You crown a happy home, though you
    Are only One.)

But when he's grown shall you be here
    To share his fun,
And talk of times when he (the Dear!)
    Was hardly One?

Dear Child, 'tis your poor lot to be
    My little Son;
I'm glad, though I am old, you see,—
    While you are One.

Frederick Locker-Lampson [1821–1895]

TO A NEW–BORN CHILD

SMALL traveler from an unseen shore,
By mortal eye ne'er seen before,
　　To you, good-morrow.
You are as fair a little dame
As ever from a glad world came
　　To one of sorrow.

We smile above you, but you fret;
We call you gentle names, and yet
　　Your cries redouble.
'Tis hard for little babes to prize
The tender love that underlies
　　A life of trouble.

And have you come from Heaven to earth?
That were a road of little mirth,
　　A doleful travel.
"Why did I come?" you seem to cry,
But that's a riddle you and I
　　Can scarce unravel.

Perhaps you really wished to come,
But now you are so far from home
　　Repent the trial.
What! did you leave celestial bliss
To bless us with a daughter's kiss?
　　What self-denial!

Have patience for a little space,
You might have come to a worse place,
　　Fair Angel-rover.
No wonder now you would have stayed,
But hush your cries, my little maid,
　　The journey's over.

For, utter stranger as you are,
There yet are many hearts ajar
　　For your arriving,
And trusty friends and lovers true
Are waiting, ready-made for you,
　　Without your striving.

The earth is full of lovely things,
And if at first you miss your wings,
    You'll soon forget them;
And others, of a rarer kind
Will grow upon your tender mind—
    If you will let them—

Until you find that your exchange
Of Heaven for earth expands your range
    E'en as a flier,
And that your mother, you and I,
If we do what we should, may fly
    Than Angels higher.

              Cosmo Monkhouse [1840-1901]

BABY MAY

CHEEKS as soft as July peaches,
Lips whose dewy scarlet teaches
Poppies paleness—round large eyes
Ever great with new surprise,
Minutes filled with shadeless gladness,
Minutes just as brimmed with sadness,
Happy smiles and wailing cries,
Crows and laughs and tearful eyes,
Lights and shadows swifter born
Than on wind-swept Autumn corn,
Ever some new tiny notion
Making every limb all motion—
Catching up of legs and arms,
Throwings back and small alarms,
Clutching fingers—straightening jerks,
Twining feet whose each toe works,
Kickings up and straining risings,
Mother's ever new surprisings,
Hands all wants and looks all wonder
At all things the heavens under,
Tiny scorns of smiled reprovings
That have more of love than lovings,

Mischiefs done with such a winning
Archness, that we prize such sinning,
Breakings dire of plates and glasses,
Graspings small at all that passes,
Pullings off of all that's able
To be caught from tray or table;
Silences—small meditations,
Deep as thoughts of cares for nations,
Breaking into wisest speeches
In a tongue that nothing teaches,
All the thoughts of whose possessing
Must be wooed to light by guessing;
Slumbers—such sweet angel-seemings,
That we'd ever have such dreamings,
Till from sleep we see thee breaking,
And we'd always have thee waking;
Wealth for which we know no measure,
Pleasure high above all pleasure,
Gladness brimming over gladness,
Joy in care—delight in sadness,
Loveliness beyond completeness,
Sweetness distancing all sweetness,
Beauty all that beauty may be—
That's May Bennett, that's my baby.

William Cox Bennett [1820–1895]

ALICE

Of deepest blue of summer skies
Is wrought the heaven of her eyes.

Of that fine gold the autumns wear
Is wrought the glory of her hair.

Of rose leaves fashioned in the south
Is shaped the marvel of her mouth.

And from the honeyed lips of bliss
Is drawn the sweetness of her kiss,

'Mid twilight thrushes that rejoice
Is found the cadence of her voice,

Of winds that wave the western fir
Is made the velvet touch of her.

Of all earth's songs God took the half
To make the ripple of her laugh.

I hear you ask, "Pray who is she?"—
This maid that is so dear to me.

"A reigning queen in Fashion's whirl?"
Nay, nay!   She is my baby girl.

Herbert Bashford [1871–1928]

SONGS FOR FRAGOLETTA

I

FRAGOLETTA, blessed one!
What think you of the light of the sun?
Do you think the dark was best,
Lying snug in mother's breast?
Ah! I knew that sweetness, too,
Fragoletta, before you!
But, Fragoletta, now you're born,
You must learn to love the morn,
Love the lovely working light,
Love the miracle of sight,
Love the thousand things to do—
Little girl, I envy you!—
Love the thousand things to see,
Love your mother, and—love me!
And some night, Fragoletta, soon,
I'll take you out to see the moon;
And for the first time, child of ours,
You shall—think of it!—look on flowers,
And smell them, too, if you are good,
And hear the green leaves in the wood
Talking, talking, all together
In the happy windy weather;
And if the journey's not too far
For little limbs so lately made,
Limb upon limb like petals laid,
We'll go and picnic in a star.

II

Blue eyes, looking up at me,
I wonder what you really see,
Lying in your cradle there,
Fragrant as a branch of myrrh?
Helpless little hands and feet,
O so helpless!   O so sweet!
Tiny tongue that cannot talk,
Tiny feet that cannot walk,
Nothing of you that can do
Aught, except those eyes of blue.
How they open, how they close!—
Eyelids of the baby-rose.
Open and shut—so blue, so wise,
Baby-eyelids, baby-eyes.

III

That, Fragoletta, is the rain
Beating upon the window-pane;
But lo! The golden sun appears,
To kiss away the window's tears.
That, Fragoletta, is the wind,
That rattles so the window-blind;
And yonder shining thing's a star,
Blue eyes—you seem ten times as far.
That, Fragoletta, is a bird
That speaks, yet never says a word;
Upon a cherry tree it sings,
Simple as all mysterious things;
Its little life to peck and pipe,
As long as cherries ripe and ripe,
And minister unto the need
Of baby-birds that feed and feed.
This, Fragoletta, is a flower,
Open and fragrant for an hour,
A flower, a transitory thing,
Each petal fleeting as a wing,
All a May morning blows and blows,
And then for everlasting goes.

IV

Blue eyes, against the whiteness pressed
Of little mother's hallowed breast,
The while your trembling lips are fed,
Look up at mother's bended head,
All benediction over you—
O blue eyes looking into blue!

Fragoletta is so small,
We wonder that she lives at all—
Tiny alabaster girl,
Hardly bigger than a pearl;
That is why we take such care,
Lest some one run away with her.

                    Richard Le Gallienne [1866–

CHOOSING A NAME

I HAVE got a new-born sister:
I was nigh the first that kissed her.
When the nursing-woman brought her
To papa, his infant daughter,
How papa's dear eyes did glisten!
She will shortly be to christen;
And papa has made the offer,
I shall have the naming of her.

Now I wonder what would please her,—
Charlotte, Julia, or Louisa?
Ann and Mary, they're too common;
Joan's too formal for a woman;
Jane's a prettier name beside;
But we had a Jane that died.
They would say, if 'twas Rebecca,
That she was a little Quaker.
Edith's pretty, but that looks
Better in old English books;

Ellen's left off long ago;
Blanche is out of fashion now.
None that I have named as yet
Is so good as Margaret.
Emily is neat and fine;
What do you think of Caroline?
How I'm puzzled and perplexed
What to choose or think of next!
I am in a little fever
Lest the name that I should give her
Should disgrace her or defame her;—
I will leave papa to name her.

Mary Lamb [1764–1847]

WEIGHING THE BABY

"How many pounds does the baby weigh—
    Baby who came but a month ago?
How many pounds from the crowning curl
    To the rosy point of the restless toe?"

Grandfather ties the 'kerchief knot,
    Tenderly guides the swinging weight,
And carefully over his glasses peers
    To read the record, "only eight."

Softly the echo goes around:
    The father laughs at the tiny girl;
The fair young mother sings the words,
    While grandmother smooths the golden curl.

And stooping above the precious thing,
    Nestles a kiss within a prayer,
Murmuring softly "Little one,
    Grandfather did not weigh you fair."

Nobody weighed the baby's smile,
    Or the love that came with the helpless one;
Nobody weighed the threads of care,
    From which a woman's life is spun.

No index tells the mighty worth
　　Of a little baby's quiet breath—
A soft, unceasing metronome,
　　Patient and faithful until death.

Nobody weighed the baby's soul,
　　For here on earth no weights there be
That could avail; God only knows
　　Its value in eternity.

Only eight pounds to hold a soul
　　That seeks no angel's silver wing,
But shrines it in this human guise,
　　Within so frail and small a thing!

Oh, mother! laugh your merry note,
　　Be gay and glad, but don't forget
From baby's eyes looks out a soul
　　That claims a home in Eden yet.

Ethel Lynn Beers [1827–1879]

ÉTUDE RÊALISTE

I

A BABY's feet, like seashells pink,
　　Might tempt, should heaven see meet,
An angel's lips to kiss, we think,
　　A baby's feet.

Like rose-hued sea-flowers toward the heat
　　They stretch and spread and wink
Their ten soft buds that part and meet.

No flower-bells that expand and shrink
　　Gleam half so heavenly sweet,
As shine on life's untrodden brink
　　A baby's feet.

II

A baby's hands, like rosebuds furled,
   Where yet no leaf expands,
Ope if you touch, though close upcurled,—
      A baby's hands.

Then, even as warriors grip their brands
   When battle's bolt is hurled,
They close, clenched hard like tightening bands.

No rosebuds yet by dawn impearled
   Match, even in loveliest lands,
The sweetest flowers in all the world,—
      A baby's hands.

III

A baby's eyes, ere speech begin,
   Ere lips learn words or sighs,
Bless all things bright enough to win
      A baby's eyes.

Love, while the sweet thing laughs and lies,
   And sleep flows out and in,
Sees perfect in them Paradise!

Their glance might cast out pain and sin,
   Their speech make dumb the wise,
By mute glad godhead felt within
      A baby's eyes.

           Algernon Charles Swinburne [1837-1909]

LITTLE FEET

Two little feet, so small that both may nestle
    In one caressing hand,—
Two tender feet upon the untried border
    Of life's mysterious land.

Dimpled, and soft, and pink as peach-tree blossoms,
    In April's fragrant days,
How can they walk among the briery tangles,
    Edging the world's rough ways?

These rose-white feet, along the doubtful future,
    Must bear a mother's load;
Alas! since Woman has the heavier burden,
    And walks the harder road.

Love, for a while, will make the path before them
    All dainty, smooth, and fair,—
Will cull away the brambles, letting only
    The roses blossom there.

But when the mother's watchful eyes are shrouded
    Away from sight of men,
And these dear feet are left without her guiding,
    . Who shall direct them then?

How will they be allured, betrayed, deluded,
    Poor little untaught feet!
Into what dreary mazes will they wander,
    What dangers will they meet?

Will they go stumbling blindly in the darkness
    Of Sorrow's tearful shades?
Or find the upland slopes of Peace and Beauty,
    Whose sunlight never fades?

Will they go toiling up Ambition's summit,
    The common world above?
Or in some nameless vale, securely sheltered,
    Walk side by side with Love?

Some feet there be which walk Life's track unwounded,
    Which find but pleasant ways:
Some hearts there be to which this life is only
    A round of happy days.

But these are few. Far more there are who wander
　　Without a hope or friend,—
Who find their journey full of pains and losses,
　　And long to reach the end.

How shall it be with her, the tender stranger,
　　Fair-faced and gentle-eyed,
Before whose unstained feet the world's rude highway
　　Stretches so fair and wide?

Ah! who may read the future? For our darling
　　We crave all blessings sweet,
And pray that He who feeds the crying ravens
　　Will guide the baby's feet.

Elizabeth Akers [1832-1911]

THE BABIE

NAE shoon to hide her tiny taes,
　　Nae stockin' on her feet;
Her supple ankles white as snaw,
　　Or early blossoms sweet.

Her simple dress o' sprinkled pìnk,
　　Her double, dimplit chin,
Her puckered lips, an' baumy mou',
　　With na ane tooth within.

Her een sae like her mither's een,
　　Twa gentle, liquid things;
Her face is like an angel's face,—
　　We're glad she has nae wings.

She is the buddin' of our luve,
　　A giftie God gied us:
We maun na luve the gift owre weel,
　　'Twad be nae blessin' thus.

We still maun luve the Giver mair,
　　An' see Him in the given;
An' sae she'll lead us up to Him,
　　Our babie straight frae Heaven.

Jeremiah Eames Rankin [1828-1904]

LITTLE HANDS

Soft little hands that stray and clutch,
Like fern fronds curl and uncurl bold,
While baby faces lie in such
Close sleep as flowers at night that fold,
What is it you would clasp and hold,
Wandering outstretched with wilful touch?
O fingers small of shell-tipped rose,
How should you know you hold so much?
Two full hearts beating you inclose,
Hopes, fears, prayers, longings, joys and woes,—
All yours to hold, O little hands!
More, more than wisdom understands
And love, love only knows.

Laurence Binyon [1869–

BARTHOLOMEW

Bartholomew is very sweet,
From sandy hair to rosy feet.

Bartholomew is six months old,
And dearer far than pearls or gold.

Bartholomew has deep blue eyes,
Round pieces dropped from out the skies.

Bartholomew is hugged and kissed:
He loves a flower in either fist.

Bartholomew's my saucy son:
No mother has a sweeter one!

Norman Gale [1862–

THE STORM–CHILD

My child came to me with the equinox,
The wild wind blew him to my swinging door,
With flakes of tawny foam from off the shore,
And shivering spindrift whirled across the rocks.
Flung down the sky, the wheeling swallow-flocks

Cried him a greeting, and the lordly woods,
Waving lean arms of welcome one by one,
Cast down their russet cloaks and golden hoods,
And bid their dancing leaflets trip and run
Before the tender feet of this my son.

Therefore the sea's swift fire is in his veins,
And in his heart the glory of the sea;
Therefore the storm-wind shall his comrade be,
That strips the hills and sweeps the cowering plains.
October, shot with flashing rays and rains,
Inhabits all his pulses; he shall know
The stress and splendor of the roaring gales,
The creaking boughs shall croon him fairy tales,
And the sea's kisses set his blood aglow,
While in his ears the eternal bugles blow.
May Byron [1861-

"ON PARENT KNEES"

On parent knees, a naked new-born child,
Weeping thou sat'st while all around thee smiled:
So live, that, sinking to thy life's last sleep,
Calm thou may'st smile, while all around thee weep.
William Jones [1746-1794]

"PHILIP, MY KING"

" Who bears upon his baby brow the round and top of sovereignty."

Look at me with thy large brown eyes,
    Philip, my king!
Round whom the enshadowing purple lies
Of babyhood's royal dignities.
Lay on my neck thy tiny hand
    With love's invisible scepter laden;
I am thine Esther to command
    Till thou shalt find a queen-handmaiden,
        Philip, my king.

O the day when thou goest a-wooing,
       Philip, my king!
When those beautiful lips are suing,
And some gentle heart's bars undoing,
Thou dost enter, love-crowned, and there
   Sittest love-glorified.   Rule kindly,
Tenderly, over thy kingdom fair,
    For we that love, ah! we love so blindly,
       Philip, my king.

Up from thy sweet mouth,—up to thy brow,
       Philip, my king!
The spirit that there lies sleeping now
May rise like a giant and make men bow
As to one heaven-chosen among his peers.
   My Saul, than thy brethren taller and fairer,
Let me behold thee in future years!—
    Yet thy head needeth a circlet rarer,
       Philip, my king.

—A wreath not of gold, but palm.   One day,
       Philip, my king!
Thou too must tread, as we trod, a way
Thorny and cruel and cold and gray:
Rebels within thee, and foes without,
   Will snatch at thy crown.   But march on, glorious,
Martyr, yet monarch! till angels shout,
    As thou sittest at the feet of God victorious,
       "Philip, the king!"
         Dinah Maria Mulock Craik [1826–1887]

THE KING OF THE CRADLE

Draw back the cradle curtains, Kate,
   While watch and ward you're keeping,
Let's see the monarch in his state,
   And view him while he's sleeping.
He smiles and clasps his tiny hand,
   With sunbeams o'er him gleaming,—
A world of baby fairyland
   He visits while he's dreaming.

Monarch of pearly powder-puff,
  Asleep in nest so cosy,
Shielded from breath of breezes rough
  By curtains warm and rosy:
He slumbers soundly in his cell,
  As weak as one decrepid,
Though King of Coral, Lord of Bell,
  And Knight of Bath that's tepid.

Ah, lucky tyrant! Happy lot!
  Fair watchers without number,
Who sweetly sing beside his cot,
  And hush him off to slumber;
White hands in wait to smooth so neat
  His pillow when its rumpled—
A couch of rose leaves soft and sweet,
  Not one of which is crumpled!

Will yonder dainty dimpled hand—
  Size, nothing and a quarter—
E'er grasp a saber, lead a band
  To glory and to slaughter?
Or, may I ask, will those blue eyes—
  In baby patois, "peepers"—
E'er in the House of Commons rise,
  And try to catch the Speaker's?

Will that smooth brow o'er Hansard frown,
  Confused by lore statistic?
Or will those lips e'er stir the town
  From pulpit ritualistic?
Will e'er that tiny Sybarite
  Become an author noted?
That little brain the world's delight,
  Its works by all men quoted?

Though rosy, dimpled, plump, and round
  Though fragile, soft, and tender,
Sometimes, alas! it may be found
  The thread of life is slender!

A little shoe, a little glove—
  Affection never waning—
The shattered idol of our love
  Is all that is remaining!

Then does one chance, in fancy, hear,
  Small feet in childish patter,
Tread soft as they a grave draw near,
  And voices hush their chatter;
'Tis small and new; they pause in fear,
  Beneath the gray church tower,
To consecrate it with a tear,
  And deck it with a flower.

Who can predict the future, Kate—
  Your fondest aspiration!
Who knows the solemn laws of fate,
  That govern all creation?
Who knows what lot awaits your boy—
  Of happiness or sorrow?
Sufficient for to-day is joy,
  Leave tears, Sweet, for to-morrow!

          Joseph Ashby-Sterry [1838-1917]

THE FIRSTBORN

So fair, so dear, so warm upon my bosom,
And in my hands the little rosy feet.
Sleep on, my little bird, my lamb, my blossom;
  Sleep on, sleep on, my sweet.

What is it God hath given me to cherish,
This living, moving wonder which is mine—
Mine only? Leave it with me or I perish,
  Dear Lord of love divine.

Dear Lord, 'tis wonderful beyond all wonder,
This tender miracle vouchsafed to me,
One with myself, yet just so far asunder
  That I myself may see.

Flesh of my flesh, and yet so subtly linking
New selfs with old, all things that I have been
With present joys beyond my former thinking
    And future things unseen.

There life began, and here it links with heaven,
The golden chain of years scarce dipped adown
From birth, ere once again a hold is given
    And nearer to God's Throne.

Seen, held in arms and clasped around so tightly,—
My love, my bird, I will not let thee go.
Yet soon the little rosy feet must lightly
    Go pattering to and fro.

Mine, Lord, all mine Thy gift and loving token.
Mine—yes or no, unseen its soul divine?
Mine by the chain of love with links unbroken,
    Dear Saviour, Thine and mine.
        John Arthur Goodchild [1851–

NO BABY IN THE HOUSE

No baby in the house, I know,
  'Tis far too nice and clean.
No toys, by careless fingers strewn,
  Upon the floors are seen.
No finger-marks are on the panes,
  No scratches on the chairs;
No wooden men set up in rows,
  Or marshaled off in pairs;
No little stockings to be darned,
  All ragged at the toes;
No pile of mending to be done,
  Made up of baby-clothes;
No little troubles to be soothed;
  No little hands to fold;
No grimy fingers to be washed;
  No stories to be told;

No tender kisses to be given;
  No nicknames, "Dove" and "Mouse";
No merry frolics after tea,—
  No baby in the house!

Clara Dolliver [18 ═

OUR WEE WHITE ROSE

From "The Mother's Idol Broken"

ALL in our marriage garden
  Grew, smiling up to God,
A bonnier flower than ever
  Sucked the green warmth of the sod;
O, beautiful unfathomably
  Its little life unfurled;
And crown of all things was our wee
  White Rose of all the world.

From out a balmy bosom
  Our bud of beauty grew;
It fed on smiles for sunshine,
  On tears for daintier dew:
Aye nestling warm and tenderly,
  Our leaves of love were curled
So close and close about our wee
  White Rose of all the world.

With mystical faint fragrance
  Our house of life she filled;
Revealed each hour some fairy tower
  Where wingèd hopes might build!
We saw—though none like us might see—
  Such precious promise pearled
Upon the petals of our wee
  White Rose of all the world.

But evermore the halo
  Of angel-light increased,
Like the mystery of moonlight
  That folds some fairy feast.

Snow-white, snow-soft, snow-silently
  Our darling bud uncurled,
And dropped in the grave—God's lap—our wee
  White Rose of all the world.

Our Rose was but in blossom,
  Our life was but in spring,
When down the solemn midnight
  We heard the spirits sing,
"Another bud of infancy
  With holy dews impearled!"
And in their hands they bore our wee
  White Rose of all the world.

You scarce could think so small a thing
  Could leave a loss so large;
Her little light such shadow fling
  From dawn to sunset's marge.
In other springs our life may be
  In bannered bloom unfurled,
But never, never match our wee
  White Rose of all the world.

Gerald Massey [1828–1907]

INTO THE WORLD AND OUT

INTO the world he looked with sweet surprise;
The children laughed so when they saw his eyes.

Into the world a rosy hand in doubt
He reached—a pale hand took one rosebud out.

"And that was all—quite all!" No, surely! But
The children cried so when his eyes were shut.

Sarah M. B. Piatt [1836–1919]

"BABY SLEEPS"

She is not dead, but sleepeth.—LUKE viii. 52.

THE baby wept;
The mother took it from the nurse's arms,
And hushed its fears, and soothed its vain alarms,
      And baby slept.

Again it weeps,
And God doth take it from the mother's arms,
From present griefs, and future unknown harms,
And baby sleeps.

Samuel Hinds [1793–1872]

BABY BELL

I

HAVE you not heard the poets tell
How came the dainty Baby Bell
Into this world of ours?
The gates of heaven were left ajar:
With folded hands and dreamy eyes,
Wandering out of Paradise,
She saw this planet, like a star,
Hung in the glistening depths of even—
Its bridges, running to and fro,
O'er which the white-winged Angels go,
Bearing the holy Dead to heaven.
She touched a bridge of flowers—those feet,
So light they did not bend the bells
Of the celestial asphodels,
They fell like dew upon the flowers:
Then all the air grew strangely sweet.
And thus came dainty Baby Bell
Into this world of ours.

II

She came and brought delicious May;
The swallows built beneath the eaves;
Like sunlight, in and out the leaves
The robins went, the livelong day;
The lily swung its noiseless bell;
And on the porch the slender vine
Held out its cups of fairy wine.
How tenderly the twilights fell!
Oh, earth was full of singing-birds
And opening springtide flowers,
When the dainty Baby Bell
Came to this world of ours.

III

O Baby, dainty Baby Bell,
How fair she grew from day to day!
What woman-nature filled her eyes,
What poetry within them lay—
Those deep and tender twilight eyes,
So full of meaning, pure and bright
As if she yet stood in the light
Of those oped gates of Paradise.
And so we loved her more and more:
Ah, never in our hearts before
Was love so lovely born:
We felt we had a link between
This real world and that unseen—
The land beyond the morn;
And for the love of those dear eyes,
For love of her whom God led forth,
(The mother's being ceased on earth
When Baby came from Paradise,)—
For love of Him who smote our lives,
And woke the chords of joy and pain,
We said, *Dear Christ!*—our hearts bowed down
Like violets after rain.

IV

And now the orchards, which were white
And pink with blossoms when she came,
Were rich in autumn's mellow prime;
The clustered apples burnt like flame,
The folded chestnut burst its shell,
The grapes hung purpling, range on range;
And time wrought just as rich a change
In little Baby Bell.
Her lissome form more perfect grew,
And in her features we could trace,
In softened curves, her mother's face.
Her angel-nature ripened too:
We thought her lovely when she came,
But she was holy, saintly now . . .
Around her pale angelic brow
We saw a slender ring of flame.

V

God's hand had taken away the seal
That held the portals of her speech;
And oft she said a few strange words
Whose meaning lay beyond our reach.
She never was a child to us,
We never held her being's key;
We could not teach her holy things
Who was Christ's self in purity.

VI

It came upon us by degrees,
We saw its shadow ere it fell—
The knowledge that our God had sent
His messenger for Baby Bell.
We shuddered with unlanguaged pain,
And all our hopes were changed to fears,
And all our thoughts ran into tears
Like sunshine into rain.
We cried aloud in our belief,
"Oh, smite us gently, gently, God!
Teach us to bend and kiss the rod,
And perfect grow through grief."
Ah! how we loved her, God can tell;
Her heart was folded deep in ours.
Our hearts are broken, Baby Bell!

VII

At last he came, the messenger,
The messenger from unseen lands:
And what did dainty Baby Bell?
She only crossed her little hands,
She only looked more meek and fair!
We parted back her silken hair,
We wove the roses round her brow—
White buds, the summer's drifted snow—
Wrapped her from head to foot in flowers . . .
And thus went dainty Baby Bell
Out of this world of ours.

Thomas Bailey Aldrich [1837–1907]

IN THE NURSERY

MOTHER GOOSE'S MELODIES

MISTRESS MARY, quite contrary,
How does your garden grow?
With cockle-shells, and silver bells,
And pretty maids all in a row.

———

THERE was an old woman who lived in a shoe,
She had so many children she didn't know what to do;
She gave them some broth without any bread;
Then whipped them all soundly and put them to bed.

———

PETER, Peter, pumpkin eater,
Had a wife and couldn't keep her;
He put her in a pumpkin shell
And there he kept her very well.

———

RUB-a-dub-dub,
Three men in a tub,
And who do you think they be?
The butcher, the baker,
The candlestick-maker;
Turn 'em out, knaves all three!

———

I'LL tell you a story
About Jack a Nory—
And now my story's begun;
I'll tell you another
About Johnny, his brother—
And now my story is done.

HICKORY, dickory, dock,
The mouse ran up the clock;
The clock struck one,
The mouse ran down,
Hickory, dickory, dock.

———

A DILLAR, a dollar,
A ten o'clock scholar,
What makes you come so soon?
You used to come at ten o'clock
But now you come at noon.

———

THERE was a little man,
And he had a little gun,
And his bullets were made of lead, lead, lead;
He shot Johnny Sprig
Through the middle of his wig,
And knocked it right off his head, head, head.

———

THERE was an old woman, and what do you think?
She lived upon nothing but victuals and drink:
Victuals and drink were the chief of her diet:
Yet this little old woman could never be quiet.

She went to a baker to buy her some bread,
And when she came home, her husband was dead;
She went to the clerk to toll the bell,
And when she came back her husband was well.

———

IF I had as much money as I could spend,
I never would cry old chairs to mend;
Old chairs to mend, old chairs to mend;
I never would cry old chairs to mend.

If I had as much money as I could tell,
I never would cry old clothes to sell;
Old clothes to sell, old clothes to sell;
I never would cry old clothes to sell.

ONE misty, moisty morning,
　When cloudy was the weather,
I met a little old man
　Clothed all in leather;
He began to bow and scrape,
　And I began to grin,—
How do you do, and how do you do,
　And how do you do again?

———

IF all the world were apple-pie,
And all the sea were ink,
And all the trees were bread and cheese,
What should we have to drink?

———

PEASE-PUDDING hot,
　Pease-pudding cold,
Pease-pudding in the pot,
　Nine days old.
Some like it hot,
　Some like it cold,
Some like it in the pot,
　Nine days old.

———

HEY, diddle, diddle,
　The cat and the fiddle,
The cow jumped over the moon;
　The little dog laughed
　To see such sport,
And the dish ran away with the spoon.

———

LITTLE Jack Horner sat in the corner
　Eating a Christmas pie;
He put in his thumb, and pulled out a plum,
　And said, "What a good boy am I!"

LITTLE Miss Muffet,
    Sat on a tuffet,
Eating of curds and whey;
    There came a great spider
    That sat down beside her,
And frightened Miss Muffet away.

———

THERE was a crooked man, and he went a crooked mile.
He found a crooked sixpence against a crooked stile:
He bought a crooked cat, which caught a crooked mouse,
And they all lived together in a little crooked house.

———

LITTLE Polly Flinders,
    Sat among the cinders,
Warming her pretty little toes;
    Her mother came and caught her,
    And whipped her little daughter
For spoiling her nice new clothes.

———

BARBER, barber, shave a pig,
    How many hairs will make a wig?
"Four-and-twenty, that's enough."
    Give the barber a pinch of snuff.

———

LITTLE Boy Blue, come blow up your horn,
The sheep's in the meadow, the cow's in the corn;
But where is the boy that looks after the sheep?
He's under a hay-cock, fast asleep.
Will you awake him?   No, not I;
For if I do, he'll be sure to cry.

———

THERE was a man of our town,
    And he was wondrous wise,
He jumped into a bramble bush,
    And scratched out both his eyes:

But when he saw his eyes were out,
    With all his might and main,
He jumped into another bush,
    And scratched 'em in again.

———

THE north wind doth blow,
    And we shall have snow,
And what will poor Robin do then,
        Poor thing?
He'll sit in a barn,
    And to keep himself warm,
Will hide his head under his wing,
        Poor thing!

———

HIGGLEBY, piggleby, my black hen,
She lays eggs for gentlemen;
Sometimes nine, and sometimes ten,
Higgleby, piggleby, my black hen.

———

THREE wise men of Gotham
    Went to sea in a bowl;
If the bowl had been stronger,
    My song had been longer.

———

THERE was an old woman lived under a hill,
And if she's not gone, she lives there still.

———

PUSSY-CAT, pussy-cat, where have you been?
I've been to London to look at the Queen.
Pussy-cat, pussy-cat, what did you there?
I frightened a little mouse under the chair.

———

THERE were two blackbirds sitting on a hill,
The one named Jack, the other named Jill;
Fly away, Jack! Fly away, Jill!
Come again, Jack! Come again, Jill!

Goosey, goosey, gander,
Whither shall I wander,
Up stairs, down stairs,
And in my lady's chamber.
There I met an old man
Who would not say his prayers;
I took him by his left leg
And threw him down the stairs.

———

Baa, baa, black sheep, have you any wool?
Yes, sir; yes, sir, three bags full.
One for my master, one for my dame,
And one for the little boy that lives in the lane.

———

Bye, baby bunting,
Daddy's gone a-hunting
To get a little rabbit-skin
To wrap the baby bunting in.

———

Old King Cole was a merry old soul,
And a merry old soul was he;
He called for his pipe, and he called for his bowl,
And he called for his fiddlers three.
Every fiddler, he had a fiddle, and a very fine fiddle had he;
Twee tweedle dee, tweedle dee, went the fiddlers.
Oh, there's none so rare, as can compare
With King Cole and his fiddlers three!

———

Ride a cock-horse to Banbury Cross,
To see a fine lady ride on a white horse,
Rings on her fingers, and bells on her toes,
She shall have music wherever she goes.

———

Hector Protector was dressed all in green;
Hector Protector was sent to the Queen.
The Queen did not like him, no more did the King;
So Hector Protector was sent back again.

PETER PIPER picked a peck of pickled peppers;
A peck of pickled peppers Peter Piper picked;
If Peter Piper picked a peck of pickled peppers,
Where's the peck of pickled peppers Peter Piper picked?

———

JACK SPRAT could eat no fat,
  His wife could eat no lean,
And so, betwixt them both, you see,
  They licked the platter clean.

———

THE lion and the unicorn
  Were fighting for the crown;
The lion beat the unicorn
  All round about the town.
Some gave them white bread,
  And some gave them brown;
Some gave them plum cake,
  And sent them out of town.

———

As Tommy Snooks and Bessy Brooks
  Were walking out one Sunday,
Says Tommy Snooks to Bessy Brooks,
  "To-morrow will be Monday."

———

CURLY locks!   Curly locks!
  Wilt thou be mine?
Thou shalt not wash dishes
  Nor yet feed the swine;
But sit on a cushion
  And sew a fine seam,
And feed upon strawberries,
  Sugar and cream.

———

BLOW, wind, blow! and go, mill, go!
  That the miller may grind his corn;
That the baker may take it and into rolls make it,
  And send us some hot in the morn.

Six little mice sat down to spin,
Pussy passed by, and she peeped in.
"What are you at, my little men?"
"Making coats for gentlemen."
"Shall I come in and bite off your threads?"
"No, no, Miss Pussy, you'll snip off our heads."
"Oh, no, I'll not, I'll help you to spin."
"That may be so, but you don't come in!"

Bobby Shaftoe's gone to sea,
Silver buckles at his knee;
When he comes back, he'll marry me,
    Bonny Bobby Shaftoe.

Bobby Shaftoe's fat and fair,
Combing down his yellow hair;
He's my love for evermair,
    Bonny Bobby Shaftoe.

Rock-a-bye, baby, thy cradle is green;
Father's a nobleman, mother's a queen;
And Betty's a lady, and wears a gold ring;
And Johnny's a drummer, and drums for the King.

Hush-a-bye, baby, on the tree-top,
When the wind blows the cradle will rock;
When the bough breaks, the cradle will fall,
Down will come baby, bough, cradle, and all.

To market, to market, to buy a fat pig,
Home again, home again, jiggety-jig;
To market, to market, to buy a fat hog,
Home again, home again, jiggety-jog;
To market, to market, to buy a plum bun,
Home again, home again, market is done.

JACK AND JILL

JACK and Jill went up the hill,
To fetch a pail of water;
Jack fell down and broke his crown
And Jill came tumbling after.

Up Jack got and home did trot
As fast as he could caper,
And went to bed to mend his head
With vinegar and brown paper.

THE QUEEN OF HEARTS

THE Queen of Hearts
She made some tarts,
All on a summer's day;
The Knave of Hearts
He stole those tarts,
And with them ran away.

The King of Hearts
Called for the tarts,
And beat the Knave full sore;
The Knave of Hearts
Brought back the tarts,
And vowed he'd steal no more!

LITTLE BO-PEEP

LITTLE Bo-peep has lost her sheep,
And can't tell where to find them;
Leave them alone, and they'll come home,
And bring their tails behind them.

Little Bo-peep fell fast asleep,
And dreamed she heard them bleating;
But when she awoke, she found it a joke,
For they were still a-fleeting.

Then up she took her little crook,
  Determined for to find them;
She found them indeed, but it made her heart bleed,
  For they'd left their tails behind them!

It happened one day, as Bo-peep did stray,
  Unto a meadow hard by,
There she espied their tails side by side,
  All hung on a tree to dry.

She heaved a sigh, and wiped her eye,
  And over the hillocks she raced;
And tried what she could, as a shepherdess should,
  That each tail should be properly placed.

MARY'S LAMB

Mary had a little lamb,
  Its fleece was white as snow,
And every where that Mary went
  The lamb was sure to go;
He followed her to school one day—
  That was against the rule,
It made the children laugh and play,
  To see a lamb at school.

And so the Teacher turned him out,
  But still he lingered near,
And waited patiently about,
  Till Mary did appear;
And then he ran to her, and laid
  His head upon her arm,
As if he said—"I'm not afraid—
  You'll keep me from all harm."

"What makes the lamb love Mary so?"
  The eager children cry—
"O, Mary loves the lamb, you know,"
  The Teacher did reply;—

"And you each gentle animal
  In confidence may bind,
And make them follow at your call,
  If you are always *kind*."
                    Sarah Josepha Hale [1788-1879]

THE STAR

TWINKLE, twinkle, little star,
How I wonder what you are,
Up above the world so high,
Like a diamond in the sky.

When the blazing sun is set,
And the grass with dew is wet,
Then you show your little light,
Twinkle, twinkle, all the night.

Then the traveler in the dark
Thanks you for your tiny spark,
He could not see where to go
If you did not twinkle so.

In the dark blue sky you keep,
And often through my curtains peep,
For you never shut your eye
Till the sun is in the sky.

As your bright and tiny spark
Lights the traveler in the dark,
Though I know not what you are,
Twinkle, twinkle, little star.
                    Jane Taylor [1783–1824]

"SING A SONG OF SIXPENCE"

SING a song of sixpence,
  A pocket full of rye;
Four-and-twenty blackbirds
  Baked in a pie;

When the pie was opened
    The birds began to sing;
Wasn't that a dainty dish
    To set before the King?

The King was in his counting-house,
    Counting out his money;
The Queen was in the parlor,
    Eating bread and honey;

The maid was in the garden
    Hanging out the clothes;
When down came a blackbird,
    And nipped off her nose.

SIMPLE SIMON

SIMPLE Simon met a pieman
    Going to the fair;
Says Simple Simon to the pieman,
    "Let me taste your ware."

Says the pieman to Simple Simon,
    "Show me first your penny";
Says Simple Simon to the pieman.
    "Indeed I have not any."

Simple Simon went a-fishing
    For to catch a whale;
All the water he had got
    Was in his mother's pail.

Simple Simon went to look
    If plums grew on a thistle;
He pricked his fingers very much,
    Which made poor Simon whistle

A PLEASANT SHIP

I SAW a ship a-sailing,
A-sailing on the sea,
And oh! it was all laden
With pretty things for thee!

There were comfits in the cabin,
And apples in the hold;
The sails were made of silk,
And the masts were made of gold.

The four-and-twenty sailors
That stood between the decks
Were four-and-twenty white mice,
With chains about their necks.

The captain was a duck,
With a packet on his back,
And when the ship began to move,
The captain said "Quack! Quack!"

"I HAD A LITTLE HUSBAND"

I HAD a little husband
    No bigger than my thumb;
I put him in a pint pot,
    And there I bade him drum.

I bought a little horse,
    That galloped up and down;
I bridled him and saddled him,
    And sent him out of town.

I gave him some garters,
    To garter up his hose,
And a little handkerchief,
    To wipe his pretty nose.

"WHEN I WAS A BACHELOR"

WHEN I was a bachelor
    I lived by myself;
And all the bread and cheese I got
    I put upon the shelf.

The rats and the mice
    They made such a strife,
I was forced to go to London
    To buy me a wife.

The streets were so bad,
  And the lanes were so narrow,
I was forced to bring my wife home
  In a wheelbarrow.

The wheelbarrow broke,
  And my wife had a fall,
Down came wheelbarrow,
  Little wife and all.

"JOHNNY SHALL HAVE A NEW BONNET"

JOHNNY shall have a new bonnet,
  And Johnny shall go to the fair,
And Johnny shall have a blue ribbon
  To tie up his bonny brown hair.

And why may not I love Johnny,
  And why may not Johnny love me?
And why may not I love Johnny
  As well as another body?

And here's a leg for a stocking,
  And here's a foot for a shoe;
And he has a kiss for his daddy,
  And one for his mammy, too.

And why may not I love Johnny,
  And why may not Johnny love me?
And why may not I love Johnny,
  As well as another body?

THE CITY MOUSE AND THE GARDEN MOUSE

THE city mouse lives in a house;—
  The garden mouse lives in a bower,
He's friendly with the frogs and toads,
  And sees the pretty plants in flower.

The city mouse eats bread and cheese;—
  The garden mouse eats what he can;
We will not grudge him seeds and stocks,
  Poor little timid furry man.
                Christina Georgina Rossetti [1830–1894]

ROBIN REDBREAST

LITTLE Robin Redbreast sat upon a tree,
Up went pussy-cat, and down went he;
Down came pussy-cat, and away Robin ran;
Said little Robin Redbreast, "Catch me if you can."

Little Robin Redbreast jumped upon a wall,
Pussy-cat jumped after him, and almost got a fall;
Little Robin chirped and sang, and what did pussy say?
Pussy-cat said naught but "Mew," and Robin flew away.

SOLOMON GRUNDY

SOLOMON Grundy,
Born on a Monday,
Christened on Tuesday,
Married on Wednesday,
Took ill on Thursday,
Worse on Friday,
Died on Saturday,
Buried on Sunday,
This is the end of
Solomon Grundy.

"MERRY ARE THE BELLS"

MERRY are the bells, and merry would they ring,
Merry was myself, and merry could I sing;
With a merry ding-dong, happy, gay, and free,
And a merry sing-song, happy let us be!

Waddle goes your gait, and hollow are your hose:
Noddle goes your pate, and purple is your nose:
Merry is your sing-song, happy, gay, and free;
With a merry ding-dong, happy let us be!

Merry have we met, and merry have we been;
Merry let us part, and merry meet again;
With our merry sing-song, happy, gay, and free,
With a merry ding-dong, happy let us be!

"WHEN GOOD KING ARTHUR RULED THIS LAND"

WHEN good King Arthur ruled this land,
  He was a goodly king;
He stole three pecks of barley meal,
  To make a bag-pudding.

A bag-pudding the queen did make,
  And stuffed it well with plums:
And in it put great lumps of fat,
  As big as my two thumbs.

The king and queen did eat thereof,
  And noblemen beside;
And what they could not eat that night,
  The queen next morning fried.

THE BELLS OF LONDON

GAY go up, and gay go down,
To ring the bells of London town.

Bull's eyes and targets,
Say the bells of Saint Marg'ret's.

Brickbats and tiles,
Say the bells of Saint Giles'.

Half-pence and farthings,
Say the bells of Saint Martin's.

Oranges and lemons,
Say the bells of Saint Clement's.

Pancakes and fritters,
Say the bells of Saint Peter's.

Two sticks and an apple,
Say the bells of Whitechapel.

Old Father Baldpate,
Say the slow bells at Aldgate.

Pokers and tongs,
Say the bells of Saint John's.

Kettles and pans,
Say the bells of Saint Ann's.

You owe me ten shillings,
Say the bells of Saint Helen's.

When will you pay me?
Say the bells at Old Bailey.

When I grow rich,
Say the bells at Shoreditch.

Pray, when will that be?
Say the bells of Stepney.

I am sure I don't know,
Says the great bell at Bow.

THE OWL, THE EEL AND THE WARMING–PAN

THE owl and the eel and the warming-pan,
They went to call on the soap-fat man.
The soap-fat man he was not within:
He'd gone for a ride on his rolling-pin.
So they all came back by the way of the town,
And turned the meeting-house upside down.

Laura E. Richards [1850–

THE COW

THANK you, pretty cow, that made
Pleasant milk to soak my bread,
Every day, and every night,
Warm, and fresh, and sweet, and white.

Do not chew the hemlock rank,
Growing on the weedy bank;
But the yellow cowslips eat,
They will make it very sweet.

Where the purple violet grows,
Where the bubbling water flows,
Where the grass is fresh and fine,
Pretty cow, go there and dine.

Ann Taylor [1782–1866]

THE LAMB

LITTLE Lamb, who made thee?
Dost thou know who made thee,
Gave thee life, and bade thee feed
By the stream and o'er the mead;
Gave thee clothing of delight,
Softest clothing, woolly, bright;
Gave thee such a tender voice,
Making all the vales rejoice?
    Little Lamb, who made thee?
    Dost thou know who made thee?

Little Lamb, I'll tell thee,
Little Lamb, I'll tell thee;
He is callèd by thy name,
For He calls Himself a Lamb.
He is meek, and He is mild;
He became a little child.
I a child, and thou a lamb,
We are callèd by His name.
    Little Lamb, God bless thee!
    Little Lamb, God bless thee.
           William Blake [1757–1827]

LITTLE RAINDROPS

OH, where do you come from,
   You little drops of rain,
Pitter patter, pitter patter,
   Down the window-pane?

They won't let me walk,
   And they won't let me play,
And they won't let me go
   Out of doors at all to-day.

They put away my playthings
   Because I broke them all,
And then they locked up all my bricks,
   And took away my ball.

Tell me, little raindrops,
　Is that the way you play,
Pitter patter, pitter patter,
　All the rainy day?

They say I'm very naughty,
　But I've nothing else to do
But sit here at the window;
　I should like to play with you.

The little raindrops cannot speak,
　But "pitter, patter pat"
Means, "We can play on *this* side:
　Why can't you play on *that?*"

"MOON, SO ROUND AND YELLOW"

Moon, so round and yellow,
　Looking from on high,
How I love to see you
　Shining in the sky.
Oft and oft I wonder,
　When I see you there,
How they get to light you,
　Hanging in the air:

Where you go at morning,
　When the night is past,
And the sun comes peeping
　O'er the hills at last.
Sometime I will watch you
　Slyly overhead,
When you think I'm sleeping
　Snugly in my bed.

Matthias Barr [1831–?]

THE HOUSE THAT JACK BUILT

This is the house that Jack built.

　This is the malt
That lay in the house that Jack built.

This is the rat
That ate the malt
That lay in the house that Jack built.

This is the cat
That killed the rat
That ate the malt
That lay in the house that Jack built.

This is the dog
That worried the cat
That killed the rat
That ate the malt
That lay in the house that Jack built.

This is the cow with the crumpled horn
That tossed the dog
That worried the cat
That killed the rat
That ate the malt
That lay in the house that Jack built.

This is the maiden all forlorn
That milked the cow with the crumpled horn
That tossed the dog
That worried the cat
That killed the rat
That ate the malt
That lay in the house that Jack built.

This is the man all tattered and torn
That kissed the maiden all forlorn
That milked the cow with the crumpled horn
That tossed the dog
That worried the cat
That killed the rat
That ate the malt
That lay in the house that Jack built.

This is the priest all shaven and shorn
That married the man all tattered and torn
That kissed the maiden all forlorn
That milked the cow with the crumpled horn

That tossed the dog
That worried the cat
That killed the rat
That ate the malt
That lay in the house that Jack built.

This is the cock that crowed in the morn
That waked the priest all shaven and shorn
That married the man all tattered and torn
That kissed the maiden all forlorn
That milked the cow with the crumpled horn
    That tossed the dog
    That worried the cat
    That killed the rat
    That ate the malt
That lay in the house that Jack built.

This is the farmer sowing his corn
That kept the cock that crowed in the morn
That waked the priest all shaven and shorn
That married the man all tattered and torn
That kissed the maiden all forlorn
That milked the cow with the crumpled horn
    That tossed the dog
    That worried the cat
    That killed the rat
    That ate the malt
That lay in the house that Jack built.

OLD MOTHER HUBBARD

OLD Mother Hubbard
Went to the cupboard,
To get her poor dog a bone:
    But when she got there
    The cupboard was bare,
And so the poor dog had none.

She went to the baker's
    To buy him some bread,
But when she came back
    The poor dog was dead.

She went to the joiner's
  To buy him a coffin,
But when she came back
  The poor dog was laughing.

She took a clean dish
  To get him some tripe,
But when she came back
  He was smoking a pipe.

She went to the fishmonger's
  To buy him some fish,
But when she came back
  He was licking the dish.

She went to the tavern
  For white wine and red,
But when she came back
  The dog stood on his head.

She went to the hatter's
  To buy him a hat,
But when she came back
  He was feeding the cat.

She went to the barber's
  To buy him a wig,
But when she came back
  He was dancing a jig.

She went to the fruiterer's
  To buy him some fruit,
But when she came back
  He was playing the flute.

She went to the tailor's
  To buy him a coat,
But when she came back
  He was riding a goat.

She went to the cobbler's
  To buy him some shoes,
But when she came back
  He was reading the news.

She went to the seamstress
  To buy him some linen,
But when she came back
  The dog was spinning.

She went to the hosier's
  To buy him some hose,
But when she came back
  He was dressed in his clothes.

The dame made a curtesy,
  The dog made a bow,
The dame said, "Your servant,"
  The dog said, "Bow-wow."

This wonderful dog
  Was Dame Hubbard's delight;
He could sing, he could dance,
  He could read, he could write.

She gave him rich dainties
  Whenever he fed,
And built him a monument
  When he was dead.

THE DEATH AND BURIAL OF COCK ROBIN

Who killed Cock Robin?
  "I," said the Sparrow,
  "With my bow and arrow,
I killed Cock Robin."

Who saw him die?
  "I," said the Fly,
  "With my little eye,
I saw him die."

Who caught his blood?
  "I," said the Fish,
  "With my little dish,
I caught his blood."

Who'll make his shroud?
  "I," said the Beetle,
  "With my thread and needle,
I'll make his shroud."

Who'll dig his grave?
  "I," said the Owl,
  "With my spade and trowel,
I'll dig his grave."

Who'll be the parson?
  "I," said the Rook,
  "With my little book.
I'll be the parson."

Who'll be the clerk?
  "I," said the Lark,
  "I'll say Amen in the dark;
I'll be the clerk."

Who'll be chief mourner?
  "I," said the Dove,
  "I mourn for my love;
I'll be chief mourner."

Who'll bear the torch?
  "I," said the Linnet,
  "I'll come in a minute,
I'll bear the torch."

Who'll sing his dirge?
  "I," said the thrush,
  "As I sing in the bush
I'll sing his dirge."

Who'll bear the pall?
  "We," said the Wren,
  Both the Cock and the Hen;
"We'll bear the pall."

Who'll carry his coffin?
  "I," said the Kite,
  "If it be in the night,
I'll carry his coffin."

Who'll toll the bell?
  "I," said the Bull,
  "Because I can pull,
I'll toll the bell."

All the birds of the air
  Fell to sighing and sobbing
When they heard the bell toll
  For poor Cock Robin.

BABY–LAND

"WHICH is the way to Baby-land?"
  "Any one can tell;
    Up one flight,
    To your right;
  Please to ring the bell."

"What can you see in Baby-land?"
  "Little folks in white—
    Downy heads,
    Cradle-beds,
  Faces pure and bright!"

"What do they do in Baby-land?"
  "Dream and wake and play,
    Laugh and crow,
    Shout and grow;
  Jolly times have they!"

"What do they say in Baby-land?"
  "Why, the oddest things;
    Might as well
    Try to tell
  What a birdie sings!"

"Who is the Queen of Baby-land?"
  "Mother, kind and sweet;
    And her love,
    Born above,
  Guides the little feet."

George Cooper [1840–1927]

THE FIRST TOOTH

THERE once was a wood, and a very thick wood,
So thick that to walk was as much as you could;
But a sunbeam got in, and the trees understood.

I went to this wood, at the end of the snows,
And as I was walking I saw a primrose;
Only one!   Shall I show you the place where it grows?

There once was a house, and a very dark house,
As dark, I believe, as the hole of a mouse,
Or a tree in my wood, at the thick of the boughs.

I went to this house, and I searched it aright,
I opened the chambers, and I found a light;
Only one!   Shall I show you this little lamp bright?

There once was a cave, and this very dark cave
One day took a gift from an incoming wave;
And I made up my mind to know what the sea gave.

I took a lit torch, I walked round the ness
When the water was lowest; and in a recess
In my cave was a jewel.   Will nobody guess?

O there was a baby, he sat on my knee,
With a pearl in his mouth that was precious to me,
His little dark mouth like my cave of the sea!

I said to my heart, "And my jewel is bright!
He blooms like a primrose!   He shines like a light!"
Put your hand in his mouth!   Do you feel?   He can bite!
                    William Brighty Rands [1823–1882]

BABY'S BREAKFAST

BABY wants his breakfast,
  Oh! what shall I do?
Said the cow, "I'll give him
  Nice fresh milk—moo-*oo!*"

Said the hen, "Cut-*dah* cut!
  I have laid an egg
For the Baby's breakfast—
  Take it now, I beg!"

And the buzzing bee said,
  "Here is honey sweet.
Don't you think the Baby
  Would like that to eat?"

Then the baker kindly
  Brought the Baby's bread.
"Breakfast is all ready,"
  Baby's mother said;

"But before the Baby
  Eats his dainty food,
Will he not say 'Thank you!'
  To his friends so good?"

Then the bonny Baby
  Laughed and laughed away.
That was all the "Thank you"
  He knew how to say.

Emilie Poulsson [1853–1939]

THE MOON

O, LOOK at the moon!
  She is shining up there;
O mother, she looks
  Like a lamp in the air.

Last week she was smaller,
  And shaped like a bow;
But now she's grown bigger,
  And round as an O.

Pretty moon, pretty moon,
  How you shine on the door,
And make it all bright
  On my nursery floor!

You shine on my playthings,
  And show me their place,
And I love to look up
  At your pretty bright face.

And there is a star
  Close by you, and maybe
That small twinkling star
  Is your little baby.

Eliza Lee Follen [1787–1859]

BABY AT PLAY

BROW bender, Eye peeper,
Nose smeller, Mouth eater,
Chin chopper,
Knock at the door—peep in,
Lift up the latch—walk in.

HERE sits the Lord Mayor, here sit his two men,
Here sits the cock, and here sits the hen;
Here sit the chickens, and here they go in,
Chippety, chippety, chippety, chin.

This little pig went to market;
This little pig stayed at home;
This little pig got roast beef;
This little pig got none;
This little pig cried wee, wee, all the way home.

One, two,
  Buckle my shoe;
Three, four,
  Shut the door;
Five, six,
  Pick up sticks;
Seven, eight,
  Lay them straight;
Nine, ten,
  A good fat hen;
Eleven, twelve,
  Who will delve?

Thirteen, fourteen,
    Maids a-courting;
Fifteen, sixteen,
    Maids a-kissing;
Seventeen, eighteen,
    Maids a-waiting;
Nineteen, twenty,
    My stomach's empty.

THE DIFFERENCE

EIGHT fingers,
    Ten toes,
Two eyes,
    And one nose.
Baby said
    When she smelt the rose,
"Oh! what a pity
    I've only one nose!"

Ten teeth
    In even rows,
Three dimples,
    And one nose.
Baby said
    When she smelt the snuff,
"Deary me!
    One nose is enough."

                    Laura E. Richards [1850–

FOOT SOLDIERS

'TIS all the way to Toe-town,
    Beyond the Knee-high hill,
That Baby has to travel down
    To see the soldiers drill.

One, two, three, four, five, a-row—
    A captain and his men—
And on the other side, you know,
    Are six, seven, eight, nine, ten.

            John Banister Tabb [1845–1909]

TOM THUMB'S ALPHABET

A WAS an Archer, who shot at a frog;
B was a Butcher, who had a great dog;
C was a Captain, all covered with lace;
D was a Drunkard, and had a red face;
E was an Esquire, with pride on his brow;
F was a Farmer, and followed the plow;
G was a Gamester, who had but ill luck;
H was a Hunter, who hunted a buck;
I was an Innkeeper, who loved to bouse;
J was a Joiner, who built up a house;
K was a King, so mighty and grand;
L was a Lady, who had a white hand;
M was a Miser, and hoarded his gold;
N was a Nobleman, gallant and bold;
O was an Oysterman, who went about town;
P was a Parson, and wore a black gown;
Q was a Quack, with a wonderful pill;
R was a Robber, who wanted to kill;
S was a Sailor, who spent all he got;
T was a Tinker, and mended a pot;
U was an Usurer, a miserable elf;
V was a Vintner, who drank all himself;
W was a Watchman, who guarded the door;
X was Expensive, and so became poor;
Y was a Youth, that did not love school;
Z was a Zany, a poor harmless fool.

GRAMMAR IN RHYME

THREE little words, you often see,
Are articles A, An, and The.
A Noun is the name of anything,
As School, or Garden, Hoop, or Swing.
Adjectives tell the kind of Noun,
As Great, Small, Pretty, White, or Brown.
Instead of Nouns the Pronouns stand,
Her head, His face, Your arm, My hand.

Verbs tell of something being done—
To Read, Count, Laugh, Sing, Jump, or Run.
How things are done the Adverbs tell,
As Slowly, Quickly, Ill, or Well.
Conjunctions join the words together—
As men And women, wind Or weather.
The Preposition stands before
A noun, as In or Through a door,
The Interjection shows surprise,
As Oh! how pretty!   Ah! how wise!
The Whole are called nine parts of speech,
Which reading, writing, speaking teach.

DAYS OF THE MONTH

THIRTY days hath September,
April, June, and November;
All the rest have thirty-one;
February twenty-eight alone,—
Except in leap year, at which time
February's days are twenty-nine.

THE GARDEN YEAR

JANUARY brings the snow,
Makes our feet and fingers glow.

February brings the rain,
Thaws the frozen lake again.

March brings breezes, loud and shrill,
To stir the dancing daffodil.

April brings the primrose sweet,
Scatters daisies at our feet.

May brings flocks of pretty lambs
Skipping by their fleecy dams.

June brings tulips, lilies, roses,
Fills the children's hands with posies.

Hot July brings cooling showers,
Apricots, and gillyflowers.

August brings the sheaves of corn,
Then the harvest home is borne.

Warm September brings the fruit;
Sportsmen then begin to shoot.

Fresh October brings the pheasant;
Then to gather nuts is pleasant.

Dull November brings the blast;
Then the leaves are whirling fast.

Chill December brings the sleet,
Blazing fire, and Christmas treat.

Sara Coleridge [1802–1852]

RIDDLES

THERE was a girl in our town,
Silk an' satin was her gown,
Silk an' satin, gold an' velvet,
Guess her name, three times I've telled it.   (Ann.)

As soft as silk, as white as milk,
As bitter as gall, a thick green wall,
And a green coat covers me all.   (A walnut.)

Make three fourths of a cross,
      And a circle complete;
And let two semicircles
      On a perpendicular meet;
Next add a triangle
      That stands on two feet;
Next two semicircles,
      And a circle complete.   (TOBACCO.)

Flour of England, fruit of Spain,
Met together in a shower of rain;
Put in a bag tied round with a string,
If you'll tell me this riddle, I'll give you a ring.
                                    (A plum-pudding.)

In marble walls as white as milk,
Lined with a skin as soft as silk,
Within a fountain crystal clear,
A golden apple doth appear.
No doors there are to this stronghold,
Yet thieves break in and steal the gold. (An egg.)

Little Nanny Etticoat,
In a white petticoat,
And a red nose;
The longer she stands,
The shorter she grows. (A candle.)

Long legs, crooked thighs,
Little head and no eyes. (A pair of tongs.)

Thirty white horses upon a red hill,
Now they tramp, now they champ, now they stand still.
(The teeth.)

Formed long ago, yet made to-day,
    Employed while others sleep;
What few would like to give away,
    Nor any wish to keep. (A bed.)

Lives in winter,
Dies in summer,
And grows with its root upwards. (An icicle.)

Elizabeth, Lizzy, Betsy and Bess,
All went together to seek a bird's nest;
They found a nest with five eggs in it;
They each took one and left four in it.

Thomas a Tattamus took two T's,
To tie two tups to two tall trees,
To frighten the terrible Thomas a Tattamus!
Tell me how many T's there are in all THAT!

Old Mother Twitchett had but one eye,
And a long tail which she let fly;
And every time she went over a gap,
She left a bit of her tail in a trap. (A needle and thread.)

As I went through a garden gap,
Who should I meet but Dick Red-Cap!
A stick in his hand, a stone in his throat,
If you'll tell me this riddle, I'll give you a groat.

                                        (A cherry).

Humpty Dumpty sat on a wall,
Humpty Dumpty had a great fall;
All the king's horses and all the king's men
Cannot put Humpty Dumpty together again.   (An egg.)

As I was going to St. Ives,
I met a man with seven wives,
Every wife had seven sacks,
Every sack had seven cats,
Every cat had seven kits—
Kits, cats, sacks, and wives,
How many were going to St. Ives?   (One.)

Two legs sat upon three legs,
With one leg in his lap;
In comes four legs
And runs away with one leg;
Up jumps two legs,
Catches up three legs,
Throws it after four legs,
And makes him drop one leg.

          (A man, a stool, a leg of mutton, and a dog.)

PROVERBS

IF wishes were horses,
  Beggars would ride;
If turnips were watches,
  I'd wear one by my side.

A MAN of words, and not of deeds,
Is like a garden full of weeds;
For when the weeds begin to grow,
Then doth the garden overflow.

HE that would thrive
Must rise at five;
He that hath thriven
May lie till seven;
And he that by the plough would thrive,
Himself must either hold or drive.

A SWARM of bees in May
Is worth a load of hay;
A swarm of bees in June
Is worth a silver spoon;
A swarm of bees in July
Is not worth a fly.

THEY that wash on Monday
Have all the week to dry;
They that wash on Tuesday
Are not so much awry;
They that wash on Wednesday
Are not so much to blame;
They that wash on Thursday,
Wash for shame;
They that wash on Friday,
Wash in need;
And they that wash on Saturday,
Oh, they are slovens, indeed.

NEEDLES and pins, needles and pins,
When a man marries, his trouble begins.

FOR every evil under the sun,
There is a remedy, or there is none.
If there be one, try and find it;
If there be none, never mind it.

TOMMY's tears, and Mary's fears,
Will make them old before their years.

IF "ifs" and "ands"
Were pots and pans,
There would be no need for tinkers!

For want of a nail, the shoe was lost;
For want of the shoe, the horse was lost;
For want of the horse, the rider was lost;
For want of the rider, the battle was lost;
For want of the battle, the kingdom was lost;
And all from the want of a horseshoe nail.

KIND HEARTS

Kind hearts are the gardens,
    Kind thoughts are the roots,
Kind words are the blossoms,
    Kind deeds are the fruits;
Love is the sweet sunshine
    That warms into life,
For only in darkness
    Grow hatred and strife.

WEATHER WISDOM

A sunshiny shower
Won't last half an hour.

    Rain before seven,
    Fair by eleven.

The South wind brings wet weather,
The North wind wet and cold together;
The West wind always brings us rain,
The East wind blows it back again.

    March winds and April showers
    Bring forth May flowers.

Evening red and morning gray
Set the traveller on his way,
But evening gray and morning red,
Bring the rain upon his head.

        Rainbow at night
        Is the sailor's delight;
        Rainbow at morning,
        Sailors, take warning.

OLD SUPERSTITIONS

SEE a pin and pick it up,
All the day you'll have good luck;
See a pin and let it lay,
Bad luck you will have all day.

CUT your nails on Monday, cut them for news;
Cut them on Tuesday, a pair of new shoes;
Cut them on Wednesday, cut them for health;
Cut them on Thursday, cut them for wealth;
Cut them on Friday, cut them for woe;
Cut them on Saturday, a journey you'll go;
Cut them on Sunday, you'll cut them for evil,
For all the next week you'll be ruled by the devil.

MARRY Monday, marry for wealth;
Marry Tuesday, marry for health;
Marry Wednesday, the best day of all;
Marry Thursday, marry for crosses;
Marry Friday, marry for losses;
Marry Saturday, no luck at all.

SNEEZE on a Monday, you sneeze for danger;
Sneeze on a Tuesday, you'll kiss a stranger;
Sneeze on a Wednesday, you sneeze for a letter;
Sneeze on a Thursday, for something better;
Sneeze on a Friday, you sneeze for sorrow;
Sneeze on a Saturday, your sweetheart to-morrow;
Sneeze on a Sunday, your safety seek—
The devil will have you the whole of the week.

MONDAY's child is fair of face,
Tuesday's child is full of grace,
Wednesday's child is full of woe,
Thursday's child has far to go,
Friday's child is loving and giving,
Saturday's child works hard for its living,
And a child that's born on the Sabbath day
Is fair and wise and good and gay.

THE ROAD TO SLUMBERLAND

WYNKEN, BLYNKEN, AND NOD

DUTCH LULLABY

WYNKEN, Blynken, and Nod one night
  Sailed off in a wooden shoe,—
Sailed on a river of crystal light
  Into a sea of dew.
"Where are you going, and what do you wish?"
  The old moon asked the three.
"We have come to fish for the herring fish
  That live in this beautiful sea;
  Nets of silver and gold have we!"
      Said Wynken,
      Blynken,
      And Nod.

The old moon laughed and sang a song,
  As they rocked in the wooden shoe;
And the wind that sped them all night long
  Ruffled the waves of dew.
The little stars were the herring fish
  That lived in that beautiful sea—
"Now cast your nets wherever you wish,—
  Never afeard are we!"
  So cried the stars to the fishermen three,
      Wynken,
      Blynken,
      And Nod.

All night long their nets they threw
  To the stars in the twinkling foam,—
Then down from the skies came the wooden shoe,
  Bringing the fishermen home:

'Twas all so pretty a sail, it seemed
    As if it could not be;
And some folk thought 'twas a dream they'd dreamed
    Of sailing that beautiful sea;
    But I shall name you the fishermen three:
            Wynken,
            Blynken,
            And Nod.

Wynken and Blynken are two little eyes,
    And Nod is a little head,
And the wooden shoe that sailed the skies
    Is a wee one's trundle-bed;
So shut your eyes while Mother sings
    Of wonderful sights that be,
And you shall see the beautiful things
    As you rock in the misty sea
    Where the old shoe rocked the fishermen three:—
            Wynken,
            Blynken,
            And Nod.

Eugene Field [1850–1895]

THE SUGAR–PLUM TREE

HAVE you ever heard of the Sugar-Plum Tree?
    'Tis a marvel of great renown!
It blooms on the shore of the Lollypop sea
    In the garden of Shut-Eye Town;
The fruit that it bears is so wondrously sweet
    (As those who have tasted it say)
That good little children have only to eat
    Of that fruit to be happy next day.

When you've got to the tree, you would have a hard time
    To capture the fruit which I sing;
The tree is so tall that no person could climb
    To the boughs where the sugar-plums swing!
But up in that tree sits a chocolate cat,
    And a gingerbread dog prowls below—
And this is the way you contrive to get at
    Those sugar-plums tempting you so:

You say but the word to that gingerbread dog
  And he barks with such terrible zest
That the chocolate cat is at once all agog,
  As her swelling proportions attest.
And the chocolate cat goes cavorting around
  From this leafy limb unto that,
And the sugar-plums tumble, of course, to the ground—
  Hurrah for that chocolate cat!

There are marshmallows, gumdrops, and peppermint canes,
  With stripings of scarlet or gold,
And you carry away of the treasure that rains,
  As much as your apron can hold!
So come, little child, cuddle closer to me
  In your dainty white nightcap and gown,
And I'll rock you away to that Sugar-Plum Tree
  In the garden of Shut-Eye Town.

Eugene Field [1850–1895]

WHEN THE SLEEPY MAN COMES

WHEN the Sleepy Man comes with the dust on his eyes,
  (Oh, weary, my Dearie, so weary!)
He shuts up the earth, and he opens the skies.
  (So hush-a-by, weary my Dearie!)

He smiles through his fingers, and shuts up the sun;
  (Oh, weary, my Dearie, so weary!)
The stars that he loves he lets out one by one.
  (So hush-a-by, weary my Dearie!)

He comes from the castles of Drowsy-boy Town;
  (Oh, weary, my Dearie, so weary!)
At the touch of his hand the tired eyelids fall down.
  (So hush-a-by, weary my Dearie!)

He comes with a murmur of dream in his wings;
  (Oh, weary, my Dearie, so weary!)
And whispers of mermaids and wonderful things.
  (So hush-a-by, weary my Dearie!)

Then the top is a burden, the bugle a bane;
    (Oh, weary, my Dearie, so weary!)
When one would be faring down Dream-a-way Lane.
    (So hush-a-by, weary my Dearie!)

When one would be wending in Lullaby Wherry,
    (Oh, weary, my Dearie, so weary!)
To Sleepy Man's Castle, by Comforting Ferry.
    (So hush-a-by, weary my Dearie!)
               Charles G. D. Roberts [1860–

AULD DADDY DARKNESS

AULD Daddy Darkness creeps frae his hole,
Black as a blackamoor, blin' as a mole:
Stir the fire till it lowes, let the bairnie sit,
Auld Daddy Darkness is no wantit yit.

See him in the corners hidin' frae the licht,
See him at the window gloomin' at the nicht;
Turn up the gas licht, close the shutters a',
An' Auld Daddy Darkness will flee far awa'.

Awa' to hide the birdie within its cosy nest,
Awa' to lap the wee flooers on their mither's breast,
Awa' to loosen Gaffer Toil frae his daily ca',
For Auld Daddy Darkness is kindly to a'.

He comes when we're weary to wean's frae oor waes,
He comes when the bairnies are getting aff their claes;
To cover them sae cosy, an' bring bonnie dreams,
So Auld Daddy Darkness is better than he seems.

Steek yer een, my wee tot, ye'll see Daddy then;
He's in below the bed claes, to cuddle ye he's fain;
Noo nestle to his bosie, sleep and dream yer fill,
Till Wee Davie Daylicht comes keekin' owre the hill.
               James Ferguson [18 – ?]

WILLIE WINKIE

Wee Willie Winkie rins through the town,
Upstairs and doon stairs, in his nicht-gown,
Tirlin' at the window, cryin' at the lock,
"Are the weans in their bed?—for it's noo ten o'clock."

Hey, Willie Winkie! are ye comin' ben?
The cat's singin' gay thrums to the sleepin' hen,
The doug's speldered on the floor, and disna gie a cheep;
But here's a waukrife laddie, that winna fa' asleep.

Onything but sleep, ye rogue!—glowrin' like the moon,
Rattlin' in an airn jug wi' an airn spoon,
Rumblin', tumblin' roun' about, crawin' like a cock,
Skirlin' like a kenna-what—wauknin' sleepin' folk!

Hey, Willie Winkie! the wean's in a creel!
Waumblin' aff a bodie's knee like a vera eel,
Ruggin' at the cat's lug, and ravellin' a' her thrums:
Hey, Willie Winkie!—See, there he comes!

William Miller [1810–1872]

THE SANDMAN

The rosy clouds float overhead,
    The sun is going down;
And now the sandman's gentle tread
    Comes stealing through the town.
"White sand, white sand," he softly cries,
    And as he shakes his hand,
Straightway there lies on babies' eyes
    His gift of shining sand.
Blue eyes, gray eyes, black eyes, and brown,
As shuts the rose, they softly close, when he goes through
        the town.

From sunny beaches far away—
    Yes, in another land—
He gathers up at break of day
    His store of shining sand.

No tempests beat that shore remote,
    No ships may sail that way;
His little boat alone may float
    Within that lovely bay.
Blue eyes, gray eyes, black eyes, and brown,
As shuts the rose, they softly close, when he goes through
        the town.

He smiles to see the eyelids close
    Above the happy eyes;
And every child right well he knows,—
    Oh, he is very wise!
But if, as he goes through the land,
    A naughty baby cries,
His other hand takes dull gray sand
    To close the wakeful eyes.
Blue eyes, gray eyes, black eyes, and brown,
As shuts the rose, they softly close, when he goes through
        the town.

So when you hear the sandman's song
    Sound through the twilight sweet,
Be sure you do not keep him long
    A-waiting in the street.
Lie softly down, dear little head,
    Rest quiet, busy hands,
Till, by your bed his good-night said,
    He strews the shining sands.
Blue eyes, gray eyes, black eyes, and brown,
As shuts the rose, they softly close, when he goes through
        the town.

                    Margaret Thomson Janvier [1845–1913]

THE DUSTMAN

WHEN the toys are growing weary,
    And the twilight gathers in;
When the nursery still echoes
    With the children's merry din;

Then unseen, unheard, unnoticed
   Comes an old man up the stair,
Lightly to the children passes,
   Lays his hand upon their hair.

Softly smiles the good old Dustman;
   In their eyes the dust he throws,
Till their little heads are falling,
   And their weary eyes must close.
Then the Dustman very gently
   Takes each little dimpled hand
Leads them through the sweet green shadows,
   Far away in slumberland.

           Frederic Edward Weatherly [1848–1929]

SEPHESTIA'S LULLABY

From "Menaphon"

WEEP not, my wanton, smile upon my knee;
When thou art old there's grief enough for thee.
   Mother's wag, pretty boy,
   Father's sorrow, father's joy;
   When thy father first did see
   Such a boy by him and me,
   He was glad, I was woe;
   Fortune changèd made him so,
   When he left his pretty boy,
   Last his sorrow, first his joy.

Weep not, my wanton, smile upon my knee;
When thou art old there's grief enough for thee.
   Streaming tears that never stint,
   Like pearl-drops from a flint,
   Fell by course from his eyes,
   That one another's place supplies;
   Thus he grieved in every part,
   Tears of blood fell from his heart,
   When he left his pretty boy,
   Father's sorrow, father's joy.

Weep not, my wanton, smile upon my knee;
When thou art old there's grief enough for thee.
　　The wanton smiled, father wept,
　　Mother cried, baby leapt;
　　More he crowed, more we cried,
　　Nature could not sorrow hide:
　　He must go, he must kiss
　　Child and mother, baby bliss,
　　For he left his pretty boy,
　　Father's sorrow, father's joy.
Weep not, my wanton, smile upon my knee,
When thou art old there's grief enough for thee.

Robert Greene [1560?–1592]

"GOLDEN SLUMBERS KISS YOUR EYES"

From "Patient Grissel"

　GOLDEN slumbers kiss your eyes,
　Smiles awake you when you rise.
　Sleep, pretty wantons, do not cry,
　And I will sing a lullaby.
　Rock them, rock them, lullaby.

　Care is heavy, therefore sleep you,
　You are care, and care must keep you.
　Sleep, pretty wantons, do not cry,
　And I will sing a lullaby.
　Rock them, rock them, lullaby.

Thomas Dekker [1570?–1641?]

"SLEEP, BABY, SLEEP"

SLEEP, baby, sleep! what ails my dear,
　What ails my darling thus to cry?
Be still, my child, and lend thine ear,
　To hear me sing thy lullaby.
My pretty lamb, forbear to weep;
Be still, my dear; sweet baby, sleep.

Thou blessed soul, what canst thou fear?
　What thing to thee can mischief do?
Thy God is now thy father dear,
　His holy Spouse thy mother too.
Sweet baby, then forbear to weep;
Be still, my babe; sweet baby, sleep.

Though thy conception was in sin,
　A sacred bathing thou hast had;
And though thy birth unclean hath been,
　A blameless babe thou art now made.
Sweet baby, then forbear to weep;
Be still, my babe; sweet baby, sleep.

While thus thy lullaby I sing,
　For thee great blessings ripening be;
Thine Eldest Brother is a king,
　And hath a kingdom bought for thee.
Sweet baby, then forbear to weep;
Be still, my babe; sweet baby, sleep.

Sweet baby, sleep, and nothing fear;
　For whosoever thee offends
By thy protector threatened are,
　And God and angels are thy friends.
Sweet baby, then forbear to weep;
Be still, my babe; sweet baby, sleep.

When God with us was dwelling here,
　In little babes He took delight;
Such innocents as thou, my dear,
　Are ever precious in His sight.
Sweet baby, then forbear to weep;
Be still, my babe; sweet baby, sleep.

A little infant once was He;
　And strength in weakness then was laid
Upon His Virgin Mother's knee,
　That power to thee might be conveyed.
Sweet baby, then forbear to weep;
Be still, my babe; sweet baby, sleep.

In this thy frailty and thy need
    He friends and helpers doth prepare,
Which thee shall cherish, clothe, and feed,
    For of thy weal they tender are.
Sweet baby, then forbear to weep;
Be still, my babe; sweet baby, sleep.

The King of Kings when He was born,
    Had not so much for outward ease;
By Him such dressings were not worn,
    Nor such like swaddling-clothes as these.
Sweet baby, then forbear to weep;
Be still, my babe; sweet baby sleep.

Within a manger lodged thy Lord,
    Where oxen lay and asses fed:
Warm rooms we do to thee afford,
    An easy cradle for a bed.
Sweet baby, then forbear to weep;
Be still, my babe; sweet baby, sleep.

The wants that He did then sustain
    Have purchased wealth, my babe, for thee,
And by His torments and His pain
    Thy rest and ease securèd be.
My baby, then forbear to weep;
Be still, my babe; sweet baby, sleep.

Thou hast, yet more, to perfect this
    A promise and an earnest got
Of gaining everlasting bliss,
    Though thou, my babe, perceiv'st it not.
Sweet baby, then forbear to weep;
Be still, my babe; sweet baby, sleep.

George Wither [1588–1667]

MOTHER'S SONG

My heart is like a fountain true
That flows and flows with love to you.
As chirps the lark unto the tree
So chirps my pretty babe to me.
And it's O! sweet, sweet! and a lullaby.

There's not a rose where'er I seek,
As comely as my baby's cheek.
There's not a comb of honey-bee,
So full of sweets as babe to me.
And it's O! sweet, sweet! and a lullaby.

There's not a star that shines on high,
Is brighter than my baby's eye.
There's not a boat upon the sea,
Can dance as baby does to me.
And it's O! sweet, sweet! and a lullaby.

No silk was ever spun so fine
As is the hair of baby mine.
My baby smells more sweet to me
Than smells in spring the elder tree.
And it's O! sweet, sweet! and a lullaby.

A little fish swims in the well,
So in my heart does baby dwell.
A little flower blows on the tree,
My baby is the flower to me.
And it's O! sweet, sweet! and a lullaby.

The Queen has sceptre, crown and ball,
You are my sceptre, crown and all.
For all her robes of royal silk,
More fair your skin, as white as milk.
And it's O! sweet, sweet! and a lullaby.

Ten thousand parks where deer do run,
Ten thousand roses in the sun,
Ten thousand pearls beneath the sea,
My babe more precious is to me.
And it's O! sweet, sweet! and a lullaby.

Unknown

A LULLABY

Upon my lap my sovereign sits
And sucks upon my breast;
Meanwhile his love sustains my life
And gives my body rest.
　Sing lullaby, my little boy,
　Sing lullaby, mine only joy!

When thou hast taken thy repast,
Repose, my babe, on me;
So may thy mother and thy nurse
Thy cradle also be.
   Sing lullaby, my little boy,
   Sing lullaby, mine only joy!

I grieve that duty doth not work
All that my wishing would,
Because I would not be to thee
But in the best I should.
   Sing lullaby, my little boy,
   Sing lullaby, mine only joy!

Yet as I am, and as I may,
I must and will be thine,
Though all too little for thy self
Vouchsafing to be mine.
   Sing lullaby, my little boy,
   Sing lullaby, mine only joy!

          Richard Rowlands [fl. 1565–1620)

A CRADLE HYMN

HUSH! my dear, lie still and slumber,
   Holy angels guard thy bed!
Heavenly blessings without number
   Gently falling on thy head.

Sleep, my babe; thy food and raiment,
   House and home, thy friends provide;
All without thy care or payment:
   All thy wants are well supplied.

How much better thou'rt attended
   Than the Son of God could be,
When from heaven He descended
   And became a child like thee!

Soft and easy is thy cradle:
   Coarse and hard thy Saviour lay,
When His birthplace was a stable
   And His softest bed was hay.

Blessèd babe! what glorious features—
  Spotless fair, divinely bright!
Must He dwell with brutal creatures?
  How could angels bear the sight?

Was there nothing but a manger
  Cursèd sinners could afford
To receive the heavenly stranger?
  Did they thus affront their Lord?

Soft, my child: I did not chide thee,
  Though my song might sound too hard;
'Tis thy mother sits beside thee,
  And her arms shall be thy guard.

Yet to read the shameful story
  How the Jews abused their King,
How they served the Lord of Glory,
  Makes me angry while I sing.

See the kinder shepherds round Him,
  Telling wonders from the sky!
Where they sought Him, there they found **Him,**
  With His Virgin mother by.

See the lovely babe a-dressing;
  Lovely infant, how He smiled!
When He wept, the mother's blessing
  Soothed and hushed the holy child.

Lo, He slumbers in His manger,
  Where the hornèd oxen fed;
Peace, my darling; here's no danger,
  Here's no ox anear thy bed.

'Twas to save thee, child, from dying,
  Save my dear from burning flame,
Bitter groans and endless crying,
  That thy blest Redeemer came.

May'st thou live to know and fear Him,
    Trust and love Him all thy days;
Then go dwell forever near Him,
    See His face, and sing His praise!

Isaac Watts [1674–1748]

CRADLE SONG

SLEEP, sleep, beauty bright,
    Dreaming in the joys of night;
Sleep, sleep; in thy sleep
    Little sorrows sit and weep.

Sweet babe, in thy face
    Soft desires I can trace,
Secret joys and secret smiles,
    Little pretty infant wiles.

As thy softest limbs I feel
    Smiles as of the morning steal
O'er thy cheek, and o'er thy breast
    Where thy little heart doth rest.

O the cunning wiles that creep
    In thy little heart asleep!
When thy little heart doth wake,
    Then the dreadful night shall break.

William Blake [1757–1827]

LULLABY

BALOO, loo, lammy, now baloo, my dear,
Does wee lammy ken that its daddy's no here?
Ye're rocking full sweetly on mammy's warm knee,
But daddy's a-rocking upon the salt sea.

Now hushaby, lammy, now hushaby, dear;
Now hushaby, lammy, for mother is near.
The wild wind is raving, and mammy's heart's sair;
The wild wind is raving, and ye dinna care.

Sing baloo, loo, lammy, sing baloo, my dear;
Sing baloo, loo, lammy, for mother is here.
My wee bairnie's dozing, it's dozing now fine,
And O may its wakening be blither than mine!

Carolina Nairne [176$-1845]

LULLABY OF AN INFANT CHIEF

O, HUSH thee, my babie, thy sire was a knight,
Thy mother a lady, both lovely and bright;
The woods and the glens, from the towers which we see,
They are all belonging, dear babie, to thee.
O ho ro, i ri ri, cadul gu lo.

O, fear not the bugle, though loudly it blows,
It calls but the warders that guard thy repose;
Their bows would be bended, their blades would be red,
Ere the step of a foeman draws near to thy bed.
O ho ro, i ri ri, cadul gu lo.

O, hush thee, my babie, the time soon will come,
When thy sleep shall be broken by trumpet and drum;
Then hush thee, my darling, take rest while you may,
For strife comes with manhood, and waking with day.
O ho ro, i ri ri, cadul gu lo.

Walter Scott [1771-1832]

GOOD-NIGHT

LITTLE baby, lay your head
On your pretty cradle-bed;
Shut your eye-peeps, now the day
And the light are gone away;
All the clothes are tucked in tight;
Little baby dear, good-night.

Yes, my darling, well I know
How the bitter wind doth blow;
And the winter's snow and rain
Patter on the window-pane:
But they cannot come in here,
To my little baby dear;

For the window shutteth fast,
Till the stormy night is past;
And the curtains warm are spread
Round about her cradle bed:
So till morning shineth bright,
Little baby dear, good-night.

Jane Taylor [1783–1824]

"LULLABY, O LULLABY"

LULLABY! O lullaby!
Baby, hush that little cry!
  Light is dying,
  Bats are flying,
Bees to-day with work have done;
So, till comes the morrow's sun,
Let sleep kiss those bright eyes dry!
  Lullaby! O lullaby.

Lullaby! O lullaby!
Hushed are all things far and nigh;
  Flowers are closing,
  Birds reposing,
All sweet things with life are done.
Sweet, till dawns the morning sun,
Sleep, then kiss those blue eyes dry.
  Lullaby! O lullaby!

William Cox Bennett [1820–1895]

LULLABY

From "The Princess"

SWEET and low, sweet and low,
  Wind of the western sea,
Low, low, breathe and blow,
  Wind of the western sea!
Over the rolling waters go,
Come from the dying moon, and blow,
  Blow him again to me;
While my little one, while my pretty one, sleeps.

Sleep and rest, sleep and rest,
    Father will come to thee soon;
Rest, rest, on mother's breast,
    Father will come to thee soon;
Father will come to his babe in the nest,
Silver sails all out of the west
        Under the silver moon:
Sleep, my little one, sleep, my pretty one, sleep.
                        Alfred Tennyson [1809–1892]

THE COTTAGER TO HER INFANT

THE days are cold, the nights are long,
The north-wind sings a doleful song;
Then hush again upon my breast;
All merry things are now at rest,
    Save thee, my pretty love!

The kitten sleeps upon the hearth;
The crickets long have ceased their mirth;
There's nothing stirring in the house
Save one *wee*, hungry, nibbling mouse;
    Then why so busy thou?

Nay! start not at that sparkling light;
'Tis but the moon that shines so bright
On the window-pane bedropped with rain:
There, little darling! sleep again,
    And wake when it is day!
                        Dorothy Wordsworth [1804–1847]

TROT, TROT!

EVERY evening Baby goes
    Trot, trot, to town,
Across the river, through the fields,
    Up hill and down.

Trot, trot, the Baby goes,
    Up hill and down,

To buy a feather for her hat,
  To buy a woolen gown.

Trot, trot, the Baby goes;
  The birds fly down, alack!
"You cannot have our feathers, dear,"
  They say, "so please trot back."

Trot, trot, the Baby goes;
  The lambs come bleating near.
"You cannot have our wool," they say,
  "But we are sorry, dear."

Trot, trot, the Baby goes,
  Trot, trot, to town;
She buys a red rose for her hat,
  She buys a cotton gown.
        Mary F. Butts [1836–1902]

HOLY INNOCENTS

SLEEP, little Baby, sleep;
  The holy Angels love thee,
And guard thy bed, and keep
  A blessed watch above thee.
No spirit can come near
  Nor evil beast to harm thee:
Sleep, Sweet, devoid of fear
  Where nothing need alarm thee.

The Love which doth not sleep,
  The eternal Arms surround thee:
The Shepherd of the sheep
  In perfect love hath found thee.
Sleep through the holy night,
  Christ-kept from snare and sorrow,
Until thou wake to light
  And love and warmth to-morrow.
    Christina Georgina Rossetti [1830–1894]

LULLABY

From "The Mistress of the Manse"

ROCKABY, lullaby, bees in the clover!
Crooning so drowsily, crying so low,
Rockaby, lullaby, dear little rover!
 Down into wonderland,
 Down to the under-land
  Go, oh go!
Down into wonderland go!

Rockaby, lullaby, rain on the clover!
(Tears on the eyelids that waver and weep!)
Rockaby, lullaby—bending it over!
 Down on the mother-world,
 Down on the other world,
  Sleep, oh sleep!
Down on the mother-world sleep!

Rockaby, lullaby, dew on the clover!
Dew on the eyes that will sparkle at dawn!
Rockaby, lullaby, dear little rover!
 Into the stilly world,
 Into the lily world,
  Gone! oh gone!
Into the lily world gone!
    Josiah Gilbert Holland [1819–1881]

CRADLE SONG

From "Bitter-Sweet"

WHAT is the little one thinking about?
Very wonderful things, no doubt!
 Unwritten history!
 Unfathomed mystery!
Yet he laughs and cries, and eats and drinks,
And chuckles and crows, and nods and winks,

As if his head were as full of kinks
And curious riddles as any sphinx!
  Warped by colic, and wet by tears,
  Punctured by pins, and tortured by fears,
  Our little nephew will lose two years;
    And he 'll never know
    Where the summers go;—
He need not laugh, for he 'll find it so!

Who can tell what a baby thinks?
Who can follow the gossamer links
  By which the mannikin feels his way
Out from the shore of the great unknown,
Blind, and wailing, and alone,
  Into the light of day?—
Out from the shore of the unknown sea,
Tossing in pitiful agony;—
Of the unknown sea that reels and rolls,
Specked with the barks of little souls,—
Barks that were launched on the other side,
And slipped from Heaven on an ebbing tide!
  What does he think of his mother 's eyes?
What does he think of his mother 's hair?
  What of the cradle-roof, that flies
Forward and backward through the air?
  What does he think of his mother 's breast,
Bare and beautiful, smooth and white,
Seeking it ever with fresh delight,—
  Cup of his life, and couch of his rest?
What does he think when her quick embrace
Presses his hand and buries his face
Deep where the heart-throbs sink and swell
With a tenderness she can never tell,
  Though she murmur the words
  Of all the birds,—
Words she has learned to murmur well?
  Now he thinks he 'll go to sleep!
  I can see the shadow creep
  Over his eyes, in soft eclipse,
  Over his brow, and over his lips,

Out to his little finger-tips!
Softly sinking, down he goes!
Down he goes! down he goes!
See! he is hushed in sweet repose!
                    Josiah Gilbert Holland [1819–1881]

AN IRISH LULLABY

I'VE found my bonny babe a nest
        On Slumber Tree,
I'll rock you there to rosy rest,
        Asthore Machree!
Oh, lulla lo! sing all the leaves
        On Slumber Tree,
Till everything that hurts or grieves
        Afar must flee.

I've put my pretty child to float
        Away from me,
Within the new moon's silver boat
        On Slumber Sea.
And when your starry sail is o'er
        From Slumber Sea,
My precious one, you'll step to shore
        On Mother's knee.
                    Alfred Perceval Graves [1846–1931]

CRADLE SONG

I

LORD Gabriel, wilt thou not rejoice
When at last a little boy's
        Cheek lies heavy as a rose,
        And his eyelids close?

Gabriel, when that hush may be,
This sweet hand all heedfully
        I'll undo, for thee alone,
        From his mother's own.

Then the far blue highways paven
With the burning stars of heaven,
    He shall gladden with the sweet
    Hasting of his feet—

Feet so brightly bare and cool,
Leaping, as from pool to pool;
    From a little laughing boy
    Splashing rainbow joy!

Gabriel, wilt thou understand
How to keep his hovering hand—
    Never shut, as in a bond,
    From the bright beyond?—

Nay, but though it cling and close
Tightly as a climbing rose,
    Clasp it only so—aright,
    Lest his heart take fright.

(Dormi, dormi tu:
The dusk is hung with blue.)

II

Lord Michael, wilt not thou rejoice
When at last a little boy's
    Heart, a shut-in murmuring bee,
    Turns him unto thee?

Wilt thou heed thine armor well—
To take his hand from Gabriel,
    So his radiant cup of dream
    May not spill a gleam?

He will take thy heart in thrall,
Telling o'er thy breastplate, all
    Colors, in his bubbling speech,
    With his hand to each.

(Dormi, dormi tu.
Sapphire is the blue:
Pearl and beryl, they are called,
Chrysoprase and emerald,

Sard and amethyst.
Numbered so, and kissed.)

Ah, but find some angel word
For thy sharp, subduing sword!
   Yea, Lord Michael, make no doubt
   He will find it out:

(Dormi, dormi tu!
His eyes will look at you.)

III

Last, a little morning space,
Lead him to that leafy place
   Where Our Lady sits awake,
   For all mothers' sake.

Bosomed with the Blessèd One,
He shall mind her of her Son,
   Once so folded from all harms,
   In her shrining arms.

(In her veil of blue,
Dormi, dormi tu.)

   So;—and fare thee well.
   Softly,—Gabriel . . .
When the first faint red shall come,
Bid the Day-star lead him home,
   For the bright world's sake—
   To my heart, awake.
         Josephine Preston Peabody [1874-1922]

MOTHER–SONG FROM "PRINCE LUCIFER"

   WHITE little hands!
    Pink little feet!
   Dimpled all over,
    Sweet, sweet, sweet!
   What dost thou wail for?
    The unknown? the unseen?
   The ills that are coming,
    The joys that have been?

Cling to me closer,
　Closer and closer,
Till the pain that is purer
　Hath banished the grosser.
Drain, drain at the stream, love,
　Thy hunger is freeing,
That was born in a dream, love,
　Along with thy being!

Little fingers that feel
　For their home on my breast,
Little lips that appeal
　For their nurture, their rest!
Why, why dost thou weep, dear?
　Nay, stifle thy cries,
Till the dew of thy sleep, dear,
　Lies soft on thine eyes.

Alfred Austin [1835–1913]

KENTUCKY BABE

Used by Permission of the White-Smith Music Publishing Co.

'SKEETERS am a hummin' on de honeysuckle vine,—
　Sleep, Kentucky Babe!
Sandman am a comin' to dis little coon of mine,—
　Sleep, Kentucky Babe!
Silv'ry moon am shinin' in de heabens up above,
Bobolink am pinin' fo' his little lady love:
　　Yo' is mighty lucky,
　　Babe of old Kentucky,—
　　Close yo' eyes in sleep.

　　Fly away,
Fly away, Kentucky Babe, fly away to rest,
　Fly away,
Lay yo' kinky, woolly head on yo' mammy's breast,—
　　Um—Um—,
　　Close yo' eyes in sleep.

Daddy's in de cane-brake wid his little dog and gun,—
　Sleep, Kentucky Babe!
'Possum fo' yo' breakfast when yo' sleepin' time is done,—
　Sleep, Kentucky Babe!

Bogie man 'll catch yo' sure unless yo' close yo' eyes,
Waitin' jes outside de doo' to take yo' by surprise:
Bes' be keepin' shady,
Little colored lady,—
Close yo' eyes in sleep.

Richard Henry Buck [1869–

MINNIE AND WINNIE

MINNIE and Winnie slept in a shell.
Sleep, little ladies!   And they slept well.

Pink was the shell within, silver without;
Sounds of the great sea wandered about.

Sleep, little ladies!   Wake not soon!
Echo on echo dies to the moon.

Two bright stars peeped into the shell.
"What are they dreaming of?   Who can tell?"

Started a green linnet out of the croft;
Wake, little ladies!   The sun is aloft.

Alfred Tennyson [1809–1892]

BED–TIME SONG

SLEEP, my baby, while I sing
Bed-time news of everything.
Chickens run to mother hen;
Piggy curls up in the pen.
In the field, all tired with play,
Quiet now the lambkins stay.
Kittens cuddle in a heap—
Baby, too, must go to sleep!

Sleep, my baby, while I sing
Bed-time news of everything.
Now the cows from pasture come;
Bees fly home with drowsy hum.
Little birds are in the nest,
Under mother-bird's soft breast.
Over all soft shadows creep—
Baby now must go to sleep.

Sleep, my baby, while I sing
Bed-time news of everything.
Sleepy flowers seem to nod,
Drooping toward the dewy sod;
While the big sun's fading light
Bids my baby dear good-night.
Mother loving watch will keep;
Baby now must go to sleep.

Emilie Poulsson [1853–1939]

TUCKING THE BABY IN

THE dark-fringed eyelids slowly close
    On eyes serene and deep;
Upon my breast my own sweet child
    Has gently dropped to sleep;
I kiss his soft and dimpled cheek,
    I kiss his rounded chin,
Then lay him on his little bed,
    And tuck my baby in.

How fair and innocent he lies;
    Like some small angel strayed,
His face still warmed by God's own smile,
    That slumbers unafraid;
Or like some new embodied soul,
    Still pure from taint of sin—
My thoughts are reverent as I stoop
    To tuck my baby in.

What toil must stain these tiny hands
    That now lie still and white?
What shadows creep across the face
    That shines with morning light?
These wee pink shoeless feet—how far
    Shall go their lengthening tread,
When they no longer cuddled close
    May rest upon this bed?

O what am I that I should train
    An angel for the skies;
Or mix the potent draught that feeds
    The soul within these eyes?

I reach him up to the sinless Hands
  Before his cares begin,—
Great Father, with Thy folds of love,
  O tuck my baby in.

Curtis May [18 ⌐

"JENNY WI' THE AIRN TEETH"

WHAT a plague is this o' mine,
  Winna steek an e'e;
Though I hap him o'er the heid,
  As cosy as can be.
Sleep an' let me to my wark—
  A' thae claes to airn—
Jenny wi' the airn teeth,
  Come an' tak' the bairn!

Tak' him to your ain den,
  Whaur the bogie bides,
But first put baith your big teeth
  In his wee plump sides;
Gie your auld gray pow a shake,
  Rive him frae my grup,
Tak' him whaur nae kiss is gaun
  When he waukens up.

Whatna noise is that I hear
  Coomin' doon the street?
Weel I ken the dump, dump,
  O' her beetle feet;
Mercy me! she's at the door!
  Hear her lift the sneck;
Wheesht, an' cuddle mammy noo,
  Closer roun' the neck.

Jenny wi' the airn teeth,
  The bairn has aff his claes;
Sleepin' safe an' soun', I think—
  Dinna touch his taes.

Sleepin' bairns are no for you,
  Ye may turn aboot,
An' tak' awa' wee Tam next door—
  I hear him screichin' oot.

Dump, dump, awa' she gangs
  Back the road she cam',
I hear her at the ither door,
  Speirin' after Tam;
He's a crabbit, greetin' thing—
  The warst in a' the toon,
Little like my ain wee wean—
  Losh, he's sleepin' soun'!

Mithers hae an awfu' wark
  Wi' their bairns at nicht,
Chappin' on the chair wi' tangs,
  To gie the rogues a fricht;
Aulder bairns are fleyed wi' less,
  Weel eneuch we ken,
Bigger bogies, bigger Jennies,
  Frichten muckle men.
            Alexander Anderson [1845-1909]

CUDDLE DOON

THE bairnies cuddle doon at nicht
  Wi' muckle faucht an' din;
"O, try an' sleep, ye waukrife rogues,
  Your father's comin' in."
They never heed a word I speak;
  I try to gie a froon,
But aye I hap them up, an' cry,
  "O bairnies, cuddle doon."

Wee Jamie wi' the curly heid—
  He aye sleeps next the wa'—
Bangs up an' cries, "I want a piece;"
  The rascal starts them a'.

I rin an' fetch them pieces, drinks,
   They stop awee the soun';
Then draw the blankets up an' cry,
   "Noo, weanies, cuddle doon."

But ere five minutes gang, wee Rab
   Cries oot, frae 'neath the claes,
"Mither, mak' Tam gie ower at once—
   He's kittlin' wi' his taes."
The mischief's in that Tam for tricks,
   He'd bother half the toon;
But aye I hap them up an' cry,
   "O bairnies, cuddle doon."

At length they hear their father's fit,
   An', as he steeks the door,
They turn their faces to the wa',
   While Tam pretends to snore.
"Hae a' the weans been gude?" he asks,
   As he pits aff his shoon;
"The bairnies, John, are in their beds,
   An' lang since cuddled doon."

An' just afore we bed oorsel's,
   We look at oor wee lambs;
Tam has his airm roun' wee Rab's neck,
   An' Rab his airm roun' Tam's.
I lift wee Jamie up the bed,
   An' as I straik each croon,
I whisper, till my heart fills up,
   "O bairnies, cuddle doon."

The bairnies cuddle doon at nicht
   Wi' mirth that's dear to me;
But sune the big warl's cark an' care
   Will quaten doon their glee.
Yet, come what will to ilka ane,
   May He who sits aboon
Aye whisper, though their pows be bauld,
   "O bairnies, cuddle doon."

               Alexander Anderson [1845–1909]

BEDTIME

'Tis bedtime; say your hymn, and bid "Good-night;
God bless Mamma, Papa, and dear ones all."
Your half-shut eyes beneath your eyelids fall,
Another minute, you will shut them quite.
Yes, I will carry you, put out the light,
And tuck you up, although you are so tall!
What will you give me, sleepy one, and call
My wages, if I settle you all right?

I laid her golden curls upon my arm,
I drew her little feet within my hand,
Her rosy palms were joined in trustful bliss,
Her heart next mine beat gently, soft and warm
She nestled to me, and, by Love's command,
Paid me my precious wages—"Baby's Kiss."
Francis Robert St. Clair Erskine [1833–1890]

THE DUTY OF CHILDREN

HAPPY THOUGHT

THE world is so full of a number of things,
I'm sure we should all be as happy as kings.

Robert Louis Stevenson [1850–1894]

WHOLE DUTY OF CHILDREN

A CHILD should always say what's true
And speak when he is spoken to,
And behave mannerly at table;
At least as far as he is able.

Robert Louis Stevenson [1850–1894]

POLITENESS

GOOD little boys should never say
  "I will," and "Give me these";
O, no! that never is the way,
  But "Mother, if you please."

And "If you please," to Sister Ann
  Good boys to say are ready;
And, "Yes, sir," to a Gentleman,
  And, "Yes, ma'am," to a Lady.

Elizabeth Turner ? –1846]

RULES OF BEHAVIOR

HEARTS, like doors, will ope with ease
To very, very little keys,
And don't forget that two of these
Are "I thank you" and "If you please."

Come when you're called,
  Do what you're bid,
Close the door after you,
  Never be chid.

Seldom "can't,"
  Seldom "don't;"
Never "shan't,"
  Never "won't."

LITTLE FRED

WHEN little Fred
  Was called to bed,
He always acted right;
  He kissed Mama,
  And then Papa,
And wished them all good-night.

He made no noise,
  Like naughty boys,
But gently up the stairs
  Directly went,
  When he was sent,
And always said his prayers.

THE LOVABLE CHILD

FRISKY as a lambkin,
  Busy as a bee—
That's the kind of little girl
  People like to see.

Modest as a violet,
  As a rosebud sweet—
That's the kind of little girl
  People like to meet.

Bright as is a diamond,
  Pure as any pearl—
Everyone rejoices in
  Such a little girl.

Happy as a robin,
  Gentle as a dove—
That's the kind of little girl
  Everyone will love.

Fly away and seek her,
  Little song of mine,
For I choose that very girl
  As my Valentine.

Emilie Poulsson [1853–1939]

GOOD AND BAD CHILDREN

CHILDREN, you are very little,
And your bones are very brittle;
If you would grow great and stately,
You must try to walk sedately.

You must still be bright and quiet,
And content with simple diet;
And remain, through all bewild'ring,
Innocent and honest children.

Happy hearts and happy faces,
Happy play in grassy places—
That was how, in ancient ages,
Children grew to kings and sages.

But the unkind and the unruly,
And the sort who eat unduly,
They must never hope for glory—
Theirs is quite a different story!

Cruel children, crying babies,
All grow up as geese and gabies,
Hated, as their age increases,
By their nephews and their nieces.

Robert Louis Stevenson [1850–1894]

REBECCA'S AFTER–THOUGHT

YESTERDAY, Rebecca Mason,
  In the parlor by herself,
Broke a handsome china basin,
  Placed upon the mantel-shelf.

Quite alarmed, she thought of going
　　Very quietly away,
Not a single person knowing,
　　Of her being there that day.

But Rebecca recollected
　　She was taught deceit to shun;
And the moment she reflected,
　　Told her mother what was done;

Who commended her behavior,
Loved her better, and forgave her.

　　　　　　　　Elizabeth Turner [? —1846]

KINDNESS TO ANIMALS

LITTLE children, never give
Pain to things that feel and live;
Let the gentle robin come
For the crumbs you save at home,—
As his meat you throw along
He'll repay you with a song;
Never hurt the timid hare
Peeping frcm her green grass lair,
Let her come and sport and play
On the lawn at close of day;
The little lark goes soaring high
To the bright windows of the sky,
Singing as if 'twere always spring,
And fluttering on an untired wing,—
Oh! let him sing his happy song,
Nor do these gentle creatures wrong.

A RULE FOR BIRDS' NESTERS

THE robin and the red-breast,
　　The sparrow and the wren;
If ye take out o' their nest,
　　Ye'll never thrive again!

The robin and the red-breast,
The martin and the swallow;
If ye touch one o' their eggs,
Bad luck will surely follow!

"SING ON, BLITHE BIRD"

I'VE plucked the berry from the bush, the brown nut from
the tree,
But heart of happy little bird ne'er broken was by me.
I saw them in their curious nests, close couching, slyly peer
With their wild eyes, like glittering beads, to note if harm
were near;
I passed them by, and blessed them all; I felt that it was
good
To leave unmoved the creatures small whose home was in
the wood.

And here, even now, above my head, a lusty rogue doth
sing;
He pecks his swelling breast and neck, and trims his little
wing.
He will not fly; he knows full well, while chirping on that
spray,
I would not harm him for the world, or interrupt his lay.
Sing on, sing on, blithe bird! and fill my heart with summer
gladness;
It has been aching many a day with measures full of sadness!
William Motherwell [1797–1835]

"I LIKE LITTLE PUSSY"

I LIKE little Pussy, her coat is so warm;
And if I don't hurt her she'll do me no harm.
So I'll not pull her tail, nor drive her away,
But Pussy and I very gently will play.

She shall sit by my side, and I'll give her some food;
And she'll love me because I am gentle and good.
I'll pat little Pussy and then she will purr,
And thus show her thanks for my kindness to her.

I'll not pinch her ears, nor tread on her paw,
Lest I should provoke her to use her sharp claw;
I never will vex her, nor make her displeased,
For Pussy can't bear to be worried or teased.
Jane Taylor [1783–1824]

LITTLE THINGS

LITTLE drops of water,
   Little grains of sand,
Make the mighty ocean
   And the pleasant land.

So the little moments,
   Humble though they be,
Make the mighty ages
   Of eternity.

So our little errors
   Lead the soul away
From the path of virtue,
   Far in sin to stray.

Little deeds of kindness,
   Little words of love,
Help to make earth happy
   Like the heaven above.
Julia Fletcher Carney [1823–1908]

THE LITTLE GENTLEMAN

From " Little Derwent's Breakfast "

TAKE your meals, my little man,
Always like a gentleman;
Wash your face and hands with care,
Change your shoes, and brush your hair;
Then so fresh, and clean, and neat,
Come and take your proper seat:
Do not loiter and be late,
Making other people wait;

Do not rudely point or touch:
Do not eat and drink too much:
Finish what you have, before
You even ask, or send for more:
Never crumble or destroy
Food that others might enjoy;
They who idly *crumbs* will waste
Often want a loaf to taste!
Never spill your milk or tea,
Never rude or noisy be;
Never choose the daintiest food,
Be content with what is good:
Seek in all things that you can
To be a little gentleman.

THE CRUST OF BREAD

I MUST not throw upon the floor
　The crust I cannot eat;
For many little hungry ones
　Would think it quite a treat.

My parents labor very hard
　To get me wholesome food;
Then I must never waste a bit
　That would do others good.

For wilful waste makes woeful want,
　And I may live to say,
Oh! how I wish I had the bread
　That once I threw away!

"HOW DOTH THE LITTLE BUSY BEE"

How doth the little busy bee
　Improve each shining hour,
And gather honey all the day
　From every opening flower!

How skilfully she builds her cell!
   How neat she spreads the wax!
And labors hard to store it well
   With the sweet food she makes.

In works of labor or of skill,
   I would be busy too;
For Satan finds some mischief still
   For idle hands to do.

In books, or work, or healthful play,
   Let my first years be passed,
That I may give for every day
   Some good account at last.

Isaac Watts [1674–1748]

THE BROWN THRUSH

THERE'S a merry brown thrush sitting up in the tree.
"He's singing to me!   He's singing to me!"
   And what does he say, little girl, little boy?
   "Oh, the world's running over with joy!
      Don't you hear?   Don't you see?
      Hush!   Look!   In my tree,
      I'm as happy as happy can be!"

And the brown thrush keeps singing, "A nest do you see,
And five eggs, hid by me in the juniper-tree?
   Don't meddle!   Don't touch! little girl, little boy,
   Or the world will lose some of its joy!
      Now I'm glad!   Now I'm free!
      And I always shall be,
      If you never bring sorrow to me."

So the merry brown thrush sings away in the tree,
To you and to me, to you and to me;
   And he sings all the day, little girl, little boy,
   "Oh, the world's running over with joy!
      But long it won't be,
      Don't you know?   Don't you see?
      Unless we're as good as can be."

Lucy Larcom [1824–1893]

THE SLUGGARD

'Tis the voice of a sluggard; I heard him complain,
"You have waked me too soon; I must slumber again";
As the door on its hinges, so he on his bed
Turns his sides, and his shoulders, and his heavy head.

"A little more sleep, and a little more slumber";
Thus he wastes half his days, and his hours without number;
And when he gets up, he sits folding his hands
Or walks about saunt'ring, or trifling he stands.

I passed by his garden, and saw the wild brier
The thorn and the thistle grow broader and higher;
The clothes that hang on him are turning to rags;
And his money still wastes till he starves or he begs.

I made him a visit, still hoping to find
That he took better care for improving his mind;
He told me his dreams, talked of eating and drinking,
But he scarce reads his Bible, and never loves thinking.

Said I then to my heart, "Here's a lesson for me;
That man's but a picture of what I might be;
But thanks to my friends for their care in my breeding,
Who taught me betimes to love working and reading."
                              Isaac Watts [1674–1748]

THE VIOLET

Down in a green and shady bed
  A modest violet grew;
Its stalk was bent, it hung its head,
  As if to hide from view.

And yet it was a lovely flower,
  Its colors bright and fair;
It might have graced a rosy bower,
  Instead of hiding there.

Yet there it was content to bloom,
  In modest tints arrayed;
And there diffused a sweet perfume,
  Within the silent shade.

Then let me to the valley go,
  This pretty flower to see;
That I may also learn to grow
  In sweet humility.

Jane Taylor [1783–1824]

DIRTY JIM

THERE was one little Jim,
'Tis reported of him,
  And must be to his lasting disgrace,
That he never was seen
With hands at all clean,
  Nor yet ever clean was his face.

His friends were much hurt
To see so much dirt,
  And often they made him quite clean;
But all was in vain,
He got dirty again,
  And not at all fit to be seen.

It gave him no pain
To hear them complain,
  Nor his own dirty clothes to survey;
His indolent mind
No pleasure could find
  In tidy and wholesome array.

The idle and bad,
Like this little lad,
  May love dirty ways, to be sure;
But good boys are seen,
To be decent and clean,
  Although they are ever so poor.

Jane Taylor [1783–1824]

THE PIN

"DEAR me! what signifies a pin,
  Wedged in a rotten board?
I'm certain that I won't begin,
  At ten years old, to hoard;
I never will be called a miser,
That I'm determined," said Eliza.

So onward tripped the little maid,
  And left the pin behind,
Which very snug and quiet lay,
  To its hard fate resigned;
Nor did she think (a careless chit)
'Twas worth her while to stoop for it.

Next day a party was to ride,
  To see an air balloon;
And all the company beside
  Were dressed and ready soon;
But she a woeful case was in,
For want of just a single pin.

In vain her eager eyes she brings,
  To every darksome crack;
There was not one, and yet her things
  Were dropping off her back.
She cut her pincushion in two,
But no, not one had fallen through.

At last, as hunting on the floor,
  Over a crack she lay,
The carriage rattled to the door,
  Then rattled fast away;
But poor Eliza was not in,
For want of just—a single pin!

There's hardly anything so small,
  So trifling or so mean,
That we may never want at all,
  For service unforeseen;

And wilful waste, depend upon't,
Brings, almost always, woeful want!
Ann Taylor [1782–1866]

JANE AND ELIZA

THERE were two little girls, neither handsome nor plain,
One's name was Eliza, the other's was Jane;
They were both of one height, as I've heard people say,
And both of one age, I believe, to a day.

'Twas fancied by some, who but slightly had seen them,
There was not a pin to be chosen between them;
But no one for long in this notion persisted,
So great a distinction there *really* existed.

Eliza knew well that she could not be pleasing,
While fretting and fuming, while sulking or teasing;
And therefore in company artfully tried,
Not to *break* her bad habits, but only to *hide*.

So, when she was out, with much labor and pain,
She contrived to look *almost* as pleasant as Jane;
But then you might see that, in forcing a smile,
Her mouth was uneasy, and ached all the while.

And in spite of her care it would sometimes befall
That some cross event happened to ruin it all;
And because it might chance that her share was the worst,
Her temper broke loose, and her dimples dispersed.

But Jane, who had nothing she wanted to hide,
And therefore these troublesome arts never tried,
Had none of the care and fatigue of concealing,
But her face always showed what her bosom was feeling.

At home or abroad there was peace in her smile,
A cheerful good nature that needed no guile.
And Eliza worked hard, but could never obtain
The affection that freely was given to Jane.
Ann Taylor [1782–1866]

MEDDLESOME MATTY

ONE ugly trick has often spoiled
    The sweetest and the best;
Matilda, though a pleasant child,
    One ugly trick possessed,
Which, like a cloud before the skies,
Hid all her better qualities.

Sometimes she'd lift the tea-pot lid,
    To peep at what was in it;
Or tilt the kettle, if you did
    But turn your back a minute.
In vain you told her not to touch,
Her trick of meddling grew so much.

Her grandmamma went out one day,
    And by mistake she laid
Her spectacles and snuff-box gay
    Too near the little maid;
"Ah! well," thought she, "I'll try them on,
As soon as grandmamma is gone."

Forthwith she placed upon her nose
    The glasses large and wide;
And looking round, as I suppose,
    The snuff-box too she spied:
"Oh! what a pretty box is that;
I'll open it," said little Matt.

"I know that grandmamma would say,
    'Don't meddle with it, dear';
But then, she's far enough away,
    And no one else is near:
Besides, what can there be amiss
In opening such a box as this?"

So thumb and finger went to work
    To move the stubborn lid,
And presently a mighty jerk
    The mighty mischief did;

For all at once, ah! woeful case,
The snuff came puffing in her face.

Poor eyes, and nose, and mouth, beside,
    A dismal sight presented;
In vain, as bitterly she cried,
    Her folly she repented.
In vain she ran about for ease;
She could do nothing now but sneeze.

She dashed the spectacles away,
    To wipe her tingling eyes,
And as in twenty bits they lay,
    Her grandmamma she spies.
"Heydey! and what's the matter now?"
Cried grandmamma, with lifted brow.

Matilda, smarting with the pain,
    And tingling still, and sore,
Made many a promise to refrain
    From meddling evermore.
And 'tis a fact, as I have heard,
She ever since has kept her word.
                    Ann Taylor [1782–1866]

CONTENTED JOHN

ONE honest John Tomkins, a hedger and ditcher,
Although he was poor, did not want to be richer;
For all such vain wishes in him were prevented
By a fortunate habit of being contented.

Though cold were the weather, or dear were the food,
John never was found in a murmuring mood;
For this he was constantly heard to declare,—
What he could not prevent he would cheerfully bear.

"For why should I grumble and murmur?" he said;
"If I cannot get meat, I'll be thankful for bread;
And, though fretting may make my calamities deeper,
It can never cause bread and cheese to be cheaper."

If John was afflicted with sickness or pain,
He wished himself better, but did not complain,
Nor lie down to fret in despondence and sorrow,
But said that he hoped to be better to-morrow.

If any one wronged him or treated him ill,
Why, John was good-natured and sociable still;
For he said that revenging the injury done
Would be making two rogues when there need be but one.

And thus honest John, though his station was humble,
Passed through this sad world without even a grumble;
And I wish that some folks, who are greater and richer,
Would copy John Tomkins, the hedger and ditcher.

Jane Taylor [1783–1824]

FRIENDS

How good to lie a little while
    And look up through the tree!
The Sky is like a kind big smile
    Bent sweetly over me.

The Sunshine flickers through the lace
    Of leaves above my head,
And kisses me upon the face
    Like Mother, before bed.

The Wind comes stealing o'er the grass
    To whisper pretty things;
And though I cannot see him pass,
    I feel his careful wings.

So many gentle Friends are near
    Whom one can scarcely see,
A child should never feel a fear,
    Wherever he may be.

Abbie Farwell Brown [1875–1927]

ANGER

ANGER in its time and place
May assume a kind of grace.
It must have some reason in it,
And not last beyond a minute.
If to further lengths it go,
It does into malice grow.
'Tis the difference that we see
'Twixt the serpent and the bee.
If the latter you provoke,
It inflicts a hasty stroke,
Puts you to some little pain,
But it *never stings again.*
Close in tufted bush or brake
Lurks the poison-swellèd snake
Nursing up his cherished wrath;
In the purlieus of his path,
In the cold, or in the warm,
Mean him good, or mean him harm,
Wheresoever fate may bring you,
The vile snake will *always sting you.*

Charles and Mary Lamb

"THERE WAS A LITTLE GIRL"

THERE was a little girl, who had a little curl
   Right in the middle of her forehead,
And when she was good, she was very, very good
   But when she was bad she was horrid.

She stood on her head, on her little trundle-bed,
   With nobody by for to hinder;
She screamed and she squalled, she yelled and she bawled,
   And drummed her little heels against the winder.

Her mother heard the noise, and thought it was the boys
   Playing in the empty attic,
She rushed upstairs, and caught her unawares,
   And spanked her, most emphatic.

Henry Wadsworth Longfellow? [1807–1882]
On the authority of his son, Ernest W.
Longfellow, *Random Memories*, p. 15.

THE REFORMATION OF GODFREY GORE

GODFREY GORDON GUSTAVUS GORE—
No doubt you have heard the name before—
Was a boy who never would shut a door!

The wind might whistle, the wind might roar,
And teeth be aching and throats be sore,
But still he never would shut the door.

His father would beg, his mother implore,
"Godfrey Gordon Gustavus Gore,
We really *do* wish you would shut the door!"

Their hands they wrung, their hair they tore;
But Godfrey Gordon Gustavus Gore
Was deaf as the buoy out at the Nore.

When he walked forth the folks would roar,
"Godfrey Gordon Gustavus Gore,
Why don't you think to shut the door?"

They rigged out a Shutter with sail and oar,
And threatened to pack off Gustavus Gore
On a voyage of penance to Singapore.

But he begged for mercy, and said, "No more!
Pray do not send me to Singapore
On a Shutter, and then I will shut the door!"

"You will?" said his parents; "then keep on shore!
But mind you do!   For the plague is sore
Of a fellow that never will shut the door,
Godfrey Gordon Gustavus Gore!"

William Brighty Rands [1823–1882]

THE BEST FIRM

A PRETTY good firm is "Watch & Waite,"
And another is "Attit, Early & Layte;"
And still another is "Doo & Dairet;"
But the best is probably "Grinn & Barrett."

Walter G. Doty [1876–

A LITTLE PAGE'S SONG
(*13th Century*)

God's lark at morning I would be!
I'd set my heart within a tree
Close to His bed and sing to Him
   Right merrily
   A sunrise hymn.

At night I'd be God's troubadour!
Beneath His starry walls I'd pour
Across the moat such roundelays
   He'd love me sure—
   And maybe praise!

              William Alexander Percy [1885–

HOW THE LITTLE KITE LEARNED TO FLY

"I never can do it," the little kite said,
As he looked at the others high over his head;
"I know I should fall if I tried to fly."
"Try," said the big kite; "only try!
Or I fear you never will learn at all."
But the little kite said, "I'm afraid I'll fall."

The big kite nodded: "Ah well, goodby;
I'm off;" and he rose toward the tranquil sky.
Then the little kite's paper stirred at the sight,
And trembling he shook himself free for flight.
First whirling and frightened, then braver grown,
Up, up he rose through the air alone,
Till the big kite looking down could see
The little one rising steadily.

Then how the little kite thrilled with pride,
As he sailed with the big kite side by side!
While far below he could see the ground,
And the boys like small spots moving round.
They rested high in the quiet air,
And only the birds and the clouds were there.
"Oh, how happy I am!" the little kite cried,
"And all because I was brave, and tried."

              Unknown

THE BUTTERFLY AND THE BEE

METHOUGHT I heard a butterfly
  Say to a laboring bee:
"Thou hast no colors of the sky
  On painted wings like me."

"Poor child of vanity! those dyes,
  And colors bright and rare,"
With mild reproof, the bee replies,
"Are all beneath my care.

"Content I toil from morn till eve,
  And, scorning idleness,
To tribes of gaudy sloth I leave
  The vanity of dress."

William Lisle Bowles [1762-1850]

THE BUTTERFLY

THE butterfly, an idle thing,
Nor honey makes, nor yet can sing,
  As do the bee and bird;
Nor does it, like the prudent ant,
Lay up the grain for times of want,
  A wise and cautious hoard.

My youth is but a summer's day:
Then like the bee and ant I'll lay
  A store of learning by;
And though from flower to flower I rove,
My stock of wisdom I'll improve,
  Nor be a butterfly.

Adelaide O'Keefe [1776-1855]

MORNING

THE lark is up to meet the sun,
  The bee is on the wing,
The ant her labor has begun,
  The woods with music ring.

Shall birds and bees and ants be wise,
  While I my moments waste?
Oh, let me with the morning rise,
  And to my duties haste.

Why should I sleep till beams of morn
  Their light and glory shed?
Immortal beings were not born
  To waste their time in bed.

Jane Taylor [1783-1824]

BUTTERCUPS AND DAISIES

BUTTERCUPS and daisies,
  Oh, the pretty flowers;
Coming ere the spring time,
  To tell of sunny hours,
While the trees are leafless,
  While the fields are bare,
Buttercups and daisies
  Spring up here and there.

Ere the snow-drop peepeth,
  Ere the crocus bold,
Ere the early primrose
  Opes its paly gold,—
Somewhere on the sunny bank
  Buttercups are bright;
Somewhere midst the frozen grass
  Peeps the daisy white.

Little hardy flowers,
  Like to children poor,
Playing in their sturdy health
  By their mother's door.
Purple with the north-wind,
  Yet alert and bold;
Fearing not, and caring not,
  Though they be a-cold!

What to them is winter!
    What are stormy showers!
Buttercups and daisies
    Are these human flowers!
He who gave them hardships
    And a life of care,
Gave them likewise hardy strength
    And patient hearts to bear.

                    Mary Howitt [1799–1888]

THE ANT AND THE CRICKET

A SILLY young cricket, accustomed to sing
Through the warm, sunny months of gay summer and spring,
Began to complain, when he found that at home
His cupboard was empty and winter was come.
    Not a crumb to be found
    On the snow-covered ground;
    Not a flower could he see,
    Not a leaf on a tree:
"Oh, what will become," says the cricket, " of me?"

At last by starvation and famine made bold,
All dripping with wet and all trembling with cold,
Away he set off to a miserly ant,
To see if, to keep him alive, he would grant
    Him shelter from rain:
    A mouthful of grain
    He wished only to borrow,
    He'd repay it to-morrow:
If not, he must die of starvation and sorrow.

Says the ant to the cricket, "I'm your servant and friend,
But we ants never borrow, we ants never lend;
But tell me, dear sir, did you lay nothing by
When the weather was warm?" Said the cricket, "Not I.
    My heart was so light
    That I sang day and night,
    For all nature looked gay."
    "You sang, sir, you say?
Go then," said the ant, "and dance winter away."

Thus ending, he hastily lifted the wicket
And out of the door turned the poor little cricket.
Though this is a fable, the moral is good:
If you live without work, you must live without food.

Unknown

AFTER WINGS

THIS was your butterfly, you see,—
  His fine wings made him vain:
The caterpillars crawl, but he
  Passed them in rich disdain.—
My pretty boy says, "Let him be
  Only a worm again!"

O child, when things have learned to wear
  Wings once, they must be fain
To keep them always high and fair:
  Think of the creeping pain
Which even a butterfly must bear
  To be a worm again!

Sarah M. B. Piatt [1836–1919]

DEEDS OF KINDNESS

SUPPOSE the little Cowslip
  Should hang its golden cup
And say, "I'm such a little flower
  I'd better not grow up!"
How many a weary traveller
  Would miss its fragrant smell,
How many a little child would grieve
  To lose it from the dell!

Suppose the glistening Dewdrop
  Upon the grass should say,
"What can a little dewdrop do?
  I'd better roll away!"
The blade on which it rested,
  Before the day was done,
Without a drop to moisten it,
  Would wither in the sun.

Suppose the little Breezes,
  Upon a summer's day,
Should think themselves too small to cool
  The traveller on his way:
Who would not miss the smallest
  And softest ones that blow,
And think they made a great mistake
  If they were acting so?

How many deed of kindness
  A little child can do,
Although it has but little strength
  And little wisdom too!
It wants a loving spirit
  Much more than strength, to prove
How many things a child may do
  For others by its love.

Epes Sargent [1813–1880]

THE LION AND THE MOUSE

A LION with the heat oppressed,
One day composed himself to rest:
But while he dozed as he intended,
A mouse, his royal back ascended;
Nor thought of harm, as Æsop tells,
Mistaking him for someone else;
And travelled over him, and round him,
And might have left him as she found him
Had she not—tremble when you hear—
Tried to explore the monarch's ear!
Who straightway woke, with wrath immense,
And shook his head to cast her thence.
"You rascal, what are you about?"
Said he, when he had turned her out,
"I'll teach you soon," the lion said,
"To make a mouse-hole in my head!"
So saying, he prepared his foot
To crush the trembling tiny brute;

But she (the mouse) with tearful eye,
Implored the lion's clemency,
Who thought it best at last to give
His little prisoner a reprieve.

'Twas nearly twelve months after this,
The lion chanced his way to miss;
When pressing forward, heedless yet,
He got entangled in a net.
With dreadful rage, he stamped and tore,
And straight commenced a lordly roar;
When the poor mouse, who heard the noise,
Attended, for she knew his voice.
Then what the lion's utmost strength
Could not effect, she did at length;
With patient labor she applied
Her teeth, the network to divide;
And so at last forth issued he,
A *lion*, by a mouse set free.

Few are so small or weak, I guess,
But may assist us in distress,
Nor shall we ever, if we're wise,
The meanest, or the least despise.

Jeffreys Taylor [1792–1853]

THE BOY AND THE WOLF

A LITTLE Boy was set to keep
A little flock of goats or sheep;
He thought the task too solitary,
And took a strange perverse vagary:
To call the people out of fun,
To see them leave their work and run,
He cried and screamed with all his might,—
"Wolf! wolf!" in a pretended fright.
Some people, working at a distance,
Came running in to his assistance.
They searched the fields and bushes round,
The Wolf was nowhere to be found.

The Boy, delighted with his game,
A few days after did the same,
And once again the people came.
The trick was many times repeated,
At last they found that they were cheated.
One day the Wolf appeared in sight,
The Boy was in a real fright,
He cried, "Wolf! wolf!"—the neighbors heard,
But not a single creature stirred.
"We need not go from our employ,—
'Tis nothing but that idle boy."
The little Boy cried out again,
"Help, help! the Wolf!" he cried in vain.
At last his master came to beat him.
He came too late, the Wolf had eat him.

This shows the bad effect of lying,
And likewise of continual crying.
If I had heard you scream and roar,
For nothing, twenty times before,
Although you might have broke your arm,
Or met with any serious harm,
Your cries could give me no alarm;
They would not make me move the faster,
Nor apprehend the least disaster;
I should be sorry when I came,
But you yourself would be to blame.

John Hookham Frere [1769–1846]

THE STORY OF AUGUSTUS, WHO WOULD NOT HAVE ANY SOUP

Augustus was a chubby lad;
Fat, ruddy cheeks Augustus had;
And everybody saw with joy
The plump and hearty, healthy boy.
He ate and drank as he was told,
And never let his soup get cold.

But one day, one cold winter's day,
He screamed out— "Take the soup away!
O take the nasty soup away!
I won't have any soup to-day."

Next day begins his tale of woes;
Quite lank and lean Augustus grows.
Yet, though he feels so weak and ill,
The naughty fellow cries out still—
"Not any soup for me, I say:
O take the nasty soup away!
I won't have any soup to-day."

The third day comes; O what a sin!
To make himself so pale and thin.
Yet, when the soup is put on table,
He screams, as loud as he is able,—
"Not any soup for me, I say:
O take the nasty soup away!
I won't have any soup to-day."

Look at him, now the fourth day's come!
He scarcely weighs a sugar-plum;
He's like a little bit of thread,
And on the fifth day, he was—dead!
From the German of Heinrich Hoffman [1798–1874]

THE STORY OF LITTLE SUCK–A–THUMB

ONE day, mamma said: "Conrad dear,
I must go out and leave you here.
But mind now, Conrad, what I say,
Don't suck your thumb while I'm away.
The great tall tailor always comes
To little boys that suck their thumbs;
And ere they dream what he's about,
He takes his great sharp scissors out
And cuts their thumbs clean off,—and then,
You know, they never grow again."

Mamma had scarcely turned her back,
The thumb was in, alack! alack!
The door flew open, in he ran,
The great, long, red-legged scissors-man.
Oh, children, see! the tailor's come
And caught our little Suck-a-Thumb.
Snip! snap! snip! the scissors go;
And Conrad cries out— "Oh! oh! oh!"

Snip! snap! snip!   They go so fast,
That both his thumbs are off at last.
Mamma comes home; there Conrad stands,
And looks quite sad, and shows his hands;—
"Ah!" said mamma, "I knew he'd come
To naughty little Suck-a-Thumb."
       From the German of Heinrich Hoffman [1798–1874]

WRITTEN IN A LITTLE LADY'S LITTLE ALBUM

HEARTS good and true
Have wishes few
In narrow circles bounded,
And hope that lives
On what God gives
Is Christian hope well founded.

Small things are best;
Grief and unrest
To rank and wealth are given;
But little things
On little wings
Bear little souls to heaven.
       Frederick William Faber [1814–1863]

MY LADY WIND

My Lady Wind, my Lady Wind,
Went round about the house to find
A chink to set her foot in;
She tried the keyhole in the door,
She tried the crevice in the floor,
And drove the chimney soot in.

And then one night when it was dark
She blew up such a tiny spark
    That all the town was bothered;
From it she raised such flame and smoke
That many in great terror woke,
    And many more were smothered.

And thus when once, my little dears,
A whisper reaches itching ears—
    The same will come, you'll find:
Take my advice, restrain the tongue,
Remember what old nurse has sung
    Of busy Lady Wind.

Unknown

TO A CHILD

SMALL service is true service while it lasts:
Of humblest friends, bright creature! scorn not one:
The daisy, by the shadow that it casts,
Protects the lingering dewdrop from the sun.

William Wordsworth [1770–1850]

A FAREWELL

MY fairest child, I have no song to give you;
    No lark could pipe to skies so dull and gray:
Yet, if you will, one quiet hint I'll leave you
        For every day.

I'll tell you how to sing a clearer carol
    Than lark who hails the dawn on breezy down;
To earn yourself a purer poet's laurel
        Than Shakespeare's crown.

Be good, sweet maid, and let who will be clever;
    Do noble things, not dream them, all day long:
And so make Life, and Death, and that For Ever
        One grand sweet song.

Charles Kingsley [1819–1875]

RHYMES OF CHILDHOOD

REEDS OF INNOCENCE

PIPING down the valleys wild,
  Piping songs of pleasant glee,
On a cloud I saw a child,
  And he laughing said to me:

"Pipe a song about a lamb!"
  So I piped with merry cheer.
"Piper, pipe that song again;"
  So I piped: he wept to hear.

"Drop thy pipe, thy happy pipe;
  Sing thy songs of happy cheer!"
So I sang the same again,
  While he wept with joy to hear.

"Piper, sit thee down and write
  In a book that all may read."
So he vanished from my sight;
  And I plucked a hollow reed,

And I made a rural pen,
  And I stained the water clear,
And I wrote my happy songs
  Every child may joy to hear.
                William Blake [1757–1827]

THE WONDERFUL WORLD

GREAT, wide, beautiful, wonderful World,
With the wonderful water round you curled,
And the wonderful grass upon your breast,
World, you are beautifully dressed.

The wonderful air is over me,
And the wonderful wind is shaking the tree—
It walks on the water, and whirls the mills,
And talks to itself on the tops of the hills.

You friendly Earth, how far do you go,
With the wheat-fields that nod and the rivers that flow,
With cities and gardens, and cliffs and isles,
And people upon you for thousands of miles?

Ah! you are so great, and I am so small,
I tremble to think of you, World, at all;
And yet, when I said my prayers to-day,
A whisper inside me seemed to say,
"You are more than the Earth, though you are such a dot:
You can love and think, and the Earth cannot!"

William Brighty Rands [1823–1882]

THE WORLD'S MUSIC

THE world's a very happy place,
   Where every child should dance and sing,
And always have a smiling face,
   And never sulk for anything.

I waken when the morning's come,
   And feel the air and light alive
With strange sweet music like the hum
   Of bees about their busy hive.

The linnets play among the leaves
   At hide-and-seek, and chirp and sing;
While, flashing to and from the eaves,
   The swallows twitter on the wing.

The twigs that shake, and boughs that sway;
   And tall old trees you could not climb;
And winds that come, but cannot stay,
   Are gaily singing all the time.

From dawn to dark the old mill-wheel
  Makes music, going round and round;
And dusty-white with flour and meal,
  The miller whistles to its sound.

And if you listen to the rain
  When leaves and birds and bees are dumb,
You hear it pattering on the pane
  Like Andrew beating on his drum.

The coals beneath the kettle croon,
  And clap their hands and dance in glee;
And even the kettle hums a tune
  To tell you when it's time for tea.

The world is such a happy place,
  That children, whether big or small,
Should always have a smiling face,
  And never, never sulk at all.
                    Gabriel Setoun [1861–

A BOY'S SONG

WHERE the pools are bright and deep,
Where the gray trout lies asleep,
Up the river and over the lea,
That's the way for Billy and me.

Where the blackbird sings the latest,
Where the hawthorn blooms the sweetest,
Where the nestlings chirp and flee,
That's the way for Billy and me.

Where the mowers mow the cleanest,
Where the hay lies thick and greenest,
There to track the homeward bee,
That's the way for Billy and me.

Where the hazel bank is steepest,
Where the shadow falls the deepest,
Where the clustering nuts fall free,
That's the way for Billy and me.

Why the boys should drive away
Little sweet maidens from the play,
Or love to banter and fight so well,
That's the thing I never could tell.

But this I know, I love to play
Through the meadow, among the hay;
Up the water and over the lea,
That's the way for Billy and me.

James Hogg [1770–1835]

GOING DOWN HILL ON A BICYCLE

A BOY'S SONG

WITH lifted feet, hands still,
I am poised, and down the hill
Dart, with heedful mind;
The air goes by in a wind.

Swifter and yet more swift,
Till the heart with a mighty lift
Makes the lungs laugh, the throat cry:—
"O bird, see; see, bird, I fly.

"Is this, is this your joy?
O bird, then I, though a boy,
For a golden moment share
Your feathery life in air!"

Say, heart, is there aught like this
In a world that is full of bliss?
'Tis more than skating, bound
Steel-shod to the level ground.

Speed slackens now, I float
Awhile in my airy boat;
Till, when the wheels scarce crawl,
My feet to the treadles fall.

Alas, that the longest hill
Must end in a vale; but still,
Who climbs with toil, wheresoe'er,
Shall find wings waiting there.
                    Henry Charles Beeching [1859–1919]

PLAYGROUNDS

In summer I am very glad
    We children are so small,
For we can see a thousand things
    That men can't see at all.

They don't know much about the moss
    And all the stones they pass:
They never lie and play among
    The forests in the grass:

They walk about a long way off;
    And, when we're at the sea,
Let father stoop as best he can
    He can't find things like me.

But, when the snow is on the ground
    And all the puddles freeze,
I wish that I were very tall,
    High up above the trees.
                    Laurence Alma-Tadema [18 –

"WHO HAS SEEN THE WIND?"

Who has seen the wind?
    Neither I nor you:
But when the leaves hang trembling,
    The wind is passing through.

Who has seen the wind?
    Neither you nor I:
But when the trees bow down their heads,
    The wind is passing by.
                    Christina Georgina Rossetti [1830–1894]

THE WIND'S SONG

O WINDS that blow across the sea,
    What is the story that you bring?
Leaves clap their hands on every tree
    And birds about their branches sing.

You sing to flowers and trees and birds
    Your sea-songs over all the land.
Could you not stay and whisper words
    A little child might understand?

The roses nod to hear you sing;
    But though I listen all the day,
You never tell me anything
    Of father's ship so far away.

Its masts are taller than the trees;
    Its sails are silver in the sun;
There's not a ship upon the seas
    So beautiful as father's one.

With wings spread out it flies so fast
    It leaves the waves all white with foam.
Just whisper to me, blowing past,
    If you have seen it sailing home.

I feel your breath upon my cheek,
    And in my hair, and on my brow.
Dear winds, if you could only speak,
    I know that you would tell me now.

My father's coming home, you'd say,
    With precious presents, one, two, three;
A shawl for mother, beads for May,
    And eggs and shells for Rob and me.

The winds sing songs where'er they roam;
    The leaves all clap their little hands;
For father's ship is coming home
    With wondrous things from foreign lands.
                                Gabriel Setoun [1861–

THE PIPER ON THE HILL

A CHILD'S SONG

THERE sits a piper on the hill
  Who pipes the livelong day,
And when he pipes both loud and shrill,
  The frightened people say:
"The wind, the wind is blowing up
  'Tis rising to a gale."
The women hurry to the shore
  To watch some distant sail.
The wind, the wind, the wind, the wind,
  Is blowing to a gale.

But when he pipes all sweet and low,
  The piper on the hill,
I hear the merry women go
  With laughter, loud and shrill:
"The wind, the wind is coming south
  'Twill blow a gentle day."
They gather on the meadow-land
  To toss the yellow hay.
The wind, the wind, the wind, the wind,
  Is blowing south to-day.

And in the morn, when winter comes,
  To keep the piper warm,
The little Angels shake their wings
  To make a feather storm:
"The snow, the snow has come at last!"
  The happy children call,
And "ring around" they dance in glee,
  And watch the snowflakes fall.
The wind, the wind, the wind, the wind,
  Has spread a snowy pall.

But when at night the piper plays,
  I have not any fear,
Because God's windows open wide
  The pretty tune to hear;

And when each crowding spirit looks,
    From its star window-pane,
A watching mother may behold
    Her little child again.
The wind, the wind, the wind, the wind,
    May blow her home again.
           Dora Sigerson Shorter [1862–1918]

THE WIND AND THE MOON

SAID the Wind to the Moon, "I will blow you out;
    You stare
    In the air
    Like a ghost in a chair,
Always looking what I am about—
I hate to be watched; I'll blow you out."

The Wind blew hard, and out went the Moon.
    So, deep
    On a heap
    Of clouds to sleep,
Down lay the Wind, and slumbered soon,
Muttering low, "I've done for that Moon."

He turned in his bed; she was there again!
    On high
    In the sky,
    With her one ghost eye,
The Moon shone white and alive and plain.
Said the Wind, "I will blow you out again."

The Wind blew hard, and the Moon grew dim.
    "With my sledge,
    And my wedge,
    I have knocked off her edge!
If only I blow right fierce and grim,
The creature will soon be dimmer than dim."

He blew and he blew, and she thinned to a thread.
    "One puff
    More 's enough
    To blow her to snuff!
One good puff more where the last was bred,
And glimmer, glimmer, glum will go the thread."

He blew a great blast, and the thread was gone.
    In the air
    Nowhere
    Was a moonbeam bare;
Far off and harmless the shy stars shone—
Sure and certain the Moon was gone!

The Wind he took to his revels once more;
    On down,
    In town,
    Like a merry-mad clown,
He leaped and halloed with whistle and roar—
"What's that?"   The glimmering thread once more!

He flew in a rage—he danced and blew;
    But in vain
    Was the pain
    Of his bursting brain;
For still the broader the Moon-scrap grew,
The broader he swelled his big cheeks and blew.

Slowly she grew—till she filled the night,
    And shone
    On her throne
    In the sky alone,
A matchless, wonderful silvery light,
Radiant and lovely, the queen of the night.

Said the Wind: "What a marvel of power am I!
    With my breath,
    Good faith!
    I blew her to death—
First blew her away right out of the sky—
Then blew her in; what strength have I!"

But the Moon she knew nothing about the affair;
    For high
    In the sky,
    With her one white eye,
Motionless, miles above the air,
She had never heard the great Wind blare.

George Macdonald [1824–1905]

CHILD'S SONG IN SPRING

THE silver birch is a dainty lady,
    She wears a satin gown;
The elm tree makes the old churchyard shady,
    She will not live in town.

The English oak is a sturdy fellow,
    He gets his green coat late;
The willow is smart in a suit of yellow,
    While brown the beech trees wait.

Such a gay green gown God gives the larches—
    As green as He is good!
The hazels hold up their arms for arches
    When Spring rides through the wood.

The chestnut's proud, and the lilac's pretty,
    The poplar's gentle and tall,
But the plane tree's kind to the poor dull city—
    I love him best of all!

Edith Nesbit [1858–1924]

BABY SEED SONG

LITTLE brown brother, oh! little brown brother,
    Are you awake in the dark?
Here we lie cosily, close to each other:
    Hark to the song of the lark—
"Waken!" the lark says, "waken and dress you;
    Put on your green coats and gay,
Blue sky will shine on you, sunshine caress you—
    Waken! 'tis morning—'tis May!"

Little brown brother, oh! little brown brother,
 What kind of flower will you be?
I'll be a poppy—all white, like my mother;
 Do be a poppy like me.
What! you're a sun-flower? How I shall miss you
 When you're grown golden and high!
But I shall send all the bees up to kiss you;
 Little brown brother, good-bye.

     Edith Nesbit [1858–1924]

LITTLE DANDELION

Gay little Dandelion
 Lights up the meads,
Swings on her slender foot,
 Telleth her beads,
Lists to the robin's note
 Poured from above;
Wise little Dandelion
 Asks not for love.

Cold lie the daisy banks
 Clothed but in green,
Where, in the days agone,
 Bright hues were seen.
Wild pinks are slumbering,
 Violets delay;
True little Dandelion
 Greeteth the May.

Brave little Dandelion!
 Fast falls the snow,
Bending the daffodil's
 Haughty head low.
Under that fleecy tent,
 Careless of cold,
Blithe little Dandelion
 Counteth her gold.

Meek little Dandelion
 Groweth more fair,
Till dies the amber dew
 Out from her hair.

High rides the thirsty sun,
　Fiercely and high;
Faint little Dandelion
　Closeth her eye.

Pale little Dandelion,
　In her white shroud,
Heareth the angel-breeze
　Call from the cloud;
Tiny plumes fluttering
　Make no delay;
Little winged Dandelion
　Soareth away.

Helen Barron Bostwick [1826– ?]

LITTLE WHITE LILY

From " Within and Without "

LITTLE White Lily sat by a stone,
Drooping and waiting till the sun shone.
Little White Lily sunshine has fed;
Little White Lily is lifting her head.

Little White Lily said: "It is good,
Little White Lily's clothing and food."
Little White Lily dressed like a bride!
Shining with whiteness, and crownèd beside!

Little White Lily drooping with pain,
Waiting and waiting for the wet rain,
Little White Lily holdeth her cup;
Rain is fast falling and filling it up.

Little White Lily said: "Good again,
When I am thirsty to have the nice rain.
Now I am stronger, now I am cool;
Heat cannot burn me, my veins are so full."

Little White Lily smells very sweet;
On her head sunshine, rain at her feet.
Thanks to the sunshine, thanks to the rain,
Little White Lily is happy again.

George Macdonald [1824–190-]

WISHING

RING–TING! I wish I were a Primrose,
A bright yellow Primrose, blowing in the Spring!
  The stooping bough above me,
  The wandering bee to love me,
The fern and moss to creep across,
    And the Elm-tree for our King!

Nay,—stay! I wish I were an Elm-tree,
A great lofty Elm-tree, with green leaves gay!
  The winds would set them dancing,
  The sun and moonshine glance in,
The Birds would house among the boughs,
    And sweetly sing!

O—no! I wish I were a Robin,
A Robin or a little Wren, everywhere to go;
  Through forest, field, or garden,
  And ask no leave or pardon,
Till Winter comes with icy thumbs
    To ruffle up our wing.

Well—tell! Where should I fly to,
Where go to sleep in the dark wood or dell?
  Before a day was over,
  Home comes the rover,
For Mother's kiss,—sweeter this
    Than any other thing!
                    William Allingham [1824–1889]

IN THE GARDEN

I SPIED beside the garden bed
    A tiny lass of ours,
Who stopped and bent her sunny head
    Above the red June flowers.

Pushing the leaves and thorns apart,
    She singled out a rose,
And in its inmost crimson heart,
    Enraptured, plunged her nose.

"O dear, dear rose, come, tell me true—
  Come, tell me true," said she,
"If I smell just as sweet to you
  As you smell sweet to me!"

Ernest Crosby [1856–1907]

THE GLADNESS OF NATURE

Is this a time to be cloudy and sad,
  When our mother Nature laughs around;
When even the deep blue heavens look glad,
  And gladness breathes from the blossoming ground?

There are notes of joy from the hang-bird and wren,
  And the gossip of swallows through all the sky;
The ground-squirrel gaily chirps by his den,
  And the wilding bee hums merrily by.

The clouds are at play in the azure space
  And their shadows at play on the bright-green vale,
And here they stretch to the frolic chase,
  And there they roll on the easy gale.

There's a dance of leaves in that aspen bower,
  There's a titter of winds in that beechen tree,
There's a smile on the fruit, and a smile on the flower,
  And a laugh from the brook that runs to the sea.

And look at the broad-faced sun, how he smiles
  On the dewy earth that smiles in his ray,
On the leaping waters and gay young isles;
  Ay, look, and he'll smile thy gloom away.

William Cullen Bryant [1794–1878]

GLAD DAY

Here's another day, dear,
Here's the sun again
Peeping in his pleasant way
Through the window pane.

Rise and let him in, dear,
Hail him "hip hurray!"
Now the fun will all begin.
Here's another day!

Down the coppice path, dear,
Through the dewy glade,
(When the Morning took her bath
What a splash she made!)
Up the wet wood-way, dear,
Under dripping green
Run to meet another day,
Brightest ever seen.

Mushrooms in the field, dear,
Show their silver gleam.
What a dainty crop they yield
Firm as clouted cream,
Cool as balls of snow, dear,
Sweet and fresh and round!
Ere the early dew can go
We must clear the ground.

Such a lot to do, dear,
Such a lot to see!
How we ever can get through
Fairly puzzles me.
Hurry up and out, dear,
Then—away! away!
In and out and round about,
Here's another day!

W. Graham Robertson [1867

THE TIGER

TIGER! Tiger! burning bright,
In the forests of the night,
What immortal hand or eye
Could frame thy fearful symmetry?

In what distant deeps or skies
Burnt the fire of thine eyes?
On what wings dare he aspire?
What the hand dare seize the fire?

And what shoulder, and what art,
Could twist the sinews of thy heart?
And when thy heart began to beat,
What dread hand and what dread feet?

What the hammer? what the chain?
In what furnace was thy brain?
What the anvil? what dread grasp
Dare its deadly terrors clasp?

When the stars threw down their spears,
And watered heaven with their tears,
Did He smile His work to see?
Did He who made the Lamb, make thee?

Tiger! Tiger! burning bright,
In the forests of the night,
What immortal hand or eye
Dare frame thy fearful symmetry?
                    William Blake [1757–1827]

ANSWER TO A CHILD'S QUESTION

Do you ask what the birds say? The Sparrow, the Dove,
The Linnet and Thrush say, "I love and I love!"
In the winter they're silent—the wind is so strong;
What it says, I don't know, but it sings a loud song.
But green leaves, and blossoms, and sunny warm weather,
And singing, and loving—all come back together.
But the Lark is so brimful of gladness and love,
The green fields below him, the blue sky above,
That he sings, and he sings, and for ever sings he—
"I love my Love, and my Love loves me!"
                    Samuel Taylor Coleridge [1772–1834]

HOW THE LEAVES CAME DOWN

I'LL tell you how the leaves came down.
    The great Tree to his children said:
"You're getting sleepy, Yellow and Brown,
    Yes, very sleepy, little Red.
    It is quite time to go to bed."

"Ah!" begged each silly, pouting leaf,
    "Let us a little longer stay;
Dear Father Tree, behold our grief!
    'Tis such a very pleasant day,
    We do not want to go away."

So, just for one more merry day
    To the great Tree the leaflets clung,
Frolicked and danced, and had their way,
    Upon the autumn breezes swung,
    Whispering all their sports among—

"Perhaps the great Tree will forget,
    And let us stay until the spring,
If we all beg, and coax, and fret."
    But the great Tree did no such thing;
    He smiled to hear them whispering.

"Come, children, all to bed," he cried;
    And ere the leaves could urge their prayer,
He shook his head, and far and wide,
    Fluttering and rustling everywhere,
    Down sped the leaflets through the air.

I saw them; on the ground they lay,
    Golden and red, a huddled swarm,
Waiting till one from far away,
    White bedclothes heaped upon her arm,
    Should come to wrap them safe and warm.

The great bare Tree looked down and smiled.
    "Goodnight, dear little leaves," he said.
And from below each sleepy child
    Replied, "Goodnight," and murmurèd,
    "It is *so* nice to go to bed!"

Susan Coolidge [1835-1905]

A LEGEND OF THE NORTHLAND

Away, away in the Northland,
  Where the hours of the day are few,
And the nights are so long in winter
  That they cannot sleep them through;

Where they harness the swift reindeer
  To the sledges, when it snows;
And the children look like bear's cubs
  In their funny, furry clothes:

They tell them a curious story—
  I don't believe 'tis true;
And yet you may learn a lesson
  If I tell the tale to you.

Once, when the good Saint Peter
  Lived in the world below,
And walked about it, preaching,
  Just as he did, you know,

He came to the door of a cottage,
  In traveling round the earth,
Where a little woman was making cakes,
  And baking them on the hearth;

And being faint with fasting,
  For the day was almost done,
He asked her, from her store of cakes,
  To give him a single one.

So she made a very little cake,
  But as it baking lay,
She looked at it, and thought it seemed
  Too large to give away.

Therefore she kneaded another,
  And still a smaller one;
But it looked, when she turned it over,
  As large as the first had done.

Then she took a tiny scrap of dough,
   And rolled and rolled it flat;
And baked it thin as a wafer—
   But she couldn't part with that.

For she said, "My cakes that seem too small
   When I eat of them myself,
Are yet too large to give away."
   So she put them on the shelf.

Then good Saint Peter grew angry,
   For he was hungry and faint;
And surely such a woman
   Was enough to provoke a saint.

And he said, "You are far too selfish
   To dwell in a human form,
To have both food and shelter,
   And fire to keep you warm.

"Now, you shall build as the birds do,
   And shall get your scanty food
By boring, and boring, and boring,
   All day in the hard, dry wood."

Then up she went through the chimney,
   Never speaking a word,
And out of the top flew a woodpecker,
   For she was changed to a bird.

She had a scarlet cap on her head,
   And that was left the same,
But all the rest of her clothes were burned
   Black as a coal in the flame.

And every country school-boy
   Has seen her in the wood,
Where she lives in the trees till this very day,
   Boring and boring for food.

And this is the lesson she teaches:
   Live not for yourself alone,
Lest the needs you will not pity
   Shall one day be your own.

Give plenty of what is given to you,
    Listen to pity's call;
Don't think the little you give is great,
    And the much you get is small.

Now, my little boy, remember that,
    And try to be kind and good,
When you see the woodpecker's sooty dress,
    And see her scarlet hood.

You mayn't be changed to a bird though you live
    As selfishly as you can;
But you will be changed to a smaller thing—
    A mean and selfish man.

Phœbe Cary [1824–1871]

THE CRICKET'S STORY

THE high and mighty lord of Glendare,
The owner of acres both broad and fair,
Searched, once on a time, his vast domains,
His deep, green forest, and yellow plains,
For some rare singer, to make complete
The studied charms of his country-seat;
But found, for all his pains and labors,
No sweeter songster than had his neighbors.

Ah, what shall my lord of the manor do?
He pondered the day and the whole night through.
He called on the gentry of hill-top and dale;
And at last on Madame the Nightingale,—
Inviting, in his majestical way,
Her pupils to sing at his grand soiree,
That perchance among them my lord might find
Some singer to whom his heart inclined.
What wonder, then, when the evening came,
And the castle gardens were all aflame
With the many curious lights that hung
O'er the ivied porches, and flared among
The grand old trees and the banners proud,
That many a heart beat high and loud,

While the famous choir of Glendare Bog,
Established and led by the Brothers Frog,
Sat thrumming as hoarsely as they were able,
In front of the manager's mushroom table!

The overture closed with a crash—then, hark!
Across the stage comes the sweet-voiced Lark.
She daintily sways, with an airy grace,
And flutters a bit of gossamer lace,
While the leafy alcove echoes and thrills
With her liquid runs and lingering trills.
Miss Goldfinch came next, in her satin gown,
And shaking her feathery flounces down,
With much expression and feeling sung
Some "Oh's" and "Ah's" in a foreign tongue;
While to give the affair a classic tone,
Miss Katydid rendered a song of her own,
In which each line closed as it had begun,
With some wonderful deed which she had done.
Then the Misses Sparrow, so prim and set,
Twittered and chirped through a long duet;
And poor little Wren, who tried with a will,
But who couldn't tell "Heber" from "Ortonville,"
Unconscious of sarcasm, piped away
And courtesied low o'er a huge bouquet
Of crimson clover-heads, culled by the dozen,
By some brown-coated, plebeian cousin.

But you should have heard the red Robin sing
His English ballad, "Come, beautiful Spring!"
And Master Owlet's melodious tune,
"O, meet me under the silvery moon!"
Then, as flighty Miss Humming-bird didn't care
To sing for the high and mighty Glendare,
The close of the evening's performance fell
To the fair young Nightingale, Mademoiselle.
Ah! the wealth of each wonderful note
That came from the depths of her tiny throat!
She carolled, she trilled, and she held her breath,
Till she seemed to hang at the point of death:

She ran the chromatics through every key,
And ended triumphant on upper C;
Airing the graces her mother had taught her
In a manner quite worthy of Madame's daughter.

But his lordship glared down the leafy aisle
With never so much as a nod or smile,
Till, out in the shade of a blackberry thicket,
He all of a sudden spied little Miss Cricket;
And, roused from his gloom, like an angry bat,
He sternly demanded, "Who is that?"
"Miss Cricket, my lord, may it please you so,
A charity scholar—ahem!—you know—
Quite worthy, of course, but we couldn't bring"—
Thundered His Mightiness, "Let her sing!"
The Nightingale opened her little eyes
Extremely wide in her blank surprise;
But catching a glimpse of his lordship's rage,
Led little Miss Cricket upon the stage,
Where she modestly sang, in her simple measures,
Of "Home, sweet Home," and its humble pleasures.
And the lord of Glendare cried out in his glee,
"This little Miss Cricket shall sing for me!"

Of course, of comment there was no need;
But the world said, "Really!" and "Ah, indeed!"
Yet, notwithstanding, we find it true
As his lordship does will the neighbors do;
So this is the way, as the legends tell,
In the very beginning it befell
That the Crickets came, in the evening's gloom,
To sing at our hearths of "Home, sweet Home."

Emma Huntington Nason [1845–1921]

THE SINGING–LESSON

A NIGHTINGALE made a mistake;
    She sang a few notes out of tune;
Her heart was ready to break,
    And she hid away from the moon.

She wrung her claws, poor thing!
  But was far too proud to weep;
She tucked her head under her wing,
  And pretended to be asleep.

A lark, arm in arm with a thrush,
  Came sauntering up to the place;
The nightingale felt herself blush,
  Though feathers hid her face.
She knew they had heard her song,
  She felt them snicker and sneer;
She thought that life was too long,
  And wished she could skip a year.

"Oh, Nightingale," cooed a dove—
  "Oh, Nightingale, what's the use?
You bird of beauty and love,
  Why behave like a goose?
Don't skulk away from our sight,
  Like a common, contemptible fowl;
You bird of joy and delight,
  Why behave like an owl?

"Only think of all you have done,
  Only think of all you can do;
A false note is really fun
  From such a bird as you!
Lift up your proud little crest,
  Open your musical beak;
Other birds have to do their best—
  You need only to speak."

The nightingale shyly took
  Her head from under her wing,
And, giving the dove a look,
  Straightway began to sing.
There was never a bird could pass;
  The night was divinely calm,
And the people stood on the grass
  To hear that wonderful psalm.

The nightingale did not care;
　　She only sang to the skies;
Her song ascended there,
　　And there she fixed her eyes.
The people that stood below
　　She knew but little about;
And this tale has a moral, I know,
　　If you'll try to find it out.

Jean Ingelow [1820–1897]

CHANTICLEER

OF all the birds from East to West
　　That tuneful are and dear,
I love that farmyard bird the best,
　　They call him Chanticleer.

Gold plume and copper plume,
　　Comb of scarlet gay;
'Tis he that scatters night and gloom,
　　And whistles back the day!

He is the sun's brave herald
　　That, ringing his blithe horn,
Calls round a world dew-pearled
　　The heavenly airs of morn.

O clear gold, shrill and bold!
　　He calls through creeping mist
The mountains from the night and cold
　　To rose and amethyst.

He sets the birds to singing,
　　And calls the flowers to rise;
The morning cometh, bringing
　　Sweet sleep to heavy eyes.

Gold plume and silver plume,
　　Comb of coral gay;
'Tis he packs off the night and gloom,
　　And summons home the day!

Black fear he sends it flying,
   Black care he drives afar;
And creeping shadows sighing
   Before the morning star.

The birds of all the forest
   Have dear and pleasant cheer,
But yet I hold the rarest
   The farmyard Chanticleer.

Red cock or black cock,
   Gold cock or white,
The flower of all the feathered flock,
   He whistles back the light!
       Katherine Tynan Hinkson [1861–1931]

"WHAT DOES LITTLE BIRDIE SAY?"

From "Sea Dreams"

WHAT does little birdie say
In her nest at peep of day?
Let me fly, says little birdie,
Mother, let me fly away.
Birdie, rest a little longer,
Till the little wings are stronger.
So she rests a little longer,
Then she flies away.

What does little baby say,
In her bed at peep of day?
Baby says, like little birdie,
Let me rise and fly away.
Baby, sleep a little longer,
Till the little limbs are stronger,
If she sleeps a little longer,
Baby too shall fly away.
       Alfred Tennyson [1809–1892]

NURSE'S SONG

WHEN the voices of children are heard on the green
  And laughing is heard on the hill,
My heart is at rest within my breast,
  And everything else is still.

"Then come home, my children, the sun is gone down,
  And the dews of the night arise;
Come, come, leave off play, and let us away
  Till the morning appears in the skies."

"No, no, let us play, for it is yet day,
  And we cannot go to sleep;
Besides in the sky the little birds fly,
  And the hills are all covered with sheep."

"Well, well, go and play till the light fades away,
  And then go home to bed."
The little ones leaped and shouted and laughed;
  And all the hills echoèd.

William Blake [1757–1827]

JACK FROST

THE door was shut, as doors should be,
  Before you went to bed last night;
Yet Jack Frost has got in, you see,
  And left your window silver white.

He must have waited till you slept;
  And not a single word he spoke,
But pencilled o'er the panes and crept
  Away again before you woke.

And now you cannot see the hills
  Nor fields that stretch beyond the lane;
But there are fairer things than these
  His fingers traced on every pane.

Rocks and castles towering high;
  Hills and dales, and streams and fields;
And knights in armor riding by,
  With nodding plumes and shining shields.

And here are little boats, and there
  Big ships with sails spread to the breeze;
And yonder, palm trees waving fair
  On islands set in silver seas.

And butterflies with gauzy wings;
  And herds of cows and flocks of sheep;
And fruit and flowers and all the things
  You see when you are sound asleep.

For creeping softly underneath
  The door when all the lights are out,
Jack Frost takes every breath you breathe,
  And knows the things you think about.

He paints them on the window pane
  In fairy lines with frozen steam;
And when you wake you see again
  The lovely things you saw in dream.

                    Gabriel Setoun [1861–

OCTOBER'S PARTY

October gave a party;
  The leaves by hundreds came—
The Chestnuts, Oaks, and Maples,
  And leaves of every name.
The Sunshine spread a carpet,
  And everything was grand,
Miss Weather led the dancing,
  Professor Wind the band.

The Chestnuts came in yellow,
  The Oaks in crimson dressed;
The lovely Misses Maple
  In scarlet looked their best;

All balanced to their partners,
  And gaily fluttered by;
The sight was like a rainbow
  New fallen from the sky.

Then, in the rustic hollow,
  At hide-and-seek they played,
The party closed at sundown,
  And everybody stayed.
Professor Wind played louder;
  They flew along the ground;
And then the party ended
  In jolly "hands around."

George Cooper [1840–1927]

THE SHEPHERD

How sweet is the Shepherd's sweet lot!
From the morn to the evening he strays;
He shall follow his sheep all the day,
And his tongue shall be fillèd with praise.
For he hears the lamb's innocent call,
And he hears the ewe's tender reply;
He is watchful, while they are in peace,
For they know when their Shepherd is nigh.

William Blake [1757–1827]

NIKOLINA

O TELL me, little children, have you seen her—
The tiny maid from Norway, Nikolina?
O, her eyes are blue as cornflowers, mid the corn,
And her cheeks are rosy red as skies of morn!

Nikolina! swift she turns if any call her,
As she stands among the poppies, hardly taller,
Breaking off their scarlet cups for you,
With spikes of slender larkspur, burning blue.

In her little garden many a flower is growing—
Red, gold, and purple in the soft wind blowing,
But the child that stands amid the blossoms gay
Is sweeter, quainter, brighter e'en than they.

Celia Thaxter [1835–1894]

LITTLE GUSTAVA

LITTLE Gustava sits in the sun,
Safe in the porch, and the little drops run
From the icicles under the eaves so fast,
For the bright spring sun shines warm at last,
    And glad is little Gustava.

She wears a quaint little scarlet cap,
And a little green bowl she holds in her lap,
Filled with bread and milk to the brim,
And a wreath of marigolds round the rim:
    "Ha! ha!" laughs little Gustava.

Up comes her little gray coaxing cat
With her little pink nose, and she mews, "What's that?"
Gustava feeds her,—she begs for more;
And a little brown hen walks in at the door:
    "Good day!" cries little Gustava.

She scatters crumbs for the little brown hen.
There comes a rush and a flutter, and then
Down fly her little white doves so sweet,
With their snowy wings and crimson feet:
    "Welcome!" cries little Gustava.

So dainty and eager they pick up the crumbs.
But who is this through the doorway comes?
Little Scotch terrier, little dog Rags,
Looks in her face, and his funny tail wags:
    "Ha! ha!" laughs little Gustava.

"You want some breakfast too?" and down
She sets her bowl on the brick floor brown;
And little dog Rags drinks up her milk,
While she strokes his shaggy locks like silk:
    "Dear Rags!" says little Gustava.

Waiting without stood sparrow and crow,
Cooling their feet in the melting snow:
"Won't you come in, good folk?" she cried.
But they were too bashful, and stood outside
    Though "Pray come in!" cried Gustava.

So the last she threw them, and knelt on the mat
With doves and biddy and dog and cat.
And her mother came to the open house-door:
"Dear little daughter, I bring you some more.
   My merry little Gustava!"

Kitty and terrier, biddy and doves,
All things harmless Gustava loves.
The shy, kind creatures 'tis joy to feed,
And oh, her breakfast is sweet indeed
   To happy little Gustava!

Celia Thaxter [1835–1894]

PRINCE TATTERS

LITTLE Prince Tatters has lost his cap!
   Over the hedge he threw it;
Into the river it fell "kerslap!"
   Stupid old thing to do it!
Now Mother may sigh and Nurse may fume
For the gay little cap with its eagle plume.
"One cannot be thinking all day of such matters!
Trifles are trifles!" says little Prince Tatters.

Little Prince Tatters has lost his coat!
   Playing, he did not need it;
"Left it *right there*, by the nanny-goat,
   And nobody never seed it!"
Now Mother and Nurse may search till night
For the little new coat with its buttons bright;
But—"Coat-sleeves or shirt-sleeves, how little it matters!
Trifles are trifles!" says little Prince Tatters.

Little Prince Tatters has LOST HIS BALL!
   Rolled away down the street!
Somebody'll *have to find it*, that's all,
   Before he can sleep or eat.
Now raise the neighborhood, quickly, do!
And send for the crier and constable too!
"Trifles are trifles; but serious matters,
They must be *seen to*," says little Prince Tatters.

Laura E. Richards [1850–

THE LITTLE BLACK BOY

My mother bore me in the southern wild,
   And I am black, but oh, my soul is white!
White as an angel is the English child,
   But I am black, as if bereaved of light.

My mother taught me underneath a tree,
   And, sitting down before the heat of day,
She took me on her lap and kissèd me,
   And, pointing to the East, began to say:

"Look on the rising sun,—there God does live,
   And gives His light, and gives His heat away;
And flowers and trees and beasts and men receive
   Comfort in morning, joy in the noonday.

"And we are put on earth a little space,
   That we may learn to bear the beams of love;
And these black bodies and this sunburnt face
   Are but a cloud, and like a shady grove.

"For, when our souls have learned the heat to bear,
   The cloud will vanish, we shall hear His voice,
Saying: 'Come out from the grove, My love and care,
   And round My golden tent like lambs rejoice.'"

Thus did my mother say, and kissèd me;
   And thus I say to little English boy.
When I from black, and he from white cloud free,
   And round the tent of God like lambs we joy,

I'll shade him from the heat, till he can bear
   To lean in joy upon our Father's knee;
And then I'll stand and stroke his silver hair,
   And be like him, and he will then love me.
                  William Blake [1757–1827]

THE BLIND BOY

O SAY what is that thing called Light,
   Which I must ne'er enjoy;
What are the blessings of the sight,
   O tell your poor blind boy!

You talk of wondrous things you see,
   You say the sun shines bright;
I feel him warm, but how can he,
   Or make it day or night?

My day or night myself I make
   Whene'er I sleep or play;
And could I ever keep awake
   With me 'twere always day.

With heavy sighs I often hear
   You mourn my hapless woe;
But sure with patience I can bear
   A loss I ne'er can know.

Then let not what I cannot have
   My cheer of mind destroy:
Whilst thus I sing, I am a king,
   Although a poor blind boy.
                    Colley Cibber [1671-1757]

BUNCHES OF GRAPES

"BUNCHES of grapes," says Timothy,
   "Pomegranates pink," says Elaine;
"A junket of cream and a cranberry tart
   For me," says Jane.

"Love-in-a-mist," says Timothy,
   "Primroses pale," says Elaine;

"A nosegay of pinks and mignonette
  For me," says Jane.

"Chariots of gold," says Timothy,
  "Silvery wings," says Elaine;
"A bumpety ride in a wagon of hay
  For me," says Jane.

Walter de la Mare [1873–

MY SHADOW

I HAVE a little shadow that goes in and out with me,
And what can be the use of him is more than I can see.
He is very, very like me from the heels up to the head;
And I see him jump before me, when I jump into my bed.

The funniest thing about him is the way he likes to grow —
Not at all like proper children, which is always very slow;
For he sometimes shoots up taller like an India-rubber ball,
And he sometimes gets so little that there's none of him
    at all.

He hasn't got a notion of how children ought to play,
And can only make a fool of me in every sort of way.
He stays so close beside me, he's a coward you can see;
I'd think shame to stick to nursie as that shadow sticks to
    me!

One morning, very early, before the sun was up,
I rose and found the shining dew on every buttercup;
But my lazy little shadow, like an arrant sleepy-head,
Had stayed at home behind me and was fast asleep in bed.

Robert Louis Stevenson [1850–1894]

THE LAND OF COUNTERPANE

WHEN I was sick and lay a-bed,
I had two pillows at my head,
And all my toys beside me lay
To keep me happy all the day.

And sometimes for an hour or so
I watched my leaden soldiers go,
With different uniforms and drills,
Among the bed-clothes, through the hills;

And sometimes sent my ships in fleets
All up and down among the sheets;
Or brought my trees and houses out,
And planted cities all about.

I was the giant great and still
That sits upon the pillow-hill,
And sees before him, dale and plain,
The pleasant land of counterpane.

Robert Louis Stevenson [1850–1894]

THE LAND OF STORY-BOOKS

AT evening when the lamp is lit,
Around the fire my parents sit;
They sit at home and talk and sing,
And do not play at anything.

Now, with my little gun, I crawl
All in the dark along the wall,
And follow round the forest track
Away behind the sofa back.

There, in the night, where none can spy,
All in my hunter's camp I lie,
And play at books that I have read
Till it is time to go to bed.

These are the hills, these are the woods,
These are my starry solitudes;
And there the river by whose brink
The roaring lions come to drink.

I see the others far away
As if in firelit camp they lay,
And I, like to an Indian scout,
Around their party prowled about.

So, when my nurse comes in for me,
Home I return across the sea,
And go to bed with backward looks
At my dear land of Story-books.

Robert Louis Stevenson [1850–1894]

THE GARDENER

THE gardener does not love to talk,
He makes me keep the gravel walk;
And when he puts his tools away,
He locks the door and takes the key.

Away behind the currant row
Where no one else but cook may go,
Far in the plots, I see him dig,
Old and serious, brown and big.

He digs the flowers, green, red, and blue,
Nor wishes to be spoken to.
He digs the flowers and cuts the hay,
And never seems to want to play.

Silly gardener! summer goes,
And winter comes with pinching toes,
When in the garden bare and brown
You must lay your barrow down.

Well now, and while the summer stays,
To profit by these garden days
O how much wiser you would be
To play at Indian wars with me!

Robert Louis Stevenson [1850–1894]

FOREIGN LANDS

UP into the cherry tree
Who should climb but little me?
I held the trunk with both my hands
And looked abroad on foreign lands.

I saw the next door garden lie,
Adorned with flowers, before my eye,
And many pleasant places more
That I had never seen before.

I saw the dimpling river pass
And be the sky's blue looking-glass;
The dusty roads go up and down
With people tramping in to town.

If I could find a higher tree,
Farther and farther I should see,
To where the grown-up river slips
Into the sea among the ships;

To where the roads on either hand
Lead onward into fairy land,
Where all the children dine at five,
And all the playthings come alive.
Robert Louis Stevenson [1850-1894]

MY BED IS A BOAT

My bed is like a little boat;
   Nurse helps me in when I embark;
She girds me in my sailor's coat
   And starts me in the dark.

At night, I go on board and say
   Good night to all my friends on shore;
I shut my eyes and sail away
   And see and hear no more.

And sometimes things to bed I take,
   As prudent sailors have to do;
Perhaps a slice of wedding-cake,
   Perhaps a toy or two.

All night across the dark we steer;
   But when the day returns at last,
Safe in my room, beside the pier,
   I find my vessel fast.
Robert Louis Stevenson [1850-1894]

THE PEDDLER'S CARAVAN

I WISH I lived in a caravan,
With a horse to drive, like a peddler-man!
Where he comes from nobody knows,
Or where he goes to, but on he goes!

His caravan has windows two,
And a chimney of tin, that the smoke comes through;
He has a wife, with a baby brown,
And they go riding from town to town.

Chairs to mend, and delf to sell!
He clashes the basins like a bell;
Tea-trays, baskets ranged in order,
Plates, with alphabets round the border!

The roads are brown, and the sea is green,
But his house is like a bathing-machine;
The world is round, and he can ride,
Rumble and slash, to the other side!

With the peddler-man I should like to roam,
And write a book when I came home;
All the people would read my book,
Just like the Travels of Captain Cook!
                    William Brighty Rands [1823–1882]

MR. COGGS

A WATCH will tell the time of day,
Or tell it nearly, any way,
Excepting when it's overwound,
Or when you drop it on the ground.

If any of our watches stop,
We haste to Mr. Coggs's shop;
For though to scold us he pretends,
He's quite among our special friends.

He fits a dice-box in his eye,
And takes a long and thoughtful spy,
And prods the wheels, and says, "Dear, dear!
More carelessness, I greatly fear."

And then he lays the dice-box down
And frowns a most prodigious frown;
But if we ask him what's the time,
He'll make his gold repeater chime.
                    Edward Verrall Lucas [1868–

THE BUILDING OF THE NEST

THEY'LL come again to the apple tree—
  Robin and all the rest—
When the orchard branches are fair to see,
  In the snow of the blossoms dressed;
And the prettiest thing in the world will be
  The building of the nest.

Weaving it well, so round and trim,
  Hollowing it with care,—
Nothing too far away for him,
  Nothing for her too fair,—
Hanging it safe on the topmost limb,
  Their castle in the air.

Ah! mother bird, you'll have weary days
  When the eggs are under your breast,
And shadow may darken the dancing rays
  When the wee ones leave the nest;
But they'll find their wings in a glad amaze.
  And God will see to the rest.

So come to the trees with all your train
  When the apple blossoms blow;
Through the April shimmer of sun and rain,
  Go flying to and fro;
And sing to our hearts as we watch again
  Your fairy building grow.

                    Margaret Sangster [1838-1912]

"THERE WAS A JOLLY MILLER"

From "Love in a Village"

THERE was a jolly miller once lived on the river Dee;
He danced and sang from morn till night, no lark so blithe
    as he;
And this the burden of his song forever used to be:—
I care for nobody, no not I, if nobody cares for me.

"I live by my mill, God bless her! she's kindred, child, and
    wife;
I would not change my station for any other in life;
No lawyer, surgeon, or doctor e'er had a groat from me;
I care for nobody, no not I, if nobody cares for me."

When spring begins his merry career, oh, how his heart
    grows gay;
No summer's drought alarms his fear, nor winter's cold
    decay;
No foresight mars the miller's joy, who's wont to sing and
    say,
"Let others toil from year to year, I live from day to day."

Thus, like the miller, bold and free, let us rejoice and sing;
The days of youth are made for glee, and time is on the wing;
This song shall pass from me to thee, along the jovial ring;
Let heart and voice and all agree to say, "Long live the king."

Isaac Bickerstaff [? –1812?]

ONE AND ONE

Two little girls are better than one,
Two little boys can double the fun,
Two little birds can build a fine nest,
Two little arms can love mother best.
Two little ponies must go to a span;
Two little pockets has my little man;
Two little eyes to open and close,
Two little ears and one little nose,
Two little elbows, dimpled and sweet,
Two little shoes on two little feet,
Two little lips and one little chin,
Two little cheeks with a rose shut in;
Two little shoulders, chubby and strong,
Two little legs running all day long.
Two little prayers does my darling say,
Twice does he kneel by my side each day,
Two little folded hands, soft and brown,
Two little eyelids cast meekly down,

And two little angels guard him in bed,
"One at the foot, and one at the head."

Mary Mapes Dodge [1831–1905]

A NURSERY SONG

Oʜ, Peterkin Pout and Gregory Grout
　Are two little goblins black.
Full oft from my house I've driven them out,
　But somehow they still come back.

They clamber up to the baby's mouth,
　And pull the corners down;
They perch aloft on the baby's brow,
　And twist it into a frown.

Chorus:

And one says "Must!" and t'other says "Can't!"
And one says "Shall!" and t'other says "Shan't!"
Oh, Peterkin Pout and Gregory Grout,
I pray you now from my house keep out!

But Samuel Smile and Lemuel Laugh
　Are two little fairies bright;
They're always ready for fun and chaff,
　And sunshine is their delight.

And when they creep into Baby's eyes,
　Why, there the sunbeams are;
And when they peep through her rosy lips,
　Her laughter rings near and far.

Chorus:

And one says "Please!" and t'other says "Do!"
And both together say "I love you!"
So, Lemuel Laugh and Samuel Smile,
Come in, my dears, and tarry awhile!

Laura E. Richards [1850–

A MORTIFYING MISTAKE

I STUDIED my tables over and over, and backward and
    forward, too;
But I couldn't remember six times nine, and I didn't know
    what to do,
Till sister told me to play with my doll, and not to bother
    my head.
"If you call her 'Fifty-four' for a while, you'll learn it by
    heart," she said.

So I took my favorite, Mary Ann (though I thought 'twas
    a dreadful shame
To give such a perfectly lovely child such a perfectly horrid
    name),
And I called her my dear little "Fifty-four" a hundred
    times, till I knew
The answer of six times nine as well as the answer of two
    times two.

Next day Elizabeth Wigglesworth, who always acts so
    proud,
Said, "Six times nine is fifty-two," and I nearly laughed
    aloud!
But I wished I hadn't when teacher said, "Now, Dorothy,
    tell if you can."
For I thought of my doll and—sakes alive!—I answered,
    "*Mary Ann!*"

Anna Maria Pratt [18 –

THE RAGGEDY MAN

O THE Raggedy Man! He works fer Pa;
An' he's the goodest man ever you saw!
He comes to our house every day,
An' waters the horses, an' feeds 'em hay;
An' he opens the shed—an' we all ist laugh
When he drives out our little old wobble-ly calf;

An' nen—ef our hired girl says he can—
He milks the cow fer 'Lizabuth Ann.—
  Ain't he a' awful good Raggedy Man?
    Raggedy! Raggedy! Raggedy Man!

W'y, the Raggedy Man— he's ist so good
He splits the kindlin' an' chops the wood;
An' nen he spades in our garden, too,
An' does most things 'at boys can't do.—
He clumbed clean up in our big tree
An' shooked a' apple down fer me—
An' nother'n', too, fer 'Lizabuth Ann—
An' nother'n', too, fer the Raggedy Man.—
  Ain't he a' awful kind Raggedy Man?
    Raggedy! Raggedy! Raggedy Man!

An' the Raggedy Man, he knows most rhymes
An' tells 'em, ef I be good, sometimes:
Knows 'bout Giunts, an' Griffuns, an' Elves,
An' the Squidgicum-Squees 'at swallers therselves!
An', wite by the pump in our pasture-lot,
He showed me the hole 'at the Wunks is got,
'At lives 'way deep in the ground, an' can
Turn into me, er 'Lizabuth Ann!
Er Ma, er Pa, er the Raggedy Man!
  Ain't he a funny old Raggedy Man?
    Raggedy! Raggedy! Raggedy Man!

The Raggedy Man—one time when he
Was makin' a little bow-n'-orry fer me,
Says, "When *you're* big like your Pa is,
Air you go' to keep a fine store like his—
An' be a rich merchunt—an' wear fine clothes?—
Er what *air* you go' to be, goodness knows?"
An' nen he laughed at 'Lizabuth Ann,
An' I says " 'M go' to be a Raggedy Man!—
  I'm ist go' to be a nice Raggedy Man!"
    Raggedy! Raggedy! Raggedy Man!
                    James Whitcomb Riley [1849-1916]

THE MAN IN THE MOON

SAID the Raggedy Man, on a hot afternoon,
    "My!
        Sakes!
            What a lot o' mistakes
Some little folks makes on The Man in the Moon!
But people that's b'en up to *see* him, like *me*,
And calls on him frequent and intimutly,
Might drop a few facts that would interest you
        Clean!
            Through!—
                If you wanted 'em to—
Some *actual* facts that might interest you!

"O The Man in the Moon has a crick in his back;
        Whee!
            Whimm!
                Ain't you sorry for him?
And a mole on his nose that is purple and black;
And his eyes are so weak that they water and run
If he dares to *dream* even he looks at the sun,—
So he jes' dreams of stars, as the doctors advise—
        My!
            Eyes!
                But isn't he wise—
To jes' dream of stars, as the doctors advise?

"And The Man in the Moon has a boil on his ear,—
        Whee!
            Whing!
                What a singular thing!
I know! but these facts are authentic, my dear,—
There's a boil on his ear; and a corn on his chin,—
He calls it a dimple—but dimples stick in—
Yet it might be a dimple turned over, you know!
        Whang!
            Ho!
                Why, certainly so!—
It might be a dimple turned over, you know!

"And The Man in the Moon has a rheumatic knee,—
            Gee!
                  Whizz!
                        What a pity that is!
And his toes have worked round where his heels ought
      to be.
So whenever he wants to go North he goes *South*,
And comes back with porridge crumbs all round his
      mouth,
And he brushes them off with a Japanese fan.
            Whing!
                  Whann!
                        What a marvelous man!
What a very remarkably marvelous man!

"And The Man in the Moon," sighed the Raggedy Man,
            "Gits!
                  So!
                        Sullonesome, you know,—
Up there by hisse'f sence creation began!—
That when I call on him and then come away,
He grabs me and holds me and begs me to stay,—
Till—*Well!* if it wasn't fer *Jimmy-cum-Jim*,
            Dadd!
                  Limb!
                        I'd go pardners with him—
Jes' jump my job here and be pardners with *him!"*
                        James Whitcomb Riley [1849-1916]

LITTLE ORPHANT ANNIE

LITTLE Orphant Annie's come to our house to stay,
An' wash the cups an' saucers up, an' brush the crumbs
      away,
An' shoo the chickens off the porch, an' dust the hearth,
      an' sweep,
An' make the fire, an' bake the bread, an' earn her board
      an'-keep;

An' all us other children, when the supper things is done,
We set around the kitchen fire an' has the mostest fun
A-list'nin' to the witch-tales 'at Annie tells about,
An' the Gobble-uns 'at gits you
      Ef you
         Don't
            Watch
               Out!

Onc't they was a little boy wouldn't say his prayers—
An' when he went to bed at night, away up stairs,
His Mammy heered him holler, an' his Daddy heered him
    bawl,
An' when they turn't the kivvers down, he wasn't there at
    all!
An' they seeked him in the rafter-room, an' cubby-hole,
    an' press,
An' seeked him up the chimbly-flue, an' ever'wheres, I guess;
But all they ever found was thist his pants an' roundabout:
An' the Gobble-uns 'll git you
      Ef you
         Don't
            Watch
               Out!

An' one time a little girl 'ud allus laugh an' grin,
An' make fun of ever' one, an' all her blood-an'-kin;
An' onc't when they was "company," an' ole folks was
    there,
She mocked 'em an' shocked 'em, an' said she didn't care!
An' thist as she kicked her heels, an' turn't to run an' hide,
They was two great big Black Things a-standin' by her
    side,
An' they snatched her through the ceilin' 'fore she knowed
    what she's about!
An' the Gobble-uns 'll git you
      Ef you
         Don't
            Watch
               Out!

An' little Orphant Annie says, when the blaze is blue,
An' the lamp-wick sputters, an' the wind goes *woo-oo!*
An' you hear the crickets quit, an' the moon is gray,
An' the lightnin'-bugs in dew is all squenched away,—
You better mind yer parents, an' yer teachers fond and
    dear,
An' churish them 'at loves you, an' dry the orphant's tear,
An' he'p the pore an' needy ones 'at clusters all about,
Er the Gobble-uns 'll git you
    Ef you
      Don't
        Watch
          Out!

James Whitcomb Riley [1849–1916]

OUR HIRED GIRL

Our hired girl, she's 'Lizabuth Ann;
   An' she can cook best things to eat!
She ist puts dough in our pie-pan,
   An' pours in somepin' 'at's good an' sweet;
An' nen she salts it all on top
With cinnamon; an' nen she'll stop
   An' stoop an' slide it, ist as slow,
In th' old cook-stove, so's 'twon't slop
   An' git all spilled; nen bakes it, so
   It's custard-pie, first thing you know!
    An' nen she'll say,
     "Clear out o' my way!
   They's time fer work, an' time fer play!
    Take yer dough, an' run, child, run!
   Er I cain't git no cookin' done!"

When our hired girl 'tends like she's mad,
   An' says folks got to walk the chalk
When *she's* around, er wisht they had!
   I play out on our porch an' talk
To Th' Raggedy Man 'at mows our lawn;
An' he says, "*Whew!*" an' nen leans on
   His old crook-scythe, and blinks his eyes,
An' sniffs all 'round an' says, "I swawn!

Ef my old nose don't tell me lies,
 It 'pears like I smell custard-pies!"
  An' nen *he'll* say,
  "Clear out o' my way!
They's time fer work, an' time fer play!
 Take yer dough, an' run, child, run!
 Er she cain't git no cookin' done!"

Wunst our hired girl, when she
 Got the supper, an' we all et,
An' it wuz night, an' Ma an' me
 An' Pa went wher' the "Social" met,—
An' nen when we come home, an' see
A light in the kitchen door, an' we
 Heerd a maccordeun, Pa says, "Lan'-
O'-Gracious, who can *her* beau be?"
  An' I marched in, an' 'Lizabuth Ann
  Wuz parchin' corn fer The Raggedy Man!
  Better say,
  "Clear out o' the way!
They's time fer work, an' time fer play!
 Take the hint, an' run, child, run!
 Er we cain't git no courtin' done!"
     James Whitcomb Riley [1849-1916]

SEEIN' THINGS

I AIN'T afeard uv snakes, or toads, or bugs, or worms, or
 mice,
An' things 'at girls are skeered uv I think are awful nice!
I'm pretty brave, I guess; an' yet I hate to go to bed,
For, when I'm tucked up warm an' snug an' when my
 prayers are said,
Mother tells me "Happy Dreams!" an' takes away the light,
An' leaves me lyin' all alone an' seein' things at night!

Sometimes they're in the corner, sometimes they're by the
 door,
Sometimes they're all a-standin' in the middle uv the floor;
Sometimes they are a-sittin' down, sometimes they're
 walkin' round
So softly and so creepylike they never make a sound!

Sometimes they are as black as ink, an' other times they're
    white—
But the color ain't no difference when you see things at
    night!

Once, when I licked a feller 'at had just moved on our street,
An' father sent me up to bed without a bite to eat,
I woke up in the dark an' saw things standin' in a row,
A-lookin' at me cross-eyed an' p'intin' at me—so!
Oh, my! I wuz so skeered that time I never slep' a mite—
It's almost alluz when I'm bad I see things at night!

Lucky thing I ain't a girl, or I'd be skeered to death!
Bein' I'm a boy, I duck my head an' hold my breath;
An' I am, oh, *so* sorry I'm a naughty boy, an' then
I promise to be better an' I say my prayers again!
Gran'ma tells me that's the only way to make it right
When a feller has been wicked an' sees things at night!

An' so, when other naughty boys would coax me into sin,
I try to skwush the Tempter's voice 'at urges me within;
An' when they's pie for supper, or cakes 'at's big an' nice,
I want to—but I do not pass my plate f'r them things
    twice!
No, ruther let Starvation wipe me slowly out o' sight
Than I should keep a-livin' on an' seein' things at night!

                        Eugene Field [1850–1895]

THE DUEL

    THE gingham dog and the calico cat
    Side by side on the table sat;
      'Twas half past twelve, and (what do you think!)
      Nor one nor t'other had slept a wink!
        The old Dutch clock and the Chinese plate
        Appeared to know as sure as fate
      There was going to be a terrible spat.
           (I wasn't there: I simply state
           What was told to me by the Chinese plate!)

    The gingham dog went, "Bow-wow-wow!"
    And the calico cat replied, "Mee-ow!"
    The air was littered, an hour or so,

With bits of gingham and calico,
 While the old Dutch clock in the chimney-place
 Up with its hands before its face,
 For it always dreaded a family row!
  (*Now mind; I'm only telling you*
  What the old Dutch clock declares is true!)

The Chinese plate looked very blue,
And wailed, "Oh, dear! what shall we do!"
But the gingham dog and the calico cat
Wallowed this way and tumbled that,
 Employing every tooth and claw
 In the awfullest way you ever saw—
And, oh! how the gingham and calico flew!
  (*Don't fancy I exaggerate—*
  I got my news from the Chinese plate!)

Next morning, where the two had sat
They found no trace of dog or cat:
And some folks think unto this day
That burglars stole that pair away!
 But the truth about the cat and pup
 Is this: they ate each other up!
Now what do you really think of that!
  (*The old Dutch clock it told me so,*
  And that is how I came to know.)
       Eugene Field [1850–1895]

HOLY THURSDAY

'Twas on a Holy Thursday, their innocent faces clean,
Came children walking two and two, in red, and blue, and
 green;
Gray-headed beadles walked before, with wands as white as
 snow,
Till into the high dome of Paul's they like Thames waters
 flow.

Oh what a multitude they seemed, these flowers of London
 town!
Seated in companies they sit, with radiance all their own.

The hum of multitudes was there, but multitudes of lambs,
Thousands of little boys and girls raising their innocent
　　hands.

Now like a mighty wind they raise to heaven the voice of
　　song,
Or like harmonious thunderings the seats of heaven among:
Beneath them sit the aged men, wise guardians of the poor.
Then cherish pity, lest you drive an angel from your door.

William Blake [1757–1827]

A STORY FOR A CHILD

LITTLE one, come to my knee!
　　Hark, how the rain is pouring
Over the roof, in the pitch-black night,
　　And the wind in the woods a-roaring!

Hush, my darling, and listen,
　　Then pay for the story with kisses;
Father was lost in the pitch-black night,
　　In just such a storm as this is!

High up on the lonely mountains,
　　Where the wild men watched and waited;
Wolves in the forest, and bears in the bush,
　　And I on my path belated.

The rain and the night together
　　Came down, and the wind came after,
Bending the props of the pine-tree roof,
　　And snapping many a rafter.

I crept along in the darkness,
　　Stunned, and bruised, and blinded,—
Crept to a fir with thick-set boughs,
　　And a sheltering rock behind it.

There, from the blowing and raining,
　　Crouching, I sought to hide me:
Something rustled, two green eyes shone,
　　And a wolf lay down beside me.

Little one, be not frightened;
    I and the wolf together,
Side by side, through the long, long night,
    Hid from the awful weather.

His wet fur pressed against me;
    Each of us warmed the other;
Each of us felt, in the stormy dark,
    That beast and man was brother.

And when the falling forest
    No longer crashed in warning,
Each of us went from our hiding-place
    Forth in the wild, wet morning.

Darling, kiss me payment!
    Hark, how the wind is roaring;
Father's house is a better place
    When the stormy rain is pouring!

                    Bayard Taylor [1825-1878]

THE SPIDER AND THE FLY

"WILL you walk into my parlor?" said the Spider to the
    Fly.
"'Tis the prettiest little parlor that ever you did spy;
The way into my parlor is up a winding stair,
And I have many curious things to show when you are
    there."
"Oh no, no," said the little Fly, "to ask me is in vain;
For who goes up your winding stair can ne'er come down
    again."

"I'm sure you must be weary, dear, with soaring up so high;
Will you rest upon my little bed?" said the Spider to the
    Fly.
"There are pretty curtains drawn around, the sheets are
    fine and thin;
And if you like to rest a while, I'll snugly tuck you in!"
"Oh no, no," said the little Fly, "for I've often heard it said,
They never, never wake again, who sleep upon your bed!"

Said the cunning Spider to the Fly, "Dear friend, what can
    I do
To prove the warm affection I 've always felt for you?
I have, within my pantry, good store of all that 's nice;
I 'm sure you 're very welcome—will you please to take a
    slice?"
"Oh no, no," said the little Fly, "kind sir, that cannot be,
I 've heard what 's in your pantry, and I do not wish to see!"

"Sweet creature," said the Spider, "you 're witty and
    you 're wise;
How handsome are your gauzy wings, how brilliant are
    your eyes!
I have a little looking-glass upon my parlor shelf;
If you 'll step in one moment, dear, you shall behold your-
    self."
"I thank you, gentle sir," she said, "for what you 're
    pleased to say,
And bidding you good morning now, I 'll call another day."

The Spider turned him round about, and went into his den,
For well he knew the silly Fly would soon be back again;
So he wove a subtle web in a little corner sly,
And set his table ready to dine upon the Fly.
Then he came out to his door again, and merrily did sing,—
"Come hither, hither, pretty Fly, with the pearl and silver
    wing;
Your robes are green and purple, there 's a crest upon your
    head;
Your eyes are like the diamond bright, but mine are dull as
    lead."

Alas, alas! how very soon this silly little Fly,
Hearing his wily, flattering words, came slowly flitting by:
With buzzing wings she hung aloft, then near and nearer
    drew,—
Thinking only of her brilliant eyes, and green and purple
    hue;
Thinking only of her crested head—poor foolish thing! At
    last,
Up jumped the cunning Spider, and fiercely held her fast.

He dragged her up his winding stair, into his dismal den
Within his little parlor—but she ne'er came out again!

And now, dear little children, who may this story read,
To idle, silly, flattering words, I pray you ne'er give heed;
Unto an evil counsellor close heart, and ear, and eye,
And take a lesson from this tale of the Spider and the Fly.
Mary Howitt [1799–1888]

BALLAD OF THE TEMPEST

WE were crowded in the cabin,
    Not a soul would dare to sleep,—
It was midnight on the waters,
    And a storm was on the deep.

'Tis a fearful thing in winter
    To be shattered by the blast,
And to hear the rattling trumpet
    Thunder, "Cut away the mast!"

So we shuddered there in silence,—
    For the stoutest held his breath,
While the hungry sea was roaring
    And the breakers talked with death.

As thus we sat in darkness,
    Each one busy with his prayers,
"We are lost!" the captain shouted,
    As he staggered down the stairs.

But his little daughter whispered,
    As she took his icy hand,
"Isn't God upon the ocean,
    Just the same as on the land?"

Then we kissed the little maiden,
    And we spake in better cheer,
And we anchored safe in harbor
    When the morn was shining clear.
James Thomas Fields [1816–1881]

THE NIGHTINGALE AND GLOW-WORM

A NIGHTINGALE, that all day long
Had cheered the village with his song,
Nor yet at eve his note suspended,
Nor yet when eventide was ended,
Began to feel, as well he might,
The keen demands of appetite;
When, looking eagerly around,
He spied far off, upon the ground,
A something shining in the dark,
And knew the glow-worm by his spark;
So, stooping down from hawthorn top,
He thought to put him in his crop.
The worm, aware of his intent,
Harangued him thus, right eloquent:
"Did you admire my lamp," quoth he,
"As much as I your minstrelsy,
You would abhor to do me wrong,
As much as I to spoil your song;
For 'twas the self-same Power Divine
Taught you to sing, and me to shine;
That you with music, I with light,
Might beautify and cheer the night."
The songster heard his short oration,
And warbling out his approbation,
Released him, as my story tells,
And found a supper somewhere else.
      Hence jarring sectaries may learn
Their real interest to discern;
That brother should not war with brother,
And worry and devour each other;
But sing and shine by sweet consent,
Till life's poor transient night is spent,
Respecting in each other's case
The gifts of nature and of grace.
      Those Christians best deserve the name
Who studiously make peace their aim;

Peace both the duty and the prize
Of him that creeps and him that flies.
William Cowper [1731–1808]

SIR LARK AND KING SUN: A PARABLE

From " Adela Cathcart "

"GOOD morrow, my lord!" in the sky alone,
Sang the lark, as the sun ascended his throne.
"Shine on me, my lord; I only am come,
Of all your servants, to welcome you home.
I have flown right up, a whole hour, I swear,
To catch the first shine of your golden hair."

"Must I thank you, then," said the king, "Sir Lark,
For flying so high and hating the dark?
You ask a full cup for half a thirst:
Half was love of me, and half love to be first.
There's many a bird makes no such haste,
But waits till I come: that's as much to my taste."

And King Sun hid his head in a turban of cloud,
And Sir Lark stopped singing, quite vexed and cowed;
But he flew up higher, and thought, "Anon
The wrath of the king will be over and gone;
And his crown, shining out of its cloudy fold,
Will change my brown feathers to a glory of gold."

So he flew—with the strength of a lark he flew;
But, as he rose, the cloud rose too;
And not one gleam of the golden hair
Came through the depths of the misty air;
Till, weary with flying, with sighing sore,
The strong sun-seeker could do no more.

His wings had had no chrism of gold:
And his feathers felt withered and worn and old;
He faltered, and sank, and dropped like a stone.
And there on her nest, where he left her, alone
Sat his little wife on her little eggs,
Keeping them warm with wings and legs.

Did I say alone? Ah, no such thing!
Full in her face was shining the king.
"Welcome, Sir Lark! You look tired," said he;
"*Up* is not always the best way to me.
While you have been singing so high and away,
I've been shining to your little wife all day."

He had set his crown all about the nest,
And out of the midst shone her little brown breast;
And so glorious was she in russet gold,
That for wonder and awe Sir Lark grew cold.
He popped his head under her wing, and lay
As still as a stone, till King Sun was away.

George Macdonald [1824–1905]

THE COURTSHIP, MERRY MARRIAGE, AND PIC-
NIC DINNER OF COCK ROBIN AND JENNY
WREN

IT was a merry time
  When Jenny Wren was young,
So neatly as she danced,
  And so sweetly as she sung,
Robin Redbreast lost his heart:
  He was a gallant bird;
He doffed his hat to Jenny,
  And thus to her he said:—

"My dearest Jenny Wren,
  If you will but be mine,
You shall dine on cherry pie,
  And drink nice currant wine.
I'll dress you like a Goldfinch,
  Or like a Peacock gay;
So if you'll have me, Jenny,
  Let us appoint the day."

Jenny blushed behind her fan,
  And thus declared her mind:
"Then let it be to-morrow, Bob,
  I take your offer kind—

Cherry pie is very good!
    So is currant wine!
But I will wear my brown gown,
    And never dress too fine."

Robin rose up early
    At the break of day;
He flew to Jenny Wren's house,
    To sing a roundelay.
He met the Cock and Hen,
    And bid the Cock declare,
This was his wedding-day
    With Jenny Wren, the fair.

The Cock then blew his horn,
    To let the neighbors know,
This was Robin's wedding-day,
    And they might see the show.
And first came Parson Rook,
    With his spectacles and band,
And one of Mother Hubbard's books
    He held within his hand.

Then followed him the Lark,
    For he could sweetly sing,
And he was to be clerk
    At Cock Robin's wedding.
He sang of Robin's love
    For little Jenny Wren;
And when he came unto the end,
    Then he began again.

Then came the bride and bridegroom;
    Quite plainly was she dressed,
And blushed so much, her cheeks were
    As red as Robin's breast.
But Robin cheered her up;
    "My pretty Jen," said he,
"We're going to be married
    And happy we shall be."

The Goldfinch came on next,
　To give away the bride;
The Linnet, being bride's maid,
　Walked by Jenny's side;
And, as she was a-walking,
　She said, "Upon my word,
I think that your Cock Robin
　Is a very pretty bird."

The Bulfinch walked by Robin,
　And thus to him did say,
"Pray, mark, friend Robin Redbreast,
　That Goldfinch, dressed so gay;
What though her gay apparel
　Becomes her very well,
Yet Jenny's modest dress and look
　Must bear away the bell."

The Blackbird and the Thrush,
　And charming Nightingale,
Whose sweet jug sweetly echoes
　Through every grove and dale;
The Sparrow and Tom Tit,
　And many more, were there:
All came to see the wedding
　Of Jenny Wren, the fair.

"O then," says Parson Rook,
　"Who gives this maid away?"
"I do," says the Goldfinch,
　"And her fortune I will pay:
Here's a bag of grain of many sorts,
　And other things beside;
Now happy be the bridegroom,
　And happy be the bride!"

"And will your have her, Robin,
　To be your wedded wife?"
"Yes, I will," says Robin,
　"And love her all my life."

"And will you have him, Jenny,
    Your husband now to be?"
"Yes, I will," says Jenny,
    "And love him heartily."

Then on her finger fair
    Cock Robin put the ring;
"You're married now," says Parson Rook,
    While the Lark aloud did sing:
"Happy be the bridegroom,
    And happy be the bride!
And may not man, nor bird, nor beast,
    This happy pair divide."

The birds were asked to dine;
    Not Jenny's friends alone,
But every pretty songster
    That had Cock Robin known.
They had a cherry pie,
    Beside some currant wine,
And every guest brought something,
    That sumptuous they might dine.

Now they all sat or stood
    To eat and to drink;
And every one said what
    He happened to think:
They each took a bumper,
    And drank to the pair:
Cock Robin, the bridegroom,
    And Jenny Wren, the fair.

The dinner-things removed,
    They all began to sing;
And soon they made the place
    Near a mile round to ring.
The concert it was fine;
    And every bird tried
Who best could sing for Robin
    And Jenny Wren, the bride.

Then in came the Cuckoo and made a great rout;
He caught hold of Jenny and pulled her about.
Cock Robin was angry, and so was the Sparrow,
Who fetched in a hurry his bow and his arrow.

His aim then he took, but he took it not right;
His skill was not good, or he shot in a fright;
For the Cuckoo he missed, but Cock Robin killed!—
And all the birds mourned that his blood was so spilled.

Unknown

THE BABES IN THE WOOD

Now ponder well, you parents dear,
   These words, which I shall write;
A doleful story you shall hear,
   In time brought forth to light.
A gentleman of good account
   In Norfolk dwelt of late,
Who did in honor far surmount
   Most men of his estate.

Sore sick was he, and like to die,
   No help his life could save;
His wife by him as sick did lie,
   And both possessed one grave.
No love between these two was lost,
   Each was to other kind;
In love they lived, in loved they died,
   And left two babes behind:

The one a fine and pretty boy,
   Not passing three years old;
The other a girl more young than he,
   And framed in beauty's mold.
The father left his little son,
   As plainly does appear,
When he to perfect age should come,
   Three hundred pounds a year.

And to his little daughter Jane
   Five hundred pounds in gold,
To be paid down on marriage-day,
   Which might not be controlled:
But if the children chance to die,
   Ere they to age should come,
Their uncle should possess their wealth;
   For so the will did run.

"Now, brother," said the dying man,
   "Look to my children dear;
Be good unto my boy and girl,
   No friends else have they here:
To God and you I recommend
   My children dear this day;
But little while be sure we have
   Within this world to stay.

"You must be father and mother both,
   And uncle all in one;
God knows what will become of them,
   When I am dead and gone."
With that bespake their mother dear,
   "O brother kind," quoth she,
"You are the man must bring our babes
   To wealth or misery.

"And if you keep them carefully
   Then God will you reward;
But if you otherwise should deal,
   God will your deeds regard."
With lips as cold as any stone,
   They kissed their children small:
"God bless you both, my children dear;"
   With that the tears did fall.

These speeches then their brother spake
   To this sick couple there,
"The keeping of your little ones,
   Sweet sister, do not fear;

God never prosper me nor mine,
  Nor aught else that I have,
If I do wrong your children dear,
  When you are laid in grave."

The parents being dead and gone,
  The children home he takes,
And brings them straight into his house,
  Where much of them he makes.
He had not kept these pretty babes
  A twelvemonth and a day,
But, for their wealth, he did devise
  To make them both away.

He bargained with two ruffians strong,
  Which were of furious mood,
That they should take these children young,
  And slay them in a wood.
He told his wife an artful tale,
  He would the children send
To be brought up in fair London,
  With one that was his friend.

Away then went these pretty babes,
  Rejoicing at that tide,
Rejoicing with a merry mind,
  They should on cock-horse ride.
They prate and prattle pleasantly,
  As they rode on the way,
To those that should their butchers be,
  And work their lives' decay:

So that the pretty speech they had,
  Made Murder's heart relent;
And they that undertook the deed,
  Full sore did now repent.
Yet one of them more hard of heart,
  Did vow to do his charge,
Because the wretch that hired him,
  Had paid him very large.

The other won't agree thereto,
    So here they fall to strife;
With one another they did fight,
    About the children's life:
And he that was of mildest mood,
    Did slay the other there,
Within an unfrequented wood;
    The babes did quake for fear!

He took the children by the hand,
    Tears standing in their eye,
And bade them straightway follow him,
    And look they did not cry:
And two long miles he led them on,
    While they for food complain:
"Stay here," quoth he, "I'll bring you bread,
    When I come back again."

These pretty babes, with hand in hand,
    Went wandering up and down,
But never more could see the man
    Approaching from the town;
Their pretty lips with black-berries
    Were all besmeared and dyed,
And, when they saw the darksome night,
    They sat them down and cried.

Thus wandered these poor innocents,
    Till death did end their grief;
In one another's arms they died,
    As wanting due relief:
No burial this pretty pair
    Of any man receives,
Till Robin-red-breast piously
    Did cover them with leaves.

And now the heavy wrath of God
    Upon their uncle fell;
Yea, fearful fiends did haunt his house,
    His conscience felt an hell:

His barns were fired, his goods consumed,
　His lands were barren made,
His cattle died within the field,
　And nothing with him stayed.

And in a voyage to Portugal
　Two of his sons did die;
And, to conclude, himself was brought
　To want and misery:
He pawned and mortgaged all his land
　Ere seven years came about,
And now at length his wicked act
　Did by this means come out:

The fellow, that did take in hand
　These children for to kill,
Was for a robbery judged to die,
　Such was God's blessed will:
Who did confess the very truth
　As here hath been displayed:
Their uncle having died in jail,
　Where he for debt was laid.

You that executors be made,
　And overseers eke
Of children that be fatherless,
　And infants mild and meek;
Take you example by this thing,
　And yield to each his right,
Lest God with such like misery
　Your wicked minds requite.

Unknown

GOD'S JUDGMENT ON A WICKED BISHOP

THE summer and autumn had been so wet,
That in winter the corn was growing yet:
'Twas a piteous sight to see, all around,
The grain lie rotting on the ground.

Every day the starving poor
Crowded around Bishop Hatto's door;
For he had a plentiful last-year's store,
And all the neighborhood could tell
His granaries were furnished well.

At last Bishop Hatto appointed a day
To quiet the poor without delay;
He bade them to his great barn repair,
And they should have food for the winter there.

Rejoiced such tidings good to hear,
The poor folk flocked from far and near;
The great barn was full as it could hold
Of women and children, and young and old.

Then, when he saw it could hold no more,
Bishop Hatto he made fast the door;
And, while for mercy on Christ they call,
He set fire to the barn, and burnt them all.

"I' faith, 'tis an excellent bonfire!" quoth he;
"And the country is greatly obliged to me
For ridding it, in these times forlorn,
Of rats that only consume the corn."

So then to his palace returnèd he,
And he sat down to supper merrily,
And he slept that night like an innocent man;
But Bishop Hatto never slept again.

In the morning, as he entered the hall,
Where his picture hung against the wall,
A sweat like death all over him came,
For the rats had eaten it out of the frame.

As he looked, there came a man from his farm,—
He had a countenance white with alarm:
"My Lord, I opened your granaries this morn,
And the rats had eaten all your corn."

Another came running presently,
And he was pale as pale could be.
"Fly! my Lord Bishop, fly!" quoth he,
"Ten thousand rats are coming this way,—
The Lord forgive you for yesterday!"

"I'll go to my tower in the Rhine," replied he;
"'Tis the safest place in Germany,—
The walls are high, and the shores are steep,
And the tide is strong, and the water deep."

Bishop Hatto fearfully hastened away,
And he crossed the Rhine without delay,
And reached his tower, and barred with care
All the windows, and doors, and loop-holes there.

He laid him down and closed his eyes,
But soon a scream made him arise;
He started, and saw two eyes of flame
On his pillow, from whence the screaming came.

He listened and looked,—it was only the cat;
But the Bishop he grew more fearful for that,
For she sat screaming, mad with fear,
At the army of rats that were drawing near.

For they have swum over the river so deep,
And they have climbed the shores so steep,
And now by thousands up they crawl
To the holes and the windows in the wall.

Down on his knees the Bishop fell,
And faster and faster his beads did he tell,
As louder and louder, drawing near,
The saw of their teeth without he could hear.

And in at the windows, and in at the door,
And through the walls by thousands they pour;
And down from the ceiling and up through the floor,
From the right and the left, from behind and before,
From within and without, from above and below,—
And all at once to the Bishop they go.

They have whetted their teeth against the stones,
And now they pick the Bishop's bones;
They gnawed the flesh from every limb,
For they were sent to do judgment on him!

Robert Southey [1774–1843]

THE PIED PIPER OF HAMELIN

A CHILD'S STORY

I

HAMELIN Town's in Brunswick,
By famous Hanover city;
  The river Weser, deep and wide,
  Washes its wall on the southern side;
  A pleasanter spot you never spied;
But, when begins my ditty,
  Almost five hundred years ago,
  To see the townsfolk suffer so
From vermin was a pity.

II

  Rats!
They fought the dogs and killed the cats,
  And bit the babies in the cradles,
And ate the cheeses out of the vats,
  And licked the soup from the cooks' own ladles,
Split open the kegs of salted sprats,
Made nests inside men's Sunday hats,
And even spoiled the women's chats
  By drowning their speaking
  With shrieking and squeaking
In fifty different sharps and flats.

III

At last the people in a body
  To the Town Hall came flocking:
"'Tis clear," cried they, "our Mayor's a noddy;
  And as for our Corporation,—shocking

To think we buy gowns lined with ermine
For dolts that can't or won't determine
What's best to rid us of our vermin!
You hope, because you're old and obese,
To find in the furry civic robe ease?
Rouse up, sirs! Give your brains a racking,
To find the remedy we're lacking,
Or, sure as fate, we'll send you packing!"
At this the Mayor and Corporation
Quaked with a mighty consternation.

IV

An hour they sat in council,—
   At length the Mayor broke silence:
"For a guilder I'd my ermine gown sell;
   I wish I were a mile hence!
It's easy to bid one rack one's brain,—
I'm sure my poor head aches again,
I've scratched it so, and all in vain.
Oh for a trap, a trap, a trap!"
Just as he said this, what should hap
At the chamber-door but a gentle tap?
"Bless us," cried the Mayor, "what's that?"
(With the Corporation as he sat,
Looking little though wondrous fat;
Nor brighter was his eye, nor moister
Than a too-long-opened oyster,
Save when at noon his paunch grew mutinous
For a plate of turtle green and glutinous)
"Only a scraping of shoes on the mat?
Anything like the sound of a rat
Makes my heart go pit-a-pat!"

V

"Come in!" the Mayor cried, looking bigger:
And in did come the strangest figure!
His queer long coat from heel to head
Was half of yellow and half of red,
And he himself was tall and thin,
With sharp blue eyes, each like a pin.

And light loose hair, yet swarthy skin,
No tuft on cheek nor beard on chin,
But lips where smiles went out and in;
There was no guessing his kith and kin:
And nobody could enough admire
The tall man and his quaint attire.
Quoth one: "It's as my great-grandsire,
Starting up at the Trump of Doom's tone,
Had walked this way from his painted tombstone!"

VI

He advanced to the council-table:
And, "Please your honors," said he, " I'm able,
By means of a secret charm, to draw
All creatures living beneath the sun,
That creep or swim or fly or run,
After me so as you never saw!
And I chiefly use my charm
On creatures that do people harm,
The mole and toad and newt and viper;
And people call me the Pied Piper."
(And here they noticed round his neck
A scarf of red and yellow stripe,
To match with his coat of the self-same check,
And at the scarf's end hung a pipe;
And his fingers, they noticed, were ever straying
As if impatient to be playing
Upon this pipe, as low it dangled
Over his vesture so old-fangled.)
"Yet," said he, "poor piper as I am,
In Tartary I freed the Cham,
Last June, from his huge swarms of gnats;
I eased in Asia the Nizam
Of a monstrous brood of vampire-bats;
And as for what your brain bewilders,—
If I can rid your town of rats,
Will you give me a thousand guilders?"
"One? fifty thousand!" was the exclamation
Of the astonished Mayor and Corporation.

VII

Into the street the Piper stepped,
  Smiling first a little smile,
As if he knew what magic slept
  In his quiet pipe the while;
Then, like a musical adept,
To blow the pipe his lips he wrinkled,
And green and blue his sharp eyes twinkled,
Like a candle-flame where salt is sprinkled;
And ere three shrill notes the pipe uttered,
You heard as if an army muttered;
And the muttering grew to a grumbling;
And the grumbling grew to a mighty rumbling;
And out of the houses the rats came tumbling.
Great rats, small rats, lean rats, brawny rats,
Brown rats, black rats, gray rats, tawny rats,
Grave old plodders, gay young friskers,
  Fathers, mothers, uncles, cousins,
Cocking tails and pricking whiskers;
  Families by tens and dozens,
Brothers, sisters, husbands, wives,—
Followed the Piper for their lives.
From street to street he piped advancing,
And step for step they followed dancing,
Until they came to the river Weser,
Wherein all plunged and perished!
—Save one who, stout as Julius Cæsar,
Swam across and lived to carry
(As he, the manuscript he cherished)
To Rat-land home his commentary,
Which was: "At the first shrill notes of the pipe,
I heard a sound as of scraping tripe,
And putting apples, wondrous ripe,
Into a cider-press's gripe,—
And a moving away of pickle-tub-boards,
And a leaving ajar of conserve-cupboards,
And a drawing the corks of train-oil-flasks,
And a breaking the hoops of butter-casks;

And it seemed as if a voice
(Sweeter far than by harp or by psaltery
Is breathed) called out, 'Oh rats, rejoice!
The world is grown to one vast drysaltery!
So munch on, crunch on, take your nuncheon,
Breakfast, supper, dinner, luncheon!'
And just as a bulky sugar-puncheon,
Already staved, like a great sun shone
Glorious scarce an inch before me,
Just as methought it said, 'Come, bore me!'—
I found the Weser rolling o'er me."

VIII

You should have heard the Hamelin people
Ringing the bells till they rocked the steeple;
"Go," cried the Mayor, "and get long poles!
Poke out the nests and block up the holes!
Consult with carpenters and builders,
And leave in our town not even a trace
Of the rats!"—when suddenly, up the face
Of the Piper perked in the market-place,
With a "First, if you please, my thousand guilders!"

IX

A thousand guilders! the Mayor looked blue;
So did the Corporation too.
For council-dinners made rare havoc
With Claret, Moselle, Vin-de-Grave, Hock;
And half the money would replenish
Their cellar's biggest butt with Rhenish.
To pay this sum to a wandering fellow
With a gypsy coat of red and yellow!
"Beside," quoth the Mayor, with a knowing wink,
"Our business was done at the river's brink;
We saw with our eyes the vermin sink,
And what's dead can't come to life, I think.
So, friend, we're not the folks to shrink
From the duty of giving you something to drink,
And a matter of money to put in your poke;

But as for the guilders, what we spoke
Of them, as you very well know, was in joke.
Beside, our losses have made us thrifty;
A thousand guilders! Come, take fifty!"

X

The Piper's face fell, and he cried,
"No trifling! I can't wait! beside,
I've promised to visit by dinner time
Bagdat, and accept the prime
Of the Head Cook's pottage, all he's rich in,
For having left, in the Caliph's kitchen,
Of a nest of scorpions no survivor:
With him I proved no bargain-driver;
With you, don't think I'll bate a stiver!
And folks who put me in a passion
May find me pipe after another fashion."

XI

"How?" cried the Mayor, "d'ye think I brook
Being worse treated than a Cook?
Insulted by a lazy ribald
With idle pipe and vesture piebald?
You threaten us, fellow?   Do your worst,
Blow your pipe there till you burst!"

XII

Once more he stepped into the street;
   And to his lips again
Laid his long pipe of smooth straight cane;
   And ere he blew three notes (such sweet
Soft notes as yet musician's cunning
Never gave the enraptured air)
There was a rustling that seemed like a bustling
Of merry crowds justling at pitching and hustling;
Small feet were pattering, wooden shoes clattering,
Little hands clapping, and little tongues chattering;
And, like fowls in a farm-yard when barley is scattering,
Out came the children running:

All the little boys and girls,
With rosy cheeks and flaxen curls,
And sparkling eyes and teeth like pearls,
Tripping and skipping, ran merrily after
The wonderful music with shouting and laughter.

XIII

The Mayor was dumb, and the Council stood
As if they were changed into blocks of wood,
Unable to move a step, or cry
To the children merrily skipping by,—
And could only follow with the eye
That joyous crowd at the Piper's back.
But how the Mayor was on the rack,
And the wretched Council's bosoms beat,
As the Piper turned from the High Street
To where the Weser rolled its waters
Right in the way of their sons and daughters!
However, he turned from south to west,
And to Koppelberg Hill his steps addressed,
And after him the children pressed;
Great was the joy in every breast.
"He never can cross that mighty top!
He's forced to let the piping drop,
And we shall see our children stop!"
When, lo, as they reached the mountain-side,
A wondrous portal opened wide,
As if a cavern was suddenly hollowed;
And the Piper advanced and the children followed;
And when all were in, to the very last,
The door in the mountain-side shut fast.
Did I say, all? No! One was lame,
And could not dance the whole of the way;
And in after years, if you would blame
His sadness, he was used to say,—
"It's dull in our town since my playmates left!
I can't forget that I'm bereft
Of all the pleasant sights they see,
Which the Piper also promised me;

For he led us, he said, to a joyous land,
Joining the town and just at hand,
Where waters gushed, and fruit-trees grew,
And flowers put forth a fairer hue,
And everything was strange and new;
The sparrows were brighter than peacocks here,
And their dogs outran our fallow deer,
And honey-bees had lost their stings,
And horses were born with eagles' wings;
And just as I became assured
My lame foot would be speedily cured,
The music stopped and I stood still,
And found myself outside the hill,
Left alone against my will,
To go now limping as before,
And never hear of that country more!"

XIV

Alas, alas for Hamelin!
    There came into many a burgher's pate
    A text which says that heaven's gate
    Opes to the rich at as easy rate
As the needle's eye takes a camel in!
The Mayor sent East, West, North and South,
To offer the Piper, by word of mouth,
    Wherever it was men's lot to find him,
Silver and gold to his heart's content,
If he'd only return the way he went,
    And bring the children behind him.
But when they saw 'twas a lost endeavor,
And piper and dancers were gone forever,
They made a decree that lawyers never
    Should think their records dated duly
If, after the day of the month and year,
These words did not as well appear,
"And so long after what happened here
    On the Twenty-second of July,
Thirteen hundred and seventy-six:"
And the better in memory to fix

The place of the children's last retreat,
They called it, the Pied Piper's Street—
Where any one playing on pipe or tabor
Was sure for the future to lose his labor.
Nor suffered they hostlery or tavern
   To shock with mirth a street so solemn;
But opposite the place of the cavern
   They wrote the story on a column,
And on the great church-window painted
The same, to make the world acquainted
How their children were stolen away,
And there it stands to this very day.
And I must not omit to say
That in Transylvania there's a tribe
Of alien people who ascribe
The outlandish ways and dress
On which their neighbors lay such stress,
To their fathers and mothers having risen
Out of some subterraneous prison
Into which they were trepanned
Long time ago in a mighty band
Out of Hamelin town in Brunswick land,
But how or why, they don't understand.

XV

So, Willy, let me and you be wipers
Of scores out with all men—especially pipers!
And, whether they pipe us free fróm rats or fróm mice,
If we've promised them aught, let us keep our promise!
              Robert Browning [1812–1889]

THE GLAD EVANGEL

A CAROL

HE came all so still
    Where His mother was,
As dew in April
    That falleth on the grass.

He came all so still
    Where His mother lay,
As dew in April
    That falleth on the spray.

He came all so still
    To His mother's bower,
As dew in April
    That falleth on the flower.

Mother and maiden
    Was never none but she!
Well might such a lady
    God's mother be.

Unknown

"GOD REST YOU MERRY, GENTLEMEN"

GOD rest you merry, gentlemen,
    Let nothing you dismay,
For Jesus Christ, our Saviour,
    Was born upon this day,
To save us all from Satan's power
    When we were gone astray.
        O tidings of comfort and joy!
        For Jesus Christ, our Saviour,
        Was born on Christmas Day.

In Bethlehem, in Jewry,
  This blessèd babe was born,
And laid within a manger,
  Upon this blessèd morn;
The which His mother, Mary,
  Nothing did take in scorn.

From God our Heavenly Father,
  A blessèd angel came;
And unto certain shepherds
  Brought tidings of the same:
How that in Bethlehem was born
  The Son of God by name.

"Fear not," then said the angel,
  "Let nothing you affright,
This day is born a Saviour
  Of virtue, power, and might,
So frequently to vanquish all
  The friends of Satan quite."

The shepherds at these tidings
  Rejoicèd much in mind,
And left their flocks a-feeding
  In tempest, storm, and wind,
And went to Bethlehem straightway
  This blessèd babe to find.

But when to Bethlehem they came,
  Whereat this infant lay,
They found Him in a manger,
  Where oxen feed on hay,
His mother Mary kneeling,
  Unto the Lord did pray.

Now to the Lord sing praises,
  All you within this place,
And with true love and brotherhood
  Each other now embrace;
This holy tide of Christmas
  All others doth deface.

O tidings of comfort and joy!
For Jesus Christ, our Saviour,
Was born in Christmas Day.

Unknown

"O LITTLE TOWN OF BETHLEHEM"

O LITTLE town of Bethlehem,
  How still we see thee lie!
Above thy deep and dreamless sleep
  The silent stars go by;
Yet in thy dark streets shineth
  The everlasting Light;
The hopes and fears of all the years
  Are met in thee to-night.

For Christ is born of Mary,
  And, gathered all above,
While mortals sleep, the angels keep
  Their watch of wondering love.
O morning stars, together
  Proclaim the holy birth!
And praises sing to God the King,
  And peace to men on earth.

How silently, how silently,
  The wondrous gift is given!
So God imparts to human hearts
  The blessings of His heaven.
No ear may hear His coming,
  But in this world of sin,
Where meek souls will receive Him still,
  The dear Christ enters in.

O holy Child of Bethlehem!
  Descend to us, we pray;
Cast out our sin, and enter in,
  Be born in us to-day.

We hear the Christmas angels
  The great glad tidings tell;
Oh come to us, abide with us,
  Our Lord Emmanuel!

Phillips Brooks [1835–1893]

A CHRISTMAS HYMN

Old Style: 1837

IT was the calm and silent night!
  Seven hundred years and fifty-three
Had Rome been growing up to might,
  And now was Queen of land and sea.
No sound was heard of clashing wars;
  Peace brooded o'er the hushed domain;
Apollo, Pallas, Jove and Mars,
  Held undisturbed their ancient reign,
    In the solemn midnight
      Centuries ago.

'Twas in the calm and silent night!
  The senator of haughty Rome
Impatient urged his chariot's flight,
  From lordly revel rolling home.
Triumphal arches gleaming swell
  His breast with thoughts of boundless sway;
What recked the Roman what befell
  A paltry province far away,
    In the solemn midnight
      Centuries ago!

Within that province far away
  Went plodding home a weary boor:
A streak of light before him lay,
  Fall'n through a half-shut stable door
Across his path. He passed—for naught
  Told what was going on within;
How keen the stars! his only thought;
  The air how calm and cold and thin,
    In the solemn midnight
      Centuries ago!

O strange indifference!—low and high
   Drowsed over common joys and cares:
The earth was still—but knew not why;
   The world was listening—unawares.
How calm a moment may precede
   One that shall thrill the world for ever!
To that still moment none would heed,
   Man's doom was linked, no more to sever,
      In the solemn midnight
        Centuries ago.

It *is* the calm and solemn night!
   A thousand bells ring out, and throw
Their joyous peals abroad, and smite
   The darkness, charmed and holy now.
The night that erst no name had worn,
   To it a happy name is given;
For in that stable lay new-born
   The peaceful Prince of Earth and Heaven,
      In the solemn midnight
        Centuries ago.
                Alfred Domett [1811–1887]

"WHILE SHEPHERDS WATCHED THEIR FLOCKS BY NIGHT"

WHILE shepherds watched their flocks by night,
   All seated on the ground,
The angel of the Lord came down,
   And glory shone around.

"Fear not," said he, for mighty dread
   Had seized their troubled mind;
"Glad tidings of great joy I bring
   To you and all mankind.

"To you, in David's town, this day
   Is born, of David's line,
The Saviour, who is Christ the Lord,
   And this shall be the sign:

"The heavenly babe you there shall find
    To human view displayed,
All meanly wrapped in swaddling bands,
    And in a manger laid."

Thus spake the seraph; and forthwith
    Appeared a shining throng
Of angels, praising God, who thus
    Addressed their joyful song:

"All glory be to God on high,
    And to the earth be peace;
Good will henceforth from Heaven to men
    Begin and never cease."

                    Nahum Tate [1652–1715]

CHRISTMAS CAROLS

It came upon the midnight clear,
    That glorious song of old,
From angels bending near the earth
    To touch their harps of gold:
"Peace on the earth, good will to men
    From heaven's all-gracious King"—
The world in solemn stillness lay
    To hear the angels sing.

Still through the cloven skies they come
    With peaceful wings unfurled,
And still their heavenly music floats
    O'er all the weary world;
Above its sad and lowly plains
    They bend on hovering wing,
And ever o'er its Babel-sounds
    The blessèd angels sing.

But with the woes of sin and strife
    The world has suffered long;
Beneath the angel-strain have rolled
    Two thousand years of wrong;

And man, at war with man, hears not
   The love-song which they bring;—
Oh, hush the noise, ye men of strife,
   And hear the angels sing!

And ye, beneath life's crushing load,
   Whose forms are bending low,
Who toil along the climbing way
   With painful steps and slow,
Look now! for glad and golden hours
   Come swiftly on the wing;—
Oh, rest beside the weary road
   And hear the angels sing!

For lo! the days are hastening on
   By prophet bards foretold,
When with the ever circling years
   Comes round the age of gold;
When Peace shall over all the earth
   Its ancient splendors fling,
And the whole world give back the song
   Which now the angels sing.
            Edmund Hamilton Sears [1810–1876]

THE ANGELS

From "Flowers of Sion"

RUN, shepherds, run where Bethlehem blest appears.
We bring the best of news; be not dismayed:
A Saviour there is born more old than years,
Amidst heaven's rolling heights this earth who stayed.
In a poor cottage inned, a virgin maid,
A weakling did him bear, who all upbears;
There is he poorly swaddled, in manger laid,
To whom too narrow swaddlings are our spheres:
Run, shepherds, run, and solemnize his birth.
This is that night—no, day, grown great with bliss,
In which the power of Satan broken is:
In heaven be glory, peace unto the earth!

Thus singing, through the air the angels swarm,
And cope of stars re-echoèd the same.
William Drummond [1585-1649]

THE BURNING BABE

As I in hoary winter's night
  Stood shivering in the snow,
Surprised I was with sudden heat
  Which made my heart to glow;
And lifting up a fearful eye
  To view what fire was near,
A pretty babe all burning bright
  Did in the air appear;
Who, scorchèd with excessive heat,
  Such floods of tears did shed,
As though His floods should quench His flames,
  Which with His tears were bred:
"Alas!" quoth He, "but newly born
  In fiery heats I fry,
Yet none approach to warm their hearts
  Or feel my fire but I!

"My faultless breast the furnace is;
  The fuel, wounding thorns;
Love is the fire, and sighs the smoke;
  The ashes, shames and scorns;
The fuel Justice layeth on,
  And Mercy blows the coals,
The metal in this furnace wrought
  Are men's defilèd souls:
For which, as now on fire I am
  To work them to their good,
So will I melt into a bath,
  To wash them in my blood."
With this He vanished out of sight
  And swiftly shrunk away,
And straight I callèd unto mind
  That it was Christmas Day.
Robert Southwell [1561?-1595]

TRYSTE NOËL

THE Ox he openeth wide the Doore,
  And from the Snowe he calls her inne,
And he hath seen her Smile therefor,
  Our Ladye without Sinne.
    Now soone from Sleep
    A Starre shall leap,
And soone arrive both King and Hinde:
      Amen, Amen:
But O, the Place co'd I but finde!

The Ox hath hushed his voyce and bent
  Trewe eyes of Pitty ore the Mow,
And on his lovelie Neck, forspent,
  The Blessed layes her Browe.
    Around her feet
    Full Warme and Sweete
His bowerie Breath doth meeklie dwell:
      Amen, Amen:
But sore am I with Vaine Travèl!

The Ox is host in Judah stall
  And Host of more than onelie one,
For close she gathereth withal
  Our Lorde her littel Sonne.
    Glad Hinde and King
    Their Gyfte may bring,
But wo'd to-night my Teares were there,
      Amen, Amen:
Between her Bosom and His hayre!
      Louise Imogen Guiney [1861-1920]

CHRISTMAS CAROL

As Joseph was a-waukin',
  He heard an angel sing,
"This night shall be the birthnight
  Of Christ our heavenly King.

"His birth-bed shall be neither
  In housen nor in hall,
Nor in the place of paradise,
  But in the oxen's stall.

"He neither shall be rockèd
  In silver nor in gold,
But in the wooden manger
  That lieth in the mould.

"He neither shall be washen
  With white wine nor with red,
But with the fair spring water
  That on you shall be shed.

"He neither shall be clothèd
  In purple nor in pall,
But in the fair, white linen
  That usen babies all."

As Joseph was a-waukin',
  Thus did the angel sing,
And Mary's son at midnight
  Was born to be our King.

Then be you glad, good people,
  At this time of the year;
And light you up your candles,
  For His star it shineth clear.

Unknown

"BRIGHTEST AND BEST OF THE SONS OF THE MORNING"

Brightest and best of the Sons of the morning!
  Dawn on our darkness and lend us thine aid!
Star of the East, the horizon adorning,
  Guide where our Infant Redeemer is laid!

Cold on His cradle the dewdrops are shining,
  Low lies His head with the beasts of the stall;
Angels adore Him in slumber reclining,
  Maker and Monarch and Saviour of all!

Say, shall we yield Him, in costly devotion,
  Odors of Edom and offerings divine?
Gems of the mountain and pearls of the ocean,
  Myrrh from the forest, or gold from the mine?

Vainly we offer each ample oblation;
  Vainly with gifts would His favor secure:
Richer by far is the heart's adoration;
  Dearer to God are the prayers of the poor.

Brightest and best of the Sons of the morning!
  Dawn on our darkness and lend us thine aid!
Star of the East, the horizon adorning,
  Guide where our Infant Redeemer is laid!
                    Reginald Heber [1783–1826]

CHRISTMAS BELLS

I HEARD the bells on Christmas Day
Their old, familiar carols play,
        And wild and sweet
        The words repeat
Of peace on earth, good-will to men!

And thought how, as the day had come,
The belfries of all Christendom
        Had rolled along
        The unbroken song
Of peace on earth, good-will to men!

Till, ringing, singing on its way,
The world revolved from night to day,
        A voice, a chime,
        A chant sublime
Of peace on earth, good-will to men!

Then from each black, accursed mouth
The cannon thundered in the South,
        And with the sound
        The carols drowned
Of peace on earth, good-will to men!

It was as if an earthquake rent
The hearth-stones of a continent,
      And made forlorn
         The households born
Of peace on earth, good-will to men!

And in despair I bowed my head;
"There is no peace on earth," I said,
      "For hate is strong,
         And mocks the song
Of peace on earth, good-will to men!"

Then pealed the bells more loud and deep:
"God is not dead, nor doth He sleep!
      The Wrong shall fail,
         The Right prevail,
With peace on earth, good-will to men!"
                    Henry Wadsworth Longfellow [1807–1882]

A CHRISTMAS CAROL

THE Christ-child lay on Mary's lap,
   His hair was like a light.
(O weary, weary were the world,
   But here is all aright.)

The Christ-child lay on Mary's breast,
   His hair was like a star.
(O stern and cunning are the kings,
   But here the true hearts are.)

The Christ-child lay on Mary's heart,
   His hair was like a fire.
(O weary, weary is the world,
   But here the world's desire.)

The Christ-child stood at Mary's knee,
   His hair was like a crown,
And all the flowers looked up at Him,
   And all the stars looked down.
                    Gilbert Keith Chesterton [1874–1936]

THE HOUSE OF CHRISTMAS

THERE fared a mother driven forth
Out of an inn to roam;
In the place where she was homeless
All men are at home.
The crazy stable close at hand,
With shaking timber and shifting sand,
Grew a stronger thing to abide and stand
Than the square stones of Rome.

For men are homesick in their homes,
And strangers under the sun,
And they lay their heads in a foreign land
Whenever the day is done.
Here we have battle and blazing eyes,
And chance and honor and high surprise,
But our homes are under miraculous skies
Where the yule tale was begun.

A Child in a foul stable,
Where the beasts feed and foam,
Only where He was homeless
Are you and I at home;
We have hands that fashion and heads that know,
But our hearts we lost—how long ago!
In a place no chart nor ship can show
Under the sky's dome.

This world is wild as an old wives' tale,
And strange the plain things are,
The earth is enough and the air is enough
For our wonder and our war;
But our rest is as far as the fire-drake swings
And our peace is put in impossible things
Where clashed and thundered unthinkable wings
Round an incredible star.

To an open house in the evening
Home shall men come,

To an older place than Eden
And a taller town than Rome.
To the end of the way of the wandering star,
To the things that cannot be and that are,
To the place where God was homeless
And all men are at home.

Gilbert Keith Chesterton [1874–1936]

THE FEAST OF THE SNOW

THERE is heard a hymn when the panes are dim,
    And never before or again,
When the nights are strong with a darkness long,
    And the dark is alive with rain.

Never we know but in sleet and snow
    The place where the great fires are,
That the midst of earth is a raging mirth,
    And the heart of the earth a star.

And at night we win to the ancient inn,
    Where the Child in the frost is furled,
We follow the feet where all souls meet,
    At the inn at the end of the world.

The gods lie dead where the leaves lie red,
    For the flame of the sun is flown;
The gods lie cold where the leaves are gold,
    And a Child comes forth alone.

Gilbert Keith Chesterton [1874–1936]

MARY'S BABY

JOSEPH, mild and noble, bent above the straw:
A pale girl, a frail girl, suffering he saw;
"O my Love, my Mary, my bride, I pity thee!"
"Nay, Dear," said Mary, "all is well with me!"
    "*Baby, my baby, O my babe,*" she sang.
    Suddenly the golden night all with music rang.

Angels leading shepherds, shepherds leading sheep:
The silence of worship broke the mother's sleep.
All the meek and lowly of all the world were there;
Smiling, she showed them that her Child was fair,
  "*Baby, my baby*," kissing Him she said.
  Suddenly a flaming star through the heavens sped.

Three old men and weary knelt them side by side,
The world's wealth forswearing, majesty and pride;
Worldly might and wisdom before the Babe bent low:
Weeping, maid Mary said, "I love Him so!"
  "*Baby, my baby*," and the Baby slept.
  Suddenly on Calvary all the olives wept.

Shaemas OSheel [1886–

GATES AND DOORS

A BALLAD OF CHRISTMAS EVE

THERE was a gentle hostler
  (And blessed be his name!)
He opened up the stable
  The night Our Lady came.
Our Lady and St. Joseph,
  He gave them food and bed,
And Jesus Christ has given him
  A glory round his head.

*So let the gate swing open
  However poor the yard,
Lest weary people visit you
  And find their passage barred.
Unlatch the door at midnight
  And let your lantern's glow
Shine out to guide the traveler's feet
  To you across the snow.*

There was a courteous hostler
  (He is in Heaven to-night)
He held Our Lady's bridle
  And helped her to alight.

He spread clean straw before her
 Whereon she might lie down,
And Jesus Christ has given him
 An everlasting crown.

Unlock the door this evening
 And let your gate swing wide,
Let all who ask for shelter
 Come speedily inside.
What if your yard be narrow?
 What if your house be small?
There is a Guest is coming
 Will glorify it all.

There was a joyous hostler
 Who knelt on Christmas morn
Beside the radiant manger
 Wherein his Lord was born.
His heart was full of laughter,
 His soul was full of bliss
When Jesus, on His Mother's lap,
 Gave him His hand to kiss.

Unbar your heart this evening
 And keep no stranger out,
Take from your soul's great portal
 The barrier of doubt.
To humble folk and weary
 Give hearty welcoming,
Your breast shall be to-morrow
 The cradle of a King.

Joyce Kilmer [1886–1918]

THE THREE KINGS

THREE Kings came riding from far away,
 Melchior and Gaspar and Baltasar;
Three Wise Men out of the East were they,
And they travelled by night and they slept by day,
 For their guide was a beautiful, wonderful star.

The star was so beautiful, large and clear,
    That all the other stars of the sky
Became a white mist in the atmosphere;
And by this they knew that the coming was near
    Of the Prince foretold in the prophecy.

Three caskets they bore on their saddle-bows,
    Three caskets of gold with golden keys;
Their robes were of crimson silk, with rows
Of bells and pomegranates and furbelows,
    Their turbans like blossoming almond-trees.

And so the Three Kings rode into the West,
    Through the dusk of night, over hill and dell,
And sometimes they nodded with beard on breast,
And sometimes talked, as they paused to rest,
    With the people they met at some wayside well.

"Of the child that is born," said Baltasar,
    "Good people, I pray you, tell us the news,
For we in the East have seen his star,
And have ridden fast, and have ridden far,
    To find and worship the King of the Jews."

And the people answered, "You ask in vain;
    We know of no king but Herod the Great!"
They thought the Wise Men were men insane,
As they spurred their horses across the plain
    Like riders in haste, and who cannot wait.

And when they came to Jerusalem,
    Herod the Great, who had heard this thing,
Sent for the Wise Men and questioned them;
And said, "Go down unto Bethlehem,
    And bring me tidings of this new king."

So they rode away, and the star stood still,
    The only one in the gray of morn;
Yes, it stopped,—it stood still of its own free will,
Right over Bethlehem on the hill,
    The city of David, where Christ was born.

And the Three Kings rode through the gate and the guard,
  Through the silent street, till their horses turned
And neighed as they entered the great inn-yard;
But the windows were closed, and the doors were barred,
  And only a light in the stable burned.

And cradled there in the scented hay,
  In the air made sweet by the breath of kine,
The little child in the manger lay,
The Child that would be King one day
  Of a kingdom not human, but divine.

His mother, Mary of Nazareth,
  Sat watching beside his place of rest,
Watching the even flow of his breath,
For the joy of life and the terror of death
  Were mingled together in her breast.

They laid their offerings at his feet:
  The gold was their tribute to a King;
The frankincense, with its odor sweet,
Was for the Priest, the Paraclete;
  The myrrh for the body's burying.

And the mother wondered and bowed her head,
  And sat as still as a statue of stone;
Her heart was troubled yet comforted,
Remembering what the Angel had said
  Of an endless reign and of David's throne.

Then the Kings rode out of the city gate,
  With a clatter of hoofs in proud array;
But they went not back to Herod the Great,
For they knew his malice and feared his hate,
  And returned to their homes by another way.

                    Henry Wadsworth Longfellow [1807–1882]

LULLABY IN BETHLEHEM

THERE hath come an host to see Thee,
  Baby dear,
Bearded men with eyes of flame
  And lips of fear,

For the heavens, they say, have broken
Into blinding gulfs of glory,
And the Lord, they say, hath spoken
In a little wondrous story,
Baby dear.

There have come three kings to greet Thee,
Baby dear,
Crowned with gold, and clad in purple,
They draw near.
They have brought rare silks to bind Thee,
At Thy feet, behold, they spread them,
From their thrones they sprang to find Thee,
And a blazing star hath led them,
Baby dear.

I have neither jade nor jasper,
Baby dear,
Thou art all my hope and glory,
And my fear,
Yet for all the gems that strew Thee,
And the costly gowns that fold Thee,
Yea, though all the world should woo Thee,
Thou art mine—and fast I hold Thee,
Baby dear.

Henry Howarth Bashford [1880–

A CHILD'S SONG OF CHRISTMAS

My counterpane is soft as silk,
My blankets white as creamy milk.
    The hay was soft to Him, I know,
    Our little Lord of long ago.

Above the roofs the pigeons fly
In silver wheels across the sky.
    The stable-doves they cooed to them,
    Mary and Christ in Bethlehem.

Bright shines the sun across the drifts,
And bright upon my Christmas gifts.
    They brought Him incense, myrrh, and gold,
    Our little Lord who lived of old.

Oh, soft and clear our mother sings
Of Christmas joys and Christmas things.
   God's holy angels sang to them,
   Mary and Christ in Bethlehem.

Our hearts they hold all Christmas dear,
And earth seems sweet and heaven seems near,
   Oh, heaven was in His sight, I know,
   That little Child of long ago.

Marjorie L. C. Pickthall [1883-1922]

JEST 'FORE CHRISTMAS

FATHER calls me William, sister calls me Will,
Mother calls me Willie, but the fellers call me Bill!
Mighty glad I ain't a girl—ruther be a boy,
Without them sashes, curls, an' things that's worn by
    Fauntleroy!
Love to chawnk green apples an' go swimmin' in the lake—
Hate to take the castor-ile they give for belly-ache!
'Most all the time, the whole year round, there ain't no
    flies on me,
But jest 'fore Christmas I'm as good as I kin be!

Got a yeller dog named Sport, sick him on the cat;
First thing she knows she doesn't know where she is at!
Got a clipper sled, an' when us kids goes out to slide,
'Long comes the grocery cart, an' we all hook a ride!
But sometimes when the grocery man is worrited an' cross,
He reaches at us with his whip, an' larrups up his hoss,
An' then I laff an' holler, "Oh, ye never teched *me!*"
But jest 'fore Christmas I'm as good as I kin be!

Gran'ma says she hopes that when I git to be a man,
I'll be a missionarer like her oldest brother, Dan,
As was et up by the cannibuls that lives in Ceylon's Isle,
Where every prospeck pleases, an' only man is vile!
But gran'ma she has never been to see a Wild West show,
Nor read the Life of Daniel Boone, or else I guess she'd
    know

That Buff'lo Bill and cow-boys is good enough for me!
Excep' jest 'fore Christmas, when I'm good as I kin be!

And then old Sport he hangs around, so solemn-like an' still,
His eyes they keep a-sayin': "What's the matter, little
    Bill?"
The old cat sneaks down off her perch an' wonders what's
    become
Of them two enemies of hern that used to make things hum!
But I am so perlite an' 'tend so earnestly to biz,
That mother says to father: "How improved our Willie is!"
But father, havin' been a boy hisself, suspicions me
When jest 'fore Christmas, I'm as good as I kin be!

For Christmas, with its lots an' lots of candies, cakes an'
    toys,
Was made, they say, for proper kids an' not for naughty
    boys;
So wash yer face an' bresh yer hair, an' mind yer p's an' q's,
An' don't bust out yer pantaloons, an' don't wear out yer
    shoes;
Say "Yessum" to the ladies, an' "Yessur" to the men,
An' when they's company, don't pass yer plate for pie
    again;
But, thinking of the things yer'd like to see upon that tree,
Jest 'fore Christmas be as good as yer kin be!

                         Eugene Field [1850–1895]

A VISIT FROM ST. NICHOLAS

'Twas the night before Christmas, when all through the
    house
Not a creature was stirring, not even a mouse;
The stockings were hung by the chimney with care,
In hopes that St. Nicholas soon would be there;
The children were nestled all snug in their beds,
While visions of sugar-plums danced in their heads;
And mamma in her 'kerchief, and I in my cap,
Had just settled our brains for a long winter's nap,
When out on the lawn there arose such a clatter,
I sprang from the bed to see what was the matter.

Away to the window I flew like a flash,
Tore open the shutters and threw up the sash.
The moon on the breast of the new-fallen snow
Gave the lustre of mid-day to objects below,
When, what to my wondering eyes should appear,
But a miniature sleigh, and eight tiny reindeer,
With a little old driver, so lively and quick,
I knew in a moment it must be St. Nick.
More rapid than eagles his coursers they came,
And he whistled, and shouted, and called them by name;
"Now, *Dasher!* now, *Dancer!* now, *Prancer* and *Vixen!*
On, *Comet !* on *Cupid!* on, *Donder* and *Blitzen!*
To the top of the porch! to the top of the wall!
Now dash away! dash away! dash away all!"
As dry leaves that before the wild hurricane fly,
When they meet with an obstacle, mount to the sky,
So up to the house-top the coursers they flew,
With the sleigh full of toys, and St. Nicholas too.
And then, in a twinkling, I heard on the roof
The prancing and pawing of each little hoof.
As I drew in my head, and was turning around,
Down the chimney St. Nicholas came with a bound.
He was dressed all in fur, from his head to his foot,
And his clothes were all tarnished with ashes and soot;
A bundle of toys he had flung on his back,
And he looked like a peddler just opening his pack.
His eyes—how they twinkled! his dimples how merry!
His cheeks were like roses, his nose like a cherry!
His droll little mouth was drawn up like a bow,
And the beard of his chin was as white as the snow;
The stump of a pipe he held tight in his teeth,
And the smoke it encircled his head like a wreath;
He had a broad face and a little round belly,
That shook, when he laughed, like a bowlful of jelly.
He was chubby and plump, a right jolly old elf,
And I laughed when I saw him, in spite of myself;
A wink of his eye and a twist of his head,
Soon gave me to know I had nothing to dread;
He spoke not a word, but went straight to his work,
And filled all the stockings; then turned with a jerk,

And laying his finger aside of his nose,
And giving a nod, up the chimney he rose;
He sprang to his sleigh, to his team gave a whistle,
And away they all flew like the down of a thistle.
But I heard him exclaim, ere he drove out of sight,
"Happy Christmas to all, and to all a good-night."
                              Clement Clarke Moore [1779–1863]

CEREMONIES FOR CHRISTMAS

Come, bring with a noise,
    My merry, merry boys,
The Christmas log to the firing;
    While my good dame, she
    Bids ye all be free;
And drink to your hearts' desiring.

    With the last year's brand
    Light the new block, and
For good success in his spending,
    On your psaltries play,
    That sweet luck may
Come while the log is a-tending.

    Drink now the strong beer,
    Cut the white loaf here,
The while the meat is a-shredding;
    For the rare mince-pie
    And the plums stand by
To fill the paste that's a-kneading.
                              Robert Herrick [1591–1674]

ON THE MORNING OF CHRIST'S NATIVITY

This is the month, and this the happy morn
Wherein the Son of Heaven's Eternal King,
Of wedded maid and virgin mother born,
Our great redemption from above did bring;

For so the holy sages once did sing
That he our deadly forfeit should release,
And with his Father work us a perpetual peace.

That glorious Form, that Light unsufferable,
And that far-beaming blaze of Majesty
Wherewith he wont at Heaven's high council-ta
To sit the midst of Trinal Unity,
He laid aside; and, here with us to be,
Forsook the courts of everlasting day,
And chose with us a darksome house of mortal clay.

Say, Heavenly Muse, shall not thy sacred vein
Afford a present to the Infant God?
Hast thou no verse, no hymn, or solemn strain
To welcome him to this his new abode,
Now while the heaven, by the sun's team untrod,
Hath took no print of the approaching light,
And all the spangled host keep watch in squadrons bright?

See how from far, upon the eastern road,
The star-led wizards haste with odors sweet!
O run, prevent them with thy humble ode
And lay it lowly at his blessed feet;
Have thou the honor first thy Lord to greet,
And join thy voice unto the angel choir
From out his secret altar touched with hallowed fire.

THE HYMN

It was the winter wild
While the heaven-born Child
All meanly wrapped in the rude manger lies;
Nature in awe to Him
Had doffed her gaudy trim,
With her great Master so to sympathize:
It was no season then for her
To wanton with the sun, her lusty paramour.

Only with speeches fair
She woos the gentle air

To hide her guilty front with innocent snow;
And on her naked shame,
Pollute with sinful blame,
The saintly veil of maiden white to throw;
Confounded, that her Maker's eyes
Should look so near upon her foul deformities.

But he, her fears to cease,
Sent down the meek-eyed Peace;
She, crowned with olive green, came softly sliding
Down through the turning sphere,
His ready harbinger,
With turtle wing and amorous clouds dividing;
And waving wide her myrtle wand,
She strikes a universal peace through sea and land.

No war, or battle's sound
Was heard the world around:
The idle spear and shield were high uphung;
The hookèd chariot stood
Unstained with hostile blood;
The trumpet spake not to the armèd throng;
And kings sat still with awful eye,
As if they surely knew their sovereign Lord was by.

But peaceful was the night
Wherein the Prince of Light
His reign of peace upon the earth began:
The winds, with wonder whist,
Smoothly the waters kissed,
Whispering new joys to the mild oceàn—
Who now hath quite forgot to rave,
While birds of calm sit brooding on the charmèd wave.

The stars, with deep amaze,
Stand fixed in steadfast gaze,
Bending one way their precious influence;
And will not take their flight
For all the morning light,
Or Lucifer that often warned them thence;
But in their glimmering orbs did glow
Until their Lord himself bespake, and bid them go.

And though the shady gloom
Had given day her room,
The sun himself withheld his wonted speed,
And hid his head for shame,
As his inferior flame
The new-enlightened world no more should need;
He saw a greater Sun appear
Than his bright throne, or burning axletree, could bear.

The shepherds on the lawn
Or ere the point of dawn
Sat simply chatting in a rustic row;
Full little thought they then
That the mighty Pan
Was kindly come to live with them below;
Perhaps their loves, or else their sheep,
Was all that did their silly thoughts so busy keep.

When such music sweet
Their hearts and ears did greet
As never was by mortal finger strook—
Divinely-warbled voice
Answering the stringèd noise,
As all their souls in blissful rapture took:
The air, such pleasure loth to lose,
With thousand echoes still prolongs each heavenly close.

Nature, that heard such sound
Beneath the hollow round
Of Cynthia's seat the airy region thrilling,
Now was almost won
To think her part was done,
And that her reign had here its last fulfilling;
She knew such harmony alone
Could hold all heaven and earth in happier union.

At last surrounds their sight
A globe of circular light
That with long beams the shamefaced night arrayed;
The helmèd Cherubim
And sworded Seraphim
Are seen in glittering ranks with wings displayed,

Harping in loud and solemn choir
With unexpressive notes, to Heaven's new-born Heir.

Such music (as 'tis said)
Before was never made
But when of old the sons of morning sung,
While the Creator great
His constellations set
And the well-balanced world on hinges hung;
And cast the dark foundations deep,
And bid the weltering waves their oozy channel keep.

Ring out, ye crystal spheres!
Once bless our human ears,
If ye have power to touch our senses so;
And let your silver chime
Move in melodious time;
And let the bass of Heaven's deep organ blow;
And with your ninefold harmony
Make up full consort to the angelic symphony.

For if such holy song
Enwrap our fancy long,
Time will run back, and fetch the age of gold;
And speckled vanity
Will sicken soon and die,
And leprous sin will melt from earthly mould;
And Hell itself will pass away,
And leave her dolorous mansions to the peering day.

Yea, Truth and Justice then
Will down return to men,
Orbed in a rainbow; and, like glories wearing,
Mercy will sit between
Throned in celestial sheen,
With radiant feet the tissued clouds down steering;
And Heaven, as at some festival,
Will open wide the gates of her high palace hall.

But wisest Fate says No;
This must not yet be so;

The Babe yet lies in smiling infancy
That on the bitter cross
Must redeem our loss;
So both himself and us to glorify:
Yet first, to those ychained in sleep
The wakeful trump of doom must thunder through the
    deep;

With such a horrid clang
As on Mount Sinai rang
While the red fire and smouldering clouds outbrake:
The agèd Earth aghast
With terror of that blast
Shall from the surface to the centre shake,
When, at the world's last sessiòn,
The dreadful Judge in middle air shall spread His throne.

And then at last our bliss
Full and perfect is,
But now begins; for from this happy day
The old Dragon under ground,
In straiter limits bound,
Not half so far casts his usurpèd sway;
And, wroth to see his kingdom fail,
Swinges the scaly horror of his folded tail.

The oracles are dumb;
No voice or hideous hum
Runs through the archèd roof in words deceiving.
Apollo from his shrine
Can no more divine,
With hollow shriek the steep of Delphos leaving:
No nightly trance or breathèd spell
Inspires the pale-eyed priest from the prophetic cell.

The lonely mountains o'er
And the resounding shore
A voice of weeping heard, and loud lament;
From haunted spring and dale
Edged with poplar pale
The parting Genius is with sighing sent;

With flower-inwoven tresses torn
The Nymphs in twilight shade of tangled thickets mourn.

In consecrated earth
And on the holy hearth
The Lars and Lemures moan with midnight plaint;
In urns, and altars round
A drear and dying sound
Affrights the Flamens at their service quaint;
And the chill marble seems to sweat,
While each peculiar Power foregoes his wonted seat.

Peor and Baälim
Forsake their temples dim,
With that twice-battered god of Palestine;
And moonèd Ashtaroth
Heaven's queen and mother both,
Now sits not girt with tapers' holy shine;
The Lybic Hammon shrinks his horn:
In vain the Tyrian maids their wounded Thammuz mourn.

And sullen Moloch, fled,
Hath left in shadows dread
His burning idol all of blackest hue;
In vain with cymbals' ring
They call the grisly king,
In dismal dance about the furnace blue;
The brutish gods of Nile as fast,
Isis, and Orus, and the dog Anubis, haste.

Nor is Osiris seen
In Memphian grove, or green,
Trampling the unshowered grass with lowings loud:
Nor can he be at rest
Within his sacred chest;
Naught but profoundest Hell can be his shroud;
In vain with timbrelled anthems dark
The sable stolèd sorcerers bear his worshiped ark.

He feels from Juda's land
The dreaded Infant's hand;

The rays of Bethlehem blind his dusky eyen;
Nor all the gods beside
Longer dare abide
Nor Typhon huge ending in snaky twine:
Our Babe, to show his Godhead true,
Can in His swaddling bands control the damnèd crew.

So, when the sun in bed
Curtained with cloudy red
Pillows his chin upon an orient wave,
The flocking shadows pale
Troop to the infernal jail,
Each fettered ghost slips to his several grave:
And the yellow-skirted fays
Fly after the night-steeds, leaving their moon-loved maze.

But see! the Virgin blest
Hath laid her Babe to rest;
Time is, our tedious song should here have ending:
Heaven's youngest teemèd star
Hath fixed her polished car,
Her sleeping Lord with hand-maid lamp attending:
And all about the courtly stable
Bright-harnessed Angels sit in order serviceable.

John Milton [1608–1674]

FAIRYLAND

THE FAIRY BOOK

In summer, when the grass is thick, if mother has the time,
She shows me with her pencil how a poet makes a rhyme,
And often she is sweet enough to choose a leafy nook,
Where I cuddle up so closely when she reads the Fairy-
book.

In winter, when the corn's asleep, and birds are not in
song,
And crocuses and violets have been away too long,
Dear mother puts her thimble by in answer to my look,
And I cuddle up so closely when she reads the Fairy-
book.

And mother tells the servants that of course they must
contrive
To manage all the household things from four till half-
past five,
For we really cannot suffer interruption from the cook,
When we cuddle close together with the happy Fairy-
book.

Norman Gale [1862–

FAIRY SONGS

I

From "A Midsummer-Night's Dream"

Over hill, over dale,
　　Through bush, through brier,
Over park, over pale,
　　Through flood, through fire,

I do wander everywhere,
Swifter than the moonè's sphere;
And I serve the fairy queen,
To dew her orbs upon the green:
The cowslips tall her pensioners be;
In their gold coats spots you see;
Those be rubies, fairy favors,
In those freckles live their savors:
I must go seek some dew-drops here,
And hang a pearl in every cowslip's ear.

II

From "A Midsummer-Night's Dream"

You spotted snakes with double tongue,
    Thorny hedgehogs, be not seen;
Newts and blind-worms, do no wrong;
    Come not near our fairy queen.

    Philomel, with melody,
    Sing in our sweet lullaby;
Lulla, lulla, lullaby; lulla, lulla, lullaby!
    Never harm,
    Nor spell nor charm,
    Come our lovely lady nigh;
    So, good night, with lullaby.

Weaving spiders, come not here;
    Hence, you long-legged spinners, hence!
Beetles black, approach not near;
    Worm nor snail, do no offence.

    Philomel, with melody,
    Sing in our sweet lullaby;
Lulla, lulla, lullaby; lulla, lulla, lullaby!
    Never harm,
    Nor spell nor charm,
    Come our lovely lady nigh;
    So, good-night, with lullaby.

III

From "The Tempest"

Come unto these yellow sands,
    And then take hands:
Court'sied when you have, and kissed,—
    The wild waves whist,—
Foot it featly here and there;
And, sweet sprites, the burthen bear.
        Hark, hark!
            Bow, wow,
        The watch-dogs bark:
            Bow, wow.
        Hark, hark!   I hear
    The strain of strutting chanticleer
    Cry, Cock-a-diddle-dow!

IV

From "The Tempest"

Where the bee sucks, there suck I:
    In a cowslip's bell I lie;
There I couch when owls do cry.
On the bat's back I do fly
After summer merrily:
    Merrily, merrily, shall I live now,
    Under the blossom that hangs on the bough.
            William Shakespeare [1564–1616]

QUEEN MAB

From "The Satyr"

This is Mab, the Mistress-Fairy,
That doth nightly rob the dairy
And can hurt or help the churning,
As she please without discerning.

She that pinches country wenches
If they rub not clean their benches,

And with sharper nails remembers
When they rake not up their embers:
But if so they chance to feast her,
In a shoe she drops a tester.

This is she that empties cradles,
Takes out children, puts in ladles:
Trains forth old wives in their slumber
With a sieve the holes to number;
And then leads them from her burrows,
Home through ponds and water-furrows.

She can start our Franklins' daughters,
In their sleep, with shrieks and laughters:
And on sweet Saint Anna's night
Feed them with a promised sight,
Some of husbands, some of lovers,
Which an empty dream discovers.

Ben Jonson [1573?–1637]

THE ELF AND THE DORMOUSE

UNDER a toadstool crept a wee Elf,
Out of the rain, to shelter himself.

Under the toadstool sound asleep,
Sat a big Dormouse all in a heap.

Trembled the wee Elf, frightened, and yet
Fearing to fly away lest he get wet.

To the next shelter—maybe a mile!
Sudden the wee Elf smiled a wee smile,

Tugged till the toadstool toppled in two.
Holding it over him, gayly he flew.

Soon he was safe home, dry as could be.
Soon woke the Dormouse—"Good gracious me!

"Where is my toadstool?" loud he lamented.
—And that's how umbrellas first were invented.

Oliver Herford [1863–1935]

"OH! WHERE DO FAIRIES HIDE THEIR HEADS?"

Oh! where do fairies hide their heads,
    When snow lies on the hills,
When frost has spoiled their mossy beds,
    And crystallized their rills?
Beneath the moon they cannot trip
    In circles o'er the plain;
And draughts of dew they cannot sip,
    Till green leaves come again.

Perhaps, in small, blue diving-bells
    They plunge beneath the waves,
Inhabiting the wreathèd shells
    That lie in coral caves.
Perhaps, in red Vesuvius
    Carousals they maintain;
And cheer their little spirits thus,
    Till green leaves come again.

When they return, there will be mirth
    And music in the air.
And fairy wings upon the earth,
    And mischief everywhere.
The maids, to keep the elves aloof,
    Will bar the doors in vain;
No key-hole will be fairy-proof,
    When green leaves come again.
                    Thomas Haynes Bayly [1797–1839]

FAIRY SONG

From "Amyntas"

We the Fairies, blithe and antic,
Of dimensions not gigantic,
Though the moonshine mostly keep us,
Oft in orchards frisk and peep us.

Stolen sweets are always sweeter,
Stolen kisses much completer,
Stolen looks are nice in chapels,
Stolen, stolen be your apples.

When to bed the world is bobbing,
Then's the time for orchard-robbing;
Yet the fruit were scarce worth peeling
Were it not for stealing, stealing.

Translated by Leigh Hunt from the Latin of Thomas Randolph
[1605–1635]

DREAM SONG

I COME from woods enchaunted,
Starlit and pixey-haunted,
 Where 'twixt the bracken and the trees
 The goblins lie and take their ease
By winter moods undaunted.

There down the golden gravel
The laughing rivers travel;
 Elves wake at nights and whisper low
 Between the bracken and the snow
Their dreamings to unravel.

Twisted and lank and hairy,
With wanton eyes and wary,
 They stretch and chuckle in the wind,
 For one has found a mermaid kind,
And one has kissed a fairy.

They know no melancholy,
But fashion crowns of holly,
 And gather sleep within the brake
 To deck a kingdom when they wake,
And bless the dreamer's folly.

Ah! would that I might follow
The servants of Apollo!
 But it is sweet to heap the hours
 With quiet dreams and poppy-flowers,
Down in the pixies' hollow.
     Richard Middleton [1882–1911]

FAIRY SONG

SHED no tear! O, shed no tear!
The flower will bloom another year.
Weep no more! O, weep no more!
Young buds sleep in the root's white core.
Dry your eyes! O, dry your eyes!
For I was taught in Paradise
To ease my breast of melodies,—

                    Shed no tear.

Overhead! look overhead!
'Mong the blossoms white and red,—
Look up, look up! I flutter now
On this flush pomegranate bough.
See me! 'tis this silvery bill
Ever cures the good man's ill,—
Shed no tear! O, shed no tear!
The flower will bloom another year.
Adieu, adieu—I fly—adieu!
I vanish in the heaven's blue,—

                    Adieu, adieu!
            John Keats [1795–1821]

QUEEN MAB

A LITTLE fairy comes at night,
  Her eyes are blue, her hair is brown,
With silver spots upon her wings,
  And from the moon she flutters down.

She has a little silver wand,
  And when a good child goes to bed
She waves her hand from right to left,
  And makes a circle round its head.

And then it dreams of pleasant things,
  Of fountains filled with fairy fish,
And trees that bear delicious fruit,
  And bow their branches at a wish:

Of arbors filled with dainty scents
    From lovely flowers that never fade;
Bright flies that glitter in the sun,
    And glow-worms shining in the shade:

And talking birds with gifted tongues,
    For singing songs and telling tales,
And pretty dwarfs to show the way
    Through fairy hills and fairy dales.

But when a bad child goes to bed,
    From left to right she weaves her rings,
And then it dreams all through the night
    Of only ugly horrid things!

Then lions come with glaring eyes,
    And tigers growl, a dreadful noise,
And ogres draw their cruel knives,
    To shed the blood of girls and boys.

Then stormy waves rush on to drown,
    Or raging flames come scorching round,
Fierce dragons hover in the air,
    And serpents crawl along the ground.

Then wicked children wake and weep,
    And wish the long black gloom away;
But good ones love the dark, and find
    The night as pleasant as the day.
                    Thomas Hood [1799–1845]

THE FAIRIES OF THE CALDON–LOW

A MIDSUMMER LEGEND

"AND where have you been, my Mary,
    And where have you been from me?"
"I've been to the top of the Caldon-Low,
    The midsummer night to see!"

"And what did you see, my Mary,
    All up on the Caldon-Low?"
"I saw the glad sunshine come down,
    And I saw the merry winds blow."

"And what did you hear, my Mary,
    All up on the Caldon-Hill?"
"I heard the drops of the water made,
    And the ears of the green corn fill."

"Oh, tell me all, my Mary—
    All—all that ever you know;
For you must have seen the fairies
    Last night on the Caldon-Low!"

"Then take me on your knee, mother,
    And listen, mother of mine:
A hundred fairies danced last night,
    And the harpers they were nine.

"And their harp-strings rang so merrily
    To their dancing feet so small;
But, oh! the words of their talking
    Were merrier far than all!"

"And what were the words, my Mary,
    That you did hear them say?"
"I'll tell you all, my mother,
    But let me have my way.

"Some of them played with the water,
    And rolled it down the hill;
'And this,' they said, 'shall speedily turn
    The poor old miller's mill.

"'For there has been no water
    Ever since the first of May;
And a busy man will the miller be
    At the dawning of the day!

" 'Oh! the miller, how he will laugh,
    When he sees the mill-dam rise!
The jolly old miller, how he will laugh,
    Till the tears fill both his eyes!'

"And some they seized the little winds,
    That sounded over the hill,
And each put a horn into his mouth,
    And blew both loud and shrill:

" 'And there,' said they, 'the merry winds go
    Away from every horn;
And they shall clear the mildew dank
    From the blind old widow's corn:

" 'Oh, the poor blind widow—
    Though she has been blind so long,
She'll be merry enough when the mildew's gone,
    And the corn stands tall and strong!'

"And some they brought the brown linseed
    And flung it down the Low:
'And this,' said they, ' by the sunrise
    In the weaver's croft shall grow!

" 'Oh, the poor lame weaver!
    How will he laugh outright
When he sees his dwindling flax-field
    All full of flowers by night!'

"And then outspoke a brownie,
    With a long beard on his chin:
'I have spun up all the tow,' said he,
    'And I want some more to spin.

" 'I've spun a piece of hempen cloth
    And I want to spin another—
A little sheet for Mary's bed,
    And an apron for her mother!'

"With that I could not help but laugh,
    And I laughed out loud and free;
And then on the top of the Caldon-Low
    There was no one left but me.

"And all on the top of the Caldon-Low
    The mists were cold and gray,
And nothing I saw but the mossy stones
    That round about me lay.

"But, coming down from the hill-top,
    I heard, afar below,
How busy the jolly miller was,
    And how merry the wheel did go!

"And I peeped into the widow's field,
    And, sure enough, was seen
The yellow ears of the mildewed corn
    All standing stout and green.

"And down the weaver's croft I stole,
    To see if the flax were sprung;
And I met the weaver at his gate
    With the good news on his tongue!

"Now, this is all I heard, mother,
    And all that I did see;
So, prithee, make my bed, mother,
    For I'm tired as I can be!"
                            Mary Howitt [1799–1888]

THE FAIRIES

Up the airy mountain,
    Down the rushy glen,
We daren't go a-hunting
    For fear of little men;
Wee folk, good folk,
    Trooping all together;
Green jacket, red cap,
    And white owl's feather!

Down along the rocky shore
  Some make their home,
They live on crispy pancakes
  Of yellow tide-foam;
Some in the reeds
  Of the black mountain lake,
With frogs for their watch-dogs,
  All night awake.

High on the hill-top
  The old King sits;
He is now so old and gray
  He's nigh lost his wits.
With a bridge of white mist
  Columbkill he crosses,
On his stately journeys
  From Slieveleague to Rosses;
Or going up with music
  On cold starry nights
To sup with the Queen
  Of the gay Northern Lights.

They stole little Bridget
  For seven years long;
When she came down again
  Her friends were all gone.
They took her lightly back,
  Between the night and morrow,
They thought that she was fast asleep,
  But she was dead with sorrow.
They have kept her ever since
  Deep within the lake,
On a bed of flag-leaves,
  Watching till she wake.

By the craggy hill-side,
  Through the mosses bare,
They have planted thorn-trees
  For pleasure here and there.

If any man so daring
　　As dig them up in spite,
He shall find their sharpest thorns
　　In his bed at night.

Up the airy mountain,
　　Down the rushy glen,
We daren't go a-hunting
　　For fear of little men;
Wee folk, good folk,
　　Trooping all together;
Green jacket, red cap,
　　And white owl's feather!
William Allingham [1824–1889]

THE FAIRY THRALL

On gossamer nights when the moon is low,
　　And stars in the mist are hiding,
Over the hill where the foxgloves grow
　　You may see the fairies riding.
　　　Kling! Klang! Kling!
　　　Their stirrups and their bridles ring,
　　And their horns are loud and their bugles blow,
　　When the moon is low.

They sweep through the night like a whistling wind,
　　They pass and have left no traces;
But one of them lingers far behind
　　The flight of the fairy faces.
　　　She makes no moan,
　　　She sorrows in the dark alone,
　　She wails for the love of human kind,
　　Like a whistling wind.

"Ah! why did I roam where the elfins ride,
　　Their glimmering steps to follow?
They bore me far from my loved one's side,
　　To wander o'er hill and hollow.

Kling! Klang! Kling!
Their stirrups and their bridles ring,
But my heart is cold in the cold night-tide,
Where the elfins ride."

Mary C. G. Byron [1861–

FAREWELL TO THE FAIRIES

FAREWELL, rewards and fairies!
 Good housewives now may say,
For now foul sluts in dairies
 Do fare as well as they.
And though they sweep their hearths no less
 Than maids were wont to do,
Yet who of late, for cleanliness,
 Finds sixpence in her shoe?

Lament, lament, old abbeys,
 The fairies' lost command!
They did but change priests' babies,
 But some have changed your land;
And all your children sprung from thence,
 Are now grown Puritanes;
Who live as changelings ever since,
 For love of your demains.

At morning and at evening both
 You merry were and glad;
So little care of sleep or sloth
 These pretty ladies had;
When Tom came home from labor,
 Or Ciss to milking rose,
Then merrily merrily went their tabor
 And nimbly went their toes.

Witness those rings and roundelays
 Of theirs, which yet remain,
Were footed in Queen Mary's days
 On many a grassy plain;

But since of late, Elizabeth,
  And later, James came in,
They never danced on any heath
  As when the time hath been.

By which we note the fairies
  Were of the old profession;
Their songs were *Ave-Maries*,
  Their dances were procession.
But now, alas! they all are dead,
  Or gone beyond the seas;
Or farther for religion fled;
  Or else they take their ease.

A tell-tale in their company
  They never could endure;
And whoso kept not secretly
  Their mirth, was punished sure;
It was a just and Christian deed
  To pinch such black and blue:
Oh, how the Commonwealth doth need
  Such justices as you!
                    Richard Corbet [1582–1635]

THE FAIRY FOLK

COME cuddle close in daddy's coat
  Beside the fire so bright,
And hear about the fairy folk
  That wander in the night.
For when the stars are shining clear
  And all the world is still,
They float across the silver moon
  From hill to cloudy hill.

Their caps of red, their cloaks of green,
  Are hung with silver bells,
And when they're shaken with the wind
  Their merry ringing swells.
And riding on the crimson moth,
  With black spots on her wings,
They guide them down the purple sky
  With golden bridle rings.

They love to visit girls and boys
  To see how sweet they sleep,
To stand beside their cosy cots
  And at their faces peep.
For in the whole of fairy-land
  They have no finer sight
Than little children sleeping sound
  With faces rosy bright.

On tip-toe crowding round their heads,
  When bright the moonlight beams,
They whisper little tender words
  That fill their minds with dreams;
And when they see a sunny smile,
  With lightest finger tips
They lay a hundred kisses sweet
  Upon the ruddy lips.

And then the little spotted moths
  Spread out their crimson wings,
And bear away the fairy crowd
  With shaking bridle rings.
Come, bairnies, hide in daddy's coat,
  Beside the fire so bright—
Perhaps the little fairy folk
  Will visit you to-night.

                          Robert Bird [1867

THE FAIRY BOOK

WHEN Mother takes the Fairy Book
  And we curl up to hear,
'Tis "All aboard for Fairyland!"
  Which seems to be so near.

For soon we reach the pleasant place
  Of Once Upon a Time,
Where birdies sing the hour of day,
  And flowers talk in rhyme;

Where Bobby is a velvet Prince,
  And where I am a Queen;

Where one can talk with animals,
   And walk about unseen;

Where Little People live in nuts,
   And ride on butterflies,
And wonders kindly come to pass
   Before your very eyes;

Where candy grows on every bush,
   And playthings on the trees,
And visitors pick basketfuls
   As often as they please.

It is the nicest time of day—
   Though Bedtime is so near,—
When Mother takes the Fairy Book
   And we curl up to hear.

       Abbie Farwell Brown [1875–1927]

THE VISITOR

THE white goat Amaryllis,
   She wandered at her will
At time of daffodillies
   Afar and up the hill:
We hunted and we holloa'd
   And back she came at dawn,
But what d'you think had followed?—
   A little, pagan Faun!

His face was like a berry,
   His ears were high and pricked:
Tip-tap—his hoofs came merry
   As up the path he clicked;
A junket for his winning
   We set in dairy delf;
He eat it—peart and grinning
   As Christian as yourself!

He stayed about the steading
   A fortnight, say, or more;
A blanket for his bedding
   We spread beside the door;

And when the cocks crowed clearly
  Before the dawn was ripe,
He'd call the milkmaids cheerly
  Upon a reedy pipe!

That fortnight of his staying
  The work went smooth as silk:
The hens were all in laying,
  The cows were all in milk;
And then—and then one morning
  The maids woke up at day
Without his oaten warning,—
  And found he'd gone away.

He left no trace behind him;
  But still the milkmaids deem
That they, perhaps, may find him
  With butter and with cream:
Beside the door they set them
  In bowl and golden pat,
But no one comes to get them—
  Unless, maybe, the cat.

The white goat Amaryllis,
  She wanders at her will
At time of daffodillies,
  Away up Woolcombe hill;
She stays until the morrow,
  Then back she comes at dawn;
But never—to our sorrow—
  The little, pagan Faun.
            Patrick R. Chalmers [18

THE LITTLE ELF

I MET a little Elf-man, once,
  Down where the lilies blow.
I asked him why he was so small,
  And why he didn't grow.

He slightly frowned, and with his eye
   He looked me through and through.
"I'm quite as big for me," said he,
   "As you are big for you."
          John Kendrick Bangs [1862–1922]

THE SATYRS AND THE MOON

WITHIN the wood behind the hill
   The moon got tangled in the trees.
Her splendor made the branches thrill
   And thrilled the breeze.

The satyrs in the grotto bent
   Their heads to see the wondrous sight.
"It is a god in banishment
   That stirs the night."

The little satyr looked and guessed:
   "It is an apple that one sees,
Brought from that garden of the West—
   Hesperides."

"It is a cyclops' glaring eye."
   "A temple dome from Babylon."
"A Titan's cup of ivory."
   "A little sun."

The tiny satyr jumped for joy,
   And kicked his hoofs in utmost glee.
"It is a wondrous silver toy—
   Bring it to me!"

A great wind whistled through the blue
   And caught the moon and tossed it high;
A bubble of pale fire it flew
   Across the sky.

The satyrs gasped and looked and smiled,
   And wagged their heads from side to side,
Except their shaggy little child,
   Who cried and cried.
          Herbert S. Gorman [1893–

THE CHILDREN

THE CHILDREN

WHEN the lessons and tasks are all ended,
   And the school for the day is dismissed,
The little ones gather around me,
   To bid me good night and be kissed;
Oh, the little white arms that encircle
   My neck in their tender embrace!
Oh, the smiles that are halos of heaven,
   Shedding sunshine of love on my face!

And when they are gone, I sit dreaming
   Of my childhood too lovely to last,—
Of joy that my heart will remember,
   While it wakes to the pulse of the past,
Ere the world and its wickedness made me
   A partner of sorrow and sin,
When the glory of God was about me,
   And the glory of gladness within.

All my heart grows as weak as a woman's,
   And the fountain of feeling will flow,
When I think of the paths steep and stony,
   Where the feet of the dear ones must go,—
Of the mountains of sin hanging o'er them,
   Of the tempest of fate blowing wild;—
Oh, there's nothing on earth half so holy
   As the innocent heart of a child!

They are idols of hearts and of households;
   They are angels of God in disguise;
His sunlight still sleeps in their tresses,
   His glory still shines in their eyes;

Those truants from home and from heaven,—
  They have made me more manly and mild;
And I know now how Jesus could liken
  The kingdom of God to a child.

I ask not a life for the dear ones,
  All radiant, as others have done,
But that life may have just enough shadow
  To temper the glare of the sun;
I would pray God to guard them from evil,
  But my prayer would bound back to myself;—
Ah! a seraph may pray for a sinner,
  But a sinner must pray for himself.

The twig is so easily bended,
  I have banished the rule and the rod
I have taught them the goodness of knowledge,
  They have taught me the goodness of God:
My heart is the dungeon of darkness
  Where I shut them for breaking a rule;
My frown is sufficient correction;
  My love is the law of the school.

I shall leave the old house in the autumn,
  To traverse its threshold no more;
Ah, how I shall sigh for the dear ones
  That meet me each morn at the door!
I shall miss the "good nights" and the kisses,
  And the gush of their innocent glee,
The group on the green, and the flowers
  That are brought every morning for me.

I shall miss them at morn and at even,
  Their song in the school and the street;
I shall miss the low hum of their voices,
  And the tread of their delicate feet.
When the lessons of life are all ended,
  And death says: "The school is dismissed!"
May the little ones gather around me,
  To bid me good night and be kissed!
                    Charles Monroe Dickinson [1842–1924]

THE CHILDREN'S HOUR

BETWEEN the dark and the daylight,
  When the night is beginning to lower,
Comes a pause in the day's occupations,
  That is known as the Children's Hour.

I hear in the chamber above me
  The patter of little feet,
The sound of a door that is opened,
  And voices soft and sweet.

From my study I see in the lamplight,
  Descending the broad hall stair,
Grave Alice, and laughing Allegra,
  And Edith with golden hair.

A whisper, and then a silence:
  Yet I know by their merry eyes
They are plotting and planning together
  To take me by surprise.

A sudden rush from the stairway,
  A sudden raid from the hall!
By three doors left unguarded
  They enter my castle wall!

They climb up into my turret
  O'er the arms and back of my chair;
If I try to escape, they surround me;
  They seem to be everywhere.

They almost devour me with kisses,
  Their arms about me entwine,
Till I think of the Bishop of Bingen
  In his Mouse-Tower on the Rhine!

Do you think, O blue-eyed banditti,
  Because you have scaled the wall,
Such an old mustache as I am
  Is not a match for you all!

I have you fast in my fortress,
  And will not let you depart,
But put you down into the dungeon
  In the round-tower of my heart.

And there will I keep you forever,
  Yes, forever and a day,
Till the walls shall crumble to ruin,
  And moulder in dust away.
                Henry Wadsworth Longfellow [1807–1882]

LAUS INFANTIUM

IN praise of little children I will say
God first made man, then found a better way
For woman, but his third way was the best.
Of all created things, the loveliest
And most divine are children. Nothing here
Can be to us more gracious or more dear.
And though, when God saw all his works were good,
There was no rosy flower of babyhood,
'Twas said of children in a later day
That none could enter Heaven save such as they.

The earth, which feels the flowering of a thorn,
Was glad, O little child, when you were born;
The earth, which thrills when skylarks scale the blue,
Soared up itself to God's own Heaven in you;
And Heaven, which loves to lean down and to glass
Its beauty in each dewdrop on the grass,—
Heaven laughed to find your face so pure and fair,
And left, O little child, its reflex there.
                William Canton [1845–

THE DESIRE

  GIVE me no mansions ivory white
  Nor palaces of pearl and gold;
  Give me a child for all delight,
    Just four years old.

Give me no wings of rosy shine
Nor snowy raiment, fold on fold,
Give me a little boy all mine,
    Just four years old.

Give me no gold and starry crown
Nor harps, nor palm branches unrolled;
Give me a nestling head of brown,
    Just four years old.

Give me a cheek that's like the peach,
Two arms to clasp me from the cold;
And all my heaven's within my reach,
    Just four years old.

Dear God, You give me from Your skies
A little paradise to hold,
As Mary once her Paradise,
    Just four years old.
              Katherine Tynan Hinkson [1861–1931]

A CHILD'S LAUGHTER

ALL the bells of heaven may ring,
All the birds of heaven may sing,
All the wells on earth may spring,
All the winds on earth may bring
    All sweet sounds together;
Sweeter far then all things heard,
Hand of harper, tone of bird,
Sound of woods at sundawn stirred,
Welling water's winsome word,
    Wind in warm, wan weather.

One thing yet there is, that none,
Hearing ere its chime be done,
Knows not well the sweetest one
Heard of man beneath the sun,
    Hoped in heaven hereafter;
Soft and strong and loud and light,

Very sound of very light,
Heard from morning's rosiest height,
When the soul of all delight,
 Fills a child's clear laughter.

Golden bells of welcome rolled
Never forth such note, nor told
Hours so blithe in tones so bold,
As the radiant mouth of gold
 Here that rings forth heaven.
If the golden-crested wren
Were a nightingale—why, then
Something seen and heard of men
Might be half as sweet as when
 Laughs a child of seven.
    Algernon Charles Swinburne [1837–1909]

SEVEN YEARS OLD

SEVEN white roses on one tree,
Seven white loaves of blameless leaven,
Seven white sails on one soft sea,
Seven white swans on one lake's lea,
Seven white flowerlike stars in Heaven,
All are types unmeet to be
For a birthday's crown of seven.

Not the radiance of the roses,
Not the blessing of the bread,
Not the breeze that ere day grows is
Fresh for sails and swans, and closes
Wings above the sun's grave spread
When the starshine on the snows is
Sweet as sleep on sorrow shed.

Nothing sweeter, nothing best,
Holds so good and sweet a treasure
As the love wherewith once blest
Joy grows holy, grief takes rest,
Life, half tired with hours to measure,
Fills his eyes and lips and breast
With most light and breath of pleasure;

As the rapture unpolluted,
As the passion undefiled,
By whose force all pains heart-rooted
Are transfigured and transmuted,
Recompensed and reconciled,
Through the imperial, undisputed,
Present godhead of a child.

Brown bright eyes and fair bright head,
Worth a worthier crown than this is,
Worth a worthier song instead,
Sweet grave wise round mouth, full fed
With the joy of love, whose bliss is
More than mortal wine and bread,
Lips whose words are sweet as kisses.

Little hands so glad of giving,
Little heart so glad of love,
Little soul so glad of living,
While the strong swift hours are weaving
Light with darkness woven above,
Time for mirth and time for grieving,
Plume of raven and plume of dove.

I can give you but a word
Warm with love therein for leaven,
But a song that falls unheard
Yet on ears of sense unstirred
Yet by song so far from Heaven,
Whence you came the brightest bird,
Seven years since, of seven times seven.

Algernon Charles Swinburne [1837–1909]

CREEP AFORE YE GANG

CREEP awa', my bairnie, creep afore ye gang,
Cock ye baith your lugs to your auld Grannie's sang:
  Gin ye gang as far ye will think the road lang,
  Creep awa', my bairnie, creep afore ye gang.

Creep awa', my bairnie, ye're ower young to learn
To tot up and down yet, my bonnie wee bairn;
  Better creepin' cannie, than fa'in' wi' a bang,
  Duntin' a' your wee brow,—creep afore ye gang.

Ye'll creep, an' ye'll hotch, an' ye'll nod to your mither,
Watchin' ilka step o' your wee dousy brither;
  Rest ye on the floor till your wee limbs grow strang,
  An' ye'll be a braw chiel yet,—creep afore ye gang.

The wee birdie fa's when it tries ower soon to flee,
Folks are sure to tumble, when they climb ower hie;
  They wha canna walk right are sure to come to wrang,
  Creep awa', my bairnie, creep afore ye gang.
James Ballantine [1808–1877]

CASTLES IN THE AIR

THE bonnie, bonnie bairn who sits poking in the ase,
Glowering in the fire wi' his wee round face,
Laughing at the fuffin' lowe—what sees he there?
Ha! the young dreamer's bigging castles in the air.

His wee chubby face and his touzie curly pow
Are laughing and nodding to the dancing lowe;
He'll brown his rosy cheeks, and singe his sunny hair,
Glowering at the imps wi' their castles in the air.

He sees muckle castles towering to the moon;
He sees little sodgers pu'ing them a' doun;
Warlds whommlin' up and doun, bleezing wi' a flare,—
See how he loups as they glimmer in the air!

For a' sae sage he looks, what can the laddie ken?
He's thinking upon naething, like mony mighty men:
A wee thing mak's us think, a sma' thing mak's us stare,—
There are mair folk than him bigging castles in the air.

Sic a night in winter may weel mak' him cauld:
His chin upon his buffy hand will soon mak' him auld;
His brow is brent sae braid—O pray that daddy Care
Wad let the wean alane wi' his castles in the air!

He'll glower at the fire, and he'll keek at the light;
But mony sparkling stars are swallowed up by Night:
Aulder e'en than his are glamored by a glare,—
Hearts are broken, heads are turned, wi' castles in the air.

James Ballantine [1808–1877]

UNDER MY WINDOW

UNDER my window, under my window,
    All in the Midsummer weather,
Three little girls with fluttering curls
    Flit to and fro together:—
There's Bell with her bonnet of satin sheen,
And Maud with her mantle of silver-green,
    And Kate with her scarlet feather.

Under my window, under my window,
    Leaning stealthily over,
Merry and clear, the voice I hear
    Of each glad-hearted rover.
Ah! sly little Kate, she steals my roses;
And Maud and Bell twine wreaths and posies,
    As merry as bees in clover.

Under my window, under my window,
    In the blue Midsummer weather,
Stealing slow, on a hushed tiptoe,
    I catch them all together:—
Bell with her bonnet of satin sheen,
And Maud with her mantle of silver-green,
    And Kate with her scarlet feather.

Under my window, under my window,
    And off through the orchard closes;
While Maud she flouts, and Bell she pouts,
    They scamper and drop their posies;
But dear little Kate takes naught amiss,
And leaps in my arms with a loving kiss,
    And I give her all my roses.

Thomas Westwood [1814?–1888]

LITTLE BELL

He prayeth well who loveth well
Both man and bird and beast.
THE ANCIENT MARINER

PIPED the blackbird on the beechwood spray·
"Pretty maid, slow wandering this way,
  What's your name?" quoth he—
"What's your name?   Oh stop and straight unfold,
Pretty maid with showery curls of gold,"—
  "Little Bell," said she.

Little Bell sat down beneath the rocks—
Tossed aside her gleaming golden locks—
  "Bonny bird," quoth she,
"Sing me your best song before I go."
"Here's the very finest song I know,
  Little Bell," said he.

And the blackbird piped; you never heard
Half so gay a song from any bird—
  Full of quips and wiles,
Now so round and rich, now soft and slow.
All for love of that sweet face below,
  Dimpled o'er with smiles.

And the while the bonny bird did pour
His full heart out freely o'er and o'er
  'Neath the morning skies,
In the little childish heart below
All the sweetness seemed to grow and grow,
And shine forth in happy overflow
  From the blue, bright eyes.

Down the dell she tripped and through the glade,
Peeped the squirrel from the hazel shade,
  And from out the tree
Swung, and leaped, and frolicked, void of fear,—
While bold blackbird piped that all might hear—
  "Little Bell," piped he.

Little Bell sat down amid the fern—
"Squirrel, to your task return—
　　Bring me nuts," quoth she.
Up, away the frisky squirrel hies—
Golden wood-lights glancing in his eyes—
　　And adown the tree,
Great ripe nuts, kissed brown by July sun,
In the little lap dropped one by one—
Hark, how blackbird pipes to see the fun!
　　"Happy Bell," pipes he.

Little Bell looked up and down the glade—
"Squirrel, squirrel, if you're not afraid,
　　Come and share with me!"
Down came squirrel eager for his fare—
Down came bonny blackbird I declare;
Little Bell gave each his honest share—
　　Ah the merry three!
And the while these frolic playmates twain
Piped and frisked from bough to bough again,
　　'Neath the morning skies,
In the little childish heart below
All the sweetness seemed to grow and grow,
And shine out in happy overflow
　　From her blue, bright eyes.

By her snow-white cot at close of day,
Knelt sweet Bell, with folded palms to pray—
　　Very calm and clear
Rose the praying voice to where, unseen,
In blue heaven, an angel shape serene
　　Paused awhile to hear—
"What good child is this," the angel said,
"That, with happy heart, beside her bed
　　Prays so lovingly?"
Low and soft, oh! very low and soft,
Crooned the blackbird in the orchard croft,
　　"Bell, dear Bell!" crooned he.

"Whom God's creatures love," the angel fair
Murmured, "God doth bless with angels' care;

Child, thy bed shall be
Folded safe from harm—Love deep and kind
Shall watch around and leave good gifts behind,
    Little Bell, for thee!"

Thomas Westwood [1814?–1888]

THE BAREFOOT BOY

BLESSINGS on thee, little man,
Barefoot boy, with cheek of tan!
With thy turned-up pantaloons,
And thy merry whistled tunes;
With thy red lip, redder still
Kissed by strawberries on the hill;
With the sunshine on thy face,
Through thy torn brim's jaunty grace;
From my heart I give thee joy,—
I was once a barefoot boy!
Prince thou art,—the grown-up man
Only is republican.
Let the million-dollared ride!
Barefoot, trudging at his side,
Thou hast more than he can buy
In the reach of ear and eye,—
Outward sunshine, inward joy:
Blessings on thee, barefoot boy!

Oh for boyhood's painless play,
Sleep that wakes in laughing day,
Health that mocks the doctor's rules,
Knowledge never learned of schools,
Of the wild bee's morning chase,
Of the wild flower's time and place,
Flight of fowl and habitude
Of the tenants of the wood;
How the tortoise bears his shell,
How the woodchuck digs his cell,
And the ground-mole sinks his well;
How the robin feeds her young,
How the oriole's nest is hung;

Where the whitest lilies blow,
Where the freshest berries grow,
Where the ground-nut trails its vine,
Where the wood-grape's clusters shine;
Of the black wasp's cunning way,
Mason of his walls of clay,
And the architectural plans
Of gray hornet artisans!
For, eschewing books and tasks,
Nature answers all he asks;
Hand in hand with her he walks,
Face to face with her he talks,
Part and parcel of her joy,—
Blessings on the barefoot boy!

Oh for boyhood's time of June,
Crowding years in one brief moon,
When all things I heard or saw,
Me, their master, waited for.
I was rich in flowers and trees,
Humming-birds and honey-bees;
For my sport the squirrel played,
Plied the snouted mole his spade;
For my taste the blackberry cone
Purpled over hedge and stone;
Laughed the brook for my delight
Through the day and through the night,
Whispering at the garden wall,
Talked with me from fall to fall;
Mine the sand-rimmed pickerel pond
Mine the walnut slopes beyond,
Mine, on bending orchard trees,
Apples of Hesperides!
Still as my horizon grew,
Larger grew my riches too;
All the world I saw or knew
Seemed a complex Chinese toy,
Fashioned for a barefoot boy!

Oh for festal dainties spread,
Like my bowl of milk and bread;

Pewter spoon and bowl of wood,
On the door-stone, gray and rude!
O'er me, like a regal tent,
Cloudy-ribbed, the sunset bent,
Purple-curtained, fringed with gold,
Looped in many a wind-swung fold;
While for music came the play
Of the pied frogs' orchestra;
And, to light the noisy choir,
Lit the fly his lamp of fire.
I was monarch: pomp and joy
Waited on the barefoot boy!

Cheerily, then, my little man,
Live and laugh, as boyhood can!
Though the flinty slopes be hard,
Stubble-speared the new-mown sward,
Every morn shall lead thee through
Fresh baptisms of the dew;
Every evening from thy feet
Shall the cool wind kiss the heat:
All too soon these feet must hide
In the prison cells of pride,
Lose the freedom of the sod,
Like a colt's for work be shod,
Made to tread the mills of toil,
Up and down in ceaseless moil:
Happy if their track be found
Never on forbidden ground;
Happy if they sink not in
Quick and treacherous sands of sin.
Ah! that thou couldst know thy joy,
Ere it passes, barefoot boy!
                    John Greenleaf Whittier [1807–1892]

THE HERITAGE

THE rich man's son inherits lands,
   And piles of brick and stone, and gold,
And he inherits soft white hands,

And tender flesh that fears the cold,
  Nor dares to wear a garment old;
A heritage, it seems to me,
One scarce would wish to hold in fee.

The rich man's son inherits cares;
  The bank may break, the factory burn,
A breath may burst his bubble shares,
  And soft white hands could hardly earn
  A living that would serve his turn;
A heritage, it seems to me,
One scarce would wish to hold in fee.

The rich man's son inherits wants,
  His stomach craves for dainty fare;
With sated heart, he hears the pants
  Of toiling hinds with brown arms bare,
  And wearies in his easy-chair;
A heritage, it seems to me,
One scarce would wish to hold in fee.

What doth the poor man's son inherit?
  Stout muscles and a sinewy heart,
A hardy frame, a hardier spirit,
  King of two hands, he does his part
  In every useful toil and art;
A heritage, it seems to me,
A king might wish to hold in fee.

What doth the poor man's son inherit?
  Wishes o'erjoyed with humble things,
A rank adjudged by toil-won merit,
  Content that from employment springs,
  A heart that in his labor sings;
A heritage, it seems to me,
A king might wish to hold in fee.

What doth the poor man's son inherit?
  A patience learned of being poor,
Courage, if sorrow come, to bear it,

A fellow-feeling that is sure
  To make the outcast bless his door;
A heritage, it seems to me,
A king might wish to hold in fee.

O rich man's son! there is a toil
  That with all others level stands;
Large charity doth never soil,
  But only whiten, soft white hands;
  This is the best crop from thy lands,
A heritage, it seems to me,
Worth being rich to hold in fee.

O poor man's son! scorn not thy state;
  There is worse weariness than thine,
In merely being rich and great;
  Toil only gives the soul to shine,
  And makes rest fragrant and benign;
A heritage, it seems to me,
Worth being poor to hold in fee.

Both, heirs to some six feet of sod,
  Are equal in the earth at last;
Both, children of the same dear God,
  Prove title to your heirship vast
  By record of a well-filled past;
A heritage, it seems to me,
Well worth a life to hold in fee.

James Russell Lowell [1819–1891]

LETTY'S GLOBE

OR SOME IRREGULARITIES IN A FIRST LESSON IN GEOGRAPHY

WHEN Letty had scarce passed her third glad year,
And her young artless words began to flow,
One day we gave the child a colored sphere
Of the wide Earth, that she might mark and know,
By tint and outline, all its sea and land.
She patted all the world; old Empires peeped
Between her baby fingers; her soft hand
Was welcome at all frontiers. How she leaped,

And laughed and prattled in her world-wide bliss!
But when we turned her sweet unlearnèd eye
On our own Isle, she raised a joyous cry,—
"O yes! I see it, Letty's home is there!"
And while she hid all England with a kiss,
Bright over Europe fell her golden hair.

Charles Tennyson Turner [1808–1879]

DOVE'S NEST

"Sylvia, hush!" I said, "come here,
Come see a fairy-tale, my dear!
Tales told are good, tales seen are best!"
The dove was brooding on the nest
In the lowest crotch of the apple tree.
I lifted her up so quietly,
That when she could have touched the bird
The soft gray creature had not stirred.
It looked at us with a wild dark eye.
But, "Birdie, fly!" was Sylvia's cry,
Impatient Sylvia, "Birdie, fly."
Ah, well: but when I touched the nest,
The child recoiled upon my breast.
Was ever such a startling thing?
Sudden silver and purple wing,
The dove was out, away, across,
Struggling heart-break on the grass.
And there in the cup within the tree
Two milk-white eggs were ours to see.
Was ever thing so pretty? Alack,
"Birdie!" Sylvia cried, "come back!"

Joseph Russell Taylor [1868–1933]

THE ORACLE

I lay upon the summer grass.
    A gold-haired, sunny child came by,
And looked at me, as loath to pass,
    With questions in her lingering eye.

She stopped and wavered, then drew near,
    (Ah! the pale gold around her head!)
And o'er my shoulder stopped to peer.
    "Why do you read?" she said.

"I read a poet of old time,
    Who sang through all his living hours—
Beauty of earth—the streams, the flowers—
    And stars, more lovely than his rhyme.

"And now I read him, since men go,
    Forgetful of these sweetest things;
Since he and I love brooks that flow,
    And dawns, and bees, and flash of wings!"

She stared at me with laughing look,
    Then clasped her hands upon my knees:
"How strange to read it in a book!
    I could have told you all of these!"
                    Arthur Davison Ficke [1883–

TO A LITTLE GIRL

You taught me ways of gracefulness and fashions of address,
The mode of plucking pansies and the art of sowing cress,
And how to handle puppies, with propitiatory pats
For mother dogs, and little acts of courtesy to cats.

O connoisseur of pebbles, colored leaves and trickling rills,
Whom seasons fit as do the sheaths that wrap the daffodils,
Whose eyes' divine expectancy foretells some starry goal,
You taught me here docility—and how to save my soul.
                    Helen Parry Eden [18

TO A LITTLE GIRL

    Her eyes are like forget-me-nots,
        So loving, kind and true;
    Her lips are like a pink sea-shell
        Just as the sun shines through;

Her hair is like the waving grain
In summer's golden light;
And, best of all, her little soul
Is, like a lily, white.

Gustav Kobbé [1857–1918]

A PARENTAL ODE TO MY SON

AGED THREE YEARS AND FIVE MONTHS

THOU happy, happy elf!
(But stop,—first let me kiss away that tear!)
　Thou tiny image of myself!
(My love, he's poking peas into his ear!)
Thou merry, laughing sprite,
With spirits feather-light,
Untouched by sorrow, and unsoiled by sin,—
(My dear, the child is swallowing a pin!)

Thou little tricksy Puck!
With antic toys so funnily bestuck,
Light as the singing bird that wings the air,—
(The door! the door! he'll tumble down the stair!)
Thou darling of thy sire!
(Why, Jane, he'll set his pinafore afire!)
　Thou imp of mirth and joy!
In Love's dear chain so strong and bright a link,
　Thou idol of thy parents,—(Drat the boy!
There goes my ink!)

　Thou cherub,—but of earth;
Fit playfellow for Fays, by moonlight pale,
　In harmless sport and mirth,
(That dog will bite him, if he pulls its tail!)
　Thou human humming-bee, extracting honey
From every blossom in the world that blows,
　Singing in youth's Elysium ever sunny.—
(Another tumble! That's his precious nose!)

Thy father's pride and hope!
(He'll break the mirror with that skipping-rope!)

With pure heart newly stamped from nature's mint,
(Where *did* he learn that squint?)
Thou young domestic dove!
(He'll have that jug off with another shove!)
Dear nursling of the hymeneal nest!
(Are these torn clothes his best?)
Little epitome of man!
(He'll climb upon the table, that's his plan!)
Touched with the beauteous tints of dawning life,—
    (He's got a knife!)

Thou enviable being!
No storms, no clouds, in thy blue sky foreseeing,
    Play on, play on,
    My elfin John!
Toss the light ball, bestride the stick,—
(I knew so many cakes would make him sick!)
    With fancies, buoyant as the thistle-down,
Prompting the face grotesque, and antic brisk,
With many a lamb-like frisk!
    (He's got the scissors, snipping at your gown!)

Thou pretty opening rose!
(Go to your mother, child, and wipe your nose!)
Balmy and breathing music like the South,—
(He really brings my heart into my mouth!)
Fresh as the morn, and brilliant as its star,—
(I wish that window had an iron bar!)
Bold as the hawk, yet gentle as the dove;—
(I'll tell you what, my love,
I cannot write unless he's sent above.)
                              Thomas Hood [1799–1845]

A NEW POET

I WRITE. He sits beside my chair,
    And scribbles, too, in hushed delight,
He dips his pen in charmèd air:
    What is it he pretends to write?

He toils and toils; the paper gives
   No clue to aught he thinks. What then?
His little heart is glad; he lives
   The poems that he cannot pen.

Strange fancies throng that baby brain.
   What grave, sweet looks! What earnest eyes!
He stops—reflects—and now again
   His unrecording pen he plies.

It seems a satire on myself,—
   These dreamy nothings scrawled in air,
This thought, this work! Oh tricksy elf,
   Wouldst drive thy father to despair?

Despair! Ah, no; the heart, the mind
   Persists in hoping,—schemes and strives
That there may linger with our kind
   Some memory of our little lives.

Beneath his rock in the early world
   Smiling the naked hunter lay,
And sketched on horn the spear he hurled,
   The urus which he made his prey.

Like him I strive in hope my rhymes
   May keep my name a little while,—
O child, who knows how many times
   We two have made the angels smile!
                    William Canton [1845–

TO LAURA W——, TWO YEARS OLD

   Bright be the skies that cover thee,
      Child of the sunny brow,—
   Bright as the dream flung over thee
      By all that meets thee now,—
   Thy heart is beating joyously,
      Thy voice is like a bird's,
   And sweetly breaks the melody
      Of thy imperfect words.

I know no fount that gushes out
As gladly as thy tiny shout.

I would that thou might'st ever be
   As beautiful as now,
That time might ever leave as free
   Thy yet unwritten brow.
I would life were all poetry
   To gentle measure set,
That naught but chastened melody
   Might stain thine eye of jet,
Nor one discordant note be spoken,
Till God the cunning harp hath broken.

I would—but deeper things than these
   With woman's lot are wove:
Wrought of intensest sympathies,
   And nerved by purest love;
By the strong spirit's discipline,
   By the fierce wrong forgiven,
By all that wrings the heart of sin,
   Is woman won to heaven.
"Her lot is on thee," lovely child—
God keep thy spirit undefiled!

I fear thy gentle loveliness,
   Thy witching tone and air,
Thine eye's beseeching earnestness
   May be to thee a snare.
The silver stars may purely shine,
   The waters taintless flow:
But they who kneel at woman's shrine
   Breathe on it as they bow.
Peace may fling back the gift again,
But the crushed flower will leave a stain.

What shall preserve thee, beautiful child?
   Keep thee as thou art now?
Bring thee, a spirit undefiled,
   At God's pure throne to bow?

The world is but a broken reed,
  And life grows early dim—
Who shall be near thee in thy need,
  To lead thee up to Him?
He who himself was "undefiled?"
With Him we trust thee, beautiful child!
            Nathaniel Parker Willis [1806–1867]

TO ROSE

ROSE, when I remember you,
Little lady, scarcely two,
I am suddenly aware
Of the angels in the air.
All your softly gracious ways
Make an island in my days
Where my thoughts fly back to be
Sheltered from too strong a sea.
All your luminous delight
Shines before me in the night
When I grope for sleep and find
Only shadows in my mind.

Rose, when I remember you,
White and glowing, pink and new,
With so swift a sense of fun
Although life has just begun;
With so sure a pride of place
In your very infant face,
I should like to make a prayer
To the angels in the air:
"If an angel ever brings
Me a baby in her wings,
Please be certain that it grows
. Very, very much like Rose."
            Sara Teasdale [1884–1933]

TO CHARLOTTE PULTENEY

TIMELY blossom, Infant fair,
Fondling of a happy pair,
Every morn and every night
Their solicitous delight,
Sleeping, waking, still at ease,
Pleasing, without skill to please;
Little gossip, blithe and hale,
Tattling many a broken tale,
Singing many a tuneless song,
Lavish of a heedless tongue;
Simple maiden, void of art,
Babbling out the very heart,
Yet abandoned to thy will,
Yet imagining no ill,
Yet too innocent to blush;
Like the linnet in the bush
To the mother-linnet's note
Moduling her slender throat;
Chirping forth thy pretty joys,
Wanton in the change of toys,
Like the linnet green, in May
Flitting to each bloomy spray;
Wearied then and glad of rest,
Like the linnet in the nest:—
This thy present happy lot,
This, in time will be forgot:
Other pleasures, other cares,
Ever-busy Time prepares;
And thou shalt in thy daughter see,
This picture, once, resembled thee.

                    Ambrose Philips [1675?-1749]

THE PICTURE OF LITTLE T. C. IN A
PROSPECT OF FLOWERS

SEE with what simplicity
This nymph begins her golden days!
In the green grass she loves to lie,
And there with her fair aspect tames

The wilder flowers, and gives them names;
But only with the roses plays,
    And them does tell
What color best becomes them, and what smell.

Who can foretell for what high cause
This darling of the gods was born?
Yet this is she whose chaster laws
The wanton Love shall one day fear,
And, under her command severe,
See his bow broke, and ensigns torn.
    Happy who can
Appease this virtuous enemy of man!

O then let me in time compound
And parley with those conquering eyes,
Ere they have tried their force to wound,
Ere with their glancing wheels they drive
In triumph over hearts that strive,
And them that yield but more despise:
    Let me be laid
Where I may see the glories from some shade.

Meantime, whilst every verdant thing
Itself does at thy beauty charm,
Reform the errors of the Spring;
Make that the tulips may have share
Of sweetness, seeing they are fair,
And roses of their thorns disarm;
    But most procure
That violets may a longer age endure.

But O young beauty of the woods,
Whom Nature courts with fruits and flowers,
Gather the flowers, but spare the buds;
Lest Flora, angry at thy crime
To kill her infants in their prime,
Do quickly make the example yours;
    And, ere we see,
Nip, in the blossom, all our hopes and thee.
        Andrew Marvell [1621–1678]

TO HARTLEY COLERIDGE

SIX YEARS OLD

O THOU! whose fancies from afar are brought:
Who of thy words dost make a mock apparel,
And fittest to unutterable thought
The breeze-like motion and the self-born carol;
Thou fairy voyager! that dost float
In such clear water, that thy boat
May rather seem
To brood on air than on an earthly stream;
Suspended in a stream as clear as sky,
Where earth and heaven do make one imagery:
O blessed vision! happy child!
Thou art so exquisitely wild,
I think of thee with many fears
For what may be thy lot in future years.
I thought of times when Pain might be thy guest,
Lord of thy house and hospitality;
And Grief, uneasy lover! never rest
But when she sate within the touch of thee.
O too industrious folly!
O vain and causeless melancholy!
Nature will either end thee quite;
Or, lengthening out thy season of delight,
Preserve for thee, by individual right,
A young lamb's heart among the full-grown flocks.
What hast thou to do with sorrow,
Or the injuries of to-morrow?
Thou art a dew-drop, which the morn brings forth,
Ill-fitted to sustain unkindly shocks,
Or to be trailed along the soiling earth;
A gem that glitters while it lives,
And no forewarning gives;
But, at the touch of wrong, without a strife,
Slips in a moment out of life.

William Wordsworth [1770–1850]

TO A CHILD OF QUALITY

FIVE YEARS OLD, 1704, THE AUTHOR THEN FORTY

LORDS, knights, and squires, the numerous band
  That wear the fair Miss Mary's fetters,
Were summoned by her high command
  To show their passions by their letters.

My pen amongst the rest I took,
  Lest those bright eyes, that cannot read,
Should dart their kindling fires, and look
  The power they have to be obeyed.

Nor quality, nor reputation,
  Forbids me yet my flame to tell;
Dear Five-years-old befriends my passion,
  And I may write till she can spell.

For, while she makes her silkworms' beds
  With all the tender things I swear;
Whilst all the house my passion reads,
  In papers round her baby's hair;

She may receive and own my flame;
  For, though the strictest prudes should know it,
She'll pass for a most virtuous dame,
  And I for an unhappy poet.

Then too, alas! when she shall tear
  The rhymes some younger rival sends,
She'll give me leave to write, I fear,
  And we shall still continue friends.

For, as our different ages move,
  'Tis so ordained (would Fate but mend it!),
That I shall be past making love
  When she begins to comprehend it.

Matthew Prior [1664–1721]

EX ORE INFANTIUM

LITTLE Jesus, wast Thou shy
Once, and just so small as I?
And what did it feel like to be
Out of Heaven, and just like me?
Didst Thou sometimes think of *there*,
And ask where all the angels were?
I should think that I would cry
For my house all made of sky;
I would look about the air,
And wonder where my angels were;
And at waking 'twould distress me—
Not an angel there to dress me!

Hadst Thou ever any toys,
Like us little girls and boys?
And didst Thou play in Heaven with all
The angels, that were not too tall,
With stars for marbles?   Did the things
Play *Can you see me?* through their wings?

Didst Thou kneel at night to pray,
And didst Thou join Thy hands, this way?
And did they tire sometimes, being young,
And make the prayer seem very long?
And dost Thou like it best, that we
Should join our hands to pray to Thee?
I used to think, before I knew,
The prayer not said unless we do.
And did Thy Mother at the night
Kiss Thee, and fold the clothes in right?
And didst Thou feel quite good in bed,
Kissed, and sweet, and Thy prayers said?

Thou canst not have forgotten all
That it feels like to be small:
And Thou know'st I cannot pray
To Thee in my father's way—
When Thou wast so little, say,
Could'st Thou talk Thy Father's way?—
So, a little Child, come down
And hear a child's tongue like Thy own;

Take me by the hand and walk,
And listen to my baby-talk.
To Thy Father show my prayer
(He will look, Thou art so fair),
And say: "O Father, I, Thy Son,
Bring the prayer of a little one."

And He will smile, that children's tongue
Has not changed since Thou wast young!
Francis Thompson [1859–1907]

OBITUARY

FINDING Francesca full of tears, I said,
"Tell me thy trouble."   "Oh, my dog is dead!
Murdered by poison!—no one knows for what!—
Was ever dog born capable of that?"
"Child,"—I began to say, but checked my thought,—
"A better dog can easily be bought."
For no—what animal could him replace?
Those loving eyes!   That fond, confiding face!
Those dear, dumb touches!   Therefore I was dumb.
From word of mine could any comfort come?
A bitter sorrow 'tis to lose a brute
Friend, dog or horse, for grief must then be mute,—
So many smile to see the rivers shed
Of tears for one poor, speechless creature dead.
When parents die there's many a word to say—
Kind words, consoling—one can always pray;
When children die 'tis natural to tell
Their mother, "Certainly, with them 'tis well!"
But for a dog, 'twas all the life he had,
Since death is end of dogs, or good or bad.
This was his world; he was contented here;
Imagined nothing better, naught more dear,
Than his young mistress; sought no brighter sphere;
Having no sin, asked not to be forgiven;
Ne'er guessed at God nor ever dreamed of heaven.
Now he has passed away, so much of love
Goes from our life, without one hope above!
When a dog dies there's nothing to be said
But—kiss me, darling!—dear old Smiler's dead.
Thomas William Parsons [1819–1892]

THE CHILD'S HERITAGE

Oh, there are those, a sordid clan,
  With pride in gaud and faith in gold,
Who prize the sacred soul of man
  For what his hands have sold.

And these shall deem thee humbly bred:
  They shall not hear, they shall not see
The kings among the lordly dead
  Who walk and talk with thee!

A tattered cloak may be thy dole,
  And thine the roof that Jesus had:
The broidered garment of the soul
  Shall keep thee purple-clad!

The blood of men hath dyed its brede,
  And it was wrought by holy seers
With sombre dream and golden deed,
  And pearled with women's tears.

With Eld thy chain of days is one:
  The seas are still Homeric seas;
Thy skies shall glow with Pindar's sun,
  The stars of Socrates!

Unaged the ancient tide shall surge,
  The old Spring burn along the bough:
For thee, the new and old converge
  In one eternal Now!

I give thy feet the hopeful sod,
  Thy mouth, the priceless boon of breath;
The glory of the search for God
  Be thine in life and death!

Unto thy flesh, the soothing dust;
  Thy soul, the gift of being free:
The torch my fathers gave in trust,
  Thy father gives to thee!

                    John G. Neihardt [1881-

A GIRL OF POMPEII

A PUBLIC haunt they found her in:
   She lay asleep, a lovely child;
   The only thing left undefiled
Where all things else bore taint of sin.

Her supple outlines fixed in clay
   The universal law suspend,
   And turn Time's chariot back, and blend
A thousand years with yesterday.

A sinless touch, austere yet warm,
   Around her girlish figure pressed,
   Caught the sweet imprint of her breast,
And held her, surely clasped, from harm.

Truer than work of sculptor's art
   Comes this dear maid of long ago,
   Sheltered from woeful chance, to show
A spirit's lovely counterpart,

And bid mistrustful men be sure
   That form shall fate of flesh escape,
   And, quit of earth's corruptions, shape
Itself, imperishably pure.
           Edward Sandford Martin [1856–1939]

ON THE PICTURE OF A "CHILD TIRED OF PLAY"

TIRED of play! Tired of play!
What hast thou done this live-long day!
The bird is silent and so is the bee,
The shadow is creeping up steeple and tree;
The doves have flown to the sheltering eaves,
And the nests are dark with the drooping leaves;
Twilight gathers, and day is done,—
How hast thou spent it, restless one?

Playing! And what hast thou done beside
To tell thy mother at eventide?

What promise of morn is left unbroken?
What kind word to thy playmate spoken?
Whom hast thou pitied, and whom forgiven?
How with thy faults has duty striven?
What hast thou learned by field and hill,
By greenwood path and by singing rill?

There will come an eve to a longer day
That will find thee tired,—but not with play!
And thou wilt learn, as thou learnest now,
With wearied limbs and aching brow,
And wish the shadows would faster creep
And long to go to thy quiet sleep.

Well will it be for thee then if thou
Art as free from sin and shame as now!
Well for thee if thy tongue can tell
A tale like this, of a day spent well!
If thine open hand hath relieved distress,
And thy pity hath sprung to wretchedness—
If thou hast forgiven the sore offence
And humbled thy heart with penitence;

If Nature's voices have spoken to thee
With her holy meanings, eloquently—
If every creature hath won thy love,
From the creeping worm to the brooding dove—
If never a sad, low-spoken word
Hath plead with thy human heart unheard—
Then, when the night steals on, as now
It will bring relief to thine aching brow,
And, with joy and peace at the thought of rest,
Thou wilt sink to sleep on thy mother's breast.
Nathaniel Parker Willis [1806–1867]

THE REVERIE OF POOR SUSAN

At the corner of Wood Street, when daylight appears,
Hangs a Thrush that sings loud, it has sung for three years:
Poor Susan has passed by the spot, and has heard
In the silence of morning the song of the Bird.

'Tis a note of enchantment; what ails her? She sees
A mountain ascending, a vision of trees;
Bright volumes of vapor through Lothbury glide,
And a river flows on through the vale of Cheapside.

Green pastures she views in the midst of the dale,
Down which she so often has tripped with her pail;
And a single small cottage, a nest like a dove's,
The one only dwelling on earth that she loves.

She looks, and her heart is in heaven: but they fade,
The mist and the river, the hill and the shade:
The stream will not flow, and the hill will not rise,
And the colors have all passed away from her eyes!

William Wordsworth [1770–1850]

CHILDREN'S SONG

SOMETIMES wind and sometimes rain,
Then the sun comes back again;
Sometimes rain and sometimes snow,
Goodness, how we'd like to know
Why the weather alters so.

When the weather's really good
We go nutting in the wood;
When it rains we stay at home,
And then sometimes other some
Of the neighbors' children come.

Sometimes we have jam and meat,
All the things we like to eat;
Sometimes we make do with bread
And potatoes boiled instead.
Once when we were put to bed
We had nowt and mother cried,
But that was after father died.

So, sometimes wind and sometimes rain,
Then the sun comes back again;
Sometimes rain and sometimes snow,
Goodness, how we'd like to know
If things will *always* alter so.

Ford Madox Ford [1873–

THE MITHERLESS BAIRN

WHEN a' other bairnies are hushed to their hame
By aunty, or cousin, or frecky grand-dame,
Wha stands last and lanely, an' naebody carin'?
'Tis the puir doited loonie,—the mitherless bairn!

The mitherless bairn gangs to his lane bed;
Nane covers his cauld back, or haps his bare head;
His wee hackit heelies are hard as the airn,
An' litheless the lair o' the mitherless bairn.

Aneath his cauld brow siccan dreams hover there,
O' hands that wont kindly to kame his dark hair;
But mornin' brings clutches, a' reckless an' stern,
That lo'e na the locks o' the mitherless bairn!

Yon sister that sang o'er his saftly rocked bed
Now rests in the mools where her mammie is laid;
The father toils sair their wee bannock to earn,
An' kens na the wrangs o' his mitherless bairn.

Her spirit, that passed in yon hour o' his birth,
Still watches his wearisome wanderings on earth;
Recording in heaven the blessings they earn
Wha couthilie deal wi' the mitherless bairn!

O, speak him na harshly,—he trembles the while,
He bends to your bidding, and blesses your smile;
In their dark hour o' anguish the heartless shall learn
That God deals the blow, for the mitherless bairn!
                              William Thom [1798?–1848]

THE CRY OF THE CHILDREN

Do ye hear the children weeping, O my brothers,
    Ere the sorrow comes with years?
They are leaning their young heads against their mothers,
    And *that* cannot stop their tears.

The young lambs are bleating in the meadows,
　　The young birds are chirping in the nest,
The young fawns are playing with the shadows,
　　The young flowers are blowing toward the west—
But the young, young children, O my brothers,
　　They are weeping bitterly!
They are weeping in the playtime of the others,
　　In the country of the free.

Do you question the young children in the sorrow,
　　Why their tears are falling so?
The old man may weep for his to-morrow
　　Which is lost in Long Ago;
The old tree is leafless in the forest,
　　The old year is ending in the frost,
The old wound, if stricken, is the sorest,
　　The old hope is hardest to be lost:
But the young, young children, O my brothers,
　　Do you ask them why they stand
Weeping sore before the bosoms of their mothers,
　　In our happy Fatherland?

They look up with their pale and sunken faces,
　　And their looks are sad to see,
For the man's hoary anguish draws and presses
　　Down the cheeks of infancy;
"Your old earth," they say, "is very dreary;
　　Our young feet," they say, "are very weak;
Few paces have we taken, yet are weary—
　　Our grave-rest is very far to seek:
Ask the aged why they weep, and not the children
　　For the outside earth is cold,
And we young ones stand without, in our bewildering,
　　And the graves are for the old.

"True," say the children, "it may happen
　　That we die before our time:
Little Alice died last year—her grave is shapen
　　Like a snowball, in the rime.
We looked into the pit prepared to take her:
　　Was no room for any work in the close clay!

From the sleep wherein she lieth none will wake her,
    Crying, 'Get up, little Alice! it is day.'
If you listen by that grave, in sun and shower,
    With your ear down, little Alice never cries;
Could we see her face, be sure we should not know her,
    For the smile has time for growing in her eyes:
And merry go her moments, lulled and stilled in
        The shroud by the kirk-chime.
It is good when it happens," say the children,
        "That we die before our time."

Alas, alas, the children! they are seeking
        Death in life, as best to have!
They are binding up their hearts away from breaking,
        With a cerement from the grave.
Go out, children, from the mine and from the city,
    Sing out, children, as the little thrushes do;
Pluck your handfuls of the meadow cowslips pretty;
    Laugh aloud, to feel your fingers let them through!
But they answer, "Are your cowslips of the meadows
        Like our weeds anear the mine?
Leave us quiet in the dark of the coal-shadows,
        From your pleasures fair and fine!

"For oh," say the children, "we are weary,
        And we cannot run or leap;
If we cared for any meadows, it were merely
        To drop down in them and sleep.
Our knees tremble sorely in the stooping,
    We fall upon our faces, trying to go;
And, underneath our heavy eyelids drooping,
    The reddest flower would look as pale as snow.
For, all day, we drag our burden tiring,
        Through the coal-dark, underground;
Or, all day, we drive the wheels of iron
        In the factories, round and round.

"For, all day, the wheels are droning, turning;
        Their wind comes in our faces,
Till our hearts turn, our heads, with pulses burning,
        And the walls turn in their places:

Turns the sky in the high window blank and reeling,
   Turns the long light that drops adown the wall,
Turn the black flies that crawl along the ceiling:
   All are turning, all the day, and we with all.
And all day, the iron wheels are droning;
    And sometimes we could pray,
'O ye wheels, (breaking out in a mad moaning)
    'Stop! be silent for to-day!' "

Ay, be silent!   Let them hear each other breathing
    For a moment, mouth to mouth!
Let them touch each other's hands, in a fresh wreathing
    Of their tender human youth!
Let them feel that this cold metallic motion
    Is not all the life God fashions or reveals:
Let them prove their living souls against the notion
    That they live in you, or under you, O wheels!
Still, all day, the iron wheels go onward,
    Grinding life down from its mark;
And the children's souls, which God is calling sunward,
    Spin on blindly in the dark.

Now tell the poor young children, O my brothers,
    To look up to Him and pray;
So the blessèd One, who blesseth all the others,
    Will bless them another day.
They answer, " Who is God that He should hear us,
    While the rushing of the iron wheels is stirred?
When we sob aloud, the human creatures near us
    Pass by, hearing not, or answer not a word!
And *we* hear not (for the wheels in their resounding)
    Strangers speaking at the door:
Is it likely God, with angels singing round Him,
    Hears our weeping any more?

"Two words, indeed, of praying we remember,
    And at midnight's hour of harm,
'Our Father,' looking upward in the chamber,
    We say softly for a charm.
We know no other words except 'Our Father,'
    And we think that, in some pause of angels' song,

God may pluck them with the silence sweet to gather,
    And hold both within his right hand which is strong.
'Our Father!' If He heard us, He would surely
      (For they call Him good and mild)
Answer, smiling down the steep world very purely,
      'Come and rest with me, my child.'

"But no!" say the children, weeping faster,
      "He is speechless as a stone;
And they tell us, of His image is the master
      Who commands us to work on.
Go to!" say the children,—"Up in Heaven,
    Dark, wheel-like, turning clouds are all we find.
Do not mock us; grief has made us unbelieving:
    We look up for God, but tears have made us blind."
Do you hear the children weeping and disproving,
      O my brothers, what ye preach?
For God's possible is taught by His world's loving,
      And the children doubt of each.

And well may the children weep before you!
      They are weary ere they run;
They have never seen the sunshine, nor the glory
      Which is brighter than the sun.
They know the grief of man, without its wisdom;
    They sink in man's despair, without its calm;
Are slaves, without the liberty in Christdom,
    Are martyrs, by the pang without the palm:
Are worn as if with age, yet unretrievingly
      The harvest of its memories cannot reap,—
Are orphans of the earthly love and heavenly.
      Let them weep! let them weep!

They look up, with their pale and sunken faces,
      And their look is dread to see,
For they mind you of their angels in high places,
      With eyes turned on Deity.
"How long," they say, "how long, O cruel nation,
    Will you stand, to move the world, on a child's heart,—
Stifle down with a mailèd heel its palpitation,
    And tread onward to your throne amid the mart?

Our blood splashes upward, O gold-heaper,
    And your purple shows your path;
But the child's sob in the silence curses deeper
    Than the strong man in his wrath!"
                    Elizabeth Barrett Browning [1806–1861]

THE SHADOW–CHILD

Why do the wheels go whirring round,
    Mother, mother?
Oh, mother, are they giants bound,
    And will they growl forever?
Yes, fiery giants underground,
    Daughter, little daughter,
Forever turn the wheels around,
    And rumble-grumble ever.

Why do I pick the threads all day,
    Mother, mother?
While sunshine children are at play?
    And must I work forever?
Yes, shadow-child; the live-long day,
    Daughter, little daughter,
Your hands must pick the threads away,
    And feel the sunshine never.

Why do the birds sing in the sun,
    Mother, mother?
If all day long I run and run,
    Run with the wheels forever?
The birds may sing till day is done,
    Daughter, little daughter,
But with the wheels your feet must run—
    Run with the wheels forever.

Why do I feel so tired each night,
    Mother, mother?
The wheels are always buzzing bright;
    Do they grow sleepy never?
Oh, baby thing, so soft and white,
    Daughter, little daughter,
The big wheels grind us in their might,
    And they will grind forever.

And is the white thread never spun,
  Mother, mother?
And is the white cloth never done,
  For you and me done never?
Oh, yes, our thread will all be spun,
  Daughter, little daughter,
When we lie down out in the sun,
  And work no more forever.

And when will come that happy day,
  Mother, mother?
Oh, shall we laugh and sing and play
  Out in the sun forever?
Nay, shadow-child, we'll rest all day,
  Daughter, little daughter,
Where green grass grows and roses gay,
  There in the sun forever.

                              Harriet Monroe [1860–1936]

MOTHER WEPT

MOTHER wept, and father sighed;
  With delight aglow
Cried the lad, "To-morrow," cried,
  "To the pit I go."

Up and down the place he sped,—
  Greeted old and young;
Far and wide the tidings spread;
  Clapt his hands and sung.

Came his cronies; some to gaze
  Wrapped in wonder; some
Free with counsel; some with praise:
  Some with envy dumb.

"May he," many a gossip cried,
  "Be from peril kept."
Father hid his face and sighed,
  Mother turned and wept.

                      Joseph Skipsey [1832–1903]

DUTY

So nigh is grandeur to our dust,
    So near is God to man,
When Duty whispers low, "Thou must,"
    The youth replies, "I can."
                    Ralph Waldo Emerson [1803-1882]

LUCY GRAY

OR SOLITUDE

OFT I had heard of Lucy Gray:
    And, when I crossed the wild,
I chanced to see, at break of day,
    The solitary child.

No mate, no comrade Lucy knew;
    She dwelt on a wide moor,
The sweetest thing that ever grew
    Beside a human door!

You yet may spy the fawn at play,
    The hare upon the green;
But the sweet face of Lucy Gray
    Will never more be seen.

"To-night will be a stormy night,—
    You to the town must go;
And take a lantern, Child, to light
    Your mother through the snow."

"That, Father, will I gladly do:
    'Tis scarcely afternoon,—
The minster-clock has just struck two,
    And yonder is the moon!"

At this the Father raised his hook,
    And snapped a fagot-brand.
He plied his work; —and Lucy took
    The lantern in her hand.

Not blither is the mountain roe:
  With many a wanton stroke
Her feet disperse the powdery snow,
  That rises up like smoke.

The storm came on before its time:
  She wandered up and down:
And many a hill did Lucy climb:
  But never reached the town.

The wretched parents all that night
  Went shouting far and wide;
But there was neither sound nor sight
  To serve them for a guide.

At daybreak on the hill they stood
  That overlooked the moor;
And thence they saw the bridge of wood,
  A furlong from their door.

They wept,—and, turning homeward, cried,
  "In heaven we all shall meet;"
When in the snow the mother spied
  The print of Lucy's feet.

Then downwards from the steep hill's edge
  They tracked the footmarks small:
And through the broken hawthorn-hedge,
  And by the low stone-wall;

And then an open field they crossed—
  The marks were still the same—
They tracked them on, nor ever lost;
  And to the bridge they came.

They followed from the snowy bank
  Those footmarks, one by one,
Into the middle of the plank;
  And further there were none!

—Yet some maintain that to this day
  She is a living child;
That you may see sweet Lucy Gray
  Upon the lonesome wild.

O'er rough and smooth she trips along,
  And never looks behind;
And sings a solitary song
  That whistles in the wind.

William Wordsworth [1770–1850]

IN THE CHILDREN'S HOSPITAL

EMMIE

OUR doctor had called in another, I never had seen him before,
But he sent a chill to my heart when I saw him come in at the door,
Fresh from the surgery-schools of France and of other lands—
Harsh red hair, big voice, big chest, big merciless hands!
Wonderful cures he had done, O yes, but they said too of him
He was happier using the knife than in trying to save the limb,
And that I can well believe, for he looked so coarse and so red,
I could think he was one of those who would break their jests on the dead,
And mangle the living dog that had loved him and fawned at his knee—
Drenched with the hellish oorali—that ever such things should be!

Here was a boy—I am sure that some of our children would die
But for the voice of love, and the smile, and the comforting eye—
Here was a boy in the ward, every bone seemed out of its place—
Caught in a mill and crushed—it was all but a hopeless case:

And he handled him gently enough; but his voice and his
    face were not kind,
And it was but a hopeless case, he had seen it and made up
    his mind,
And he said to me roughly "The lad will need little more of
    your care."
"All the more need," I told him, "to seek the Lord Jesus
    in prayer;
They are all His children here, and I pray for them all as
    my own:"
But he turned to me, "Ay, good woman, can prayer set a
    broken bone?"
Then he muttered half to himself, but I know that I heard
    him say,
"All very well—but the good Lord Jesus has had his day."

Had? has it come? It has only dawned. It will come by
    and by.
O, how could I serve in the wards if the hope of the world
    were a lie?
How could I bear with the sights and the loathsome smells
    of disease
But that He said "Ye do it to me, when ye do it to these"?

So he went. And we passed to this ward where the younger
    children are laid:
Here is the cot of our orphan, our darling, our meek little
    maid;
Empty you see just now! We have lost her who loved her
    so much—
Patient of pain though as quick as a sensitive plant to the
    touch;
Hers was the prettiest prattle, it often moved me to
    tears,
Hers was the gratefullest heart I have found in a child of
    her years—
Nay you remember our Emmie; you used to send her the
    flowers;
How she would smile at 'em, play with 'em, talk to 'em
    hours after hours!

They that can wander at will where the works of the Lord
    are revealed
Little guess what joy can be got from a cowslip out of the
    field;
Flowers to these "spirits in prison" are all they can know of
    the spring,
They freshen and sweeten the wards like the waft of an
    angel's wing;
And she lay with a flower in one hand and her thin hands
    crossed on her breast—
Wan, but as pretty as heart can desire, and we thought her
    at rest,
Quietly sleeping—so quiet, our doctor said, "Poor little
    dear,
Nurse, I must do it to-morrow; she'll never live through it,
    I fear."

I walked with our kindly old doctor as far as the head of the
    stair,
Then I returned to the ward; the child didn't see I was there.

Never since I was nurse, had I been so grieved and so vexed!
Emmie had heard him.   Softly she called from her cot to
    the next,
"He says I shall never live through it; O Annie, what shall
    I do?"
Annie considered.   "If I," said the wise little Annie, "was
    you,
I should cry to the dear Lord Jesus to help me, for, Emmie,
    you see,
It's all in the picture there: 'Little children should come to
    Me.' "—
(Meaning the print that you gave us, I find that it always
    can please
Our children, the dear Lord Jesus with children about His
    knees.)
"Yes, and I will," said Emmie, "but then if I call to the
    Lord,
How should He know that it's me? such a lot of beds in the
    ward?"

That was a puzzle for Annie.   Again she considered and
    said:
"Emmie, you put out your arms, and you leave 'em outside
    on the bed—
The Lord has so *much* to see to! but, Emmie, you tell it Him
    plain,
It's the little girl with her arms lying out on the counter-
    pane."

I had sat three nights by the child—I could not watch her
    for four—
My brain had begun to reel—I felt I could do it no
    more.
That was my sleeping-night, but I thought that it never
    would pass.
There was a thunderclap once, and a clatter of hail on the
    glass,
And there was a phantom cry that I heard as I tossed
    about,
The motherless bleat of a lamb in the storm and the dark-
    ness without;
My sleep was broken besides with dreams of the dreadful
    knife
And fears for our delicate Emmie who scarce would escape
    with her life;
Then in the gray of the morning it seemed she stood by me
    and smiled,
And the doctor came at his hour, and we went to see the
    child.

He had brought his ghastly tools: we believed her asleep
    again—
Her dear, long, lean, little arms lying out on the counter-
    pane;—
Say that His day is done! Ah, why should we care what they
    say?
The Lord of the children had heard her, and Emmie had
    passed away.

                  Alfred Tennyson [1809-1892]

"IF I WERE DEAD"

"If I were dead, you'd sometimes say, Poor Child!"
The dear lips quivered as they spake,
And the tears brake
From eyes which, not to grieve me, brightly smiled.
Poor Child, poor Child!
I seem to hear your laugh, your talk, your song.
It is not true that Love will do no wrong.
Poor Child!
And did you think, when you so cried and smiled,
How I, in lonely nights, should lie awake,
And of those words your full avengers make?
Poor Child, poor Child!
And now, unless it be
That sweet amends thrice told are come to thee,
O God, have Thou *no* mercy upon me!
Poor Child!

Coventry Patmore [1823–1896]

THE TOYS

My little Son, who looked from thoughtful eyes
And moved and spoke in quiet grown-up wise,
Having my law the seventh time disobeyed,
I struck him, and dismissed
With hard words and unkissed,
—His Mother, who was patient, being dead.
Then, fearing lest his grief should hinder sleep,
I visited his bed,
But found him slumbering deep,
With darkened eyelids, and their lashes yet
From his late sobbing wet.
And I, with moan,
Kissing away his tears, left others of my own;
For, on a table drawn beside his head,
He had put, within his reach,
A box of counters and a red-veined stone,
A piece of glass abraded by the beach,

And six or seven shells,
A bottle with bluebells,
And two French copper coins, ranged there with careful art,
To comfort his sad heart.
So when that night I prayed
To God, I wept, and said:
Ah, when at last we lie with trancèd breath,
Not vexing Thee in death,
And Thou rememberest of what toys
We made our joys,
How weakly understood
Thy great commanded good,
Then, fatherly not less
Than I whom Thou hast moulded from the clay,
Thou'lt leave Thy wrath, and say,
"I will be sorry for their childishness."

Coventry Patmore [1823-1896]

A SONG OF TWILIGHT

OH, to come home once more, when the dusk is falling,
    To see the nursery lighted and the children's table spread;
"Mother, mother, mother!" the eager voices calling,
    "The baby was so sleepy that he had to go to bed!"

Oh, to come home once more, and see the smiling faces,
    Dark head, bright head, clustered at the pane;
Much the years have taken, when the heart its path retraces,
    But until time is not for me, the image will remain.

Men and women now they are, standing straight and steady,
    Grave heart, gay heart, fit for life's emprise;
Shoulder set to shoulder, how should they be but ready!
    The future shines before them with the light of their own
        eyes.

Still each answers to my call; no good has been denied me,
    My burdens have been fitted to the little strength that's
        mine,
Beauty, pride and peace have walked by day beside me,
    The evening closes gently in, and how can I repine?

But oh, to see once more, when the early dusk is falling,
  The nursery windows glowing and the children's table spread;
"Mother, mother, mother!" the high child-voices calling,
  "He couldn't stay awake for you, he had to go to bed!"
                                                    Unknown

LITTLE BOY BLUE

THE little toy dog is covered with dust,
  But sturdy and stanch he stands;
And the little toy soldier is red with rust,
  And his musket moulds in his hands.
Time was when the little toy dog was new,
  And the soldier was passing fair;
And that was the time when our Little Boy Blue
  Kissed them and put them there.

"Now, don't you go till I come," he said,
  "And don't you make any noise!"
So, toddling off to his trundle-bed,
  He dreamt of the pretty toys;
And, as he was dreaming, an angel song
  Awakened our Little Boy Blue—
Oh! the years are many, the years are long,
  But the little toy friends are true!

Ay, faithful to Little Boy Blue they stand,
  Each in the same old place,
Awaiting the touch of a little hand,
  The smile of a little face;
And they wonder, as waiting the long years through
  In the dust of that little chair,
What has become of our Little Boy Blue,
  Since he kissed them and put them there.
                          Eugene Field [1850–1895]

THE DISCOVERER

    I HAVE a little kinsman
    Whose earthly summers are but three,
    And yet a voyager is he
    Greater then Drake or Frobisher,

Than all their peers together!
He is a brave discoverer,
And, far beyond the tether
Of them who seek the frozen Pole,
Has sailed where the noiseless surges roll.
Ay, he has travelled whither
A winged pilot steered his bark
Through the portals of the dark,
Past hoary Mimir's well and tree,
    Across the unknown sea.

Suddenly, in his fair young hour,
Came one who bore a flower,
And laid it in his dimpled hand
    With this command:
"Henceforth thou art a rover!
Thou must make a voyage far,
Sail beneath the evening star,
And a wondrous land discover."
—With his sweet smile innocent
    Our little kinsman went.

Since that time no word
From the absent has been heard.
    Who can tell
How he fares, or answer well
What the little one has found
Since he left us, outward bound?
Would that he might return!
Then should we learn
From the pricking of his chart
How the skyey roadways part.
Hush! does not the baby this way bring,
To lay beside this severed curl,
    Some starry offering
Of chrysolite or pearl?

    Ah, no! not so!
We may follow on his track,
    But he comes not back.

And yet I dare aver
He is a brave discoverer
Of climes his elders do not know.
He has more learning than appears
On the scroll of twice three thousand years,
More than in the groves is taught,
Or from furthest Indies brought;
He knows, perchance, how spirits fare,—
What shapes the angels wear,
What is their guise and speech
In those lands beyond our reach,—
And his eyes behold
Things that shall never, never be to mortal hearers told.
Edmund Clarence Stedman [1833–1908]

A CHRYSALIS

My little Mädchen found one day
A curious something in her play,
That was not fruit, nor flower, nor seed;
It was not anything that grew,
Or crept, or climbed, or swam, or flew;
Had neither legs nor wings, indeed;
And yet she was not sure, she said,
Whether it was alive or dead.

She brought in her tiny hand
To see if I would understand,
And wondered when I made reply,
"You've found a baby butterfly."
"A butterfly is not like this,"
With doubtful look she answered me.
So then I told her what would be
Some day within the chrysalis;
How, slowly, in the dull brown thing
Now still as death, a spotted wing,
And then another, would unfold,
Till from the empty shell would fly
A pretty creature, by and by,
All radiant in blue and gold.

"And will it, truly?" questioned she—
Her laughing lips and eager eyes
All in a sparkle of surprise—
"And shall your little Mädchen see?"
"She shall!" I said. How could I tell
That ere the worm within its shell
Its gauzy, splendid wings had spread,
My little Mädchen would be dead?

To-day the butterfly has flown,—
She was not here to see it fly,—
And sorrowing I wonder why
The empty shell is mine alone.
Perhaps the secret lies in this:
I too had found a chrysalis,
And Death that robbed me of delight
Was but the radiant creature's flight!

Mary Emily Bradley [1835–1898]

MATER DOLOROSA

I'D a dream to-night
  As I fell asleep,
O! the touching sight
  Makes me still to weep:
Of my little lad,
Gone to leave me sad,
Ay, the child I had,
  But was not to keep.

As in heaven high,
  I my child did seek,
There in train came by
  Children fair and meek,
Each in lily white,
With a lamp alight;
Each was clear to sight,
  But they did not speak.

Then, a little sad,
   Came my child in turn,
But the lamp he had,
   O it did not burn!
He, to clear my doubt,
Said, half-turned about,
   "Your tears put it out;
      Mother, never mourn."

William Barnes [1801–1886]

THE LITTLE GHOST

THE stars began to peep
   Gone was the bitter day.
She heard the milky ewes
   Bleat to their lambs astray.
Her heart cried for her lamb
   Lapped cold in the churchyard sod,
She could not think on the happy children
   At play with the Lamb of God.

She heard the calling ewes
   And the lambs' answer, alas!
She heard her heart's blood drip in the night
   As the ewes' milk on the grass.
Her tears that burnt like fire
   So bitter and slow ran down
She could not think on the new-washed children
   Playing by Mary's gown.

Oh who is this comes in
   Over her threshold stone?
And why is the old dog wild with joy
   Who all day long made moan?
This fair little radiant ghost,
   Her one little son of seven,
New 'scaped from the band of merry children
   In the nurseries of Heaven.

He was all clad in white
  Without a speck or stain;
His curls had a ring of light
  That rose and fell again.
"Now come with me, my own mother,
  And you shall have great ease,
For you shall see the lost children
  Gathered to Mary's knees."

Oh, lightly sprang she up
  Nor waked her sleeping man,
And hand in hand with the little ghost
  Through the dark night she ran.
She is gone swift as a fawn,
  As a bird homes to its nest,
She has seen them lie, the sleepy children
  Twixt Mary's arm and breast.

At morning she came back;
  Her eyes were strange to see.
She will not fear the long journey,
  However long it be.
As she goes in and out
  She sings unto hersel';
For she has seen the mothers' children
  And knows that it is well.

Katherine Tynan Hinkson [1861–1931]

MOTHERHOOD

THE night throbs on; O, let me pray, dear lad!
Crush off his name a moment from my mouth.
To Thee my eyes would turn, but they go back,
Back to my arm beside me, where he lay—
So little, Lord, so little and so warm!

I cannot think that Thou hadst need of him!
He was so little, Lord, he cannot sing,
He cannot praise Thee; all his life had learned
Was to hold fast my kisses in the night.

Give him to me—he is not happy there!
He had not felt this life; his lovely eyes
Just knew me for his mother, and he died.

Hast Thou an angel there to mother him?
I say he loves me best—if he forgets,
If Thou allow it that my child forgets
And runs not out to meet me when I come—

What are my curses to Thee? Thou hast heard
The curse of Abel's mother, and since then
We have not ceased to threaten at Thy throne,
To threat and pray Thee that Thou hold them still
In memory of us.

            See Thou tend him well,
Thou God of all the mothers. If he lack
One of his kisses—ah, my heart, my heart,
Do angels kiss in heaven? Give him back!

Forgive me, Lord, but I am sick with grief,
And tired of tears, and cold to comforting.
Thou art wise, I know, and tender, aye, and good,
Thou hast my child, and he is safe in Thee,
And I believe—

Ah, God, my child shall go
Orphaned among the angels! All alone.
So little and alone! He knows not Thee,
He only knows his mother—give him back.

            Josephine Daskam Bacon [1876–

THE MOTHER'S PRAYER

THE good Lord gave, the Lord has taken from me,
    Blessed be His name, His holy will be done.
The mourners all have gone, all save I, his mother,
    The little grave lies lonely in the sun.

Nay! I would not follow, though they did beseech me,
　For the angels come now waiting for my dead.
Heaven's door is open, so my whispers soar there,
　While the gentle angels lift him from his bed.

Oh Lord, when Thou gavest he was weak and helpless,
　Could not rise nor wander from my shielding arm;
Lovely is he now and strong with four sweet summers,
　Laughing, running, tumbling, hard to keep from harm.

If some tender mother, whose babe on earth is living,
　Takes his little hand to guide his stranger feet
'Mid the countless hosts that cross the floor of heaven,
　Thou wilt not reprove her for Thy pity sweet.

If upon her breast she holds his baby beauty,
　All his golden hair will fall about her hand,
Laughing let her fingers pull it into ringlets—
　Long and lovely ringlets.　She will understand.

Wilful are his ways and full of merry mischief;
　If he prove unruly, lay the blame on me.
Never did I chide him for his noise or riot,
　Smiled upon his folly, glad his joy to see.

Each eve shall I come beside his bed so lowly;
　"Hush-a-by, my baby," softly shall I sing,
So, if he be frightened, full of sleep and anger,
　The song he loved shall reach him and sure comfort bring.

Lord, if in my praying, Thou shouldst hear me weeping,
　Ever was I wayward, always full of tears,
Take no heed of this grief.　Sweet the gift Thou gavest
　All the cherished treasure of those golden years.

Do not, therefore, hold me to Thy will ungrateful:
　Soon I shall stand upright, smiling, strong, and brave,
With a son in heaven the sad earth forgetting,
　But 'tis lonely yet, Lord, by the little grave.
　Oh, 'tis lonely, lonely, by the little grave!
　　　　　　　　　Dora Sigerson Shorter [1862–1918]

DA LEETLA BOY

Da spreeng ees com'; but oh, da joy
　　Eet ees too late!
He was so cold, my leetla boy,
　　He no could wait.

I no can count how manny week,
How manny day, dat he ees seeck;
How manny night I seet an' hold
Da leetla hand dat was so cold.
He was so patience, oh, so sweet!
Eet hurts my throat for theenk of eet;
An' all he evra ask ees w'en
Ees gona com' da spreeng agen.
Wan day, wan brighta sunny day,
He see, across da alleyway,
Da leetla girl dat's livin' dere
Ees raise her window for da air,
An' put outside a leetla pot
Of—w'at-you-call?—forgat-me-not.
So smalla flower, so leetla theeng!
But steell eet mak' hees hearta seeng:
"Oh, now, at las', ees com' da spreeng!
Da leetla plant ees glad for know
Da sun ees com' for mak' eet grow.
So, too, I am grow warm and strong."
So lika dat he seeng hees song.
But, ah! da night com' down an' den
Da weenter ees sneak back agen,
An' een da alley all da night
Ees fall da snow, so cold, so white,
An' cover up da leetla pot
Of—w'at-you-call?—forgat-me-not.
All night da leetla hand I hold
Ees grow so cold, so cold, so cold!

Da spreeng ees com'; but, oh, da joy
　　Eet ees too late!
He was so cold, my leetla boy,
　　He no could wait.

　　　　　Thomas Augustin Daly [:871–

ON THE MOOR

I

I MET a child upon the moor
    A-wading down the heather;
She put her hand into my own,
    We crossed the fields together.

I led her to her father's door—
    A cottage midst the clover.
I left her—and the world grew poor
    To me, a childless rover.

II

I met a maid upon the moor,
    The morrow was her wedding.
Love lit her eyes with lovelier hues
    Than the eve-star was shedding.

She looked a sweet good-bye to me,
    And o'er the stile went singing.
Down all the lonely night I heard
    But bridal bells a-ringing.

III

I met a mother on the moor,
    By a new grave a-praying.
The happy swallows in the blue
    Upon the winds were playing.

"Would I were in his grave," I said,
    "And he beside her standing!"
There was no heart to break if death
    For me had made demanding.
        Cale Young Rice [1872–

EPITAPH OF DIONYSIA

HERE doth Dionysia lie:
She whose little wanton foot,
Tripping (ah, too carelessly!)
Touched this tomb, and fell into 't.

Trip no more shall she, nor fall.
And her trippings were so few!
Summers only eight in all
Had the sweet child wandered through.

But, already, life's few suns
Love's strong seeds had ripened warm.
All her ways were winning ones;
All her cunning was to charm.

And the fancy, in the flower,
While the flesh was in the bud,
Childhood's dawning sex did dower
With warm gusts of womanhood.

Oh what joys by hope begun,
Oh what kisses kissed by thought,
What love-deeds by fancy done,
Death to endless dust hath wrought!

Had the fates been kind as thou,
Who, till now, was never cold,
Once Love's aptest scholar, now
Thou hadst been his teacher bold;

But, if buried seeds upthrow
Fruits and flowers; if flower and fruit
By their nature fitly show
What the seeds are, whence they shoot,

Dionysia, o'er this tomb,
Where thy buried beauties be,
From their dust shall spring and bloom
Loves and graces like to thee.

Unknown

FOR CHARLIE'S SAKE

THE night is late, the house is still;
The angels of the hour fulfil
Their tender ministries, and move
From couch to couch in cares of love.

They drop into thy dreams, sweet wife,
The happiest smile of Charlie's life,
And lay on baby's lips a kiss,
Fresh from his angel-brother's bliss;
And, as they pass, they seem to make
A strange, dim hymn, "For Charlie's sake."

My listening heart takes up the strain,
And gives it to the night again,
Fitted with words of lowly praise,
And patience learned of mournful days,
And memories of the dead child's ways.
His will be done, His will be done!
Who gave and took away my son,
In "the far land" to shine and sing
Before the Beautiful, the King,
Who every day doth Christmas make,
All starred and belled for Charlie's sake.

For Charlie's sake I will arise;
I will anoint me where he lies,
And change my raiment, and go in
To the Lord's house, and leave my sin
Without, and seat me at his board,
Eat, and be glad, and praise the Lord.
For wherefore should I fast and weep,
And sullen moods of mourning keep?
I cannot bring him back, nor he,
For any calling, come to me.
The bond the angel Death did sign,
God sealed—for Charlie's sake, and mine.

I'm very poor—this slender stone
Marks all the narrow field I own;
Yet, patient husbandman, I till
With faith and prayers, that precious hill,
Sow it with penitential pains,
And, hopeful, wait the latter rains;
Content if, after all, the spot
Yield barely one forget-me-not—
Whether or figs or thistles make
My crop, content for Charlie's sake.

I have no houses, builded well—
Only that little lonesome cell,
Where never romping playmates come,
Nor bashful sweethearts, cunning-dumb—
An April burst of girls and boys,
Their rainbowed cloud of glooms and joys
Born with their songs, gone with their toys;
Nor ever is its stillness stirred
By purr of cat, or chirp of bird,
Or mother's twilight legend, told
Of Horner's pie, or Tiddler's gold,
Or fairy hobbling to the door,
Red-cloaked and weird, banned and poor,
To bless the good child's gracious eyes,
The good child's wistful charities,
And crippled changeling's hunch to make
Dance on his crutch, for good child's sake.

How is it with the child? 'Tis well;
Nor would I any miracle
Might stir my sleeper's tranquil trance,
Or plague his painless countenance:
I would not any seer might place
His staff on my immortal's face,
Or lip to lip, and eye to eye,
Charm back his pale mortality.
No, Shunamite! I would not break
God's stillness. Let them weep who wake.

For Charlie's sake my lot is blest:
No comfort like his mother's breast,
No praise like hers; no charm expressed
In fairest forms hath half her zest.
For Charlie's sake this bird's caressed
That death left lonely in the nest;
For Charlie's sake my heart is dressed,
As for its birthday, in its best;
For Charlie's sake we leave the rest
To Him who gave, and who did take,
And saved us twice, for Charlie's sake.
                    John Williamson Palmer [1825–1906]

"ARE THE CHILDREN AT HOME?"

EACH day, when the glow of sunset
  Fades in the western sky,
And the wee ones, tired of playing,
  Go tripping lightly by,
I steal away from my husband,
  Asleep in his easy-chair,
And watch from the open doorway
  Their faces fresh and fair.

Alone in the dear old homestead
  That once was full of life,
Ringing with girlish laughter,
  Echoing boyish strife,
We two are waiting together;
  And oft, as the shadows come,
With tremulous voice he calls me,
  "It is night! are the children home?"

"Yes, love!" I answer him gently,
  "They're all home long ago;"—
And I sing, in my quivering treble,
  A song so soft and low,
Till the old man drops to slumber,
  With his head upon his hand,
And I tell to myself the number
  At home in the better land.

At home, where never a sorrow
  Shall dim their eyes with tears!
Where the smile of God is on them
  Through all the summer years!
I know,—yet my arms are empty,
  That fondly folded seven,
And the mother-heart within me
  Is almost starved for heaven.

Sometimes, in the dusk of evening,
  I only shut my eyes,
And the children are all about me,
  A vision from the skies:

The babes whose dimpled fingers
  Lost the way to my breast,
And the beautiful ones, the angels,
  Passed to the world of the blest.

With never a cloud upon them,
  I see their radiant brows;
My boys that I gave to freedom,—
  The red sword sealed their vows!
In a tangled Southern forest,
  Twin brothers bold and brave,
They fell; and the flag they died for,
  Thank God! floats over their grave.

A breath, and the vision is lifted
  Away on wings of light,
And again we two are together,
  All alone in the night.
They tell me his mind is failing,
  But I smile at idle fears;
He is only back with the children,
  In the dear and peaceful years.

And still, as the summer sunset
  Fades away in the west,
And the wee ones, tired of playing,
  Go trooping home to rest,
My husband calls from his corner,
  "Say, love, have the children come?"
And I answer, with eyes uplifted,
  "Yes, dear! they are all at home."
                    Margaret Sangster [1838–1912]

THE MORNING–GLORY

WE wreathed about our darling's head
  The morning-glory bright;
Her little face looked out beneath,
  So full of life and light,

So lit as with a sunrise,
  That we could only say,
"She is the morning-glory true,
  And her poor types are they."

So always from that happy time
  We called her by their name,
And very fitting did it seem—
  For, sure as morning came,
Behind her cradle bars she smiled
  To catch the first faint ray,
As from the trellis smiles the flower
  And opens to the day.

But not so beautiful they rear
  Their airy cups of blue,
As turned her sweet eyes to the light,
  Brimmed with sleep's tender dew;
And not so close their tendrils fine
  Round their supports are thrown,
As those dear arms whose outstretched plea
  Clasped all hearts to her own.

We used to think how she had come,
  Even as comes the flower,
The last and perfect added gift
  To crown Love's morning hour;
And how in her was imaged forth
  The love we could not say,
As on the little dewdrops round
  Shines back the heart of day.

We never could have thought, O God,
  That she must wither up,
Almost before a day was flown,
  Like the morning-glory's cup;
We never thought to see her droop
  Her fair and noble head,
Till she lay stretched before our eyes,
  Wilted, and cold, and dead!

The morning-glory's blossoming
　　Will soon be coming round—
We see the rows of heart-shaped leaves
　　Upspringing from the ground;
The tender things the winter killed
　　Renew again their birth,
But the glory of our morning
　　Has passed away from earth.

O Earth! in vain our aching eyes
　　Stretch over thy green plain!
Too harsh thy dews, too gross thine air
　　Her spirit to sustain;
But up in groves of Paradise
　　Full surely we shall see
Our morning-glory beautiful
　　Twine round our dear Lord's knee.

　　　　　　Maria White Lowell [1821–1855]

SHE CAME AND WENT

As a twig trembles, which a bird
　　Lights on to sing, then leaves unbent,
So is my memory thrilled and stirred;—
　　I only know she came and went.

As clasps some lake, by gusts unriven,
　　The blue dome's measureless content,
So my soul held that moment's heaven;—
　　I only know she came and went.

As, at one bound, our swift spring heaps
　　The orchards full of bloom and scent,
So clove her May my wintry sleeps;—
　　I only know she came and went.

An angel stood and met my gaze,
　　Through the low doorway of my tent;
The tent is struck, the vision stays;—
　　I only know she came and went.

Oh, when the room grows slowly dim,
  And life's last oil is nearly spent,
One gush of light these eyes will brim,
  Only to think she came and went.
      James Russell Lowell [1819–1891]

THE FIRST SNOW–FALL

THE snow had begun in the gloaming,
  And busily all the night
Had been heaping field and highway
  With a silence deep and white.

Every pine and fir and hemlock
  Wore ermine too dear for an earl,
And the poorest twig on the elm-tree
  Was ridged inch deep with pearl.

From sheds new-roofed with Carrara
  Came Chanticleer's muffled crow,
The stiff rails softened to swan's-down,
  And still fluttered down the snow.

I stood and watched by the window
  The noiseless work of the sky,
And the sudden flurries of snow-birds,
  Like brown leaves whirling by.

I thought of a mound in sweet Auburn
  Where a little headstone stood;
How the flakes were folding it gently,
  As did robins the babes in the wood.

Up spoke our own little Mabel,
  Saying, "Father, who makes it snow?"
And I told of the good All-father
  Who cares for us here below.

Again I looked at the snow-fall,
  And thought of the leaden sky
That arched o'er our first great sorrow,
  When that mound was heaped so high.

I remembered the gradual patience
  That fell from that cloud like snow,
Flake by flake, healing and hiding
  The scar that renewed our woe.

And again to the child I whispered,
  "The snow that husheth all,
Darling, the merciful Father
  Alone can make it fall!"

Then, with eyes that saw not, I kissed her;
  And she, kissing back, could not know
That *my* kiss was given to her sister,
  Folded close under deepening snow.
           James Russell Lowell [1819–1891]

"WE ARE SEVEN"

A simple Child,
  That lightly draws its breath,
And feels its life in every limb,
  What should it know of death?

I met a little cottage Girl:
  She was eight years old, she said:
Her hair was thick with many a curl
  That clustered round her head.

She had a rustic, woodland air,
  And she was wildly clad:
Her eyes were fair, and very fair;
  —Her beauty made me glad.

"Sisters and brothers, little Maid,
  How many may you be?"
"How many? Seven in all," she said,
  And wondering looked at me.

"And where are they? I pray you tell."
  She answered, "Seven are we;
And two of us at Conway dwell,
  And two are gone to sea;

"Two of us in the church-yard lie,
  My sister and my brother;
And, in the church-yard cottage, I
  Dwell near them with my mother."

"You say that two at Conway dwell,
  And two are gone to sea,
Yet ye are seven!—I pray you tell,
  Sweet Maid, how this may be."

Then did the little Maid reply,
  "Seven boys and girls are we;
Two of us in the church-yard lie
  Beneath the church-yard tree."

"You run about, my little Maid;
  Your limbs they are alive;
If two are in the church-yard laid,
  Then ye are only five."

"Their graves are green, they may be seen,"
  The little Maid replied:
"Twelve steps or more from my mother's door,
  And they are side by side.

"My stockings there I often knit,
  My kerchief there I hem;
And there upon the ground I sit,
  And sing a song to them.

"And often after sunset, Sir,
  When it is light and fair,
I take my little porringer,
  And eat my supper there.

"The first that died was sister Jane;
  In bed she moaning lay,
Till God released her of her pain;
  And then she went away.

"So in the church-yard she was laid;
  And, when the grass was dry,
Together round her grave we played,
  My brother John and I.

"And when the ground was white with snow,
  And I could run and slide,
My brother John was forced to go,
  And he lies by her side."

"How many are you, then," said I,
  "If they two are in heaven?"
Quick was the little Maid's reply,
  "O Master! we are seven."

"But they are dead; those two are dead!
  Their spirits are in heaven!"
'Twas throwing words away; for still
The little Maid would have her will,
  And said, "Nay, we are seven!"

                    William Wordsworth [1770–1850]

MY CHILD

I CANNOT make him dead!
  His fair sunshiny head
Is ever bounding round my study chair;
  Yet when my eyes, now dim
  With tears, I turn to him,
The vision vanishes,—he is not there!

I walk my parlor floor,
  And, through the open door,
I hear a footfall on the chamber stair;
  I'm stepping toward the hall
  To give my boy a call;
And then bethink me that—he is not there'

I thread the crowded street;
  A satchelled lad I meet,

With the same beaming eyes and colored hair;
    And, as he's running by,
    Follow him with my eye,
Scarcely believing that—he is not there!

    I know his face is hid
    Under the coffin-lid;
Closed are his eyes; cold is his forehead fair;
    My hand that marble felt;
    O'er it in prayer I knelt;
Yet my heart whispers that—he is not there!

    I cannot make him dead!
    When passing by the bed,
So long watched over with parental care,
    My spirit and my eye,
    Seek him inquiringly,
Before the thought comes that—he is not there!

    When, at the cool gray break
    Of day, from sleep I wake,
With my first breathing of the morning air
    My soul goes up, with joy,
    To Him who gave my boy;
Then comes the sad thought that—he is not there!

    When at the day's calm close,
    Before we seek repose,
I'm with his mother, offering up our prayer;
    Whate'er I may be saying,
    I am, in spirit, praying
For our boy's spirit, though—he is not there!

    Not there!—Where, then, is he?
    The form I used to see
Was but the raiment that he used to wear.
    The grave, that now doth press
    Upon that cast-off dress,
Is but his wardrobe locked;—*he* is not there!

He lives!—In all the past
He lives; nor, to the last,
Of seeing him again will I despair;
In dreams I see him now;
And on his angel brow,
I see it written, "Thou shalt see me *there!*"

Yes, we all live to God!
Father, thy chastening rod
So help us, thine afflicted ones, to bear,
That, in the spirit-land,
Meeting at thy right hand,
'Twill be our heaven to find that—he is there!
John Pierpont [1785-1866]

THE CHILD'S WISH GRANTED

Do you remember, my sweet, absent son,
How in the soft June days forever done
You loved the heavens so warm and clear and high;
And when I lifted you, soft came your cry,—
"Put me 'way up—'way, 'way up in blue sky"?

I laughed and said I could not;—set you down,
Your gray eyes wonder-filled beneath that crown
Of bright hair gladdening me as you raced by.
Another Father now, more strong than I,
Has borne you voiceless to your dear blue sky.
George Parsons Lathrop [1851-1898]

CHALLENGE

THIS little child, so white, so calm,
Decked for her grave,
Encountered death without a qualm.
Are you as brave?

So small, and armed with naught beside
Her mother's kiss,
Alone she stepped, unterrified,
Into the abyss.

"Ah," you explain, "she did not know—
    This babe of four—
Just what it signifies to go."
    Do you know more?

Kenton Foster Murray [18 -

TIRED MOTHERS

A LITTLE elbow leans upon your knee,
    Your tired knee that has so much to bear;
A child's dear eyes are looking lovingly
    From underneath a thatch of tangled hair.
Perhaps you do not heed the velvet touch
    Of warm, moist fingers, folding yours so tight;
You do not prize this blessing overmuch,—
    You almost are too tired to pray to-night.

But it *is* blessedness! A year ago
    I did not see it as I do to-day,—
We are so dull and thankless; and too slow
    To catch the sunshine till it slips away.
And now it seems surpassing strange to me
    That, while I wore the badge of motherhood,
I did not kiss more oft and tenderly
    The little child that brought me only good.

And if some night when you sit down to rest,
    You miss this elbow from your tired knee,—
This restless, curling head from off your breast,—
    This lisping tongue that chatters constantly;
If from your own the dimpled hands had slipped,
    And ne'er would nestle in your palm again;
If the white feet into their grave had tripped,
    I could not blame you for your heartache then!

I wonder so that mothers ever fret
    At little children clinging to their gown;
Or that the footprints, when the days are wet,
    Are ever black enough to make them frown.

If I could find a little muddy boot,
  Or cap, or jacket, on my chamber-floor,—
If I could kiss a rosy, restless foot,
  And hear its patter in my house once more,—

If I could mend a broken cart to-day,
  To-morrow make a kite to reach the sky,
There is no woman in God's world could say
  She was more blissfully content than I.
But ah! the dainty pillow next my own
  Is never rumpled by a shining head;
My singing birdling from its nest has flown,
  The little boy I used to kiss is dead.
                    May Riley Smith [1842–1927]

MY DAUGHTER LOUISE

In the light of the moon, by the side of the water,
  My seat on the sand and her seat on my knees,
We watch the bright billows, do I and my daughter,
  My sweet little daughter Louise.
We wonder what city the pathway of glory,
  That broadens away to the limitless west,
Leads up to—she minds her of some pretty story
  And says: "To the city that mortals love best."
Then I say: "It must lead to the far away city,
  The beautiful City of Rest."

In the light of the moon, by the side of the water,
  Stand two in the shadow of whispering trees,
And one loves my daughter, my beautiful daughter,
  My womanly daughter Louise.
She steps to the boat with a touch of his fingers,
  And out on the diamonded pathway they move;
The shallop is lost in the distance, it lingers,
  It waits, but I know that its coming will prove
That it went to the walls of the wonderful city,
  The magical City of Love.

In the light of the moon, by the side of the water,
   I wait for her coming from over the seas;
I wait but to welcome the dust of my daughter,
   To weep for my daughter Louise.
The path, as of old, reaching out in its splendor,
   Gleams bright, like a way that an angel has trod;
I kiss the cold burden its billows surrender,
   Sweet clay to lie under the pitiful sod:
But she rests, at the end of the path, in the city
   Whose "builder and maker is God."

             Homer Greene [1853–1940]

"I AM LONELY"

From "The Spanish Gypsy"

THE world is great: the birds all fly from me,
The stars are golden fruit upon a tree
All out of reach: my little sister went,
       And I am lonely.

The world is great: I tried to mount the hill
Above the pines, where the light lies so still,
But it rose higher: little Lisa went
       And I am lonely.

The world is great: the wind comes rushing by.
I wonder where it comes from; sea birds cry
And hurt my heart: my little sister went,
       And I am lonely.

The world is great: the people laugh and talk,
And make loud holiday: how fast they walk!
I'm lame, they push me: little Lisa went,
       And I am lonely.

             George Eliot [1819–1880]

SONNETS

From "Mimma Bella"

I

HAVE dark Egyptians stolen Thee away,
Oh Baby, Baby, in whose cot we peer
As down some empty gulf that opens sheer
And fathomless, illumined by no ray?

And wilt thou come, on some far distant day,
With unknown face, and say, "Behold! I'm here,
The child you lost;" while we in sudden fear,
Dumb with great doubt, shall find no word to say?
One darker than dark gipsy holds thee fast;
One whose strong fingers none has forced apart
Since first they closed on things that were too fair;
Nor shall we see thee other than thou wast,
But such as thou art printed in the heart,
In changeless baby loveliness still there.

II

Two springs she saw—two radiant Tuscan springs,
What time the wild red tulips are aflame
In the new wheat, and wreaths of young vine frame
The daffodils that every light breeze swings;
And the anemones that April brings
Make purple pools, as if Adonis came
Just there to die; and Florence scrolls her name
In every blossom Primavera flings.
Now, when the scented iris, straight and tall,
Shall hedge the garden gravel once again
With pale blue flags, at May's exulting call,
And when the amber roses, wet with rain,
Shall tapestry the old gray villa wall,
We, left alone, shall seek one bud in vain.

IV

Oh, rosy as the lining of a shell
Were the wee hands that now are white as snows;
And like pink coral, with their elfin toes,
The feet that on life's brambles never fell.
And with its tiny smile, adorable
The mouth that never knew life's bitter sloes;
And like the incurved petal of a rose
The little ear, now deaf in Death's strong spell.
Now, while the seasons in their order roll,
And sun and rain pour down from God's great dome,
And deathless stars shine nightly overhead,
Near other children, with her little doll,

She waits the wizard that will never come
To wake the sleep-struck playground of the dead.

VI

Oh, bless the law that veils the Future's face;
For who could smile into a baby's eyes,
Or bear the beauty of the evening skies,
If he could see what cometh on apace?
The ticking of the death-watch would replace
The baby's prattle, for the over-wise;
The breeze's murmur would become the cries
Of stormy petrels where the breakers race.
We live as moves the walker in his sleep,
Who walks because he sees not the abyss
His feet are skirting as he goes his way:
If we could see the morrow from the steep
Of our security, the soul would miss
Its footing, and fall headlong from to-day.

VIII

One day, I mind me, now that she is dead,
When nothing warned us of the dark decree,
I crooned, to lull her, in a minor key,
Such fancies as first came into my head.
I crooned them low, beside her little bed;
And the refrain was somehow "Come with me,
And we will wander by the purple sea;"
I crooned it, and—God help me!—felt no dread.
O Purple Sea, beyond the stress of storms,
Where never ripple breaks upon the shore
Of Death's pale Isles of Twilight as they dream,
Give back, give back, O Sea of Nevermore,
The frailest of the unsubstantial forms
That leave the shores that are for those that seem!

XX

What essences from Idumean palm,
What ambergris, what sacerdotal wine,
What Arab myrrh, what spikenard, would be thine,
If I could swathe thy memory in such balm!

Oh, for wrecked gold, from depths for ever calm,
To fashion for thy name a fretted shrine;
Oh, for strange gems, still locked in virgin mine,
To stud the pyx, where thought would bring sweet psalm!
I have but this small rosary of rhyme,—
No rubies but heart's drops, no pearls but tears,
To lay upon the altar of thy name,
O Mimma Bella;—on the shrine that Time
Makes ever holier for the soul, while years
Obliterate the rolls of human fame.

Eugene Lee-Hamilton [1845–1907]

ROSE–MARIE OF THE ANGELS

LITTLE Sister Rose-Marie,
Will thy feet as willing-light
Run through Paradise, I wonder,
As they run the blue skies under,
Willing feet, so airy-light?

Little Sister Rose-Marie,
Will thy voice as bird-note clear
Lift and ripple over Heaven
As its mortal sound is given,
Swift bird-voice, so young and clear?

How God will be glad of thee,
Little Sister Rose-Marie!

Adelaide Crapsey [1878–1914]

MAIDENHOOD

MAIDENHOOD

MAIDEN! with the meek, brown eyes
In whose orbs a shadow lies
Like the dusk in evening skies!

Thou whose locks outshine the sun,
Golden tresses, wreathed in one,
As the braided streamlets run!

Standing, with reluctant feet,
Where the brook and river meet,
Womanhood and childhood fleet!

Gazing, with a timid glance,
On the brooklet's swift advance,
On the river's broad expanse!

Deep and still, that gliding stream
Beautiful to thee must seem,
As the river of a dream.

Then why pause with indecision,
When bright angels in thy vision
Beckon thee to fields Elysian?

Seest thou shadows sailing by,
As the dove, with startled eye,
Sees the falcon's shadow fly?

Hearest thou voices on the shore,
That our ears perceive no more,
Deafened by the cataract's roar?

Oh, thou child of many prayers!
Life hath quicksands,—Life hath snares!
Care and age come unawares!

Like the swell of some sweet tune,
Morning rises into noon,
May glides onward into June.

Childhood is the bough, where slumbered
Birds and blossoms many-numbered;—
Age, that bough with snows encumbered.

Gather, then, each flower that grows,
When the young heart overflows,
To embalm that tent of snows.

Bear a lily in thy hand;
Gates of brass cannot withstand
One touch of that magic wand.

Bear through sorrow, wrong, and ruth,
In thy heart the dew of youth,
On thy lips the smile of truth.

Oh, that dew, like balm, shall steal
Into wounds that cannot heal,
Even as sleep our eyes doth seal;

And that smile, like sunshine, dart
Into many a sunless heart
For a smile of God thou art.
                    Henry Wadsworth Longfellow [1807–1882]

TO THE VIRGINS, TO MAKE MUCH OF TIME

GATHER ye rosebuds while ye may,
    Old Time is still a-flying:
And this same flower that smiles to-day
    To-morrow will be dying.

The glorious lamp of heaven, the sun,
  The higher he's a-getting,
The sooner will his race be run,
  And nearer he's to setting,

That age is best which is the first,
  When youth and blood are warmer;
But being spent, the worse, and worst
  Times still succeed the former.

Then be not coy, but use your time,
  And while ye may, go marry:
For having lost but once your prime,
  You may for ever tarry.
                    Robert Herrick [1591–1674]

TO MISTRESS MARGARET HUSSEY

Merry Margaret
As midsummer flower,
Gentle as falcon,
Or hawk of the tower:
With solace and gladness,
Much mirth and no madness,
All good and no badness;
So joyously,
So maidenly,
So womanly
Her demeaning
In every thing,
Far, far passing
That I can indite,
Or suffice to write
Of merry Margaret
As midsummer flower,
Gentle as falcon,
Or hawk of the tower,
As patient and still
And as full of good will
As fair Isaphill,

Coliander,
Sweet pomander,
Good Cassander;
Steadfast of thought,
Well made, well wrought,
Far may be sought,
Ere that ye can find
So courteous, so kind,
As merry Margaret,
This midsummer flower,
Gentle as falcon,
Or hawk of the tower.

John Skelton [1460?-1529]

ON HER COMING TO LONDON

WHAT'S she, so late from Penshurst come,
More gorgeous than the mid-day sun,
   That all the world amazes?
Sure 'tis some angel from above,
Or 'tis the Cyprian Queen of Love
   Attended by the Graces.

Or is't not Juno, Heaven's great dame,
Or Pallas armed, as on she came
   To assist the Greeks in fight,
Or Cynthia, that huntress bold,
Or from old Tithon's bed so cold,
   Aurora chasing night?

No, none of those, yet one that shall
Compare, perhaps exceed them all,
   For beauty, wit, and birth;
As good as great, as chaste as fair,
A brighter nymph none breathes the air,
   Or treads upon the earth.

'Tis Dorothèe, a maid high-born,
   And lovely as the blushing morn,

Of noble Sidney's race;
Oh! could you see into her mind,
The beauties there locked-up outshine
 The beauties of her face.

Fair Dorothea, sent from heaven
To add more wonders to the seven,
 And glad each eye and ear,
Crown of her sex, the Muse's port,
The glory of our English court,
 The brightness of our sphere.

To welcome her the Spring breathes forth
Elysian sweets, March strews the earth
 With violets and posies,
The sun renews his darting fires,
April puts on her best attires,
 And May her crown of roses.

Go, happy maid, increase the store
Of graces born with you, and more
 Add to their number still;
So neither all-consuming age,
Nor envy's blast, nor fortune's rage
 Shall ever work you ill.

     Edmund Waller [1606–1687]

"O, SAW YE BONNY LESLEY"

O SAW ye bonny Lesley
 As she gaed owre the Border?
She's gane, like Alexander,
 To spread her conquests farther.

To see her is to love her,
 And love but her for ever;
For nature made her what she is,
 And ne'er made sic anither!

Thou art a queen, fair Lesley,
   Thy subjects we, before thee;
Thou art divine, fair Lesley,
   The hearts o' men adore thee.

The deil he couldna scaith thee,
   Or aught that wad belang thee;
He'd look into thy bonny face,
   And say, "I canna wrang thee!"

The powers aboon will tent thee;
   Misfortune sha' na steer thee;
Thou'rt like themselves sae lovely
   That ill they'll ne'er let near thee.

Return again, fair Lesley,
   Return to Caledonie!
That we may brag we hae a lass
   There's nane again sae bonny.
                    Robert Burns [1759–1796]

TO A YOUNG LADY

SWEET stream, that winds through yonder glade,
Apt emblem of a virtuous maid!—
Silent and chaste she steals along,
Far from the world's gay busy throng:
With gentle yet prevailing force,
Intent upon her destined course;
Graceful and useful all she does,
Blessing and blest where'er she goes;
Pure-bosomed as that watery glass,
And Heaven reflected in her face!
                    William Cowper [1731–180c]

RUTH

SHE stood breast high among the corn,
Clasped by the golden light of morn,
Like the sweetheart of the sun,
Who many a glowing kiss had won.

On her cheek an autumn flush,
Deeply ripened;—such a blush
In the midst of brown was born,
Like red poppies grown with corn.

Round her eyes her tresses fell,
Which were blackest none could tell.
But long lashes veiled a light,
That had else been all too bright.

And her hat, with shady brim,
Made her tressy forehead dim;
Thus she stood amid the stooks,
Praising God with sweetest looks:

Sure, I said, Heaven did not mean,
Where I reap thou shouldst but glean;
Lay thy sheaf adown and come,
Share my harvest and my home.

Thomas Hood [1799–1845]

THE SOLITARY REAPER

BEHOLD her, single in the field,
Yon solitary Highland Lass!
Reaping and singing by herself;
Stop here, or gently pass!
Alone she cuts and binds the grain,
And sings a melancholy strain;
O listen! for the Vale profound
Is overflowing with the sound.

No Nightingale did ever chaunt
More welcome notes to weary bands
Of Travellers in some shady haunt,
Among Arabian sands:
A voice so thrilling ne'er was heard
In spring-time from the Cuckoo-bird,
Breaking the silence of the seas
Among the farthest Hebrides.

Will no one tell me what she sings?
Perhaps the plaintive numbers flow
For old, unhappy, far-off things,
And battles long ago:
Or is it some more humble lay,
Familiar matter of to-day?
Some natural sorrow, loss, or pain,
That has been, and may be again!

Whate'er the theme, the Maiden sang
As if her song could have no ending;
I saw her singing at her work,
And o'er the sickle bending;—
I listened, motionless and still;
And, as I mounted up the hill,
The music in my heart I bore,
Long after it was heard no more.
William Wordsworth [1770–1850]

THE THREE COTTAGE GIRLS

I

How blest the Maid whose heart—yet free
From Love's uneasy sovereignty—
Beats with a fancy running high,
Her simple cares to magnify;
Whom Labor, never urged to toil,
Hath cherished on a healthful soil;
Who knows not pomp, who heeds not pelf;
Whose heaviest sin it is to look
Askance upon her pretty Self
Reflected in some crystal brook;
Whom grief hath spared—who sheds no tear
But in sweet pity; and can hear
Another's praise from envy clear.

II

Such (but O lavish Nature! why
That dark unfathomable eye,
Where lurks a Spirit that replies
To stillest mood of softest skies,

Yet hints at peace to be o'erthrown,
Another's first, and then her own?)
Such haply, yon Italian Maid,
Our Lady's laggard Votaress,
Halting beneath the chestnut shade
To accomplish there her loveliness:
Nice aid maternal fingers lend;
A Sister serves with slacker hand;
Then, glittering like a star, she joins the festal band.

III

How blest (if truth may entertain
Coy fancy with a bolder strain)
The Helvetian Girl—who daily braves,
In her light skiff, the tossing waves,
And quits the bosom of the deep
Only to climb the rugged steep!
—Say whence that modulated shout!
From Wood-nymph of Diana's throng?
Or does the greeting to a rout
Of giddy Bacchanals belong?
Jubilant outcry! rock and glade
Resounded—but the voice obeyed
The breath of an Helvetian Maid.

IV

Her beauty dazzles the thick wood;
Her courage animates the flood;
Her steps the elastic greensward meets
Returning unreluctant sweets;
The mountains (as ye heard) rejoice
Aloud, saluted by her voice!
Blithe Paragon of Alpine grace,
Be as thou art—for through thy veins
The blood of Heroes runs its race!
And nobly wilt thou brook the chains
That, for the virtuous, Life prepares;
The fetter which the Matron wears;
The patriot Mother's weight of anxious cares!

V

"Sweet Highland Girl! a very shower
Of beauty was thy earthly dower,"
When thou didst flit before mine eyes,
Gay Vision under sullen skies,
While Hope and Love around thee played,
Near the rough falls of Inversneyd!
Have they, who nursed the blossom, seen
No breach of promise in the fruit?
Was joy, in following joy, as keen
As grief can be in grief's pursuit?
When youth had flown did hope still bless
Thy goings—or the cheerfulness
Of innocence survive to mitigate distress?

VI

But from our course why turn—to tread
A way with shadows overspread;
Where what we gladliest would believe
Is feared as what may most deceive?
Bright Spirit, not with amaranth crowned
But heath-bells from thy native ground,
Time cannot thin thy flowing hair,
Nor take one ray of light from Thee;
For in my Fancy thou dost share
The gift of immortality;
And there shall bloom, with Thee allied,
The Votaress by Lugano's side;
And that intrepid Nymph, on Uri's steep descried!
                    William Wordsworth [1770–1850]

BLACKMWORE MAIDENS

THE primrwose in the sheäde do blow,
    The cowslip in the zun,
The thyme upon the down do grow,
    The clote where streams do run;

An' where do pretty maïdens grow
An' blow, but where the tower
Do rise among the bricken tuns,
In Blackmwore by the Stour.

If you could zee their comely gait,
An' pretty feäces' smiles,
A-trippèn on so light o' waïght,
An' steppèn off the stiles;
A-gwaïn to church, as bells do swing
An' ring within the tower,
You'd own the pretty maïdens' pleäce
Is Blackmwore by the Stour.

If you vrom Wimborne took your road,
To Stower or Paladore,
An' all the farmers' housen showed
Their daughters at the door;
You'd cry to bachelors at hwome—
"Here, come: 'ithin an hour
You'll vind ten maïdens to your mind,
In Blackmwore by the Stour."

An' if you looked 'ithin their door,
To zee em in their pleäce,
A-doèn housework up avore
Their smilèn mother's feäce;
You'd cry—"Why, if a man would wive
An' thrive, 'ithout a dower,
Then let en look en out a wife
In Blackmwore by the Stour."

As I upon my road did pass
A school-house back in Maÿ,
There out upon the beäten grass
Wer maïdens at their plaÿ;
An' as the pretty souls did tweil
An' smile, I cried, "The flower
O' beauty, then, is still in bud
In Blackmwore by the Stour."

William Barnes [1801–1886]

A PORTRAIT

" One name is Elizabeth "
BEN JONSON

I will paint her as I see her.
  Ten times have the lilies blown
  Since she looked upon the sun.

And her face is lily-clear,
  Lily-shaped, and dropped in duty
  To the law of its own beauty.

Oval cheeks encolored faintly,
  Which a trail of golden hair
  Keeps from fading off to air:

And a forehead fair and saintly,
  Which two blue eyes undershine,
  Like meek prayers before a shrine.

Face and figure of a child,—
  Though too calm, you think, and tender,
  For the childhood you would lend her.

Yet child-simple, undefiled,
  Frank, obedient, waiting still
  On the turnings of your will.

Moving light, as all young things,
  As young birds, or early wheat
  When the wind blows over it.

Only, free from flutterings
  Of loud mirth that scorneth measure—
  Taking love for her chief pleasure.

Choosing pleasures, for the rest,
  Which come softly—just as she,
  When she nestles at your knee.

Quiet talk she liketh best,
  In a bower of gentle looks,—
  Watering flowers, or reading books.

And her voice, it murmurs lowly,
   As a silver stream may run,
   Which yet feels (you feel) the sun.

And her smile it seems half holy,
   As if drawn from thoughts more far
   Than our common jestings are.

And if any poet knew her,
   He would sing of her with falls
   Used in lovely madrigals.

And if any painter drew her,
   He would paint her unaware
   With a halo round her hair.

And if reader read the poem,
   He would whisper—"You have done a
   Consecrated little Una!"

And a dreamer (did you show him
   That same picture) would exclaim,
   "'Tis my angel, with a name!"

And a stranger,—when he sees her
   In the street even—smileth stilly,
   Just as you would at a lily.

And all voices that address her,
   Soften, sleeken every word,
   As if speaking to a bird.

And all fancies yearn to cover
   The hard earth, whereon she passes,
   With the thymy-scented grasses.

And all hearts do pray, "God love her!"
   Ay and always, in good sooth,
   We may all be sure HE DOTH.
       Elizabeth Barrett Browning [1806–1861]

TO A CHILD OF FANCY

THE nests are in the hedgerows,
The lambs are on the grass;
With laughter sweet as music
The hours lightfooted pass,
My darling child of fancy,
My winsome prattling lass.

Blue eyes, with long brown lashes,
Thickets of golden curl,
Red little lips disclosing
Twin rows of fairy pearl,
Cheeks like the apple blossom,
Voice lightsome as the merle.

A whole Spring's fickle changes,
In every short-lived day,
A passing cloud of April,
A flowery smile of May,
A thousand quick mutations
From graver moods to gay.

Far off, I see the season
When thy childhood's course is run,
And thy girlhood opens wider
Beneath the growing sun,
And the rose begins to redden,
But the violets are done.

And further still the summer,
When thy fair tree, fully grown,
Shall bourgeon, and grow splendid
With blossoms of its own,
And the fruit begins to gather,
But the buttercups are mown.

If I should see thy autumn,
'Twill not be close at hand,
But with a spirit vision,
From some far-distant land.

Or, perhaps, I hence may see thee
Amongst the angels stand.

I know not what of fortune
The future holds for thee,
Nor if skies fair or clouded
Wait thee in days to be,
But neither joy nor sorrow
Shall sever thee from me.

Dear child, whatever changes
Across our lives may pass,
I shall see thee still for ever,
Clearly as in a glass,
The same sweet child of fancy,
The same dear winsome lass.

Lewis Morris [1833–1907]

DAISY

WHERE the thistle lifts a purple crown
  Six foot out of the turf,
And the harebell shakes on the windy hill—
  O the breath of the distant surf!—

The hills look over on the South,
  And southward dreams the sea;
And, with the sea-breeze hand in hand,
  Came innocence and she.

Where 'mid the gorse the raspberry
  Red for the gatherer springs,
Two children did we stray and talk
  Wise, idle, childish things.

She listened with big-lipped surprise,
  Breast-deep 'mid flower and spine:
Her skin was like a grape, whose veins
  Run snow instead of wine.

She knew not those sweet words she spake,
  Nor knew her own sweet way;
But there's never a bird, so sweet a song
  Thronged in whose throat that day!

Oh, there were flowers in Storrington
  On the turf and on the spray;
But the sweetest flower on Sussex hills
  Was the Daisy-flower that day!

Her beauty smoothed earth's furrowed face!
  She gave me tokens three:—
A look, a word of her winsome mouth,
  And a wild raspberry.

A berry red, a guileless look,
  A still word,—strings of sand!
And yet they made my wild, wild heart
  Fly down to her little hand.

For standing artless as the air,
  And candid as the skies,
She took the berries with her hand,
  And the love with her sweet eyes.

The fairest things have fleetest end:
  Their scent survives their close,
But the rose's scent is bitterness
  To him that loved the rose!

She looked a little wistfully,
  Then went her sunshine way:—
The sea's eye had a mist on it,
  And the leaves fell from the day.

She went her unremembering way,
  She went and left in me
The pang of all the partings gone,
  And partings yet to be.

She left me marveling why my soul
   Was sad that she was glad;
At all the sadness in the sweet,
   The sweetness in the sad.

Still, still I seemed to see her, still
   Look up with soft replies,
And take the berries with her hand,
   And the love with her lovely eyes.

Nothing begins, and nothing ends,
   That is not paid with moan;
For we are born in others' pain,
   And perish in our own.
          Francis Thompson [1859?-1907]

TO PETRONILLA WHO HAS PUT UP HER HAIR

YESTERDAY it blew alway,
   Yesterday is dead,
Now forever must it stay
   Coiled about your head,
Tell me Whence the great Command
   Hitherward has sped.
"Silly boy, as if I knew,"
   Petronilla said.

Nay, but I am very sure,
   Since you left my side,
Something has befallen you,
   You are fain to hide,
Homage has been done to you,
   Innocents have died.
"Silly boy, and what of that?"
   Petronilla cried.

Petronilla, much I fear
   Scarcely have you wept
All those merry yesterdays,
   Slaughtered whilst you slept,
Slain to bind that pretty crown
   Closer round your head.
"Silly boy, as if I cared,"
   Petronilla said.
       Henry Howarth Bashford [1880-

THE GYPSY GIRL

Passing I saw her as she stood beside
A lonely stream between two barren wolds;
Her loose vest hung in rudely gathered folds
On her swart bosom, which in maiden pride
Pillowed a string of pearls; among her hair
Twined the light bluebell and the stone-crop gay;
And not far thence the small encampment lay,
Curling its wreathèd smoke into the air.
She seemed a child of some sun-favored clime;
So still, so habited to warmth and rest;
And in my wayward musings on past time,
When my thought fills with treasured memories,
That image nearest borders on the blest
Creations of pure art that never dies.

Henry Alford [1810–1871]

FANNY

A SOUTHERN BLOSSOM

Come and see her as she stands,
Crimson roses in her hands;
        And her eyes
Are as dark as Southern night,
Yet than Southern dawn more bright,
And a soft, alluring light
        In them lies.

None deny if she beseech
With that pretty, liquid speech
        Of the South.
All her consonants are slurred,
And the vowels are preferred;
There's a poem in each word
        From that mouth.

Even Cupid is her slave;
Of her arrows, half he gave

Her one day
In a merry, playful hour.
Dowered with these and beauty's dower,
Strong indeed her magic power,
        So they say.

Venus, not to be outdone
By her generous little son,
        Shaped the mouth
Very like to Cupid's bow.
Lack-a-day! Our North can show
No such lovely flowers as grow
        In the South!
                        Anne Reeve Aldrich [1866-1892]

SOMEBODY'S CHILD

Just a picture of Somebody's child,—
    Sweet face set in golden hair,
Violet eyes, and cheeks of rose,
    Rounded chin, with a dimple there,

Tender eyes where the shadows sleep,
    Lit from within by a secret ray,—
Tender eyes that will shine like stars
    When love and womanhood come this way:

Scarlet lips with a story to tell,—
    Blessed be he who shall find it out,
Who shall learn the eyes' deep secret well,
    And read the heart with never a doubt.

Then you will tremble, scarlet lips,
    Then you will crimson, loveliest cheeks:
Eyes will brighten and blushes will burn
    When the one true lover bends and speaks.

But she's only a child now, as you see,
    Only a child in her careless grace:
When Love and Womanhood come this way
    Will anything sadden the flower-like face?
                    Louise Chandler Moulton [1835-1908]

EMILIA

HALFWAY up the Hemlock valley turnpike,
    In the bend of Silver Water's arm,
Where the deer come trooping down at even,
    Drink the cowslip pool, and fear no harm,
            Dwells Emilia,
    Flower of the fields of Camlet Farm.

Sitting sewing by the western window
    As the too brief mountain sunshine flies,
Hast thou seen a slender-shouldered figure
    With a chestnut braid, Minerva-wise,
            Round her temples,
    Shadowing her gray, enchanted eyes?

When the freshets flood the Silver Water,
    When the swallow flying northward braves
Sleeting rains that sweep the birchen foothills
    Where the windflowers' pale plantation waves—
            (Fairy gardens
    Springing from the dead leaves in their graves),—

Falls forgotten, then, Emilia's needle;
    Ancient ballads, fleeting through her brain,
Sing the cuckoo and the English primrose,
    Outdoors calling with a quaint refrain;
            And a rainbow
    Seems to brighten through the gusty rain.

Forth she goes, in some old dress and faded,
    Fearless of the showery shifting wind;
Kilted are her skirts to clear the mosses,
    And her bright braids in a 'kerchief pinned,
            Younger sister
    Of the damsel-errant Rosalind.

While she helps to serve the harvest supper
    In the lantern-lighted village hall,
Moonlight rises on the burning woodland,
    Echoes dwindle from the distant Fall.
            Hark, Emilia!
    In her ear the airy voices call.

Hidden papers in the dusty garret,
   Where her few and secret poems lie,—
Thither flies her heart to join her treasure,
   While she serves, with absent-musing eye,
       Mighty tankards
   Foaming cider in the glasses high.

"Would she mingle with her young companions!"
   Vainly do her aunts and uncles say;
Ever, from the village sports and dances,
   Early missed, Emilia slips away.
       Whither vanished?
   With what unimagined mates to play?

Did they seek her, wandering by the water,
   They should find her comrades shy and strange:
Queens and princesses, and saints and fairies,
   Dimly moving in a cloud of change:—
       Desdemona;
   Mariana of the Moated Grange.

Up this valley to the fair and market
   When young farmers from the southward ride,
Oft they linger at a sound of chanting
   In the meadows by the turnpike side;
       Long they listen,
   Deep in fancies of a fairy bride.

                  Sarah N. Cleghorn [1876-

TO A GREEK GIRL

   With breath of thyme and bees that hum,
   Across the years you seem to come,—
   Across the years with nymph-like head,
   And wind-blown brows unfilleted;
   A girlish shape that slips the bud
      In lines of unspoiled symmetry;
   A girlish shape that stirs the blood
      With pulse of Spring, Autonoë!

Where'er you pass,—where'er you go,
I hear the pebbly rillet flow;
Where'er you go,—where'er you pass,
There comes a gladness on the grass;
You bring blithe airs where'er you tread,—
    Blithe airs that blow from down and sea;
You wake in me a Pan not dead,—
    Not wholly dead!—Autonoë!

How sweet with you on some green sod
To wreathe the rustic garden-god;
How sweet beneath the chestnut's shade
With you to weave a basket-braid;
To watch across the stricken chords
    Your rosy-twinkling fingers flee;
To woo you in soft woodland words,
    With woodland pipe, Autonoë!

In vain,—in vain! The years divide:
Where Thamis rolls a murky tide,
I sit and fill my painful reams,
And see you only in my dreams;—
A vision, like Alcestis, brought
    From under-lands of Memory,—
A dream of Form in days of Thought,—
    A dream,—a dream, Autonoë!
                    Austin Dobson [1840–1921]

"CHAMBER SCENE"

AN EXQUISITE PICTURE IN THE STUDIO OF A YOUNG ARTIST AT ROME

SHE rose from her untroubled sleep,
    And put away her soft brown hair,
And, in a tone as low and deep
    As love's first whisper, breathed a prayer--
Her snow-white hands together pressed,
    Her blue eyes sheltered in the lid,
The folded linen on her breast,
    Just swelling with the charms it hid;

And from her long and flowing dress
  Escaped a bare and slender foot,
Whose shape upon the earth did press
  Like a new snow-flake, white and "mute";
And there, from slumber pure and warm,
  Like a young spirit fresh from heaven,
She bowed her slight and graceful form,
  And humbly prayed to be forgiven.

Oh God! if souls unsoiled as these
  Need daily mercy from Thy throne;
If she upon her bended knees,
  Our loveliest and our purest one,—
She, with a face so clear and bright,
We deem her some stray child of light;—
If she, with those soft eyes in tears,
Day after day in her first years,
  Must kneel and pray for grace from Thee,
  What far, far deeper need have we!
How hardly, if she win not heaven,
Will *our* wild errors be forgiven!
             Nathaniel Parker Willis [1806–1867]

"AH, BE NOT FALSE"

AH, be not false, sweet Splendor!
  Be true, be good;
Be wise as thou art tender;
  Be all that Beauty should.

Not lightly be thy citadel subdued;
  Not ignobly, not untimely,
Take praise in solemn mood;
  Take love sublimely.
            Richard Watson Gilder [1844–1909]

A LIFE-LESSON

THERE! little girl, don't cry!
  They have broken your doll, I know;
    And your tea-set blue,
    And your play-house, too,
  Are things of the long ago;

But childish troubles will soon pass by.—
There! little girl, don't cry!

There! little girl, don't cry!
They have broken your slate, I know;
And the glad, wild ways
Of your school-girl days
Are things of the long ago;
But life and love will soon come by.—
There! little girl, don't cry!

There! little girl, don't cry!
They have broken your heart, I know;
And the rainbow gleams
Of your youthful dreams
Are things of the long ago;
But Heaven holds all for which you sigh.—
There! little girl, don't cry!

James Whitcomb Riley [1849–1916]

THE MAN

THE BREAKING

THE LORD GOD SPEAKS TO A YOUTH

Bend now thy body to the common weight:
  (But oh, that vine-clad head, those limbs of morn!
Those proud young shoulders, I myself made straight!
  How shall ye wear the yoke that must be worn?)

Look thou, my son, what wisdom comes to thee:
  (But oh, that singing mouth, those radiant eyes!
Those dancing feet—that I myself made free!
  How shall I sadden them to make them wise?)

Nay, then, thou shalt! Resist not—have a care!
  (Yea, I must work my plans who sovereign sit;
Yet do not tremble so! I cannot bear—
  Though I am God—to see thee so submit!)
        Margaret Steele Anderson [1869–1921]

THE FLIGHT OF YOUTH

There are gains for all our losses,
  There are balms for all our pain:
But when youth, the dream, departs,
It takes something from our hearts,
  And it never comes again.

We are stronger, and are better,
  Under manhood's sterner reign:
Still we feel that something sweet
Followed youth, with flying feet,
  And will never come again.

Something beautiful is vanished,
And we sigh for it in vain:
We behold it everywhere,
On the earth, and in the air,
But it never comes again.

Richard Henry Stoddard [1825–1903]

"DAYS OF MY YOUTH"

DAYS of my youth,
Ye have glided away;
Hairs of my youth,
Ye are frosted and gray;
Eyes of my youth,
Your keen sight is no more;
Cheeks of my youth,
Ye are furrowed all o'er;
Strength of my youth,
All your vigor is gone;
Thoughts of my youth,
Your gay visions are flown.

Days of my youth,
I wish not your recall;
Hairs of my youth,
I'm content ye should fall;
Eyes of my youth,
You much evil have seen;
Cheeks of my youth,
Bathed in tears have you been;
Thoughts of my youth,
You have led me astray;
Strength of my youth,
Why lament your decay?

Days of my age,
Ye will shortly be past;
Pains of my age,
Yet awhile ye can last;

Joys of my age,
    In true wisdom delight;
Eyes of my age,
    Be religion your light;
Thoughts of my age,
    Dread ye not the cold sod;
Hopes of my age,
    Be ye fixed on your God.

                St. George Tucker [1752–1827]

AVE ATQUE VALE

FAREWELL, my Youth! for now we needs must part,
For here the paths divide;
Here hand from hand must sever, heart from heart,—
    Divergence deep and wide.

You'll wear no withered roses for my sake,
Though I go mourning for you all day long,
Finding no magic more in bower or brake,
    No melody in song.

Gray Eld must travel in my company
To seal this severance more fast and sure.
A joyless fellowship, i' faith, 'twill be,
Yet must we fare together, I and he,
Till I shall tread the footpath way no more.

But when a blackbird pipes among the boughs,
On some dim, iridescent day in spring,
Then I may dream you are remembering
    Our ancient vows.

Or when some joy foregone, some fate forsworn,
Looks through the dark eyes of the violet,
I may re-cross the set, forbidden bourne,
    I may forget
Our long, long parting for a little while,
Dream of the golden splendors of your smile,
    Dream you remember yet.

                Rosamund Marriott Watson [1863–1911]

TO YOUTH

WHERE art thou gone, light-ankled Youth?
  With wing at either shoulder,
And smile that never left thy mouth
  Until the Hours grew colder:

Then somewhat seemed to whisper near
  That thou and I must part;
I doubted it; I felt no fear,
  No weight upon the heart.

If aught befell it, Love was by
  And rolled it off again;
So, if there ever was a sigh,
  'Twas not a sigh of pain.

I may not call thee back; but thou
  Returnest when the hand
Of gentle Sleep waves o'er my brow
  His poppy-crested wand;

Then smiling eyes bend over mine,
  Then lips once pressed invite;
But sleep hath given a silent sign,
  And both, alas! take flight.
                    Walter Savage Landor [1775–1864]

STANZAS WRITTEN ON THE ROAD BETWEEN FLORENCE AND PISA

OH, talk not to me of a name great in story;
The days of our youth are the days of our glory;
And the myrtle and ivy of sweet two-and-twenty
Are worth all your laurels, though ever so plenty.

What are garlands and crowns to the brow that is wrinkled?
'Tis but as a dead-flower with May-dew besprinkled:
Then away with all such from the head that is hoary!
What care I for the wreaths that can *only* give glory?

Oh FAME!—if I e'er took delight in thy praises,
'Twas less for the sake of thy high-sounding phrases,
Than to see the bright eyes of the dear one discover,
She thought that I was not unworthy to love her.

There chiefly I sought thee, *there* only I found thee;
Her glance was the best of the rays that surround thee;
When it sparkled o'er aught that was bright in my story,
I knew it was love, and I felt it was glory.

George Gordon Byron [1788–1824]

STANZAS FOR MUSIC

THERE's not a joy the world can give like that it takes away,
When the glow of early thought declines in feeling's dull decay;
'Tis not on youth's smooth cheek the blush alone, which fades so fast,
But the tender bloom of heart is gone, ere youth itself be past.

Then the few whose spirits float above the wreck of happiness
Are driven o'er the shoals of guilt or ocean of excess:
The magnet of their course is gone, or only points in vain
The shore to which their shivered sail shall never stretch again.

Then the mortal coldness of the soul like death itself comes down;
It cannot feel for others' woes, it dare not dream its own;
That heavy chill has frozen o'er the fountain of our tears,
And though the eye may sparkle still, 'tis where the ice appears.

Though wit may flash from fluent lips, and mirth distract the breast,
Through midnight hours that yield no more their former hope of rest;
'Tis but as ivy-leaves around the ruined turret wreathe,
All green and wildly fresh without, but worn and gray beneath.

Oh could I feel as I have felt,—or be what I have been,
Or weep as I could once have wept o'er many a vanished
    scene;
As springs in deserts found seem sweet, all brackish though
    they be,
So, midst the withered waste of life, those tears would flow
    to me.

George Gordon Byron [1788–1824]

"WHEN AS A LAD"

WHEN, as a lad, at break of day
I watched the fishers sail away,
My thoughts, like flocking birds, would follow
Across the curving sky's blue hollow,
    And on and on—
    Into the very heart of dawn!

For long I searched the world! Ah me!
I searched the sky, I searched the sea,
With much of useless grief and rueing,
Those wingèd thoughts of mine pursuing—
    So dear were they,
    So lovely and so far away!

I seek them still and always will
Until my laggard heart is still,
And I am free to follow, follow,
Across the curving sky's blue hollow,
    Those thoughts too fleet
    For any save the soul's swift feet!

Isabel Ecclestone Mackay [1875–

"AROUND THE CHILD"

AROUND the child bend all the three
Sweet Graces—Faith, Hope, Charity.
Around the man bend other faces—
Pride, Envy, Malice, are his Graces.

Walter Savage Landor [1775–1864]

ALADDIN

When I was a beggarly boy,
  And lived in a cellar damp,
I had not a friend nor a toy,
  But I had Aladdin's lamp;
When I could not sleep for the cold,
  I had fire enough in my brain,
And builded, with roofs of gold,
  My beautiful castles in Spain!

Since then I have toiled day and night,
  I have money and power good store,
But I'd give all my lamps of silver bright
  For the one that is mine no more.
Take, Fortune, whatever you choose;
  You gave, and may snatch again;
I have nothing 'twould pain me to lose,
  For I own no more castles in Spain!
                    James Russell Lowell [1819–1891]

THE QUEST

It was a heavenly time of life
  When first I went to Spain,
The lovely land of silver mists,
  The land of golden grain.

My little ship through unknown seas
  Sailed many a changing day;
Sometimes the chilling winds came up
  And blew across her way;

Sometimes the rain came down and hid
  The shining shores of Spain,
The beauty of the silver mists
  And of the golden grain.

But through the rains and through the winds,
  Upon the untried sea,
My fairy ship sailed on and on,
  With all my dreams and me.

And now, no more a child, I long
  For that sweet time again,
When on the far horizon bar
  Rose up the shores of Spain.

O lovely land of silver mists,
  O land of golden grain,
I look for you with smiles, with tears,
  But look for you in vain!
                    Ellen Mackay Hutchinson Cortissoz [?–1933]

MY BIRTH–DAY

"My birth-day"—what a different sound
  That word had in my youthful ears!
And how, each time the day comes round,
  Less and less white its mark appears!
When first our scanty years are told,
It seems like pastime to grow old;
And, as Youth counts the shining links
  That Time around him binds so fast,
Pleased with the task, he little thinks
  How hard that chain will press at last.
Vain was the man, and false as vain,
  Who said— " were he ordained to run
His long career of life again,
  He would do all that he had done."

Ah, 'tis not thus the voice, that dwells
  In sober birth-days, speaks to me;
Far otherwise—of time it tells
  Lavished unwisely, carelessly;
Of counsel mocked: of talents, made
  Haply for high and pure designs,
But oft, like Israel's incense, laid
  Upon unholy, earthly shrines;

Of nursing many a wrong desire;
    Of wandering after Love too far,
And taking every meteor-fire
    That crossed my pathway, for a star.
All this it tells, and, could I trace
    The imperfect picture o'er again,
With power to add, retouch, efface
    The lights and shades, the joy and pain,
How little of the past would stay!
How quickly all should melt away—
All—but that Freedom of the Mind,
    Which hath been more than wealth to me;
Those friendships, in my boyhood twined,
    And kept till now unchangingly;
And that dear home, that saving-ark,
    Where Love's true light at last I've found,
Cheering within, when all grows dark,
    And comfortless, and stormy round!

Thomas Moore [1779–1852]

SONNET

ON HIS HAVING ARRIVED TO THE AGE OF TWENTY-THREE

How soon hath Time, the subtle thief of youth,
    Stolen on his wing my three-and-twentieth year!
    My hasting days fly on with full career,
    But my late spring no bud or blossom shew'th.
Perhaps my semblance might deceive the truth
    That I to manhood am arrived so near;
    And inward ripeness doth much less appear,
    That some more timely-happy spirits endu'th.
Yet, be it less or more, or soon or slow,
    It shall be still in strictest measure even
    To that same lot, however mean or high,
Toward which Time leads me, and the will of Heaven:
    All is, if I have grace to use it so,
    As ever in my great Task-master's eye.

John Milton [1608–1674]

ON THIS DAY I COMPLETE MY THIRTY–SIXTH YEAR

'Tis time this heart should be unmoved,
Since others it hath ceased to move:
Yet, though I cannot be beloved,
Still let me love!

My days are in the yellow leaf;
The flowers and fruits of love are gone;
The worm, the canker, and the grief
Are mine alone!

The fire that on my bosom preys
Is lone as some volcanic isle;
No torch is kindled at its blaze—
A funeral pile.

The hope, the fear, the jealous care,
The exalted portion of the pain
And power of love, I cannot share,
But wear the chain.

But 'tis not *thus*—and 'tis not *here*—
Such thoughts should shake my soul, nor *now*,
Where glory decks the hero's bier,
Or binds his brow.

The sword, the banner, and the field,
Glory and Greece, around me see!
The Spartan, borne upon his shield,
Was not more free.

Awake! (not Greece—she *is* awake!)
Awake, my spirit!   Think through *whom*
Thy life-blood tracks its parent lake,
And then strike home!

Tread those reviving passions down,
Unworthy manhood!—unto thee
Indifferent should the smile or frown
Of beauty be.

If thou regret'st thy youth, *why live?*
    The land of honorable death
Is here:—up to the field, and give
        Away thy breath!

Seek out—less often sought than found—
    A soldier's grave, for thee the best;
Then look around, and choose thy ground,
        And take thy rest.

                George Gordon Byron [1788–1824]

GROWING GRAY

"On a l' age de son cœur."
                            A. D' HOUDETOT

A LITTLE more toward the light;—
Me miserable! Here's one that's white;
            And one that's turning;
Adieu to song and "salad days;"
My Muse, let's go at once to Jay's,
            And order mourning.

We must reform our rhymes, my Dear,—
Renounce the gay for the severe,—
            Be grave, not witty;
We have, no more, the right to find
That Pyrrha's hair is neatly twined,—
            That Chloe's pretty.

Young Love's for us a farce that's played;
Light canzonet and serenade
            No more may tempt us;
Gray hairs but ill accord with dreams;
From aught but sour didactic themes
            Our years exempt us.

Indeed! you really fancy so?
You think for one white streak we grow
            At once satiric?
A fiddlestick! Each hair's a string
To which our ancient Muse shall sing
            A younger lyric.

The heart's still sound.   Shall "cakes and ale"
Grow rare to youth because *we* rail
   At schoolboy dishes?
Perish the thought!   'Tis ours to chant
When neither Time nor Tide can grant
   Belief with wishes.

          Austin Dobson [1840–1921]

THE ONE WHITE HAIR

THE wisest of the wise
Listen to pretty lies
   And love to hear 'em told.
Doubt not that Solomon
Listened to many a one,—
Some in his youth, and more when he grew old.

I never was among
The choir of Wisdom's song,
   But pretty lies loved I
As much as any king,
When youth was on the wing,
And (must it then be told?) when youth had quite gone by.

Alas! and I have not
The pleasant hour forgot
   When one pert lady said,
"O Walter! I am quite
Bewildered with affright!
I see (sit quiet now) a white hair on your head!"

Another more benign
Snipped it away from mine,
   And in her own dark hair
Pretended it was found . . .
   She leaped, and twirled it round . . .
Fair as she was, she never was *so* fair!

          Walter Savage Landor [1775–1864]

BALLADE OF MIDDLE AGE

OUR youth began with tears and sighs,
    With seeking what we could not find;
Our verses all were threnodies,
    In elegiacs still we whined;
    Our ears were deaf, our eyes were blind,
We sought and knew not what we sought.
    We marvel, now we look behind:
Life's more amusing than we thought!

Oh, foolish youth, untimely wise!
    Oh, phantoms of the sickly mind!
What? not content with seas and skies,
    With rainy clouds and southern wind,
    With common cares and faces kind,
With pains and joys each morning brought?
    Ah, old, and worn, and tired we find
Life's more amusing than we thought!

Though youth "turns spectre-thin and dies,"
    To mourn for youth we're not inclined;
We set our souls on salmon flies,
    We whistle where we once repined.
    Confound the woes of human-kind!
By Heaven we're "well deceived," I wot;
    Who hum, contented or resigned,
"Life's more amusing than we thought"!

ENVOY

    O nate mecum, worn and lined
Our faces show, but *that* is naught;
    Our hearts are young 'neath wrinkled rind:
Life's more amusing than we thought!
                        Andrew Lang [1844–1912]

MIDDLE AGE

WHEN that my days were fewer,
    Some twenty years ago,
And all that is was newer,
    And time itself seemed slow,

With ardor all impassioned,
  I let my hopes fly free,
And deemed the world was fashioned
  My playing-field to be.

The cup of joy was filled then
  With Fancy's sparkling wine;
And all the things I willed then
  Seemed destined to be mine.
Friends had I then in plenty,
  And every friend was true;
Friends always are at twenty,
  And on to twenty-two.

The men whose hair was sprinkled
  With little flecks of gray,
Whose faded brows were wrinkled—
  Sure they had had their day.
And though we bore no malice,
  We knew their hearts were cold,
For they had drained their chalice,
  And now were spent and old.

At thirty, we admitted,
  A man may be alive,
But slower, feebler witted;
  And done at thirty-five.
If Fate prolongs his earth-days,
  His joys grow fewer still;
And after five more birthdays
  He totters down the hill.

We were the true immortals
  Who held the earth in fee;
For us were flung the portals
  Of fame and victory.
The days were bright and breezy,
  And gay our banners flew,
And every peak was easy
  To scale at twenty-two.

And thus we spent our gay time
  As having much to spend;
Swift, swift, that pretty playtime
  Flew by and had its end.
And lo! without a warning
  I woke, as others do,
One fine mid-winter morning,
  A man of forty-two.

And now I see how vainly
  Is youth with ardor fired;
How fondly, how insanely
  I formerly aspired.
A boy may still detest age,
  But as for me I know,
A man has reached his best age
  At forty-two or so.

For youth it is the season
  Of restlessness and strife;
Of passion and unreason,
  And ignorance of life.
Since, though his cheeks have roses,
  No boy can understand
That everything he knows is
  A graft at second hand.

But *we* have toiled and wandered
  With weary feet and numb;
Have doubted, sifted, pondered,—
  How else should knowledge come?
Have seen, too late for heeding,
  Our hopes go out in tears,
Lost in the dim receding,
  Irrevocable years.

Yet, though with busy fingers
  No more we wreathe the flowers,
An airy perfume lingers,
  A brightness still is ours.

And though no rose our cheeks have,
  The sky still shines as blue;
And still the distant peaks have
  The glow of twenty-two.
      Rudolph Chambers Lehmann [1856–1929]

TO CRITICS

WHEN I was seventeen I heard
  From each censorious tongue,
"I'd not do that if I were you;
  You see you're rather young."

Now that I number forty years,
  I'm quite as often told
Of this or that I shouldn't do
  Because I'm quite too old.

O carping world! If there's an age
  Where youth and manhood keep
An equal poise, alas! I must
  Have passed it in my sleep.
      Walter Learned [1847–1915]

THE RAINBOW

MY heart leaps up when I behold
  A rainbow in the sky:
So was it when my life began;
So is it now I am a man;
So be it when I shall grow old,
    Or let me die!
The Child is father of the Man;
And I could wish my days to be
Bound each to each by natural piety.
      William Wordsworth [1770–1850]

LEAVETAKING

PASS, thou wild light,
Wild light on peaks that so

Grieve to let go
  The day.
Lovely thy tarrying, lovely too is night:
  Pass thou away.

Pass, thou wild heart,
Wild heart of youth that still
Hast half a will
  To stay.
I grow too old a comrade, let us part:
  Pass thou away.

William Watson [1858–1935]

EQUINOCTIAL

THE sun of life has crossed the line;
  The summer-shine of lengthened light
Faded and failed, till, where I stand,
  'Tis equal day and equal night.

One after one, as dwindling hours,
  Youth's glowing hopes have dropped away,
And soon may barely leave the gleam
  That coldly scores a winter's day.

I am not young; I am not old;
  The flush of morn, the sunset calm,
Paling and deepening, each to each,
  Meet midway with a solemn charm.

One side I see the summer fields,
  Not yet disrobed of all their green;
While westerly, along the hills,
  Flame the first tints of frosty sheen.

Ah, middle-point, where cloud and storm
  Make battle-ground of this my life!
Where, even-matched, the night and day
  Wage round me their September strife!

I bow me to the threatening gale:
    I know when that is overpast,
Among the peaceful harvest days,
    An Indian Summer comes at last!
           Adeline D. T. Whitney [1824–1906]

"BEFORE THE BEGINNING OF YEARS"

From " Atalanta in Calydon"

BEFORE the beginning of years,
    There came to the making of man
Time, with a gift of tears;
    Grief, with a glass that ran;
Pleasure, with pain for leaven;
    Summer, with flowers that fell;
Remembrance, fallen from heaven;
    And madness, risen from hell;
Strength, without hands to smite;
    Love, that endures for a breath;
Night, the shadow of light;
    And life, the shadow of death.

And the high gods took in hand
    Fire, and the falling of tears,
And a measure of sliding sand
    From under the feet of the years;
And froth and drift of the sea;
    And dust of the laboring earth;
And bodies of things to be
    In the houses of death and of birth;
And wrought with weeping and laughter,
    And fashioned with loathing and love,
With life before and after,
    And death beneath and above,
For a day and a night and a morrow,
    That his strength might endure for a span,
With travail and heavy sorrow,
    The holy spirit of man.

From the winds of the north and the south
　They gathered as unto strife;
They breathed upon his mouth,
　They filled his body with life;
Eyesight and speech they wrought
　For the veils of the soul therein,
A time for labor and thought,
　A time to serve and to sin;
They gave him light in his ways,
　And love, and a space for delight,
And beauty and length of days,
　And night, and sleep in the night.
His speech is a burning fire;
　With his lips he travaileth;
In his heart is a blind desire,
　In his eyes foreknowledge of death;
He weaves, and is clothed with derision'
　Sows, and he shall not reap;
His life is a watch or a vision
　Between a sleep and a sleep.

Algernon Charles Swinburne [1837–1909]

MAN

WEIGHING the steadfastness and state
Of some mean things which here below reside,
Where birds, like watchful clocks, the noiseless date
　And intercourse of times divide,
Where bees at night get home and hive, and flowers,
　　Early as well as late,
Rise with the sun, and set in the same bowers;

　I would, said I, my God would give
The staidness of these things to man! for these
To His divine appointments ever cleave,
　And no new business breaks their peace;
The birds nor sow nor reap, yet sup and dine,
　　The flowers without clothes live,
Yet Solomon was never dressed so fine.

Man hath still either toys, or care;
He hath no root, nor to one place is tied,
But ever restless and irregular
  About this earth doth run and ride;
He knows he hath a home, but scarce knows where;
      He says it is so far,
That he hath quite forgot how to go there.

He knocks at all doors, strays and roams;
Nay, hath not so much wit as some stones have,
Which in the darkest nights point to their homes
  By some hid sense their Maker gave;
Man is the shuttle, to whose winding quest
      And passage through these looms
God ordered motion, but ordained no rest.

Henry Vaughan [1622–1695]

THE PULLEY

WHEN God at first made Man,
Having a glass of blessings standing by—
Let us (said He) pour on him all we can;
Let the world's riches, which dispersèd lie,
      Contract into a span.

So strength first made a way,
Then beauty flowed, then wisdom, honor, pleasure:
When almost all was out, God made a stay,
Perceiving that, alone of all His treasure,
      Rest in the bottom lay.

For if I should (said He)
Bestow this jewel also on My creature,
He would adore My gifts instead of Me,
And rest in Nature, not the God of Nature:
      So both should losers be.

Yet let him keep the rest,
But keep them with repining restlessness;
Let him be rich and weary, that at least,
If goodness lead him not, yet weariness
      May toss him to My breast.

George Herbert [1593–1633]

ODE ON THE INTIMATIONS OF IMMORTALITY
FROM RECOLLECTIONS OF EARLY CHILDHOOD

I

THERE was a time when meadow, grove, and stream,
The earth, and every common sight,
  To me did seem
  Apparelled in celestial light,
The glory and the freshness of a dream.
It is not now as it hath been of yore;—
  Turn wheresoe'er I may,
   By night or day,
The things which I have seen I now can see no more.

II

  The Rainbow comes and goes,
  And lovely is the Rose;
  The Moon doth with delight
Look round her when the heavens are bare;
  Waters on a starry night
  Are beautiful and fair;
 The sunshine is a glorious birth;
 But yet I know, where'er I go,
That there hath passed away a glory from the earth.

III

Now, while the Birds thus sing a joyous song,
  And while the young Lambs bound
  As to the tabor's sound,
To me alone there came a thought of grief:
A timely utterance gave that thought relief,
  And I again am strong.
The Cataracts blow their trumpets from the steep:
No more shall grief of mine the season wrong;
I hear the Echoes through the mountains throng,
The Winds come to me from the fields of sleep,

And all the earth is gay;
　　Land and Sea
Give themselves up to jollity,
　　And with the heart of May
Doth every Beast keep holiday;—
　　　Thou Child of Joy,
Shout round me, let me hear thy shouts, thou happy Shep-
herd-boy!

IV

Ye blessèd Creatures, I have heard the call
　　Ye to each other make; I see
The heavens laugh with you in your jubilee;
　　My heart is at your festival,
　　　My head hath its coronal,
The fulness of your bliss, I feel—I feel it all.
　　　O evil day! if I were sullen
　　　While Earth herself is adorning
　　　　This sweet May morning,
　　　And the Children are culling
　　　　On every side,
　　In a thousand valleys far and wide,
　　　Fresh flowers; while the sun shines warm,
And the Babe leaps up on his Mother's arm:—
　　　I hear, I hear, with joy I hear!
　　　—But there's a Tree, of many, one,
A single Field which I have looked upon,
Both of them speak of something that is gone:
　　　The Pansy at my feet
　　　Doth the same tale repeat:
Whither is fled the visionary gleam?
Where is it now, the glory and the dream?

V

Our birth is but a sleep and a forgetting:
The Soul that rises with us, our life's Star,
　　　Hath had elsewhere its setting,
　　　And cometh from afar:
　　　Not in entire forgetfulness,
　　　And not in utter nakedness,

But trailing clouds of glory do we come
      From God, who is our home:
Heaven lies about us in our infancy!
Shades of the prison-house begin to close
      Upon the growing Boy,
But he beholds the light, and whence it flows,
      He sees it in his joy;
The Youth, who daily farther from the East
      Must travel, still is Nature's Priest,
      And by the vision spendid
      Is on his way attended;
At length the Man perceives it die away,
And fade into the light of common day.

VI

Earth fills her lap with pleasures of her own;
Yearnings she hath in her own natural kind,
And even with something of a Mother's mind,
      And no unworthy aim,
      The homely Nurse doth all she can,
To make her Foster-child, her Inmate Man,
      Forget the glories he hath known,
And that imperial palace whence he came.

VII

Behold the Child among his new-born blisses,
A six years' darling of a pigmy size!
See, where 'mid work of his own hand he lies,
Fretted by sallies of his Mother's kisses,
With light upon him from his Father's eyes!
See, at his feet, some little plan or chart,
Some fragment from his dream of human life,
Shaped by himself with newly-learnèd art;
      A wedding or a festival,
      A mourning or a funeral;
      And this hath now his heart,
      And unto this he frames his song:
      Then will he fit his tongue
To dialogues of business, love, or strife:
      But it will not be long

Ere this be thrown aside,
And with new joy and pride
The little Actor cons another part;
Filling from time to time his "humorous stage"
With all the Persons, down to palsied Age,
That Life brings with her in her equipage;
As if his whole vocation
Were endless imitation.

VIII

Thou, whose exterior semblance doth belie
Thy Soul's immensity;
Thou best Philosopher, who yet dost keep
Thy heritage, thou Eye among the blind,
That, deaf and silent, read'st the eternal deep,
Haunted for ever by the eternal mind,—
Mighty Prophet! Seer blest!
On whom those truths do rest,
Which we are toiling all our lives to find,
In darkness lost, the darkness of the grave:
Thou, over whom thy Immortality
Broods like the Day, a master o'er a Slave,
A Presence which is not to be put by;
Thou little Child, yet glorious in the might
Of heaven-born freedom on thy being's height,
Why with such earnest pains dost thou provoke
The years to bring the inevitable yoke,
Thus blindly with thy blessedness at strife?
Full soon thy Soul shall have her earthly freight,
And custom lie upon thee with a weight
Heavy as frost, and deep almost as life!

IX

O joy! that in our embers
Is something that doth live,
That nature yet remembers
What was so fugitive!
The thought of our past years in me doth breed
Perpetual benediction: not indeed

For that which is most worthy to be blest—
Delight and liberty, the simple creed
Of Childhood, whether busy or at rest,
With new-fledged hope still fluttering in his breast:—
     Not for these I raise
     The song of thanks and praise;
But for those obstinate questionings
     Of sense and outward things,
     Fallings from us, vanishings;
  Blank misgivings of a Creature
Moving about in worlds not realized,
High instincts before which our mortal Nature
Did tremble like a guilty thing surprised:
     But for those first affections,
     Those shadowy recollections,
      Which, be they what they may,
Are yet the fountain-light of all our day,
Are yet a master-light of all our seeing;
     Uphold us, cherish, and have power to make
Our noisy years seem moments in the being
Of the eternal Silence: truths that wake,
      To perish never;
Which neither listlessness, nor mad endeavor,
     Nor Man nor Boy,
Nor all that is at enmity with joy,
Can utterly abolish or destroy!
     Hence, in a season of calm weather,
     Though inland far we be,
Our Souls have sight of that immortal sea
     Which brought us hither,
     Can in a moment travel thither
And see the children sport upon the shore,
And hear the mighty waters rolling evermore.

x

Then sing, ye Birds, sing, sing a joyous song!
     And let the young Lambs bound
     As to the tabor's sound!
     We in thought will join your throng,

Ye that pipe and ye that play,
Ye that through your hearts to-day
Feel the gladness of the May!
What though the radiance which was once so bright
Be now for ever taken from my sight,
Though nothing can bring back the hour
Of splendor in the grass, of glory in the flower;
We will grieve not, rather find
Strength in what remains behind;
In the primal sympathy
Which having been must ever be;
In the soothing thoughts that spring
Out of human suffering;
In the faith that looks through death,
In years that bring the philosophic mind.

XI

And O, ye Fountains, Meadows, Hills, and Groves,
Forebode not any severing of our loves!
Yet in my heart of hearts I feel your might;
I only have relinquished one delight
To live beneath your more habitual sway.
I love the Brooks, which down their channels fret,
Even more than when I tripped lightly as they:
The innocent brightness of a new-born Day
Is lovely yet;
The Clouds that gather round the setting sun
Do take a sober coloring from an eye
That hath kept watch o'er man's mortality;
Another race hath been, and other palms are won.
Thanks to the human heart by which we live,
Thanks to its tenderness, its joys, and fears,
To me the meanest flower that blows can give
Thoughts that do often lie too deep for tears.
                    William Wordsworth [1770–1850]

THE WOMAN

WOMAN

Not she with traitorous kiss her Saviour stung,
Not she denied him with unholy tongue;
She, while apostles shrank, could dangers brave,
Last at the cross and earliest at the grave.

Eaton Stannard Barrett [1786–1820]

WOMAN

There in the fane a beauteous creature stands,
The first best work of the Creator's hands,
Whose slender limbs inadequately bear
A full-orbed bosom and a weight of care;
Whose teeth like pearls, whose lips like cherries, show,
And fawn-like eyes still tremble as they glow.

From the Sanskrit of Calidasa

SIMPLEX MUNDITIIS

From "Epicœne"

Still to be neat, still to be dressed
As you were going to a feast;
Still to be powdered, still perfumed:
Lady, it is to be presumed,
Though art's hid causes are not found,
All is not sweet, all is not sound.

Give me a look, give me a face,
That makes simplicity a grace;
Robes loosely flowing, hair as free:
Such sweet neglect more taketh me
Than all the adulteries of art;
They strike mine eyes, but not my heart.

Ben Jonson [1573?–1637]

DELIGHT IN DISORDER

A SWEET disorder in the dress
Kindles in clothes a wantonness:
A lawn about the shoulders thrown
Into a fine distraction:
An erring lace, which here and there
Enthrals the crimson stomacher:
A cuff neglectful, and thereby
Ribbons to flow confusedly:
A winning wave, deserving note,
In the tempestuous petticoat:
A careless shoe-string, in whose tie
I see a wild civility:
Do more bewitch me than when art
Is too precise in every part.
Robert Herrick [1591–1674]

A PRAISE OF HIS LADY

GIVE place, you ladies, and begone!
    Boast not yourselves at all!
For here at hand approacheth one
    Whose face will stain you all.

The virtue of her lively looks
    Excels the precious stone;
I wish to have none other books
    To read or look upon.

In each of her two crystal eyes
    Smileth a naked boy;
It would you all in heart suffice
    To see that lamp of joy.

I think Nature hath lost the mould
    Where she her shape did take;
Or else I doubt if Nature could
    So fair a creature make.

She may be well compared
  Unto the Phœnix kind,
Whose like was never seen nor heard,
  That any man can find.

In life she is Diana chaste,
  In truth Penelope;
In word and eke in deed steadfast.
  What will you more we say?

If all the world were sought so far,
  Who could find such a wight?
Her beauty twinkleth like a star
  Within the frosty night.

Her roseal color comes and goes
  With such a comely grace,
More ruddier, too, than doth the rose
  Within her lively face.

At Bacchus' feast none shall her meet,
  Nor at no wanton play,
Nor gazing in an open street,
  Nor gadding as a stray.

The modest mirth that she doth use
  Is mixed with shamefastness;
All vice she doth wholly refuse,
  And hateth idleness.

O Lord! it is a world to see
  How virtue can repair,
And deck her in such honesty,
  Whom Nature made so fair.

Truly she doth so far exceed
  Our women nowadays,
As doth the gillyflower a weed;
  And more a thousand ways.

How might I do to get a graff
    Of this unspotted tree?
For all the rest are plain but chaff,
    Which seem good corn to be.

This gift alone I shall her give:
    When death doth what he can,
Her honest fame shall ever live
    Within the mouth of man.
                    John Heywood [1497?–1580?]

ON A CERTAIN LADY AT COURT

I KNOW a thing that's most uncommon;
    (Envy, be silent and attend!)
I know a reasonable woman,
    Handsome and witty, yet a friend.

Not warped by passion, awed by rumor;
    Not grave through pride, nor gay through folly;
An equal mixture of good-humor
    And sensible soft melancholy.

"Has she no faults then (Envy says), Sir?"
    Yes, she has one, I must aver:
When all the world conspires to praise her,
    The woman's deaf, and does not hear.
                    Alexander Pope [1688–1744]

PERFECT WOMAN

SHE was a phantom of delight
When first she gleamed upon my sight;
A lovely apparition, sent
To be a moment's ornament;
Her eyes as stars of twilight fair;
Like twilight's, too, her dusky hair;
But all things else about her drawn
From May-time and the cheerful dawn;
A dancing shape, an image gay,
To haunt, to startle. and waylay.

I saw her upon nearer view,
A Spirit, yet a Woman too!
Her household motions light and free,
And steps of virgin liberty;
A countenance in which did meet
Sweet records, promises as sweet;
A creature not too bright or good
For human nature's daily food;
For transient sorrows, simple wiles,
Praise, blame, love, kisses, tears, and smiles.

And now I see with eye serene
The very pulse of the machine;
A being breathing thoughtful breath,
A traveller between life and death;
The reason firm, the temperate will,
Endurance, foresight, strength, and skill;
A perfect Woman, nobly planned,
To warn, to comfort, and command;
And yet a Spirit still, and bright
With something of angelic light.

William Wordsworth [1770-1850]

THE SOLITARY-HEARTED

SHE was a queen of noble Nature's crowning,
A smile of hers was like an act of grace;
She had no winsome looks, no pretty frowning,
Like daily beauties of the vulgar race:
But if she smiled, a light was on her face,
A clear, cool kindliness, a lunar beam
Of peaceful radiance, silvering o'er the stream
Of human thought with unabiding glory;
Not quite a waking truth, not quite a dream,
A visitation, bright and transitory.

But she is changed,—hath felt the touch of sorrow,
No love hath she, no understanding friend;
O grief! when Heaven is forced of earth to borrow
What the poor niggard earth has not to lend;

But when the stalk is snapped, the rose must bend.
The tallest flower that skyward rears its head
Grows from the common ground, and there must shed
Its delicate petals.   Cruel fate, too surely,
That they should find so base a bridal bed,
Who lived in virgin pride, so sweet and purely.

She had a brother, and a tender father,
And she was loved, but not as others are
From whom we ask return of love,—but rather
As one might love a dream; a phantom fair
Of something exquisitely strange and rare,
Which all were glad to look on, men and maids,
Yet no one claimed—as oft, in dewy glades,
The peering primrose, like a sudden gladness,
Gleams on the soul, yet unregarded fades;—
The joy is ours, but all its own the sadness.

'Tis vain to say—her worst of grief is only
The common lot, which all the world have known;
To her 'tis more, because her heart is lonely,
And yet she hath no strength to stand alone,—
Once she had playmates, fancies of her own,
And she did love them.   They are passed away
As Fairies vanish at the break of day;
And like a spectre of an age departed,
Or unsphered Angel wofully astray,
She glides along—the solitary-hearted.

Hartley Coleridge [1796–1849]

OF THOSE WHO WALK ALONE

WOMEN there are on earth, most sweet and high,
    Who lose their own, and walk bereft and lonely,
Loving that one lost heart until they die,
        Loving it only.

And so they never see beside them grow
    Children, whose coming is like breath of flowers;
Consoled by subtler loves the angels know
        Through childless hours.

Good deeds they do: they comfort and they bless
  In duties others put off till the morrow;
Their look is balm, their touch is tenderness
    To all in sorrow.

Betimes the world smiles at them, as 'twere shame,
  This maiden guise, long after youth's departed;
But in God's Book they bear another name—
    "The faithful-hearted."

Faithful in life, and faithful unto death,
  Such souls, in sooth, illume with lustre splendid
That glimpsed, glad land wherein, the Vision saith,
    Earth's wrongs are ended.
                    Richard Burton [1861-1940]

"SHE WALKS IN BEAUTY"

SHE walks in beauty, like the night
  Of cloudless climes and starry skies;
And all that's best of dark and bright
  Meet in her aspect and her eyes:
Thus mellowed to that tender light
  Which heaven to gaudy day denies.

One shade the more, one ray the less,
  Had half impaired the nameless grace
Which waves in every raven tress
  Or softly lightens o'er her face;
Where thoughts serenely sweet express
  How pure, how dear their dwelling-place.

And on that cheek, and o'er that brow
  So soft, so calm, yet eloquent,
The smiles that win, the tints that glow,
  But tell of days in goodness spent,
A mind at peace with all below,
  A heart whose love is innocent!
                George Gordon Byron [1788-1824]

PRELUDES

From "The Angel in the House"

I

UNTHRIFT

Ah, wasteful woman, she that may
  On her sweet self set her own price,
Knowing man cannot choose but pay,
  How has she cheapened paradise;
How given for nought her priceless gift,
  How spoiled the bread, and spilled the wine,
Which, spent with due, respective thrift,
  Had made brutes men, and men divine.

II

HONOR AND DESERT

O Queen, awake to thy renown,
  Require what 'tis our wealth to give,
And comprehend and wear the crown
  Of thy despised prerogative!
I, who in manhood's name at length
  With glad songs come to abdicate
The gross regality of strength,
  Must yet in this thy praise abate,
That, through thine erring humbleness
  And disregard of thy degree,
Mainly, has man been so much less
  Than fits his fellowship with thee.

High thoughts had shaped the foolish brow,
  The coward had grasped the hero's sword,
The vilest had been great, hadst thou,
  Just to thyself, been worth's reward.
But lofty honors undersold
  Seller and buyer both disgrace;
And favors that make folly bold
  Banish the light from virtue's face.

III

THE ROSE OF THE WORLD

Lo, when the Lord made North and South,
　And sun and moon ordainèd, He,
Forthbringing each by word of mouth
　In order of its dignity
Did man from the crude clay express
　By sequence, and all else decreed,
He formed the woman; nor might less
　Than Sabbath such a work succeed.

And still with favor singled out,
　Marred less than man by mortal fall,
Her disposition is devout,
　Her countenance angelical:
The best things that the best believe
　Are in her face so kindly writ
The faithless, seeing her, conceive
　Not only heaven, but hope of it;
No idle thought her instinct shrouds,
　But fancy chequers settled sense,
Like alteration of the clouds
　On noonday's azure permanence.

Pure dignity, composure, ease,
　Declare affections nobly fixed,
And impulse sprung from due degrees
　Of sense and spirit sweetly mixed.
Her modesty, her chiefest grace,
　The cestus clasping Venus' side,
How potent to deject the face
　Of him who would affront its pride!

Wrong dares not in her presence speak,
　Nor spotted thought its taint disclose
Under the protest of a cheek
　Outbragging Nature's boast, the rose.
In mind and manners how discreet;
　How artless in her very art;
How candid in discourse; how sweet
　The concord of her lips and heart!

How simple and how circumspect;
  How subtle and how fancy-free;
Though sacred to her love, how decked
  With unexclusive courtesy;
How quick in talk to see from far
  The way to vanquish or evade;
How able her persuasions are
  To prove, her reasons to persuade.

How (not to call true instinct's bent
  And woman's very nature, harm),
How amiable and innocent
  Her pleasure in her power to charm;
How humbly careful to attract,
  Though crowned with all the soul desires,
Connubial aptitude exact,
  Diversity that never tires!

IV

THE TRIBUTE

Boon Nature to the woman bows;
  She walks in earth's whole glory clad,
And, chiefest far herself of shows,
  All others help her and are glad:
No splendor 'neath the sky's proud dome
  But serves her for familiar wear;
The far-fetched diamond finds its home
  Flashing and smouldering in her hair;
For her the seas their pearls reveal;
  Art and strange lands her pomp supply
With purple, chrome, and cochineal,
  Ochre, and lapis lazuli;
The worm its golden woof presents;
  Whatever runs, flies, dives. or delves,
All doff for her their ornaments,
  Which suit her better than themselves;
And all, by this their power to give,
  Proving her right to take, proclaim
Her beauty's clear prerogative
  To profit so by Eden's blame.

V

NEAREST THE DEAREST

Till Eve was brought to Adam, he
  A solitary desert trod,
Though in the great society
  Of nature, angels, and of God.
If one slight column counterweighs
  The ocean, 'tis the Maker's law,
Who deems obedience better praise
  Than sacrifice of erring awe.

VI

THE FOREIGN LAND

A woman is a foreign land,
  Of which, though there he settle young,
A man will ne'er quite understand
  The customs, politics, and tongue.
The foolish hie them post-haste through,
  See fashions odd and prospects fair,
Learn of the language, "How d'ye do,"
  And go and brag they have been there.
The most for leave to trade apply,
  For once, at Empire's seat, her heart,
Then get what knowledge ear and eye
  Glean chancewise in the life-long mart.
And certain others, few and fit,
  Attach them to the Court, and see
The Country's best, its accent hit,
  And partly sound its polity.

Coventry Patmore [1823–1896]

A HEALTH

I FILL this cup to one made up
  Of loveliness alone,
A woman, of her gentle sex
  The seeming paragon;

To whom the better elements
  And kindly stars have given
A form so fair, that, like the air,
  'Tis less of earth than heaven.

Her every tone is music's own,
  Like those of morning birds,
And something more than melody
  Dwells ever in her words;
The coinage of her heart are they,
  And from her lips each flows
As one may see the burdened bee
  Forth issue from the rose.

Affections are as thoughts to her,
  The measures of her hours;
Her feelings have the fragrancy,
  The freshness of young flowers;
And lovely passions, changing oft,
  So fill her, she appears
The image of themselves by turns,—
  The idol of past years!

Of her bright face one glance will trace
  A picture on the brain,
And of her voice in echoing hearts
  A sound must long remain;
But memory, such as mine of her,
  So very much endears,
When death is nigh my latest sigh
  Will not be life's, but hers.

I fill this cup to one made up
  Of loveliness alone,
A woman, of her gentle sex
  The seeming paragon—
Her health! and would on earth there stood
  Some more of such a frame,
That life might be all poetry,
  And weariness a name.

                    Edward Coote Pinkney [1802–1828]

OUR SISTER

HER face was very fair to see,
So luminous with purity:—
It had no roses, but the hue
Of lilies lustrous with their dew—
Her very soul seemed shining through!

Her quiet nature seemed to be
Tuned to each season's harmony.
The holy sky bent near to her;
She saw a spirit in the stir
Of solemn woods.   The rills that beat
Their mosses with voluptuous feet,
Went dripping music through her thought.
Sweet impulse came to her unsought
From graceful things, and beauty took
A sacred meaning in her look.

In the great Master's steps went she
With patience and humility.
The casual gazer could not guess
Half of her veilèd loveliness;
Yet ah! what precious things lay hid
Beneath her bosom's snowy lid:—
What tenderness and sympathy,
What beauty of sincerity,
What fancies chaste, and loves, that grew
In heaven's own stainless light and dew!

True woman was she day by day
In suffering, toil, and victory.
Her life, made holy and serene
By faith, was hid with things unseen.
She knew what they alone can know
Who live above but dwell below.
                    Horatio Nelson Powers [1826–1890]

FROM LIFE

HER thoughts are like a flock of butterflies.
    She has a merry love of little things,
    And a bright flutter of speech, whereto she brings
A threefold eloquence—voice, hands and eyes.
Yet under all a subtle silence lies
    As a bird's heart is hidden by its wings;
    And you shall search through many wanderings
The fairyland of her realities.

She hides herself behind a busy brain—
    A woman, with a child's laugh in her blood;
    A maid, wearing the shadow of motherhood—
Wise with the quiet memory of old pain,
As the soft glamor of remembered rain
    Hallows the gladness of a sunlit wood.
                                    Brian Hooker [1880–

THE ROSE OF THE WORLD

WHO dreamed that beauty passes like a dream?
    For these red lips, with all their mournful pride,
    Mournful that no new wonder may betide,
    Troy passed away in one high funeral gleam,
    And Usna's children died.

We and the laboring world are passing by:
    Amid men's souls, that waver and give place,
    Like the pale waters in their wintry race,
    Under the passing stars, foam of the sky,
    Lives on this lonely face.

Bow down, archangels, in your dim abode:
    Before you were, or any hearts to beat,
    Weary and kind one lingered by His seat;
    He made the world to be a grassy road
    Before her wandering feet.
                        William Butler Yeats [1865–1939]

DAWN OF WOMANHOOD

Thus will I have the woman of my dream.
  Strong must she be and gentle, like a star
Her soul burn whitely; nor its arrowy beam

May any cloud of superstition mar:
  True to the earth she is, patient and calm.
Her tranquil eyes shall penetrate afar

Through centuries, and her maternal arm
  Enfold the generations yet unborn;
Nor she, by passing glamor nor alarm,

Will from the steadfast way of life be drawn.
  Gray-eyed and fearless, I behold her gaze
Outward into the furnace of the dawn.

Sacred shall be the purport of her days,
  Yet human; and the passion of the earth
Shall be for her adornment and her praise.

She is most often joyous, with a mirth
  That rings true-tempered holy womanhood.
She cannot fear the agonies of birth,

Nor sit in pallid lethargy and brood
  Upon the coming seasons of her pain:
By her the mystery is understood

Of harvest, and fulfilment in the grain.
  Yea, she is wont to labor in the field,
Delights to heap, at sunset, on the wain

Festoons and coronals of the golden yield.
  A triumph is the labor of her soul,
Sublime along eternity revealed.

Lo, everlastingly in her control,
  Under the even measure of her breath,
Like crested waves the onward centuries roll.

Nor to far heaven her spirit wandereth,
  Nor lifteth she her voice in barren prayer,
Nor trembleth at appearances of death.

She, godlike in her womanhood, will fare
    Calm-visaged and heroic to the end.
The homestead is her most especial care;

She loves the sacred hearth: she will defend
    Her gods from desecration of the vile.
Fierce, like a wounded tigress, she can rend

Whatever may have entered to defile.
    I see her in the evening by the fire,
And in her eyes, illumined from the pile

Of blazing logs, a motherly desire
    Glows like the moulded passion of a rose;
Beautiful is her presence in the bower:

Her spirit is the spirit of repose.
    Mankind shall hold her motherhood in awe:
Woman is she indeed, and not of those

That he with sacramental gold must draw
    Discreetly to his chamber in the night,
Or bind to him with fetters of the law.

He holds her by a spiritual right.
    With diamond and with pearl he need not sue;
Nor will she deck herself for his delight:

Beauty is the adornment of the true.
    She shall possess for ornament and gem
A flower, the glowworm, or the drop of dew:

More innocently fair than all of them,
    It will not even shame her if she make
A coronal of stars her diadem.

Though she is but a vision, I can take
    Courage from her.   I feel her arrowy beam
Already, for her spirit is awake,

And passes down the future like a gleam,—
Thus have I made the woman of my dream.

                        Harold Monro [1879–1932]

THE SHEPHERDESS

SHE walks—the lady of my delight—
    A shepherdess of sheep.
Her flocks are thoughts. She keeps them white;
    She guards them from the steep.
She feeds them on the fragrant height,
    And folds them in for sleep.

She roams maternal hills and bright,
    Dark valleys safe and deep.
Into that tender breast at night
    The chastest stars may peep.
She walks—the lady of my delight—
    A shepherdess of sheep.

She holds her little thoughts in sight,
    Though gay they run and leap.
She is so circumspect and right;
    She has her soul to keep.
She walks—the lady of my delight—
    A shepherdess of sheep.

Alice Meynell [1853–1922]

A PORTRAIT

MOTHER and maid and soldier, bearing best
    Her girl's lithe body under matron gray,
    And opening new eyes on each new day
With faith concealed and courage unconfessed;
Jealous to cloak a blessing in a jest,
    Clothe beauty carefully in disarray,
    And love absurdly, that no word betray
The worship all her deeds make manifest:

Armored in smiles, a motley Britomart—
    Her lance is high adventure, tipped with scorn;
    Her banner to the suns and winds unfurled,
Washed white with laughter; and beneath her heart,
    Shrined in a garland of laborious thorn,
    Blooms the unchanging Rose of all the World.

Brian Hooker [1880–

THE WIFE

THE little Dreams of Maidenhood—
 I put them all away
As tenderly as mother would
 The toys of yesterday,
When little children grow to men
 Too over-wise for play.

The little dreams I put aside—
 I loved them every one,
And yet since moon-blown buds must hide
 Before the noon-day sun,
I close them wistfully away
 And give the key to none.

O little Dreams of Maidenhood—
 Lie quietly, nor care
If some day in an idle mood
 I, searching unaware
Through some closed corner of my heart,
 Should laugh to find you there.

Theodosia Garrison [1874–

"TRUSTY, DUSKY, VIVID, TRUE"

TRUSTY, dusky, vivid, true,
With eyes of gold and bramble-dew,
Steel true and blade straight
The great Artificer made my mate.

Honor, anger, valor, fire,
A love that life could never tire,
Death quench, or evil stir,
The mighty Master gave to her.

Teacher, tender comrade, wife,
A fellow-farer true through life,
Heart-whole and soul-free,
The August Father gave to me.

Robert Louis Stevenson [1850–1894]

THE SHRINE

THERE is a shrine whose golden gate
 Was opened by the Hand of God;
It stands serene, inviolate,
 Though millions have its pavement trod;
As fresh, as when the first sunrise
Awoke the lark in Paradise.

'Tis compassed with the dust and toil
 Of common days, yet should there fall
A single speck, a single soil
 Upon the whiteness of its wall,
The angels' tears in tender rain
Would make the temple theirs again.

Without, the world is tired and old,
 But, once within the enchanted door,
The mists of time are backward rolled,
 And creeds and ages are no more;
But all the human-hearted meet
In one communion vast and sweet.

I enter—all is simply fair,
 Nor incense-clouds, nor carven throne;
But in the fragrant morning air
 A gentle lady sits alone;
My mother—ah! whom should I see
Within, save ever only thee?

     Digby Mackworth Dolben [1848–1867]

THE VOICE

As I went down the hill I heard
 The laughter of the countryside;
For, rain being past, the whole land stirred
 With new emotion, like a bride.
I scarce had left the grassy lane,
 When something made me catch my breath:
A woman called, and called again,
 Elizabeth! Elizabeth!

It was my mother's name.   A part
　　Of wounded memory sprang to tears,
And the few violets of my heart
　　Shook in the wind of happier years.
Quicker than magic came the face
　　That once was sun and moon for me;
The garden shawl, the cap of lace,
　　The collie's head against her knee.

Mother, who findest out a way
　　To pass the sentinels, and stand
Behind my chair at close of day,
　　To touch me—almost—with thy hand,
Deep in my breast, how sure, how clear,
　　The lamp of love burns on till death!—
How trembles if I chance to hear
　　Elizabeth!   Elizabeth!
　　　　　　　　Norman Gale [1862–

MOTHER

I HAVE praised many loved ones in my song,
　　And yet I stand
Before her shrine, to whom all things belong,
　　With empty hand.

Perhaps the ripening future holds a time
　　For things unsaid;
Not now; men do not celebrate in rhyme
　　Their daily bread.
　　　　　　　　Theresa Helburn [1888–

AD MATREM

OFT in the after days, when thou and I
Have fallen from the scope of human view,
When, both together, under the sweet sky,
We sleep beneath the daisies and the dew,
Men will recall thy gracious presence bland,
Conning the pictured sweetness of thy face;
Will pore o'er paintings by thy plastic hand,
And vaunt thy skill and tell thy deeds of grace.
Oh, may they then, who crown thee with true bays
Saying, "What love unto her son she bore!"

Make this addition to thy perfect praise,
"Nor ever yet was mother worshipped more!"
So shall I live with Thee, and thy dear fame
Shall link my love unto thine honored name.

Julian Fane [1827–1870]

C. L. M.

In the dark womb where I began,
My mother's life made me a man.
Through all the months of human birth
Her beauty fed my common earth.
I cannot see, nor breathe, nor stir,
But through the death of some of her.

Down in the darkness of the grave
She cannot see the life she gave.
For all her love, she cannot tell
Whether I use it ill or well,
Nor knock at dusty doors to find
Her beauty dusty in the mind.

If the grave's gates could be undone,
She would not know her little son,
I am so grown. If we should meet,
She would pass by me in the street,
Unless my soul's face let her see
My sense of what she did for me.

What have I done to keep in mind
My debt to her and womankind?
What woman's happier life repays
Her for those months of wretched days?
For all my mouthless body leeched
Ere Birth's releasing hell was reached?

What have I done, or tried, or said
In thanks to that dear woman dead?
Men triumph over women still,
Men trample women's rights at will,
And man's lust roves the world untamed. . .
O grave, keep shut lest I be shamed.

John Masefield [1878–

STEPPING WESTWARD

STEPPING WESTWARD

"What, you are stepping westward?"—"Yea."
—'Twould be a wildish destiny,
If we, who thus together roam
In a strange Land, and far from home,
Were in this place the guests of Chance:
Yet who would stop, or fear to advance
Though home or shelter he had none,
With such a sky to lead him on?

The dewy ground was dark and cold;
Behind, all gloomy to behold;
And stepping westward seemed to be
A kind of heavenly destiny:
I liked the greeting; 'twas a sound
Of something without place or bound;
And seemed to give me spiritual right
To travel through that region bright.

The voice was soft, and she who spake
Was walking by her native lake:
The salutation had to me
The very sound of courtesy:
Its power was felt; and while my eye
Was fixed upon the glowing Sky,
The echo of the voice enwrought
A human sweetness with the thought
Of travelling through the world that lay
Before me in my endless way.

$\qquad\qquad\qquad$ *William Wordsworth* [1770–1850]

A FAREWELL TO ARMS

(TO QUEEN ELIZABETH)

His golden locks Time hath to silver turned;
 O Time too swift, O swiftness never ceasing!
His youth 'gainst time and age hath ever spurned,
 But spurned in vain; youth waneth by increasing:
Beauty, strength, youth, are flowers but fading seen;
Duty, faith, love, are roots, and ever green.

His helmet now shall make a hive for bees;
 And lovers' sonnets turned to holy psalms,
A man-at-arms must now serve on his knees,
 And feed on prayers, which are Age his alms:
But though from court to cottage he depart,
His Saint is sure of his unspotted heart.

And when he saddest sits in homely cell,
 He'll teach his swains this carol for a song,—
"Blest be the hearts that wish my sovereign well,
 Curst be the souls that think her any wrong."
Goddess, allow this aged man his right
To be your beadsman now that was your knight.
      George Peele [1558?–1597?]

THE WORLD

The World's a bubble, and the life of Man
   Less than a span:
In his conception wretched,—from the womb,
   So to the tomb;
Curst from his cradle, and brought up to years
   With cares and fears.
Who then to frail mortality shall trust,
But limns the water, or but writes in dust.

Yet whilst with sorrow here we live oppressed,
   What life is best?
Courts are but only superficial schools
   To dandle fools;

The rural parts are turned into a den
   Of savage men;
And where's the city from all vice so free,
But may be termed the worst of all the three?

Domestic cares afflict the husband's bed,
   Or pains his head:
Those that live single, take it for a curse,
   Or do things worse:
Some would have children; those that have them moan
   Or wish them gone:
What is it, then, to have, or have no wife,
But single thraldom, or a double strife?

Our own affections still at home to please
   Is a disease;
To cross the seas to any foreign soil,
   Peril and toil;
Wars with their noise affright us; when they cease,
   We are worse in peace:
—What then remains, but that we still should cry
For being born, or, being born, to die?

      Francis Bacon [1561–1626]

"WHEN THAT I WAS AND A LITTLE TINY BOY"

From "Twelfth Night"

When that I was and a little tiny boy,
 With hey, ho, the wind and the rain,
A foolish thing was but a toy,
 For the rain it raineth every day.

But when I came to man's estate,
 With hey, ho, the wind and the rain,
'Gainst knaves and thieves men shut their gate,
 For the rain it raineth every day.

But when I came, alas! to wive,
 With hey, ho, the wind and the rain,
By swaggering could I never thrive,
 For the rain it raineth every day.

But when I came unto my beds,
  With hey, ho, the wind and the rain,
With toss-pots still had drunken heads;
  For the rain it raineth every day.

A great while ago the world begun,
  With hey, ho, the wind and the rain,
But that's all one, our play is done,
  And we'll strive to please you every day.
                    William Shakespeare [1564-1616]

OF THE LAST VERSES IN THE BOOK

WHEN we for age could neither read nor write,
The subject made us able to indite;
The soul, with nobler resolutions decked,
The body stooping does herself erect.
No mortal parts are requisite to raise
Her that, unbodied, can her Maker praise.

The seas are quiet when the winds give o'er;
So calm are we when passions are no more.
For then we know how vain it was to boast
Of fleeting things, so certain to be lost.
Clouds of affection from our younger eyes
Conceal that emptiness which age descries.

The soul's dark cottage, battered and decayed,
Lets in new light through chinks that Time has made:
Stronger by weakness, wiser, men become
As they draw near to their eternal home.
Leaving the old, both worlds at once they view
That stand upon the threshold of the new.
                    Edmund Waller [1606-1687]

A LAMENT

THE NIGHT BEFORE HIS EXECUTION

MY prime of youth is but a frost of cares;
  My feast of joy is but a dish of pain;
My crop of corn is but a field of tares;
  And all my good is but vain hope of gain·

The day is fled, and yet I saw no sun;
And now I live, and now my life is done!

The spring is past, and yet it is not sprung;
    The fruit is dead, and yet the leaves be green;
My youth is gone, and yet I am but young;
    I saw the world, and yet I was not seen;
My thread is cut, and yet it is not spun;
And now I live, and now my life is done!

I sought my death, and found it in my womb;
    I looked for life, and saw it was a shade;
I trod the earth, and knew it was my tomb;
    And now I die, and now I am but made;
The glass is full, and now my glass is run;
And now I live, and now my life is done!
                    Chidiock Tichborne [1558?–1586]

TOMORROW

In the down-hill of life, when I find I'm declining,
    May my fate no less fortunate be
Than a snug elbow-chair will afford for reclining,
    And a cot that o'erlooks the wide sea;
With an ambling pad-pony to pace o'er the lawn,
    While I carol away idle sorrow,
And blithe as the lark that each day hails the dawn,
    Look forward with hope for Tomorrow.

With a porch at my door, both for shelter and shade too,
    As the sunshine or rain may prevail,
And a small spot of ground for the use of the spade too,
    With a barn for the use of the flail:
A cow for my dairy, a dog for my game,
    And a purse when a friend wants to borrow;
I'll envy no Nabob his riches or fame,
    Nor what honors may wait him Tomorrow.

From the bleak northern blast may my cot be completely
    Secured by a neighboring hill;
And at night may repose steal upon me more sweetly
    By the sound of a murmuring rill.

And while peace and plenty I find at my board,
　　With a heart free from sickness and sorrow,
With my friends may I share what Today may afford,
　　And let them spread the table Tomorrow.

And when I at last must throw off this frail covering,
　　Which I've worn for three-score years and ten,
On the brink of the grave I'll not seek to keep hovering,
　　Nor my thread wish to spin o'er again;
But my face in the glass I'll serenely survey,
　　And with smiles count each wrinkle and furrow;
And this old worn-out stuff, which is threadbare Today,
　　May become everlasting Tomorrow.
　　　　　　　　　John Collins [1742?–1808]

LATE WISDOM

WE'VE trod the maze of error round,
　　Long wandering in the winding glade;
And now the torch of truth is found,
　　It only shows us where we strayed:
By long experience taught, we know—
　　Can rightly judge of friends and foes;
Can all the worth of these allow,
　　And all the faults discern in those.

Now, 'tis our boast that we can quell
　　The wildest passions in their rage,
Can their destructive force repel,
　　And their impetuous wrath assuage.—
Ah, Virtue! dost thou arm when now
　　This bold rebellious race are fled?
When all these tyrants rest, and thou
　　Art warring with the mighty dead?
　　　　　　　　George Crabbe [1754–1832]

YOUTH AND AGE

VERSE, a breeze 'mid blossoms straying,
　　Where Hope clung feeding like a bee,—
Both were mine! Life went a-maying
　　With Nature, Hope, and Poesy
　　　　　　When I was young!

When I was young?—Ah, woful When!
Ah, for the change 'twixt Now and Then!
This breathing house not built with hands,
This body that does me grievous wrong,
O'er aery cliffs and glittering sands,
How lightly *then* it flashed along:—
Like those trim skiffs, unknown of yore,
On winding lakes and rivers wide,
That ask no aid of sail or oar,
That fear no spite of wind or tide!
Naught cared this body for wind or weather
When Youth and I lived in't together.

Flowers are lovely; Love is flower-like;
Friendship is a sheltering tree;
Oh! the joys that came down shower-like,
Of Friendship, Love, and Liberty
            Ere I was old!

Ere I was old? Ah, woful Ere,
Which tells me, Youth's no longer here!
O Youth! for years so many and sweet,
'Tis known that Thou and I were one.
I'll think it but a fond conceit—
It cannot be that Thou art gone!
Thy vesper-bell hath not yet tolled:—
And thou wert aye a masker bold!
What strange disguise hast now put on
To make believe that thou art gone?
I see these locks in silvery slips,
This drooping gait, this altered size:
But Springtide blossoms on thy lips,
And tears take sunshine from thine eyes!
Life is but thought: so think I will
That Youth and I are house-mates still.

Dewdrops are the gems of morning,
But the tears of mournful eve!
Where no hope is, life's a warning
That only serves to make us grieve
            When we are old.

That only serves to make us grieve
With oft and tedious taking-leave,
Like some poor nigh-related guest,
That may not rudely be dismissed,
Yet hath outstayed his welcome while,
And tells the jest without the smile.

Samuel Taylor Coleridge [1772–1834]

THE OLD MAN'S COMFORTS

AND HOW HE GAINED THEM

"You are old, Father William," the young man cried;
  "The few locks which are left you are gray;
You are hale, Father William,—a hearty old man:
  Now tell me the reason, I pray."

"In the days of my youth," Father William replied,
  "I remembered that youth would fly fast,
And abused not my health and my vigor at first,
  That I never might need them at last."

"You are old, Father William," the young man cried,
  "And pleasures with youth pass away;
And yet you lament not the days that are gone:
  Now tell me the reason, I pray."

"In the days of my youth," Father William replied,
  "I remembered that youth could not last;
I thought of the future, whatever I did,
  That I never might grieve for the past."

"You are old, Father William," the young man cried,
  "And life must be hastening away;
You are cheerful, and love to converse upon death:
  Now tell me the reason, I pray."

"I am cheerful, young man," Father William replied;
  "Let the cause thy attention engage;
In the days of my youth, I remembered my God,
  And He hath not forgotten my age."

Robert Southey [1774–1843]

TO AGE

WELCOME, old friend! These many years
   Have we lived door by door:
The Fates have laid aside their shears
   Perhaps for some few more.

I was indocile at an age
   When better boys were taught,
But thou at length hast made me sage,
   If I am sage in aught.

Little I know from other men,
   Too little they from me,
But thou hast pointed well the pen
   That writes these lines to thee.

Thanks for expelling Fear and Hope,
   One vile, the other vain;
One's scourge, the other's telescope,
   I shall not see again:

Rather what lies before my feet
   My notice shall engage.—
He who hath braved Youth's dizzy heat
   Dreads not the frost of Age.
                    Walter Savage Landor [1775–1864]

LATE LEAVES

THE leaves are falling; so am I;
The few late flowers have moisture in the eye;
      So have I too.
Scarcely on any bough is heard
Joyous, or even unjoyous, bird
      The whole wood through.

Winter may come: he brings but nigher
His circle (yearly narrowing) to the fire

Where old friends meet.
Let him; now heaven is overcast,
And spring and summer both are past,
And all things sweet.
Walter Savage Landor [1775–1864]

YEARS

YEARS, many parti-colored years,
Some have crept on, and some have flown
Since first before me fell those tears
I never could see fall alone.

Years, not so many, are to come,
Years not so varied, when from you
One more will fall: when, carried home,
I see it not, nor hear *Adieu*.
Walter Savage Landor [1775–1864]

THE RIVER OF LIFE

THE more we live, more brief appear
Our life's succeeding stages:
A day to childhood seems a year,
And years like passing ages.

The gladsome current of our youth,
Ere passion yet disorders,
Steals, lingering like a river smooth
Along its grassy borders.

But as the careworn cheek grows wan,
And sorrow's shafts fly thicker,
Ye Stars, that measure life to man,
Why seem your courses quicker?

When joys have lost their bloom and breath,
And life itself is vapid,
Why, as we reach the Falls of Death,
Feel we its tide more rapid?

It may be strange—yet who would change
    Time's course to slower speeding,
When one by one our friends have gone
    And left our bosoms bleeding?

    Heaven gives our years of fading strength
        Indemnifying fleetness;
    And those of youth, a seeming length,
        Proportioned to their sweetness.

Thomas Campbell [1777–1844]

"LONG TIME A CHILD"

Long time a child, and still a child, when years
Had painted manhood on my cheek, was I,—
For yet I lived like one not born to die;
A thriftless prodigal of smiles and tears,
No hope I needed, and I knew no fears.
But sleep, though sweet, is only sleep; and waking,
I waked to sleep no more; at once o'ertaking
The vanguard of my age, with all arrears
Of duty on my back.   Nor child, nor man,
Nor youth, nor sage, I find my head is gray,
For I have lost the race I never ran:
A rathe December blights my lagging May;
And still I am a child, though I be old:
Time is my debtor for my years untold.

Hartley Coleridge [1796–1849]

THE WORLD I AM PASSING THROUGH

Few, in the days of early youth,
Trusted like me in love and truth.
I've learned sad lessons from the years;
But slowly, and with many tears;
For God made me to kindly view
The world that I was passing through.

How little did I once believe
That friendly tones could e'er deceive!
That kindness, and forbearance long,
Might meet ingratitude and wrong!
I could not help but kindly view
The world that I was passing through.

And though I've learned some souls are base,
I would not, therefore, hate the race;
I still would bless my fellow men,
And trust them, though deceived again.
God help me still to kindly view
The world that I am passing through!

Through weary conflicts I have passed,
And struggled into rest at last;
Such rest as when the rack has broke
A joint, or nerve, at every stroke.
The wish survives to kindly view
The world that I am passing through.

From all that fate has brought to me
I strive to learn humility,
And trust in Him who rules above,
Whose universal law is love.
Thus only can I kindly view
The world that I am passing through.

When I approach the setting sun,
And feel my journey nearly done,
May earth be veiled in genial light,
And her last smile to me seem bright!
Help me till then to kindly view
The world that I am passing through!

And all who tempt a trusting heart
From faith and hope to drift apart,—
May they themselves be spared the pain
Of losing power to trust again!
God help us all to kindly view
The world that we are passing through!

Lydia Maria Child [1802–1880]

TERMINUS

Iᴛ is time to be old,
To take in sail:—
The god of bounds,
Who sets to seas a shore,
Came to me in his fatal rounds,
And said: "No more!
No farther shoot
Thy broad ambitious branches, and thy root.
Fancy departs: no more invent;
Contract thy firmament
To compass of a tent.
There's not enough for this and that,
Make thy option which of two;
Economize the failing river,
Not the less revere the Giver,
Leave the many and hold the few.
Timely wise accept the terms,
Soften the fall with wary foot;
A little while
Still plan and smile,
And,—fault of novel germs,—
Mature the unfallen fruit.
Curse, if thou wilt, thy sires,
Bad husbands of their fires,
Who, when they gave thee breath,
Failed to bequeath
The needful sinew stark as once,
The Baresark marrow to thy bones,
But left a legacy of ebbing veins,
Inconstant heat and nerveless reins,—
Amid the Muses, left thee deaf and dumb,
Amid the Gladiators, halt and numb."

As the bird trims her to the gale,
I trim myself to the storm of time,
I man the rudder, reef the sail,
Obey the voice at eve obeyed at prime:

"Lowly faithful, banish fear,
Right onward drive unharmed;
The port, well worth the cruise, is near,
And every wave is charmed."
Ralph Waldo Emerson [1803–1882]

RABBI BEN EZRA

Grow old along with me!
The best is yet to be,
The last of life, for which the first was made:
Our times are in his hand
Who saith "A whole I planned,
Youth shows but half; trust God: see all, nor be afraid!"

Not that, amassing flowers,
Youth sighed, "Which rose make ours,
Which lily leave and then as best recall?"
Not that, admiring stars,
It yearned, "Nor Jove, nor Mars;
Mine be some figured flame which blends, transcends them
all!"

Not for such hopes and fears
Annulling youth's brief years,
Do I remonstrate: folly wide the mark!
Rather I prize the doubt
Low kinds exist without,
Finished and finite clods, untroubled by a spark.

Poor vaunt of life indeed,
Were man but formed to feed
On joy, to solely seek and find and feast:
Such feasting ended, then
As sure an end to men;
Irks care the crop-full bird? Frets doubt the maw-crammed
beast?

Rejoice we are allied
To that which doth provide

And not partake, effect and not receive!
    A spark disturbs our clod;
    Nearer we hold of God
Who gives, than of his tribes that take, I must believe.

    Then, welcome each rebuff
    That turns earth's smoothness rough,
Each sting that bids nor sit nor stand but go!
    Be our joys three-parts pain!
    Strive, and hold cheap the strain;
Learn, nor account the pang; dare, never grudge the throe!

    For thence,—a paradox
    Which comforts while it mocks,—
Shall life succeed in that it seems to fail:
    What I aspired to be,
    And was not, comforts me:
A brute I might have been, but would not sink i' the scale.

    What is he but a brute
    Whose flesh has soul to suit,
Whose spirit works lest arms and legs want play?
    To man, propose this test—
    Thy body at its best,
How far can that project thy soul on its lone way?

    Yet gifts should prove their use:
    I own the Past profuse
Of power each side, perfection every turn:
    Eyes, ears took in their dole,
    Brain treasured up the whole:
Should not the heart beat once "How good to live and
    learn"?

    Not once beat "Praise be thine!
    I see the whole design,
I, who saw power, see now Love perfect too:
    Perfect I call thy plan:
    Thanks that I was a man!
Maker, remake, complete,—I trust what thou shalt do!"

For pleasant is this flesh;
    Our soul, in its rose-mesh
Pulled ever to the earth, still yearns for rest:
    Would we some prize might hold
    To match those manifold
Possessions of the brute,—gain most, as we did best!

    Let us not always say,
    "Spite of this flesh to-day
I strove, made head, gained ground upon the whole!"
    As the bird wings and sings,
    Let us cry, "All good things
Are ours, nor soul helps flesh more, now, than flesh helps
      soul!"

    Therefore I summon age
    To grant youth's heritage,
Life's struggle having so far reached its term:
    Thence shall I pass, approved
    A man, for aye removed
From the developed brute; a God though in the germ.

    And I shall thereupon
    Take rest, ere I be gone
Once more on my adventure brave and new:
    Fearless and unperplexed,
    When I wage battle next,
What weapons to select, what armor to indue.

    Youth ended, I shall try
    My gain or loss thereby;
Leave the fire ashes, what survives is gold:
    And I shall weigh the same,
    Give life its praise or blame:
Young, all lay in dispute; I shall know, being old.

    For note, when evening shuts,
    A certain moment cuts
The deed off, calls the glory from the gray:
    A whisper from the west
    Shoots—"Add this to the rest,
Take it and try its worth: here dies another day."

So, still within this life,
Though lifted o'er its strife,
Let me discern, compare, pronounce at last,
"This rage was right i' the main,
That acquiescence vain:
The Future I may face now I have proved the Past."

For more is not reserved
To man, with soul just nerved
To act to-morrow what he learns to-day:
Here, work enough to watch
The Master work, and catch
Hints of the proper craft, tricks of the tool's true play.

As it was better, youth
Should strive, through acts uncouth,
Toward making, than repose on aught found made:
So, better, age, exempt
From strife, should know, than tempt
Further.   Thou waitedest age: wait death nor be afraid!

Enough now, if the Right
And Good and Infinite
Be named here, as thou callest thy hand thine own,
With knowledge absolute,
Subject to no dispute
From fools that crowded youth, nor let thee feel alone.

Be there, for once and all,
Severed great minds from small,
Announced to each his station in the Past!
Was I, the world arraigned,
Were they, my soul disdained,
Right?   Let age speak the truth and give us peace at last!

Now, who shall arbitrate?
Ten men love what I hate,
Shun what I follow, slight what I receive;
Ten, who in ears and eyes
Match me: we all surmise,
They this thing, and I that: whom shall my soul believe?

Not on the vulgar mass
Called "work," must sentence pass,
Things done, that took the eye and had the price;
O'er which, from level stand,
The low world laid its hand,
Found straightway to its mind, could value in a trice:

But all, the world's coarse thumb
And finger failed to plumb,
So passed in making up the main account;
All instincts immature,
All purposes unsure,
That weighed not as his work, yet swelled the man's amount:

Thoughts hardly to be packed
Into a narrow act,
Fancies that broke through language and escaped;
All I could never be,
All, men ignored in me,
This, I was worth to God, whose wheel the pitcher shaped.

Ay, note that Potter's wheel,
That metaphor! and feel
Why time spins fast, why passive lies our clay,—
Thou, to whom fools propound,
When the wine makes its round,
"Since life fleets, all is change; the Past gone, seize to-day!"

Fool! All that is, at all,
Lasts ever, past recall;
Earth changes, but thy soul and God stand sure:
What entered into thee,
That was, is, and shall be:
Time's wheel runs back or stops: Potter and clay endure.

He fixed thee 'mid this dance
Of plastic circumstance,
This Present, thou, forsooth, would fain arrest:
Machinery just meant
To give thy soul its bent,
Try thee and turn thee forth, sufficiently impressed.

What though the earlier grooves
Which ran the laughing loves
Around thy base, no longer pause and press?
What though, about thy rim,
Scull-things in order grim
Grow out, in graver mood, obey the sterner stress?

Look not thou down but up!
To uses of a cup,
The festal board, lamp's flash and trumpet's peal,
The new wine's foaming flow,
The Master's lips a-glow!
Thou, heaven's consummate cup, what needest thou with
earth's wheel?

But I need, now as then,
Thee, God, who mouldest men;
And since, not even while the whirl was worst,
Did I,—to the wheel of life
With shapes and colors rife,
Bound dizzily,—mistake my end, to slake thy thirst:

So, take and use thy work:
Amend what flaws may lurk,
What strain o' the stuff, what warpings past the aim!
My times be in thy hand!
Perfect the cup as planned!
Let age approve of youth, and death complete the same!
                              Robert Browning [1812–1889]

HUMAN LIFE

Sad is our youth, for it is ever going,
Crumbling away beneath our very feet;
Sad is our life, for onward it is flowing,
In current unperceived because so fleet;
Sad are our hopes for they were sweet in sowing,
But tares, self-sown, have overtopped the wheat;
Sad are our joys, for they were sweet in blowing;
And still, O still, their dying breath is sweet:

And sweet is youth, although it hath bereft us
Of that which made our childhood sweeter still;
And sweet our life's decline, for it hath left us
A nearer Good to cure an older Ill:
And sweet are all things, when we learn to prize them
Not for their sake, but His who grants them or denies them.

Aubrey Thomas de Vere [1814–1902]

YOUNG AND OLD

From "The Water Babies"

WHEN all the world is young, lad,
    And all the trees are green;
And every goose a swan, lad,
    And every lass a queen;
Then hey for boot and horse, lad,
    And round the world away;
Young blood must have its course, lad,
    And every dog his day.

When all the world is old, lad,
    And all the trees are brown;
And all the sport is stale, lad,
    And all the wheels run down:
Creep home, and take your place there,
    The spent and maimed among:
God grant you find one face there
    You loved when all was young.

Charles Kingsley [1819–1875]

THE ISLE OF THE LONG AGO

Oh, a wonderful stream is the River Time,
    As it flows through the realm of Tears,
With a faultless rhythm and a musical rhyme,
And a broader sweep and a surge sublime
    As it blends with the ocean of Years.

How the winters are drifting like flakes of snow!
  And the summers like buds between;
And the year in the sheaf—so they come and they go
On the River's breast with its ebb and flow,
  As they glide in the shadow and sheen.

There's a magical Isle up the River Time
  Where the softest of airs are playing;
There's a cloudless sky and a tropical clime,
And a voice as sweet as a vesper chime,
  And the Junes with the roses are staying.

And the name of this Isle is the Long Ago,
  And we bury our treasures there;
There are brows of beauty and bosoms of snow—
They are heaps of dust, but we loved them so!
  There are trinkets and tresses of hair.

There are fragments of song that nobody sings,
  And a part of an infant's prayer,
There's a harp unswept and a lute without strings,
There are broken vows and pieces of rings,
  And the garments that *she* used to wear.

There are hands that are waved when the fairy shore
  By the mirage is lifted in air;
And we sometimes hear through the turbulent roar
Sweet voices we heard in the days gone before,
  When the wind down the River is fair.

Oh, remembered for aye be the blessed Isle
  All the day of our life till night,
And when evening comes with its beautiful smile,
And our eyes are closing in slumber awhile,
  May that "Greenwood" of soul be in sight.

        Benjamin Franklin Taylor [1819–1887]

GROWING OLD

WHAT is it to grow old?
Is it to lose the glory of the form,
The lustre of the eye?

Is it for beauty to forego her wealth?
—Yes, but not this alone.

Is it to feel our strength—
Not our bloom only, but our strength—decay?
Is it to feel each limb
Grow stiffer, every function less exact,
Each nerve more loosely strung?

Yes, this, and more; but not—
Ah, 'tis not what in youth we dreamed 'twould be!
'Tis not to have our life
Mellowed and softened as with sunset glow,
A golden day's decline.

'Tis not to see the world
As from a height, with rapt prophetic eyes,
And heart profoundly stirred;
And weep, and feel the fulness of the past,
The years that are no more.

It is to spend long days
And not once feel that we were ever young;
It is to add, immured
In the hot prison of the present, month
To month with weary pain.

It is to suffer this,
And feel but half, and feebly, what we feel.
Deep in our hidden heart
Festers the dull remembrance of a change,
But no emotion—none.

It is!—last stage of all—
When we are frozen up within, and quite
The phantom of ourselves,
To hear the world applaud the hollow ghost
Which blessed the living man.

Matthew Arnold [1822-1888]

PAST

THE clocks are chiming in my heart
Their cobweb chime;
Old murmurings of days that die,
The sob of things a-drifting by.
The clocks are chiming in my heart!

The stars have twinkled, and gone out—
Fair candles blown!
The hot desires burn low, and wan
Those ashy fires, that flamed anon.
The stars have twinkled, and gone out.

John Galsworthy [1867–1933]

TWILIGHT

WHEN I was young the twilight seemed too long.
How often on the western window-seat
    I leaned my book against the misty pane
    And spelled the last enchanting lines again,
The while my mother hummed an ancient song,
Or sighed a little and said: "The hour is sweet!"
When I, rebellious, clamored for the light.

But now I love the soft approach of night,
    And now with folded hands I sit and dream
    While all too fleet the hours of twilight seem;
And thus I know that I am growing old.

O granaries of Age!   O manifold
And royal harvest of the common years!
There are in all thy treasure-house no ways
But lead by soft descent and gradual slope
To memories more exquisite than hope.
Thine is the Iris born of olden tears,
And thrice more happy are the happy days
That live divinely in the lingering rays.

A. Mary F. Robinson [1857–

YOUTH AND AGE

Youth hath many charms,—
  Hath many joys, and much delight;
Even its doubts, and vague alarms,
  By contrast make it bright:
And yet—and yet—forsooth,
  I love Age as well as Youth!

Well, since I love them both,
  The good of both I will combine,—
In women, I will look for Youth,
  And look for Age, in wine:
And then—and then—I'll bless
  This twain that gives me happiness!
                    George Arnold [1834–1865]

FORTY YEARS ON

Forty years on, when afar and asunder
  Parted are those who are singing today,
When you look back, and forgetfully wonder
  What you were like in your work and your play;
Then, it may be, there will often come o'er you
  Glimpses of notes like the catch of a song—
Visions of boyhood shall float them before you,
  Echoes of dreamland shall bear them along.
  Follow up! Follow up! Follow up! Follow up!
    Till the field ring again and again,
    With the tramp of the twenty-two men,
      Follow up! Follow up!

Routs and discomfitures, rushes and rallies,
  Bases attempted, and rescued, and won,
Strife without anger, and art without malice,—
  How will it seem to you forty years on?

Then, you will say, not a feverish minute
    Strained the weak heart, and the wavering knee,
Never the battle raged hottest, but in it
    Neither the last nor the faintest were we!
        Follow up! Follow up!

O the great days, in the distance enchanted,
    Days of fresh air, in the rain and the sun,
How we rejoiced as we struggled and panted—
    Hardly believable, forty years on!
How we discoursed of them, one with another,
    Auguring triumph, or balancing fate,
Loved the ally with the heart of a brother,
    Hated the foe with a playing at hate!
        Follow up! Follow up!

Forty years on, growing older and older,
    Shorter in wind, and in memory long,
Feeble of foot and rheumatic of shoulder,
    What will it help you that once you were strong?
God gives us bases to guard or beleaguer,
    Games to play out, whether earnest or fun,
Fights for the fearless, and goals for the eager,
    Twenty, and thirty, and forty years on!
        Follow up! Follow up!
          Edward Ernest Bowen [1836–1901]

DREGS

THE fire is out, and spent the warmth thereof,
(This is the end of every song man sings!)
The golden wine is drunk, the dregs remain,
Bitter as wormwood and as salt as pain;
And health and hope have gone the way of love
Into the drear oblivion of lost things.
Ghosts go along with us until the end;
This was a mistress, this, perhaps, a friend.
With pale, indifferent eyes, we sit and wait
For the dropped curtain and the closing gate:
This is the end of all the songs man sings.
        Ernest Dowson [1867–1900]

THE PARADOX OF TIME

A VARIATION ON RONSARD

" Le temps s'en va, le temps s'en va, ma dame!
Las! le temps non: mais nous nous en allons!"

TIME goes, you say? Ah no!
Alas, Time stays, *we* go;
    Or else, were this not so,
What need to chain the hours,
For Youth were always ours?
    Time goes, you say?—ah no!

Ours is the eyes' deceit
Of men whose flying feet
    Lead through some landscape low;
We pass, and think we see
The earth's fixed surface flee:—
    Alas, Time stays—we go!

Once in the days of old,
Your locks were curling gold,
    And mine had shamed the crow.
Now, in the self-same stage,
We've reached the silver age;
    Time goes, you say?—ah no!

Once, when my voice was strong,
I filled the woods with song
    To praise your " rose" and "snow";
My bird, that sang, is dead;
Where are your roses fled?
    Alas, Time stays—we go!

See, in what traversed ways,
What backward Fate delays
    The hopes we used to know;
Where are our old desires?—
Ah, where those vanished fires?
    Time goes, you say?—ah no!

How far, how far, O Sweet,
The past behind our feet
  Lies in the even-glow!
Now, on the forward way,
Let us fold hands, and pray;
  Alas, Time stays,—*we* go!
                    Austin Dobson [1840–1921]

AGE

SNOW and stars, the same as ever
  In the days when I was young,—
But their silver song, ah never,
  Never now is sung!

Cold the stars are, cold the earth is,
  Everything is grim and cold!
Strange and drear the sound of mirth is—
  Life and I are old!
                    William Winter [1836–1917]

OMNIA SOMNIA

DAWN drives the dreams away, yet some abide.
  Once, in a tide of pale and sunless weather,
I dreamed I wandered on a bare hillside,
  When suddenly the birds sang all together.

Still it was Winter, even in the dream;
  There was no leaf nor bud nor young grass springing;
The skies shone cold above the frost-bound stream:
  It was not Spring, and yet the birds were singing.

Blackbird and thrush and plaintive willow-wren,
  Chaffinch and lark and linnet, all were calling;
A golden web of music held me then,
  Innumerable voices, rising, falling.

O, never do the birds of April sing
  More sweet than in that dream I still remember:
Perchance the heart may keep its songs of Spring
  Even through the wintry dream of life's December.
                    Rosamund Marriott Watson [1863–1911]

THE YEAR'S END

FULL happy is the man who comes at last
  Into the safe completion of his year;
Weathered the perils of his spring, that blast
  How many blossoms promising and dear!
And of his summer, with dread passions fraught
  That oft, like fire through the ripening corn,
Blight all with mocking death and leave distraught
  Loved ones to mourn the ruined waste forlorn.
But now, though autumn gave but harvest slight,
  Oh, grateful is he to the powers above
For winter's sunshine, and the lengthened night
  By hearth-side genial with the warmth of love.
Through silvered days of vistas gold and green
Contentedly he glides away, serene.

Timothy Cole [1852–1931]

AN OLD MAN'S SONG

YE are young, ye are young,
  I am old, I am old;
And the song has been sung
  And the story been told.

Your locks are as brown
  As the mavis in May,
Your hearts are as warm
  As the sunshine to-day,
But mine white and cold
  As the snow on the brae.

And Love, like a flower,
  Is growing for you,
Hands clasping, lips meeting,
  Hearts beating so true;
While Fame like a star
In the midnight afar
  Is flashing for you.

For you the To-come,
　　But for me the Gone-by,
You are panting to live,
　　I am waiting to die;
The meadow is empty,
　　No flower groweth high,
And naught but a socket
　　The face of the sky.

Yea, howso we dream,
　　Or how bravely we do;
The end is the same,
　　Be we traitor or true:
And after the bloom
　　And the passion is past,
Death cometh at last.
　　　　　　Richard Le Gallienne [1866‑

SONGS OF SEVEN

SEVEN TIMES ONE.—EXULTATION

THERE'S no dew left on the daisies and clover,
　　There's no rain left in heaven;
I've said my "seven times" over and over,
　　Seven times one are seven.

I am old, so old, I can write a letter;
　　My birthday lessons are done;
The lambs play always, they know no better;
　　They are only one times one.

O moon! in the night I have seen you sailing
　　And shining so round and low;
You were bright! ah, bright! but your light is failing,—
　　You are nothing now but a bow.

You moon, have you done something wrong in heaven
　　That God has hidden your face?
I hope if you have, you will soon be forgiven,
　　And shine again in your place.

O velvet bee, you're a dusty fellow,
  You've powdered your legs with gold!
O brave marsh marybuds, rich and yellow,
  Give me your money to hold!

O columbine, open your folded wrapper,
  Where two twin turtle-doves dwell?
O cuckoopint, toll me the purple clapper
  That hangs in your clear green bell!

And show me your nest with the young ones in it;
  I will not steal them away;
I am old! you may trust me, linnet, linnet,—
  I am seven times one to-day.

SEVEN TIMES TWO.—ROMANCE

You bells in the steeple, ring, ring out your changes,
  How many soever they be,
And let the brown meadow-lark's note as he ranges
  Come over, come over to me.

Yet birds' clearest carol by fall or by swelling
  No magical sense conveys,
And bells have forgotten their old art of telling
  The fortune of future days

"Turn again, turn again," once they rang cheerily,
  While a boy listened alone;
Made his heart yearn again, musing so wearily
  All by himself on a stone.

Poor bells! I forgive you; your good days are over,
  And mine, they are yet to be;
No listening, no longing shall aught, aught discover:
  You leave the story to me.

The foxglove shoots out of the green matted heather
  Preparing her hoods of snow;
She was idle, and slept till the sunshiny weather:
  Oh! children take long to grow.

I wish and I wish that the spring would go faster,
   Nor long summer bide so late;
And I could grow on like the foxglove and aster,
   For some things are ill to wait.

I wait for the day when dear hearts shall discover,
   While dear hands are laid on my head;
"The child is a woman, the book may close over,
   For all the lessons are said."

I wait for my story,—the birds cannot sing it,
   Not one, as he sits on the tree;
The bells cannot ring it, but long years, oh, bring it!
   Such as I wish it to be.

SEVEN TIMES THREE.—LOVE

I LEANED out of window, I smelt the white clover,
   Dark, dark was the garden, I saw not the gate;
"Now, if there be footsteps, he comes, my one lover,—
   Hush, nightingale, hush! O sweet nightingale, wait
      Till I listen and hear
      If a step draweth near,
      For my love he is late!

"The skies in the darkness stoop nearer and nearer,
   A cluster of stars hangs like fruit in the tree,
The fall of the water comes sweeter, comes clearer:
   To what art thou listening, and what dost thou see?
      Let the star-clusters grow,
      Let the sweet waters flow,
      And cross quickly to me.

"You night-moths that hover, where honey brims over
   From sycamore blossoms, or settle or sleep;
You glowworms, shine out, and the pathway discover
   To him that comes darkling along the rough steep.
      Ah, my sailor, make haste,
      For the time runs to waste,
      And my love lieth deep,—

"Too deep for swift telling; and yet, my one lover,
  I've conned thee an answer, it waits thee to-night."
By the sycamore passed he, and through the white
      clover,
    Then all the sweet speech I had fashioned took flight;
      But I'll love him more, more
      Than e'er wife loved before,
      Be the days dark or bright.

SEVEN TIMES FOUR.—MATERNITY

HEIGH–HO! daisies and buttercups!
  Fair yellow daffodils, stately and tall!
When the wind wakes how they rock in the grasses,
  And dance with the cuckoo-buds slender and small!
Here's two bonny boys, and here's mother's own lasses,
  Eager to gather them all.

Heigh-ho! daisies and buttercups;
  Mother shall thread them a daisy chain;
Sing them a song of the pretty hedge-sparrow,
  That loved her brown little ones, loved them full fain;
Sing, "Heart, thou art wide though the house be but nar-
      row,"—
    Sing once, and sing it again.

Heigh-ho! daisies and buttercups!
  Sweet wagging cowslips, they bend and they bow;
A ship sails afar over warm ocean waters,
  And haply one musing doth stand at her prow.
O bonny brown sons, and O sweet little daughters,
  Maybe he thinks of you now.

Heigh-ho! daisies and buttercups!
  Fair yellow daffodils, stately and tall!
A sunshiny world full of laughter and leisure,
  And fresh hearts unconscious of sorrow and thrall!
Send down on their pleasure smiles passing its measure,
  God that is over us all!

SEVEN TIMES FIVE.—WIDOWHOOD

I SLEEP and rest, my heart makes moan
　　Before I am well awake;
"Let me bleed!　O let me alone,
　　Since I must not break!"

For children wake, though fathers sleep
　　With a stone at foot and at head:
O sleepless God, forever keep,
　　Keep both living and dead!

I lift mine eyes, and what to see
　　But a world happy and fair!
I have not wished it to mourn with me,—
　　Comfort is not there.

Oh, what anear but golden brooms,
　　But a waste of reedy rills!
Oh, what afar but the fine glooms
　　On the rare blue hills!

I shall not die, but live forlore,—
　　How bitter it is to part!
Oh, to meet thee, my love, once more!
　　O my heart, my heart!

No more to hear, no more to see!
　　Oh, that an echo might wake
And waft one note of thy psalm to me
　　Ere my heart-strings break!

I should know it how faint soe'er,
　　And with angel voices blent;
Oh, once to feel thy spirit anear;
　　I could be content!

Or once between the gates of gold,
　　While an entering angel trod,
But once,—thee sitting to behold
　　On the hills of God!

SEVEN TIMES SIX.—GIVING IN MARRIAGE

To bear, to nurse, to rear,
　To watch, and then to lose:
To see my bright ones disappear,
　Drawn up like morning dews,—
To bear, to nurse, to rear,
　To watch and then to lose:
This have I done when God drew near
　Among his own to choose.

To hear, to heed, to wed,
　And with thy lord depart
In tears, that he, as soon as shed,
　Will let no longer smart,—
To hear, to heed, to wed,
　This while thou didst I smiled,
For now it was not God who said,
　"Mother, give ME thy child."

O fond, O fool, and blind!
　To God I gave with tears;
But when a man like grace would find,
　My soul put by her fears,—
O fond, O fool, and blind!
　God guards in happier spheres;
That man will guard where he did bind
　Is hope for unknown years.

To hear, to heed, to wed,
　Fair lot that maidens choose,
Thy mother's tenderest words are said,
　Thy face no more she views;
Thy mother's lot, my dear,
　She doth in naught accuse;
Her lot to bear, to nurse, to rear,
　To love,—and then to lose.

SEVEN TIMES SEVEN.—LONGING FOR HOME

　A SONG of a boat:—
There was once a boat on a billow:
Lightly she rocked to her port remote,

And the foam was white in her wake like snow,
And her frail mast bowed when the breeze would blow,
   And bent like a wand of willow.

I shaded mine eyes one day when a boat
   Went curtsying over the billow,
I marked her course till a dancing mote,
   She faded out on the moonlit foam,
   And I stayed behind in the dear-loved home;
And my thoughts all day were about the boat,
   And my dreams upon the pillow.

I pray you hear my song of a boat
   For it is but short:—
My boat you shall find none fairer afloat,
   In river or port.
Long I looked out for the lad she bore,
   On the open desolate sea,
And I think he sailed to the heavenly shore,
   For he came not back to me—
                            Ah me!

   A song of a nest:—
   There was once a nest in a hollow:
Down in the mosses and knot-grass pressed,
Soft and warm and full to the brim—
Vetches leaned over it purple, and dim,
   With buttercup buds to follow.

I pray you hear my song of a nest,
   For it is not long:—
You shall never light in a summer quest
   The bushes among—
Shall never light on a prouder sitter,
   A fairer nestful, nor ever know
A softer sound than their tender twitter,
   That wind-like did come and go.

I had a nestful once of my own,
   Ah, happy, happy I!
Right dearly I loved them; but when they were grown
   They spread out their wings to fly—

Oh, one after one they flew away
    Far up to the heavenly blue,
To the better country, the upper day,
    And—I wish I was going too.

I pray you what is the nest to me,
    My empty nest?
And what is the shore where I stood to see
    My boat sail down to the west?
Can I call that home where I anchor yet,
    Though my good man has sailed?
Can I call that home where my nest was set,
    Now all its hope hath failed?

Nay, but the port where my sailor went,
    And the land where my nestlings be:
There is the home where my thoughts are sent
    The only home for me—
                  Ah me!
          Jean Ingelow [1820–1897]

AUSPEX

    My heart, I cannot still it,
    Nest that had song-birds in it;
    And when the last shall go,
    The dreary days, to fill it,
    Instead of lark or linnet,
    Shall whirl dead leaves and snow.

    Had they been swallows only,
    Without the passion stronger
    That skyward longs and sings,—
    Woe's me, I shall be lonely
    When I can feel no longer
    The impatience of their wings!

    A moment, sweet delusion,
    Like birds the brown leaves hover;
    But it will not be long
    Before their wild confusion
    Fall wavering down to cover
    The poet and his song.
        James Russell Lowell [1819–1891]

LOOKING BACKWARD

THE RETREAT

HAPPY those early days, when I
Shined in my Angel-infancy!
Before I understood this place
Appointed for my second race,
Or taught my soul to fancy aught
But a white, celestial thought;
When yet I had not walked above
A mile or two from my first Love,
And looking back, at that short space,
Could see a glimpse of His bright face;
When on some gilded cloud or flower
My gazing soul would dwell an hour,
And in those weaker glories spy
Some shadows of eternity;
Before I taught my tongue to wound
My Conscience with a sinful sound,
Or had the black art to dispense
A several sin to every sense;
But felt through all this fleshly dress
Bright shoots of everlastingness.

O how I long to travel back,
And tread again that ancient track!
That I might once more reach that plain
Where first I left my glorious train;
From whence the enlightened spirit sees
That shady City of Palm-trees.
But ah! my soul with too much stay
Is drunk, and staggers in the way!
Some men a forward motion love,
But I by backward steps would move;
And, when this dust falls to the urn,
In that state I came, return.

Henry Vaughan [1622–1695]

434

A SUPERSCRIPTION

Look in my face; my name is Might-have-been;
I am also called No-more, Too-late, Farewell;
Unto thine ear I hold the dead-sea shell
Cast up thy Life's foam-fretted feet between;
Unto thine eyes the glass where that is seen
Which had Life's form and Love's, but by my spell
Is now a shaken shadow intolerable,
Of ultimate things unuttered the frail screen.
Mark me, how still I am! But should there dart
One moment through thy soul the soft surprise
Of that winged Peace which lulls the breath of sighs,—
Then shalt thou see me smile, and turn apart
Thy visage to mine ambush at thy heart
Sleepless with cold commemorative eyes.

Dante Gabriel Rossetti [1828–1882]

THE CHILD IN THE GARDEN

When to the garden of untroubled thought
I came of late, and saw the open door,
And wished again to enter, and explore
The sweet, wild ways with stainless bloom inwrought,
And bowers of innocence with beauty fraught,
It seemed some purer voice must speak before
I dared to tread that garden loved of yore,
That Eden lost unknown and found unsought.
Then just within the gate I saw a child,—
A stranger-child, yet to my heart most dear,—
Who held his hands to me and softly smiled
With eyes that knew no shade of sin or fear;
"Come in," he said, "and play awhile with me;
I am the little child you used to be."

Henry Van Dyke [1852–1933]

CASTLES IN THE AIR

My thoughts by night are often filled
    With visions false as fair:
For in the Past alone I build
    My castles in the air.

I dwell not now on what may be;
   Night shadows o'er the scene;
But still my fancy wanders free
   Through that which might have been.

           Thomas Love Peacock [1785–1866]

SOMETIMES

ACROSS the fields of yesterday
   He sometimes comes to me,
A little lad just back from play—
   The lad I used to be.

And yet he smiles so wistfully
   Once he has crept within,
I wonder if he hopes to see
   The man I might have been.

           Thomas S. Jones, Jr. [1882–1932]

THE LITTLE GHOSTS

WHERE are they gone, and do you know
   If they come back at fall o' dew,
The little ghosts of long ago,
   That long ago were you?

And all the songs that ne'er were sung,
   And all the dreams that ne'er came true,
Like little children dying young—
   Do they come back to you?

           Thomas S. Jones, Jr. [1882–1932]

MY OTHER ME

CHILDREN, do you ever,
   In walks by land or sea,
Meet a little maiden
   Long time lost to me?

She is gay and gladsome,
   Has a laughing face,
And a heart as sunny;
   And her name is Grace.

Naught she knows of sorrow,
　　Naught of doubt or blight;
Heaven is just above her—
　　All her thoughts are white.

Long time since I lost her,
　　That other Me of mine;
She crossed, into Time's shadow
　　Out of Youth's sunshine.

Now the darkness keeps her;
　　And, call her as I will,
The years that lie between us
　　Hide her from me still.

I am dull and pain-worn,
　　And lonely as can be—
Oh, children, if you meet her,
　　Send back my other Me!
Grace Denio Litchfield [1849–

A SHADOW BOAT

UNDER my keel another boat
　Sails as I sail, floats as I float;
Silent and dim and mystic still,
　It steals through that weird nether-world,
Mocking my power, though at my will
　The foam before its prow is curled,
　Or calm it lies, with canvas furled.

Vainly I peer, and fain would see
　What phantom in that boat may be;
Yet half I dread, lest I with ruth
　Some ghost of my dead past divine,
Some gracious shape of my lost youth,
　Whose deathless eyes once fixed on mine
　Would draw me downward through the brine!
Arlo Bates [1850–1918]

A LAD THAT IS GONE

Sing me a song of a lad that is gone;
Say, could that lad be I?
Merry of soul he sailed on a day
Over the sea to Skye.

Mull was astern, Rum on the port,
Eigg on the starboard bow;
Glory of youth glowed in his soul:
Where is that glory now?

Sing me a song of a lad that is gone;
Say, could that lad be I?
Merry of soul he sailed on a day
Over the sea to Skye.

Give me again all that was there,
Give me the sun that shone!
Give me the eyes, give me the soul,
Give me the lad that's gone!

Sing me a song of a lad that is gone;
Say, could that lad be I?
Merry of soul he sailed on a day
Over the sea to Skye.

Billow and breeze, islands and seas,
Mountains of rain and sun,
All that was good, all that was fair,
All that was me is gone.

Robert Louis Stevenson [1850–1894]

CARCASSONNE *

"I'M growing old, I've sixty years;
I've labored all my life in vain.
In all that time of hopes and fears,
I've failed my dearest wish to gain.

* For the original of this poem see page 3844.

I see full well that here below
  Bliss unalloyed there is for none;
My prayer would else fulfilment know—
  Never have I seen Carcassonne!

"You see the city from the hill,
  It lies beyond the mountains blue;
And yet to reach it one must still
  Five long and weary leagues pursue,
And, to return, as many more.
  Had but the vintage plenteous grown—
But, ah! the grape withheld its store.
  I shall not look on Carcassonne!

"They tell me every day is there
  Not more or less than Sunday gay;
In shining robes and garments fair
  The people walk upon their way.
One gazes there on castle walls
  As grand as those of Babylon,
A bishop and two generals!
  What joy to dwell in Carcassonne!

"The vicar's right: he says that we
  Are ever wayward, weak, and blind;
He tells us in his homily
  Ambition ruins all mankind;
Yet could I there two days have spent,
  While still the autumn sweetly shone,
Ah, me! I might have died content
  When I had looked on Carcassonne.

"Thy pardon, Father, I beseech,
  In this my prayer if I offend;
One something sees beyond his reach
  From childhood to his journey's end.
My wife, our little boy, Aignan,
  Have travelled even to Narbonne;
My grandchild has seen Perpignan;
  And I—have not seen Carcassonne!"

So crooned, one day, close by Limoux,
    A peasant, double-bent with age.
"Rise up, my friend," said I; "with you
    I'll go upon this pilgrimage."
We left, next morning, his abode,
    But (Heaven forgive him!) half-way on
The old man died upon the road.
    He never gazed on Carcassonne.

Translated by John R. Thompson from the French of
    Gustave Nadaud [1820– ?]

CHILDHOOD

OLD Sorrow I shall meet again,
    And Joy, perchance—but never, never,
Happy Childhood, shall we twain
    See each other's face forever!

And yet I would not call thee back,
    Dear Childhood, lest the sight of me,
Thine old companion, on the rack
    Of Age, should sadden even thee.

John Banister Tabb [1845–1909]

THE WASTREL

ONCE, when I was little, as the summer night was falling,
    Among the purple upland fields I lost my barefoot way;
The road to home was hidden fast, and frightful shadows, crawling
    Along the sky-line, swallowed up the last kind light of day;
        And then I seemed to hear you
        In the twilight, and be near you;
    Seemed to hear your dear voice calling—
    Through the meadows, calling, calling—
        And I followed and I found you,
        Flung my tired arms around you,
And rested on the mother-breast, returned, tired out from play.

Down the days from that day, though I trod strange
    paths unheeding,
  Though I chased the jack-o'-lanterns of so many mad-
    dened years,
Though I never looked behind me, where the home-lights
    were receding,
  Though I never looked enough ahead to ken the Inn of
    Fears;
    Still I knew your heart was near me,
    That your ear was strained to hear me,
  That your love would need no pleading
  To forgive me, but was pleading
    Of its self that, in disaster,
    I should run to you the faster
And be sure that I was dearer for your sacrifice of tears.

Now on life's last Summertime the long last dusk is falling,
  And I, who trod one way so long, can tread no other way
Until at death's dim crossroads I watch, hesitant, the
    crawling
  Night-passages that maze me with the ultimate dismay.
    Then when Death and Doubt shall blind me—
    Even then—I know you'll find me:
I shall hear you, Mother, calling—
Hear you calling—calling—calling:
    I shall fight and follow—find you
    Though the grave-clothes swathe and bind you,
And I know your love will answer: "Here's my laddie
  home from play!"

               Reginald Wright Kauffman [1877–

TROIA FUIT

  THE world was wide when I was young,
  My schoolday hills and dales among;
  But, oh, it needs no Puck to put,
  With whipping wing and flying foot,
  A girdle 'round the narrow sphere
  In which I labor now and here!

Life's face was fair when careless I
First loved beneath an April sky,
And wept those fine-imagined woes
That Youth at nineteen thinks it knows;
Now love and woe both run so deep
I have not any time to weep.

No matter; though at last we see
That what was could not always be,
It girds our loins and steels our hands
In duller days and smaller lands
To recollect the country where
The world was wide and life was fair.

Reginald Wright Kauffman [1877–

TEMPLE GARLANDS

THERE is a temple in my heart
    Where moth or rust can never come,
A temple swept and set apart,
    To make my soul a home.

And round about the doors of it
    Hang garlands that forever last,
That gathered once are always sweet;
    The roses of the Past!

A. Mary F. Robinson [1857–

TIME LONG PAST

LIKE the ghost of a dear friend dead
    Is Time long past.
A tone which is now forever fled,
A hope which is now forever past,
A love so sweet it could not last,
    Was Time long past.

There were sweet dreams in the night
    Of Time long past:
And, was it sadness or delight,
Each day a shadow onward cast
Which made us wish it yet might last,—
    That Time long past.

There is regret, almost remorse,
    For Time long past.
'Tis like a child's belovèd corse
A father watches, till at last
Beauty is like remembrance, cast
    From Time long past.
        Percy Bysshe Shelley [1792–1822]

"I REMEMBER, I REMEMBER"

I REMEMBER, I remember
The house where I was born,
The little window where the sun
Came peeping in at morn;
He never came a wink too soon
Nor brought too long a day;
But now, I often wish the night
Had borne my breath away.

I remember, I remember
The roses, red and white,
The violets, and the lily-cups—
Those flowers made of light!
The lilacs where the robin built,
And where my brother set
The laburnum on his birthday,—
The tree is living yet!

I remember, I remember
Where I was used to swing,
And thought the air must rush as fresh
To swallows on the wing;
My spirit flew in feathers then
That is so heavy now,
The summer pools could hardly cool
The fever on my brow.

I remember, I remember
The fir-trees dark and high;
I used to think their slender tops
Were close against the sky:

It was a childish ignorance,
But now 'tis little joy
To know I'm farther off from Heaven
Than when I was a boy.

Thomas Hood [1799–1845]

MY LOST YOUTH

OFTEN I think of the beautiful town
    That is seated by the sea;
Often in thought go up and down
The pleasant streets of that dear old town,
    And my youth comes back to me.
        And a verse of a Lapland song
        Is haunting my memory still:
        "A boy's will is the wind's will,
And the thoughts of youth, are long, long thoughts."

I can see the shadowy lines of its trees,
    And catch, in sudden gleams,
The sheen of the far-surrounding seas,
And islands that were the Hesperides
    Of all my boyish dreams.
        And the burden of that old song,
        It murmurs and whispers still:
        "A boy's will is the wind's will,
And the thoughts of youth are long, long thoughts."

I remember the black wharves and the slips,
    And the sea-tides tossing free;
And Spanish sailors with bearded lips,
And the beauty and mystery of the ships,
    And the magic of the sea.
        And the voice of that wayward song
        Is singing and saying still:
        "A boy's will is the wind's will,
And the thoughts of youth are long, long thoughts."

I remember the bulwarks by the shore,
    And the fort upon the hill;
The sunrise gun, with its hollow roar,
The drum-beat repeated o'er and o'er,

And the bugle wild and shrill.
  And the music of that old song
  Throbs in my memory still:
  "A boy's will is the wind's will,
And the thoughts of youth are long, long thoughts."

I remember the sea-fight far away,
  How it thundered o'er the tide!
And the dead captains, as they lay
In their graves, o'erlooking the tranquil bay
  Where they in battle died.
    And the sound of that mournful song
    Goes through me with a thrill:
    "A boy's will is the wind's will,
And the thoughts of youth are long, long thoughts."

I can see the breezy dome of groves,
  The shadows of Deering's Woods;
And the friendships old and the early loves
Come back with a Sabbath sound, as of doves
  In quiet neighborhoods.
    And the verse of that sweet old song,
    It flutters and murmurs still:
    "A boy's will is the wind's will,
And the thoughts of youth are long, long thoughts."

I remember the gleams and glooms that dart
  Across the school-boy's brain;
The song and the silence in the heart,
That in part are prophecies, and in part
  Are longings wild and vain.
    And the voice of that fitful song
    Sings on, and is never still:
    "A boy's will is the wind's will,
And the thoughts of youth are long, long thoughts."

There are things of which I may not speak;
  There are dreams that cannot die;
There are thoughts that make the strong heart weak,
And bring a pallor into the cheek,

And a mist before the eye.
   And the words of that fatal song
   Come over me like a chill:
   "A boy's will is the wind's will,
And the thoughts of youth are long, long thoughts "

Strange to me are the forms I meet
   When I visit the dear old town;
But the native air is pure and sweet,
And the trees that o'ershadow each well-known street.
   As they balance up and down,
      Are singing the beautiful song,
      Are sighing and whispering still:
      "A boy's will is the wind's will,
And the thoughts of youth are long, long thoughts."

And Deering's Woods are fresh and fair,
   And with joy that is almost pain
My heart goes back to wander there,
And among the dreams of the days that were
   I find my lost youth again.
      And the strange and beautiful song,
      The groves are repeating it still:
      "A boy's will is the wind's will,
And the thoughts of youth are long, long thoughts."
                    Henry Wadsworth Longfellow [1807–1882]

"VOICE OF THE WESTERN WIND"

VOICE of the western wind!
   Thou singest from afar,
Rich with the music of a land
   Where all my memories are;
But in thy song I only hear
   The echo of a tone
That fell divinely on my ear
   In days forever flown.

Star of the western sky!
   Thou beamest from afar,
With lustre caught from eyes I knew
   Whose orbs were each a star;

But, oh, those orbs—too wildly bright—
No more eclipse thine own,
And never shall I find the light
Of days forever flown!
Edmund Clarence Stedman [1833–1908]

"LANGSYNE, WHEN LIFE WAS BONNIE"

LANGSYNE, when life was bonnie,
   An' a' the skies were blue,
When ilka thocht took blossom,
   An' hung its heid wi' dew,
When winter wasna winter,
   Though snaws cam' happin' doon,
Langsyne, when life was bonnie,
   Spring gaed a twalmonth roun'.

Langsyne, when life was bonnie,
   An' a' the days were lang;
When through them ran the music
   That comes to us in sang,
We never wearied liltin'
   The auld love-laden tune;
Langsyne, when life was bonnie,
   Love gaed a twalmonth roun'.

Langsyne, when life was bonnie,
   An' a' the warld was fair,
The leaves were green wi' simmer,
   For autumn wasna there.
But listen hoo they rustle,
   Wi' an eerie, weary soun',
For noo, alas, 'tis winter
   That gangs a twalmonth roun'.
Alexander Anderson [1845–1909]

THE SHOOGY-SHOO

I DO be thinking, lassie, of the old days now;
For oh! your hair is tangled gold above your Irish brow;
And oh! your eyes are fairy flax! no other eyes so blue;
Come nestle in my arms, and swing upon the shoogy-shoo.

Sweet and slow, swinging low, eyes of Irish blue,
All my heart is swinging, dear, swinging here with you;
Irish eyes are like the flax, and mine are wet with dew,
Thinking of the old days upon the shoogy-shoo.

When meadow-larks would singing be in old Glentair,
Was one sweet lass had eyes of blue and tangled golden hair;
She was a wee bit girleen then, dear heart, the like of you,
When we two swung the braes among, upon the shoogy-
shoo.

Ah well, the world goes up and down, and some sweet day
Its shoogy-shoo will swing us two where sighs will pass away;
So nestle close your bonnie head, and close your eyes so
true,
And swing with me, and memory, upon the shoogy-shoo.

Sweet and slow, swinging low, eyes of Irish blue,
All my heart is swinging, dear, swinging here with you;
Irish eyes are like the flax, and mine are wet with dew,
Thinking of the old days upon the shoogy-shoo.
Winthrop Packard [1862–

BABYLON

"We shall meet again in Babylon."

I'M going softly all my years in wisdom if in pain—
For, oh, the music stirs my blood as once it did before,
And still I hear in Babylon, in Babylon, in Babylon,
The dancing feet in Babylon, of those who took my floor.

I'm going silent all my years, but garnered in my brain
Is that swift wit which used to flash and cut them like a
sword—
And now I hear in Babylon, in Babylon, in Babylon,
The foolish tongues in Babylon, of those who took my
word.

I'm going lonely all my days, who was the first to crave
The second, fierce, unsteady voice, that struggled to speak
free—
And now I watch in Babylon, in Babylon, in Babylon,
The pallid loves in Babylon of men who once loved me.

I'm sleeping early by a flame as one content and gray,
But, oh, I dream a dream of dreams beneath a winter
  moon,
I breathe the breath of Babylon, of Babylon, of Babylon,
The scent of silks in Babylon that floated to a tune.

A band of years has flogged me out—an exile's fate is mine,
To sit with mumbling crones and still a heart that cries
  with youth.
But, oh, to walk in Babylon, in Babylon, in Babylon,
The happy streets in Babylon, when once the dream was
  truth.

        Viola Taylor [18

THE ROAD OF REMEMBRANCE

The old wind stirs the hawthorn tree;
 The tree is blossoming;
Northward the road runs to the sea,
 And past the House of Spring.

The folk go down it unafraid;
 The still roofs rise before;
When you were lad and I was maid,
 Wide open stood the door.

Now, other children crowd the stair,
 And hunt from room to room;
Outside, under the hawthorn fair,
 We pluck the thorny bloom.

Out in the quiet road we stand,
 Shut in from wharf and mart,
The old wind blowing up the land,
 The old thoughts at our heart.

    Lizette Woodworth Reese [1856–1935]

THE TRIUMPH OF FORGOTTEN THINGS

There is a pity in forgotten things,
 Banished the heart they can no longer fill,
Since restless Fancy, spreading swallow wings,
 Must seek new pleasures still!

There is a patience, too, in things forgot;
　　They wait—they find the portal long unused;
And knocking there, it shall refuse them not,—
　　　Nor aught shall be refused!

Ah, yes! though we, unheeding years on years,
　　In alien pledges spend the heart's estate,
They bide some blessed moment of quick tears—
　　　Some moment without date—

Some gleam on flower, or leaf, or beaded dew,
　　Some tremble at the ear of memoried sound
Of mother-song,—they seize the slender clew,—
　　　The old loves gather round!

When that which lured us once now lureth not,
　　But the tired hands their garnered dross let fall,
This is the triumph of the things forgot—
　　　To hear the tired heart call!

And they are with us at Life's farthest reach,
　　A light when into shadow all else dips,
As, in the stranger's land, their native speech
　　　Returns to dying lips!

Edith M. Thomas [1854–1925]

IN THE TWILIGHT

Men say the sullen instrument,
　　That, from the Master's bow,
　　With pangs of joy or woe,
Feels music's soul through every fibre sent,
　　Whispers the ravished strings
More than he knew or meant;
　　Old summers in its memory glow;
　　The secrets of the wind it sings;
　　It hears the April-loosened springs;
　　　And mixes with its mood
　　　All it dreamed when it stood
　　　In the murmurous pine-wood
　　　　　Long ago!

The magical moonlight then
  Steeped every bough and cone;
The roar of the brook in the glen
  Came dim from the distance blown;
The wind through its glooms sang low,
  And it swayed to and fro,
    With delight as it stood,
    In the wonderful wood,
        Long ago!

O my life, have we not had seasons
  That only said, Live and rejoice?
That asked not for causes and reasons,
  But made us all feeling and voice?
When we went with the winds in their blowing,
  When Nature and we were peers,
And we seemed to share in the flowing
  Of the inexhaustible years?
    Have we not from the earth drawn juices
    Too fine for earth's sordid uses?
      Have I heard, have I seen
      All I feel, all I know?
      Doth my heart overween?
      Or could it have been
          Long ago?

Sometimes a breath floats by me,
  An odor from Dreamland sent,
That makes the ghost seem nigh me
  Of a splendor that came and went,
Of a life lived somewhere, I know not
  In what diviner sphere,
Of memories that stay not and go not,
  Like music heard once by an ear
    That cannot forget or reclaim it,
    A something so shy, it would shame it
    To make it a show,
    A something too vague, could I name it,
      For others to know,

As if I had lived it or dreamed it,
As if I had acted or schemed it,
      Long ago!

And yet, could I live it over,
  This life that stirs in my brain,
Could I be both maiden and lover,
Moon and tide, bee and clover,
  As I seem to have been, once again,
Could I but speak it and show it,
  This pleasure more sharp than pain,
  That baffles and lures me so,
The world should once more have a poet,
    Such as it had
    In the ages glad,
        Long ago!
          James Russell Lowell [1819–1891]

AN IMMORALITY

Sing we for love and idleness,
Naught else is worth the having.
Though I have been in many a land,
There is naught else in living.

And I would rather have my sweet,
Though rose-leaves die of grieving,
Than do high deeds in Hungary
To pass all men's believing.

          Ezra Pound [1885–

THREE SEASONS

"A cup for hope!" she said,
In springtime ere the bloom was old:
The crimson wine was poor and cold
  By her mouth's richer red.

"A cup for love!" how low,
How soft the words; and all the while
Her blush was rippling with a smile
  Like summer after snow.

"A cup for memory!"
Cold cup that one must drain alone:
While autumn winds are up and moan
   Across the barren sea.

   Hope, memory, love:
Hope for fair morn, and love for day,
And memory for the evening gray
   And solitary dove.

Christina Georgina Rossetti [1830–1894]

THE OLD FAMILIAR FACES

I HAVE had playmates, I have had companions,
In my days of childhood, in my joyful schooldays,—
All, all are gone, the old familiar faces.

I have been laughing, I have been carousing,
Drinking late, sitting late, with my bosom cronies,—
All, all are gone, the old familiar faces.

I loved a Love once, fairest among women:
Closed are her doors on me, I must not see her,—
All, all are gone, the old familiar faces.

I have a friend, a kinder friend has no man:
Like an ingrate, I left my friend abruptly;
Left him, to muse on the old familiar faces.

Ghost-like, I paced round the haunts of my childhood.
Earth seemed a desert I was bound to traverse,
Seeking to find the old familiar faces.

Friend of my bosom, thou more than a brother,
Why wert not thou born in my father's dwelling?
So might we talk of the old familiar faces—

How some they have died, and some they have left me,
And some are taken from me; all are departed,—
All, all are gone, the old familiar faces.

Charles Lamb [1775–1834]

THE LIGHT OF OTHER DAYS

OFT in the stilly night,
　Ere Slumber's chain hath bound me,
Fond memory brings the light
　Of other days around me:
　　The smiles, the tears,
　　Of boyhood's years,
　The words of love then spoken;
　　The eyes that shone,
　　Now dimmed and gone,
　The cheerful hearts now broken!
Thus in the stilly night,
　Ere Slumber's chain hath bound me,
Sad Memory brings the light
　Of other days around me.

When I remember all
　The friends, so linked together,
I've seen around me fall,
　Like leaves in wintry weather,
　　I feel like one
　　Who treads alone
　Some banquet-hall deserted,
　　Whose lights are fled,
　　Whose garlands dead,
　And all but he departed!
Thus in the stilly night,
　Ere Slumber's chain hath bound me,
Sad Memory brings the light
　Of other days around me.

Thomas Moore [1779–1852]

"TEARS, IDLE TEARS"

From "The Princess"

TEARS, idle tears, I know not what they mean,
Tears from the depth of some divine despair
Rise in the heart and gather to the eyes,
In looking on the happy Autumn-fields,
And thinking of the days that are no more.

Fresh as the first beam glittering on a sail,
That brings our friends up from the underworld,
Sad as the last which reddens over one
That sinks with all we love below the verge;
So sad, so fresh, the days that are no more.

Ah, sad and strange as in dark summer dawns
The earliest pipe of half-awakened birds
To dying ears, when unto dying eyes
The casement slowly grows a glimmering square;
So sad, so strange, the days that are no more.

Dear as remembered kisses after death,
And sweet as those by hopeless fancy feigned
On lips that are for others; deep as love,
Deep as first love, and wild with all regret;
O Death in Life, the days that are no more!
                    Alfred Tennyson [1809–1892]

THE PET NAME

" . . . *the name*
Which from their *lips seemed a caress.*"
—MISS MILFORD'S "DRAMATIC SCENES"

I HAVE a name, a little name,
    Uncadenced for the ear,
Unhonored by ancestral claim,
Unsanctified by prayer and psalm
    The solemn font anear.

It never did to pages wove
    For gay romance belong;
It never dedicate did move
As "Sacharissa" unto love,
    "Orinda" unto song.

Though I write books, it will be read
    Upon the leaves of none,
And afterward, when I am dead,
Will ne'er be graved for sight or tread,
    Across my funeral-stone.

This name, whoever chance to call,
    Perhaps your smile may win:
Nay, do not smile! mine eyelids fall
Over mine eyes and feel withal
    The sudden tears within.

Is there a leaf, that greenly grows
    Where summer meadows bloom,
But gathereth the winter snows,
And changeth to the hue of those,
    If lasting till they come?

Is there a word, or jest, or game,
    But time incrusteth round
With sad associate thoughts the same?
And so to me my very name
    Assumes a mournful sound.

My brother gave that name to me
    When we were children twain,
When names acquired baptismally
Were hard to utter, as to see
    That life had any pain.

No shade was on us then, save one
    Of chestnuts from the hill;
And through the word our laugh did run
As part thereof: the mirth being done,
    He calls me by it still.

Nay, do not smile! I hear in it
    What none of you can hear,—
The talk upon the willow seat,
The bird and wind that did repeat
    Around, our human cheer.

I hear the birthday's noisy bliss
    My sisters' woodland glee,
My father's praise I did not miss
When stooping down, he cared to kiss
    The poet at his knee,—

And voices which, to name me, aye
   Their tenderest tones were keeping,—
To some I nevermore can say
An answer till God wipes away
   In heaven these drops of weeping.

My name to me a sadness wears:
   No murmurs cross my mind—
Now God be thanked for these thick tears,
Which show, of those departed years,
   Sweet memories left behind.

Now God be thanked for years enwrought
   With love which softens yet:
Now God be thanked for every thought
Which is so tender it has caught
   Earth's guerdon of regret.

Earth saddens, never shall remove
   Affections purely given;
And e'en that mortal grief shall prove
The immortality of love,
   And heighten it with Heaven.
         Elizabeth Barrett Browning [1806–1861]

THREESCORE AND TEN

WHO reach their threescore years and ten,
   As I have mine, without a sigh,
Are either more or less than men—
      Not such am I.

I am not of them; life to me
   Has been a strange, bewildering dream,
Wherein I knew not things that be
      From things that seem.

I thought, I hoped, I knew one thing,
   And had one gift, when I was young—
The impulse and the power to sing,
      And so I sung.

To have a place in the high choir
  Of poets, and deserve the same—
What more could mortal man desire
    Than poet's fame?

I sought it long, but never found;
  The choir so full was and so strong
The jubilant voices there, they drowned
    My simple song.

Men would not hear me then, and now
  I care not, I accept my fate,
When white hairs thatch the furrowed brow
    Crowns come too late!

The best of life went long ago
  From me; it was not much at best;
Only the love that young hearts know,
    The dear unrest.

Back on my past, through gathering tears,
  Once more I cast my eyes, and see
Bright shapes that in my better years
    Surrounded me!

They left me here, they left me there,
  Went down dark pathways, one by one—
The wise, the great, the young, the fair;
    But I went on.

And I go on!   And bad or good,
  The old allotted years of men
I have endured as best I could,
    Threescore and ten!
                    Richard Henry Stoddard [1825–1903]

RAIN ON THE ROOF

WHEN the humid shadows hover
  Over all the starry spheres,
And the melancholy darkness
  Gently weeps in rainy tears,

What a bliss to press the pillow
  Of a cottage-chamber bed,
And to listen to the patter
  Of the soft rain overhead!

Every tinkle on the shingles
  Has an echo in the heart;
And a thousand dreamy fancies
  Into busy being start,
And a thousand recollections
  Weave their air-threads into woof,
As I listen to the patter
  Of the rain upon the roof.

Now in memory comes my mother,
  As she used, in years agone,
To regard the darling dreamers
  Ere she left them till the dawn;
And I feel her fond look on me,
  As I list to this refrain
Which is played upon the shingles
  By the patter of the rain.

Then my little seraph sister,
  With her wings and waving hair,
And her star-eyed cherub brother—
  A serene angelic pair—
Glide around my wakeful pillow,
  With their praise or mild reproof,
As I listen to the murmur
  Of the soft rain on the roof.

And another comes, to thrill me
  With her eyes' delicious blue;
And I mind not, musing on her,
  That her heart was all untrue:
I remember but to love her
  With a passion kin to pain,
And my heart's quick pulses vibrate
  To the patter of the rain.

Art hath naught of tone or cadence
    That can work with such a spell
In the soul's mysterious fountains,
    Whence the tears of rapture well,
As that melody of nature,
    That subdued, subduing strain
Which is played upon the shingles
    By the patter of the rain.

             Coates Kinney [1826–1904]

ALONE BY THE HEARTH

HERE, in my snug little fire-lit chamber,
    Sit I alone:
And, as I gaze in the coals, I remember
    Days long agone.
Saddening it is when the night has descended,
    Thus to sit here,
Pensively musing on episodes ended
    Many a year.

Still in my visions a golden-haired glory
    Flits to and fro;
She whom I loved—but 'tis just the old story:
    Dead, long ago.
'Tis but a wraith of love; yet I linger
    (Thus passion errs),
Foolishly kissing the ring on my finger—
    Once it was hers.

Nothing has changed since her spirit departed,
    Here, in this room
Save I, who, weary, and half broken-hearted,
    Sit in the gloom.
Loud 'gainst the window the winter rain dashes,
    Dreary and cold;
Over the floor the red fire-light flashes
    Just as of old.

Just as of old—but the embers are scattered,
    Whose ruddy blaze
Flashed o'er the floor where the fairy feet pattered
    In other days!
Then, her dear voice, like a silver chime ringing,
    Melted away;
Often these walls have re-echoed her singing,
    Now hushed for aye!

Why should love bring naught but sorrow, I wonder?
    Everything dies!
Time and death, sooner or later, must sunder
    Holiest ties.
Years have rolled by; I am wiser and older—
    Wiser, but yet
Not till my heart and its feelings grow colder,
    Can I forget.

So, in my snug little fire-lit chamber,
    Sit I alone;
And, as I gaze in the coals, I remember
    Days long agone!

             George Arnold [1834–1865]

THE OLD MAN DREAMS

Oʜ for one hour of youthful joy!
    Give back my twentieth spring!
I'd rather laugh, a bright-haired boy,
    Than reign, a gray-beard king.

Off with the spoils of wrinkled age!
    Away with Learning's crown!
Tear out life's Wisdom-written page,
    And dash its trophies down!

One moment let my life-blood stream
    From boyhood's fount of flame!
Give me one giddy, reeling dream
    Of life all love and fame!

My listening angel heard the prayer,
    And, calmly smiling, said,
"If I but touch thy silvered hair,
    Thy hasty wish hath sped.

"But is there nothing in thy track
    To bid thee fondly stay,
While the swift seasons hurry back
    To find the wished-for day?"

"Ah, truest soul of womankind!
    Without thee what were life?
One bliss I cannot leave behind:
    I'll take—my—precious—wife!"

The angel took a sapphire pen
    And wrote in rainbow dew,
The man would be a boy again,
    And be a husband, too!

"And is there nothing yet unsaid,
    Before the change appears?
Remember, all their gifts have fled
    With those dissolving years."

"Why, yes;" for memory would recall
    My fond paternal joys;
"I could not bear to leave them all—
    I'll take—my—girl—and—boys."

The smiling angel dropped his pen,—
    "Why, this will never do;
The man would be a boy again,
    And be a father, too!"

And so I laughed,—my laughter woke
    The household with its noise,—
And wrote my dream, when morning broke,
    To please the gray-haired boys.
            Oliver Wendell Holmes [1809–1894]

THE GARRET*

AFTER BÉRANGER

WITH pensive eyes the little room I view,
  Where, in my youth, I weathered it so long;
With a wild mistress, a stanch friend or two,
  And a light heart still breaking into song:
Making a mock of life, and all its cares,
  Rich in the glory of my rising sun,
Lightly I vaulted up four pair of stairs,
  In the brave days when I was twenty-one.

Yes; 'tis a garret—let him know't who will—
  There was my bed—full hard it was and small;
My table there—and I decipher still
  Half a lame couplet charcoaled on the wall.
Ye joys, that Time hath swept with him away,
  Come to mine eyes, ye dreams of love and fun;
For you I pawned my watch how many a day,
  In the brave days when I was twenty-one.

And see my little Jessy, first of all;
  She comes with pouting lips and sparkling eyes:
Behold, how roguishly she pins her shawl
  Across the narrow casement, curtain-wise;
Now by the bed her petticoat glides down,
  And when did woman look the worse in none?
I have heard since who paid for many a gown,
  In the brave days when I was twenty-one.

One jolly evening, when my friends and I
  Made happy music with our songs and cheers,
A shout of triumph mounted up thus high,
  And distant cannon opened on our ears:
We rise,—we join in the triumphant strain,—
  Napoleon conquers—Austerlitz is won—
Tyrants shall never tread us down again,
  In the brave days when I was twenty-one.

* For the original of this poem see page 3839.

Let us begone—the place is sad and strange—
How far, far off, these happy times appear;
All that I have to live I'd gladly change
For one such month as I have wasted here—
To draw long dreams of beauty, love, and power,
From founts of hope that never will outrun,
And drink all life's quintessence in an hour,
Give me the days when I was twenty-one!
William Makepeace Thackeray [1811–1863]

AULD LANG SYNE

SHOULD auld acquaintance be forgot,
And never brought to min'?
Should auld acquaintance be forgot,
And days o' lang syne?

For auld lang syne, my dear,
For auld lang syne,
We'll tak a cup o' kindness yet
For auld lang syne.

We twa hae rin about the braes,
And pu'd the gowans fine;
But we've wandered monie a weary fit
Sin' auld lang syne.

We twa hae paidl't i' the burn,
Frae mornin' sun till dine;
But seas between us braid hae roared
Sin' auld lang syne.

And here's a hand, my trusty fiere,
And gie's a hand o' thine;
And we'll tak a right guid willie-waught
For auld lang syne.

And surely ye'll be your pint-stowp,
And surely I'll be mine,
And we'll tak a cup o' kindness yet
For auld lang syne!
Robert Burns [1759–1796]

ROCK ME TO SLEEP

BACKWARD, turn backward, O Time, in your flight,
Make me a child again, just for to-night!
Mother, come back from the echoless shore,
Take me again to your heart as of yore;
Kiss from my forehead the furrows of care,
Smooth the few silver threads out of my hair;
Over my slumbers your loving watch keep;—
Rock me to sleep, mother,—rock me to sleep!

Backward, flow backward, O tide of the years!
I am so weary of toil and of tears,—
Toil without recompense, tears all in vain,—
Take them, and give me my childhood again!
I have grown weary of dust and decay,—
Weary of flinging my soul-wealth away;
Weary of sowing for others to reap;—
Rock me to sleep, mother,—rock me to sleep!

Tired of the hollow, the base, the untrue,
Mother, O mother, my heart calls for you!
Many a summer the grass has grown green,
Blossomed and faded, our faces between:
Yet, with strong yearning and passionate pain,
Long I to-night for your presence again.
Come from the silence so long and so deep;—
Rock me to sleep, mother,— rock me to sleep!

Over my heart, in the days that are flown,
No love like mother-love ever has shone;
No other worship abides and endures,—
Faithful, unselfish, and patient, like yours:
None like a mother can charm away pain
From the sick soul and the world-weary brain.
Slumber's soft calms o'er my heavy lids creep;—
Rock me to sleep, mother,—rock me to sleep!

Come, let your brown hair, just lighted with gold,
Fall on your shoulders again as of old;

Let it drop over my forehead to-night,
Shading my faint eyes away from the light;
For with its sunny-edged shadows once more
Haply will throng the sweet visions of yore;
Lovingly, softly, its bright billows sweep;—
Rock me to sleep, mother,—rock me to sleep!

Mother, dear mother, the years have been long
Since I last listened your lullaby song:
Sing, then, and unto my soul it shall seem
Womanhood's years have been only a dream.
Clasped to your heart in a loving embrace,
With your light lashes just sweeping my face,
Never hereafter to wake or to weep;—
Rock me to sleep, mother,—rock me to sleep!

Elizabeth Akers [1832–1911]

THE BUCKET

How dear to this heart are the scenes of my childhood,
    When fond recollection presents them to view!
The orchard, the meadow, the deep-tangled wild-wood,
    And every loved spot which my infancy knew!
The wide-spreading pond, and the mill that stood by it,
    The bridge, and the rock where the cataract fell,
The cot of my father, the dairy-house nigh it,
    And e'en the rude bucket that hung in the well—
The old oaken bucket, the iron-bound bucket,
The moss-covered bucket which hung in the well.

That moss-covered vessel I hailed as a treasure,
    For often at noon, when returned from the field,
I found it the source of an exquisite pleasure,
    The purest and sweetest that nature can yield.
How ardent I seized it, with hands that were glowing,
    And quick to the white-pebbled bottom it fell;
Then soon, with the emblem of truth overflowing,
    And dripping with coolness, it rose from the well—
The old oaken bucket, the iron-bound bucket,
The moss-covered bucket arose from the well.

How sweet from the green mossy brim to receive it,
  As poised on the curb it inclined to my lips!
Not a full blushing goblet would tempt me to leave it,
  The brightest that beauty or revelry sips.
And now, far removed from the loved habitation,
  The tear of regret will intrusively swell,
As fancy reverts to my father's plantation,
  And sighs for the bucket that hangs in the well—
The old oaken bucket, the iron-bound bucket,
The moss-covered bucket that hangs in the well!

                                Samuel Woodworth [1785–1842]

THE GRAPE-VINE SWING

LITHE and long as the serpent train,
  Springing and clinging from tree to tree,
Now darting upward, now down again,
  With a twist and a twirl that are strange to see;
Never took serpent a deadlier hold,
  Never the cougar a wilder spring,
Strangling the oak with the boa's fold,
  Spanning the beach with the condor's wing.

Yet no foe that we fear to seek,—
  The boy leaps wild to thy rude embrace;
Thy bulging arms bear as soft a cheek
  As ever on lover's breast found place;
On thy waving train is a playful hold
  Thou shalt never to lighter grasp persuade;
While a maiden sits in thy drooping fold,
  And swings and sings in the noonday shade!

O giant strange of our Southern woods!
  I dream of thee still in the well-known spot,
Though our vessel strains o'er the ocean floods,
  And the Northern forest beholds thee not;
I think of thee still with a sweet regret,
  As the cordage yields to my playful grasp,—
Dost thou spring and cling in our woodlands yet?
  Does the maiden still swing in thy giant clasp?

                        William Gilmore Simms [1806–1870]

THE OLD SWIMMIN'-HOLE

Oh! the old swimmin'-hole! whare the crick so still and deep
Looked like a baby-river that was laying half asleep,
And the gurgle of the worter round the drift jest below
Sounded like the laugh of something we onc't ust to know
Before we could remember anything but the eyes
Of the angels lookin' out as we left Paradise;
But the merry days of youth is beyond our controle,
And it's hard to part ferever with the old swimmin'-hole.

Oh! the old swimmin'-hole!   In the happy days of yore,
When I ust to lean above it on the old sickamore,
Oh! it showed me a face in its warm sunny tide
That gazed back at me so gay and glorified,
It made me love myself as I leaped to caress
My shadder smilin' up at me with sich tenderness.
But them days is past and gone, and old Time's tuck his toll
From the old man come back to the old swimmin'-hole.

Oh! the old swimmin'-hole!   In the long, lazy days
When the hum-drum of school made so many run-a-ways,
How pleasant was the journey down the old dusty lane,
Whare the tracks of our bare feet was all printed so plane
You could tell by the dent of the heel and the sole
They was lots o' fun on hand at the old swimmin'-hole.
But the lost joys is past!   Let your tears in sorrow roll
Like the rain that ust to dapple up the old swimmin'-hole.

Thare the bulrushes growed, and the cattails so tall,
And the sunshine and shadder fell over it all;
And it mottled the worter with amber and gold
Tel the glad lilies rocked in the ripples that rolled;
And the snake-feeder's four gauzy wings fluttered by
Like the ghost of a daisy dropped out of the sky,
Or a wownded apple-blossom in the breeze's controle
As it cut acrost some orchurd to'rds the old swimmin'-hole.

Oh! the old swimmin'-hole!   When I last saw the place,
The scenes was all changed, like the change in my face;

The bridge of the railroad now crosses the spot
Whare the old divin'-log lays sunk and fergot.
And I stray down the banks whare the trees ust to be—
But never again will theyr shade shelter me!
And I wish in my sorrow I could strip to the soul,
And dive off in my grave like the old swimmin'-hole.

James Whitcomb Riley [1849–1916]

FORTY YEARS AGO

I'VE wandered to the village, Tom, I've sat beneath the tree,
Upon the schoolhouse playground, that sheltered you and
     me;
But none were there to greet me, Tom; and few were left
     to know,
Who played with us upon that green some forty years ago.

The grass is just as green, Tom; barefooted boys at play
Were sporting, just as we did then, with spirits just as gay.
But the "master" sleeps upon the hill, which, coated o'er
     with snow,
Afforded us a sliding-place some forty years ago.

The old schoolhouse is altered some; the benches are re-
     placed
By new ones, very like the same our jackknives once defaced;
But the same old bricks are in the wall, the bell swings to
     and fro;
Its music's just the same, dear Tom, 'twas forty years ago.

The boys were playing some old game, beneath that same
     old tree;
I have forgot the name just now—you've played the same
     with me,
On that same spot; 'twas played with knives, by throwing
     so and so;
The loser had a task to do, there, forty years ago.

The river's running just as still; the willows on its side
Are larger than they were, Tom; the stream appears less
     wide;

But the grape-vine swing is ruined now, where once we
    played the beau,
And swung our sweethearts—pretty girls—just forty years
    ago.

The spring that bubbled 'neath the hill, close by the spread-
    ing beech,
Is very low—'twas then so high that we could scarcely
    reach;
And, kneeling down to get a drink, dear Tom, I started so,
To see how sadly I am changed since forty years ago.

Near by that spring, upon an elm, you know I cut your name,
Your sweetheart's just beneath it, Tom, and you did mine
    the same;
Some heartless wretch has peeled the bark, 'twas dying sure
    but slow,
Just as she died, whose name you cut, some forty years
    ago.

My lids have long been dry, Tom, but tears came to my
    eyes;
I thought of her I loved so well, those early broken ties;
I visited the old churchyard, and took some flowers to
    strow
Upon the graves of those we loved some forty years ago.

Some are in the churchyard laid, some sleep beneath the sea,
And none are left of our old class, excepting you and me;
But when our time shall come, Tom, and we are called to go,
I hope we'll meet with those we loved some forty years ago.

                                            Unknown
            [Sometimes called "Twenty Years Ago." Claimed
            for A. J. Gault (1818–1903) by his family]

                        BEN BOLT

Don't you remember sweet Alice, Ben Bolt,—
    Sweet Alice whose hair was so Brown,
Who wept with delight when you gave her a smile,
    And trembled with fear at your frown?

In the old churchyard in the valley, Ben Bolt,
    In a corner obscure and alone,
They have fitted a slab of the granite so gray,
    And Alice lies under the stone.

Under the hickory tree, Ben Bolt,
    Which stood at the foot of the hill,
Together we've lain in the noonday shade,
    And listened to Appleton's mill.
The mill-wheel has fallen to pieces, Ben Bolt,
    The rafters have tumbled in,
And a quiet which crawls round the walls as you gaze
    Has followed the olden din.

Do you mind of the cabin of logs, Ben Bolt.
    At the edge of the pathless wood,
And the button-ball tree with its motley limbs,
    Which nigh by the doorstep stood?
The cabin to ruin has gone, Ben Bolt,
    The tree you would seek for in vain;
And where once the lords of the forest waved
    Are grass and the golden grain.

And don't you remember the school, Ben Bolt,
    With the master so cruel and grim,
And the shaded nook in the running brook
    Where the children went to swim?
Grass grows on the master's grave, Ben Bolt,
    The spring of the brook is dry,
And of all the boys who were schoolmates then
    There are only you and I.

There is change in the things I loved, Ben Bolt,
    They have changed from the old to the new;
But I feel in the deeps of my spirit the truth,
    There never was change in you.
Twelvemonths twenty have passed, Ben Bolt,
    Since first we were friends—yet I hail
Your presence a blessing, your friendship a truth,
    Ben Bolt of the salt-sea gale.

Thomas Dunn English [1819–1902]

"BREAK, BREAK, BREAK"

BREAK, break, break,
　　On thy cold gray stones, O Sea!
And I would that my tongue could utter
　　The thoughts that arise in me.

O, well for the fisherman's boy,
　　That he shouts with his sister at play!
O, well for the sailor lad,
　　That he sings in his boat on the bay!

And the stately ships go on,
　　To their haven under the hill;
But O for the touch of a vanished hand,
　　And the sound of a voice that is still!

Break, break, break,
　　At the foot of thy crags, O Sea!
But the tender grace of a day that is dead
　　Will never come back to me.

　　　　　　　　Alfred Tennyson [1809–1892]

PART II

POEMS OF LOVE

EROS

THE sense of the world is short,—
Long and various the report,—
    To love and be beloved;
Men and gods have not outlearned it;
And, how oft soe'er they've turned it,
    'Tis not to be improved.

Ralph Waldo Emerson [1803–1882]

"NOW WHAT IS LOVE"

"NOW WHAT IS LOVE"

Now what is Love, I pray thee, tell?
  It is that fountain and that well
  Where pleasure and repentance dwell;
  It is, perhaps, the saucing bell
  That tolls all into heaven or hell;
  And this is Love, as I hear tell.

Yet what is Love, I prithee, say?
  It is a work on holiday,
  It is December matched with May,
  When lusty bloods in fresh array
  Hear ten months after of the play;
  And this is Love, as I hear say.

Yet what is Love, good shepherd, sain?
  It is a sunshine mixed with rain,
  It is a toothache or like pain,
  It is a game where none hath gain;
  The lass saith no, yet would full fain;
  And this is Love, as I hear sain.

Yet, shepherd, what is Love, I pray?
  It is a yes, it is a nay,
  A pretty kind of sporting fray,
  It is a thing will soon away.
  Then, nymphs, take vantage while ye may;
  And this is Love, as I hear say.

Yet what is Love, good shepherd, show?
  A thing that creeps, it cannot go,
  A prize that passeth to and fro,
  A thing for one, a thing for moe,
  And he that proves shall find it so;
  And shepherd, this is Love, I trow.

                    Walter Raleigh [1552?–1618]

WOOING SONG

From " Christ's Victory "

LOVE is the blossom where there blows
Every thing that lives or grows:
Love doth make the Heavens to move,
And the Sun doth burn in love:
Love the strong and weak doth yoke,
And makes the ivy climb the oak,
Under whose shadows lions wild,
Softened by love, grow tame and mild:
Love no medicine can appease,
He burns fishes in the seas:
Not all the skill his wounds can stench,
Not all the sea his fire can quench.
Love did make the bloody spear
Once a leavy coat to wear,
While in his leaves there shrouded lay
Sweet birds, for love that sing and play
And of all love's joyful flame
I the bud and blossom am.
        Only bend thy knee to me,
        Thy wooing shall thy winning be!

See, see the flowers that below
Now as fresh as morning blow;
And of all the virgin rose
That as bright Aurora shows;
How they all unleavèd die,
Losing their virginity!
Like unto a summer shade,
But now born, and now they fade.
Every thing doth pass away;
There is danger in delay:
Come, come, gather then the rose,
Gather it, or it you lose!
All the sand of Tagus' shore
Into my bosom casts his ore:
All the valleys' swimming corn
To my house is yearly borne:

Every grape of every vine
Is gladly bruised to make me wine:
While ten thousand kings, as proud,
To carry up my train have bowed,
And a world of ladies send me
In my chambers to attend me:
All the stars in Heaven that shine,
And ten thousand more, are mine:
    Only bend thy knee to me,
    Thy wooing shall thy winning be.

        Giles Fletcher [1549?–1611]

ROSALIND'S MADRIGAL

From " Rosalind"

LOVE in my bosom like a bee
    Doth suck his sweet:
Now with his wings he plays with me,
    Now with his feet.
Within mine eyes he makes his nest,
His bed amidst my tender breast;
My kisses are his daily feast,
And yet he robs me of my rest:
    Ah! wanton, will ye?

And if I sleep, then percheth he
    With pretty flight,
And makes his pillow of my knee
    The livelong night.
Strike I my lute, he tunes the string;
He music plays if so I sing;
He lends me every lovely thing,
Yet cruel he my heart doth sting:
    Whist, wanton, still ye!

Else I with roses every day
    Will whip you hence,
And bind you, when you long to play,
    For your offence.

I'll shut mine eyes to keep you in;
I'll make you fast it for your sin;
I'll count your power not worth a pin.
—Alas! what hereby shall I win
        If he gainsay me?

What if I beat the wanton boy
        With many a rod?
He will repay me with annoy,
        Because a god.
Then sit thou safely on my knee;
Then let thy bower my bosom be;
Lurk in mine eyes, I like of thee;
O Cupid, so thou pity me,
        Spare not, but play thee!

                    Thomas Lodge [1558?–1625]

SONG

From "Hymen's Triumph"

LOVE is a sickness full of woes,
    All remedies refusing;
A plant that with most cutting grows,
    Most barren with best using.
            Why so?
More we enjoy it, more it dies;
If not enjoyed, it sighing cries—
            Heigh ho!

Love is a torment of the mind,
    A tempest everlasting;
And Jove hath made it of a kind
    Not well, nor full nor fasting.
            Why so?
More we enjoy it, more it dies;
If not enjoyed, it sighing cries—
            Heigh ho!

                    Samuel Daniel [1562–1619]

LOVE'S PERJURIES

From "Love's Labor's Lost"

ON a day, alack the day!
Love, whose month is ever May,
Spied a blossom passing fair
Playing in the wanton air:
Through the velvet leaves the wind,
All unseen, 'gan passage find;
That the lover, sick to death,
Wished himself the heaven's breath.
Air, quoth he, thy cheeks may blow;
Air, would I might triumph so!
But, alack, my hand is sworn
Ne'er to pluck thee from thy thorn:
Vow, alack, for youth unmeet;
Youth so apt to pluck a sweet.
Do not call it sin in me
That I am forsworn for thee:
Thou for whom e'en Jove would swear
Juno but an Ethiope were,
And deny himself for Jove,
Turning mortal for thy love.

William Shakespeare [1564–1616]

VENUS' RUNAWAY

From "The Hue and Cry After Cupid"

BEAUTIES, have ye seen this toy,
Callèd Love, a little boy,
Almost naked, wanton, blind;
Cruel now, and then as kind?
If he be amongst ye, say?
He is Venus' runaway.

She that will but now discover
Where the wingèd wag doth hover,
Shall to-night receive a kiss,
How or where herself would wish:

But who brings him to his mother,
Shall have that kiss, and another.

He hath marks about him plenty:
You shall know him among twenty.
All his body is a fire,
And his breath a flame entire,
That, being shot like lightning in,
Wounds the heart, but not the skin.

At his sight, the sun hath turned,
Neptune in the waters burned;
Hell hath felt a greater heat;
Jove himself forsook his seat:
From the centre to the sky,
Are his trophies rearèd high.

Wings he hath, which though ye clip,
He will leap from lip to lip,
Over liver, lights, and heart,
But not stay in any part;
But if chance his arrow misses,
He will shoot himself in kisses.

He doth bear a golden bow,
And a quiver, hanging low,
Full of arrows, that outbrave
Dian's shafts; where, if he have
Any head more sharp than other,
With that first he strikes his mother.

Still the fairest are his fuel.
When his days are to be cruel,
Lovers' hearts are all his food,
And his baths their warmest blood:
Naught but wounds his hands doth season,
And he hates none like to Reason.

Trust him not; his words, though sweet,
Seldom with his heart do meet.

All his practice is deceit;
Every gift it is a bait;
Not a kiss but poison bears;
And most treason in his tears.

Idle minutes are his reign;
Then, the straggler makes his gain
By presenting maids with toys,
And would have ye think them joys:
'Tis the ambition of the elf
To have all childish as himself.

If by these ye please to know him,
Beauties, be not nice, but show him.
Though ye had a will to hide him,
Now, we hope, ye'll not abide him;
Since you hear his falser play,
And that he's Venus' runaway.

Ben Jonson [1573?-1637]

WHAT IS LOVE?

From " The Captain "

TELL me, dearest, what is love?
'Tis a lightning from above;
'Tis an arrow, 'tis a fire,
'Tis a boy they call Desire.
    'Tis a grave,
    Gapes to have
Those poor fools that long to prove.

Tell me more, are women true?
Yes, some are, and some as you.
Some are willing, some are strange,
Since you men first taught to change.
    And till troth
    Be in both,
All shall love, to love anew.

Tell me more yet, can they grieve?
Yes, and sicken sore, but live,
And be wise, and delay,
When you men are wise as they.
    Then I see,
      Faith will be
Never till they both believe.

John Fletcher [1579–1625]

LOVE'S EMBLEMS

From "Valentinian"

Now the lusty spring is seen;
  Golden yellow, gaudy blue,
  Daintily invite the view:
Everywhere on every green
Roses blushing as they blow,
  And enticing men to pull,
Lilies whiter than the snow,
  Woodbines of sweet honey full:
    All love's emblems, and all cry,
    "Ladies, if not plucked, we die."

Yet the lusty spring hath stayed;
  Blushing red and purest white
  Daintily to love invite
Every woman, every maid:
Cherries kissing as they grow,
  And inviting men to taste,
Apples even ripe below,
  Winding gently to the waist:
    All love's emblems, and all cry,
    "Ladies, if not plucked, we die."

John Fletcher [1579–1625]

THE POWER OF LOVE

From "Valentinian"

HEAR, ye ladies that despise
  What the mighty Love has done;
Fear examples and be wise:
  Fair Callisto was a nun;

Leda, sailing on the stream
  To deceive the hopes of man,
Love accounting but a dream,
    Doted on a silver swan;
      Danaë, in a brazen tower,
       Where no love was, loved a shower.

Hear, ye ladies that are coy,
  What the mighty Love can do;
Fear the fierceness of the boy:
  The chaste Moon he makes to woo;
Vesta, kindling holy fires,
  Circled round about with spies,
Never dreaming loose desires,
    Doting at the altar dies;
      Ilion, in a short hour, higher
       He can build, and once more fire.

John Fletcher [1579-1625]

ADVICE TO A LOVER

THE sea hath many thousand sands,
The sun hath motes as many;
The sky is full of stars, and Love
As full of woes as any:
Believe me, that do know the elf,
And make no trial by thyself!

It is in truth a pretty toy
For babes to play withal:
But O, the honies of our youth
Are oft our age's gall:
Self-proof in time will make thee know
He was a prophet told thee so:

A prophet that, Cassandra-like,
Tells truth without belief;
For headstrong Youth will run his race,
Although his goal be grief:—
Love's Martyr, when his heat is past,
Proves Care's Confessor at the last.

Unknown

LOVE'S HOROSCOPE

Love, brave Virtue's younger brother,
Erst hath made my heart a mother,
She consults the anxious spheres,
To calculate her young son's years;
She asks if sad or saving powers
Gave omen to his infant hours;
She asks each star that then stood by
If poor Love shall live or die.

Ah, my heart! is that the way?
Are these the beams that rule thy day?
Thou know'st a face in whose each look
Beauty lays ope Love's fortune-book,
On whose fair revolutions wait
The obsequious motions of Love's fate.
Ah, my heart! her eyes and she
Have taught thee new astrology.
Howe'er Love's native hours were set,
Whatever starry synod met,
'Tis in the mercy of her eye,
If poor Love shall live or die.

If those sharp rays, putting on
Points of death, bid Love be gone;—
Though the heavens in council sate
To crown an uncontrollèd fate;
Though their best aspects twined upon
The kindest constellation,
Cast amorous glances on its birth,
And whispered the confederate earth
To pave his paths with all the good
That warms the bed of youth and blood:—
Love has no plea against her eye;
Beauty frowns, and Love must die.

But if her milder influence move,
And gild the hopes of humble Love;—
Though heaven's inauspicious eye
Lay black on Love's nativity;

Though every diamond in Jove's crown
Fixed his forehead to a frown;—
Her eye a strong appeal can give,
Beauty smiles, and Love shall live.

O, if Love shall live, O where,
But in her eye, or in her ear,
In her breast, or in her breath,
Shall I hide poor Love from death?
For in the life aught else can give,
Love shall die, although he live.

Or, if Love shall die, O where,
But in her eye, or in her ear,
In her breath, or in her breast,
Shall I build his funeral nest?
While Love shall thus entombèd lie,
Love shall live, although he die!

Richard Crashaw [1613?–1649]

"AH, HOW SWEET IT IS TO LOVE!"

From "Tyrannic Love"

Ah, how sweet it is to love!
    Ah, how gay is young Desire!
And what pleasing pains we prove
    When we first approach Love's fire!
Pains of Love be sweeter far
Than all other pleasures are.

Sighs which are from lovers blown
    Do but gently heave the heart:
Even the tears they shed alone
    Cure, like trickling balm, their smart:
Lovers, when they lose their breath,
Bleed away in easy death.

Love and Time with reverence use,
    Treat them like a parting friend;
Nor the golden gifts refuse
    Which in youth sincere they send:

For each year their price is more,
And they less simple than before.

Love, like spring-tides full and high,
   Swells in every youthful vein;
But each tide does less supply,
   Till they quite shrink in again:
If a flow in age appear,
'Tis but rain, and runs not clear.

John Dryden [1631-1700]

SONG

LOVE still has something of the sea,
   From whence his Mother rose;
No time his slaves from doubt can free,
   Nor give their thoughts repose.

They are becalmed in clearest days,
   And in rough weather tossed;
They wither under cold delays,
   Or are in tempests lost.

One while they seem to touch the port,
   Then straight into the main
Some angry wind, in cruel sport,
   The vessel drives again.

At first Disdain and Pride they fear,
   Which if they chance to 'scape,
Rivals and Falsehood soon appear,
   In a more dreadful shape.

By such degrees to joy they come,
   And are so long withstood,
So slowly they receive the sum,
   It hardly does them good.

'Tis cruel to prolong a pain;
   And to defer a joy,
Believe me, gentle Celemene,
   Offends the wingèd boy.

An hundred thousand oaths your fears,
    Perhaps, would not remove;
And if I gazed a thousand years,
    I could no deeper love.
                        Charles Sedley [1639?–1710]

THE VINE
From "Sunday Up the River"

THE wine of Love is music,
    And the feast of Love is song:
And when Love sits down to the banquet,
    Love sits long:

Sits long and arises drunken,
    But not with the feast and the wine;
He reeleth with his own heart,
    That great, rich Vine.
                        James Thomson [1834–1882]

SONG

FAIN would I change that note
    To which fond love hath charmed me,
Long, long to sing by rote,
    Fancying that that harmed me:
Yet when this thought doth come,—
Love is the perfect sum
    Of all delight.
I have no other choice
Either for pen or voice
    To sing or write.

O love, they wrong thee much
    That say thy sweet is bitter
When thy rich fruit is such
    As nothing can be sweeter.
Fair house of joy and bliss
Where truest pleasure is,
    I do adore thee:
I know thee what thou art,
I serve thee with my heart,
    And fall before thee.
                        Unknown

CUPID STUNG

CUPID once upon a bed
Of roses laid his weary head;
Luckless urchin, not to see
Within the leaves a slumbering bee.
The bee awaked—with anger wild
The bee awaked, and stung the child.
Loud and piteous are his cries;
To Venus quick he runs, he flies;
"Oh Mother! I am wounded through—
I die with pain—in sooth I do!
Stung by some little angry thing,
Some serpent on a tiny wing—
A bee it was—for once, I know,
I heard a rustic call it so."
Thus he spoke, and she the while
Heard him with a soothing smile;
Then said, "My infant, if so much
Thou feel the little wild bee's touch,
How must the heart, ah, Cupid! be,
The hapless heart that's stung by thee!"

                              Thomas Moore [1779–1852]

CUPID DROWNED

T'OTHER day, as I was twining
Roses, for a crown to dine in,
What, of all things, 'mid the heap,
Should I light on, fast asleep,
But the little desperate elf,
The tiny traitor, Love, himself!
By the wings I picked him up
Like a bee, and in a cup
Of my wine I plunged and sank him,
Then what d'ye think I did?—I drank him.
Faith, I thought him dead. Not he!
There he lives with ten-fold glee;

And now this moment with his wings
I feel him tickling my heart-strings.

Leigh Hunt [1784–1859]

SONG

From "The Heir of Vironi"

Oh! say not woman's love is bought
  With vain and empty treasure.
Oh! say not woman's heart is caught
  By every idle pleasure.
When first her gentle bosom knows
  Love's flame, it wanders never;
Deep in her heart the passion glows,
  She loves, and loves for ever.

Oh! say not woman's false as fair,
  That, like the bee, she ranges,
Still seeking flowers more sweet and rare,
  As fickle fancy changes.
Ah no! the love that first can warm
  Will leave her bosom never;
No second passion e'er can charm,
  She loves, and loves for ever.

Isaac Pocock [1782–1835]

"IN THE DAYS OF OLD"

From "Crotchet Castle"

In the days of old
Lovers felt true passion,
Deeming years of sorrow
By a smile repaid:
Now the charms of gold,
Spells of pride and fashion,
Bid them say Good-morrow
To the best-loved Maid.

Through the forests wild,
O'er the mountains lonely,
They were never weary
Honor to pursue:

If the damsel smiled
Once in seven years only,
All their wanderings dreary
Ample guerdon knew.

Now one day's caprice
Weighs down years of smiling,
Youthful hearts are rovers,
Love is bought and sold.
Fortune's gifts may cease,
Love is less beguiling:
Wiser were the lovers
In the days of old.

Thomas Love Peacock [1785–1866]

SONG

How delicious is the winning
Of a kiss at Love's beginning,
When two mutual hearts are sighing
For the knot there's no untying!

Yet remember, 'midst your wooing,
Love has bliss, but Love has ruing;
Other smiles may make you fickle,
Tears for other charms may trickle.

Love he comes, and Love he tarries,
Just as fate or fancy carries;
Longest stays, when sorest chidden;
Laughs and flies, when pressed and bidden.

Bind the sea to slumber stilly,
Bind its odor to the lily,
Bind the aspen ne'er to quiver,
Then bind Love to last forever!

Love's a fire that needs renewal
Of fresh beauty for its fuel:
Love's wing moults when caged and captured,
Only free, he soars enraptured.

Can you keep the bee from ranging,
Or the ringdove's neck from changing?
No! nor fettered Love from dying
In the knot there's no untying.

Thomas Campbell [1777–1844]

STANZAS

COULD Love for ever
Run like a river,
And Time's endeavor
  Be tried in vain—
No other pleasure
With this could measure.
And like a treasure
  We'd hug the chain.
But since our sighing
Ends not in dying,
And, formed for flying,
  Love plumes his wing;
Then for this reason
Let's love a season;
But let that season
  Be only Spring.

When lovers parted
Feel broken-hearted,
And, all hopes thwarted,
  Expect to die;
A few years older,
Ah! how much colder
They might behold her
  For whom they sigh!
When linked together,
In every weather,
They pluck Love's feather
  From out his wing—
He'll stay for ever,
But sadly shiver

Without his plumage,
When past the Spring.

Like Chiefs of Faction,
His life is action—
A formal paction
    That curbs his reign,
Obscures his glory,
Despot no more, he
Such territory
    Quits with disdain.
Still, still advancing,
With banners glancing,
His power enhancing,
    He must move on—
Repose but cloys him,
Retreat destroys him,
Love brooks not a
    Degraded throne.

Wait not, fond lover!
Till years are over,
And then recover,
    As from a dream.
While each bewailing
The other's failing,
With wrath and railing,
    All hideous seem—
While first decreasing,
Yet not quite ceasing,
Wait not till teasing
    All passion blight:
If once diminished
Love's reign is finished—
Then part in friendship,—
    And bid good-night.

So shall Affection
To recollection
The dear connection

Bring back with joy:
You had not waited
Till, tired or hated,
Your passions sated
    Began to cloy.
Your last embraces
Leave no cold traces—
The same fond faces
    As through the past;
And eyes, the mirrors
Of your sweet errors,
Reflect but rapture—
    Not least though last.

True, separations
Ask more than patience;
What desperations
    From such have risen!
But yet remaining,
What is 't but chaining
Hearts which, once waning,
    Beat 'gainst their prison?
Time can but cloy love,
And use destroy love:
The wingèd boy, Love,
    Is but for boys—
You 'll find it torture
Though sharper, shorter,
To wean and not
    Wear out your joys.

George Gordon Byron [1788-1824]

"THEY SPEAK O' WILES"

THEY speak o' wiles in woman's smiles,
    An' ruin in her ee;
I ken they bring a pang at whiles
    That's unco' sair to dree;

But mind ye this, the half-ta'en kiss,
  The first fond fa'in' tear,
Is, heaven kens, fu' sweet amends,
  An' tints o' heaven here.

When two leal hearts in fondness meet,
  Life's tempests howl in vain;
The very tears o' love are sweet
  When paid with tears again.

Shall hapless prudence shake its pow?
  Shall cauldrife caution fear?
Oh, dinna, dinna droun the lowe
  That lights a heaven here!

William Thom [1798?–1848]

"LOVE WILL FIND OUT THE WAY"

OVER the mountains
  And over the waves,
Under the fountains
  And under the graves,
Under floods that are deepest,
  Which Neptune obey,
Over rocks that are steepest,
  Love will find out the way.

Where there is no place
  For the glow-worm to lie,
Where there is no space
  For receipt of a fly,
Where the midge dares not venture,
  Lest herself fast she lay,
If Love come, he will enter,
  And find out the way.

You may esteem him
  A child for his might,
Or you may deem him
  A coward from his flight:

But if she whom Love doth honor
    Be concealed from the day,
Set a thousand guards upon her,
    Love will find out the way.

Some think to lose him,
    By having him confined,
And some do suppose him,
    Poor thing, to be blind;
But if ne'er so close ye wall him,
    Do the best that you may,
Blind Love, if so ye call him,
    Will find out the way.

You may train the eagle
    To stoop to your fist,
Or you may inveigle
    The phoenix of the east;
The tiger, ye may move her
    To give over her prey;
But you'll ne'er stop a lover—
    He will find out the way.

Unknown

A WOMAN'S SHORTCOMINGS

She has laughed as softly as if she sighed,
    She has counted six, and over,
Of a purse well filled, and a heart well tried—
    Oh, each a worthy lover!
They "give her time"; for her soul must slip
    Where the world has set the grooving;
She will lie to none with her fair red lip:
    But love seeks truer loving.

She trembles her fan in a sweetness dumb,
    As her thoughts were beyond recalling;
With a glance for *one*, and a glance for *some*,
    From her eyelids rising and falling;

Speaks common words with a blushful air,
　Hears bold words, unreproving;
But her silence says—what she never will swear—
　And love seeks better loving.

Go, lady! lean to the night-guitar,
　And drop a smile to the bringer;
Then smile as sweetly, when he is far,
　At the voice of an in-door singer.
Bask tenderly beneath tender eyes;
　Glance lightly, on their removing;
And join new vows to old perjuries—
　But dare not call it loving!

Unless you can think, when the song is done,
　No other is soft in the rhythm;
Unless you can feel, when left by One,
　That all men else go with him;
Unless you can know, when unpraised by his breath,
　That your beauty itself wants proving;
Unless you can swear "For life, for death!"—
　Oh, fear to call it loving!

Unless you can muse in a crowd all day
　On the absent face that fixed you;
Unless you can love, as the angels may,
　With the breadth of heaven betwixt you;
Unless you can dream that his faith is fast,
　Through behoving and unbehoving;
Unless you can *die* when the dream is past—
　Oh, never call it loving!
　　　　　Elizabeth Barrett Browning [1806–1861]

"LOVE HATH A LANGUAGE"
From "To My Son"

Love hath a language for all years—
　Fond hieroglyphs, obscure and old—
Wherein the heart reads, writ in tears,
　The tale which never yet was told.

Love hath his meter too, to trace
  Those bounds which never yet were given,—
To measure that which mocks at space,
  Is deep as death, and high as heaven.

Love hath his treasure hoards, to pay
  True faith, or goodly service done,—
Dear priceless nothings, which outweigh
  All riches that the sun shines on.

       Helen Selina Sheridan [1807–1867]

SONG

From " Maud "

O, LET the solid ground,
  Not fail beneath my feet
Before my life has found
  What some have found so sweet;
Then let come what come may,
What matter if I go mad,
I shall have had my day.

Let the sweet heavens endure,
  Not close and darken above me
Before I am quite quite sure
  That there is one to love me!
Then let come what come may
To a life that has been so sad,
I shall have had my day.

       Alfred Tennyson [1809–1892]

AMATURUS

SOMEWHERE beneath the sun,
  These quivering heart-strings prove it,
Somewhere there must be one
  Made for this soul to move it;

Some one that hides her sweetness
    From neighbors whom she slights,
Nor can attain completeness,
    Nor give her heart its rights;
Some one whom I could court
    With no great change of manner,
Still holding reason's fort,
    Though waving fancy's banner;
A lady, not so queenly
    As to disdain my hand,
Yet born to smile serenely
    Like those that rule the land;
Noble, but not too proud;
    With soft hair simply folded,
And bright face crescent-browed,
    And throat by Muses moulded;
And eyelids lightly falling
    On little glistening seas,
Deep-calm, when gales are brawling,
    Though stirred by every breeze;
Swift voice, like flight of dove
    Through minster-arches floating,
With sudden turns, when love
    Gets overnear to doting;
Keen lips, that shape soft sayings
    Like crystals of the snow,
With pretty half-betrayings
    Of things one may not know;
Fair hand whose touches thrill,
    Like golden rod of wonder,
Which Hermes wields at will
    Spirit and flesh to sunder;
Light foot, to press the stirrup
    In fearlessness and glee,
Or dance, till finches chirrup,
    And stars sink to the sea.

Forth, Love, and find this maid,
    Wherever she be hidden:
Speak, Love, be not afraid,
    But plead as thou art bidden;

And say, that he who taught thee
    His yearning want and pain,
Too dearly, dearly bought thee
    To part with thee in vain.
                    William Johnson-Cory [1823–1892]

THE SURFACE AND THE DEPTHS

LOVE took my life and thrilled it
    Through all its strings,
Played round my mind and filled it
    With sound of wings;
But to my heart he never came
To touch it with his golden flame.

Therefore it is that singing
    I do rejoice,
Nor heed the slow years bringing
    A harsher voice;
Because the songs which he has sung
Still leave the untouched singer young.

But whom in fuller fashion
    The Master sways,
For him, swift-winged with passion,
    Fleet the brief days.
Betimes the enforced accents come,
And leave him ever after dumb.
                    Lewis Morris [1833–1907]

A BALLAD OF DREAMLAND

I HID my heart in a nest of roses,
    Out of the sun's way, hidden apart;
In a softer bed then the soft white snow's is,
    Under the roses I hid my heart.
    Why would it sleep not? why should it start,
When never a leaf of the rose-tree stirred?
    What made sleep flutter his wings and part?
Only the song of a secret bird.

Lie still, I said, for the wind's wing closes,
    And mild leaves muffle the keen sun's dart;
Lie still, for the wind on the warm seas dozes,
    And the wind is unquieter yet than thou art.
    Does a thought in thee still as a thorn's wound smart?
Does the fang still fret thee of hope deferred?
    What bids the lips of thy sleep dispart?
Only the song of a secret bird.

The green land's name that a charm encloses,
    It never was writ in the traveller's chart,
And sweet on its trees as the fruit that grows is,
    It never was sold in the merchant's mart.
    The swallows of dreams through its dim fields dart,
And sleep's are the tunes in its tree-tops heard;
    No hound's note wakens the wildwood hart,
Only the song of a secret bird.

ENVOI

In the world of dreams I have chosen my part,
    To sleep for a season and hear no word
Of true love's truth or of light love's art,
    Only the song of a secret bird.
                    Algernon Charles Swinburne [1837–1909]

ENDYMION

THE rising moon has hid the stars;
Her level rays, like golden bars,
        Lie on the landscape green,
        With shadows brown between.

And silver white the river gleams,
As if Diana, in her dreams
        Had dropped her silver bow
        Upon the meadows low.

On such a tranquil night as this,
She woke Endymion with a kiss,
　　When, sleeping in the grove,
　　He dreamed not of her love.

Like Dian's kiss, unasked, unsought,
Love gives itself, but is not bought;
　　Nor voice, nor sound betrays
　　Its deep, impassioned gaze.

It comes,—the beautiful, the free,
The crown of all humanity,—
　　In silence and alone
　　To seek the elected one.

It lifts the boughs, whose shadows deep
Are life's oblivion, the soul's sleep,
　　And kisses the closed eyes
　　Of him who slumbering lies.

O weary hearts! O slumbering eyes!
O drooping souls, whose destinies
　　Are fraught with fear and pain,
　　Ye shall be loved again!

No one is so accursed by fate,
No one so utterly desolate,
　　But some heart, though unknown,
　　Responds unto his own.

Responds,—as if with unseen wings,
An angel touched its quivering strings;
　　And whispers, in its song,
　　"Where hast thou stayed so long?"
　　　　Henry Wadsworth Longfellow [1807–1882]

FATE

Two shall be born, the whole wide world apart,
And speak in different tongues and have no thought
Each of the other's being, and no heed.
And these, o'er unknown seas, to unknown lands
Shall cross, escaping wreck, defying death;
And all unconsciously shape every act
And bend each wandering step to this one end—
That, one day, out of darkness they shall meet
And read life's meaning in each other's eyes.

And two shall walk some narrow way of life
So nearly side by side that, should one turn
Ever so little space to left or right,
They needs must stand acknowledged, face to face.
And, yet, with wistful eyes that never meet
And groping hands that never clasp and lips
Calling in vain to ears that never hear,
They seek each other all their weary days
And die unsatisfied—and this is Fate!

Susan Marr Spalding [1841-1908]

"GIVE ALL TO LOVE"

GIVE all to love;
Obey thy heart;
Friends, kindred, days,
Estate, good fame,
Plans, credit, and the Muse,—
Nothing refuse.

'Tis a brave master;
Let it have scope:
Follow it utterly,
Hope beyond hope:
High and more high

It dives into noon,
With wing unspent,
Untold intent;
But it is a god,
Knows its own path
And the outlets of the sky.

It was never for the mean;
It requireth courage stout.
Souls above doubt,
Valor unbending,
It will reward,—
They shall return
More than they were,
And ever ascending.

Leave all for love;
Yet, hear me, yet,
One word more thy heart behoved,
One pulse more of firm endeavor,—
Keep thee to-day,
To-morrow, forever,
Free as an Arab
Of thy beloved.

Cling with life to the maid;
But when the surprise,
First vague shadow of surmise,
Flits across her bosom young,
Of a joy apart from thee,
Free be she, fancy-free;
Nor thou detain her vesture's hem,
Nor the palest rose she flung
From her summer diadem.

Though thou loved her as thyself,
As a self of purer clay,
Though her parting dims the day,
Stealing grace from all alive;

Heartily know,
When half-gods go,
The gods arrive.
Ralph Waldo Emerson [1803–1882]

"O, LOVE IS NOT A SUMMER MOOD"

O, LOVE is not a summer mood,
    Nor flying phantom of the brain,
Nor youthful fever of the blood,
        Nor dream, nor fate, nor circumstance.
        Love is not born of blinded chance,
        Nor bred in simple ignorance.

Love is the flower of maidenhood;
    Love is the fruit of mortal pain;
And she hath winter in her blood.
        True love is steadfast as the skies,
        And once alight, she never flies;
        And love is strong, and love is wise.
Richard Watson Gilder [1844–1909]

WHEN WILL LOVE COME?

SOME find Love late, some find him soon,
    Some with the rose in May,
Some with the nightingale in June,
    And some when skies are gray;
Love comes to some with smiling eyes,
    And comes with tears to some;
For some Love sings, for some Love sighs,
    For some Love's lips are dumb.

How will you come to me, fair Love?
    Will you come late or soon?
With sad or smiling skies above,
    By light of sun or moon?

Will you be sad, will you be sweet,
  Sing, sigh, Love, or be dumb?
Will it be summer when we meet,
  Or autumn ere you come?
            Pakenham Beatty [1855-

"AWAKE, MY HEART"

AWAKE, my heart, to be loved, awake, awake!
The darkness silvers away, the morn doth break,
It leaps in the sky: unrisen lustres slake
The o'ertaken moon. Awake, O heart, awake!

She too that loveth awaketh and hopes for thee:
Her eyes already have sped the shades that flee,
Already they watch the path thy feet shall take:
Awake, O heart, to be loved, awake, awake!

And if thou tarry from her,—if this could be,—
She cometh herself, O heart, to be loved, to thee;
For thee would unashamèd herself forsake:
Awake, to be loved, my heart, awake, awake!

Awake! The land is scattered with light, and see,
Uncanopied sleep is flying from field and tree;
And blossoming boughs of April in laughter shake:
Awake, O heart, to be loved, awake, awake!

Lo, all things wake and tarry and look for thee:
She looketh and saith, "O sun, now bring him to me.
Come, more adored, O adored, for his coming's sake,
And awake, my heart, to be loved, awake, awake!"
            Robert Bridges [1844-1930]

THE SECRET

NIGHTINGALES warble about it
  All night under blossom and star;
The wild swan is dying without it,
  And the eagle crieth afar;

The sun, he doth mount but to find it,
　　Searching the green earth o'er;
But more doth a man's heart mind it—
　　O more, more, more!

Over the gray leagues of ocean
　　The infinite yearneth alone;
The forests with wandering emotion
　　The thing they know not intone;
Creation arose but to see it,
　　A million lamps in the blue;
But a lover, he shall be it,
　　If one sweet maid is true.

George Edward Woodberry [1855–1930]

THE ROSE OF STARS

When Love, our great Immortal,
　　Put on mortality,
And down from Eden's portal
　　Brought this sweet life to be,
At the sublime archangel
　　He laughed with veilèd eyes,
For he bore within his bosom
　　The seed of Paradise.

He hid it in his bosom,
　　And there such warmth it found,
It brake in bud and blossom,
　　And the rose fell on the ground;
As the green light on the prairie,
　　As the red light on the sea,
Through fragrant belts of summer
　　Came this sweet life to be.

And the grave archangel seeing,
　　Spread his mighty wings for flight,
But the glow hung round him fleeing
　　Like the rose of an Arctic night;

And sadly moving heavenward
  By Venus and by Mars,
He heard the joyful planets
  Hail Earth, the Rose of Stars.
                    George Edward Woodberry [1855–1930]

SONG OF EROS

From " Agathon "

WHEN love in the faint heart trembles,
  And the eyes with tears are wet,
O, tell me what resembles
  Thee, young Regret?
Violets with dewdrops drooping,
  Lilies o'erfull of gold,
Roses in June rains stooping,
  That weep for the cold,
Are like thee, young Regret.

Bloom, violets, lilies, and roses!
  But what, young Desire,
Like thee, when love discloses
  Thy heart of fire?
The wild swan unreturning,
  The eagle alone with the sun,
The long-winged storm-gulls burning
  Seaward when day is done,
Are like thee, young Desire.
                    George Edward Woodberry [1855-1930]

LOVE IS STRONG

A VIEWLESS thing is the wind,
  But its strength is mightier far
Than a phalanxed host in battle line,
  Than the limbs of a Samson are.

And a viewless thing is Love,
　　And a name that vanisheth;
But her strength is the wind's wild strength above,
　　For she conquers shame and Death.

Richard Burton [1861–1940]

'LOVE ONCE WAS LIKE AN APRIL DAWN"

LOVE once was like an April dawn:
　　Song throbbed within the heart by rote,
And every tint of rose or fawn
　　Was greeted by a joyous note.
　　　　How eager was my thought to see
　　　　Into that morning mystery!

Love now is like an August noon,
　　No spot is empty of its shine;
The sun makes silence seem a boon,
　　And not a voice so dumb as mine.
　　　　Yet with what words I'd welcome thee—
　　　　Couldst thou return, dear mystery!

Robert Underwood Johnson [1853–1937]

THE GARDEN OF SHADOW

LOVE heeds no more the sighing of the wind
Against the perfect flowers: thy garden's close
Is grown a wilderness, where none shall find
One strayed, last petal of one last year's rose.

O bright, bright hair! O mouth like a ripe fruit!
Can famine be so nigh to harvesting?
Love, that was songful, with a broken lute
In grass of graveyards goeth murmuring.

Let the wind blow against the perfect flowers,
And all thy garden change and glow with spring:
Love is grown blind with no more count of hours
Nor part in seed-time nor in harvesting.

Ernest Dowson [1867–1900]

THE CALL

LOVE comes laughing up the valleys,
    Hand in hand with hoyden Spring;
All the Flower-People nodding,
    All the Feathered-Folk a-wing.

"Higher! Higher!" call the thrushes;
    "Wilder! Freer!" breathe the trees;
And the purple mountains beckon
    Upward to their mysteries.

Always farther leagues to wander,
    Peak to peak and slope to slope;
Lips to sing and feet to follow,
    Eyes to dream and heart to hope!

Tarry? Nay, but who can tarry?
    All the world is on the wing;
Love comes laughing up the valleys,
    Hand in hand with hoyden Spring.
                    Reginald Wright Kauffman [1877–

THE HIGHWAY

ALL day long on the highway
The King's fleet couriers ride;
    You may hear the tread of their horses sped
Over the country side.
    They ride for life and they ride for death
    And they override who tarrieth.
With show of color and flush of pride
They stir the dust on the highway.

Let them ride on the highway wide.
Love walks in little paths aside.

All day long on the highway
Is a tramp of an army's feet;
    You may see them go in a marshaled row

With the tale of their arms complete:
   They march for war and they march for peace,
   For the lust of gold and fame's increase,
For victories sadder than defeat
They raise the dust on the highway.

All the armies of earth defied,
Love dwells in little paths aside.

All day long on the highway
Rushes an eager band,
   With straining eyes for a worthless prize
That slips from the grasp like sand.
   And men leave blood where their feet have stood
   And bow them down unto brass and wood—
Idols fashioned by their own hand—
Blind in the dust of the highway.

Power and gold and fame denied,
Love laughs glad in the paths aside.

Louise Driscoll [1875–

SONG

   Take it, love!
   'Twill soon be over,
   With the thickening of the clover,
   With the calling of the plover,
   Take it, take it, lover.

   Take it, boy!
   The blossom's falling,
   And the farewell cuckoo's calling,
   While the sun and showers are one,
   Take your love out in the sun.

   Take it, girl!
   And fear no after,
   Take your fill of all this laughter,
   Laugh or not, the tears will fall,
   Take the laughter first of all.

Richard Le Gallienne [1866–

"NEVER GIVE ALL THE HEART"

NEVER give all the heart, for love
Will hardly seem worth thinking of
To passionate women, if it seem
Certain, and they never dream
That it fades out from kiss to kiss;
For everything that's lovely is
But a brief, dreamy, kind delight.
O never give the heart outright
For they, for all smooth lips can say,
Have given their hearts up to the play,
And who can play it well enough
If deaf and dumb and blind with love?
He that made this knows all the cost,
For he gave all his heart and lost.

William Butler Yeats [1865-1939]

SONG

I CAME to the door of the House of Love
  And knocked as the starry night went by;
And my true love cried "Who knocks?" and I said
  "It is I."

And Love looked down from a lattice above
  Where the roses were dry as the lips of the dead:
"There is not room in the House of Love
  For you both," he said.

I plucked a leaf from the porch and crept
  Away through a desert of scoffs and scorns
To a lonely place where I prayed and wept
  And wove me a crown of thorns.

I came once more to the House of Love
  And knocked, ah, softly and wistfully,
And my true love cried "Who knocks?" and I said
  "None now but thee."

And the great doors opened wide apart
    And a voice rang out from a glory of light,
"Make room, make room for a faithful heart
    In the House of Love, to-night."

Alfred Noyes [1880–

"CHILD, CHILD"

CHILD, child, love while you can
The voice and the eyes and the soul of a man,
Never fear though it break your heart—
Out of the wound new joy will start;
Only love proudly and gladly and well
Though love be heaven or love be hell.

Child, child, love while you may,
For life is short as a happy day;
Never fear the thing you feel—
Only by love is life made real;
Love, for the deadly sins are seven,
Only through love will you enter heaven.

Sara Teasdale [1884–1933]

WISDOM

THE young girl questions: "Whether were it better
To lie for ever, a warm slug-a-bed,
Or to rise up and bide by Fate and Chance,
    The rawness of the morning,
    The gibing and the scorning
Of the stern Teacher of my ignorance?"
    "I know not," Wisdom said.

The young girl questions: "Friend, shall I die calmer,
If I've lain for ever, sheets above the head,
Warm in a dream, or rise to take the worst
    Of peril in the highways
    Of straying in the by-ways,
Of hunger for the truth, of drought and thirst?"
    "We do not know," he said,
    "Nor may till we be dead."

Ford Madox Ford [1873–

EPILOGUE

FROM "EMBLEMS OF LOVE"

WHAT shall we do for Love these days?
How shall we make an altar-blaze
To smite the horny eyes of men
With the renown of our Heaven,
And to the unbelievers prove
Our service to our dear god, Love?
What torches shall we lift above
The crowd that pushes through the mire,
To amaze the dark heads with strange fire?
I should think I were much to blame,
If never I held some fragrant flame
Above the noises of the world,
And openly 'mid men's hurrying stares,
Worshipped before the sacred fears
That are like flashing curtains furled
Across the presence of our lord Love.
Nay, would that I could fill the gaze
Of the whole earth with some great praise
Made in a marvel for men's eyes,
Some tower of glittering masonries,
Therein such a spirit flourishing
Men should see what my heart can sing:
All that Love hath done to me
Built into stone, a visible glee;
Marble carried to gleaming height
As moved aloft by inward delight;
Not as with toil of chisels hewn,
But seeming poised in a mighty tune.
For of all those who have been known
To lodge with our kind host, the sun,
I envy one for just one thing:
In Cordova of the Moors
There dwelt a passion-minded King,
Who set great bands of marble-hewers
To fashion his heart's thanksgiving
In a tall palace, shapen so

All the wondering world might know
The joy he had of his Moorish lass.
His love, that brighter and larger was
Than the starry places, into firm stone
He sent, as if the stone were glass
Fired and into beauty blown.

   Solemn and invented gravely
In its bulk the fabric stood,
Even as Love, that trusteth bravely
In its own exceeding good
To be better than the waste
Of time's devices; grandly spaced,
Seriously the fabric stood.
But over it all a pleasure went
Of carven delicate ornament,
Wreathing up like ravishment,
Mentioning in sculptures twined
The blitheness Love hath in his mind;
And like delighted senses were
The windows, and the columns there
Made the following sight to ache
As the heart that did them make.
Well I can see that shining song
Flowering there, the upward throng
Of porches, pillars and windowed walls,
Spires like piercing panpipe calls,
Up to the roof's snow-cloud flight;
All glancing in the Spanish light
White as water of arctic tides,
Save an amber dazzle on sunny sides.
You had said, the radiant sheen
Of that palace might have been
A young god's fantasy, ere he came
His serious worlds and suns to frame;
Such an immortal passion
Quivered among the slim hewn stone.
And in the nights it seemed a jar
Cut in the substance of a star,
Wherein a wine, that will be poured
Some time for feasting Heaven, was stored.

But within this fretted shell,
The wonder of Love made visible,
The King a private gentle mood
There placed, of pleasant quietude.
For right amidst there was a court,
Where always muskèd silences
Listened to water and to trees;
And herbage of all fragrant sort,—
Lavender, lad's-love, rosemary,
Basil, tansy, centaury,—
Was the grass of that orchard, hid
Love's amazements all amid.
Jarring the air with rumor cool,
Small fountains played into a pool
With sound as soft as the barley's hiss
When its beard just sprouting is;
Whence a young stream, that trod on moss,
Prettily rimpled the court across.
And in the pool's clear idleness,
Moving like dreams through happiness,
Shoals of small bright fishes were;
In and out weed-thickets bent
Perch and carp, and sauntering went
With mounching jaws and eyes a-stare;
Or on a lotus leaf would crawl
A brindled loach to bask and sprawl,
Tasting the warm sun ere it dipped
Into the water; but quick as fear
Back his shining brown head slipped
To crouch on the gravel of his lair,
Where the cooled sunbeams, broke in wrack,
Spilt shattered gold about his back.
So within that green-veiled air,
Within that white-walled quiet, where
Innocent water thought aloud,—
Childish prattle that must make
The wise sunlight with laughter shake
On the leafage overbowed,—
Often the King and his love-lass
Let the delicious hours pass.

All the outer world could see
Graved and sawn amazingly
Their love's delighted riotise,
Fixed in marble for all men's eyes;
But only these twain could abide
In the cool peace that withinside
Thrilling desire and passion dwelt;
They only knew the still meaning spelt
By Love's flaming script, which is
God's word written in ecstasies.

  And where is now that palace gone,
All the magical skilled stone,
All the dreaming towers wrought
By Love as if no more than thought
The unresisting marble was?
How could such a wonder pass?
Ah, it was but built in vain
Against the stupid horns of Rome,
That pushed down into the common loam
The loveliness that shone in Spain.
But we have raised it up again!
A loftier palace, fairer far,
Is ours, and one that fears no war.
Safe in marvellous walls we are;
Wondering sense like builded fires,
High amazement of desires,
Delight and certainty of love,
Closing around, roofing above
Our unapproached and perfect hour
Within the splendors of love's power.

Lascelles Abercrombie [1881–1938]

ON HAMPSTEAD HEATH

AGAINST the green flame of the hawthorn-tree,
His scarlet tunic burns;
And livelier than the green sap's mantling glee
The Spring fire tingles through him headily
As quivering he turns

And stammers out the old amazing tale
Of youth and April weather;
While she, with half-breathed jests that, sobbing, fail,
Sits, tight-lipped, quaking, eager-eyed and pale,
Beneath her purple feather.

Wilfrid Wilson Gibson [1878–

ONCE ON A TIME

Once on a time, once on a time,
    Before the Dawn began,
There was a nymph of Dian's train
    Who was beloved of Pan;
Once on a time a peasant lad
    Who loved a lass at home;
Once on a time a Saxon king
    Who loved a queen of Rome.

The world has but one song to sing,
    And it is ever new,
The first and last of all the songs
    For it is ever true—
A little song, a tender song,
    The only song it hath;
"There was a youth of Ascalon
    Who loved a girl of Gath."

A thousand thousand years have gone,
    And æons still shall pass,
Yet shall the world forever sing
    Of him who loved a lass—
An olden song, a golden song,
    And sing it unafraid:
"There was a youth, once on a time,
    Who dearly loved a maid."

Kendall Banning [1879–

IN PRAISE OF HER

FIRST SONG

From " Astrophel and Stella "

DOUBT you to whom my Muse these notes intendeth,
Which now my breast, o'ercharged, to music lendeth?
  To you! to you! all song of praise is due;
Only in you my song begins and endeth.

Who hath the eyes which marry state with pleasure?
Who keeps the key of Nature's chiefest treasure?
  To you! to you! all song of praise is due;
Only for you the heaven forgat all measure.

Who hath the lips where wit in fairness reigneth?
Who womankind at once both decks and staineth?
  To you! to you! all song of praise is due;
Only by you Cupid his crown maintaineth.

Who hath the feet, whose step all sweetness planteth?
Who else, for whom Fame worthy trumpets wanteth?
  To you! to you! all song of praise is due;
Only to you her sceptre Venus granteth.

Who hath the breast, whose milk doth passions nourish?
Whose grace is such, that when it chides doth cherish?
  To you! to you! all song of praise is due;
Only through you the tree of life doth flourish.

Who hath the hand, which without stroke subdueth?
Who long-dead beauty with increase reneweth?
  To you! to you! all song of praise is due;
Only at you all envy hopeless rueth.

Who hath the hair, which loosest fastest tieth?
Who makes a man live then glad when he dieth?
  To you! to you! all song of praise is due;
Only of you the flatterer never lieth.

Who hath the voice, which soul from senses sunders?
Whose force but yours the bolts of beauty thunders?
  To you! to you! all song of praise is due;
Only with you not miracles are wonders.

Doubt you to whom my Muse these notes intendeth,
Which now my breast, o'ercharged, to music lendeth?
  To you! to you! all song of praise is due;
Only in you my song begins and endeth.

Philip Sidney [1554–1586]

SILVIA

From "The Two Gentlemen of Verona"

Who is Silvia? What is she?
  That all our swains commend her?
Holy, fair, and wise is she;
  The heaven such grace did lend her,
That she might admirèd be.

Is she kind as she is fair?
  For beauty lives with kindness:
Love doth to her eyes repair,
  To help him of his blindness;
And, being helped, inhabits there.

Then to Silvia let us sing,
  That Silvia is excelling;
She excels each mortal thing
  Upon the dull earth dwelling:
To her let us garlands bring.

William Shakespeare [1564–1616]

CUPID AND CAMPASPE
From "Alexander and Campaspe"

CUPID and my Campaspe played
At cards for kisses; Cupid paid:
He stakes his quiver, bow, and arrows,
His mother's doves, and team of sparrows;
Loses them too; then down he throws
The coral of his lip, the rose
Growing on's cheek (but none knows how);
With these, the crystal of his brow,
And then the dimple on his chin;
All these did my Campaspe win:
And last he set her both his eyes—
She won, and Cupid blind did rise.
    O Love! has she done this to thee?
    What shall, alas! become of me?

John Lyly [1554?-1606]

APOLLO'S SONG
From "Midas"

MY Daphne's hair is twisted gold,
Bright stars apiece her eyes do hold,
My Daphne's brow enthrones the Graces,
My Daphne's beauty stains all faces,
On Daphne's cheek grow rose and cherry,
On Daphne's lip a sweeter berry,
Daphne's snowy hand but touched does melt,
And then no heavenlier warmth is felt,
My Daphne's voice tunes all the spheres,
My Daphne's music charms all ears.
Fond am I thus to sing her praise;
These glories now are turned to bays.

John Lyly [1554?-1606]

"FAIR IS MY LOVE FOR APRIL'S IN HER FACE"
From "Perimedes"

FAIR is my love for April's in her face,
    Her lovely breasts September claims his part,
And lordly July in her eyes takes place,
    But cold December dwelleth in her heart;

Blest be the months that set my thoughts on fire,
Accurst that month that hindereth my desire.

Like Phoebus' fire, so sparkle both her eyes,
   As air perfumed with amber is her breath,
Like swelling waves her lovely breasts do rise,
   As earth, her heart, cold, dateth me to death:
Aye me, poor man, that on the earth do live,
When unkind earth death and despair doth give!

In pomp sits mercy seated in her face,
   Love 'twixt her breasts his trophies doth imprint,
Her eyes shine favor, courtesy, and grace,
   But touch her heart, ah, that is framed of flint!
Therefore my harvest in the grass bears grain;
The rock will wear, washed with a winter's rain.

               Robert Greene [1560?–1592]

SAMELA

From " Menaphon "

LIKE to Diana in her summer weed,
   Girt with a crimson robe of brightest dye,
      Goes fair Samela;
Whiter than be the flocks that straggling feed,
When washed by Arethusa's Fount they lie,
      Is fair Samela.

As fair Aurora in her morning-gray,
Decked with the ruddy glister of her love,
      Is fair Samela;
Like lovely Thetis on a calmèd day,
Whenas her brightness Neptune's fancy move,
      Shines fair Samela.

Her tresses gold, her eyes like glassy streams,
Her teeth are pearl, the breasts are ivory
      Of fair Samela;
Her cheeks like rose and lily yield forth gleams;
Her brows bright arches framed of ebony:
      Thus fair Samela

Passeth fair Venus in her bravest hue,
And Juno in the show of majesty,
　　For she's Samela;
Pallas, in wit,—all three, if you well view,
For beauty, wit, and matchless dignity
　　Yield to Samela.

Robert Greene [1560?–1592]

DAMELUS' SONG OF HIS DIAPHENIA

DIAPHENIA like the daffadowndilly,
White as the sun, fair as the lily,
　Heigh ho, how I do love thee!
I do love thee as my lambs
Are belovèd of their dams;—
　How blest were I if thou would'st prove me.

Diaphenia like the spreading roses,
That in thy sweets all sweets encloses,
　Fair sweet, how I do love thee!
I do love thee as each flower
Loves the sun's life-giving power;
　For dead, thy breath to life might move me.

Diaphenia like to all things blessèd,
When all thy praises are expressèd,
　Dear joy, how I do love thee!
As the birds do love the spring,
Or the bees their careful king:
　Then in requite, sweet virgin, love me!

Henry Constable [1562–1613]

MADRIGAL

MY love in her attire doth show her wit,
　It doth so well become her;
For every season she hath dressings fit,
　For Winter, Spring, and Summer.

No beauty she doth miss
When all her robes are on:
But Beauty's self she is
When all her robes are gone.

Unknown

ON CHLORIS WALKING IN THE SNOW

I SAW fair Chloris walk alone,
Whilst feathered rain came softly down,
As Jove descended from his tower
To court her in a silver shower.
The wanton snow flew on her breast
Like little birds unto their nest,
But, overcome with whiteness there,
For grief it thawed into a tear;
Thence falling on her garment's hem,
To deck her, froze into a gem.

William Strode [1602–1645]

"THERE IS A LADY SWEET AND KIND"

THERE is a lady sweet and kind,
Was never face so pleased my mind;
I did but see her passing by,
And yet I love her till I die.

Her gesture, motion, and her smiles,
Her wit, her voice my heart beguiles,
Beguiles my heart, I know not why,
And yet I love her till I die.

Cupid is wingèd and doth range,
Her country so my love doth change:
But change she earth, or change she sky,
Yet I will love her till I die.

Unknown

CHERRY–RIPE

THERE is a garden in her face
    Where roses and white lilies blow;
A heavenly paradise is that place,
    Wherein all pleasant fruits do flow:
        There cherries grow which none may buy
        Till "Cherry-ripe" themselves do cry.

Those cherries fairly do enclose
    Of orient pearl a double row,
Which when her lovely laughter shows,
    They look like rose-buds filled with snow;
        Yet them nor peer nor prince can buy
        Till "Cherry-ripe" themselves do cry.

Her eyes like angels watch them still;
    Her brows like bended bows do stand,
Threatening with piercing frowns to kill
    All that attempt with eye or hand
        Those sacred cherries to come nigh,
        Till "Cherry-ripe" themselves do cry.

                    Thomas Campion [? –1619]

AMARILLIS

I CARE not for these ladies,
That must be wooed and prayed:
Give me kind Amarillis,
The wanton countrymaid.
Nature art disdaineth,
Her beauty is her own.
Her when we court and kiss,
She cries, Forsooth, let go!
But when we come where comfort is,
She never will say No.

If I love Amarillis,
She gives me fruit and flowers:
But if we love these ladies,
We must give golden showers.

Give them gold, that sell love,
Give me the Nut-brown lass,
Who, when we court and kiss,
She cries, Forsooth, let go:
But when we come where comfort is,
She never will say No.

These ladies must have pillows,
And beds by strangers wrought;
Give me a bower of willows,
Of moss and leaves unbought,
And fresh Amarillis,
With milk and honey fed;
Who, when we court and kiss,
She cries, Forsooth, let go:
But when we come where comfort is,
She never will say No!

Thomas Campion [? —1619]

ELIZABETH OF BOHEMIA

You meaner beauties of the night,
  That poorly satisfy our eyes
More by your number than your light,
  You common people of the skies;
  What are you when the moon shall rise?

You curious chanters of the wood,
  That warble forth Dame Nature's lays,
Thinking your passions understood
  By your weak accents; what's your praise
  When Philomel her voice shall raise?

You violets that first appear,
  By your pure purple mantles known
Like the proud virgins of the year,
  As if the spring were all your own;
  What are you when the rose is blown?

So, when my mistress shall be seen
    In form and beauty of her mind,
By virtue first, then choice, a Queen,
    Tell me, if she were not designed
    Th' eclipse and glory of her kind.

                        Henry Wotton [1568-1639]

HER TRIUMPH

From "A Celebration of Charis"

SEE the Chariot at hand here of Love,
    Wherein my Lady rideth!
Each that draws is a swan or a dove,
    And well the car Love guideth.
As she goes, all hearts do duty
            Unto her beauty;
And, enamored, do wish, so they might
            But enjoy such a sight,
That they still were to run by her side,
Through swords, through seas, whither she would ride

Do but look on her eyes, they do light
    All that Love's world compriseth!
Do but look on her hair, it is bright
    As Love's star when it riseth!
Do but mark, her forehead's smoother
            Than words that soothe her!
And from her arched brows such a grace
            Sheds itself through the face,
As alone there triumphs to the life
All the gain, all the good, of the elements' strife.

Have you seen but a bright lily grow
    Before rude hands have touched it?
Have you marked but the fall o' the snow
    Before the soil hath smutched it?
Have you felt the wool of beaver,
            Or swan's down ever?

Or have smelt o' the bud o' the brier?
Or the nard in the fire?
Or have tasted the bag o' the bee?
O so white, O so soft, O so sweet is she!

Ben Jonson [1573?-1637]

OF PHYLLIS

IN petticoat of green,
Her hair about her eyne,
Phyllis beneath an oak
Sat milking her fair flock:
Among that sweet-strained moisture, rare delight,
Her hand seemed milk in milk, it was so white.

William Drummond [1585-1649]

A WELCOME

Welcome, welcome, do I sing,
Far more welcome than the spring;
He that parteth from you never
Shall enjoy a spring forever.

He that to the voice is near,
Breaking from your ivory pale,
Need not walk abroad to hear
The delightful nightingale.

He that looks still on your eyes,
Though the winter have begun
To benumb our arteries,
Shall not want the summer's sun.

He that still may see your cheeks,
Where all rareness still reposes,
Is a fool if e'er he seeks
Other lilies, other roses.

He to whom your soft lip yields,
   And perceives your breath in kissing,
All the odors of the fields
   Never, never shall be missing.

He that question would anew
   What fair Eden was of old,
Let him rightly study you,
   And a brief of that behold.

Welcome, welcome, then I sing,
Far more welcome than the spring;
He that parteth from you never,
Shall enjoy a spring forever.
        William Browne [1591–1643?]

THE COMPLETE LOVER

FOR her gait, if she be walking;
Be she sitting, I desire her
For her state's sake; and admire her
For her wit if she be talking;
   Gait and state and wit approve her;
   For which all and each I love her.

Be she sullen, I commend her
For a modest. Be she merry,
For a kind one her prefer I.
Briefly, everything doth lend her
   So much grace, and so approve her,
   That for everything I love her.
        William Browne [1591–1643?]

RUBIES AND PEARLS

SOME asked me where the rubies grew,
   And nothing I did say,
But with my finger pointed to
   The lips of Julia.

Some asked how pearls did grow, and where;
   Then spoke I to my girl,
To part her lips, and showed them there
   The quarrelets of pearl.

                    Robert Herrick [1591–1674]

UPON JULIA'S CLOTHES

WHEN as in silks my Julia goes,
Then, then (me thinks) how sweetly flows
That liquefaction of her clothes.

Next, when I cast mine eyes and see
That brave vibration each way free;
O how that glittering taketh me!

                    Robert Herrick [1591–1674]

TO CYNTHIA ON CONCEALMENT OF HER BEAUTY

Do not conceal those radiant eyes,
The starlight of serenest skies;
Lest, wanting of their heavenly light,
They turn to chaos' endless night!

Do not conceal those tresses fair,
The silken snares of thy curled hair;
Lest, finding neither gold nor ore,
The curious silk-worm work no more.

Do not conceal those breasts of thine,
More snow-white than the Apennine;
Lest, if there be like cold and frost,
The lily be for ever lost.

Do not conceal that fragrant scent,
Thy breath, which to all flowers hath lent
Perfumes; lest, it being suppressed,
No spices grow in all the East.

Do not conceal thy heavenly voice,
Which makes the hearts of gods rejoice;
Lest, music hearing no such thing,
The nightingale forget to sing.

Do not conceal, nor yet eclipse,
Thy pearly teeth with coral lips;
Lest that the seas cease to bring forth
Gems which from thee have all their worth.

Do not conceal no beauty, grace,
That's either in thy mind or face;
Lest virtue overcome by vice
Make men believe no Paradise.

Francis Kynaston [1587-1642]

SONG

Ask me no more where Jove bestows,
When June is past, the fading rose;
For in your beauty's orient deep
These flowers, as in their causes, sleep.

Ask me no more whither do stray
The golden atoms of the day;
For in pure love heaven did prepare
Those powders to enrich your hair.

Ask me no more whither doth haste
The nightingale when May is past;
For in your sweet dividing throat
She winters and keeps warm her note.

Ask me no more where those stars 'light
That downwards fall in dead of night;
For in your eyes they sit, and there
Fixèd become as in their sphere.

Ask me no more if east or west
The Phœnix builds her spicy nest;
For unto you at last she flies,
And in your fragrant bosom dies.

Thomas Carew [1598?-1639?]

A DEVOUT LOVER

I HAVE a mistress, for perfections rare
In every eye, but in my thoughts most fair.
Like tapers on the altar shine her eyes;
Her breath is the perfume of sacrifice;
And wheresoe'er my fancy would begin,
Still her perfection lets religion in.
We sit and talk, and kiss away the hours
As chastely as the morning dews kiss flowers:
I touch her, like my beads, with devout care,
And come unto my courtship as my prayer.

Thomas Randolph [1605–1635]

ON A GIRDLE

THAT which her slender waist confined
Shall now my joyful temples bind;
No monarch but would give his crown
His arms might do what this has done.

It was my Heaven's extremest sphere,
The pale which held that lovely deer:
My joy, my grief, my hope, my love,
Did all within this circle move.

A narrow compass! and yet there
Dwelt all that's good, and all that's fair!
Give me but what this ribbon bound,
Take all the rest the sun goes round!

Edmund Waller [1606–1687]

CASTARA

LIKE the violet, which alone
    Prospers in some happy shade,
My Castara lives unknown,
    To no looser eye betrayed:
        For she's to herself untrue
        Who delights i' the public view.

Such is her beauty as no arts
   Have enriched with borrowed grace.
Her high birth no pride imparts,
   For she blushes in her place.
      Folly boasts a glorious blood;
      She is noblest, being good.

Cautious, she knew never yet
   What a wanton courtship meant;
Nor speaks loud to boast her wit,
   In her silence, eloquent.
      Of herself survey she takes,
      But 'tween men no difference makes.

She obeys with speedy will
   Her grave parents' wise commands;
And so innocent, that ill
   She nor acts, nor understands.
      Women's feet run still astray
      If to ill they know the way.

She sails by that rock, the court,
   Where oft virtue splits her mast;
And retiredness thinks the port
   Where her fame may anchor cast.
      Virtue safely cannot sit
      Where vice is enthroned for wit.

She holds that day's pleasure best
   Where sin waits not on delight;
Without mask, or ball, or feast,
   Sweetly spends a winter's night.
      O'er that darkness whence is thrust
      Prayer and sleep, oft governs lust.

She her throne makes reason climb,
   While wild passions captive lie;
And, each article of time,
   Her pure thoughts to heaven fly;
      All her vows religious be,
      And she vows her love to me.

               William Habington [1605-1654]

TO ARAMANTHA

THAT SHE WOULD DISHEVEL HER HAIR

ARAMANTHA, sweet and fair,
Ah, braid no more that shining hair!
As my curious hand or eye
Hovering round thee, let it fly.

Let it fly as unconfined
As its calm ravisher the wind,
Who hath left his darling, th' east,
To wanton in that spicy nest.

Every tress must be confessed;
But neatly tangled at the best;
Like a clew of golden thread
Most excellently ravellèd.

Do not, then, wind up that light
In ribbons, and o'er-cloud in night,
Like the sun in's early ray;
But shake your head and scatter day.

Richard Lovelace [1618-1658]

CHLOE DIVINE

CHLOE's a Nymph in flowery groves,
    A Nereid in the streams;
Saint-like she in the temple moves,
    A woman in my dreams.

Love steals artillery from her eyes,
    The Graces point her charms;
Orpheus is rivalled in her voice,
    And Venus in her arms.

Never so happily in one
    Did heaven and earth combine;
And yet 'tis flesh and blood alone
    That makes her so divine.

Thomas D'Urfey [1653-1723]

MY PEGGY

My Peggy is a young thing,
  Just entered in her teens,
Fair as the day, and sweet as May,
Fair as the day, and always gay:
    My Peggy is a young thing,
      And I'm na very auld,
    Yet weel I like to meet her at
      The wauking o' the fauld.

My Peggy speaks sae sweetly
  Whene'er we meet alane,
I wish nae mair to lay my care,
I wish nae mair o' a' that's rare:
    My Peggy speaks sae sweetly,
      To a' the lave I'm cauld;
    But she gars a' my spirits glow
      At wauking o' the fauld.

My Peggy smiles sae kindly
  Whene'er I whisper love,
That I look doun on a' the toun,
That I look doun upon a croun:
    My Peggy smiles sae kindly,
      It makes me blithe and bauld,
    And naething gi'es me sic delight
      As waulking o' the fauld.

My Peggy sings sae saftly,
  When on my pipe I play;
By a' the rest it is confessed,
By a' the rest that she sings best:
    My Peggy sings sae saftly,
      And in her sangs are tauld,
    Wi' innocence the wale o' sense,
      At wauking o' the fauld.
              Allan Ramsay [1686–1758]

SONG

From "Acis and Galatea"

O RUDDIER than the cherry!
O sweeter than the berry!
    O nymph more bright
    Than moonshine night,
Like kidlings blithe and merry!
Ripe as the melting luster;
    Yet hard to tame
    As raging flame,
And fierce as storms that bluster!

John Gay [1685–1732]

"TELL ME, MY HEART, IF THIS BE LOVE"

WHEN Delia on the plain appears,
Awed by a thousand tender fears
I would approach, but dare not move:
Tell me, my heart, if this be love?

Whene'er she speaks, my ravished ear
No other voice than hers can hear,
No other wit but hers approve:
Tell me, my heart, if this be love?

If she some other youth commend,
Though I was once his fondest friend,
His instant enemy I prove:
Tell me, my heart, if this be love?

When she is absent, I no more
Delight in all that pleased before—
The clearest spring, or shadiest grove:
Tell me, my heart, if this be love?

When fond of power, of beauty vain,
Her nets she spread for every swain,
I strove to hate, but vainly strove:
Tell me, my heart, if this be love?

George Lyttleton [1709–1773]

THE FAIR THIEF

BEFORE the urchin well could go,
She stole the whiteness of the snow;
And more, that whiteness to adorn,
She stole the blushes of the morn;
Stole all the sweetness ether sheds
On primrose buds and violet beds.

Still to reveal her artful wiles
She stole the Graces' silken smiles;
She stole Aurora's balmy breath;
And pilfered orient pearl for teeth;
The cherry, dipped in morning dew,
Gave moisture to her lips, and hue.

These were her infant spoils, a store;
And she, in time, still pilfered more!
At twelve, she stole from Cyprus' queen
Her air and love-commanding mien;
Stole Juno's dignity; and stole
From Pallas sense to charm the soul.

Apollo's wit was next her prey;
Her next, the beam that lights the day;
She sang;—amazed, the Sirens heard,
And to assert their voice appeared.
She played;—the Muses from their hill,
Wondered who thus had stole their skill.

Great Jove approved her crimes and art;
And, t'other day, she stole my heart!
If lovers, Cupid, are thy care,
Exert thy vengeance on this Fair:
To trial bring her stolen charms,
And let her prison be my arms!

Charles Wyndham [1710–1763]

AMORET

IF rightly tuneful bards decide,
    If it be fixed in Love's decrees,
That Beauty ought not to be tried
    But by its native power to please,
Then tell me, youths and lovers, tell—
What fair can Amoret excel?

Behold that bright unsullied smile,
    And wisdom speaking in her mien:
Yet—she so artless all the while,
    So little studious to be seen—
We naught but instant gladness know,
Nor think to whom the gift we owe.

But neither music, nor the powers
    Of youth and mirth and frolic cheer,
Add half the sunshine to the hours,
    Or make life's prospect half so clear,
As memory brings it to the eye
From scenes where Amoret was by.

This, sure, is Beauty's happiest part;
    This gives the most unbounded sway;
This shall enchant the subject heart
    When rose and lily fade away;
And she be still, in spite of Time,
Sweet Amoret, in all her prime.

Mark Akenside [1721–1770]

SONG

THE shape alone let others prize,
    The features of the fair:
I look for spirit in her eyes,
    And meaning in her air.

A damask cheek, an ivory arm,
  Shall ne'er my wishes win:
Give me an animated form,
  That speaks a mind within.

A face where awful honor shines,
  Where sense and sweetness move,
And angel innocence refines
  The tenderness of love.

These are the soul of beauty's frame;
  Without whose vital aid
Unfinished all her features seem,
  And all her roses dead.

But ah! where both their charms unite,
  How perfect is the view,
With every image of delight,
  With graces ever new:

Of power to charm the greatest woe,
  The wildest rage control,
Diffusing mildness o'er the brow,
  And rapture through the soul.

Their power but faintly to express
  All language must despair;
But go, behold Arpasia's face,
  And read it perfect there.

                        Mark Akenside [1721-1770]

KATE OF ABERDEEN

THE silver moon's enamored beam
  Steals softly through the night,
To wanton with the winding stream,
  And kiss reflected light.
To beds of state go balmy sleep
  ('Tis where you've seldom been),
May's vigil while the shepherds keep
  With Kate of Aberdeen.

Upon the green the virgins wait,
  In rosy chaplets gay,
Till morn unbar her golden gate,
  And give the promised May.
Methinks I hear the maids declare,
  The promised May, when seen,
Not half so fragrant, half so fair,
  As Kate of Aberdeen.

Strike up the tabor's boldest notes,
  We'll rouse the nodding grove;
The nested birds shall raise their throats,
  And hail the maid of love;
And see—the matin lark mistakes,
  He quits the tufted green:
Fond bird! 'tis not the morning breaks,—
  'Tis Kate of Aberdeen.

Now lightsome o'er the level mead,
  Where midnight fairies rove,
Like them the jocund dance we'll lead,
  Or tune the reed to love:
For see the rosy May draws nigh,
  She claims a virgin Queen;
And hark, the happy shepherds cry,
  'Tis Kate of Aberdeen.
                John Cunningham [1729–1773]

SONG

WHO has robbed the ocean cave,
  To tinge thy lips with coral hue?
Who from India's distant wave
  For thee those pearly treasures drew?
    Who from yonder orient sky
    Stole the morning of thine eye?

A thousand charms, thy form to deck,
  From sea, and earth, and air are torn;
Roses bloom upon thy cheek,
  On thy breath their fragrance borne.

Guard thy bosom from the day,
Lest thy snows should melt away.

But one charm remains behind,
    Which mute earth can ne'er impart;
Nor in ocean wilt thou find,
    Nor in the circling air, a heart.
        Fairest! wouldst thou perfect be,
        Take, oh, take that heart from me.

John Shaw [1559–1625]

CHLOE

IT was the charming month of May,
When all the flowers were fresh and gay;
One morning, by the break of day,
    The youthful, charming Chloe
From peaceful slumber she arose,
Girt on her mantle and her hose,
And o'er the flowery mead she goes,
    The youthful, charming Chloe.
        Lovely was she by the dawn,
            Youthful Chloe, charming Chloe,
        Tripping o'er the pearly lawn,
            The youthful, charming Chloe.

The feathered people you might see,
Perched all around on every tree,
In notes of sweetest melody
    They hail the charming Chloe;
Till, painting gay the eastern skies,
The glorious sun began to rise,
Out-rivalled by the radiant eyes
    Of youthful, charming Chloe.
        Lovely was she by the dawn,
            Youthful Chloe, charming Chloe,
        Tripping o'er the pearly lawn,
            The youthful, charming Chloe.

Robert Burns [1759–1796]

"O MALLY'S MEEK, MALLY'S SWEET"

As I was walking up the street,
  A barefit maid I chanced to meet;
But O the road was very hard
  For that fair maiden's tender feet.
    O Mally's meek, Mally's sweet,
      Mally's modest and discreet,
    Mally's rare, Mally's fair,
      Mally's every way complete.

It were more meet that those fine feet
  Were weel laced up in silken shoon,
And 'twere more fit that she should sit
  Within yon chariot gilt aboon.

Her yellow hair, beyond compare,
  Comes trinkling down her swan-white neck,
And her two eyes, like stars in skies,
  Would keep a sinking ship frae wreck.
    O Mally's meek, Mally's sweet,
      Mally's modest and discreet,
    Mally's rare, Mally's fair,
      Mally's every way complete.

                    Robert Burns [1759–1796]

THE LOVER'S CHOICE

You, Damon, covet to possess
The nymph that sparkles in her dress;
Would rustling silks and hoops invade,
And clasp an armful of brocade.

Such raise the price of your delight
Who purchase both their red and white,
And, pirate-like, surprise your heart
With colors of adulterate art.

Me, Damon, me the maid enchants
Whose cheeks the hand of nature paints;
A modest blush adorns her face,
Her air an unaffected grace.

No art she knows, or seeks to know;
No charm to wealthy pride will owe;
No gems, no gold she needs to wear;
She shines intrinsically fair.

Thomas Bedingfield [? –1613]

RONDEAU REDOUBLÉ

My day and night are in my lady's hand;
  I have no other sunrise than her sight;
For me her favor glorifies the land;
  Her anger darkens all the cheerful light.
  Her face is fairer than the hawthorn white,
When all a-flower in May the hedgerows stand;
  While she is kind, I know of no affright;
My day and night are in my lady's hand.

All heaven in her glorious eyes is spanned;
  Her smile is softer than the summer's night,
Gladder than daybreak on the Faery strand;
  I have no other sunrise than her sight.
  Her silver speech is like the singing flight
Of runnels rippling o'er the jewelled sand;
  Her kiss a dream of delicate delight;
For me her favor glorifies the land.

What if the Winter chase the Summer bland!
  The gold sun in her hair burns ever bright.
If she be sad, straightway all joy is banned;
  Her anger darkens all the cheerful light.
  Come weal or woe, I am my lady's knight
And in her service every ill withstand;
  Love is my Lord in all the world's despite
And holdeth in the hollow of his hand
          My day and night.

John Payne [1842–1916]

"MY LOVE SHE'S BUT A LASSIE YET"

My love she's but a lassie yet,
A lightsome lovely lassie yet;
  It scarce wad do
  To sit an' woo
Down by the stream sae glassy yet.

But there's a braw time coming yet,
When we may gang a-roaming yet;
  An' hint wi' glee
  O' joys to be,
When fa's the modest gloaming yet.

She's neither proud nor saucy yet,
She's neither plump nor gaucy yet;
  But just a jinking,
  Bonny blinking,
Hilty-skilty lassie yet.

But O, her artless smile's mair sweet
Than hinny or than marmalete;
  An' right or wrang,
  Ere it be lang,
I'll bring her to a parley yet.

I'm jealous o' what blesses her,
The very breeze that kisses her,
  The flowery beds
  On which she treads,
Though wae for ane that misses her.

Then O, to meet my lassie yet,
Up in yon glen sae grassy yet;
  For all I see
  Are naught to me,
Save her that's but a lassie yet.

      James Hogg [1770–1835]

JESSIE, THE FLOWER O' DUNBLANE

THE sun has gane down o'er the lofty Benlomond
 And left the red clouds to preside o'er the scene,
While lanely I stray, in the calm simmer gloamin',
 To muse on sweet Jessie, the Flower o' Dunblane.

How sweet is the brier, wi' its saft fauldin' blossom,
 And sweet is the birk, wi' its mantle o' green;
Yet sweeter and fairer, and dear to this bosom,
 Is lovely young Jessie, the Flower o' Dunblane.

She's modest as ony, and blithe as she's bonnie;
 For guileless simplicity marks her its ain;
And far be the villain, divested of feeling,
 Wha'd blight in its bloom the sweet Flower o' Dunblane.

Sing on, thou sweet mavis, thy hymn to the e'ening!
 Thou'rt dear to the echoes of Calderwood glen;
Sae dear to this bosom, sae artless and winning,
 Is charming young Jessie, the Flower o' Dunblane.

How lost were my days till I met wi' my Jessie!
 The sports o' the city seemed foolish and vain;
I ne'er saw a nymph I would ca' my dear lassie
 Till charmed wi' sweet Jessie, the Flower o' Dunblane.

Though mine were the station o' loftiest grandeur,
 Amidst its profusion I'd languish in pain,
And reckon as naething the height o' its splendor,
 If wanting sweet Jessie, the Flower o' Dunblane.

Robert Tannahill [1774-1810]

MARGARET AND DORA

MARGARET's beauteous—Grecian arts
 Ne'er drew form completer,
Yet why, in my hearts of hearts,
 Hold I Dora's sweeter?

Dora's eyes of heavenly blue
   Pass all painting's reach,
Ringdoves' notes are discord to
   The music of her speech.

Artists! Margaret's smile receive,
   And on canvas show it;
But for perfect worship leave
   Dora to her poet.

Thomas Campbell [1777

DAGONET'S CANZONET

A QUEEN lived in the South;
And music was her mouth,
And sunshine was her hair,
By day, and all the night
The drowsy embers there
Remembered still the light;
   My soul, was she not fair!

But for her eyes—they made
An iron man afraid;
Like sky-blue pools they were,
Watching the sky that knew
Itself transmuted there
Light blue, or deeper blue;
   My soul, was she not fair!

The lifting of her hands
Made laughter in the lands
Where the sun is, in the South:
But my soul learnt sorrow there
In the secrets of her mouth,
Her eyes, her hands, her hair:
   O soul, was she not fair!

Ernest Rhys [1859–1941]

STANZAS FOR MUSIC

THERE be none of Beauty's daughters
    With a magic like thee;
And like music on the waters
    Is thy sweet voice to me:
When, as if its sound were causing
The charmèd occan's pausing,
The waves lie still and gleaming,
And the lulled winds seem dreaming.

And the midnight moon is weaving
    Her bright chain o'er the deep,
Whose breast is gently heaving,
    As an infant's asleep:
So the spirit bows before thee,
To listen and adore thee;
With a full but soft emotion,
Like the swell of Summer's ocean.

George Gordon Byron [1788–1824]

"FLOWERS I WOULD BRING"

FLOWERS I would bring if flowers could make thee fairer,
And music, if the Muse were dear to thee;
(For loving these would make thee love the bearer)
But sweetest songs forget their melody,
And loveliest flowers would but conceal the wearer:—
A rose I marked, and might have plucked; but she
Blushed as she bent, imploring me to spare her,
Nor spoil her beauty by such rivalry.
Alas! and with what gifts shall I pursue thee,
What offerings bring, what treasures lay before thee;
When earth with all her floral train doth woo thee,
And all old poets and old songs adore thee;
And love to thee is naught; from passionate mood
Secured by joy's complacent plenitude!

Aubrey Thomas de Vere [1814–1902]

" IT IS NOT BEAUTY I DEMAND "

It is not Beauty I demand,
  A crystal brow, the moon's despair,
Nor the snow's daughter, a white hand,
  Nor mermaid's yellow pride of hair:

Tell me not of your starry eyes,
  Your lips that seem on roses fed,
Your breasts, where Cupid tumbling lies
  Nor sleeps for kissing of his bed:—

A bloomy pair of vermeil cheeks
  Like Hebe's in her ruddiest hours,
A breath that softer music speaks
  Than summer winds a-wooing flowers,—

These are but gauds: nay, what are lips?
  Coral beneath the ocean-stream,
Whose brink when your adventurer sips
  Full oft he perisheth on them.

And what are cheeks but ensigns oft
  That wave hot youth to fields of blood?
Did Helen's breast, though ne'er so soft,
  Do Greece or Ilium any good?

Eyes can with baleful ardor burn;
  Poison can breathe, that erst perfumed;
There's many a white hand holds an urn
  With lovers' hearts to dust consumed.

For crystal brows—there's naught within;
  They are but empty cells for pride;
He who the Siren's hair would win
  Is mostly strangled in the tide.

Give me, instead of Beauty's bust,
  A tender heart, a loyal mind
Which with temptation I could trust,
  Yet never linked with error find,—

One in whose gentle bosom I
  Could pour my secret heart of woes,
Like the care-burthened honey-fly
  That hides his murmurs in the rose,—

My earthly Comforter! whose love
  So indefeasible might be
That, when my spirit won above,
  Hers could not stay, for sympathy.

George Darley [1795–1846]

SONG

She is not fair to outward view
  As many maidens be,
Her loveliness I never knew
  Until she smiled on me;
Oh! then I saw her eye was bright,
A well of love, a spring of light.

But now her looks are coy and cold,
  To mine they ne'er reply,
And yet I cease not to behold
  The love-light in her eye:
Her very frowns are fairer far
Than smiles of other maidens are.

Hartley Coleridge [1796–1849]

SONG

A violet in her lovely hair,
A rose upon her bosom fair!
  But O, her eyes
A lovelier violet disclose,
And her ripe lips the sweetest rose
  That's 'neath the skies.

A lute beneath her graceful hand
Breathes music forth at her command;

But still her tongue
Far richer music calls to birth
Than all the minstrel power on earth
Can give to song.

And thus she moves in tender light,
The purest ray, where all is bright,
Serene, and sweet;
And sheds a graceful influence round,
That hallows e'en the very ground
Beneath her feet!

Charles Swain [1801–1874]

EILEEN AROON

WHEN like the early rose,
Eileen Aroon!
Beauty in childhood blows,
Eileen Aroon!
When, like a diadem,
Buds blush around the stem,
Which is the fairest gem? —
Eileen Aroon!

Is it the laughing eye,
Eileen Aroon!
Is it the timid sigh,
Eileen Aroon!
Is it the tender tone,
Soft as the stringed harp's moan?
O, it is truth alone, —
Eileen Aroon!

When like the rising day,
Eileen Aroon!
Love sends his early ray,
Eileen Aroon!
What makes his dawning glow,
Changeless through joy or woe?
Only the constant know: —
Eileen Aroon!

I know a valley fair,
  Eileen Aroon!
I knew a cottage there,
  Eileen Aroon!
Far in that valley's shade
I knew a gentle maid,
Flower of a hazel glade,—
  Eileen Aroon!

Who in the song so sweet?
  Eileen Aroon!
Who in the dance so fleet?
  Eileen Aroon!
Dear were her charms to me
Dearer her laughter free,
Dearest her constancy,—
  Eileen Aroon!

Were she no longer true,
  Eileen Aroon!
What should her lover do?
  Eileen Aroon!
Fly with his broken chain
Far o'er the sounding main,
Never to love again,—
  Eileen Aroon!

Youth must with time decay,
  Eileen Aroon!
Beauty must fade away,
  Eileen Aroon!
Castles are sacked in war,
Chieftains are scattered far,
Truth is a fixèd star,—
  Eileen Aroon!

Gerald Griffin [1803–1840]

ANNIE LAURIE

Maxwelton braes are bonnie
Where early fa's the dew,
And it's there that Annie Laurie
Gie'd me her promise true—

Gie'd me her promise true,
  Which ne'er forgot will be;
And for bonnie Annie Laurie
  I'd lay me doun and dee.

Her brow is like the snaw-drift;
  Her throat is like the swan;
Her face it is the fairest
  That e'er the sun shone on—
That e'er the sun shone on—
  And dark blue is her ee;
  And for bonnie Annie Laurie
  I'd lay me doun and dee.

Like dew on the gowan lying
  Is the fa' o' her fairy feet;
And like the winds in summer sighing,
  Her voice is low and sweet—
Her voice is low and sweet—
  And she's a' the world to me;
And for bonnie Annie Laurie
  I'd lay me doun and dee.

William Douglas [1672?–1748]

TO HELEN

HELEN, thy beauty is to me
  Like those Nicæan barks of yore,
That gently, o'er a perfumed sea,
  The weary, wayworn wanderer bore
  To his own native shore.

On desperate seas long wont to roam,
  Thy hyacinth hair, thy classic face,
Thy Naiad airs, have brought me home
  To the glory that was Greece
  And the grandeur that was Rome.

Lo! in yon brilliant window-niche
  How statue-like I see thee stand,
The agate lamp within thy hand!
  Ah, Psyche, from the regions which
  Are Holy Land!

Edgar Allan Poe [1809–1849]

"A VOICE BY THE CEDAR TREE"

From "Maud"

I

A VOICE by the cedar tree,
In the meadow under the Hall!
She is singing an air that is known to me,
A passionate ballad gallant and gay,
A martial song like a trumpet's call!
Singing alone in the morning of life,
In the happy morning of life and of May,
Singing of men that in battle array,
Ready in heart and ready in hand,
March with banner and bugle and fife
To the death, for their native land.

II

Maud with her exquisite face,
And wild voice pealing up to the sunny sky,
And feet like sunny gems on an English green,
Maud in the light of her youth and her grace,
Singing of Death, and of Honor that cannot die,
Till I well could weep for a time so sordid and mean,
And myself so languid and base.

III

Silence, beautiful voice!
Be still, for you only trouble the mind
With a joy in which I cannot rejoice,
A glory I shall not find.
Still! I will hear you no more,
For your sweetness hardly leaves me a choice
But to move to the meadow and fall before
Her feet on the meadow grass, and adore,
Not her, who is neither courtly nor kind,
Not her, not her, but a voice.

Alfred Tennyson [1809–1892]

SONG

NAY but you, who do not love her,
  Is she not pure gold, my mistress?
Holds earth aught—speak truth—above her?
  Aught like this tress, see, and this tress,
And this last fairest tress of all,
So fair, see, ere I let it fall?

Because you spend your lives in praising;
  To praise, you search the wide world over:
Then why not witness, calmly gazing,
  If earth holds aught—speak truth—above her?
Above this tress, and this, I touch
But cannot praise, I love so much!

Robert Browning [1812–1889]

THE HENCHMAN

My lady walks her morning round,
My lady's page her fleet greyhound,
My lady's hair the fond winds stir,
And all the birds make songs for her.

Her thrushes sing in Rathburn bowers,
And Rathburn side is gay with flowers;
But ne'er like hers, in flower or bird,
Was beauty seen or music heard.

The distance of the stars is hers;
The least of all her worshipers,
The dust beneath her dainty heel,
She knows not that I see or feel.

Oh, proud and calm!—she cannot know
Where'er she goes with her I go;
Oh, cold and fair!—she cannot guess
I kneel to share her hound's caress!

Gay knights beside her hunt and hawk,
I rob their ears of her sweet talk:

Her suitors come from east and west,
I steal her smiles from every guest.

Unheard of her, in loving words,
I greet her with the song of birds;
I reach her with her green-armed bowers,
I kiss her with the lips of flowers.

The hound and I are on her trail,
The wind and I uplift her veil;
As if the calm, cold moon she were,
And I the tide, I follow her.

As unrebuked as they, I share
The license of the sun and air,
And in a common homage hide
My worship from her scorn and pride.

World-wide apart, and yet so near,
I breathe her charmèd atmosphere,
Wherein to her my service brings
The reverence due to holy things.

Her maiden pride, her haughty name,
My dumb devotion shall not shame;
The love that no return doth crave
To knightly levels lifts the slave.

No lance have I, in joust or fight,
To splinter in my lady's sight;
But, at her feet, how blest were I
For any need of hers to die!

John Greenleaf Whittier [1807–1892]

LOVELY MARY DONNELLY

Oh, lovely Mary Donnelly, it's you I love the best!
If fifty girls were round you I'd hardly see the rest.
Be what it may the time of day, the place be where it will,
Sweet looks of Mary Donnelly, they bloom before me still.

Her eyes like mountain water that's flowing on a rock,
How clear they are, how dark they are! they give me many
a shock.
Red rowans warm in sunshine and wetted with a shower,
Could ne'er express the charming lip that has me in its
power.

Her nose is straight and handsome, her eyebrows lifted up,
Her chin is very neat and pert, and smooth like a china cup,
Her hair's the brag of Ireland, so weighty and so fine;
It's rolling down upon her neck, and gathered in a twine.

The dance o' last Whit-Monday night exceeded all before;
No pretty girl for miles about was missing from the floor;
But Mary kept the belt of love, and O but she was gay!
She danced a jig, she sung a song, that took my heart away.

When she stood up for dancing, her steps were so complete,
The music nearly killed itself to listen to her feet;
The fiddler moaned his blindness, he heard her so much
praised,
But blessed his luck he wasn't deaf when once her voice she
raised.

And evermore I'm whistling or lilting what you sung,
Your smile is always in my heart, your name beside my
tongue;
But you've as many sweethearts as you'd count on both
your hands,
And for myself there's not a thumb or little finger stands.

Oh, you're the flower o' womankind in country or in town;
The higher I exalt you, the lower I'm cast down.
If some great lord should come this way, and see your beauty
bright,
And you to be his lady, I'd own it was but right.

O might we live together in a lofty palace hall,
Where joyful music rises, and where scarlet curtains fall!
O might we live together in a cottage mean and small,
With sods of grass the only roof, and mud the only wall!

O lovely Mary Donnelly, your beauty's my distress:
It's far too beauteous to be mine, but I'll never wish it less.
The proudest place would fit your face, and I am poor and
    low;
But blessings be about you, dear, wherever you may go!

William Allingham [1824–1889]

LOVE IN THE VALLEY

UNDER yonder beech-tree single on the green-sward,
    Couched with her arms behind her golden head,
Knees and tresses folded to slip and ripple idly,
    Lies my young love sleeping in the shade.
Had I the heart to slide an arm beneath her,
    Press her parting lips as her waist I gather slow,
Waking in amazement she could not but embrace me:
    Then would she hold me and never let me go?

Shy as the squirrel and wayward as the swallow,
    Swift as the swallow along the river's light
Circleting the surface to meet his mirrored winglets,
    Fleeter she seems in her stay than in her flight.
Shy as the squirrel that leaps among the pine-tops,
    Wayward as the swallow overhead at set of sun,
She whom I love is hard to catch and conquer,
    Hard, but O the glory of the winning were she won!

When her mother tends her before the laughing mirror,
    Tying up her laces, looping up her hair,
Often she thinks, were this wild thing wedded,
    More love should I have, and much less care.
When her mother tends her before the lighted mirror,
    Loosening her laces, combing down her curls,
Often she thinks, were this wild thing wedded,
    I should miss but one for many boys and girls.

Heartless she is as the shadow in the meadows,
    Flying to the hills on a blue and breezy noon.
No, she is athirst and drinking up her wonder:
    Earth to her is young as the slip of the new moon

Deals she an unkindness, 'tis but her rapid measure,
  Even as in a dance; and her smile can heal no less:
Like the swinging May-cloud that pelts the flowers with
    hailstones
  Off a sunny border, she was made to bruise and bless.

Lovely are the curves of the white owl sweeping
  Wavy in the dusk lit by one large star.
Lone on the fir-branch, his rattle-note unvaried,
  Brooding o'er the gloom, spins the brown eve-jar.
Darker grows the valley, more and more forgetting:
  So were it with me if forgetting could be willed.
Tell the grassy hollow that holds the bubbling well-spring,
  Tell it to forget the source that keeps it filled.

Stepping down the hill with her fair companions,
  Arm in arm, all against the raying West,
Boldly she sings, to the merry tune she marches;
  Brave in her shape, and sweeter unpossessed.
Sweeter, for she is what my heart first awaking
  Whispered the world was; morning light is she.
Love that so desires would fain keep her changeless;
  Fain would fling the net, and fain have her free.

Happy happy time, when the white star hovers
  Low over dim fields fresh with bloomy dew,
Near the face of dawn, that draws athwart the darkness,
  Threading it with color, like yewberries the yew.
Thicker crowd the shades as the grave East deepens
  Glowing, and with crimson a long cloud swells.
Maiden still the morn is; and strange she is, and secret;
  Strange her eyes; her cheeks are cold as cold sea-shells.

Sunrays, leaning on our southern hills and lighting
  Wild cloud-mountains that drag the hills along,
Oft ends the day of your shifting brilliant laughter
  Chill as a dull face frowning on a song.
Ay, but shows the South-west a ripple-feathered bosom
  Blown to silver while the clouds are shaken and ascend
Scaling the mid-heavens as they stream, there comes a sunset
  Rich, deep like love in beauty without end.

When at dawn she sighs, and like an infant to the window
   Turns grave eyes craving light, released from dreams,
Beautiful she looks, like a white water-lily
   Bursting out of bud in havens of the streams.
When from bed she rises clothed from neck to ankle
   In her long nightgown sweet as boughs of May,
Beautiful she looks, like a tall garden-lily
   Pure from the night, and splendid for the day.

Mother of the dews, dark eye-lashed twilight,
   Low-lidded twilight, o'er the valley's brim,
Rounding on thy breast sings the dew-delighted skylark,
   Clear as though the dewdrops had their voice in him.
Hidden where the rose-flush drinks the rayless planet,
   Fountain-full he pours the spraying fountain-showers.
Let me hear her laughter, I would have her ever
   Cool as dew in twilight, the lark above the flowers.

All the girls are out with their baskets for the primrose;
   Up lanes, woods through, they troop in joyful bands.
My sweet leads: she knows not why, but now she loiters,
   Eyes the bent anemones, and hangs her hands.
Such a look will tell that the violets are peeping,
   Coming the rose: and unaware a cry
Springs in her bosom for odors and for color,
   Covert and the nightingale; she knows not why.

Kerchiefed head and chin she darts between her tulips,
   Streaming like a willow gray in arrowy rain:
Some bend beaten cheek to gravel, and their angel
   She will be; she lifts them, and on she speeds again.
Black the driving rain cloud breasts the iron gateway:
   She is forth to cheer a neighbor lacking mirth.
So when sky and grass met rolling dumb for thunder
   Saw I once a white dove, sole light of earth.

Prim little scholars are the flowers of her garden,
   Trained to stand in rows, and asking if they please.
I might love them well but for loving more the wild ones:
   O my wild ones! they tell me more than these.

You, my wild one, you tell of honied field-rose,
  Violet, blushing eglantine in life; and even as they,
They by the wayside are earnest of your goodness,
  You are of life's, on the banks that line the way.

Peering at her chamber the white crowns the red rose,
  Jasmine winds the porch with stars two and three.
Parted is the window; she sleeps; the starry jasmine
  Breathes a falling breath that carries thoughts of me.
Sweeter unpossessed, have I said of her my sweetest?
  Not while she sleeps: while she sleeps the jasmine breathes,
Luring her to love: she sleeps; the starry jasmine
  Bears me to her pillow under white rose-wreaths.

Yellow with birdfoot-trefoil are the grass-glades;
  Yellow with cinquefoil of the dew-gray leaf;
Yellow with stonecrop; the moss-mounds are yellow;
  Blue-necked the wheat sways, yellowing to the sheaf.
Green-yellow bursts from the copse the laughing yaffle;
  Sharp as a sickle is the edge of shade and shine:
Earth in her heart laughs looking at the heavens,
  Thinking of the harvest: I look and think of mine.

This I may know: her dressing and undressing
  Such a change of light shows as when the skies in sport
Shift from cloud to moonlight; or edging over thunder
  Slips a ray of sun; or sweeping into port
White sails furl; or on the ocean borders
  White sails lean along the waves leaping green.
Visions of her shower before me, but from eyesight
  Guarded she would be like the sun were she seen.

Front door and back of the mossed old farmhouse
  Open with the morn, and in a breezy link
Freshly sparkles garden to stripe-shadowed orchard,
  Green across a rill where on sand the minnows wink.
Busy in the grass the early sun of summer
  Swarms, and the blackbird's mellow fluting notes
Call my darling up with round and roguish challenge:
  Quaintest, richest carol of all the singing throats!

Cool was the woodside; cool as her white dairy
    Keeping sweet the cream-pan; and there the boys from
        school,
Cricketing below, rushed brown and red with sunshine;
    O the dark translucence of the deep-eyed cool!
Spying from the farm, herself she fetched a pitcher
    Full of milk, and tilted for each in turn the beak.
Then a little fellow, mouth up and on tiptoe,
    Said, "I will kiss you": she laughed and leaned her cheek.

Doves of the fir-wood walling high our red roof
    Through the long noon coo, crooning through the coo.
Loose droop the leaves, and down the sleepy roadway
    Sometimes pipes a chaffinch; loose droops the blue.
Cows flap a slow tail knee-deep in the river,
    Breathless, given up to sun and gnat and fly.
Nowhere is she seen; and if I see her nowhere,
    Lightning may come, straight rains and tiger sky.

O the golden sheaf, the rustling treasure-armful!
    O the nutbrown tresses nodding interlaced!
O the treasure-tresses one another over
    Nodding! O the girdle slack about the waist!
Slain are the poppies that shot their random scarlet
    Quick amid the wheat-ears: wound about the waist,
Gathered, see these brides of Earth one blush of ripeness!
    O the nutbrown tresses nodding interlaced.

Large and smoky red the sun's cold disk drops,
    Clipped by naked hills, on violet shaded snow:
Eastward large and still lights up a bower of moonrise,
    Whence at her leisure steps the moon aglow.
Nightlong on black print-branches our beech-tree
    Gazes in this whiteness: nightlong could I.
Here may life on death or death on life be painted.
    Let me clasp her soul to know she cannot die!

Gossips count her faults; they scour a narrow chamber
    Where there is no window, read not heaven or her.
"When she was a tiny," one agèd woman quavers,
    Plucks at my heart and leads me by the ear.

Faults she had once as she learned to run and tumbled:
  Faults of feature some see, beauty not complete.
Yet, good gossips, beauty that makes holy
  Earth and air, may have faults from head to feet.

Hither she comes; she comes to me; she lingers,
  Deepens her brown eyebrows, while in new surprise
High rise the lashes in wonder of a stranger;
  Yet am I the light and living of her eyes.
Something friends have told her fills her heart to brimming,
  Nets her in her blushes, and wounds her, and tames.—
Sure of her haven, O like a dove alighting,
  Arms up, she dropped: our souls were in our names.

Soon will she lie like a white frost sunrise.
  Yellow oats and brown wheat, barley pale as rye,
Long since your sheaves have yielded to the thresher,
  Felt the girdle loosened, seen the tresses fly.
Soon will she lie like a blood-red sunset.
  Swift with the to-morrow, green-winged Spring!
Sing from the South-west, bring her back the truants,
  Nightingale and swallow, song and dipping wing.

Soft new beech-leaves, up to beamy April
  Spreading bough on bough a primrose mountain, you,
Lucid in the moon, raise lilies to the skyfields,
  Youngest green transfused in silver shining through:
Fairer than the lily, than the wild white cherry:
  Fair as in image my seraph love appears
Borne to me by dreams when dawn is at my eyelids:
  Fair as in the flesh she swims to me on tears.

Could I find a place to be alone with heaven,
  I would speak my heart out: heaven is my need.
Every woodland tree is flushing like the dogwood,
  Flashing like the whitebeam, swaying like the reed.
Flushing like the dogwood crimson in October;
  Streaming like the flag-reed South-west blown;
Flashing as in gusts the sudden-lighted whitebeam:
  All seem to know what is for heaven alone.

George Meredith [1828-1909]

MARIAN

SHE can be as wise as we,
  And wiser when she wishes;
She can knit with cunning wit,
  And dress the homely dishes.
She can flourish staff or pen,
  And deal a wound that lingers;
She can talk the talk of men,
  And touch with thrilling fingers.

Match her ye across the sea,
  Natures fond and fiery;
Ye who zest the turtle's nest
  With the eagle's eyrie.
Soft and loving is her soul,
  Swift and lofty soaring;
Mixing with its dove-like cole
  Passionate adoring.

Such a she who'll match with me?
  In flying or pursuing,
Subtle wiles are in her smiles
  To set the world a-wooing.
She is steadfast as a star,
  And yet the maddest maiden:
She can wage a gallant war,
  And give the peace of Eden.

                        George Meredith [1828–1909]

PRAISE OF MY LADY

MY lady seems of ivory
Forehead, straight nose, and cheeks that be
Hollowed a little mournfully.
      Beata mea Domina!

Her forehead, overshadowed much
By bows of hair, has a wave such
As God was good to make for me.
      Beata mea Domina!

Not greatly long my lady's hair,
Nor yet with yellow color fair,
But thick and crispèd wonderfully:
  Beata mea Domina !

Heavy to make the pale face sad,
And dark, but dead as though it had
Been forged by God most wonderfully
  Beata mea Domina !

Of some strange metal, thread by thread,
To stand out from my lady's head,
Not moving much to tangle me.
  Beata mea Domina !

Beneath her brows the lids fall slow,
The lashes a clear shadow throw
Where I would wish my lips to be.
  Beata mea Domina !

Her great eyes, standing far apart,
Draw up some memory from her heart,
And gaze out very mournfully;
  Beata mea Domina !

So beautiful and kind they are,
But most times looking out afar,
Waiting for something, not for me.
  Beata mea Domina !

I wonder if the lashes long
Are those that do her bright eyes wrong,
For always half tears seem to be
  Beata mea Domina !

Lurking below the underlid,
Darkening the place where they lie hid:
If they should rise and flow for me!
  Beata mea Domina !

Her full lips being made to kiss,
Curled up and pensive each one is;
This makes me faint to stand and see.
  Beata mea Domina !

Her lips are not contented now,
Because the hours pass so slow
Towards a sweet time: (pray for me),
    Beata mea Domina !

Nay, hold thy peace! for who can tell?
But this at least I know full well,
Her lips are parted longingly,
    Beata mea Domina !

So passionate and swift to move,
To pluck at any flying love,
That I grow faint to stand and see.
    Beata mea Domina !

Yea! there beneath them is her chin,
So fine and round, it were a sin
To feel no weaker when I see
    Beata mea Domina !

God's dealings; for with so much care
And troublous, faint lines wrought in there,
He finishes her face for me.
    Beata mea Domina !

Of her long neck what shall I say?
What things about her body's sway,
Like a knight's pennon or slim tree
    Beata mea Domina !

Set gently waving in the wind;
Or her long hands that I may find
On some day sweet to move o'er me?
    Beata mea Domina !

God pity me though, if I missed
The telling, how along her wrist
The veins creep, dying languidly
    Beata mea Domina !

Inside her tender palm and thin.
Now give me pardon, dear, wherein
My voice is weak and vexes thee.
    Beata mea Domina !

All men that see her any time,
I charge you straightly in this rhyme,
What, and wherever you may be,
  Beata mea Domina !

To kneel before her; as for me
I choke and grow quite faint to see
My lady moving graciously.
  Beata mea Domina !
   William Morris [1834–1896]

MADONNA MIA

UNDER green apple boughs
That never a storm will rouse,
My lady hath her house
 Between two bowers;
In either of the twain
Red roses full of rain;
She hath for bondwomen
 All kind of flowers.

She hath no handmaid fair
To draw her curled gold hair
Through rings of gold that bear
 Her whole hair's weight;
She hath no maids to stand
Gold-clothed on either hand;
In all that great green land
 None is so great.

She hath no more to wear
But one white hood of vair
Drawn over eyes and hair,
 Wrought with strange gold,
Made for some great queen's head,
Some fair great queen since dead;
And one strait gown of red
 Against the cold.

Beneath her eyelids deep
Love lying seems asleep,
Love, swift to wake, to weep,
    To laugh, to gaze;
Her breasts are like white birds,
And all her gracious words
As water-grass to herds
    In the June-days.

To her all dews that fall
And rains are musical;
Her flowers are fed from all,
    Her joys from these;
In the deep-feathered firs
Their gift of joy is hers,
In the least breath that stirs
    Across the trees.

She grows with greenest leaves,
Ripens with reddest sheaves,
Forgets, remembers, grieves,
    And is not sad;
The quiet lands and skies
Leave light upon her eyes;
None knows her, weak or wise,
    Or tired or glad.

None knows, none understands,
What flowers are like her hands;
Though you should search all lands
    Wherein time grows,
What snows are like her feet,
Though his eyes burn with heat
Through gazing on my sweet,—
    Yet no man knows.

Only this thing is said;
That white and gold and red,
God's three chief words, man's bread
    And oil and wine,

Were given her for dowers,
And kingdom of all hours,
And grace of goodly flowers
    And various vine.

This is my lady's praise:
God after many days
Wrought her in unknown ways,
    In sunset lands;
This is my lady's birth;
God gave her might and mirth.
And laid his whole sweet earth
    Between her hands.

Under deep apple boughs
My lady hath her house;
She wears upon her brows
    The flower thereof;
All saying but what God saith
To her is as vain breath;
She is more strong than death,
    Being strong as love.
            Algernon Charles Swinburne [1837-1909]

"MEET WE NO ANGELS, PANSIE?"

CAME, on a Sabbath morn, my sweet,
    In white, to find her lover;
The grass grew proud beneath her feet,
    The green elm-leaves above her:—
        Meet we no angels, Pansie?

She said, "We meet no angels now";
    And soft lights streamed upon her;
And with white hand she touched a bough;
    She did it that great honor:—
        What! meet no angels, Pansie?

O sweet brown hat, brown hair, brown eyes,
  Down-dropped brown eyes, so tender!
Then what said I?—gallant replies
  Seem flattery, and offend her:—
    But,—meet we no angels, Pansie?

          Thomas Ashe [1836–1889]

TO DAPHNE

LIKE apple-blossoms, white and red;
  Like hues of dawn, which fly too soon;
Like bloom of peach, so softly spread;
  Like thorn of May and rose of June—
Oh, sweet! oh, fair! beyond compare,
    Are Daphne's cheeks,
Are Daphne's blushing cheeks, I swear.

That pretty rose, which comes and goes
  Like April sunshine in the sky,
I can command it when I choose—
  See how it rises if I cry:
Oh, sweet! oh, fair! beyond compare,
    Are Daphne's cheeks,
Are Daphne's blushing cheeks, I swear.

Ah! when it lies round lips and eyes,
  And fades away, again to spring,
No lover, sure, could ask for more
  Than still to cry, and still to sing:
Oh, sweet! oh, fair! beyond compare,
    Are Daphne's cheeks,
Are Daphne's blushing cheeks, I swear.

          Walter Besant [1836–1901]

"GIRL OF THE RED MOUTH"

GIRL of the red mouth,
  Love me! Love me!
Girl of the red mouth,
  Love me!

'Tis by its curve, I know,
Love fashioneth his bow,
And bends it—ah, even so!
  Oh, girl of the red mouth, love me!

Girl of the blue eye,
  Love me! Love me!
Girl of the dew eye,
  Love me!
Worlds hang for lamps on high;
And thought's world lives in thy
Lustrous and tender eye—
  Oh, girl of the blue eye, love me!

Girl of the swan's neck,
  Love me! Love me!
Girl of the swan's neck,
  Love me!
As a marble Greek doth grow
To his steed's back of snow,
Thy white neck sits thy shoulder so,—
  Oh, girl of the swan's neck, love me!

Girl of the low voice,
  Love me! Love me!
Girl of the sweet voice,
  Love me!
Like the echo of a bell,—
Like the bubbling of a well,—
Sweeter! Love within doth dwell,—
  Oh, girl of the low voice, love me!
     Martin MacDermott [1823–1905]

THE DAUGHTER OF MENDOZA

O LEND to me, sweet nightingale,
  Your music by the fountain,
And lend to me your cadences,
  O river of the mountain!

That I may sing my gay brunette,
A diamond spark in coral set,
Gem for a prince's coronet—
    The daughter of Mendoza.

How brilliant is the morning star,
    The evening star how tender,—
The light of both is in her eyes,
    Their softness and their splendor.
But for the lash that shades their light
They were too dazzling for the sight,
And when she shuts them, all is night—
    The daughter of Mendoza.

O ever bright and beauteous one,
    Bewildering and beguiling,
The lute is in thy silvery tones,
    The rainbow in thy smiling;
And thine, is, too, o'er hill and dell,
The bounding of the young gazelle,
The arrow's flight and ocean's swell—
    Sweet daughter of Mendoza!

What though, perchance, we no more meet,—
    What though too soon we sever?
Thy form will float like emerald light
    Before my vision ever.
For who can see and then forget
The glories of my gay brunette—
Thou art too bright a star to set,
    Sweet daughter of Mendoza!

Mirabeau Bonaparte Lamar [1798–1859]

'IF SHE BE MADE OF WHITE AND RED"

If she be made of white and red,
As all transcendent beauty shows;
If heaven be blue above her head,
And earth be golden, as she goes:
Nay, then thy deftest words restrain;
Tell not that beauty, it is vain.

If she be filled with love and scorn,
As all divinest natures are;
If 'twixt her lips such words are born,
As can but Heaven or Hell confer:
Bid Love be still, nor ever speak,
Lest he his own rejection seek.

Herbert P. Horne [1864–

THE LOVER'S SONG

LEND me thy fillet, Love!
    I would no longer see:
Cover mine eyelids close awhile,
    And make me blind like thee.

Then might I pass her sunny face,
    And know not it was fair;
Then might I hear her voice, nor guess
    Her starry eyes were there.

Ah! banished so from stars and sun—
    Why need it be my fate?
If only she might dream me good
    And wise, and be my mate!

Lend her thy fillet, Love!
    Let her no longer see:
If there is hope for me at all,
    She must be blind like thee.

Edward Rowland Sill [1841–1887]

"WHEN FIRST I SAW HER"

WHEN first I saw her, at the stroke
The heart of nature in me spoke;
The very landscape smiled more sweet,
Lit by her eyes, pressed by her feet;
She made the stars of heaven more bright
By sleeping under them at night;
And fairer made the flowers of May
By being lovelier than they.

O, soft, soft, where the sunshine spread,
Dark in the grass I laid my head;
And let the lights of earth depart
To find her image in my heart;
Then through my being came and went
Tones of some heavenly instrument,
As if where its blind motions roll
The world should wake and be a soul.

George Edward Woodberry [1855–1930]

MY APRIL LADY

WHEN down the stair at morning
   The sunbeams round her float,
Sweet rivulets of laughter
   Are rippling in her throat;
The gladness of her greeting
   Is gold without alloy;
And in the morning sunlight
   I think her name is Joy.

When in the evening twilight
   The quiet book-room lies,
We read the sad old ballads,
   While from her hidden eyes
The tears are falling, falling,
   That give her heart relief;
And in the evening twilight,
   I think her name is Grief.

My little April lady,
   Of sunshine and of showers
She weaves the old spring magic,
   And breaks my heart in flowers!
But when her moods are ended,
   She nestles like a dove;
Then, by the pain and rapture,
   I know her name is Love.

Henry Van Dyke [1852–1933]

THE MILKMAID

A NEW SONG TO AN OLD TUNE

Across the grass I see her pass;
  She comes with tripping pace,—
A maid I know,—and March winds blow
  Her hair across her face;—
      With a hey, Dolly! ho, Dolly!
        Dolly shall be mine,
      Before the spray is white with May,
        Or blooms the eglantine.

The March winds blow.   I watch her go:
  Her eye is brown and clear;
Her cheek is brown, and soft as down,
  (To those who see it near!)—
      With a hey, Dolly! ho, Dolly!
        Dolly shall be mine,
      Before the spray is white with May,
        Or blooms the eglantine.

What has she not that those have got,—
  The dames that walk in silk!
If she undo her kerchief blue,
  Her neck is white as milk.
      With a hey, Dolly! ho, Dolly!
        Dolly shall be mine,
      Before the spray is white with May,
        Or blooms the eglantine.

Let those who will be proud and chill!
  For me, from June to June,
My Dolly's words are sweet as curds—
  Her laugh is like a tune;—
      With a hey, Dolly! ho, Dolly!
        Dolly shall be mine,
      Before the spray is white with May,
        Or blooms the eglantine.

Break, break to hear, O crocus-spear!
  O tall Lent-lilies flame!
There'll be a bride at Easter-tide,
  And Dolly is her name.
    With a hey, Dolly! ho, Dolly!
      Dolly shall be mine,
    Before the spray is white with May,
      Or blooms the eglantine.

                    Austin Dobson [1840–1921]

SONG

THIS peach is pink with such a pink
  As suits the peach divinely;
The cunning color rarely spread
  Fades to the yellow finely;
But where to spy the truest pink
Is in my Love's soft cheek, I think.

The snowdrop, child of windy March,
  Doth glory in her whiteness;
Her golden neighbors, crocuses,
  Unenvious praise her brightness!
But I do know where, out of sight,
My sweetheart keeps a warmer white.

                    Norman Gale [1862–

IN FEBRUARY

My Lady's birthday crowns the growing year;
A flower of Spring before the Spring is here;
To sing of her and this fair day to keep
The very Loves forsake their Winter sleep;
Where'er she goes their circling wings they spread,
And shower celestial roses o'er her head.
I, too, would chant her worth and dare to raise
A hymn to what's beyond immortal praise.
Go, little verse, and lay in vesture meet
Of poesy, my homage at her feet.

                    Henry Simpson [1868–

"LOVE, I MARVEL WHAT YOU ARE"

LOVE, I marvel what you are!
Heaven in a pearl of dew,
Lilies hearted with a star—
All are you.

Spring along your forehead shines
And the summer blooms your breast.
Graces of autumnal vines
Round you rest.

Birds about a limpid rose
Making song and light of wing
While the warm wind sunny blows,—
So you sing.

Darling, if the little dust,
That I know is merely I,
Have availed to win your trust,
Let me die.

Trumbull Stickney [1874–1904]

BALLADE OF MY LADY'S BEAUTY

SQUIRE ADAM had two wives, they say,
  Two wives had he for his delight;
He kissed and clypt them all the day,
  And clypt and kissed them all the night.
  Now Eve like ocean foam was white,
And Lilith, roses dipped in wine,
  But though they were a goodly sight,
No lady is so fair as mine.

To Venus some folk tribute pay,
  And Queen of Beauty she is hight,
And Sainte Marie the world doth sway,
  In cerule napery bedight.
  My wonderment these twain invite,
Their comeliness it is divine;
  And yet I say in their despite,
No lady is so fair as mine.

Dame Helen caused a grievous fray,
　　For love of her brave men did fight,
The eyes of her made sages fey
　　And put their hearts in woeful plight.
　　To her no rhymes will I indite,
For her no garlands will I twine;
　　Though she be made of flowers and light,
No lady is so fair as mine.

L'ENVOI

Prince Eros, Lord of lovely might,
　　Who on Olympus doth recline,
Do I not tell the truth aright?
　　No lady is so fair as mine.

Joyce Kilmer [1886–1918]

URSULA

I SEE her in the festal warmth to-night,
Her rest all grace, her motion all delight.
Endowed with all the woman's arts that please,
In her soft gown she seems a thing of ease,
Whom sorrow may not reach or evil blight.

To-morrow she will toil from floor to floor
To smile upon the unreplying poor,
To stay the tears of widows, and to be
Confessor to men's erring hearts . . . ah me!
She knows not I am beggar at her door.

Robert Underwood Johnson [1853–1937]

VILLANELLE OF HIS LADY'S TREASURES

I TOOK her dainty eyes, as well
　　As silken tendrils of her hair:
And so I made a Villanelle!

I took her voice, a silver bell,
　　As clear as song, as soft as prayer;
I took her dainty eyes as well.

It may be, said I, who can tell,
   These things shall be my less despair?
And so I made a Villanelle!

I took her whiteness virginal
   And from her cheeks two roses rare:
I took her dainty eyes as well.

I said: "It may be possible
   Her image from my heart to tear!"
And so I made a Villanelle!

I stole her laugh, most musical:
   I wrought it in with artful care;
I took her dainty eyes as well;
And so I made a Villanelle.

Ernest Dowson [1867–1900]

SONG

   LOVE, by that loosened hair
   Well now I know
   Where the lost Lilith went
   So long ago.

   Love, by those starry eyes
   I understand
   How the sea maidens lure
   Mortals from land.

   Love, by that welling laugh
   Joy claims his own
   Sea-born and wind-wayward
   Child of the sun.

Bliss Carman [1861–1929]

SONG

O, LIKE a queen's her happy tread,
And like a queen's her golden head!
But O, at last, when all is said,
   Her woman's heart for me!

We wandered where the river gleamed
'Neath oaks that mused and pines that dreamed,
A wild thing of the woods she seemed,
        So proud, and pure, and free!

All heaven drew nigh to hear her sing,
When from her lips her soul took wing;
The oaks forgot their pondering,
        The pines their reverie.

And O, her happy, queenly tread,
And O, her queenly golden head!
But O, her heart, when all is said,
        Her woman's heart for me!

William Watson [1858–1935]

ANY LOVER, ANY LASS

WHY are her eyes so bright, so bright,
    Why do her lips control
The kisses of a summer night,
    When I would love her soul?

God set her brave eyes wide apart
    And painted them with fire;
They stir the ashes of my heart
    To embers of desire.

Her lips so tenderly are wrought
    In so divine a shape,
That I am servant to my thought
    And can no wise escape.

Her body is a flower, her hair
    About her neck doth play;
I find her colors everywhere,
    They are the pride of day.

Her little hands are soft, and when
    I see her fingers move
I know in very truth that men
    Have died for less than love.

Ah, dear, live, lovely thing! my eyes
   Have sought her like a prayer;
It is my better self that cries
   "Would she were not so fair!"

Would I might forfeit ecstasy
   And find a calmer place,
Where I might undesirous see
   Her too desired face:

Nor find her eyes so bright, so bright,
   Nor hear her lips unroll
Dream after dream the lifelong night,
   When I would love her soul.

             Richard Middleton [1882-1911]

SONGS ASCENDING

Love has been sung a thousand ways—
   So let it be;
The songs ascending in your praise
Through all my days
   Are three.

Your cloud-white body first I sing;
   Your love was heaven's blue,
And I, a bird, flew carolling
In ring on ring
   Of you.

Your nearness is the second song;
   When God began to be,
And bound you strongly, right or wrong,
With his own thong,
   To me.

But oh, the song, eternal, high,
   That tops these two!—
You live forever, you who die,
I am not I
   But you.

             Witter Bynner [1881-

SONG

"OH! Love," they said, "is King of Kings,
    And Triumph is his crown.
Earth fades in flame before his wings,
    And Sun and Moon bow down."—
But that, I knew, would never do;
    And Heaven is all too high.
So whenever I meet a Queen, I said,
    I will not catch her eye.

"Oh! Love," they said, and "Love," they said,
    "The gift of Love is this;
A crown of thorns about thy head,
    And vinegar to thy kiss!"—
But Tragedy is not for me;
    And I'm content to be gay.
So whenever I spied a Tragic Lady,
    I went another way.

And so I never feared to see
    You wander down the street,
Or come across the fields to me
    On ordinary feet.
For what they'd never told me of,
    And what I never knew;
It was that all the time, my love,
    Love would be merely you.

                        Rupert Brooke [1887–1915]

SONG

How do I love you?
    I do not know.
Only because of you
    Gladly I go.

Only because of you
    Labor is sweet,
And all the song of you
    Sings in my feet.

Only the thought of you
  Trembles and lies
Just where the world begins—
  Under my eyes.

Irene Rutherford McLeod [1891–

TO ... IN CHURCH

IF I was drawn here from a distant place,
'Twas not to pray nor hear our friend's address,
But, gazing once more on your winsome face,
To worship there Ideal Loveliness.
On that pure shrine that has too long ignored
The gifts that once I brought so frequently
I lay this votive offering, to record
How sweet your quiet beauty seemed to me.
Enchanting girl, my faith is not a thing
By futile prayers and vapid psalm-singing
To vent in crowded nave and public pew.
My creed is simple: that the world is fair,
And beauty the best thing to worship there,
And I confess it by adoring you.

Alan Seeger [1888–1916]

AFTER TWO YEARS

SHE is all so slight
And tender and white
  As a May morning.
She walks without hood
At dusk. It is good
  To hear her sing.

It is God's will
That I shall love her still
  As He loves Mary.
And night and day
I will go forth to pray
  That she love me.

She is as gold
Lovely, and far more cold.
  Do thou pray with me,
For if I win grace
To kiss twice her face
  God has done well to me.
                        Richard Aldington [1892-

PRAISE

DEAR, they are praising your beauty,
The grass and the sky:
The sky in a silence of wonder,
The grass in a sigh.

I too would sing for your praising,
Dearest, had I
Speech as the whispering grass,
Or the silent sky.

These have an art for the praising
Beauty so high.
Sweet, you are praised in a silence,
Sung in a sigh.
                        Seumas O'Sullivan [1879-

PLAINTS AND PROTESTATIONS

"FORGET NOT YET"

THE LOVER BESEECHETH HIS MISTRESS NOT TO FORGET HIS STEADFAST FAITH AND TRUE INTENT

FORGET not yet the tried intent
Of such a truth as I have meant;
My great travail so gladly spent,
Forget not yet!

Forget not yet when first began
The weary life ye know, since when
The suit, the service, none tell can;
Forget not yet!

Forget not yet the great assays,
The cruel wrong, the scornful ways,
The painful patience in delays,
Forget not yet!

Forget not! O, forget not this!—
How long ago hath been, and is,
The mind that never meant amiss—
Forget not yet!

Forget not then thine own approved,
The which so long hath thee so loved,
Whose steadfast faith yet never moved:
Forget not this!

Thomas Wyatt [1503?-1542]

FAWNIA

From "Pandosto"

AH! were she pitiful as she is fair,
Or but as mild as she is seeming so,
Then were my hopes greater than my despair,
Then all the world were heaven, nothing woe.

583

Ah! were her heart relenting as her hand,
That seems to melt even with the mildest touch,
Then knew I where to seat me in a land
Under wide heavens, but yet there is not such.
So as she shows she seems the budding rose,
Yet sweeter far than is an earthly flower;
Sovereign of beauty, like the spray she grows;
Compassed she is with thorns and cankered flower.
   Yet were she willing to be plucked and worn,
    She would be gathered, though she grew on thorn.

Ah! when she sings, all music else be still,
For none must be comparèd to her note;
Ne'er breathed such glee from Philomela's bill,
Nor from the morning-singer's swelling throat.
Ah! when she riseth from her blissful bed
She comforts all the world as doth the sun,
And at her sight the night's foul vapor's fled;
When she is set the gladsome day is done.
   O glorious sun, imagine me the west,
    Shine in my arms, and set thou in my breast!

Robert Greene [1560?–1592]

THE PASSIONATE SHEPHERD TO HIS LOVE

COME live with me and be my Love,
And we will all the pleasures prove
That hills and valleys, dales and fields,
Or woods or steepy mountain yields.

And we will sit upon the rocks,
And see the shepherds feed their flocks
By shallow rivers, to whose falls
Melodious birds sing madrigals.

And I will make thee beds of roses
And a thousand fragrant posies;
A cap of flowers, and a kirtle
Embroidered all with leaves of myrtle.

A gown made of the finest wool
Which from our pretty lambs we pull;
Fair-linèd slippers for the cold,
With buckles of the purest gold.

A belt of straw and ivy-buds
With coral clasps and amber studs:
And if these pleasures may thee move,
Come live with me and be my Love.

The shepherd swains shall dance and sing
For thy delight each May morning:
If these delights thy mind may move,
Then live with me and be my Love.

Christopher Marlowe [1564–1593]

THE NYMPH'S REPLY TO THE PASSIONATE
SHEPHERD

IF all the world and love were young,
And truth in every shepherd's tongue.
These pretty pleasures might me move
To live with thee, and be thy Love.

But Time drives flocks from field to fold;
When rivers rage and rocks grow cold;
And Philomel becometh dumb;
The rest complains of cares to come.

The flowers do fade, and wanton fields
To wayward Winter reckoning yields:
A honey tongue, a heart of gall,
Is fancy's spring, but sorrow's fall.

Thy gowns, thy shoes, thy beds of roses,
Thy cap, thy kirtle, and thy posies,
Soon break, soon wither,—soon forgotten,
In folly ripe, in reason rotten.

Thy belt of straw and ivy-buds,
Thy coral clasps and amber studs,—
All these in me no means can move
To come to thee and be thy Love.

But could youth last, and love still breed,
Had joys no date, nor age no need,
Then these delights my mind might move
To live with thee and be thy Love.

Walter Raleigh [1552?–1618]

"WRONG NOT, SWEET EMPRESS OF MY HEART"

WRONG not, sweet empress of my heart,
    The merit of true passion,
With thinking that he feels no smart,
    That sues for no compassion.

Silence in love bewrays more woe
    Than words, though ne'er so witty:
A beggar that is dumb, you know,
    May challenge double pity.

Then wrong not, dearest to my heart,
    My true, though secret passion;
He smarteth most that hides his smart,
    And sues for no compassion.

Walter Raleigh [1552?–1618]

TO HIS COY LOVE

I PRAY thee, leave, love me no more,
    Call home the heart you gave me!
I but in vain that saint adore
    That can but will not save me.
These poor half-kisses kill me quite—
    Was ever man thus servèd:
Amidst an ocean of delight
    For pleasure to be starvèd!

Show me no more those snowy breasts
   With azure riverets branchèd,
Where, whilst mine eye with plenty feasts,
   Yet is my thirst not stanchèd;
O Tantalus, thy pains ne'er tell!
   By me thou art prevented:
'Tis nothing to be plagued in Hell,
   But thus in Heaven tormented.

Clip me no more in those dear arms,
   Nor thy life's comfort call me,
O these are but too powerful charms,
   And do but more enthral me!
But see how patient I am grown
   In all this coil about thee:
Come, nice thing, let my heart alone,
   I cannot live without thee!

Michael Drayton [1563–1631]

HER SACRED BOWER

WHERE she her sacred bower adorns,
   The rivers clearly flow,
The groves and meadows swell with flowers,
   The winds all gently blow.
Her sun-like beauty shines so fair,
   Her spring can never fade:
Who then can blame the life that strives
   To harbor in her shade?

Her grace I sought, her love I wooed;
   Her love thought to obtain;
No time, no toil, no vow, no faith,
   Her wishèd grace can gain.
Yet truth can tell my heart is hers
   And her will I adore;
And from that love when I depart,
   Let heaven view me no more!

Her roses with my prayers shall spring;
    And when her trees I praise,
Their boughs shall blossom, mellow fruit
    Shall strew her pleasant ways.
The words of hearty zeal have power
    High wonders to effect;
O, why should then her princely ear
    My words or zeal neglect?

If she my faith misdeems, or worth,
    Woe worth my hapless fate!
For though time can my truth reveal,
    That time will come too late.
And who can glory in the worth
    That cannot yield him grace?
Content in everything is not,
    Nor joy in every place.

But from her Bower of Joy since I
    Must now excluded be,
And she will not relieve my cares,
    Which none can help but she;
My comfort in her love shall dwell,
    Her love lodge in my breast,
And though not in her bower, yet I
    Shall in her temple rest.

Thomas Campion [? - 1619]

TO LESBIA *

AFTER CATULLUS

MY sweetest Lesbia, let us live and love,
And though the sager sort our deeds reprove,
Let us not weigh them. Heaven's great lamps do dive
Into their west, and straight again revive:
But soon as once set is our little light,
Then must we sleep one ever-during night.

If all would lead their lives in love like me,
Then bloody swords and armor should not be;
No drum nor trumpet peaceful sleeps should move,
Unless alarm came from the Camp of Love:

* For the original of this poem see page 3827.

But fools do live and waste their little light,
And seek with pain their ever-during night.

When timely death my life and fortune ends,
Let not my hearse be vexed with mourning friends;
But let all lovers, rich in triumph, come
And with sweet pastimes grace my happy tomb:
And, Lesbia, close up thou my little light,
And crown with love my ever-during night.

Thomas Campion [? –1619]

"LOVE ME OR NOT"

LOVE me or not, love her I must or die:
Leave her or not, follow her needs must I.
O that her grace would my wished comforts give!
How rich in her, how happy should I live!

All my desire, all my delight should be
Her to enjoy, her to unite to me;
Envy should cease, her would I love alone:
Who loves by looks, is seldom true to one.

Could I enchant, and that it lawful were,
Her would I charm softly that none should hear;
But love enforced rarely yields firm content:
So would I love that neither should repent.

Thomas Campion [? –1619]

"THERE IS NONE, O NONE BUT YOU"

THERE is none, O none but you,
   That from me estrange the sight,
Whom mine eyes affect to view,
   And chainèd ears hear with delight.

Other beauties others move:
   In you I all graces find;
Such is the effect of Love,
   To make them happy that are kind.

Women in frail beauty trust,
  Only seem you fair to me:
Still prove truly kind and just,
  For that may not dissembled be.

Sweet, afford me then your sight,
  That, surveying all your looks,
Endless volumes I may write,
  And fill the world with envied books:

Which, when after-ages view,
  All shall wonder and despair,—
Woman, to find a man so true,
  Or man, a woman half so fair!

Thomas Campion [? –1619]

OF CORINNA'S SINGING

WHEN to her lute Corinna sings,
Her voice revives the leaden strings,
And doth in highest notes appear,
As any challenged echo clear:
But when she doth of mourning speak,
E'en with her sighs, the strings do break.

And as her lute doth live or die,
Led by her passion, so must I!
For when of pleasure she doth sing,
My thoughts enjoy a sudden spring:
But if she doth of sorrow speak,
E'en from my heart the strings do break.

Thomas Campion [? –1619]

"WERE MY HEART AS SOME MEN'S ARE"

WERE my heart as some men's are, thy errors would not
    move me;
But thy faults I curious find, and speak because I love thee:
Patience is a thing divine, and far, I grant, above me.

Foes sometimes befriend us more, our blacker deeds ob-
    jecting,
Than the obsequious bosom-guest with false respect af-
    fecting:
Friendship is the Glass of Truth, our hidden stains detecting.

When I use of eyes enjoy, and inward light of reason,
Thy observer will I be and censor, but in season:
Hidden mischief to conceal in State and Love is treason.

              Thomas Campion [? —1619]

"KIND ARE HER ANSWERS"

    KIND are her answers,
    But her performance keeps no day;
    Breaks time, as dancers
    From their own music when they stray.
    All her free favors
    And smooth words wing my hopes in vain.
O, did ever voice so sweet but only feign?
    Can true love yield such delay,
    Converting joy to pain?

    Lost is our freedom
    When we submit to women so:
    Why do we need 'em
    When, in their best, they work our woe?
    There is no wisdom
    Can alter ends by fate prefixed.
O, why is the good of man with evil mixed?
    Never were days yet called two
    But one night went betwixt.

              Thomas Campion [? —1619]

TO CELIA

From "The Forest"

    DRINK to me only with thine eyes,
      And I will pledge with mine;
    Or leave a kiss but in the cup
      And I'll not look for wine.

The thirst that from the soul doth rise
  Doth ask a drink divine;
But might I of Jove's nectar sup,
  I would not change for thine.

I sent thee late a rosy wreath,
  Not so much honoring thee
As giving it a hope that there
  It could not withered be;
But thou thereon didst only breathe,
  And sent'st it back to me;
Since when it grows, and smells, I swear,
  Not of itself but thee!

            Ben Jonson [1573?-1637]

SONG

From " The Forest "

O, DO not wanton with those eyes,
  Lest I be sick with seeing;
Nor cast them down, but let them rise,
  Lest shame destroy their being.

O, be not angry with those fires,
  For then their threats will kill me;
Nor look too kind on my desires,
  For then my hopes will spill me.

O, do not steep them in thy tears,
  For so will sorrow slay me;
Nor spread them as distract with fears;
  Mine own enough betray me.

            Ben Jonson [1573?-1637]

SONG

Go and catch a falling star,
  Get with child a mandrake root,
Tell me where all past years are,
  Or who cleft the Devil's foot;

Teach me to hear mermaid's singing,
Or to keep off envy's stinging,
      And find
      What wind
Serves to advance an honest mind.

If thou be'st born to strange sights,
  Things invisible go see,
Ride ten thousand days and nights
  Till Age snow white hairs on thee;
Thou, when thou return'st, wilt tell me
All strange wonders that befell thee,
      And swear
      No where
Lives a woman true and fair.

If thou find'st one, let me know;
  Such a pilgrimage were sweet.
Yet do not; I would not go,
  Though at next door we might meet.
Though she were true when you met her,
And last till you write your letter,
      Yet she
      Will be
False, ere I come, to two or three.

              John Donne [1573–1631]

THE MESSAGE

SEND home my long-strayed eyes to me,
Which, O! too long have dwelt on thee:
But if from you they've learned such ill,
    To sweetly smile,
    And then beguile,
Keep the deceivers, keep them still.

Send home my harmless heart again,
Which no unworthy thought could stain:
But if it has been taught by thine
    To forfeit both
    Its word and oath,
Keep it, for then 'tis none of mine.

Yet send me back my heart and eyes,
For I'll know all thy falsities;
That I one day may laugh, when thou
    Shalt grieve and mourn—
    Of one the scorn,
Who proves as false as thou art now.

               John Donne [1573–1631]

SONG

LADIES, though to your conquering eyes
Love owes his chiefest victories,
And borrows those bright arms from you
With which he does the world subdue,
Yet you yourselves are not above
The empire nor the griefs of love.

Then rack not lovers with disdain,
Lest Love on you revenge their pain:
You are not free because you're fair:
The Boy did not his Mother spare.
Beauty's but an offensive dart:
It is no armor for the heart.

            George Etherege [1635?–1691]

TO A LADY ASKING HIM HOW LONG HE WOULD LOVE HER

IT is not, Celia, in our power
    To say how long our love will last;
It may be we within this hour
    May lose those joys we now do taste:
The Blessèd, that immortal be,
From change in love are only free.

Then since we mortal lovers are,
    Ask not how long our love will last;
But while it does, let us take care
    Each minute be with pleasure passed:
Were it not madness to deny
To live because we're sure to die?

            George Etherege [1635?–1691]

TO ÆNONE

WHAT conscience, say, is it in thee,
  When I a heart had one,
To take away that heart from me,
  And to retain thy own?

For shame or pity now incline
  To play a loving part;
Either to send me kindly thine,
  Or give me back my heart.

Covet not both; but if thou dost
  Resolve to part with neither,
Why, yet to show that thou art just,
  Take me and mine together!
                    Robert Herrick [1591–1674]

TO ANTHEA, WHO MAY COMMAND HIM ANYTHING

BID me to live, and I will live
  Thy Protestant to be;
Or bid me love, and I will give
  A loving heart to thee.

A heart as soft, a heart as kind,
  A heart as sound and free
As in the whole world thou canst find,
  That heart I'll give to thee.

Bid that heart stay, and it will stay
  To honor thy decree;
Or bid it languish quite away,
  And 't shall do so for thee.

Bid me to weep, and I will weep,
  While I have eyes to see;
And having none, yet will I keep
  A heart to weep for thee.

Bid me despair, and I'll despair,
   Under that cypress tree;
Or bid me die, and I will dare
   E'en death, to die for thee.

Thou art my life, my love, my heart,
   The very eyes of me;
And hast command of every part,
   To live and die for thee.

                    Robert Herrick [1591–1674]

THE BRACELET: TO JULIA

WHY I tie about thy wrist,
Julia, this my silken twist;
For what other reason is't
But to show thee how, in part,
Thou my pretty captive art?
But thy bond-slave is my heart:
'Tis but silk that bindeth thee,
Knap the thread and thou art free;
But 'tis otherwise with me:
I am bound and fast bound, so
That from thee I cannot go;
If I could, I would not so.

                    Robert Herrick [1591–1674]

TO THE WESTERN WIND

SWEET western wind, whose luck it is,
   Made rival with the air,
To give Perenna's lip a kiss,
   And fan her wanton hair:

Bring me but one, I'll promise thee,
   Instead of common showers,
Thy wings shall be embalmed by me,
   And all beset with flowers.

                    Robert Herrick [1591–1674]

TO MY INCONSTANT MISTRESS

WHEN thou, poor Excommunicate
  From all the joys of Love, shalt see
The full reward and glorious fate
  Which my strong faith shall purchase me,
  Then curse thine own Inconstancy.

A fairer hand than thine shall cure
  That heart which thy false oaths did wound;
And to my soul a soul more pure
  Than thine shall by Love's hand be bound,
  And both with equal glory crowned.

Then shalt thou weep, entreat, complain
  To Love, as I did once to thee:
When all thy tears shall be as vain
  As mine were then: for thou shalt be
  Damned for thy false Apostasy.
                    Thomas Carew [1598?· 1639?]

PERSUASIONS TO ENJOY

IF the quick spirits in your eye
Now languish and anon must die;
If every sweet and every grace
Must fly from that forsaken face:
      Then, Celia, let us reap our joys
      Ere Time such goodly fruit destroys.

Or, if that golden fleece must grow
For ever free from agèd snow;
If those bright suns must know no shade,
Nor your fresh beauties ever fade:
      Then fear not, Celia, to bestow
      What, still being gathered, still must grow.

Thus either Time his sickle brings
In vain, or else in vain his wings.
                    Thomas Carew [1598?–1639?]

MEDIOCRITY IN LOVE REJECTED

GIVE me more love, or more disdain:
   The torrid, or the frozen zone
Bring equal ease unto my pain;
   The temperate affords me none:
Either extreme, of love or hate,
Is sweeter than a calm estate.

Give me a storm; if it be love,
   Like Danaë in that golden shower,
I'll swim in pleasure; if it prove
   Disdain, that torrent will devour
My vulture-hopes; and he's possessed
Of heaven, that's but from hell released.

Then crown my joys, or cure my pain:
Give me more love, or more disdain.
             Thomas Carew [1598?–1639?]

THE MESSAGE

YE little birds that sit and sing
   Amidst the shady valleys,
And see how Phillis sweetly walks
   Within her garden-alleys;
Go, pretty birds, about her bower;
Sing, pretty birds, she may not lower;
Ah me! methinks I see her frown!
   Ye pretty wantons, warble.

Go tell her through your chirping bills,
   As you by me are bidden,
To her is only known my love,
   Which from the world is hidden.
Go, pretty birds, and tell her so,
See that your notes strain not too low,
For still methinks I see her frown;
   Ye pretty wantons, warble.

Go tune your voices' harmony
    And sing, I am her lover;
Strain loud and sweet, that every note
    With sweet content may move her:
And she that hath the sweetest voice,
Tell her I will not change my choice:
—Yet still methinks I see her frown!
        Ye pretty wantons, warble.

O fly! make haste! see, see, she falls
    Into a pretty slumber!
Sing round about her rosy bed
    That waking she may wonder:
Say to her, 'tis her lover true
That sendeth love to you, to you!
And when you hear her kind reply,
        Return with pleasant warblings.
                        Thomas Heywood [? —1650?]

"HOW CAN THE HEART FORGET HER"

At her fair hands how have I grace entreated
With prayers oft repeated!
Yet still my love is thwarted:
Heart, let her go, for she'll not be converted—
        Say, shall she go?
        O no, no, no, no, no!
She is most fair, though she be marble-hearted.

How often have my sighs declared my anguish,
Wherein I daily languish!
Yet still she doth procure it:
Heart, let her go, for I cannot endure it—
        Say, shall she go?
        O no, no, no, no, no!
She gave the wound, and she alone must cure it.

But shall I still a true affection owe her,
Which prayers, sighs, tears do show her,

And shall she still disdain me?
Heart, let her go, if they no grace can gain me—
    Say, shall she go?
    O no, no, no, no, no!
She made me hers, and hers she will retain me.

But if the love that hath and still doth burn me
No love at length return me,
Out of my thoughts I'll set her:
Heart, let her go, O heart I pray thee, let her!
    Say, shall she go?
    O no, no, no, no, no!
Fixed in the heart, how can the heart forget her?

Francis Davison [fl. 1602]

TO ROSES IN THE BOSOM OF CASTARA

YE blushing virgins happy are
    In the chaste nunnery of her breasts—
For he'd profane so chaste a fair,
    Whoe'er should call them Cupid's nests.

Transplanted thus how bright ye grow!
    How rich a perfume do ye yield!
In some close garden cowslips so
    Are sweeter than in the open field.

In those white cloisters live secure
    From the rude blasts of wanton breath!—
Each hour more innocent and pure,
    Till you shall wither into death.

Then that which living gave you room,
    Your glorious sepulcher shall be.
There wants no marble for a tomb
    Whose breast hath marble been to me.

William Habington [1605–1654]

TO FLAVIA

'TIS not your beauty can engage
    My wary heart;
The sun, in all his pride and rage,
    Has not that art;

And yet he shines as bright as you,
If brightness could our souls subdue.

'Tis not the pretty things you say,
   Nor those you write,
Which can make Thyrsis' heart your prey:
   For that delight,
The graces of a well-taught mind,
In some of our own sex we find.

No, Flavia, 'tis your love I fear;
   Love's surest darts,
Those which so seldom fail him, are
   Headed with hearts:
Their very shadows make us yield;
Dissemble well, and win the field!

Edmund Waller [1606–1687]

"LOVE NOT ME FOR COMELY GRACE"

Love not me for comely grace,
For my pleasing eye or face;
Nor for any outward part,
No, nor for a constant heart:
      For these may fail or turn to ill,
      So thou and I shall sever.
Keep, therefore, a true woman's eye,
And love me still, but know not why;
      So hast thou the same reason still
      To doat upon me ever.

Unknown

"WHEN, DEAREST, I BUT THINK OF THEE"

When, dearest, I but think of thee,
Methinks all things that lovely be
   Are present, and my soul delighted:
For beauties that from worth arise
Are, like the grace of deities,
   Still present with us, though unsighted.

Thus while I sit and sigh the day
With all his borrowed lights away,
　　Till night's black wings do overtake me,
Thinking on thee, thy beauties then,
As sudden lights do sleepy men,
　　So they by their bright rays awake me.

Thus absence dies, and dying proves
No absence can subsist with loves
　　That do partake of fair perfection:
Since in the darkest night they may
By their quick motion find a way
　　To see each other by reflection.

The waving sea can with each flood
Bathe some high promont that hath stood
　　Far from the main up in the river:
O think not then but love can do
As much! for that's an ocean too,
　　Which flows not every day, but ever!

John Suckling [1609–1642]
or Owen Feltham [1602?–1668]

A DOUBT OF MARTYRDOM

O FOR some honest lover's ghost,
　　Some kind unbodied post
　　　　Sent from the shades below!
　　　　I strangely long to know
Whether the noble chaplets wear
Those that their mistress' scorn did bear
　　　　Or those that were used kindly.

For whatsoe'er they tell us here
　　To make those sufferings dear,
　　　　'Twill there, I fear, be found
　　　　That to the being crowned
To have loved alone will not suffice,
Unless we also have been wise
　　　　And have our loves enjoyed.

What posture can we think him in
  That, here unloved, again
    Departs, and's thither gone
    Where each sits by his own?
Or how can that Elysium be
Where I my mistress still must see
    Circled in other's arms?

For there the judges all are just,
  And Sophonisba must
    Be his whom she held dear,
    Not his who loved her here.
The sweet Philoclea, since she died,
Lies by her Pirocles his side,
    Not by Amphialus.

Some bays, perchance, or myrtle bough
  For difference crowns the brow
    Of those kind souls that were
    The noble martyrs here:
And if that be the only odds
(As who can tell?), ye kinder gods,
    Give me the woman here!

John Suckling [1609–1642]

TO CHLOE

WHO FOR HIS SAKE WISHED HERSELF YOUNGER

CHLOE, why wish you that your years
  Would backwards run till they meet mine,
That perfect likeness, which endears
  Things unto things, might us combine?
Our ages so in date agree,
That twins do differ more than we.

There are two births; the one when light
  First strikes the new awakened sense;
The other when two souls unite,
  And we must count our life from thence:

When you loved me and I loved you
Then both of us were born anew.

Love then to us new souls did give
    And in those souls did plant new powers;
Since when another life we live,
    The breath we breathe is his, not ours:
Love makes those young whom age doth chill,
And whom he finds young keeps young still.

Love, like that angel that shall call
    Our bodies from the silent grave,
Unto one age doth raise us all;
    None too much, none too little have;
Nay, that the difference may be none,
He makes two, not alike, but one.

And now since you and I are such,
    Tell me what's yours, and what is mine?
Our eyes, our ears, our taste, smell, touch,
    Do, like our souls, in one combine;
So, by this, I as well may be
Too old for you, as you for me.

                    William Cartwright [1611–1643]

"I'LL NEVER LOVE THEE MORE"

My dear and only Love, I pray
    This little world of thee
Be governed by no other sway
    Than purest monarchy;
For if confusion have a part,
    Which virtuous souls abhor,
And hold a synod in thy heart,
    I'll never love thee more.

Like Alexander I will reign,
    And I will reign alone;
My thoughts did evermore disdain
    A rival on my throne.

He either fears his fate too much,
   Or his deserts are small,
That dares not put it to the touch
   To gain or lose it all.

But I must rule and govern still,
   And always give the law,
And have each subject at my will
   And all to stand in awe.
But 'gainst my batteries if I find
   Thou kick, or vex me sore,
As that thou set me up a blind,
   I'll never love thee more!

Or in the empire of thy heart,
   Where I should solely be,
If others do pretend a part
   And dare to vie with me,
Or if committees thou erect,
   And go on such a score,
I'll laugh and sing at thy neglect,
   And never love thee more.

But if thou wilt be faithful, then,
   And constant of thy word,
I'll make thee glorious by my pen
   And famous by my sword;
I'll serve thee in such noble ways
   Were never heard before;
I'll crown and deck thee all with bays,
   And love thee evermore.
                 James Graham [1612–1650]

TO ALTHEA, FROM PRISON

WHEN Love with unconfinèd wings
   Hovers within my gates,
And my divine Althea brings
   To whisper at the grates;

When I lie tangled in her hair
  And fettered to her eye,
The birds that wanton in the air
  Know no such liberty.

When flowing cups run swiftly round
  With no allaying Thames,
Our careless heads with roses bound,
  Our hearts with loyal flames;
When thirsty grief in wine we steep,
  When healths and draughts go free—
Fishes that tipple in the deep
  Know no such liberty.

When, like committed linnets, I
  With shriller throat shall sing
The sweetness, mercy, majesty,
  And glories of my King;
When I shall voice aloud how good
  He is, how great should be,
Enlargèd winds, that curl the flood,
  Know no such liberty.

Stone walls do not a prison make,
  Nor iron bars a cage;
Minds innocent and quiet take
  That for an hermitage;
If I have freedom in my love
  And in my soul am free,
Angels alone, that soar above,
  Enjoy such liberty.

Richard Lovelace [1618–1658]

WHY I LOVE HER

'Tis not her birth, her friends, nor yet her treasure,
Nor do I covet her for sensual pleasure,
Nor for that old morality
Do I love her, 'cause she loves me.

Sure he that loves his lady 'cause she's fair,
Delights his eye, so loves himself, not her.
Something there is moves me to love, and I
Do know I love, but know not how, nor why.

Alexander Brome [1620–1666]

TO HIS COY MISTRESS

HAD we but world enough, and time,
This coyness, Lady, were no crime.
We would sit down and think which way
To walk and pass our long love's day.
Thou by the Indian Ganges' side
Shouldst rubies find: I by the tide
Of Humber would complain.   I would
Love you ten years before the Flood,
And you should, if you please, refuse
Till the conversion of the Jews.
My vegetable love should grow
Vaster than empires, and more slow;
An hundred years should go to praise
Thine eyes and on thy forehead gaze;
Two hundred to adore each breast,
But thirty thousand to the rest;
An age at least to every part,
And the last age should show your heart.
For, Lady, you deserve this state,
Nor would I love at lower rate.
  But at my back I always hear
Time's wingèd chariot hurrying near;
And yonder all before us lie
Deserts of vast eternity.
Thy beauty shall no more be found,
Nor, in thy marble vault, shall sound
My echoing song: then worms shall try
That long preserved virginity,
And your quaint honor turn to dust,
And into ashes all my lust:
The grave's a fine and private place,
But none, I think, do there embrace.

Now therefore, while the youthful hue
Sits on thy skin like morning dew,
And while thy willing soul transpires
At every pore with instant fires,
Now let us sport us while we may,
And now, like amorous birds of prey,
Rather at once our time devour
Than languish in his slow-chapt power.
Let us roll all our strength and all
Our sweetness up into one ball,
And tear our pleasures with rough strife
Through the iron gates of life:
Thus, though we cannot make our sun
Stand still, yet we will make him run.

Andrew Marvell [1621–1678]

A DEPOSITION FROM BEAUTY

THOUGH when I loved thee thou wert fair,
    Thou art no longer so;
These glories all the pride they wear
    Unto opinion owe.
Beauties, like stars, in borrowed luster shine;
And 'twas my love that gave thee thine.

The flames that dwelt within thine eye
    Do now with mine expire;
Thy brightest graces fade and die
    At once with my desire.
Love's fires thus mutual influence return;
Thine cease to shine, when mine to burn.

Then, proud Celinda, hope no more
    To be implored or wooed,
Since by thy scorn thou dost restore
    Thy wealth my love bestowed:
And thy despised disdain too late shall find
That none are fair but who are kind.

Thomas Stanley [1625–1678]

"LOVE IN THY YOUTH, FAIR MAID"

Love in thy youth, fair maid, be wise,
  Old Time will make thee colder,
And though each morning new arise,
  Yet we each day grow older.

Thou as heaven art fair and young,
  Thine eyes like twin stars shining;
But ere another day be sprung,
  All these will be declining;

Then winter comes with all his fears,
  And all thy sweets shall borrow;
Too late then wilt thou shower thy tears,
  And I, too late, shall sorrow.

Unknown

TO CELIA

When, Celia, must my old day set,
  And my young morning rise
In beams of joy so bright as yet
  Ne'er blessed a lover's eyes?
My state is more advanced than when
  I first attempted thee:
I sued to be a servant then,
  But now to be made free.

I've served my time faithful and true,
  Expecting to be placed
In happy freedom, as my due,
  To all the joys thou hast:
Ill husbandry in love is such
  A scandal to love's power,
We ought not to misspend so much
  As one poor short-lived hour.

Yet think not, sweet, I'm weary grown,
  That I pretend such haste;
Since none to surfeit e'er was known
  Before he had a taste:

My infant love could humbly wait
　　When, young, it scarce knew how
To plead; but grown to man's estate,
　　He is impatient now.

Charles Cotton [1630 -1687]

TO CELIA

NOT, Celia, that I juster am
　　Or better than the rest!
For I would change each hour, like them,
　　Were not my heart at rest.

But I am tied to very thee
　　By every thought I have;
Thy face I only care to see,
　　Thy heart I only crave.

All that in woman is adored
　　In thy dear self I find—
For the whole sex can but afford
　　The handsome and the kind.

Why then should I seek further store,
　　And still make love anew?
When change itself can give no more,
　　'Tis easy to be true!

Charles Sedley [1639 -1701]

A SONG

MY dear mistress has a heart
　　Soft as those kind looks she gave me;
When with love's resistless art,
　　And her eyes, she did enslave me.
But her constancy's so weak,
　　She's so wild and apt to wander,
That my jealous heart would break
　　Should we live one day asunder.

Melting joys about her move,
  Killing pleasures, wounding blisses;
She can dress her eyes in love,
  And her lips can arm with kisses.
Angels listen when she speaks;
  She's my delight, all mankind's wonder;
But my jealous heart would break
  Should we live one day asunder.

John Wilmot [1647–1680]

LOVE AND LIFE

ALL my past life is mine no more;
  The flying hours are gone,
Like transitory dreams given o'er,
Whose images are kept in store
  By memory alone.

The time that is to come is not;
  How can it then be mine?
The present moment's all my lot;
And that, as fast as it is got,
  Phillis, is only thine.

Then talk not of inconstancy,
  False hearts, and broken vows;
If I by miracle can be
This live-long minute true to thee,
  'Tis all that Heaven allows.

John Wilmot [1647–1680]

CONSTANCY

I CANNOT change as others do,
  Though you unjustly scorn;
Since that poor swain that sighs for you
  For you alone was born.
No, Phillis, no; your heart to move
  A surer way I'll try;
And, to revenge my slighted love,
  Will still live on, will still live on and die.

When, killed with grief, Amyntas lies,
   And you to mind shall call
The sighs that now unpitied rise,
   The tears that vainly fall—
That welcome hour that ends this smart,
   Will then begin your pain;
For such a faithful tender heart
Can never break, can never break in vain.

John Wilmot [1647–1680]

SONG

Too late, alas! I must confess,
   You need not arts to move me;
Such charms by nature you possess,
   'Twere madness not to love ye.

Then spare a heart you may surprise,
   And give my tongue the glory
To boast, though my unfaithful eyes
   Betray a tender story.

John Wilmot [1647–1680]

SONG

Come, Celia, let's agree at last
   To love and live in quiet;
Let's tie the knot so very fast
   That time shall ne'er untie it.
Love's dearest joys they never prove,
   Who free from quarrels live;
'Tis sure a godlike part of love
   Each other to forgive.

When least I seemed concerned I took
   No pleasure, nor had rest;
And when I feigned an angry look,
   Alas!   I loved you best.
Say but the same to me, you'll find
   How blest will be our fate;
Sure to be grateful, to be kind,
   Can never be too late.

John Sheffield [1648–1721]

THE ENCHANTMENT

I DID but look and love awhile,
  'Twas but for one half-hour;
Then to resist I had no will,
  And now I have no power.

To sigh and wish is all my ease;
  Sighs which do heat impart
Enough to melt the coldest ice,
  Yet cannot warm your heart.

O would your pity give my heart
  One corner of your breast,
'Twould learn of yours the winning art,
  And quickly steal the rest.

Thomas Otway [1652–1685]

SONG

ONLY tell her that I love:
  Leave the rest to her and Fate:
Some kind planet from above
May perhaps her pity move:
  Lovers on their stars must wait.—
Only tell her that I love!

Why, O why should I despair!
  Mercy's pictured in her eye:
If she once vouchsafe to hear,
Welcome Hope and farewell Fear!
  She's too good to let me die.—
Why, O why should I despair?

John Cutts [1661–1707]

"FALSE THOUGH SHE BE"

FALSE though she be to me and love,
  I'll ne'er pursue revenge;
For still the charmer I approve,
  Though I deplore her change.

In hours of bliss we oft have met:
  They could not always last;
And though the present I regret,
  I'm grateful for the past.

William Congreve [1670–1729]

TO SILVIA

From "The Cautious Lovers"

SILVIA, let us from the crowd retire,
  For what to you and me
(Who but each other do desire)
  Is all that here we see?

Apart we'll live, though not alone;
  For who *alone* can call
Those who in deserts live with one
  If in that one they've all?

The world a vast meander is,
  Where hearts confusedly stray;
Where few do hit, whilst thousands miss,
  The happy mutual way.

Anne Finch [? –1720]

"WHY, LOVELY CHARMER"

WHY, lovely charmer, tell me why,
So very kind, and yet so shy?
Why does that cold, forbidding air
Give damps of sorrow and despair?
Or why that smile my soul subdue,
And kindle up my flames anew?

In vain you strive with all your art,
By turns to fire and freeze my heart;
When I behold a face so fair,
So sweet a look, so soft an air,
My ravished soul is charmed all o'er,
I cannot love thee less or more.

Unknown

AGAINST INDIFFERENCE

MORE love or more disdain I crave;
  Sweet, be not still indifferent:
O send me quickly to my grave,
  Or else afford me more content!
Or love or hate me more or less,
For love abhors all lukewarmness.

Give me a tempest if 'twill drive
  Me to the place where I would be;
Or if you'll have me still alive,
  Confess you will be kind to me.
Give hopes of bliss or dig my grave:
More love or more disdain I crave.
                    Charles Webbe [c. 1678]

A SONG TO AMORET

IF I were dead, and, in my place,
  Some fresher youth designed
To warm thee, with new fires; and **grace**
  Those arms I left behind:

Were he as faithful as the Sun,
  That's wedded to the Sphere;
His blood as chaste and temperate run,
  As April's mildest tear;

Or were he rich; and, with his heap
  And spacious share of earth,
Could make divine affection cheap,
  And court his golden birth;

For all these arts, I'd not believe
  (No! though he should be thine!),
The mighty Amorist could give
  So rich a heart as mine!

Fortune and beauty thou might'st find,
    And greater men than I;
But my true resolvèd mind
    They never shall come nigh.

For I not for an hour did love,
    Or for a day desire,
But with my soul had from above
    This endless holy fire.

Henry Vaughan [1622–1695]

THE LASS OF RICHMOND HILL

On Richmond Hill there lives a lass
    More bright than May-day morn,
Whose charms all other maids surpass,—
    A rose without a thorn.

This lass so neat, with smiles so sweet,
    Has won my right good-will;
I'd crowns resign to call her mine,
    Sweet lass of Richmond Hill.

Ye zephyrs gay, that fan the air,
    And wanton through the grove,
O, whisper to my charming fair,
    I die for her I love.

How happy will the shepherd be
    Who calls this nymph his own!
O, may her choice be fixed on me!
    Mine's fixed on her alone.

James Upton [1670–1749]

SONG

From "Sunday Up the River"

Let my voice ring out and over the earth,
    Through all the grief and strife,
With a golden joy in a silver mirth:
    Thank God for life!

Let my voice swell out through the great abyss
　　To the azure dome above,
With a chord of faith in the harp of bliss:
　　Thank God for Love!

Let my voice thrill out beneath and above,
　　The whole world through:
O my Love and Life, O my Life and Love,
　　Thank God for you!

James Thomson [1834–1882]

GIFTS
From "Sunday Up the River"

GIVE a man a horse he can ride,
　　Give a man a boat he can sail;
And his rank and wealth, his strength and health,
　　On sea nor shore shall fail.

Give a man a pipe he can smoke,
　　Give a man a book he can read:
And his home is bright with a calm delight,
　　Though the room be poor indeed.

Give a man a girl he can love,
　　As I, O my love, love thee;
And his heart is great with the pulse of Fate,
　　At home, on land, on sea.

James Thomson [1834–1882]

AMYNTA

MY sheep I neglected, I broke my sheep-crook,
And all the gay haunts of my youth I forsook;
No more for Amynta fresh garlands I wove;
For ambition, I said would soon cure me of love.

Oh, what had my youth with ambition to do?
Why left I Amynta?　Why broke I my vow?
Oh, give me my sheep, and my sheep-hook restore,
And I'll wander from love and Amynta no more.

Through regions remote in vain do I rove,
And bid the wide ocean secure me from love!
O fool! to imagine that aught could subdue
A love so well founded, a passion so true!

Alas! 'tis too late at thy fate to repine;
Poor shepherd, Amynta can never be thine:
Thy tears are all fruitless, thy wishes are vain,
The moments neglected return not again.

Gilbert Elliot [1722–1777]

"O NANCY! WILT THOU GO WITH ME"

O NANCY, wilt thou go with me,
    Nor sigh to leave the flaunting town:
Can silent glens have charms for thee,
    The lowly cot, the russet gown?
No longer dressed in silken sheen,
    No longer decked with jewels rare,
Say, canst thou quit each courtly scene
    Where thou wert fairest of the fair?

O Nancy! when thou'rt far away,
    Wilt thou not cast a wish behind?
Say, canst thou face the parching ray,
    Nor shrink before the wintry wind?
O! can that soft and gentle mien
    Extremes of hardship learn to bear,
Nor, sad, regret each courtly scene
    Where thou wert fairest of the fair?

O Nancy! canst thou love so true,
    Through perils keen with me to go,
Or when thy swain mishap shall rue,
    To share with him the pang of woe?
Say, should disease or pain befall,
    Wilt thou assume the nurse's care;
Nor wistful those gay scenes recall
    Where thou wert fairest of the fair?

And when at last thy love shall die,
    Wilt thou receive his parting breath?
Wilt thou repress each struggling sigh,
    And cheer with smiles the bed of death?
And wilt thou o'er his breathless clay
    Strew flowers and drop the tender tear?
Nor *then* regret those scenes so gay
    Where thou wert fairest of the fair?

          Thomas Percy [1729–1811]

CAVALIER'S SONG

IF doughty deeds my lady please,
    Right soon I'll mount my steed;
And strong his arm and fast his seat,
    That bears frae me the meed.
I'll wear thy colors in my cap,
    Thy picture in my heart;
And he that bends not to thine eye
    Shall rue it to his smart!
      Then tell me how to woo thee, Love;
        O tell me how to woo thee!
      For thy dear sake nae care I'll take,
        Though ne'er another trow me.

If gay attire delight thine eye
    I'll dight me in array;
I'll tend thy chamber door all night,
    And squire thee all the day.
If sweetest sounds can win thine ear,
    These sounds I'll strive to catch;
Thy voice I'll steal to woo thysel',
    That voice that nane can match.
      Then tell me how to woo thee, Love;
        O tell me how to woo thee!
      For thy dear sake nae care I'll take
        Though ne'er another trow me.

But if fond love thy heart can gain,
    I never broke a vow;
Nae maiden lays her skaith to me,
    I never loved but you.

For you alone I ride the ring,
  For you I wear the blue;
For you alone I strive to sing,
  O tell me how to woo!
    Then tell me how to woo thee, Love;
      O tell me how to woo thee!
    For thy dear sake nae care I'll take
      Though ne'er another trow me.

Robert Cunninghame-Graham [? –1797?]

"MY HEART IS A LUTE"

Alas, that my heart is a lute,
  Whereon you have learned to play!
For a many years it was mute,
  Until one summer's day
You took it, and touched it, and made it thrill,
And it thrills and throbs, and quivers still!

I had known you, dear, so long!
  Yet my heart did not tell me why
It should burst one morn into song,
  And wake to new life with a cry,
Like a babe that sees the light of the sun,
And for whom this great world has just begun.

Your lute is enshrined, cased in,
  Kept close with love's magic key,
So no hand but yours can win
  And wake it to minstrelsy;
Yet leave it not silent too long, nor alone,
Lest the strings should break, and the music be done.

Anne Barnard [1750–1825]

SONG

From "The Duenna"

Had I a heart for falsehood framed,
  I ne'er could injure you;
For though your tongue no promise claimed,
  Your charms would make me true:

Then, lady, dread not here deceit,
  Nor fear to suffer wrong,
For friends in all the aged you'll meet,
  And lovers in the young.

But when they find that you have blessed
  Another with your heart,
They'll bid aspiring passion rest,
  And act a brother's part:
Then, lady, dread not here deceit
  Nor fear to suffer wrong;
For friends in all the aged you'll meet,
  And brothers in the young.

Richard Brinsley Sheridan [1751–1816]

MEETING

My Damon was the first to wake
  The gentle flame that cannot die;
My Damon is the last to take
  The faithful bosom's softest sigh:
The life between is nothing worth,
  O cast it from thy thought away!
Think of the day that gave it birth,
  And this its sweet returning day.

Buried be all that has been done,
  Or say that naught is done amiss;
For who the dangerous path can shun
  In such bewildering world as this?
But love can every fault forgive,
  Or with a tender look reprove;
And now let naught in memory live
  But that we meet, and that we love.

George Crabbe [1754–1832]

"O WERE MY LOVE YON LILAC FAIR"

O were my Love yon lilac fair,
  Wi' purple blossoms to the spring,
And I a bird to shelter there,
  When wearied on my little wing;

How I wad mourn when it was torn
   By autumn wild and winter rude!
But I wad sing on wanton wing
   When youthfu' May its bloom renewed.

O gin my Love were yon red rose
   That grows upon the castle wa',
And I mysel a drap o' dew,
   Into her bonnie breast to fa';
O there, beyond expression blest,
   I'd feast on beauty a' the night;
Sealed on her silk-saft faulds to rest,
   Till fleyed awa' by Phœbus' light.

               Robert Burns [1759–1796]

"BONNIE WEE THING"

BONNIE wee thing! cannie wee thing!
   Lovely wee thing! wert thou mine,
I wad wear thee in my bosom,
   Lest my jewel I should tine.
Wishfully I look, and languish
   In that bonnie face o' thine;
And my heart it stounds wi' anguish,
   Lest my wee thing be na mine.

Wit and grace, and love and beauty,
   In ae constellation shine;
To adore thee is my duty,
   Goddess o' this soul o' mine!
Bonnie wee thing, cannie wee thing,
   Lovely wee thing, wert thou mine,
I wad wear thee in my bosom,
   Lest my jewel I should tine.

               Robert Burns [1759–1796]

ROSE AYLMER

AH, what avails the sceptered race!
   Ah, what the form divine!
What every virtue, every grace!
   Rose Aylmer, all were thine.

Rose Aylmer, whom these wakeful eyes
    May weep, but never see,
A night of memories and sighs
    I consecrate to thee.
           Walter Savage Landor [1775–1864]

"TAKE BACK THE VIRGIN PAGE"

WRITTEN ON RETURNING A BLANK BOOK

TAKE back the Virgin Page
    White and unwritten still;
Some hand more calm and sage
    The leaf must fill.
Thoughts came as pure as light—
    Pure as even *you* require:
But oh! each word I write
    Love turns to fire.

Yet let me keep the book:
    Oft shall my heart renew,
When on its leaves I look,
    Dear thoughts of you.
Like you, 'tis fair and bright;
    Like you, too bright and fair
To let wild passion write
    One wrong wish there.

Haply, when from those eyes
    Far, far away I roam,
Should calmer thoughts arise
    Towards you and home;
Fancy may trace some line
    Worthy those eyes to meet,
Thoughts that not burn, but shine,
    Pure, calm, and sweet.

And as o'er ocean far
    Seamen their records keep,
Led by some hidden star

Through the cold deep;
So may the words I write
Tell through what storms I stray,
You still the unseen light
Guiding my way.

Thomas Moore [1779–1852]

"BELIEVE ME, IF ALL THOSE ENDEARING YOUNG CHARMS"

BELIEVE me, if all those endearing young charms,
  Which I gaze on so fondly to-day,
Were to change by to-morrow, and fleet in my arms,
  Like fairy-gifts fading away,
Thou wouldst still be adored, as this moment thou art,
  Let thy loveliness fade as it will,
And around the dear ruin each wish of my heart
  Would entwine itself verdantly still.

It is not while beauty and youth are thine own,
  And thy cheeks unprofaned by a tear,
That the fervor and faith of a soul may be known,
  To which time will but make thee more dear!
No, the heart that has truly loved never forgets,
  But as truly loves on to the close,
As the sunflower turns to her god when he sets
  The same look which she turned when he rose!

Thomas Moore [1779–1852]

THE NUN

IF you become a nun, dear,
  A friar I will be;
In any cell you run, dear,
  Pray look behind for me.
The roses all turn pale, too;
The doves all take the veil, too;
  The blind will see the show;
What! you become a nun, my dear,
  I 'll not believe *i*t, no!

If you become a nun, dear,
  The bishop Love will be:
The Cupids every one, dear,
  Will chant, "We trust in thee!"
The incense will go sighing.
The candles fall a-dying,
  The water turn to wine:
What! you go take the vows, my dear?
  You may—but they'll be mine.

Leigh Hunt [1784–1859]

ONLY OF THEE AND ME

ONLY of thee and me the night wind sings,
  Only of us the sailors speak at sea,
The earth is filled with wondered whisperings
  Only of thee and me.

Only of thee and me the breakers chant,
  Only of us the stir in bush and tree;
The rain and sunshine tell the eager plant
  Only of thee and me.

Only of thee and me, till all shall fade;
  Only of us the whole world's thoughts can be—
For we are Love, and God Himself is made
  Only of thee and me.

Louis Untermeyer [1885–

TO ———

ONE word is too often profaned
  For me to profane it,
One feeling too falsely disdained
  For thee to disdain it.
One hope is too like despair
  For prudence to smother,
And Pity from thee more dear
  Than that from another.

I can give not what men call love;
  But wilt thou accept not
The worship the heart lifts above
  And the Heavens reject not:
The desire of the moth for the star,
  Of the night for the morrow,
The devotion to something afar
  From the sphere of our sorrow?
                    Percy Bysshe Shelley [1792–1822]

FROM THE ARABIC

My faint spirit was sitting in the light
    Of thy looks, my love;
  It panted for thee like the hind at noon
    For the brooks, my love.
Thy barb, whose hoofs outspeed the tempest's flight,
    Bore thee far from me;
  My heart, for my weak feet were weary soon,
    Did companion thee.

Ah! fleeter far than fleetest storm or steed,
    Or the death they bear,
  The heart which tender thought clothes like a dove
    With the wings of care;
In the battle, in the darkness, in the need,
    Shall mine cling to thee,
  Nor claim one smile for all the comfort, love,
    It may bring to thee.
                    Percy Bysshe Shelley [1792–1822]

THE WANDERING KNIGHT'S SONG

My ornaments are arms,
  My pastime is in war,
My bed is cold upon the wold,
  My lamp yon star.

My journeyings are long,
  My slumbers short and broken;
From hill to hill I wander still,
  Kissing thy token.

I ride from land to land,
  I sail from sea to sea;
Some day more kind I fate may find,
  Some night, kiss thee.
John Gibson Lockhart [1794–1854]

SONG

LOVE'S on the highroad,
Love's in the byroad—
  Love's on the meadow, and Love's in the mart!
And down every byway
Where I've taken my way
  I've met Love a-smiling—for Love's in my heart!
Dana Burnet [1888–

THE SECRET LOVE

You and I have found the secret way,
None can bar our love or say us nay:
All the world may stare and never know
You and I are twined together so.

You and I for all his vaunted width
Know the giant Space is but a myth;
Over miles and miles of pure deceit
You and I have found our lips can meet.

You and I have laughed the leagues apart
In the soft delight of heart to heart.
If there's a gulf to meet or limit set,
You and I have never found it yet.

You and I have trod the backward way
To the happy heart of yesterday,
To the love we felt in ages past.
You and I have found it still to last.

You and I have found the joy had birth
In the angel childhood of the earth,
Hid within the heart of man and maid.
You and I of Time are not afraid.

You and I can mock his fabled wing,
For a kiss is an immortal thing.
And the throb wherein those old lips met
Is a living music in us yet.

A. E. (George William Russell) [1867–1935]

THE FLOWER OF BEAUTY

SWEET in her green dell the flower of beauty slumbers,
  Lulled by the faint breezes sighing through her hair;
Sleeps she, and hears not the melancholy numbers
  Breathed to my sad lute amid the lonely air?

Down from the high cliffs the rivulet is teeming
  To wind round the willow-banks that lure him from
    above:
Oh that, in tears from my rocky prison streaming,
  I too could glide to the bower of my love!

Ah, where the woodbines with sleepy arms have wound
    her,
  Opes she her eyelids at the dream of my lay,
Listening like the dove, while the fountains echo round her,
  To her lost mate's call in the forest far away?

Come, then, my bird! for the peace thou ever bearest,
  Still Heaven's messenger of comfort be to me;
Come! this fond bosom, my faithfulest, my fairest,
  Bleeds with its death-wound,—but deeper yet for thee.

George Darley [1795–1846]

MY SHARE OF THE WORLD

I AM jealous: I am true:
Sick at heart for love of you,
  O my share of the world!
I am cold, O, cold as stone
To all men save you alone.

Seven times slower creeps the day
When your face is far away,
  O my share of the world!

Seven times darker falls the night.
When you gladden not my sight.

Measureless my joy and pride
Would you choose me for your bride,
    O my share of the world!
For your face is my delight,
Morn and even, noon and night.

To the dance and to the wake
Still I go but for your sake,
    O my share of the world!
Just to see your face awhile,
Meet your eyes and win your smile.

And the gay word on my lip
Never lets my secret slip
    To my share of the world!
Light my feet trip over the green—
But my heart cries in the keen!

My poor mother sighs anew
When my looks go after you,
    O my share of the world!
And my father's brow grows black
When you smile and turn your back.

I would part with wealth and ease,
I would go beyond the seas,
    For my share of the world!
I would leave my hearth and home
If he only whispered "Come!"

Houseless under sun and dew,
I would beg my bread with you,
    O my share of the world!
Houseless in the snow and storm,
Your heart's love would keep me warm.

I would pray and I would crave
To be with you in the grave,
    O my share of the world!

I would go through fire and flood,
I would give up all but God
For my share of the world!
                    Alice Furlong [1875–

SONG

A LAKE and a fairy boat
  To sail in the moonlight clear,—
And merrily we would float
  From the dragons that watch us here!

Thy gown should be snow-white silk,
  And strings of orient pearls,
Like gossamers dipped in milk,
  Should twine with thy raven curls.

Red rubies should deck thy hands,
  And diamonds be thy dower—
But fairies have broke their wands,
  And wishing has lost its power!
                    Thomas Hood [1799–1845]

"SMILE AND NEVER HEED ME"

THOUGH, when other maids stand by,
I may deign thee no reply,
Turn not then away, and sigh,—
    Smile, and never heed me!
If our love, indeed, be such
As must thrill at every touch,
Why should others learn as much?—
    Smile, and never heed me!

Even if, with maiden pride,
I should bid thee quit my side,
Take this lesson for thy guide,—
    Smile, and never heed me!

But when stars and twilight meet,
And the dew is falling sweet,
And thou hear'st my coming feet,—
 Then—thou then—mayst heed me!
    Charles Swain [1801–1874]

ARE THEY NOT ALL MINISTERING SPIRITS?

WE see them not—we cannot hear
 The music of their wing—
Yet know we that they sojourn near,
 The Angels of the spring!

They glide along this lovely ground
 When the first violet grows;
Their graceful hands have just unbound
 The zone of yonder rose.

I gather it for thy dear breast,
 From stain and shadow free:
That which an Angel's touch hath blest
 Is meet, my love, for thee!
    Robert Stephen Hawker [1803–1875]

MAIDEN EYES

YOU never bade me hope, 'tis true;
 I asked you not to swear:
But I looked in those eyes of blue,
 And read a promise there.

The vow should bind, with maiden sighs
 That maiden lips have spoken:
But that which looks from maiden eyes
 Should last of all be broken.
    Gerald Griffin [1803–1840]

HALLOWED PLACES

I PASS my days among the quiet places
  Made sacred by your feet.
The air is cool in the fresh woodland spaces,
  The meadows very sweet.

The sunset fills the wide sky with its splendor,
  The glad birds greet the night;
I stop and listen for a voice strong, tender,
  I wait those dear eyes' light.

You are the heart of every gleam of glory,
  Your presence fills the air,
About you gathers all the fair year's story;
  I read you everywhere.

Alice Freeman Palmer [1855–1902]

THE LADY'S "YES"

"YES," I answered you last night;
  "No," this morning, sir, I say:
Colors seen by candle-light
  Will not look the same by day.

When the viols played their best,
  Lamps above, and laughs below,
Love me sounded like a jest,
  Fit for *yes* or fit for *no*.

Call me false or call me free,
  Vow, whatever light may shine,—
No man on your face shall see
  Any grief for change on mine.

Yet the sin is on us both;
  Time to dance is not to woo;
Wooing light makes fickle troth,
  Scorn of *me* recoils on *you*.

Learn to win a lady's faith
  Nobly, as the thing is high,
Bravely, as for life and death,
  With a loyal gravity.

Lead her from the festive boards,
  Point her to the starry skies,
Guard her, by your truthful words,
  Pure from courtship's flatteries.

By your truth she shall be true,
  Ever true, as wives of yore;
And her *yes*, once said to you,
  SHALL be Yes for evermore.
                    Elizabeth Barrett Browning [1806–1861]

SONG

From "The Miller's Daughter"

IT is the miller's daughter,
  And she is grown so dear, so dear,
That I would be the jewel
  That trembles in her ear;
For hid in ringlets day and night,
I'd touch her neck so warm and white.

And I would be the girdle
  About her dainty, dainty waist,
And her heart would beat against me,
  In sorrow and in rest;
And I should know if it beat right,
I'd clasp it round so close and tight.

And I would be the necklace,
  And all day long to fall and rise
Upon her balmy bosom
  With her laughter or her sighs;

And I would lie so light, so light,
I scarce should be unclasped at night.
Alfred Tennyson [1809–1892]

LILIAN

AIRY, fairy Lilian,
Flitting, fairy Lilian,
When I ask her if she love me,
Clasps her tiny hand above me,
  Laughing all she can;
She'll not tell me if she love me,
  Cruel little Lilian.

When my passion seeks
Pleasance in love-sighs,
She, looking through and through me,
Thoroughly to undo me,
  Smiling, never speaks:
So innocent-arch, so cunning-simple,
From beneath her gathered wimple
  Glancing with black-beaded eyes,
Till the lightning laughters dimple
  The baby-roses in her cheeks;
  Then away she flies.

Prithee weep, May Lilian!
  Gaiety without eclipse
Wearieth me, May Lilian:
Through my very heart it thrilleth,
  When from crimson-threaded lips
Silver-treble laughter thrilleth:
Prithee weep, May Lilian!

  Praying all I can,
If prayers will not hush thee,
  Airy Lilian,
Like a rose-leaf I will crush thee,
  Fairy Lilian.
Alfred Tennyson [1809–1892]

BUGLE SONG

From "The Princess"

THE splendor falls on castle walls
 And snowy summits old in story:
The long light shakes across the lakes,
 And the wild cataract leaps in glory.
Blow, bugle, blow, set the wild echoes flying,
Blow, bugle; answer, echoes, dying, dying, dying.

O hark, O hear! how thin and clear,
 And thinner, clearer, farther going!
O sweet and far from cliff and scar
 The horns of Elfland faintly blowing!
Blow, let us hear the purple glens replying:
Blow, bugle; answer, echoes, dying, dying, dying.

O love, they die in yon rich sky,
 They faint on hill or field or river:
Our echoes roll from soul to soul,
 And grow for ever and for ever.
Blow, bugle, blow, set the wild echoes flying,
And answer, echoes, answer, dying, dying, dying.

Alfred Tennyson [1809–1892]

RONSARD TO HIS MISTRESS

*" Quand vous serez bien vieille, le soir à la chandelle
Assise auprès du feu devisant et filant,
Dires, chantant mes vers en vous esmerveillant,
Ronsard m'a célébré du temps que j'étois belle."*

SOME winter night, shut snugly in
 Beside the fagot in the hall,
I think I see you sit and spin,
 Surrounded by your maidens all.
Old tales are told, old songs are sung,
 Old days come back to memory;
You say, "When I was fair and young,
 A poet sang of me!"

For the original of this poem see page 594.

There's not a maiden in your hall,
  Though tired and sleepy ever so,
But wakes, as you my name recall,
  And longs the history to know.
And, as the piteous tale is said,
  Of lady cold and lover true,
Each, musing, carries it to bed,
  And sighs and envies you!

"Our lady's old and feeble now,"
  They'll say: "she once was fresh and fair,
And yet she spurned her lover's vow,
  And heartless left him to despair:
The lover lies in silent earth,
  No kindly mate the lady cheers;
She sits beside a lonely hearth,
  With threescore and ten years!"

Ah! dreary thoughts and dreams are those,
  But wherefore yield me to despair,
While yet the poet's bosom glows,
  While yet the dame is peerless fair!
Sweet lady mine! while yet 'tis time
  Requite my passion and my truth,
And gather in their blushing prime
  The roses of your youth!

William Makepeace Thackeray [1811–1863]

"WHEN YOU ARE OLD"*
After Pierre de Ronsard

WHEN you are old and gray and full of sleep,
And nodding by the fire, take down this book,
And slowly read and dream of the soft look
Your eyes had once, and of their shadows deep;

How many loved your moments of glad grace,
And loved your beauty with love false or true,
But one man loved the pilgrim soul in you,
And loved the sorrows of your changing face.

*For the original of this poem see page 3847.

And bending down beside the glowing bars
Murmur, a little sadly, how love fled
And paced upon the mountains overhead
And hid his face amid a crowd of stars.
> *William Butler Yeats* [1865–1939]

SONG

From " Pippa Passes "

You'll love me yet!—and I can tarry
  Your love's protracted growing:
June reared that bunch of flowers you carry,
  From seeds of April's sowing.

I plant a heartfull now: some seed
  At least is sure to strike,
And yield—what you'll not pluck indeed,
  Not love, but, may be, like.

You'll look at least on love's remains,
  A grave's one violet:
Your look?—that pays a thousand pains.
  What's death?   You'll love me yet!
> *Robert Browning* [1812–1889]

LOVE IN A LIFE

Room after room,
I hunt the house through
We inhabit together.
Heart, fear nothing, for, heart, thou shalt find her—
Next time, herself!—not the trouble behind her
Left in the curtain, the couch's perfume!
As she brushed it, the cornice-wreath blossomed anew:
Yon looking-glass gleamed at the wave of her feather.

Yet the day wears,
And door succeeds door;
I try the fresh fortune—
Range the wide house from the wing to the center.

Still the same chance! she goes out as I enter.
Spend my whole day in the quest,—who cares?
But 'tis twilight, you see,—with such suites to explore,
Such closets to search, such alcoves to importune!

Robert Browning [1812–1889]

LIFE IN A LOVE

Escape me?
　　Never—
　　　Beloved!
While I am I, and you are you,
　　So long as the world contains us both,
　　Me the loving and you the loth,
While the one eludes, must the other pursue.
My life is a fault at last, I fear:
　　It seems too much like a fate, indeed!
　　Though I do my best I shall scarce succeed.
But what if I fail of my purpose here?
It is but to keep the nerves at strain,
　　To dry one's eyes and laugh at a fall,
And, baffled, get up and begin again,—
　　So the chase takes up one's life, that's all.
While, look but once from your farthest bound
　　At me so deep in the dust and dark,
No sooner the old hope drops to ground
　　Than a new one, straight to the self-same mark,
　　　I shape me—
　　　Ever
　　　Removed!

Robert Browning [1812–1889]

THE WELCOME

Come in the evening, or come in the morning;
Come when you're looked for, or come without warning:
Kisses and welcome you'll find here before you,
And the oftener you come here the more I'll adore you!
Light is my heart since the day we were plighted;
Red is my cheek that they told me was blighted;

The green of the trees looks far greener than ever,
And the linnets are singing,"True lovers don't sever!"

I'll pull you sweet flowers, to wear if you choose them,—
Or, after you've kissed them, they'll lie on my bosom;
I'll fetch from the mountain its breeze to inspire you;
I'll fetch from my fancy a tale that won't tire you.
Oh! your step's like the rain to the summer-vexed farmer,
Or saber and shield to a knight without armor;
I'll sing you sweet songs till the stars rise above me,
Then, wandering, I'll wish you in silence to love me.

We'll look through the trees at the cliff and the eyrie;
We'll tread round the rath on the track of the fairy;
We'll look on the stars, and we'll list to the river,
Till you ask of your darling what gift you can give her:
Oh! she'll whisper you—"Love, as unchangeably beaming,
And trust, when in secret, most tunefully streaming;
Till the starlight of heaven above us shall quiver,
As our souls flow in one down eternity's river."

So come in the evening, or come in the morning;
Come when you're looked for, or come without warning:
Kisses and welcome you'll find here before you,
And the oftener you come here the more I'll adore you!
Light is my heart since the day we were plighted;
Red is my cheek that they told me was blighted;
The green of the trees looks far greener than ever,
And the linnets are singing, "True lovers don't sever!"

Thomas Osborne Davis [1814–1845]

URANIA

She smiles and smiles, and will not sigh,
While we for hopeless passion die;
Yet she could love, those eyes declare,
Were but men nobler than they are.

Eagerly once her gracious ken
Was turned upon the sons of men;

But light the serious visage grew—
She looked, and smiled, and saw them through.

Our petty souls, our strutting wits,
Our labored, puny passion-fits—
Ah, may she scorn them still, till we
Scorn them as bitterly as she!

Yet show her once, ye heavenly Powers,
One of some worthier race than ours!
One for whose sake she once might prove
How deeply she who scorns can love.

His eyes be like the starry lights;
His voice like sounds of summer nights;
In all his lovely mien let pierce
The magic of the universe!

And she to him will reach her hand,
And gazing in his eyes will stand,
And know her friend, and weep for glee,
And cry, Long, long I've looked for thee!

Then will she weep—with smiles, till then
Coldly she mocks the sons of men.
Till then her lovely eyes maintain
Their pure, unwavering, deep disdain.

Matthew Arnold [1822–1888]

THREE SHADOWS

I LOOKED and saw your eyes in the shadow of your hair,
  As a traveler sees the stream in the shadow of the wood;—
And I said, " My faint heart sighs, ah me! to linger there,
  To drink deep and to dream in that sweet solitude."

I looked and saw your heart in the shadow of your eyes,
  As a seeker sees the gold in the shadow of the stream;
And I said, "Ah, me! what art should win the immortal
    prize,
  Whose want must make life cold and Heaven a hollow
    dream?"

I looked and saw your love in the shadow of your heart,
  As a diver sees the pearl in the shadow of the sea;
And I murmured, not above my breath, but all apart,—
  "Ah! you can love, true girl, and is your love for me?"
                    Dante Gabriel Rossetti [1828–1882]

SINCE WE PARTED

SINCE we parted yester eve,
I do love thee, love, believe,
Twelve times dearer, twelve hours longer,—
One dream deeper, one night stronger,
One sun surer,—thus much more
Than I loved thee, love, before.
              Edward Robert Bulwer Lytton [1831–1891]

A MATCH

IF love were what the rose is,
  And I were like the leaf,
Our lives would grow together
In sad or singing weather,
Blown fields or flowerful closes,
  Green pleasure or gray grief;
If love were what the rose is,
  And I were like the leaf.

If I were what the words are,
  And love were like the tune,
With double sound and single
Delight our lips would mingle,
With kisses glad as birds are
  That get sweet rain at noon;
If I were what the words are,
  And love were like the tune.

If you were life, my darling,
  And I your love were death,
We'd shine and snow together
Ere March made sweet the weather

With daffodil and starling
   And hours of fruitful breath;
If you were life, my darling,
   And I your love were death.

If you were thrall to sorrow,
   And I were page to joy,
We'd play for lives and seasons
With loving looks and treasons
And tears of night and morrow
   And laughs of maid and boy;
If you were thrall to sorrow,
   And I were page to joy.

If you were April's lady,
   And I were lord in May,
We'd throw with leaves for hours
And draw for days with flowers,
Till day like night were shady
   And night were bright like day;
If you were April's lady,
   And I were lord in May.

If you were queen of pleasure,
   And I were king of pain,
We'd hunt down love together,
Pluck out his flying-feather,
And teach his feet a measure,
   And find his mouth a rein;
If you were queen of pleasure,
   And I were king of pain.
            Algernon Charles Swinburne [1837–1909]

A BALLAD OF LIFE

I FOUND in dreams a place of wind and flowers,
   Full of sweet trees and color of glad grass,
      In midst whereof there was
A lady clothed like summer with sweet hours,

Her beauty, fervent as a fiery moon
  Made my blood burn and swoon
    Like a flame rained upon.
Sorrow had filled her shaken eyelids' blue,
And her mouth's sad red heavy rose all through
    Seemed sad with glad things gone.

She held a little cithern by the strings,
  Shaped heartwise, strung with subtle-colored hair
    Of some dead lute player
That in dead years had done delicious things.
The seven strings were named accordingly;
  The first string charity,
    The second tenderness,
The rest were pleasure, sorrow, sleep, and sin,
And loving kindness, that is pity's kin
    And is most pitiless.

There were three men with her, each garmented
  With gold, and shod with gold upon the feet;
    And with plucked ears of wheat.
The first man's hair was wound upon his head:
His face was red, and his mouth curled and sad;
  All his gold garment had
    Pale stains of dust and rust.
A riven hood was pulled across his eyes;
The token of him being upon this wise
    Made for a sign of Lust.

The next was Shame, with hollow heavy face
  Colored like green wood when flame kindles it.
    He hath such feeble feet
They may not well endure in any place.
His face was full of gray old miseries.
  And all his blood's increase
    Was even increase of pain.
The last was Fear, that is akin to Death;
He is Shame's friend, and always as Shame saith
    Fear answers him again.

My soul said in me: This is marvelous,
   Seeing the air's face is not so delicate
   Nor the sun's grace so great,
If sin and she be kin or amorous.
And seeing where maidens served her on their knees,
   I bade one crave of these
     To know the cause thereof.
Then Fear said: I am Pity that was dead.
And Shame said: I am Sorrow comforted.
    And Lust said: I am Love.

Thereat her hands began a lute-playing
   And her sweet mouth a song in a strange tongue;
   And all the while she sung
There was no sound but long tears following
Long tears upon men's faces, waxen white
   With extreme sad delight.
    But those three following men
Became as men raised up among the dead;
Great glad mouths open, and fair cheeks made red
    With child's blood come again.

Then I said: Now assuredly I see
   My lady is perfect, and transfigureth
   All sin and sorrow and death,
Making them fair as her own eyelids be,
Or lips wherein my whole soul's life abides;
   Or as her sweet white sides
    And bosom carved to kiss.
Now therefore, if her pity further me,
Doubtless for her sake all my days shall be
    As righteous as she is.

Forth, ballad, and take roses in both arms,
   Even till the top rose touch thee in the throat
Where the least thornprick harms;
   And girdled in thy golden singing-coat,
Come thou before my lady and say this:

Borgia, thy gold hair's color burns in me,
   Thy mouth makes beat my blood in feverish rhymes;
Therefore so many as these roses be,
   Kiss me so many times.
Then it may be, seeing how sweet she is,
   That she will stoop herself none otherwise
     Than a blown vine-branch doth,
And kiss thee with soft laughter on thine eyes,
   Ballad, and on thy mouth.

               Algernon Charles Swinburne [1837–1909]

A LEAVE–TAKING

LET us go hence, my songs; she will not hear.
Let us go hence together without fear;
Keep silence now, for singing time is over,
And over all old things and all things dear.
She loves not you nor me as all we love her.
Yea, though we sang as angels in her ear,
     She would not hear.

Let us rise up and part; she will not know.
Let us go seaward as the great winds go,
Full of blown sand and foam; what help is there?
There is no help, for all these things are so,
And all the world is bitter as a tear,
And how these things are, though ye strove to show,
     She would not know.

Let us go home and hence; she will not weep.
We gave love many dreams and days to keep,
Flowers without scent, and fruits that would not grow,
Saying, "If thou wilt, thrust in thy sickle and reap."
All is reaped now; no grass is left to mow;
And we that sowed, though all we fell on sleep,
     She would not weep.

Let us go hence and rest; she will not love.
She shall not hear us if we sing hereof,
Nor see love's ways how sore they are and steep.
Come hence, let be, lie still; it is enough.
Love is a barren sea, bitter and deep;
And though she saw all heaven in flower above,
    She would not love.

Let us give up, go down; she will not care.
Though all the stars made gold of all the air,
And the sea moving saw before it move
One moon-flower making all the foam-flowers fair;
Though all those waves went over us, and drove
Deep down the stifling lips and drowning hair,
    She would not care.

Let us go hence, go hence; she will not see.
Sing all once more together; surely she,
She too, remembering days and words that were,
Will turn a little towards us, sighing; but we,
We are hence, we are gone, as though we had not been there.
Nay, and though all men seeing had pity on me,
    She would not see.

                    Algernon Charles Swinburne [1837–1909]

A LYRIC

THERE's nae lark loves the lift, my dear,
    There's nae ship loves the sea,
There's nae bee loves the heather-bells,
    That loves as I love thee, my love,
    That loves as I love thee.

The whin shines fair upon the fell,
    The blithe broom on the lea:
The muirside wind is merry at heart:
    It's a' for love of thee, my love,
    It's a' for love of thee.

                    Algernon Charles Swinburne [1837–1909]

MAUREEN

O, you plant the pain in my heart with your wistful eyes,
        Girl of my choice, Maureen!
Will you drive me mad for the kisses your shy, sweet mouth
    denies,
            Maureen?

Like a walking ghost I am, and no words to woo,
        White rose of the West, Maureen:
For it's pale you are, and the fear that's on you is over me
    too,
            Maureen!

Sure it's one complaint that's on us, asthore, this day,
        Bride of my dreams, Maureen:
The smart of the bee that stung us his honey must cure,
    they say,
            Maureen!

I'll coax the light to your eyes, and the rose to your face,
        Mavourneen, my own Maureen!
When I feel the warmth of your breast, and your nest is my
    arm's embrace,
            Maureen!

O where was the King o' the World that day—only me?
        My one true love, Maureen!
And you the Queen with me there, and your throne in my
    heart, machree,
            Maureen!

                                    John Todhunter [1839–1916]

A LOVE SYMPHONY

        Along the garden ways just now
            I heard the flowers speak;
        The white rose told me of your brow,
            The red rose of your cheek;

The lily of your bended head,
  The bindweed of your hair;
Each looked its loveliest and said
  You were more fair.

I went into the wood anon,
  And heard the wild birds sing,
How sweet you were, they warbled on,
  Piped, trilled, the selfsame thing.
Thrush, blackbird, linnet, without pause
  The burden did repeat,
And still began again because
  You were more sweet.

And then I went down to the sea,
  And heard it murmuring too,
Part of an ancient mystery,
  All made of me and you:
How many a thousand years ago
  I loved, and you were sweet—
Longer I could not stay, and so
  I fled back to your feet.

                Arthur O'Shaughnessy [1844–1881]

LOVE ON THE MOUNTAIN

My love comes down from the mountain
  Through the mists of dawn;
I look, and the star of the morning
  From the sky is gone.

My love comes down from the mountain,
  At dawn, dewy sweet;
Did you step from the star to the mountain,
  O little white feet?

O whence came your twining tresses
  And your shining eyes,
But out of the gold of the morning
  And the blue of the skies?

The misty mountain is burning
  In the sun's red fire,
And the heart in my breast is burning
  And lost in desire.

I follow you into the valley
  But no word can I say;
To the East or the West I will follow
  Till the dusk of my day.
               Thomas Boyd [1867-

KATE TEMPLE'S SONG

ONLY a touch, and nothing more:
Ah! but never so touched before!
Touch of lip, was it? Touch of hand?
Either is easy to understand.
Earth may be smitten with fire or frost—
Never the touch of true love lost.

Only a word, was it? Scarce a word!
Musical whisper, softly heard,
Syllabled nothing—just a breath—
'Twill outlast life and 'twill laugh at death.
Love with so little can do so much—
Only a word, sweet! Only a touch!
          Mortimer Collins [1827-1876]

MY QUEEN

WHEN and how shall I earliest meet her?
  What are the words she first will say?
By what name shall I learn to greet her?
  I know not now; it will come some day!
With the selfsame sunlight shining upon her,
  Shining down on her ringlets' sheen,
She is standing somewhere—she I shall honor,
  She that I wait for, my queen, my queen!

Whether her hair be golden or raven,
     Whether her eyes be hazel or blue,
I know not now; but 'twill be engraven
     Some day hence as my loveliest hue.
Many a girl I have loved for a minute,
     Worshipped many a face I have seen:
Ever and aye there was something in it,
     Something that could not be hers, my queen!

I will not dream of her tall and stately,
     She that I love may be fairy light;
I will not say she must move sedately,—
     Whatever she does it will then be right.
She may be humble or proud, my lady,
     Or that sweet calm which is just between;
And whenever she comes she will find me ready
     To do her homage, my queen, my queen!

But she must be courteous, she must be holy,
     Pure in her spirit, this maiden I love;
Whether her birth be noble or lowly
     I care no more than the spirits above.
But I'll give my heart to my lady's keeping,
     And ever her strength on mine shall lean;
And the stars may fall, and the saints be weeping
     Ere I cease to love her, my queen, my queen!

Unknown

"DARLING, TELL ME YES"

ONE little minute more, Maud,
     One little whisper more;
I have a word to speak, Maud,
     I never breathed before.
What can it be but *love*, Maud;
     And do I rightly guess
'Tis pleasant to your ear, Maud?
     O darling! tell me *yes!*

The burden of my heart, Maud,
  There's little need to tell;
There's little need to say, Maud,
  I've loved you long and well.
There's language in a sigh, Maud,
  One's meaning to express,
And yours—was it for *me*, Maud?
  O darling! tell me *yes !*

My eyes have told my love, Maud,
  And on my burning cheek,
You've read the tender thought, Maud,
  My lips refused to speak.
I gave you all my heart, Maud,
  'Tis needless to confess;
And did you give me yours, Maud?
  O darling! tell me *yes !*

'Tis sad to starve a love, Maud,
  So worshipful and true;
I know a little cot, Maud,
  Quite large enough for two;
And you will be my wife, Maud?
  So may you ever bless
Through all your sunny life, Maud,
  The day you answered *yes !*
              John Godfrey Saxe [1816–1887]

"DO I LOVE THEE?"

Do I love thee? Ask the bee
If she loves the flowery lea,
Where the honeysuckle blows
And the fragrant clover grows.
      As she answers, Yes or No,
      Darling! take my answer so.

Do I love thee? Ask the bird
When her matin song is heard,

If she loves the sky so fair,
Fleecy cloud and liquid air.
        As she answers, Yes or No,
        Darling! take my answer so.

Do I love thee? Ask the flower
If she loves the vernal shower,
Or the kisses of the sun,
Or the dew, when day is done.
        As she answers, Yes or No,
        Darling! take my answer so.

John Godfrey Saxe [1816–1887]

"O WORLD, BE NOBLER"

O WORLD, be nobler, for her sake!
  If she but knew thee what thou art,
What wrongs are borne, what deeds are done
In thee, beneath thy daily sun,
  Know'st thou not that her tender heart
For pain and very shame would break?
O World, be nobler, for her sake!

Laurence Binyon [1869–

"IN THE DARK, IN THE DEW"

In the dark, in the dew,
I am smiling back at you;
But you cannot see the smile,
And you're thinking all the while
How I turn my face from you,
In the dark, in the dew.

In the dark, in the dew,
All my love goes out to you,
Flutters like a bird in pain,
Dies and comes to life again;
While you whisper, "Sweetest, hark:
Someone's sighing in the dark,
In the dark, in the dew!"

In the dark, in the dew,
All my heart cries out to you,
As I cast it at your feet,
Sweet indeed, but not too sweet;
Wondering will you hear it beat,
Beat for you, and bleed for you,
In the dark, in the dew!

Mary Newmarch Prescott [1849–1888]

NANNY

OH, for an hour when the day is breaking,
Down by the shore where the tide is making,
Fair as a white cloud, thou, love, near me,
None but the waves and thyself to hear me!
Oh, to my breast how these arms would press thee!
Wildly my heart in its joy would bless thee!
Oh, how the soul thou has won would woo thee,
Girl of the snow neck, closer to me!

Oh, for an hour as the day advances,
Out where the breeze on the broom-bush dances,
Watching the lark, with the sun-ray o'er us,
Winging the notes of his Heaven-taught chorus!
Oh, to be there, and my love before me,
Soft as a moonbeam smiling o'er me!
Thou would'st but love, and I would woo thee,
Girl of the dark eye, closer to me!

Oh, for an hour where the sun first found us,
Out in the eve with its red sheets round us,
Brushing the dew from the gale's soft winglets,
Pearly and sweet, with thy long dark ringlets!
Oh, to be there on the sward beside thee,
Telling my tale, though I know you'd chide me!
Sweet were thy voice, though it should undo me,—
Girl of the dark locks, closer to me!

Oh, for an hour by night or by day, love,
Just as the Heavens and thou might say, love!

Far from the stare of the cold-eyed many,
Bound in the breath of my dove-souled Nanny!
Oh, for the pure chains that have bound me,
Warm from thy red lips circling round me!
Oh, in my soul, as the light above me,
Queen of the pure hearts, do I love thee!

Francis Davis [1810–1885]

A TRIFLE

I KNOW not why, but even to me
My songs seem sweet when read to thee.

Perhaps in this the pleasure lies—
I read my thoughts within thine eyes,

And so dare fancy that my art
May sink as deeply as thy heart.

Perhaps I love to make my words
Sing round thee like so many birds,

Or, maybe, they are only sweet
As they seem offerings at thy feet.

Or haply, Lily, when I speak,
I think, perchance, they touch thy cheek,

Or with a yet more precious bliss,
Die on thy red lips in a kiss.

Each reason here—I cannot tell—
Or all perhaps may solve the spell.

But if she watch when I am by,
Lily may deeper see than I.

Henry Timrod [1829–1867]

ROMANCE

I WILL make you brooches and toys for your delight
Of bird-song at morning and star-shine at night.
I will make a palace fit for you and me,
Of green days in forests and blue days at sea.

I will make my kitchen, and you shall keep your room,
Where white flows the river and bright blows the broom,
And you shall wash your linen and keep your body white
In rainfall at morning and dewfall at night.

And this shall be for music when no one else is near
The fine song for singing, the rare song to hear!
That only I remember, that only you admire,
Of the broad road that stretches and the roadside fire.

Robert Louis Stevenson [1850–1894]

"OR EVER THE KNIGHTLY YEARS WERE GONE"

Or ever the knightly years were gone
  With the old world to the grave,
I was a King in Babylon
  And you were a Christian Slave.

I saw, I took, I cast you by,
  I bent and broke your pride.
You loved me well, or I heard them lie,
  But your longing was denied.
Surely I knew that by and by
  You cursed your gods and died.

And a myriad suns have set and shone
  Since then upon the grave
Decreed by the King in Babylon
  To her that had been his Slave.

The pride I trampled is now my scathe,
  For it tramples me again.
The old resentment lasts like death,
  For you love, yet you refrain.
I break my heart on your hard unfaith,
  And I break my heart in vain.

Yet not for an hour do I wish undone
  The deed beyond the grave,
When I was a King in Babylon
  And you were a Virgin Slave.

William Ernest Henley [1849–1903]

RUS IN URBE

Poets are singing the whole world over
   Of May in melody, joys for June;
Dusting their feet in the careless clover,
   And filling their hearts with the blackbird's tune.
The "brown bright nightingale" strikes with pity
   The sensitive heart of a count or clown;
But where is the song for our leafy city,
   And where the rhymes for our lovely town?

"O for the Thames, and its rippling reaches,
   Where almond rushes, and breezes sport!
Take me a walk under Burnham Beeches;
   Give me a dinner at Hampton Court!"
Poets, be still, though your hearts I harden;
   We've flowers by day and have scents at dark,
The limes are in leaf in the cockney garden,
   And lilacs blossom in Regent's Park.

"Come for a blow," says a reckless fellow,
   Burned red and brown by passionate sun;
"Come to the downs, where the gorse is yellow;
   The season of kisses has just begun!
Come to the fields where bluebells shiver,
   Hear cuckoo's carol, or plaint of dove;
Come for a row on the silent river;
   Come to the meadows and learn to love!"

Yes, I will come when this wealth is over
   Of softened color and perfect tone—
The lilac's better than fields of clover;
   I'll come when blossoming May has flown.
When dust and dirt of a trampled city
   Have dragged the yellow laburnum down,
I'll take my holiday—more's the pity—
   And turn my back upon London town.

Margaret! am I so wrong to love it,
   This misty town that your face shines through?
A crown of blossom is waved above it;
   But heart and life of the whirl—'tis you!

Margaret! pearl! I have sought and found you;
  And, though the paths of the wind are free,
I'll follow the ways of the world around you,
  And build my nest on the nearest tree!

Clement Scott [1841–1904]

MY ROAD

THERE'S a road to heaven, a road to hell,
A road for the sick and one for the well;
There's a road for the false and a road for the true,
But the road for me is the road to you.

There's a road through prairie and forest and glen,
A road to each place in human ken;
There's a road over earth and a road over sea,
But the road to you is the road for me.

There's a road for animal, bird, and beast,
A road for the greatest, a road for the least;
There's a road that is old and a road that is new,
But the road for me is the road to you.

There's a road for the heart and a road for the soul,
There's a road for a part and a road for the whole;
There's a road for love,—which few ever see,—
'Tis the road to you and the road for me.

Oliver Opdyke [1878–

A WHITE ROSE

THE red rose whispers of passion,
  And the white rose breathes of love;
Oh, the red rose is a falcon,
  And the white rose is a dove.

But I send you a cream white rosebud
  With a flush on its petal tips;
For the love that is purest and sweetest
  Has a kiss of desire on the lips.

John Boyle O'Reilly [1844–1890]

"SOME DAY OF DAYS"

SOME day, some day of days, threading the street
    With idle, heedless pace,
    Unlooking for such grace
    I shall behold your face!
Some day, some day of days, thus may we meet.

Perchance the sun may shine from skies of May,
    Or winter's icy chill
    Touch whitely vale and hill.
    What matter?   I shall thrill
Through every vein with summer on that day.

Once more life's perfect youth will all come back,
    And for a moment there
    I shall stand fresh and fair,
    And drop the garment care;
Once more my perfect youth will nothing lack.

I shut my eyes now, thinking how 'twill be—
    How face to face each soul
    Will slip its long control,
    Forget the dismal dole
Of dreary Fate's dark, separating sea;

And glance to glance, and hand to hand in greeting,
    The past with all its fears,
    Its silences and tears,
    Its lonely, yearning years,
Shall vanish in the moment of that meeting.
                          Nora Perry [1832–1896]

THE TELEPHONE

"WHEN I was just as far as I could walk
From here to-day,
There was an hour
All still
When leaning with my bead against a flower

I heard you talk.
Don't say I didn't, for I heard you say—
You spoke from that flower on the window sill—
Do you remember what it was you said?"

"First tell me what it was you thought you heard."

"Having found the flower and driven a bee away,
I leaned my head,
And holding by the stalk,
I listened and I thought I caught the word—
What was it? Did you call me by my name?
Or did you say—
Someone said 'Come'—I heard it as I bowed."

"I may have thought as much, but not aloud."

"Well, so I came."
Robert Frost [1875–

WHERE LOVE IS

By the rosy cliffs of Devon, on a green hill's crest,
I would build me a house as a swallow builds its nest;
I would curtain it with roses, and the wind should breathe
    to me
The sweetness of the roses and the saltness of the sea.

Where the Tuscan olives whiten in the hot blue day,
I would hide me from the heat in a little hut of gray,
While the singing of the husbandmen should scale my lat-
    tice green
From the golden rows of barley that the poppies blaze be-
    tween.

Narrow is the street, Dear, and dingy are the walls
Wherein you wait my coming as the twilight falls.
All day with dreams I gild the grime till at your step I start—
Ah Love, my country in your arms—my home upon your
    heart!
Amelia Josephine Burr [1878–

THAT DAY YOU CAME

SUCH special sweetness was about
   That day God sent you here,
I knew the lavender was out,
   And it was mid of year.

Their common way the great winds blew,
   The ships sailed out to sea;
Yet ere that day was spent I knew
   Mine own had come to me.

As after song some snatch of tune
   Lurks still in grass or bough,
So, somewhat of the end o' June
   Lurks in each weather now.

The young year sets the buds astir,
   The old year strips the trees;
But ever in my lavender
   I hear the brawling bees.

Lizette Woodworth Reese [1856–1935]

AMANTIUM IRÆ

WHEN this, our rose, is faded,
   And these, our days, are done,
In lands profoundly shaded
   From tempest and from sun:
Ah, once more come together,
   Shall we forgive the past,
And safe from worldly weather
   Possess our souls at last?

Or in our place of shadows
   Shall still we stretch an hand
To green, remembered meadows,
   Of that old pleasant land?

And vainly there foregathered,
  Shall we regret the sun?
The rose of love, ungathered?
  The bay, we have not won?

Ah, child! the world's dark marges
  May lead to Nevermore,
The stately funeral barges
  Sail for an unknown shore,
And love we vow to-morrow,
  And pride we serve to-day:
What if they both should borrow
  Sad hues of yesterday?

Our pride! Ah, should we miss it,
  Or will it serve at last?
Our anger, if we kiss it,
  Is like a sorrow past.
While roses deck the garden,
  While yet the sun is high,
Doff sorry pride for pardon,
  Or ever love go by.

              Ernest Dowson [1867–1900]

IN A ROSE GARDEN

A HUNDRED years from now, dear heart,
  We shall not care at all.
It will not matter then a whit,
  The honey or the gall.
The summer days that we have known
Will all forgotten be and flown;
The garden will be overgrown
  Where now the roses fall.

A hundred years from now, dear heart,
  We shall not mind the pain;
The throbbing crimson tide of life
  Will not have left a stain.

The song we sing together, dear,
The dream we dream together here,
Will mean no more than means a tear
    Amid a summer rain.

A hundred years from now, dear heart,
    The grief will all be o'er;
The sea of care will surge in vain
    Upon a careless shore.
These glasses we turn down to-day
Here at the parting of the way—
We shall be wineless then as they,
    And shall not mind it more.

A hundred years from now, dear heart,
    We'll neither know nor care
What came of all life's bitterness,
    Or followed love's despair.
Then fill the glasses up again,
And kiss me through the rose-leaf rain;
We'll build one castle more in Spain,
    And dream one more dream there.

                    John Bennett [1865–

" GOD BLESS YOU, DEAR, TO–DAY "

If there be graveyards in the heart
    From which no roses spring,
A place of wrecks and old gray tombs
    From which no birds take wing,
Where linger buried hopes and dreams
    Like ghosts among the graves,
Why, buried hopes are dismal things,
    And lonely ghosts are knaves!

If there come dreary winter days,
    When summer roses fall
And lie, forgot, in withered drifts
    Along the garden wall;

If all the wreaths a lover weaves
  Turn thorns upon the brow,—
Then out upon the silly fool
  Who makes not merry now!

For if we cannot keep the past,
  Why care for what's to come?
The instant's prick is all that stings,
  And then the place is numb.
If Life's a lie, and Love's a cheat,
  As I have heard men say,
Then here's a health to fond deceit—
  God bless you, dear, to-day!

John Bennett [1865–

TO–DAY

I BRING you all my olden days,
  My childhood's morning glow;
I love you down the meadow ways
  Where early blossoms blow:
And up deep lanes of long-gone-by,
  Shining with dew-drops yet,—
I wander still, till you and I
  Over the world are met.

I bring you all my lonely days,
  My heart that hungered so;
I love you through the wistful haze
  Of autumns burning low;
And on pale seas, beneath wan sky,
  By weary tides beset,
I voyage still, till you and I
  Over the world are met.

I bring you all my happy days,—
  Armfuls of flowers—oh,
I love you as the sunlight stays
  On mountains heaped with snow:
And where the dearest dream-buds lie,
  With tears and dew-drops wet,
I toss to-day; for you and I
  Over the world are met!

Benjamin R. C. Low [1880–1941]

TO ARCADY

ACROSS the hills of Arcady
    Into the Land of Song—
Ah, dear, if you will go with me
    The way will not be long!

It will not lead through solitudes
    Of wind-blown woods or sea;
Dear, no! the city's weariest moods
    May scarce veil Arcady.

'Tis in no unfamiliar land
    Lit by some distant star.
No!   Arcady is where you stand,
    And Song is where you are!

So walk but hand in hand with me—
    No road can lead us wrong;
These are the hills of Arcady—
    Here is the Land of Song!

Charles Buxton Going [1863–

WILD WISHES

I WISH, because the sweetness of your passing
    Makes all the earth a garden where you tread,
That I might be the meanest of your roses,
    To pave your path with petals passion-red!

I wish, because the softness of your breathing
    Stirs the white jasmine at your window frame,
That I might be the fragrance of a flower,
    To stir the night breeze with your dearest name!

I wish, because the glory of your dreaming
    Strews all the field of heaven with throbbing stars,
That I might storm the portals of your slumber,
    And soar with you beyond night's golden bars!

I wish to be the day you die, Beloved,
    Though at its close my foolish heart must break!
But most of all, I wish, my dearest darling,
    To be the Blessed Morning when you wake!

Ethel M. Hewitt [18 –

"BECAUSE OF YOU"

SWEET have I known the blossoms of the morning
    Tenderly tinted to their hearts of dew:
But now my flowers have found a fuller fragrance,
    Because of you.

Long have I worshiped in my soul's enshrining
    High visions of the noble and the true—
Now all my aims and all my prayers are purer,
    Because of you.

Wise have I seen the uses of life's labor;
    To all its puzzles found some answering clue.
But now my life has learned a nobler meaning,
    Because of you.

In the past days I chafed at pain and waiting,
    Grasping at gladness as the children do;
Now it is sweet to wait and joy to suffer,
    Because of you.

In the long years of silences that part us
    Dimmed by my tears and darkened to my view,
Close shall I hold my memories and my madness,
    Because of you.

Whether our lips shall touch or hands shall hunger,
    Whether our love be fed or joys be few,
Life will be sweeter and more worth the living,
    Because of you.

Sophia Almon Hensley [1866–

THEN

I GIVE thee treasures hour by hour,
   That old-time princes asked in vain,
And pined for in their useless power,
   Or died of passion's eager pain.

I give thee love as God gives light,
   Aside from merit, or from prayer,
Rejoicing in its own delight,
   And freer than the lavish air.

I give thee prayers, like jewels strung
   On golden threads of hope and fear;
And tenderer thoughts than ever hung
   In a sad angel's pitying tear.

As earth pours freely to the sea
   Her thousand streams of wealth untold,
So flows my silent life to thee,
   Glad that its very sands are gold.

What care I for thy carelessness?
   I give from depths that overflow,
Regardless that their power to bless
   Thy spirit cannot sound or know.

Far lingering on a distant dawn,
   My triumph shines, more sweet than late;
When, from these mortal mists withdrawn,
   Thy heart shall know me—I can wait.

Rose Terry Cooke [1827-1892]

THE MISSIVE

I THAT tremble at your feet
   Am a rose;
Nothing dewier or more sweet
   Buds or blows;
He that plucked me, he that threw me
Breathed in fire his whole soul through me.

How the cold air is infused
   With the scent!
See, this satin leaf is bruised—
   Bruised and bent,
Lift me, lift the wounded blossom,
Soothe it at your rosier bosom!

Frown not with averted eyes!
   Joy's a flower
That is born a god, and dies
   In an hour.
Take me, for the Summer closes,
And your life is but a rose's.

        Edmund Gosse [1849–1928]

PLYMOUTH HARBOR

OH, what know they of harbors
   Who toss not on the sea!
They tell of fairer havens
   But none so fair there be

As Plymouth town outstretching
   Her quiet arms to me;
Her breast's broad welcome spreading
   From Mewstone to Penlee.

Ah, with this home-thought, darling,
   Come crowding thoughts of thee.
Oh, what know they of harbors
   Who toss not on the sea!

        Mrs. Ernest Radford [1858–

THE SERF'S SECRET

I KNOW a secret, such a one
The hawthorn blossoms spider-spun,
The dew-damp daisies in the grass
Laugh up to greet me as I pass
To meet the upland sun.

It is that I would rather be
The little page, on bended knee,
Who stoops to gather up her train
Beneath the porch-lamp's ruby rain
Than hold a realm in fee.

It is that in her scornful eye,
Too hid for courtly sneer to spy,
I saw, one day, a look which said
That I, and only I, might shed
Love-light across her sky.

I know a secret, such a one
The hawthorn blossoms spider-spun,
The dew-damp daisies in the grass
Laugh up to greet me as I pass
To meet the upland sun.

William Vaughn Moody [1869–1910]

"O, INEXPRESSIBLE AS SWEET"

O, INEXPRESSIBLE as sweet,
    Love takes my voice away;
I cannot tell thee when we meet
    What most I long to say.

But hadst thou hearing in thy heart
    To know what beats in mine,
Then shouldst thou walk, where'er thou art,
    In melodies divine.

So warbling birds lift higher notes
    Than to our ears belong;
The music fills their throbbing throats,
    But silence steals the song.

George Edward Woodberry [1855–1930]

THE CYCLAMEN

OVER the plains where Persian hosts
    Laid down their lives for glory
Flutter the cyclamens, like ghosts
    That witness to their story.

Oh, fair! Oh, white! Oh, pure as snow!
On countless graves how sweet they grow!

Or crimson, like the cruel wounds
    From which the life-blood, flowing,
Poured out where now on grassy mounds
    The low, soft winds are blowing:
Oh, fair! Oh, red! Like blood of slain;
Not even time can cleanse that stain.

But when my dear these blossoms holds,
    All loveliness her dower,
All woe and joy the past enfolds
    In her find fullest flower.
Oh, fair! Oh, pure! Oh, white and red!
If she but live, what are the dead!

Arlo Bates [1850–1918]

THE WEST–COUNTRY LOVER

THEN, lady, at last thou art sick of my sighing?
Good-bye!
So long as I sue, thou wilt still be denying?
Good-bye!
Ah, well! shall I vow then to serve thee forever,
And swear no unkindness our kinship can sever?
Nay, nay, dear my lass! here's an end of endeavor.
Good-bye!

Yet let no sweet ruth for my misery grieve thee.
Good-bye!
The man who has loved knows as well how to leave thee.
Good-bye!
The gorse is enkindled, there's bloom on the heather,
And love is my joy, and so too is fair weather;
I still ride abroad, though we ride not together.
Good-bye!

My horse is my mate; let the wind be my master.
Good-bye!
Though Care may pursue, yet my hound follows faster.
Good-bye!

The red deer's a-tremble in coverts unbroken.
He hears the hoof-thunder; he scents the death-token.
Shall I mope at home, under vows never spoken?
Good-bye!

The brown earth's my book, and I ride forth to read it.
Good-bye!
The stream runneth fast, but my will shall outspeed it.
Good-bye!
I love thee, dear lass, but I hate the hag Sorrow.
As sun follows rain, and to-night has its morrow,
So I'll taste of joy, though I steal, beg, or borrow!
Good-bye!

Alice Brown [1857–

"BE YE IN LOVE WITH APRIL–TIDE"

BE ye in love with April-tide?
        I' faith, in love am I!
    For now 'tis sun, and now 'tis shower,
        And now 'tis frost and now 'tis flower,
And now 'tis Laura laughing-eyed,
        And now 'tis Laura shy!

Ye doubtful days, O slower glide!
        Still smile and frown, O sky!
    Some beauty unforeseen I trace
    In every change of Laura's face;—
Be ye in love with April-tide?
        I' faith, in love am I!

Clinton Scollard [1860–1932]

UNITY

HEART of my heart, the world is young:
    Love lies hidden in every rose!
Every song that the skylark sung
    Once, we thought, must come to a close:
Now we know the spirit of song,
    Song that is merged in the chant of the whole,
Hand in hand as we wander along,
    What should we doubt of the years that roll?

Heart of my heart, we can not die!
 Love triumphant in flower and tree,
Every life that laughs at the sky
 Tells us nothing can cease to be;
One, we are one with a song to-day,
 One with the clover that scents the wold,
One with the Unknown, far away,
 One with the stars, when earth grows old.

Heart of my heart, we are one with the wind,
 One with the clouds that are whirled o'er the lea,
One in many, O broken and blind,
 One as the waves are at one with the sea!
Ay! when life seems scattered apart,
 Darkens, ends as a tale that is told,
One, we are one, O heart of my heart,
 One, still one, while the world grows old.

      Alfred Noyes [1880–

THE QUEEN

He loves not well whose love is bold!
 I would not have thee come too nigh:
The sun's gold would not seem pure gold
 Unless the sun were in the sky:
To take him thence and chain him near
Would make his glory disappear.

He keeps his state,—keep thou in thine,
 And shine upon me from afar!
So shall I bask in light divine,
 That falls from love's own guiding star;
So shall thy eminence be high,
And so my passion shall not die;

But all my life shall reach its hands
 Of lofty longing toward thy face,
And be as one who, speechless, stands
 In rapture at some perfect grace!
My love, my hope, my all shall be
To look to heaven and look to thee!

Thy eyes shall be the heavenly lights,
  Thy voice the gentle summer breeze,—
What time it sways, on moonlit nights,
  The murmuring tops of leafy trees;
And I shall touch thy beauteous form
In June's red roses, rich and warm.

But thou thyself shall come not down
  From that pure region far above;
But keep thy throne and wear thy crown,
  Queen of my heart and queen of love!
A monarch in thy realm complete,
And I a monarch—at thy feet!

William Winter [1836–1917]

A LOVER'S ENVY

I ENVY every flower that blows
Beside the pathway where she goes,
    And every bird that sings to her,
    And every breeze that brings to her
      The fragrance of the rose.

I envy every poet's rhyme
That moves her heart at eventime,
    And every tree that wears for her
    Its brightest bloom, and bears for her
      The fruitage of its prime.

I envy every Southern night
That paves her path with moonbeams white,
    And silvers all the leaves for her,
    And in their shadow weaves for her
      A dream of dear delight.

I envy none whose love requires
Of her a gift, a task that tires:
    I only long to live to her,
    I only ask to give to her
      All that her heart desires.

Henry Van Dyke [1852–1933]

STAR SONG

WHEN sunset flows into golden glows
  And the breath of the night is new,
Love, find afar eve's eager star—
  That is my thought of you.

O tear-wet eye that scans the sky
  Your lonely lattice through:
Choose any one, from sun to sun—
  That is my thought of you.

And when you wake at the morning's break
  To rival rose and dew,
The star that stays till the leaping rays—
  That is my thought of you.

Ay, though by day they seem away
  Beyond or cloud or blue,
From dawn to night unquenched their light—
  As are my thoughts of you.

        Robert Underwood Johnson [1853–

"MY HEART SHALL BE THY GARDEN"

MY heart shall be thy garden. Come, my own,
  Into thy garden; thine be happy hours
  Among my fairest thoughts, my tallest flowers,
From root to crowning petal, thine alone.
Thine is the place from where the seeds are sown
  Up to the sky inclosed, with all its showers.
  But ah, the birds, the birds! Who shall build bowers
To keep these thine? O friend, the birds have flown.

For as these come and go, and quit our pine
  To follow the sweet season, or, new-comers,
    Sing one song only from our alder-trees,
My heart has thoughts, which, though thine eyes hold mine,
  Flit to the silent world and other summers,
    With wings that dip beyond the silver seas.

        Alice Meynell [1853–1922]

AT NIGHT

HOME, home from the horizon far and clear,
    Hither the soft wings sweep;
Flocks of the memories of the day draw near
    The dovecote doors of sleep.

Oh which are they that come through sweetest light
    Of all these homing birds?
Which with the straightest and the swiftest flight?
    Your words to me, your words!

             Alice Meynell [1850–1922]

SONG

      SONG is so old,
        Love is so new—
    Let me be still
      And kneel to you.

    Let me be still
      And breathe no word,
    Save what my warm blood
      Sings unheard.

    Let my warm blood
      Sing low of you—
    Song is so fair,
      Love is so new!

          Hermann Hagedorn [1882–

"ALL LAST NIGHT"

ALL last night I had quiet
    In a fragrant dream and warm:
She had become my Sabbath,
    And round my neck, her arm.

I knew the warmth in my dreaming;
    The fragrance, I suppose,
Was her hair about me,
    Or else she wore a rose.

Her hair, I think; for likest
   Woodruffe 'twas, when Spring
Loitering down wet woodways
   Treads it sauntering.

No light, nor any speaking;
   Fragrant only and warm.
Enough to know my lodging,
   The white Sabbath of her arm.

Lascelles Abercrombie [1881–1938]

THE LAST WORD

WHEN I have folded up this tent
   And laid the soiled thing by,
I shall go forth 'neath different stars,
   Under an unknown sky.

And yet whatever house I find
   Beneath the grass or snow
Will ne'er be tenantless of love
   Or lack the face I know.

O lips—wild roses wet with rain!
   Blown hair of drifted brown!
O passionate eyes! O panting heart—
   When in that colder town

I lie, the one inhabitant,
   My hands across my breast,
How warm through all eternity
   The summer of my rest!

To each frail root beneath the ground
   That thrusts its flower above,
I shall impart a fiercer sap—
   I who have known your love!

And growing things will lean to me
   To learn what love hath won,
Till I shall whisper to the dust
   That secret of the Sun.

Yea, though my spirit never wake
  To hear the voice I knew,
Even an endless sleep would be
  Stirred by the dreams of You!

Frederic Lawrence Knowles [1869–1905]

"HEART OF MY HEART"

HEART of my heart, my life, my light!
  If you were lost what should I do?
I dare not let you from my sight
  Lest Death should fall in love with you.

Such countless terrors lie in wait!
  The gods know well how dear you are!
What if they left me desolate
  And plucked and set you for their star!

Then hold me close, the gods are strong,
  And perfect joy so rare a flower
No man may hope to keep it long—
  And I may lose you any hour.

Then kiss me close, my star, my flower!
  So shall the future grant me this:
That there was not a single hour
  We might have kissed, and did not kiss!

Unknown

MY LADDIE

OH, my laddie, my laddie,
  I lo'e your very plaidie,
  I lo'e your very bonnet
Wi' the silver buckle on it,
  I lo'e your collie Harry,
  I lo'e the kent ye carry;
But oh! it's past my power to tell
How much, how much I lo'e yoursel!

Oh, my dearie, my dearie,
I could luik an' never weary
At your een sae blue an' laughin',
That a heart o' stane wad saften,
While your mouth sae proud an' curly
Gars my heart gang tirlie-wirlie;
But oh! yoursel, your very sel,
I lo'e ten thousand times as well!

Oh! my darlin', my darlin',
Let's flit whaur flits the starlin',
Let's loll upo' the heather
A' this bonny, bonny weather;
Ye shall fauld me in your plaidie,
My luve, my luve, my laddie;
An' close, an' close into your ear
I'll tell ye how I lo'e ye, dear.

Amélie Rives [1863–

THE SHADED POOL

A LAUGHING knot of village maids
Goes gaily tripping to the brook,
For water-nymphs they mean to be,
And seek some still, secluded nook.
Here Laura goes, my own delight,
And Colin's love, the madcap Jane,
And half a score of goddesses
Trip over daisies in the plain:
Already now they loose their hair
And peep from out the tangled gold,
Or speed the flying foot to reach
The brook that's only summer-cold;
The lovely locks stream out behind
The shepherdesses on the wing,
And Laura's is the wealth I love,
And Laura's is the gold I sing.

A-row upon the bank they pant,
And all unlace the country shoe;
Their fingers tug the garter-knots
To loose the hose of varied hue.

The flashing knee at last appears,
The lower curves of youth and grace,
Whereat the girls intently scan
The mazy thickets of the place.
But who's to see except the thrush
Upon the wild crab-apple tree?
Within his branchy haunt he sits—
A very Peeping Tom is he!
Now music bubbles in his throat,
And now he pipes the scene in song—
The virgins slipping from their robes,
The cheated stockings lean and long,
The swift-descending petticoat,
The breasts that heave because they ran,
The rounded arms, the brilliant limbs,
The pretty necklaces of tan.
Did ever amorous God in Greece,
In search of some young mouth to kiss,
By any river chance upon
A sylvan scene as bright as this?
But though each maid is pure and fair,
For one alone my heart I bring,
And Laura's is the shape I love,
And Laura's is the snow I sing.

And now upon the brook's green brink,
A milk-white bevy, lo, they stand,
Half shy, half frightened, reaching back
The beauty of a poising hand!
How musical their little screams
When ripples kiss their shrinking feet
And then the brook embraces all
Till gold and white and water meet!
Within the streamlet's soft cool arms
Delight and love and gracefulness
Sport till a flock of tiny waves
Swamps all the beds of floating cress;
And on his shining face are seen
Great yellow lilies drifting down
Beyond the ringing apple-tree,
Beyond the empty homespun gown.

Did ever Orpheus with his lute,
When making melody of old,
E'er find a stream in Attica
So ripely full of pink and gold?

At last they climb the sloping bank
And shake upon the thirsty soil
A treasury of diamond-drops
Not gained by aught of grimy toil.
Again the garters clasp the hose,
Again the velvet knee is hid,
Again the breathless babble tells
What Colin said, what Colin did.
In grace upon the grass they lie
And spread their tresses to the sun,
And rival, musical as they,
The blackbird's alto shake and run.
Did ever Love, on hunting bent,
Come idly humming through the hay,
And, to his sudden joyfulness,
Find fairer game at close of day?
Though every maid's a lily-rose,
And meet to sway a sceptred king,
Yet Laura's is the face I love,
And Laura's are the lips I sing.

Norman Gale [1862–

GOOD-NIGHT

GOOD-NIGHT. Good-night. Ah, good the night
That wraps thee in its silver light.
Good-night. No night is good for me
That does not hold a thought of thee.
  Good-night.

Good-night. Be every night as sweet
As that which made our love complete,
Till that last night when death shall be
One brief "Good-night," for thee and me.
  Good-night.

S. Weir Mitchell [1829–1914]

THE MYSTIC

By seven vineyards on one hill
    We walked. The native wine
In clusters grew beside us two,
    For your lips and for mine,

When, "Hark!" you said,—"Was that a bell
    Or a bubbling spring we heard?"
But I was wise and closed my eyes
    And listened to a bird;

For as summer leaves are bent and shake
    With singers passing through,
So moves in me continually
    The wingèd breath of you.

You tasted from a single vine
    And took from that your fill—
But I inclined to every kind,
    All seven on one hill.

                    Witter Bynner [1881–

"I AM THE WIND"

I AM the wind that wavers,
    You are the certain land;
I am the shadow that passes
    Over the sand.

I am the leaf that quivers,
    You the unshaken tree;
You are the stars that are steadfast,
    I am the sea.

You are the light eternal,
    Like a torch I shall die. . . .
You are the surge of deep music,
    I—but a cry!

                    Zoë Akins [1886–

"I LOVE MY LIFE, BUT NOT TOO WELL"

I LOVE my life, but not too well
    To give it to thee like a flower,
So it may pleasure thee to dwell
    Deep in its perfume but an hour.
I love my life, but not too well.

I love my life, but not too well
    To sing it note by note away,
So to thy soul the song may tell
    The beauty of the desolate day.
I love my life, but not too well.

I love my life, but not too well
    To cast it like a cloak on thine,
Against the storms that sound and swell
    Between thy lonely heart and mine.
I love my life, but not too well.

Harriet Monroe [1860–1936]

"THIS IS MY LOVE FOR YOU"

I HAVE brought the wine
And the folded raiment fine,
Pilgrim staff and shoe—
This is my love for you.

I will smooth your bed,
Lay away your coverlid,
Sing the whole day through.
This is my love for you.

Mayhap in the night,
When the dark beats back the light,
I shall struggle too . . .
This is my love for you.

In your dream, once more,
Will a star lead to my door?
To stars and dreams be true!
This is my love for you . . .

Grace Fallow Norton [1876–

MY LADY'S LIPS

LIPS AND EYES

From "Blurt, Master Constable"

LOVE for such a cherry lip
  Would be glad to pawn his arrows;
Venus here to take a sip
  Would sell her doves and team of sparrows.
    But they shall not so;
      Hey nonny, nonny no!
    None but I this lip must owe;
      Hey nonny, nonny no!

Did Jove see this wanton eye,
  Ganymede must wait no longer;
Phœbe here one night did lie,
  Would change her face and look much younger.
    But they shall not so;
      Hey nonny, nonny no!
    None but I this lip must owe;
      Hey nonny, nonny no!
        Thomas Middleton [1570?-1627]

THE KISS

From "Cynthia's Revels"

O THAT joy so soon should waste!
  Or so sweet a bliss
  As a kiss
Might not for ever last!
So sugared, so melting, so soft, so delicious,
  The dew that lies on roses,
  When the morn herself discloses,
Is not so precious.

O, rather than I would it smother,
Were I to taste such another,
   It should be my wishing
   That I might die with kissing.

          Ben Jonson [1573?–1637]

"TAKE, O TAKE THOSE LIPS AWAY"

TAKE, O take those lips away,
   That so sweetly were forsworn,
And those eyes, the break of day,
   Lights that do mislead the morn;
But my kisses bring again,
Seals of love, but sealed in vain.

Hide, O hide those hills of snow,
   Which thy frozen bosom bears,
On whose tops the pinks that grow
   Are of those that April wears!
But first set my poor heart free,
Bound in those icy chains by thee.

The first stanza from " Measure for Measure," by
          William Shakespeare [1564–1616]
The second stanza from " The Bloody Brothers," by
          John Fletcher [1579–1625]

A STOLEN KISS

Now gentle sleep hath closèd up those eyes
Which, waking, kept my boldest thoughts in awe;
And free access unto that sweet lip lies,
From which I long the rosy breath to draw.
Methinks no wrong it were, if I should steal
From those two melting rubies one poor kiss;
None sees the theft that would the thief reveal,
Nor rob I her of aught that she can miss;
Nay, should I twenty kisses take away,
There would be little sign I had done so;
Why then should I this robbery delay?
O, she may wake, and therewith angry grow!
Well if she do, I'll back restore that one,
And twenty hundred thousand more for loan.

          George Wither [1588–1667]

SONG

My Love bound me with a kiss
   That I should no longer stay;
When I felt so sweet a bliss
   I had less power to part away:
Alas! that women do not know
Kisses make men loath to go.

Yes, she knows it but too well,
   For I heard when Venus' dove
In her ear did softly tell
   That kisses were the seals of love:
O muse not then though it be so,
Kisses make men loath to go.

Wherefore did she thus inflame
   My desires, heat my blood,
Instantly to quench the same
   And starve whom she had given food?
Ay, ay, the common sense can show,
Kisses make men loath to go.

Had she bid me go at first
   I would ne'er have grieved my heart
Hope delayed had been the worst;
   But ah to kiss and then to part!
How deep it struck, speak, gods! you know
Kisses make men loath to go.

Unknown

TO ELECTRA

I DARE not ask a kiss,
   I dare not beg a smile,
Lest having that, or this,
   I might grow proud the while.

No, no, the utmost share
   Of my desire shall be
Only to kiss that air
   That lately kissèd thee.

Robert Herrick [1591–1674]

"COME, CHLOE, AND GIVE ME SWEET KISSES"

Come, Chloe, and give me sweet kisses,
　For sweeter sure never girl gave;
But why in the midst of my blisses,
　Do you ask me how many I'd have?
I'm not to be stinted in pleasure,
　Then, prithee, my charmer, be kind,
For whilst I love thee above measure,
　To numbers I'll ne'er be confined.

Count the bees that on Hybla are playing,
　Count the flowers that enamel its fields,
Count the flocks that on Tempe are straying,
　Or the grain that rich Sicily yields,
Go number the stars in the heaven,
　Count how many sands on the shore,
When so many kisses you've given,
　I still shall be craving for more.

To a heart full of love, let me hold thee,
　To a heart that, dear Chloe, is thine;
In my arms I'll for ever enfold thee,
　And twist round thy limbs like a vine.
What joy can be greater than this is?
　My life on thy lips shall be spent!
But the wretch that can number his kisses,
　With few will be ever content.
　　　　　　　Charles Hanbury Williams [1708–1759]

A RIDDLE

I am just two and two, I am warm, I am cold,
And the parent of numbers that cannot be told,
I am lawful, unlawful—a duty, a fault—
I am often sold dear, good for nothing when bought;
An extraordinary boon, and a matter of course,
And yielded with pleasure when taken by force.
　　　　　　　William Cowper [1731–1800]

TO A KISS

Soft child of love, thou balmy bliss,
Inform me, O delicious kiss,
Why thou so suddenly art gone,
Lost in the moment thou art won?

Yet go! For wherefore should I sigh?
On Delia's lips, with raptured eye,
On Delia's blushing lips I see
A thousand full as sweet as thee.

John Wolcot [1738–1819]

SONG

Often I have heard it said
That her lips are ruby-red.
Little heed I what they say,
I have seen as red as they.
Ere she smiled on other men,
Real rubies were they then.

When she kissed me once in play,
Rubies were less bright than they,
And less bright than those which shone
In the palace of the Sun.
Will they be as bright again?
Not if kissed by other men.

Walter Savage Landor [1775–1864]

THE FIRST KISS OF LOVE

'Α βάρβιτος δὲ χορδαῖς
'Ερωτα μοῦνον ἠχεῖ—Anacreon

Away with your fictions of flimsy romance,
   Those tissues of falsehood which folly has wove!
Give me the mild beam of the soul-breathing glance,
   Or the rapture which dwells on the first kiss of love.

Ye rhymers, whose bosoms with phantasy glow,
Whose pastoral passions are made for the grove;
From what blest inspiration your sonnets would flow,
Could you ever have tasted the first kiss of love!

If Apollo should e'er his assistance refuse,
Or the Nine be disposed from your service to rove,
Invoke them no more, bid adieu to the muse,
And try the effect of the first kiss of love.

I hate you, ye cold compositions of art!
Though prudes may condemn me, and bigots reprove,
I court the effusions that spring from the heart,
Which throbs with delight to the first kiss of love.

Your shepherds, your flocks, those fantastical themes,
Perhaps may amuse, yet they never can move:
Arcadia displays but a region of dreams;
What are visions like these to the first kiss of love?

Oh! cease to affirm that man, since his birth,
From Adam till now, has with wretchedness strove;
Some portion of Paradise still is on earth,
And Eden revives in the first kiss of love.

When age chills the blood, when our pleasures are past-
For years fleet away with the wings of the dove—
The dearest remembrance will still be the last,
Our sweetest memorial the first kiss of love.

George Gordon Byron [1788–1824]

"JENNY KISSED ME"

JENNY kissed me when we met,
Jumping from the chair she sat in;
Time, you thief, who love to get
Sweets into your list, put that in!
Say I'm weary, say I'm sad,
Say that health and wealth have missed me,
Say I'm growing old, but add,
Jenny kissed me.

Leigh Hunt [1784–1859]

"I FEAR THY KISSES, GENTLE MAIDEN"

I FEAR thy kisses, gentle maiden:
Thou needest not fear mine;
My spirit is too deeply laden
Ever to burthen thine.

I fear thy mien, thy tones, thy motion;
Thou needest not fear mine;
Innocent is the heart's devotion
With which I worship thine.

Percy Bysshe Shelley [1792–1822]

LOVE'S PHILOSOPHY

THE fountains mingle with the river,
    And the rivers with the ocean,
The winds of heaven mix forever
    With a sweet emotion;
Nothing in the world is single;
    All things by a law divine
In one another's being mingle;—
    Why not I with thine?

See the mountains kiss high heaven,
    And the waves clasp one another;
No sister flower would be forgiven
    If it disdained its brother;
And the sunlight clasps the earth,
    And the moonbeams kiss the sea;
What are all these kissings worth,
    If thou kiss not me?

Percy Bysshe Shelley [1792–1822]

SONG

From "In a Gondola"

THE moth's kiss, first!
Kiss me as if you made believe
You were not sure, this eve,

How my face, your flower, had pursed
Its petals up; so, here and there
You brush it, till I grow aware
Who wants me, and wide ope I burst.

The bee's kiss, now!
Kiss me as if you entered gay
My heart at some noonday,
A bud that dares not disallow
The claim, so all is rendered up,
And passively its shattered cup
Over your head to sleep I bow.

Robert Browning [1812-1889]

SUMMUM BONUM

ALL the breath and the bloom of the year in the bag of one
    bee:
  All the wonder and wealth of the mine in the heart of one
    gem:
In the core of one pearl all the shade and the shine of the sea:
  Breath and bloom, shade and shine,—wonder, wealth,
    and—how far above them—
      Truth, that's brighter than gem,
      Trust, that's purer than pearl,—
Brightest truth, purest trust in the universe—all were for me
      In the kiss of one girl.

Robert Browning [1812-1889]

THE FIRST KISS

IF only in dreams may man be fully blest,
  Is heaven a dream? Is she I clasped a dream?
  Or stood she here even now where dewdrops gleam
And miles of furze shine golden down the West?
I seem to clasp her still—still on my breast
  Her bosom beats,—I see the blue eyes beam:—
  I think she kissed these lips, for now they seem
Scarce mine: so hallowed of the lips they pressed!

Yon thicket's breath—can that be eglantine?
    Those birds—can they be morning's choristers?
    Can this be earth? Can these be banks of furze?
Like burning bushes fired of God they shine!
I seem to know them, though this body of mine
    Passed into spirit at the touch of hers!
                    Theodore Watts-Dunton [1836–1914]

TO MY LOVE

KISS me softly and speak to me low;
    Malice has ever a vigilant ear;
    What if Malice were lurking near?
        Kiss me, dear!
Kiss me softly and speak to me low.

Kiss me softly and speak to me low;
    Envy, too, has a watchful ear;
    What if Envy should chance to hear?
        Kiss me, dear!
Kiss me softly and speak to me low.

Kiss me softly and speak to me low;
    Trust me, darling, the time is near
    When lovers may love with never a fear;
        Kiss me, dear!
Kiss me softly and speak to me low.
                    John Godfrey Saxe [1816–1887]

TO LESBIA

GIVE me kisses! Do not stay,
Counting in that careful way.
All the coins your lips can print
Never will exhaust the mint.
        Kiss me, then,
Every moment—and again!

Give me kisses! Do not stop,
Measuring nectar by the drop.

Though to millions they amount,
They will never drain the fount.
     Kiss me, then,
Every moment—and again!

Give me kisses! All is waste
Save the luxury we taste;
And for kissing,—kisses live
Only when we take or give.
     Kiss me, then,
Every moment—and again!

Give me kisses! Though their worth
Far exceeds the gems of earth,
Never pearls so rich and pure
Cost so little, I am sure.
     Kiss me, then,
Every moment—and again!

Give me kisses! Nay, 'tis true
I am just as rich as you;
And for every kiss I owe,
I can pay you back, you know,
     Kiss me, then,
Every moment—and again!

         John Godfrey Saxe [1816–1887]

MAKE BELIEVE

Kiss me, though you make believe;
  Kiss me, though I almost know
You are kissing to deceive:
  Let the tide one moment flow
Backward ere it rise and break,
Only for poor pity's sake!

Give me of your flowers one leaf,
  Give me of your smiles one smile,
Backward roll this tide of grief
  Just a moment, though, the while,

I should feel and almost know
You are trifling with my woe.

Whisper to me sweet and low;
  Tell me how you sit and weave
Dreams about me, though I know
  It is only make believe!
Just a moment, though 'tis plain
You are jesting with my pain.

Alice Cary [1820–1871]

KISSING'S NO SIN

SOME say that kissing's a sin;
  But I think it's nane ava,
For kissing has wonn'd in this warld
  Since ever that there was twa.

O, if it wasna lawfu'
  Lawyers wadna allow it;
If it wasna holy,
  Ministers wadna do it.

If it wasna modest,
  Maidens wadna tak' it;
If it wasna plenty,
  Puir folk wadna get it.

Unknown

TO ANNE

How many kisses do I ask?
Now you set me to my task.
First, sweet Anne, will you tell me
How many waves are in the sea?
How many stars are in the sky?
How many lovers you make sigh?
How many sands are on the shore?
I shall want just one kiss more.

William Stirling-Maxwell [1818–1878]

SONG

THERE is many a love in the land, my love,
But never a love like this is;
Then kill me dead with your love, my love,
And cover me up with kisses.

So kill me dead and cover me deep
Where never a soul discovers;
Deep in your heart to sleep, to sleep,
In the darlingest tomb of lovers.

Joaquin Miller [1839–1913]

PHILLIS AND CORYDON

PHILLIS took a red rose from the tangles of her hair,—
Time, the Golden Age; the place, Arcadia, anywhere,—

Phillis laughed, the saucy jade: "Sir Shepherd, wilt have this,
Or"—Bashful god of skipping lambs and oaten reeds!—"a kiss?"

Bethink thee, gentle Corydon! A rose lasts all night long,
A kiss but slips from off your lips like a thrush's evening song.

A kiss that goes, where no one knows! A rose, a crimson rose!
Corydon made his choice and took—Well, which do you suppose?

Arthur Colton [1868–

AT HER WINDOW

"HARK, HARK, THE LARK"

From "Cymbeline"

HARK, hark! the lark at heaven's gate sings,
  And Phœbus 'gins arise,
His steeds to water at those springs
  On chaliced flowers that lies;
And winking Mary-buds begin
  To ope their golden eyes:
With everything that pretty bin,
  My lady sweet, arise:
    Arise, arise.

William Shakespeare [1564-1616]

"SLEEP, ANGRY BEAUTY"

SLEEP, angry beauty, sleep and fear not me!
  For who a sleeping lion dares provoke?
It shall suffice me here to sit and see
  Those lips shut up, that never kindly spoke:
What sight can more content a lover's mind
Than beauty seeming harmless, if not kind?

My words have charmed her, for secure she sleeps,
  Though guilty much of wrong done to my love;
And in her slumber, see! she close-eyed weeps:
  Dreams often more than waking passions move.
Plead, Sleep, my cause, and make her soft like thee:
That she is peace may wake and pity me.

Thomas Campion [? –1619]

MATIN SONG

RISE, Lady Mistress, rise!
  The night hath tedious been;
No sleep hath fallen into mine eyes
  Nor slumbers made me sin.

694

Is not she a saint then, say,
Thoughts of whom keep sin away?

Rise, Madam! rise and give me light,
  Whom darkness still will cover,
And ignorance, darker than night,
  Till thou smile on thy lover.
All want day till thy beauty rise;
For the gray morn breaks from thine eyes.

Nathaniel Field [1587–1633]

THE NIGHT–PIECE: TO JULIA

HER eyes the glow-worm lend thee,
The shooting stars attend thee;
    And the elves also,
    Whose little eyes glow
Like the sparks of fire, befriend thee.

No Will-o'-the-wisp mislight thee,
Nor snake or slow-worm bite thee;
    But on, on thy way
    Not making a stay,
Since ghost there's none to affright thee.

Let not the dark thee cumber:
What though the moon does slumber?
    The stars of the night
    Will lend thee their light
Like tapers clear without number.

Then, Julia, let me woo thee,
Thus, thus to come unto me;
    And when I shall meet
    Thy silvery feet,
My soul I'll pour into thee.

Robert Herrick [1591–1674]

MORNING

THE lark now leaves his watery nest,
  And climbing shakes his dewy wings,
He takes your window for the east,
  And to implore your light, he sings;

Awake, awake, the morn will never rise,
Till she can dress her beauty at your eyes.

The merchant bows unto the seaman's star,
    The ploughman from the sun his season takes;
But still the lover wonders what they are,
    Who look for day before his mistress wakes;
Awake, awake, break through your veils of lawn!
Then draw your curtains and begin the dawn.

                    William D'Avenant [1606–1668]

MATIN–SONG

From "The Rape of Lucrece"

PACK, clouds, away, and welcome, day,
    With night we banish sorrow.
Sweet air, blow soft; mount, lark, aloft
    To give my Love good-morrow!
Wings from the wind to please her mind
    Notes from the lark I'll borrow:
Bird, prune thy wing, nightingale, sing,
    To give my Love good-morrow;
        To give my Love good-morrow
        Notes from them both I'll borrow.

Wake from thy nest, Robin-red-breast,
    Sing, birds, in every furrow;
And from each hill, let music shrill
    Give my fair Love good-morrow!
Blackbird and thrush in every bush,
    Stare, linnet, and cock-sparrow,
You pretty elves, amongst yourselves
    Sing my fair Love good-morrow;
        To give my Love good-morrow
        Sing, birds, in every furrow!

                    Thomas Heywood [? –1650?]

THE ROSE

SWEET, serene, sky-like flower,
    Haste to adorn her bower;
From thy long-cloudy bed,
    Shoot forth thy damask head.

New-startled blush of Flora,
The grief of pale Aurora
(Who will contest no more),
Haste, haste to strew her floor!

Vermilion ball that's given
From lip to lip in Heaven;
Love's couch's coverled,
Haste, haste to make her bed.

Dear offspring of pleased Venus
And jolly, plump Silenus,
Haste, haste to deck the hair
Of the only sweetly fair!

See! rosy is her bower,
Her floor is all this flower
Her bed a rosy nest
By a bed of roses pressed.

But early as she dresses,
Why fly you her bright tresses?
Ah! I have found, I fear,—
Because her cheeks are near.

Richard Lovelace [1618-1658]

SONG

SEE, see, she wakes! Sabina wakes!
And now the sun begins to rise;
Less glorious is the morn that breaks
From his bright beams, than her fair eyes.

With light united, day they give;
But different fates ere night fulfil;
How many by his warmth will live!
How many will her coldness kill!

William Congreve [1670-1729]

MARY MORISON

O MARY, at thy window be,
It is the wished, the trysted hour!
Those smiles and glances let me see,
That make the miser's treasure poor:

How blithely wad I bide the stour
  A weary slave frae sun to sun,
Could I the rich reward secure,
  The lovely Mary Morison!

Yestreen, when to the trembling string
  The dance gaed through the lighted ha',
To thee my fancy took its wing,
  I sat, but neither heard nor saw:
Though this was fair, and that was braw,
  And yon the toast of a' the town,
I sighed, and said amang them a',
  "Ye arena Mary Morison."

O Mary, canst thou wreck his peace,
  Wha for thy sake wad gladly die?
Or canst thou break that heart of his,
  Whase only faut is loving thee?
If love for love thou wiltna gie,
  At least be pity to me shown;
A thought ungentle canna be
  The thought o' Mary Morison.
                    Robert Burns [1759–1796]

WAKE, LADY!

Up! quit thy bower! late wears the hour,
Long have the rooks cawed round the tower;
O'er flower and tree loud hums the bee,
And the wild kid sports merrily.
The sun is bright, the sky is clear:
Wake, lady, wake! and hasten here.

Up! maiden fair, and bind thy hair,
And rouse thee in the breezy air!
The lulling stream that soothed thy dream
Is dancing in the sunny beam.
Waste not these hours, so fresh and gay;
Leave thy soft couch, and haste away!

Up!   Time will tell the morning bell
Its service-sound has chimèd well;

The aged crone keeps house alone,
The reapers to the fields are gone.
Lose not these hours, so cool and gay:
Lo! while thou sleep'st they haste away!

Joanna Baillie [1762-1851]

THE SLEEPING BEAUTY

SLEEP on, and dream of Heaven awhile—
Though shut so close thy laughing eyes,
Thy rosy lips still wear a smile
And move, and breathe delicious sighs!

Ah, now soft blushes tinge her cheeks
And mantle o'er her neck of snow:
Ah, now she murmurs, now she speaks
What most I wish—and fear to know!

She starts, she trembles, and she weeps!
Her fair hands folded on her breast:
—And now, how like a saint she sleeps!
A seraph in the realms of rest!

Sleep on secure! Above control
Thy thoughts belong to Heaven and thee:
And may the secret of thy soul
Remain within its sanctuary!

Samuel Rogers [1763-1855]

"THE YOUNG MAY MOON"

THE young May moon is beaming, love,
The glow-worm's lamp is gleaming, love;
    How sweet to rove
    Through Morna's grove,
When the drowsy world is dreaming, love!
Then awake!—the heavens look bright, my dear,
'Tis never too late for delight, my dear;
    And the best of all ways
    To lengthen our days
Is to steal a few hours from the night, my dear!

Now all the world is sleeping, love,
But the Sage, his star-watch keeping, love,
And I, whose star
More glorious far
Is the eye from that casement peeping, love.
Then awake!—till rise of sun, my dear,
The Sage's glass we'll shun, my dear,
Or in watching the flight
Of bodies of light
He might happen to take thee for one, my dear!

Thomas Moore [1779–1852]

"ROW GENTLY HERE"

Row gently here,
My gondolier,
So softly wake the tide,
That not an ear,
On earth, may hear,
But hers to whom we glide.
Had Heaven but tongues to speak, as well
As starry eyes to see,
Oh think what tales 'twould have to tell
Of wandering youths like me!

Now rest thee here,
My gondolier;
Hush, hush, for up I go,
To climb yon light
Balcony's height,
While thou keep'st watch below.
Ah! did we take for Heaven above
But half such pains as we
Take, day and night, for woman's love,
What angels we should be!

Thomas Moore [1779–1852]

MORNING SERENADE

Awake! the dawn is on the hills!
Behold, at her cool throat a rose,
Blue-eyed and beautiful she goes,
Leaving her steps in daffodils.—

Awake! arise! and let me see
    Thine eyes, whose deeps epitomize
All dawns that were or are to be,
    O love, all Heaven in thine eyes!—
Awake! arise! come down to me!

Behold! the dawn is up: behold!
    How all the birds around her float,
    Wild rills of music, note on note,
Spilling the air with mellow gold.—
Arise! awake! and, drawing near,
    Let me but hear thee and rejoice!
Thou, who keep'st captive, sweet and clear,
    All song, O love, within thy voice!
Arise! awake! and let me hear!

See, where she comes, with limbs of day,
    The dawn! with wild-rose hands and feet,
    Within whose veins the sunbeams beat,
And laughters meet of wind and ray.
Arise! come down! and, heart to heart,
    Love, let me clasp in thee all these—
The sunbeam, of which thou art part,
    And all the rapture of the breeze!—
Arise! come down! loved that thou art!

                    Madison Cawein [1865–1914]

SERENADE

SOFTLY, O midnight Hours!
    Move softly o'er the bowers
Where lies in happy sleep a girl so fair!
    For ye have power, men say,
    Our hearts in sleep to sway,
And cage cold fancies in a moonlight snare.
    Round ivory neck and arm
    Enclasp a separate charm;
Hang o'er her poised, but breathe nor sigh nor prayer:
    Silently ye may smile,
    But hold your breath the while,
And let the wind sweep back your cloudy hair!

    Bend down your glittering urns,
    Ere yet the dawn returns,

And star with dew the lawn her feet shall tread;
   Upon the air rain balm,
   Bid all the woods be calm,
Ambrosial dreams with healthful slumbers wed;
   That so the Maiden may
   With smiles your care repay,
When from her couch she lifts her golden head;
   Waking with earliest birds,
   Ere yet the misty herds
Leave warm 'mid the gray grass their dusky bed.

Aubrey Thomas De Vere [1814–1902]

LINES TO AN INDIAN AIR

I ARISE from dreams of thee
In the first sweet sleep of night,
When the winds are breathing low,
And the stars are shining bright.
I arise from dreams of thee,
And a spirit in my feet
Has led me—who knows how?
To thy chamber window, sweet!

The wandering airs they faint
On the dark, the silent stream;
The champak odors fail
Like sweet thoughts in a dream;
The nightingale's complaint,
It dies upon her heart,
As I must die on thine,
O belovèd as thou art!

O lift me from the grass!
I die, I faint, I fail!
Let thy love in kisses rain
On my lips and eyelids pale.
My cheek is cold and white, alas!
My heart beats loud and fast;
Oh! press it close to thine again,
Where it must break at last.

Percy Bysshe Shelley [1792–1822]

GOOD-NIGHT

GOOD-NIGHT? ah! no; the hour is ill
   Which severs those it should unite;
Let us remain together still,
   Then it will be *good* night.

How can I call the lone night good,
   Though thy sweet wishes wing its flight?
Be it not said, thought, understood,
   Then it will be *good* night.

To hearts which near each other move
   From evening close to morning light,
The night *is* good; because, my love,
   They never *say* good-night.

              Percy Bysshe Shelley [1792-1822]

SERENADE

From "Sylvia"

AWAKE thee, my lady-love,
   Wake thee and rise!
The sun through the bower peeps
   Into thine eyes!

Behold how the early lark
   Springs from the corn!
Hark, hark how the flower-bird
   Winds her wee horn!

The swallow's glad shriek is heard
   All through the air;
The stock-dove is murmuring
   Loud as she dare!

Apollo's winged bugleman
   Cannot contain,
But peals his loud trumpet-call
   Once and again!

Then wake thee, my lady-love—
    Bird of my bower!
The sweetest and sleepiest
    Bird at this hour!
                George Darley [1795–1846]

SERENADE

AH, sweet, thou little knowest how
    I wake and passionate watches keep;
And yet, while I address thee now,
    Methinks thou smilest in thy sleep.
'Tis sweet enough to make me weep,
    That tender thought of love and thee,
That while the world is hushed so deep,
    Thy soul's perhaps awake to me!

Sleep on, sleep on, sweet bride of sleep!
    With golden visions for thy dower,
While I this midnight vigil keep,
    And bless thee in thy silent bower;
To me 'tis sweeter than the power
    Of sleep, and fairy dreams unfurled,
That I alone, at this still hour,
    In patient love outwatch the world.
                Thomas Hood [1799–1845]

SERENADE

LOOK out upon the stars, my love,
    And shame them with thine eyes,
On which, than on the lights above,
    There hang more destinies.
Night's beauty is the harmony
    Of blending shades and light:
Then, lady, up,—look out, and be
    A sister to the night!

Sleep not!—thine image wakes for aye
    Within my watching breast;
Sleep not!—from her soft sleep should fly,
    Who robs all hearts of rest.

Nay, lady, from thy slumbers break,
    And make this darkness gay,
With looks whose brightness well might make
    Of darker nights a day.
                    Edward Coote Pinkney [1802–1828]

SERENADE

HIDE, happy damask, from the stars,
    What sleep enfolds behind your veil,
But open to the fairy cars
    On which the dreams of midnight sail;
And let the zephyrs rise and fall
    About her in the curtained gloom,
And then return to tell me all
    The silken secrets of the room.

Ah! dearest! may the elves that sway
    Thy fancies come from emerald plots,
Where they have dozed and dreamed all day
    In hearts of blue forget-me-nots.
And one perhaps shall whisper thus:
    Awake! and light the darkness, Sweet!
While thou art reveling with us,
    He watches in the lonely street.
                    Henry Timrod [1829–1867]

SERENADE

From "The Spanish Student"

STARS of the summer night!
    Far in yon azure deeps,
Hide, hide your golden light!
    She sleeps!
My lady sleeps!
    Sleeps!

Moon of the summer night!
    Far down yon western steeps,
Sink, sink in silver light!

> She sleeps!
> My lady sleeps!
> Sleeps!
>
> Wind of the summer night!
>   Where yonder woodbine creeps,
> Fold, fold thy pinions light!
>   She sleeps!
> My lady sleeps!
>   Sleeps!
>
> Dreams of the summer night!
>   Tell her, her lover keeps
> Watch! while in slumbers light
>   She sleeps!
> My lady sleeps!
>   Sleeps!

Henry Wadsworth Longfellow [1807–1882]

"COME INTO THE GARDEN, MAUD"

From "Maud"

COME into the garden, Maud,
    For the black bat, night, has flown,
Come into the garden, Maud,
    I am here at the gate alone;
And the woodbine spices are wafted abroad,
    And the musk of the rose is blown.

For a breeze of morning moves,
    And the planet of Love is on high,
Beginning to faint in the light that she loves
    On a bed of daffodil sky,
To faint in the light of the sun she loves,
    To faint in his light, and to die.

All night have the roses heard
    The flute, violin, bassoon;
All night has the casement jessamine stirred
    To the dancers dancing in tune;
Till a silence fell with the waking bird,
    And a hush with the setting moon.

I said to the lily, "There is but one
  With whom she has heart to be gay.
When will the dancers leave her alone?
  She is weary of dance and play."
Now half to the setting moon are gone,
  And half to the rising day;
Low on the sand and loud on the stone
  The last wheel echoes away.

I said to the rose, "The brief night goes
  In babble and revel and wine.
O young lord-lover, what sighs are those,
  For one that will never be thine?
But mine, but mine," so I sware to the rose,
  "For ever and ever, mine."

And the soul of the rose went into my blood,
  As the music clashed in the hall:
And long by the garden lake I stood,
  For I heard your rivulet fall
From the lake to the meadow and on to the wood,
  Our wood, that is dearer than all;

From the meadow your walks have left so sweet
  That whenever a March-wind sighs
He sets the jewel-print of your feet
  In violets blue as your eyes,
To the woody hollows in which we meet
  And the valleys of Paradise.

The slender acacia would not shake
  One long milk-bloom on the tree;
The white lake-blossom fell into the lake
  As the pimpernel dozed on the lea;
But the rose was awake all night for your sake,
  Knowing your promise to me;
The lilies and roses were all awake,
  They sighed for the dawn and thee.

Queen rose of the rosebud garden of girls,
    Come hither, the dances are done,
In gloss of satin and glimmer of pearls,
    Queen lily and rose in one;
Shine out, little head, sunning over with curls,
    To the flowers, and be their sun.

There has fallen a splendid tear
    From the passion-flower at the gate.
She is coming, my dove, my dear;
    She is coming, my life, my fate;
The red rose cries, "She is near, she is near";
    And the white rose weeps, "She is late";
The larkspur listens, "I hear, I hear";
    And the lily whispers, "I wait."

She is coming, my own, my sweet;
    Were it ever so airy a tread,
My heart would hear her and beat,
    Were it earth in an earthy bed;
My dust would hear her and beat,
    Had I lain for a century dead;
Would start and tremble under her feet,
    And blossom in purple and red.

                    Alfred Tennyson [1809–1892]

AT HER WINDOW

*Ah, Minstrel, how strange is
    The carol you sing!
Let Psyche, who ranges
    The garden of spring,
Remember the changes
    December will bring.*

BEATING Heart! we come again
    Where my Love reposes:
This is Mabel's window-pane;
    These are Mabel's roses.

Is she nested? Does she kneel
    In the twilight stilly,
Lily clad from throat to heel,
    She, my virgin Lily?

Soon the wan, the wistful stars,
  Fading, will forsake her;
Elves of light, on beamy bars,
  Whisper then, and wake her.

Let this friendly pebble plead
  At her flowery grating;
If she hear me will she heed?
  Mabel, I am waiting.

Mabel will be decked anon,
  Zoned in bride's apparel;
Happy zone! Oh hark to yon
  Passion-shaken carol!

Sing thy song, thou trancèd thrush,
  Pipe thy best, thy clearest;—
Hush, her lattice moves, oh hush—
  Dearest Mabel!—dearest. . . .

      Frederick Locker-Lampson [1821–1895]

BEDOUIN SONG

FROM the Desert I come to thee
  On a stallion shod with fire;
And the winds are left behind
  In the speed of my desire.
Under thy window I stand,
  And the midnight hears my cry:
I love thee, I love but thee,
  With a love that shall not die
    Till the sun grows cold,
    And the stars are old,
    And the leaves of the Judgment
      Book unfold!

Look from thy window and see
  My passion and my pain;
I lie on the sands below,
  And I faint in thy disdain.

Let the night-winds touch thy brow
  With the heat of my burning sigh,
And melt thee to hear the vow
  Of a love that shall not die
    Till the sun grows cold,
    And the stars are old,
    And the leaves of the Judgment
      Book unfold !

My steps are nightly driven,
  By the fever in my breast,
To hear from thy lattice breathed
  The word that shall give me rest.
Open the door of thy heart,
  And open thy chamber door,
And my kisses shall teach thy lips
  The love that shall fade no more
    Till the sun grows cold,
    And the stars are old,
    And the leaves of the Judgment
      Book unfold !
          Bayard Taylor [1825–1878]

NIGHT AND LOVE

From " Ernest Maltravers "

WHEN stars are in the quiet skies,
  Then most I pine for thee;
Bend on me, then, thy tender eyes,
  As stars look on the sea!

For thoughts, like waves that glide by night,
  Are stillest when they shine;
Mine earthly love lies hushed in light
  Beneath the heaven of thine.

There is an hour when angels keep
  Familiar watch o'er men,
When coarser souls are wrapped in sleep—
  Sweet spirit, meet me then

There is an hour when holy dreams
   Through slumber fairest glide;
And in that mystic hour it seems
   Thou shouldst be by my side.

My thoughts of thee too sacred are
   For daylight's common beam:
I can but know thee as my star,
   My angel and my dream!
     Edward George Earle Bulwer Lytton [1803–1873]

NOCTURNE

UP to her chamber window
   A slight wire trellis goes,
And up this Romeo's ladder
   Clambers a bold white rose.

I lounge in the ilex shadows,
   I see the lady lean,
Unclasping her silken girdle,
   The curtain's folds between.

She smiles on her white-rose lover,
   She reaches out her hand
And helps him in at the window—
   I see it where I stand!

To her scarlet lip she holds him,
   And kisses him many a time—
Ah, me! it was he that won her
   Because he dared to climb!
     Thomas Bailey Aldrich [1837–1907]

PALABRAS CARIÑOSAS

SPANISH AIR

GOOD-NIGHT! I have to say good-night
To such a host of peerless things!
Good-night unto the slender hand
All queenly with its weight of rings;

Good-night to fond, uplifted eyes,
Good-night to chestnut braids of hair,
Good-night unto the perfect mouth,
And all the sweetness nestled there—
  The snowy hand detains me, then
  I'll have to say Good-night again!

But there will come a time, my love,
When, if I read our stars aright,
I shall not linger by this porch
With my farewells. Till then, good-night!
You wish the time were now? And I.
You do not blush to wish it so?
You would have blushed yourself to death
To own so much a year ago—
  What, both these snowy hands! ah, then
  I'll have to say Good-night again!

                    Thomas Bailey Aldrich [1837–1907]

SERENADE

THE western wind is blowing fair
  Across the dark Ægean sea,
And at the secret marble stair
  My Tyrian galley waits for thee.
Come down! the purple sail is spread,
  The watchman sleeps within the town;
O leave thy lily-flowered bed,
  O Lady mine, come down, come down!

She will not come, I know her well,
  Of lover's vows she hath no care,
And little good a man can tell
  Of one so cruel and so fair.
True love is but a woman's toy,
  They never know the lover's pain,
And I, who love as loves a boy,
  Must love in vain, must love in vain.

O noble pilot, tell me true,
   Is that the sheen of golden hair?
Or is it but the tangled dew
   That binds the passion-flowers there?
Good sailor, come and tell me now,
   Is that my Lady's lily hand?
Or is it but the gleaming prow,
   Or is it but the silver sand?

No! no! 'tis not the tangled dew,
   'Tis not the silver-fretted sand,
It is my own dear Lady true
   With golden hair and lily hand!
O noble pilot, steer for Troy!
   Good sailor, ply the laboring oar!
This is the Queen of life and joy
   Whom we must bear from Grecian shore!

The waning sky grows faint and blue;
   It wants an hour still of day;
Aboard! aboard! my gallant crew,
   O Lady mine, away! away!
O noble pilot, steer for Troy!
   Good sailor, ply the laboring oar!
O loved as only loves a boy!
   O loved for ever, evermore!

                 Oscar Wilde [1856–1900]

THE LITTLE RED LARK

O SWAN of slenderness,
Dove of tenderness,
   Jewel of joys, arise!
The little red lark,
Like a soaring spark
   Of song, to his sunburst flies;
But till thou art arisen,
Earth is a prison,
   Full of my lonesome sighs:
Then awake and discover,
To thy fond lover,
   The morn of thy matchless eyes.

The dawn is dark to me,
Hark! oh, hark to me,
  Pulse of my heart, I pray!
  And out of thy hiding
With blushes gliding,
  Dazzle me with thy day.
Ah, then once more to thee
Flying I'll pour to thee
  Passion so sweet and gay,
The larks shall listen,
And dew-drops glisten,
  Laughing on every spray.

              Alfred Perceval Graves [1846–1931]

SERENADE

By day my timid passions stand
  Like begging children at your gate,
Each with a mute, appealing hand
  To ask a dole of Fate;
But when night comes, released from doubt,
  Like merry minstrels they appear,
The stars ring out their hopeful shout,
  Beloved, can you hear?

They dare not sing to you by day
  Their all-desirous song, or take
The world with their adventurous lay
  For your enchanted sake.
But when the night-wind wakes and thrills
  The shadows that the night unbars,
Their music fills the dreamy hills,
  And folds the friendly stars.

Beloved, can you hear? They sing
  Words that no mortal lips can sound;
Love through the world has taken wing,
  My passions are unbound.
And now, and now, my lips, my eyes,
  Are stricken dumb with hope and fear,
It is my burning soul that cries,
  Beloved, can you hear?

              Richard Middleton [1882–1911]

THE COMEDY OF LOVE

A LOVER'S LULLABY

Sing lullaby, as women do,
  Wherewith they bring their babes to rest;
And lullaby can I sing too,
  As womanly as can the best.
With lullaby they still the child;
And if I be not much beguiled,
Full many a wanton babe have I,
Which must be stilled with lullaby.

First lullaby my youthful years,
  It is now time to go to bed:
For crookèd age and hoary hairs
  Have won the haven within my head.
With lullaby, then, youth be still;
With lullaby content thy will;
Since courage quails and comes behind,
Go sleep, and so beguile thy mind!

Next lullaby my gazing eyes,
  Which wonted were to glance apace;
For every glass may now suffice
  To show the furrows in thy face.
With lullaby then wink awhile;
With lullaby your looks beguile;
Let no fair face, nor beauty bright,
Entice you eft with vain delight.

And lullaby my wanton will;
  Let reason's rule now reign thy thought;
Since all too late I find by skill
  How dear I have thy fancies bought;

With lullaby now take thine ease,
With lullaby thy doubts appease;
For trust to this, if thou be still,
My body shall obey thy will.

Thus lullaby my youth, mine eyes,
    My will, my ware, and all that was:
I can no more delays devise;
    But welcome pain, let pleasure pass.
With lullaby now take your leave;
With lullaby your dreams deceive;
And when you rise with waking eye,
Remember then this lullaby.

George Gascoigne [1525?-1577]

PHILLIDA AND CORIDON

In the merry month of May,
In a morn by break of day,
Forth I walked by the wood-side
When as May was in his pride:
There I spièd all alone
Phillida and Coridon.
Much ado there was, God wot!
He would love and she would not.
She said, Never man was true;
He said, None was false to you.
He said, He had loved her long;
She said, Love should have no wrong.
Coridon would kiss her then;
She said, Maids must kiss no men
Till they did for good and all;
Then she made the shepherd call
All the heavens to witness truth
Never loved a truer youth.
Thus with many a pretty oath,
Yea and nay, and faith and troth,
Such as silly shepherds use
When they will not Love abuse,

Love, which had been long deluded,
Was with kisses sweet concluded;
And Phillida, with garlands gay,
Was made the Lady of the May.

Nicholas Breton [1545?–1626?]

"CRABBÈD AGE AND YOUTH"

From "The Passionate Pilgrim"

CRABBÈD Age and Youth
Cannot live together:
Youth is full of pleasance,
Age is full of care;
Youth like summer morn,
Age like winter weather;
Youth like summer brave,
Age like winter bare.
Youth is full of sport,
Age's breath is short;
Youth is nimble, Age is lame;
Youth is hot and bold,
Age is weak and cold;
Youth is wild, and Age is tame.
Age, I do abhor thee;
Youth, I do adore thee;
O, my Love, my Love is young!
Age, I do defy thee:
O, sweet shepherd, hie thee!
For methinks thou stay'st too long.

William Shakespeare [1564–1616]

"IT WAS A LOVER AND HIS LASS"

From "As You Like It"

IT was a lover and his lass,
  With a hey, and a ho, and a hey nonino,
That o'er the green corn-field did pass,
  In the spring time, the only pretty ring time,
When birds do sing, hey ding a ding, ding;
Sweet lovers love the spring.

Between the acres of the rye,
　　With a hey, and a ho, and a hey nonino,
These pretty country folks would lie,
　　In the spring time, the only pretty ring time,
When birds do sing, hey ding a ding, ding;
Sweet lovers love the spring.

This carol they began that hour,
　　With a hey, and a ho, and a hey nonino,
How that life was but a flower
　　In the spring time, the only pretty ring time,
When birds do sing, hey ding a ding, ding;
Sweet lovers love the spring.

And, therefore, take the present time
　　With a hey, and a ho, and a hey nonino,
For love is crownèd with the prime
　　In the spring time, the only pretty ring time,
When birds do sing, hey ding a ding, ding;
Sweet lovers love the spring.

William Shakespeare [1564–1616]

"I LOVED A LASS"

I LOVED a lass, a fair one,
　　As fair as e'er was seen;
She was indeed a rare one,
　　Another Sheba Queen:
But, fool as then I was,
　　I thought she loved me too:
But now, alas! she's left me,
　　Falero, lero, loo!

Her hair like gold did glister,
　　Each eye was like a star,
She did surpass her sister,
　　Which passed all others far;
She would me honey call,
　　She'd—O she'd kiss me too!
But now, alas! she's left me,
　　Falero, lero, loo!

Many a merry meeting
  My love and I have had;
She was my only sweeting,
  She made my heart full glad;
The tears stood in her eyes
  Like to the morning dew:
But now, alas! she's left me,
  Falero, lero, loo!

Her cheeks were like the cherry,
  Her skin was white as snow;
When she was blithe and merry
  She angel-like did show;
Her waist exceeding small,
  The fives did fit her shoe:
But now, alas! she's left me,
  Falero, lero, loo!

In summer time or winter
  She had her heart's desire;
I still did scorn to stint her
  From sugar, sack, or fire;
The world went round about,
  No cares we ever knew:
But now, alas! she's left me,
  Falero, lero, loo!

To maidens' vows and swearing
  Henceforth no credit give;
You may give them the hearing,
  But never them believe;
They are as false as fair,
  Unconstant, frail, untrue:
For mine, alas! hath left me,
  Falero, lero, loo!
                    George Wither [1588–1667]

TO CHLORIS
From *The Mulberry Garden.* Act iii, sc. 2.

Ah, Chloris! that I now could sit
  As unconcerned as when
Your infant beauty could beget
  No pleasure, nor no pain!

When I the dawn used to admire,
    And praised the coming day,
I little thought the growing fire
    Must take my rest away.

Your charms in harmless childhood lay
    Like metals in the mine;
Age from no face took more away
    Than youth concealed in thine.
But as your charms insensibly
    To their perfection pressed,
Fond love as unperceived did fly,
    And in my bosom rest.

My passion with your beauty grew,
    And Cupid at my heart,
Still as his mother favored you,
    Threw a new flaming dart:
Each gloried in their wanton part;
    To make a lover, he
Employed the utmost of his art—
    To make a beauty, she.

Though now I slowly bend to love,
    Uncertain of my fate,
If your fair self my chains approve,
    I shall my freedom hate.
Lovers, like dying men, may well
    At first disordered be,
Since none alive can truly tell
    What fortune they may see.

Sir Charles Sedley [1639–1701]

SONG

THE merchant, to secure his treasure,
    Conveys it in a borrowed name:
Euphelia serves to grace my measure;
    But Chloe is my real flame.

My softest verse, my darling lyre,
    Upon Euphelia's toilet lay;
When Chloe noted her desire
    That I should sing, that I should play.

My lyre I tune, my voice I raise;
  But with my numbers mix my sighs:
And while I sing Euphelia's praise,
  I fix my soul on Chloe's eyes.

Fair Chloe blushed: Euphelia frowned:
  I sung, and gazed: I played, and trembled:
And Venus to the Loves around
  Remarked, how ill we all dissembled.
                    Matthew Prior]1664-1721]

PIOUS SELINDA

Pious Selinda goes to prayers,
  If I but ask her favor;
And yet the silly fool's in tears
  If she believes I'll leave her;
Would I were free from this restraint,
  Or else had hopes to win her:
Would she could make of me a saint,
  Or I of her a sinner.
                    William Congreve [1670-1729]

FAIR HEBE

Fair Hebe I left, with a cautious design
To escape from her charms, and to drown them in wine,
I tried it; but found, when I came to depart,
The wine in my head, and still love in my heart.

I repaired to my Reason, entreated her aid;
Who paused on my case and each circumstance weighed,
Then gravely pronounced, in return to my prayer,
That "Hebe was fairest of all that was fair!"

"That's a truth," replied I, "I've no need to be taught;
I came for your counsel to find out a fault."
"If that's all," quoth Reason, "return as you came;
To find fault with Hebe, would forfeit my name."

What hopes then, alas! of relief from my pain,
While, like lightning, she darts through each throbbing vein?
My Senses surprised, in her favor took arms;
And Reason confirms me a slave to her charms.

John West [1693–1766]

A MAIDEN'S IDEAL OF A HUSBAND

From " The Contrivances "

GENTEEL in personage,
Conduct, and equipage,
Noble by heritage,
    Generous and free:
Brave, not romantic;
Learned, not pedantic;
Frolic, not frantic;
    This must he be.

Honor maintaining,
Meanness disdaining,
Still entertaining,
    Engaging and new.
Neat, but not finical;
Sage, but not cynical;
Never tyrannical,
    But ever true.

Henry Carey [? –1743]

"PHILLADA FLOUTS ME"

O WHAT a plague is love!
    How shall I bear it?
She will inconstant prove,
    I greatly fear it.
She so torments my mind
    That my strength faileth,
And wavers with the wind
    As a ship saileth.

Please her the best I may,
She loves still to gainsay;
Alack and well-a-day!
  Phillada flouts me.

At the fair yesterday
  She did pass by me;
She looked another way
  And would not spy me:
I wooed her for to dine,
  But could not get her;
Will had her to the wine—
  He might entreat her.
With Daniel she did dance,
On me she looked askance:
O thrice unhappy chance!
  Phillada flouts me.

Fair maid, be not so coy,
  Do not disdain me!
I am my mother's joy:
  Sweet, entertain me!
She'll give me, when she dies,
  All that is fitting:
Her poultry and her bees,
  And her goose sitting,
A pair of mattress beds,
And a bag full of shreds;
And yet, for all this guedes,
  Phillada flouts me!

She hath a clout of mine
  Wrought with blue coventry,
Which she keeps for a sign
  Of my fidelity:
But i' faith, if she flinch
  She shall not wear it;
To Tib, my t'other wench,
  I mean to bear it.

And yet it grieves my heart
So soon from her to part:
Death strike me with his dart!
  Phillada flouts me.

Thou shalt eat crudded cream
  All the year lasting,
And drink the crystal stream
  Pleasant in tasting;
Whig and whey whilst thou lust,
  And bramble-berries,
Pie-lid and pastry-crust,
  Pears, plums, and cherries.
Thy raiment shall be thin,
Made of a weevil's skin—
Yet all's not worth a pin!
  Phillada flouts me.

In the last month of May
  I made her posies;
I heard her often say
  That she loved roses.
Cowslips and gillyflowers
  And the white lily
I brought to deck the bowers
  For my sweet Philly.
But she did all disdain,
And threw them back again;
Therefore 'tis flat and plain
  Phillada flouts me.

Fair maiden, have a care,
  And in time take me;
I can have those as fair
  If you forsake me:
For Doll the dairy-maid
  Laughed at me lately,
And wanton Winifred
  Favors me greatly.

One throws milk on my clothes,
T'other plays with my nose;
What wanting signs are those?
    Phillada flouts me.

I cannot work nor sleep
    At all in season:
Love wounds my heart so deep
    Without all reason
I 'gin to pine away
    In my love's shadow,
Like as a fat beast may,
    Penned in a meadow,
I shall be dead, I fear,
Within this thousand year:
And all for that my dear
    Phillada flouts me.

Unknown

"WHEN MOLLY SMILES"

WHEN Molly smiles beneath her cow,
I feel my heart—I can't tell how;
When Molly is on Sunday dressed,
On Sundays I can take no rest.

What can I do? On worky days
I leave my work on her to gaze.
What shall I say? At sermons, I
Forget the text when Molly's by.

Good master curate, teach me how
To mind your preaching and my plow:
And if for this you'll raise a spell,
A good fat goose shall thank you well.

Unknown

CONTENTIONS

IT was a lordling's daughter, the fairest one of three,
That likèd of her master as well as well might be;
Till looking on an Englishman, the fair'st that eye could see
    Her fancy fell a-turning.

Long was the combat doubtful that love with love did fight,
To leave the master loveless, or kill the gallant knight:
To put in practice either, alas! it was a spite
    Unto the silly damsel.

But one must be refusèd: more mickle was the pain,
That nothing could be usèd to turn them both to gain;
For of the two the trusty knight was wounded with disdain:
    Alas! she could not help it.

Thus art with arms contending was victor of the day,
Which by a gift of learning did bear the maid away;
Then lullaby, the learned man hath got the lady gay;
    For now my song is ended.

          Unknown

"I ASKED MY FAIR, ONE HAPPY DAY"

AFTER LESSING

I ASKED my fair, one happy day,
What I should call her in my lay;
    By what sweet name from Rome or Greece;
Lalage, Neæra, Chloris,
Sappho, Lesbia, or Doris,
    Arethusa or Lucrece.

"Ah!" replied my gentle fair,
"Belovèd, what are names but air?
    Choose thou whatever suits the line;
Call me Sappho, call me Chloris,
Call me Lalage or Doris,
    Only—only call me thine."

        Samuel Taylor Coleridge [1772-1834]

THE EXCHANGE

WE pledged our hearts, my love and I,—
    I in my arms the maiden clasping:
I could not tell the reason why,
    But oh! I trembled like an aspen.

Her father's love she bade me gain;
   I went, and shook like any reed!
I strove to act the man—in vain!
   We had exchanged our hearts indeed.
             Samuel Taylor Coleridge [1772–1834]

"COMIN' THROUGH THE RYE"

Comin' through the rye, poor body,
   Comin' through the rye,
She draiglet a' her petticoatie,
   Comin' through the rye.

      Oh Jenny's a' wat poor body,
        Jenny's seldom dry;
        She draiglet a' her petticoatie,
          Comin' through the rye.

Gin a body meet a body,
   Comin' through the rye,
Gin a body kiss a body,
   Need a body cry?

Gin a body meet a body
   Comin' through the glen,
Gin a body kiss a body,
   Need the warld ken?
             Robert Burns [1759–1796]

"GREEN GROW THE RASHES, O!"

There's naught but care on every han',
In every hour that passes, O!
What signifies the life o' man,
An' 'twere na for the lasses, O?

      Green grow the rashes, O!
      Green grow the rashes, O!
      The sweetest hours that e'er I spend,
      Are spent amang the lasses, O!

The warl'ly race may riches chase,
An' riches still may fly them, O!
An' though at last they catch them fast,
Their hearts can ne'er enjoy them, O!

Gie me a canny hour at e'en;
My arms about my dearie, O!
An' warl'ly cares, an' warl'ly men,
May a' gae tapsalteerie, O!

For you sae douce, ye sneer at this;
Ye'er naught but senseless asses, O!
The wisest man the warl' e'er saw
He dearly loved the lasses, O!

Auld Nature swears the lovely dears
Her noblest work she classes, O!
Her 'prentice han' she tried on man,
An' then she made the lasses, O!

Robert Burns [1759–1796]

DEFIANCE

CATCH her and hold her if you can—
See, she defies you with her fan,
Shuts, opens, and then holds it spread
In threatening guise above your head.
Ah! why did you not start before
She reached the porch and closed the door?
Simpleton! will you never learn
That girls and time will not return;
Of each you should have made the most;
Once gone, they are forever lost.
In vain your knuckles knock your brow,
In vain will you remember how
Like a slim brook the gamesome maid
Sparkled, and ran into the shade.

Walter Savage Landor [1775–1864]

OF CLEMENTINA

In Clementina's artless mien
   Lucilla asks me what I see,
And are the roses of sixteen
     Enough for me?

Lucilla asks, if that be all,
   Have I not culled as sweet before:
Ah yes, Lucilla! and their fall
     I still deplore.

I now behold another scene,
   Where Pleasure beams with Heaven's own light,
More pure, more constant, more serene,
     And not less bright.

Faith, on whose breast the Loves repose,
   Whose chain of flowers no force can sever,
And Modesty who, when she goes,
     Is gone for ever.
         Walter Savage Landor [1775–1864]

"THE TIME I'VE LOST IN WOOING"

The time I've lost in wooing,
In watching and pursuing
   The light that lies
   In woman's eyes,
Has been my heart's undoing.
Though Wisdom oft has sought me,
I scorned the lore she brought me,—
   My only books
   Were women's looks,
And folly's all they taught me.

Her smile when Beauty granted,
I hung with gaze enchanted,

Like him the sprite
Whom maids by night
Oft meet in glen that's haunted.
Like him, too, Beauty won me;
But when the spell was on me,
If once their ray
Was turned away,
O! winds could not outrun me.

And are those follies going?
And is my proud heart growing
Too cold or wise
For brilliant eyes
Again to set it glowing?
No—vain, alas! th' endeavor
From bonds so sweet to sever;—
Poor Wisdom's chance
Against a glance
Is now as weak as ever.

Thomas Moore [1779–1852]

DEAR FANNY

"SHE has beauty, but you must keep your heart cool;
    She has wit, but you mustn't be caught so":
Thus Reason advises, but Reason's a fool,
    And 'tis not the first time I have thought so,
        Dear Fanny,
    'Tis not the first time I have thought so.

"She is lovely; then love her, nor let the bliss fly;
    'Tis the charm of youth's vanishing season";
Thus Love has advised me, and who will deny
    That Love reasons better than Reason,
        Dear Fanny
    Love reasons much better than Reason.

Thomas Moore [1779–1852]

A CERTAIN YOUNG LADY

THERE'S a certain young lady,
Who's just in her hey-day,
　　And full of all mischief, I ween;
　　　So teasing! so pleasing!
　　　Capricious! delicious!
　　And you know very well whom I mean.

With an eye dark as night,
Yet than noonday more bright,
　　Was ever a black eye so keen?
　　　It can thrill with a glance,
　　　With a beam can entrance,
　　And you know very well whom I mean.

With a stately step—such as
You'd expect in a duchess—
　　And a brow might distinguish a queen,
　　　With a mighty proud air,
　　　That says "touch me who dare,"
　　And you know very well whom I mean.

With a toss of the head
That strikes one quite dead,
　　But a smile to revive one again;
　　　That toss so appalling!
　　　That smile so enthralling!
　　And you know very well whom I mean.

Confound her! de'il take her!—
A cruel heart-breaker—
　　But hold! see that smile so serene.
　　　God love her! God bless her!
　　　May nothing distress her!
　　You know very well whom I mean.

Heaven help the adorer
Who happens to bore her,

The lover who wakens her spleen;
 But too blest for a sinner
 Is he who shall win her,
And you know very well whom I mean.
Washington Irving [1783–1859]

"WHERE BE YOU GOING, YOU DEVON MAID"

WHERE be you going, you Devon maid?
 And what have ye there in the basket?
Ye tight little fairy, just fresh from the dairy,
 Will ye give me some cream if I ask it?

I love your hills and I love your dales,
 And I love your flocks a-bleating;
But oh, on the heather to lie together,
 With both our hearts a-beating!

I'll put your basket all safe in a nook;
 Your shawl I'll hang on a willow;
And we will sigh in the daisy's eye,
 And kiss on a grass-green pillow.
John Keats [1795–1821]

LOVE IN A COTTAGE

THEY may talk of love in a cottage,
 And bowers of trellised vine,—
Of nature bewitchingly simple,
 And milkmaids half divine;
They may talk of the pleasure of sleeping
 In the shade of a spreading tree,
And a walk in the fields at morning,
 By the side of a footstep free!

But give me a sly flirtation
 By the light of a chandelier,—
With music to play in the pauses,
 And nobody very near;

Or a seat on a silken sofa,
　　With a glass of pure old wine,
And mamma too blind to discover
　　The small white hand in mine.

Your love in a cottage is hungry,
　　Your vine is a nest for flies,—
Your milkmaid shocks the Graces,
　　And simplicity talks of pies!
You lie down to your shady slumber
　　And wake with a bug in your ear,
And your damsel that walks in the morning
　　Is shod like a mountaineer.

True love is at home on a carpet,
　　And mightily likes his ease;—
And true love has an eye for a dinner,
　　And starves beneath shady trees.
His wing is the fan of a lady,
　　His foot's an invisible thing,
And his arrow is tipped with a jewel,
　　And shot from a silver string.
　　　　　　　Nathaniel Parker Willis [1806–1867]

SONG OF THE MILKMAID

From "Queen Mary"

SHAME upon you, Robin,
　　Shame upon you now!
Kiss me would you? with my hands
　　Milking the cow?
　　Daisies grow again,
　　Kingcups blow again,
And you came and kissed me milking the cow.

Robin came behind me,
　　Kissed me well, I vow;
Cuff him could I? with my hands

Milking the cow?
Swallows fly again,
Cuckoos cry again,
And you came and kissed me milking the cow.

Come, Robin, Robin,
Come and kiss me now;
Help it can I? with my hands
Milking the cow?
Ringdoves coo again,
All things woo again,
Come behind and kiss me milking the cow!

Alfred Tennyson [1809–1892]

"WOULDN'T YOU LIKE TO KNOW"

I KNOW a girl with teeth of pearl,
And shoulders white as snow;
    She lives,—ah well,
    I must not tell,—
Wouldn't you like to know?

Her sunny hair is wondrous fair,
And wavy in its flow;
    Who made it less
    One little tress,—
Wouldn't you like to know?

Her eyes are blue (celestial hue!)
And dazzling in their glow;
    On whom they beam
    With melting gleam,—
Wouldn't you like to know?

Her lips are red and finely wed,
Like roses ere they blow;
    What lover sips
    Those dewy lips,—
Wouldn't you like to know?

Her fingers are like lilies fair
When lilies fairest grow;
    Whose hand they press
     With fond caress,—
Wouldn't you like to know?

Her foot is small, and has a fall
Like snowflakes on the snow;
    And where it goes
     Beneath the rose,—
Wouldn't you like to know?

She has a name, the sweetest name
That language can bestow.
    'Twould break the spell
     If I should tell,—
Wouldn't you like to know?

John Godfrey Saxe [1816–1887]

"SING HEIGH-HO!"

THERE sits a bird on every tree;
    Sing heigh-ho!
There sits a bird on every tree,
And courts his love as I do thee;
    Sing heigh-ho, and heigh-ho!
   Young maids must marry.

There grows a flower on every bough;
    Sing heigh-ho!
There grows a flower on every bough,
Its petals kiss—I'll show you how:
    Sing heigh-ho, and heigh-ho!
   Young maids must marry.

From sea to stream the salmon roam;
    Sing heigh-ho!
From sea to stream the salmon roam;
Each finds a mate and leads her home;
    Sing heigh-ho, and heigh-ho!
   Young maids must marry.

The sun's a bridegroom, earth a bride;
    Sing heigh-ho!
They court from morn till eventide:
The earth shall pass, but love abide.
    Sing heigh-ho, and heigh-ho!
    Young maids must marry.

Charles Kingsley [1819-1875]

THE GOLDEN FISH

LOVE is a little golden fish,
    Wondrous shy . . . ah, wondrous shy . . .
You may catch him if you wish;
He might make a dainty dish . . .
    But I . . .
    Ah, I've other fish to fry!

For when I try to snare this prize,
    Earnestly and patiently,
All my skill the rogue defies,
Lurking safe in Aimée's eyes . . .
    So, you see,
    I am caught and Love goes free!

George Arnold [1834-1865]

THE COURTIN'

GOD makes sech nights, all white an' still
    Fur 'z you can look or listen,
Moonshine an' snow on field an' hill,
    All silence an' all glisten.

Zekle crep' up quite unbeknown
    An' peeked in thru' the winder,
An' there sot Huldy all alone,
    'ith no one nigh to hender.

A fireplace filled the room's one side,
    With half a cord o' wood in—
There warn't no stoves (tell comfort died)
    To bake ye to a puddin'.

The wa'nut logs shot sparkles out
   Towards the pootiest, bless her!
An' leetle flames danced all about
   The chiny on the dresser.

Agin the chimbley crook-necks hung,
   An' in amongst 'em rusted
The ole queen's-arm thet gran'ther Young
   Fetched back f'om Concord busted.

The very room, coz she was in,
   Seemed warm f'om floor to ceilin',
An' she looked full ez rosy agin
   Ez the apples she was peelin'.

'Twas kin' o' kingdom-come to look
   On sech a blessèd cretur,
A dogrose blushin' to a brook
   Ain't modester nor sweeter.

He was six foot o' man, A 1,
   Clear grit an' human natur';
None couldn't quicker pitch a ton,
   Nor dror a furrer straighter.

He'd sparked it with full twenty gals,
   He'd squired 'em, danced 'em, druv 'em,
Fust this one, an' then thet, by spells—
   All is, he couldn't love 'em.

But long o' her his veins 'ould run
   All crinkly like curled maple,
The side she breshed felt full o' sun
   Ez a south slope in Ap'il.

She thought no v'ice hed sech a swing
   Ez hisn in the choir;
My! when he made Ole Hundred ring,
   She *knowed* the Lord was nigher.

An' she'd blush scarlit, right in prayer,
  When her new meetin'-bunnet
Felt somehow thru' its crown a pair
  O' blue eyes sot upun it.

Thet night, I tell ye, she looked *some!*
  She seemed to've gut a new soul,
For she felt sartin-sure he'd come,
  Down to her very shoe-sole.

She heered a foot, an' knowed it tu,
  A-raspin' on the scraper,—
All ways to once her feelin's flew
  Like sparks in burnt-up paper.

He kin' o' l'itered on the mat,
  Some doubtfle o' the sekle,
His heart kep' goin' pitty-pat,
  But hern went pity Zekle.

An' yit she gin her cheer a jerk
  Ez though she wished him furder,
An' on her apples kep' to work,
  Parin' away like murder.

"You want to see my Pa, I s'pose?"
  "Wal . . . no . . . I come dasignin'"
"To see my Ma? She's sprinklin' clo'es
  Agin to-morrer's i'nin'."

To say why gals acts so or so,
  Or don't, 'ould be presumin';
Mebby to mean *yes* an' say *no*
  Comes nateral to women.

He stood a spell on one foot fust,
  Then stood a spell on t'other,
An' on which one he felt the wust
  He couldn't ha' told ye nuther.

Says he, "I'd better call ag'in";
    Says she, "Think likely, Mister";
Thet last word pricked him like a pin,
    An' . . . Wal, he up an' kissed her.

When Ma bimeby upon 'em slips,
    Huldy sot pale ez ashes,
All kin' o' smily roun' the lips
    An' teary roun' the lashes.

For she was jes' the quiet kind
    Whose naturs never vary,
Like streams that keep a summer mind
    Snow-hid in Jenooary.

The blood clost roun' her heart felt glued
    Too tight for all expressin',
Tell mother see how metters stood
    And gin 'em both her blessin'.

Then her red come back like the tide
    Down to the Bay o' Fundy,
An' all I know is they was cried
    In meetin' come nex' Sunday.
                    James Russell Lowell [1819–1891]

L'EAU DORMANTE

CURLED up and sitting on her feet,
    Within the window's deep embrasure,
Is Lydia; and across the street,
    A lad, with eyes of roguish azure,
Watches her buried in her book.
In vain he tries to win a look,
And from the trellis over there
Blows sundry kisses through the air,
Which miss the mark, and fall unseen,
Uncared for. Lydia is thirteen.

My lad, if you, without abuse,
  Will take advice from one who's wiser,
And put his wisdom to more use
  Than ever yet did your adviser;
If you will let, as none will do,
Another's heartbreak serve for two,
You'll have a care, some four years hence,
How you lounge there by yonder fence
And blow those kisses through that screen—
For Lydia will be seventeen.
               Thomas Bailey Aldrich [1837–1907]

A PRIMROSE DAME

She has a primrose at her breast,
  I almost wish I were a Tory.
I like the Radicals the best;
She has a primrose at her breast;
Now is it chance she so is dressed,
  Or must I tell a story?
She has a primrose at her breast,
  I almost wish I *were* a Tory.
               Gleason White [1851–1898]

IF

Oh, if the world were mine, Love,
           I'd give the world for thee!
Alas! there is no sign, Love,
           Of that contingency.

Were I a king,—which isn't
           To be considered now,—
A diadem had glistened
           Upon that lovely brow.

Had fame with laurels crowned me,—
           She hasn't, up to date,—
Nor time nor change had found me
           To love and thee ingrate.

If Death threw down his gage, Love,
Though life is dear to me,
I'd die, e'en of old age, Love,
To win a smile from thee.

But being poor, we part, dear,
And love, sweet love, must die;
Thou wilt not break thy heart, dear,
No more, I think, shall I!
James Jeffrey Roche [1847–1908]

DON'T

YOUR eyes were made for laughter;
Sorrow befits them not;
Would you be blithe hereafter,
Avoid the lover's lot.

The rose and lily blended
Possess your cheeks so fair;
Care never was intended
To leave his furrows there.

Your heart was not created
To fret itself away,
By being unduly mated
To common human clay.

But hearts were made for loving—
Confound philosophy!
Forget what I've been proving,
Sweet Phyllis, and love me!
James Jeffrey Roche [1847–1908]

AN IRISH LOVE–SONG

IN the years about twenty
(When kisses are plenty)
The love of an Irish lass fell to my fate—
So winsome and sightly,
So saucy and sprightly,
The priest was a prophet that christened her Kate.

Soft gray of the dawning,
Bright blue of the morning,
'The sweet of her eye there was nothing to mate;
A nose like a fairy's,
A cheek like a cherry's,
And a smile—well, her smile was like—nothing but Kate.

To see her was passion,
To love her, the fashion;
What wonder my heart was unwilling to wait!
And, daring to love her,
I soon did discover
A Katherine masking in mischievous Kate.

No Katy unruly
But Katherine, truly—
Fond, serious, patient, and even sedate;
With a glow in her gladness
That banishes sadness—
Yet stay! Should I credit the sunshine to *Kate?*

Love cannot outlive it,
Wealth cannot o'ergive it—
The saucy surrender she made at the gate.
O Time, be but human,
Spare the girl in the woman!
You gave me my Katherine—leave me my Kate!

Robert Underwood Johnson [1853–1937]

GROWING OLD

SWEET sixteen is shy and cold,
Calls me "sir," and thinks me old;
Hears in an embarrassed way
All the compliments I pay;

Finds my homage quite a bore,
Will not smile on me, and more
To her taste she finds the noise
And the chat of callow boys.

Not the lines around my eye,
Deepening as the years go by;
Not white hairs that strew my head,
Nor my less elastic tread;

Cares I find, nor joys I miss,
Make me feel my years like this:—
Sweet sixteen is shy and cold,
Calls me "sir," and thinks me old.

Walter Learned [1847–1915]

TIME'S REVENGE

WHEN I was ten and she fifteen—
    Ah, me! how fair I thought her.
She treated with disdainful mien
    The homage that I brought her,
And, in a patronizing way,
Would of my shy advances say:
    "It's really quite absurd, you see;
    He's very much too young for me."

I'm twenty now, she twenty-five—
    Well, well! how old she's growing.
I fancy that my suit might thrive
    If pressed again; but, owing
To great discrepancy in age,
Her marked attentions don't engage
    My young affections, for, you see,
    She's really quite too old for me.

Walter Learned [1847–1915]

IN EXPLANATION

HER lips were so near
    That—what else could I do?
You'll be angry, I fear.
But her lips were so near—
Well, I can't make it clear,
    Or explain it to you.
But—her lips were so near
    That—what else could I do?

Walter Learned [1847–1915]

OMNIA VINCIT

Long from the lists of love I stood aloof
My heart was steeled and I was beauty-proof;
Yet I, unscathed in many a peril past,
Lo! here am I defeated at the last.

My practice was, in easy-chair reclined,
Superior-wise to speak of womankind,
Waving away the worn-out creed of love
To join the smoke that wreathed itself above.

Love, I said in my wisdom, Love is dead,
For all his fabled triumphs—and instead
We find a calm affectionate respect,
Doled forth by Intellect to Intellect.

Yet when Love, taking vengeance, smote me sore,
My Siren called me from no classic shore;
It was no Girton trumpet that laid low
The walls of this Platonic Jericho.

For when my peace of mind at length was stole,
I thought no whit of Intellect or Soul,
Nay! I was cast in pitiful distress
By brown eyes wide with truth and tenderness.

Alfred Cochrane [1865-

A PASTORAL

Along the lane beside the mead
    Where cowslip-gold is in the grass
I matched the milkmaid's easy speed,
    A tall and springing country lass:
But though she had a merry plan
    To shield her from my soft replies,
Love played at Catch-me-if-you-Can
    In Mary's eyes.

A mile or twain from Varley bridge
   I plucked a dock-leaf for a fan,
And drove away the constant midge,
   And cooled her forehead's strip of tan.
But though the maiden would not spare
   My hand her pretty finger-tips,
Love played at Kiss-me-if-you-Dare
     On Mary's lips.

Since time was short and blood was bold,
   I drew me closer to her side,
And watched her freckles change from gold
   To pink beneath a blushing tide.
But though she turned her face away,
   How much her panting heart confessed!
Love played at Find-me-for-you-May
     In Mary's breast.

Norman Gale [1862=

A ROSE

'TWAS a Jacqueminot rose
     That she gave me at parting;
Sweetest flower that blows,
'Twas a Jacqueminot rose.
 In the love garden close,
     With the swift blushes starting,
'Twas a Jacqueminot rose
     That she gave me at parting.

If she kissed it, who knows—
     Since I will not discover,
And love is that close,
If she kissed it, who knows?
Or if not the red rose
     Perhaps then the lover!
If she kissed it, who knows,
     Since I will not discover.

Yet at least with the rose
　　Went a kiss that I'm wearing!
More I will not disclose,
Yet at least with the rose
Went whose kiss no one knows,—
　　Since I'm only declaring,
"Yet at least with the rose
　　Went a kiss that I'm wearing."

Arlo Bates [1850–1918]

"WOOED AND MARRIED AND A'"

THE bride cam' out o' the byre,
　　And oh, as she dighted her cheeks:
"Sirs, I'm to be married the night,
　　And ha'e neither blankets nor sheets;
Ha'e neither blankets nor sheets,
　　Nor scarce a coverlet too;
The bride that has a' thing to borrow,
　　Has e'en right muckle ado!"
　　　　Wooed and married, and a',
　　　　Married and wooed and a'!
　　　　And was she nae very weel aff,
　　　　That was wooed and married and a'?

Out spake the bride's father,
　　As he cam' in frae the pleugh:
"Oh, haud your tongue, my dochter,
　　And ye'se get gear eneugh;
The stirk stands i' the tether,
　　And our braw bawsint yaud,
Will carry ye hame your corn—
　　What wad ye be at, ye jaud?"

Out spake the bride's mither:
　　"What deil needs a' this pride?
I had nae a plack in my pouch
　　That night I was a bride:

My gown was linsey woolsey,
    And ne'er a sark ava;
And ye ha'e ribbons and buskins,
    Mair than ane or twa."

Out spake the bride's brither,
    As he cam' in wi' the kye:
"Poor Willie wad ne'er ha'e ta'en ye,
    Had he kent ye as weel as I;
For ye're baith proud and saucy
    And no for a puir man's wife;
Gin I canna get a better,
    I'se ne'er tak' ane i' my life."

Out spake the bride's sister,
    As she cam' in frae the byre:
"O gin I were but married,
    It's a' that I desire;
But we puir folk maun live single,
    And do the best we can;
I dinna ken what I should want,
    If I could get but a man!"

Alexander Ross [1699–1784]

"OWRE THE MUIR AMANG THE HEATHER"

Comin' through the craigs o' Kyle,
    Amang the bonnie bloomin' heather,
There I met a bonnie lassie,
    Keepin' a' her ewes thegither.

Owre the muir amang the heather,
    Owre the muir amang the heather;
There I met a bonnie lassie,
    Keepin' a' her ewes thegither.

Says I, My dear, where is thy hame,—
    In muir or dale, pray tell me whether?
She says, I tent the fleecy flocks
    That feed amang the bloomin' heather.

We laid us down upon a bank,
　　Sae warm and sunny was the weather:
She left her flocks at large to rove
　　Amang the bonnie bloomin' heather.

While thus we lay, she sung a sang,
　　Till echo rang a mile and farther;
And aye the burden of the sang
　　Was, Owre the muir amang the heather.

She charmed my heart, and aye sinsyne
　　I couldna think on ony ither;
By sea and sky! she shall be mine,
　　The bonnie lass amang the heather.

Jean Glover [1758–1801]

MARRIAGE AND THE CARE O'T

QUOTH Rab to Kate, My sonsy dear,
I've wooed ye mair than ha' a year,
An' if ye'd wed me ne'er cou'd speer,
　　Wi' blateness, an' the care o't.
Now to the point: sincere I'm wi't:
Will ye be my ha'f-marrow, sweet?
Shake han's, and say a bargain be't
　　An' ne'er think on the care o't.

Na, na, quo' Kate, I winna wed,
O' sic a snare I'll aye be rede;
How mony, thochtless, are misled
　　By marriage, an' the care o't!
A single life's a life o' glee,
A wife ne'er think to mak' o' me,
Frae toil an' sorrow I'll keep free,
　　An' a' the dool an' care o't.

Weel, weel, said Robin, in reply,
Ye ne'er again shall me deny,
Ye may a toothless maiden die

For me, I'll tak' nae care o't.
Fareweel for ever!—aff I hie;—
Sae took his leave without a sigh;
Oh! stop, quo' Kate, I'm yours, I'll try
    The married life, an' care o't.

Rab wheel't about, to Kate cam' back,
An' ga'e her mou' a hearty smack,
Syne lengthened out a lovin' crack
    'Bout marriage an' the care o't.
Though as she thocht she didna speak,
An' lookit unco mim an' meek,
Yet blithe was she wi' Rab to cleek,
    In marriage, wi' the care o't.
            Robert Lochore [1762–1852]

THE WOMEN FOLK

O SAIRLY may I rue the day
    I fancied first the womenkind;
For aye sinsyne I ne'er can ha'e
    Ae quiet thought or peace o' mind!
They ha'e plagued my heart, an' pleased my e'e,
    An' teased an' flattered me at will,
But aye, for a' their witchery,
    The pawky things! I lo'e them still.
      O, the women folk! O, the women folk,
        But they ha'e been the wreck o' me;
      O, weary fa' the women folk,
        For they winna let a body be!

I ha'e thought an' thought, but darena tell,
    I've studied them wi' a' my skill,
I've lo'ed them better than mysel',
    I've tried again to like them ill.
Wha sairest strives, will sairest rue,
    To comprehend what nae man can;
When he has done what man can do,
    He'll end at last where he began.

That they ha'e gentle forms an' meet,
  A man wi' half a look may see;
An' gracefu' airs, an' faces sweet,
  An' waving curls aboon the bree!
An' smiles as saft as the young rose-bud,
  An' e'en sae pawky, bright, an' rare,
Wad lure the laverock frae the clud—
  But, laddie, seek to ken nae mair!

James Hogg [1770–1835]

"LOVE IS LIKE A DIZZINESS"

I LATELY lived in quiet ease,
  An' never wished to marry, O!
But when I saw my Peggy's face,
  I felt a sad quandary, O!
Though wild as ony Athol deer,
  She has trepanned me fairly, O!
Her cherry cheeks an' een sae clear
  Torment me late an' early, O!
    O, love, love, love!
      Love is like a dizziness;
    It winna let a poor body
      Gang about his biziness!

To tell my feats this single week
  Wad mak a daft-like diary, O!
I drave my cart out owre a dike,
  My horses in a miry, O!
I wear my stockings white an' blue,
  My love's sae fierce an' fiery, O!
I drill the land that I should pleugh,
  An' pleugh the drills entirely, O!

Ae morning, by the dawn o' day,
  I rase to theek the stable, O!
I cuist my coat, an' plied away
  As fast as I was able, O!

I wrought that morning out an' out,
   As I'd been redding fire, O!
When I had done an' looked about,
   Gudefaith, it was the byre, O!

Her wily glance I'll ne'er forget,
   The dear, the lovely blinkin' o't
Has pierced me through an' through the heart,
   An' plagues me wi' the prinkling o't.
I tried to sing, I tried to pray,
   I tried to drown 't wi' drinkin' o't,
I tried wi' sport to drive 't away,
   But ne'er can sleep for thinkin' o't.

Nae man can tell what pains I prove,
   Or how severe my pliskie, O!
I swear I'm sairer drunk wi' love
   Than ever I was wi' whiskey, O!
For love has raked me fore an' aft,
   I scarce can lift a leggie, O!
I first grew dizzy, then gaed daft,
   An' soon I'll dee for Peggy, O!

James Hogg [1770–1835]

"BEHAVE YOURSEL' BEFORE FOLK"

BEHAVE yoursel' before folk,
   Behave yoursel' before folk,
And dinna be sae rude to me,
   As kiss me sae before folk.

It wadna gi'e me meikle pain,
   Gin we were seen and heard by nane,
To tak' a kiss, or grant you ane;
   But guidsake! no before folk.
    Behave yoursel' before folk.
    Behave yoursel' before folk;
    Whate'er ye do, when out o' view,
     Be cautious aye before folk.

Consider, lad, how folk will crack,
And what a great affair they'll mak'
O' naething but a simple smack,
   That's gi'en or ta'en before folk.
     Behave yoursel' before folk,
     Behave yoursel' before folk;
    Nor gi'e the tongue o' auld or young
     Occasion to come o'er folk.

It's no through hatred o' a kiss,
That I sae plainly tell you this;
But, losh! I tak' it sair amiss
   To be sae teased before folk.
     Behave yoursel' before folk,
     Behave yoursel' before folk;
    When we're our lane ye may tak' ane,
     But fient a ane before folk.

I'm sure wi' you I've been as free
As ony modest lass should be;
But yet it doesna do to see
   Sic freedom used before folk.
     Behave yoursel' before folk,
     Behave yoursel' before folk;
    I'll ne'er submit again to it—
     So mind you that—before folk.

Ye tell me that my face is fair;
It may be sae—I dinna care—
But ne'er again gar't blush sae sair
   As ye ha'e done before folk.
     Behave yoursel' before folk,
     Behave yoursel' before folk;
    Nor heat my cheeks wi' your mad freaks,
     But aye be douce before folk.

Ye tell me that my lips are sweet,
Sic tales, I doubt, are a' deceit;
At ony rate, it's hardly meet

To pree their sweets before folk.
    Behave yoursel' before folk,
    Behave yoursel' before folk;
Gin that's the case, there's time, and place,
    But surely no before folk.

But, gin you really do insist
That I should suffer to be kissed,
Gae, get a license frae the priest,
    And mak' me yours before folk.
    Behave yoursel' before folk,
    Behave yoursel' before folk;
And when we're ane, baith flesh and bane,
    Ye may tak' ten—before folk.

Alexander Rodger [1784–1846]

RORY O'MORE; OR, GOOD OMENS

YOUNG Rory O'More courted Kathleen bawn,
He was bold as a hawk,—she as soft as the dawn;
He wished in his heart pretty Kathleen to please,
And he thought the best way to do that was to tease.
"Now, Rory, be aisy," sweet Kathleen would cry
(Reproof on her lip, but a smile in her eye),
"With your tricks I don't know, in troth, what I'm about,
Faith, you've teased till I've put on my cloak inside out."
"Och! jewel," says Rory, "that same is the way
You've thrated my heart for this many a day;
And 'tis plazed that I am, and why not, to be sure?
For 'tis all for good luck," says bold Rory O'More.

"Indeed, then," says Kathleen, "don't think of the like,
For I half gave a promise to soothering Mike;
The ground that I walk on he loves, I'll be bound."
"Faith," says Rory, "I'd rather love you than the ground."
"Now, Rory, I'll cry if you don't let me go;
Sure I drame ev'ry night that I'm hating you so!"
"Oh," says Rory, "that same I'm delighted to hear,
For drames always go by conthrairies, my dear;

So, jewel, keep draming that same till you die,
And bright mornin' will give dirty night the black lie!
And 'tis plazed that I am, and why not, to be sure?
Since 'tis all for good luck," says bold Rory O'More.

"Arrah, Kathleen, my darlint, you've teased me enough,
Sure I've thrashed for your sake Dinny Grimes and Jim Duff;
And I've made myself, drinkin' your health, quite a baste,
So I think, after that, I may talk to the praste."
Then Rory, the rogue, stole his arm round her neck,
So soft and so white, without freckle or speck,
And he looked in her eyes that were beaming with light,
And he kissed her sweet lips;—don't you think he was right?
"Now, Rory, leave off, sir; you'll hug me no more;
That's eight times to-day that you've kissed me before."
"Then here goes another," says he, "to make sure,
For there's luck in odd numbers," says Rory O'More.

Samuel Lover [1797–1868]

ASK AND HAVE

"Oh, 'tis time I should talk to your mother,
    Sweet Mary," says I;
"Oh, don't talk to my mother," says Mary,
    Beginning to cry:
"For my mother says men are deceivers,
    And never, I know, will consent;
She says girls in a hurry to marry,
    At leisure repent."

"Then, suppose I would talk to your father,
    Sweet Mary," says I;
"Oh, don't talk to my father," says Mary,
    Beginning to cry:
"For my father he loves me so dearly,
    He'll never consent I should go—
If you talk to my father," says Mary,
    "He'll surely say, 'No.'"

"Then how shall I get you, my jewel?
　　Sweet Mary," says I;
"If your father and mother's so cruel,
　　Most surely I'll die!"
"Oh, never say die, dear," says Mary;
　"A way now to save you I see;
　Since my parents are both so contrary—
　　You'd better ask me!"

　　　　　　　　Samuel Lover [1797–1868]

KITTY OF COLERAINE

As beautiful Kitty one morning was tripping,
　With a pitcher of milk, from the fair of Coleraine,
When she saw me she stumbled, the pitcher down tumbled,
　And all the sweet buttermilk watered the plain.

"Oh! what shall I do now—'twas looking at you, now;
　Sure, sure, such a pitcher I'll ne'er meet again!
'Twas the pride of my dairy! Oh! Barney MacCleary,
　You're sent as a plague to the girls of Coleraine."

I sat down beside her, and gently did chide her,
　That such a misfortune should give her such pain;
A kiss then I gave her, and, ere I did leave her,
　She vowed for such pleasure she'd break it again.

'Twas hay-making season—I can't tell the reason—
　Misfortunes will never come single, 'tis plain;
For very soon after poor Kitty's disaster
　The devil a pitcher was whole in Coleraine.

　　　　　　　Charles Dawson Shanly [1811–1875]

THE PLAIDIE

UPON ane stormy Sunday,
　　Coming adoon the lane,
Were a score of bonnie lassies—
　　And the sweetest I maintain,
　　　Was Caddie,
　That I took un'neath my plaidie,
　　To shield her from the rain.

She said the daisies blushed
　For the kiss that I had ta'en;
I wadna hae thought the lassie
　Wad sae of a kiss complain;
　　"Now, laddie!
I winna stay under your plaidie,
　If I gang hame in the rain!"

But, on an after Sunday,
　When cloud there was not ane,
This self-same winsome lassie
　(We chanced to meet in the lane)
　　Said, "Laddie,
Why dinna ye wear your plaidie?
　Wha kens but it may rain?"

Charles Sibley [?]

KITTY NEIL

"Ah, sweet Kitty Neil, rise up from that wheel,
　Your neat little foot will be weary from spinning;
Come trip down with me to the sycamore-tree,
　Half the parish is there, and the dance is beginning.
The sun is gone down, but the full harvest-moon
　Shines sweetly and cool on the dew-whitened valley,
While all the air rings with the soft, loving things
　Each little bird sings in the green shaded alley."

With a blush and a smile, Kitty rose up the while,
　Her eye in the glass, as she bound her hair, glancing·
'Tis hard to refuse when a young lover sues,
　So she couldn't but choose to go off to the dancing.
And now on the green the glad groups are seen,
　Each gay-hearted lad with the lass of his choosing;
And Pat, without fail, leads out sweet Kitty Neil,—
　Somehow, when he asked, she ne'er thought of refusing.

Now, Felix Magee puts his pipes to his knee,
　And with flourish so free sets each couple in motion;
With a cheer and a bound, the lads patter the ground,
　The maids move around just like swans on the ocean:

Cheeks bright as the rose—feet light as the doe's,
    Now coyly retiring, now boldly advancing—
Search the world all around, from the sky to the ground,
    No such sight can be found as an Irish lass dancing!

Sweet Kate! who could view your bright eyes of deep blue,
    Beaming humidly through their dark lashes so mildly,
Your fair-turnèd arm, heaving breast, rounded form,
    Nor feel his heart warm, and his pulses throb wildly?
Young Pat feels his heart, as he gazes, depart,
    Subdued by the smart of such painful yet sweet love;
The sight leaves his eye, as he cries with a sigh,
    "Dance light, for my heart it lies under your feet, love!"
                  John Francis Waller [1810–1894]

"THE DULE'S I' THIS BONNET O' MINE"

THE dule's i' this bonnet o' mine;
    My ribbins'll never be reet;
Here, Mally, aw'm like to be fine,
    For Jamie'll be comin' to-neet;
He met me i' th' lone t'other day,—
    Aw're gooin' for wayter to th' well,—
An' he begged that aw'd wed him i' May;—
    Bi th' mass, iv he'll let me, aw will!

When he took my two honds into his,
    Good Lord, heaw they trembled between;
An' aw durstn't look up in his face,
    Becose on him seein' my e'en;
My cheek went as red as a rose;—
    There's never a mortal can tell
Heaw happy aw felt; for, thea knows,
    One couldn't ha' axed him theirsel'.

But th' tale wur at th' end o' my tung,—
    To let it eawt wouldn't be reet,—
For aw thought to seem forrud wur wrung,
    So aw towd him aw'd tell him to-neet;
But Mally, thae knows very weel,—

Though it isn't a thing one should own,—
    Iv aw'd th' pikein' o' th' world to mysel',
      Aw'd oather ha' Jamie or noan.

Neaw, Mally, aw've towd tho my mind;
    What would to do iv't wur thee?
"Aw'd tak him just while he're inclined,
    An' a farrantly bargain he'd be;
For Jamie's as gradely a lad
    As ever stepped eawt into th' sun;—
Go, jump at thy chance, an' get wed,
    An' mak th' best o' th' job when it's done!"

Eh, dear, but it's time to be gwon,—
    Aw shouldn't like Jamie to wait;
Aw connut for shame be too soon,
    An' aw wouldn't for th' world be too late;
Aw'm a' ov a tremble to th' heel,—
    Dost think 'at my bonnet'll do?—
"Be off, lass,—thae looks very weel;
    He wants noan o' th' bonnet, thae foo!"

                Edwin Waugh [1817–1890]

THE OULD PLAID SHAWL

NOT far from old Kinvara, in the merry month of May,
When birds were singing cheerily, there came across my way,
As if from out the sky above an angel chanced to fall,
A little Irish cailin in an ould plaid shawl.

She tripped along right joyously, a basket on her arm;
And oh! her face; and oh! her grace, the soul of saint would
    charm:
Her brown hair rippled o'er her brow, but greatest charm
    of all
Was her modest blue eyes beaming 'neath her ould plaid
    shawl.

I courteously saluted her—"God save you, miss," says I;
"God save you kindly, sir," said she, and shyly passed me
    by;

Off went my heart along with her, a captive in her thrall,
Imprisoned in the corner of her ould plaid shawl.

Enchanted with her beauty rare, I gazed in pure delight,
Till round an angle of the road she vanished from my sight;
But ever since I sighing say, as I that scene recall,
"The grace of God about you and your ould plaid shawl."

I've heard of highway robbers that with pistols and with knives,
Make trembling travelers yield them up their money or their lives,
But think of me that handed out my heart and head and all
To a simple little cailin in an ould plaid shawl.

Oh! graceful the mantillas that the signorinas wear,
And tasteful are the bonnets of Parisian ladies fair,
But never cloak, or hood, or robe, in palace, bower, or hall,
Clad half such witching beauty as that ould plaid shawl.

Oh! some men sigh for riches, and some men live for fame,
And some on history's pages hope to win a glorious name:
My aims are not ambitious, and my wishes are but small—
You might wrap them all together in an ould plaid shawl.

I'll seek her all through Galway, and I'll seek her all through Clare,
I'll search for tale or tidings of my traveler everywhere,
For peace of mind I'll never find until my own I call
That little Irish cailin in her ould plaid shawl.

Francis A. Fahy [1854–

LITTLE MARY CASSIDY

OH, 'tis little Mary Cassidy's the cause of all my misery,
    And the raison that I am not now the boy I used to be;
Oh, she bates the beauties all that we read about in history,
    And sure half the country-side is as hot for her as me.

Travel Ireland up and down, hill, village, vale and town—
    Fairer than the Cailin Donn, you're looking for in vain;
Oh, I'd rather live in poverty with little Mary Cassidy
    Than emperor, without her, be of Germany or Spain.

'Twas at the dance at Darmody's that first I caught a sight
    of her,
    And heard her sing the "Droighnean Donn," till tears
    came in my eyes,
And ever since that blessed hour I'm dreaming day and
    night of her;
    The devil a wink of sleep at all I get from bed to rise.
Cheeks like the rose in June, song like the lark in tune,
    Working, resting, night or noon, she never leaves my
    mind;
Oh, till singing by my cabin fire sits little Mary Cassidy,
    'Tis little aise or happiness I'm sure I'll ever find.

What is wealth, what is fame, what is all that people fight
    about
    To a kind word from her lips or a love-glance from her eye?
Oh, though troubles throng my breast, sure they'd soon go
    to the right-about
    If I thought the curly head of her would rest there by and
    by.
Take all I own to-day, kith, kin, and care away,
    Ship them all across the say, or to the frozen zone:
Lave me an orphan bare—but lave me Mary Cassidy,
    I never would feel lonesome with the two of us alone.

Francis A. Fahy [1854–

THE ROAD

"Now where are ye goin'," ses I, "wid the shawl
An' cotton umbrella an' basket an' all?
Would ye not wait for McMullen's machine,
Wid that iligant instep befittin' a queen?
    Oh, you wid the wind-soft gray eye wid a wile in it,
    You wid the lip wid the troublesome smile in it,
    Sure, the road's wet, ivery rain-muddied mile in it—"
"*Ah, the Saints'll be kapin' me petticoats clean!*"

"But," ses I, "would ye like it to meet Clancy's bull,
Or the tinks poachin' rabbits above Slieve-na-coul?
An' the ford at Kilmaddy is big wid the snows,
An' the whisht Little People that wear the green close,
   They'd run from the bog to be makin' a catch o' ye,
   The king o' them's wishful o' weddin' the match o' ye,
   'Twould be long, if they did, ere ye lifted the latch o' ye—"
"What fairy's to touch her that sings as she goes!"

"Ah, where are ye goin'," ses I, "wid the shawl,
An' the gray eyes a-dreamin' beneath it an' all?
The road by the mountain's a long one, depend
Ye'll be done for, alannah, ere reachin' the end;
   Ye'll be bate wid the wind on each back-breakin' bit on it,
   Wet wid the puddles and lamed wid the grit on it,—
   Since lonesome ye're layin' yer delicut fit on it—"
"Sure whin's a road lonesome that's stepped wid a friend?"

      That's stepped wid a friend?
      Who did Bridgy intend?
Still 'twas me that went wid her right on to the end!
         Patrick R. Chalmers [18

TWICKENHAM FERRY

"Аноy! and O-ho! and it's who's for the ferry?"
   (The briar's in bud and the sun going down)
"And I'll row ye so quick and I'll row ye so steady,
   And 'tis but a penny to Twickenham Town."
The ferryman's slim and the ferryman's young,
With just a soft tang in the turn of his tongue;
And he's fresh as a pippin and brown as a berry,
   And 'tis but a penny to Twickenham Town.

"Ahoy! and O-ho! and it's I'm for the ferry,"
   (The briar's in bud and the sun going down)
"And it's late as it is and I haven't a penny—
   Oh! how can I get me to Twickenham Town?"
She'd a rose in her bonnet, and oh! she looked sweet
As the little pink flower that grows in the wheat,

With her cheeks like a rose and her lips like a cherry—
    It's sure but you're welcome to Twickenham Town.

"Ahoy! and O-ho!"—You're too late for the ferry,
    (The briar's in bud and the sun has gone down)
And he's not rowing quick and he's not rowing steady;
    It seems quite a journey to Twickenham Town.
"Ahoy! and O-ho!" you may call as you will;
    The young moon is rising o'er Petersham Hill;
And, with Love like a rose in the stern of the wherry,
    There's danger in crossing to Twickenham Town.

        Théophile Marzials [1850–

THE HUMOR OF LOVE

SONG

I PRITHEE send me back my heart,
  Since I cannot have thine:
For if from yours you will not part,
  Why then shouldst thou have mine?

Yet now I think on't, let it lie,
  To find it were in vain,
For thou hast a thief in either eye
  Would steal it back again.

Why should two hearts in one breast lie,
  And yet not lodge together?
O love, where is thy sympathy,
  If thus our breasts thou sever?

But love is such a mystery,
  I cannot find it out:
For when I think I'm best resolved,
  I then am most in doubt.

Then farewell care, and farewell woe!
  I will no longer pine;
For I'll believe I have her heart,
  As much as she hath mine.

John Suckling [1609-1642]

A BALLAD UPON A WEDDING

I TELL thee, Dick, where I have been,
Where I the rarest things have seen;
  Oh, things without compare!
Such sights again cannot be found
In any place on English ground,
  Be it at wake or fair.

At Charing Cross, hard by the way
Where we (thou know'st) do sell our hay,
   There is a house with stairs;
And there did I see coming down
Such folk as are not in our town,
   Forty at least, in pairs.

Amongst the rest, one pest'lent fine
(His beard no bigger, though, than thine)
   Walked on before the rest;
Our landlord looks like nothing to him;
The king (God bless him!) 'twould undo him
   Should he go still so drest.

At Course-a-park, without all doubt,
He should have first been taken out
   By all the maids i' th' town:
Though lusty Roger there had been,
Or little George upon the green,
   Or Vincent of the Crown.

But wot you what? The youth was going
To make an end of all his wooing;
   The parson for him staid:
Yet by his leave (for all his haste),
He did not so much wish all past,
   (Perchance) as did the maid.

The maid (and thereby hangs a tale)
For such a maid no Whitsun-ale
   Could ever yet produce:
No grape that's kindly ripe, could be
So round, so plump, so soft, as she,
   Nor half so full of juice.

Her finger was so small, the ring
Would not stay on which they did bring;
   It was too wide a peck:
And to say truth (for out it must)
It looked like the great collar (just)
   About our young colt's neck.

Her feet beneath her petticoat
Like little mice stole in and out,
   As if they feared the light:
But oh, she dances such a way!
No sun upon an Easter-day
   Is half so fine a sight.

Her cheeks so rare a white was on,
No daisy makes comparison;
   Who sees them is undone;
For streaks of red were mingled there,
Such as are on a Cath'rine pear,
   The side that's next the sun.

Her lips were red; and one was thin
Compared to that was next her chin
   (Some bee had stung it newly);
But, Dick, her eyes so guard her face,
I durst no more upon them gaze,
   Than on the sun in July.

Her mouth so small, when she does speak,
Thou'dst swear her teeth her words did break,
   That they might passage get;
But she so handled still the matter,
They came as good as ours, or better,
   And are not spent a whit.

Passion o' me! how I run on!
There's that that would be thought upon,
   I trow, besides the bride:
The business of the kitchen's great,
For it is fit that men should eat;
   Nor was it there denied.

Just in the nick the cook knocked thrice,
And all the waiters in a trice
   His summons did obey;
Each serving-man, with dish in hand,
Marched boldly up, like our trained-band,
   Presented, and away.

When all the meat was on the table,
What man of knife, or teeth, was able
    To stay to be intreated?
And this the very reason was,
Before the parson could say grace,
    The company was seated.

Now hats fly off, and youths carouse;
Healths first go round, and then the house,
    The bride's come thick and thick;
And when 'twas named another's health,
Perhaps he made it hers by stealth,
    (And who could help it, Dick?)

O' th' sudden up they rise and dance;
Then sit again, and sigh, and glance;
    Then dance again, and kiss.
Thus sev'ral ways the time did pass,
Till ev'ry woman wished her place,
    And ev'ry man wished his.

By this time all were stol'n aside
To counsel and undress the bride;
    But that he must not know:
But yet 'twas thought he guessed her mind,
And did not mean to stay behind
    Above an hour or so.

                                John Suckling [1609–1642]

TO CHLOE JEALOUS

DEAR Chloe, how blubbered is that pretty face!
    Thy cheek all on fire, and thy hair all uncurled:
Prithee quit this caprice; and (as old Falstaff says),
    Let us e'en talk a little like folks of this world.

How canst thou presume thou hast leave to destroy
  The beauties which Venus but lent to thy keeping?
Those looks were designed to inspire love and joy:
  More ordinary eyes may serve people for weeping.

To be vexed at a trifle or two that I writ,
  Your judgment at once, and my passion you wrong:
You take that for fact, which will scarce be found wit:
  Od's life! must one swear to the truth of a song?

What I speak, my fair Chloe, and what I write, shows
  The difference there is betwixt nature and art:
I court others in verse, but I love thee in prose:
  And they have my whimsies, but thou hast my heart.

The god of us verse-men (you know, Child) the sun,
  How after his journeys he sets up his rest;
If at morning o'er earth 'tis his fancy to run;
  At night he reclines on his Thetis's breast.

So when I am wearied with wandering all day,
  To thee, my delight, in the evening I come:
No matter what beauties I saw in my way:
  They were but my visits, but thou art my home.

Then finish, dear Chloe, this pastoral war;
  And let us, like Horace and Lydia, agree:
For thou art a girl as much brighter than her,
  As he was a poet sublimer than me.

Matthew Prior [1664–1721]

JACK AND JOAN

  Jack and Joan they think no ill,
  But loving live, and merry still;
  Do their week-days' work, and pray
  Devoutly on the holy day:
  Skip and trip it on the green,
  And help to choose the Summer Queen:

Lash out, at a country feast,
Their silver penny with the best.

Well can they judge of nappy ale,
And tell at large a winter tale;
Climb up to the apple loft,
And turn the crabs till they be soft.
Tib is all the father's joy,
And little Tom the mother's boy.
All their pleasure is content;
And care, to pay their yearly rent.

Joan can call by name her cows,
And deck her windows with green boughs;
She can wreaths and tuttyes make,
And trim with plums a bridal cake.
Jack knows what brings gain or loss;
And his long flail can stoutly toss:
Makes the hedge which others break;
And ever thinks what he doth speak.

Now, you courtly dames and knights,
That study only strange delights;
Though you scorn the home-spun gray,
And revel in your rich array:
Though your tongues dissemble deep,
And can your heads from danger keep;
Yet, for all your pomp and train,
Securer lives the silly swain.

Thomas Campion [? -1619]

PHILLIS AND CORYDON

Phillis kept sheep along the western plains,
   And Corydon did feed his flocks hard by:
This shepherd was the flower of all the swains
   That traced the downs of fruitful Thessaly;
And Phillis, that did far her flocks surpass
In silver hue, was thought a bonny lass.

A bonny lass, quaint in her country 'tire,
    Was lovely Phillis,—Corydon swore so;
Her locks, her looks, did set the swain on fire,
    He left his lambs, and he began to woo;
He looked, he sighed, he courted with a kiss,
No better could the silly swad than this.

He little knew to paint a tale of love,
    Shepherds can fancy, but they cannot say:
Phillis 'gan smile, and wily thought to prove
    What uncouth grief poor Corydon did pay;
She asked him how his flocks or he did fare,
Yet pensive thus his sighs did tell his care.

The shepherd blushed when Phillis questioned so,
    And swore by Pan it was not for his flocks:
" 'Tis love, fair Phillis, breedeth all this woe,
    My thoughts are trapped within thy lovely locks;
Thine eye hath pierced, thy face hath set on fire;
Fair Phillis kindleth Corydon's desire."

"Can shepherds love?" said Phillis to the swain.
    "Such saints as Phillis," Corydon replied.
"Men when they lust can many fancies feign,"
    Said Phillis. This not Corydon denied,
That lust had lies; "But love," quoth he, "says truth:
Thy shepherd loves, then, Phillis, what ensu'th?"

Phillis was won, she blushed and hung her head;
    The swain stepped to, and cheered her with a kiss:
With faith, with troth, they struck the matter dead;
    So usèd they when men thought not amiss:
Thus love begun and ended both in one;
Phillis was loved, and she liked Corydon.

                    Robert Greene [1560?–1592]

SALLY IN OUR ALLEY

OF all the girls that are so smart
    There's none like pretty Sally;
She is the darling of my heart,
    And she lives in our alley.

There is no lady in the land
　　Is half so sweet as Sally;
She is the darling of my heart,
　　And she lives in our alley.

Her father he makes cabbage-nets,
　　And through the streets does cry 'em;
Her mother she sells laces long
　　To such as please to buy 'em;
But sure such folks could ne'er beget
　　So sweet a girl as Sally!
She is the darling of my heart,
　　And she lives in our alley.

When she is by, I leave my work,
　　I love her so sincerely;
My master comes like any Turk,
　　And bangs me most severely:
But let him bang his bellyful,
　　I'll bear it all for Sally;
She is the darling of my heart,
　　And she lives in our alley.

Of all the days that's in the week
　　I dearly love but one day—
And that's the day that comes betwixt
　　A Saturday and Monday;
For then I'm dressed all in my best
　　To walk abroad with Sally;
She is the darling of my heart,
　　And she lives in our alley.

My master carries me to church,
　　And often am I blamèd
Because I leave him in the lurch
　　As soon as text is namèd;
I leave the church in sermon-time
　　And slink away to Sally;
She is the darling of my heart,
　　And she lives in our alley.

When Christmas comes about again,
    O, then I shall have money;
I'll hoard it up, and box it all,
    I'll give it to my honey:
I would it were ten thousand pound,
    I'd give it all to Sally;
She is the darling of my heart,
    And she lives in our alley.

My master and the neighbors all
    Make game of me and Sally,
And, but for her, I'd better be
    A slave and row a galley;
But when my seven long years are out,
    O, then I'll marry Sally;
O, then we'll wed, and then we'll bed—
    But not in our alley!

                    Henry Carey [? −1743]

THE COUNTRY WEDDING

WELL met, pretty nymph, says a jolly young swain
To a lovely young shepherdess crossing the plain;
Why so much in haste?—now the month it was May—
May I venture to ask you, fair maiden, which way?
Then straight to this question the nymph did reply,
With a blush on her cheek, and a smile in her eye,
I came from the village, and homeward I go,
And now, gentle shepherd, pray why would you know?

I hope, pretty maid, you won't take it amiss,
If I tell you my reason for asking you this;
I would see you safe home—(now the swain was in love!)
Of such a companion if you would approve.
Your offer, kind shepherd, is civil, I own;
But I see no great danger in going alone;
Nor yet can I hinder, the road being free
For one as another, for you as for me.

No danger in going alone, it is true,
But yet a companion is pleasanter, too;
And if you could like—(now the swain he took heart)—
Such a sweetheart as me, why we never would part.
O that's a long word, said the shepherdess then,
I've often heard say there's no minding you men.
You'll say and unsay, and you'll flatter, 'tis true!
Then to leave a young maiden's the first thing you do.

O judge not so harshly, the shepherd replied,
To prove what I say, I will make you my bride.
To-morrow the parson—(well-said, little swain!)—
Shall join both our hands, and make one of us twain.
Then what the nymph answered to this isn't said,
The very next morn, to be sure, they were wed.
Sing hey-diddle,—ho-diddle,—hey-diddle-down,—
Now when shall we see such a wedding in town?

Unknown

"O MERRY MAY THE MAID BE"

O MERRY may the maid be
    That marries wi' the miller,
For, foul day and fair day,
    He's aye bringing till her,—
Has aye a penny in his purse
    For dinner or for supper;
And, gin she please, a good fat cheese
    And lumps of yellow butter.

When Jamie first did woo me,
    I speired what was his calling;
"Fair maid," says he, "O come and see,
    Ye're welcome to my dwalling."
Though I was shy, yet could I spy
    The truth o' what he told me,
And that his house was warm and couth,
    And room in it to hold me.

Behind the door a bag o' meal,
  And in the kist was plenty
O' guid hard cakes his mither bakes,
  And bannocks werena scanty.
A guid fat sow, a sleeky cow
  Was standing in the byre,
Whilst lazy puss with mealy mouse
  Was playing at the fire.

" Guid signs are these," my mither says,
  And bids me tak' the miller;
For, fair day and foul day,
  He's aye bringing till her;
For meal and maut she doesna want,
  Nor anything that's dainty;
And now and then a kecking hen,
  To lay her eggs in plenty.

In winter, when the wind and rain
  Blaws o'er the house and byre,
He sits beside a clean hearth-stane,
  Before a rousing fire.
With nut-brown ale he tells his tale,
  Which rows him o'er fu' nappy:—
Wha'd be a king—a petty thing,
  When a miller lives so happy?
                    John Clerk [1684–1755]

THE LASS O' GOWRIE

'Twas on a simmer's afternoon,
A wee afore the sun gaed doun,
A lassie wi' a braw new goun
  Cam' owre the hills to Gowrie.
The rosebud washed in simmer's shower
Bloomed fresh within the sunny bower;
But Kitty was the fairest flower
  That e'er was seen in Gowrie.

To see her cousin she cam' there;
And oh! the scene was passing fair,
For what in Scotland can compare
    Wi' the Carse o' Gowrie?
The sun was setting on the Tay,
The blue hills melting into gray,
The mavis and the blackbird's lay
    Were sweetly heard in Gowrie.

O lang the lassie I had wooed,
And truth and constancy had vowed,
But could nae speed wi' her I lo'ed
    Until she saw fair Gowrie.
I pointed to my faither's ha'—
Yon bonnie bield ayont the shaw,
Sae loun that there nae blast could blaw:—
    Wad she no bide in Gowrie?

Her faither was baith glad and wae;
Her mither she wad naething say;
The bairnies thocht they wad get play
    If Kitty gaed to Gowrie.
She whiles did smile, she whiles did greet;
The blush and tear were on her cheek;
She naething said, and hung her head;—
    But now she's Leddy Gowrie.

Carolina Nairne [1766-1845]

THE CONSTANT SWAIN AND VIRTUOUS
MAID

Soon as the day begins to waste,
Straight to the well-known door I haste,
    And rapping there, I'm forced to stay
While Molly hides her work with care,
Adjusts her tucker and her hair,
    And nimble Becky scours away.

Entering, I see in Molly's eyes
A sudden smiling joy arise,

As quickly checked by virgin shame:
She drops a curtsey, steals a glance,
Receives a kiss, one step advance.—
    If such I love, am I to blame?

I sit, and talk of twenty things,
Of South Sea stock, or death of kings,
    While only "Yes" or "No," says Molly;
As cautious she conceals her thoughts,
As others do their private faults:—
    Is this her prudence, or her folly?

Parting, I kiss her lip and cheek,
I hang about her snowy neck,
    And cry, "Farewell, my dearest Molly!"
Yet still I hang and still I kiss,
Ye learnèd sages, say, is this
    In me the effect of love, or folly?

No—both by sober reason move,—
She prudence shows, and I true love—
    No charge of folly can be laid.
Then (till the marriage-rites proclaimed
Shall join our hands) let us be named
    The constant swain, the virtuous maid.

Unknown

" WHEN THE KYE COMES HAME "

COME, all ye jolly shepherds
    That whistle through the glen,
I'll tell ye of a secret
    That courtiers dinna ken:
What is the greatest bliss
    That the tongue o' man can name?
'Tis to woo a bonnie lassie
    When the kye comes hame.
        When the kye comes hame,
            When the kye comes hame,
        'Tween the gloamin and the mirk,
            When the kye comes hame.

'Tis not beneath the coronet,
   Nor canopy of state,
'Tis not on couch of velvet,
   Nor arbor of the great—
'Tis beneath the spreading birk,
   In the glen without the name,
Wi' a bonnie, bonnie lassie,
   When the kye comes hame.

There the blackbird bigs his nest
   For the mate he lo'es to see,
And on the topmost bough,
   O, a happy bird is he!
Then he pours his melting ditty,
   And love is a' the theme,
And he'll woo his bonnie lassie
   When the kye comes hame.

When the blewart bears a pearl,
   And the daisy turns a pea,
And the bonnie lucken gowan
   Has fauldit up her e'e,
Then the laverock frae the blue lift
   Draps down, and thinks nae shame
To woo his bonnie lassie
   When the kye comes hame.

See yonder pawkie shepherd
   That lingers on the hill—
His ewes are in the fauld,
   And his lambs are lying still;
Yet he downa gang to bed,
   For his heart is in a flame
To meet his bonnie lassie
   When the kye comes hame.

When the little wee bit heart
   Rises high in the breast,
And the little wee bit starn
   Rises red in the east,

O there's a joy sae dear,
    That the heart can hardly frame,
Wi' a bonnie, bonnie lassie,
    When the kye comes hame.

Then since all nature joins
    In this love without alloy,
O, wha wad prove a traitor
    To Nature's dearest joy?
Or wha wad choose a crown,
    Wi' its perils and its fame,
And miss his bonnie lassie
    When the kye comes hame?
        When the kye comes hame,
            When the kye comes hame
            'Tween the gloamin' and the mirk,
            When the kye comes hame!
                    James Hogg [1770–1835]

THE LOW–BACKED CAR

WHEN first I saw sweet Peggy,
    'Twas on a market day,
A low-backed car she drove, and sat
    Upon a truss of hay;
But when that hay was blooming grass
    And decked with flowers of Spring,
No flower was there that could compare
    With the blooming girl I sing.
As she sat in the low-backed car,
The man at the turnpike bar
        Never asked for the toll,
        But just rubbed his ould poll,
And looked after the low-backed car.

In battle's wild commotion,
    The proud and mighty Mars,
With hostile scythes, demands his tithes
    Of death—in warlike cars:

While Peggy, peaceful goddess,
   Has darts in her bright eye,
That knock men down in the market town,
   As right and left they fly;—
While she sits in her low-backed car,
Than battle more dangerous far,—
     For the doctor's art
     Cannot cure the heart
That is hit from that low-backed car.

Sweet Peggy round her car, sir,
   Has strings of ducks and geese,
But the scores of hearts she slaughters
   By far outnumber these;
While she among her poultry sits,
   Just like a turtle-dove,
Well worth the cage, I do engage,
   Of the blooming god of Love!
While she sits in her low-backed car,
The lovers come near and far,
     And envy the chicken
     That Peggy is pickin',
As she sits in her low-backed car.

O, I'd rather own that car, sir,
   With Peggy by my side,
Than a coach-and-four, and goold galore,
   And a lady for my bride;
For the lady would sit forninst me,
   On a cushion made with taste,
While Peggy would sit beside me,
   With my arm around her waist,—
While we drove in the low-backed car,
To be married by Father Mahar,
     O, my heart would beat high
     At her glance and her sigh,—
Though it beat in a low-backed car!

             Samuel Lover [1797–1868]

THE PRETTY GIRL OF LOCH DAN

THE shades of eve had crossed the glen
   That frowns o'er infant Avonmore,
When, nigh Loch Dan, two weary men,
   We stopped before a cottage door.

"God save all here!" my comrade cries,
   And rattles on the raised latch-pin;
"God save you kindly!" quick replies
   A clear sweet voice, and asks us in.

We enter; from the wheel she starts,
   A rosy girl with soft black eyes;
Her fluttering curtsey takes our hearts,
   Her blushing grace and pleased surprise.

Poor Mary, she was quite alone,
   For, all the way to Glenmalure,
Her mother had that morning gone,
   And left the house in charge with her.

But neither household cares, nor yet
   The shame that startled virgins feel,
Could make the generous girl forget
   Her wonted hospitable zeal.

She brought us, in a beechen bowl,
   Sweet milk that smacked of mountain thyme,
Oat cake, and such a yellow roll
   Of butter,—it gilds all my rhyme!

And, while we ate the grateful food
   (With weary limbs on bench reclined),
Considerate and discreet, she stood
   Apart, and listened to the wind.

Kind wishes both our souls engaged,
   From breast to breast spontaneous ran
The mutual thought,—we stood and pledged
   THE MODEST ROSE ABOVE LOCH DAN.

"The milk we drink is not more pure,
  Sweet Mary,—bless those budding charms!—
Than your own generous heart, I'm sure,
  Nor whiter than the breast it warms!"

She turned and gazed, unused to hear
  Such language in that homely glen;
But, Mary, you have naught to fear,
  Though smiled on by two stranger-men.

Not for a crown would I alarm
  Your virgin pride by word or sign,
Nor need a painful blush disarm
  My friend of thoughts as pure as mine.

Her simple heart could not but feel
  The words we spoke were free from guile;
She stooped, she blushed, she fixed her wheel,—
  'Tis all in vain,—she can't but smile!

Just like sweet April's dawn appears
  Her modest face,—I see it yet,—
And though I lived a hundred years
  Methinks I never could forget

The pleasure that, despite her heart,
  Fills all her downcast eyes with light;
The lips reluctantly apart,
  The white teeth struggling into sight,

The dimples eddying o'er her cheek,—
  The rosy cheek that won't be still:—
O, who could blame what flatterers speak,
  Did smiles like this reward their skill?

For such another smile, I vow,
  Though loudly beats the midnight rain,
I'd take the mountain-side e'en now,
  And walk to Luggelaw again!

                    Samuel Ferguson [1810–1886]

MUCKLE-MOUTH MEG

FROWNED the Laird on the Lord: "So, red-handed I catch
    thee?
Death-doomed by our Law of the Border!
We've a gallows outside and a chiel to dispatch thee:
    Who trespasses—hangs: all's in order."

He met frown with smile, did the young English gallant:
    Then the Laird's dame: "Nay, Husband, I beg!
He's comely: be merciful! Grace for the callant
    —If he marries our Muckle-mouth Meg!"

"No mile-wide-mouthed monster of yours do I marry:
    Grant rather the gallows!" laughed he.
"Foul fare kith and kin of you—why do you tarry?"
    "To tame your fierce temper!" quoth she.

"Shove him quick in the Hole, shut him fast for a week:
    Cold, darkness, and hunger work wonders:
Who lion-like roars, now mouse-fashion will squeak,
    And 'it rains' soon succeed to 'it thunders.'"

A week did he bide in the cold and dark
    —Not hunger: for duly at morning
In flitted a lass, and a voice like a lark
    Chirped, "Muckle-mouth Meg still ye're scorning?

"Go hang, but here's parritch to hearten ye first!"
    "Did Meg's muckle-mouth boast within some
Such music as yours, mine should match it or burst:
    No frog-jaws! So tell folk, my Winsome!"

Soon week came to end, and, from Hole's door set wide,
    Out he marched, and there waited the lassie:
"Yon gallows, or Muckle-mouth Meg for a bride!
    Consider! Sky's blue and turf's grassy:

"Life's sweet; shall I say ye wed Muckle-mouth Meg?"
    "Not I," quoth the stout heart: "too eerie
The mouth that can swallow a bubblyjock's egg:
    Shall I let it munch mine? Never, Dearie!"

"Not Muckle-mouth Meg?   Wow, the obstinate man!
    Perhaps he would rather wed me!"
"Ay, would he—with just for a dowry your can!"
    "I'm Muckle-mouth Meg," chirruped she.

"Then so—so—so—so—" as he kissed her apace—
    "Will I widen thee out till thou turnest
From Margaret Minnikin-mou', by God's grace,
    To Muckle-mouth Meg in good earnest!"

                    Robert Browning [1812–1889]

MUCKLE–MOU'D MEG

"OH, what hae ye brought us hame now, my brave lord,
    Strappit flaught owre his braid saddle-bow?
Some bauld Border reiver to feast at our board,
    An' harry our pantry, I trow.
He's buirdly an' stalwart in lith an' in limb;
    Gin ye were his master in war
The field was a saft enough litter for him,
    Ye needna hae brought him sae far.
Then saddle an' munt again, harness an' dunt again,
An' when ye gae hunt again, strike higher game."

"Hoot, whisht ye, my dame, for he comes o' gude kin,
    An' boasts o' a lang pedigree;
This night he maun share o' our gude cheer within,
    At morning's gray dawn he maun dee.
He's gallant Wat Scott, heir o' proud Harden Ha',
    Wha ettled our lands clear to sweep;
But now he is snug in auld Elibank's paw,
    An' shall swing frae our donjon-keep.
Though saddle an' munt again, harness an' dunt again,
I'll ne'er when I hunt again strike higher game."

"Is this young Wat Scott? an' wad ye rax his craig,
    When our daughter is fey for a man?
Gae, gaur the loun marry our muckle-mou'd Meg,
    Or we'll ne'er get the jaud aff our han'!"

"Od! hear our gudewife, she wad fain save your life;
　Wat Scott, will ye marry or hang?"
But Meg's muckle mou set young Wat's heart agrue.
　Wat swore to the woodie he'd gang.
Ne'er saddle nor munt again, harness nor dunt again,
Wat ne'er shall hunt again, ne'er see his hame.

Syne muckle-mou'd Meg pressed in close to his side,
　An' blinkit fu' sleely and kind,
But aye as Wat glowered at his braw proffered bride,
　He shook like a leaf in the wind.
"A bride or a gallows, a rope or a wife!"
　The morning dawned sunny and clear—
Wat boldly strode forward to part wi' his life,
　Till he saw Meggy shedding a tear;
Then saddle an' munt again, harness an' dunt again,
Fain wad Wat hunt again, fain wad be hame.

Meg's tear touched his bosom, the gibbet frowned high,
　An' slowly Wat strode to his doom;
He gae a glance round wi' a tear in his eye,
　Meg shone like a star through the gloom.
She rushed to his arms, they were wed on the spot,
　An' lo'ed ither muckle and lang;
Nae bauld border laird had a wife like Wat Scott;
　'Twas better to marry than hang.
So saddle an' munt again, harness an' dunt again,
Elibank hunt again, Wat's snug at hame.
　　　　　　　　　　　James Ballantine [1808–1877]

GLENLOGIE

THREESCORE o' nobles rade to the king's ha',
But bonnie Glenlogie's the flower o' them a',
Wi' his milk-white steed and his bonnie black e'e,
"Glenlogie, dear mither, Glenlogie for me!"

"O haud your tongue, dochter, ye'll get better than he";
"O say na sae, mither, for that canna be;
Though Doumlie is richer, and greater than he,
Yet if I maun tak' him, I'll certainly dee.

"Where will I get a bonnie boy, to win hose and shoon,
Will gae to Glenlogie, and come again soon?"
"O here am I, a bonnie boy, to win hose and shoon,
Will gae to Glenlogie and come again soon."

When he gaed to Glenlogie, 'twas "Wash and go dine";
'Twas "Wash ye, my pretty boy, wash and go dine."
"O 'twas ne'er my father's fashion, and it ne'er shall be mine
To gar a lady's errand wait till I dine.

"But there is, Glenlogie, a letter for thee."
The first line that he read, a low smile ga'e he;
The next line that he read, the tear blindit his e'e:
But the last line he read, he gart the table flee.

"Gar saddle the black horse, gar saddle the brown;
Gar saddle the swiftest steed e'er rade frae a town";
But lang ere the horse was brought round to the green,
O bonnie Glenlogie was two mile his lane.

When he cam' to Glenfeldy's door, sma' mirth was there;
Bonnie Jean's mither was tearing her hair;
"Ye're welcome, Glenlogie, ye're welcome," said she,
"Ye're welcome, Glenlogie, your Jeanie to see."

Pale and wan was she, when Glenlogie gaed ben,
But red rosy grew she whene'er he sat down;
She turned awa' her head, but the smile was in her e'e,
"O binna feared, mither, I'll maybe no dee."

Unknown

LOCHINVAR

From "Marmion"

O, YOUNG Lochinvar is come out of the west,
Through all the wide Border his steed was the best;
And, save his good broadsword, he weapon had none,
He rode all unarmed, and he rode all alone.
So faithful in love, and so dauntless in war,
There never was knight like the young Lochinvar.

He stayed not for brake, and he stopped not for stone,
He swam the Eske river where ford there was none;
But, ere he alighted at Netherby gate,
The bride had consented, the gallant came late;
For a laggard in love, and a dastard in war,
Was to wed the fair Ellen of brave Lochinvar.

So boldly he entered the Netherby Hall,
Among bridesmen, and kinsmen, and brothers, and all.
Then spoke the bride's father, his hand on his sword,
(For the poor craven bridegroom said never a word),
"O come ye in peace here, or come ye in war,
Or to dance at our bridal, young Lord Lochinvar?"

"I long wooed your daughter, my suit you denied;—
Love swells like the Solway, but ebbs like its tide,—
And now am I come, with this lost love of mine,
To lead but one measure, drink one cup of wine.
There are maidens in Scotland more lovely by far,
That would gladly be bride to the young Lochinvar."

The bride kissed the goblet; the knight took it up,
He quaffed off the wine, and he threw down the cup.
She looked down to blush, and she looked up to sigh,
With a smile on her lips, and a tear in her eye.
He took her soft hand, ere her mother could bar,—
"Now tread we a measure!" said young Lochinvar.

So stately his form, and so lovely her face,
That never a hall such a galliard did grace;
While her mother did fret, and her father did fume.
And the bridegroom stood dangling his bonnet and plume;
And the bride-maidens whispered, "'Twere better by far,
To have matched our fair cousin with young Lochinvar."

One touch to her hand, and one word in her ear,
When they reached the hall-door, and the charger stood near'
So light to the croupe the fair lady he swung,
So light to the saddle before her he sprung!

"She is won! we are gone! over bank, bush, and scaur;
They'll have fleet steeds that follow," quoth young Lochinvar.

There was mounting 'mong Græmes of the Netherby clan;
Forsters, Fenwicks, and Musgraves, they rode and they ran:
There was racing and chasing on Cannobie Lee,
But the lost bride of Netherby ne'er did they see.
So daring in love, and so dauntless in war,
Have ye e'er heard of gallant like young Lochinvar?

                    Walter Scott [1771–1832]

JOCK OF HAZELDEAN

"WHY weep ye by the tide, ladie?
   Why weep ye by the tide?
I'll wed ye to my youngest son,
   And ye sall be his bride:
And ye sall be his bride, ladie,
   Sae comely to be seen"—
But aye she loot the tears down fa'
   For Jock of Hazeldean.

"Now let this wilfu' grief be done,
   And dry that cheek so pale;
Young Frank is chief of Errington
   And lord of Langley-dale;
His step is first in peaceful ha',
   His sword in battle keen"—
But aye she loot the tears down fa'
   For Jock of Hazeldean.

"A chain of gold ye sall not lack,
   Nor braid to bind your hair,
Nor mettled hound, nor managed hawk,
   Nor palfrey fresh and fair;
And you the foremost o' them a'
   Shall ride our forest-queen"—
But aye she loot the tears down fa'
   For Jock of Hazel · ·

The kirk was decked at morning-tide,
    The tapers glimmered fair;
The priest and bridegroom wait the bride,
    And dame and knight are there:
They sought her baith by bower and ha';
    The ladie was not seen!
She's o'er the Border, and awa'
    Wi' Jock of Hazeldean.

Walter Scott [1771–1832]

CANDOR

OCTOBER—A WOOD

"I KNOW what you're going to say," she said,
    And she stood up, looking uncommonly tall:
    "You are going to speak of the hectic fall,
And say you're sorry the summer's dead,
    And no other summer was like it, you know,
    And can I imagine what made it so.
Now aren't you, honestly?" "Yes," I said.

"I know what you're going to say," she said:
    "You are going to ask if I forget
    That day in June when the woods were wet,
And you carried me"—here she drooped her head—
    "Over the creek; you are going to say,
    Do I remember that horrid day.
Now aren't you, honestly?" "Yes," I said.

"I know what you're going to say," she said:
    "You are going to say that since that time
    You have rather tended to run to rhyme,
And"—her clear glance fell, and her cheek grew red—
    "And have I noticed your tone was queer.
    Why, everybody has seen it here!
Now aren't you, honestly?" "Yes," I said.

"I know what you're going to say," I said:
    "You're going to say you've been much annoyed;
    And I'm short of tact—you will say, devoid—

And I'm clumsy and awkward; and call me Ted;
   And I bear abuse like a dear old lamb;
   And you'll have me, anyway, just as I am.
Now aren't you, honestly?" "Ye-es," she said.

Henry Cuyler Bunner [1855–1896]

"DO YOU REMEMBER"

Do you remember when you heard
My lips breathe love's first faltering word?
   You do, sweet—don't you?
When, having wandered all the day,
Linked arm in arm, I dared to say,
   "You'll love me—won't you?"

And when you blushed and could not speak,
I fondly kissed your glowing cheek,
   Did that affront you?
Oh, surely not—your eye expressed
No wrath—but said, perhaps in jest,
   "You'll love me—won't you?"

I'm sure my eyes replied, "I will."
And you believe that promise still,
   You do, sweet—don't you?
Yes, yes! when age has made our eyes
Unfit for questions or replies,
   You'll love me—won't you?

Thomas Haynes Bayly [1797–1839]

BECAUSE

Sweet Nea!—for your lovely sake
   I weave these rambling numbers,
Because I've lain an hour awake,
   And can't compose my slumbers;
Because your beauty's gentle light
   Is round my pillow beaming,
And flings, I know not why, to-night,
   Some witchery o'er my dreaming!

Because we've passed some joyous days,
   And danced some merry dances;
Because we love old Beaumont's plays,
   And old Froissart's romances!
Because whene'er I hear your words
   Some pleasant feeling lingers;
Because I think your heart has cords
   That vibrate to your fingers.

Because you've got those long, soft curls,
   I've sworn should deck my goddess;
Because you're not, like other girls,
   All bustle, blush, and bodice!
Because your eyes are deep and blue,
   Your fingers long and rosy;
Because a little child and you
   Would make one's home so cosy!

Because your little tiny nose
   Turns up so pert and funny;
Because I know you choose your beaux
   More for their mirth than money;
Because I think you'd rather twirl
   A waltz, with me to guide you,
Than talk small nonsense with an earl,
   And a coronet beside you!

Because you don't object to walk,
   And are not given to fainting;
Because you have not learned to talk
   Of flowers, and Poonah-painting;
Because I think you'd scarce refuse
   To sew one on a button;
Because I know you sometimes choose
   To dine on simple mutton!

Because I think I'm just so weak
   As, some of those fine morrows,
To ask you if you'll let me speak
   My story—and *my* sorrows;

Because the rest's a simple thing,
  A matter quickly over
A church—a priest—a sigh—a ring—
  And a chaise-and-four to Dover.

Edward Fitzgerald [1809–1883]

LOVE AND AGE

From " Gryll Grange "

I PLAYED with you 'mid cowslips blowing,
  When I was six and you were four;
When garlands weaving, flower-balls throwing,
  Were pleasures soon to please no more.
Through groves and meads, o'er grass and heather,
  With little playmates, to and fro,
We wandered hand in hand together;
  But that was sixty years ago.

You grew a lovely roseate maiden,
  And still our early love was strong;
Still with no care our days were laden,
  They glided joyously along;
And I did love you very dearly—
  How dearly, words want power to show;
I thought your heart was touched as nearly;
  But that was fifty years ago.

Then other lovers came around you,
  Your beauty grew from year to year,
And many a splendid circle found you
  The center of its glittering sphere.
I saw you then, first vows forsaking,
  On rank and wealth your hand bestow;
O, then, I thought my heart was breaking,—
  But that was forty years ago.

And I lived on, to wed another:
  No cause she gave me to repine;
And when I heard you were a mother,
  I did not wish the children mine.

My own young flock, in fair progression,
  Made up a pleasant Christmas row:
My joy in them was past expression;—
  But that was thirty years ago.

You grew a matron plump and comely,
  You dwelt in fashion's brightest blaze;
My earthly lot was far more homely;
  But I too had my festal days.
No merrier eyes have ever glistened
  Around the hearth-stone's wintry glow,
Than when my youngest child was christened:—
  But that was twenty years ago.

Time passed. My eldest girl was married,
  And I am now a grandsire gray;
One pet of four years old I've carried
  Among the wild-flowered meads to play.
In our old fields of childish pleasure,
  Where now, as then, the cowslips blow,
She fills her basket's ample measure,—
  And that is not ten years ago.

But though first love's impassioned blindness
  Has passed away in colder light,
I still have thought of you with kindness,
  And shall do, till our last good-night.
The ever-rolling silent hours
  Will bring a time we shall not know,
When our young days of gathering flowers
  Will be an hundred years ago.
                    Thomas Love Peacock [1785–1866]

TO HELEN

  I**f** wandering in a wizard's car
    Through yon blue ether, I were able
  To fashion of a little star
    A taper for my Helen's table;—

"What then?" she asks me with a laugh—
    Why, then, with all heaven's luster glowing,
It would not gild her path with half
    The light her love o'er mine is throwing!

Winthrop Mackworth Praed [1802–1839]

AT THE CHURCH GATE

From "Pendennis"

ALTHOUGH I enter not,
Yet round about the spot
    Ofttimes I hover;
And near the sacred gate,
With longing eyes I wait,
    Expectant of her.

The Minster bell tolls out
Above the city's rout,
    And noise and humming;
They've hushed the Minster bell:
The organ 'gins to swell;
    She's coming, she's coming!

My lady comes at last,
Timid, and stepping fast
    And hastening hither,
With modest eyes downcast;
She comes—she's here—she's past!
    May heaven go with her!

Kneel undisturbed, fair Saint!
Pour out your praise or plaint
    Meekly and duly;
I will not enter there,
To sully your pure prayer
    With thoughts unruly.

But suffer me to pace
Round the forbidden place,
    Lingering a minute,

Like outcast spirits, who wait,
And see, through heaven's gate,
Angels within it.
William Makepeace Thackeray [1811–1863]

MABEL, IN NEW HAMPSHIRE

FAIREST of the fairest, rival of the rose,
That is Mabel of the Hills, as everybody knows.

Do you ask me near what stream this sweet floweret grows?
That's an ignorant question, sir, as everybody knows.

Ask you what her age is, reckoned as time goes?
Just the age of beauty, as everybody knows.

Is she tall as Rosalind, standing on her toes?
She is just the perfect height, as everybody knows.

What's the color of her eyes, when they ope or close?
Just the color they should be, as everybody knows.

Is she lovelier dancing, or resting in repose?
Both are radiant pictures, as everybody knows.

Do her ships go sailing on every wind that blows?
She is richer far than that, as everybody knows.

Has she scores of lovers, heaps of bleeding beaux?
That question's quite superfluous, as everybody knows.

I could tell you something, if I only chose!—
But what's the use of telling what everybody knows?
James Thomas Fields [1816–1881]

TOUJOURS AMOUR

PRITHEE tell me, Dimple-Chin,
At what age does Love begin?
Your blue eyes have scarcely seen
Summers three, my fairy queen,

But a miracle of sweets,
Soft approaches, sly retreats,
Show the little archer there,
Hidden in your pretty hair;
When didst learn a heart to win?
Prithee tell me, Dimple-Chin!

"Oh!" the rosy lips reply,
"I can't tell you if I try.
'Tis so long I can't remember:
Ask some younger lass than I!"

Tell, O tell me, Grizzled-Face,
Do your heart and head keep pace?
When does hoary Love expire,
When do frosts put out the fire?
Can its embers burn below
All that chill December snow?
Care you still soft hands to press,
Bonny heads to smooth and bless?
When does Love give up the chase?
Tell, O tell me, Grizzled-Face!

"Ah!" the wise old lips reply,
"Youth may pass and strength may die;
But of Love I can't foretoken:
Ask some older sage than I!"
                    Edmund Clarence Stedman [1833–1908]

THE DOORSTEP

THE conference-meeting through at last,
    We boys around the vestry waited
To see the girls come tripping past,
    Like snow-birds willing to be mated.

Not braver he that leaps the wall
    By level musket-flashes bitten,
Than I, that stepped before them all
    Who longed to see me get the mitten.

But no! she blushed and took my arm:
  We let the old folks have the highway,
And started toward the Maple Farm
  Along a kind of lovers' by-way.

I can't remember what we said,—
  'Twas nothing worth a song or story;
Yet that rude path by which we sped
  Seemed all transformed and in a glory.

The snow was crisp beneath our feet,
  The moon was full, the fields were gleaming;
By hood and tippet sheltered sweet,
  Her face with youth and health was beaming.

The little hand outside her muff
  (O sculptor! if you could but mold it)
So lightly touched my jacket-cuff,
  To keep it warm I had to hold it.

To have her with me there alone,—
  'Twas love and fear and triumph blended:
At last we reached the foot-worn stone
  Where that delicious journey ended.

The old folks, too, were almost home:
  Her dimpled hand the latches fingered,
We heard the voices nearer come,
  Yet on the doorstep still we lingered.

She shook her ringlets from her hood,
  And with a "Thank you, Ned!" dissembled;
But yet I knew she understood
  With what a daring wish I trembled.

A cloud passed kindly overhead,
  The moon was slyly peeping through it,
Yet hid its face, as if it said—
  "Come, now or never! do it! *do it!*"

My lips till then had only known
　　The kiss of mother and of sister,—
But somehow, full upon her own
　　Sweet, rosy, darling mouth,—I kissed her!

Perhaps 'twas boyish love: yet still,
　　O listless woman! weary lover!
To feel once more that fresh, wild thrill
　　I'd give—but who can live youth over?
　　　　　　　Edmund Clarence Stedman [1833–1908]

THE WHITE FLAG

I SENT my love two roses,—one
　　As white as driven snow,
And one a blushing royal red,
　　A flaming Jacqueminot.

I meant to touch and test my fate;
　　That night I should divine,
The moment I should see my love,
　　If her true heart were mine.

For if she holds me dear, I said,
　　She'll wear my blushing rose;
If not, she'll wear my cold Lamarque,
　　As white as winter's snows.

My heart sank when I met her: sure
　　I had been overbold,
For on her breast my pale rose lay
　　In virgin whiteness cold.

Yet with low words she greeted me,
　　With smiles divinely tender;
Upon her cheek the red rose dawned,—
　　The white rose meant surrender.
　　　　　　　John Hay [1838–1905]

A SONG OF THE FOUR SEASONS

WHEN Spring comes laughing
  By vale and hill,
By wind-flower walking
  And daffodil,—
Sing stars of morning,
  Sing morning skies,
Sing blue of speedwell,—
  And my Love's eyes.

When comes the Summer,
  Full-leaved and strong,
And gay birds gossip
  The orchard long,—
Sing hid, sweet honey
  That no bee sips;
Sing red, red roses,—
  And my Love's lips.

When Autumn scatters
  The leaves again,
And piled sheaves bury
  The broad-wheeled wain,—
Sing flutes of harvest
  Where men rejoice;
Sing rounds of reapers,—
  And my Love's voice.

But when comes Winter
  With hail and storm,
And red fire roaring
  And ingle warm,—
Sing first sad going
  Of friends that part;
Then sing glad meeting,—
  And my Love's heart.

Austin Dobson [1840–1921]

THE LOVE–KNOT

TYING her bonnet under her chin,
She tied her raven ringlets in;
But not alone in the silken snare
Did she catch her lovely floating hair,
For, tying her bonnet under her chin,
She tied a young man's heart within.

They were strolling together up the hill,
Where the wind came blowing merry and chill;
And it blew the curls, a frolicsome race,
All over the happy peach-colored face.
Till, scolding and laughing, she tied them in,
Under her beautiful, dimpled chin.

And it blew a color, bright as the bloom
Of the pinkest fuchsia's tossing plume,
All over the cheeks of the prettiest girl
That ever imprisoned a romping curl,
Or, in tying her bonnet under her chin,
Tied a young man's heart within.

Steeper and steeper grew the hill,
Madder, merrier, chillier still
The western wind blew down, and played
The wildest tricks with the little maid,
As, tying her bonnet under her chin,
She tied a young man's heart within.

O western wind, do you think it was fair
To play such tricks with her floating hair?
To gladly, gleefully, do your best
To blow her against the young man's breast,
Where he as gladly folded her in,
And kissed her mouth and her dimpled chin?

Ah! Ellery Vane, you little thought,
An hour ago, when you besought

This country lass to walk with you,
After the sun had dried the dew,
What terrible danger you'd be in,
As she tied her bonnet under her chin!

Nora Perry [1832–1896]

RIDING DOWN

Oh, did you see him riding down,
And riding down, while all the town
Came out to see, came out to see,
And all the bells rang mad with glee?

Oh, did you hear those bells ring out,
The bells ring out, the people shout,
And did you hear that cheer on cheer
That over all the bells rang clear?

And did you see the waving flags,
The fluttering flags, the tattered flags,
Red, white, and blue, shot through and **through**,
Baptized with battle's deadly dew?

And did you hear the drums' gay beat,
The drums' gay beat, the bugles sweet,
The cymbals' clash, the cannons' crash,
That rent the sky with sound and flash?

And did you see me waiting there,
Just waiting there, and watching there,
One little lass, amid the mass
That pressed to see the hero pass?

And did you see him smiling down,
And smiling down, as riding down
With slowest pace, with stately grace,
He caught the vision of a face,—

My face uplifted red and white,
Turned red and white with sheer delight,

To meet the eyes, the smiling eyes,
Outflashing in their swift surprise?

Oh, did you see how swift it came,
How swift it came like sudden flame,
That smile to me, to only me.
The little lass who blushed to see?

And at the windows all along,
Oh, all along, a lovely throng
Of faces fair, beyond compare,
Beamed out upon him riding there!

Each face was like a radiant gem,
A sparkling gem, and yet for them
No swift smile came like sudden flame,
No arrowy glance took certain aim.

He turned away from all their grace,
From all that grace of perfect face,
He turned to me, to only me,
The little lass who blushed to see!

Nora Perry [1832-1896]

"FORGETTIN'"

THE night when last I saw my lad
　　His eyes were bright an' wet.
He took my two hands in his own,
　　"'Tis well," says he, "we're met.
Asthore machree! the likes o' me
　　I bid ye now forget."

Ah, sure the same's a thriflin' thing,
　　'Tis more I'd do for him!
I mind the night I promised well,
　　Away on Ballindim.—
An' every little while or so
　　I thry forgettin' Jim.

It shouldn't take that long to do,
　　An' him not very tall:

'Tis quare the way I'll hear his voice,
  A boy that's out o' call,—
An' whiles I'll see him stand as plain
  As e'er a six-fut wall.

Och, never fear, my jewel!
  I'd forget ye now this minute,
If I only had a notion
  O' the way I should begin it;
But first an' last it isn't known
  The heap o' throuble's in it.

Meself began the night ye went
  An' hasn't done it yet;
I'm nearly fit to give it up,
  For where's the use to fret?—
An' the memory's fairly spoilt on me
  Wid mindin' to forget.

                    Moira O'Neill [18

"ACROSS THE FIELDS TO ANNE"

How often in the summer-tide,
His graver business set aside,
Has stripling Will, the thoughtful-eyed,
  As to the pipe of Pan,
Stepped blithesomely with lover's pride
  Across the fields to Anne.

It must have been a merry mile,
This summer stroll by hedge and stile,
With sweet foreknowledge all the while
  How sure the pathway ran
To dear delights of kiss and smile,
  Across the fields to Anne.

The silly sheep that graze to-day,
I wot, they let him go his way,
Nor once looked up, as who would say:
  "It is a seemly man."
For many lads went wooing aye
  Across the fields to Anne.

The oaks, they have a wiser look;
Mayhap they whispered to the brook:
"The world by him shall yet be shook,
    It is in nature's plan;
Though now he fleets like any rook
    Across the fields to Anne."

And I am sure, that on some hour
Coquetting soft 'twixt sun and shower,
He stooped and broke a daisy-flower
    With heart of tiny span,
And bore it as a lover's dower
    Across the fields to Anne.

While from her cottage garden-bed
She plucked a jasmin's goodlihede,
To scent his jerkin's brown instead;
    Now since that love began,
What luckier swain than he who sped
    Across the fields to Anne?

The winding path whereon I pace,
The hedgerows green, the summer's grace,
Are still before me face to face;
    Methinks I almost can
Turn port and join the singing race
    Across the fields to Anne.

                    Richard Burton [1861–1940]

PAMELA IN TOWN

The fair Pamela came to town,
    To London town, in early summer;
And up and down and round about
    The beaux discussed the bright newcomer,
With "Gadzooks, sir," and "Ma'am, my duty,"
And "Odds my life, but 'tis a Beauty!"

To Ranelagh went Mistress Pam,
    Sweet Mistress Pam so fair and merry,
With cheeks of cream and roses blent,
    With voice of lark and lip of cherry.

Then all the beaux vowed 'twas their duty
To win and wear this country Beauty.

And first Frank Lovelace tried his wit,
    With whispers bold and eyes still bolder;
The warmer grew his saucy flame,
    Cold grew the charming fair and colder.
'Twas "icy bosom"—"cruel beauty"—
"To love, sweet Mistress, 'tis a duty."

Then Jack Carew his arts essayed,
    With honeyed sighs and feignèd weeping.
Good lack! his billets bound the curls
    That pretty Pam she wore a-sleeping.
Next day these curls had richer beauty,
So well Jack's fervor did its duty.

Then Cousin Will came up to view
    The way Pamela ruled the fashion;
He watched the gallants crowd about,
    And flew into a rustic passion,—
Left "Squire, his mark," on divers faces,
And pinked Carew beneath his laces.

Alack! one night at Ranelagh
    The pretty Sly-boots fell a-blushing;
And all the mettled bloods looked round
    To see what caused that telltale flushing.
Up stepped a grizzled Poet Fellow
To dance with Pam a saltarello.

Then Jack and Frank and Will resolved,
    With hand on sword and cutting glances,
That they would lead that Graybeard forth
    To livelier tunes and other dances.
But who that saw Pam's eyes a-shining
With love and joy would see her pining!

And —oons! Their wrath cooled as they looked-—
    That Poet stared as fierce as any!
He was a mighty proper man,
    With blade on hip and inches many;

The beaux all vowed it was their duty
To toast some newer, softer Beauty.

Sweet Pam she bridled, blushed and smiled—
   The wild thing loved and could but show it!
Mayhap some day you'll see in town
   Pamela and her grizzled Poet.
Forsooth he taught the rogue her duty,
And won her faith, her love, her beauty.

               Ellen Mackay Hutchinson Cortissoz [?–1933]

YES?

Is it true, then, my girl, that you mean it—
   The word spoken yesterday night?
Does that hour seem so sweet now between it
   And this has come day's sober light?
Have you woke from a moment of rapture
   To remember, regret, and repent,
And to hate, perchance, him who has trapped your
   Unthinking consent?

Who was he, last evening—this fellow
   Whose audacity lent him a charm?
Have you promised to wed Pulchinello?
   For life taking Figaro's arm?
Will you have the Court fool of the papers,
   The clown in the journalists' ring,
Who earns his scant bread by his capers,
   To be your heart's king?

When we met quite by chance at the theatre
   And I saw you home under the moon,
I'd no thought, love, that mischief would be at her
   Tricks with my tongue quite so soon;
That I should forget fate and fortune
   Make a difference 'twixt Sèvres and delf—
That I'd have the calm nerve to importune
   You, sweet, for yourself.

It's appalling, by Jove, the audacious
  Effrontery of that request!
But you—you grew suddenly gracious,
  And hid your sweet face on my breast.
Why you did it I cannot conjecture;
  I surprised you, poor child, I dare say,
Or perhaps—does the moonlight affect your
  Head often that way?

.   .   .   .

You're released! With some wooer replace me
  More worthy to be your life's light;
From the tablet of memory efface me,
  If you don't mean your Yes of last night.
But—unless you are anxious to see me a
  Wreck of the pipe and the cup
In my birthplace and graveyard, Bohemia—
  Love, don't give me up!

Henry Cuyler Bunner [1855–1896]

THE PRIME OF LIFE

Just as I thought I was growing old,
  Ready to sit in my easy chair,
To watch the world with a heart grown cold,
  And smile at a folly I would not share,

Rose came by with a smile for me,
  And I am thinking that forty year
Isn't the age that it seems to be,
  When two pretty brown eyes are near.

Bless me! of life it is just the prime,
  A fact that I hope she will understand;
And forty year is a perfect rhyme
  To dark brown eyes and a pretty hand.

These gray hairs are by chance, you see—
  Boys are sometimes gray, I am told:
Rose came by with a smile for me,
  Just as I thought I was getting old.

Walter Learned [1847–1915]

THOUGHTS ON THE COMMANDMENTS

"LOVE your neighbor as yourself,"—
　So the parson preaches:
That's one half the Decalogue,—
　So the prayer-book teaches.
Half my duty I can do
　With but little labor,
For with all my heart and soul
　I do love my neighbor.

Mighty little credit, that,
　To my self-denial,
Not to love her, though, might be
　Something of a trial.
Why, the rosy light, that peeps
　Through the glass above her,
Lingers round her lips,—you see
　E'en the sunbeams love her.

So to make my merit more,
　I'll go beyond the letter:—
Love my neighbor as myself?
　Yes, and ten times better.
For she's sweeter than the breath
　Of the Spring, that passes
Through the fragrant, budding woods,
　O'er the meadow-grasses.

And I've preached the word I know,
　For it was my duty
To convert the stubborn heart
　Of the little beauty.
Once again success has crowned
　Missionary labor,
For her sweet eyes own that she
　Also loves her neighbor.

George Augustus Baker [1849–1906]

THE IRONY OF LOVE

"SIGH NO MORE, LADIES"

From "Much Ado About Nothing"

SIGH no more, ladies, sigh no more,
  Men were deceivers ever;
One foot in sea, and one on shore;
  To one thing constant never.
    Then sigh not so,
    But let them go,
  And be you blithe and bonny,
Converting all your sounds of woe
  Into Hey nonny, nonny.

Sing no more ditties, sing no moe
  Of dumps so dull and heavy;
The fraud of men was ever so,
  Since summer first was leavy.
    Then sigh not so,
    But let them go,
  And be you blithe and bonny,
Converting all your sounds of woe
  Into Hey nonny, nonny.
           William Shakespeare [1564-1616]

A RENUNCIATION

IF women could be fair, and yet not fond,
Or that their love were firm, not fickle still,
I would not marvel that they make men bond
By service long to purchase their good will;
But when I see how frail those creatures are,
I muse that men forget themselves so far.

To mark the choice they make, and how they change,
How oft from Phœbus they do flee to Pan;
Unsettled still, like haggards wild they range,
These gentle birds that fly from man to man;
Who would not scorn and shake them from the fist,
And let them fly, fair fools, which way they list?

Yet for disport we fawn and flatter both,
To pass the time when nothing else can please,
And train them to our lure with subtle oath,
Till, weary of their wiles, ourselves we ease;
And then we say when we their fancy try,
To play with fools, O what a fool was I!

Edward Vere [1550–1604]

A SONG

Ye happy swains, whose hearts are free
    From Love's imperial chain,
Take warning, and be taught by me,
    To avoid the enchanting pain;
Fatal the wolves to trembling flocks,
    Fierce winds to blossoms prove,
To careless seamen, hidden rocks,
    To human quiet, love.

Fly the fair sex, if bliss you prize;
    The snake's beneath the flower:
Who ever gazed on beauteous eyes,
    That tasted quiet more?
How faithless is the lovers' joy!
    How constant is their care
The kind with falsehood to destroy,
    The cruel, with despair.

George Etherege [1635?–1691]

TO HIS FORSAKEN MISTRESS

I do confess thou'rt smooth and fair,
    And I might have gone near to love thee,
Had I not found the slightest prayer
    That lips could speak, had power to move thee:

But I can let thee now alone
As worthy to be loved by none.

I do confess thou'rt sweet; yet find
    Thee such an unthrift of thy sweets,
Thy favors are but like the wind
    That kisseth everything it meets:
And since thou canst with more than one,
Thou'rt worthy to be kissed by none.

The morning rose that untouched stands
    Armed with her briers, how sweet her smell!
But plucked and strained through ruder hands,
    Her sweets no longer with her dwell:
But scent and beauty both are gone,
And leaves fall from her, one by one.

Such fate ere long will thee betide
    When thou hast handled been awhile,
With sere flowers to be thrown aside;
    And I shall sigh, while some will smile,
To see thy love to every one
Hath brought thee to be loved by none.

                    Robert Ayton [1570–1638]

TO AN INCONSTANT

I LOVED thee once; I'll love no more,—
    Thine be the grief as is the blame;
Thou art not what thou wast before,
    What reason I should be the same?
        He that can love unloved again,
        Hath better store of love than brain:
    God send me love my debts to pay,
    While unthrifts fool their love away!

Nothing could have my love o'erthrown,
    If thou hadst still continued mine;
Yea, if thou hadst remained thy own,
    I might perchance have yet been thine.

But thou thy freedom didst recall,
   That it thou might elsewhere enthrall:
And then how could I but disdain
A captive's captive to remain?

When new desires had conquered thee,
   And changed the object of thy will,
It had been lethargy in me,
   Not constancy, to love thee still.
      Yea, it had been a sin to go
      And prostitute affection so,
   Since we are taught no prayers to say
To such as must to others pray.

Yet do thou glory in thy choice,
   Thy choice of his good fortune boast;
I'll neither grieve nor yet rejoice,
   To see him gain what I have lost:
      The height of my disdain shall be,
      To laugh at him, to blush for thee;
   To love thee still, but go no more
A-begging at a beggar's door.

                    Robert Ayton [1570–1638]

ADVICE TO A GIRL

NEVER love unless you can
Bear with all the faults of man!
Men sometimes will jealous be,
Though but little cause they see,
And hang the head, as discontent,
And speak what straight they will repent.

Men, that but one Saint adore,
Make a show of love to more;
Beauty must be scorned in none,
Though but truly served in one:
For what is courtship but disguise?
True hearts may have dissembling eyes.

Men, when their affairs require,
Must awhile themselves retire;
Sometimes hunt, and sometimes hawk,
And not ever sit and talk:—
If these and such-like you can bear,
Then like, and love, and never fear!

Thomas Campion [? —1619]

SONG

THAT WOMEN ARE BUT MEN'S SHADOWS

From "The Forest"

FOLLOW a shadow, it still flies you;
  Seem to fly it, it will pursue:
So court a mistress, she denies you;
  Let her alone, she will court you.
    Say, are not women truly, then,
    Styled but the shadows of us men?

At morn and even, shades are longest;
  At noon they are or short or none:
So men at weakest, they are strongest,
  But grant us perfect, they're not known.
    Say, are not women truly then,
    Styled but the shadows of us men?

Ben Jonson [1573?—1637]

TRUE BEAUTY

MAY I find a woman fair
And her mind as clear as air!
If her beauty go alone,
'Tis to me as if 'twere none.

May I find a woman rich,
And not of too high a pitch!
If that pride should cause disdain,
Tell me, Lover, where's thy gain?

May I find a woman wise,
And her falsehood not disguise!
Hath she wit as she hath will,
Double-armed she is to ill.

May I find a woman kind,
And not wavering like the wind!
How should I call that love mine
When 'tis his, and his, and thine?

May I find a woman true!
There is beauty's fairest hue:
There is beauty, love, and wit.
Happy he can compass it!

         Francis Beaumont [1584–1616]

THE INDIFFERENT

NEVER more will I protest
To love a woman but in jest:
For as they cannot be true,
So to give each man his due,
    When the wooing fit is past,
    Their affection cannot last.

Therefore if I chance to meet
With a mistress fair and sweet,
She my service shall obtain,
Loving her for love again:
    Thus much liberty I crave
    Not to be a constant slave.

But when we have tried each other,
If she better like another,
Let her quickly change for me;
Then to change am I as free.
    He or she that loves too long
    Sell their freedom for a song.

         Francis Beaumont [1584–1616]

THE LOVER'S RESOLUTION

SHALL I, wasting in despair,
Die because a woman's fair?
Or make pale my cheeks with care
'Cause another's rosy are?
Be she fairer than the day,
Or the flowery meads in May,
  If she think not well of me,
    What care I how fair she be?

Shall my silly heart be pined
'Cause I see a woman kind?
Or a well disposèd nature
Joinèd with a lovely feature?
Be she meeker, kinder, than
Turtle-dove or pelican,
  If she be not so to me,
    What care I how kind she be?

Shall a woman's virtues move
Me to perish for her love?
Or her well-deservings known
Make me quite forget my own?
Be she with that goodness blest
Which may merit name of Best,
  If she be not such to me,
    What care I how good she be?

'Cause her fortune seems too high,
Shall I play the fool and die?
She that bears a noble mind,
If not outward helps she find,
Thinks what with them he would do
That without them dares her woo;
  And unless that mind I see,
    What care I how great she be?

Great, or good, or kind, or fair,
I will ne'er the more despair·

If she love me, this believe,
I will die ere she shall grieve;
If she slight me when I woo,
I can scorn and let her go;
    For if she be not for me,
    What care I for whom she be?

George Wither [1588–1667]

HIS FURTHER RESOLUTION

SHALL I (like a hermit) dwell
On a rock or in a cell;
Calling home the smallest part
That is missing of my heart,
To bestow it where I may
Meet a rival every day?
    If she undervalue me,
    What care I how fair she be!

Were her tresses angel-gold;
If a stranger may be bold,
Unrebuked, and unafraid,
To convert them to a braid;
And, with little more ado,
Work them into bracelets, too!
    If the mine be grown so free,
    What care I how rich it be!

Were her hands as rich a prize
As her hair or precious eyes;
If she lay them out to take
Kisses for good manners' sake!
And let every lover slip
From her hand unto her lip!
    If she seem not chaste to me,
    What care I how chaste she be!

No! She must be perfect snow
In effect as well as show!
Warming but as snowballs do:

Not like fire by burning, too!
But when she by change hath got
To her heart a second lot;
   Then if others share with me,
   Farewell her! whate'er she be!

Unknown

SONG

From " Britannia's Pastorals "

SHALL I tell you whom I love?
   Hearken then awhile to me;
And if such a woman move
   As I now shall versify,
Be assured 'tis she or none,
That I love, and love alone.

Nature did her so much right
   As she scorns the help of art;
In as many virtues dight
   As e'er yet embraced a heart:
So much good so truly tried,
Some for less were deified.

Wit she hath, without desire
   To make known how much she hath;
And her anger flames no higher
   Than may fitly sweeten wrath.
Full of pity as may be,
Though perhaps not so to me.

Reason masters every sense,
   And her virtues grace her birth;
Lovely as all excellence,
   Modest in her most of mirth,
Likelihood enough to prove
Only worth could kindle love.

Such she is: and if you know
   Such a one as I have sung;
Be she brown, or fair, or so
   That she be but somewhat young;

Be assured 'tis she, or none,
That I love, and love alone.
William Browne '1591–1643?]

TO DIANEME

Sweet, be not proud of those two eyes,
Which, star-like, sparkle in their skies;
Nor be you proud that you can see
All hearts your captives, yours yet free;
Be you not proud of that rich hair,
Which wantons with the love-sick air;
Whenas that ruby which you wear,
Sunk from the tip of your soft ear,
Will last to be a precious stone
When all your world of beauty's gone.
Robert Herrick [1591–1674]

INGRATEFUL BEAUTY THREATENED

Know, Celia, since thou art so proud,
'Twas I that gave thee thy renown.
Thou hadst in the forgotten crowd
Of common beauties lived unknown,
Had not my verse extolled thy name,
And with it imped the wings of Fame.

That killing power is none of thine;
I gave it to thy voice and eyes;
Thy sweets, thy graces, all are mine;
Thou art my star, shin'st in my skies;
Then dart not from thy borrowed sphere
Lightning on him that fixed thee there.

Tempt me with such affrights no more,
Lest what I made I uncreate;
Let fools thy mystic form adore,
I know thee in thy mortal state.
Wise poets, that wrapped Truth in tales,
Knew her themselves through all her veils.
Thomas Carew [1598?–1639?]

DISDAIN RETURNED

HE that loves a rosy cheek,
   Or a coral lip admires,
Or from star-like eyes doth seek
   Fuel to maintain his fires:
As old Time makes these decay,
So his flames must waste away.

But a smooth and steadfast mind,
   Gentle thoughts, and calm desires,
Hearts with equal love combined,
   Kindle never-dying fires:—
Where these are not, I despise
Lovely cheeks, or lips, or eyes.

No tears, Celia, now shall win
   My resolved heart to return;
I have searched thy soul within,
   And find naught but pride and scorn;
I have learned thy arts, and now
Can disdain as much as thou.

Some power, in my revenge, convey
That love to her I cast away.
           Thomas Carew [1598?–1639?]

"LOVE WHO WILL, FOR I'LL LOVE NONE"

LOVE who will, for I'll love none,
   There's fools enough beside me:
Yet if each woman have not one,
   Come to me where I hide me,
And if she can the place attain,
For once I'll be her fool again.

It is an easy place to find,
   And women sure should know it;
Yet thither serves not every wind,
   Nor many men can show it:

It is the storehouse, where doth lie
All woman's truth and constancy.

If the journey be so long,
   No woman will adventer;
But dreading her weak vessel's wrong,
   The voyage will not enter:
Then may she sigh and lie alone,
In love with all, yet loved of none.
               William Browne [1591–1643]

VALERIUS ON WOMEN

SHE that denies me I would have;
      Who craves me I despise:
Venus hath power to rule mine heart,
      But not to please mine eyes.

Temptations offered I still scorn;
      Denied, I cling them still;
I'll neither glut mine appetite,
      Nor seek to starve my will.

Diana, double-clothed, offends;
      So Venus, naked quite:
The last begets a surfeit, and
      The other no delight.

That crafty girl shall please me best,
      That no, for yea, can say;
And every wanton willing kiss
      Can season with a nay.
               Thomas Heywood [? –1650?]

DISPRAISE OF LOVE, AND LOVERS' FOLLIES

IF love be life, I long to die,
   Live they that list for me;
And he that gains the most thereby,
   A fool at least shall be.

But he that feels the sorest fits,
'Scapes with no less than loss of wits.
　　Unhappy life they gain,
　　Which love do entertain.

In day by feignèd looks they live,
　　By lying dreams in night;
Each frown a deadly wound doth give,
　　Each smile a false delight.
If 't hap their lady pleasant seem,
It is for others' love they deem:
　　If void she seem of joy,
　　Disdain doth make her coy.

Such is the peace that lovers find,
　　Such is the life they lead,
Blown here and there with every wind,
　　Like flowers in the mead;
Now war, now peace, now war again,
Desire, despair, delight, disdain:
　　Though dead in midst of life,
　　In peace, and yet at strife.

Francis Davison [fl. 1602]

THE CONSTANT LOVER

OUT upon it, I have loved
　　Three whole days together!
And am like to love three more,
　　If it prove fair weather.

Time shall moult away his wings,
　　Ere he shall discover
In the whole wide world again
　　Such a constant lover.

But the spite on't is, no praise
　　Is due at all to me:
Love with me had made no stays,
　　Had it any been but she.

Had it any been but she,
    And that very face,
There had been at least ere this
    A dozen in her place.

John Suckling [1609–1642]

SONG

From "Aglaura"

WHY so pale and wan, fond lover?
    Prithee, why so pale?
Will, when looking well can't move her,
    Looking ill prevail?
    Prithee, why so pale?

Why so dull and mute, young sinner?
    Prithee, why so mute?
Will, when speaking well can't win her,
    Saying nothing do't?
    Prithee, why so mute?

Quit, quit, for shame, this will not move:
    This cannot take her.
If of herself she will not love,
    Nothing can make her:
    The devil take her!

John Suckling [1609–1642]

WISHES TO HIS SUPPOSED MISTRESS

WHOE'ER she be,
That not impossible She
That shall command my heart and me:

Where'er she lie,
Locked up from mortal eye
In shady leaves of destiny:

Till that ripe birth
Of studied Fate stand forth,
And teach her fair steps tread our earth:

Till that divine
Idea take a shrine
Of crystal flesh, through which to shine:

Meet you her, my Wishes,
Bespeak her to my blisses,
And be ye called my absent kisses.

I wish her Beauty
That owes not all its duty
To gaudy tire, or glistering shoe-tie:

Something more than
Taffeta or tissue can,
Or rampant feather, or rich fan.

More than the spoil
Of shop, or silkworm's toil,
Or a bought blush, or a set smile.

A Face that's best
By its own beauty dressed,
And can alone commend the rest

A Face, made up
Out of no other shop
Than what Nature's white hand sets ope.

A Cheek, where youth
And blood, with pen of truth,
Write what the reader sweetly ru'th.

A Cheek, where grows
More than a morning rose,
Which to no box its being owes.

Lips, where all day
A lover's kiss may play,
Yet carry nothing thence away.

Looks, that oppress
Their richest tires, but dress
And clothe their simplest nakedness.

Eyes, that displace
The neighbor diamond, and outface
That sunshine by their own sweet grace.

Tresses, that wear
Jewels but to declare
How much themselves more precious are:

Whose native ray
Can tame the wanton day
Of gems that in their bright shades play.

Each ruby there,
Or pearl that dare appear,
Be its own blush, be its own tear.

A well-tamed Heart,
For whose more noble smart
Love may be long choosing a dart.

Eyes, that bestow
Full quivers on Love's bow,
Yet pay less arrows than they owe.

Smiles, that can warm
The blood, yet teach a charm,
That chastity shall take no harm.

Blushes, that bin
The burnish of no sin,
Nor flames of aught too hot within.

Joys, that confess
Virtue their mistress,
And have no other head to dress.

Fears, fond and slight
As the coy bride's, when night,
First does the longing lover right.

Days that need borrow
No part of their good-morrow
From a fore-spent night of sorrow.

Days that, in spite
Of darkness, by the light
Of a clear mind, are day all night.

Nights, sweet as they,
Made short by lovers' play,
Yet long by the absence of the day.

Life, that dares send
A challenge to his end,
And when it comes, say, "Welcome, friend!"

Sydneian showers
Of sweet discourse, whose powers
Can crown old Winter's head with flowers.

Soft silken hours,
Open suns, shady bowers;
'Bove all, nothing within that lowers.

Whate'er delight
Can make Day's forehead bright,
Or give down to the wings of Night.

In her whole frame
Have Nature all the name;
Art and Ornament, the shame!

Her flattery,
Picture and Poesy:
Her counsel her own virtue be.

I wish her store
Of worth may leave her poor
Of wishes; and I wish—no more.

Now, if Time knows
That Her, whose radiant brows
Weave them a garland of my vows;

Her, whose just bays
My future hopes can raise,
A trophy to her present praise;

Her, that dares be
What these lines wish to see;
I seek no further, it is She.

'Tis She, and here,
Lo! I unclothe and clear
My Wishes' cloudy character.

May She enjoy it
Whose merit dare apply it,
But modesty dares still deny it!

Such worth as this is
Shall fix my flying Wishes,
And determine them to kisses.

Let her full glory,
My fancies, fly before ye;
Be ye my fictions—but her Story!

Richard Crashaw [1613?–1649]

SONG

From "Abdelazer"

LOVE in fantastic triumph sate
　　Whilst bleeding hearts around him flowed,
For whom fresh pains he did create
　　And strange tyrannic power he showed:
From thy bright eyes he took his fires,
　　Which round about in sport he hurled;
But 'twas from mine he took desires
　　Enough t' undo the amorous world.

From me he took his sighs and tears,
  From thee his pride and cruelty;
From me his languishments and fears,
  And every killing dart from thee.
Thus thou and I the god have armed
  And set him up a deity;
But my poor heart alone is harmed,
  Whilst thine the victor is, and free!

Aphra Behn [1640–1689]

LES AMOURS

SHE that I pursue, still flies me;
  Her that follows me, I fly;
She that I still court, denies me;
  Her that courts me, I deny;
Thus in one web we're subtly wove,
And yet we mutiny in love.

She that can save me, must not do it;
  She that cannot, fain would do;
Her love is bound, yet I still woo it;
  Hers by love is bound in woe:
Yet how can I of love complain,
Since I have love for love again?

This is thy work, imperious Child,
  Thine's this labyrinth of love,
That thus hast our desires beguiled,
  Nor seest how thine arrows rove.
Then, prithee, to compose this stir,
Make her love me, or me love her.

But, if irrevocable are
  Those keen shafts that wound us so,
Let me prevail with thee thus far,
  That thou once more take thy bow;
Wound her hard heart, and by my troth,
I'll be content to take them both.

Charles Cotton [1630–1687]

RIVALS

Of all the torments, all the cares,
  With which our lives are cursed;
Of all the plagues a lover bears,
  Sure rivals are the worst!
By partners in each other kind
  Afflictions easier grow;
In love alone we hate to find
  Companions of our woe.

Sylvia, for all the pangs you see
  Are laboring in my breast,
I beg not you would favor me,
  Would you but slight the rest!
How great soe'er your rigors are,
  With them alone I'll cope;
I can endure my own despair,
  But not another's hope.

William Walsh [1663–1708]

"I LATELY VOWED, BUT 'TWAS IN HASTE"

I lately vowed, but 'twas in haste,
  That I no more would court
The joys which seem when they are past
  As dull as they are short.

I oft to hate my mistress swear,
  But soon my weakness find:
I make my oaths when she's severe,
  But break them when she's kind.

John Oldmixon [1673–1742]

THE TOUCH-STONE

A fool and knave with different views
  For Julia's hand apply;
The knave to mend his fortune sues,
  The fool to please his eye.

Ask you how Julia will behave,
   Depend on't for a rule,
If she's a fool she'll wed the knave—
   If she's a knave, the fool.
               Samuel Bishop [1731-1795]

AIR

From " The Duenna "

I NE'ER could any luster see
In eyes that would not look on me;
I ne'er saw nectar on a lip,
But where my own did hope to sip.
Has the maid who seeks my heart
Cheeks of rose, untouched by art?
I will own the color true
When yielding blushes aid their hue.

Is her hand so soft and pure?
I must press it, to be sure;
Nor can I be certain then,
Till it, grateful, press again.
Must I, with attentive eye,
Watch her heaving bosom sigh?
I will do so, when I see
That heaving bosom sigh for me.
      Richard Brinsley Sheridan [1751-1816]

"I TOOK A HANSOM ON TO-DAY"

I TOOK a hansom on to-day,
   For a round I used to know—
That I used to take for a woman's sake
   In a fever of to-and-fro.

There were the landmarks one and all—
   What did they stand to show?
Street and square and river were there—
   Where was the ancient woe?

Never a hint of a challenging hope
    Nor a hope laid sick and low,
But a longing dead as its kindred sped
    A thousand years ago!
                William Ernest Henley [1849–1903]

DA CAPO

SHORT and sweet, and we've come to the end of it—
    Our poor little love lying cold.
Shall no sonnet, then, ever be penned of it?
    Nor the joys and pains of it told?
How fair was its face in the morning,
    How close its caresses at noon,
How its evening grew chill without warning,
            Unpleasantly soon!

I can't say just how we began it—
    In a blush, or a smile, or a sigh;
Fate took but an instant to plan it;
    It needs but a moment to die.
Yet—remember that first conversation,
    When the flowers you had dropped at your feet
I restored.   The familiar quotation
            Was—"Sweets to the sweet."

Oh, their delicate perfume has haunted
    My senses a whole season through.
If there *was* one soft charm that you wanted
    The violets lent it to you.
I whispered you, life was but lonely:
    A cue which you graciously took;
And your eyes learned a look for me only—
            A very nice look.

And sometimes your hand would touch *my* hand,
    With a sweetly particular touch;
You said many things in a sigh, and
    Made a look express wondrously much.
We smiled for the mere sake of smiling,
    And laughed for no reason but fun;
Irrational joys; but beguiling—
            And all that is done!

We were idle, and played for a moment
   At a game that now neither will press:
I cared not to find out what "No" meant;
   Nor your lips to grow yielding with "Yes."
Love is done with and dead; if there lingers
   A faint and indefinite ghost,
It is laid with this kiss on your fingers—
      A jest at the most.

'Tis a commonplace, stale situation,
   Now the curtain comes down from above
On the end of our little flirtation—
   A travesty romance; for Love,
If he climbed in disguise to your lattice,
   Fell dead of the first kisses' pain:
But one thing is left us now; that is—
      Begin it again.

Henry Cuyler Bunner [1855–1896]

SONG AGAINST WOMEN

WHY should I sing of women
   And the softness of night,
When the dawn is loud with battle
   And the day's teeth bite,
And there's a sword to lay my hand to
   And a man's fight?

Why should I sing of women? . . .
   There's life in the sun,
And red adventure calling
   Where the roads run,
And cheery brews at the tavern
   When the day's done.

I've sung of a hundred women
   In a hundred lands:
But all their love is nothing
   But drifting sands.
I'm sick of their tears and kisses
   And their pale hands.

I've sung of a hundred women
   And their bought lips;
But out on the clean horizon
   I can hear the whips
Of the white waves lashing the bulwarks
   Of great, strong ships:

And the trails that run to the westward
   Are shot with fire,
And the winds hurl from the headland
   With ancient ire;
And all my body itches
   With an old desire.

So I'll deal no more in women
   And the softness of night,
But I'll follow the red adventure
   And the wind's flight;
And I'll sing of the sea and of battle
   And of men's might.

Willard Huntington Wright [1888–1939]

SONG OF THYRSIS

THE turtle on yon withered bough,
That lately mourned her murdered mate,
Has found another comrade now—
Such changes all await!
Again her drooping plume is drest,
Again she's willing to be blest
And takes her lover to her nest.

If nature has decreed it so
With all above, and all below,
Let us like them forget our woe,
   And not be killed with sorrow.
If I should quit your arms to-night
And chance to die before 'twas light,
I would advise you—and you might—
   Love again to-morrow.

Philip Freneau [1752–1832]

THE TEST

I HELD her hand, the pledge of bliss,
  Her hand that trembled and withdrew;
She bent her head before my kiss . . .
  My heart was sure that hers was true.
Now I have told her I must part,
  She shakes my hand, she bids adieu,
Nor shuns the kiss. Alas, my heart!
  Hers never was the heart for you.
                    Walter Savage Landor [1775-1864]

"THE FAULT IS NOT MINE"

THE fault is not mine if I love you too much,
  I loved you too little too long,
Such ever your graces, your tenderness such,
  And the music the heart gave the tongue.

A time is now coming when Love must be gone,
  Though he never abandoned me yet.
Acknowledge our friendship, our passion disown,
  Our follies (ah can you?) forget.
                    Walter Savage Landor [1775-1864]

THE SNAKE

My love and I, the other day,
Within a myrtle arbor lay,
When near us, from a rosy bed,
A little Snake put forth its head.

"See," said the maid, with laughing eyes—
"Yonder the fatal emblem lies!
Who could expect such hidden harm
Beneath the rose's velvet charm?"

Never did moral thought occur
  In more unlucky hour than this;
For oh! I just was leading her
  To talk of love and think of bliss.

I rose to kill the snake, but she
In pity prayed it might not be.
"No," said the girl—and many a spark
   Flashed from her eyelid as she said it—
"Under the rose, or in the dark,
   One might, perhaps, have cause to dread it;
But when its wicked eyes appear,
   And when we know for what they wink so,
One must be very simple, dear,
   To let it sting one—don't you think so?"
                         Thomas Moore [1779–1852]

"WHEN I LOVED YOU"

WHEN I loved you, I can't but allow
   I had many an exquisite minute;
But the scorn that I feel for you now
   Hath even more luxury in it!

Thus, whether we're on or we're off,
   Some witchery seems to await you;
To love you is pleasant enough,
   And oh! 'tis delicious to hate you!
                         Thomas Moore [1779–1852]

A TEMPLE TO FRIENDSHIP

"A TEMPLE to Friendship," said Laura, enchanted,
   "I'll build in this garden,—the thought is divine!"
Her temple was built, and she now only wanted
   An image of Friendship to place on the shrine.
She flew to a sculptor, who set down before her
   A Friendship, the fairest his art could invent;
But so cold and so dull, that the youthful adorer
   Saw plainly this was not the idol she meant.

"O never," she cried, "could I think of enshrining
   An image whose looks are so joyless and dim:—
But yon little god, upon roses reclining,
   We'll make, if you please, sir, a Friendship of him."

So the bargain was struck. With the little god laden
  She joyfully flew to her shrine in the grove:
"Farewell," said the sculptor, "you're not the first maiden
  Who came but for Friendship and took away Love!"

Thomas Moore [1779–1852]

THE GLOVE AND THE LIONS

KING FRANCIS was a hearty king, and loved a royal sport,
And one day, as his lions fought, sat looking on the court.
The nobles filled the benches, and the ladies in their pride,
And 'mongst them sat the Count de Lorge, with one for
    whom he sighed:
And truly 'twas a gallant thing to see that crowning show,
Valor and love, and a king above, and the royal beasts below.

Ramped and roared the lions, with horrid laughing jaws;
They bit, they glared, gave blows like beams, a wind went
    with their paws;
With wallowing might and stifled roar they rolled on one
    another,
Till all the pit with sand and mane was in a thunderous
    smother;
The bloody foam above the bars came whisking through the
    air;
Said Francis then, "Faith, gentlemen, we're better here than
    there."

De Lorge's love o'erheard the King, a beauteous lively dame,
With smiling lips and sharp bright eyes, which always
    seemed the same;
She thought, " The Count, my lover, is brave as brave can
    be;
He surely would do wondrous things to show his love of me;
King, ladies, lovers, all look on; the occasion is divine;
I'll drop my glove to prove his love; great glory will be
    mine."

She dropped her glove, to prove his love, then looked at him
    and smiled;
He bowed, and in a moment leaped among the lions wild;

The leap was quick, return was quick, he has regained his
    place,
Then threw the glove, but not with love, right in the lady's
    face.
"By Heaven," said Francis, "rightly done!" and he rose
    from where he sat;
"No love," quoth he, "but vanity, sets love a task like that."
                Leigh Hunt [1784–1859]

TO WOMAN

Woman! experience might have told me
That all must love thee who behold thee;
Surely experience might have taught
Thy firmest promises are naught;
But, placed in all thy charms before me,
All I forget, but to adore thee.
Oh, Memory! thou choicest blessing,
When joined with hope, when still possessing;
But how much cursed by every lover,
When hope is fled, and passion's over!
Woman, that fair and fond deceiver,
How prompt are striplings to believe her!
How throbs the pulse when first we view
The eye that rolls in glossy blue,
Or sparkles black, or mildly throws
A beam from under hazel brows!
How quick we credit every oath,
And hear her plight the willing troth!
Fondly we hope 'twill last for aye,
When, lo! she changes in a day.
This record will forever stand,
"Woman, thy vows are traced in sand."
              George Gordon Byron [1788–1824]

LOVE'S SPITE

You take a town you cannot keep;
    And, forced in turn to fly,
O'er ruins you have made shall leap
    Your deadliest enemy!

Her love is yours—and be it so—
But can you keep it? No, no, no!

Upon her brow we gazed with awe,
    And loved, and wished to love, in vain
But when the snow begins to thaw
    We shun with scorn the miry plain.
Women with grace may yield: but she
Appeared some Virgin Deity.

Bright was her soul as Dian's crest
    Whitening on Vesta's fane its sheen:
Cold looked she as the waveless breast
    Of some stone Dian at thirteen.
Men loved: but hope they deemed to be
A sweet Impossibility!

> *Aubrey Thomas De Vere* [1814–1902]

LADY CLARA VERE DE VERE

LADY Clara Vere de Vere,
    Of me you shall not win renown:
You thought to break a country heart
    For pastime, ere you went to town.
At me you smiled, but unbeguiled
    I saw the snare, and I retired:
The daughter of a hundred earls,
    You are not one to be desired.

Lady Clara Vere de Vere,
    I know you proud to bear your name,
Your pride is yet no mate for mine,
    Too proud to care from whence I came.
Nor would I break for your sweet sake
    A heart that dotes on truer charms.
A simple maiden in her flower
    Is worth a hundred coats-of-arms.

Lady Clara Vere de Vere,
    Some meeker pupil you must find,
For, were you queen of all that is,
    I could not stoop to such a mind.

You sought to prove how I could love,
  And my disdain is my reply.
The lion on your old stone gates
  Is not more cold to you than I.

Lady Clara Vere de Vere,
  You put strange memories in my head.
Not thrice your branching limes have blown
  Since I beheld young Laurence dead.
O, your sweet eyes, your low replies!
  A great enchantress you may be;
But there was that across his throat
  Which you had hardly cared to see.

Lady Clara Vere de Vere,
  When thus he met his mother's view,
She had the passions of her kind,
  She spake some certain truths of you.
Indeed I heard one bitter word
  That scarce is fit for you to hear;
Her manners had not that repose
  Which stamps the caste of Vere de Vere.

Lady Clara Vere de Vere,
  There stands a specter in your hall;
The guilt of blood is at your door;
  You changed a wholesome heart to gall.
You held your course without remorse,
  To make him trust his modest worth,
And, last, you fixed a vacant stare,
  And slew him with your noble birth.

Trust me, Clara Vere de Vere,
  From yon blue heavens above us bent,
The gardener Adam and his wife
  Smile at the claims of long descent.
Howe'er it be, it seems to me,
  'Tis only noble to be good.
Kind hearts are more than coronets,
  And simple faith than Norman blood.

I know you, Clara Vere de Vere;
　You pine among your halls and towers:
The languid light of your proud eyes
　Is wearied of the rolling hours.
In glowing health, with boundless wealth,
　But sickening of a vague disease,
You know so ill to deal with time,
　You needs must play such pranks as these.

Clara, Clara Vere de Vere,
　If time be heavy on your hands,
Are there no beggars at your gate,
　Nor any poor about your lands?
O, teach the orphan-boy to read,
　Or teach the orphan-girl to sew,
Pray Heaven for a human heart,
　And let the foolish yeoman go.

Alfred Tennyson [1809–1892]

SHADOWS

THEY seemed, to those who saw them meet,
　The casual friends of every day;
Her smile was undisturbed and sweet,
　His courtesy was free and gay.

But yet if one the other's name
　In some unguarded moment heard,
The heart you thought so calm and tame
　Would struggle like a captured bird:

And letters of mere formal phrase
　Were blistered with repeated tears,—
And this was not the work of days,
　But had gone on for years and years!

Alas, that love was not too strong
　For maiden shame and manly pride!
Alas, that they delayed so long
　The goal of mutual bliss beside!

Yet what no chance could then reveal,
  And neither would be first to own,
Let fate and courage now conceal,
  When truth could bring remorse alone.
                    Richard Monckton Milnes [1809-1885]

SORROWS OF WERTHER

WERTHER had a love for Charlotte
  Such as words could never utter;
Would you know how first he met her?
  She was cutting bread and butter.

Charlotte was a married lady,
  And a moral man was Werther,
And, for all the wealth of Indies,
  Would do nothing for to hurt her.

So he sighed and pined and ogled,
  And his passion boiled and bubbled,
Till he blew his silly brains out,
  And no more was by it troubled.

Charlotte, having seen his body
  Borne before her on a shutter,
Like a well-conducted person,
  Went on cutting bread and butter.
                    William Makepeace Thackeray [1811-1863]

THE AGE OF WISDOM

Ho, pretty page, with the dimpled chin,
  That never has known the barber's shear,
All your wish is woman to win,
This is the way that boys begin,—
  Wait till you come to Forty Year.

Curly gold locks cover foolish brains,
  Billing and cooing is all your cheer;
Sighing, and singing of midnight strains,
Under Bonnybell's window-panes,—
  Wait till you come to Forty Year.

Forty times over let Michaelmas pass,
    Grizzling hair the brain does clear—
Then you know a boy is an ass,
Then you know the worth of a lass,
    Once you have come to Forty Year.

Pledge me round; I bid ye declare,
    All good fellows whose beards are gray,
Did not the fairest of the fair
Common grow and wearisome ere
    Ever a month was passed away?

The reddest lips that ever have kissed,
    The brightest eyes that ever have shone,
May pray and whisper, and we not list,
Or look away and never be missed,
    Ere yet ever a month is gone.

Gillian's dead, God rest her bier,
    How I loved her twenty years syne!
Marian's married, but I sit here,
Alone and merry at Forty Year,
    Dipping my nose in the Gascon wine.
                William Makepeace Thackeray [1811–1863]

ANDREA DEL SARTO

CALLED "THE FAULTLESS PAINTER"

BUT do not let us quarrel any more,
No, my Lucrezia; bear with me for once:
Sit down and all shall happen as you wish.
You turn your face, but does it bring your heart?
I'll work then for your friend's friend, never fear,
Treat his own subject after his own way,
Fix his own time, accept too his own price,
And shut the money into this small hand
When next it takes mine.   Will it? tenderly?
Oh, I'll content him,—but to-morrow, Love!
I often am much wearier than you think,
This evening more than usual, and it seems

As if—forgive now—should you let me sit
Here by the window, with your hand in mine,
And look a half-hour forth on Fiesole,
Both of one mind, as married people use,
Quietly, quietly the evening through,
I might get up to-morrow to my work
Cheerful and fresh as ever.   Let us try.
To-morrow how you shall be glad for this!
Your soft hand is a woman of itself,
And mine the man's bared breast she curls inside.
Don't count the time lost neither; you must serve
For each of the five pictures we require;
It saves a model.   So! keep looking so—
My serpentining beauty, rounds on rounds!
—How could you ever prick those perfect ears,
Even to put the pearl there! oh, so sweet—
My face, my moon, my everybody's moon,
Which everybody looks on and calls his,
And, I suppose, is looked on by in turn,
While she looks—no one's: very dear, no less.
You smile? why, there's my picture ready made,
There's what we painters call our harmony!
A common grayness silvers everything,—
All in a twilight, you and I alike
—You, at the point of your first pride in me
 (That's gone you know),—but I, at every point;
My youth, my hope, my art, being all toned down
To yonder sober pleasant Fiesole.
There's the bell clinking from the chapel-top;
That length of convent wall across the way
Holds the trees safer, huddled more inside;
The last monk leaves the garden; days decrease,
And autumn grows, autumn in everything.
Eh? the whole seems to fall into a shape
As if I saw alike my work and self
And all that I was born to be and do,
A twilight-piece.   Love, we are in God's hand.
How strange now looks the life he makes us lead;
So free we seem, so fettered fast we are!
I feel he laid the fetter; let it lie!

This chamber for example--turn your head--
All that's behind us! You don't understand
Nor care to understand about my art,
But you can hear at least when people speak:
And that cartoon, the second from the door
—It is the thing, Love! so such thing should be—
Behold Madonna!—I am bold to say.
I can do with my pencil what I know,
What I see, what at bottom of my heart
I wish for, if I ever wish so deep—
Do easily, too—when I say, perfectly,
I do not boast, perhaps: yourself are judge,
Who listened to the Legate's talk last week,
And just as much they used to say in France.
At any rate 'tis easy, all of it!
No sketches first, no studies, that's long past:
I do what many dream of all their lives,
—Dream? strive to do, and agonize to do,
And fail in doing. I could count twenty such
On twice your fingers, and not leave this town,
Who strive—you don't know how the others strive
To paint a little thing like that you smeared
Carelessly passing with your robes afloat,—
Yet do much less, so much less, Someone says,
(I know his name, no matter)—so much less!
Well, less is more, Lucrezia: I am judged.
There burns a truer light of God in them,
In their vexed beating stuffed and stopped-up brain,
Heart, or whate'er else, than goes on to prompt
This low-pulsed forthright craftsman's hand of mine.
Their works drop groundward, but themselves, I know,
Reach many a time a heaven that's shut to me,
Enter and take their place there sure enough,
Though they come back and cannot tell the world.
My works are nearer heaven, but I sit here.
The sudden blood of these men! at a word—
Praise them, it boils, or blame them, it boils too.
I, painting from myself and to myself,
Know what I do, am unmoved by men's blame
Or their praise either.   Somebody remarks

Morello's outline there is wrongly traced,
His hue mistaken; what of that? or else,
Rightly traced and well ordered; what of that?
Speak as they please, what does the mountain care?
Ah, but a man's reach should exceed his grasp,
Or what's a heaven for?   All is silver-gray,
Placid and perfect with my art; the worse!
I know both what I want and what might gain;
And yet how profitless to know, to sigh
" Had I been two, another and myself,
Our head would have o'erlooked the world!" No doubt.
Yonder's a work now, of that famous youth
The Urbinate who died five years ago.
('Tis copied, George Vasari sent it me.)
Well, I can fancy how he did it all,
Pouring his soul, with kings and popes to see,
Reaching, that heaven might so replenish him,
Above and through his art—for it gives way;
That arm is wrongly put—and there again—
A fault to pardon in the drawing's lines,
Its body, so to speak: its soul is right,
He means right,—that, a child may understand.
Still, what an arm! and I could alter it:
But all the play, the insight and the stretch—
Out of me, out of me!   And wherefore out?
Had you enjoined them on me, given me soul,
We might have risen to Rafael, I and you!
Nay, Love, you did give all I asked, I think—
More than I merit, yes, by many times.
But had you—oh, with the same perfect brow,
And perfect eyes, and more than perfect mouth,
And the low voice my soul hears, as a bird
The fowler's pipe, and follows to the snare—
Had you, with these the same, but brought a mind!
Some women do so.   Had the mouth there urged,
"God and the glory! never care for gain.
The present by the future, what is that?
Live for fame, side by side with Agnolo!
Rafael is waiting: up to God, all three!"
I might have done it for you.   So it seems:

Perhaps not. All is as God overrules.
Beside, incentives come from the soul's self;
The rest avail not. Why do I need you?
What wife had Rafael, or has Agnolo?
In this world, who can do a thing, will not;
And who would do it, cannot, I perceive:
Yet the will's somewhat—somewhat, too, the power—
And thus we half-men struggle. At the end,
God I conclude, compensates, punishes.
'Tis safer for me, if the award be strict,
That I am something underrated here,
Poor this long while, despised, to speak the truth.
I dared not, do you know, leave home all day,
For fear of chancing on the Paris lords.
The best is when they pass and look aside;
But they speak sometimes; I must bear it all.
Well may they speak! That Francis, that first time,
And that long festal year at Fontainebleau!
I surely then could sometimes leave the ground,
Put on the glory, Rafael's daily wear,
In that humane great monarch's golden look,—
One finger in his beard or twisted curl
Over his mouth's good mark that made the smile,
One arm about my shoulder, round my neck,
The jingle of his gold chain in my ear,
I painting proudly with his breath on me,
All his court round him, seeing with his eyes,
Such frank French eyes, and such a fire of souls
Profuse, my hand kept plying by those hearts,—
And, best of all, this, this, this face beyond,
This in the background, waiting on my work,
To crown the issue with a last reward!
A good time, was it not, my kingly days?
And had you not grown restless . . . but I know—
'Tis done and past; 'twas right, my instinct said;
Too live the life grew, golden and not gray,
And I'm the weak-eyed bat no sun should tempt
Out of the grange whose four walls make his world.
How could it end in any other way?
You called me, and I came home to your heart.

The triumph was,—to reach and stay there; since
I reached it ere the triumph, what is lost?
Let my hands frame your face in your hair's gold,
You beautiful Lucrezia that are mine!
"Rafael did this, Andrea painted that;
The Roman's is the better when you pray,
But still the other's Virgin was his wife"—
Men will excuse me.   I am glad to judge
Both pictures in your presence; clearer grows
My better fortune, I resolve to think.
For do you know, Lucrezia, as God lives,
Said one day Agnolo, his very self
To Rafael . . . I have known it all these years . . .
(When the young man was flaming out his thoughts
Upon a palace-wall for Rome to see,
Too lifted up in heart because of it)
"Friend, there's a certain sorry little scrub
Goes up and down our Florence, none cares how,
Who, were he set to plan and execute
As you are, pricked on by your popes and kings,
Would bring the sweat into that brow of yours!"
To Rafael's!   And indeed the arm is wrong.
I hardly dare . . . yet, only you to see,
Give the chalk here—quick, thus the line should go!
Ay, but the soul! he's Rafael! rub it out!
Still, all I care for, if he spoke the truth,
(What he? why, who but Michel Agnolo?
Do you forget already words like those?)
If really there was such a chance, so lost,—
Is, whether you're—not grateful—but more pleased.
Well, let me think so.   And you smile indeed!
This hour has been an hour!   Another smile?
If you would sit thus by me every night
I should work better, do you comprehend?
I mean that I should earn more, give you more.
See, it is settled dusk now; there's a star;
Morello's gone, the watch-lights show the wall,
The cue-owls speak the name we call them by.
Come from the window, love,—come in, at last,
Inside the melancholy little house

We built to be so gay with.   God is just.
King Francis may forgive me: oft at nights
When I look up from painting, eyes tired out,
The walls become illumined, brick from brick
Distinct, instead of mortar, fierce bright gold,
That gold of his I did cement them with!
Let us but love each other.   Must you go?
That Cousin here again? he waits outside?
Must see you—you, and not with me?   Those loans?
More gaming debts to pay? you smiled for that?
Well, let smiles buy me! have you more to spend?
While hand and eye and something of a heart
Are left me, work's my ware, and what's it worth?
I'll pay my fancy.   Only let me sit
The gray remainder of the evening out,
Idle, you call it, and muse perfectly
How I could paint, were I but back in France,
One picture, just one more,—the Virgin's face,
Not yours this time!   I want you at my side
To hear them—that is Michel Agnolo—
Judge all I do and tell you of its worth.
Will you?   To-morrow, satisfy your friend.
I take the subjects for his corridor,
Finish the portrait out of hand—there, there,
And throw him in another thing or two
If he demurs; the whole should prove enough
To pay for this same Cousin's freak.   Beside,
What's better and what's all I care about,
Get you the thirteen scudi for the ruff!
Love, does that please you?   Ah, but what does he,
The Cousin! what does he to please you more?

I am grown peaceful as old age to-night.
I regret little, I would change still less.
Since there my past life lies, why alter it?
The very wrong to Francis!—it is true
I took his coin, was tempted and complied,
And built this house and sinned, and all is said.
My father and my mother died of want.
Well, had I riches of my own? you see

How one gets rich!　Let each one bear his lot.
They were born poor, lived poor, and poor they died:
And I have labored somewhat in my time
And not been paid profusely.　Some good son
Paint my two hundred pictures—let him try!
No doubt, there's something strikes a balance.　Yes,
You loved me quite enough, it seems to-night.
This must suffice me here.　What would one have?
In heaven, perhaps, new chances, one more chance—
Four great walls in the New Jerusalem,
Meted on each side by the angel's reed,
For Leonard, Rafael, Agnolo, and me
To cover,—the three first without a wife,
While I have mine!　So—still they overcome
Because there's still Lucrezia,—as I choose.

Again the Cousin's whistle!　Go, my love.

Robert Browning [1812–1889]

MY LAST DUCHESS

FERRARA

THAT'S my last Duchess painted on the wall,
Looking as if she were alive.　I call
That piece a wonder, now: Frà Pandolf's hands
Worked busily a day, and there she stands.
Will't please you sit and look at her?　I said
"Frà Pandolf" by design, for never read
Strangers like you that pictured countenance,
The depth and passion of its earnest glance,
But to myself they turned (since none puts by
The curtain I have drawn for you, but I)
And seemed as they would ask me, if they durst,
How such a glance came there; so, not the first
Are you to turn and ask thus.　Sir, 'twas not
Her husband's presence only, called that spot
Of joy into the Duchess' cheek: perhaps
Frà Pandolf chanced to say, "Her mantle laps
Over my lady's wrist too much," or "Paint

Must never hope to reproduce the faint
Half-flush that dies along her throat": such stuff
Was courtesy, she thought, and cause enough
For calling up that spot of joy. She had
A heart—how shall I say?—too soon made glad,
Too easily impressed: she liked whate'er
She looked on, and her looks went everywhere.
Sir, 'twas all one! My favor at her breast,
The dropping of the daylight in the West,
The bough of cherries some officious fool
Broke in the orchard for her, the white mule
She rode with round the terrace—all and each
Would draw from her alike the approving speech,
Or blush, at least. She thanked men,—good! but thanked
Somehow—I know not how—as if she ranked
My gift of a nine-hundred-years-old name
With anybody's gift. Who'd stoop to blame
This sort of trifling? Even had you skill
In speech—(which I have not)—to make your will
Quite clear to such an one, and say, "Just this
Or that in you disgusts me; here you miss,
Or there exceed the mark"—and if she let
Herself be lessoned so, nor plainly set
Her wits to yours, forsooth, and made excuse,
—E'en then would be some stooping; and I choose
Never to stoop. Oh sir, she smiled, no doubt,
Whene'er I passed her; but who passed without
Much the same smile? This grew; I gave commands;
Then all smiles stopped together. There she stands
As if alive. Will't please you rise? We'll meet
The company below, then. I repeat,
The Count your master's known munificence
Is ample warrant that no just pretense
Of mine for dowry will be disallowed;
Though his fair daughter's self, as I avowed
At starting, is my object. Nay, we'll go
Together down, sir. Notice Neptune, though,
Taming a sea-horse, thought a rarity,
Which Claus of Innsbruck cast in bronze for me!

Robert Browning [1812–1889]

ADAM, LILITH, AND EVE

ONE day, it thundered and lightened.
Two women, fairly frightened,
Sank to their knees, transformed, transfixed,
At the feet of the man who sat betwixt;
And "Mercy!" cried each—"if I tell the truth
Of a passage in my youth!"

Said This: "Do you mind the morning
I met your love with scorning?
As the worst of the venom left my lips,
I thought, 'If, despite this lie, he strips
The mask from my soul with a kiss—I crawl
His slave,—soul, body, and all!'"

Said That: "We stood to be married;
The priest, or some one, tarried;
'If Paradise-door prove locked?' smiled you.
I thought, as I nodded, smiling too,
'Did one, that's away, arrive—nor late
Nor soon should unlock Hell's gate!'"

It ceased to lighten and thunder.
Up started both in wonder,
Looked around and saw that the sky was clear,
Then laughed "Confess you believed us, Dear!"
"I saw through the joke!" the man replied
They re-seated themselves beside.

Robert Browning [1812–1889]

THE LOST MISTRESS

ALL's over, then: does truth sound bitter
    As one at first believes?
Hark, 'tis the sparrows' good-night twitter
    About your cottage eaves!

And the leaf-buds on the vine are woolly,
    I noticed that, to-day;
One day more bursts them open fully
    —You know the red turns gray.

To-morrow we meet the same then, dearest?
  May I take your hand in mine?
Mere friends are we,—well, friends the merest
  Keep much that I resign:

For each glance of the eye so bright and black,
  Though I keep with heart's endeavor,—
Your voice, when you wish the snowdrops back,
  Though it stay in my soul forever!—

Yet I will but say what mere friends say,
  Or only a thought stronger;
I will hold your hand but as long as all may,
  Or so very little longer!

Robert Browning [1812–1889]

FRIEND AND LOVER

WHEN Psyche's friend becomes her lover,
  How sweetly these conditions blend!
But, oh, what anguish to discover
  Her lover has become—her friend!

Mary Ainge de Vere [1844–1920]

LOST LOVE

WHO wins his Love shall lose her,
  Who loses her shall gain,
For still the spirit wooes her,
  A soul without a stain;
And Memory still pursues her
  With longings not in vain!

He loses her who gains her,
  Who watches day by day
The dust of time that stains her,
  The griefs that leave her gray,
The flesh that yet enchains her
  Whose grace hath passed away!

Oh, happier he who gains not
  The Love some seem to gain:
The joy that custom stains not
  Shall still with him remain,

The loveliness that wanes not,
  The Love that ne'er can wane.

In dreams she grows not older
  The lands of Dream among,
Though all the world wax colder,
  Though all the songs be sung,
In dreams doth he behold her
  Still fair and kind and young.

Andrew Lang [1844–1912]

VOBISCUM EST IOPE

WHEN thou must home to shades of underground,
And there arrived, a new admirèd guest,
The beauteous spirits do engirt thee round,
White Iope, blithe Helen, and the rest,
To hear the stories of thy finished love
From that smooth tongue whose music hell can move;

Then wilt thou speak of banqueting delights,
Of masques and revels which sweet youth did make,
Of tourneys and great challenges of knights,
And all these triumphs for thy beauty's sake:
When thou hast told these honors done to thee,
Then tell, O tell, how thou didst murder me!

Thomas Campion [? –1619]

FOUR WINDS

"FOUR winds blowing through the sky,
You have seen poor maidens die,
Tell me then what I shall do
That my lover may be true."
Said the wind from out the south,
"Lay no kiss upon his mouth,"
And the wind from out the west,
"Wound the heart within his breast,"
And the wind from out the east,
"Send him empty from the feast,"
And the wind from out the north,

"In the tempest thrust him forth;
    When thou art more cruel than he,
    Then will Love be kind to thee."

Sara Teasdale [1884–1933]

TO MANON

AS TO HIS CHOICE OF HER

IF I had chosen thee, thou shouldst have been
A virgin proud, untamed, immaculate,
Chaste as the morning star, a saint, a queen,
Scarred by no wars, no violence of hate.
Thou shouldst have been of soul commensurate
With thy fair body, brave and virtuous
And kind and just; and if of poor estate,
At least an honest woman for my house.
I would have had thee come of honored blood
And honorable nurture.   Thou shouldst bear
Sons to my pride and daughters to my heart,
And men should hold thee happy, wise, and good.
Lo, thou art none of this, but only fair,
Yet must I love thee, dear, and as thou art.

Wilfrid Scawen Blunt [1840–1922]

CROWNED

YOU came to me bearing bright roses,
    Red like the wine of your heart;
You twisted them into a garland
    To set me aside from the mart.
Red roses to crown me your lover,
    And I walked aureoled and apart.

Enslaved and encircled, I bore it,
    Proud token of my gift to you.
The petals waned paler, and shriveled,
    And dropped; and the thorns started through.
Bitter thorns to proclaim me your lover,
    A diadem woven with rue.

Amy Lowell [1874–1925]

HEBE

I SAW the twinkle of white feet,
    I saw the flash of robes descending;
Before her ran an influence fleet,
    That bowed my heart like barley bending.

As, in bare fields, the searching bees
    Pilot to blooms beyond our finding,
It led me on, by sweet degrees
    Joy's simple honey-cells unbinding.

Those Graces were that seemed grim Fates;
    With nearer love the sky leaned o'er me;
The long-sought Secret's golden gates
    On musical hinges swung before me.

I saw the brimmed bowl in her grasp
    Thrilling with godhood; like a lover
I sprang the proffered life to clasp;—
    The beaker fell; the luck was over.

The Earth has drunk the vintage up;
    What boots it patch the goblet's splinters?
Can Summer fill the icy cup
    Whose treacherous crystal is but Winter's?

O spendthrift haste! await the Gods;
    Their nectar crowns the lips of Patience;
Haste scatters on unthankful sods
    The immortal gift in vain libations.

Coy Hebe flies from those that woo,
    And shuns the hands would seize upon her;
Follow thy life, and she will sue
    To pour for thee the cup of honor.

               James Russell Lowell [1819–1891]

"JUSTINE, YOU LOVE ME NOT!"

" Helas ! vous ne m'aimez pas."—PIRON

I KNOW, Justine, you speak me fair
 As often as we meet;
And 'tis à luxury, I swear,
 To hear a voice so sweet;
And yet it does not please me quite,
 The civil way you've got;
For me you're something too polite—
 Justine, you love me not!

I know Justine, you never scold
 At aught that I may do:
If I am passionate or cold,
 'Tis all the same to you.
"A charming temper," say the men,
 "To smooth a husband's lot":
I wish 'twere ruffled now and then—
 Justine you love me not!

I know, Justine, you wear a smile
 As beaming as the sun;
But who supposes all the while
 It shines for only one?
Though azure skies are fair to see,
 A transient cloudy spot
In yours would promise more to me—
 Justine, you love me not!

I know, Justine, you make my name
 Your eulogistic theme,
And say—if any chance to blame—
 You hold me in esteem.
Such words, for all their kindly scope,
 Delight me not a jot;
Just as you would have praised the Pope—
 Justine, you love me not!

I know, Justine—for I have heard
  What friendly voices tell—
You do not blush to say the word,
  "You like me passing well";
And thus the fatal sound I hear
  That seals my lonely lot:
There's nothing now to hope or fear—
  Justine, you love me not!

John Godfrey Saxe [1816–1887]

SNOWDROP

WHEN, full of warm and eager love,
  I clasp you in my fond embrace,
You gently push me back and say,
  "Take care, my dear, you'll spoil my lace."

You kiss me just as you would kiss
  Some woman friend you chanced to see;
You call me "dearest."—All love's forms
  Are yours, not its reality.

Oh, Annie! cry, and storm, and rave!
  Do anything with passion in it!
Hate me an hour, and then turn round
  And love me truly, just one minute.

William Wetmore Story [1819–1895]

WHEN THE SULTAN GOES TO ISPAHAN

When the Sultan Shah-Zaman
Goes to the city Ispahan,
Even before he gets so far
As the place where the clustered palm-trees are,
At the last of the thirty palace-gates,
The flower of the harem, Rose-in-Bloom,
Orders a feast in his favorite room—
Glittering squares of colored ice,

Sweetened with syrop, tinctured with spice,
Creams, and cordials, and sugared dates,
Syrian apples, Othmanee quinces,
Limes, and citrons, and apricots,
And wines that are known to Eastern princes;
And Nubian slaves, with smoking pots
Of spicèd meats and costliest fish
And all that the curious palate could wish,
Pass in and out of the cedarn doors;
Scattered over mosaic floors
Are anemones, myrtles, and violets,
And a musical fountain throws its jets
Of a hundred colors into the air.
The dusk Sultana loosens her hair,
And stains with the henna-plant the tips
Of her pointed nails, and bites her lips
Till they bloom again; but, alas, *that* rose
Not for the Sultan buds and blows,
Not for the Sultan Shah-Zaman
When he goes to the city Ispahan.

Then at a wave of her sunny hand
The dancing-girls of Samarcand
Glide in like shapes from fairy-land,
Making a sudden mist in air
Of fleecy veils and floating hair
And white arms lifted. Orient blood
Runs in their veins, shines in their eyes.
And there, in this Eastern Paradise,
Filled with the breath of sandal-wood,
And Khoten musk, and aloes and myrrh,
Sits Rose-in-Bloom on a silk divan,
Sipping the wines of Astrakhan;
And her Arab lover sits with her.
That's when the Sultan Shah-Zaman
Goes to the city Ispahan.

Now, when I see an extra light,
Flaming, flickering on the night
From my neighbor's casement opposite,

I know as well as I know to pray,
I know as well as a tongue can say,
That the innocent Sultan Shah-Zaman
Has gone to the city Ispahan.

Thomas Bailey Aldrich [1837–1907]

THE SHADOW DANCE

She sees her image in the glass,—
  How fair a thing to gaze upon!
  She lingers while the moments run,
With happy thoughts that come and pass,

Like winds across the meadow grass
  When the young June is just begun:
She sees her image in the glass,—
  How fair a thing to gaze upon!

What wealth of gold the skies amass!
  How glad are all things 'neath the sun!
  How true the love her love has won!
She recks not that this hour will pass,—
She sees her image in the glass.

Louise Chandler Moulton [1835–1908]

"ALONG THE FIELD AS WE CAME BY"

Along the field as we came by
A year ago, my love and I,
The aspen over stile and stone
Was talking to itself alone.
"Oh, who are these that kiss and pass?
A country lover and his lass;
Two lovers looking to be wed;
And time shall put them both to bed,
But she shall lie with earth above,
And he beside another love."

And sure enough beneath the tree
There walks another love with me,
And overhead the aspen heaves
Its rainy-sounding silver leaves;
And I spell nothing in their stir,
But now perhaps they speak to her,
And plain for her to understand
They talk about a time at hand
When I shall sleep with clover clad,
And she beside another lad.

Alfred Edward Housman [1859–1936]

"WHEN I WAS ONE–AND–TWENTY"

WHEN I was one-and-twenty
  I heard a wise man say,
"Give crowns and pounds and guineas
  But not your heart away;
Give pearls away and rubies
  But keep your fancy free."
But I was one-and-twenty,
  No use to talk to me.

When I was one-and-twenty
  I heard him say again,
"The heart out of the bosom
  Was never given in vain;
'Tis paid with sighs a plenty
  And sold for endless rue."
And I am two-and-twenty,
  And oh, 'tis true, 'tis true.

Alfred Edward Housman [1859–1936]

"GRIEVE NOT, LADIES"

OH, grieve not, Ladies, if at night
  Ye wake to feel your beauty going;
It was a web of frail delight,
  Inconstant as an April snowing.

In other eyes, in other lands,
    In deep fair pools new beauty lingers;
But like spent water in your hands
    It runs from your reluctant fingers.

You shall not keep the singing lark
    That owes to earlier skies its duty.
Weep not to hear along the dark
    The sound of your departing beauty.

The fine and anguished ear of night
    Is tuned to hear the smallest sorrow:
Oh, wait until the morning light!
    It may not seem so gone to-morrow.

But honey-pale and rosy-red!
    Brief lights that make a little shining!
Beautiful looks about us shed—
    They leave us to the old repining.

Think not the watchful, dim despair
    Has come to you the first, sweet-hearted!
For oh, the gold in Helen's hair!
    And how she cried when that departed!

Perhaps that one that took the most,
    The swiftest borrower, wildest spender,
May count, as we would not, the cost—
    And grow more true to us and tender.

Happy are we if in his eyes
    We see no shadow of forgetting.
Nay—if our star sinks in those skies
    We shall not wholly see its setting.

Then let us laugh as do the brooks,
    That such immortal youth is ours,
If memory keeps for them our looks
    As fresh as are the springtime flowers.

So grieve not, Ladies, if at night
  Ye wake to feel the cold December!
Rather recall the early light,
   And in your loved one's arms, remember.

Anna Hempstead Branch [18 –1937]

SUBURB

Dull and hard the low wind creaks
Among the rustling pampas plumes.
Drearily the year consumes
Its fifty-two insipid weeks.

Most of the gray-green meadow land
Was sold in parsimonious lots;
The dingy houses stand
Pressed by some stout contractor's hand
Tightly together in their plots.

Through builded banks the sullen river
Gropes, where its houses crouch and shiver.
Over the bridge the tyrant train
Shrieks, and emerges on the plain.

In all the better gardens you may pass,
(Product of many careful Saturdays),
Large red geraniums and tall pampas grass
Adorn the plots and mark the gravelled ways.

Sometimes in the background may be seen
A private summer-house in white or green.
Here on warm nights the daughter brings
Her vacillating clerk,
To talk of small exciting things
And touch his fingers through the dark.

He, in the uncomfortable breach
Between her trilling laughters,
Promises, in halting speech,
Hopeless immense Hereafters.

She trembles like the pampas plumes.
Her strained lips haggle.   He assumes
The serious quest. . . .

Now as the train is whistling past
He takes her in his arms at last.

It's done.   She blushes at his side
Across the lawn—a bride, a bride.

. . . .

The stout contractor will design,
The lazy laborers will prepare,
Another villa on the line;
In the little garden-square
Pampas grass will rustle there.

Harold Monro [1879–1932]

THE BETROTHED

*"You must choose between me and your cigar"—Breach of Promise
case, circa 1885.*

OPEN the old cigar-box, get me a Cuba stout,
For things are running crossways, and Maggie and I are out.

We quarreled about Havanas—we fought o'er a good
    cheroot—
And I know she is exacting, and she says I am a brute.

Open the old cigar-box—let me consider a space,
In the soft blue veil of the vapor, musing on Maggie's face.

Maggie is pretty to look at—Maggie's a loving lass,
But the prettiest cheeks must wrinkle, the truest of loves
    must pass.

There's peace in a Laranaga, there's calm in a Henry Clay,
But the best cigar in an hour is finished and thrown away—

Thrown away for another as perfect and ripe and brown—
But I never could throw away Maggie for fear o' the talk o'
    the town!

Maggie, my wife at fifty—gray and dour and old—
With never another Maggie to purchase for love or gold.

And the light of Days that have Been, the dark of the Days
that Are,
And Love's torch stinking and stale, like the butt of a dead
cigar—

The butt of a dead cigar you are bound to keep in your
pocket—
With never a new one to light, though it's charred and black
to the socket.

Open the old cigar-box—let me consider awhile;
Here is a mild Manilla—there is a wifely smile.

Which is the better portion—bondage bought with a ring,
Or a harem of dusky beauties, fifty tied in a string?

Counselors cunning and silent—comforters true and tried,
And never a one of the fifty to sneer at a rival bride.

Thought in the early morning, solace in time of woes,
Peace in the hush of the twilight, balm ere my eyelids close.

This will the fifty give me, asking naught in return,
With only a Suttee's passion—to do their duty and burn.

This will the fifty give me. When they are spent and dead,
Five times other fifties shall be my servants instead.

The furrows of far-off Java, the isles of the Spanish Main,
When they hear that my harem is empty, will send me my
brides again.

I will take no heed to their raiment, nor food for their mouths
withal,
So long as the gulls are nesting, so long as the showers fall.

I will scent 'em with best vanilla, with tea will I temper their
    hides,
And the Moor and the Mormon shall envy who read of the
    tale of my brides.

For Maggie has written a letter to give me my choice between
The wee little whimpering Love and the great god Nick
    o' Teen.

And I have been servant of Love for barely a twelvemonth
    clear,
But I have been Priest of Partagas a matter of seven year;

And the gloom of my bachelor days is flecked with the cheery
    light
Of stumps that I burned to Friendship, and Pleasure, and
    Work, and Fight.

And I turn my eyes to the future that Maggie and I must
    prove,
But the only light on the marshes is the Will-o'-the-Wisp of
    Love.

Will it see me safe through my journey, or leave me bogged
    in the mire?
Since a puff of tobacco can cloud it, shall I follow the fitful
    fire?

Open the old cigar-box—let me consider anew—
Old friends, and who is Maggie, that I should abandon *you?*

A million surplus Maggies are willing to bear the yoke;
And a woman is only a woman, but a good cigar is a Smoke.

Light me another Cuba—I hold to my first-sworn vows,
If Maggie will have no rival, I'll have no Maggie for spouse!
                                    Rudyard Kipling [1865–1936]

LOVE'S SADNESS

"THE NIGHT HAS A THOUSAND EYES"

THE night has a thousand eyes,
  And the day but one;
Yet the light of the bright world dies
  With the dying sun.

The mind has a thousand eyes,
  And the heart but one;
Yet the light of a whole life dies
  When love is done.

Francis William Bourdillon [1852–1921]

"I SAW MY LADY WEEP"

I SAW my Lady weep,
And Sorrow proud to be advancèd so
In those fair eyes where all perfections keep.
  Her face was full of Woe,
But such a Woe (believe me) as wins more hearts
Than Mirth can do with her enticing parts.

  Sorrow was there made fair,
And Passion, wise; Tears, a delightful thing;
Silence, beyond all speech, a wisdom rare:
  She made her sighs to sing,
And all things with so sweet a sadness move
As made my heart at once both grieve and love.

  O fairer than aught else
The world can show, leave off in time to grieve!
Enough, enough: your joyful look excels:
  Tears kill the heart, believe.
O strive not to be excellent in Woe,
Which only breeds your beauty's overthrow.

Unknown

863

LOVE'S YOUNG DREAM

OH! the days are gone, when Beauty bright
    My heart's chain wove;
When my dream of life, from morn till night,
    Was love, still love.
     New hope may bloom,
     And days may come,
    Of milder, calmer beam,
But there's nothing half so sweet in life
    As love's young dream;
No, there's nothing half so sweet in life
    As love's young dream.

Though the bard to purer fame may soar,
    When wild youth's past;
Though he win the wise, who frowned before,
    To smile at last;
     He'll never meet
     A joy so sweet,
    In all his noon of fame,
As when first he sung to woman's ear
    His soul-felt flame,
And, at every close, she blushed to hear
    The one loved name.

No,—that hallowed form is ne'er forgot
    Which first love traced;
Still it lingering haunts the greenest spot
    On memory's waste.
     'Twas odor fled
     As soon as shed;
    'Twas morning's wingèd dream;
'Twas a light that ne'er can shine again
    On life's dull stream;
Oh! 'twas light that ne'er can shine again
    On life's dull stream.

Thomas Moore [1779–1852]

"NOT OURS THE VOWS"

NOT ours the vows of such as plight
  Their troth in sunny weather,
While leaves are green, and skies are bright,
  To walk on flowers together.

But we have loved as those who tread
  The thorny path of sorrow,
With clouds above, and cause to dread
  Yet deeper gloom to-morrow.

That thorny path, those stormy skies,
  Have drawn our spirits nearer;
And rendered us, by sorrow's ties,
  Each to the other dearer.

Love, born in hours of joy and mirth,
  With mirth and joy may perish;
That to which darker hours gave birth
  Still more and more we cherish.

It looks beyond the clouds of time,
  And through death's shadowy portal;
Made by adversity sublime,
  By faith and hope immortal.

Bernard Barton [1784–1849]

THE GRAVE OF LOVE

I DUG, beneath the cypress shade,
  What well might seem an elfin's grave;
And every pledge in earth I laid,
  That erst thy false affection gave.

I pressed them down the sod beneath;
  I placed one mossy stone above;
And twined the rose's fading wreath
  Around the sepulcher of love.

Frail as thy love, the flowers were dead
    Ere yet the evening sun was set:
But years shall see the cypress spread,
    Immutable as my regret.
          Thomas Love Peacock [1785–1866]

"WE'LL GO NO MORE A ROVING"

So, we'll go no more a roving
    So late into the night,
Though the heart be still as loving,
    And the moon be still as bright.

For the sword outwears its sheath,
    And the soul wears out the breast,
And the heart must pause to breathe,
    And Love itself have rest.

Though the night was made for loving,
    And the day returns too soon,
Yet we'll go no more a roving
    By the light of the moon.
          George Gordon Byron [1788–1824]

SONG

Sing the old song, amid the sounds dispersing
    That burden treasured in your hearts too long;
        Sing it, with voice low-breathed, but never name her:
She will not hear you, in her turrets nursing
    High thoughts, too high to mate with mortal song—
        Bend o'er her, gentle Heaven, but do not claim her!

In twilight caves, and secret lonelinesses,
    She shades the bloom of her unearthly days;
        And the soft winds alone have power to woo her:
Far off we catch the dark gleam of her tresses;
    And wild birds haunt the wood-walks where she strays,
        Intelligible music warbling to her.

That Spirit charged to follow and defend her,—
    He also, doubtless, suffers this love-pain;
        And she, perhaps, is sad, hearing his sighing:
    And yet that face is not so sad as tender;
        Like some sweet singer's, when her sweetest strain
        From the heaved heart is gradually dying!

Aubrey Thomas De Vere [1814–1902]

THE QUESTION

I DREAMED that, as I wandered by the way,
    Bare Winter suddenly was changed to Spring;
And gentle odors led my steps astray,
    Mixed with a sound of waters murmuring
Along a shelving bank of turf, which lay
    Under a copse, and hardly dared to fling
Its green arms round the bosom of the stream,
But kissed it and then fled, as thou mightest in dream.

There grew pied wind-flowers and violets;
    Daisies, those pearled Arcturi of the earth,
The constellated flower that never sets;
    Faint oxlips; tender bluebells, at whose birth
The sod scarce heaved; and that tall flower that wets—
    Like a child, half in tenderness and mirth—
Its mother's face with heaven-collected tears
When the low wind, its playmate's voice, it hears.

And in the warm hedge grew lush eglantine,
    Green cowbind and the moonlight-colored may,
And cherry-blossoms, and white cups whose wine
    Was the bright dew yet drained not by the day;
And wild roses, and ivy serpentine,
    With its dark buds and leaves wandering astray;
And flowers, azure, black, and streaked with gold,
Fairer than any wakened eyes behold.

And nearer to the river's trembling edge
    There grew broad flag-flowers, purple pranked with white,
And starry river-buds among the sedge,
    And floating water-lilies, broad and bright,

Which lit the oak that overhung the hedge
    With moonlight beams of their own watery light;
And bulrushes, and reeds of such deep green
As soothed the dazzled eye with sober sheen.

Methought that of these visionary flowers
    I made a nosegay, bound in such a way
That the same hues which in their natural bowers
    Were mingled or opposed, the like array
Kept these imprisoned children of the Hours
    Within my hand;—and then, elate and gay,
I hastened to the spot whence I had come,
That I might there present it—O! to whom?

Percy Bysshe Shelley [1792–1822]

THE WANDERER

LOVE comes back to his vacant dwelling,—
    The old, old Love that we knew of yore!
    We see him stand by the open door,
With his great eyes sad, and his bosom swelling.

He makes as though in our arms repelling,
    He fain would lie as he lay before;—
Love comes back to his vacant dwelling,—
    The old, old Love that we knew of yore!

Ah, who shall keep us from over-spelling
    That sweet forgotten, forbidden lore!
    E'en as we doubt in our hearts once more,
With a rush of tears to our eyelids welling,
Love comes back to his vacant dwelling.

Austin Dobson [1840–1921]

EGYPTIAN SERENADE

SING again the song you sung
When we were together young—
When there were but you and I
Underneath the summer sky.

Sing the song, and o'er and o'er
Though I know that nevermore
Will it seem the song you sung
When we were together young.

George William Curtis [1824–1892]

THE WATER LADY

ALAS, the moon should ever beam
To show what man should never see!
I saw a maiden on a stream,
And fair was she!

I stayed awhile, to see her throw
Her tresses back, that all beset
The fair horizon of her brow
With clouds of jet.

I stayed a little while to view
Her cheek, that wore, in place of red,
The bloom of water, tender blue,
Daintily spread.

I stayed to watch, a little space,
Her parted lips if she would sing;
The waters closed above her face
With many a ring.

And still I stayed a little more:
Alas, she never comes again!
I throw my flowers from the shore,
And watch in vain.

I know my life will fade away,
I know that I must vainly pine,
For I am made of mortal clay,
But she's divine!

Thomas Hood [1799–1845]

"TRIPPING DOWN THE FIELD-PATH"

TRIPPING down the field-path,
  Early in the morn,
There I met my own love
  'Midst the golden corn;
Autumn winds were blowing,
  As in frolic chase,
All her silken ringlets
  Backward from her face;
Little time for speaking
  Had she, for the wind,
Bonnet, scarf, or ribbon,
  Ever swept behind.

Still some sweet improvement
  In her beauty shone;
Every graceful movement
  Won me,—one by one!
As the breath of Venus
  Seemed the breeze of morn,
Blowing thus between us,
  'Midst the golden corn.
Little time for wooing
  Had we, for the wind
Still kept on undoing
  What we sought to bind.

Oh! that autumn morning
  In my heart it beams,
Love's last look adorning
  With its dream of dreams:
Still, like waters flowing
  In the ocean shell,
Sounds of breezes blowing
  In my spirit dwell;
Still I see the field-path;—
  Would that I could see
Her whose graceful beauty
  Lost is now to me!

Charles Swain [1801–1874]

LOVE NOT

LOVE not, love not, ye hapless sons of clay!
  Hope's gayest wreaths are made of earthly flowers—
Things that are made to fade and fall away,
  When they have blossomed but a few short hours.
          Love not, love not!

Love not, love not! The thing you love may die—
  May perish from the gay and gladsome earth;
The silent stars, the blue and smiling sky,
  Beam on its grave as once upon its birth.
          Love not, love not!

Love not, love not! The thing you love may change,
  The rosy lip may cease to smile on you;
The kindly beaming eye grow cold and strange;
  The heart still warmly beat, yet not be true.
          Love not, love not!

Love not, love not! O warning vainly said
  In present years, as in the years gone by!
Love flings a halo round the dear one's head,
  Faultless, immortal—till they change or die!
          Love not, love not!
          Caroline Elizabeth Sarah Norton [1808–1877]

"A PLACE IN THY MEMORY"

A PLACE in thy memory, Dearest!
    Is all that I claim:
To pause and look back when thou hearest
    The sound of my name.
Another may woo thee, nearer;
    Another may win and wear:
I care not though he be dearer,
    If I am remembered there.

Remember me, not as a lover
    Whose hope was crossed,
Whose bosom can never recover
    The light it hath lost!

As the young bride remembers the mother
    She loves, though she never may see,
As a sister remembers a brother,
    O Dearest, remember me!

Could I be thy true lover, Dearest!
    Couldst thou smile on me,
I would be the fondest and nearest
    That ever loved thee:
But a cloud on my pathway is glooming
    That never must burst upon thine;
And heaven, that made thee all blooming,
    Ne'er made thee to wither on mine.

Remember me then! O remember
    My calm light love!
Though bleak as the blasts of November
    My life may prove.
That life will, though lonely, be sweet
    If its brightest enjoyment should be
A smile and kind word when we meet,
    And a place in thy memory.

                          Gerald Griffin [1803–1840]

INCLUSIONS

Oh, wilt thou have my hand, Dear, to lie along in thine?
As a little stone in a running stream, it seems to lie and pine.
Now drop the poor pale hand, Dear, unfit to plight with
    thine.

Oh, wilt thou have my cheek, Dear, drawn closer to thine
    own?
My cheek is white, my cheek is worn, by many a tear run
    down.
Now leave a little space, Dear, lest it should wet thine own.

Oh, must thou have my soul, Dear, commingled with thy
    soul?—

Red grows the cheek, and warm the hand; the part is in the
    whole;
Nor hands nor cheeks keep separate, when soul is joined to
    soul.

Elizabeth Barrett Browning [1806–1861]

MARIANA

Mariana in the moated grange.—MEASURE FOR MEASURE

WITH blackest moss the flower-plots
    Were thickly crusted, one and all:
The rusted nails fell from the knots
    That held the pear to the gable-wall.
The broken sheds looked sad and strange:
    Unlifted was the clinking latch;
    Weeded and worn the ancient thatch
Upon the lonely moated grange.
      She only said, "My life is dreary,
        He cometh not," she said;
      She said, "I am aweary, aweary,
        I would that I were dead!"

Her tears fell with the dews at even;
    Her tears fell ere the dews were dried;
She could not look on the sweet heaven,
    Either at morn or eventide.
After the flitting of the bats,
    When thickest dark did trance the sky,
    She drew her casement-curtain by,
And glanced athwart the glooming flats.
      She only said, "The night is dreary,
        He cometh not," she said;
      She said, "I am aweary, aweary,
        I would that I were dead!"

Upon the middle of the night,
    Waking she heard the night-fowl crow:
The cock sung out an hour ere light:
    From the dark fen the oxen's low

Came to her: without hope of change,
    In sleep she seemed to walk forlorn,
    Till cold winds woke the gray-eyed morn
About the lonely moated grange.
        She only said, "The day is dreary,
            He cometh not," she said;
        She said, "I am aweary, aweary,
            I would that I were dead!"

About a stone-cast from the wall
    A sluice with blackened waters slept,
And o'er it many, round and small,
    The clustered marish-mosses crept.
Hard by a poplar shook alway,
    All silver-green with gnarlèd bark:
    For leagues no other tree did mark
The level waste, the rounding gray.
        She only said, "My life is dreary,
            He cometh not," she said;
        She said, "I am aweary, aweary,
            I would that I were dead!"

And ever when the moon was low,
    And the shrill winds were up and away,
In the white curtain, to and fro,
    She saw the gusty shadow sway.
But when the moon was very low,
    And wild winds bound within their cell,
    The shadow of the poplar fell
Upon her bed, across her brow.
        She only said, "The night is dreary
            He cometh not," she said;
        She said, "I am aweary, aweary,
            I would that I were dead!"

All day within the dreamy house,
    The doors upon their hinges creaked;
The blue fly sung in the pane; the mouse
    Behind the moldering wainscot shrieked,

Or from the crevice peered about.
  Old faces glimmered through the doors,
  Old footsteps trod the upper floors,
Old voices called her from without.
    She only said, "My life is dreary,
      He cometh not," she said;
    She said, "I am aweary, aweary,
      I would that I were dead!"

The sparrow's chirrup on the roof,
  The slow clock ticking, and the sound
Which to the wooing wind aloof
  The poplar made, did all confound
Her sense; but most she loathed the hour
  When the thick-moted sunbeam lay
  Athwart the chambers, and the day
Was sloping toward his western bower.
    Then, said she, "I am very dreary,
      He will not come," she said;
    She wept, "I am aweary, aweary,
      O God, that I were dead!"
          Alfred Tennyson [1809–1892]

"ASK ME NO MORE"

From "The Princess"

ASK me no more: the moon may draw the sea;
  The cloud may stoop from heaven and take the shape,
  With fold to fold, of mountain or of cape;
But O too fond, when have I answered thee?
    Ask me no more.

Ask me no more: what answer should I give?
  I love not hollow cheek or faded eye:
  Yet, O my friend, I will not have thee die!
Ask me no more, lest I should bid thee live;
    Ask me no more.

Ask me no more: thy fate and mine are sealed;
I strove against the stream and all in vain;
Let the great river take me to the main.
No more, dear love, for at a touch I yield;
    Ask me no more.
                        Alfred Tennyson [1809–1892]

A WOMAN'S LAST WORD

LET's contend no more, Love,
    Strive nor weep:
All be as before, Love,
    —Only sleep!

What so wild as words are?
    I and thou
In debate, as birds are,
    Hawk on bough!

See the creature stalking
    While we speak!
Hush and hide the talking,
    Cheek on cheek!

What so false as truth is,
    False to thee?
Where the serpent's tooth is
    Shun the tree—

Where the apple reddens
    Never pry—
Lest we lose our Edens,
    Eve and I!

Be a god and hold me
    With a charm!
Be a man and fold me
    With thine arm!

Teach me, only teach, Love!
    As I ought
I will speak thy speech, Love,
    Think thy thought—

Meet, if thou require it,
    Both demands,
Laying flesh and spirit
    In thy hands.

That shall be to-morrow
    Not to-night:
I must bury sorrow
    Out of sight:

—Must a little weep, Love,
    (Foolish me!)
And so fall asleep, Love
    Loved by thee.

Robert Browning [1812–1889]

THE LAST RIDE TOGETHER

I SAID—Then, dearest, since 'tis so,
Since now at length my fate I know,
Since nothing all my love avails,
Since all, my life seemed meant for, fails,
    Since this was written and needs must be—
My whole heart rises up to bless
Your name in pride and thankfulness!
Take back the hope you gave,—I claim
Only a memory of the same,
—And this beside, if you will not blame;
    Your leave for one more last ride with me.

My mistress bent that brow of hers;
Those deep dark eyes where pride demurs
When pity would be softening through,
Fixed me a breathing-while or two

With life or death in the balance: right!
The blood replenished me again;
My last thought was at least not vain:
I and my mistress, side by side
Shall be together, breathe and ride,
So, one day more am I deified.
　　Who knows but the world may end to-night?

Hush! if you saw some western cloud
All billowy-bosomed, over-bowed
By many benedictions—sun's
And moon's and evening-star's at once—
　　And so, you, looking and loving best,
Conscious grew, your passion drew
Cloud, sunset, moonrise, star-shine too,
Down on you, near and yet more near,
Till flesh must fade for heaven was here!—
Thus leant she and lingered—joy and fear!
　　Thus lay she a moment on my breast.

Then we began to ride. My soul
Smoothed itself out, a long-cramped scroll
Freshening and fluttering in the wind.
Past hopes already lay behind.
　　What need to strive with a life awry?
Had I said that, had I done this,
So might I gain, so might I miss.
Might she have loved me? just as well
She might have hated, who can tell!
Where had I been now if the worst befell?
　　And here we are riding, she and I.

Fail I alone, in words and deeds?
Why, all men strive, and who succeeds?
We rode; it seemed my spirit flew,
Saw other regions, cities new,
　　As the world rushed by on either side.
I thought,—All labor, yet no less
Bear up beneath their unsuccess.

Look at the end of work, contrast
The petty done, the undone vast,
This present of theirs with the hopeful past!
    I hoped she would love me; here we ride.

What hand and brain went ever paired?
What heart alike conceived and dared?
What act proved all its thought had been?
What will but felt the fleshly screen?
    We ride and I see her bosom heave.
There's many a crown for who can reach.
Ten lines, a statesman's life in each!
The flag stuck on a heap of bones,
A soldier's doing! what atones?
They scratch his name on the Abbey-stones.
    My riding is better, by their leave.

What does it all mean, poet? Well,
Your brains beat into rhythm, you tell
What we felt only; you expressed
You hold things beautiful the best,
    And place them in rhyme so, side by side.
'Tis something, nay 'tis much: but then,
Have you yourself what's best for men?
Are you—poor, sick, old ere your time—
Nearer one whit your own sublime
Than we who never have turned a rhyme?
    Sing, riding's a joy! For me, I ride.

And you, great sculptor—so, you gave
A score of years to Art, her slave,
And that's your Venus, whence we turn
To yonder girl that fords the burn!
    You acquiesce, and shall I repine?
What, man of music, you grown gray
With notes and nothing else to say,
Is this your sole praise from a friend,
"Greatly his opera's strains intend,
But in music we know how fashions end!"
    I gave my youth: but we ride, in fine.

Who knows what's fit for us? Had fate
Proposed bliss here should sublimate
My being—had I signed the bond—
Still one must lead some life beyond,
   Have a bliss to die with, dim-descried.
This foot once planted on the goal,
This glory-garland round my soul,
Could I descry such? Try and test!
I sink back shuddering from the quest.
Earth being so good, would heaven seem best?
   Now, heaven and she are beyond this ride.

And yet—she has not spoke so long!
What if heaven be that, fair and strong
At life's best, with our eyes upturned
Whither life's flower is first discerned,
   We, fixed so, ever should so abide?
What if we still ride on, we two,
With life forever old yet new,
Changed not in kind but in degree,
The instant made eternity,—
And heaven just prove that I and she
   Ride, ride together, forever ride?

                     Robert Browning [1812–1889]

YOUTH AND ART

It once might have been, once only:
   We lodged in a street together,
You, a sparrow on the housetop lonely,
   I, a lone she-bird of his feather.

Your trade was with sticks and clay,
   You thumbed, thrust, patted, and polished,
Then laughed, "They will see some day
   Smith made, and Gibson demolished."

My business was song, song, song;
   I chirped, cheeped, trilled, and twittered,
"Kate Brown's on the boards ere long,
   And Grisi's existence embittered!"

I earned no more by a warble
  Than you by a sketch in plaster;
You wanted a piece of marble,
  I needed a music-master.

We studied hard in our styles,
  Chipped each at a crust like Hindoos,
For air, looked out on the tiles,
  For fun, watched each other's windows.

You lounged, like a boy of the South,
  Cap and blouse—nay, a bit of beard too;
Or you got it, rubbing your mouth
  With fingers the clay adhered to.

And I—soon managed to find
  Weak points in the flower-fence facing,
Was forced to put up a blind,
  And be safe in my corset-lacing.

No harm! It was not my fault
  If you never turned your eye's tail up,
As I shook upon E *in alt.*,
  Or ran the chromatic scale up:

For spring bade the sparrows pair,
  And the boys and girls gave guesses,
And stalls in our street looked rare
  With bulrush and water-cresses.

Why did not you pinch a flower
  In a pellet of clay and fling it?
Why did not I put a power
  Of thanks in a look, or sing it?

I did look, sharp as a lynx
  (And yet the memory rankles),
When models arrived, some minx
  Tripped up-stairs, she and her ankles.

But I think I gave you as good!
    "That foreign fellow,—who can know
How she pays, in a playful mood,
    For his tuning her that piano?"

Could you say so, and never say,
    "Suppose we join hands and fortunes,
And I fetch her from over the way,
    Her, piano, and long tunes and short tunes"?

No, no: you would not be rash,
    Nor I rasher and something over:
You've to settle yet Gibson's hash,
    And Grisi yet lives in clover.

But you meet the Prince at the Board,
    I'm queen myself at *bals-paré*,
I've married a rich old lord,
    And you're dubbed knight and an R. A.

Each life unfulfilled, you see;
    It hangs still, patchy and scrappy:
We have not sighed deep, laughed free,
    Starved, feasted, despaired,—been happy.

And nobody calls you a dunce,
    And people suppose me clever:
This could but have happened once,
    And we missed it, lost it forever.

                          Robert Browning [1812–1889]

TWO IN THE CAMPAGNA

I WONDER do you feel to-day
    As I have felt since, hand in hand,
We sat down on the grass, to stray
    In spirit better through the land,
This morn of Rome and May?

For me, I touched a thought, I know,
  Has tantalized me many times,
(Like turns of thread the spiders throw
  Mocking across our path) for rhymes
To catch at and let go.

Help me to hold it! First it left
  The yellowing fennel, run to seed
There, branching from the brickwork's cleft,
  Some old tomb's ruin: yonder weed
Took up the floating weft,

Where one small orange cup amassed
  Five beetles,—blind and green they grope
Among the honey-meal: and last,
  Everywhere on the grassy slope
I traced it. Hold it fast!

The champaign with its endless fleece
  Of feathery grasses everywhere!
Silence and passion, joy and peace,
  And everlasting wash of air—
Rome's ghost since her decease.

Such life here, through such lengths of hours
  Such miracles performed in play,
Such primal naked forms of flowers,
  Such letting Nature have her way
While Heaven looks from its towers!

How say you? Let us, O my dove,
  Let us be unashamed of soul,
As earth lies bare to heaven above!
  How is it under our control
To love or not to love?

I would that you were all to me,
  You that are just so much, no more.
Nor yours, nor mine,—nor slave nor free!
  Where does the fault lie? What the core
Of the wound, since wound must be?

I would I could adopt your will,
  See with your eyes, and set my heart
Beating by yours, and drink my fill
  At your soul's springs,—your part, my part
In life, for good and ill.

No. I yearn upward, touch you close,
  Then stand away. I kiss your cheek,
Catch your soul's warmth,—I pluck the rose
  And love it more than tongue can speak—
Then the good minute goes.

Already how am I so far
  Out of that minute? Must I go
Still like the thistle-ball, no bar,
  Onward, whenever light winds blow,
Fixed by no friendly star?

Just when I seemed about to learn!
  Where is the thread now? Off again!
The old trick! Only I discern—
  Infinite passion, and the pain
Of finite hearts that yearn.

                    Robert Browning [1812–1889]

ONE WAY OF LOVE

ALL June I bound the rose in sheaves.
Now, rose by rose, I strip the leaves
And strew them where Pauline may pass.
She will not turn aside? Alas!
Let them lie. Suppose they die?
The chance was they might take her eye.

How many a month I strove to suit
These stubborn fingers to the lute!
To-day I venture all I know.
She will not hear my music? So!
Break the string; fold music's wing:
Suppose Pauline had bade me sing!

My whole life long I learned to love.
This hour my utmost art I prove
And speak my passion—heaven or hell?
She will not give me heaven? 'Tis well!
Lose who may—I still can say,
Those who win heaven, blest are they!

Robert Browning [1812-1889]

"NEVER THE TIME AND THE PLACE"

NEVER the time and the place
    And the loved one all together!
This path—how soft to pace!
    This May—what magic weather!
Where is the loved one's face?
In a dream that loved one's face meets mine,
    But the house is narrow, the place is bleak
Where, outside, rain and wind combine
    With a furtive ear, if I strive to speak,
    With a hostile eye at my flushing cheek,
With a malice that marks each word, each sign!
O enemy sly and serpentine,
        Uncoil thee from the waking man!
            Do I hold the Past
            Thus firm and fast
        Yet doubt if the Future hold I can?
    This path so soft to pace shall lead
    Through the magic of May to herself indeed!
    Or narrow if needs the house must be,
    Outside are the storms and strangers: we—
    Oh, close, safe, warm sleep I and she,
    —I and she!

Robert Browning [1812-1889]

SONG

From " The Saint's Tragedy "

OH! that we two were Maying
Down the stream of the soft spring breeze;
Like children with violets playing
In the shade of the whispering trees.

Oh! that we two sat dreaming
On the sward of some sheep-trimmed down,
Watching the white mist steaming
Over river and mead and town.

Oh! that we two lay sleeping
In our nest in the churchyard sod,
With our limbs at rest on the quiet earth's breast,
And our souls at home with God!

Charles Kingsley [1819–1875]

FOR HE HAD GREAT POSSESSIONS

AH! marvel not if when I come to die
   And follow Death the way my fancies went
Year after fading year, the last mad sky
   Finds me impenitent;
For though my heart went doubting through the night,
   With many a backward glance at heaven's face,
Yet found I many treasures of delight
   Within this pleasant place.

I shall not grieve because the girls were fair
   And kinder than the world, nor shall I weep
Because with crying lips and clinging hair
   They stole away my sleep.
For lacking this I might not yet have known
   How high the heart could climb, or waking seen
The mountains bare their silver breasts of stone
   From their chaste robes of green.

Though it were all a sin, within the mirth
   And pain of life I found a song above
Our songs, in her who scattered on the earth
   Her glad largesse of love;
And though she held some dream that was not ours
   In some far place that was not for our feet,
Where blew across the gladder, madder flowers
   A wind more bitter-sweet.

Ah! who shall hearten when the music stops,
   For joy of silence? While they dreamed above

She showed me love upon the mountain tops
  And in the valleys, love.
And while the wise found heaven with their charts
  And lore of souls, she made an earth for me
More sweet than all, and from our beating hearts
  She called the pulsing sea.

So marvel not if in the days when death
  Shall make my body mine, I do not cry
For hours and treasure lost, but with my breath
  Praise my mortality.
For lo! this place is fair, and losing all
  That I have won and dreamed beneath her kiss,
I would not see the light of morning fall
  On any world but this.

Richard Middleton [1882–1911]

WINDLE–STRAWS

SHE kissed me on the forehead,
  She spoke not any word,
The silence flowed between us,
  And I nor spoke nor stirred.

So hopeless for my sake it was,
  So full of ruth, so sweet,
My whole heart rose and blessed her,
  —Then died before her feet.

Edward Dowden [1843–1913]

JESSIE

WHEN Jessie comes with her soft breast,
  And yields the golden keys,
Then is it as if God caressed
  Twin babes upon His knees—
Twin babes that, each to other pressed,
Just feel the Father's arms, wherewith they both are blessed.

But when I think if we must part,
  And all this personal dream be fled—
O then my heart! O then my useless heart!
  Would God that thou wert dead—

A clod insensible to joys and ills—
A stone remote in some bleak gully of the hills!
                    Thomas Edward Brown [1830–1897]

THE CHESS-BOARD

My little love, do you remember,
  Ere we were grown so sadly wise,
Those evenings in the bleak December,
Curtained warm from the snowy weather,
When you and I played chess together,
  Checkmated by each other's eyes?

Ah! still I see your soft white hand
Hovering warm o'er Queen and Knight;
  Brave Pawns in valiant battle stand;
The double Castles guard the wings;
The Bishop, bent on distant things,
Moves, sliding, through the fight.

Our fingers touch; our glances meet,
And falter; falls your golden hair
  Against my cheek; your bosom sweet
Is heaving.   Down the field, your Queen
Rides slow, her soldiery all between,
  And checks me unaware.

Ah me! the little battle's done:
Dispersed is all its chivalry.
Full many a move, since then, have we
'Mid Life's perplexing chequers made,
And many a game with Fortune played;—
  What is it we have won?
  This, this at least,—if this alone:

That never, never, never more,
As in those old still nights of yore
  (Ere we were grown so sadly wise),
  Can you and I shut out the skies,

Shut out the world and wintry weather,
And, eyes exchanging warmth with eyes,
Play chess, as then we played together!
Edward Robert Bulwer Lytton [1831–1891]

AUX ITALIENS

AT Paris it was, at the Opera there;—
And she looked like a queen in a book that night,
With the wreath of pearl in her raven hair,
And the brooch on her breast, so bright.

Of all the operas that Verdi wrote,
The best, to my taste, is the Trovatore;
And Mario can soothe with a tenor note
The souls in Purgatory.

The moon on the tower slept soft as snow:
And who was not thrilled in the strangest way,
As we heard him sing, while the gas burned low,
"Non ti scordar di me"?

The Emperor there, in his box of state,
Looked grave, as if he had just then seen
The red flag wave from the city-gate
Where his eagles in bronze had been.

The Empress, too, had a tear in her eye.
You'd have said that her fancy had gone back again,
For one moment, under the old blue sky,
To the old glad life in Spain.

Well! there in our front-row box we sat,
Together, my bride-betrothed and I;
My gaze was fixed on my opera-hat,
And hers on the stage hard by.

And both were silent, and both were sad.
Like a queen she leaned on her full white arm,
With that regal, indolent air she had;
So confident of her charm!

I have not a doubt she was thinking then
  Of her former lord, good soul that he was!
Who died the richest and roundest of men,
  The Marquis of Carabas.

I hope that, to get to the kingdom of heaven,
  Through a needle's eye he had not to pass.
I wish him well, for the jointure given
  To my lady of Carabas.

Meanwhile, I was thinking of my first love,
  As I had not been thinking of aught for years,
Till over my eyes there began to move
  Something that felt like tears.

I thought of the dress that she wore last time,
  When we stood, 'neath the cypress-trees, together,
In that lost land, in that soft clime,
  In the crimson evening weather;

Of that muslin dress (for the eve was hot),
  And her warm white neck in its golden chain,
And her full, soft hair, just tied in a knot,
  And falling loose again;

And the jasmine-flower in her fair young breast,
  (O the faint, sweet smell of that jasmine-flower!)
And the one bird singing alone to his nest,
  And the one star over the tower.

I thought of our little quarrels and strife,
  And the letter that brought me back my ring.
And it all seemed then, in the waste of life,
  Such a very little thing!

For I thought of her grave below the hill,
  Which the sentinel cypress-tree stands over;
And I thought . . . "were she only living still,
  How I could forgive her, and love her!"

And I swear, as I thought of her thus, in that hour,
 And of how, after all, old things were best,
That I smelt the smell of that jasmine-flower
 Which she used to wear in her breast.

It smelt so faint, and it smelt so sweet,
 It made me creep, and it made me cold!
Like the scent that steals from the crumbling sheet
 Where a mummy is half unrolled.

And I turned, and looked. She was sitting there
 In a dim box, over the stage; and dressed
In that muslin dress with that full soft hair,
 And that jasmine in her breast!

I was here; and she was there;
 And the glittering horseshoe curved between:—
From my bride-betrothed, with her raven hair,
 And her sumptuous scornful mien,

To my early love, with her eyes downcast,
 And over her primrose face the shade
(In short from the Future back to the Past),
 There was but a step to be made.

To my early love from my future bride
 One moment I looked. Then I stole to the door,
I traversed the passage; and down at her side
 I was sitting, a moment more.

My thinking of her, or the music's strain,
 Or something which never will be expressed,
Had brought her back from the grave again,
 With the jasmine in her breast.

She is not dead, and she is not wed!
 But she loves me now, and she loved me then!
And the very first word that her sweet lips said,
 My heart grew youthful again.

The Marchioness there, of Carabas,
   She is wealthy, and young, and handsome still,
And but for her . . . well, we'll let that pass,
   She may marry whomever she will.

But I will marry my own first love,
   With her primrose face: for old things are best,
And the flower in her bosom, I prize it above
   The brooch in my lady's breast.

The world is filled with folly and sin,
   And Love must cling where it can, I say:
For Beauty is easy enough to win;
   But one isn't loved every day.

And I think, in the lives of most women and men,
   There's a moment when all would go smooth and even,
If only the dead could find out when
   To come back, and be forgiven.

But O the smell of that jasmine-flower!
   And O that music! and O the way
That voice rang out from the donjon tower,
  Non ti scordar di me,
    Non ti scordar di me!
            Edward Robert Bulwer Lytton [1831–1891]

SONG

    I saw the day's white rapture
      Die in the sunset's flame,
    But all her shining beauty
      Lives like a deathless name.

    Our lamps of joy are wasted,
      Gone is Love's hallowed light;
    But you and I remember
      Through every starlit night.
            Charles Hanson Towne [1877–

THE LONELY ROAD

I THINK thou waitest, Love, beyond the Gate—
    Eager, with wind-stirred ripples in thy hair;
I have not found thee, and the hour is late,
    And harsh the weight I bear.

Far have I sought, and flung my wealth of years
    Like a young traveler, gay at careless inns—
See how the wine-stain whitens 'neath the tears
    My burden wins!

And wilt thou know me, Love, with bended back,
    Or wilt thou scorn me, in so drear a guise?
I have a wealth of sorrows in my pack,
    One lonely prize—

Thy dream—and dross of sin. . . . O, dim the fields—
    I may not find thee in so dark a land—
Yet I await what hope the turning yields
    And beg with empty hand.
                    Kenneth Rand [1891–

EVENSONG

BEAUTY calls and gives no warning,
Shadows rise and wander on the day.
In the twilight, in the quiet evening,
We shall rise and smile and go away.
Over the flaming leaves
Freezes the sky.
It is the season grieves,
Not you, not I.
All our spring-times, all our summers,
We have kept the longing warm within.
Now we leave the after-comers
To attain the dreams we did not win.
Oh, we have wakened, Sweet, and had our birth,
And that's the end of earth;
And we have toiled and smiled and kept the light,
And that's the end of night.
                    Ridgely Torrence [1875–

THE NYMPH'S SONG TO HYLAS

From "The Life and Death of Jason"

I KNOW a little garden-close
Set thick with lily and red rose,
Where I would wander if I might
From dewy dawn to dewy night,
And have one with me wandering.

And though within it no birds sing,
And though no pillared house is there,
And though the apple boughs are bare
Of fruit and blossom, would to God,
Her feet upon the green grass trod,
And I beheld them as before!

There comes a murmur from the shore,
And in the close two fair streams are,
Drawn from the purple hills afar,
Drawn down unto the restless sea;
Dark hills whose heath-bloom feeds no bee,
Dark shore no ship has ever seen,
Tormented by the billows green,
Whose murmur comes unceasingly
Unto the place for which I cry.

For which I cry both day and night,
For which I let slip all delight,
Whereby I grow both deaf and blind,
Careless to win, unskilled to find,
And quick to lose what all men seek.

Yet tottering as I am, and weak,
Still have I left a little breath
To seek within the jaws of death
An entrance to that happy place;
To seek the unforgotten face
Once seen, once kissed, once reft from me
Anigh the murmuring of the sea.

William Morris [1834-1896]

NO AND YES

IF I could choose my paradise,
  And please myself with choice of bliss,
Then I would have your soft blue eyes
  And rosy little mouth to kiss!
Your lips, as smooth and tender, child,
As rose-leaves in a coppice wild.

If fate bade choose some sweet unrest,
  To weave my troubled life a snare,
Then I would say "her maiden breast
  And golden ripple of her hair";
And weep amid those tresses, child,
Contented to be thus beguiled.

            Thomas Ashe [1836–1889]

LOVE IN DREAMS

LOVE hath his poppy-wreath,
  Not Night alone.
I laid my head beneath
  Love's lilied throne:
Then to my sleep he brought
  This anodyne—
The flower of many a thought
  And fancy fine:
A form, a face, no more;
  Fairer than truth;
A dream from death's pale shore;
  The soul of youth:
A dream so dear, so deep,
  All dreams above,
That still I pray to sleep—
  Bring Love back, Love!

    John Addington Symonds [1840–1893]

"A LITTLE WHILE I FAIN WOULD
LINGER YET"

A LITTLE while (my life is almost set!)
  I fain would pause along the downward way,
  Musing an hour in this sad sunset-ray,

While, Sweet! our eyes with tender tears are wet:
A little hour I fain would linger yet.

A little while I fain would linger yet,
   All for love's sake, for love that cannot tire;
   Though fervid youth be dead, with youth's desire,
And hope has faded to a vague regret,
A little while I fain would linger yet.

A little while I fain would linger here:
   Behold! who knows what strange, mysterious bars
   'Twixt souls that love may rise in other stars?
Nor can love deem the face of death is fair:
A little while I still would linger here.

A little while I yearn to hold thee fast,
   Hand locked in hand, and loyal heart to heart;
   (O pitying Christ! those woeful words, "We part!")
So, ere the darkness fall, the light be past,
A little while I fain would hold thee fast.

A little while, when light and twilight meet,—
   Behind, our broken years; before, the deep
   Weird wonder of the last unfathomed sleep,—
A little while I still would clasp thee, Sweet,
A little while, when night and twilight meet.

A little while I fain would linger here;
   Behold! who knows what soul-dividing bars
   Earth's faithful loves may part in other stars?
Nor can love deem the face of death is fair:
A little while I still would linger here.

               Paul Hamilton Hayne [1830–1886]

SONG

I MADE another garden, yea,
   For my new Love:
I left the dead rose where it lay
   And set the new above.

Why did my Summer not begin?
　　Why did my heart not haste?
My old Love came and walked therein,
　　And laid the garden waste.

She entered with her weary smile,
　　Just as of old;
She looked around a little while
　　And shivered with the cold:
Her passing touch was death to all,
　　Her passing look a blight;
She made the white rose-petals fall,
　　And turned the red rose white.

Her pale robe clinging to the grass
　　Seemed like a snake
That bit the grass and ground, alas!
　　And a sad trail did make.
She went up slowly to the gate,
　　And there, just as of yore,
She turned back at the last to wait
　　And say farewell once more.

　　　　　　Arthur O'Shaughnessy [1844–1881]

SONG

HAS summer come without the rose,
　　Or left the bird behind?
Is the blue changed above thee,
　　O world! or am I blind?
Will you change every flower that grows,
　　Or only change this spot,
Where she who said, I love thee,
　　Now says, I love thee not?

The skies seemed true above thee,
　　The rose true on the tree;
The bird seemed true the summer through,
　　But all proved false to me.

World! is there one good thing in you,
    Life, love, or death—or what?
Since lips that sang, I love thee,
    Have said, I love thee not?

I think the sun's kiss will scarce fall
    Into one flower's gold cup;
I think the bird will miss me,
    And give the summer up.
O sweet place! desolate in tall
    Wild grass, have you forgot
How her lips loved to kiss me,
    Now that they kiss me not?

Be false or fair above me,
    Come back with any face,
Summer!—do I care what you do?
    You cannot change one place—
The grass, the leaves, the earth, the dew,
    The grave I make the spot—
Here, where she used to love me,
    Here, where she loves me not.
        Arthur O'Shaughnessy [1844–1881]

AFTER

A LITTLE time for laughter,
    A little time to sing,
    A little time to kiss and cling,
And no more kissing after.

A little while for scheming
    Love's unperfected schemes;
    A little time for golden dreams,
Then no more any dreaming.

A little while 'twas given
    To me to have thy love;
    Now, like a ghost, alone I move
About a ruined heaven.

A little time for speaking
  Things sweet to say and hear;
  A time to seek, and find thee near,
Then no more any seeking.

A little time for saying
  Words the heart breaks to say;
  A short sharp time wherein to pray,
Then no more need of praying;

But long, long years to weep in,
  And comprehend the whole
  Great grief that desolates the soul,
And eternity to sleep in.

      Philip Bourke Marston [1850–1887]

AFTER SUMMER

WE'LL not weep for summer over,—
  No, not we:
Strew above his head the clover,—
  Let him be!

Other eyes may weep his dying,
  Shed their tears
There upon him, where he's lying
  With his peers.

Unto some of them he proffered
  Gifts most sweet;
For our hearts a grave he offered,—
  Was this meet?

All our fond hopes, praying, perished
  In his wrath,—
All the lovely dreams we cherished
  Strewed his path.

Shall we in our tombs, I wonder,
  Far apart,
Sundered wide as seas can sunder
  Heart from heart,

Dream at all of all the sorrows
  That were ours,—
Bitter nights, more bitter morrows;
  Poison-flowers

Summer gathered, as in madness,
  Saying, "See,
These are yours, in place of gladness,—
  Gifts from me"?

Nay, the rest that will be ours
  Is supreme,—
And below the poppy flowers
  Steals no dream.

          Philip Bourke Marston [1850–1887]

ROCOCO

TAKE hand and part with laughter;
  Touch lips and part with tears;
Once more and no more after,
  Whatever comes with years.
We twain shall not remeasure
  The ways that left us twain;
Nor crush the lees of pleasure
  From sanguine grapes of pain.

We twain once well in sunder,
  What will the mad gods do
For hate with me, I wonder,
  Or what for love with you?
Forget them till November,
  And dream there's April yet,
Forget that I remember,
  And dream that I forget.

Time found our tired love sleeping,
  And kissed away his breath;
But what should we do weeping,
  Though light love sleep to death?

We have drained his lips at leisure,
  Till there's not left to drain
A single sob of pleasure,
  A single pulse of pain.

Dream that the lips once breathless
  Might quicken if they would;
Say that the soul is deathless;
  Dream that the gods are good;
Say March may wed September,
  And time divorce regret;
But not that you remember,
  And not that I forget.

We have heard from hidden places
  What love scarce lives and hears:
We have seen on fervent faces
  The pallor of strange tears:
We have trod the wine-vat's treasure,
  Whence, ripe to steam and stain,
Foams round the feet of pleasure
  The blood-red must of pain.

Remembrance may recover
  And time bring back to time
The name of your first lover,
  The ring of my first rhyme:
But rose-leaves of December
  The frosts of June shall fret,
The day that you remember,
  The day that I forget.

The snake that hides and hisses
  In heaven we twain have known;
The grief of cruel kisses,
  The joy whose mouth makes moan;
The pulses' pause and measure,
  Where in one furtive vein
Throbs through the heart of pleasure
  The purpler blood of pain.

We have done with tears and treasons
 And love for treason's sake;
Room for the swift new seasons,
 The years that burn and break,
Dismantle and dismember
 Men's days and dreams, Juliette;
For love may not remember,
 But time will not forget.

Life treads down love in flying,
 Time withers him at root;
Bring all dead things and dying,
 Reaped sheaf and ruined fruit,
Where, crushed by three days' pressure
 Our three days' love lies slain;
And earlier leaf of pleasure,
 And latter flower of pain.

Breathe close upon the ashes,
 It may be flame will leap;
Unclose the soft close lashes,
 Lift up the lids and weep.
Light love's extinguished ember,
 Let one tear leave it wet
For one that you remember
 And ten that you forget.
    Algernon Charles Swinburne [1837–1909]

RONDEL

THESE many years since we began to be,
What have the Gods done with us? what with me,
What with my love? They have shown me fates and fears,
Harsh springs, and fountains bitterer than the sea,
Grief a fixed star, and joy a vane that veers,
    These many years.

With her, my Love,—with her have they done well?
But who shall answer for her? who shall tell
Sweet things or sad, such things as no man hears?
May no tears fall, if no tears ever fell,

From eyes more dear to me than starriest spheres,
   These many years!

But if tears ever touched, for any grief,
Those eyelids folded like a white-rose leaf,
Deep double shells where through the eye-flower peers,
Let them weep once more only, sweet and brief,
Brief tears and bright, for one who gave her tears
   These many years!
     Algernon Charles Swinburne [1837–1909]

THE OBLATION

Ask nothing more of me, sweet;
 All I can give you I give.
  Heart of my heart, were it more,
 More would be laid at your feet:
  Love that should help you to live,
   Song that should spur you to soar.

All things were nothing to give
 Once to have sense of you more,
  Touch you and taste of you, sweet,
Think you and breathe you and live,
  Swept of your wings as they soar,
   Trodden by chance of your feet.

I that have love and no more
 Give you but love of you, sweet:
  He that hath more, let him give;
He that hath wings, let him soar,
 Mine is the heart at your feet
  Here, that must love you to live.
     Algernon Charles Swinburne [1837–1909]

THE SONG OF THE BOWER

From "The House of Life"

Say, is it day, is it dusk in thy bower,
 Thou whom I long for, who longest for me?
Oh! be it light, be it night, 'tis Love's hour,
 Love's that is fettered as Love's that is free.

Free Love has leaped to that innermost chamber,
    Oh! the last time, and the hundred before:
Fettered Love, motionless, can but remember,
    Yet something that sighs from him passes the door.

Nay, but my heart when it flies to thy bower,
    What does it find there that knows it again?
There it must droop like a shower-beaten flower,
    Red at the rent core and dark with the rain.
Ah! yet what shelter is still shed above it,—
    What waters still image its leaves torn apart?
Thy soul is the shade that clings round it to love it,
    And tears are its mirror deep down in thy heart.

What were my prize, could I enter thy bower,
    This day, to-morrow, at eve or at morn?
Large lovely arms and a neck like a tower,
    Bosom then heaving that now lies forlorn.
Kindled with love-breath, (the sun's kiss is colder!)
    Thy sweetness all near me, so distant to-day;
My hand round thy neck and thy hand on my shoulder,
    My mouth to thy mouth as the world melts away.

What is it keeps me afar from thy bower,—
    My spirit, my body, so fain to be there?
Waters engulfing or fires that devour?—
    Earth heaped against me or death in the air?
Nay, but in day-dreams, for terror, for pity,
    The trees wave their heads with an omen to tell;
Nay, but in night-dreams, throughout the dark city,
    The hours, clashed together, lose count in the bell.

Shall I not one day remember thy bower,
    One day when all days are one day to me?—
Thinking, "I stirred not, and yet had the power,"
    Yearning, "Ah God, if again it might be!"
Peace, peace! such a small lamp illumes, on this highway,
    So dimly so few steps in front of my feet,—
Yet shows me that her way is parted from my way. . . .
    Out of sight, beyond light, at what goal may we meet?
         Dante Gabriel Rossetti [1828–1882]

SONG

WE break the glass, whose sacred wine
  To some belovèd health we drain,
Lest future pledges, less divine,
  Should e'er the hallowed toy profane;
And thus I broke a heart that poured
  Its tide of feelings out for thee,
In draughts, by after-times deplored,
  Yet dear to memory.

But still the old, impassioned ways
  And habits of my mind remain,
And still unhappy light displays
  Thine image chambered in my brain,
And still it looks as when the hours
  Went by like flights of singing birds,
Or that soft chain of spoken flowers
  And airy gems,—thy words.

Edward Coote Pinkney [1802–1828]

MAUD MULLER

MAUD MULLER on a summer's day
Raked the meadow sweet with hay.

Beneath her torn hat glowed the wealth
Of simple beauty and rustic health.

Singing, she wrought, and her merry glee
The mock-bird echoed from his tree.

But when she glanced to the far-off town,
White from its hill-slope looking down,

The sweet song died, and a vague unrest
And a nameless longing filled her breast,—

A wish that she hardly dared to own,
For something better than she had known

The Judge rode slowly down the lane,
Smoothing his horse's chestnut mane.

He drew his bridle in the shade
Of the apple-trees, to greet the maid,

And asked a draught from the spring that flowed
Through the meadow across the road.

She stooped where the cool spring bubbled up,
And filled for him her small tin cup,

And blushed as she gave it, looking down
On her feet so bare, and her tattered gown.

"Thanks!" said the Judge; "a sweeter draught
From a fairer hand was never quaffed."

He spoke of the grass and flowers and trees,
Of the singing birds and the humming bees;

Then talked of the haying, and wondered whether
The cloud in the west would bring foul weather.

And Maud forgot her brier-torn gown,
And her graceful ankles bare and brown;

And listened, while a pleased surprise
Looked from her long-lashed hazel eyes.

At last, like one who for delay
Seeks a vain excuse, he rode away.

Maud Muller looked and sighed: "Ah me!
That I the Judge's bride might be!

"He would dress me up in silks so fine,
And praise and toast me at his wine.

"My father should wear a broadcloth coat;
My brother should sail a painted boat.

"I'd dress my mother so grand and gay,
And the baby should have a new toy each day.

"And I'd feed the hungry and clothe the poor,
And all should bless me who left our door."

The Judge looked back as he climbed the hill,
And saw Maud Muller standing still.

"A form more fair, a face more sweet,
Ne'er hath it been my lot to meet.

"And her modest answer and graceful air
Show her wise and good as she is fair.

"Would she were mine, and I to-day,
Like her, a harvester of hay;

"No doubtful balance of rights and wrongs,
Nor weary lawyers with endless tongues,

"But low of cattle and song of birds,
And health and quiet and loving words."

But he thought of his sisters, proud and cold,
And his mother, vain of her rank and gold.

So, closing his heart, the Judge rode on,
And Maud was left in the field alone.

But the lawyers smiled that afternoon,
When he hummed in court an old love-tune;

And the young girl mused beside the well
Till the rain on the unraked clover fell.

He wedded a wife of richest dower,
Who lived for fashion, as he for power.

Yet oft, in his marble hearth's bright glow,
He watched a picture come and go;

And sweet Maud Muller's hazel eyes
Looked out in their innocent surprise.

Oft, when the wine in his glass was red,
He longed for the wayside well instead;

And closed his eyes on his garnished rooms
To dream of meadows and clover-blooms.

And the proud man sighed, with a secret pain,
"Ah, that I were free again!

"Free as when I rode that day,
Where the barefoot maiden raked her hay."

She wedded a man unlearned and poor,
And many children played round her door.

But care and sorrow, and childbirth pain,
Left their traces on heart and brain.

And oft, when the summer sun shone hot
On the new-mown hay in the meadow lot,

And she heard the little spring brook fall
Over the roadside, through the wall,

In the shade of the apple-tree again
She saw a rider draw his rein;

And, gazing down with timid grace,
She felt his pleased eyes read her face.

Sometimes her narrow kitchen walls
Stretched away into stately halls;

The weary wheel to a spinet turned,
The tallow candle an astral burned,

And for him who sat by the chimney lug,
Dozing and grumbling o'er pipe and mug,

A manly form at her side she saw,
And joy was duty and love was law.

Then she took up her burden of life again,
Saying only, "It might have been."

Alas for maiden, alas for Judge,
For rich repiner and household drudge!

God pity them both! and pity us all,
Who vainly the dreams of youth recall.

For of all sad words of tongue or pen,
The saddest are these: "It might have been!"

Ah, well! for us all some sweet hope lies
Deeply buried from human eyes;

And, in the hereafter, angels may
Roll the stone from its grave away!

John Greenleaf Whittier [1807–1892]

LA GRISETTE

AH, Clemence! when I saw thee last
    Trip down the Rue de Seine,
And turning, when thy form had passed,
    I said, "We meet again,"—
I dreamed not in that idle glance
    Thy latest image came,
And only left to memory's trance
    A shadow and a name.

The few strange words my lips had taught
    Thy timid voice to speak,
Their gentler signs, which often brought
    Fresh roses to thy cheek,
The trailing of thy long loose hair
    Bent o'er my couch of pain,
All, all returned, more sweet, more fair;
    Oh, had we met again!

I walked where saint and virgin keep
   The vigil lights of Heaven,
I knew that thou hadst woes to weep,
   And sins to be forgiven;
I watched where Genevieve was laid,
   I knelt by Mary's shrine,
Beside me low, soft voices prayed;
   Alas! but where was thine?

And when the morning sun was bright,
   When wind and wave were calm,
And flamed, in thousand-tinted light,
   The rose of Notre Dame,
I wandered through the haunts of men,
   From Boulevard to Quai,
Till, frowning o'er Saint Etienne,
   The Pantheon's shadow lay.

In vain, in vain; we meet no more,
   Nor dream what fates befall;
And long upon the stranger's shore
   My voice on thee may call,
When years have clothed the line in moss
   That tells thy name and days,
And withered, on thy simple cross,
   The wreaths of Père-la-Chaise!
Oliver Wendell Holmes [1809–1894]

THE DARK MAN

ROSE o' the World, she came to my bed
And changed the dreams of my heart and head;
For joy of mine she left grief of hers,
And garlanded me with a crown of furze.

Rose o' the World, they go out and in,
And watch me dream amd my mother spin;
And they pity the tears on my sleeping face
While my soul's away in a fairy place.

Rose o' the World, they have words galore,
And wide's the swing of my mother's door:
And soft they speak of my darkened eyes—
But what do they know, who are all so wise?

Rose o' the World, the pain you give
Is worth all days that a man may live—
Worth all shy prayers that the colleens say
On the night that darkens the wedding-day.

Rose o' the World, what man would wed
When he might dream of your face instead?
Might go to the grave with the blessèd pain
Of hungering after your face again?

Rose o' the World, they may talk their fill,
For dreams are good, and my life stands still
While their lives' red ashes the gossips stir;
But my fiddle knows—and I talk to her.

Nora Hopper [1871–1906]

EURYDICE

HE came to call me back from death
   To the bright world above.
I hear him yet with trembling breath
   Low calling, "O sweet love!
Come back!   The earth is just as fair;
The flowers, the open skies are there;
   Come back to life and love!"

Oh! all my heart went out to him,
   And the sweet air above.
With happy tears my eyes were dim;
   I called him, "O sweet love!
I come, for thou art all to me.
Go forth, and I will follow thee,
   Right back to life and love!"

I followed through the cavern black;
  I saw the blue above.
Some terror turned me to look back:
  I heard him wail, "O love!
What hast thou done! What hast thou done!"
And then I saw no more the sun,
    And lost were life and love.

Francis William Bourdillon [1852–1921]

A WOMAN'S THOUGHT

I AM a woman—therefore I may not
  Call to him, cry to him,
  Fly to him,
  Bid him delay not!

Then when he comes to me, I must sit quiet;
  Still as a stone—
  All silent and cold.
    If my heart riot—
  Crush and defy it!
  Should I grow bold,
  Say one dear thing to him,
  All my life fling to him,
  Cling to him—
  What to atone
  Is enough for my sinning!
  This were the cost to me,
  This were my winning—
  That he were lost to me.

Not as a lover
At last if he part from me,
Tearing my heart from me,
Hurt beyond cure,—
Calm and demure
Then must I hold me,
In myself fold me,
Lest he discover;

Showing no sign to him
By look of mine to him
What he has been to me—
How my heart turns to him,
Follows him, yearns to him,
Prays him to love me.

Pity me, lean to me,
Thou God above me!

Richard Watson Gilder [1844–1909]

LAUS VENERIS

A PICTURE BY BURNE-JONES

PALLID with too much longing,
White with passion and prayer,
Goddess of love and beauty,
She sits in the picture there,—

Sits with her dark eyes seeking
Something more subtle still
Than the old delights of loving
Her measureless days to fill.

She has loved and been loved so often
In her long, immortal years,
That she tires of the worn-out rapture,
Sickens of hopes and fears.

No joys or sorrows move her,
Done with her ancient pride;
For her head she found too heavy
The crown she has cast aside.

Clothed in her scarlet splendor,
Bright with her glory of hair,
Sad that she is not mortal,—
Eternally sad and fair,

Longing for joys she knows not,
Athirst with a vain desire,
There she sits in the picture,
Daughter of foam and fire.
Louise Chandler Moulton [1835–1908]

ADONAIS

SHALL we meet no more, my love, at the binding of the
sheaves,
In the happy harvest-fields, as the sun sinks low,
When the orchard paths are dim with the drift of fallen
leaves,
And the reapers sing together, in the mellow, misty eves:
O, happy are the apples when the south winds blow!

Love met us in the orchard, ere the corn had gathered
plume,—
O, happy are the apples when the south winds blow!
Sweet as summer days that die when the months are in the
bloom,
And the peaks are ripe with sunset, like the tassels of the
broom,
In the happy harvest-fields as the sun sinks low.

Sweet as summer days that die, leafing sweeter each to
each,—
O, happy are the apples when the south winds blow!
All the heart was full of feeling: love had ripened into speech,
Like the sap that turns to nectar in the velvet of the peach,
In the happy harvest-fields as the sun sinks low.

Sweet as summer days that die at the ripening of the corn,—
O, happy are the apples when the south winds blow!
Sweet as lovers' fickle oaths, sworn to faithless maids for-
sworn,
When the musty orchard breathes like a mellow drinking-
horn,
Over happy harvest-fields as the sun sinks low.

Love left us at the dying of the mellow autumn eves,—
  O, happy are the apples when the south winds blow!
When the skies are ripe and fading, like the colors of the
      leaves,
And the reapers kiss and part, at the binding of the sheaves,
  In the happy harvest-fields as the sun sinks low.

Then the reapers gather home, from the gray and misty
      meres;—
  O, happy are the apples when the south winds blow!
Then the reapers gather home, and they bear upon their
      spears,
One whose face is like the moon, fallen gray among the
      spheres,
  With the daylight's curse upon it, as the sun sinks low.

Faint as far-off bugles blowing, soft and low the reapers
      sung;—
  O, happy are the apples when the south winds blow!
Sweet as summer in the blood, when the heart is ripe and
      young,
Love is sweetest in the dying, like the sheaves he lies among,
  In the happy harvest-fields as the sun sinks low.

                    William Wallace Harney [1831–1912]

FACE TO FACE

IF my face could only promise that its color would remain;
If my heart were only certain it would hide the moment's
      pain;
I would meet you and would greet you in the old familiar
      tone,
And naught should ever show you the wrong that you have
      done.

If my trembling hand were steady, if my smiles had not all
      fled;
If my eyes spoke not so plainly of the tears they often shed;
I would meet you and would greet you at the old trysting
      place,
And perchance you'd deem me happy if you met me face to
      face.

If the melody of Springtime awoke no wild refrain,
If the Autumn's gold burthen awoke no living pain,
I would meet you and would greet you, as years ago we met,
Before our hearts were shipwrecked on the ocean of regret.

If my woman's soul were stronger, if my heart were not so
          true,
I should long have ceased remembering the love I had for
          you;
But I dare not meet or greet you, in the old familiar way,
Until we meet in Heaven, where all tears have passed away.

Frances Cochrane [18 –

ASHORE

OUT I came from the dancing-place,
The night-wind met me face to face,—

A wind off the harbor, cold and keen,
"I know," it whistled, "where thou hast been."

A faint voice fell from the stars above—
"Thou? whom we lighted to shrines of Love!"

I found when I reached my lonely room
A faint sweet scent in the unlit gloom.

And this was the worst of all to bear,
For some one had left white lilac there.

The flower you loved, in times that were.

Laurence Hope [1865–1904]

KHRISTNA AND HIS FLUTE

BE still, my heart, and listen,
     For sweet and yet acute
I hear the wistful music
     Of Khristna and his flute.
Across the cool, blue evenings,
     Throughout the burning days,
Persuasive and beguiling,
     He plays and plays and plays.

Ah, none may hear such music
  Resistant to its charms,
The household work grows weary,
  And cold the husband's arms.
I must arise and follow,
  To seek, in vain pursuit,
The blueness and the distance,
  The sweetness of that flute!

In linked and liquid sequence,
  The plaintive notes dissolve
Divinely tender secrets
  That none but he can solve.
O Khristna, I am coming,
  I can no more delay.
"My heart has flown to join thee,"
  How shall my footsteps stay?

Beloved, such thoughts have peril;
  The wish is in my mind
That I had fired the jungle,
  And left no leaf behind,—
Burnt all bamboos to ashes,
  And made their music mute,—
To save thee from the magic
  Of Khristna and his flute.

          Laurence Hope [1865-1904]

IMPENITENTIA ULTIMA

BEFORE my light goes out forever, if God should give me
    choice of graces,
  I would not reck of length of days, nor crave for
    things to be;
But cry: "One day of the great lost days, one face of all the
    faces,
  Grant me to see and touch once more and nothing more
    to see!

"For, Lord, I was free of all Thy flowers, but I chose the
    world's sad roses,
  And that is why my feet are torn and mine eyes are
    blind with sweat,
But at Thy terrible judgment seat, when this my tired life
    closes,
  I am ready to reap whereof I sowed, and pay my righteous
    debt.

"But once, before the sand is run and the silver thread is
    broken,
  Give me a grace and cast aside the veil of dolorous years,
Grant me one hour of all mine hours, and let me see for a
    token
  Her pure and pitiful eyes shine out, and bathe her feet
    with tears."

Her pitiful hands should calm and her hair stream down and
    blind me,
  Out of the sight of night, and out of the reach of fear,
And her eyes should be my light whilst the sun went out
    behind me,
  And the viols in her voice be the last sound in mine ear.

Before the ruining waters fall and my life be carried under,
  And Thine anger cleave me through, as a child cuts down
    a flower,
I will praise Thee, Lord, in hell, while my limbs are racked
    asunder,
  For the last sad sight of her face and the little grace of an
    hour.

Ernest Dowson [1867–1900]

NON SUM QUALIS ERAM BONAE SUB REGNO CYNARAE

LAST night, ah, yesternight, betwixt her lips and mine
There fell thy shadow, Cynara! thy breath was shed
Upon my soul between the kisses and the wine;
And I was desolate and sick of an old passion,
    Yea, I was desolate and bowed my head.
I have been faithful to thee, Cynara! in my fashion.

All night upon mine heart I felt her warm heart beat,
Night-long within mine arms in love and sleep she lay;
Surely the kisses of her bought red mouth were sweet;
But I was desolate and sick of an old passion,
     When I awoke and found the dawn was gray:
I have been faithful to thee, Cynara! in my fashion.

I have forgot much, Cynara! gone with the wind,
Flung roses, roses riotously with the throng,
Dancing, to put thy pale, lost lilies out of mind;
But I was desolate and sick of an old passion,
     Yea, all the time, because the dance was long:
I have been faithful to thee, Cynara! in my fashion.

I cried for madder music and for stronger wine,
But when the feast is finished and the lamps expire,
Then falls thy shadow, Cynara! the night is thine;
And I am desolate and sick of an old passion,
     Yea, hungry for the lips of my desire:
I have been faithful to thee, Cynara! in my fashion.

          Ernest Dowson [1867–1900]

QUID NON SPEREMUS, AMANTES?

WHY is there in the least touch of her hands
  More grace than other women's lips bestow,
If love is but a slave to fleshly bands
  Of flesh to flesh, wherever love may go?

Why choose vain grief and heavy-hearted hours
  For her lost voice, and dear remembered hair,
If love may cull his honey from all flowers,
  And girls grow thick as violets, everywhere?

Nay! She is gone, and all things fall apart;
  Or she is cold, and vainly have we prayed;
And broken is the summer's splendid heart,
  And hope within a deep, dark grave is laid.

As man aspires and falls, yet a soul springs
    Out of his agony of flesh at last,
So love that flesh enthralls, shall rise on wings
    Soul-centered, when the rule of flesh is past.

Then, most High Love, or wreathed with myrtle sprays,
    Or crownless and forlorn, nor less a star,
Thee may I serve and follow all my days,
    Whose thorns are sweet as never roses are!

Ernest Dowson [1867-1900]

"SO SWEET LOVE SEEMED"

So sweet love seemed that April morn,
When first we kissed beside the thorn,
So strangely sweet, it was not strange
We thought that love could never change.

But I can tell—let truth be told—
That love will change in growing old;
Though day by day is naught to see,
So delicate his motions be.

And in the end 'twill come to pass
Quite to forget what once he was,
Nor even in fancy to recall
The pleasure that was all in all.

His little spring, that sweet we found,
So deep in summer floods is drowned,
I wonder, bathed in joy complete,
How love so young could be so sweet.

Robert Bridges [1844-1930]

AN OLD TUNE *

AFTER GÉRARD DE NERVAL

THERE is an air for which I would disown
    Mozart's, Rossini's, Weber's melodies,—
A sweet sad air that languishes and sighs,
    And keeps its secret charm for me alone.

* For the original of this poem see page 3842

Whene'er I hear that music vague and old,
     Two hundred years are mist that rolls away;
The thirteenth Louis reigns, and I behold
     A green land golden in the dying day.

An old red castle, strong with stony towers,
     And windows gay with many-colored glass;
Wide plains, and rivers flowing among flowers,
     That bathe the castle basement as they pass.

In antique weed, with dark eyes and gold hair,
     A lady looks forth from her window high;
It may be that I knew and found her fair,
     In some forgotten life, long time gone by.

Andrew Lang [1844–1912]

REFUGE

SET your face to the sea, fond lover,—
     Cold in darkness the sea-winds blow!
Waves and clouds and the night will cover
     All your passion and all your woe:
Sobbing waves, and the death within them,
     Sweet as the lips that once you pressed—
Pray that your hopeless heart may win them!
     Pray that your weary life may rest!

Set your face to the stars, fond lover,—
     Calm, and silent, and bright, and true!—
They will pity you, they will hover
     Softly over the deep for you.
Winds of heaven will sigh your dirges,
     Tears of heaven for you be spent,
And sweet for you will the murmuring surges
     Pour the wail of their low lament.

Set your face to the lonely spaces,
     Vast and gaunt, of the midnight sky!
There, with the drifting cloud, your place is,
     There with the griefs that cannot die.

Love is a mocking fiend's derision,
  Peace a phantom, and faith a snare!
Make the hope of your heart a vision—
  Look to heaven, and find it there!
                    William Winter [1836–

MIDSUMMER

AFTER the May time and after the June time
  Rare with blossoms and perfume sweet,
Cometh the round world's royal noon time,
  The red midsummer of blazing heat,
When the sun, like an eye that never closes,
  Bends on the earth its fervid gaze,
And the winds are still, and the crimson roses
  Droop and wither and die in its rays.

Unto my heart has come this season,
  O, my lady, my worshiped one,
When, over the stars of Pride and Reason,
  Sails Love's cloudless, noonday sun.
Like a great red ball in my bosom burning
  With fires that nothing can quench or tame,
It glows till my heart itself seems turning
  Into a liquid lake of flame.

The hopes half shy and the sighs all tender,
  The dreams and fears of an earlier day,
Under the noontide's royal splendor,
  Droop like roses, and wither away.
From the hills of Doubt no winds are blowing,
  From the isles of Pain no breeze is sent,—
Only the sun in a white heat glowing
  Over an ocean of great content.

Sink, O my soul, in this golden glory!
  Die, O my heart, in thy rapture-swoon!
For the Autumn must come with its mournful story.
  And Love's midsummer will fade too soon.
                    Ella Wheeler Wilcox [1850–1919]

ASHES OF ROSES

Soft on the sunset sky
  Bright daylight closes,
Leaving when light doth die,
Pale hues that mingling lie—
  Ashes of roses.

When love's warm sun is set,
  Love's brightness closes;
Eyes with hot tears are wet,
In hearts there linger yet
  Ashes of roses.

Elaine Goodale Eastman [1863-

SYMPATHY

The color gladdens all your heart;
  You call it Heaven, dear, but I—
Now Hope and I are far apart—
  Call it the sky.

I know that Nature's tears have wet
  The world with sympathy; but you,
Who know not any sorrow yet,
  Call it the dew.

Althea Gyles [?]

THE LOOK

Strephon kissed me in the spring,
  Robin in the fall,
But Colin only looked at me
  And never kissed at all.

Strephon's kiss was lost in jest,
  Robin's lost in play,
But the kiss in Colin's eyes
  Haunts me night and day.

Sara Teasdale [1884-1933]

"WHEN MY BELOVED SLEEPING LIES"

WHEN my beloved sleeping lies
I cannot look at him for tears,
Such mournful peace is on his eyes.

A look of lonely death he wears,
And graven very calm and deep
Lie all the sorrows of old years.

He is so passionless in sleep,
With all his strength relaxed to rest;
I cannot see him and not weep.

For weakness life has not confessed
And shadowed scars of old mistakes,
I take his head upon my breast,
And hold my dearest till he wakes.

Irene Rutherford McLeod [1891–

LOVE AND LIFE

"GIVE me a fillet, Love," quoth I,
"To bind my Sweeting's heart to me,
So ne'er a chance of earth or sky
Shall part us ruthlessly:
A fillet, Love, but not to chafe
My Sweeting's soul, to cause her pain;
But just to bind her close and safe
Through snow and blossom and sun and rain:
    A fillet, boy!"
    Love said, "Here's joy."

"Give me a fetter, Life," quoth I,
"To bind to mine my Sweeting's heart,
So Death himself must fail to pry
With Time the two apart:
A fetter, Life, that each shall wear,
Whose precious bondage each shall know.
I prithee, Life, no more forbear—
Why dost thou wait and falter so?

Haste, Life—be brief!"
Said Life:—"Here's grief."
Julie Mathilde Lippman [1864–

LOVE'S PRISONER

Sweet love has twined his fingers in my hair,
And laid his hand across my wondering eyes.
  I cannot move save in the narrow space
  Of his strong arms' embrace,
Nor see but only in my own heart where
      His image lies.
      How can I tell,
  Emprisonèd so well,
If in the outer world be sunset or sunrise?
Sweet Love has laid his hand across my eyes.

Sweet Love has loosed his fingers from my hair,
His lifted hand has left my eyelids wet.
  I cannot move save to pursue his fleet
    And unreturning feet,
Nor see but in my ruined heart, and there
      His face lies yet.
      How should I know,
  Distraught and blinded so,
If in the outer world be sunrise or sunset?
Sweet Love has freed my eyes, but they are wet.
    Mariana Griswold Van Rensselaer [1851–1934]

ROSIES

There's a rosie-show in Derry,
  An' a rosie-show in Down;
An' 'tis like there's wan, I'm thinkin',
  'll be held in Randalstown;
But if I had the choosin'
  Av a rosie-prize the day,
'Twould be a pink wee rosie
  Like he plucked whin rakin' hay:

Yon pink wee rosie in my hair—
He fixed it troth—an' kissed it there!
White gulls wor wheelin' roun' the sky
         Down by—down by.

Ay, there's rosies sure in Derry,
   An' there's famous wans in Down;
Och there's rosies all a-hawkin'
   Through the heart av London town!
But if I had the liftin'
   Or the buyin' av a few,
I'd choose jist pink wee rosies
   That's all drenchin' wid the dew—
Yon pink wee rosies wid the tears!
Och wet, wet tears!—ay, troth, 'tis years
Since we kep' rakin' in the hay
         Thon day—thon day!

Agnes I. Hanrahan [18

AT THE COMEDY

LAST night, in snowy gown and glove,
   I saw you watch the play
Where each mock hero won his love
   In the old unlifelike way.

(And, oh, were life their little scene
   Where love so smoothly ran,
How different, Dear, this world had been
   Since this old world began!)

For you, who saw them gayly win
   Both hand and heart away,
Knew well where dwelt the mockery in
   That foolish little play.

("If love were all—if love were all,"
   The viols sobbed and cried,
"Then love were best whate'er befall!"
   Low, low, the flutes replied.)

And you, last night, did you forget,
  So far from me, so near?
For watching there your eyes were wet
  With just an idle tear!

(*And down the great dark curtain fell*
  Upon their foolish play:
But you and I knew—Oh, too well !—
  Life went another way !)
                    Arthur Stringer [1874⁻

"SOMETIME IT MAY BE"

SOMETIME it may be you and I
In that deserted yard shall lie
Where memories fade away;
Caring no more for our old dreams,
Busy with new and alien themes,
The saints and sages say.

But let our graves be side by side,
So passers-by at even-tide
May pause a moment's space:
"Ah, they were lovers who lie here!
Else why these low graves laid so near,
In this forgotten place?"
                    Arthur Colton [1868⁻

"I HEARD A SOLDIER"

I HEARD a soldier sing some trifle
  Out in the sun-dried veldt alone:
He lay and cleaned his grimy rifle
  Idly, behind a stone.

"If after death, love, comes a waking,
  And in their camp so dark and still
The men of dust hear bugles, breaking
  Their halt upon the hill.

"To me the slow and silver pealing
　　That then the last high trumpet pours
Shall softer than the dawn come stealing,
　　For, with its call, comes yours!"

What grief of love had he to stifle,
　　Basking so idly by his stone,
That grimy soldier with his rifle
　　Out in the veldt, alone?

Herbert Trench [1865–1923]

THE LAST MEMORY

WHEN I am old, and think of the old days,
And warm my hands before a little blaze,
Having forgotten love, hope, fear, desire,
I shall see, smiling out of the pale fire,
One face, mysterious and exquisite;
And I shall gaze, and ponder over it,
Wondering, was it Leonardo wrought
That stealthy ardency, where passionate thought
Burns inward, a revealing flame, and glows
To the last ecstasy, which is repose?
Was it Bronzino, those Borghese eyes?
And, musing thus among my memories,
O unforgotten! you will come to seem,
As pictures do, remembered, some old dream.
And I shall think of you as something strange,
And beautiful, and full of helpless change,
Which I beheld and carried in my heart;
But you, I loved, will have become a part
Of the eternal mystery, and love
Like a dim pain; and I shall bend above
My little fire, and shiver, being cold,
When you are no more young, and I am old.

Arthur Symons [1865–

"DOWN BY THE SALLEY GARDENS"

DOWN by the salley gardens my love and I did meet;
She passed the salley gardens with little snow-white feet.
She bid me take love easy, as the leaves grow on the tree;
But I, being young and foolish, with her would not agree.

In a field by the river my love and I did stand,
And on my leaning shoulder she laid her snow-white hand.
She bid me take life easy, as the grass grows on the weirs;
But I was young and foolish, and now am full of tears.

William Butler Yeats [1865–1939]

ASHES OF LIFE

Love has gone and left me, and the days are all alike.
    Eat I must, and sleep I will—and would that night were
      here!
But ah, to lie awake and hear the slow hours strike!
    Would that it were day again, with twilight near!

Love has gone and left me, and I don't know what to do;
    This or that or what you will is all the same to me;
But all the things that I begin I leave before I'm through—
    There's little use in anything as far as I can see.

Love has gone and left me, and the neighbors knock and
      borrow,
    And life goes on forever like the gnawing of a mouse.
And to-morrow and to-morrow and to-morrow and to-
      morrow
    There's this little street and this little house.

Edna St. Vincent Millay [1892–

A FAREWELL

Thou wilt not look on me?
Ah, well! the world is wide;
The rivers still are rolling free,
Song and the sword abide;
And who sets forth to sail the sea
Shall follow with the tide.

Thrall of my darkling day,
I vassalage fulfil:
Seeking the myrtle and the bay,
(They thrive when hearts are chill!)
The straitness of the narrowing way,
The house where all is still.

Alice Brown [1857–

THE PARTED LOVERS

SONG

From "Twelfth Night"

O MISTRESS mine, where are you roaming?
O, stay and hear; your true Love's coming,
   That can sing both high and low:
Trip no further, pretty Sweeting;
Journeys end in lovers meeting,
   Every wise man's son doth know.

What is love? 'tis not hereafter;
Present mirth hath present laughter;
   What's to come is still unsure:
In delay there lies no plenty:
Then come kiss me, Sweet-and-twenty,
   Youth's a stuff will not endure.

William Shakespeare [1564–1616]

"GO, LOVELY ROSE"

Go, lovely Rose—
Tell her that wastes her time and me,
   That now she knows,
When I resemble her to thee,
How sweet and fair she seems to be.

Tell her that's young,
And shuns to have her graces spied,
   That hadst thou sprung
In deserts, where no men abide,
Thou must have uncommended died.

Small is the worth
Of beauty from the light retired:
   Bid her come forth,
Suffer herself to be desired,
And not blush so to be admired.

Then die—that she
The common fate of all things rare
  May read in thee;
How small a part of time they share
That are so wondrous sweet and fair!
Edmund Waller [1606–1687]

TO THE ROSE: A SONG

Go, happy Rose, and, interwove
With other flowers, bind my love.
Tell her, too, she must not be
Longer flowing, longer free,
That so oft has fettered me.

Say, if she's fretful, I have bands
Of pearl and gold to bind her hands;
Tell her, if she struggle still,
I have myrtle rods at will
For to tame, though not to kill.

Take thou my blessing thus, and go
And tell her this,—but do not so!—
Lest a handsome anger fly
Like a lightning from her eye,
And burn thee up, as well as I!
Robert Herrick [1591–1674]

MEMORY

From "Britannia's Pastorals"

MARINA'S gone, and now sit I,
  As Philomela (on a thorn,
Turned out of nature's livery),
  Mirthless, alone, and all forlorn:
Only she sings not, while my sorrows can
Breathe forth such notes as fit a dying swan.

So shuts the marigold her leaves
  At the departure of the sun;
So from the honeysuckle sheaves
  The bee goes when the day is done;

So sits the turtle when she is but one,
And so all woe, as I since she is gone.

To some few birds, kind Nature hath
    Made all the summer as one day:
Which once enjoyed, cold winter's wrath
    As night, they sleeping pass away.
Those happy creatures are, that know not yet
The pain to be deprived or to forget.

I oft have heard men say there be
    Some that with confidence profess
The helpful Art of Memory:
    But could they teach Forgetfulness,
I'd learn; and try what further art could do
To make me love her and forget her too.

Sad melancholy, that persuades
    Men from themselves, to think they be
Headless, or other bodies' shades,
    Hath long and bootless dwelt with me;
For could I think she some idea were,
I still might love, forget, and have her here.

But such she is not: nor would I,
    For twice as many torments more,
As her bereavèd company
    Hath brought to those I felt before,
For then no future time might hap to know
That she deserved, or I did love her so.

Ye hours, then, but as minutes be!
    (Though so I shall be sooner old)
Till I those lovely graces see,
    Which, but in her, can none behold;
Then be an age! that we may never try
More grief in parting, but grow old and die.
                    William Browne [1591–1643?]

TO LUCASTA, GOING TO THE WARS

TELL me not, Sweet, I am unkind,
    That from the nunnery
Of thy chaste breast and quiet mind
    To war and arms I fly.

True, a new mistress now I chase,
    The first foe in the field;
And with a stronger faith embrace
    A sword, a horse, a shield.

Yet this inconstancy is such
    As thou too shalt adore;
I could not love thee, Dear, so much,
    Loved I not Honor more.

                Richard Lovelace [1618–1658]

TO LUCASTA, GOING BEYOND THE SEAS

IF to be absent were to be
    Away from thee;
Or that when I am gone
    You or I were alone;
Then, my Lucasta, might I crave
Pity from blustering wind or swallowing wave.

But I'll not sigh one blast or gale
    To swell my sail,
Or pay a tear to 'suage
    The foaming blue god's rage;
For whether he will let me pass
Or no, I'm still as happy as I was.

Though seas and land be twixt us both,
    Our faith and troth,
Like separated souls,
    All time and space controls:
Above the highest sphere we meet
Unseen, unknown; and greet as Angels greet.

So then we do anticipate
Our after-fate,
And are alive in the skies,
If thus our lips and eyes
Can speak like spirits unconfined
In Heaven, their earthy bodies left behind.

Richard Lovelace [1618–1658]

SONG TO A FAIR YOUNG LADY, GOING OUT OF THE TOWN IN THE SPRING

Ask not the cause why sullen Spring
So long delays her flowers to bear;
Why warbling birds forget to sing,
And winter storms invert the year:
Chloris is gone; and fate provides
To make it Spring where she resides.

Chloris is gone, the cruel fair;
She cast not back a pitying eye:
But left her lover in despair
To sigh, to languish, and to die:
Ah! how can those fair eyes endure
To give the wounds they will not cure?

Great God of Love, why hast thou made
A face that can all hearts command,
That all religions can invade,
And change the laws of every land?
Where thou hadst placed such power before,
Thou shouldst have made her mercy more.

When Chloris to the temple comes,
Adoring crowds before her fall;
She can restore the dead from tombs
And every life but mine recall,
I only am by Love designed
To be the victim for mankind.

John Dryden [1631–1700]

SONG

To all you ladies now at land
  We men at sea indite;
But first would have you understand
  How hard it is to write:
The Muses now, and Neptune too,
We must implore to write to you—
    With a fa, la, la, la, la.

For though the Muses should prove kind,
  And fill our empty brain,
Yet if rough Neptune rouse the wind
  To wave the azure main,
Our paper, pen, and ink, and we,
Roll up and down our ships at sea—
    With a fa, la, la, la, la.

Then if we write not by each post,
  Think not we are unkind;
Nor yet conclude our ships are lost
  By Dutchmen or by wind:
Our tears we'll send a speedier way,
The tide shall bring them twice a day—
    With a fa, la, la, la, la.

The King with wonder and surprise
  Will swear the seas grow bold,
Because the tides will higher rise
  Than e'er they did of old:
But let him know it is our tears
Bring floods of grief to Whitehall stairs—
    With a fa, la, la, la, la.

Should foggy Opdam chance to know
  Our sad and dismal story,
The Dutch would scorn so weak a foe,
  And quit their fort at Goree:

For what resistance can they find
From men who've left their hearts behind?—
   With a fa, la, la, la, la.

Let wind and weather do its worst,
   Be you to us but kind;
Let Dutchmen vapor, Spaniards curse,
   No sorrow we shall find:
'Tis then no matter how things go,
Or who's our friend, or who's our foe—
   With a fa, la, la, la, la.

To pass our tedious hours away
   We throw a merry main,
Or else at serious ombre play:
   But why should we in vain
Each other's ruin thus pursue?
We were undone when we left you—
   With a fa, la, la, la, la.

But now our fears tempestuous grow
   And cast our hopes away;
Whilst you, regardless of our woe,
   Sit careless at a play:
Perhaps permit some happier man
To kiss your hand, or flirt your fan—
   With a fa, la, la, la, la.

When any mournful tune you hear,
   That dies in every note
As if it sighed with each man's care
   For being so remote,
Think then how often love we've made
To you, when all those tunes were played—
   With a fa, la, la, la, la.

In justice you cannot refuse
   To think of our distress,
When we for hopes of honor lose
   Our certain happiness:

All those designs are but to prove
Ourselves more worthy of your love—
    With a fa, la, la, la, la.

And now we've told you all our loves,
    And likewise all our fears,
In hopes this declaration moves
    Some pity for our tears:
Let's hear of no inconstancy—
We have too much of that at sea—
    With a fa, la, la, la, la.

Charles Sackville [1638–1706]

SONG

In vain you tell your parting lover,
You wish fair winds may waft him over.
Alas! what winds can happy prove
That bear me far from what I love?
Alas! what dangers on the main
Can equal those that I sustain
From slighted vows, and cold disdain?

Be gentle, and in pity choose
To wish the wildest tempests loose:
That, thrown again upon the coast,
Where first my shipwrecked heart was lost,
I may once more repeat my pain;
Once more in dying notes complain
Of slighted vows and cold disdain.

Matthew Prior [1664–1721]

BLACK–EYED SUSAN

All in the Downs the fleet was moored,
    The streamers waving in the wind,
When black-eyed Susan came aboard;
    "O! where shall I my true-love find?
Tell me, ye jovial sailors, tell me true
If my sweet William sails among the crew."

William, who high upon the yard
   Rocked with the billow to and fro,
Soon as her well-known voice he heard
   He sighed, and cast his eyes below:
The cord slides swiftly through his glowing hands,
And, quick as lightning, on the deck he stands.

So the sweet lark, high poised in air,
   Shuts close his pinions to his breast
If chance his mate's shrill call he hear,
   And drops at once into her nest:—
The noblest captain in the British fleet
Might envy William's lip those kisses sweet.

"O Susan, Susan, lovely dear,
   My vows shall ever true remain;
Let me kiss off that falling tear;
   We only part to meet again.
Change as ye list, ye winds; my heart shall be
The faithful compass that still points to thee.

"Believe not what the landmen say
   Who tempt with doubts thy constant mind:
They'll tell thee, sailors, when away,
   In every port a mistress find:
Yes, yes, believe them when they tell thee so,
For Thou art present wheresoe'er I go.

"If to far India's coast we sail,
   Thy eyes are seen in diamonds bright,
Thy breath is Afric's spicy gale,
   Thy skin is ivory so white.
Thus every beauteous object that I view
Wakes in my soul some charm of lovely Sue.

"Though battle call me from thy arms
   Let not my pretty Susan mourn;
Though cannons roar, yet, safe from harms,
   William shall to his Dear return.
Love turns aside the balls that round me fly,
Lest precious tears should drop from Susan's eye."

The boatswain gave the dreadful word,
    The sails their swelling bosom spread,
No longer must she stay aboard;
    They kissed, she sighed, he hung his head.
Her lessening boat unwilling rows to land;
    "Adieu!" she cries; and waved her lily hand.

John Gay [1685-1732]

IRISH MOLLY O

Oh! who is that poor foreigner that lately came to town,
And like a ghost that cannot rest still wanders up and down?
A poor, unhappy Scottish youth;—if more you wish to know,
His heart is breaking all for love of Irish Molly O!

    She's modest, mild, and beautiful, the fairest I have
        known—
    The primrose of Ireland—all blooming here alone—
    The primrose of Ireland, for wheresoe'er I go,
    The only one entices me is Irish Molly O!

When Molly's father heard of it, a solemn oath he swore,
That if she'd wed a foreigner he'd never see her more.
He sent for young MacDonald and he plainly told him so—
"I'll never give to such as you my Irish Molly O!"

MacDonald heard the heavy news, and grievously did say—
"Farewell, my lovely Molly, since I'm banished far away,
A poor forlorn pilgrim I must wander to and fro,
And all for the sake of my Irish Molly O!

"There is a rose in Ireland, I thought it would be mine:
But now that she is lost to me, I must for ever pine,
Till death shall come to comfort me, for to the grave I'll go,
And all for the sake of my Irish Molly O!

"And now that I am dying, this one request I crave,
To place a marble tombstone above my humble grave!
And on the stone these simple words I'd have engraven so—
" ' MacDonald lost his life for love of Irish Molly O!' "

Unknown

SONG

AT setting day and rising morn,
  Wi' soul that still shall love thee,
I'll ask o' Heaven thy safe return,
  Wi' a' that can improve thee.
I'll visit aft the birken bush
  Where first thou kindly tauld me
Sweet tales o' love, and hid my blush,
  Whilst round thou didst infauld me.

To a' our haunts I will repair,
  By greenwood, shaw, or fountain,
Or where the summer day I'd share
  Wi' thee upon yon mountain:
There will I tell the trees an' flooers,
  From thoughts unfeigned an' tender;
By vows you're mine, by love is yours
  A heart that cannot wander.

Allan Ramsay [1686-1758]

LOCHABER NO MORE

FAREWELL to Lochaber, an' farewell my Jean,
Where heartsome wi' thee I hae mony day been;
For Lochaber no more, Lochaber no more!
We'll maybe return to Lochaber no more!
These tears that I shed, they are a' for my dear,
An' no for the dangers attending on weir,
Though borne on rough seas to a far bloody shore,
Maybe to return to Lochaber no more.

Though hurricanes rise, an' rise every wind,
They'll ne'er mak' a tempest like that in my mind;
Though loudest o' thunders on louder waves roar,
That's naething like leaving my love on the shore.
To leave thee behind me my heart is sair pained;
By ease that's inglorious no fame can be gained;

An' beauty an' love's the reward o' the brave,
An' I must deserve it before I can crave.

Then glory, my Jeanie, maun plead my excuse;
Since honor commands me, how can I refuse?
Without it I ne'er can have merit for thee,
An' without thy favor I'd better not be,
I gae, then, my lass, to win honor an' fame,
An' if I should luck to come gloriously hame,
I'll bring a heart to thee wi' love running o'er,
An' then I'll leave thee an' Lochaber no more.

Allan Ramsay [1686–1758]

WILLIE AND HELEN

"WHAREFORE sou'd ye talk o' love,
    Unless it be to pain us?
Wharefore sou'd ye talk o' love
    Whan ye say the sea maun twain us?"

"It's no because my love is light,
    Nor for your angry deddy;
It's a' to buy ye pearlins bright,
    An' to busk ye like a leddy."

"O Willy, I can caird an' spin,
    Sae ne'er can want for cleedin';
An' gin I hae my Willy's heart,
    I hae a' the pearls I'm heedin'.

"Will it be time to praise this cheek
    Whan years an' tears hae blenched it?
Will it be time to talk o' love
    Whan cauld an' care hae quenched it?"

He's laid ae han' about her waist—
    The ither's held to heaven;
An' his luik was like the luik o' man
    Wha's heart in twa is riven.

Hew Ainslie [1792–1878]

ABSENCE

WITH leaden foot Time creeps along
    While Delia is away:
With her, nor plaintive was the song,
    Nor tedious was the day.

Ah, envious Power! reverse my doom;
    Now double thy career,
Strain every nerve, stretch every plume,
    And rest them when she's here!

Richard Jago [1715–1781]

"MY MOTHER BIDS ME BIND MY HAIR"

MY mother bids me bind my hair
    With bands of rosy hue;
Tie up my sleeves with ribbons rare,
    And lace my bodice blue!

"For why," she cries, "sit still and weep,
    While others dance and play?"
Alas! I scarce can go, or creep,
    While Lubin is away!

'Tis sad to think the days are gone
    When those we love were near!
I sit upon this mossy stone,
    And sigh when none can hear:

And while I spin my flaxen thread,
    And sing my simple lay,
The village seems asleep, or dead,
    Now Lubin is away!

Anne Hunter [1742–1821]

"BLOW HIGH! BLOW LOW!"

BLOW high, blow low! let tempest tear
    The mainmast by the board!
My heart (with thoughts of thee, my dear!
    And love well stored)

Shall brave all danger, scorn all fear,
　The roaring wind, the raging sea,
　　In hopes, on shore,
　　To be once more
　Safe moored with thee.

Aloft, while mountain-high we go,
　The whistling winds that scud along,
And the surge roaring from below,
　　Shall my signal be
　　To think on thee.
　And this shall be my Song,
Blow high, blow low! let tempest tear. . . .

And on that night (when all the crew
　The memory of their former lives,
O'er flowing cans of flip renew,
　And drink their sweethearts and their wives),
　　I'll heave a sigh,
　　And think of thee.
　And, as the ship toils through the sea,
　The burden of my Song shall be,
Blow high, blow low! let tempest tear. . . .
　　　　　　　Charles Dibdin [1745–1814]

THE SILLER CROUN

" AND ye sall walk in silk attire,
　And siller ha'e to spare,
Gin ye'll consent to be his bride,
　Nor think o' Donald mair."

Oh, wha wad buy a silken goun
　Wi' a puir broken heart?
Or what's to me a siller croun,
　Gin' frae my luve I part?

The mind wha's every wish is pure
　Far dearer is to me;
And ere I'm forced to break my faith,
　I'll lay me doun and dee.

For I ha'e pledged my virgin troth
   Brave Donald's fate to share;
And he has gi'en to me his heart,
   Wi' a' its virtues rare.

His gentle manners wan my heart,
   He gratefu' took the gift;
Could I but think to tak' it back,
   It wad be waur than theft.

For langest life can ne'er repay
   The love he bears to me;
And ere I'm forced to break my troth
   I'll lay me doun and dee.

                    Susanna Blamire [1747-1794]

"MY NANNIE'S AWA'"

Now in her green mantle blithe Nature arrays,
An' listens the lambkins that bleat o'er the braes,
While birds warble welcome in ilka green shaw;
But to me it's delightless—my Nannie's awa'.

The snaw-drap an' primrose our woodlands adorn,
An' violets bathe in the weet o' the morn;
They pain my sad bosom, sae sweetly they blaw,
They mind me o' Nannie—an' Nannie's awa'.

Thou laverock that springs frae the dews of the lawn,
The shepherd to warn o' the gray-breaking dawn,
An' thou mellow mavis that hails the night-fa',
Give over for pity—my Nannie's awa'.

Come, autumn, sae pensive, in yellow an' gray,
An' soothe me wi' tidings o' Nature's decay;
The dark, dreary winter, an' wild-driving snaw
Alane can delight me—now Nannie's awa'.

                    Robert Burns [1759-1796]

"AE FOND KISS"

AE fond kiss, and then we sever;
Ae fareweel, alas, for ever!
Deep in heart-wrung tears I'll pledge thee,
Warring sighs and groans I'll wage thee!

Who shall say that Fortune grieves him
While the star of Hope she leaves him?
Me, nae cheerfu' twinkle lights me,
Dark despair around benights me.

I'll ne'er blame my partial fancy;
Naething could resist my Nancy;
But to see her was to love her,
Love but her, and love for ever.

Had we never loved sae kindly,
Had we never loved sae blindly,
Never met, or never parted,
We had ne'er been broken-hearted.

Fare thee weel, thou first and fairest!
Fare thee weel, thou best and dearest!
Thine be ilka joy and treasure,
Peace, enjoyment, love, and pleasure!

Ae fond kiss, and then we sever!
Ae fareweel, alas, for ever!
Deep in heart-wrung tears I'll pledge thee,
Warring sighs and groans I'll wage thee!

Robert Burns [1759–1796]

"THE DAY RETURNS"

THE day returns, my bosom burns,
  The blissful day we twa did meet;
Though winter wild in tempest toiled,
  Ne'er summer sun was half sae sweet.

Than a' the pride that loads the tide,
    And crosses o'er the sultry line,—
Than kingly robes, and crowns and globes,
    Heaven gave me more,—it made thee mine.

While day and night can bring delight,
    Or Nature aught of pleasure give,—
While joys above my mind can move,
    For thee, and thee alone, I live.
When that grim foe of life below
    Comes in between to make us part,
The iron hand that breaks our band,
    It breaks my bliss,—it breaks my heart.
                    Robert Burns [1759-1796]

MY BONNIE MARY

Go fetch to me a pint o' wine,
    And fill it in a silver tassie,
That I may drink, before I go,
    A service to my bonnie lassie.
The boat rocks at the pier o' Leith,
    Fu' loud the wind blaws frae the ferry,
The ship rides by the Berwick-law,
    And I maun leave my bonnie Mary.

The trumpets sound, the banners fly,
    The glittering spears are rankèd ready;
The shouts o' war are heard afar,
    The battle closes thick and bloody;
But it's no the roar o' sea or shore
    Wad mak me langer wish to tarry;
Nor shout o' war that's heard afar—
    It's leaving thee, my bonnie Mary!
                    Robert Burns [1759-1796]

A RED, RED ROSE

O, MY luve's like a red, red rose
    That's newly sprung in June;
O, my luve's like the melodie
    That's sweetly played in tune.

As fair thou art, my bonnie lass,
 So deep in luve am I;
And I will luve thee still, my dear,
 Till a' the seas gang dry.

Till a' the seas gang dry, my dear,
 And the rocks melt wi' the sun;
I will luve thee still, my dear,
 While the sands o' life shall run.

And fare-thee-weel, my only luve!
 And fare-thee-weel a while!
And I will come again, my luve,
 Though it were ten thousand mile.
      Robert Burns [1759–1796]

I LOVE MY JEAN

OF a' the airts the wind can blaw
 I dearly like the west,
For there the bonnie lassie lives,
 The lassie I lo'e best:
There's wild woods grow, and rivers row,
 And monie a hill between;
But day and night my fancy's flight
 Is ever wi' my Jean.

I see her in the dewy flowers,
 I see her sweet and fair:
I hear her in the tunefu' birds,
 I hear her charm the air:
There's not a bonnie flower that springs
 By fountain, shaw, or green,
There's not a bonnie bird that sings
 But minds me o' my Jean.

O blaw ye westlin winds, blaw saft
 Amang the leafy trees;
Wi' balmy gale, frae hill and dale
 Bring hame the laden bees;

And bring the lassie back to me
   That's aye sae neat and clean;
Ae smile o' her wad banish care,
   Sae charming is my Jean.

What sighs and vows amang the knowes
   Hae passed atween us twa!
How fond to meet, how wae to part
   That night she gaed awa!
The Powers aboon can only ken
   To whom the heart is seen,
That nane can be sae dear to me
   As my sweet lovely Jean!
     The first two stanzas by Robert Burns [1759–1796]
       The last two by John Hamilton [1761–1814]

THE ROVER'S ADIEU

From " Rokeby "

" A WEARY lot is thine, fair maid,
  · A weary lot is thine!
To pull the thorn thy brow to braid,
   And press the rue for wine.
A lightsome eye, a soldier's mien,
   A feather of the blue,
A doublet of the Lincoln green—
   No more of me ye knew,
      My Love!
   No more of me ye knew.

"This morn is merry June, I trow,
   The rose is budding fain;
But she shall bloom in winter snow
   Ere we two meet again."
—He turned his charger as he spake
   Upon the river shore,
He gave the bridle-reins a shake,
   Said "Adieu for evermore,
      My Love!
   And adieu for evermore."
         Walter Scott [1771–1832]

"LOUDOUN'S BONNIE WOODS AND BRAES"

"LOUDOUN'S bonnie woods and braes,
  I maun lea' them a', lassie;
Wha can thole when Britain's faes
  Wad gi'e Britons law, lassie?
Wha wad shun the field o' danger?
Wha frae fame wad live a stranger?
Now when freedom bids avenge her,
  Wha wad shun her ca', lassie?
Loudoun's bonnie woods and braes
Hae seen our happy bridal days,
And gentle Hope shall soothe thy waes
  When I am far awa', lassie."

"Hark! the swelling bugle sings,
  Yielding joy to thee, laddie,
But the dolefu' bugle brings
  Waefu' thoughts to me, laddie.
Lanely I maun climb the mountain,
Lanely stray beside the fountain,
Still the weary moments countin',
  Far frae love and thee, laddie.
O'er the gory fields of war,
When Vengeance drives his crimson car,
Thou'lt maybe fa', frae me afar,
  And nane to close thy e'e, laddie."

"O! resume thy wonted smile!
  O! suppress thy fears, lassie!
Glorious honor crowns the toil
  That the soldier shares, lassie;
Heaven will shield thy faithful lover
Till the vengeful strife is over;
Then we'll meet nae mair to sever;
  Till the day we dee, lassie.
'Midst our bonnie woods and braes
We'll spend our peaceful, happy days,
As blithe's yon lightsome lamb that plays
  On Loudoun's flowery lea, lassie."

Robert Tannahill [1774–1810]

"FARE THEE WELL"

FARE thee well! and if for ever,
  Still for ever, fare *thee well:*
Even though unforgiving, never
  'Gainst thee shall my heart rebel.

Would that breast were bared before thee
  Where thy head so oft hath lain,
While that placid sleep came o'er thee
  Which thou ne'er canst know again:

Would that breast, by thee glanced over,
  Every inmost thought could show!
Then thou wouldst at last discover
  'Twas not well to spurn it so.

Though the world for this commend thee,—
  Though it smile upon the blow,
Even its praises must offend thee,
  Founded on another's woe:

Though my many faults defaced me,
  Could no other arm be found
Than the one which once embraced me,
  To inflict a cureless wound?

Yet, oh yet, thyself deceive not;
  Love may sink by slow decay,
But by sudden wrench, believe not
  Hearts can thus be torn away:

Still thine own its life retaineth;—
  Still must mine, though bleeding, beat;
And the undying thought which paineth
  Is—that we no more may meet.

These are words of deeper sorrow
  Than the wail above the dead;
Both shall live, but every morrow
  Wake us from a widowed bed.

And when thou wouldst solace gather,
　　When our child's first accents flow,
Wilt thou teach her to say "Father!"
　　Though his care she must forego?

When her little hands shall press thee,
　　When her lip to thine is pressed,
Think of him whose prayer shall bless thee,
　　Think of him thy love had blessed!

Should her lineaments resemble
　　Those thou nevermore may'st see,
Then thy heart will softly tremble
　　With a pulse yet true to me.

All my faults perchance thou knowest,
　　All my madness none can know;
All my hopes, where'er thou goest,
　　Whither, yet with *thee* they go.

Every feeling hath been shaken;
　　Pride, which not a world could bow,
Bows to thee,—by thee forsaken,
　　Even my soul forsakes me now:

But 'tis done,—all words are idle,—
　　Words from me are vainer still;
But the thoughts we cannot bridle
　　Force their way without the will.

Fare thee well!—thus disunited,
　　Torn from every nearer tie,
Seared in heart, and lone, and blighted,
　　More than this I scarce can die.

　　　　　　　　George Gordon Byron [1788–1824]

"MAID OF ATHENS, ERE WE PART"

　　MAID of Athens, ere we part,
　　　Give, oh, give me back my heart!

Or, since that has left my breast,
Keep it now, and take the rest!
Hear my vow before I go,
Ζώη μοῦ, σᾶς ἀγαπῶ.

By those tresses unconfined,
Wooed by each Ægean wind;
By those lids whose jetty fringe
Kiss thy soft cheeks' blooming tinge;
By those wild eyes like the roe,
Ζώη μοῦ, σᾶς ἀγαπῶ.

By that lip I long to taste;
By that zone-encircled waist;
By all the token-flowers that tell
What words can never speak so well;
By love's alternate joy and woe,
Ζώη μοῦ, σᾶς ἀγαπῶ.

Maid of Athens! I am gone:
Think of me, sweet! when alone.
Though I fly to Istambol,
Athens holds my heart and soul:
Can I cease to love thee? No!
Ζώη μοῦ, σᾶς ἀγαπῶ.

George Gordon Byron [1788–1824]

"WHEN WE TWO PARTED"

WHEN we two parted
In silence and tears,
Half broken-hearted,
To sever for years,
Pale grew thy cheek and cold,
Colder thy kiss;
Truly that hour foretold
Sorrow to this!

The dew of the morning
Sunk chill on my brow;
It felt like the warning
Of what I feel now.

Thy vows are all broken,
And light is thy fame:
I hear thy name spoken
And share in its shame.

They name thee before me,
A knell to mine ear;
A shudder comes o'er me—
Why wert thou so dear?
They know not I knew thee
Who knew thee too well:
Long, long shall I rue thee
Too deeply to tell.

In secret we met:
In silence I grieve
That thy heart could forget,
Thy spirit deceive.
If I should meet thee
After long years,
How should I greet thee?—
With silence and tears.

George Gordon Byron [1788–1824]

"GO, FORGET ME"

Go, forget me! Why should sorrow
  O'er that brow a shadow fling?
Go, forget me,—and to-morrow
  Brightly smile and sweetly sing.
Smile—though I shall not be near thee.
Sing—though I shall never hear thee.
  May thy soul with pleasure shine,
  Lasting as the gloom of mine.

Like the sun, thy presence glowing
  Clothes the meanest things in light;
And when thou, like him, art going,
  Loveliest objects fade in night.
All things looked so bright about thee,
That they nothing seem without thee;

By that pure and lucid mind
Earthly things are too refined.

Go, thou vision, wildly gleaming,
  Softly on my soul that fell;
Go, for me no longer beaming—
  Hope and Beauty, fare ye well!
Go, and all that once delighted
Take—and leave me, all benighted,
  Glory's burning, generous swell,
  Fancy, and the poet's shell.

Charles Wolfe [1791–1823]

LAST NIGHT

I SAT with one I love last night,
She sang to me an olden strain;
In former times it woke delight,
    Last night—but pain.

Last night we saw the stars arise,
But clouds soon dimmed the ether blue:
And when we sought each other's eyes
    Tears dimmed them too!

We paced along our favorite walk,
But paced in silence broken-hearted:
Of old we used to smile and talk;
    Last night—we parted.

George Darley [1795–1846]

ADIEU

LET time and chance combine, combine,
  Let time and chance combine;
The fairest love from heaven above,
  That love of yours was mine,
    My dear,
  That love of yours was mine.

The past is fled and gone, and gone,
　The past is fled and gone;
If naught but pain to me remain,
　I'll fare in memory on,
　　　My dear,
　I'll fare in memory on.

The saddest tears must fall, must fall,
　The saddest tears must fall;
In weal or woe, in this world below,
　I love you ever and all,
　　　My dear,
　I love you ever and all.

A long road full of pain, of pain,
　A long road full of pain;
One soul, one heart, sworn ne'er to part,—
　We ne'er can meet again,
　　　My dear,
　We ne'er can meet again.

Hard fate will not allow, allow,
　Hard fate will not allow;
We blessed were as the angels are,—
　Adieu forever now,
　　　My dear,
　Adieu forever now.

　　　　　　　　　Thomas Carlyle [1795–1881]

JEANIE MORRISON

I'VE wandered east, I've wandered west,
　Through mony a weary way;
But never, never can forget
　The luve o' life's young day!
The fire that's blawn on Beltane e'en,
　May weel be black gin Yule;
But blacker fa' awaits the heart
　Where first fond luve grows cule.

O dear, dear Jeanie Morrison,
　　The thochts o' bygane years
Still fling their shadows owre my path,
　　And blind my een wi' tears:
They blind my een wi' saut, saut tears,
　　And sair and sick I pine,
As Memory idly summons up
　　The blithe blinks o' langsyne.

'Twas then we luvit ilk ither weel,
　　'Twas then we twa did part;
Sweet time, sad time!—twa bairns at schule,
　　Twa bairns, and but ae heart!
'Twas then we sat on ae laigh bink,
　　To leir ilk ither lear;
And tones, and looks, and smiles were shed,
　　Remembered evermair.

I wonder, Jeanie, aften yet,
　　When sitting on that bink,
Cheek touchin' cheek, loof locked in loof,
　　What our wee heads could think!
When baith bent doun owre ae braid page,
　　Wi' ae buik on our knee,
Thy lips were on thy lesson, but
　　My lesson was in thee.

Oh, mind ye how we hung our heads,
　　How cheeks brent red wi' shame,
Whene'er the schule-weans, laughin', said,
　　We cleek'd thegither hame?
And mind ye o' the Saturdays
　　(The schule then skail't at noon),
When we ran aff to speel the braes—
　　The broomy braes o' June?

My head rins round and round about,
　　My heart flows like a sea,
As, ane by ane, the thochts rush back
　　O' schule-time and o' thee.

Oh, mornin' life! Oh, mornin' luve!
  Oh, lichtsome days and lang,
When hinnied hopes around our hearts,
  Like simmer blossoms, sprang!

Oh, mind ye, luve, how aft we left
  The deavin' dinsome toun,
To wander by the green burnside,
  And hear its waters croon?
The simmer leaves hung owre our heads,
  The flowers burst round our feet,
And in the gloamin' o' the wud
  The throssil whusslit sweet.

The throssil whusslit in the wud,
  The burn sung to the trees,
And we, with Nature's heart in tune,
  Concerted harmonies;
And on the knowe abune the burn
  For hours thegither sat
In the silentness o' joy, till baith
  Wi' very gladness grat.

Ay, ay, dear Jeanie Morrison,
  Tears trinkled doun your cheek,
Like dew-beads on a rose, yet nane
  Had ony power to speak!
That was a time, a blessèd time,
  When hearts were fresh and young,
When freely gushed all feelings forth,
  Unsyllabled—unsung!

I marvel, Jeanie Morrison,
  Gin I hae been to thee
As closely twined wi' earliest thochts
  As ye hae been to me?
Oh! tell me gin their music fills
  Thine ear as it does mine;
Oh! say gin e'er your heart grows great
  Wi' dreamings o' langsyne?

I've wandered east, I've wandered west,
  I've borne a weary lot;
But in my wanderings, far or near,
  Ye never were forgot.
The fount that first burst frae this heart,
  Still travels on its way;
And channels deeper as it rins
  The luve o' life's young day.

O dear, dear Jeanie Morrison,
  Since we were sindered young,
I've never seen your face, nor heard
  The music o' your tongue;
But I could hug all wretchedness,
  And happy could I dee,
Did I but ken your heart still dreamed
  O' bygane days and me!

                    William Motherwell [1797–1835]

THE SEA–LANDS

Would I were on the sea-lands,
  Where winds know how to sting;
And in the rocks at midnight
  The lost long murmurs sing.

Would I were with my first love
  To hear the rush and roar
Of spume below the doorstep
  And winds upon the door.

My first love was a fair girl
  With ways forever new;
And hair a sunlight yellow,
  And eyes a morning blue.

The roses, have they tarried
  Or are they dun and frayed?

If we had stayed together,
  Would love, indeed, have stayed?

Ah, years are filled with learning,
  And days are leaves of change!
And I have met so many
  I knew . . . and found them strange.

But on the sea-lands tumbled
  By winds that sting and blind,
The nights we watched, so silent,
  Come back, come back to mind . . .

I mind about my first love,
  And hear the rush and roar
Of spume below the doorstep
  And winds upon the door.

Orrick Johns [1887–

FAIR INES

O SAW ye not fair Ines?
  She's gone into the West,
To dazzle when the sun is down,
  And rob the world of rest:
She took our daylight with her,
  The smiles that we love best,
With morning blushes on her cheek,
  And pearls upon her breast.

O turn again, fair Ines,
  Before the fall of night,
For fear the Moon should shine alone,
  And stars unrivaled bright;
And blessèd will the lover be
  That walks beneath their light,
And breathes the love against thy cheek
  I dare not even write!

Would I had been, fair Ines,
    That gallant cavalier,
Who rode so gaily by thy side,
    And whispered thee so near!
Were there no bonny dames at home,
    Or no true lovers here,
That he should cross the seas to win
    The dearest of the dear?

I saw thee, lovely Ines,
    Descend along the shore,
With bands of noble gentlemen,
    And banners waved before;
And gentle youth and maidens gay,
    And snowy plumes they wore:
It would have been a beauteous dream,—
    If it had been no more!

Alas, alas! fair Ines,
    She went away with song,
With Music waiting on her steps,
    And shoutings of the throng;
But some were sad, and felt no mirth,
    But only Music's wrong,
In sounds that sang Farewell, farewell,
    To her you've loved so long.

Farewell, farewell, fair Ines!
    That vessel never bore
So fair a lady on its deck,
    Nor danced so light before,—
Alas for pleasure on the sea,
    And sorrow on the shore!
The smile that blessed one lover's heart
    Has broken many more!
                                    Thomas Hood [1799–1845]

A VALEDICTION

God be with thee, my belovèd,—God be with thee!
    Else alone thou goest forth,
    Thy face unto the north,

Moor and pleasance all around thee and beneath thee
    Looking equal in one snow;
    While I, who try to reach thee,
    Vainly follow, vainly follow
    With the farewell and the hollo,
    And cannot reach thee so.
    Alas, I can but teach thee!
God be with thee, my belovèd,—God be with thee!

Can I teach thee, my belovèd,—can I teach thee?
    If I said, "Go left or right,"
    The counsel would be light,
The wisdom, poor of all that could enrich thee;
    My right would show like left;
    My raising would depress thee,
    My choice of light would blind thee,
    Of way—would leave behind thee,
    Of end—would leave bereft.
    Alas, I can but bless thee!
May God teach thee, my belovèd,—may God teach thee!

Can I bless thee, my belovèd,—can I bless thee?
    What blessing word can I
    From mine own tears keep dry?
What flowers grow in my field wherewith to dress thee?
    My good reverts to ill;
    My calmnesses would move thee,
    My softnesses would prick thee,
    My bindings up would break thee,
    My crownings curse and kill.
    Alas, I can but love thee!
May God bless thee, my belovèd,—may God bless thee!

Can I love thee, my belovèd,—can I love thee?
    And is *this* like love, to stand
    With no help in my hand,
When strong as death I fain would watch above thee?
    My love-kiss can deny
    No tear that falls beneath it;

Mine oath of love can swear thee
From no ill that comes near thee,
And thou diest while I breathe it,
And *I*—I can but die!
May God love thee, my belovèd,—may God love thee!

Elizabeth Barrett Browning [1806–1861]

FAREWELL

Thou goest; to what distant place
    Wilt thou thy sunlight carry?
I stay with cold and clouded face:
    How long am I to tarry?
Where'er thou goest, morn will be;
Thou leavest night and gloom to me.

The night and gloom I can but take;
    I do not grudge thy splendor:
Bid souls of eager men awake;
    Be kind and bright and tender.
Give day to other worlds; for me
It must suffice to dream of thee.

John Addington Symonds [1840–1893]

"I DO NOT LOVE THEE"

I do not love thee!—no! I do not love thee!
And yet when thou art absent I am sad;
    And envy even the bright blue sky above thee,
Whose quiet stars may see thee and be glad.

I do not love thee!—yet, I know not why,
Whate'er thou dost seems still well done, to me:
    And often in my solitude I sigh
That those I do love are not more like thee!

I do not love thee!—yet, when thou art gone,
I hate the sound (though those who speak be near)
    Which breaks the lingering echo of the tone
Thy voice of music leaves upon my ear.

I do not love thee!—yet thy speaking eyes,
With their deep, bright, and most expressive blue,
  Between me and the midnight heaven arise,
Oftener than any eyes I ever knew.

I know I do not love thee!—yet, alas!
Others will scarcely trust my candid heart;
  And oft I catch them smiling as they pass,
Because they see me gazing where thou art.
                    Caroline Elizabeth Sarah Norton [1808–1870]

THE PALM–TREE AND THE PINE

BENEATH an Indian palm a girl
  Of other blood reposes,
Her cheek is clear and pale as pearl,
  Amid that wild of roses.

Beside a northern pine a boy
  Is leaning fancy-bound,
Nor listens where with noisy joy
  Awaits the impatient hound.

Cool grows the sick and feverish calm,—
  Relaxed the frosty twine,—
The pine-tree dreameth of the palm,
  The palm-tree of the pine.

As soon shall nature interlace
  Those dimly-visioned boughs,
As these young lovers face to face
  Renew their early vows!
                    Richard Monckton Milnes [1809–1885]

"O SWALLOW, SWALLOW, FLYING SOUTH"

From "The Princess"

O SWALLOW, Swallow, flying, flying South,
Fly to her, and fall upon her gilded eaves,
And tell her, tell her what I tell to thee.

O, tell her, Swallow, thou that knowest each,
That bright and fierce and fickle is the South,
And dark and true and tender is the North.

O Swallow, Swallow, if I could follow, and light
Upon her lattice, I would pipe and trill,
And cheep and twitter twenty million loves.

O, were I thou that she might take me in,
And lay me on her bosom, and her heart
Would rock the snowy cradle till I died!

Why lingereth she to clothe her heart with love,
Delaying as the tender ash delays
To clothe herself, when all the woods are green?

O, tell her, Swallow, that thy brood is flown;
Say to her, I do but wanton in the South,
But in the North long since my nest is made.

O, tell her, brief is life but love is long,
And brief the sun of summer in the North,
And brief the moon of beauty in the South.

O Swallow, flying from the golden woods,
Fly to her, and pipe and woo her, and make her mine,
And tell her, tell her, that I follow thee.
Alfred Tennyson [1809–1892]

THE FLOWER'S NAME

HERE'S the garden she walked across,
    Arm in my arm, such a short while since:
Hark, now I push its wicket, the moss
    Hinders the hinges and makes them wince!
She must have reached this shrub ere she turned,
    As back with that murmur the wicket swung;
For she laid the poor snail, my chance foot spurned,
    To feed and forget it the leaves among.

Down this side of the gravel-walk
  She went while her robe's edge brushed the box:
And here she paused in her gracious talk
  To point me a moth on the milk-white phlox.
Roses, ranged in valiant row,
  I will never think that she passed you by!
She loves you, noble roses, I know;
  But yonder see where the rock-plants lie!

This flower she stopped at, finger on lip,
  Stooped over, in doubt, as settling its claim;
Till she gave me, with pride to make no slip,
  Its soft meandering Spanish name:
What a name! Was it love or praise?
  Speech half-asleep, or song half-awake?
I must learn Spanish, one of these days,
  Only for that slow sweet name's sake.

Roses, if I live and do well,
  I may bring her, one of these days,
To fix you fast with as fine a spell,
  Fit you each with his Spanish phrase:
But do not detain me now; for she lingers
  There, like sunshine over the ground,
And ever I see her soft white fingers
  Searching after the bud she found.

Flower, you Spaniard, look that you grow not,
  Stay as you are and be loved forever!
Bud, if I kiss you, 'tis that you blow not,
  Mind, the shut pink mouth opens never!
For while it pouts, her fingers wrestle,
  Twinkling the audacious leaves between,
Till round they turn, and down they nestle—
  Is not the dear mark still to be seen?

Where I find her not, beauties vanish;
  Whither I follow her, beauties flee;
Is there no method to tell her in Spanish
  June's twice June since she breathed it with me?

Come, bud, show me the least of her traces,
Treasure my lady's lightest footfall!
—Ah, you may flout and turn up your faces,—
Roses, you are not so fair after all!

Robert Browning [1812–1889]

TO MARGUERITE

YES: in the sea of life enisled,
    With echoing straits between us thrown,
Dotting the shoreless watery wild,
    We mortal millions live *alone*.
The islands feel the enclasping flow,
And then their endless bounds they know.

But when the moon their hollows lights,
    And they are swept by balms of spring,
And in their glens, on starry nights,
    The nightingales divinely sing;
And lovely notes, from shore to shore,
Across the sounds and channels pour;

O then a longing like despair
    Is to their farthest caverns sent!
For surely once, they feel, we were
    Parts of a single continent.
Now round us spreads the watery plain—
O might our marges meet again!

Who ordered that their longing's fire
    Should be, as soon as kindled, cooled?
Who renders vain their deep desire?—
    A God, a God their severance ruled;
And bade betwixt their shores to be
The unplumbed, salt, estranging sea.

Matthew Arnold [1822–1888]

SEPARATION

STOP!—not to me, at this bitter departing,
    Speak of the sure consolations of time!
Fresh be the wound, still-renewed be its smarting,
    So but thy image endure in its prime.

But, if the steadfast commandment of Nature
   Wills that remembrance should always decay—
If the loved form and the deep-cherished feature
   Must, when unseen, from the soul fade away—

Me let no half-effaced memories cumber!
   Fled, fled at once, be all vestige of thee!
Deep be the darkness and still be the slumber—
   Dead be the past and its phantoms to me!

Then, when we meet, and thy look strays towards me,
   Scanning my face and the changes wrought there:
Who, let me say, *is this stranger regards me,*
   With the gray eyes, and the lovely brown hair?
             Matthew Arnold [1822–1888]

LONGING

COME to me in my dreams, and then
By day I shall be well again!
For then the night will more than pay
The hopeless longing of the day.

Come, as thou cam'st a thousand times,
A messenger from radiant climes,
And smile on thy new world, and be
As kind to others as to me!

Or, as thou never cam'st in sooth,
Come now, and let me dream it truth;
And part my hair, and kiss my brow,
And say: *My love! why sufferest thou?*

Come to me in my dreams, and then
By day I shall be well again!
For then the night will more than pay
The hopeless longing of the day
           Matthew Arnold [1822–1888]

DIVIDED

I

An empty sky, a world of heather,
  Purple of foxglove, yellow of broom;
We two among them wading together,
  Shaking out honey, treading perfume.

Crowds of bees are giddy with clover,
  Crowds of grasshoppers skip at our feet,
Crowds of larks at their matins hang over,
  Thanking the Lord for a life so sweet.

Flusheth the rise with her purple favor,
  Gloweth the cleft with her golden ring,
'Twixt the two brown butterflies waver,
  Lightly settle, and sleepily swing.

We two walk till the purple dieth,
  And short dry grass under foot is brown,
But one little streak at a distance lieth
  Green like a ribbon to prank the down.

II

Over the grass we stepped unto it,
  And God He knoweth how blithe we were!
Never a voice to bid us eschew it:
  Hey the green ribbon that showed so fair!

Hey the green ribbon! we kneeled beside it,
  We parted the grasses dewy and sheen:
Drop over drop there filtered and slided
  A tiny bright beck that trickled between.

Tinkle, tinkle, sweetly it sung to us,
  Light was our talk as of fairy bells;—
Fairy wedding-bells faintly rung to us
  Down in their fortunate parallels.

Hand in hand, while the sun peered over,
   We lapped the grass on that youngling spring;
Swept back its rushes, smoothed its clover,
   And said, "Let us follow it westering."

III

A dappled sky, a world of meadows,
   Circling above us the black rooks fly
Forward, backward; io their dark shadows
   Flit on the blossoming tapestry;—

Flit on the beck; for her long grass parteth
   As hair from a maid's bright eyes blown back:
And, lo, the sun like a lover darteth
   His flattering smile on her wayward track.

Sing on! we sing in the glorious weather
   Till one steps over the tiny strand,
So narrow, in sooth, that still together
   On either brink we go hand in hand.

The beck grows wider, the hands must sever.
   On either margin, our songs all done,
We move apart, while she singeth ever,
   Taking the course of the stooping sun.

He prays, "Come over,"—I may not follow;
   I cry, "Return,"—but he cannot come:
We speak, we laugh, but with voices hollow;
   Our hands are hanging, our hearts are numb.

IV

A breathing sigh, a sigh for answer,
   A little talking of outward things:
The careless beck is a merry dancer,
   Keeping sweet time to the air she sings.

A little pain when the beck grows wider;
   "Cross to me now; for her wavelets swell";
"I may not cross,"—and the voice beside her
   Faintly reacheth, though heeded well.

No backward path; ah! no returning;
　　No second crossing that ripple's flow:
"Come to me now, for the west is burning;
　　Come ere it darkens."—"Ah, no! ah, no!"

Then cries of pain, and arms outreaching,—
　　The beck grows wider and swift and deep:
Passionate words as of one beseeching:
　　The loud beck drowns them: we walk, and weep.

V

A yellow moon in splendor drooping,
　　A tired queen with her state oppressed,
Low by rushes and swordgrass stooping,
　　Lies she soft on the waves at rest.

The desert heavens have felt her sadness;
　　Her earth will weep her some dewy tears;
The wild beck ends her tune of gladness,
　　And goeth stilly as soul that fears.

We two walk on in our grassy places
　　On either marge of the moonlit flood,
With the moon's own sadness in our faces,
　　Where joy is withered, blossom and bud.

VI

A shady freshness, chafers whirring;
　　A little piping of leaf-hid birds;
A flutter of wings, a fitful stirring;
　　A cloud to the eastward snowy as curds.

Bare grassy slopes, where kids are tethered,
　　Round valleys like nests all ferny-lined,
Round hills, with fluttering tree-tops feathered,
　　Swell high in their freckled robes behind.

A rose-flush tender, a thrill, a quiver,
　　When golden gleams to the tree-tops glide;
A flashing edge for the milk-white river,
　　The beck, a river—with still sleek tide.

Broad and white, and polished as silver,
  On she goes under fruit-laden trees:
Sunk in leafage cooeth the culver,
  And 'plaineth of love's disloyalties.

Glitters the dew, and shines the river,
  Up comes the lily and dries her bell;
But two are walking apart forever,
  And wave their hands for a mute farewell.

VII

A braver swell, a swifter sliding;
  The river hasteth, her banks recede.
Wing-like sails on her bosom gliding
  Bear down the lily, and drown the reed.

Stately prows are rising and bowing
  (Shouts of mariners winnow the air),
And level sands for banks endowing
  The tiny green ribbon that showed so fair.

While, O my heart! as white sails shiver,
  And clouds are passing, and banks stretch wide,
How hard to follow, with lips that quiver,
  That moving speck on the far-off side.

Farther, farther; I see it, know it—
  My eyes brim over, it melts away:
Only my heart to my heart shall show it
  As I walk desolate day by day.

VIII

And yet I know past all doubting, truly,—
  A knowledge greater than grief can dim,—
I know, as he loved, he will love me duly,—
  Yea, better, e'en better than I love him.

And as I walk by the vast calm river,
  The awful river so dread to see,
I say, "Thy breadth and thy depth forever
  Are bridged by his thoughts that cross to me."
                    Jean Ingelow [1820–1897]

MY PLAYMATE

THE pines were dark on Ramoth hill,
　　Their song was soft and low;
The blossoms in the sweet May wind
　　Were falling like the snow.

The blossoms drifted at our feet,
　　The orchard birds sang clear;
The sweetest and the saddest day
　　It seemed of all the year.

For, more to me than birds or flowers,
　　My playmate left her home,
And took with her the laughing spring,
　　The music and the bloom.

She kissed the lips of kith and kin,
　　She laid her hand in mine:
What more could ask the bashful boy
　　Who fed her father's kine?

She left us in the bloom of May:
　　The constant years told o'er
Their seasons with as sweet May morns,
　　But she came back no more.

I walk, with noiseless feet, the round
　　Of uneventful years;
Still o'er and o'er I sow the spring
　　And reap the autumn ears.

She lives where all the golden year
　　Her summer roses blow;
The dusky children of the sun
　　Before her come and go.

There haply with her jeweled hands
　　She smooths her silken gown,—
No more the homespun lap wherein
　　I shook the walnuts down.

My Playmate

The wild grapes wait us by the brook,
   The brown nuts on the hill,
And still the May-day flowers make sweet
   The woods of Follymill.

The lilies blossom in the pond,
   The bird builds in the tree,
The dark pines sing on Ramoth hill
   The slow song of the sea.

I wonder if she thinks of them,
   And how the old time seems,—
If ever the pines of Ramoth wood
   Are sounding in her dreams.

I see her face, I hear her voice:
   Does she remember mine?
And what to her is now the boy
   Who fed her father's kine?

What cares she that the orioles build
   For other eyes than ours,—
That other laps with nuts are filled,
   And other hands with flowers?

O playmate in the golden time!
   Our mossy seat is green,
Its fringing violets blossom yet,
   The old trees o'er it lean.

The winds so sweet with birch and fern
   A sweeter memory blow;
And there in spring the veeries sing
   The song of long ago.

And still the pines of Ramoth wood
   Are moaning like the sea,—
The moaning of the sea of change
   Between myself and thee!

       John Greenleaf Whittier [1807–1892]

A FAREWELL

WITH all my will, but much against my heart,
We two now part.
My Very Dear,
Our solace is, the sad road lies so clear.
It needs no art,
With faint, averted feet
And many a tear,
In our opposèd paths to persevere.
Go thou to East, I West.
We will not say
There's any hope, it is so far away.
But, O, my Best,
When the one darling of our widowhead,
The nursling Grief
Is dead,
And no dews blur our eyes
To see the peach-bloom come in evening skies,
Perchance we may,
Where now this night is day,
And even through faith of still averted feet,
Making full circle of our banishment,
Amazèd meet;
The bitter journey to the bourne so sweet
Seasoning the termless feast of our content
With tears of recognition never dry.

                              Coventry Patmore [1823–1896]

DEPARTURE

IT was not like your great and gracious ways!
Do you, that have naught other to lament,
Never, my Love, repent
Of how, that July afternoon,
You went,
With sudden, unintelligible phrase,
And frightened eye,
Upon your journey of so many days

Without a single kiss, or a good-bye?
I knew, indeed, that you were parting soon;
And so we sate, within the low sun's rays,
You whispering to me, for your voice was weak,
Your harrowing praise.
Well, it was well
To hear you such things speak,
And I could tell
What made your eyes a glowing gloom of love,
As a warm South-wind sombers a March grove.

And it was like your great and gracious ways
To turn your talk on daily things, my Dear,
Lifting the luminous, pathetic lash
To let the laughter flash,
Whilst I drew near,
Because you spoke so low that I could scarcely hear.
But all at once to leave me at the last,
More at the wonder than the loss aghast,
With huddled, unintelligible phrase,
And frightened eye,
And go your journey of all days
With not one kiss, or a good-bye,
And the only loveless look the look with which you passed:
'Twas all unlike your great and gracious ways.

Coventry Patmore [1823–1896]

A SONG OF PARTING

My dear, the time has come to say
    Farewell to London town,
Farewell to each familiar street,
    The room where we looked down
Upon the people going by,
    The river flowing fast:
The innumerable shine of lamps,
    The bridges and—our past.

Our past of London days and nights,
    When every night we dreamed

Of Love and Art and Happiness,
    And every day it seemed
Ah! little room, you held my life,
    In you I found my all;
A white hand on the mantelpiece,
    A shadow on the wall.

My dear, what dinners we have had,
    What cigarettes and wine
In faded corners of Soho,
    Your fingers touching mine!
And now the time has come to say
    Farewell to London town;
The prologue of our play is done,
    So ring the curtain down.

There lies a crowded life ahead
    In field and sleepy lane,
A fairer picture than we saw
    Framed in our window-pane.
There'll be the stars on summer nights,
    The white moon through the trees,
Moths, and the song of nightingales
    To float along the breeze.

And in the morning we shall see
    The swallows in the sun,
And hear the cuckoo on the hill
    Welcome a day begun.
And life will open with the rose
    For me, sweet, and for you,
And on our life and on the rose
    How soft the falling dew!

So let us take this tranquil path,
    But drop a parting tear
For town, whose greatest gift to us
    Was to be lovers here.

            H. C. Compton Mackenzie [1883-

SONG

From "The Earthly Paradise"

FAIR is the night, and fair the day,
Now April is forgot of May,
Now into June May falls away:
Fair day! fair night!   O give me back
The tide that all fair things did lack
Except my Love, except my Sweet!

Blow back, O wind! thou art not kind,
Though thou art sweet: thou hast no mind
Her hair about my Sweet to bind.
O flowery sward! though thou art bright,
I praise thee not for thy delight,—
Thou hast not kissed her silver feet.

Thou know'st her not, O rustling tree!
What dost thou then to shadow me,
Whose shade her breast did never see?
O flowers! in vain ye bow adown:
Ye have not felt her odorous gown
Brush past your heads my lips to meet.

Flow on, great river! thou mayst deem
That far away, a summer stream,
Thou saw'st her limbs amidst the gleam,
And kissed her foot, and kissed her knee:
Yet get thee swift unto the sea!
With naught of true thou wilt me greet.

And Thou that men call by my name!
O helpless One! hast thou no shame
That thou must even look the same
As while agone, as while agone
When Thou and She were left alone,
And hands and lips and tears did meet?

Grow weak and pine, lie down to die,
O body! in thy misery,

Because short time and sweet goes by.
O foolish heart! how weak thou art:
Break, break, because thou needs must part
From thine own Love, from thine own Sweet!

William Morris [1834–1896]

AT PARTING

FOR a day and a night Love sang to us, played with us,
   Folded us round from the dark and the light;
And our hearts were fulfilled of the music he made with us,
Made with our hearts and our lips while he stayed with us,
   Stayed in mid passage his pinions from flight
        For a day and a night.

From his foes that kept watch with his wings had he hidden
   us,
   Covered us close from the eyes that would smite,
From the feet that had tracked and the tongues that had
    chidden us
Sheltering in shade of the myrtles forbidden us
   Spirit and flesh growing one with delight
        For a day and a night.

But his wings will not rest and his feet will not stay for us:
   Morning is here in the joy of its might;
With his breath has he sweetened a night and a day for us:
Now let him pass, and the myrtles make way for us;
   Love can but last in us here at his height
        For a day and a night.

Algernon Charles Swinburne [1837–1909]

"IF SHE BUT KNEW"

IF she but knew that I am weeping
    Still for her sake,
That love and sorrow grow with keeping
    Till they must break,
My heart that breaking will adore her,
    Be hers and die;
If she might hear me once implore her,
    Would she not sigh?

If she but knew that it would save me
　　Her voice to hear,
Saying she pitied me, forgave me,
　　Must she forbear?
If she were told that I was dying,
　　Would she be dumb?
Could she content herself with sighing?
　　Would she not come?

Arthur O'Shaughnessy [1844–1881]

KATHLEEN MAVOURNEEN

KATHLEEN MAVOURNEEN! the gray dawn is breaking,
　The horn of the hunter is heard on the hill;
The lark from her light wing the bright dew is shaking,—
　Kathleen Mavourneen! what, slumbering still?
Oh, hast thou forgotten how soon we must sever?
　Oh! hast thou forgotten this day we must part?
It may be for years, and it may be forever!
　Oh, why art thou silent, thou voice of my heart?
Oh! why art thou silent, Kathleen Mavourneen?

Kathleen Mavourneen, awake from thy slumbers!
　The blue mountains glow in the sun's golden light;
Ah, where is the spell that once hung on my numbers?
　Arise in thy beauty, thou star of my night!
Mavourneen, Mavourneen, my sad tears are falling,
　To think that from Erin and thee I must part!
It may be for years, and it may be forever!
　Then why art thou silent, thou voice of my heart?
Then why art thou silent, Kathleen Mavourneen?

Louisa Macartney Crawford [1790–1858]

ROBIN ADAIR

WHAT'S this dull town to me?
　Robin's not near,—
He whom I wished to see,
　Wished for to hear;

Where's all the joy and mirth
Made life a heaven on earth?
O, they're all fled with thee,
  Robin Adair!

What made the assembly shine?
  Robin Adair:
What made the ball so fine?
  Robin was there:
What, when the play was o'er,
What made my heart so sore?
O, it was parting with
  Robin Adair!

But now thou art far from me,
  Robin Adair;
But now I never see
  Robin Adair;
Yet him I loved so well
Still in my heart shall dwell;
O, I can ne'er forget
  Robin Adair!

Welcome on shore again,
  Robin Adair!
Welcome once more again,
  Robin Adair!
I feel thy trembling hand;
Tears in thy eyelids stand,
To greet thy native land,
  Robin Adair!

Long I ne'er saw thee, love,
  Robin Adair;
Still I prayed for thee, love,
  Robin Adair;
When thou wert far at sea,
Many made love to me,
But still I thought on thee,
  Robin Adair!

Come to my heart again,
  Robin Adair;
Never to part again,
  Robin Adair;
And if thou still art true,
I will be constant too,
And will wed none but you,
  Robin Adair!

        Caroline Keppel [1735– ?]

"IF YOU WERE HERE"

A SONG IN WINTER

O LOVE, if you were here
  This dreary, weary day,—
If your lips, warm and dear,
  Found some sweet word to say,—
Then hardly would seem drear
  These skies of wintry gray.

But you are far away,—
  How far from me, my dear!
What cheer can warm the day?
  My heart is chill with fear,
Pierced through with swift dismay;
  A thought has turned Life sere:

If you, from far away,
  Should come not back, my dear:
If I no more might lay
  My hand on yours, nor hear
That voice, now sad, now gay,
  Caress my listening ear;

If you, from far away,
  Should come no more, my dear,—
Then with what dire dismay
  Year joined to hostile year
Would frown, if I should stay
  Where memories mock and jeer!

But I would come away
    To dwell with you, my dear;
Through unknown worlds to stray,—
    Or sleep; nor hope, nor fear,
Nor dream beneath the clay
    Of all our days that were.

Philip Bourke Marston [1850–1887]

"COME TO ME, DEAREST"

COME to me, dearest, I'm lonely without thee;
Daytime and night-time, I'm thinking about thee;
Night-time and daytime, in dreams I behold thee;
Unwelcome the waking which ceases to fold thee.
Come to me, darling, my sorrows to lighten,
Come in thy beauty to bless and to brighten;
Come in thy womanhood, meekly and lowly,
Come in thy lovingness, queenly and holy.

Swallows will flit round the desolate ruin,
Telling of spring and its joyous renewing;
And thoughts of thy love and its manifold treasure,
Are circling my heart with a promise of pleasure.
O Spring of my spirit, O May of my bosom,
Shine out on my soul, till it bourgeon and blossom;
The waste of my life has a rose-root within it,
And thy fondness alone to the sunshine can win it.

Figure that moves like a song through the even;
Features lit up by a reflex of heaven;
Eyes like the skies of poor Erin, our mother,
Where shadow and sunshine are chasing each other;
Smiles coming seldom, but childlike and simple,
Planting in each rosy cheek a sweet dimple;—
O, thanks to the Saviour, that even thy seeming
Is left to the exile to brighten his dreaming.

You have been glad when you knew I was gladdened;
Dear, are you sad now to hear I am saddened?

Our hearts ever answer in tune and in time, love,
As octave to octave, and rhyme unto rhyme, love:
I cannot weep but your tears will be flowing,
You cannot smile but my cheek will be glowing;
I would not die without you at my side, love,
You will not linger when I shall have died, love.

Come to me, dear, ere I die of my sorrow,
Rise on my gloom like the sun of to-morrow;
Strong, swift, and fond are the words which I speak, love,
With a song on your lip and a smile on your cheek, love.
Come, for my heart in your absence is weary,—
Haste, for my spirit is sickened and dreary,—
Come to my arms which alone should caress thee,
Come to the heart which is throbbing to press thee!

Joseph Brenan [1829–1857]

SONG

'TIS said that absence conquers love!
　But, oh! believe it not;
I've tried, alas! its power to prove,
　But thou art not forgot.
Lady, though fate has bid us part,
　Yet still thou art as dear,
As fixed in this devoted heart,
　As when I clasped thee here.

I plunge into the busy crowd,
　And smile to hear thy name;
And yet, as if I thought aloud,
　They know me still the same;
And when the wine-cup passes round,
　I toast some other fair,—
But when I ask my heart the sound,
　Thy name is echoed there.

And when some other name I learn,
　And try to whisper love,
Still will my heart to thee return
　Like the returning dove.

In vain! I never can forget,
  And would not be forgot;
For I must bear the same regret,
  Whate'er may be my lot.

E'en as the wounded bird will seek
  Its favorite bower to die,
So, lady! I would hear thee speak,
  And yield my parting sigh.
'Tis said that absence conquers love!
  But, oh! believe it not;
I've tried, alas! its power to prove,
  But thou art not forgot.

Frederick William Thomas [1811–1864]

PARTING

Too fair, I may not call thee mine:
  Too dear, I may not see
Those eyes with bridal beacons shine;
  Yet, Darling, keep for me—
Empty and hushed, and safe apart,—
One little corner of thy heart.

Thou wilt be happy, dear! and bless
  Thee: happy mayst thou be.
I would not make thy pleasure less;
  Yet, Darling, keep for me—
My life to light, my lot to leaven,—
One little corner of thy Heaven.

Good-by, dear heart! I go to dwell
  A weary way from thee;
Our first kiss is our last farewell;
  Yet, Darling, keep for me—
Who wander outside in the night,—
One little corner of thy light.

Gerald Massey [1828–1907]

THE PARTING HOUR

Not yet, dear love, not yet: the sun is high;
  You said last night, "At sunset I will go."
Come to the garden, where when blossoms die
  No word is spoken; it is better so:
    Ah! bitter word "Farewell."

Hark! how the birds sing sunny songs of spring!
  Soon they will build, and work will silence them;
So we grow less light-hearted as years bring
  Life's grave responsibilities—and then
    The bitter word "Farewell."

The violets fret to fragrance 'neath your feet,
  Heaven's gold sunlight dreams aslant your hair:
No flower for me! your mouth is far more sweet.
  O, let my lips forget, while lingering there,
    Love's bitter word "Farewell."

Sunset already! have we sat so long?
  The parting hour, and so much left unsaid!
The garden has grown silent—void of song,
  Our sorrow shakes us with a sudden dread!
    Ah! bitter word "Farewell."

                    Olive Custance [1874–

A SONG OF AUTUMN

All through the golden weather
  Until the autumn fell,
Our lives went by together
  So wildly and so well.

But autumn's wind uncloses
  The heart of all your flowers;
I think, as with the roses,
  So hath it been with ours.

Like some divided river
   Your ways and mine will be,
To drift apart for ever,
   For ever till the sea.

And yet for one word spoken,
   One whisper of regret,
The dream had not been broken,
   And love were with us yet.
             Rennell Rodd [1858–

THE GIRL I LEFT BEHIND ME

THE dames of France are fond and free,
   And Flemish lips are willing,
And soft the maids of Italy,
   And Spanish eyes are thrilling;
Still, though I bask beneath their smile,
   Their charms fail to bind me,
And my heart falls back to Erin's Isle,
   To the girl I left behind me.

For she's as fair as Shannon's side,
   And purer than its water,
But she refused to be my bride
   Though many a year I sought her;
Yet, since to France I sailed away,
   Her letters oft remind me
That I promised never to gainsay
   The girl I left behind me.

She says, "My own dear love, come home,
   My friends are rich and many,
Or else abroad with you I'll roam,
   A soldier stout as any;
If you'll not come, nor let me go,
   I'll think you have resigned me,"—
My heart nigh broke when I answered "No,"
   To the girl I left behind me.

For never shall my true love brave
  A life of war and toiling,
And never as a skulking slave
  I'll tread my native soil on;
But, were it free or to be freed,
  The battle's close would find me
To Ireland bound, nor message need
  From the girl I left behind me.

Unknown

"WHEN WE ARE PARTED"

WHEN we are parted let me lie
  In some far corner of thy heart,
  Silent, and from the world apart,
Like a forgotten melody:
Forgotten of the world beside,
  Cherished by one, and one alone,
  For some loved memory of its own;
So let me in thy heart abide
        When we are parted.

When we are parted, keep for me
  The sacred stillness of the night;
  That hour, sweet Love, is mine by right;
Let others claim the day of thee!
The cold world sleeping at our feet,
  My spirit shall discourse with thine;—
  When stars upon thy pillow shine,
At thy heart's door I stand and beat,
        Though we are parted.

Hamilton Aidé [1826–1906]

REMEMBER OR FORGET

I SAT beside the streamlet,
  I watched the water flow,
  As we together watched it
    One little year ago:

The soft rain pattered on the leaves,
    The April grass was wet.
Ah! folly to remember;
    'Tis wiser to forget.

The nightingales made vocal
    June's palace paved with gold;
I watched the rose you gave me
    Its warm red heart unfold;
But breath of rose and bird's song
    Were fraught with wild regret.
'Tis madness to remember;
    'Twere wisdom to forget.

I stood among the gold corn,
    Alas! no more, I knew,
To gather gleaner's measure
    Of the love that fell from you.
For me, no gracious harvest—
    Would God we ne'er had met!
'Tis hard, Love, to remember,
    But 'tis harder to forget.

The streamlet now is frozen,
    The nightingales are fled,
The cornfields are deserted,
    And every rose is dead.
I sit beside my lonely fire,
    And pray for wisdom yet:
For calmness to remember,
    Or courage to forget.
                    Hamilton Aidé [1826–1906]

NANCY DAWSON

NANCY DAWSON, Nancy Dawson,
    Not so very long ago
        Some one wronged you from sheer love, dear;
        Little thinking it would crush, dear,
    All I cherished in you so.

But now, what's the odds, my Nancy?
Where's the guinea, there's the fancy.
Are you Nancy, that old Nancy?
   Nancy Dawson.

Nancy Dawson, Nancy Dawson,
 I forget you, what you were;
  Till I feel the sad hours creep, dear,
   O'er my heart; as o'er my cheek, dear,
 Once of old, that old, old hair:
And then, unawares, my Nancy,
I remember, and I fancy
You are Nancy, that old Nancy;
   Nancy Dawson.
     Herbert P. Horne [1864–

MY LITTLE LOVE

GOD keep you safe, my little love,
 All through the night.
Rest close in His encircling arms
 Until the light.
My heart is with you as I kneel to pray,
"Good night! God keep you in His care alway."

Thick shadows creep like silent ghosts
 About my bed.
I lose myself in tender dreams
 While overhead
The moon comes stealing through the window bars.
A silver sickle gleaming 'mid the stars.

For I, though I am far away,
 Feel safe and strong,
To trust you thus, dear love, and yet
 The night is long.
I say with sobbing breath the old fond prayer,
"Good night! Sweet dreams! God keep you everywhere!"
    Charles B. Hawley [1858–

FOR EVER

THRICE with her lips she touched my lips,
  Thrice with her hand my hand,
And three times thrice looked towards the sea,
  But never to the land:
Then, "Sweet," she said, "no more delay,
For Heaven forbids a longer stay."

I, with my passion in my heart,
  Could find no words to waste;
But striving often to depart,
  I strained her to my breast:
Her wet tears washed my weary cheek;
I could have died, but could not speak.

The anchor swings, the sheet flies loose
  And, bending to the breeze,
The tall ship, never to return,
  Flies through the foaming seas:
Cheerily ho! the sailors cry;—
My sweet love lessening to my eye.

O Love, turn towards the land thy sight!
  No more peruse the sea;
Our God, who severs thus our hearts,
  Shall surely care for thee:
For me let waste-wide ocean swing,
I too lie safe beneath His wing.

William Caldwell Roscoe [1823–1859]

AUF WIEDERSEHEN

THE little gate was reached at last,
  Half hid in lilacs down the lane;
She pushed it wide, and, as she passed,
A wistful look she backward cast,
  And said,—"*Auf wiedersehen !*"

With hand on latch, a vision white
  Lingered reluctant, and again
Half doubting if she did aright,
Soft as the dews that fell that night,
   She said,—"*Auf wiedersehen !*"

The lamp's clear gleam flits up the stair;
  I linger in delicious pain;
Ah, in that chamber, whose rich air
To breathe in thought I scarcely dare,
   Thinks she,—"*Auf wiedersehen ?*" . . .

'Tis thirteen years; once more I press
  The turf that silences the lane;
I hear the rustle of her dress,
I smell the lilacs, and—ah, yes,
   I hear,—"*Auf wiedersehen !*"

Sweet piece of bashful maiden art!
  The English words had seemed too fain,
But these—they drew us heart to heart,
Yet held us tenderly apart;
   She said,—"*Auf wiedersehen !*"
          James Russell Lowell [1819–1891]

"FOREVER AND A DAY"

I LITTLE know or care
If the blackbird on the bough
Is filling all the air
With his soft crescendo now;
  For she is gone away,
  And when she went she took
  The springtime in her look,
  The peachblow on her cheek,
  The laughter from the brook,
  The blue from out the May—
  And what she calls a week
  Is forever and a day!

It's little that I mind
How the blossoms, pink or white,
At every touch of wind
Fall a-trembling with delight;
　For in the leafy lane,
　Beneath the garden-boughs,
　And through the silent house
　One thing alone I seek.
　Until she come again
　The May is not the May,
　And what she calls a week
　Is forever and a day!
　　　　Thomas Bailey Aldrich [1837-1907]

OLD GARDENS

THE white rose tree that spent its musk
　For lovers' sweeter praise,
The stately walks we sought at dusk,
　Have missed thee many days.

Again, with once-familiar feet,
　I tread the old parterre—
But, ah, its bloom is now less sweet
　Than when thy face was there.

I hear the birds of evening call;
　I take the wild perfume;
I pluck a rose—to let it fall
　And perish in the gloom.
　　　　Arthur Upson [1877-1908]

FERRY HINKSEY

　BEYOND the ferry water
　That fast and silent flowed,
　She turned, she gazed a moment,
　Then took her onward road

Between the winding willows
To a city white with spires;
It seemed a path of pilgrims
To the home of earth's desires.

Blue shade of golden branches
Spread for her journeying,
Till he that lingered lost her
Among the leaves of Spring.

Laurence Binyon [1869–

WEARYIN' FER YOU

JEST a-wearyin' fer you—
All the time a-feelin' blue;
Wishin' fer you—wonderin' when
You'll be comin' home again;
Restless—don't know *what* to do—
    Jest a-wearyin' fer you!

Keep a-mopin' day by day:
Dull—in everybody's way;
Folks they smile an' pass along
Wonderin' what on earth is wrong;
'Twouldn't help 'em if they knew—
    Jest a-wearyin' fer you.

Room's so lonesome, with your chair
Empty by the fireplace there,
Jest can't stand the sight o' it!
Go outdoors an' roam a bit:
But the woods is lonesome, too,
    Jest a-wearyin' fer you.

Comes the wind with sounds that' jes'
Like the rustlin' o' your dress;
An' the dew on flower an' tree
Tinkles like your steps to me!
Violets, like your eyes so blue—
    Jest a-wearyin' fer you!

Mornin' comes, the birds awake
(Them that sung so fer your sake!),
But there's sadness in the notes
That come thrillin' from their throats!
Seem to feel your absence, too—
    Jest a-wearyin' fer you.

Evenin' comes: I miss you more
When the dark is in the door;
'Pears jest like *you* orter be
There to open fer me!
Latch goes tinklin'—thrills me through,
    Sets me wearyin' fer you!

. . . .

Jest a-wearyin' fer you—
All the time a-feelin' blue!
Wishin' fer you—wonderin' when
You'll be comin' home again;
Restless—don't know *what* to do—
    Jest a-wearyin' fer you!

Frank L. Stanton [1857–1927]

THE LOVERS OF MARCHAID

DOMINIC came riding down, sworded, straight and splendid,
Drave his hilt against her door, flung a golden chain.
Said: "I'll teach your lips a song sweet as his that's ended,
Ere the white rose call the bee, the almond flower again."

But he only saw her head bent within the gloom
Over heaps of bridal thread bright as apple-bloom,
Silver silk like rain that spread across the driving loom.

Dreaming Fanch, the cobbler's son, took his tools and laces,
Wrought her shoes of scarlet dye, shoes as pale as snow;
"They shall lead her wildrose feet all the fairy paces
Danced along the road of love, the road such feet should
    go"—

But he only saw her eyes turning from his gift
Out towards the silver skies where the white clouds drift,
Where the wild gerfalcon flies, where the last sails lift.

Bran has built his homestead high where the hills may shield
    her,
Where the young bird waits the spring, where the dawns
    are fair,
Said: "I'll name my trees for her, since I may not yield her
Stars of morning for her feet, of evening for her hair."

But he did not see them ride, seven dim sail and more,
All along the harbor-side, white from shore to shore,
Nor heard the voices of the tide crying at her door.

Jean-Marie has touched his pipe down beside the river
When the young fox bends the fern, when the folds are
    still,
Said: "I send her all the gifts that my love may give
    her,—
Golden notes like golden birds to seek her at my will."

But he only found the waves, heard the sea-gull's cry,
In and out the ocean caves, underneath the sky,
All above the wind-washed graves where dead seamen lie.

Marjorie L. C. Pickthall [1883–1922]

SONG

SHE'S somewhere in the sunlight strong,
    Her tears are in the falling rain,
She calls me in the wind's soft song,
    And with the flowers she comes again.

Yon bird is but her messenger,
    The moon is but her silver car;
Yea! sun and moon are sent by her,
    And every wistful waiting star.

Richard Le Gallienne [1866–

THE LOVER THINKS OF HIS LADY IN THE NORTH

Now many are the stately ships that northward steam away,
And gray sails northward blow black hulls, and many more
    are they;
And myriads of viking gulls flap to the northern seas:
But Oh my thoughts that go to you are more than all of
    these!

The winds blow to the northward like a million eager wings,
The driven sea a million white-capped waves to northward
    flings:
I send you thoughts more many than the waves that fleck
    the sea,
More eager than tempestuous winds, O Love long leagues
    from me!

O Love, long leagues from me, I would I trod the drenchèd
    deck
Of some ship speeding to the North and staunch against all
    wreck,
I would I were a sea-gull strong of wing and void of fear:
Unfaltering and fleet I'd fly the long way to my Dear!

O if I were the sea, upon your northern land I'd beat
Until my waves flowed over all, and kissed your wandering
    feet;
And if I were the winds, I'd waft you perfumes from the
    South,
And give my pleadings to your ears, my kisses to your mouth.

Though many ships are sailing, never one will carry me,
I may not hurry northward with the gulls, the winds, the sea;
But fervid thoughts they say can flash across long leagues of
    blue—
Ah, so my love and longing must be known, Dear Heart, to
    you!

Shaemas O Sheel [1886–

CHANSON DE ROSEMONDE

THE dawn is lonely for the sun,
　And chill and drear;
The one lone star is pale and wan
　As one in fear.

But when day strides across the hills,
　The warm blood rushes through
　The bared soft bosom of the blue
And all the glad east thrills.

Oh, come, my King!　The hounds of joy
　Are waiting for thy horn
To chase the doe of heart's desire
　Across the heights of morn.
Oh, come, my Sun, and let me know
　The rapture of the day!
Oh, come, my love!　Oh, come, my love!
　Thou art so long away!

Richard Hovey [1864–1900]

AD DOMNULAM SUAM

LITTLE lady of my heart!
　Just a little longer,
Love me: we will pass and part,
　Ere this love grow stronger.

I have loved thee, Child! too well,
　To do aught but leave thee:
Nay! my lips should never tell
　Any tale to grieve thee.

Little lady of my heart!
　Just a little longer
I may love thee: we will part
　Ere my love grow stronger.

Soon thou leavest fairy-land;
　Darker grow thy tresses:
Soon no more of hand in hand;
　Soon no more caresses!

Little lady of my heart!
　　　Just a little longer
Be a child; then we will part,
　　　Ere this love grow stronger.
　　　　　　　　Ernest Dowson [1867–1900]

MARIAN DRURY

MARIAN DRURY, Marian Drury,
　　How are the marshes full of the sea!
Acadie dreams of your coming home
　　All year through, and her heart gets free,—

Free on the trail of the wind to travel,
　　Search and course with the roving tide,
All year long where his hands unravel
　　Blossom and berry the marshes hide.

Marian Drury, Marian Drury,
　　How are the marshes full of the surge!
April over the Norland now
　　Walks in the quiet from verge to verge.

Burying, brimming, the building billows
　　Fret the long dikes with uneasy foam.
Drenched with gold weather, the idling willows
　　Kiss you a hand from the Norland home.

Marian Drury, Marian Drury,
　　How are the marshes full of the sun!
Blomidon waits for your coming home,
　　All day long where the white wings run.

All spring through they falter and follow,
　　Wander, and beckon the roving tide,
Wheel and float with the veering swallow,
　　Lift you a voice from the blue hillside.

Marian Drury, Marian Drury,
　　How are the marshes full of the rain!
April over the Norland now
　　Bugles for rapture, and rouses pain,—

Halts before the forsaken dwelling,
  Where in the twilight, too spent to roam,
Love, whom the fingers of death are quelling,
  Cries you a cheer from the Norland home.

Marian Drury, Marian Drury,
  How are the marshes filled with you!
Grand Pré dreams of your coming home,—
  Dreams while the rainbirds all night through,

Far in the uplands calling to win you,
  Tease the brown dusk on the marshes wide;
And never the burning heart within you
  Stirs in your sleep by the roving tide.

                          Bliss Carman [1861–1929]

LOVE'S ROSARY

ALL day I tell my rosary
        For now my love's away:
To-morrow he shall come to me
        About the break of day;
A rosary of twenty hours,
        And then a rose of May;
A rosary of fettered flowers,
        And then a holy-day.

All day I tell my rosary,
        My rosary of hours:
And here's a flower of memory,
        And here's a hope of flowers,
And here's an hour that yearns with pain
        For old forgotten years,
An hour of loss, an hour of gain,
        And then a shower of tears.

All day I tell my rosary,
        Because my love's away;
And never a whisper comes to me,
        And never a word to say;

But, if it's parting more endears,
    God bring him back, I pray;
Or my heart will break in the darkness
    Before the break of day.

All day I tell my rosary,
    My rosary of hours,
Until an hour shall bring to me
    The hope of all the flowers . . .
I tell my rosary of hours,
    For O, my love's away;
And—a dream may bring him back to me
    About the break of day.

Alfred Noyes [1880–

WHEN SHE COMES HOME

WHEN she comes home again! A thousand ways
I fashion, to myself, the tenderness
Of my glad welcome: I shall tremble—yes;
And touch her, as when first in the old days
I touched her girlish hand, nor dared upraise
Mine eyes, such was my faint heart's sweet distress
Then silence: and the perfume of her dress:
The room will sway a little, and a haze
Cloy eyesight—soul-sight, even—for a space;
And tears—yes; and the ache here in the throat,
To know that I so ill deserve the place
Her arms make for me; and the sobbing note
I stay with kisses, ere the tearful face
Again is hidden in the old embrace.

James Whitcomb Riley [1849–1916]

THE TRAGEDY OF LOVE

SONG

My silks and fine array,
　My smiles and languished air,
By Love are driven away;
　And mournful lean Despair
Brings me yew to deck my grave:
Such end true lovers have.

His face is fair as heaven
　When springing buds unfold:
O why to him was't given,
　Whose heart is wintry cold?
His breast is Love's all-worshipped tomb,
Where all Love's pilgrims come.

Bring me an ax and spade,
　Bring me a winding-sheet;
When I my grave have made,
　Let winds and tempests beat:
Then down I'll lie, as cold as clay:
True love doth pass away!

William Blake [1757-1827]

THE FLIGHT OF LOVE

When the lamp is shattered
The light in the dust lies dead—
When the cloud is scattered,
The rainbow's glory is shed.
When the lute is broken,
Sweet tones are remembered not;
When the lips have spoken,
Loved accents are soon forgot.

As music and splendor
Survive not the lamp and the lute,
The heart's echoes render
No song when the spirit is mute—
No song but sad dirges,
Like the wind through a ruined cell,
Or the mournful surges
That ring the dead seaman's knell.

When hearts have once mingled,
Love first leaves the well-built nest;
The weak one is singled
To endure what it once possessed.
O Love! who bewailest
The frailty of all things here,
Why choose you the frailest
For your cradle, your home, and your bier?

Its passions will rock thee
As the storms rock the ravens on high;
Bright reason will mock thee,
Like the sun from a wintry sky.
From thy nest every rafter
Will rot, and thine eagle home
Leave thee naked to laughter,
When leaves fall and cold winds come.

Percy Bysshe Shelley [1792–1822]

"FAREWELL! IF EVER FONDEST PRAYER"

FAREWELL! if ever fondest prayer
    For other's weal availed on high,
Mine will not all be lost in air,
    But waft thy name beyond the sky.
'Twere vain to speak, to weep, to sigh:
    Oh! more than tears of blood can tell,
When wrung from guilt's expiring eye,
    Are in that word—Farewell!—Farewell!

These lips are mute, these eyes are dry:
  But in my breast and in my brain
Awake the pangs that pass not by,
  The thought that ne'er shall sleep again.
My soul nor deigns nor dares complain,
  Though grief and passion there rebel:
I only know we loved in vain—
  I only feel—Farewell!—Farewell!

George Gordon Byron [1788–1824]

PORPHYRIA'S LOVER

THE rain set early in to-night,
  The sullen wind was soon awake,
It tore the elm-tops down for spite,
  And did its worst to vex the lake:
  I listened with heart fit to break.
When glided in Porphyria; straight
  She shut the cold out and the storm,
And kneeled and made the cheerless grate
  Blaze up, and all the cottage warm;
  Which done, she rose, and from her form
Withdrew the dripping cloak and shawl,
  And laid her soiled gloves by, untied
Her hat and let the damp hair fall,
  And, last, she sat down by my side
  And called me.   When no voice replied,
She put my arm about her waist,
  And made her smooth white shoulder bare,
And all her yellow hair displaced,
  And, stooping, made my cheek lie there,
  And spread, o'er all, her yellow hair,
Murmuring how she loved me—she
  Too weak, for all her heart's endeavor,
To set its struggling passion free
  From pride, and vainer ties dissever,
  And give herself to me for ever.
But passion sometimes would prevail,
  Nor could to-night's gay feast restrain
A sudden thought of one so pale

For love of her, and all in vain:
  So, she was come through wind and rain.
Be sure I looked up at her eyes
  Happy and proud; at last I knew
Porphyria worshipped me; surprise
  Made my heart swell, and still it grew
  While I debated what to do.
That moment she was mine, mine, fair,
  Perfectly pure and good: I found
A thing to do, and all her hair
  In one long yellow string I wound
  Three times her little throat around,
And strangled her. No pain felt she;
  I am quite sure she felt no pain.
As a shut bud that holds a bee,
  I warily oped her lids: again
  Laughed the blue eyes without a stain.
And I untightened next the tress
  About her neck; her cheek once more
Blushed bright beneath my burning kiss:
  I propped her head up as before,
  Only, this time my shoulder bore
Her head, which droops upon it still:
  The smiling rosy little head,
So glad it has its utmost will,
  That all it scorned at once is fled,
  And I, its love, am gained instead!
Porphyria's love: she guessed not how
  Her darling one wish would be heard.
And thus we sit together now,
  And all night long we have not stirred,
  And yet God has not said a word!

                    Robert Browning [1812–1889]

MODERN BEAUTY

I AM the torch, she saith, and what to me
If the moth die of me? I am the flame
Of Beauty, and I burn that all may see
Beauty, and I have neither joy nor shame.

But live with that clear light of perfect fire
Which is to men the death of their desire.

I am Yseult and Helen, I have seen
Troy burn, and the most loving knight lies dead.
The world has been my mirror, time has been
My breath upon the glass; and men have said,
Age after age, in rapture and despair,
Love's poor few words, before my image there.

I live, and am immortal; in my eyes
The sorrow of the world, and on my lips
The joy of life, mingle to make me wise;
Yet now the day is darkened with eclipse:
Who is there lives for beauty?   Still am I
The torch, but where's the moth that still dares die?
Arthur Symons [1865–

LA BELLE DAME SANS MERCI

O WHAT can ail thee, knight-at-arms,
    Alone and palely loitering?
The sedge has withered from the lake,
    And no birds sing.

O what can ail thee, knight-at-arms
    So haggard and so woe-begone?
The squirrel's granary is full,
    And the harvest's done.

I see a lily on thy brow
    With anguish moist and fever-dew,
And on thy cheeks a fading rose
    Fast withereth too.

I met a lady in the meads,
    Full beautiful—a fairy's child,
Her hair was long, her foot was light,
    And her eyes were wild.

I made a garland for her head,
    And bracelets too, and fragrant zone;
She looked at me as she did love,
    And made sweet moan.

I set her on my pacing steed
    And nothing else saw all day long,
For sidelong would she bend, and sing
    A fairy's song.

She found me roots of relish sweet,
    And honey wild and manna-dew,
And sure in language strange she said,
    "I love thee true."

She took me to her elfin grot,
    And there she wept and sighed full sore;
And there I shut her wild, wild eyes
    With kisses four.

And there she lullèd me asleep,
    And there I dreamed—Ah! woe betide!
The latest dream I ever dreamed
    On the cold hill's side.

I saw pale kings and princes too,
    Pale warriors, death-pale were they all:
They cried—"La belle dame sans merci
    Hath thee in thrall!"

I saw their starved lips in the gloam
    With horrid warning gapèd wide,
And I awoke and found me here
    On the cold hill's side.

And this is why I sojourn here
    Alone and palely loitering,
Though the sedge is withered from the lake,
    And no birds sing.

                   John Keats [1795–1821]

TANTALUS—TEXAS

"If I may trust your love," she cried,
"And you would have me for a bride,
Ride over yonder plain, and bring
Your flask full from the Mustang spring;
Fly, fast as western eagle's wing,
     O'er the Llano Estacado!"

He heard, and bowed without a word,
His gallant steed he lightly spurred!
He turned his face, and rode away
Toward the grave of dying day,
And vanished with its parting ray
     On the Llano Estacado.

Night came, and found him riding on,
Day came, and still he rode alone.
He spared not spur, he drew not rein,
Across that broad, unchanging plain,
Till he the Mustang spring might gain,
     On the Llano Estacado.

A little rest, a little draught,
Hot from his hand, and quickly quaffed,
His flask was filled, and then he turned.
Once more his steed the maguey spurned,
Once more the sky above him burned,
     On the Llano Estacado.

How hot the quivering landscape glowed!
His brain seemed boiling as he rode—
Was it a dream, a drunken one,
Or was he really riding on?
Was that a skull that gleamed and shone
     On the Llano Estacado?

"Brave steed of mine, brave steed!" he cried,
"So often true, so often tried,

Bear up a little longer yet!"
His mouth was black with blood and sweat—
Heaven! how he longed his lips to wet
 On the Llano Estacado.

And still, within his breast, he held
The precious flask so lately filled.
Oh, for a drink! But well he knew
If empty it should meet her view,
Her scorn—but still his longing grew
 On the Llano Estacado.

His horse went down. He wandered on,
Giddy, blind, beaten, and alone.
While upon cushioned couch you lie,
Oh, think how hard it is to die,
Beneath the cruel, cloudless sky
 On the Llano Estacado.

At last he staggered, stumbled, fell,
His day was done, he knew full well,
And raising to his lips the flask,
The end, the object of his task,
Drank to her—more she could not ask.
 Ah, the Llano Estacado!

That night in the Presidio,
Beneath the torchlight's wavy glow,
She danced—and never thought of him,
The victim of a woman's whim,
Lying, with face upturned and grim,
 On the Llano Estacado.

     Joaquin Miller [1839-1913]

ENCHAINMENT

I WENT to her who loveth me no more,
 And prayed her bear with me, if so she might;
For I had found day after day too sore,
 And tears that would not cease night after night.

And so I prayed her, weeping, that she bore
To let me be with her a little; yea,
   To soothe myself a little with her sight,
Who loved me once, ah! many a night and day.

Then she who loveth me no more, maybe
   She pitied somewhat: and I took a chain
To bind myself to her, and her to me;
   Yea, so that I might call her mine again.
Lo! she forbade me not; but I and she
Fettered her fair limbs, and her neck more fair,
   Chained the fair wasted white of love's domain,
And put gold fetters on her golden hair.

Oh! the vain joy it is to see her lie
   Beside me once again; beyond release,
Her hair, her hand, her body, till she die,
   All mine, for me to do with what I please!
For, after all, I find no chain whereby
To chain her heart to love me as before,
   Nor fetter for her lips, to make them cease
From saying still she loveth me no more.

          Arthur O'Shaughnessy [1844–1881]

AULD ROBIN GRAY

WHEN the sheep are in the fauld, and the kye at hame,
And a' the warld to rest are gane,
The waes o' my heart fa' in showers frae my e'e,
While my gudeman lies sound by me.

Young Jamie lo'ed me weel, and sought me for his bride;
But saving a croun he had naething else beside:
To make the croun a pund, young Jamie gaed to sea;
And the croun and the pund were baith for me.

He hadna been awa' a week but only twa,
When my father brak his arm, and the kye was stown awa';
My mother she fell sick,—and my Jamie at the sea—
And auld Robin Gray came a-courtin' me.

My father couldna work, and my mother couldna spin;
I toiled day and night, but their bread I couldna win;
Auld Rob maintained them baith, and wi' tears in his e'e
Said, "Jennie, for their sakes, O, marry me!"

My heart it said nay; I looked for Jamie back;
But the wind it blew high, and the ship it was a wrack;
His ship it was a wrack—Why didna Jamie dee?
Or why do I live to cry, Wae's me!

My father urged me sair: my mother didna speak;
But she looked in my face till my heart was like to break:
They gi'ed him my hand, though my heart was in the sea;
Sae auld Robin Gray he was gudeman to me.

I hadna been a wife a week but only four,
When mournfu' as I sat on the stane at the door,
I saw my Jamie's wraith,—for I couldna think it he,
Till he said, "I'm come hame to marry thee."

O, sair, sair did we greet, and muckle did we say;
We took but ae kiss, and we tore ourselves away:
I wish that I were dead, but I'm no like to dee;
And why was I born to say, Wae's me!

I gang like a ghaist, and I carena to spin;
I daurna think on Jamie, for that wad be a sin;
But I'll do my best a gude wife aye to be,
For auld Robin Gray he is kind unto me.

                        Anne Barnard [1750–1825]

LOST LIGHT

My heart is chilled and my pulse is slow,
But often and often will memory go,
Like a blind child lost in a waste of snow,
Back to the days when I loved you so—
       The beautiful long ago.

I sit here dreaming them through and through,
The blissful moments I shared with you—

The sweet, sweet days when our love was new,
When I was trustful and you were true—
    Beautiful days, but few!

Blest or wretched, fettered or free,
Why should I care how your life may be,
Or whether you wander by land or sea?
I only know you are dead to me,
    Ever and hopelessly.

Oh, how often at day's decline
I pushed from my window the curtaining vine,
To see from your lattice the lamp-light shine—
Type of a message that, half divine,
    Flashed from your heart to mine.

Once more the starlight is silvering all;
The roses sleep by the garden wall;
The night bird warbles his madrigal,
And I hear again through the sweet air fall
    The evening bugle-call.

But summers will vanish and years will wane,
And bring no light to your window pane;
Nor gracious sunshine nor patient rain
Can bring dead love back to life again:
    I call up the past in vain.

My heart is heavy, my heart is old,
And that proves dross which I counted gold;
I watch no longer your curtain's fold;
The window is dark and the night is cold,
    And the story forever told.
            Elizabeth Akers [1832–1911]

A SIGH

It was nothing but a rose I gave her,—
    Nothing but a rose
Any wind might rob of half its savor,
    Any wind that blows.

When she took it from my trembling fingers
    With a hand as chill —
Ah, the flying touch upon them lingers,
    Stays, and thrills them still!

Withered, faded, pressed between the pages,
    Crumpled fold on fold,—
Once it lay upon her breast, and ages
    Cannot make it old!

Harriet Prescott Spofford [1835–1921]

HEREAFTER

Love, when all the years are silent, vanished quite and laid
    to rest,
When you and I are sleeping, folded breathless breast to
    breast,
When no morrow is before us, and the long grass tosses o'er
    us,
And our grave remains forgotten, or by alien footsteps
    pressed—

Still that love of ours will linger, that great love enrich the
    earth,
Sunshine in the heavenly azure, breezes blowing joyous
    mirth;
Fragrance fanning off from flowers, melody of summer
    showers,
Sparkle of the spicy wood-fires round the happy autumn
    hearth.

That's our love.   But you and I, dear—shall we linger with
    it yet,
Mingled in one dew-drop, tangled in one sunbeam's golden
    net—
On the violet's purple bosom, I the sheen, but you the blos-
    som,
Stream on sunset winds, and be the haze with which some
    hill is wet?

Or, belovèd—if ascending—when we have endowed the
world
With the best bloom of our being, whither will our way be
whirled,
Through what vast and starry spaces, toward what awful,
holy places,
With a white light on our faces, spirit over spirit furled?

Only this our yearning answers: wheresoe'er that way defile,
Not a film shall part us through the eons of that mighty
while,
In the fair eternal weather, even as phantoms still together,
Floating, floating, one forever, in the light of God's great
smile.

Harriet Prescott Spofford [1835–1921]

ENDYMION

THE apple trees are hung with gold,
   And birds are loud in Arcady,
The sheep lie bleating in the fold,
The wild goat runs across the wold,
But yesterday his love he told,
   I know he will come back to me.
O rising moon! O Lady moon!
   Be you my lover's sentinel,
   You cannot choose but know him well,
For he is shod with purple shoon,
You cannot choose but know my love,
   For he a shepherd's crook doth bear,
And he is soft as any dove,
   And brown and curly is his hair.

The turtle now has ceased to call
   Upon her crimson-footed groom,
The gray wolf prowls about the stall,
The lily's singing seneschal
Sleeps in the lily-bell, and all
   The violet hills are lost in gloom.

O risen moon! O holy moon!
   Stand on the top of Helice,
And if my own true love you see,
Ah! if you see the purple shoon,
The hazel crook, the lad's brown hair,
   The goat-skin wrapped about his arm,
Tell him that I am waiting where
   The rushlight glimmers in the Farm.

The falling dew is cold and chill,
   And no bird sings in Arcady,
The little fauns have left the hill,
Even the tired daffodil
Has closed its gilded doors, and still
   My lover comes not back to me.
False moon! False moon! O waning moon!
   Where is my own true lover gone,
   Where are the lips vermilion,
The shepherd's crook, the purple shoon?
Why spread that silver pavilion,
   Why wear that veil of drifting mist?
Ah! thou hast young Endymion,
   Thou hast the lips that should be kissed!

Oscar Wilde [1856–1900]

"LOVE IS A TERRIBLE THING"

I WENT out to the farthest meadow,
I lay down in the deepest shadow;

And I said unto the earth, "Hold me,"
And unto the night, "O enfold me!"

And unto the wind petulantly
I cried, "You know not for you are free!"

And I begged the little leaves to lean
Low and together for a safe screen;

Then to the stars I told my tale:
"That is my home-light, there in the vale,

"And O, I know that I shall return,
But let me lie first mid the unfeeling fern;

"For there is a flame that has blown too near,
And there is a name that has grown too dear,
And there is a fear" . . . .

And to the still hills and cool earth and far sky I made moan,
"The heart in my bosom is not my own!

"O would I were free as the wind on wing;
Love is a terrible thing!"

Grace Fallow Norton [1876–

THE BALLAD OF THE ANGEL

"Who is it knocking in the night,
   That fain would enter in?"
"The ghost of Lost Delight am I,
   The sin you would not sin,
Who comes to look in your two eyes
   And see what might have been."

"Oh, long ago and long ago
   I cast you forth," he said,
"For that your eyes were all too blue,
   Your laughing mouth too red,
And my torn soul was tangled in
   The tresses of your head."

"Now mind you with what bitter words
   You cast me forth from you?"
"I bade you back to that fair Hell
   From whence your breath you drew,
And with great blows I broke my heart
   Lest it might follow too.

"Yea, from the grasp of your white hands
   I freed my hands that day,
And have I not climbed near to God
   As these His henchmen may?"
"Ah, man,—ah, man! 'twas my two hands
   That led you all the way."

"I hid my eyes from your two eyes
　　That they might see aright."
"Yet think you 'twas a star that led
　　Your feet from height to height?
It was the flame of my two eyes
　　That drew you through the night."

With trembling hands he threw the door,
　　Then fell upon his knee:
"O, Vision armed and cloaked in light,
　　Why do you honor me?"
"The Angel of your Strength am I
　　Who was your sin," quoth she.

"For that you slew me long ago
　　My hands have raised you high;
For that mine eyes you closed, mine eyes
　　Are lights to lead you by;
And 'tis my touch shall swing the gates
　　Of Heaven when you die!"

　　　　　　Theodosia Garrison [1874–

"LOVE CAME BACK AT FALL O' DEW"

Love came back at fall o' dew,
　　Playing his old part;
But I had a word or two,
　　That would break his heart.

"He who comes at candlelight,
　　That should come before,
Must betake him to the night
　　From a barrèd door."

This the word that made us part
　　In the fall o' dew;
This the word that brake his heart—
　　Yet it brake mine, too!

　　　　　　Lizette Woodworth Reese [1856–1935]

I SHALL NOT CARE

WHEN I am dead and over me bright April
    Shakes out her rain-drenched hair,
Though you should lean above me broken-hearted,
    I shall not care.

I shall have peace, as leafy trees are peaceful
    When rain bends down the bough,
And I shall be more silent and cold-hearted
    Than you are now.   *Sara Teasdale* [1884–1933]

OUTGROWN

NAY, you wrong her, my friend, she's not fickle; her love she
    has simply outgrown:
One can read the whole matter, translating her heart by the
    light of one's own.

Can you bear me to talk with you frankly? There is much
    that my heart would say;
And you know we were children together, have quarreled
    and "made up" in play.

And so, for the sake of old friendship, I venture to tell you
    the truth,—
As plainly, perhaps, and as bluntly, as I might in our earlier
    youth.

Five summers ago, when you wooed her, you stood on the
    selfsame plane,
Face to face, heart to heart, never dreaming your souls
    should be parted again.

She loved you at that time entirely, in the bloom of her life's
    early May;
And it is not her fault, I repeat it, that she does not love you
    to-day.

Nature never stands still, nor souls either: they ever go up
    or go down;
And hers has been steadily soaring—but how has it been
    with your own?

She has struggled and yearned and aspired, grown purer and
    wiser each year:
The stars are not farther above you in yon luminous atmos-
    phere!

For she whom you crowned with fresh roses, down yonder,
    five summers ago,
Has learned that the first of our duties to God and ourselves
    is to grow.

Her eyes they are sweeter and calmer: but their vision is
    clearer as well;
Her voice has a tenderer cadence, but is pure as a silver bell.

Her face has the look worn by those who with God and his
    angels have talked:
The white robes she wears are less white than the spirits
    with whom she has walked.

And you? Have you aimed at the highest? Have you, too,
    aspired and prayed?
Have you looked upon evil unsullied? Have you conquered
    it undismayed?

Have you, too, grown purer and wiser, as the months and
    the years have rolled on?
Did you meet her this morning rejoicing in the triumph of
    victory won?

Nay, hear me! The truth cannot harm you. When to-day
    in her presence you stood
Was the hand that you gave her as white and clean as that
    of her womanhood?

Go measure yourself by her standard; look back on the years
    that have fled:
Then ask, if you need, why she tells you that the love of her
    girlhood is dead.

She cannot look down to her lover: her love, like her soul,
    aspires;
He must stand by her side, or above her, who would kindle
    its holy fires.

Now farewell! For the sake of old friendship I have ven-
tured to tell you the truth,
As plainly, perhaps, and as bluntly as I might in our earlier
youth.

Julia C. R. Dorr [1825–1913]

A TRAGEDY

AMONG his books he sits all day
To think and read and write;
He does not smell the new-mown hay,
The roses red and white.

I walk among them all alone,
His silly, stupid wife;
The world seems tasteless, dead and done—
An empty thing is life.

At night his window casts a square
Of light upon the lawn;
I sometimes walk and watch it there
Until the chill of dawn.

I have no brain to understand
The books he loves to read;
I only have a heart and hand
He does not seem to need.

He calls me "Child"—lays on my hair
Thin fingers, cold and mild;
Oh! God of Love, who answers prayer,
I wish I were a child!

And no one sees and no one knows
(He least would know or see),
That ere Love gathers next year's rose
Death will have gathered me.

Edith Nesbit [1858–1924]

LEFT BEHIND

IT was the autumn of the year;
The strawberry-leaves were red and sere;
October's airs were fresh and chill,
When, pausing on the windy hill,
The hill that overlooks the sea,
You talked confidingly to me,—
Me whom your keen, artistic sight
Has not yet learned to read aright,
Since I have veiled my heart from you,
And loved you better than you knew.

You told me of your toilsome past;
The tardy honors won at last,
The trials borne, the conquests gained,
The longed-for boon of Fame attained;
I knew that every victory
But lifted you away from me,
That every step of high emprise
But left me lowlier in your eyes;
I watched the distance as it grew,
And loved you better than you knew.

You did not see the bitter trace
Of anguish sweep across my face;
You did not hear my proud heart beat,
Heavy and slow, beneath your feet;
You thought of triumphs still unwon,
Of glorious deeds as yet undone;
And I, the while you talked to me,
I watched the gulls float lonesomely,
Till lost amid the hungry blue,
And loved you better than you knew.

You walk the sunny side of fate;
The wise world smiles, and calls you great;
The golden fruitage of success
Drops at your feet in plenteousness;
And you have blessings manifold:—
Renown and power and friends and gold,—

They build a wall between us twain,
Which may not be thrown down again,
Alas! for I, the long years through,
Have loved you better than you knew.

Your life's proud aim, your art's high truth,
Have kept the promise of your youth;
And while you won the crown, which now
Breaks into bloom upon your brow,
My soul cried strongly out to you
Across the ocean's yearning blue,
While, unremembered and afar,
I watched you, as I watch a star
Through darkness struggling into view,
And loved you better than you knew.

I used to dream in all these years
Of patient faith and silent tears,
That Love's strong hand would put aside
The barriers of place and pride,
Would reach the pathless darkness through,
And draw me softly up to you;
But that is past. If you should stray
Beside my grave, some future day,
Perchance the violets o'er my dust
Will half betray their buried trust,
And say, their blue eyes full of dew,
"She loved you better than you knew."

Elizabeth Akers [1832–1911]

THE FORSAKEN MERMAN

Come, dear children, let us away;
    Down and away below!
Now my brothers call from the bay,
Now the great winds shoreward blow,
Now the salt tides seaward flow;
Now the wild white horses play,
Champ and chafe and toss in the spray.
    Children dear, let us away!
        This way, this way!

Call her once before you go.—
    Call once yet!
In a voice that she will know:
    "Margaret! Margaret!"
Children's voices should be dear
(Call once more) to a mother's ear;
Children's voices, wild with pain,—
    Surely she will come again!
Call her once and come away;
    This way, this way!
"Mother dear, we cannot stay!
The wild white horses foam and fret."
    Margaret! Margaret!

Come, dear children, come away down;
    Call no more!
One last look at the white-walled town,
And the little gray church on the windy shore;
    Then come down!
She will not come, though you call all day;
    Come away, come away!

Children dear, was it yesterday
We heard the sweet bells over the bay?
In the caverns where we lay,
Through the surf and through the swell,
The far-off sound of a silver bell?
Sand-strewn caverns, cool and deep,
Where the winds are all asleep;
Where the spent lights quiver and gleam,
Where the salt weed sways in the stream,
Where the sea-beasts, ranged all round,
Feed in the ooze of their pasture-ground;
Where the sea-snakes coil and twine,
Dry their mail and bask in the brine;
Where great whales come sailing by,
Sail and sail, with unshut eye,
Round the world for ever and aye?
    When did music come this way?
    Children dear, was it yesterday?

Children dear, was it yesterday
(Call yet once) that she went away?
Once she sate with you and me,
On a red gold throne in the heart of the sea,
And the youngest sate on her knee.
She combed its bright hair, and she tended it well,
When down swung the sound of the far-off bell.
She sighed, she looked up through the clear green sea;
She said: "I must go, for my kinsfolk pray
In the little gray church on the shore to-day.
'Twill be Easter-time in the world,—ah me!
And I lose my poor soul, Merman, here with thee."
I said: "Go up, dear heart, through the waves:
Say thy prayer, and come back to the kind sea-caves!"
She smiled, she went up through the surf in the bay.
    Children dear, was it yesterday?

    Children dear, were we long alone?
"The sea grows stormy, the little ones moan;
Long prayers," I said, "in the world they say;
Come!" I said, and we rose through the surf in the bay.
We went up the beach, by the sandy down
Where the sea-stocks bloom, to the white-walled town,
Through the narrow paved streets, where all was still,
To the little gray church on the windy hill.
From the church came a murmur of folk at their prayers,
But we stood without in the cold blowing airs.
We climbed on the graves, on the stones worn with
      rains,
And we gazed up the aisle through the small leaded
      panes.
  She sate by the pillar; we saw her clear:
  "Margaret, hist! come quick, we are here!
  Dear heart," I said, "we are long alone;
  The sea grows stormy, the little ones moan."
But, ah, she gave me never a look,
For her eyes were sealed to the holy book!
    Loud prays the priest; shut stands the door.
    Come away, children, call no more!
    Come away, come down, call no more!

Down, down, down!
Down to the depths of the sea!
She sits at her wheel in the humming town,
   Singing most joyfully.
Hark what she sings: "O joy, O joy,
From the humming street, and the child with its toy!
From the priest, and the bell, and the holy well;
      From the wheel where I spun,
      And the blessed light of the sun!"
      And so she sings her fill,
      Singing most joyfully,
      Till the spindle drops from her hand,
      And the whizzing wheel stands still.
She steals to the window, and looks at the sand,
      And over the sand at the sea;
      And her eyes are set in a stare,
      And anon there breaks a sigh,
      And anon there drops a tear,
      From a sorrow-clouded eye,
      And a heart sorrow-laden,
         A long, long sigh;
For the cold strange eyes of a little Mermaiden,
And the gleam of her golden hair.

      Come away, away, children;
      Come, children, come down!
      The hoarse wind blows colder;
      Lights shine in the town.
      She will start from her slumber
      When gusts shake the door;
      She will hear the winds howling,
      Will hear the waves roar.
      We shall see, while above us
      The waves roar and whirl,
      A ceiling of amber,
      A pavement of pearl.
      Singing: "Here came a mortal,
      But faithless was she!
      And alone dwell for ever
      The kings of the sea."

But, children, at midnight,
When soft the winds blow,
When clear falls the moonlight,
When spring-tides are low;
When sweet airs come seaward
From heaths starred with broom,
And high rocks throw mildly
On the blanched sands a gloom;
Up the still, glistening beaches,
Up the creeks we will hie;
Over banks of bright seaweed
The ebb-tide leaves dry.
We will gaze, from the sand-hills,
At the white, sleeping town;
At the church on the hillside—
And then come back down.
Singing: "There dwells a loved one,
But cruel is she!
She left lonely for ever
The kings of the sea."

Matthew Arnold [1822–1888]

THE PORTRAIT

MIDNIGHT past! Not a sound of aught
　　Through the silent house, but the wind at his prayers.
I sat by the dying fire, and thought
　　Of the dear dead woman up-stairs.

A night of tears! for the gusty rain
　　Had ceased, but the eaves were dripping yet;
And the moon looked forth, as though in pain,
　　With her face all white and wet:

Nobody with me, my watch to keep,
　　But the friend of my bosom, the man I love:
And grief had sent him fast to sleep
　　In the chamber up above.

Nobody else, in the country place
   All round, that knew of my loss beside,
But the good young Priest with the Raphael-face,
   Who confessed her when she died.

That good young Priest is of gentle nerve,
   And my grief had moved him beyond control;
For his lip grew white, as I could observe,
   When he speeded her parting soul.

I sat by the dreary hearth alone:
   I thought of the pleasant days of yore:
I said, "The staff of my life is gone:
   The woman I loved is no more.

"On her cold dead bosom my portrait lies,
   Which next to her heart she used to wear—
Haunting it o'er with her tender eyes
   When my own face was not there.

"It is set all round with rubies red,
   And pearls which a Peri might have kept.
For each ruby there my heart hath bled:
   For each pearl my eyes have wept."

And I said—"The thing is precious to me:
   They will bury her soon in the churchyard clay;
It lies on her heart, and lost must be
   If I do not take it away."

I lighted my lamp at the dying flame,
   And crept up the stairs that creaked for fright,
Till into the chamber of death I came,
   Where she lay all in white.

The moon shone over her winding-sheet,
   There stark she lay on her carven bed:
Seven burning tapers about her feet,
   And seven about her head.

As I stretched my hand, I held my breath;
  I turned as I drew the curtains apart:
I dared not look on the face of death:
  I knew where to find her heart.

I thought at first, as my touch fell there,
  It had warmed that heart to life, with love;
For the thing I touched was warm, I swear,
  And I could feel it move.

'Twas the hand of a man, that was moving slow
  O'er the heart of the dead,—from the other side:
And at once the sweat broke over my brow:
  "Who is robbing the corpse?" I cried.

Opposite me by the tapers' light,
  The friend of my bosom, the man I loved,
Stood over the corpse, and all as white,
  And neither of us moved.

"What do you here, my friend?". . .   The man
  Looked first at me, and then at the dead.
"There is a portrait here," he began:
  "There is.   It is mine," I said.

Said the friend of my bosom, "Yours, no doubt,
  The portrait was, till a month ago,
When this suffering angel took that out,
  And placed mine there, I know."

"This woman, she loved me well," said I.
  "A month ago," said my friend to me:
"And in your throat," I groaned, "you lie!"
  He answered, . . . "Let us see."

"Enough!" I returned, "let the dead decide:
  And whosesoever the portrait prove,
His shall it be, when the cause is tried,
  Where Death is arraigned by Love."

We found the protrait there, in its place:
　We opened it by the tapers' shine:
The gems were all unchanged: the face
　Was—neither his nor mine.

"One nail drives out another, at least!
　The face of the portrait there," I cried,
"Is our friend's, the Raphael-faced young Priest,
　Who confessed her when she died."

The setting is all of rubies red,
　And pearls which a Peri might have kept.
For each ruby there my heart hath bled:
　For each pearl my eyes have wept.

Edward Robert Bulwer Lytton [1831–1891]

THE ROSE AND THORN

She's loveliest of the festal throng
　In delicate form and Grecian face,—
A beautiful, incarnate song,
　A marvel of harmonious grace;
And yet I know the truth I speak:
　From those gay groups she stands apart,
A rose upon her tender cheek,
　A thorn within her heart.

Though bright her eyes' bewildering gleams,
　Fair tremulous lips and shining hair,
A something born of mournful dreams
　Breathes round her sad enchanted air;
No blithesome thoughts at hide and seek
　From out her dimples smiling start;
If still the rose be on her cheek,
　A thorn is in her heart.

Young lover, tossed 'twixt hope and fear,
　Your whispered vow and yearning eyes
Yon marble Clytie pillared near
　Could move as soon to soft replies:

Or, if she thrill at words you speak,
   Love's memory prompts the sudden start;
The rose has paled upon her cheek,
    The thorn has pierced her heart.
           Paul Hamilton Hayne [1830–1886]

TO HER—UNSPOKEN

Go to him, ah, go to him, and lift your eyes aglow to him;
   Fear not royally to give whatever he may claim;
All your spirit's treasury scruple not to show to him.
   He is noble; meet him with a pride too high for shame.

Say to him, ah, say to him, that soul and body sway to him;
   Cast away the cowardice that counsels you to flight,
Lest you turn at last to find that you have lost the way to
    him,
   Lest you stretch your arms in vain across a starless night.

Be to him, ah, be to him, the key that sets joy free to him;
   Teach him all the tenderness that only love can know,
And if ever there should come a memory of me to him,
   Bid him judge me gently for the sake of long ago.
           Amelia Josephine Burr [1878–

A LIGHT WOMAN

So far as our story approaches the end,
   Which do you pity the most of us three?—
My friend, or the mistress of my friend
   With her wanton eyes, or me?

My friend was already too good to lose,
   And seemed in the way of improvement yet,
When she crossed his path with her hunting-noose,
   And over him drew her net.

When I saw him tangled in her toils,
   A shame, said I, if she adds just him
To her nine-and-ninety other spoils,
   The hundredth for a whim!

And before my friend be wholly hers,
　　How easy to prove to him, I said,
An eagle's the game her pride prefers,
　　Though she snaps at a wren instead!

So, I gave her eyes my own eyes to take,
　　My hand sought hers as in earnest need,
And round she turned for my noble sake,
　　And gave me herself indeed.

The eagle am I, with my fame in the world,
　　The wren is he, with his maiden face.
·—You look away and your lip is curled?
　　Patience, a moment's space!

For see, my friend goes shaking and white;
　　He eyes me as the basilisk:
I have turned, it appears, his day to night,
　　Eclipsing his sun's disk.

And I did it, he thinks, as a very thief:
　　" Though I love her—that, he comprehends—
One should master one's passions, (love, in chief)
　　And be loyal to one's friends!"

And she,—she lies in my hand as tame
　　As a pear late basking over a wall;
Just a touch to try and off it came;
　　'Tis mine,—can I let it fall?

With no mind to eat it, that's the worst!
　　Were it thrown in the road, would the case assist?
'Twas quenching a dozen blue-flies' thirst
　　When I gave its stalk a twist.

And I,—what I seem to my friend, you see:
　　What I soon shall seem to his love, you guess:
What I seem to myself, do you ask of me?
　　No hero, I confess.

'Tis an awkward thing to play with souls,
  And matter enough to save one's own:
Yet think of my friend, and the burning coals
  He played with for bits of stone!

One likes to show the truth for the truth;
  That the woman was light is very true:
But suppose she says,—Never mind that youth!
  What wrong have I done to you?

Well, anyhow, here the story stays,
  So far at least as I understand;
And, Robert Browning, you writer of plays,
  Here's a subject made to your hand!
                    Robert Browning [1812–1889]

FROM THE TURKISH

THE chain I gave was fair to view,
  The lute I added sweet in sound,
The heart that offered both was true,
  And ill deserved the fate it found.

These gifts were charmed by secret spell
  Thy truth in absence to divine;
And they have done their duty well,
  Alas! they could not teach thee thine.

That chain was firm in every link,
  But not to bear a stranger's touch;
That lute was sweet—till thou couldst think
  In other hands its notes were such.

Let him, who from thy neck unbound
  The chain which shivered in his grasp,
Who saw that lute refuse to sound,
  Restring the chords, renew the clasp.

When thou wert changed, they altered too;
  The chain is broke, the music mute:
'Tis past—to them and thee adieu—
  False heart, frail chain, and silent lute.
                    George Gordon Byron [1788–1824]

A SUMMER WOOING

THE wind went wooing the rose,
  For the rose was fair.
How the rough wind won her, who knows?
  But he left her there.
Far away from her grave he blows:
  Does the free wind care?

Louise Chandler Moulton [1835-1908]

BUTTERFLIES

AT sixteen years she knew no care;
  How could she, sweet and pure as light?
And there pursued her everywhere
  Butterflies all white.

A lover looked. She dropped her eyes
  That glowed like pansies wet with dew;
And lo, there came from out the skies
  Butterflies all blue.

Before she guessed her heart was gone;
  The tale of love was swiftly told;
And all about her wheeled and shone
  Butterflies all gold.

Then he forsook her one sad morn;
  She wept and sobbed, "Oh, love, come back!"
There only came to her forlorn
  Butterflies all black.

John Davidson [1857-1909]

UNSEEN SPIRITS

THE shadows lay along Broadway,
  'Twas near the twilight-tide,
And slowly there a lady fair
  Was walking in her pride.
Alone walked she; but, viewlessly,
  Walked spirits at her side.

Peace charmed the street beneath her feet,
  And Honor charmed the air;
And all astir looked kind on her,
  And called her good as fair,—
For all God ever gave to her
  She kept with chary care.

She kept with care her beauties rare
  From lovers warm and true,
For her heart was cold to all but gold,
  And the rich came not to woo—
But honored well are charms to sell
  If priests the selling do.

Now walking there was one more fair—
  A slight girl, lily-pale;
And she had unseen company
  To make the spirit quail:
'Twixt Want and Scorn she walked forlorn,
  And nothing could avail.

No mercy now can clear her brow
  For this world's peace to pray;
For, as love's wild prayer dissolved in air,
  Her woman's heart gave way!—
But the sin forgiven by Christ in heaven
  By man is cursed alway!
                    Nathaniel Parker Willis [1806–1867]

"GRANDMITHER, THINK NOT I FORGET"

GRANDMITHER, think not I forget, when I come back to town,
An' wander the old ways again, an' tread them up and down.
I never smell the clover bloom, nor see the swallows pass,
Without I mind how good ye were unto a little lass.
I never hear the winter rain a-pelting all night through,
Without I think and mind me of how cold it falls on you.
And if I come not often to your bed beneath the thyme,
Mayhap 'tis that I'd change wi' ye, and gie my bed for thine,
              Would like to sleep in thine.

I never hear the summer winds among the roses blow,
Without I wonder why it was ye loved the lassie so.
Ye gave me cakes and lollipops and pretty toys a store,—
I never thought I should come back and ask ye now for more.
Grandmither, gie me your still, white hands, that lie upon
    your breast,
For mine do beat the dark all night, and never find me
    rest;
They grope among the shadows, an' they beat the cold black
    air,
They go seekin' in the darkness, an' they never find him
    there,
        They never find him there.

Grandmither, gie me your sightless eyes, that I may never
    see
His own a-burnin' full o' love that must not shine for me.
Grandmither, gie me your peaceful lips, white as the kirk-
    yard snow,
For mine be tremblin' wi' the wish that he must never
    know.
Grandmither, gie me your clay-stopped ears, that I may
    never hear
My lad a-singin' in the night when I am sick wi' fear;
A-singin' when the moonlight over a' the land is white—
Ah, God! I'll up an' go to him a-singin' in the night,
        A-callin' in the night.

Grandmither, gie me your clay-cold heart that has forgot to
    ache,
For mine be fire within my breast and yet it cannot break.
Wi' every beat it's callin' for things that must not be,—
An' can ye not let me creep in an' rest awhile by ye?
A little lass afeard o' dark slept by ye years agone—
Ah, she has found what night can hold 'twixt sundown an'
    the dawn!
So when I plant the rose an' rue above your grave for ye,
Ye'll know it's under rue an' rose that I would like to be,
        That I would like to be.
             Willa Sibert Cather [1875—

LITTLE WILD BABY

THROUGH the fierce fever I nursed him, and then he said
I was the woman—I!—that he would wed;
He sent a boat with men for his own white priest,
And he gave my father horses, and made a feast.
I am his wife: if he has forgotten me,
I will not live for scorning eyes to see.
(*Little wild baby, that knowest not where thou art going,*
Lie still ! lie still !   Thy mother will do the rowing.)

Three moons ago—it was but three moons ago—
He took his gun, and started across the snow;
For the river was frozen, the river that still goes down
Every day, as I watch it, to find the town;
The town whose name I caught from his sleeping lips,
A place of many people and many ships.
(*Little wild baby, that knowest not where thou art going,*
Lie still ! lie still !   Thy mother will do the rowing.)

I to that town am going, to search the place,
With his little white son in my arms, till I see his face.
Only once shall I need to look in his eyes,
To see if his soul, as I knew it, lives or dies.
If it lives, we live, and if it is dead, we die,
And the soul of my baby will never ask me why.
(*Little wild baby, that knowest not where thou art going,*
Lie still ! lie still !   Thy mother will do the rowing.)

I have asked about the river: one answered me,
That after the town it goes to find the sea;
That great waves, able to break the stoutest bark,
Are there, and the sea is very deep and dark.
If he is happy without me, so best, so best;
I will take his baby and go away to my rest.
(*Little wild baby, that knowest not where thou art going,*
Lie still ! lie still !   Thy mother will do the rowing.
The river flows swiftly, the sea is dark and deep:
Little wild baby, lie still !   Lie still and sleep.)

                    Margaret Thomson Janvier [1845-1913]

A CRADLE SONG

Come little babe, come silly soul,
Thy father's shame, thy mother's grief,
Born as I doubt to all our dole,
And to thyself unhappy chief:
    Sing lullaby, and lap it warm,
    Poor soul that thinks no creature harm.

Thou little think'st and less dost know
The cause of this thy mother's moan;
Thou want'st the wit to wail her woe,
And I myself am all alone:
    Why dost thou weep? why dost thou wail?
    And know'st not yet what thou dost ail.

Come, little wretch—ah, silly heart!
Mine only joy, what can I more?
If there be any wrong thy smart,
That may the destinies implore:
    'Twas I, I say, against my will,
    I wail the time, but be thou still.

And dost thou smile? O, thy sweet face!
Would God Himself He might thee see!—
No doubt thou wouldst soon purchase grace,
I know right well, for thee and me:
    But come to mother, babe, and play,
    For father false is fled away.

Sweet boy, if it by fortune chance
Thy father home again to send,
If death do strike me with his lance,
Yet may'st thou me to him commend:
    If any ask thy mother's name,
    Tell how by love she purchased blame.

Then will his gentle heart soon yield:
I know him of a noble mind:
Although a lion in the field,
A lamb in town thou shalt him find:

Ask blessing, babe, be not afraid,
His sugared words hath me betrayed.

Then may'st thou joy and be right glad;
Although in woe I seem to moan,
Thy father is no rascal lad,
A noble youth of blood and bone:
    His glancing looks, if he once smile,
    Right honest women may beguile.

Come, little boy, and rock asleep;
Sing lullaby and be thou still;
I, that can do naught else but weep,
Will sit by thee and wail my fill:
    God bless my babe, and lullaby
    From this thy father's quality.
                    Nicholas Breton [1545?–1626?]

LADY ANNE BOTHWELL'S LAMENT

Balow, my babe, lie still and sleep!
It grieves me sore to see thee weep.
Wouldst thou be quiet I'se be glad,
Thy mourning makes my sorrow sad:
Balow my boy, thy mother's joy,
Thy father breeds me great annoy—
            Balow, la-low!

When he began to court my love,
And with his sugared words me move,
His feignings false and flattering cheer
To me that time did not appear:
But now I see most cruelly
He cares ne for my babe nor me—
            Balow, la-low!

Lie still, my darling, sleep awhile,
And when thou wak'st thou'll sweetly smile:
But smile not as thy father did,
To cozen maids: nay, God forbid!

But yet I fear thou wilt go near
Thy father's heart and face to bear—
    Balow, la-low!

I cannot choose but ever will
Be loving to thy father still;
Where'er he go, where'er he ride,
My love with him doth still abide;
In weal or woe, where'er he go,
My heart shall ne'er depart him fro—
    Balow, la-low!

But do not, do not, pretty mine,
To feignings false thy heart incline!
Be loyal to thy lover true,
And never change her for a new:
If good or fair, of her have care
For women's banning's wondrous sair—
    Balow, la-low!

Bairn, by thy face I will beware;
Like Sirens' words, I'll come not near;
My babe and I together will live;
He'll comfort me when cares do grieve.
My babe and I right soft will lie,
And ne'er respect man's cruelty—
    Balow, la-low!

Farewell, farewell, the falsest youth
That ever kissed a woman's mouth!
I wish all maids be warned by me
Never to trust man's courtesy;
For if we do but chance to bow,
They'll use us then they care not how—
    Balow, la-low!

Unknown

A WOMAN'S LOVE

A SENTINEL angel, sitting high in glory,
Heard this shrill wail ring out from Purgatory:
"Have mercy, mighty angel, hear my story!

"I loved,—and, blind with passionate love, I fell.
Love brought me down to death, and death to Hell;
For God is just, and death for sin is well.

"I do not rage against His high decree,
Nor for myself do ask that grace shall be;
But for my love on earth who mourns for me.

"Great Spirit!   Let me see my love again
And comfort him one hour, and I were fain
To pay a thousand years of fire and pain."

Then said the pitying angel, "Nay, repent
That wild vow!   Look, the dial-finger's bent
Down to the last hour of thy punishment!"

But still she wailed, "I pray thee, let me go!
I cannot rise to peace and leave him so.
O, let me soothe him in his bitter woe!"

The brazen gates ground sullenly ajar,
And upwards, joyous, like a rising star,
She rose and vanished in the ether far.

But soon adown the dying sunset sailing,
And like a wounded bird her pinions trailing,
She fluttered back, with broken-hearted wailing,

She sobbed, "I found him by the summer sea
Reclined, his head upon a maiden's knee,—
She curled his hair and kissed him.   Woe is me!"

She wept, "Now let my punishment begin!
I have been fond and foolish.   Let me in
To expiate my sorrow and my sin."

The angel answered, "Nay, sad soul, go higher!
To be deceived in your true heart's desire
Was bitterer than a thousand years of fire!"

John Hay [1838–1905]

A TRAGEDY

SHE was only a woman, famished for loving,
  Mad with devotion, and such slight things;
And he was a very great musician,
  And used to finger his fiddle-strings.

Her heart's sweet gamut is cracking and breaking
  For a look, for a touch,—for such slight things;
But he's such a very great musician
  Grimacing and fingering his fiddle-strings.
        Théophile Marzials [1850–

"MOTHER, I CANNOT MIND MY WHEEL"

MOTHER, I cannot mind my wheel;
  My fingers ache, my lips are dry:
O, if you felt the pain I feel!
  But O, who ever felt as I?

No longer could I doubt him true—
  All other men may use deceit;
He always said my eyes were blue,
  And often swore my lips were sweet.
        Walter Savage Landor [1775–1864]

AIRLY BEACON

AIRLY Beacon, Airly Beacon;
  O the pleasant sight to see
Shires and towns from Airly Beacon,
  While my love climbed up to me!

Airly Beacon, Airly Beacon;
  O the happy hours we lay
Deep in fern on Airly Beacon,
  Courting through the summer's day!

Airly Beacon, Airly Beacon;
  O the weary haunt for me,
All alone on Airly Beacon,
  With his baby on my knee!
        Charles Kingsley [1819–1875]

A SEA CHILD

THE lover of child Marjory
    Had one white hour of life brim full;
Now the old nurse, the rocking sea,
    Hath him to lull.

The daughter of child Marjory
    Hath in her veins, to beat and run,
The glad indomitable sea,
    The strong white sun.

Bliss Carman [1861–1929]

FROM THE HARBOR HILL

"Is it a sail?" she asked.
    "No," I said.
"Only a white sea-gull with its pinions spread."

    "Is it a spar?" she asked.
    "No," said I.
"Only the slender light-house tower against the sky."

    "Flutters a pennant there?"
    "No," I said.
"Only a shred of cloud in the sunset red."

    "Surely a hull, a hull!"
    "Where?" I cried.
"Only a rock half-bared by the ebbing tide."

    "Wait you a ship?" I asked.
    "Aye!" quoth she.
"The *Harbor Belle;* her mate comes home to marry me.

    "Surely the good ship hath
        Met no harm?"
Was it the west wind wailed or the babe on her arm?

    "The *Harbor Belle!*" she urged.
    Naught said I.—
For I knew o'er the grave o' the *Harbor Belle* the sea-gulls fly.

Gustav Kobbé [1857–1918]

ALLAN WATER

On the banks of Allan Water,
When the sweet spring-time did fall,
Was the miller's lovely daughter,
    Fairest of them all.

For his bride a soldier sought her,
And a winning tongue had he,
On the banks of Allan Water,
    None so gay as she.

On the banks of Allan Water,
When brown autumn spread his store,
There I saw the miller's daughter,
    But she smiled no more.

For the summer grief had brought her,
And the soldier false was he,
On the banks of Allan Water,
    None so sad as she.

On the banks of Allan Water,
When the winter snow fell fast,
Still was seen the miller's daughter,
    Chilling blew the blast.

But the miller's lovely daughter,
Both from cold and care was free;
On the banks of Allan Water,
    There a corse lay she.
                    Matthew Gregory Lewis [1775–1818]

FORSAKEN

O WALY waly up the bank,
    And waly waly down the brae,
And waly waly yon burn-side
    Where I and my Love wont to gae!

I leaned my back unto an aik,
  I thought it was a trusty tree;
But first it bowed, and syne it brak,
  Sae my true Love did lichtly me.

O waly waly, but love be bonny
  A little while when it is new;
But when 'tis auld, it waxeth cauld
  And fades awa' like morning dew.
O wherefore should I busk my head?
  Or wherefore should I kame my hair?
For my true Love has me forsook,
  And says he'll never loe me mair.

Now Arthur-seat sall be my bed;
  The sheets shall ne'er be pressed by me:
Saint Anton's well sall be my drink,
  Since my true Love has forsaken me.
Martinmas wind, when wilt thou blaw
  And shake the green leaves aff the tree?
O gentle Death, when wilt thou come?
  For of my life I am wearie.

'Tis not the frost, that freezes fell,
  Nor blawing snaw's inclemencie;
'Tis not sic cauld that makes me cry,
  But my Love's heart grown cauld to me.
When we cam in by Glasgow town
  We were a comely sight to see;
My Love was clad in black velvet.
  And I mysel in cramasie.

But had I wist, before I kissed,
  That love had been sae ill to win;
I had locked my heart in a case of gowd
  And pinned it with a siller pin.
And, O! if my young babe were born,
  And sat upon the nurse's knee,
And I mysel were dead and gane,
  And the green grass growing over me!

                                Unknown

BONNIE DOON

YE banks and braes o' bonnie Doon,
How can ye bloom sae fair!
How can ye chant, ye little birds,
And I sae fu' o' care!

Thou'll break my heart, thou bonnie bird
That sings upon the bough;
Thou minds me o' the happy days
When my fause Luve was true.

Thou'll break my heart, thou bonnie bird
That sings beside thy mate;
For sae I sat, and sae I sang,
And wist na o' my fate.

Aft hae I roved by bonnie Doon
To see the woodbine twine,
And ilka bird sang o' its love;
And sae did I o' mine.

Wi' lightsome heart I pu'd a rose,
Frae aff its thorny tree;
And my fause luver staw the rose,
But left the thorn wi' me.

Robert Burns [1759–1796]

THE TWO LOVERS

THE lover of her body said:
"She is more beautiful than night, —
But like the kisses of the dead
Is my despair and my delight."

The lover of her soul replied:
"She is more wonderful than death, —
But bitter as the aching tide
Is all the speech of love she saith."

The lover of her body said:
  "To know one secret of her heart,
For all the joy that I have had,
  Is past the reach of all my art."

The lover of her soul replied:
  "The secrets of her heart are mine,—
Save how she lives, a riven bride,
  Between the dust and the divine."

The lover of her body sware:
  "Though she should hate me, wit you well,
Rather than yield one kiss of her
  I give my soul to burn in hell."

The lover of her soul cried out:
  "Rather than leave her to your greed,
I would that I were walled about
  With death,—and death were death indeed!"

The lover of her body wept,
  And got no good of all his gain,
Knowing that in her heart she kept
  The penance of the other's pain.

The lover of her soul went mad,
  But when he did himself to death,
Despite of all the woe he had,
  He smiled as one who vanquisheth.
               Richard Hovey [1864–1900]

THE VAMPIRE

AS SUGGESTED BY THE PAINTING BY PHILIP BURNE-JONES

A FOOL there was and he made his prayer
      (Even as you and I!)
To a rag and a bone and a hank of hair
(We called her the woman who did not care),
But the fool he called her his lady fair
      (Even as you and I!)

Oh the years we waste and the tears we waste,
  And the work of our head and hand,
Belong to the woman who did not know
(And now we know that she never could know)
  And did not understand.

A fool there was and his goods he spent
      (Even as you and I!)
Honor and faith and a sure intent
(And it wasn't the least what the lady meant),
But a fool must follow his natural bent
      (Even as you and I!)

Oh the toil we lost and the spoil we lost,
  And the excellent things we planned,
Belong to the woman who didn't know why
(And now we know she never knew why)
  And did not understand.

The fool was stripped to his foolish hide
      (Even as you and I!)
Which she might have seen when she threw him aside,—
(But it isn't on record the lady tried)
So some of him lived but the most of him died—
      (Even as you and I!)

And it isn't the shame and it isn't the blame
  That stings like a white-hot brand.
It's coming to know that she never knew why
(Seeing at last she could never know why)
  And never could understand.
                    Rudyard Kipling [1865–1936]

AGATHA

SHE wanders in the April woods,
    That glisten with the fallen shower;
She leans her face against the buds,
    She stops, she stoops, she plucks a flower.
    She feels the ferment of the hour:

She broodeth when the ringdove broods;
　　The sun and flying clouds have power
Upon her cheek and changing moods.
　　She cannot think she is alone,
　　　　As o'er her senses warmly steal
Floods of unrest she fears to own.
　　And almost dreads to feel.

Along the summer woodlands wide
　　Anew she roams, no more alone;
The joy she feared is at her side,
　　Spring's blushing secret now is known.
The primrose and its mates have flown,
The thrush's ringing note hath died;
　　But glancing eye and glowing tone
Fall on her from her god, her guide.
　　She knows not, asks not, what the goal,
　　　　She only feels she moves towards bliss,
And yields her pure unquestioning soul
　　To touch and fondling kiss.

And still she haunts those woodland ways,
　　Though all fond fancy finds there now
To mind of spring or summer days,
　　Are sodden trunk and songless bough.
The past sits widowed on her brow,
Homeward she wends with wintry gaze,
　　To walls that house a hollow vow,
To hearth where love hath ceased to blaze:
　　Watches the clammy twilight wane,
　　　　With grief too fixed for woe or tear;
　　And, with her forehead 'gainst the pane,
　　　　Envies the dying year.

Alfred Austin [1835-1913]

"A ROSE WILL FADE"

You were always a dreamer, Rose—red Rose,
　　As you swung on your perfumed spray,
Swinging, and all the world was true,
Swaying, what did it trouble you?
　　A rose will fade in a day.

Why did you smile to his face, red Rose,
  As he whistled across your way?
And all the world went mad for you,
All the world it knelt to woo.
    A rose will bloom in a day.

I gather your petals, Rose—red Rose,
  The petals he threw away.
And all the world derided you;
Ah! the world, how well it knew
    A rose will fade in a day!

               Dora Sigerson Shorter [1862–1918]

AFFAIRE D'AMOUR

ONE pale November day
  Flying Summer paused,
      They say:
  And growing bolder,
  O'er rosy shoulder
    Threw her lover such a glance
    That Autumn's heart began to dance.
    (O happy lover!)

A leafless peach-tree bold
  Thought for him she smiled,
      I'm told;
  And, stirred by love,
  His sleeping sap did move,
Decking each naked branch with green
To show her that her look was seen!
    (Alas, poor lover!)

But Summer, laughing fled,
  Nor knew he loved her!
     'Tis said
  The peach-tree sighed,
  And soon he gladly died:
And Autumn, weary of the chase,
Came on at Winter's sober pace
    (O careless lover!)

               Margaret Deland [1857–

A CASUAL SONG

SHE sang of lovers met to play
"Under the may bloom, under the may,"
But when I sought her face so fair,
I found the set face of Despair.

She sang of woodland leaves in spring,
And joy of young love dallying;
But her young eyes were all one moan,
And Death weighed on her heart like stone.

I could not ask, I know not now,
The story of that mournful brow;
It haunts me as it haunted then,
A flash from fire of hellbound men.

Roden Noel [1834–1894]

THE WAY OF IT

THE wind is awake, pretty leaves, pretty leaves,
Heed not what he says; he deceives, he deceives:
          Over and over
          To the lowly clover
He has lisped the same love (and forgotten it, too)
He will soon be lisping and pledging to you.

The boy is abroad, pretty maid, pretty maid,
Beware his soft words; I'm afraid, I'm afraid:
          He has said them before
          Times many a score,
Ay, he died for a dozen ere his beard pricked through,
And the very same death he will die for you.

The way of the boy is the way of the wind,
As light as the leaves is dainty maid-kind;
          One to deceive,
          And one to believe—
That is the way of it, year to year;
But I know you will learn it too late, my dear.

John Vance Cheney [1848–1922]

"WHEN LOVELY WOMAN STOOPS TO FOLLY"

From "The Vicar of Wakefield"

WHEN lovely woman stoops to folly
    And finds too late that men betray,—
What charm can soothe her melancholy,
    What art can wash her guilt away?

The only art her guilt to cover,
    To hide her shame from every eye,
To give repentance to her lover
    And wring his bosom, is—to die.

                    Oliver Goldsmith [1728-1774]

FOLK-SONG

BACK she came through the trembling dusk;
    And her mother spoke and said:
"What is it makes you late to-day,
And why do you smile and sing as gay
    As though you just were wed?"
*"Oh mother, my hen that never had chicks
    Has hatched out six!"*

Back she came through the flaming dusk;
    And her mother spoke and said:
"What gives your eyes that dancing light,
What makes your lips so strangely bright,
    And why are your cheeks so red?"
*"Oh mother, the berries I ate in the lane
    Have left a stain."*

Back she came through the faltering dusk;
    And her mother spoke and said:
"You are weeping; your footstep is heavy with care—
What makes you totter and cling to the stair,
    And why do you hang your head?"
*"Oh mother—oh mother—you never can know—
    I loved him so!"*

                    Louis Untermeyer [1885-

A VERY OLD SONG

"DAUGHTER, thou art come to die:
  Sound be thy sleeping, lass."
"Well: without lament or cry,
  Mother, let me pass."

"What things on mould were best of all?
  (Soft be thy sleeping, lass.)"
"The apples reddening till they fall
In the sun beside the convent wall.
  Let me pass."

"Whom on earth hast thou loved best?
  (Sound be thy sleeping, lass.)"
"Him that shared with me thy breast;
Thee and a knight last year our guest.
He hath an heron to his crest.
  Let me pass."

"What leavest thou of fame or hoard?
  (Soft be thy sleeping, lass.)"
"My far-blown shame for thy reward;
To my brother, gold to get him a sword.
  Let me pass."

"But what wilt leave thy lover, Grim?
  (Sound be thy sleeping, lass.)"
"The hair he kissed to strangle him.
  Mother, let me pass."
                              William Laird [1888–

"SHE WAS YOUNG AND BLITHE AND FAIR"

SHE was young and blithe and fair,
Firm of purpose, sweet and strong;
Perfect was her crown of hair,
Perfect most of all her song.

Yesterday beneath an oak,
She was chanting in the wood:

Wandering harmonies awoke;
Sleeping echoes understood.

To-day without a song, without a word,
She seems to drag one piteous fallen wing
Along the ground, and, like a wounded bird,
Move silent, having lost the heart to sing.

She was young and blithe and fair,
Firm of purpose, sweet and strong;
Perfect was her crown of hair,
Perfect most of all her song.

Harold Monro [1879–1932]

THE LASS THAT DIED OF LOVE

LIFE is not dear or gay
    Till lovers kiss it,
Love stole my life away
    Ere I might miss it.
In sober March I vowed
    I'd have no lover,
Love laid me in my shroud
    Ere June was over.

I felt his body take
    My body to it,
And knew my heart would break
    Ere I should rue it;
June roses are not sad
    When dew-drops steep them,
My moments were so glad
    I could not keep them.

Proud was I love had made
    Desire to fill me,
I shut my eyes and prayed
    That he might kill me.
I saw new wonders wreathe
    The stars above him.
And oh, I could not breathe
    For kissing of him.

Is love too sweet to last,
  Too fierce to cherish,
Can kisses fall too fast
  And lovers perish?
Who heeds since love disarms
  Death, ere we near him?
Within my lover's arms
  I did not fear him!

But since I died in sin
  And all unshriven,
They would not let me win
  Into their heaven;
They would not let my bier
  Into God's garden,
But bade me tarry here
  And pray for pardon.

I lie and wait for grace
  That shall surround me,
His kisses on my face,
  His arms around me;
And sinless maids draw near
  To drop above me
A virginal sad tear
  For envy of me.

Richard Middleton [1882–1911]

THE PASSION-FLOWER

My love gave me a passion-flower.
I nursed it well—so brief its hour!
My eyelids ache, my throat is dry:
He told me that it would not die.

My love and I are one, and yet
Full oft my cheeks with tears are wet—
So sweet the night is and the bower!
My love gave me a passion-flower.

So sweet! Hold fast my hands. Can God
Make all this joy revert to sod,
And leave to me but this for dower—
My love gave me a passion-flower.

Margaret Fuller [1871–

NORAH

I KNEW his house by the poplar-trees,
Green and silvery in the breeze;

"A heaven-high hedge," were the words he said,
"And holly-hocks, pink and white and red. . . ."

It seemed so far from McChesney's Hall—
Where first he told me about it all.

A long path runs inside from the gate,—
He still can take it, early or late;

But where in the world is the path for me
Except the river that runs to the sea!

Zoë Akins [1886–

OF JOAN'S YOUTH

I WOULD unto my fair restore
A simple thing:
The flushing cheek she had before!
Out-velveting
No more, no more,
On our sad shore,
The carmine grape, the moth's auroral wing.

Ah, say how winds in flooding grass
Unmoor the rose;
Or guileful ways the salmon pass
To sea, disclose;
For so, alas,
With Love, alas,
With fatal, fatal Love a girlhood goes.

Louise Imogen Guiney [1861–1920]

THERE'S WISDOM IN WOMEN

"Oh love is fair, and love is rare;" my dear one she said,
"But love goes lightly over."   I bowed her foolish head,
And kissed her hair and laughed at her.   Such a child was
    she;
So new to love, so true to love, and she spoke so bitterly.

But there's wisdom in women, of more than they have
    known,
And thoughts go blowing through them, are wiser than their
    own,
Or how should my dear one, being ignorant and young,
Have cried on love so bitterly, with so true a tongue?

Rupert Brooke [1887–1915]

GOETHE AND FREDERIKA

Wander, oh, wander, maiden sweet,
In the fairy bower, while yet you may;
See in rapture he lies at your feet;
Rest on the truth of the glorious youth,
Rest—for a summer day.
That great clear spirit of flickering fire
You have lulled awhile in magic sleep,
But you cannot fill his wide desire.
His heart is tender, his eyes are deep,
His words divinely flow;
But his voice and his glance are not for you;
He never can be to a maiden true;
Soon will he wake and go.
Well, well, 'twere a piteous thing
To chain forever that strong young wing.
Let the butterfly break for his own sweet sake
The gossamer threads that have bound him;
Let him shed in free flight his rainbow light,
And gladden the world around him.
Short is the struggle and slight is the strain;
Such a web was made to be broken,
And she that wove it may weave again

Or, if no power of love to bless
Can heal the wound in her bosom true,
It is but a lorn heart more or less,
And hearts are many and poets few,
So his pardon is lightly spoken.

Henry Sidgwick [1838–1901]

THE SONG OF THE KING'S MINSTREL

I SING no longer of the skies,
 And the swift clouds like driven ships,
For there is earth upon my eyes
 And earth between my singing lips.
Because the King loved not my song
 That he had found so sweet before,
I lie at peace the whole night long,
 And sing no more.

The King liked well my song that night;
 Upon the palace roof he lay
With his fair Queen, and as I might
 I sang, until the morning's gray
Crept o'er their faces, and the King,
 Mocked by the breaking dawn above,
Clutched at his youth and bade me sing
 A song of love.

Well it might be—the King was old,
 And though his Queen was passing fair,
His dull eyes might not catch the gold
 That tangled in her wayward hair,
It had been much to see her smile,
 But with my song I made her weep.
Our heavens last but a little while,
 So now I sleep.

More than the pleasures that I had
 I would have flung away to know
My song of love could make her sad,
 Her sweet eyes fill and tremble so.

What were my paltry store of years,
  My body's wretched life to stake,
Against the treasure of her tears,
  For my love's sake?

Not lightly is a King made wise;
  My body ached beneath his whips,
And there is earth upon my eyes,
  And earth between my singing lips.
But I sang once—and for that grace
  I am content to lie and store
The vision of her dear, wet face,
  And sing no more.

Richard Middleton [1882–1911]

ANNIE SHORE AND JOHNNIE DOON

Annie Shore, 'twas, sang last night
  Down in South End saloon;
A tawdry creature in the light,
Painted cheeks, eyes over bright,
  Singing a dance-hall tune.

I'd be forgetting Annie's singing—
  I'd not have thought again—
But for the thing that cried and fluttered
  Through all the shrill refrain:
Youth crying above foul words, cheap music,
  And innocence in pain.

They sentenced Johnnie Doon today
  For murder, stark and grim:
Death's none too dear a price, they say,
For such-like men as him to pay:
  No need to pity him!

And Johnnie Doon I'd not be pitying—
  I could forget him now—
But for the childish look of trouble
  That fell across his brow,
For the twisting hands he looked at dumbly
  As if they'd sinned, he knew not how.

Patrick Orr [18

EMMY

EMMY'S exquisite youth and her virginal air,
Eyes and teeth in the flash of a musical smile,
Come to me out of the past, and I see her there
As I saw her once for a while.

Emmy's laughter rings in my ears, as bright,
Fresh and sweet as the voice of a mountain brook,
And still I hear her telling us tales that night,
Out of Boccaccio's book.

There, in the midst of the villainous dancing-hall,
Leaning across the table, over the beer,
While the music maddened the whirling skirts of the ball,
As the midnight hour drew near,

There with the women, haggard, painted and old,
One fresh bud in a garland withered and stale,
She, with her innocent voice and her clear eyes, told
Tale after shameless tale.

And ever the witching smile, to her face beguiled,
Paused and broadened, and broke in a ripple of fun,
And the soul of a child looked out of the eyes of a child,
Or ever the tale was done.

O my child, who wronged you first, and began
First the dance of death that you dance so well?
Soul for soul: and I think the soul of a man
Shall answer for yours in hell.

Arthur Symons [1865–

THE BALLAD OF CAMDEN TOWN

I WALKED with Maisie long years back
  The streets of Camden Town,
I splendid in my suit of black,
  And she divine in brown.

Hers was a proud and noble face
  A secret heart, and eyes
Like water in a lonely place
  Beneath unclouded skies.

A bed, a chest, a faded mat,
　　And broken chairs a few,
Were all we had to grace our flat
　　In Hazel Avenue.

But I could walk to Hampstead Heath,
　　And crown her head with daisies,
And watch the streaming world beneath,
　　And men with other Maisies.

When I was ill and she was pale
　　And empty stood our store,
She left the latchkey on its nail,
　　And saw me nevermore.

Perhaps she cast herself away
　　Lest both of us should drown:
Perhaps she feared to die, as they
　　Who die in Camden Town.

What came of her? The bitter nights
　　Destroy the rose and lily,
And souls are lost among the lights
　　Of painted Piccadilly.

What came of her? The river flows
　　So deep and wide and stilly,
And waits to catch the fallen rose
　　And clasp the broken lily.

I dream she dwells in London still
　　And breathes the evening air,
And often walk to Primrose Hill,
　　And hope to meet her there.

Once more together we will live,
　　For I will find her yet:
I have so little to forgive;
　　So much, I can't forget.

　　　　　　　　James Elroy Flecker [1884–1915]

LOVE AND DEATH

HELEN OF KIRCONNELL

I WISH I were where Helen lies,
Night and day on me she cries;
O that I were where Helen lies,
   On fair Kirconnell lea!

Cursed be the heart that thought the thought,
And cursed the hand that fired the shot,
When in my arms burd Helen dropped,
   And died to succor me!

O think na ye my heart was sair,
When my Love dropped and spak nae mair!
There did she swoon wi' meikle care,
   On fair Kirconnell lea.

As I went down the water side,
None but my foe to be my guide,
None but my foe to be my guide,
   On fair Kirconnell lea;

I lighted down my sword to draw,
I hackèd him in pieces sma',
I hackèd him in pieces sma',
   For her sake that died for me.

O Helen fair, beyond compare!
I'll mak a garland o' thy hair,
Shall bind my heart for evermair,
   Until the day I dee!

O that I were where Helen lies!
Night and day on me she cries;
Out of my bed she bids me rise,
   Says, "Haste, and come to me!"

O Helen fair!   O Helen chaste!
If I were with thee, I'd be blest,
Where thou lies low and taks thy rest,
 On fair Kirconnell lea.

I wish my grave were growing green,
A winding-sheet drawn owre my e'en,
And I in Helen's arms lying,
 On fair Kirconnell lea.

I wish I were where Helen lies!
Night and day on me she cries;
And I am weary of the skies,
 For her sake that died for me.

Unknown

WILLY DROWNED IN YARROW

"WILLY's rare, and Willy's fair,
 And Willy's wondrous bonny;
And Willy hecht to marry me,
 Gin e'er he married ony.

"Yestreen I made my bed fu' braid,
 This night I'll make it narrow;
For a' the livelang winter night
 I lie twined of my marrow.

"Oh came you by yon water-side?
 Pu'd you the rose or lily?
Or came you by yon meadow green?
 Or saw you my sweet Willy?"

She sought him east, she sought him west,
 She sought him braid and narrow;
Syne in the cleaving of a craig,
 She found him drowned in Yarrow.

Unknown

ANNAN WATER

" ANNAN Water's wading deep,
   And my Love Annie's wondrous bonny;
And I am laith she should wet her feet,
   Because I love her best of ony."

He's loupen on his bonny gray,
   He rade the right gate and the ready;
For all the storm he wadna stay,
   For seeking of his bonny lady.

And he has ridden o'er field and fell,
   Through moor, and moss, and many a mire;
His spurs of steel were sair to bide,
   And from her four feet flew the fire.

"My bonny gray, now play your part!
   If ye be the steed that wins my dearie,
With corn and hay ye'll be fed for aye,
   And never spur shall make you wearie."

The gray was a mare, and a right gude mare;
   But when she wan the Annan Water,
She could not have ridden the ford that night
   Had a thousand merks been wadded at her.

"O boatman, boatman, put off your boat,
   Put off your boat for golden money!"
But for all the gold in fair Scotland,
   He dared not take him through to Annie.

"Oh, I was sworn so late yestreen,
   Not by a single oath, but mony!
I'll cross the drumly stream tonight,
   Or never could I face my honey."

The side was stey, and the bottom deep,
   From bank to brae the water pouring;
The bonny gray mare she swat for fear,
   For she heard the water-kelpy roaring.

He spurred her forth into the flood,
  I wot she swam both strong and steady;
But the stream was broad, and her strength did fail,
  And he never saw his bonny lady!

Unknown

THE LAMENT OF THE BORDER WIDOW

My love he built me a bonnie bower,
And clad it a' wi' lily flower;
A brawer bower ye ne'er did see,
Than my true-love he built for me.

There came a man, by middle day,
He spied his sport, and went away;
And brought the king that very night,
Who brake my bower, and slew my knight.

He slew my knight, to me sae dear;
He slew my knight, and poin'd his gear:
My servants all for life did flee,
And left me in extremitie.

I sewed his sheet, making my mane;
I watched the corpse, mysel alane;
I watched his body night and day;
No living creature came that way.

I took his body on my back,
And whiles I gaed, and whiles I sat;
I digged a grave, and laid him in,
And happed him with the sod sae green.

But think na ye my heart was sair,
When I laid the moul' on his yellow hair?
O, think na ye my heart was wae,
When I turned about, away to gae?

Nae living man I'll love again,
Since that my lovely knight is slain;
Wi' ae lock o' his yellow hair
I'll chain my heart for evermair.

Unknown

ASPATIA'S SONG

From "The Maid's Tragedy"

Lay a garland on my hearse
    Of the dismal yew;
Maidens, willow branches bear;
    Say, I died true.

My love was false, but I was firm
    From my hour of birth.
Upon my buried body lie
    Lightly, gentle earth!

John Fletcher [1579–1625]

A BALLAD

From the "What-d'ye-call-it"

'Twas when the seas were roaring
    With hollow blasts of wind,
A damsel lay deploring,
    All on a rock reclined.
Wide o'er the foaming billows
    She cast a wistful look;
Her head was crowned with willows,
    That trembled o'er the brook.

"Twelve months are gone and over,
    And nine long tedious days;
Why didst thou, venturous lover,
    Why didst thou trust the seas?
Cease, cease thou cruel ocean,
    And let my lover rest;
Ah! what's thy troubled motion
    To that within my breast?

"The merchant robbed of pleasure,
    Sees tempests in despair;
But what's the loss of treasure,
    To losing of my dear?

Should you some coast be laid on,
  Where gold and diamonds grow,
You'd find a richer maiden,
  But none that loves you so.

"How can they say that nature
  Has nothing made in vain;
Why then, beneath the water,
  Should hideous rocks remain?
No eyes the rocks discover
  That lurk beneath the deep,
To wreck the wandering lover,
  And leave the maid to weep."

All melancholy lying,
  Thus wailed she for her dear;
Repaid each blast with sighing,
  Each billow with a tear.
When, o'er the white wave stooping,
  His floating corpse she spied,
Then, like a lily drooping,
  She bowed her head, and died.

John Gay [1685–1732]

THE BRAES OF YARROW

THY braes were bonnie, Yarrow stream,
  When first on them I met my lover:
Thy braes how dreary, Yarrow stream,
  When now thy waves his body cover!
Forever now, O Yarrow stream!
  Thou art to me a stream of sorrow;
For never on thy banks shall I
  Behold my love, the flower of Yarrow.

He promised me a milk-white steed,
  To bear me to his father's bowers;
He promised me a little page,
  To squire me to his father's towers;

He promised me a wedding-ring,—
    The wedding-day was fixed to-morrow;
Now he is wedded to his grave,
    Alas! his watery grave, in Yarrow.

Sweet were his words when last we met:
    My passion I as freely told him:
Clasped in his arms, I little thought
    That I should never more behold him!
Scarce was he gone, I saw his ghost;
    It vanished with a shriek of sorrow;
Thrice did the water-wraith ascend,
    And gave a doleful groan through Yarrow.

His mother from the window looked,
    With all the longing of a mother;
His little sister weeping walked
    The greenwood path to meet her brother.
They sought him east, they sought him west,
    They sought him all the forest thorough;
They only saw the cloud of night,
    They only heard the roar of Yarrow!

No longer from thy window look,—
    Thou hast no son, thou tender mother!
No longer walk, thou little maid;
    Alas! thou hast no more a brother.
No longer seek him east or west,
    And search no more the forest thorough;
For, wandering in the night so dark,
    He fell a lifeless corse in Yarrow.

The tear shall never leave my cheek,
    No other youth shall be my marrow:
I'll seek thy body in the stream,
    And then with thee I'll sleep in Yarrow.
The tear did never leave her cheek,
    No other youth became her marrow;
She found his body in the stream,
    And now with him she sleeps in Yarrow.

John Logan [1748–1788]

THE CHURCHYARD ON THE SANDS

My love lies in the gates of foam,
　　The last dear wreck of shore;
The naked sea-marsh binds her home,
　　The sand her chamber door.

The gray gull flaps the written stones,
　　The ox-birds chase the tide;
And near that narrow field of bones
　　Great ships at anchor ride.

Black piers with crust of dripping green,
　　One foreland, like a hand,
O'er intervals of grass between
　　Dim lonely dunes of sand.

A church of silent weathered looks,
　　A breezy reddish tower,
A yard whose mounded resting-nooks
　　Are tinged with sorrel flower.

In peace the swallow's eggs are laid
　　Along the belfry walls;
The tempest does not reach her shade,
　　The rain her silent halls.

But sails are sweet in summer sky,
　　The lark throws down a lay;
The long salt levels steam and dry,
　　The cloud-heart melts away.

But patches of the sea-pink shine,
　　The pied crows poise and come;
The mallow hangs, the bind-weeds twine,
　　Where her sweet lips are dumb.

The passion of the wave is mute;
　　No sound or ocean shock;
No music save the trilling flute
　　That marks the curlew flock.

But yonder when the wind is keen,
  And rainy air is clear,
The merchant city's spires are seen,
  The toil of men grows near.

Along the coast-way grind the wheels
  Of endless carts of coal;
And on the sides of giant keels
  The shipyard hammers roll.

The world creeps here upon the shout,
  And stirs my heart to pain;
The mist descends and blots it out,
  And I am strong again.

Strong and alone, my dove, with thee;
  And though mine eyes be wet,
There's nothing in the world to me
  So dear as my regret.

I would not change my sorrow sweet
  For others' nuptial hours;
I love the daisies at thy feet
  More than their orange flowers.

My hand alone shall tend thy tomb
  From leaf-bud to leaf-fall,
And wreathe around each season's bloom
  Till autumn ruins all.

Let snowdrops early in the year
  Droop o'er her silent breast;
And bid the later cowslip rear
  The amber of its crest.

Come hither, linnets tufted-red;
  Drift by, O wailing tern;
Set pure vale lilies at her head,
  At her feet lady-fern.

Grow, samphire, at the tidal brink,
  Wave pansies of the shore,
To whisper how alone I think
  Of her for evermore.

Bring blue sea-hollies thorny, keen,
  Long lavender in flower;
Gray wormwood like a hoary queen,
  Stanch mullein like a tower.

O sea-wall, mounded long and low,
  Let iron bounds be thine;
Nor let the salt wave overflow
  That breast I held divine.

Nor float its sea-weed to her hair,
  Nor dim her eyes with sands;
No fluted cockle burrow where
  Sleep folds her patient hands.

Though thy crest feel the wild sea's breath,
  Though tide-weight tear thy root,
Oh, guard the treasure-house, where death
  Has bound my Darling mute.

Though cold her pale lips to reward
  With love's own mysteries,
Ah, rob no daisy from her sward,
  Rough gale of eastern seas!

Ah, render sere no silken bent
  That by her head-stone waves;
Let noon and golden summer blent
  Pervade these ocean graves.

And, ah, dear heart, in thy still nest,
  Resign this earth of woes,
Forget the ardors of the west,
  Neglect the morning glows.

Sleep and forget all things but one,
  Heard in each wave of sea,—
How lonely all the years will run
  Until I rest by thee.
          John Byrne Leicester Warren [1835–1895]

THE MINSTREL'S SONG

From "Ælla"

Oh sing unto my roundelay;
  Oh drop the briny tear with me;
Dance no more at holiday;
  Like a running river be!
    My love is dead,
    Gone to his death-bed,
    All under the willow tree!

Black his hair as the winter night,
  White his throat as the summer snow,
Red his cheek as the morning light,
  Cold he lies in the grave below.

Sweet his tongue as the throstle's note;
  Quick in dance as thought can be;
Deft his tabor, cudgel stout,
  Oh, he lies by the willow tree.

Hark! the raven flaps his wing
  In the briery dell below;
Hark! the death-owl loud doth sing,
  To the night-mares as they go.

See! the white moon shines on high;
  Whiter is my true love's shroud;
Whiter than the morning sky,
  Whiter than the evening cloud.

Here, upon my true love's grave,
  Shall the barren flowers be laid;
Not one holy saint to save
  All the coldness of a maid.

With my hands I'll twist the briers
  Round his holy corpse to gre;
Elfin fairy, light your fires,
  Here my body still shall be.

Come, with acorn-cup and thorn,
  Drain my heartès blood away;
Life and all its good I scorn,
  Dance by night, or feast by day.

Water-witches, crowned with reeds,
  Bear me to your deadly tide.
I die! I come! my true love waits!—
  Thus the damsel spake, and died.

                    Thomas Chatterton [1752–1770]

HIGHLAND MARY

YE banks and braes and streams around
  The castle o' Montgomery,
Green be your woods, and fair your flowers,
  Your waters never drumlie!
There simmer first unfauld her robes,
  And there the langest tarry;
For there I took the last fareweel
  O' my sweet Highland Mary.

How sweetly bloomed the gay green birk,
  How rich the hawthorn's blossom,
As underneath their fragrant shade
  I clasped her to my bosom!
The golden hours on angel's wings
  Flew o'er me and my dearie;
For dear to me as light and life
  Was my sweet Highland Mary.

Wi' mony a vow and locked embrace
  Our parting was fu' tender;
And, pledging aft to meet again,
  We tore oursels asunder;
But, O! fell Death's untimely frost,
  That nipped my flower sae early!
Now green's the sod, and cauld's the clay,
  That wraps my Highland Mary!

O pale, pale now, those rosy lips,
    I aft hae kissed sae fondly!
And closed for aye the sparkling glance
    That dwelt on me sae kindly;
And moldering now in silent dust
    That heart that lo'ed me dearly!
But still within my bosom's core
    Shall live my Highland Mary.

Robert Burns [1759–1796]

TO MARY IN HEAVEN

Thou lingering star, with lessening ray,
    That lov'st to greet the early morn,
Again thou usher'st in the day
    My Mary from my soul was torn.
O Mary! dear departed shade!
    Where is thy place of blissful rest?
See'st thou thy lover lowly laid?
    Hear'st thou the groans that rend his breast?

That sacred hour can I forget,
    Can I forget the hallowed grove,
Where by the winding Ayr we met,
    To live one day of parting love!
Eternity will not efface
    Those records dear of transports past;
Thy image at our last embrace,—
    Ah! little thought we 'twas our last!

Ayr, gurgling, kissed his pebbled shore,
    O'erhung with wild woods, thickening green;
The fragrant birch, and hawthorn hoar,
    Twined amorous round the raptured scene;
The flowers sprang wanton to be pressed,
    The birds sang love on every spray,—
Till soon, too soon, the glowing west
    Proclaimed the speed of wingèd day.

Still o'er these scenes my memory wakes,
    And fondly broods with miser care!
Time but the impression stronger makes,
    As streams their channels deeper wear.
My Mary! dear departed shade!
    Where is thy place of blissful rest?
See'st thou thy lover lowly laid?
    Hear'st thou the groans that rend his breast?

Robert Burns [1759-1796]

LUCY

I

STRANGE fits of passion have I known:
And I will dare to tell,
But in the lover's ear alone,
What once to me befell.

When she I loved looked every day
Fresh as a rose in June,
I to her cottage bent my way,
Beneath an evening moon.

Upon the moon I fixed my eye,
All over the wide lea;
With quickening pace my horse drew nigh
Those paths so dear to me.

And now we reached the orchard-plot;
And, as we climbed the hill,
The sinking moon to Lucy's cot
Came near, and nearer still.

In one of those sweet dreams I slept,
Kind Nature's gentlest boon!
And all the while my eyes I kept
On the descending moon.

My horse moved on; hoof after hoof
He raised, and never stopped:
When down behind the cottage roof,
At once, the bright moon dropped.

What fond and wayward thoughts will slide
Into a lover's head!
"O mercy!" to myself I cried,
"If Lucy should be dead!"

II

She dwelt among the untrodden ways
   Beside the springs of Dove,
A Maid whom there were none to praise
   And very few to love:

A violet by a mossy stone
   Half hidden from the eye!
Fair as a star, when only one
   Is shining in the sky.

She lived unknown, and few could know
   When Lucy ceased to be;
But she is in her grave, and oh,
   The difference to me!

III

I traveled among unknown men,
   In lands beyond the sea;
Nor, England! did I know till then
   What love I bore to thee.

'Tis past, that melancholy dream!
   Nor will I quit thy shore
A second time; for still I seem
   To love thee more and more.

Among thy mountains did I feel
   The joy of my desire;
And she I cherished turned her wheel
   Beside an English fire.

Thy mornings showed, thy nights concealed,
   The bowers where Lucy played;
And thine too is the last green field
   That Lucy's eyes surveyed.

IV

Three years she grew in sun and shower;
Then Nature said, "A lovelier flower
   On earth was never sown;
This child I to myself will take;
She shall be mine, and I will make
   A lady of my own.

"Myself will to my darling be
Both law and impulse: and with me
   The girl, in rock and plain,
In earth and heaven, in glade and bower,
Shall feel an overseeing power
   To kindle or restrain.

"She shall be sportive as the fawn
That wild with glee across the lawn
   Or up the mountain springs;
And hers shall be the breathing balm,
And hers the silence and the calm
   Of mute insensate things.

"The floating clouds their state shall lend
To her; for her the willow bend;
   Nor shall she fail to see
Even in the motions of the storm
Grace that shall mold the maiden's form
   By silent sympathy.

"The stars of midnight shall be dear
To her; and she shall lean her ear
   In many a secret place
Where rivulets dance their wayward round
And beauty born of murmuring sound
   Shall pass into her face.

"And vital feelings of delight
Shall rear her form to stately height,
  Her virgin bosom swell;
Such thoughts to Lucy I will give
While she and I together live
  Here in this happy dell."

Thus Nature spake—The work was done—
How soon my Lucy's race was run!
  She died, and left to me
This heath, this calm and quiet scene;
The memory of what has been,
  And never more will be.

v

A slumber did my spirit seal;
  I had no human fears:
She seemed a thing that could not feel
  The touch of earthly years.

No motion has she now, or force;
  She neither hears nor sees;
Rolled round in earth's diurnal course,
  With rocks, and stones, and trees.

William Wordsworth [1770–1850]

PROUD MAISIE

From "The Heart of Midlothian"

PROUD Maisie is in the wood,
  Walking so early;
Sweet Robin sits on the bush,
  Singing so rarely.

"Tell me, thou bonny bird,
  When shall I marry me?"
—"When six braw gentlemen
  Kirkward shall carry ye."

"Who makes the bridal bed,
  Birdie, say truly?"
—"The gray-headed sexton
  That delves the grave duly.

"The glow-worm o'er grave and stone
  Shall light thee steady;
The owl from the steeple sing
  Welcome, proud lady!"
                    Walter Scott [1771-1832]

SONG

EARL MARCH looked on his dying child,
  And, smit with grief to view her—
The youth, he cried, whom I exiled
  Shall be restored to woo her.

She's at the window many an hour
  His coming to discover;
And he looked up to Ellen's bower
  And she looked on her lover—

But ah! so pale, he knew her not,
  Though her smile on him was dwelling!
And I am then forgot—forgot?
  It broke the heart of Ellen.

In vain he weeps, in vain he sighs,
  Her cheek is cold as ashes;
Nor love's own kiss shall wake those eyes
  To lift their silken lashes.
                    Thomas Campbell [1777-1844]

THE MAID'S LAMENT

From "The Examination of Shakespeare"

I LOVED him not; and yet now he is gone
  I feel I am alone.
I checked him while he spoke; yet could he speak,
  Alas! I would not check.

For reasons not to love him once I sought,
  And wearied all my thought
To vex myself and him: I now would give
  My love, could he but live
Who lately lived for me, and when he found
  'Twas vain, in holy ground
He hid his face amid the shades of death.
  I waste for him my breath
Who wasted his for me; but mine returns,
  And this lorn bosom burns
With stifling heat, heaving it up in sleep,
  And waking me to weep
Tears that had melted his soft heart: for years
  Wept he as bitter tears.
Merciful God ! Such was his latest prayer,
  These may she never share !
Quieter is his breath, his breast more cold,
  Than daisies in the mold,
Where children spell, athwart the churchyard gate,
  His name and life's brief date.
Pray for him, gentle souls, whoe'er you be,
  And, oh! pray too for me!

Walter Savage Landor [1775–1864]

"SHE IS FAR FROM THE LAND"

SHE is far from the land where her young hero sleeps,
  And lovers are round her, sighing:
But coldly she turns from their gaze, and weeps,
  For her heart in his grave is lying.

She sings the wild songs of her dear native plains,
  Every note which he loved awaking;—
Ah! little they think, who delight in her strains,
  How the heart of the minstrel is breaking.

He had lived for his love, for his country he died,
  They were all that to life had entwined him;
Nor soon shall the tears of his country be dried,
  Nor long will his love stay behind him.

Oh! make her a grave where the sunbeams rest,
  When they promise a glorious morrow;
They'll shine o'er her sleep, like a smile from the West,
  From her own loved island of sorrow.

Thomas Moore [1779-1852]

"AT THE MID HOUR OF NIGHT"

At the mid hour of night, when stars are weeping, I fly
To the lone vale we loved, when life shone warm in thine eye;
  And I think oft, if spirits can steal from the regions of air
  To revisit past scenes of delight, thou wilt come to me
    there,
And tell me our love is remembered even in the sky.

Then I sing the wild song 'twas once such rapture to hear,
When our voices commingling breathed like one on the ear;
  And, as Echo far off through the vale my sad orison rolls,
  I think, O my love! 'tis thy voice from the Kingdom of
    Souls
Faintly answering still the notes that once were so dear.

Thomas Moore [1779-1852]

ON A PICTURE BY POUSSIN REPRESENTING SHEPHERDS IN ARCADIA

Ah, happy youths, ah, happy maid,
  Snatch present pleasure while ye may;
Laugh, dance, and sing in sunny glade,
  Your limbs are light, your hearts are gay;
Ye little think there comes a day
  ('Twill come to you, it came to me)
When love and life shall pass away:
  I, too, once dwelt in Arcady.

Or listless lie by yonder stream,
  And muse and watch the ripples play,
Or note their noiseless flow, and deem
  That life thus gently glides away—
That love is but a sunny ray
  To make our years go smiling by.
I knew that stream, I too could dream,
  I, too, once dwelt in Arcady.

Sing, shepherds, sing; sweet lady, listen;
  Sing to the music of the rill,
With happy tears her bright eyes glisten,
  For, as each pause the echoes fill,
They waft her name from hill to hill—
  So listened my lost love to me,
The voice she loved has long been still;
  I, too, once dwelt in Arcady.

John Addington Symonds [1840-1893]

THRENODY

THERE'S a grass-grown road from the valley—
A winding road and steep—
That leads to the quiet hill-top,
Where lies your love asleep. . . .
While mine is lying, God knows where,
A hundred fathoms deep.

I saw you kneel at a grave-side—
How still a grave can be,
Wrapped in the tender starlight,
Far from the moaning sea!
But through all dreams and starlight,
The breakers call to me.

Oh, steep is your way to Silence—
But steeper the ways I roam,
For never a road can take me
Beyond the wind and foam,
And never a road can reach him
Who lies so far from home.

Ruth Guthrie Harding [1882–

STRONG AS DEATH

O DEATH, when thou shalt come to me
  From out thy dark, where she is now,
Come not with graveyard smell on thee,
  Or withered roses on thy brow.

Come not, O Death, with hollow tone,
  And soundless step, and clammy hand—
Lo, I am now no less alone
  Than in thy desolate, doubtful land;

But with that sweet and subtle scent
  That ever clung about her (such
As with all things she brushed was blent);
  And with her quick and tender touch.

With the dim gold that lit her hair,
  Crown thyself, Death; let fall thy tread
So light that I may dream her there,
  And turn upon my dying bed.

And through my chilling veins shall flame
  My love, as though beneath her breath;
And in her voice but call my name,
  And I will follow thee, O Death.

Henry Cuyler Bunner [1855–1896]

"I SHALL NOT CRY RETURN"

I SHALL not cry Return! Return!
  Nor weep my years away;
But just as long as sunsets burn,
  And dawns make no delay,
I shall be lonesome—I shall miss
Your hand, your voice, your smile, your kiss.

Not often shall I speak your name,
  For what would strangers care
That once a sudden tempest came
  And swept my gardens bare,
And then you passed, and in your place
Stood Silence with her lifted face.

Not always shall this parting be,
  For though I travel slow,

I, too, may claim eternity
And find the way you go;
And so I do my task and wait
The opening of the outer gate.

Ellen M. H. Gates [1835–1920]

"OH! SNATCHED AWAY IN BEAUTY'S BLOOM"

OH! snatched away in beauty's bloom,
On thee shall press no ponderous tomb;
But on thy turf shall roses rear
Their leaves, the earliest of the year;
And the wild cypress wave in tender gloom:

And oft by yon blue gushing stream
Shall Sorrow lean her drooping head,
And feed deep thought with many a dream,
And lingering pause and lightly tread;
Fond wretch! as if her step disturbed the dead!

Away! we know that tears are vain,
That Death nor heeds nor hears distress:
Will this unteach us to complain?
Or make one mourner weep the less?
And thou,—who tell'st me to forget,
Thy looks are wan, thine eyes are wet.

George Gordon Byron [1788–1824]

TO MARY

IF I had thought thou couldst have died,
  I might not weep for thee;
But I forgot, when by thy side,
  That thou couldst mortal be:
It never through my mind had passed
  The time would e'er be o'er,
And I on thee should look my last,
  And thou shouldst smile no more!

And still upon that face I look,
　And think 'twill smile again;
And still the thought I will not brook,
　That I must look in vain.
But when I speak—thou dost not say
　What thou ne'er left'st unsaid;
And now I feel, as well I may,
　Sweet Mary, thou art dead!

If thou wouldst stay, e'en as thou art,
　All cold and all serene,
I still might press thy silent heart,
　And where thy smiles have been.
While e'en thy chill, bleak corse I have,
　Thou seemest still mine own;
But there I lay thee in thy grave,—
　And I am now alone!

I do not think, where'er thou art,
　Thou hast forgotten me;
And I, perhaps, may soothe this heart
　In thinking, too, of thee;
Yet there was round thee such a dawn
　Of light ne'er seen before,
As fancy never could have drawn,
　And never can restore!

Charles Wolfe [1791–1823]

MY HEART AND I

ENOUGH! we're tired, my heart and I.
　We sit beside the headstone thus,
　And wish that name were carved for us.
The moss reprints more tenderly
　The hard types of the mason's knife,
　As Heaven's sweet life renews earth's life
With which we're tired, my heart and I.

You see we're tired, my heart and I.
　We dealt with books, we trusted men,
　And in our own blood drenched the pen,

As if such colors could not fly.
    We walked too straight for fortune's end,
    We loved too true to keep a friend;
At last we're tired, my heart and I.

How tired we feel, my heart and I!
    We seem of no use in the world;
    Our fancies hang gray and uncurled
About men's eyes indifferently;
    Our voice which thrilled you so, will let
    You sleep; our tears are only wet:
What do we here, my heart and I?

So tired, so tired, my heart and I!
    It was not thus in that old time
    When Ralph sat with me 'neath the lime
To watch the sunset from the sky.
    "Dear love, you're looking tired," he said:
    I, smiling at him, shook my head.
'Tis now we're tired, my heart and I.

So tired, so tired, my heart and I!
    Though now none takes me on his arm
    To fold me close and kiss me warm
Till each quick breath end in a sigh
    Of happy languor.   Now, alone,
    We lean upon this graveyard stone,
Uncheered, unkissed, my heart and I.

Tired out we are, my heart and I.
    Suppose the world brought diadems
    To tempt us, crusted with loose gems
Of powers and pleasures?   Let it try.
    We scarcely care to look at even
    A pretty child, or God's blue heaven,
We feel so tired, my heart and I.

Yet who complains?   My heart and I?
    In this abundant earth no doubt
    Is little room for things worn out:

Disdain them, break them, throw them by!
  And if before the days grew rough
  We *once* were loved, used,—well enough,
I think, we've fared, my heart and I.
            Elizabeth Barrett Browning [1806–1861]

ROSALIND'S SCROLL

From "The Poet's Vow"

I LEFT thee last, a child at heart,
  A woman scarce in years:
I come to thee, a solemn corpse
  Which neither feels nor fears.
I have no breath to use in sighs;
They laid the dead-weights on mine eyes
  To seal them safe from tears.

Look on me with thine own calm look:
  I meet it calm as thou.
No look of thine can change *this* smile,
  Or break thy sinful vow:
I tell thee that my poor scorned heart
Is of thine earth—thine earth, a part:
  It cannot vex thee now.

But out, alas! these words are writ
  By a living, loving one,
Adown whose cheeks the proofs of life,
  The warm quick tears do run:
Ah, let the unloving corpse control
Thy scorn back from the loving soul
  Whose place of rest is won.

I have prayed for thee with bursting sob
  When passion's course was free;
I have prayed for thee with silent lips
  In the anguish none could see;
They whispered oft, "She sleepeth soft"—
  But I only prayed for thee.

Go to! I pray for thee no more:
   The corpse's tongue is still;
Its folded fingers point to heaven,
   But point there stiff and chill:
No farther wrong, no farther woe
Hath license from the sin below
   Its tranquil heart to thrill.

I charge thee, by the living's prayer,
   And the dead's silentness,
To wring from out thy soul a cry
   Which God shall hear and bless!
Lest Heaven's own palm droop in my hand,
And pale among the saints I stand,
   A saint companionless.
              Elizabeth Barrett Browning [1806–1861]

LAMENT OF THE IRISH EMIGRANT

I'M sittin' on the stile, Mary,
   Where we sat side by side
On a bright May mornin' long ago,
   When first you were my bride.
The corn was springin' fresh and green,
   And the lark sang loud and high,
And the red was on your lip, Mary,
   And the love-light in your eye.

The place is little changed, Mary,
   The day is bright as then,
The lark's loud song is in my ear,
   And the corn is green again;
But I miss the soft clasp of your hand,
   And your breath, warm on my cheek:
And I still keep list'nin' for the words
   You never more will speak.

'Tis but a step down yonder lane,
   And the little church stands near—
The church where we were wed, Mary;
   I see the spire from here.

But the graveyard lies between, Mary,
　　And my step might break your rest—
For I've laid you, darling, down to sleep,
　　With your baby on your breast.

I'm very lonely now, Mary,
　　For the poor make no new friends;
But, oh! they love the better still
　　The few our Father sends.
And you were all I had, Mary,
　　My blessin' and my pride:
There's nothin' left to care for now,
　　Since my poor Mary died.

Yours was the good, brave heart, Mary,
　　That still kept hoping on,
When the trust in God had left my soul,
　　And my arm's young strength was gone;
There was comfort ever on your lip,
　　And the kind look on your brow—
I bless you, Mary, for that same,
　　Though you cannot hear me now.

I thank you for the patient smile
　　When your heart was fit to break,
When the hunger pain was gnawin' there,
　　And you hid it for my sake;
I bless you for the pleasant word,
　　When your heart was sad and sore—
Oh! I'm thankful you are gone, Mary,
　　Where grief can't reach you more!

I'm biddin' you a long farewell,
　　My Mary—kind and true!
But I'll not forget you, darling,
　　In the land I'm goin' to:
They say there's bread and work for all,
　　And the sun shines always there,
But I'll not forget old Ireland,
　　Were it fifty times as fair!

And often in those grand old woods
    I'll sit, and shut my eyes,
And my heart will travel back again
    To the place where Mary lies;
And I'll think I see the little stile
    Where we sat side by side,
And the springin' corn, and the bright May morn,
    When first you were my bride.

Helen Selina Sheridan [1807–1867]

THE KING OF DENMARK'S RIDE

WORD was brought to the Danish king
    (Hurry!)
That the love of his heart lay suffering,
And pined for the comfort his voice would bring;
    (O, ride as though you were flying!)
Better he loves each golden curl
On the brow of that Scandinavian girl
Than his rich crown jewels of ruby and pearl:
    And his rose of the isles is dying!

Thirty nobles saddled with speed;
    (Hurry!)
Each one mounting a gallant steed
Which he kept for battle and days of need;
    (O, ride as though you were flying!)
Spurs were struck in the foaming flank;
Worn-out chargers staggered and sank;
Bridles were slackened, and girths were burst;
But ride as they would, the king rode first,
    For his rose of the isles lay dying!

His nobles are beaten, one by one;
    (Hurry!)
They have fainted, and faltered, and homeward gone;
His little fair page now follows alone,
    For strength and for courage trying!
The king looked back at that faithful child;
Wan was the face that answering smiled;

They passed the drawbridge with clattering din,
Then he dropped; and only the king rode in
  Where his rose of the isles lay dying!

The king blew a blast on his bugle horn;
    (Silence!)
No answer came; but faint and forlorn
An echo returned on the cold gray morn,
    Like the breath of a spirit sighing.
The castle portal stood grimly wide;
None welcomed the king from that weary ride;
For dead, in the light of the dawning day,
The pale sweet form of the welcomer lay,
  Who had yearned for his voice while dying!

The panting steed, with a drooping crest,
    Stood weary.
The king returned from her chamber of rest,
The thick sobs choking in his breast;
    And, that dumb companion eyeing,
The tears gushed forth which he strove to check;
He bowed his head on his charger's neck:
"O steed, that every nerve didst strain,
Dear steed, our ride hath been in vain
  To the halls where my love lay dying!"
        Caroline Elizabeth Sarah Norton [1808–1870]

THE WATCHER

    A ROSE for a young head,
    A ring for a bride,
    Joy for the homestead
    Clean and wide—
        Who's that waiting
        In the rain outside?

    A heart for an old friend,
    A hand for the new:
    Love can to earth lend
    Heaven's hue—
        Who's that standing
        In the silver dew?

A smile for the parting,
A tear as they go,
God's sweethearting
Ends just so—
    Who's that watching
    Where the black winds blow?

He who is waiting
In the rain outside,
He who is standing
Where the dew drops wide,
He who is watching
In the wind must ride
    (Though the pale hands cling)
    With the rose
    And the ring
    And the bride,
      Must ride
With the red of the rose,
And the gold of the ring,
And the lips and the hair of the bride.

James Stephens [1882–

THE THREE SISTERS

GONE are those three, those sisters rare
With wonder-lips and eyes ashine.
One was wise and one was fair,
And one was mine.

Ye mourners, weave for the sleeping hair
Of only two your ivy vine.
For one was wise and one was fair,
But one was mine.

Arthur Davison Ficke [1883–

BALLAD

HE said: "The shadows darken down,
    The night is near at hand.
Now who's the friend will follow me
    Into the sunless land?

"For I have vassals leal and true,
   And I have comrades kind,
And wheresoe'er my soul shall speed,
   They will not stay behind."

He sought the brother young and blithe
   Who bore his spear and shield:
"In the long chase you've followed me,
   And in the battle-field.

"Few vows you make; but true's your heart,
   And you with me will win."
He said: "God speed you, brother mine,
   But I am next of kin."

He sought the friar, the gray old priest
   Who loved his father's board.
The friar he turned him to the east
   And reverently adored.

He said: "A godless name you bear,
   A godless life you've led,
And whoso wins along with you,
   His spirit shall have dread.

"Oh, hasten, get your guilty soul
   From every burden shriven;
Yet you are bound for flame and dole,
   But I am bound for heaven."

He sought the lady bright and proud,
   Who sate at his right hand:
"Make haste, O Love, to follow me
   Into the sunless land."

She said: "And pass you in your prime?
   Heaven give me days of cheer!
And keep me from the sunless clime
   Many and many a year."

All heavily the sun sank down
   Among black clouds of fate.
There came a woman fair and wan
   Unto the castle gate.

Through gazing vassals, idle serfs,
   So silently she sped!
The winding staircase echoed not
   Unto her light, light tread.

His lady eyed her scornfully.
   She stood at his right hand;
She said: "And I will follow you
   Into the sunless land.

"There is no expiation, none.
   A bitter load I bore:
Now I shall love you nevermore,
   Never and nevermore.

"There is no touch or tone of yours
   Can make the old love wake."
She said: "But I will follow you,
   Even for the old love's sake."

Oh, he has kissed her on the brow,
   He took her by the hand:
Into the sunless land they went,
   Into the starless land.

May Kendall [1861‑

"O THAT 'TWERE POSSIBLE"

From "Maud"

O THAT 'twere possible
   After long grief and pain
To find the arms of my true love
   Round me once again!

When I was wont to meet her
In the silent moody places
Of the land that gave me birth,
We stood tranced in long embraces
Mixed with kisses sweeter, sweeter
Than anything on earth.

A shadow flits before me,
Not thou, but like to thee.
Ah, Christ, that it were possible
For one short hour to see
The souls we loved, that they might tell us
What and where they be!

Alfred Tennyson [1809–1892]

"HOME THEY BROUGHT HER WARRIOR DEAD"

From "The Princess"

HOME they brought her warrior dead;
She nor swooned, nor uttered cry.
All her maidens, watching, said,
"She must weep or she will die."

Then they praised him, soft and low,
Called him worthy to be loved,
Truest friend and noblest foe;
Yet she neither spoke nor moved.

Stole a maiden from her place,
Lightly to the warrior stepped,
Took the face-cloth from the face;
Yet she neither moved nor wept.

Rose a nurse of ninety years,
Set his child upon her knee,—
Like summer tempest came her tears,
"Sweet my child, I live for thee."

Alfred Tennyson [1809–1892]

EVELYN HOPE

BEAUTIFUL Evelyn Hope is dead!
　Sit and watch by her side an hour.
That is her book-shelf, this her bed;
　She plucked that piece of geranium-flower,
Beginning to die too, in the glass.
　Little has yet been changed, I think:
The shutters are shut, no light may pass
　Save two long rays through the hinge's chink.

Sixteen years old when she died!
　Perhaps she had scarcely heard my name;
It was not her time to love; beside,
　Her life had many a hope and aim,
Duties enough and little cares,
　And now was quiet, now astir,
Till God's hand beckoned unawares,—
　And the sweet white brow is all of her.

Is it too late, then, Evelyn Hope?
　What, your soul was pure and true,
The good stars met in your horoscope,
　Made you of spirit, fire, and dew—
And, just because I was thrice as old,
　And our paths in the world diverged so wide,
Each was naught to each, must I be told?
　We were fellow mortals, naught beside?

No, indeed! for God above
　Is great to grant, as mighty to make,
And creates the love to reward the love:
　I claim you still, for my own love's sake!
Delayed, it may be, for more lives yet,
　Through worlds I shall traverse, not a few:
Much is to learn, much to forget
　Ere the time be come for taking you.

But the time will come,—at last it will,
　When, Evelyn Hope, what meant (I shall say)
In the lower earth, in the years long still,
　That body and soul so pure and gay?

Why your hair was amber, I shall divine,
    And your mouth of your own geranium's red,—
And what you would do with me, in fine,
    In the new life come in the old one's stead.

I have lived (I shall say) so much since then,
    Given up myself so many times,
Gained me the gains of various men,
    Ransacked the ages, spoiled the climes;
Yet one thing, one, in my soul's full scope,
    Either I missed or itself missed me:
And I want and find you, Evelyn Hope!
    What is the issue? let us see!

I loved you, Evelyn, all the while!
    My heart seemed full as it could hold;
There was place and to spare for the frank young smile,
    And the red young mouth, and the hair's young gold.
So, hush,—I will give you this leaf to keep:
    See, I shut it inside the sweet, cold hand!
There, that is our secret: go to sleep!
    You will wake, and remember, and understand.
                              Robert Browning [1812–1889]

REMEMBRANCE

COLD in the earth—and the deep snow piled above thee,
    Far, far removed, cold in the dreary grave!
Have I forgot, my only Love, to love thee,
    Severed at last by Time's all-severing wave?

Now, when alone, do my thoughts no longer hover
    Over the mountains, on that northern shore,
Resting their wings where heath and fern-leaves cover
    Thy noble heart for ever, ever more?

Cold in the earth—and fifteen wild Decembers,
    From those brown hills, have melted into spring:
Faithful, indeed, is the spirit that remembers
    After such years of change and suffering!

Sweet Love of youth, forgive, if I forget thee,
    While the world's tide is bearing me along;
Other desires and other hopes beset me,
    Hopes which obscure, but cannot do thee wrong!

No later light has lightened up my heaven,
    No second morn has ever shone for me;
All my life's bliss from thy dear life was given,
    All my life's bliss is in the grave with thee.

But, when the days of golden dreams had perished,
    And even Despair was powerless to destroy;
Then did I learn how existence could be cherished,
    Strengthened, and fed without the aid of joy.

Then did I check the tears of useless passion—
    Weaned my young soul from yearning after thine;
Sternly denied its burning wish to hasten
    Down to that tomb already more than mine.

And, even yet, I dare not let it languish,
    Dare not indulge in memory's rapturous pain;
Once drinking deep of that divinest anguish,
    How could I seek the empty world again?

                                    Emily Brontë [1818–1848]

SONG

THE linnet in the rocky dells,
    The moor-lark in the air,
The bee among the heather bells
    That hide my lady fair:

The wild deer browse above her breast;
    The wild birds raise their brood;
And they, her smiles of love caressed,
    Have left her solitude.

I ween that, when the grave's dark wall
    Did first her form retain,
They thought their hearts could ne'er recall
    The light of joy again.

They thought the tide of grief would flow
  Unchecked through future years;
But where is all their anguish now,
  And where are all their tears?

Well, let them fight for honor's breath,
  Or pleasure's shade pursue:
The dweller in the land of death
  Is changed and careless too.

And, if their eyes should watch and weep
  Till sorrow's source were dry,
She would not, in her tranquil sleep,
  Return a single sigh.

Blow, west-wind, by the lonely mound,
  And murmur, summer streams!
There is no need of other sound
  To soothe my lady's dreams.

Emily Brontë [1818–1848]

SONG OF THE OLD LOVE

From "Supper at the Mill"

WHEN sparrows build, and the leaves break forth,
  My old sorrow wakes and cries,
For I know there is dawn in the far, far north,
  And a scarlet sun doth rise;
Like a scarlet fleece the snow-field spreads,
  And the icy founts run free,
And the bergs begin to bow their heads,
  · And plunge, and sail in the sea.

O my lost love, and my own, own love,
  And my love that loved me so!
Is there never a chink in the world above
  Where they listen for words from below?
Nay, I spoke once, and I grieved thee sore,
  I remember all that I said,
And now thou wilt hear me no more—no more
  Till the sea gives up her dead.

Thou didst set thy foot on the ship, and sail
    To the ice-fields and the snow;
Thou wert sad, for thy love did naught avail,
    And the end I could not know;
How could I tell I should love thee to-day,
    Whom that day I held not dear?
How could I know I should love thee away
    When I did not love thee anear?

We shall walk no more through the sodden plain
    With the faded bents o'erspread,
We shall stand no more by the seething main
    While the dark wrack drives o'erhead;
We shall part no more in the wind and the rain,
    Where thy last farewell was said;
But perhaps I shall meet thee and know thee again
    When the sea gives up her dead.

Jean Ingelow [1820–1897]

REQUIESCAT

Strew on her roses, roses,
    And never a spray of yew!
In quiet she reposes:
    Ah! would that I did too.

Her mirth the world required:
    She bathed it in smiles of glee.
But her heart was tired, tired,
    And now they let her be.

Her life was turning, turning,
    In mazes of heat and sound.
But for peace her soul was yearning,
    And now peace laps her round.

Her cabined, ample Spirit,
    It fluttered and failed for breath.
To-night it doth inherit
    The vasty hall of Death.

Matthew Arnold [1822–1888]

TOO LATE

"DOWGLAS, DOWGLAS, TENDIR AND TREU"

COULD ye come back to me, Douglas, Douglas,
    In the old likeness that I knew,
I would be so faithful, so loving, Douglas,
    Douglas, Douglas, tender and true.

Never a scornful word should grieve ye,
    I'd smile on ye sweet as the angels do:
Sweet as your smile on me shone ever,
    Douglas, Douglas, tender and true.

Oh, to call back the days that are not!
    My eyes were blinded, your words were few:
Do you know the truth now, up in heaven,
    Douglas, Douglas, tender and true?

I never was worthy of you, Douglas;
    Not half worthy the like of you:
Now all men beside seem to me like shadows—
    I love you, Douglas, tender and true.

Stretch out your hand to me, Douglas, Douglas,
    Drop forgiveness from heaven like dew;
As I lay my heart on your dead heart, Douglas,
    Douglas, Douglas, tender and true!
            Dinah Maria Mulock Craik [1826–1887]

FOUR YEARS

AT the Midsummer, when the hay was down,
Said I mournful—Though my life be in its prime,
Bare lie my meadows all shorn before their time,
O'er my sere woodlands the leaves are turning brown;
    It is the hot Midsummer, when the hay is down.

At the Midsummer, when the hay was down,
Stood she by the brooklet, young and very fair,
With the first white bindweed twisted in her hair—
Hair that drooped like birch-boughs, all in her simple gown—
    That eve in high Midsummer, when the hay was down.

At the Midsummer, when the hay was down,
Crept she a willing bride close into my breast;
Low-piled the thunder-clouds had sunk into the west,
Red-eyed the sun out-glared like knight from leaguered town;
    It was the high Midsummer, and the sun was down.

It is Midsummer—all the hay is down,
Close to her forehead press I dying eyes,
Praying God shield her till we meet in Paradise,
Bless her in love's name who was my joy and crown,
    And I go at Midsummer, when the hay is down.
               Dinah Maria Mulock Craik [1826–1887]

BARBARA

On the Sabbath-day,
Through the churchyard old and gray,
Over the crisp and yellow leaves, I held my rustling way;
And amid the words of mercy, falling on my soul like balms;
'Mid the gorgeous storms of music—in the mellow organ-
    calms,
'Mid the upward streaming prayers, and the rich and solemn
    psalms,
    I stood careless, Barbara.

My heart was otherwhere
While the organ shook the air,
And the priest, with outspread hands, blessed the people
    with a prayer;
But, when rising to go homeward, with a mild and saint-like
    shine
Gleamed a face of airy beauty with its heavenly eyes on
    mine—
Gleamed and vanished in a moment—O that face was surely
    thine
    Out of heaven, Barbara!

O pallid, pallid face!
O earnest eyes of grace!
When last I saw thee, dearest, it was in another place.
You came running forth to meet me with my love-gift on
    your wrist:

The flutter of a long white dress, then all was lost in mist—
A purple stain of agony was on the mouth I kissed,
    That wild morning, Barbara!

I searched in my despair,
Sunny noon and midnight air;
I could not drive away the thought that you were lingering
        there.
O many and many a winter night I sat when you were gone,
My worn face buried in my hands, beside the fire alone.
Within the dripping churchyard, the rain plashing on your
        stone,
    You were sleeping, Barbara.

'Mong angels, do you think
Of the precious golden link
I clasped around your happy arm while sitting by yon
        brink?
Or when that night of gliding dance, of laughter and guitars,
Was emptied of its music, and we watched, through lattice-
        bars,
The silent midnight heaven creeping o'er us with its stars,
    Till the day broke, Barbara?

In the years I've changed;
Wild and far my heart has ranged,
And many sins and errors now have been on me avenged;
But to you I have been faithful, whatsoever good I lacked:
I loved you, and above my life still hangs that love intact—
Your love the trembling rainbow, I the reckless cataract.
    Still I love you, Barbara!

Yet, love, I am unblest;
With many doubts oppressed,
I wander like a desert wind, without a place of rest.
Could I but win you for an hour from off that starry shore,
The hunger of my soul were stilled, for Death hath told you
        more
Than the melancholy world doth know; things deeper than
        all lore
    Will you teach me, Barbara?

In vain, in vain, in vain!
You will never come again.
There droops upon the dreary hills a mournful fringe of rain;
The gloaming closes slowly round, loud winds are in the tree,
Round selfish shores for ever moans the hurt and wounded
    sea,
There is no rest upon the earth, peace is with Death and thee,
    Barbara!
                       Alexander Smith [1830–1867]

SONG

When I am dead, my dearest,
    Sing no sad songs for me;
Plant thou no roses at my head,
    Nor shady cypress-tree:
Be the green grass above me
    With showers and dewdrops wet;
And if thou wilt, remember,
    And if thou wilt, forget.

I shall not see the shadows,
    I shall not feel the rain;
I shall not hear the nightingale
    Sing on, as if in pain:
And dreaming through the twilight
    That doth not rise nor set,
Haply I may remember
    And haply may forget.
             Christina Georgina Rossetti [1830–1894]

SARRAZINE'S SONG TO HER DEAD LOVER
From "Chaitivel"

Hath any loved you well, down there,
    Summer or winter through?
Down there, have you found any fair
    Laid in the grave with you?
Is death's long kiss a richer kiss
    Than mine was wont to be —
Or have you gone to some far bliss
    And quite forgotten me?

What soft enamoring of sleep
  Hath you in some soft way?
What charmed death holdeth you with deep
  Strange lure by night and day?
— A little space below the grass,
  Out of the sun and shade;
But worlds away from me, alas,
  Down there where you are laid?

My bright hair's waved and wasted gold,
  What is it now to thee —
Whether the rose-red life I hold
  Or white death holdeth me?
Down there you love the grave's own green,
  And evermore you rave
Of some sweet seraph you have seen
  Or dreamt of in the grave.

There you shall lie as you have lain,
  Though in the world above,
Another life you live again,
  Loving again your love:
Is it not sweet beneath the palm?
  Is not the warm day rife
With some long mystic golden calm
  Better than love and life?

The broad quaint odorous leaves like hands
  Weaving the fair day through,
Weave sleep no burnished bird withstands,
  While death weaves sleep for you;
And many a strange rich breathing sound
  Ravishes morn and noon:
And in that place you must have found
  Death a delicious swoon.

Hold me no longer for a word
  I used to say or sing:
Ah, long ago you must have heard
  So many a sweeter thing:
For rich earth must have reached your heart
  And turned the faith to flowers;

And warm wind stolen, part by part,
  Your soul through faithless hours.

And many a soft seed must have won
  Soil of some yielding thought,
To bring a bloom up to the sun
  That else had ne'er been brought;
And, doubtless, many a passionate hue
  Hath made that place more fair,
Making some passionate part of you
  Faithless to me down there.

Arthur O'Shaughnessy [1844–1884]

LOVE AND DEATH

IN the wild autumn weather, when the rain was on the sea,
And the boughs sobbed together, Death came and spake to
    me:
"Those red drops of thy heart I have come to take from
    thee;
As the storm sheds the rose, so thy love shall broken be,"
    Said Death to me.

Then I stood straight and fearless while the rain was in the
    wave,
And I spake low and tearless: "When thou hast made my
    grave,
Those red drops from my heart then thou shalt surely have;
But the rose keeps its bloom, as I my love will save
    All for my grave."

In the wild autumn weather a dread sword slipped from its
    sheath;
While the boughs sobbed together, I fought a fight with
    Death,
And I vanquished him with prayer, and I vanquished him
    by faith:
Now the summer air is sweet with the rose's fragrant breath
    That conquered Death.

Rosa Mulholland [18 –1921]

TO ONE IN PARADISE

Thou wast all that to me, love,
    For which my soul did pine:
A green isle in the sea, love,
    A fountain and a shrine
All wreathed with fairy fruits and flowers,
    And all the flowers were mine.

Ah, dream too bright to last!
    Ah, starry Hope, that didst arise
But to be overcast!
    A voice from out of the Future cries,
"On! on!"—but o'er the Past
    (Dim gulf!) my spirit hovering lies
Mute, motionless, aghast.

For, alas! alas! with me
    The light of Life is o'er!
No more—no more—no more—
(Such language holds the solemn sea
    To the sands upon the shore)
Shall bloom the thunder-blasted tree,
    Or the stricken eagle soar.

And all my days are trances,
    And all my nightly dreams
Are where thy dark eye glances,
    And where thy footstep gleams—
In what ethereal dances,
    By what eternal streams.

Edgar Allan Poe [1809–1849]

ANNABEL LEE

It was many and many a year ago,
    In a kingdom by the sea,
That a maiden there lived whom you may know
    By the name of Annabel Lee;
And this maiden she lived with no other thought
    Than to love and be loved by me.

I was a child and she was a child,
　　In this kingdom by the sea,
But we loved with a love that was more than love,
　　I and my Annabel Lee;
With a love that the winged seraphs of heaven
　　Coveted her and me.

And this was the reason that, long ago,
　　In this kingdom by the sea,
A wind blew out of a cloud, chilling
　　My beautiful Annabel Lee;
So that her highborn kinsmen came
　　And bore her away from me,
To shut her up in a sepulcher
　　In this kingdom by the sea.

The angels, not half so happy in heaven,
　　Went envying her and me;
Yes! that was the reason (as all men know,
　　In this kingdom by the sea)
That the wind came out of the cloud by night,
　　Chilling and killing my Annabel Lee.

But our love it was stronger by far than the love
　　Of those who were older than we,
　　Of many far wiser than we;
And neither the angels in heaven above,
　　Nor the demons down under the sea,
Can ever dissever my soul from the soul
　　Of the beautiful Annabel Lee:

For the moon never beams, without bringing me dreams
　　Of the beautiful Annabel Lee;
And the stars never rise, but I feel the bright eyes
　　Of the beautiful Annabel Lee;
And so, all the night-tide, I lie down by the side
Of my darling—my darling—my life and my bride,
　　In the sepulcher there by the sea,
　　In her tomb by the sounding sea.

　　　　　　　　　　　　Edgar Allan Poe [1809–1849]

FOR ANNIE

THANK Heaven! the crisis—
　The danger is past,
And the lingering illness
　Is over at last—
And the fever called "Living"
　Is conquered at last.

Sadly, I know
　I am shorn of my strength,
And no muscle I move
　As I lie at full length:
But no matter—I feel
　I am better at length.

And I rest so composedly
　Now, in my bed,
That any beholder
　Might fancy me dead—
Might start at beholding me,
　Thinking me dead.

The moaning and groaning,
　The sighing and sobbing,
Are quieted now,
　With that horrible throbbing
At heart—ah, that horrible,
　Horrible throbbing!

The sickness—the nausea—
　The pitiless pain—
Have ceased, with the fever
　That maddened my brain—
With the fever called "Living"
　That burned in my brain.

And O! of all tortures
　That torture the worst
Has abated—the terrible
　Torture of thirst

For the naphthaline river
    Of Passion accurst—
I have drunk of a water
    That quenches all thirst,

—Of a water that flows,
    With a lullaby sound,
From a spring but a very few
    Feet under ground—
From a cavern not very far
    Down under ground.

And ah! let it never
    Be foolishly said
That my room it is gloomy,
    And narrow my bed;
For man never slept
    In a different bed—
And, to *sleep*, you must slumber
    In just such a bed.

My tantalized spirit
    Here blandly reposes,
Forgetting, or never
    Regretting, its roses—
Its old agitations
    Of myrtles and roses:

For now, while so quietly
    Lying, it fancies
A holier odor
    About it, of pansies—
A rosemary odor,
    Commingled with pansies—
With rue and the beautiful
    Puritan pansies.

And so it lies happily,
    Bathing in many
A dream of the truth
    And the beauty of Annie—
Drowned in a bath
    Of the tresses of Annie.

She tenderly kissed me,
　　She fondly caressed,
And then I fell gently
　　To sleep on her breast—
Deeply to sleep
　　From the heaven of her breast.

When the light was extinguished,
　　She covered me warm,
And she prayed to the angels
　　To keep me from harm—
To the queen of the angels
　　To shield me from harm.

And I lie so composedly,
　　Now, in my bed
(Knowing her love),
　　That you fancy me dead—
And I rest so contentedly,
　　Now, in my bed
(With her love at my breast),
　　That you fancy me dead—
That you shudder to look at me,
　　Thinking me dead.

But my heart it is brighter
　　Than all of the many
Stars in the sky,
　　For it sparkles with Annie—
It glows with the light
　　Of the love of my Annie—
With the thought of the light
　　Of the eyes of my Annie.

Edgar Allan Poe [1809–1849]

TELLING THE BEES

HERE is the place; right over the hill
　　Runs the path I took;
You can see the gap in the old wall still,
　　And the stepping-stones in the shallow brook.

There is the house, with the gate red-barred,
  And the poplars tall;
And the barn's brown length, and the cattle-yard,
  And the white horns tossing above the wall.

There are the beehives ranged in the sun;
  And down by the brink
Of the brook are her poor flowers, weed-o'errun,
  Pansy and daffodil, rose and pink.

A year has gone, as the tortoise goes,
  Heavy and slow;
And the same rose blows, and the same sun glows,
  And the same brook sings of a year ago.

There's the same sweet clover-smell in the breeze;
  And the June sun warm
Tangles his wings of fire in the trees,
  Setting, as then, over Fernside farm.

I mind me how with a lover's care
  From my Sunday coat
I brushed off the burrs, and smoothed my hair,
  And cooled at the brookside my brow and throat.

Since we parted, a month had passed,—
  To love, a year;
Down through the beeches I looked at last
  On the little red gate and the well-sweep near.

I can see it all now,—the slantwise rain
  Of light through the leaves,
The sundown's blaze on her window-pane,
  The bloom of her roses under the eaves.

Just the same as a month before,—
  The house and the trees,
The barn's brown gable, the vine by the door,—
  Nothing changed but the hives of bees.

Before them, under the garden wall,
  Forward and back,
Went drearily singing the chore-girl small,
  Draping each hive with a shred of black.

Trembling, I listened: the summer sun
  Had the chill of snow;
For I knew she was telling the bees of one
  Gone on the journey we all must go!

Then I said to myself, "My Mary weeps
  For the dead to-day:
Haply her blind old grandsire sleeps
  The fret and the pain of his age away."

But her dog whined low; on the doorway sill
  With his cane to his chin,
The old man sat; and the chore-girl still
  Sung to the bees stealing out and in.

And the song she was singing ever since
  In my ears sounds on:—
"Stay at home, pretty bees, fly not hence!
  Mistress Mary is dead and gone!"
          John Greenleaf Whittier [1807–1892]

A TRYST

I WILL not break the tryst, my dear,
  That we have kept so long,
Though winter and its snows are here,
  And I've no heart for song.

You went into the voiceless night;
  Your path led far away.
Did you forget me, Heart's Delight,
  As night forgets the day?

Sometimes I think that you would speak
  If still you held me dear;
But space is vast, and I am weak—
  Perchance I do not hear.

Surely, howe'er remote the star
    Your wandering feet may tread,
When I shall pass the sundering bar
    Our souls must still be wed.
                    Louise Chandler Moulton [1835-1908]

LOVE'S RESURRECTION DAY

ROUND among the quiet graves,
        When the sun was low,
Love went grieving,—Love who saves:
        Did the sleepers know?

At his touch the flowers awoke,
        At his tender call
Birds into sweet singing broke,
        And it did befall

From the blooming, bursting sod
        All Love's dead arose,
And went flying up to God
        By a way Love knows.
                    Louise Chandler Moulton [1835-1908]

HEAVEN

ONLY to find Forever, blest
    By thine encircling arm;
Only to lie beyond unrest
    In passion's dreamy calm!

Only to meet and never part,
    To sleep and never wake,—
Heart unto heart and soul to soul,
    Dead for each other's sake.
                    Martha Gilbert Dickinson [18 -

JANETTE'S HAIR

OH, loosen the snood that you wear, Janette,
Let me tangle a hand in your hair—my pet;

For the world to me had no daintier sight
Than your brown hair veiling your shoulders white;
   Your beautiful dark brown hair—my pet.

It was brown with a golden gloss, Janette,
It was finer than silk of the floss—my pet;
'Twas a beautiful mist falling down to your wrist,
'Twas a thing to be braided, and jewelled, and kissed—
   'Twas the loveliest hair in the world—my pet.

My arm was the arm of a clown, Janette,
It was sinewy, bristled, and brown—my pet;
But warmly and softly it loved to caress
Your round white neck and your wealth of tress,
   Your beautiful plenty of hair—my pet.

Your eyes had a swimming glory, Janette.
Revealing the old, dear story—my pet;
They were gray with that chastened tinge of the sky
When the trout leaps quickest to snap the fly,
   And they matched with your golden hair—my pet.

Your lips—but I have no words, Janette—
They were fresh as the twitter of birds—my pet,
When the spring is young, and the roses are wet,
With the dewdrops in each red bosom set,
   And they suited your gold brown hair—my pet.

Oh, you tangled my life in your hair, Janette,
'Twas a silken and golden snare—my pet;
But, so gentle the bondage, my soul did implore
The right to continue your slave evermore,
   With my fingers enmeshed in your hair—my pet.

Thus ever I dream what you were, Janette,
With your lips, and your eyes, and your hair—my pet,
In the darkness of desolate years I moan,
And my tears fall bitterly over the stone
   That covers your golden hair—my pet.

               Charles Graham Halpine [1829–1868]

THE DYING LOVER

THE grass that is under me now
Will soon be over me, Sweet;
When you walk this way again
I shall not hear your feet.

You may walk this way again,
And shed your tears like dew;
They will be no more to me then
Than mine are now to you!

Richard Henry Stoddard [1825-1903]

"WHEN THE GRASS SHALL COVER ME"

WHEN the grass shall cover me,
Head to foot where I am lying;
When not any wind that blows,
Summer blooms nor winter snows,
Shall awake me to your sighing:
Close above me as you pass,
You will say, "How kind she was,"
You will say, "How true she was,"
When the grass grows over me.

When the grass shall cover me,
Holden close to earth's warm bosom,—
While I laugh, or weep, or sing,
Nevermore, for anything,
You will find in blade and blossom,
Sweet small voices, odorous,
Tender pleaders in my cause,
That shall speak me as I was—
When the grass grows over me.

When the grass shall cover me!
Ah, belovèd, in my sorrow
Very patient, I can wait,
Knowing that, or soon or late,

There will dawn a clearer morrow:
　　When your heart will moan "Alas!
　　Now I know how true she was;
　　Now I know how dear she was"—
When the grass grows over me!
　　　　　Ina Donna Coolbrith [1842–1928]

GIVE LOVE TO-DAY

WHEN the lean, gray grasses
　　Cover me, bury me deep,
No sea wind that passes
　　Shall break my sleep.

When you come, my lover,
　　Sorrowful-eyed to me,
Earth mine eyes will cover;
　　I shall not see.

Though with sad words splendid,
　　Praising, you call me dear,
It will be all ended;
　　I shall not hear.

You may live love's riot
　　Laughingly over my head,
But I shall lie quiet
　　With the gray dead.

Love, you will not wake me
　　With all your singing carouse,
Nor your dancing shake me
　　In my dark house.

Though you should go weeping,
　　Sorrowful for my sake,
Fain to break my sleeping,
　　I could not wake.

Now, ere time destroy us—
  Shadows beneath and above;
Death has no song joyous,
  Nor dead men love—

Now, while deep-eyed, golden,
  Love on the mountain sings,
Let him be close holden;
  Fetter his wings.

Love, nor joy nor sorrow
  Troubles the end of day.
Leave the Fates to-morrow;
  Give Love to-day.

Ethel Talbot [18 —

UNTIL DEATH

MAKE me no vows of constancy, dear friend,
  To love me, though I die, thy whole life long,
And love no other till thy days shall end—
  Nay, it were rash and wrong.

If thou canst love another, be it so;
  I would not reach out of my quiet grave
To bind thy heart, if it should choose to go—
  Love should not be a slave.

My placid ghost, I trust, will walk serene
  In clearer light than gilds those earthly morns,
Above the jealousies and envies keen,
  Which sow this life with thorns.

Thou wouldst not feel my shadowy caress;
  If, after death, my soul should linger here;
Men's hearts crave tangible, close tenderness,
  Love's presence, warm and near.

It would not make me sleep more peacefully
    That thou wert wasting all thy life in woe
For my poor sake; what love thou hast for me,
    Bestow it ere I go.

Carve not upon a stone when I am dead
    The praises which remorseful mourners give
To women's graves—a tardy recompense—
    But speak them while I live.

Heap not the heavy marble o'er my head
    To shut away the sunshine and the dew;
Let small blooms grow there, and let grasses wave,
    And raindrops filter through.

Thou wilt meet many fairer and more gay
    Than I; but, trust me, thou canst never find
One who will love and serve thee night and day
    With a more single mind.

Forget me when I die!   The violets
    Above my breast will blossom just as blue,
Nor miss thy tears; e'en nature's self forgets;
    But while I live, be true.

                    Elizabeth Akers [1832–1911]

FLORENCE VANE

I LOVED thee long and dearly,
        Florence Vane;
My life's bright dream and early
        Hath come again;
I renew in my fond vision,
        My heart's dear pain—
My hopes, and thy derision,
        Florence Vane.

The ruin, lone and hoary,
        The ruin old,
Where thou didst hark my story,
        At even told—

That spot—the hues Elysian
    Of sky and plain—
I treasure in my vision,
    Florence Vane.

Thou wast lovelier than the roses
    In their prime;
Thy voice excelled the closes
    Of sweetest rhyme;
Thy heart was as a river
    Without a main.
Would I had loved thee never,
    Florence Vane!

But, fairest, coldest wonder!
    Thy glorious clay
Lieth the green sod under—
    Alas, the day!
And it boots not to remember
    Thy disdain,
To quicken love's pale ember,
    Florence Vane.

The lilies of the valley
    By young graves weep;
The daisies love to dally
    Where maidens sleep.
May their bloom, in beauty vying,
    Never wane
Where thine earthly part is lying,
    Florence Vane!
                Philip Pendleton Cooke [1816–1850]

"IF SPIRITS WALK"

IF spirits walk, love, when the night climbs slow
The slant footpath where we were wont to go,
    Be sure that I shall take the selfsame way
    To the hill-crest, and shoreward, down the gray,
Sheer, graveled slope, where vetches straggling grow.

Look for me not when gusts of winter blow,
When at thy pane beat hands of sleet and snow;
  I would not come thy dear eyes to affray,
      If spirits walk.

But when, in June, the pines are whispering low,
And when their breath plays with thy bright hair so
  As some one's fingers once were used to play—
  That hour when birds leave song, and children pray,
Keep the old tryst, sweetheart, and thou shalt know
      If spirits walk.

Sophie Jewett [1861–1909]

REQUIESCAT

TREAD lightly, she is near,
  Under the snow;
Speak gently, she can hear
  The daisies grow.

All her bright golden hair
  Tarnished with rust,
She that was young and fair
  Fallen to dust.

Lily-like, white as snow,
  She hardly knew
She was a woman, so
  Sweetly she grew.

Coffin-board, heavy stone,
  Lie on her breast;
I vex my heart alone,
  She is at rest.

Peace, peace; she cannot hear
  Lyre or sonnet;
All my life's buried here—
  Heap earth upon it.

Oscar Wilde [1856–1900]

LYRIC

Ah, dans ces mornes séjours
Les jamais sont les toujours.—PAUL VERLAINE

You would have understood me, had you waited;
   I could have loved you, dear! as well as he:
Had we not been impatient, dear! and fated
      Always to disagree.

What is the use of speech?   Silence were fitter:
   Lest we should still be wishing things unsaid.
Though all the words we ever spake were bitter,
      Shall I reproach you dead?

Nay, let this earth, your portion, likewise cover
   All the old anger, setting us apart:
Always, in all, in truth was I your lover;
      Always, I held your heart.

I have met other women who were tender,
   As you were cold, dear! with a grace as rare.
Think you I turned to them, or made surrender,
      I who had found you fair?

Had we been patient, dear! ah, had you waited,
   I had fought death for you, better than he:
But from the very first, dear! we were fated
      Always to disagree.

Late, late, I come to you, now death discloses
   Love that in life was not to be our part:
On your low-lying mound between the roses,
      Sadly I cast my heart.

I would not waken you: nay! this is fitter;
   Death and the darkness give you unto me;
Here we who loved so, were so cold and bitter,
      Hardly can disagree.

                Ernest Dowson [1867–1900]

ROMANCE

My Love dwelt in a Northern land.
  A gray tower in a forest green
Was hers, and far on either hand
  The long wash of the waves was seen,
And leagues and leagues of yellow sand,
  The woven forest boughs between!

And through the silver Northern night
  The sunset slowly died away,
And herds of strange deer, lily-white,
  Stole forth among the branches gray;
About the coming of the light,
  They fled like ghosts before the day!

I know not if the forest green
  Still girdles round that castle gray;
I know not if the boughs between
  The white deer vanish ere the day;
Above my Love the grass is green,
  My heart is colder than the clay!

                    Andrew Lang [1844–1912]

GOOD-NIGHT

Good-night, dear friend! I say good-night to thee
  Across the moonbeams, tremulous and white,
Bridging all space between us, it may be.
  Lean low, sweet friend; it is the last good-night.

For, lying low upon my couch, and still,
  The fever flush evanished from my face,
I heard them whisper softly, " 'Tis His will;
  Angels will give her happier resting-place!"

And so from sight of tears that fell like rain,
  And sounds of sobbing smothered close and low,
I turned my white face to the window-pane,
  To say good-night to thee before I go.

Good-night! good-night!   I do not fear the end,
    The conflict with the billows dark and high;
And yet, if I could touch thy hand, my friend,
    I think it would be easier to die;

If I could feel through all the quiet waves
    Of my deep hair thy tender breath a-thrill,
I could go downward to the place of graves
    With eyes a-shine and pale lips smiling still;

Or it may be that, if through all the strife
    And pain of parting I should hear thy call,
I would come singing back to sweet, sweet life,
    And know no mystery of death at all.

It may not be.   Good-night, dear friend, good-night!
    And when you see the violets again,
And hear, through boughs with swollen buds a-white,
    The gentle falling of the April rain,

Remember her whose young life held thy name
    With all things holy, in its outward flight,
And turn sometimes from busy haunts of men
    To hear again her low good-night! good-night!
                    Hester A. Benedict [18 –

REQUIESCAT

BURY me deep when I am dead,
    Far from the woods where sweet birds sing;
Lap me in sullen stone and lead,
    Lest my poor dust should feel the Spring.

Never a flower be near me set,
    Nor starry cup nor slender stem,
Anemone nor violet,
    Lest my poor dust remember them.

And you—wherever you may fare—
    Dearer than birds, or flowers, or dew—
Never, ah me, pass never there,
    Lest my poor dust should dream of you.
                Rosamund Marriott Watson [1863– 1911]

THE FOUR WINDS

WIND of the North,
Wind of the Norland snows,
Wind of the winnowed skies and sharp, clear stars—
Blow cold and keen across the naked hills,
And crisp the lowland pools with crystal films,
And blur the casement-squares with glittering ice,
But go not near my love.

Wind of the West,
Wind of the few, far clouds,
Wind of the gold and crimson sunset lands—
Blow fresh and pure across the peaks and plains,
And broaden the blue spaces of the heavens,
And sway the grasses and the mountain pines,
But let my dear one rest.

Wind of the East,
Wind of the sunrise seas,
Wind of the clinging mists and gray, harsh rains—
Blow moist and chill across the wastes of brine,
And shut the sun out, and the moon and stars,
And lash the boughs against the dripping eaves,
Yet keep thou from my love.

But thou, sweet wind!
Wind of the fragrant South,
Wind from the bowers of jasmine and of rose!—
Over magnolia glooms and lilied lakes
And flowering forests come with dewy wings,
And stir the petals at her feet, and kiss
The low mound where she lies.

Charles Henry Lüders [1858–1891]

THE KING'S BALLAD

GOOD my King, in your garden close,
(Hark to the thrush's trilling)
Why so sad when the maiden rose
Love at your feet is spilling?

Golden the air and honey-sweet,
Sapphire the sky, it is not meet
Sorrowful faces should flowers greet,
(Hark to the thrush's trilling).

All alone walks the King to-day.
(Hark to the thrush's trilling)
Far from his throne he steals away
Loneness and quiet willing.
Roses and tulips and lilies fair
Smile for his pleasure everywhere,
Yet of their joyance he takes no share,
(Hark to the thrush's trilling).

Ladies wait in the palace, Sire,
(Hark to the thrush's trilling)
Red and white for the king's desire,
Love-warm and sweet and thrilling;
Breasts of moonshine and hair of night,
Glances amorous, soft and bright,
Nothing is lacking for your delight,
(Hark to the thrush's trilling).

Kneels the King in a grassy place,
(Hark to the thrush's trilling)
Little flowers under his face
With his warm tears are filling.
Says the King, "Here my heart lies dead
Where my fair love is burièd,
Would I were lying here instead!"
(Hark to the thrush's trilling).

Joyce Kilmer [1886–1918]

HELIOTROPE

AMID the chapel's chequered gloom
She laughed with Dora and with Flora,
And chattered in the lecture-room,—
That saucy little sophomora!

Yet while, as in her other schools,
  She was a privileged transgressor,
She never broke the simple rules
  Of one particular professor.

But when he spoke of varied lore,
  Paroxytones and modes potential,
She listened with a face that wore
  A look half fond, half reverential.
    To her, that earnest voice was sweet,
      And, though her love had no confessor,
    Her girlish heart lay at the feet
      Of that particular professor.

And he had learned, among his books
  That held the lore of ages olden,
To watch those ever-changing looks,
  The wistful eyes, the tresses golden,
    That stirred his pulse with passion's pain
      And thrilled his soul with soft desire,
    And bade fond youth return again,
      Crowned with its coronet of fire.

Her sunny smile, her winsome ways,
  Were more to him than all his knowledge,
And she preferred his words of praise
  To all the honors of the college.
    Yet "What am foolish I to him?"
      She whispered to her heart's confessor.
    "She thinks me old and gray and grim,"
      In silence pondered the professor.

Yet once when Christmas bells were rung
  Above ten thousand solemn churches,
And swelling anthems grandly sung
  Pealed through the dim cathedral arches,—
    Ere home returning, filled with hope,
      Softly she stole by gate and gable,
    And a sweet spray of heliotrope
      Left on his littered study-table.

Nor came she more from day to day
  Like sunshine through the shadows rifting:
Above her grave, far, far away,
  The ever-silent snows were drifting;
    And those who mourned her winsome face
      Found in its stead a swift successor
    And loved another in her place—
      All, save the silent old professor.

But, in the tender twilight gray,
  Shut from the sight of carping critic,
His lonely thoughts would often stray
  From Vedic verse and tongues Semitic,
    Bidding the ghost of vanished hope
      Mock with its past the sad possessor
    Of the dead spray of heliotrope
      That once she gave the old professor.
                Harry Thurston Peck [1856–1914]

"LYDIA IS GONE THIS MANY A YEAR"

Lydia is gone this many a year,
  Yet when the lilacs stir,
In the old gardens far or near,
  This house is full of her.

They climb the twisted chamber stair;
  Her picture haunts the room;
On the carved shelf beneath it there,
  They heap the purple bloom.

A ghost so long has Lydia been,
  Her cloak upon the wall,
Broidered, and gilt, and faded green,
  Seems not her cloak at all.

The book, the box on mantle laid,
  The shells in a pale row,
Are those of some dim little maid,
  A thousand years ago.

And yet the house is full of her;
  She goes and comes again;
And longings thrill, and memories stir,
  Like lilacs in the rain.

Out in their yards the neighbors walk,
  Among the blossoms tall;
Of Anne, of Phyllis do they talk,
  Of Lydia not at all.

Lizette Woodworth Reese [1856–1935]

AFTER

Oh, the littles that remain!
Scent of mint out in the lane;
Flare of window, sound of bees;—
These, but these.

Three times sitting down to bread;
One time climbing up to bed;
Table-setting o'er and o'er;
Drying herbs for winter's store;
This thing; that thing;—nothing more.

But just now out in the lane,
Oh, the scent of mint was plain!

Lizette Woodworth Reese [1856–1935]

MEMORIES

Of my ould loves, of their ould ways,
I sit an' think, these bitther days.

(I've kissed—'gainst rason an' 'gainst rhyme—
More mouths than one in my mad time!)

Of their soft ways an' words I dream,
But far off now, in faith, they seem.

Wid betther lives, wid betther men,
They've all long taken up again!

For me an' mine they're past an' done—
Aye, all but one—yes, all but one!

Since I kissed *her* 'neath Tullagh Hill
That one gerrl stays close wid me still.

Och! up to mine her face still lifts,
An' round us still the white May drifts;

An' her soft arm, in some ould way,
Is here beside me, night an' day;

But, faith, 'twas her they buried deep,
Wid all that love she couldn't keep,

Aye, deep an' cold, in Killinkere,
This many a year—this many a year!

Arthur Stringer [1874–

TO DIANE

THE ruddy poppies bend and bow,
    Diane! do you remember?
The sun you knew shines proudly now,
The lake still lists the breezes vow,
Your towers are fairer for their stains,
Each stone you smiled upon remains.
    Sing low—where is Diane?
      Diane! do you remember?

I come to find you through the years,
    Diane! do you remember?
For none may rule my love's soft fears.
The ladies now are not your peers,
I seek you through your tarnished halls,
Pale sorrow on my spirit falls,
    High, low—where is Diane?
      Diane! do you remember?

I crush the poppies where I tread,
    Diane! do you remember?
Your flower of life, so bright, so red—
She does not hear—Diane is dead.

I pace the sunny bowers alone
Where naught of her remains but stone.
　Sing low—where is Diane?
　　Diane does not remember.
Helen Hay Whitney [18   –

"MUSIC I HEARD"

Music I heard with you was more than music,
And bread I broke with you was more than bread.
Now that I am without you, all is desolate,
All that was once so beautiful is dead.

Your hands once touched this table and this silver,
And I have seen your fingers hold this glass.
These things do not remember you, beloved:
And yet your touch upon them will not pass.

For it was in my heart you moved among them,
And blessed them with your hands and with your eyes.
And in my heart they will remember always:
They knew you once, O beautiful and wise!
Conrad Aiken [1889–

HER DWELLING-PLACE

Amid the fairest things that grow
　My lady hath her dwelling-place;
Where runnels flow, and frail buds blow
　As shy and pallid as her face.

The wild, bright creatures of the wood
　About her fearless flit and spring;
To light her dusky solitude
　Comes April's earliest offering.

The calm Night from her urn of rest
　Pours downward an unbroken stream;
All day upon her mother's breast
　My lady lieth in a dream.

Love could not chill her low, soft bed
   With any sad memorial stone;
He put a red rose at her head—
   A flame as fragrant as his own.

Ada Foster Murray [1857–1936]

THE WIFE FROM FAIRYLAND

HER talk was all of woodland things,
   Of little lives that pass
Away in one green afternoon,
   Deep in the haunted grass;

For she had come from fairyland,
   The morning of a day
When the world that still was April
   Was turning into May.

Green leaves and silence and two eyes—
   'Twas so she seemed to me,
A silver shadow of the woods,
   Whisper and mystery.

I looked into her woodland eyes,
   And all my heart was hers,
And then I led her by the hand
   Home up my marble stairs;

And all my granite and my gold
   Was hers for her green eyes,
And all my sinful heart was hers
   From sunset to sunrise;

I gave her all delight and ease
   That God had given to me,
I listened to fulfil her dreams,
   Rapt with expectancy.

But all I gave, and all I did,
   Brought but a weary smile
Of gratitude upon her face;
   As though a little while,

She loitered in magnificence
  Of marble and of gold,
And waited to be home again
  When the dull tale was told.

Sometimes, in the chill galleries,
  Unseen, she deemed, unheard,
I found her dancing like a leaf
  And singing like a bird.

So lone a thing I never saw
  In lonely earth or sky,
So merry and so sad a thing,
  One sad, one laughing, eye.

There came a day when on her heart
  A wildwood blossom lay,
And the world that still was April
  Was turning into May.

In the green eyes I saw a smile
  That turned my heart to stone:
My wife that came from fairyland
  No longer was alone.

For there had come a little hand
  To show the green way home,
Home through the leaves, home through the dew,
  Home through the greenwood—home.
          Richard Le Gallienne [1866–

IN THE FALL O' YEAR

I went back an old-time lane
  In the fall o' year,
There was wind and bitter rain
  And the leaves were sere.

Once the birds were lilting high
  In a far-off May—
I remember, you and I
  Were as glad as they.

But the branches now are bare
  And the lad you knew,
Long ago was buried there—
  Long ago, with you!
             Thomas S. Jones, Jr. [1882–1932]

THE INVISIBLE BRIDE

THE low-voiced girls that go
  In gardens of the Lord,
Like flowers of the field they grow
  In sisterly accord.

Their whispering feet are white
  Along the leafy ways;
They go in whirls of light
  Too beautiful for praise.

And in their band forsooth
  Is one to set me free—
The one that touched my youth—
  The one God gave to me.

She kindles the desire
  Whereby the gods survive—
The white ideal fire
  That keeps my soul alive.

Now at the wondrous hour,
  She leaves her star supreme,
And comes in the night's still power,
  To touch me with a dream.

Sibyl of mystery
  On roads beyond our ken,
Softly she comes to me,
  And goes to God again.
             Edwin Markham [1852–1940]

RAIN ON A GRAVE

CLOUDS spout upon her
    Their waters amain
    In ruthless disdain,—
Her who but lately
    Had shivered with pain
As at touch of dishonor
If there had lit on her
So coldly, so straightly
    Such arrows of rain.

She who to shelter
    Her delicate head
Would quicken and quicken
    Each tentative tread
If drops chanced to pelt her
    That summertime spills
    In dust-paven rills
When thunder-clouds thicken
    And birds close their bills.

Would that I lay there
    And she were housed here!
Or better, together
Were folded away there
Exposed to one weather
We both,—who would stray there
When sunny the day there,
    Or evening was clear
    At the prime of the year.

Soon will be growing
    Green blades from her mound,
And daisies be showing
    Like stars on the ground,
Till she form part of them—
Ay—the sweet heart of them,
Loved beyond measure
With a child's pleasure
    All her life's round.

             Thomas Hardy [1840–1928]

PATTERNS

I walk down the garden paths,
And all the daffodils
Are blowing, and the bright blue squills.
I walk down the patterned garden-paths
In my stiff, brocaded gown.
With my powdered hair and jewelled fan,
I too am a rare
Pattern.   As I wander down
The garden paths.

My dress is richly figured,
And the train
Makes a pink and silver stain
On the gravel, and the thrift
Of the borders.
Just a plate of current fashion,
Tripping by in high-heeled, ribboned shoes.
Not a softness anywhere about me,
Only whale-bone and brocade.
And I sink on a seat in the shade
Of a lime-tree.   For my passion
Wars against the stiff brocade.
The daffodils and squills
Flutter in the breeze
As they please.
And I weep;
For the lime-tree is in blossom
And one small flower has dropped upon my bosom.

And the plashing of waterdrops
In the marble fountain
Comes down the garden-paths.
The dripping never stops.
Underneath my stiffened gown
Is the softness of a woman bathing in a marble basin,
A basin in the midst of hedges grown
So thick, she cannot see her lover hiding.

But she guesses he is near,
And the sliding of the water
Seems the stroking of a dear
Hand upon her.
What is Summer in a fine brocaded gown!
I should like to see it lying in a heap upon the ground.
All the pink and silver crumpled upon the ground.

I would be the pink and silver as I ran along the paths,
And he would stumble after,
Bewildered by my laughter.
I should see the sun flashing from his sword-hilt and the
     buckles on his shoes.
I would choose
To lead him in a maze along the patterned paths,
A bright and laughing maze for my heavy-booted lover,
Till he caught me in the shade,
And the buttons of his waistcoat bruised my body as he
     clasped me,
Aching, melting, unafraid.
With the shadows of the leaves and the sundrops,
And the plopping of the waterdrops,
All about us in the open afternoon—
I am very like to swoon
With the weight of this brocade,
For the sun sifts through the shade.

Underneath the fallen blossom
In my bosom,
Is a letter I have hid.
It was brought to me this morning by a rider from the Duke.
"Madam, we regret to inform you that Lord Hartwell
Died in action Thursday se'nnight."
As I read it in the white, morning sunlight,
The letters squirmed like snakes.
"Any answer, Madam?" said my footman.
"No," I told him.
"See that the messenger takes some refreshment.
No, no answer."
And I walked into the garden,

Up and down the patterned paths,
In my stiff, correct brocade.
The blue and yellow flowers stood up proudly in the sun,
Each one.
I stood upright too,
Held rigid to the pattern
By the stiffness of my gown.
Up and down I walked,
Up and down.

In a month he would have been my husband.
In a month, here, underneath this lime,
We would have broke the pattern;
He for me, and I for him,
He as Colonel, I as Lady,
On this shady seat.
He had a whim
That sunlight carried blessing.
And I answered, "It shall be as you have said."
Now he is dead.

In Summer and in Winter I shall walk
Up and down
The patterned garden-paths
In my stiff, brocaded gown.
The squills and daffodils
Will give place to pillared roses, and to asters, and to snow.
I shall go
Up and down,
In my gown.
Gorgeously arrayed,
Boned and stayed.
And the softness of my body will be guarded from embrace
By each button, hook, and lace.
For the man who should loose me is dead,
Fighting with the Duke in Flanders,
In a pattern called a war.
Christ!   What are patterns for?

Amy Lowell [1874–1925]

DUST

When the white flame in us is gone,
  And we that lost the world's delight
Stiffen in darkness, left alone
  To crumble in our separate night;

When your swift hair is quiet in death,
  And through the lips corruption thrust
Has stilled the labor of my breath—
  When we are dust, when we are dust!—

Not dead, not undesirous yet,
  Still sentient, still unsatisfied,
We'll ride the air, and shine, and flit,
  Around the places where we died,

And dance as dust before the sun,
  And light of foot, and unconfined,
Hurry from road to road, and run
  About the errands of the wind.

And every mote, on earth or air,
  Will speed and gleam, down later days,
And like a secret pilgrim fare
  By eager and invisible ways,

Nor ever rest, nor ever lie,
  Till, beyond thinking, out of view,
One mote of all the dust that's I
  Shall meet one atom that was you.

Then in some garden hushed from wind,
  Warm in a sunset's afterglow,
The lovers in the flowers will find
  A sweet and strange unquiet grow

Upon the peace; and, past desiring,
  So high a beauty in the air,
And such a light, and such a quiring,
  And such a radiant ecstasy there,

They'll know not if it's fire, or dew,
  Or out of earth, or in the height,
Singing, or flame, or scent, or hue,
  Or two that pass, in light, to light,

Out of the garden, higher, higher. . . .
  But in that instant they shall learn
The shattering ecstasy of our fire,
  And the weak passionless hearts will burn

And faint in that amazing glow,
  Until the darkness close above;
And they will know—poor fools, they'll know!—
  One moment, what it is to love.

Rupert Brooke [1887–1915]

BALLAD

THE roses in my garden
  Were white in the noonday sun,
But they were dyed with crimson
  Before the day was done.

All clad in golden armor,
  To fight the Saladin,
He left me in my garden,
  To weep, to sing, and spin.

When fell the dewy twilight
  I heard the wicket grate,
There came a ghost who shivered
  Beside my garden gate.

All clad in golden armor,
  But dabbled with red dew;
He did not lift his vizor,
  And yet his face I knew.

And when he left my garden
The roses all were red
And dyed in a fresh crimson;
Only my heart was dead.

The roses in my garden
Were white in the noonday sun;
But they were dyed with crimson
Before the day was done.

Maurice Baring [1874–·

"THE LITTLE ROSE IS DUST, MY DEAR"

THE little rose is dust, my dear;
The elfin wind is gone
That sang a song of silver words
And cooled our hearts with dawn.

And what is left to hope, my dear,
Or what is left to say?
The rose, the little wind and you
Have gone so far away.

Grace Hazard Conkling [18

DIRGE

NEVER the nightingale,
Oh, my dear,
Never again the lark
Thou wilt hear;
Though dusk and the morning still
Tap at thy window-sill,
Though ever love call and call
Thou wilt not hear at all,
My dear, my dear.

Adelaide Crapsey [1878–1914]

THE LITTLE RED RIBBON

THE little red ribbon, the ring and the rose!
The summertime comes, and the summertime goes —
And never a blossom in all of the land
As white as the gleam of her beckoning hand!

The long winter months, and the glare of the snows;
The little red ribbon, the ring and the rose!
And never a glimmer of sun in the skies
As bright as the light of her glorious eyes!

Dreams only are true; but they fade and are gone —
For her face is not here when I waken at dawn;
The little red ribbon, the ring and the rose
Mine only; *hers* only the dream and repose.

I am weary of waiting, and weary of tears,
And my heart wearies, too, all these desolate years,
Moaning over the one only song that it knows, —
The little red ribbon, the ring and the rose!

James Whitcomb Riley [1849–1916]

THE ROSARY

THE hours I spent with thee, dear heart,
    Are as a string of pearls to me;
I count them over, every one apart,
      My rosary.

Each hour a pearl, each pearl a prayer,
    To still a heart in absence wrung;
I tell each bead unto the end and there
      A cross is hung.

Oh memories that bless—and burn!
    Oh barren gain—and bitter loss!
I kiss each bead, and strive at last to learn
      To kiss the cross,
        Sweetheart,
          To kiss the cross.

Robert Cameron Rogers [1862–1912]

LOVE'S FULFILMENT

"MY TRUE–LOVE HATH MY HEART"

From the "Arcadia"

MY true-love hath my heart, and I have his,
　By just exchange one for the other given:
I hold his dear, and mine he cannot miss;
　There never was a better bargain driven:
His heart in me keeps him and me in one,
　My heart in him his thoughts and senses guides:
He loves my heart, for once it was his own,
　I cherish his, because in me it bides.

His heart his wound receivèd from my sight;
　My heart was wounded from his wounded heart;
For as from me, on him his hurt did light,
　So still me thought in me his heart did smart:
Both equal hurt, in this change sought our bliss,
My true love hath my heart, and I have his.

Philip Sidney [1554–1586]

SONG

O SWEET delight, O more than human bliss,
With her to live that ever loving is!
To hear her speak whose words are so well placed
That she by them, as they in her are graced:
Those looks to view that feast the viewer's eye,
How blest is he that may so live and die!

Such love as this the Golden Times did know,
When all did reap, yet none took care to sow;
Such love as this an endless summer makes,
And all distaste from frail affection takes.
So loved, so blest, in my beloved am I:
Which till their eyes ache, let iron men envy!

Thomas Campion [? –1619]

THE GOOD–MORROW

I WONDER, by my troth, what thou and I
Did, till we loved? were we not weaned till then?
But sucked on country pleasures, childishly?
Or snored we in the Seven Sleepers' den?
'Twas so; but this, all pleasures fancies be;
If ever any beauty I did see,
Which I desired, and got, 'twas but a dream of thee.

And now good-morrow to our waking souls,
Which watch not one another out of fear;
For love all love of other sights controls,
And makes one little room an everywhere.
Let sea-discoverers to new worlds have gone;
Let maps to other, worlds on worlds have shown,
Let us possess one world; each hath one, and is one.

My face in thine eye, thine in mine appears,
And true plain hearts do in the faces rest;
Where can we find two fitter hemispheres
Without sharp north, without declining west?
Whatever dies, was not mixed equally;
If our two loves be one, or thou and I
Love just alike in all, none of these loves can die.

John Donne [1573–1631]

"THERE'S GOWD IN THE BREAST"

THERE'S gowd in the breast of the primrose pale,
  An' siller in every blossom;
There's riches galore in the breeze of the vale,
  And health in the wild wood's bosom.
Then come, my love, at the hour of joy,
  When warbling birds sing o'er us;
Sweet nature for us has no alloy,
  And the world is all before us.

The courtier joys in bustle and power,
  The soldier in war-steeds bounding,
The miser in hoards of treasured ore,
  The proud in their pomp surrounding:

But we hae yon heaven sae bonnie and blue,
  And laverocks skimming o'er us;
The breezes of health, and the valleys of dew—
  Oh, the world is all before us!

James Hogg [1770–1835]

THE BEGGAR MAID

HER arms across her breast she laid;
  She was more fair than words can say:
Bare-footed came the beggar maid
  Before the king Cophetua.
In robe and crown the king stepped down,
  To meet and greet her on her way;
"It is no wonder," said the lords,
  "She is more beautiful than day."

As shines the moon in clouded skies,
  She in her poor attire was seen:
One praised her ankles, one her eyes,
  One her dark hair and lovesome mien.
So sweet a face, such angel grace,
  In all that land had never been:
Cophetua sware a royal oath:
  "This beggar maid shall be my queen!"

Alfred Tennyson [1809–1892]

REFUGE

TWILIGHT, a timid fawn, went glimmering by,
  And Night, the dark-blue hunter, followed fast,
Ceaseless pursuit and flight were in the sky,
  But the long chase had ceased for us at last.

We watched together while the driven fawn
  Hid in the golden thicket of the day.
We, from whose hearts pursuit and flight were gone,
  Knew on the hunter's breast her refuge lay.

A. E. (George William Russell) [1867–1935]

AT SUNSET

CLASP her and hold her and love her,
    Here in the arching green
Of boughs that bend above her
    With belts of blue between.

Clasp her and hold her and love her,
    Swift! Ere the splendor dies;
The blue grows black above her,
    The earth in shadow lies.

Flowers of dream enfold her.
    Soft! Let me bend above,
Clasp her and love her and hold her,
    Clasp her and hold and love.

Louis V. Ledoux [1880–

"ONE MORNING, OH! SO EARLY"

ONE morning, oh! so early, my belovèd, my belovèd,
All the birds were singing blithely, as if never they would
    cease;
'Twas a thrush sang in my garden, "Hear the story, hear the
    story!"
        And the lark sang, "Give us glory!"
        And the dove said, "Give us peace!"

Then I hearkened, oh! so early, my belovèd, my belovèd,
To that murmur from the woodland of the dove, my dear,
    the dove;
When the nightingale came after, "Give us fame to sweeten
    duty!"
        When the wren sang, "Give us beauty!"
        She made answer, "Give us love!"

Sweet is spring, and sweet the morning, my beloved, my
    belovèd;
Now for us doth spring, doth morning, wait upon the year's
    increase,

And my prayer goes up, "Oh, give us, crowned in youth with
   marriage glory,
      Give for all our life's dear story,
      Give us love, and give us peace!"
              Jean Ingelow [1820–1897]

ACROSS THE DOOR

THE fiddles were playing and playing,
   The couples were out on the floor;
From converse and dancing he drew me,
   And across the door.

Ah! strange were the dim, wide meadows,
   And strange was the cloud-strewn sky,
And strange in the meadows the corncrakes,
   And they making cry!

The hawthorn bloom was by us,
   Around us the breath of the south.
White hawthorn, strange in the night-time—
   His kiss on my mouth!
              Padraic Colum [1881–

MAY MARGARET

IF you be that May Margaret
   That lived on Kendal Green,
Then where's that sunny hair of yours
   That crowned you like a queen?
That sunny hair is dim, lad,
   They said was like a crown—
The red gold turned to gray, lad,
   The night a ship went down.

If you be yet May Margaret,
   May Margaret now as then,
Then where's that bonny smile of yours
   That broke the hearts of men?

The bonny smile is wan, lad,
　That once was glad as day—
And oh! 'tis weary smiling
　To keep the tears away.

If you be that May Margaret,
　As yet you swear to me,
Then where's that proud, cold heart of yours
　That sent your love to sea?
Ah, me! that heart is broken,
　The proud, cold heart has bled
For one light word outspoken,
　For all the love unsaid.

Then Margaret, my Margaret,
　If all you say be true,
Your hair is yet the sunniest gold,
　Your eyes the sweetest blue.
And dearer yet and fairer yet
　For all the coming years—
The fairer for the waiting,
　The dearer for the tears!

　　　　　　Théophile Marzials [1850–

RONDEL

Kissing her hair, I sat against her feet,
Wove and unwove it, wound and found it sweet;
Made fast therewith her hands, drew down her eyes,
Deep as deep flowers and dreamy like dim skies;
With her own tresses bound and found her fair,
　　　　　Kissing her hair.

Sleep were no sweeter than her face to me,
Sleep of cold sea-bloom under the cold sea;
What pain could get between my face and hers?
What new sweet thing would love not relish worse?
Unless, perhaps, white death had kissed me there,
　　　　　Kissing her hair.

　　　　　Algernon Charles Swinburne [1837–1909]

A SPRING JOURNEY

WE journeyed through broad woodland ways,
 My Love and I.
The maples set the shining fields ablaze.
 The blue May sky
Brought to us its great Spring surprise;
While we saw all things through each other's eyes.

And sometimes from a steep hillside
 Shone fair and bright
The shadbush, like a young June bride,
 Fresh clothed in white.
Sometimes came glimpses glad of the blue sea;
But I smiled only on my Love; he smiled on me.

The violets made a field one mass of blue—
 Even bluer than the sky;
The little brook took on that color too,
 And sang more merrily.
"Your dress is blue," he laughing said. "Your eyes,"
My heart sang, "sweeter than the bending skies."

We spoke of poets dead so long ago,
 And their wise words;
We glanced at apple-trees, like drifted snow;
 We watched the nesting birds,—
Only a moment! Ah, how short the day!
Yet all the winters cannot blow its sweetness quite away.
                    Alice Freeman Palmer [1855–1902]

THE BROOKSIDE

I WANDERED by the brookside,
I wandered by the mill;
I could not hear the brook flow,—
The noisy wheel was still;
There was no burr of grasshopper,
No chirp of any bird,
But the beating of my own heart
Was all the sound I heard.

I sat beneath the elm-tree;
I watched the long, long shade,
And, as it grew still longer,
I did not feel afraid;
For I listened for a footfall,
I listened for a word,—
But the beating of my own heart
Was all the sound I heard.

He came not,—no, he came not,—
The night came on alone,—
The little stars sat, one by one,
Each on his golden throne;
The evening wind passed by my cheek,
The leaves above were stirred,—
But the beating of my own heart
Was all the sound I heard.

Fast silent tears were flowing,
When something stood behind;
A hand was on my shoulder,—
I knew its touch was kind:
It drew me nearer,—nearer,—
We did not speak one word,
For the beating of our own hearts
Was all the sound we heard.

Richard Monckton Milnes [1809–1885]

SONG

For me the jasmine buds unfold
And silver daisies star the lea,
The crocus hoards the sunset gold,
And the wild rose breathes for me.
I feel the sap through the bough returning,
I share the skylark's transport fine,
I know the fountain's wayward yearning;
I love, and the world is mine!

I love, and thoughts that sometime grieved,
Still well remembered, grieve not me;
From all that darkened and deceived
Upsoars my spirit free.

For soft the hours repeat one story,
Sings the sea one strain divine,
My clouds arise all flushed with glory;
I love, and the world is mine!

Florence Earle Coates [1850–1927]

WHAT MY LOVER SAID

By the merest chance, in the twilight gloom,
In the orchard path he met me;
In the tall, wet grass, with its faint perfume,
And I tried to pass, but he made no room,
Oh, I tried, but he would not let me.
So I stood and blushed till the grass grew red,
With my face bent down above it,
While he took my hand as he whispering said—
(How the clover lifted each pink, sweet head,
To listen to all that my lover said;
Oh, the clover in bloom, I love it!)

In the high, wet grass went the path to hide,
And the low, wet leaves hung over;
But I could not pass upon either side,
For I found myself, when I vainly tried,
In the arms of my steadfast lover.
And he held me there and he raised my head,
While he closed the path before me,
And he looked down into my eyes and said—
(How the leaves bent down from the boughs o'erhead
To listen to all that my lover said,
Oh, the leaves hanging lowly o'er me!)

Had he moved aside but a little way,
I could surely then have passed him;
And he knew I never could wish to stay,
And would not have heard what he had to say,

    Could I only aside have cast him.
It was almost dark, and the moments sped,
    And the searching night wind found us,
But he drew me nearer and softly said—
(How the pure, sweet wind grew still, instead,
To listen to all that my lover said;
    Oh, the whispering wind around us!)

I am sure he knew when he held me fast,
    That I must be all unwilling;
For I tried to go, and I would have passed,
As the night was come with its dew, at last,
    And the sky with its stars was filling.
But he clasped me close when I would have fled,
    And he made me hear his story,
And his soul came out from his lips and said—
(How the stars crept out where the white moon led,
To listen to all that my lover said;
    Oh, the moon and the stars in glory!)

I know that the grass and the leaves will not tell,
    And I'm sure that the wind, precious rover,
Will carry my secret so safely and well
    That no being shall ever discover
One word of the many that rapidly fell
    From the soul-speaking lips of my lover;
    And the moon and the stars that looked over
Shall never reveal what a fairy-like spell
They wove round about us that night in the dell,
    In the path through the dew-laden clover,
Nor echo the whispers that made my heart swell
    As they fell from the lips of my lover.

                   Homer Greene [1853–1940]

MAY–MUSIC

Oh! lose the winter from thine heart, the darkness from thine
    eyes,
And from the low hearth-chair of dreams, my Love-o'-
    May, arise;

And let the maidens robe thee like a white white-lilac tree,
Oh! hear the call of Spring, fair Soul,—and wilt thou
   come with me?

          Even so, and even so!
          Whither thou goest, I will go.
          I will follow thee.

Then wilt thou see the orange trees star-flowering over Spain,
Or arched and mounded Kaiser-towns that molder mid
   Almain,
Or through the cypress-gardens go of magic Italy?
Oh! East or West or South or North, say, wilt thou come
   with me?

          Even so, or even so!
          Whither thou goest, I will go.
          I will follow thee.

But wilt thou farther come with me through hawthorn red
   and white
Until we find the wall that hides the Land of Heart's Delight?
The gates all carved with olden things are strange and
   dread to see:
But I will lift thee through, fair Soul. Arise and come with
   me!

          Even so, Love, even so!
          Whither thou goest, I will go!
          Lo, I follow thee.
                Rachel Annand Taylor [18 –

SONG

FLAME at the core of the world,
   And flame in the red rose-tree;
The one is the fire of the ancient spheres,
   The other is Junes to be;
And, oh, there's a flame that is both their flames
   Here at the heart of me!

As strong as the fires of stars,
  As the prophet rose-tree true,
The fire of my life is tender and wild,
  Its beauty is old and new;
For out of the infinite past it came
  With the love in the eyes of you!

Arthur Upson [1877–1908]

A MEMORY

The Night walked down the sky
  With the moon in her hand;
By the light of that yellow lantern
  I saw you stand.

The hair that swept your shoulders
  Was yellow, too,
Your feet as they touched the grasses
  Shamed the dew.

The Night wore all her jewels,
  And you wore none,
But your gown had the odor of lilies
  Drenched with sun.

And never was Eve of the Garden
  Or Mary the Maid
More pure than you as you stood there
  Bold, yet afraid.

And the sleeping birds woke, trembling,
  And the folded flowers were aware,
And my senses were faint with the fragrant
  Gold of your hair.

And our lips found ways of speaking
  What words cannot say,
Till a hundred nests gave music,
  And the East was gray.

Frederic Lawrence Knowles [1869–1905]

LOVE TRIUMPHANT

HELEN's lips are drifting dust;
Ilion is consumed with rust;
All the galleons of Greece
Drink the ocean's dreamless peace;
Lost was Solomon's purple show
Restless centuries ago;
Stately empires wax and wane—
Babylon, Barbary, and Spain;—
Only one thing, undefaced,
Lasts, though all the worlds lie waste
And the heavens are overturned.
—Dear, how long ago we learned!

There's a sight that blinds the sun,
Sound that lives when sounds are done,
Music that rebukes the birds,
Language lovelier than words,
Hue and scent that shame the rose,
Wine no earthly vineyard knows,
Silence stiller than the shore
Swept by Charon's stealthy oar,
Ocean more divinely free
Than Pacific's boundless sea,—
Ye who love have learned it true.
—Dear, how long ago we knew!

Frederic Lawrence Knowles [1869–1905]

LINES

LOVE within the lover's breast
Burns like Hesper in the West,
O'er the ashes of the sun,
Till the day and night are done;
Then, when dawn drives up his car—
Lo! it is the morning star.

Love! thy love pours down on mine,
As the sunlight on the vine,

As the snow rill on the vale,
As the salt breeze on the sail;
As the song unto the bird
On my lips thy name is heard.

As a dewdrop on the rose
In thy heart my passion glows;
As a skylark to the sky,
Up into thy breast I fly;
As a sea-shell of the sea
Ever shall I sing of thee.

George Meredith [1828–1909]

LOVE AMONG THE RUINS

WHERE the quiet-colored end of evening smiles
          Miles and miles
On the solitary pastures where our sheep
          Half-asleep
Tinkle homeward through the twilight, stray or stop
          As they crop—
Was the site once of a city great and gay,
          (So they say)
Of our country's very capital, its prince
          Ages since
Held his court in, gathered councils, wielding far
          Peace or war.

Now,—the country does not even boast a tree,
          As you see,
To distinguish slopes of verdure, certain rills
          From the hills
Intersect and give a name to (else they run
          Into one),
Where the domed and daring palace shot its spires
          Up like fires
O'er the hundred-gated circuit of a wall
          Bounding all,
Made of marble, men might march on nor be pressed,
          Twelve abreast.

And such plenty and perfection, see, of grass
         Never was!
Such a carpet as, this summer-time, o'erspreads
         And embeds
Every vestige of the city, guessed alone,
         Stock or stone—
Where a multitude of men breathed joy and woe
         Long ago;
Lust of glory pricked their hearts up, dread of shame
         Struck them tame;
And that glory and that shame alike, the gold
         Bought and sold.

Now,—the single little turret that remains
         On the plains,
By the caper overrooted, by the gourd
         Overscored,
While the patching houseleek's head of blossom winks
         Through the chinks—
Marks the basement whence a tower in ancient time
         Sprang sublime,
And a burning ring, all round, the chariots traced
         As they raced,
And the monarch and his minions and his dames
         Viewed the games.

And I know, while thus the quiet-colored eve
         Smiles to leave
To their folding, all our many-tinkling fleece
         In such peace,
And the slopes and rills in undistinguished gray
         Melt away—
That a girl with eager eyes and yellow hair
         Waits me there
In the turret whence the charioteers caught soul
         For the goal,
When the king looked, where she looks now, breathless, dumb,
         Till I come.

But he looked upon the city, every side,
         Far and wide,

All the mountains topped with temples, all the glades'
　　　Colonnades,
All the causeys, bridges, aqueducts,—and then,
　　　All the men!
When I do come, she will speak not, she will stand,
　　　Either hand
On my shoulder, give her eyes the first embrace
　　　Of my face,
Ere we rush, ere we extinguish sight and speech
　　　Each on each.

In one year they sent a million fighters forth
　　　South and North,
And they built their gods a brazen pillar high
　　　As the sky,
Yet reserved a thousand chariots in full force—
　　　Gold, of course.
Oh heart! oh blood that freezes, blood that burns!
　　　Earth's returns
For whole centuries of folly, noise and sin!
　　　Shut them in,
With their triumphs and their glories and the rest!
　　　Love is best!

　　　　　　Robert Browning [1812–1889]

EARL MERTOUN'S SONG

From "The Blot in the 'Scutcheon"

THERE'S a woman like a dewdrop, she's so purer than the
　　　purest;
And her noble heart's the noblest, yes, and her sure faith's
　　　the surest:
And her eyes are dark and humid, like the depth on depth
　　　of luster
Hid i' the harebell, while her tresses, sunnier than the wild-
　　　grape cluster,
Gush in golden-tinted plenty down her neck's rose-misted
　　　marble:
Then her voice's music . . . . call it the well's bubbling, the
　　　bird's warble!

And this woman says, "My days were sunless and my nights
    were moonless,
Parched the pleasant April herbage, and the lark's heart's
    outbreak tuneless,
If you loved me not!" And I who (ah, for words of flame!)
    adore her,
Who am mad to lay my spirit prostrate palpably before
    her—
I may enter at her portal soon, as now her lattice takes
    me,
And by noontide as by midnight make her mine, as hers she
    makes me!

                          Robert Browning [1812–1889]

MEETING AT NIGHT

THE gray sea and the long black land;
And the yellow half-moon large and low;
And the startled little waves that leap
In fiery ringlets from their sleep,
As I gain the cove with pushing prow,
And quench its speed in the slushy sand.

Then a mile of warm sea-scented beach;
Three fields to cross till a farm appears;
A tap at the pane, the quick sharp scratch
And blue spirt of a lighted match,
And a voice less loud, through its joys and fears,
Than the two hearts beating each to each!

                          Robert Browning [1812–1889]

PARTING AT MORNING

ROUND the cape of a sudden came the sea,
And the sun looked over the mountain's rim:
And straight was a path of gold for him,
And the need of a world of men for me.

                          Robert Browning [1812–1889]

THE TURN OF THE ROAD

Soft, gray buds on the willow,
  Warm, moist winds from the bay,
Sea-gulls out on the sandy beach,
And a road my eager feet would reach,
  That leads to the Far-away.

Dust on the wayside flower,
  The meadow-lark's luring tone
Is silent now, from the grasses tipped
With dew at the dawn, the pearls have slipped—
  Far have I fared alone.

And then, by the alder thicket
  The turn of the road—and *you!*
Though the earth lie white in the noonday heat,
Or the swift storm follow our hurrying feet
  What do we care—we two!

Alice Rollit Coe [18 –

"MY DELIGHT AND THY DELIGHT"

My delight and thy delight
Walking, like two angels white,
In the gardens of the night:

My desire and thy desire
Twining to a tongue of fire,
Leaping live, and laughing higher;

Through the everlasting strife
In the mystery of life.

Love, from whom the world begun,
Hath the secret of the sun.

Love can tell, and love alone,
Whence the million stars were strown,
Why each atom knows its own,
How, in spite of woe and death,
Gay is life, and sweet is breath:

This he taught us, this we knew,
Happy in his science true,
Hand in hand as we stood
'Neath the shadows of the wood,
Heart to heart as we lay
In the dawning of the day.

Robert Bridges [1844–1930]

"O, SAW YE THE LASS"

O, SAW ye the lass wi' the bonny blue een?
Her smile is the sweetest that ever was seen;
Her cheek like the rose is, but fresher, I ween;
She's the loveliest lassie that trips on the green.
The home of my love is below in the valley,
Where wild-flowers welcome the wandering bee;
But the sweetest of flowers in that spot that is seen
Is the maid that I love wi' the bonny blue een.

When night overshadows her cot in the glen,
She'll steal out to meet her loved Donald again;
And when the moon shines on the valley so green,
I'll welcome the lass wi' the bonny blue een.
As the dove that has wandered away from his nest
Returns to the mate his fond heart loves the best,
I'll fly from the world's false and vanishing scene,
To my dear one, the lass wi' the bonny blue een.

Richard Ryan [1796–1849]

LOVE AT SEA

IMITATED FROM THÉOPHILE GAUTIER

WE are in love's land to-day;
  Where shall we go?
Love, shall we start or stay,
  Or sail or row?
There's many a wind and way,
And never a May but May;
We are in love's hand to-day;
  Where shall we go?

Our land-wind is the breath
Of sorrows kissed to death
    And joys that were;
Our ballast is a rose;
Our way lies where God knows
    And love knows where.
        We are in love's hand to-day—

Our seamen are fledged Loves,
Our masts are bills of doves,
    Our decks fine gold;
Our ropes are dead maids' hair,
Our stores are love-shafts fair
    And manifold.
        We are in love's land to-day—

Where shall we land you, sweet?
On fields of strange men's feet,
    Or fields near home?
Or where the fire-flowers blow,
Or where the flowers of snow
    Or flowers of foam?
        We are in love's hand to-day—

Land me, she says, where love
Shows but one shaft, one dove,
    One heart, one hand,—
A shore like that, my dear,
Lies where no man will steer,
    No maiden land.
            Algernon Charles Swinburne [1837–1909]

MARY BEATON'S SONG

From "Chastelard"

BETWEEN the sunset and the sea
My love laid hands and lips on me;
Of sweet came sour, of day came night,
Of long desire came brief delight:
Ah love, and what thing came of thee
Between the sea-downs and the sea?

Between the sea-mark and the sea
Joy grew to grief, grief grew to me;
Love turned to tears, and tears to fire,
And dead delight to new desire;
Love's talk, love's touch there seemed to be
Between the sea-sand and the sea.

Between the sundown and the sea
Love watched one hour of love with me;
Then down the all-golden water-ways
His feet flew after yesterday's;
I saw them come and saw them flee
Between the sea-foam and the sea.

Between the sea-strand and the sea
Love fell on sleep, sleep fell on me;
The first star saw twain turn to one
Between the moonrise and the sun;
The next, that saw not love, saw me
Between the sea-banks and the sea.

Algernon Charles Swinburne [1837–1909]

PLIGHTED

MINE to the core of the heart, my beauty!
Mine, all mine, and for love, not duty:
Love given willingly, full and free,
Love for love's sake,—as mine to thee.
    Duty's a slave that keeps the keys,
But Love, the master, goes in and out
Of his goodly chambers with song and shout,
    Just as he please,—just as he please.

Mine, from the dear head's crown, brown-golden,
To the silken foot that's scarce beholden;
Give to a few friends hand or smile,
Like a generous lady, now and awhile,
    But the sanctuary heart, that none dare win,
Keep holiest of holiest evermore;
The crowd in the aisles may watch the door,
    The high-priest only enters in.

Mine, my own, without doubts or terrors,
With all thy goodnesses, all thy errors,
Unto me and to me alone revealed,
"A spring shut up, a fountain sealed."
　　Many may praise thee,—praise mine as thine,
Many may love thee,—I'll love them too;
But thy heart of hearts, pure, faithful, and true,
　　Must be mine, mine wholly, and only mine.

Mine!—God, I thank Thee that Thou hast given
Something all mine on this side heaven:
Something as much myself to be
As this my soul which I lift to Thee:
　　Flesh of my flesh, bone of my bone,
Life of my life, whom Thou dost make
Two to the world for the world's work's sake,—
　　But each unto each, as in Thy sight, *one*.
　　　　　Dinah Maria Mulock Craik [1826–1887]

A WOMAN'S QUESTION

Before I trust my fate to thee,
　　Or place my hand in thine,
Before I let thy future give
　　Color and form to mine,
Before I peril all for thee, question thy soul to-night for me.

I break all slighter bonds, nor feel
　　A shadow of regret:
Is there one link within the past
　　That holds thy spirit yet?
Or is thy faith as clear and free as that which I can pledge to
　　thee?

Does there within thy dimmest dreams
　　A possible future shine,
Wherein thy life could henceforth breathe,
　　Untouched, unshared by mine?
If so, at any pain or cost, O, tell me before all is lost.

Look deeper still. If thou canst feel,
  Within thy inmost soul,
That thou hast kept a portion back,
  While I have staked the whole,
Let no false pity spare the blow, but in true mercy tell me so.

Is there within thy heart a need
  That mine cannot fulfil?
One chord that any other hand
  Could better wake or still?
Speak now—lest at some future day my whole life wither and
  decay.

Lives there within thy nature hid
  The demon-spirit change,
Shedding a passing glory still
  On all things new and strange?
It may not be thy fault alone,—but shield my heart against
  thy own.

Couldst thou withdraw thy hand one day
  And answer to my claim,
That Fate, and that to-day's mistake—
  Not thou—had been to blame?
Some soothe their conscience thus; but thou wilt surely
  warn and save me now.

Nay, answer not,—I dare not hear,
  The words would come too late;
Yet I would spare thee all remorse,
  So, comfort thee, my Fate,—
Whatever on my heart may fall—remember, I would risk it
  all!

Adelaide Anne Procter [1825–1864]

"DINNA ASK ME"

O, DINNA ask me gin I lo'e ye:
  Troth, I daurna tell!
Dinna ask me gin I lo'e ye,—
  Ask it o' yoursel'.

O, dinna look sae sair at me,
  For weel ye ken me true;
O, gin ye look sae sair at me,
  I daurna look at you.

When ye gang to yon braw, braw town,
  And bonnier lassies see,
O, dinna, Jamie, look at them,
  Lest ye should mind na me.

For I could never bide the lass
  That ye'd lo'e mair than me;
And O, I'm sure my heart wad brak,
  Gin ye'd prove fause to me!

                    John Dunlop [1755–1820]

A SONG

SING me a sweet, low song of night
  Before the moon is risen,
A song that tells of the stars' delight
  Escaped from day's bright prison,
A song that croons with the cricket's voice,
  That sleeps with the shadowed trees,
A song that shall bid my heart rejoice
  At its tender mysteries!

And then when the song is ended, love,
  Bend down your head unto me,
Whisper the word that was born above
  Ere the moon had swayed the sea;
Ere the oldest star began to shine,
  Or the farthest sun to burn,—
The oldest of words, O heart of mine,
  Yet newest, and sweet to learn.

                    Hildegarde Hawthorne [18 –

THE REASON

OH, hark the pulses of the night,
  The crickets hidden in the field,
That beat out music of delight
  Till summoned dawn stands half revealed!

Oh, mark above the bearded corn
 And the green wheat and bending rye,
Tuned to the earth, and calling morn,
 The stars vibrating in the sky!

And know, divided soul of me,
 Here in the meadow, sweet in speech,
This perfect night could never be
 Were we not mated each to each.

      James Oppenheim [1882–1932]

"MY OWN CÁILIN DONN"

THE blush is on the flower, and the bloom is on the tree,
And the bonnie, bonnie sweet birds are caroling their glee;
And the dews upon the grass are made diamonds by the sun,
All to deck a path of glory for my own Cáilin Donn!

 Oh fair she is! Oh rare she is! Oh dearer still to me,
 More welcome than the green leaf to winter-stricken tree!
 More welcome than the blossom to the weary, dusty bee,
 Is the coming of my true love—my own Cáilin Donn!

O sycamore! O sycamore! wave, wave your banners green!
Let all your pennons flutter, O beech! before my queen!
Ye fleet and honeyed breezes, to kiss her hand ye run;
But my heart has passed before ye to my own Cáilin Donn.

Ring out, ring out, O linden, your merry leafy bells!
Unveil your brilliant torches, O chestnut! to the dells;
Strew, strew the glade with splendor, for morn it cometh on!
Oh, the morn of all delight to me—my own Cáilin Donn!

She is coming, where we parted, where she wanders every
  day;
There's a gay surprise before her who thinks me far away;
Oh, like hearing bugles triumph when the fight of freedom's
  won,
Is the joy around your footsteps, my own Cáilin Donn!

      George Sigerson [1839–1925]

NOCTURNE

ALL the earth a hush of white,
    White with moonlight all the skies;
Wonder of a winter night—
    And . . . your eyes.

Hues no palette dares to claim
    Where the spoils of sunken ships
Leap to light in singing flame—
    And . . . your lips.

Darkness as the shadows creep
    Where the embers sigh to rest;
Silence of a world asleep—
    And . . . your breast.

Amelia Josephine Burr [1878-

SURRENDER

As I look back upon your first embrace
I understand why from your sudden touch
Angered I sprang, and struck you in the face.
You asked at once too little and too much.
But now that of my spirit you require
Love's very soul that unto death endures,
Crown as you will the cup of your desire—
    I am all yours.

Amelia Josephine Burr [1878-

"BY YON BURN SIDE"

WE'LL meet beside the dusky glen, on yon burn side,
Where the bushes form a cosie den, on yon burn side;
    Though the broomy knowes be green,
    And there we may be seen,
Yet we'll meet—we'll meet at e'en, down by yon burn side.

I'll lead thee to the birken bower, on yon burn side,
Sae sweetly wove wi' woodbine flower, on yon burn side;
    There the busy prying eye,
    Ne'er disturbs the lover's joy,
While in ither's arms they lie, down by yon burn side.

Awa', ye rude, unfeeling crew, frae yon burn side,
Those fairy scenes are no for you, by yon burn side;
    There fancy smooths her theme,
    By the sweetly murmuring stream,
And the rock-lodged echoes skim, down by yon burn side.

Now the plantin' taps are tinged wi' goud, on yon burn side,
And gloamin' draws her foggy shroud o'er yon burn side;
    Far frae the noisy scene,
    I'll through the fields alane,
There we'll meet, my ain dear Jean, down by yon burn
    side.

Robert Tannahill [1774–1810]

A PASTORAL

FLOWER of the medlar,
    Crimson of the quince,
I saw her at the blossom-time,
    And loved her ever since!
She swept the draughty pleasance,
    The blooms had left the trees,
The whilst the birds sang canticles,
    In cherry symphonies.

Whiteness of the white rose,
    Redness of the red,
She went to cut the blush-rose buds
    To tie at the altar-head;
And some she laid in her bosom,
    And some around her brows,
And, as she passed, the lily-heads
    All becked and made their bows.

Scarlet of the poppy,
   Yellow of the corn,
The men were at the garnering,
   A-shouting in the morn;
I chased her to a pippin-tree,—
   The waking birds all whist,—
And oh! it was the sweetest kiss
   That I have ever kissed.

Marjorie, mint, and violets
   A-drying round us set,
'Twas all done in the faience-room
   A-spicing marmalet;
On one tile was a satyr,
   On one a nymph at bay,
Methinks the birds will scarce be home
   To wake our wedding-day!
                    Théophile Marzials [1850–

"WHEN DEATH TO EITHER SHALL COME"

WHEN Death to either shall come,—
   I pray it be first to me,—
Be happy as ever at home,
   If so, as I wish, it be.

Possess thy heart, my own;
   And sing to thy child on thy knee,
Or read to thyself alone
   The songs that I made for thee.
                    Robert Bridges [1844–1930]

THE RECONCILIATION
From "The Princess"

As through the land at eve we went,
   And plucked the ripened ears,
We fell out, my wife and I,
O, we fell out, I know not why,
   And kissed again with tears.

And blessings on the falling out
That all the more endears,
When we fall out with those we love
And kiss again with tears!

For when we came where lies the child
We lost in other years,
There above the little grave,
O, there above the little grave,
We kissed again with tears.

Alfred Tennyson [1809–1892]

SONG

Wait but a little while—
The bird will bring
A heart in tune for melodies
Unto the spring,
Till he who's in the cedar there
Is moved to trill a song so rare,
And pipe her fair.

Wait but a little while—
The bud will break;
The inner rose will open and glow
For summer's sake:
Fond bees will lodge within her breast
Till she herself is plucked and pressed
Where I would rest.

Wait but a little while—
The maid will grow
Gracious with lips and hands to thee,
With breast of snow.
To-day Love's mute, but time hath sown
A soul in her to match thine own,
Though yet ungrown.

Norman Gale [1862–

CONTENT

THOUGH singing but the shy and sweet
Untrod by multitudes of feet,
Songs bounded by the brook and wheat,
   I have not failed in this,
The only lure my woodland note,
To win all England's whitest throat!
O bards in gold and fire who wrote,
   Be yours all other bliss!

Norman Gale [1862–

CHE SARA SARA

PREACH wisdom unto him who understands!
   When there's such lovely longing in thine eyes,
And such a pulse in thy small clinging hands,
   What is the good of being great or wise?

What is the good of beating up the dust
   On the world's highway, vexed with droughty heat?
Oh, I grow fatalist—what must be must,
   Seeing that thou, beloved, art so sweet!

Victor Plarr [1863–

"BID ADIEU TO GIRLISH DAYS"

BID adieu, adieu, adieu,
   Bid adieu to girlish days,
Happy Love is come to woo
   Thee and woo thy girlish ways—
The zone that doth become thee fair,
The snood upon thy yellow hair.

When thou hast heard his name upon
   The bugles of the cherubim,
Begin thou softly to unzone
   Thy girlish bosom unto him,
And softly to undo the snood
That is the sign of maidenhood.

James Joyce [1882–1941]

TO F. C.

Fast falls the snow, O lady mine,
Sprinkling the lawn with crystals fine,
But by the gods we won't repine
    While we're together,
We'll chat and rhyme, and kiss and dine,
    Defying weather.

So stir the fire and pour the wine,
And let those sea-green eyes divine
Pour their love-madness into mine:
    I don't care whether
'Tis snow or sun or rain or shine
    If we're together.
           Mortimer Collins [1827–1876]

SPRING PASSION

Blue sky, green fields, and lazy yellow sun!
  Why should I hunger for the burning South,
Where beauty needs no travail to be won,
  Now I may kiss her pure impassioned mouth?

Winds rippling with the rich delight of spring!
  Why should I yearn for myriad-colored skies,
Lit by auroral suns, when I may sing
  The flame and rapture of her starry eyes?

Oh, song of birds, and flowers fair to see!
  Why should I thirst for far-off Eden-isles,
When I may hear her discourse melody,
  And bask, a dreamer, in her dreamy smiles?
           Joel Elias Spingarn [1875–1939]

ADVICE TO A LOVER

Oh, if you love her,
  Show her the best of you;
So will you move her
  To bear with the rest of you.

Coldness and jealousy
  Cannot but seem to her
Signs that a tempest lurks
  Where was sunbeam to her.
Patience and tenderness
  Still will awake in her
Hopes of new sunshine,
  Though the storm break for her;
Love, she will know, for her,
  Like the blue firmament,
Under the tempest lies
  Gentle and permanent.
Nor will she ever
  Gentleness find the less
When the storm overblown
  Leaveth clear kindliness.
Deal with her tenderly,
  Skylike above her,
Smile on her waywardness,
  Oh, if you love her!

          S. Charles Jellicoe [18 —

"YES"

THEY stood above the world,
  In a world apart;
And she dropped her happy eyes,
And stilled the throbbing pulses
  Of her happy heart.
And the moonlight fell above her,
  Her secret to discover;
  And the moonbeams kissed her hair,
As though no human lover
  Had laid his kisses there.

"Look up, brown eyes," he said,
  "And answer mine;
Lift up those silken fringes
That hide a happy light
  Almost divine."

The jealous moonlight drifted
To the finger half-uplifted,
  Where shone the opal ring—
Where the colors danced and shifted
  On the pretty, changeful thing.

Just the old, old story
  Of light and shade,
Love like the opal tender,
Like it may be to vary—
  May be to fade.
Just the old tender story,
Just a glimpse of morning glory
  In an earthly Paradise,
With shadowy reflections
  In a pair of sweet brown eyes.

Brown eyes a man might well
  Be proud to win!
Open to hold his image,
Shut under silken lashes,
  Only to shut him in.
O glad eyes, look together,
For life's dark, stormy weather
  Grows to a fairer thing
When young eyes look upon it
  Through a slender wedding ring.
        Richard Doddridge Blackmore [1825–1900]

LOVE

ALL thoughts, all passions, all delights,
Whatever stirs this mortal frame,
All are but ministers of Love,
  And feed his sacred flame.

Oft in my waking dreams do I
Live o'er again that happy hour,
When midway on the mount I lay,
    Beside the ruined tower.

The moonshine, stealing o'er the scene,
Had blended with the lights of eve;
And she was there, my hope, my joy,
        My own dear Genevieve!

She leaned against the armèd man,
The statue of the armèd Knight;
She stood and listened to my lay,
        Amid the lingering light.

Few sorrows hath she of her own,
My hope! my joy! my Genevieve!
She loves me best whene'er I sing
        The songs that make her grieve.

I played a soft and doleful air;
I sang an old and moving story—
An old rude song, that suited well
        That ruin wild and hoary.

She listened with a flitting blush,
With downcast eyes, and modest grace;
For well she knew I could not choose
        But gaze upon her face.

I told her of the Knight that wore
Upon his shield a burning brand;
And that for ten long years he wooed
        The Lady of the Land.

I told her how he pined: and ah!
The deep, the low, the pleading tone
With which I sang another's love,
        Interpreted my own.

She listened with a flitting blush,
With downcast eyes, and modest grace;
And she forgave me, that I gazed
        Too fondly on her face!

But when I told the cruel scorn
That crazed that bold and lovely Knight,
And that he crossed the mountain-woods,
    Nor rested day nor night;

That sometimes from the savage den,
And sometimes from the darksome shade,
And sometimes starting up at once
    In green and sunny glade—

There came and looked him in the face
An angel beautiful and bright;
And that he knew it was a Fiend,
    This miserable Knight!

And that, unknowing what he did,
He leaped amid a murderous band,
And saved from outrage worse than death
    The Lady of the Land;—

And how she wept and clasped his knees;
And how she tended him in vain—
And ever strove to expiate
    The scorn that crazed his brain;—

And that she nursed him in a cave;
And how his madness went away,
When on the yellow forest-leaves
    A dying man he lay;—

His dying words—but when I reached
That tenderest strain of all the ditty,
My faltering voice and pausing harp
    Disturbed her soul with pity!

All impulses of soul and sense
Had thrilled my guileless Genevieve'
The music and the doleful tale,
    The rich and balmy eve:

And hopes, and fears that kindle hope,
An undistinguishable throng,
And gentle wishes long subdued,
   Subdued and cherished long!

She wept with pity and delight,
She blushed with love and virgin-shame;
And like the murmur of a dream,
   I heard her breathe my name.

Her bosom heaved—she stepped aside,
As conscious of my look she stepped—
Then suddenly, with timorous eye
   She fled to me and wept.

She half enclosed me with her arms,
She pressed me with a meek embrace;
And bending back her head, looked up,
   And gazed upon my face.

'Twas partly love, and partly fear,
And partly 'twas a bashful art,
That I might rather feel, than see,
   The swelling of her heart.

I calmed her fears, and she was calm,
And told her love with virgin pride;
And so I won my Genevieve,
   My bright and beauteous Bride.

Samuel Taylor Coleridge [1772–1834]

NESTED

ON THE SUSSEX DOWNS

"Lured," little one? Nay, you've but heard
   Love o'er your wild downs roaming;
Not lured, my bird, my light, swift bird,
   But homing—homing.

"Caught," does she feel? Nay, no net stirred
  To catch the heart fore-fated;
Not caught, my bird, my bright, wild bird,
      But mated—mated.

And "caged," she fears? Nay, never that word
  Of where your brown head rested;
Not caged, my bird, my shy, sweet bird,
      But nested—nested!

                    Habberton Lulham [18 –

THE LETTERS

STILL on the tower stood the vane,
  A black yew gloomed the stagnant air;
I peered athwart the chancel pane,
  And saw the altar cold and bare.
A clog of lead was round my feet,
  A band of pain across my brow;
"Cold altar, heaven and earth shall meet
  Before you hear my marriage vow."

I turned and hummed a bitter song
  That mocked the wholesome human heart,
And then we met in wrath and wrong,
  We met, but only meant to part.
Full cold my greeting was and dry;
  She faintly smiled, she hardly moved;
I saw, with half-unconscious eye,
  She wore the colors I approved.

She took the little ivory chest,
  With half a sigh she turned the key,
Then raised her head with lips compressed,
  And gave my letters back to me;
And gave the trinkets and the rings,
  My gifts, when gifts of mine could please.
As looks a father on the things
  Of his dead son, I looked on these.

She told me all her friends had said;
    I raged against the public liar.
She talked as if her love were dead;
    But in my words were seeds of fire.
"No more of love, your sex is known;
    I never will be twice deceived.
Henceforth I trust the man alone;
    The woman cannot be believed.

"Through slander, meanest spawn of hell,—
    And woman's slander is the worst,—
And you, whom once I loved so well,
    Through you my life will be accursed."
I spoke with heart and heat and force,
    I shook her breast with vague alarms—
Like torrents from a mountain source
    We rushed into each other's arms.

We parted; sweetly gleamed the stars,
    And sweet the vapor-braided blue;
Low breezes fanned the belfry bars,
    As homeward by the church I drew.
The very graves appeared to smile,
    So fresh they rose in shadowed swells;
"Dark porch," I said, "and silent aisle,
    There comes a sound of marriage bells."
        Alfred Tennyson [1809–1892]

PROTHALAMION

CALM was the day, and through the trembling air
Sweet-breathing Zephyrus did softly play
A gentle spirit, that lightly did delay
Hot Titan's beams, which then did glister fair;
When I (whom sullen care,
Through discontent of my long fruitless stay
In Prince's Court, and expectation vain
Of idle hopes, which still do fly away,
Like empty shadows, did afflict my brain),
Walked forth to ease my pain

Along the shore of silver streaming Thames;
Whose rutty bank, the which his river hems,
Was painted all with variable flowers,
And all the meads adorned with dainty gems,
Fit to deck maidens' bowers,
And crown their paramours
Against the bridal day, which is not long:
   Sweet Thames! run softly, till I end my song.

There, in a meadow, by the river's side,
A flock of nymphs I chancèd to espy,
All lovely daughters of the flood thereby,
With goodly greenish locks, all loose untied,
As each had been a bride:
And each one had a little wicker basket,
Made of fine twigs, entrailèd curiously,
In which they gathered flowers to fill their flasket,
And, with fine fingers, cropped full feateously
The tender stalks on high.
Of every sort, which in that meadow grew,
They gathered some; the violet, pallid blue,
The little daisy, that at evening closes,
The virgin lily, and the primrose true,
With store of vermeil roses,
To deck their bridegroom's posies
Against the bridal day, which was not long:
   Sweet Thames! run softly, till I end my song.

With that I saw two swans of goodly hue
Come softly swimming down along the Lee;
Two fairer birds I yet did never see;
The snow, which doth the top of Pindus strew,
Did never whiter shew,
Nor Jove himself, when he a swan would be
For love of Leda, whiter did appear;
Yet Leda was, they say, as white as he,
Yet not so white as these, nor nothing near;
So purely white they were,
That even the gentle stream, the which them bare,

Seemed foul to them, and bade his billows spare
To wet their silken feathers, lest they might
Soil their fair plumes with water not so fair,
And mar their beauties bright,
That shone as heaven's light,
Against their bridal day, which was not long:
  Sweet Thames! run softly, till I end my song.

Eftsoons the nymphs, which now had flowers their fill,
Ran all in haste to see that silver brood,
As they came floating on the crystal flood;
Whom when they saw, they stood amazèd still,
Their wondering eyes to fill;
Them seemed they never saw a sight so fair
Of fowls so lovely, that they sure did deem
Them heavenly born, or to be that same pair
Which through the sky draw Venus' silver team;
For sure they did not seem
To be begot of any earthly seed,
But rather angels, or of angels' breed;
Yet were they bred of summer's heat, they say,
In sweetest season, when each flower and weed
The earth did fresh array;
So fresh they seemed as day,
Even as their bridal day, which was not long:
  Sweet Thames! run softly, till I end my song.

Then forth they all out of their baskets drew
Great store of flowers, the honor of the field,
That to the sense did fragrant odors yield,
All which upon those goodly birds they threw
And all the waves did strew,
That like old Peneus' waters they did seem,
When down along by pleasant Tempe's shore,
Scattered with flowers, through Thessaly they stream,
That they appear, through lilies' plenteous store,
Like a bride's chamber floor:
Two of those nymphs, meanwhile, two garlands bound
Of freshest flowers which in that mead they found,

The which presenting all in trim array,
Their snowy foreheads therewithal they crowned,
Whilst one did sing this lay,
Prepared against that day,
Against their bridal day, which was not long:
   Sweet Thames! run softly, till I end my song.

"Ye gentle birds! the world's fair ornament,
And heaven's glory whom this happy hour
Doth lead unto your lover's blissful bower,
Joy may you have, and gentle hearts' content
Of your love's couplement;
And let fair Venus, that is queen of love,
With her heart-quelling son upon you smile,
Whose smile, they say, hath virtue to remove
All love's dislike, and friendship's faulty guile
For ever to assoil;
Let endless peace your steadfast hearts accord,
And blessèd plenty wait upon your board;
And let your bed with pleasures chaste abound,
That fruitful issue may to you afford,
Which may your foes confound,
And make your joys redound
Upon your bridal day, which is not long":
   Sweet Thames! run softly, till I end my song.

So ended she: and all the rest around
To her redoubled that her undersong,
Which said their bridal day should not be long:
And gentle Echo from the neighbor-ground
Their accents did resound.
So forth those joyous birds did pass along,
Adown the Lee, that to them murmured low,
As he would speak, but that he lacked a tongue,
Yet did by signs his glad affection show,
Making his stream run slow.
And all the fowl which in his flood did dwell
'Gan flock about these twain, that did excel
The rest, so far as Cynthia doth shend
The lesser stars. So they, enrangèd well,

Did on those two attend,
And their best service lend
Against their wedding day, which was not long:
   Sweet Thames! run softly, till I end my song.

At length they all to merry London came,
To merry London, my most kindly nurse,
That to me gave this life's first native source;
Though from another place I take my name,
An house of ancient fame:
There when they came, whereas those bricky towers
The which on Thames' broad, aged back do ride,
Where now the studious lawyers have their bowers,
There whilom wont the Templar Knights to bide,
Till they decayed through pride:
Next whereunto there stands a stately place,
Where oft I gainèd gifts and goodly grace
Of that great lord, which therein wont to dwell,
Whose want too well now feels my friendless case;
But ah! here fits not well
Old woes, but joys, to tell
Against the bridal day, which is not long:
   Sweet Thames! run softly, till I end my song.

Yet therein now doth lodge a noble peer,
Great England's glory, and the world's wide wonder,
Whose dreadful name late through all Spain did thunder,
And Hercules' two pillars standing near
Did make to quake and fear:
Fair branch of honor, flower of chivalry!
That fillest England with thy triumph's fame,
Joy have thou of thy noble victory,
And endless happiness of thine own name,
That promiseth the same;
That through thy prowess, and victorious arms,
Thy country may be freed from foreign harms;
And great Elisa's glorious name may ring
Through all the world, filled with thy wide alarms,
Which some brave muse may sing
To ages following,

Upon the bridal day, which is not long:
   Sweet Thames! run softly, till I end my song.

From those high towers this noble lord issuing,
Like radiant Hesper, when his golden hair
In the ocean billows he hath bathèd fair,
Descended to the river's open viewing,
With a great train ensuing.
Above the rest were goodly to be seen
Two gentle knights of lovely face and feature
Beseeming well the bower of any queen,
With gifts of wit, and ornaments of nature,
Fit for so goodly stature,
That like the twins of Jove they seemed in sight,
Which deck the baldrick of the heavens bright;
They two, forth pacing to the river's side,
Received those two fair brides, their love's delight;
Which, at the appointed tide,
Each one did make his bride
Against their bridal day, which is not long:
   Sweet Thames! run softly, till I end my song.

Edmund Spenser [1552?–1599]

EPITHALAMION

YE learnèd sisters, which have oftentimes
Been to me aiding, others to adorn,
Whom ye thought worthy of your graceful rhymes,
That even the greatest did not greatly scorn
To hear their names sung in your simple lays,
But joyèd in their praise;
And when ye list your own mishaps to mourn,
Which death, or love, or fortune's wreck did raise,
Your string could soon to sadder tenor turn,
And teach the woods and waters to lament
Your doleful dreariment:
Now lay those sorrowful complaints aside;
And, having all your heads with garlands crowned,
Help me mine own love's praises to resound;
Nor let the same of any be envide:
So Orpheus did for his own bride!

So I unto myself alone will sing;
The woods shall to me answer, and my echo ring.

Early, before the world's light-giving lamp
His golden beam upon the hills doth spread,
Having dispersed the night's uncheerful damp,
Do ye awake; and, with fresh lusty-hed,
Go to the bower of my belovèd love,
My truest turtle dove;
Bid her awake; for Hymen is awake,
And long since ready forth his mask to move,
With his bright Tead that flames with many a flake,
And many a bachelor to wait on him,
In their fresh garments trim.
Bid her awake therefore, and soon her dight,
For lo! the wishèd day is come at last,
That shall, for all the pains and sorrows past,
Pay to her usury of long delight:
And, whilst she doth her dight,
Do ye to her of joy and solace sing,
That all the woods may answer, and your echo ring.

Bring with you all the Nymphs that you can hear,
Both of the rivers and the forests green,
And of the sea that neighbors to her near,
All with gay garlands goodly well beseen.
And let them also with them bring in hand
Another gay garland,
For my fair love, of lilies and of roses,
Bound truelove wise with a blue silk riband;
And let them make great store of bridal posies,
And let them eke bring store of other flowers,
To deck the bridal bowers.
And let the ground whereas her foot shall tread,
For fear the stones her tender foot should wrong,
Be strewed with fragrant flowers all along,
And diapered like the discolored mead;
Which done, do at her chamber door await,
For she will waken straight;

The whiles do ye this song unto her sing,
The woods shall to you answer, and your echo ring.

Ye Nymphs of Mulla, which with careful heed
The silver scaly trouts do tend full well,
And greedy pikes which use therein to feed
(Those trouts and pikes all others do excel);
And ye likewise, which keep the rushy lake,
Where none do fishes take;
Bind up the locks the which hang scattered light,
And in his waters, which your mirror make,
Behold your faces as the crystal bright,
That when you come whereas my love doth lie,
No blemish she may spy.
And eke, ye lightfoot maids, which keep the deer,
That on the hoary mountain used to tower;
And the wild wolves, which seek them to devour,
With your steel darts do chase from coming near;
Be also present here,
To help to deck her, and to help to sing,
That all the woods may answer, and your echo ring.

Wake, now, my love, awake! for it is time;
The rosy morn long since left Tithon's bed,
All ready to her silver coach to climb;
And Phœbus 'gins to show his glorious head.
Hark, how the cheerful birds do chant their lays
And carol of love's praise.
The merry lark her matins sings aloft;
The thrush replies; the mavis descant plays;
The ouzel shrills; the ruddock warbles soft;
So goodly all agree, with sweet consent,
To this day's merriment.
Ah! my dear love, why do ye sleep thus long,
When meeter were that ye should now awake,
To await the coming of your joyous mate,
And hearken to the birds' love-learnèd song,
The dewy leaves among!
For they of joy and pleasance to you sing,
That all the woods them answer, and their echo ring.

My love is now awake out of her dreams,
And her fair eyes, like stars that dimmèd were
With darksome cloud, now show their goodly beams
More bright than Hesperus his head doth rear.
Come now, ye damsels, daughters of delight,
Help quickly her to dight:
But first come, ye fair hours, which were begot
In Jove's sweet paradise of Day and Night;
Which do the seasons of the year allot,
And all that ever in this world is fair,
Do make and still repair:
And ye three handmaids of the Cyprian queen,
The which do still adorn her beauty's pride,
Help to adorn my beautifulest bride;
And as ye her array, still throw between
Some graces to be seen,
And, as ye use to Venus, to her sing,
The whiles the woods shall answer, and your echo ring.

Now is my love all ready forth to come:
Let all the virgins therefore well await:
And ye fresh boys, that tend upon her groom,
Prepare yourselves; for he is coming straight;
Set all your things in seemly good array,
Fit for so joyful day:
The joyfulest day that ever sun did see.
Fair Sun! show forth thy favorable ray,
And let thy life-full heat not fervent be,
For fear of burning her sunshiny face,
Her beauty to disgrace.
O fairest Phœbus! father of the Muse!
If ever I did honor thee aright,
Or sing the thing that might thy mind delight,
Do not thy servant's simple boon refuse;
But let this day, let this one day, be mine;
Let all the rest be thine.
Then I thy sovereign praises loud will sing,
That all the woods shall answer, and their echo ring.

Hark! how the Minstrels 'gin to shrill aloud
Their merry music that resounds from far,

The pipe, the tabor, and the trembling croud,
That well agree withouten breach or jar.
But, most of all, the Damsels do delight
When they their timbrels smite,
And thereunto do dance and carol sweet,
That all the senses they do ravish quite;
The whiles the boys run up and down the street,
Crying aloud with strong confusèd noise,
As if it were one voice,
Hymen, iö Hymen, Hymen, they do shout;
That even to the heavens their shouting shrill
Doth reach, and all the firmament doth fill;
To which the people standing all about,
As in approvance, do thereto applaud,
And loud advance her laud;
And evermore they Hymen, Hymen sing,
That all the woods them answer, and their echo ring.

Lo! where she comes along with portly pace,
Like Phœbe, from her chamber of the East,
Ar'sing forth to run her mighty race,
Clad all in white, that seems a virgin best.
So well it her beseems, that ye would ween
Some angel she had been.
Her long loose yellow locks like golden wire,
Sprinkled with pearl, and pearling flowers atween,
Do like a golden mantle her attire;
And, being crownèd with a garland green,
Seem like some maiden queen.
Her modest eyes, abashèd to behold
So many gazers as on her do stare,
Upon the lowly ground affixèd are;
Nor dare lift up her countenance too bold,
But blush to hear her praises sung so loud,
So far from being proud.
Nathless do ye still loud her praises sing,
That all the woods may answer, and your echo ring.

Tell me, ye merchants' daughters, did ye see
So fair a creature in your town before;

So sweet, so lovely, and so mild as she,
Adorned with beauty's grace and virtue's store?
Her goodly eyes like sapphires shining bright,
Her forehead ivory white,
Her cheeks like apples which the sun hath ruddied,
Her lips like cherries charming men to bite,
Her breast like to a bowl of cream uncrudded,
Her paps like lilies budded,
Her snowy neck like to a marble tower;
And all her body like a palace fair,
Ascending up, with many a stately stair,
To honor's seat and chastity's sweet bower.
Why stand ye still, ye virgins, in amaze,
Upon her so to gaze,
Whiles ye forget your former lay to sing,
To which the woods did answer, and your echo ring?

But if ye saw that which no eyes can see,
The inward beauty of her lively spright,
Garnished with heavenly gifts of high degree,
Much more then would ye wonder at that sight,
And stand astonished like to those which read
Medusa's mazeful head.
There dwells sweet love, and constant chastity,
Unspotted faith, and comely womanhood,
Regard of honor, and mild modesty;
There virtue reigns as queen in royal throne,
And giveth laws alone,
The which the base affections do obey,
And yield their services unto her will;
Nor thought of thing uncomely ever may
Thereto approach to tempt her mind to ill.
Had ye once seen these her celestial treasures,
And unrevealèd pleasures,
Then would ye wonder, and her praises sing,
That all the woods should answer, and your echo ring.

Open the temple gates unto my love,
Open them wide that she may enter in,
And all the posts adorn as doth behove,
And all the pillars deck with garlands trim,

For to receive this Saint with honor due,
That cometh in to you.
With trembling steps, and humble reverence,
She cometh in, before the Almighty's view;
Of her ye virgins learn obedience,
When so ye come into those holy places,
To humble your proud faces:
Bring her up to the high altar, that she may
The sacred ceremonies there partake,
The which do endless matrimony make;
And let the roaring organs loudly play
The praises of the Lord in lively notes;
The whiles, with hollow throats,
The Choristers the joyous Anthems sing,
That all the woods may answer, and their echo ring.

Behold, whiles she before the altar stands,
Hearing the holy priest that to her speaks,
And blesseth her with his two happy hands,
How the red roses flush up in her cheeks,
And the pure snow, with goodly vermill stain
Like crimson dyed in grain:
That even the Angels, which continually
About the sacred altar do remain,
Forget their service and about her fly,
Oft peeping in her face, that seems more fair,
The more they on it stare.
But her sad eyes, still fastened on the ground,
Are governèd with goodly modesty,
That suffers not one look to glance awry,
Which may let in a little thought unsound.
Why blush ye, love, to give to me your hand,
The pledge of all our band?
Sing, ye sweet Angels, Alleluja sing,
That all the woods may answer, and your echo ring.

Now all is done: bring home the bride again;
Bring home the triumph of our victory:
Bring home with you the glory of her gain;
With joyance bring her and with jollity.

Never had man more joyful day than this,
Whom heaven would heap with bliss.
Make feast therefore now all this live-long day;
This day for ever to me holy is.
Pour out the wine without restraint or stay,
Pour not by cups, but by the belly full,
Pour out to all that will,
And sprinkle all the posts and walls with wine,
That they may sweat, and drunken be withal.
Crown ye God Bacchus with a coronal,
And Hymen also crown with wreaths of vine;
And let the Graces dance unto the rest,
For they can do it best:
The whiles the maidens do their carol sing,
To which the woods shall answer, and their echo ring.

Ring ye the bells, ye young men of the town,
And leave your wonted labors for this day:
This day is holy; do ye write it down,
That ye for ever it remember may.
This day the sun is in his chiefest height,
With Barnaby the bright,
From whence declining daily by degrees,
He somewhat loseth of his heat and light,
When once the Crab behind his back he sees.
But for this time it ill ordainèd was,
To choose the longest day in all the year,
And shortest night, when longest fitter were:
Yet never day so long, but late would pass.
Ring ye the bells, to make it wear away,
And bonfires make all day;
And dance about them, and about them sing,
That all the woods may answer, and your echo ring.

Ah! when will this long weary day have end,
And lend me leave to come unto my love?
How slowly do the hours their numbers spend?
How slowly does sad Time his feathers move?
Haste thee, O fairest Planet, to thy home,
Within the Western foam:

Thy tirèd steeds long since have need of rest.
Long though it be, at last I see it gloom,
And the bright evening-star with golden crest
Appear out of the East.
Fair child of beauty! glorious lamp of love!
That all the host of heaven in ranks dost lead,
And guidest lovers through the night's sad dread,
How cheerfully thou lookest from above,
And seems to laugh atween thy twinkling light,
As joying in the sight
Of these glad many, which for joy do sing,
That all the woods them answer, and their echo ring!

Now, cease, ye damsels, your delights fore-past;
Enough is it that all the day was yours:
Now day is done, and night is nighing fast,
Now bring the bride into the bridal bowers.
The night is come, now soon her disarray,
And in her bed her lay;
Lay her in lilies and in violets,
And silken curtains over her display,
And odored sheets, and Arras coverlets.
Behold how goodly my fair love does lie,
In proud humility!
Like unto Maia, when as Jove her took
In Tempe, lying on the flowery grass,
'Twixt sleep and wake, after she weary was,
With bathing in the Acidalian brook.
Now it is night, ye damsels may be gone,
And leave my love alone,
And leave likewise your former lay to sing:
The woods no more shall answer, nor your echo ring.

Now welcome, night! thou night so long expected,
That long day's labor dost at last defray,
And all my cares, which cruel Love collected,
Hast summed in one, and cancellèd for aye:
Spread thy broad wing over my love and me,
That no man may us see;
And in thy sable mantle us enwrap,
From fear of peril and foul horror free.

Let no false treason seek us to entrap,
Nor any dread disquiet once annoy
The safety of our joy;
But let the night be calm, and quietsome,
Without tempestuous storms or sad affray:
Like as when Jove with fair Alcmena lay,
When he begot the great Tirynthian groom:
Or like as when he with thyself did lie
And begot Majesty.
And let the maids and young men cease to sing;
Nor let the woods them answer, nor their echo ring.

Let no lamenting cries, nor doleful tears,
Be heard all night within, nor yet without:
Nor let false whispers, breeding hidden fears,
Break gentle sleep with misconceivèd doubt.
Let no deluding dreams, nor dreadful sights,
Make sudden sad affrights;
Nor let house-fires, nor lightning's helpless harms,
Nor let the Puck, nor other evil sprites,
Nor let mischievous witches with their charms,
Nor let hobgoblins, names whose sense we see not,
Fray us with things that be not:
Let not the screech-owl nor the stork be heard,
Nor the night raven, that still deadly yells;
Nor damnèd ghosts, called up with mighty spells,
Nor grizzly vultures, make us once afraid:
Nor let the unpleasant choir of frogs still croaking
Make us to wish their choking.
Let none of these their dreary accents sing;
Nor let the woods them answer, nor their echo ring.

But let still Silence true night-watches keep,
That sacred Peace may in assurance reign,
And timely Sleep, when it is time to sleep,
May pour his limbs forth on your pleasant plain;
The whiles an hundred little wingèd loves,
Like divers-feathered doves,
Shall fly and flutter round about your bed,
And in the secret dark, that none reproves,
Their pretty stealths shall work, and snares shall spread

To filch away sweet snatches of delight,
Concealed through covert night.
Ye sons of Venus, play your sports at will!
For greedy pleasure, careless of your toys,
Thinks more upon her paradise of joys,
Then what ye do, albeit good or ill.
All night therefore attend your merry play,
For it will soon be day:
Now none doth hinder you, that say or sing;
Nor will the woods now answer, nor your echo ring.

Who is the same, which at my window peeps?
Or whose is that fair face that shines so bright?
Is it not Cynthia, she that never sleeps,
But walks about high heaven all the night?
O! fairest goddess, do thou not envy
My love with me to spy:
For thou likewise didst love, though now unthought,
And for a fleece of wool, which privily
The Latmian shepherd once unto thee brought,
His pleasures with thee wrought.
Therefore to us be favorable now;
And since of women's labors thou hast charge,
And generation goodly dost enlarge,
Incline thy will to effect our wishful vow,
And the chaste womb inform with timely seed,
That may our comfort breed:
Till which we cease our hopeful hap to sing;
Nor let the woods us answer, nor our echo ring.

And thou, great Juno! which with awful might
The laws of wedlock still dost patronize,
And the religion of the faith first plight
With sacred rites hast taught to solemnize;
And eke for comfort often callèd art
Of women in their smart;
Eternally bind thou this lovely band,
And all thy blessings unto us impart.
And thou, glad Genius! in whose gentle hand
The bridal bower and genial bed remain,
Without blemish or stain:

And the sweet pleasures of their love's delight
With secret aid dost succor and supply,
Till they bring forth the fruitful progeny;
Send us the timely fruit of this same night.
And thou, fair Hebe! and thou, Hymen free!
Grant that it may so be.
Till which we cease your further praise to sing;
Nor any woods shall answer, nor your echo ring.

And ye high heavens, the temple of the gods,
In which a thousand torches flaming bright
Do burn, that to us wretched earthly clods
In dreadful darkness lend desirèd light;
And all ye powers which in the same remain,
More than we men can feign,
Pour out your blessing on us plenteously,
And happy influence upon us rain,
That we may raise a large posterity,
Which from the earth, which they may long possess
With lasting happiness,
Up to your haughty palaces may mount;
And, for the guerdon of their glorious merit,
May heavenly tabernacies there inherit,
Of blessèd Saints for to increase the count.
So let us rest, sweet love, in hope of this,
And cease till then our timely joys to sing:
The woods no more us answer, nor our echo ring!

Song! made in lieu of many ornaments,
With which my love should duly have been decked,
Which cutting off through hasty accidents,
Ye would not stay your due time to expect,
But promised both to recompense;
Be unto her a goodly ornament,
And for short time an endless monument.

                 Edmund Spenser [1552?–1599]

THE KISS

Before you kissed me only winds of heaven
    Had kissed me, and the tenderness of rain—
Now you have come, how can I care for kisses
    Like theirs again?

I sought the sea, she sent her winds to meet me,
  They surged about me singing of the south—
I turned my head away to keep still holy
    Your kiss upon my mouth.

And swift sweet rains of shining April weather
  Found not my lips where living kisses are;
I bowed my head lest they put out my glory
    As rain puts out a star.

I am my love's and he is mine forever,
  Sealed with a seal and safe forevermore—
Think you that I could let a beggar enter
    Where a king stood before?
               Sara Teasdale [1884–1933]

MARRIAGE

GOING my way of old
Contented more or less
I dreamt not life could hold
Such happiness.

I dreamt not that love's way
Could keep the golden height
Day after happy day,
Night after night.
               Wilfrid Wilson Gibson [1878–

THE NEWLY-WEDDED

Now the rite is duly done,
  Now the word is spoken,
And the spell has made us one
  Which may ne'er be broken;
Rest we, dearest, in our home,
  Roam we o'er the heather:
We shall rest, and we shall roam,
  Shall we not? together.

From this hour the summer rose
  Sweeter breathes to charm us;
From this hour the winter snows
  Lighter fall to harm us:

Fair or foul—on land or sea—
    Come the wind or weather,
Best and worst, whate'er they be,
    We shall share together.

Death, who friend from friend can part,
    Brother rend from brother,
Shall but link us, heart and heart,
    Closer to each other:
We will call his anger play,
    Deem his dart a feather,
When we meet him on our way
    Hand in hand together.

Winthrop Mackworth Praed [1802–1839]

"I SAW TWO CLOUDS AT MORNING"

I SAW two clouds at morning,
    Tinged by the rising sun,
And in the dawn they floated on,
    And mingled into one:
I thought that morning cloud was blest,
It moved so sweetly to the west.

I saw two summer currents
    Flow smoothly to their meeting,
And join their course, with silent force,
    In peace each other greeting;
Calm was their course through banks of green,
While dimpling eddies played between.

Such be your gentle motion,
    Till life's last pulse shall beat;
Like summer's beam, and summer's stream,
    Float on, in joy, to meet
A calmer sea, where storms shall cease,
A purer sky, where all is peace.

John Gardiner Calkins Brainard [1796–1828]

HOLY MATRIMONY

THE voice that breathed o'er Eden,
  That earliest wedding-day,
The primal marriage blessing,
  It hath not passed away.

Still in the pure espousal
  Of Christian man and maid,
The holy Three are with us,
  The threefold grace is said.

For dower of blessèd children,
  For love and faith's sweet sake,
For high mysterious union,
  Which naught on earth may break.

Be present, awful Father,
  To give away this bride,
As Eve thou gav'st to Adam
  Out of his own pierced side:

Be present, Son of Mary,
  To join their loving hands,
As thou didst bind two natures
  In thine eternal bands:

Be present, Holiest Spirit,
  To bless them as they kneel,
As thou for Christ, the Bridegroom,
  The heavenly Spouse dost seal.

Oh, spread thy pure wing o'er them,
  Let no ill power find place,
When onward to thine altar
  The hallowed path they trace,

To cast their crowns before thee
  In perfect sacrifice,
Till to the home of gladness
  With Christ's own Bride they rise. AMEN.

John Keble [1792–1866]

THE BRIDE

BEAT on the Tom-toms, and scatter the flowers,
    Jasmine, hibiscus, vermilion and white,
This is the day, and the Hour of Hours,
    Bring forth the Bride for her Lover's delight.
Maidens no more as a maiden shall claim her,
    Near, in his Mystery, draweth Desire.
Who, if she waver a moment, shall blame her?
    She is a flower, and love is a fire.

Give her the anklets, the ring, and the necklace,
    Darken her eyelids with delicate art,
Heighten the beauty, so youthful and fleckless,
    By the Gods favored, oh, Bridegroom, thou art!
Twine in thy fingers her fingers so slender,
    Circle together the Mystical Fire,
Bridegroom,—a whisper,—be gentle and tender,
    Choti Tinchaurya knows not desire.

Bring forth the silks and the veil that shall cover
    Beauty, till yesterday careless and wild;
Red are her lips for the kiss of a lover,
    Ripe are her breasts for the lips of a child.
Center and Shrine of Mysterious Power,
    Chalice of Pleasure and Rose of Delight,
Shyly aware of the swift-coming hour,
    Waiting the shade and the silence of night.

Still must the Bridegroom his longing dissemble,
    Longing to loosen the silk-woven cord,
Ah, how his fingers will flutter and tremble,
    Fingers well skilled with the bridle and sword.
Thine is his valor, oh Bride, and his beauty,
    Thine to possess and re-issue again,
Such is thy tender and passionate duty,
    Licit thy pleasure and honored thy pain.

Choti Tinchaurya, lovely and tender,
  Still all unbroken to sorrow and strife,
Come to the Bridegroom who, silk-clad and slender,
  Brings thee the Honor and Burden of Life.
Bidding farewell to thy light-hearted playtime,
  Worship thy Lover with fear and delight;
Art thou not ever, though slave of his daytime,
  Choti Tinchaurya, queen of his night?

Laurence Hope [1865–1904]

A MARRIAGE CHARM

I SET a charm upon your hurrying breath,
I set a charm upon your wandering feet,
You shall not leave me—not for life, nor death,
Not even though you cease to love me, Sweet.

A woman's love nine Angels cannot bind,
Nor any rune that wind or water knows,
My heart were all as well set on the wind,
Or bound, to live or die, upon a rose.

I set a charm upon you, foot and hand,
That you and Knowledge, love, may never meet,
That you may never chance to understand
How strong you are, how weak your lover, Sweet.

I set my charm upon your kindly arm,
I set it as a seal upon your breast;
That you may never hear another's charm,
Nor guess another's gift outruns my best.

I bid your wandering footsteps me to follow,
Your thoughts to travel after in my track,
I am the sky that waits you, dear gray swallow,
No wind of mine shall ever blow you back.

I am your dream, Sweet; so no more of dreaming,
Your lips to mine must end this chanted charm,
Your heart to mine, 'neath nut-brown tresses streaming,
I set my love a seal upon your arm.

Nora Hopper [1871–1906]

"LIKE A LAVEROCK IN THE LIFT"

It's we two, it's we two, it's we two for aye,
All the world, and we two, and Heaven be our stay!
Like a laverock in the lift, sing, O bonny bride!
All the world was Adam once, with Eve by his side.

What's the world, my lass, my love!—what can it do?
I am thine, and thou art mine; life is sweet and new.
If the world have missed the mark, let it stand by;
For we two have gotten leave, and once more we'll try.

Like a laverock in the lift, sing, O bonny bride!
It's we two, it's we two, happy side by side.
Take a kiss from me, thy man; now the song begins:
"All is made afresh for us, and the brave heart wins."

When the darker days come, and no sun will shine,
Thou shalt dry my tears, lass, and I'll dry thine.
It's we two, it's we two, while the world's away,
Sitting by the golden sheaves on our wedding-day.

Jean Ingelow [1820–1897]

MY OWEN

Proud of you, fond of you, clinging so near to you,
Light is my heart now I know I am dear to you!
Glad is my voice now, so free it may sing for you
All the wild love that is burning within for you!
Tell me once more, tell it over and over,
The tale of that eve which first saw you my lover.
Now I need never blush
At my heart's hottest gush—
The wife of my Owen her heart may discover!

Proud of you, fond of you, having all right in you,
Quitting all else through my love and delight in you!
Glad is my heart since 'tis beating so nigh to you!
Light is my step for it always may fly to you!

Clasped in your arms where no sorrow can reach to me,
Reading your eyes till new love they shall teach to me.
Though wild and weak till now,
By that blest marriage vow,
More than the wisest know your heart shall preach to me.

Ellen Mary Patrick Downing [1828–1869]

DORIS: A PASTORAL

I SAT with Doris, the shepherd maiden;
Her crook was laden with wreathèd flowers.
I sat and wooed her through sunlight wheeling,
And shadows stealing for hours and hours.

And she, my Doris, whose lap incloses
Wild summer roses of faint perfume,
The while I sued her, kept hushed and harkened
Till shades had darkened from gloss to gloom.

She touched my shoulder with fearful finger;
She said, "We linger, we must not stay;
My flock's in danger, my sheep will wander;
Behold them yonder, how far they stray!"

I answered bolder, "Nay, let me hear you,
And still be near you, and still adore!
No wolf nor stranger will touch one yearling—
Ah! stay my darling a moment more!"

She whispered, sighing, "There will be sorrow
Beyond to-morrow, if I lose to-day;
My fold unguarded, my flock unfolded—
I shall be scolded and sent away!"

Said I, denying, "If they do miss you,
They ought to kiss you when you get home;
And well rewarded by friend and neighbor
Should be the labor from which you come."

"They might remember," she answered meekly,
  "That lambs are weakly and sheep are wild;
But if they love me it's none so fervent—
  I am a servant and not a child."

Then each hot ember glowed quick within me,
  And love did win me to swift reply:
"Ah! do but prove me, and none shall bind you,
  Nor fray nor find you until I die!"

She blushed and started, and stood awaiting,
  As if debating in dreams divine;
But I did brave them—I told her plainly,
  She doubted vainly, she must be mine.

So we, twin-hearted, from all the valley
  Did rouse and rally her nibbling ewes;
And homeward drove them, we two together,
  Through blooming heather and gleaming dews.

That simple duty such grace did lend her,
  My Doris tender, my Doris true,
That I her warder did always bless her,
  And often press her to take her due.

And now in beauty she fills my dwelling
  With love excelling, and undefiled;
And love doth guard her, both fast and fervent,
  No more a servant, nor yet a child.
                    Arthur Joseph Munby [1828–1910]

"HE'D NOTHING BUT HIS VIOLIN"

HE'D nothing but his violin,
  I'd nothing but my song,
But we were wed when skies were blue
  And summer days were long;
And when we rested by the hedge,
  The robins came and told
How they had dared to woo and win,
  When early Spring was cold.

We sometimes supped on dew-berries,
Or slept among the hay,
But oft the farmers' wives at eve
Came out to hear us play;
The rare old songs, the dear old tunes,—
We could not starve for long
While my man had his violin,
And I my sweet love-song.

The world has aye gone well with us
Old man since we were one,—
Our homeless wandering down the lanes
It long ago was done.
But those who wait for gold or gear,
For houses or for kine,
Till youth's sweet spring grows brown and sere,
And love and beauty tine,
Will never know the joy of hearts
That met without a fear,
When you had but your violin
And I a song, my dear.

Mary Kyle Dallas [1830–1897]

LOVE'S CALENDAR

THAT gusty spring, each afternoon
    By the ivied cot I passed,
And noted at that lattice soon
    Her fair face downward cast;
Still in the same place seated there,
So diligent, so very fair.

Oft-times I said I knew her not,
    Yet that way round would go,
Until, when evenings lengthened out,
    And bloomed the may-hedge row,
I met her by the wayside well,
Whose waters, maybe, broke the spell.

For, leaning on her pail, she prayed,
  I'd lift it to her head.
So did I; but I'm much afraid
  Some wasteful drops were shed,
And that we blushed, as face to face
Needs must we stand the shortest space.

Then when the sunset mellowed through
  The ears of rustling grain,
When lattices wide open flew,
  When ash-leaves fell like rain,
As well as I she knew the hour
At morn or eve I neared her bower.

And now that snow o'erlays the thatch,
  Each starlit eve within
The door she waits, I raise the latch,
  And kiss her lifted chin;
Nor do I think we've blushed again,
For Love hath made but one of twain.

William Bell Scott [1811-1890]

HOME

Two birds within one nest;
Two hearts within one breast;
Two spirits in one fair,
Firm league of love and prayer,
Together bound for aye, together blest.

An ear that waits to catch
A hand upon the latch;
A step that hastens its sweet rest to win;
A world of care without,
A world of strife shut out,
A world of love shut in.

Dora Greenwell [1821-1882]

TWO LOVERS

Two lovers by a moss-grown spring:
  They leaned soft cheeks together there,
  Mingled the dark and sunny hair,
And heard the wooing thrushes sing.

O budding time!
O love's blest prime!

Two wedded from the portal stept:
  The bells made happy carolings,
  The air was soft as fanning wings,
White petals on the pathway slept.
      O pure-eyed bride!
      O tender pride!

Two faces o'er a cradle bent:
  Two hands above the head were locked:
  These pressed each other while they rocked,
Those watched a life that love had sent.
      O solemn hour!
      O hidden power!

Two parents by the evening fire:
  The red light fell about their knees
  On heads that rose by slow degrees
Like buds upon the lily spire.
      O patient life!
      O tender strife!

The two still sat together there,
  The red light shone about their knees;
  But all the heads by slow degrees
Had gone and left that lonely pair.
      O voyage fast!
      O vanished past!

The red light shone upon the floor
  And made the space between them wide;
  They drew their chairs up side by side,
Their pale cheeks joined, and said, "Once more!"
      O memories!
      O past that is!

                    George Eliot [1819–1880]

THE LAND OF HEART'S DESIRE

"SOMEWHERE," he mused, "its dear enchantments wait,
  That land, so heavenly sweet;
Yet all the paths we follow, soon or late,
  End in the desert's heat.

"And still it lures us to the eager quest,
  And calls us day by day"—
"But I," she said, her babe upon her breast
  "*But I have found the way.*"

"Some time," he sighed, "when youth and joy are spent,
  Our feet the gates may win"—
"But I," she smiled, with eyes of deep content,
  "*But I have entered in.*"

Emily Huntington Miller [1833–1913]

MY AIN WIFE

I WADNA gi'e my ain wife
  For ony wife I see;
I wadna gi'e my ain wife
  For ony wife I see;
A bonnier yet I've never seen,
  A better canna be—
I wadna gi'e my ain wife
  For ony wife I see!

O couthie is my ingle-cheek,
  An' cheerie is my Jean;
I never see her angry look,
  Nor hear her word on ane.
She's gude wi' a' the neebors roun'
  An' aye gude wi' me—
I wadna gi'e my ain wife
  For ony wife I see.

An' O her looks sae kindlie,
  They melt my heart outright,
When o'er the baby at her breast
  She hangs wi' fond delight;

She looks intill its bonnie face,
  An' syne looks to me—
I wadna gi'e my ain wife
  For ony wife I see.

Alexander Laing [1787–1857]

THE IRISH WIFE

I WOULD not give my Irish wife
  For all the dames of the Saxon land;
I would not give my Irish wife
  For the Queen of France's hand;
For she to me is dearer
  Than castles strong, or lands, or life.
An outlaw—so I'm near her
  To love till death my Irish wife.

O what would be this home of mine,
  A ruined, hermit-haunted place,
But for the light that nightly shines
  Upon its walls from Kathleen's face!
What comfort in a mine of gold,
  What pleasure in a royal life,
If the heart within lay dead and cold,
  If I could not wed my Irish wife?

I knew the law forbade the banns;
  I knew my king abhorred her race;
Who never bent before their clans
  Must bow before their ladies' grace.
Take all my forfeited domain,
  I cannot wage with kinsmen strife:
Take knightly gear and noble name,
  And I will keep my Irish wife.

My Irish wife has clear blue eyes,
  My heaven by day, my stars by night;
And twin-like truth and fondness lies
  Within her swelling bosom white.

My Irish wife has golden hair,
    Apollo's harp had once such strings,
Apollo's self might pause to hear
    Her bird-like carol when she sings.

I would not give my Irish wife
    For all the dames of the Saxon land;
I would not give my Irish wife
    For the Queen of France's hand;
For she to me is dearer
    Than castles strong, or lands, or life:
In death I would be near her,
    And rise beside my Irish wife.
             Thomas D'Arcy McGee [1825–1868]

MY WIFE'S A WINSOME WEE THING

SHE is a winsome wee thing,
She is a handsome wee thing,
She is a bonnie wee thing,
This sweet wee wife o' mine.

I never saw a fairer,
I never lo'ed a dearer,
And niest my heart I'll wear her,
For fear my jewel tine.

She is a winsome wee thing,
She is a handsome wee thing,
She is a bonnie wee thing,
This sweet wee wife o' mine.

The warld's wrack we share o't,
The warsle and the care o't:
Wi' her I'll blithely bear it,
And think my lot divine.
             Robert Burns [1759–1796]

LETTICE

I SAID to Lettice, our sister Lettice,
    While drooped and glistened her eyelash brown,
"Your man's a poor man, a cold and dour man,
    There's many a better about our town."

She smiled securely—"He loves me purely:
   A true heart's safe, both in smile or frown;
And nothing harms me while his love warms me,
   Whether the world go up or down."

"He comes of strangers, and they are rangers,
   And ill to trust, girl, when out of sight:
Fremd folk may blame ye, and e'en defame ye,—
   A gown oft handled looks seldom white."
She raised serenely her eyelids queenly,—
   "My innocence is my whitest gown;
No harsh tongue grieves me while he believes me,
   Whether the world go up or down."

"Your man's a frail man, was ne'er a hale man,
   And sickness knocketh at every door,
And death comes making bold hearts cower, breaking—"
   Our Lettice trembled;—but once, no more.
"If death should enter, smite to the center
   Our poor home palace, all crumbling down,
He cannot fright us, nor disunite us,
   Life bears Love's cross, death brings Love's crown."
           Dinah Maria Mulock Craik [1826–1887]

"IF THOU WERT BY MY SIDE, MY LOVE"

     If thou wert by my side, my love,
       How fast would evening fail
     In green Bengala's palmy grove,
       Listening the nightingale!

     If thou, my love, wert by my side,
       My babies at my knee,
     How gayly would our pinnace glide
       O'er Gunga's mimic sea!

     I miss thee at the dawning gray,
       When, on our deck reclined,
     In careless ease my limbs I lay
       And woo the cooler wind.

I miss thee when by Gunga's stream
  My twilight steps I guide,
But most beneath the lamp's pale beam
  I miss thee from my side.

I spread my books, my pencil try,
  The lingering noon to cheer,
But miss thy kind, approving eye,
  Thy meek, attentive ear.

But when at morn and eve the star
  Beholds me on my knee,
I feel, though thou art distant far,
  Thy prayers ascend for me.

Then on! then on! where duty leads,
  My course be onward still,
O'er broad Hindostan's sultry meads,
  O'er bleak Almorah's hill.

That course nor Delhi's kingly gates,
  Nor mild Malwah detain;
For sweet the bliss us both awaits
  By yonder western main.

Thy towers, Bombay, gleam bright, they say,
  Across the dark blue sea;
But ne'er were hearts so light and gay
  As then shall meet in thee!

Reginald Heber [1783-1826]

THE SHEPHERD'S WIFE'S SONG

From "The Mourning Garment"

AH, what is love?   It is a pretty thing,
As sweet unto a shepherd as a king,
    And sweeter, too:

For kings have cares that wait upon a crown,
And cares can make the sweetest love to frown:
    Ah then, ah then,
If country loves such sweet desires do gain,
What lady would not love a shepherd swain?

His flocks are folded; he comes home at night
As merry as a king in his delight,
    And merrier, too:
For kings bethink them what the state require,
Where shepherds, careless, carol by the fire:

He kisseth first, then sits as blithe to eat
His cream and curds, as doth a king his meat,
    And blither, too:
For kings have often fears when they do sup,
Where shepherds dread no poison in their cup:

To bed he goes, as wanton then, I ween,
As is a king in dalliance with a queen;
    More wanton, too:
For kings have many griefs, affects to move,
Where shepherds have no greater grief than love:

Upon his couch of straw he sleeps as sound
As doth the king upon his bed of down;
    More sounder, too:
For cares cause kings full oft their sleep to spill,
Where weary shepherds lie and snort their fill:

Thus, with his wife, he spends the year as blithe
As doth the king at every tide or sithe,
    And blither, too:
For kings have wars and broils to take in hand,
Where shepherds laugh and love upon the land:
    Ah then, ah then,
Since country loves such sweet desires do gain,
What lady would not love a shepherd swain?

           Robert Greene [1560?–1592]

"TRUTH DOTH TRUTH DESERVE"

From the "Arcadia"

WHO doth desire that chaste his wife should be,
First be he true, for truth doth truth deserve:
Then such be he as she his worth may see,
And one man still credit with her preserve.
Not toying kind, nor causelessly unkind;
Not stirring thoughts, nor yet denying right;
Not spying faults, nor in plain errors blind;
Never hard hand, nor ever reins too light.
As far from want, as far from vain expense
(The one doth force, the latter doth entice);
Allow good company, but keep from thence
All filthy mouths that glory in their vice.
This done, thou hast no more, but leave the rest
To virtue, fortune, time, and woman's breast.

Philip Sidney [1554–1586]

THE MARRIED LOVER

From "The Angel in the House"

WHY, having won her, do I woo?
  Because her spirit's vestal grace
Provokes me always to pursue,
  But, spirit-like, eludes embrace;
Because her womanhood is such
  That, as on court-days subjects kiss
The Queen's hand, yet so near a touch
  Affirms no mean familiarness;
Nay, rather marks more fair the height
  Which can with safety so neglect
To dread, as lower ladies might,
  That grace could meet with disrespect;
Thus she with happy favor feeds
  Allegiance from a love so high
That thence no false conceit proceeds
  Of difference bridged, or state put by;

Because, although in act and word
 As lowly as a wife can be,
Her manners, when they call me lord,
 Remind me 'tis by courtesy;
Not with her least consent of will,
 Which would my proud affection hurt,
But by the noble style that still
 Imputes an unattained desert;
Because her gay and lofty brows,
 When all is won which hope can ask,
Reflect a light of hopeless snows
 That bright in virgin ether bask;
Because, though free of the outer court
 I am, this Temple keeps its shrine
Sacred to heaven; because, in short,
 She's not and never can be mine.

                    Coventry Patmore [1823–1896]

MY LOVE

NOT as all other women are
Is she that to my soul is dear;
Her glorious fancies come from far,
Beneath the silver evening-star,
And yet her heart is ever near.

Great feelings hath she of her own,
Which lesser souls may never know;
God giveth them to her alone,
And sweet they are as any tone
Wherewith the wind may choose to blow.

Yet in herself she dwelleth not,
Although no home were half so fair;
No simplest duty is forgot,
Life hath no dim and lowly spot
That doth not in her sunshine share.

She doeth little kindnesses,
Which most leave undone, or despise:

For naught that sets one heart at ease,
And giveth happiness or peace,
Is low-esteemèd in her eyes.

She hath no scorn of common things,
And, though she seem of other birth,
Round us her heart intwines and clings,
And patiently she folds her wings
To tread the humble paths of earth.

Blessing she is: God made her so,
And deeds of week-day holiness
Fall from her noiseless as the snow,
Nor hath she ever chanced to know
That aught were easier than to bless.

She is most fair, and thereunto
Her life doth rightly harmonize;
Feeling or thought that was not true
Ne'er made less beautiful the blue
Unclouded heaven of her eyes.

She is a woman: one in whom
The spring-time of her childish years
Hath never lost its fresh perfume,
Though knowing well that life hath room
For many blights and many tears.

I love her with a love as still
As a broad river's peaceful might,
Which, by high tower and lowly mill,
Seems following its own wayward will,
And yet doth ever flow aright.

And, on its full, deep breast serene,
Like quiet isles my duties lie;
It flows around them and between,
And makes them fresh and fair and green,
Sweet homes wherein to live and die.

James Russell Lowell [1819-1891]

MARGARET TO DOLCINO

Ask if I love thee? Oh, smiles cannot tell
Plainer what tears are now showing too well.
Had I not loved thee, my sky had been clear:
Had I not loved thee, I had not been here,
      Weeping by thee.

Ask if I love thee? How else could I borrow
Pride from man's slander, and strength from my sorrow?
Laugh when they sneer at the fanatic's bride,
Knowing no bliss, save to toil and abide
      Weeping by thee.
          Charles Kingsley [1819–1875]

DOLCINO TO MARGARET

The world goes up and the world goes down,
  And the sunshine follows the rain;
And yesterday's sneer, and yesterday's frown,
  Can never come over again,
    Sweet wife:
  No, never come over again.

For woman is warm, though man be cold,
  And the night will hallow the day;
Till the heart which at even was weary and old
  Can rise in the morning gay,
    Sweet wife;
  To its work in the morning gay.
          Charles Kingsley [1819–1875]

AT LAST

When first the bride and bridegroom wed,
  They love their single selves the best;
A sword is in the marriage bed,
  Their separate slumbers are not rest.
They quarrel, and make up again,
They give and suffer worlds of pain.

Both right and wrong,
They struggle long,
Till some good day, when they are old,
Some dark day, when the bells are tolled,
Death having taken their best of life,
  They lose themselves, and find each other;
They know that they are husband, wife,
  For, weeping, they are Father, Mother!

    Richard Henry Stoddard [1825–1903]

THE WIFE TO HER HUSBAND

LINGER not long. Home is not home without thee:
  Its dearest tokens do but make me mourn.
O, let its memory, like a chain about thee,
  Gently compel and hasten thy return!

Linger not long. Though crowds should woo thy staying,
  Bethink thee, can the mirth of thy friends, though dear,
Compensate for the grief thy long delaying
  Costs the fond heart that sighs to have thee here?

Linger not long. How shall I watch thy coming,
  As evening shadows stretch o'er moor and dell;
When the wild bee hath ceased her busy humming,
  And silence hangs on all things like a spell!

How shall I watch for thee, when fears grow stronger,
  As night grows dark and darker on the hill!
How shall I weep, when I can watch no longer!
  Ah! art thou absent, art thou absent still?

Yet I shall grieve not, though the eye that seeth me
  Gazeth through tears that make its splendor dull;
For oh! I sometimes fear when thou art with me,
  My cup of happiness is all too full.

Haste, haste thee home unto thy mountain dwelling,
  Haste, as a bird unto its peaceful nest!
Haste, as a skiff, through tempests wide and swelling,
  Flies to its haven of securest rest!

    Unknown

A WIFE'S SONG

O WELL I love the Spring,
   When the sweet, sweet hawthorn blows;
And well I love the Summer,
   And the coming of the rose;
But dearer are the changing leaf,
   And the year upon the wane,
For O, they bring the blessed time
   That brings him home again.

November may be dreary,
   December's days may be
As full of gloom to others
   As once they were to me;
But O, to hear the tempest
   Beat loud against the pane!
For the roaring wind and the blessed time
   That brings him home again.

William Cox Bennett [1820–1895]

THE SAILOR'S WIFE

AND are ye sure the news is true?
   And are ye sure he's weel?
Is this a time to talk o' wark?
   Ye jauds, fling by your wheel!
Is this a time to spin a thread,
   When Colin's at the door?
Rax down my cloak—I'll to the quay,
   And see him come ashore.
      For there's nae luck aboot the house,
         There's nae luck ava',
      There's little pleasure in the house,
         When our gudeman's awa'.

And gi'e to me my bigonet,
   My bishop's satin gown;
For I maun tell the baillie's wife
   That Colin's in the town.

My Turkey slippers maun gae **on,**
   My stockins pearly blue;
It's a' to pleasure our gudeman,
   For he's baith leal and true.

Rise, lass, and mak' a clean fireside,
   Put on the muckle pot;
Gi'e little Kate her button gown,
   And Jock his Sunday coat.
And mak' their shoon as black as **slaes,**
   Their hose as white as snaw;
It's a' to please my own gudeman,
   He likes to see them braw.

There's twa hens upon the bauk,
   Hae fed this month and mair;
Mak' haste and thraw their necks about
   That Colin weel may fare!
And spread the table neat and clean,
   Gar ilka thing look braw;
For wha can tell how Colin fared,
   When he was far awa'?

Sae true his heart, sae smooth his speech,
   His breath like caller air;
His very foot has music in't
   As he comes up the stair.
And will I see his face again,
   And will I hear him speak?
I'm downright dizzy wi' the thought,
   In troth I'm like to greet!

If Colin's weel, and weel content,
   I ha'e nae mair to crave;
And gin I live to keep him sae,
   I'm blest abune the lave.
And will I see his face again,
   And will I hear him speak?
I'm downright dizzy wi' the thought,
   In troth I'm like to greet!

For there's nae luck aboot the house,
  There's nae luck ava';
There's little pleasure in the house
  When our gudeman's awa'.
             William Julius Mickle [1735–1788]
                  (*or Jean Adam* (?) [1710–1765])

JERRY AN' ME

No matter how the chances are,
  Nor when the winds may blow,
My Jerry there has left the sea
  With all its luck an' woe:
For who would try the sea at all,
  Must try it luck or no.

They told him—Lor', men take no care
  How words they speak may fall—
They told him blunt, he was too old,
  Too slow with oar an' trawl,
An' this is how he left the sea
  An' luck an' woe an' all.

Take any man on sea or land
  Out of his beaten way,
If he is young 'twill do, but then,
  If he is old an' gray,
A month will be a year to him.
  Be all to him you may.

He sits by me, but most he walks
  The door-yard for a deck,
An' scans the boat a-goin' out
  Till she becomes a speck,
Then turns away, his face as wet
  As if she were a wreck.

I cannot bring him back again,
  The days when we were wed.
But he shall never know—my man—
  The lack o' love or bread,
While I can cast a stitch or fill
  A needleful o' thread.

God pity me, I'd most forgot
    How many yet there be,
Whose goodmen full as old as mine
    Are somewhere on the sea,
Who hear the breakin' bar an' think
    O' Jerry home an'—me.

Hiram Rich [1832–1901]

"DON'T BE SORROWFUL, DARLING"

O DON'T be sorrowful, darling!
    And don't be sorrowful, pray;
Taking the year together, my dear,
    There isn't more night than day.

'Tis rainy weather, my darling;
    Time's waves they heavily run;
But taking the year together, my dear,
    There isn't more cloud than sun.

We are old folks now, my darling,
    Our heads are growing gray;
But taking the year all round, my dear,
    You will always find the May.

We have had our May, my darling,
    And our roses long ago;
And the time of the year is coming, my dear,
    For the silent night and the snow.

But God is God, my darling,
    Of the night as well as the day;
And we feel and know that we can go
    Wherever He leads the way.

A God of the night, my darling,
    Of the night of death so grim;
The gate that leads out of life, good wife,
    Is the gate that leads to Him.

Rembrandt Peale [1778–1860]

WINIFREDA

Away! let naught to love displeasing,
  My Winifreda, move your care;
Let naught delay the heavenly blessing,
  Nor squeamish pride, nor gloomy fear.

What though no grants of royal donors
  With pompous titles grace our blood,
We'll shine in more substantial honors,
  And, to be noble, we'll be good.

Our name, while virtue thus we tender,
  Will sweetly sound where'er 'tis spoke;
And all the great ones, they shall wonder
  How they respect such little folk.

What though, from fortune's lavish bounty,
  No mighty treasures we possess;
We'll find, within our pittance, plenty,
  And be content without excess.

Still shall each kind returning season
  Sufficient for our wishes give;
For we will live a life of reason,
  And that's the only life to live.

Through youth and age, in love excelling,
  We'll hand in hand together tread;
Sweet-smiling peace shall crown our dwelling,
  And babes, sweet-smiling babes, our bed.

How should I love the pretty creatures,
  While round my knees they fondly clung!
To see them look their mother's features,
  To hear them lisp their mother's tongue!

And when with envy time transported
  Shall think to rob us of our joys,
You'll in your girls again be courted,
  And I'll go wooing in my boys.

                                        Unknown

AN OLD MAN'S IDYL

By the waters of Life we sat together,
    Hand in hand, in the golden days
Of the beautiful early summer weather,
    When skies were purple and breath was praise,
When the heart kept tune to the carol of birds,
    And the birds kept tune to the songs which ran
Through shimmer of flowers on grassy swards,
    And trees with voices æolian.

By the rivers of Life we walked together,
    I and my darling, unafraid;
And lighter than any linnet's feather
    The burdens of being on us weighed;
And Love's sweet miracles o'er us threw
    Mantles of joy outlasting Time,
And up from the rosy morrows grew
    A sound that seemed like a marriage chime.

In the gardens of Life we strayed together,
    And the luscious apples were ripe and red,
And the languid lilac, and honeyed heather
    Swooned with the fragrance which they shed;
And under the trees the angels walked,
    And up in the air a sense of wings
Awed us tenderly while we talked
    Softly in sacred communings.

In the meadows of Life we strayed together,
    Watching the waving harvests grow,
And under the benison of the Father
    Our hearts, like the lambs, skipped to and fro;
And the cowslip, hearing our low replies,
    Broidered fairer the emerald banks,
And glad tears shone in the daisy's eyes,
    And the timid violet glistened thanks.

Who was with us, and what was round us,
    Neither myself nor my darling guessed;
Only we knew that something crowned us
    Out from the heavens with crowns of rest;

Only we knew that something bright
    Lingered lovingly where we stood,
Clothed with the incandescent light
    Of something higher than humanhood.

Oh, the riches Love doth inherit!
    Oh, the alchemy which doth change
Dross of body and dregs of spirit
    Into sanctities rare and strange!
My flesh is feeble, and dry, and old,
    My darling's beautiful hair is gray;
But our elixir and precious gold
    Laugh at the footsteps of decay.

Harms of the world have come unto us,
    Cups of sorrow we yet shall drain;
But we have a secret which doth show us
    Wonderful rainbows in the rain.
And we hear the tread of the years move by,
    And the sun is setting behind the hills;
But my darling does not fear to die,
    And I am happy in what God wills.

So we sit by our household fires together,
    Dreaming the dreams of long ago;
Then it was balmy, sunny weather,
    And now the valleys are laid in snow;
Icicles hang from the slippery eaves,
    The wind blows cold,—'tis growing late;
Well, well! we have garnered all our sheaves,
    I and my darling, and we wait.

                    Richard Realf [1834–1878]

THE POET'S SONG TO HIS WIFE ,

        How many summers, love,
            Have I been thine?
        How many days, thou dove,
            Hast thou been mine?

Time, like the wingèd wind
　　When it bends the flowers,
Hath left no mark behind,
　　To count the hours.

Some weight of thought, though loth,
　　On thee he leaves;
Some lines of care round both
　　Perhaps he weaves;
Some fears,—a soft regret
　　For joys scarce known;
Sweet looks we half forget;—
　　All else is flown!

Ah!—With what thankless heart
　　I mourn and sing!
Look, where our children start,
　　Like sudden Spring!
With tongues all sweet and low,
　　Like a pleasant rhyme,
They tell how much I owe
　　To thee and Time!

　　　　　　　Bryan Waller Procter [1787–1874]

JOHN ANDERSON

JOHN ANDERSON my jo, John,
　When we were first acquent
Your locks were like the raven,
　Your bonnie brow was brent;
But now your brow is bald, John,
　Your locks are like the snow;
But blessings on your frosty pow,
　John Anderson my jo.

John Anderson my jo, John,
　We clamb the hill thegither,
And mony a canty day, John,
　We've had wi' ane anither:

Now we maun totter down, John,
But hand in hand we'll go,
And sleep thegither at the foot,
John Anderson my jo.

Robert Burns [1759–1796]

TO MARY

"THEE, Mary, with this ring I wed,
So, fourteen years ago, I said—
Behold another ring!—"For what?
To wed thee o'er again—why not?"

With that first ring I married Youth,
Grace, Beauty, Innocence, and Truth;
Taste long admired, sense long revered,
And all my Molly then appeared.
If she, by merit since disclosed,
Prove twice the woman I supposed,
I plead that double merit now,
To justify a double vow.

Here then, to-day, (with faith as sure,
With ardor as intense and pure,
As when, amidst the rites divine,
I took thy troth, and plighted mine),
To thee, sweet girl, my second ring
A token, and a pledge, I bring;
With this I wed, till death us part,
Thy riper virtues to my heart;
Those virtues, which, before untried,
The wife has added to the bride;
Those virtues, whose progressive claim,
Endearing wedlock's very name,
My soul enjoys, my song approves,
For Conscience' sake, as well as Love's.

For why?—They show me every hour,
Honor's high thought, Affection's power,
Discretion's deed, sound Judgment's sentence,
And teach me all things—but Repentance.

Samuel Bishop [1731–1795]

THE GOLDEN WEDDING

O Love, whose patient pilgrim feet
  Life's longest path have trod;
Whose ministry hath symbolled sweet
  The dearer love of God;
The sacred myrtle wreathes again
  Thine altar, as of old;
And what was green with summer then,
  Is mellowed now to gold.

Not now, as then, the future's face
  Is flushed with fancy's light;
But memory, with a milder grace,
  Shall rule the feast to-night.
Blest was the sun of joy that shone,
  Nor less the blinding shower;
The bud of fifty years agone
  Is love's perfected flower.

O memory, ope thy mystic door;
  O dream of youth, return;
And let the light that gleamed of yore
  Beside this altar burn.
The past is plain; 'twas love designed
  E'en sorrow's iron chain;
And mercy's shining thread has twined
  With the dark warp of pain.

So be it still.   O Thou who hast
  That younger bridal blest,
Till the May-morn of love has passed
  To evening's golden west;
Come to this later Cana, Lord,
  And, at thy touch divine,
The water of that earlier board
  To-night shall turn to wine.

                    David Gray [1837–1888]

MOGGY AND ME

Oh wha are sae happy as me an' my Moggy?
  Oh wha are sae happy as Moggy an' me?
We're baith turnin' auld, an' our walth is soon tauld,
  But contentment bides aye in our cottage sae wee.
She toils a' the day when I'm out wi' the hirsel,
  An' chants to the bairns while I sing on the brae;
An' aye her blithe smile welcomes me frae my toil,
  When down the glen I come weary an' wae.

Aboon our auld heads we've a nice little biggin,
  That keeps out the cauld when the simmer's awa;
We've twa webs o' linen o' Moggy's ain spinnin',
  As thick as silk velvet and white as the snaw;
We've kye in the byre, an' yauds in the stable,
  A grumphie sae fat that she hardly can stand;
An' something, I guess, in yon auld painted press
  To cheer up the speerits an' steady the hand.

'Tis true we hae had mony sorrows an' crosses,
  Our pouches oft toom, an' our hearts fu' o' care;
But wi' a' our crosses, our sorrows an' losses,
  Contentment, thank heaven! has aye been our share.
I've an auld roostit sword that was left by my father,
  Whilk aye has been drawn when my king had a fae;
We hae friends ane or twa that aft gie us a ca',
  To laugh when we're happy or grieve when we're wae.

Our duke may hae gowd mair than schoolmen can reckon,
  An' flunkies to watch ilka glance o' his e'e,
His lady aye braw sittin' prim in her ha';
  But are they sae happy as Moggy an' me?
A' ye wha ne'er fand the straight road to be happy,
  Wha are nae content wi' the lot that ye dree,
Come down to the dwellin' o' whilk I've been tellin',
  You'll learn it by lookin' at Moggy an' me.

James Hogg [1770-1835]

"O, LAY THY HAND IN MINE, DEAR!"

O, LAY thy hand in mine, dear!
　　We're growing old;
But Time hath brought no sign, dear,
　　That hearts grow cold.
'Tis long, long since our new love
　　Made life divine;
But age enricheth true love,
　　Like noble wine.

And lay thy cheek to mine, dear,
　　And take thy rest;
Mine arms around thee twine, dear,
　　And make thy nest.
A many cares are pressing
　　On this dear head;
But Sorrow's hands in blessing
　　Are surely laid.

O, lean thy life on mine, dear!
　　'Twill shelter thee.
Thou wert a winsome vine, dear,
　　On my young tree:
And so, till boughs are leafless,
　　And songbirds flown,
We'll twine, then lay us, griefless,
　　Together down.

Gerald Massey [1828–1907]

THE EXEQUY

ACCEPT, thou shrine of my dead saint,
Instead of dirges this complaint;
And for sweet flowers to crown thy hearse,
Receive a strew of weeping verse
From thy grieved friend, whom thou might'st see
Quite melted into tears for thee.

Dear loss! since thy untimely fate,
My task hath been to meditate
On thee, on thee: thou art the book,
The library whereon I look,
Though almost blind. For thee (loved clay)
I languish out, not live, the day,
Using no other exercise
But which I practise with mine eyes:
By which wet glasses I find out
How lazily time creeps about
To one that mourns: this, only this,
My exercise and business is:
So I compute the weary hours
With sighs dissolvèd into showers.

Nor wonder if my time go thus
Backward and most preposterous;
Thou hast benighted me; thy set
This eve of blackness did beget,
Who wast my day (though overcast
Before thou hadst thy noontide passed):
And I remember must in tears
Thou scarce hadst seen so many years
As day tells hours. By thy clear sun
My love and fortune first did run;
But thou wilt never more appear
Folded within my hemisphere,
Since both thy light and motiòn,
Like a fled star, is fallen and gone,
And 'twixt me and my soul's dear wish
The earth now interposèd is,
Which such a strange eclipse doth make
As ne'er was read in almanac.

I could allow thee for a time
To darken me and my sad clime;
Were it a month, a year, or ten,
I would thy exile live till then,
And all that space my mirth adjourn,
So thou wouldst promise to return,

And putting off thy ashy shroud
At length disperse this sorrow's cloud.
But woe is me! the longest date
Too narrow is to calculate
These empty hopes: never shall I
Be so much blest as to descry
A glimpse of thee, till that day come
Which shall the earth to cinders doom,
And a fierce fever must calcine
The body of this world—like thine,
(My little world!) That fit of fire
Once off, our bodies shall aspire
To our souls' bliss: then we shall rise
And view ourselves with clearer eyes
In that calm region where no night
Can hide us from each other's sight.

Meantime thou hast her, earth: much good
May my harm do thee! Since it stood
With Heaven's will I might not call
Her longer mine, I give thee all
My short-lived right and interest
In her whom living I loved best:
With a most free and bounteous grief
I give thee what I could not keep.
Be kind to her, and prithee look
Thou write into thy Doomsday book
Each parcel of this rarity
Which in thy casket shrined doth lie,
See that thou make thy reckoning straight,
And yield her back again by weight;
For thou must audit on thy trust
Each grain and atom of this dust,
As thou wilt answer Him that lent—
Not gave—thee my dear monument.
So close the ground, and 'bout her shade
Black curtains draw: my bride is laid.

Sleep on, my Love, in thy cold bed
Never to be disquieted!

My last good-night! Thou wilt not wake
Till I thy fate shall overtake:
Till age, or grief, or sickness must
Marry my body to that dust
It so much loves; and fill the room
My heart keeps empty in thy tomb.
Stay for me there: I will not fail
To meet thee in that hollow vale.
And think not much of my delay:
I am already on the way,
And follow thee with all the speed
Desire can make, or sorrows breed.
Each minute is a short degree
And every hour a step towards thee.
At night when I betake to rest,
Next morn I rise nearer my west
Of life, almost by eight hours' sail,
Than when sleep breathed his drowsy gale.

   Thus from the Sun my bottom steers,
And my day's compass downward bears:
Nor labor I to stem the tide
Through which to thee I swiftly glide.
'Tis true, with shame and grief I yield,
Thou, like the van, first took'st the field;
And gotten hast the victory
In thus adventuring to die
Before me, whose more years might crave
A just precedence in the grave.
But hark! my pulse, like a soft drum,
Beats my approach, tells thee I come:
And slow howe'er my marches be
I shall at last sit down by thee.

   The thought of this bids me go on
And wait my dissolution
With hope and comfort. Dear (forgive
The crime), I am content to live
Divided, with but half a heart,
Till we shall meet and never part.

Henry King [1592–1669]

LOVE SONNETS

SONNETS

From "Amoretti"

III

THE sovereign beauty which I do admire,
Witness the world how worthy to be praised!
The light whereof hath kindled heavenly fire
In my frail spirit, by her from baseness raised;
That being now with her huge brightness dazed,
Base thing I can no more endure to view:
But, looking still on her, I stand amazed
At wondrous sight of so celestial hue.
So when my tongue would speak her praises due,
It stoppèd is with thought's astonishment;
And when my pen would write her titles true,
It ravished is with fancy's wonderment:
    Yet in my heart I then both speak and write
    The wonder that my wit cannot indite.

VIII

More than most fair, full of the living fire
Kindled above unto the Maker near;
No eyes but joys, in which all powers conspire
That to the world naught else be counted dear;
Through your bright beams doth not the blinded guest
Shoot out his darts to base affections wound;
But angels come to lead frail minds to rest
In chaste desires, on heavenly beauty bound.
You frame my thoughts, and fashion me within;
You stop my tongue, and teach my heart to speak;
You calm the storm that passion did begin,
Strong through your cause, but by your virtue weak.
    Dark is the world, where your light shinèd never;
    Well is he born that may behold you ever.

XXIV

When I behold that beauty's wonderment,
And rare perfection of each goodly part,
Of Nature's still the only complement,
I honor and admire the Maker's art.
But when I feel the bitter baleful smart
Which her fair eyes un'wares do work in me,
That death out of their shiny beams do dart,
I think that I a new Pandora see,
Whom all the gods in council did agree
Into this sinful world from heaven to send,
That she to wicked men a scourge should be,
For all their faults with which they did offend.
But since ye are my scourge, I will entreat
That for my faults ye will me gently beat.

XXXIV

Like as a ship, that through the ocean wide,
By conduct of some star doth make her way,
Whenas a storm hath dimmed her trusty guide,
Out of her course doth wander far astray;
So I, whose star, that wont with her bright ray
Me to direct, with clouds is overcast,
Do wander now, in darkness and dismay,
Through hidden perils round about me placed;
Yet hope I well that, when this storm is past,
My Helicè, the lodestar of my life,
Will shine again, and look on me at last,
With lovely light to clear my cloudy grief:
Till then I wander care-full, comfortless,
In secret sorrow, and sad pensiveness.

LV

So oft as I her beauty do behold,
And therewith do her cruelty compare,
I marvel of what substance was the mould,
The which her made at once so cruel fair;
Not earth, for her high thoughts more heavenly are;
Not water, for her love doth burn like fire;

Not air, for she is not so light or rare;
Not fire, for she doth freeze with faint desire.
Then needs another element inquire
Whereof she might be made—that is, the sky;
For to the heaven her haughty looks aspire,
And eke her mind is pure immortal high.
   Then, since to heaven ye likened are the best,
   Be like in mercy as in all the rest.

LXVIII

Most glorious Lord of Life! that on this day
Didst make thy triumph over death and sin,
And, having harrowed hell, didst bring away
Captivity thence captive, us to win,
This joyous day, dear Lord, with joy begin;
And grant that we, for whom thou diddest die,
Being with thy dear blood clean washed from sin,
May live forever in felicity;
And that thy love we weighing worthily,
May likewise love thee for the same again,
And for thy sake, that all 'like dear didst buy,
With love may one another entertain!
   So let us love, dear Love, like as we ought:
   Love is the lesson which the Lord us taught.

LXX

Fresh Spring, the herald of love's mighty king,
In whose coat-armor richly are displayed
All sorts of flowers the which on earth do spring
In goodly colors gloriously arrayed;
Go to my love, where she is careless laid,
Yet in her winter's bower not well awake;
Tell her the joyous time will not be stayed,
Unless she do him by the forelock take;
Bid her therefore herself soon ready make
To wait on Love amongst his lovely crew;
Where everyone that misseth then her mate
Shall be by him amerced with penance due.
   Make haste, therefore, sweet love, whilst it is prime;
   For none can call again the passèd time.

LXXV

One day I wrote her name upon the strand,
But came the waves and washèd it away:
Again I wrote it with a second hand,
But came the tide and made my pains his prey.
"Vain man," said she, "that dost in vain essay
A mortal thing so to immortalize;
For I myself shall like to this decay,
And eke my name be wipèd out likewise."
"Not so," quoth I; "let baser things devise
To die in dust, but you shall live by fame;
My verse your virtues rare shall eternize,
And in the heavens write your glorious name:
    Where, whenas Death shall all the world subdue,
    Our love shall live, and later life renew."

LXXIX

Men call you fair, and you do credit it,
For that yourself ye daily such do see:
But the true fair, that is the gentle wit
And virtuous mind, is much more praised of me:
For all the rest, however fair it be,
Shall turn to naught and lose that glorious hue;
But only that is permanent and free
From frail corruption that doth flesh ensue.
That is true beauty; that doth argue you
To be divine, and born of heavenly seed;
Derived from that fair Spirit from whom all true
And perfect beauty did at first proceed:
    He only fair, and what he fair hath made;
    All other fair, like flowers, untimely fade.

Edmund Spenser [1552?-1599]

SONNETS
From "Astrophel and Stella"

I

Loving in truth, and fain in verse my love to show,
That She, dear She! might take some pleasure of my pain;
Pleasure might cause her read, reading might make her know,
Knowledge might pity win, and pity grace obtain:

I sought fit words to paint the blackest face of woe,
Studying inventions fine, her wits to entertain;
Oft turning others' leaves, to see if thence would flow
Some fresh and fruitful showers upon my sunburnt brain:
But words came halting forth, wanting Invention's stay.
Invention, Nature's child, fled step-dame Study's blows;
And others' feet still seemed but strangers in my way.
Thus, great with child to speak, and helpless in my throes,
   Biting my truant pen, beating myself for spite:
    "Fool!" said my Muse to me, "look in thy heart, and write!"

XXXI

With how sad steps, O Moon, thou climb'st the skies!
How silently, and with how wan a face!
What! may it be that even in heavenly place
That busy archer his sharp arrows tries?
Sure, if that long-with-love-acquainted eyes
Can judge of love, thou feel'st a lover's case;
I read it in thy looks. Thy languished grace
To me, that feel the like, thy state descries.
Then, even of fellowship, O Moon, tell me,
Is constant love deemed there but want of wit?
Are beauties there as proud as here they be?
Do they above love to be loved, and yet
   Those lovers scorn whom that love doth possess?
   Do they call virtue there, ungratefulness?

XXXIX

Come Sleep! O Sleep, the certain knot of peace,
The baiting-place of wit, the balm of woe,
The poor man's wealth, the prisoner's release,
The indifferent judge between the high and low!
With shield of proof, shield me from out the press
Of those fierce darts Despair at me doth throw:
O make in me those civil wars to cease!
I will good tribute pay if thou do so.
Take thou of me, smooth pillows, sweetest bed,
A chamber deaf to noise and blind to light,
A rosy garland, and a weary head:
And if these things, as being thine in right,

Move not thy heavy grace, thou shalt in me,
Livelier than elsewhere, Stella's image see.

LXII

Late tired with woe, even ready for to pine
With rage of love, I called my Love unkind;
She in whose eyes love, though unfelt, doth shine,
Sweet said that I true love in her should find.
I joyed; but straight thus watered was my wine,
That love she did, but loved a love not blind;
Which would not let me, whom she loved, decline
From nobler cause, fit for my birth and mind:
And therefore, by her love's authority,
Willed me these tempests of vain love to fly,
And anchor fast myself on Virtue's shore.
Alas, if this the only metal be
Of love new-coined to help my beggary,
Dear! love me not, that ye may love me more!

LXIV

No more, my Dear, no more these counsels try;
O give my passions leave to run their race!
Let Fortune lay on me her worst disgrace;
Let folk o'ercharged with brain, against me cry;
Let clouds bedim my face, break in mine eye;
Let me no steps but of lost labor trace;
Let all the earth with scorn recount my case;
But do not will me from my love to fly!
I do not envy Aristotle's wit;
Nor do aspire to Caesar's bleeding fame;
Nor aught do care, though some above me sit;
Nor hope, nor wish another course to frame,
But that which once may win thy cruel heart:
Thou art my Wit, and thou my Virtue art.

LXXIII

Love still a boy and oft a wanton is,
Schooled only by his mother's tender eye;
What wonder, then, if he his lesson miss,
When for so soft a rod dear play he try?

And yet my Star, because a sugared kiss
In sport I sucked while she asleep did lie,
Doth lower, nay chide, nay threat, for only this.—
Sweet, it was saucy Love, not humble I!
But no 'scuse serves; she makes her wrath appear
In Beauty's throne; see now, who dares come near
Those scarlet judges, threatening bloody pain!
O heavenly fool, thy most kiss-worthy face
Anger invests with such a lovely grace,
That Anger's self I needs must kiss again.

CIII

O happy Thames that didst my Stella bear!
I saw thee with full many a smiling line
Upon thy cheerful face, Joy's livery wear,
While those fair planets on thy streams did shine.
The boat for joy could not to dance forbear;
While wanton winds, with beauties so divine,
Ravished, stayed not, till in her golden hair
They did themselves, (O sweetest prison!) twine.
And fain those Æol's youths there would their stay
Have made, but forced by Nature still to fly,
First did with puffing kiss those locks display.
She so dishevelled, blushed. From window, I,
    With sight thereof, cried out, "O fair disgrace!
    Let Honor's self to thee grant highest place!"

CVII

Stella! since thou so right a Princess art
Of all the powers which life bestows on me,
That ere by them aught undertaken be,
They first resort unto that sovereign part;
Sweet! for a while give respite to my heart,
Which pants as though it still should leap to thee;
And on my thoughts give thy lieutenancy
To this great cause, which needs both use and art.
And as a Queen, who from her presence sends
Whom she employs, dismiss from thee my wit,
Till it have wrought what thy own will attends:
On servants' shame oft master's blame doth sit.

O, let not fools in me thy works reprove,
And scorning, say, "See what it is to love!"

Philip Sidney [1554–1586]

SONNETS

From "To Delia"

VI

FAIR is my Love, and cruel as she's fair:
Her brow shades frowns, although her eyes are sunny;
Her smiles are lightning, though her pride despair,
And her disdains are gall, her favors honey.
A modest maid, decked with a blush of honor,
Whose feet do tread green paths of youth and love;
The wonder of all eyes that look upon her,
Sacred on earth, designed a Saint above.
Chastity and Beauty, which were deadly foes,
Live reconcilèd friends within her brow;
And had she Pity to conjoin with those,
Then who had heard the plaints I utter now?
  O had she not been fair, and thus unkind,
  My Muse had slept, and none had known my mind.

XII

My spotless love hovers, with purest wings,
About the temple of the proudest frame,
Where blaze those lights, fairest of earthly things,
Which clear our clouded world with brightest flame.
My ambitious thoughts, confinèd in her face,
Affect no honor but what she can give;
My hopes do rest in limits of her grace;
I weigh no comfort, unless she relieve.
For she, that can my heart imparadise,
Holds in her fairest hand what dearest is.
My Fortune's Wheel's the Circle of her Eyes,
Whose rolling grace deign once a turn of bliss!
  All my life's sweet consists in her alone;
  So much I love the most unloving one.

XXX

And yet I cannot reprehend the flight
Or blame the attempt, presuming so to soar;
The mounting venture, for a high delight,
Did make the honor of the fall the more.
For who gets wealth, that puts not from the shore?
Danger hath honor; great designs, their fame;
Glory doth follow, courage goes before;
And though the event oft answers not the same,
Suffice that high attempts have never shame.
The Mean-observer (whom base safety keeps)
Lives without honor, dies without a name,
And in eternal darkness ever sleeps.
    And therefore, Delia! 'tis to me no blot
    To have attempted, though attained thee not.

XXXVI

When men shall find thy flower, thy glory pass,
And thou, with careful brow, sitting alone,
Receivèd hast this message from thy glass,
That tells the truth, and says that *All is gone;*
Fresh shalt thou see in me the wounds thou madest,
Though spent thy flame, in me the heat remaining:
I that have loved thee thus before thou fadest,
My faith shall wax, when thou art in thy waning!
The world shall find this miracle in me,
That fire can burn when all the matter's spent:
Then what my faith hath been, thyself shalt see,
And that thou wast unkind, thou may'st repent!
    Thou may'st repent that thou hast scorned my tears,
    When Winter snows upon thy golden hairs.

XXXIX

Look, Delia, how we esteem the half-blown rose
The image of thy blush, and Summer's honor!
Whilst yet her tender bud doth undisclose
That full of beauty Time bestows upon her.
No sooner spreads her glory in the air
But straight her wide-blown pomp comes to decline;

She then is scorned that late adorned the fair;
So fade the roses of those cheeks of thine.
No April can revive thy withered flowers
Whose springing grace adorns thy glory now;
Swift, speedy Time, feathered with flying hours,
Dissolves the beauty of the fairest brow.
    Then do not thou such treasure waste in vain,
    But love now, whilst thou may'st be loved again.

XLV

Beauty, sweet Love, is like the morning dew,
Whose short refresh upon the tender green
Cheers for a time, but till the sun doth show:
And straight 'tis gone, as it had never been.
Soon doth it fade, that makes the fairest flourish;
Short is the glory of the blushing rose:
The hue which thou so carefully dost nourish,
Yet which, at length, thou must be forced to lose.
When thou, surcharged with burthen of thy years,
Shalt bend thy wrinkles homeward to the earth;
When Time hath made a passport for thy fears,
Dated in Age, the Calends of our Death:
    But ah, no more! This hath been often told;
    And women grieve to think they must be old.

XLVI

I must not grieve my Love, whose eyes would read
Lines of delight, whereon her youth might smile!
Flowers have a time, before they come to seed;
And she is young, and now must sport the while.
And sport, Sweet Maid, in season of these years,
And learn to gather flowers before they wither!
And where the sweetest blossom first appears,
Let Love and Youth conduct thy pleasures thither!
Lighten forth smiles to clear the clouded air,
And calm the tempest which my sighs do raise!
Pity and smiles do best become the fair;
Pity and smiles shall yield thee lasting praise.
    I hope to say, when all my griefs are gone,
    "Happy the heart that sighed for such a one!"

L

Let others sing of Knights and Paladines
In agèd accents and untimely words,
Paint shadows in imaginary lines,
Which well the reach of their high wit records:
But I must sing of Thee, and those fair eyes!
Authentic shall my verse in time to come,
When the yet unborn shall say, *Lo, where she lies!*
Whose beauty made him speak, that else was dumb!
These are the arks, the trophies I erect,
That fortify thy name against old age;
And these thy sacred virtues must protect
Against the Dark, and Time's consuming rage.
    Though the error of my youth in them appear,
    Suffice, they showed I lived, and loved thee dear.

LI

Care-charmer Sleep, son of the sable Night,
Brother to Death, in silent darkness born:
Relieve my languish, and restore the light;
With dark forgetting of my care, return!
And let the day be time enough to mourn
The shipwreck of my ill-adventured youth:
Let waking eyes suffice to wail their scorn,
Without the torment of the night's untruth.
Cease, dreams, the images of day-desires,
To model forth the passions of the morrow;
Never let rising sun approve you liars,
To add more grief to aggravate my sorrow.
    Still let me sleep, embracing clouds in vain;
    And never wake to feel the day's disdain.

Samuel Daniel [1562–1619]

SONNETS

From " Idea "

TO THE READER OF THESE SONNETS

Into these Loves, who but for Passion looks,
At this first sight, here let him lay them by,
And seek elsewhere in turning other books,
Which better may his labor satisfy.

No far-fetched sigh shall ever wound my breast;
Love from mine eye a tear shall never wring;
Nor in "Ah me's!" my whining sonnets dressed!
A libertine, fantasticly I sing!
My verse is the true image of my mind,
Ever in motion, still desiring change;
And as thus, to variety inclined,
So in all humors sportively I range!

My Muse is rightly of the English strain,
That cannot long one fashion entertain.

IV

Bright Star of Beauty! on whose eyelids sit
A thousand nymph-like and enamored Graces,
The Goddesses of Memory and Wit,
Which there in order take their several places;
In whose dear bosom, sweet delicious Love
Lays down his quiver, which he once did bear,
Since he that blessèd paradise did prove;
And leaves his mother's lap, to sport him there.
Let others strive to entertain with words!
My soul is of a braver mettle made:
I hold that vile, which vulgar wit affords,
In me's that faith which Time cannot invade!

Let what I praise be still made good by you!
Be you most worthy, whilst I am most true!

XX

An evil Spirit (your Beauty) haunts me still,
Wherewith, alas, I have been long possessed;
Which ceaseth not to attempt me to each ill,
Nor give me once, but one poor minute's rest.
In me it speaks, whether I sleep or wake;
And when by means to drive it out I try,
With greater torments then it me doth take,
And tortures me in most extremity.
Before my face, it lays down my despairs,
And hastes me on unto a sudden death;
Now tempting me, to drown myself in tears,
And then in sighing to give up my breath.

Thus am I still provoked to every evil,
By this good-wicked Spirit, sweet Angel-Devil.

XXXVII

Dear! why should you command me to my rest,
When now the night doth summon all to sleep?
Methinks this time becometh lovers best!
Night was ordained together friends to keep.
How happy are all other living things,
Which, through the day, disjoined by several flight,
The quiet evening yet together brings,
And each returns unto his Love at night!
O thou that art so courteous else to all,
Why shouldst thou, Night, abuse me only thus!
That every creature to his kind doth call,
And yet 'tis thou dost only sever us?
   Well could I wish it would be ever day,
   If, when night comes, you bid me go away!

XL

My heart the Anvil where my thoughts do beat;
My words the Hammers fashioning my Desire;
My breast the Forge including all the heat,
Love is the Fuel which maintains the fire.
My sighs the Bellows which the flame increaseth,
Filling mine ears with noise and nightly groaning.
Toiling with pain, my labor never ceaseth;
In grievous Passions, my woes still bemoaning.
My eyes with tears against the fire striving,
Whose scorching glede my heart to cinders turneth:
But with those drops, the flame again reviving
Still more and more it to my torment burneth.
   With Sisyphus thus do I roll the stone,
   And turn the wheel with damnèd Ixion.

XLII

How many paltry, foolish, painted things,
That now in coaches trouble every street,
Shall be forgotten, whom no poet sings,
Ere they be well wrapped in their winding-sheet?

Where I to thee eternity shall give,
When nothing else remaineth of these days,
And queens hereafter shall be glad to live
Upon the alms of thy superfluous praise;
Virgins and matrons reading these my rhymes,
Shall be so much delighted with thy story,
That they shall grieve they lived not in these times,
To have seen thee, their sex's only glory:
  So shalt thou fly above the vulgar throng,
  Still to survive in my immortal song.

LXI

Since there's no help, come, let us kiss and part!
Nay, I have done.   You get no more of me!
And I am glad, yea, glad with all my heart,
That thus so cleanly I myself can free.
Shake hands for ever!   Cancel all our vows!
And when we meet at any time again,
Be it not seen in either of our brows
That we one jot of former love retain.
Now at the last gasp of Love's latest breath,
When, his pulse failing, Passion speechless lies,
When Faith is kneeling by his bed of death,
And Innocence is closing up his eyes:
  Now, if thou wouldst, when all have given him over,
  From death to life thou might'st him yet recover!

Michael Drayton [1563–1631]

SONNETS

From " Diana "

IX

My Lady's presence makes the Roses red,
Because to see her lips they blush for shame.
The Lily's leaves, for envy, pale became;
And her white hands in them this envy bred.
The Marigold the leaves abroad doth spread,
Because the sun's and her power is the same.
The Violet of purple color came,
Dyed in the blood she made my heart to shed.

In brief, all flowers from her their virtue take;
From her sweet breath, their sweet smells do proceed;
The living heat which her eyebeams doth make
Warmeth the ground, and quickeneth the seed.
  The rain, wherewith she watereth the flowers,
  Falls from mine eyes, which she dissolves in showers.

LXII

To live in hell, and heaven to behold;
To welcome life, and die a living death;
To sweat with heat, and yet be freezing cold;
To grasp at stars, and lie the earth beneath;
To tread a maze that never shall have end;
To burn in sighs, and starve in daily tears;
To climb a hill, and never to descend;
Giants to kill, and quake at childish fears;
To pine for food, and watch the Hesperian tree;
To thirst for drink, and nectar still to draw;
To live accurst, whom men hold blest to be;
And weep those wrongs which never creature saw;
  If this be love, if love in these be founded,
  My heart is love, for these in it are grounded.

Henry Constable (?) [1562–1613]

SONNETS

XVIII

SHALL I compare thee to a Summer's day?
Thou art more lovely and more temperate:
Rough winds do shake the darling buds of May,
And Summer's lease hath all too short a date:
Sometime too hot the eye of heaven shines,
And often is his gold complexion dimmed;
And every fair from fair sometime declines,
By chance or nature's changing course untrimmed:
But thy eternal Summer shall not fade
Nor lose possession of that fair thou owest;
Nor shall Death brag thou wanderest in his shade,
When in eternal lines to time thou growest:

So long as men can breathe, or eyes can see,
So long lives this, and this gives life to thee.

XXIII

As an unperfect actor on the stage,
Who with his fear is put besides his part,
Or some fierce thing replete with too much rage,
Whose strength's abundance weakens his own heart;
So I, for fear of trust, forget to say
The perfect ceremony of love's rite,
And in mine own love's strength seem to decay,
O'ercharged with burden of mine own love's might.
O, let my books be then the eloquence
And dumb presagers of my speaking breast;
Who plead for love, and look for recompense,
More than that tongue that more hath more expressed.
    O, learn to read what silent love hath writ:
    To hear with eyes belongs to love's fine wit.

XXIX

When, in disgrace with fortune and men's eyes,
I all alone beweep my outcast state,
And trouble deaf heaven with my bootless cries,
And look upon myself, and curse my fate,
Wishing me like to one more rich in hope,
Featured like him, like him with friends possessed,
Desiring this man's art and that man's scope,
With what I most enjoy contented least;
Yet in these thoughts myself almost despising,
Haply I think on thee: and then my state,
Like to the lark at break of day arising
From sullen earth, sings hymns at heaven's gate:
    For thy sweet love remembered such wealth brings
    That then I scorn to change my state with kings.

XXX

When to the sessions of sweet silent thought
I summon up remembrance of things past,
I sigh the lack of many a thing I sought,
And with old woes new wail my dear time's waste:

Then can I drown an eye, unused to flow,
For precious friends hid in death's dateless night,
And weep afresh love's long-since cancelled woe,
And moan the expense of many a vanished sight:
Then can I grieve at grievances foregone,
And heavily from woe to woe tell o'er
The sad account of fore-bemoanèd moan,
Which I new pay as if not paid before:
    But if the while I think on thee, dear friend,
    All losses are restored, and sorrows end.

XXXII

If thou survive my well-contented day
When that churl Death my bones with dust shall cover,
And shalt by fortune once more re-survey
These poor rude lines of thy deceasèd lover,
Compare them with the bettering of the time,
And though they be outstripped by every pen,
Reserve them for my love, not for their rhyme,
Exceeded by the height of happier men.
O, then vouchsafe me but this loving thought:
"Had my friend's Muse grown with this growing age,
A dearer birth than this his love had brought,
To march in ranks of better equipage:
    But since he died, and poets better prove,
    Theirs for their style I'll read, his for his love."

XXXIII

Full many a glorious morning have I seen
Flatter the mountain-tops with sovereign eye,
Kissing with golden face the meadows green,
Gilding pale streams with heavenly alchemy.
Anon permit the basest clouds to ride
With ugly rack on his celestial face,
And from the forlorn world his visage hide,
Stealing unseen to west with this disgrace:
Even so my sun one early morn did shine
With all-triumphant splendor on my brow;
But out, alack! he was but one hour mine,
The region cloud hath masked him from me now.

Yet him for this my love no whit disdaineth;
Suns of the world may stain when heaven's sun staineth.

LX

Like as the waves make towards the pebbled shore,
So do our minutes hasten to their end;
Each changing place with that which goes before,
In sequent toil all forwards do contend.
Nativity, once in the main of light,
Crawls to maturity, wherewith being crowned,
Crooked eclipses 'gainst his glory fight,
And Time that gave, doth now his gift confound.
Time doth transfix the flourish set on youth,
And delves the parallels in beauty's brow;
Feeds on the rarities of nature's truth,
And nothing stands but for his scythe to mow:
   And yet, to times in hope, my verse shall stand
   Praising thy worth, despite his cruel hand.

LXXI

No longer mourn for me when I am dead,
Than you shall hear the surly, sullen bell
Give warning to the world that I am fled
From this vile world, with vilest worms to dwell:
Nay, if you read this line, remember not
The hand that writ it; for I love you so,
That I in your sweet thoughts would be forgot,
If thinking on me then should make you woe.
O, if (I say) you look upon this verse,
When I perhaps compounded am with clay,
Do not so much as my poor name rehearse,
But let your love even with my life decay;
   Lest the wise world should look into your moan,
   And mock you with me after I am gone.

LXXIII

That time of year thou may'st in me behold
When yellow leaves, or none, or few, do hang
Upon those boughs which shake against the cold,
Bare ruined choirs, where late the sweet birds sang.

In me thou see'st the twilight of such day
As after sunset fadeth in the west,
Which by and by black night doth take away,
Death's second self, that seals up all in rest.
In me thou see'st the glowing of such fire
That on the ashes of his youth doth lie,
As the death-bed whereon it must expire,
Consumed with that which it was nourished by.
    This thou perceiv'st, which makes thy love more strong
    To love that well which thou must leave ere long.

CIV

To me, fair friend, you never can be old;
For as you were when first your eye I eyed,
Such seems your beauty still.   Three Winters cold
Have from the forests shook three Summers' pride;
Three beauteous Springs to yellow Autumn turned
In process of the seasons have I seen,
Three April perfumes in three hot Junes burned,
Since first I saw you fresh, which yet are green.
Ah! yet doth beauty, like a dial-hand,
Steal from his figure, and no pace perceived;
So your sweet hue, which methinks still doth stand,
Hath motion, and mine eye may be deceived:
    For fear of which, hear this, thou age unbred:
    Ere you were born was beauty's Summer dead.

CVI

When in the chronicle of wasted time
I see descriptions of the fairest wights,
And beauty making beautiful old rhyme
In praise of ladies dead, and lovely knights;
Then in the blazon of sweet beauty's best
Of hand, of foot, of lip, of eye, of brow,
I see their antique pen would have expressed
Even such a beauty as you master now.
So all their praises are but prophecies
Of this our time, all, you prefiguring;
And, for they looked but with divining eyes,
They had not skill enough your worth to sing:

For we, which now behold these present days,
Have eyes to wonder, but lack tongues to praise.

O, never say that I was false of heart
Though absence seemed my flame to qualify:
As easy might I from myself depart
As from my soul, which in thy breast doth lie;
That is my home of love; if I have ranged,
Like him that travels, I return again,
Just to the time, not with the time exchanged,
So that myself bring water for my stain.
Never believe, though in my nature reigned
All frailties that besiege all kinds of blood,
That it could so preposterously be stained
To leave for nothing all thy sum of good!
  For nothing this wide universe I call,
  Save thou, my rose: in it thou art my all.

Let me not to the marriage of true minds
Admit impediments.   Love is not love
Which alters when it alteration finds,
Or bends with the remover to remove:
O, no! it is an ever-fixèd mark
That looks on tempests, and is never shaken;
It is the star to every wandering bark,
Whose worth's unknown, although his height be taken.
Love's not Time's fool, though rosy lips and cheeks
Within his bending sickle's compass come;
Love alters not with his brief hours and weeks,
But bears it out even to the edge of doom:
  If this be error, and upon me proved,
  I never writ, nor no man ever loved.

My mistress' eyes are nothing like the sun;
Coral is far more red than her lips' red;
If snow be white, why then her breasts are dun;
If hairs be wires, black wires grow on her head.

I have seen roses damasked, red and white,
But no such roses see I in her cheeks;
And in some perfumes is there more delight
Than in the breath that from my mistress reeks.
I love to hear her speak,—yet well I know
That music hath a far more pleasing sound;
I grant I never saw a goddess go,—
My mistress, when she walks, treads on the ground:
   And yet, by heaven, I think my love as rare
   As any she belied with false compare.

CXLVI

Poor soul, the centre of my sinful earth,
Pressed by these rebel powers that thee array,
Why dost thou pine within and suffer dearth,
Painting thy outward walls so costly gay?
Why so large cost, having so short a lease,
Dost thou upon thy fading mansion spend?
Shall worms, inheritors of this excess,
Eat up thy charge?   Is this thy body's end?
Then, soul, live thou upon thy servant's loss,
And let that pine to aggravate thy store;
Buy terms divine in selling hours of dross;
Within be fed, without be rich no more:
   So shalt thou feed on Death, that feeds on men;
   And Death once dead, there's no more dying then.
             William Shakespeare [1564–1616]

"ALEXIS, HERE SHE STAYED"

ALEXIS, here she stayed; among these pines,
Sweet hermitress, she did alone repair;
Here did she spread the treasure of her hair,
More rich than that brought from the Colchian mines.
She set her by these muskèd eglantines,
The happy place the print seems yet to bear;
Her voice did sweeten here thy sugared lines,
To which winds, trees, beasts, birds, did lend their ear.

Me here she first perceived, and here a morn
Of bright carnations did o'erspread her face;
Here did she sigh, here first my hopes were born,
And I first got a pledge of promised grace:
    But, ah! what served it to be happy so,
    Since passèd pleasures double but new woe?
               William Drummond [1585–1649]

"WERE I AS BASE AS IS THE LOWLY PLAIN"

WERE I as base as is the lowly plain,
And you, my love, as high as heaven above,
Yet should the thoughts of me, your humble swain,
Ascend to heaven in honor of my love.
Were I as high as heaven above the plain,
And you, my love, as humble and as low
As are the deepest bottoms of the main,
Wheresoe'er you were, with you my love should go.
Were you the earth, dear love, and I the skies,
My love should shine on you, like to the sun,
And look upon you with ten thousand eyes,
Till heaven waxed blind and till the world were done.
    Wheresoe'er I am,—below, or else above you,—
    Wheresoe'er you are, my heart shall truly love you.
               Joshua Sylvester [1563–1618]

A SONNET OF THE MOON

LOOK how the pale Queen of the silent night
Doth cause the ocean to attend upon her,
And he, as long as she is in his sight,
With his full tide is ready her to honor:
But when the silver wagon of the Moon
Is mounted up so high he cannot follow,
The sea calls home his crystal waves to moan,
And with low ebb doth manifest his sorrow.
So you that are the sovereign of my heart,
Have all my joys attending on your will,
My joys low-ebbing when you do depart,
When you return, their tide my heart doth fill.

So as you come, and as you do depart,
Joys ebb and flow within my tender heart.

Charles Best [fl. 1602]

TO MARY UNWIN

Mary! I want a lyre with other strings,
Such aid from Heaven as some have feigned they drew,
An eloquence scarce given to mortals, new
And undebased by praise of meaner things;
That, ere through age or woe I shed my wings,
I may record thy worth with honor due,
In verse as musical as thou art true,
And that immortalizes whom it sings:
But thou hast little need.   There is a Book
By seraphs writ with beams of heavenly light,
On which the eyes of God not rarely look,
A chronicle of actions just and bright:
      There all thy deeds, my faithful Mary, shine;
      And, since thou own'st that praise, I spare thee mine.

William Cowper [1731–1800]

"WHY ART THOU SILENT"

Why art thou silent?   Is thy love a plant
Of such weak fibre that the treacherous air
Of absence withers what was once so fair?
Is there no debt to pay, no boon to grant?
Yet have my thoughts for thee been vigilant,
Bound to thy service with unceasing care—
The mind's least generous wish a mendicant
For naught but what thy happiness could spare.
Speak!—though this soft warm heart, once free to hold
A thousand tender pleasures, thine and mine,
Be left more desolate, more dreary cold
Than a forsaken bird's-nest filled with snow
'Mid its own bush of leafless eglantine—
Speak, that my torturing doubts their end may know!

William Wordsworth [1770–1850]

SONNETS

From "The House of Life"

IV

LOVESIGHT

WHEN do I see thee most, belovèd one?
When in the light the spirits of mine eyes
Before thy face, their altar, solemnize
The worship of that Love through thee made known?
Or when in the dusk hours, (we two alone,)
Close-kissed and eloquent of still replies
Thy twilight-hidden glimmering visage lies,
And my soul only sees thy soul its own?
O love, my love! if I no more should see
Thyself, nor on the earth the shadow of thee,
Nor image of thine eyes in any spring,—
How then should sound upon Life's darkening slope
The ground-whirl of the perished leaves of Hope,
The wind of Death's imperishable wing?

V

HEART'S HOPE

By what word's power, the key of paths untrod,
Shall I the difficult deeps of Love explore,
Till parted waves of Song yield up the shore
Even as that sea which Israel crossed dryshod?
For lo! in some poor rhythmic period,
Lady, I fain would tell how evermore
Thy soul I know not from thy body, nor
Thee from myself, neither our love from God.
Yea, in God's name, and Love's, and thine, would I
Draw from one loving heart such evidence
As to all hearts all things shall signify;
Tender as dawn's first lull-fire, and intense
As instantaneous penetrating sense,
In Spring's birth-hour, of other Springs gone by.

XV
THE BIRTH-BOND

HAVE you not noted, in some family
Where two were born of a first marriage-bed,
How still they own their gracious bond, though fed
And nursed on the forgotten breast and knee?—
How to their father's children they shall be
In act and thought of one goodwill; but each
Shall for the other have, in silence speech,
And in a word complete community?
Even so, when first I saw you, seemed it, love,
That among souls allied to mine was yet
One nearer kindred than life hinted of.
O born with me somewhere that men forget,
And though in years of sight and sound unmet,
Known for my soul's birth-partner well enough!

XIX
SILENT NOON

YOUR hands lie open in the long fresh grass,—
The finger-points look through like rosy blooms:
Your eyes smile peace.   The pasture gleams and glooms
'Neath billowing skies that scatter and amass.
All round our nest, far as the eye can pass,
Are golden kingcup-fields with silver edge
Where the cow-parsley skirts the hawthorn-hedge.
'Tis visible silence, still as the hour-glass.
Deep in the sun-searched growths the dragon-fly
Hangs like a blue thread loosened from the sky:—
So this winged hour is dropped to us from above.
Oh! clasp we to our hearts, for deathless dower,
This close-companioned inarticulate hour
When twofold silence was the song of love.

XXVI
MID-RAPTURE

THOU lovely and belovèd, thou my love;
Whose kiss seems still the first; whose summoning eyes,
Even now, as for our love-world's new sunrise,
Shed very dawn; whose voice, attuned above

All modulation of the deep-bowered dove,
Is like a hand laid softly on the soul;
Whose hand is like a sweet voice to control
Those worn tired brows it hath the keeping of:—
What word can answer to thy word,—what gaze
To thine, which now absorbs within its sphere
My worshipping face, till I am mirrored there
Light-circled in a heaven of deep-drawn rays?
    What clasp, what kiss mine inmost heart can prove,
    O lovely and belovèd, O my love?

XXXI

HER GIFTS

HIGH grace, the dower of queens; and therewithal
Some wood-born wonder's sweet simplicity;
A glance like water brimming with the sky
Or hyacinth-light where forest-shadows fall;
Such thrilling pallor of cheek as doth enthrall
The heart; a mouth whose passionate forms imply
All music and all silence held thereby;
Deep golden locks, her sovereign coronal;
A round reared neck, meet column of Love's shrine
To cling to when the heart takes sanctuary;
Hands which for ever at Love's bidding be,
And soft-stirred feet still answering to his sign:—
    These are her gifts, as tongue may tell them o'er.
    Breathe low her name, my soul; for that means more.

XXXIV

THE DARK GLASS

NOT I myself know all my love for thee:
How should I reach so far, who cannot weigh
To-morrow's dower by gage of yesterday?
Shall birth and death, and all dark names that be
As doors and windows bared to some loud sea,
Lash deaf mine ears and blind my face with spray;
And shall my sense pierce love,—the last relay
And ultimate outpost of eternity?

Lo! what am I to Love, the lord of all?
One murmuring shell he gathers from the sand,—
One little heart-flame sheltered in his hand.
Yet through thine eyes he grants me clearest call
And veriest touch of powers primordial
That any hour-girt life may understand.

XLIX

WILLOWWOOD

I SAT with Love upon a woodside well,
Leaning across the water, I and he;
Nor ever did he speak nor looked at me,
But touched his lute wherein was audible
The certain secret thing he had to tell:
Only our mirrored eyes met silently
In the low wave; and that sound came to be
The passionate voice I knew; and my tears fell.
And at their fall, his eyes beneath grew hers;
And with his foot and with his wing-feathers
He swept the spring that watered my heart's drouth.
Then the dark ripples spread to waving hair,
And as I stooped, her own lips rising there
Bubbled with brimming kisses at my mouth.

LXXVIII

BODY'S BEAUTY

OF Adam's first wife, Lilith, it is told
(The witch he loved before the gift of Eve,)
That, ere the snake's, her sweet tongue could deceive,
And her enchanted hair was the first gold.
And still she sits, young while the earth is old,
And, subtly of herself contemplative,
Draws men to watch the bright web she can weave,
Till heart and body and life are in its hold.
The rose and poppy are her flowers: for where
Is he not found, O Lilith! whom shed scent
And soft-shed kisses and soft sleep shall snare?
Lo! as that youth's eyes burned at thine, so went

Thy spell through him, and left his straight neck bent,
And round his heart one strangling golden hair.

Dante Gabriel Rossetti [1828–1882]

SONNETS

MEETING

THEY made the chamber sweet with flowers and leaves,
And the bed sweet with flowers on which I lay;
While my soul, love-bound, loitered on its way.
I did not hear the birds about the eaves,
Nor hear the reapers talk among the sheaves:
Only my soul kept watch from day to day,
My thirsty soul kept watch for one away:—
Perhaps he loves, I thought, remembers, grieves.
At length there came the step upon the stair,
Upon the lock the old familiar hand:
Then first my spirit seemed to scent the air
Of Paradise; then first the tardy sand
Of time ran golden; and I felt my hair
Put on a glory, and my soul expand.

THE FIRST DAY

I WISH I could remember the first day,
First hour, first moment of your meeting me,
If bright or dim the season, it might be
Summer or Winter for aught I can say;
So unrecorded did it slip away,
So blind was I to see and to foresee,
So dull to mark the budding of my tree
That would not blossom yet for many a May.
If only I could recollect it, such
A day of days! I let it come and go
As traceless as a thaw of bygone snow;
It seemed to mean so little, meant so much;
If only now I could recall that touch,
First touch of hand in hand—Did one but know!

REMEMBER

REMEMBER me when I am gone away,
Gone far away into the silent land;
When you can no more hold me by the hand,
Nor I half turn to go, yet turning stay.
Remember me when no more, day by day,
You tell me of our future that you planned:
Only remember me; you understand
It will be late to counsel then or pray.
Yet if you should forget me for a while
And afterwards remember, do not grieve:
For if the darkness and corruption leave
A vestige of the thoughts that once I had,
Better by far you should forget and smile
Than that you should remember and be sad.

REST

O EARTH, lie heavily upon her eyes;
Seal her sweet eyes weary of watching, Earth;
Lie close around her; leave no room for mirth
With its harsh laughter, nor for sound of sighs.
She hath no questions, she hath no replies,
Hushed in and curtained with a blessèd dearth
Of all that irked her from the hour of birth;
With stillness that is almost Paradise.
Darkness more clear than noonday holdeth her,
Silence more musical than any song;
Even her very heart has ceased to stir:
Until the morning of Eternity
Her rest shall not begin nor end, but be;
And when she wakes she will not think it long.

Christina Georgina Rossetti [1830–1894]

HOW MY SONGS OF HER BEGAN

GOD made my lady lovely to behold;—
Above the painter's dream he set her face,
And wrought her body in divinest grace;
He touched the brown hair with a sense of gold,

And in the perfect form He did enfold
What was alone as perfect, the sweet heart;
Knowledge most rare to her He did impart,
And filled with love and worship all her days.
And then God thought Him how it would be well
To give her music, and to Love He said,
"Bring thou some minstrel now that he may tell
How fair and sweet a thing My hands have made."
Then at Love's call I came, bowed down my head,
And at His will my lyre grew audible.

Philip Bourke Marston [1850–1887]

AT THE LAST

BECAUSE the shadows deepened verily,—
Because the end of all seemed near, forsooth,—
Her gracious spirit, ever quick to ruth,
Had pity on her bond-slave, even on me.
She came in with the twilight noiselessly,
Fair as a rose, immaculate as Truth;
She leaned above my wrecked and wasted youth;
I felt her presence, which I could not see.
"God keep you, my poor friend," I heard her say;
And then she kissed my dry, hot lips and eyes.
Kiss *thou* the next kiss, quiet Death, I pray;
Be instant on this hour, and so surprise
My spirit while the vision seems to stay;
Take thou the heart with the heart's Paradise.

Philip Bourke Marston [1850–1887]

TO ONE WHO WOULD MAKE A CONFESSION

OH! leave the past to bury its own dead.
The past is naught to us, the present all.
What need of last year's leaves to strew Love's bed?
What need of ghosts to grace a festival?
I would not, if I could, those days recall,
Those days not ours. For us the feast is spread,
The lamps are lit, and music plays withal.
Then let us love and leave the rest unsaid.

This island is our home.   Around it roar
Great gulfs and oceans, channels, straits and seas.
What matter in what wreck we reached the shore,
So we both reached it?   We can mock at these.
   Oh! leave the past, if past indeed there be;
   I would not know it; I would know but thee.

Wilfrid Scawen Blunt [1840–1922]

THE PLEASURES OF LOVE

I DO not care for kisses.   'Tis a debt
We paid for the first privilege of love.
These are the rains of April which have wet
Our fallow hearts and forced their germs to move.
Now the green corn has sprouted.   Each new day
Brings better pleasures, a more dear surprise,
The blade, the ear, the harvest—and our way
Leads through a region wealthy grown and wise.
We now compare our fortunes.   Each his store
Displays to kindred eyes of garnered grain,
Two happy farmers, learned in love's lore,
Who weigh and touch and argue and complain—
   Dear endless argument!   Yet sometimes we
   Even as we argue kiss.   There! Let it be.

Wilfrid Scawen Blunt [1840–1922]

"WERE BUT MY SPIRIT LOOSED UPON THE AIR"

WERE but my spirit loosed upon the air,—
By some High Power who could Life's chains unbind,
Set free to seek what most it longs to find,—
To no proud Court of Kings would I repair:
I would but climb, once more, a narrow stair,
When day was wearing late, and dusk was kind;
And one should greet me to my failings blind,
Content so I but shared his twilight there.
Nay! well I know he waits not as of old,—
I could not find him in the old-time place,—

I must pursue him, made by sorrow bold,
Through worlds unknown, in strange celestial race,
Whose mystic round no traveller has told,
From star to star, until I see his face.

Louise Chandler Moulton [1835–1908]

RENOUNCEMENT

I MUST not think of thee; and, tired yet strong,
I shun the thought that lurks in all delight—
The thought of thee—and in the blue heaven's height,
And in the dearest passage of a song.
Oh, just beyond the fairest thoughts that throng
This breast, the thought of thee waits, hidden yet bright
But it must never, never come in sight;
I must stop short of thee the whole day long.
But when sleep comes to close each difficult day,
When night gives pause to the long watch I keep,
And all my bonds I needs must loose apart,
Must doff my will as raiment laid away,—
With the first dream that comes with the first sleep
I run, I run, I am gathered to thy heart.

Alice Meynell [1850–1922]

"MY LOVE FOR THEE"

My love for thee doth march like armèd men,
Against a queenly city they would take.
Along the army's front its banners shake;
Across the mountain and the sun-smit plain
It steadfast sweeps as sweeps the steadfast rain;
And now the trumpet makes the still air quake,
And now the thundering cannon doth awake
Echo on echo, echoing loud again.
But, lo! the conquest higher than bard e'er sung:
Instead of answering cannon, proud surrender!
Joyful the iron gates are open flung
And, for the conqueror, welcome gay and tender!
    O, bright the invader's path with tribute flowers,
    While comrade flags flame forth on wall and towers!

Richard Watson Gilder [1844–1909]

SONNETS
AFTER THE ITALIAN

I KNOW not if I love her overmuch;
But this I know, that when unto her face
She lifts her hand, which rests there, still, a space,
Then slowly falls—'tis I who feel that touch.
And when she sudden shakes her head, with such
A look, I soon her secret meaning trace.
So when she runs I think 'tis I who race.
Like a poor cripple who has lost his crutch
I am if she is gone; and when she goes,
I know not why, for that is a strange art—
As if myself should from myself depart.
I know not if I love her more than those
Who long her light have known; but for the rose
She covers in her hair, I'd give my heart.

I like her gentle hand that sometimes strays,
To find the place, through the same book with mine;
I like her feet; and O, those eyes divine!
And when we say farewell, perhaps she stays
Love-lingering—then hurries on her ways,
As if she thought, "To end my pain and thine."
I like her voice better than new-made wine;
I like the mandolin whereon she plays.
And I like, too, the cloak I saw her wear,
And the red scarf that her white neck doth cover,
And well I like the door that she comes through;
I like the ribbon that doth bind her hair—
But then, in truth, I am that lady's lover,
And every new day there is something new.

Richard Watson Gilder [1844–1909]

STANZAS
From "Modern Love"

I

By this he knew she wept with waking eyes:
That, at his hand's light quiver by her head,
The strange low sobs that shook their common bed
Were called into her with a sharp surprise,

And strangled mute, like little gaping snakes,
Dreadfully venomous to him.   She lay
Stone-still, and the long darkness flowed away
With muffled pulses.   Then as midnight makes
Her giant heart of Memory and Tears
Drink the pale drug of silence, and so beat
Sleep's heavy measure, they from head to feet
Were moveless, looking through their dead black years,
By vain regret scrawled over the blank wall.
Like sculptured effigies they might be seen
Upon their marriage-tomb, the sword between;
Each wishing for the sword that severs all.

II

It ended, and the morrow brought the task.
Her eyes were guilty gates, that let him in
By shutting all too zealous for their sin:
Each sucked a secret, and each wore a mask.
But, oh, the bitter taste her beauty had!
He sickened as at breath of poison-flowers:
A languid humor stole among the hours,
And if their smiles encountered, he went mad,
And raged deep inward, till the light was brown
Before his vision, and the world forgot,
Looked wicked as some old dull murder-spot.
A star with lurid beams, she seemed to crown
The pit of infamy: and then again
He fainted on his vengefulness, and strove
To ape the magnanimity of love,
And smote himself, a shuddering heap of pain.

III

This was the woman; what now of the man?
But pass him.   If he comes beneath a heel,
He shall be crushed until he cannot feel,
Or, being callous, haply till he can.
But he is nothing:—nothing?   Only mark
The rich light striking out from her on him!
Ha! what a sense it is when her eyes swim
Across the man she singles, leaving dark

All else! Lord God, who mad'st the thing so fair,
See that I am drawn to her, even now!
It cannot be such harm on her cool brow
To plant a kiss? Yet if I meet him there!
But she is mine! Ah, no! I know too well
I claim a star whose light is overcast:
I claim a phantom-woman in the Past.
The hour has struck, though I heard not the bell!

XIV

What soul would bargain for a cure that brings
Contempt the nobler agony to kill?
Rather let me bear on the bitter ill,
And strike this rusty bosom with new stings!
It seems there is another veering fit,
Since on a gold-haired lady's eyeballs pure,
I looked with little prospect of a cure,
The while her mouth's red bow loosed shafts of wit.
Just heaven! can it be true that jealousy
Has decked the woman thus? and does her head
Swim somewhat for possessions forfeited?
Madam, you teach me many things that be.
I open an old book, and there I find,
That "Women still may love whom they deceive."
Such love I prize not, madam: by your leave,
The game you play at is not to my mind.

XVI

In our old shipwrecked days there was an hour
When in the firelight steadily aglow,
Joined slackly, we beheld the red chasm grow
Among the clicking coals. Our library-bower
That eve was left to us: and hushed we sat
As lovers to whom Time is whispering.
From sudden-opened doors we heard them sing:
The nodding elders mixed good wine with chat.
Well knew we that Life's greatest treasure lay
With us, and of it was our talk. "Ah, yes!
Love dies!" I said: I never thought it less.
She yearned to me that sentence to unsay.

Then when the fire domed blackening, I found
Her cheek was salt against my kiss, and swift
Up the sharp scale of sobs her breast did lift:—
Now am I haunted by that taste! that sound!

XXVI

Love ere he bleeds, an eagle in high skies,
Has earth beneath his wings: from reddened eve
He views the rosy dawn.   In vain they weave
The fatal web below while far he flies.
But when the arrow strikes him, there's a change.
He moves but in the track of his spent pain,
Whose red drops are the links of a harsh chain,
Binding him to the ground, with narrow range.
A subtle serpent then has Love become.
I had the eagle in my bosom erst:
Henceforward with the serpent I am cursed.
I can interpret where the mouth is dumb.
Speak, and I see the side-lie of a truth.
Perchance my heart may pardon you this deed:
But be no coward:—you that made Love bleed,
You must bear all the venom of his tooth!

XLI

How many a thing which we cast to the ground,
When others pick it up becomes a gem!
We grasp at all the wealth it is to them;
And by reflected light its worth is found.
Yet for us still 'tis nothing! and that zeal
Of false appreciation quickly fades.
This truth is little known to human shades,
How rare from their own instinct 'tis to feel!
They waste the soul with spurious desire,
That is not the ripe flame upon the bough.
We two have taken up a lifeless vow
To rob a living passion: dust for fire!
Madam is grave, and eyes the clock that tells
Approaching midnight.   We have struck despair
Into two hearts.   O, look we like a pair
Who for fresh nuptials joyfully yield all else?

XLIII

MARK where the pressing wind shoots javelin-like,
Its skeleton shadow on the broad-backed wave!
Here is a fitting spot to dig Love's grave;
Here where the ponderous breakers plunge and strike,
And dart their hissing tongues high up the sand:
In hearing of the ocean, and in sight
Of those ribbed wind-streaks running into white.
If I the death of Love had deeply planned,
I never could have made it half so sure,
As by the unblest kisses which upbraid
The full-waked sense; or failing that, degrade!
'Tis morning: but no morning can restore
What we have forfeited. I see no sin:
The wrong is mixed. In tragic life, God wot,
No villain need be! Passions spin the plot:
We are betrayed by what is false within.

XLIX

He found her by the ocean's moaning verge,
Nor any wicked change in her discerned;
And she believed his old love had returned,
Which was her exultation, and her scourge.
She took his hand, and walked with him, and seemed
The wife he sought, though shadow-like and dry.
She had one terror, lest her heart should sigh,
And tell her loudly she no longer dreamed.
She dared not say, "This is my breast: look in."
But there's a strength to help the desperate weak.
That night he learned how silence best can speak
The awful things when Pity pleads for Sin.
About the middle of the night her call
Was heard, and he came wondering to the bed.
"Now kiss me, dear! it may be, now!" she said.
Lethe had passed those lips, and he knew all.

L

Thus piteously Love closed what he begat:
The union of this ever-diverse pair!

These two were rapid falcons in a snare,
Condemned to do the flitting of the bat.
Lovers beneath the singing sky of May,
They wandered once; clear as the dew on flowers:
But they fed not on the advancing hours:
Their hearts held cravings for the buried day.
Then each applied to each that fatal knife,
Deep questioning, which probes to endless dole.
Ah, what a dusty answer gets the soul
When hot for certainties in this our life!—
In tragic hints here see what evermore
Moves dark as yonder midnight ocean's force,
Thundering like ramping hosts of warrior horse,
To throw that faint thin line upon the shore!

George Meredith [1828–1909]

LOVE IN THE WINDS

WHEN I am standing on a mountain crest,
Or hold the tiller in the dashing spray,
My love of you leaps foaming in my breast,
Shouts with the winds and sweeps to their foray;
My heart bounds with the horses of the sea,
And plunges in the wild ride of the night,
Flaunts in the teeth of tempest the large glee
That rides out Fate and welcomes gods to fight.
Ho, love, I laugh aloud for love of you,
Glad that our love is fellow to rough weather,—
No fretful orchid hothoused from the dew,
But hale and hardy as the highland heather,
    Rejoicing in the wind that stings and thrills,
    Comrade of ocean, playmate of the hills.

Richard Hovey [1864–1900]

"OH! DEATH WILL FIND ME"

OH! Death will find me, long before I tire
Of watching you; and swing me suddenly
Into the shade and loneliness and mire
Of the last land! There, waiting patiently,
One day, I think, I'll feel a cool wind blowing,
See a slow light across the Stygian tide,
And hear the Dead about me stir, unknowing,
And tremble. And *I* shall know that you have died.

And watch you, a broad-browed and smiling dream,
Pass, light as ever, through the lightless host,
Quietly ponder, start, and sway, and gleam—
Most individual and bewildering ghost!—
And turn, and toss your brown delightful head
Amusedly, among the ancient Dead.

Rupert Brooke [1887–1915]

THE BUSY HEART

Now that we've done our best and worst, and parted,
I would fill my mind with thoughts that will not rend.
(O heart, I do not dare go empty-hearted)
I'll think of Love in books, Love without end;
Women with child, content; and old men sleeping;
And wet strong ploughlands, scarred for certain grain;
And babes that weep, and so forget their weeping;
And the young heavens, forgetful after rain;
And evening hush, broken by homing wings;
And Song's nobility and Wisdom holy,
That live, we dead. I would think of a thousand things,
Lovely and durable, and taste them slowly,
One after one, like tasting a sweet food.
I have need to busy my heart with quietude.

Rupert Brooke [1887–1915]

THE HILL

BREATHLESS, we flung us on the windy hill,
Laughed in the sun, and kissed the lovely grass.
You said, "Through glory and ecstasy we pass;
Wind, sun, and earth remain, the birds sing still,
When we are old, are old. . . ." "And when we die
All's over that is ours; and life burns on
Through other lovers, other lips," said I,
—"Heart of my heart, our heaven is now, is won!"
"We are Earth's best, that learnt her lesson here.
Life is our cry. We have kept the faith!" we said;
"We shall go down with unreluctant tread
Rose-crowned into the darkness!" . . . Proud we were,
And laughed, that had such brave true things to say.
—And then you suddenly cried, and turned away.

Rupert Brooke [1887–1915]

SONNETS

From " Sonnets to Miranda "

I

DAUGHTER of her whose face, and lofty name
Prenuptial, of old States and Cities speak,
Where lands of wine look north to peak on peak
Of the overwatching Alps: through her, you claim
Kinship with vanished Power, unvanished Fame;
And midst a world grown colorless and bleak
I see the blood of Doges in your cheek,
And in your hair the Titian tints of flame.
Daughter of England too, you first drew breath
Where our coy Springs to our coy Summers yield;
And you descend from one whose lance and shield
Were with the grandsire of Elizabeth,
When the Plantagenet saw the avenger Death
Toward him spurring over Bosworth field.

II

If you had lived in that more stately time
When men remembered the great Tudor queen,
To noblest verse your name had wedded been,
And you for ever crowned with golden rhyme.
If, mid Lorenzo's Florence, made sublime
By Art's Re-Birth, you had moved, a Muse serene,
The mightiest limners had revealed your mien
To all the ages and each wondering clime.
Fled are the singers that from language drew
Its virgin secrets; and in narrow space
The mightiest limners sleep: and only He,
The Eternal Artist, still creates anew
That which is fairer than all song—the grace
That takes the world into captivity.

III

I dare but sing of you in such a strain
As may beseem the wandering harper's tongue,
Who of the glory of his Queen hath sung,
Outside her castle gates in wind and rain.

She, seated mid the noblest of her train,
In her great halls with pictured arras hung,
Hardly can know what melody hath rung
Through the forgetting night, and rung in vain.
He, with one word from her to whom he brings
The loyal heart that she alone can sway,
Would be made rich for ever; but he sings
Of queenhood too aloof, too great, to say
"Sing on, sing on, O minstrel"—though he flings
His soul to the winds that whirl his songs away.

V

I cast these lyric offerings at your feet,
And ask you but to fling them not away:
There suffer them to rest, till even they,
By happy nearness to yourself, grow sweet.
He that hath shaped and wrought them holds it meet
That you be sung, not in some artless way,
But with such pcmp and ritual as when May
Sends her full choir, the thronèd Morn to greet.
With something caught from your own lofty air,
With something learned from your own highborn grace,
Song must approach your presence; must forbear
All light and easy accost; and yet abase
Its own proud spirit in awe and reverence there,
Before the Wonder of your form and face.

VI

I move amid your throng, I watch you hold
Converse with many who are noble and fair,
Yourself the noblest and the fairest there,
Reigning supreme, crowned with that living gold.
I talk with men whose names have been enrolled
In England's book of honor; and I share
With these *one* honor—your regard; and wear
Your friendship as a jewel of worth untold.
And then I go from out your spherèd light
Into a world which still seems full of You.
I know the stars are yonder, that possess
Their ancient seats, heedless what mortals do;

But I behold in all the range of Night
Only the splendor of your loveliness.

VIII

If I had never known your face at all,
Had only heard you speak, beyond thick screen
Of leaves, in an old garden, when the sheen
Of morning dwelt on dial and ivied wall,
I think your voice had been enough to call
Yourself before me, in living vision seen,
So pregnant with your Essence had it been,
So charged with You, in each soft rise and fall.
At least I know, that when upon the night
With chanted word your voice lets loose your soul,
I am pierced, I am pierced and cloven, with Delight
That hath all Pain within it, and the whole
World's tears, all ecstasy of inward sight,
And the blind cry of all the seas that roll.

William Watson [1858–1935]

SONNETS

From "Thysia"

II

TWIN songs there are, of joyance, or of pain;
One of the morning lark in midmost sky,
When falls to earth a mist, a silver rain,
A glittering cascade of melody;
And mead and wold and the wide heaven rejoice,
And praise the Maker; but alone I kneel
In sorrowing prayer.   Then wanes the day; a voice
Trembles along the dusk, till peal on peal
It pierces every living heart that hears,
Pierces and burns and purifies like fire;
Again I kneel under the starry spheres,
And all my soul seems healed, and lifted higher,
   Nor could that jubilant song of day prevail
   Like thine of tender grief, O nightingale.

III

Bow down, my song, before her presence high,
In that far world where you must seek her now;
Say that you bring to her no sonnetry,
But plain-set anguish of the breast or brow;
Say that on earth I sang to her alone,
But now, while in her heaven she sits divine,
Turning, I tell the world my bitter moan,
Bidding it share its hopes and griefs with mine,
Versing not what I would, but what I must,
Wail of the wind, or sobbing of the wave;
Ah! say you raised my bowed head from the dust,
And held me backward from a willful grave;
    Say this, and her sweet pity will approve,
    And bind yet closer her dead bond of love.

VII

I watch beside you in your silent room;
Without, the chill rain falls, life dies away,
The dead leaves drip, and the fast-gathering gloom
Closes around this brief November day,
First day of holy death, of sacred rest;
I kiss your brow, calm, beautiful and cold,
I lay my yearning arms across your breast,
I claim our darling rapture as of old;
Dear heart, I linger but a little space,
Sweet wife, I come to your new world ere long;
This lily—keep it till our next embrace,
While the mute Angel makes our love more strong,
    While here I cling, in life's short agony,
    To God, and to your deathless memory.

XVI

Comes the New Year; wailing the north winds blow;
In her cold, lonely grave my dead love lies;
Dead lies the stiffened earth beneath the snow,
And blinding sleet blots out the desolate skies;
I stand between the living and the dead;
Hateful to me is life, hateful is death;

Her life was sad, and on that narrow bed
She will not turn, nor wake with human breath.
I kneel between the evil and the good;
The struggle o'er, this one sweet faith have I—
Though life and death be dimly understood,
She loved me; I loved her; love cannot die;
   Go then thy way with thine accustomed cheer,
   Nor heed my churlish greeting, O New Year.

XXIII

Like some lone miser, dear, behold me stand,
To count my treasures, and their worth extol:—
A last word penciled by that poor left hand;
Two kindred names on the same gentle scroll,
(I found it near your pillow,) traced below;
This little scarf you made, our latest pride;
The violet I digged so long ago,
That nestled in your bosom till you died;
But dearest to my heart, whereon it lies,
Is one warm tress of your luxuriant hair,
Still present to my touch, my lips, my eyes,
Forever changeless, and forever fair,
   And even in your grave, beauteous and free
   From the cold grasp of mutability.

XXXVI

So sang I in the springtime of my years—
"There's nothing we can call our own but love;"
So let me murmur now that winter nears,
And even in death the deathless truth approve.
Oft have I seen the slow, the broadening river
Roll its glad waters to the parent sea;
Death is the call of love to love; the giver
Claims his own gift for some new mystery.
In boundless love divine the heavens are spread,
In wedded love is earth's divinest store,
And he that liveth to himself is dead,
And he that lives for love lives evermore;
   Only in love can life's true path be trod;
   Love is self-giving; therefore love is God.

XXXVII

Hear, O Self-Giver, infinite as good;
This faith, at least, my wavering heart should hold,
Nor find in dark regret its daily food,
But catch the gleam of glories yet untold.
Yea, even on earth, beloved, as love well knew,
Brief absence brought our fond returning kiss,
So let my soul to God's great world and you
Look onward with sweet pain of secret bliss;—
O sunset sky and lonely gleaming star,
Your beauty thrills me from the bound of space,
O Love, thy loveliness shows best afar,
And only Heaven shall give thee perfect grace;
    Grant then, dear Lord, that all who love may be
    Heirs of Thy glorious Immortality.

XLV

How shall I tell the measure of my love?
'Tis vain that I have given thee vows and tears,
Or striven in verse my tenderness to prove,
Or held thy hand in journeyings through the years;
Vain that I follow now with hastening feet,
And sing thy death, still murmuring in my song,
"Only for thee I would the strain were sweet,
Only for thee I would the words were strong;"
Vain even that I closed with death, and fought
To hold thee longer in a world so dear,
Vain that I count a weary world as naught,
That I would die to bring thee back; I hear
    God answer me from heaven, O angel wife—
    "To prove thy love, live thou a nobler life."

Morton Luce [1849–

SONNETS

From "Sonnets from the Portuguese"

I

I THOUGHT once how Theocritus had sung
Of the sweet years, the dear and wished-for years,
Who each one in a gracious hand appears
To bear a gift for mortals, old or young:

And, as I mused it in his antique tongue,
I saw, in gradual vision through my tears,
The sweet, sad years, the melancholy years,
Those of my own life, who by turns had flung
A shadow across me. Straightway I was 'ware,
So weeping, how a mystic Shape did move
Behind me, and drew me backward by the hair;
And a voice said in mastery, while I strove,—
"Guess now who holds thee?"—"Death," I said. But, there,
The silver answer rang,—"Not Death, but Love."

III

Unlike are we, unlike, O princely Heart!
Unlike our uses and our destinies.
Our ministering two angels look surprise
On one another, as they strike athwart
Their wings in passing. Thou, bethink thee, **art**
A guest for queens to social pageantries,
With gages from a hundred brighter eyes
Than tears even can make mine, to play thy part
Of chief musician. What hast *thou* to do
With looking from the lattice-lights at me,
A poor, tired, wandering singer, singing through
The dark, and leaning up a cypress tree?
The chrism is on thine head,—on mine, the dew,—
And Death must dig the level where these agree.

VI

Go from me. Yet I feel that I shall stand
Henceforward in thy shadow. Nevermore
Alone upon the threshold of my door
Of individual life, I shall command
The uses of my soul, nor lift my hand
Serenely in the sunshine as before,
Without the sense of that which I forbore,—
Thy touch upon the palm. The widest land
Doom takes to part us, leaves thy heart in mine
With pulses that beat double. What I do
And what I dream include thee, as the wine
Must taste of its own grapes. And when I sue

God for myself, He hears that name of thine,
And sees within my eyes the tears of two.

VII

The face of all the world is changed, I think,
Since first I heard the footsteps of thy soul
Move still, oh, still, beside me, as they stole
Betwixt me and the dreadful outer brink
Of obvious death, where I, who thought to sink,
Was caught up into love, and taught the whole
Of life in a new rhythm.   The cup of dole
God gave for baptism, I am fain to drink,
And praise its sweetness, Sweet, with thee anear.
The name of country, heaven, are changed away
For where thou art or shalt be, there or here;
And this . . . this lute and song . . . loved yesterday,
(The singing angels know) are only dear
Because thy name moves right in what they say.

VIII

What can I give thee back, O liberal
And princely giver, who hast brought the gold
And purple of thine heart, unstained, untold,
And laid them on the outside of the wall
For such as I to take or leave withal,
In unexpected largess? Am I cold,
Ungrateful, that for these most manifold
High gifts, I render nothing back at all?
Not so; not cold,—but very poor instead.
Ask God who knows.   For frequent tears have run
The colors from my life, and left so dead
And pale a stuff, it were not fitly done
To give the same as pillow to thy head.
Go farther! let it serve to trample on.

IX

Can it be right to give what I can give?
To let thee sit beneath the fall of tears
As salt as mine, and hear the sighing years
Re-sighing on my lips renunciative

Through those infrequent smiles which fail to live
For all thy adjurations?   O my fears,
That this can scarce be right!   We are not peers
So to be lovers; and I own, and grieve,
That givers of such gifts as mine are, must
Be counted with the ungenerous.   Out, alas!
I will not soil thy purple with my dust,
Nor breathe my poison on thy Venice-glass,
Nor give thee any love—which were unjust.
Beloved, I only love thee! let it pass.

X

Yet, love, mere love, is beautiful indeed
And worthy of acceptation.   Fire is bright,
Let temple burn, or flax; an equal light
Leaps in the flame from cedar-plank or weed:
And love is fire.   And when I say at need
I love thee . . . mark! . . . *I love thee*—in thy sight
I stand transfigured, glorified aright,
With conscience of the new rays that proceed
Out of my face toward thine.   There's nothing low
In love, when love the lowest: meanest creatures
Who love God, God accepts while loving so.
And what I *feel*, across the inferior features
Of what I *am*, doth flash itself, and show
How that great work of Love enhances Nature's.

XII

Indeed this very love which is my boast,
And which, when rising up from breast to brow,
Doth crown me with a ruby large enow
To draw men's eyes and prove the inner cost,—
This love even, all my worth, to the uttermost,
I should not love withal, unless that thou
Hadst set me an example, shown me how,
When first thine earnest eyes with mine were crossed,
And love called love.   And thus, I cannot speak
Of love even, as a good thing of my own:
Thy soul hath snatched up mine all faint and weak,
And placed it by thee on a golden throne,—

And that I love (O soul, we must be meek!)
Is by thee only, whom I love alone.

XIV

If thou must love me, let it be for naught
Except for love's sake only. Do not say
"I love her for her smile—her look—her way
Of speaking gently,—for a trick of thought
That falls in well with mine, and certes brought
A sense of pleasant ease on such a day"—
For these things in themselves, Belovèd, may
Be changed, or change for thee,—and love, so wrought,
May be unwrought so. Neither love me for
Thine own dear pity's wiping my cheeks dry,—
A creature might forget to weep, who bore
Thy comfort long, and lose thy love thereby!
But love me for love's sake, that evermore
Thou may'st love on, through love's eternity.

XVII

My poet, thou canst touch on all the notes
God set between His After and Before,
And strike up and strike off the general roar
Of the rushing worlds a melody that floats
In a serene air purely. Antidotes
Of medicated music, answering for
Mankind's forlornest uses, thou canst pour
From thence into their ears. God's will devotes
Thine to such ends, and mine to wait on thine.
How, Dearest, wilt thou have me for most use?
A hope, to sing by gladly? or a fine
Sad memory, with thy songs to interfuse?
A shade, in which to sing—of palm or pine?
A grave, on which to rest from singing? Choose.

XVIII

I never gave a lock of hair away
To a man, Dearest, except this to thee,
Which now upon my fingers thoughtfully
I ring out to the full brown length and say

"Take it."   My day of youth went yesterday;
My hair no longer bounds to my foot's glee,
Nor plant I it from rose or myrtle-tree,
As girls do, any more: it only may
Now shade on two pale cheeks the mark of tears,
Taught drooping from the head that hangs aside
Through sorrow's trick.   I thought the funeral-shears
Would take this first, but Love is justified,—
Take it thou,—finding pure, from all those years,
The kiss my mother left here when she died.

XXI

Say over again, and yet once over again,
That thou dost love me.   Though the word repeated
Should seem "a cuckoo-song," as thou dost treat it,
Remember, never to the hill or plain,
Valley and wood, without her cuckoo-strain,
Comes the fresh Spring in all her green completed.
Belovèd, I, amid the darkness greeted
By a doubtful spirit-voice, in that doubt's pain
Cry: "Speak once more—thou lovest!"   Who can fear
Too many stars, though each in heaven shall roll,
Too many flowers, though each shall crown the year?
Say thou dost love me, love me, love me,—toll
The silver iterance!—only minding, Dear,
To love me also in silence with thy soul.

XXII

When our two souls stand up erect and strong,
Face to face, silent, drawing nigh and nigher,
Until the lengthening wings break into fire
At either curvèd point,—what bitter wrong
Can the earth do us, that we should not long
Be here contented?   Think.   In mounting higher,
The angels would press on us and aspire
To drop some golden orb of perfect song
Into our deep, dear silence.   Let us stay
Rather on earth, Belovèd,—where the unfit
Contrarious moods of men recoil away
And isolate pure spirits, and permit

A place to stand and love in for a day,
With darkness and the death-hour rounding it.

XXVIII

My letters! all dead paper, mute and white!
And yet they seem alive and quivering
Against my tremulous hands which loose the string
And let them drop down on my knee to-night.
This said,—he wished to have me in his sight
Once, as a friend: this fixed a day in spring
To come and touch my hand . . . a simple thing,
Yet I wept for it!—this, . . . the paper's light . . .
Said, *Dear, I love thee;* and I sank and quailed,
As if God's future thundered on my past.
This said, *I am thine,*—and so its ink has paled
With lying at my heart that beat too fast.
And this . . . O Love, thy words have ill availed,
If, what this said, I dared repeat at last!

XXXVIII

First time he kissed me, he but only kissed
The fingers of this hand wherewith I write;
And ever since, it grew more clean and white,
Slow to world-greetings, quick with its "Oh, list,"
When the angels speak. A ring of amethyst
I could not wear here, plainer to my sight,
Than that first kiss. The second passed in height
The first, and sought the forehead, and half missed,
Half falling on the hair. O beyond meed!
That was the chrism of love, which love's own crown,
With sanctifying sweetness, did precede.
The third upon my lips was folded down
In perfect, purple state; since when, indeed,
I have been proud, and said, "My love, my own!"

XLIII

How do I love thee? Let me count the ways.
I love thee to the depth and breadth and height
My soul can reach, when feeling out of sight
For the ends of Being and ideal Grace.

I love thee to the level of everyday's
Most quiet need, by sun and candle-light.
I love thee freely, as men strive for Right;
I love thee purely, as they turn from Praise.
I love thee with the passion put to use
In my old griefs, and with my childhood's faith.
I love thee with a love I seemed to lose
With my lost saints,—I love thee with the breath,
Smiles, tears, of all my life!—and, if God choose,
I shall but love thee better after death.

Elizabeth Barrett Browning [1806–1861]

ONE WORD MORE

TO E. B. B.

I

THERE they are, my fifty men and women
Naming me the fifty poems finished!
Take them, Love, the book and me together;
Where the heart lies, let the brain lie also.

II

Rafael made a century of sonnets,
Made and wrote them in a certain volume
Dinted with the silver-pointed pencil
Else he only used to draw Madonnas:
These, the world might view—but one, the volume.
Who that one, you ask? Your heart instructs you.
Did she live and love it all her lifetime?
Did she drop, his lady of the sonnets,
Die, and let it drop beside her pillow
Where it lay in place of Rafael's glory,
Rafael's cheek so duteous and so loving—
Cheek, the world was wont to hail a painter's,
Rafael's cheek, her love had turned a poet's?

III

You and I would rather read that volume,
(Taken to his beating bosom by it)
Lean and list the bosom-beats of Rafael,
Would we not? than wonder at Madonnas—
Her, San Sisto names, and Her, Foligno,
Her, that visits Florence in a vision,
Her, that's left with lilies in the Louvre—
Seen by us and all the world in circle.

IV

You and I will never read that volume.
Guido Reni, like his own eye's apple

Guarded long the treasure-book and loved it.
Guido Reni dying, all Bologna
Cried, and the world cried too, "Ours, the treasure!"
Suddenly, as rare things will, it vanished.

V

Dante once prepared to paint an angel:
Whom to please?   You whisper "Beatrice."
While he mused and traced it and retraced it,
(Peradventure with a pen corroded
Still by drops of that hot ink he dipped for,
When, his left hand i' the hair o' the wicked,
Back he held the brow and pricked its stigma,
Bit into the live man's flesh for parchment,
Loosed him, laughed to see the writing rankle,
Let the wretch go festering through Florence)--
Dante, who loved well because he hated,
Hated wickedness that hinders loving,
Dante standing, studying his angel,—
In there broke the folk of his Inferno.
Says he—"Certain people of importance"
(Such he gave his daily dreadful line to)
"Entered and would seize, forsooth, the poet."
Says the poet—"Then I stopped my painting."

VI

You and I would rather see that angel,
Painted by the tenderness of Dante,
Would we not?—than read a fresh Inferno.

VII

You and I will never see that picture.
While he mused on love and Beatrice,
While he softened o'er his outlined angel,
In they broke, those "people of importance":
We and Bice bear the loss forever.

VIII

What of Rafael's sonnets, Dante's picture?
This: no artist lives and loves, that longs not

Once, and only once, and for one only,
(Ah, the prize!) to find his love a language
Fit and fair and simple and sufficient—
Using nature that's an art to others,
Not, this one time, art that's turned his nature.
Ay, of all the artists living, loving,
None but would forego his proper dowry,—
Does he paint? he fain would write a poem,—
Does he write? he fain would paint a picture,
Put to proof art alien to the artist's,
Once, and only once, and for one only,
So to be the man and leave the artist,
Gain the man's joy, miss the artist's sorrow.

IX

Wherefore?   Heaven's gift takes earth's abatement!
He who smites the rock and spreads the water,
Bidding drink and live a crowd beneath him,
Even he, the minute makes immortal,
Proves, perchance, but mortal in the minute,
Desecrates, belike, the deed in doing.
While he smites, how can he but remember,
So he smote before, in such a peril,
When they stood and mocked—"Shall smiting help us?"
When they drank and sneered—"A stroke is easy!"
When they wiped their mouths and went their journey,
Throwing him for thanks—"But drought was pleasant."
Thus old memories mar the actual triumph;
Thus the doing savors of disrelish;
Thus achievement lacks a gracious somewhat;
O'er-importuned brows becloud the mandate,
Carelessness or consciousness—the gesture.
For he bears an ancient wrong about him,
Sees and knows again those phalanxed faces,
Hears, yet one time more, the 'customed prelude—
"How shouldst thou of all men, smite, and save us?"
Guesses what is like to prove the sequel—
"Egypt's flesh-pots—nay, the drought was better."

X

Oh, the crowd must have emphatic warrant!
Theirs, the Sinai-forehead's cloven brilliance,
Right-arm's rod-sweep, tongue's imperial fiat.
Never dares the man put off the prophet.

XI

Did he love one face from out the thousands,
(Were she Jethro's daughter, white and wifely,
Were she but the Æthiopian bondslave,)
He would envy yon dumb patient camel,
Keeping a reserve of scanty water
Meant to save his own life in the desert;
Ready in the desert to deliver
(Kneeling down to let his breast be opened)
Hoard and life together for his mistress.

XII

I shall never, in the years remaining,
Paint you pictures, no, nor carve you statues,
Make you music that should all-express me;
So it seems: I stand on my attainment.
This of verse alone, one life allows me;
Verse and nothing else have I to give you.
Other heights in other lives, God willing:
All the gifts from all the heights, your own, Love!

XIII

Yet a semblance of resource avails us—
Shade so finely touched, love's sense must seize it.
Take these lines, look lovingly and nearly,
Lines I write the first time and the last time.
He who works in fresco, steals a hair-brush,
Curbs the liberal hand, subservient proudly,
Cramps his spirit, crowds its all in little,
Makes a strange art of an art familiar,
Fills his lady's missal-marge with flowerets.
He who blows through bronze, may breathe through silver,
Fitly serenade a slumbrous princess.
He who writes, may write for once as I do.

XIV

Love, you saw me gather men and women,
Live or dead or fashioned by my fancy,
Enter each and all, and use their service,
Speak from every mouth,—the speech, a poem.
Hardly shall I tell my joys and sorrows,
Hopes and fears, belief and disbelieving:
I am mine and yours—the rest be all men's,
Karshish, Cleon, Norbert, and the fifty.
Let me speak this once in my true person,
Not as Lippo, Roland, or Andrea,
Though the fruit of speech be just this sentence:
Pray you, look on these my men and women,
Take and keep my fifty poems finished;
Where my heart lies, let my brain lie also!
Poor the speech; be how I speak, for all things.

XV

Not but that you know me!   Lo, the moon's self!
Here in London, yonder late in Florence,
Still we find her face, the thrice-transfigured.
Curving on a sky imbrued with color,
Drifted over Fiesole by twilight,
Came she, our new crescent of a hair's-breadth.
Full she flared it, lamping Samminiato,
Rounder 'twixt the cypresses and rounder,
Perfect till the nightingales applauded.
Now, a piece of her old self, impoverished,
Hard to greet, she traverses the house-roofs,
Hurries with unhandsome thrift of silver,
Goes dispiritedly, glad to finish.

XVI

What, there's nothing in the moon noteworthy?
Nay: for if that moon could love a mortal,
Use, to charm him (so to fit a fancy),
All her magic ('tis the old sweet mythos),
She would turn a new side to her mortal,
Side unseen of herdsman, huntsman, steersman—

Blank to Zoroaster on his terrace,
Blind to Galileo on his turret,
Dumb to Homer, dumb to Keats—him, even!
Think, the wonder of the moonstruck mortal—
When she turns round, comes again in heaven,
Opens out anew for worse or better!
Proves she like some portent of an iceberg
Swimming full upon the ship it founders,
Hungry with huge teeth of splintered crystals?
Proves she as the paved work of a sapphire
Seen by Moses when he climbed the mountain?
Moses, Aaron, Nadab and Abihu
Climbed and saw the very God, the Highest,
Stand upon the paved work of a sapphire.
Like the bodied heaven in his clearness
Shone the stone, the sapphire of that paved work,
When they ate and drank and saw God also!

XVII

What were seen? None knows, none ever shall know.
Only this is sure—the sight were other,
Not the moon's same side, born late in Florence,
Dying now impoverished here in London.
God be thanked, the meanest of his creatures
Boasts two soul-sides, one to face the world with,
One to show a woman when he loves her!

XVIII

This I say of me, but think of you, Love!
This to you—yourself my moon of poets!
Ah, but that's the world's side, there's the wonder,
Thus they see you, praise you, think they know you!
There, in turn I stand with them and praise you—
Out of my own self, I dare to phrase it.
But the best is when I glide from out them,
Cross a step or two of dubious twilight,
Come out on the other side, the novel
Silent silver lights and darks undreamed of,
Where I hush and bless myself with silence.

XIX

Oh, their Rafael of the dear Madonnas,
Oh, their Dante of the dread Inferno,
Wrote one song—and in my brain I sing it,
Drew one angel—borne, see, on my bosom!

Robert Browning [1812-1889]

PART III
POEMS OF NATURE

THE world is too much with us; late and soon,
Getting and spending, we lay waste our powers:
Little we see in Nature that is ours;
We have given our hearts away, a sordid boon!
This sea that bares her bosom to the moon,
The winds that will be howling at all hours,
And are up-gathered now like sleeping flowers;
For this, for everything, we are out of tune;
It moves us not.—Great God! I'd rather be
A Pagan suckled in a creed outworn;
So might I, standing on this pleasant lea,
Have glimpses that would make me less forlorn;
Have sight of Proteus rising from the sea;
Or hear old Triton blow his wreathèd horn.

William Wordsworth [1770–1850]

MOTHER NATURE

THE BOOK OF THE WORLD

OF this fair volume which we World do name,
If we the sheets and leaves could turn with care,
Of him who it corrects, and did it frame,
We clear might read the art and wisdom rare;
Find out his power which wildest powers doth tame,
His providence extending everywhere,
His justice which proud rebels doth not spare,
In every page, no, period of the same.
But silly we, like foolish children, rest
Well pleased with colored vellum, leaves of gold,
Fair dangling ribbons, leaving what is best,
On the great Writer's sense ne'er taking hold;
   Or, if by chance we stay our minds on aught,
   It is some picture on the margin wrought.
William Drummond [1585–1649]

NATURE

THE bubbling brook doth leap when I come by,
Because my feet find measure with its call;
The birds know when the friend they love is nigh,
For I am known to them, both great and small.
The flower that on the lonely hillside grows
Expects me there when spring its bloom has given;
And many a tree and bush my wanderings knows,
And e'en the clouds and silent stars of heaven;
For he who with his Maker walks aright,
Shall be their lord as Adam was before;
His ear shall catch each sound with new delight,
Each object wear the dress that then it wore;
   And he, as when erect in soul he stood,
   Hear from his Father's lips that all is good.
Jones Very [1813–1880]

COMPENSATION

In that new world toward which our feet are set,
Shall we find aught to make our hearts forget
Earth's homely joys and her bright hours of bliss?
Has heaven a spell divine enough for this?
For who the pleasure of the spring shall tell
When on the leafless stalk the brown buds swell,
When the grass brightens and the days grow long,
And little birds break out in rippling song?

O sweet the dropping eve, the blush of morn,
The starlit sky, the rustling fields of corn,
The soft airs blowing from the freshening seas,
The sunflecked shadow of the stately trees,
The mellow thunder and the lulling rain,
The warm, delicious, happy summer rain,
When the grass brightens and the days grow long,
And little birds break out in rippling song!

O beauty manifold, from morn till night,
Dawn's flush, noon's blaze and sunset's tender light!
O fair, familiar features, changes sweet
Of her revolving seasons, storm and sleet
And golden calm, as slow she wheels through space,
From snow to roses,—and how dear her face,
When the grass brightens, when the days grow long,
And little birds break out in rippling song!

O happy earth!   O home so well beloved!
What recompense have we, from thee removed?
One hope we have that overtops the whole,—
The hope of finding every vanished soul,
We love and long for daily, and for this
Gladly we turn from thee, and all thy bliss,
Even at thy loveliest, when the days are long,
And little birds break out in rippling song.

Celia Thaxter [1835-1894]

THE LAST HOUR

O joys of love and joys of fame,
  It is not you I shall regret;
  I sadden lest I should forget
The beauty woven in earth's name:

The shout and battle of the gale,
  The stillness of the sun-rising,
  The sound of some deep hidden spring,
The glad sob of the filling sail,

The first green ripple of the wheat,
  The rain-song of the lifted leaves,
  The waking birds beneath the eaves,
The voices of the summer heat.

                    Ethel Clifford [18

NATURE

O NATURE! I do not aspire
To be the highest in thy choir,—
To be a meteor in thy sky,
Or comet that may range on high;
Only a zephyr that may blow
Among the reeds by the river low;
Give me thy most privy place
Where to run my airy race.

In some withdrawn, unpublic mead
Let me sigh upon a reed,
Or in the woods, with leafy din,
Whisper the still evening in:
Some still work give me to do,—
Only—be it near to you!

For I'd rather be thy child
And pupil, in the forest wild,
Than be the king of men elsewhere,
And most sovereign slave of care;

To have one moment of thy dawn,
Than share the city's year forlorn.

Henry David Thoreau [1817–1862]

SONG OF NATURE

MINE are the night and morning,
The pits of air, the gulf of space,
The sportive sun, the gibbous moon,
The innumerable days.

I hide in the solar glory,
I am dumb in the pealing song,
I rest on the pitch of the torrent,
In slumber I am strong.

No numbers have counted my tallies,
No tribes my house can fill,
I sit by the shining Fount of Life
And pour the deluge still;

And ever by delicate powers
Gathering along the centuries
From race on race the rarest flowers,
My wreath shall nothing miss.

And many a thousand summers
My gardens ripened well,
And light from meliorating stars
With firmer glory fell.

I wrote the past in characters
Of rock and fire the scroll,
The building in the coral sea.
The planting of the coal.

And thefts from satellites and rings
And broken stars I drew,
And out of spent and agèd things
I formed the world anew;

What time the gods kept carnival,
Tricked out in star and flower,
And in cramp elf and saurian forms
They swathed their too much power.

Time and Thought were my surveyors,
They laid their courses well,
They boiled the sea, and piled the layers
Of granite, marl and shell.

But he, the man-child glorious,—
Where tarries he the while?
The rainbow shines his harbinger,
The sunset gleams his smile.

My boreal lights leap upward,
Forthright my planets roll,
And still the man-child is not born,
The summit of the whole.

Must time and tide forever run?
Will never my winds go sleep in the west?
Will never my wheels which whirl the sun
And satellites have rest?

Too much of donning and doffing,
Too slow the rainbow fades,
I weary of my robe of snow,
My leaves and my cascades;

I tire of globes and races,
Too long the game is played;
What without him is summer's pomp,
Or winter's frozen shade?

I travail in pain for him,
My creatures travail and wait;
His couriers come by squadrons,
He comes not to the gate.

Twice I have moulded an image,
And thrice outstretched my hand,
Made one of day and one of night
And one of the salt sea-sand.

One in a Judæan manger,
And one by Avon stream,
One over against the mouths of Nile,
And one in the Academe.

I moulded kings and saviors,
And bards o'er kings to rule;—
But fell the starry influence short,
The cup was never full.

Yet whirl the glowing wheels once more,
And mix the bowl again;
Seethe, Fate! the ancient elements,
Heat, cold, wet, dry, and peace, and pain.

Let war and trade and creeds and song
Blend, ripen race on race,
The sunburnt world a man shall breed
Of all the zones and countless days.

No ray is dimmed, no atom worn,
My oldest force is good as new,
And the fresh rose on yonder thorn
Gives back the bending heavens in dew.

Ralph Waldo Emerson [1803–1882]

"GREAT NATURE IS AN ARMY GAY"

GREAT nature is an army gay,
Resistless marching on its way;
I hear the bugles clear and sweet,
I hear the tread of million feet.
    Across the plain I see it pour;
It tramples down the waving grass;
Within the echoing mountain-pass
I hear a thousand cannon roar.

It swarms within my garden gate;
My deepest well it drinketh dry.
It doth not rest; it doth not wait;
By night and day it sweepeth by;
Ceaseless it marcheth by my door;
It heeds me not, though I implore.
I know not whence it comes, nor where
It goes.   For me it doth not care—
Whether I starve, or eat, or sleep,
Or live, or die, or sing, or weep.
And now the banners all are bright,
Now torn and blackened by the fight.
Sometimes its laughter shakes the sky,
Sometimes the groans of those who die.
Still through the night and through the livelong day
The infinite army marches on its remorseless way.
                    Richard Watson Gilder [1844-1909]

TO MOTHER NATURE

NATURE, in thy largess, grant
I may be thy confidant!
Taste who will life's roadside cheer
(Though my heart doth hold it dear—
Song and wine and trees and grass,
All the joys that flash and pass),
I must put within my prayer
Gifts more intimate and rare.
Show me how dry branches throw
Such blue shadows on the snow,—
Tell me how the wind can fare
On his unseen feet of air,—
Show me how the spider's loom
Weaves the fabric from her womb,—
Lead me to those brooks of morn
Where a woman's laugh is born,—
Let me taste the sap that flows
Through the blushes of a rose,

Yea, and drain the blood which runs
From the heart of dying suns,—
Teach me how the butterfly
Guessed at immortality,—
Let me follow up the track
Of Love's deathless Zodiac
Where Joy climbs among the spheres
Circled by her moon of tears,—
Tell me how, when I forget
All the schools have taught me, yet
I recall each trivial thing
In a golden, far-off Spring,—
Give me whispered hints how I
May instruct my heart to fly
Where the baffling Vision gleams
Till I overtake my dreams,
And the impossible be done
When the Wish and Deed grow one!

Frederic Lawrence Knowles [1869–1905]

QUIET WORK

ONE lesson, Nature, let me learn of thee,
One lesson which in every wind is blown,
One lesson of two duties kept at one
Though the loud world proclaim their enmity—
Of toil unsevered from tranquillity;
Of labor, that in lasting fruit outgrows
Far noisier schemes, accomplished in repose,
Too great for haste, too high for rivalry.

Yes, while on earth a thousand discords ring,
Man's fitful uproar mingling with his toil,
Still do thy sleepless ministers move on,
Their glorious tasks in silence perfecting;
Still working, blaming still our vain turmoil;
Laborers that shall not fail, when man is gone.

Matthew Arnold [1822–1888]

NATURE

As a fond mother, when the day is o'er,
  Leads by the hand her little child to bed,
  Half willing, half reluctant to be led,
And leave his broken playthings on the floor,
Still gazing at them through the open door,
  Nor wholly reassured and comforted
  By promises of others in their stead,
Which, though more splendid, may not please him more;
So Nature deals with us, and takes away
  Our playthings one by one, and by the hand
    Leads us to rest so gently, that we go
Scarce knowing if we wish to go or stay,
  Being too full of sleep to understand
    How far the unknown transcends the what we know.
            Henry Wadsworth Longfellow [1807–1882]

"AS AN OLD MERCER"

As an old mercer in some sleepy town
  Swings wide his windows new day after day,
  Sets all his wares around in arch array
  To please the taste of passers up and down,—
His hoard of handy things of trite renown,
  Of sweets and spices and of faint perfumes,
  Of silks and prints,—and at the last illumes
  His tiny panes to foil the evening's frown;
So Nature spreads her proffered treasures: such
  As daily dazzle at the morning's rise,—
  Fair show of isle and ocean merchandise,
And airy offerings filmy to the touch;
  Then, lest we like not these, in Dark's bazaars
  She nightly tempts us with her store of stars.
            Mahlon Leonard Fisher [1874–

GOOD COMPANY

To-day I have grown taller from walking with the trees,
The seven sister-poplars who go softly in a line;
And I think my heart is whiter for its parley with a star
That trembled out at nightfall and hung above the pine.

The call-note of a redbird from the cedars in the dusk
Woke his happy mate within me to an answer free and fine;
And a sudden angel beckoned from a column of blue smoke—
*Lord, who am I that they should stoop—these holy folk of
thine?*   *Karle Wilson Baker* [1878–

"HERE IS THE PLACE WHERE LOVELINESS KEEPS HOUSE"

HERE is the place where Loveliness keeps house,
Between the river and the wooded hills,
Within a valley where the Springtime spills
Her firstling wind-flowers under blossoming boughs:
Where Summer sits braiding her warm, white brows
With bramble-roses; and where Autumn fills
Her lap with asters; and old Winter frills
With crimson haw and hip his snowy blouse.
Here you may meet with Beauty. Here she sits
Gazing upon the moon, or all the day
Tuning a wood-thrush flute, remote, unseen;
Or when the storm is out, 'tis she who flits
From rock to rock, a form of flying spray,
Shouting, beneath the leaves' tumultuous green.
    Madison Cawein [1865–1914]

GOD'S WORLD

O WORLD, I cannot hold thee close enough!
Thy winds, thy wide gray skies!
Thy mists, that roll and rise!
Thy woods, this autumn day, that ache and sag
And all but cry with color! That gaunt crag
To crush! To lift the lean of that black bluff!
World, world, I cannot get thee close enough!

Long have I known a glory in it all
But never knew I this.
Here such a passion is
As stretcheth me apart. Lord, I do fear
Thou'st made the world too beautiful this year.
My soul is all but out of me—let fall
No burning leaf; prithee, let no bird call.
    Edna St. Vincent Millay [1892–

WILD HONEY

WHERE hints of racy sap and gum
Out of the old dark forest come;
Where birds their beaks like hammers wield,
And pith is pierced and bark is peeled;
Where the green walnut's outer rind
Gives precious bitterness to the wind;
There lurks the sweet creative power,
As lurks the honey in the flower.
In winter's bud that bursts in spring,
In nut of autumn's ripening,
In acrid bulb beneath the mold,
Sleeps the elixir, strong and old,
That Rosicrucians sought in vain,—
Life that renews itself again!
What bottled perfume is so good
As fragrance of split tulip-wood?
What fabled drink of god or muse
Was rich as purple mulberry juice?
And what school-polished gem of thought
Is like the rune from Nature caught?
He is a poet strong and true
Who loves wild thyme and honey-dew;
And like a brown bee works and sings
With morning freshness on his wings,
And a golden burden on his thighs,—
The pollen-dust of centuries!

Maurice Thompson [1844–1901]

PATMOS

ALL around him Patmos lies,
Who hath spirit-gifted eyes,
Who his happy sight can suit
To the great and the minute.
Doubt not but he holds in view
A new earth and heaven new;
Doubt not but his ear doth catch
Strain nor voice nor reed can match:
Many a silver, sphery note
Shall within his hearing float.

All around him Patmos lies,
Who unto God's priestess flies:
Thou, O Nature, bid him see,
Through all guises worn by thee,
A divine apocalypse.
Manifold his fellowships:
Now the rocks their archives ope;
Voiceless creatures tell their hope
In a language symbol-wrought;
Groves to him sigh out their thought;
Musings of the flower and grass
Through his quiet spirit pass.
'Twixt new earth and heaven new
He hath traced and holds the clue,
Number his delights ye may not;
Fleets the year but these decay not.
Now the freshets of the rain,
Bounding on from hill to plain,
Show him earthly streams have rise
In the bosom of the skies.
Now he feels the morning thrill,
As upmounts, unseen and still,
Dew the wing of evening drops.
Now the frost, that meets and stops
Summer's feet in tender sward,
Greets him, breathing heavenward.
Hieroglyphics writes the snow,
Through the silence falling slow;
Types of star and petaled bloom
A white missal-page illume.
By these floating symbols fine,
Heaven-truth shall be divine.

All around him Patmos lies,
Who hath spirit-gifted eyes;
He need not afar remove,
He need not the times reprove,
Who would hold perpetual lease
Of an isle in seas of peace.

Edith M. Thomas [1854–1925]

DAWN AND DARK

SONG

PHŒBUS, arise,
And paint the sable skies
With azure, white, and red:
Rouse Memnon's mother from her Tithon's bed,
That she thy càreer may with roses spread:
The nightingales thy coming each where sing,
Make an eternal Spring!
Give life to this dark world which lieth dead;
Spread forth thy golden hair
In larger locks than thou wast wont before,
And, emperor-like, decore
With diadem of pearl thy temples fair:
Chase hence the ugly night,
Which serves but to make dear thy glorious light.

This is that happy morn,
That day, long-wishèd day,
Of all my life so dark,
(If cruel stars have not my ruin sworn,
And fates not hope betray,)
Which, only white, deserves
A diamond for ever should it mark.
This is the morn should bring unto this grove
My Love, to hear and recompense my love.
Fair king, who all preserves,
But show thy blushing beams,
And thou two sweeter eyes
Shalt see, than those which by Peneus' streams
Did once thy heart surprise.
Nay, suns, which shine as clear
As thou, when two thou didst to Rome appear.
Now, Flora, deck thyself in fairest guise:
If that ye, winds, would hear

A voice surpassing far Amphion's lyre,
Your stormy chiding stay;
Let Zephyr only breathe,
And with her tresses play,
Kissing sometimes these purple ports of death.
—The winds all silent are,
And Phœbus in his chair
Ensaffroning sea and air,
Makes vanish every star:
Night like a drunkard reels
Beyond the hills, to shun his flaming wheels:
The fields with flowers are decked in every hue,
The clouds bespangle with bright gold their blue:
Here is the pleasant place,
And everything save her, who all should grace.

William Drummond [1585–1649]

HYMN OF APOLLO

THE sleepless Hours who watch me as I lie,
  Curtained with star-inwoven tapestries,
From the broad moonlight of the sky,
  Fanning the busy dreams from my dim eyes,—
Waken me when their Mother, the gray Dawn,
Tells them that dreams and that the moon is gone.

Then I arise, and climbing Heaven's blue dome,
  I walk over the mountains and the waves,
Leaving my robe upon the ocean foam;
  My footsteps pave the clouds with fire; the caves
Are filled with my bright presence, and the air
Leaves the green Earth to my embraces bare.

The sunbeams are my shafts, with which I kill
  Deceit, that loves the night and fears the day;
All men who do or even imagine ill
  Fly me, and from the glory of my ray
Good minds and open actions take new might,
Until diminished by the reign of Night.

I feed the clouds, the rainbows, and the flowers,
    With their ethereal colors; the Moon's globe,
And the pure stars in their eternal bowers,
    Are cinctured with my power as with a robe;
Whatever lamps on Earth or Heaven may shine,
Are portions of one power, which is mine.

I stand at noon upon the peak of Heaven;
    Then with unwilling steps I wander down
Into the clouds of the Atlantic even;
    For grief that I depart they weep and frown:
What look is more delightful than the smile
With which I soothe them from the western isle?

I am the eye with which the Universe
    Beholds itself, and knows it is divine;
All harmony of instrument or verse,
    All prophecy, all medicine, is mine,
All light of art or nature;—to my song
    Victory and praise in its own right belong.
                    Percy Bysshe Shelley [1792–1822]

PRELUDE

From "The New Day"

THE night was dark, though sometimes a faint star
A little while a little space made bright.
The night was dark and still the dawn seemed far,
When, o'er the muttering and invisible sea,
Slowly, within the East, there grew a light
Which half was starlight, and half seemed to be
The herald of a greater.   The pale white
Turned slowly to pale rose, and up the height
Of heaven slowly climbed.   The gray sea grew
Rose-colored like the sky.   A white gull flew
Straight toward the utmost boundary of the East
Where slowly the rose gathered and increased.
There was light now, where all was black before:
It was as on the opening of a door

By one who in his hand a lamp doth hold
(Its flame being hidden by the garment's fold),—
The still air moves, the wide room is less dim.
　More bright the East became, the ocean turned
Dark and more dark against the brightening sky—
Sharper against the sky the long sea line.
The hollows of the breakers on the shore
Were green like leaves whereon no sun doth shine,
Though sunlight make the outer branches hoar.
From rose to red the level heaven burned;
Then sudden, as if a sword fell from on high,
A blade of gold flashed on the ocean's rim.

Richard Watson Gilder [1844-1909]

DAWN ON THE HEADLAND

Dawn—and a magical stillness: on earth, quiescence profound;
　On the waters a vast Content, as of hunger appeased and stayed;
In the heavens a silence that seems not mere privation of sound,
　But a thing with form and body, a thing to be touched and weighed!

Yet I know that I dwell in the midst of the roar of the cosmic wheel,
　In the hot collision of Forces, and clangor of boundless Strife,
Mid the sound of the speed of the worlds, the rushing worlds, and the peal
　Of the thunder of Life.

William Watson [1858-1935]

THE MIRACLE OF THE DAWN

What would it mean for you and me
　If dawn should come no more!
Think of its gold along the sea,
　Its rose above the shore!
That rose of awful mystery,
　Our souls bow down before

What wonder that the Inca kneeled,
  The Aztec prayed and pled
And sacrificed to it, and sealed,—
  With rites that long are dead,—
The marvels that it once revealed
  To them it comforted.

What wonder, yea! what awe, behold!
  What rapture and what tears
Were ours, if wild its rivered gold,—
  That now each day appears,—
Burst on the world, in darkness rolled,
  Once every thousand years!

Think what it means to me and you
  To see it even as God
Evolved it when the world was new!
  When Light rose, earthquake-shod,
And slow its gradual splendor grew
  O'er deeps the whirlwind trod.

What shoutings then and cymballings
  Arose from depth and height!
What worship-solemn trumpetings,
  And thunders, burning-white,
Of winds and waves, and anthemings
  Of Earth received the Light.

Think what it meant to see the dawn!
  The dawn, that comes each day!—
What if the East should ne'er grow wan,
  Should nevermore grow gray!
That line of rose no more be drawn
  Above the ocean's spray!
                    Madison Cawein [1865–1914]

DAWN-ANGELS

ALL night I watched awake for morning,
  At last the East grew all a flame,
The birds for welcome sang, or warning,
  And with their singing morning came.

Along the gold-green heavens drifted
  Pale wandering souls that shun the light,
Whose cloudy pinions, torn and rifted,
  Had beat the bars of Heaven all night.

These clustered round the moon, but higher
  A troop of shining spirits went,
Who were not made of wind or fire,
  But some divine dream-element.

Some held the Light, while those remaining
  Shook out their harvest-colored wings,
A faint unusual music raining,
  (Whose sound was Light) on earthly things.

They sang, and as a mighty river
  Their voices washed the night away,
From East to West ran one white shiver,
  And waxen strong their song was Day.
                    A. Mary F. Robinson [1857–

MUSIC OF THE DAWN

AT SEA, OCTOBER 23, 1907

In far forests' leafy twilight, now is stealing gray dawn's
    shy light,
  And the misty air is tremulous with songs of many a bird;
While from mountain steeps descending, every streamlet's
    voice is blending
  With the anthems of great pine trees, by the breath of
    daylight stirred.

But I turn from Fancy's dreaming of the green earth, to the
    gleaming
  Of the fluttering wings of morning rushing o'er the jewelled
    deep;
And the ocean's rhythmic pounding, with each lucent wave
    resounding,
  Seems the music made when God's own hands His mighty
    harpstrings sweep.
                    Virginia Bioren Harrison [1847–

SUNRISE ON MANSFIELD MOUNTAIN

O SWIFT forerunners, rosy with the race!
Spirits of dawn, divinely manifest
Behind your blushing banners in the sky,
Daring invaders of Night's tenting-ground,—
How do ye strain on forward-bending foot,
Each to be first in heralding of joy!
With silence sandalled, so they weave their way,
And so they stand, with silence panoplied,
Chanting, through mystic symbollings of flame,
Their solemn invocation to the light.

O changeless guardians!   O ye wizard firs!
What strenuous philter feeds your potency,
That thus ye rest, in sweet wood-hardiness.
Ready to learn of all and utter naught?
What breath may move ye, or what breeze invite
To odorous hot lendings of the heart?
What wind—but all the winds are yet afar,
And e'en the little tricksy zephyr sprites,
That fleet before them, like their elfin locks,
Have lagged in sleep, nor stir nor waken yet
To pluck the robe of patient majesty.

Too still for dreaming, too divine for sleep,
So range the firs, the constant, fearless ones.
Warders of mountain secrets, there they wait,
Each with his cloak about him, breathless, calm,
And yet expectant, as who knows the dawn,
And all night thrills with memory and desire,
Searching in what has been for what shall be:
The marvel of the ne'er familiar day,
Sacred investiture of life renewed,
The chrism of dew, the coronal of flame.

Low in the valley lies the conquered rout
Of man's poor trivial turmoil, lost and drowned
Under the mist, in gleaming rivers rolled,
Where oozy marsh contends with frothing main.

And rounding all, springs one full, ambient **arch,**
One great good limpid world—so still, so still!
For no sound echoes from its crystal curve
Save four clear notes, the song of that lone bird
Who, brave but trembling, tries his morning **hymn,**
And has no heart to finish, for the awe
And wonder of this pearling globe of dawn.

Light, light eternal! veiling-place of stars!
Light, the revealer of dread beauty's face!
Weaving whereof the hills are lambent clad!
Mighty libation to the Unknown God!
Cup whereat pine-trees slake their giant **thirst**
And little leaves drink sweet delirium!
Being and breath and potion! Living soul
And all-informing heart of all that lives!
How can we magnify thine awful name
Save by its chanting: Light! and light! and **light!**
An exhalation from far sky retreats,
It grows in silence, as 'twere self-create,
Suffusing all the dusky web of night.
But one lone corner it invades not yet,
Where low above a black and rimy crag
Hangs the old moon, thin as a battered **shield,**
The holy, useless shield of long-past wars,
Dinted and frosty, on the crystal dark.
But lo! the east,—let none forget the east,
Pathway ordained of old where He should tread.
Through some sweet magic common in the skies
The rosy banners are with saffron tinct:
The saffron grows to gold, the gold is fire,
And led by silence more majestical
Than clash of conquering arms, He comes! **He comes!**
He holds his spear benignant, sceptrewise,
And strikes out flame from the adoring hills.

Alice Brown [1857–

ODE TO EVENING

If aught of oaten stop, or pastoral song,
May hope, chaste Eve, to soothe thy modest ear,
    Like thy own solemn springs,
    Thy springs and dying gales;

O Nymph reserved, while now the bright-haired sun
Sits in yon western tent, whose cloudy skirts,
    With brede ethereal wove,
    O'erhang his wavy bed:

Now air is hushed, save where the weak-eyed bat
With short shrill shriek flits by on leathern wing,
    Or where the beetle winds
    His small but sullen horn,

As oft he rises, 'midst the twilight path
Against the pilgrim borne in heedless hum:
    Now teach me, maid composed,
    To breathe some softened strain,

Whose numbers, stealing through thy darkening vale,
May not unseemly with its stillness suit,
    As, musing slow, I hail
    Thy genial loved return!

For when thy folding-star arising shows
His paly circlet, at his warning lamp
    The fragrant Hours, and Elves
    Who slept in buds the day,

And many a Nymph who wreathes her brows with sedge,
And sheds the freshening dew, and, lovelier still,
    The pensive Pleasures sweet,
    Prepare thy shadowy car:

Then lead, calm votaress, where some sheety lake
Cheers the lone heath, or some time-hallowed pile,
    Or upland fallows gray
    Reflect its last cool gleam.

Or, if chill blustering winds, or driving rain,
Prevent my willing feet, be mine the hut
    That, from the mountain's side,
    Views wilds and swelling floods,

And hamlets brown, and dim-discovered spires,
And hears their simple bell, and marks o'er all
    Thy dewy fingers draw
    The gradual dusky veil.

While Spring shall pour his showers, as of the wont,
And bathe thy breathing tresses, meekest Eve!
    While Summer loves to sport
    Beneath thy lingering light;

While sallow Autumn fills thy lap with leaves,
Or Winter, yelling through the troublous air,
    Affrights thy shrinking train,
    And rudely rends thy robes:

So long, regardful of thy quiet rule,
Shall Fancy, Friendship, Science, smiling Peace,
    Thy gentlest influence own,
    And hymn thy favorite name!
                   William Collins [1721–1759]

"IT IS A BEAUTEOUS EVENING, CALM AND FREE"

It is a beauteous evening, calm and free;
The holy time is quiet as a Nun
Breathless with adoration; the broad sun
Is sinking down in his tranquility;
The gentleness of heaven broods o'er the Sea;
Listen! the mighty Being is awake,
And doth with his eternal motion make
A sound like thunder—everlastingly.
Dear Child! dear Girl! that walkest with me here,
If thou appear untouched by solemn thought,

Thy nature is not therefore less divine:
Thou liest in Abraham's bosom all the year,
And worship'st at the Temple's inner shrine,
God being with thee when we know it not.

William Wordsworth [1770–1850]

GLOAMING

SKIES to the West are stained with madder;
Amber light on the rare blue hills;
The sough of the pines is growing sadder;
From the meadow-lands sound the whippoorwills.
    Air is sweet with the breath of clover;
    Dusk is on, and the day is over.

Skies to the East are streaked with golden;
Tremulous light on the darkening pond;
Glow-worms pale, to the dark beholden;
Twitterings hush in the hedge beyond.
    Air is sweet with the breath of clover;
    Silver the hills where the moon climbs over.

Robert Adger Bowen [1868–

EVENING MELODY

O THAT the pines which crown yon steep
    Their fires might ne'er surrender!
O that yon fervid knoll might keep,
    While lasts the world, its splendor!

Pale poplars on the breeze that lean,
    And in the sunset shiver,
O that your golden stems might screen
    For aye yon glassy river!

That yon white bird on homeward wing
    Soft-sliding without motion,
And now in blue air vanishing
    Like snow-flake lost in ocean,

Beyond our sight might never flee,
    Yet forward still be flying;
And all the dying day might be
    Immortal in its dying!

Pellucid thus in saintly trance,
    Thus mute in expectation,
What waits the earth? Deliverance?
    Ah no! Transfiguration!

She dreams of that "New Earth" divine,
    Conceived of seed immortal;
She sings "Not mine the holier shrine,
    Yet mine the steps and portal!"

          Aubrey Thomas de Vere [1814–1902]

"IN THE COOL OF THE EVENING"

In the cool of the evening, when the low sweet whispers waken,
    When the laborers turn them homeward, and the weary have their will,
When the censers of the roses o'er the forest aisles are shaken,
    Is it but the wind that cometh o'er the far green hill?

For they say 'tis but the sunset winds that wander through the heather,
    Rustle all the meadow-grass and bend the dewy fern;
They say 'tis but the winds that bow the reeds in prayer together,
    And fill the shaken pools with fire along the shadowy burn.

In the beauty of the twilight, in the Garden that He loveth,
    They have veiled His lovely vesture with the darkness of a name!
Through His Garden, through His Garden, it is but the wind that moveth,
    No more! But O the miracle, the miracle is the same.

In the cool of the evening, when the sky is an old story,
　　Slowly dying, but remembered, ay, and loved with pas-
　　　sion still . . .
Hush! . . . the fringes of His garment, in the fading golden
　　glory
　　Softly rustling as He cometh o'er the far green hill.
　　　　　　　　　　　　　　Alfred Noyes [1880–

TWILIGHT

SPIRIT of Twilight, through your folded wings
　　I catch a glimpse of your averted face,
And rapturous on a sudden, my soul sings
　　"Is not this common earth a holy place?"

Spirit of Twilight, you are like a song
　　That sleeps, and waits a singer,—like a hymn
That God finds lovely and keeps near Him long,
　　Till it is choired by aureoled cherubim.

Spirit of Twilight, in the golden gloom
　　Of dreamland dim I sought you, and I found
A woman sitting in a silent room
　　Full of white flowers that moved and made no sound.

These white flowers were the thoughts you bring to all,
　　And the room's name is Mystery where you sit, ·
Woman whom we call Twilight, when night's pall
　　You lift across our Earth to cover it.
　　　　　　　　　　　　Olive Custance [1874–

TWILIGHT AT SEA

THE twilight hours, like birds, flew by,
　　As lightly and as free,
Ten thousand stars were in the sky,
　　Ten thousand on the sea;
For every wave, with dimpled face,
　　That leaped upon the air,
Had caught a star in its embrace,
　　And held it trembling there.
　　　　　　　　　　　Amelia C. Welby [1819–1852]

"THIS IS MY HOUR"

I

THE ferries ply like shuttles in a loom,
   And many barques come in across the bay
To lights and bells that signal through the gloom
   Of twilight gray;

And like the brown soft flutter of the snow
   The wide-winged sea-birds droop from closing skies,
And hover near the water, circling low,
   As the day dies.

The city like a shadowed castle stands,
   Its turrets indistinctly touching night;
Like earth-born stars far fetched from faerie lands,
   Its lamps are bright.

This is my hour,—when wonder springs anew
   To see the towers ascending, pale and high,
And the long seaward distances of blue,
   And the dim sky.

II

This is my hour, between the day and night;
   The sun has set and all the world is still,
   The afterglow upon the distant hill
Is as a holy light.

This is my hour, between the sun and moon;
   The little stars are gathering in the sky,
   There is no sound but one bird's startled cry,—
One note that ceases soon.

The gardens and, far off, the meadow-land,
   Are like the fading depths beneath a sea,
   While over waves of misty shadows we
Drift onward, hand in hand.

This is my hour, that you have called your own;
  Its hushèd beauty silently we share, —
  Touched by the wistful wonder in the air
That leaves us so alone.

III

In rain and twilight mist the city street,
  Hushed and half-hidden, might this instant be
  A dark canal beneath our balcony,
Like one in Venice, Sweet.

The street-lights blossom, star-wise, one by one;
  A lofty tower the shadows have not hid
  Stands out—part column and part pyramid—
Holy to look upon.

The dusk grows deeper, and on silver wings
  The twilight flutters like a weary gull
  Toward some sea-island, lost and beautiful,
Where a sea-syren sings.

"This is my hour," you breathe with quiet lips;
  And filled with beauty, dreaming and devout,
  We sit in silence, while our thoughts go out—
Like treasure-seeking ships.

Zoë Akins [1886–

SONG TO THE EVENING STAR

STAR that bringest home the bee,
And sett'st the weary laborer free!
If any star shed peace, 'tis thou
  That send'st it from above,
Appearing when Heaven's breath and brow
  Are sweet as hers we love.

Come to the luxuriant skies,
Whilst the landscape's odors rise,

Whilst far-off lowing herds are heard
　　And songs when toil is done,
From cottages whose smoke unstirred
　　Curls yellow in the sun.

Star of love's soft interviews,
Parted lovers on thee muse;
Their remembrancer in Heaven
　　Of thrilling vows thou art,
Too delicious to be riven
　　By absence from the heart.

Thomas Campbell [1777-1844]

THE EVENING CLOUD

A CLOUD lay cradled near the setting sun,
　A gleam of crimson tinged its braided snow;
Long had I watched the glory moving on
　O'er the still radiance of the lake below.
Tranquil its spirit seemed, and floated slow!
　Even in its very motion there was rest;
While every breath of eve that chanced to blow
　Wafted the traveller to the beauteous west.
Emblem, methought, of the departed soul!
　To whose white robe the gleam of bliss is given,
And by the breath of mercy made to roll
　Right onwards to the golden gates of heaven,
Where to the eye of faith it peaceful lies,
And tells to man his glorious destinies.

John Wilson [1785-1854]

SONG: TO CYNTHIA

From " Cynthia's Revels "

QUEEN and huntress, chaste and fair,
　Now the sun is laid to sleep,
Seated in thy silver chair,
　State in wonted manner keep:
　　Hesperus entreats thy light,
　　Goddess excellently bright.

Earth, let not thy envious shade
Dare itself to interpose;
Cynthia's shining orb was made
Heaven to clear, when day did close:
    Bless us then with wishèd sight,
    Goddess excellently bright.

Lay thy bow of pearl apart,
And thy crystal-shining quiver;
Give unto the flying hart
Space to breathe, how short soever:
    Thou that mak'st a day of night,
    Goddess excellently bright.

Ben Jonson [1573?–1637]

MY STAR

ALL that I know
    Of a certain star
Is, it can throw
    (Like the angled spar)
Now a dart of red,
    Now a dart of blue,
Till my friends have said
    They would fain see, too,
My star that dartles the red and the blue!
Then it stops like a bird; like a flower, hangs furled:
   They must solace themselves with the Saturn above it.
What matter to me if their star is a world?
   Mine has opened its soul to me; therefore I love it.

Robert Browning [1812–1889]

NIGHT

THE sun descending in the West,
The evening star does shine;
The birds are silent in their nest,
And I must seek for mine.

The moon, like a flower
In heaven's high bower,
With silent delight
Sits and smiles on the night.

Farewell, green fields and happy grove,
Where flocks have ta'en delight;
Where lambs have nibbled, silent move
The feet of angels bright:
    Unseen, they pour blessing,
    And joy without ceasing,
    On each bud and blossom,
    On each sleeping bosom.

They look in every thoughtless nest,
Where birds are covered warm;
They visit caves of every beast,
To keep them all from harm.
    If they see any weeping
    That should have been sleeping,
    They pour sleep on their head,
    And sit down by their bed.

When wolves and tigers howl for prey
They pitying stand and weep,
Seeking to drive their thirst away,
And keep them from the sheep.
    But, if they rush dreadful,
    The angels, most heedful,
    Receive each mild spirit
    New worlds to inherit.

And there the lion's ruddy eyes
Shall flow with tears of gold:
And pitying the tender cries,
And walking round the fold,
    Saying: "Wrath by His meekness,
    And by His health, sickness,
    Are driven away
    From our immortal day.

"And now beside thee, bleating lamb,
I can lie down and sleep.
Or think on Him who bore thy name,
Graze after thee, and weep.
　For, washed in life's river,
　My bright mane for ever
　Shall shine like the gold,
　As I guard o'er the fold."

William Blake [1757–1827]

TO NIGHT

SWIFTLY walk o'er the western wave,
　　Spirit of Night!
Out of the misty eastern cave
Where, all the long and lone daylight,
Thou wovest dreams of joy and fear,
Which make thee terrible and dear,
　　Swift be thy flight!

Wrap thy form in a mantle gray,
　　Star-inwrought!
Blind with thine hair the eyes of Day;
Kiss her until she be wearied out,
Then wander o'er city, and sea, and land,
Touching all with thine opiate wand—
　　Come, long-sought!

When I arose and saw the dawn,
　　I sighed for thee;
When light rode high, and the dew was gone,
And noon lay heavy on flower and tree,
And the weary Day turned to his rest,
Lingering like an unloved guest,
　　I sighed for thee.

Thy brother Death came, and cried,
　　"Would'st thou me?"
Thy sweet child Sleep, the filmy-eyed,
Murmured like a noontide bee,

"Shall I nestle near thy side?
    Would'st thou me?"—And I replied,
      "No, not thee."

Death will come when thou art dead,
    Soon, too soon—
Sleep will come when thou art fled;
Of neither would I ask the boon
I ask of thee, belovèd Night—
Swift be thine approaching flight,
      Come soon, soon!

        Percy Bysshe Shelley [1792–1822]

TO NIGHT

MYSTERIOUS Night! when our first parent knew
Thee from report divine, and heard thy name,
Did he not tremble for this lovely frame,
This glorious canopy of light and blue?
Yet 'neath the curtain of translucent dew,
Bathed in the rays of the great setting flame,
Hesperus with the host of heaven came,
And lo! creation widened on man's view.
Who could have thought such darkness lay concealed
Within thy beams, O Sun! or who could find,
While fly, and leaf, and insect stood revealed,
That to such countless orbs thou mad'st us blind!
  Why do we, then, shun Death with anxious strife?—
  If Light can thus deceive, wherefore not Life?

        Joseph Blanco White [1775–1841]

NIGHT

MYSTERIOUS night! Spread wide thy silvery plume!
Soft as swan's down, brood o'er the sapphirine
Breadth of still shadowy waters dark as wine;
Smooth out the liquid heavens that stars illume!
Come with fresh airs breathing the faint perfume
Of deep-walled gardens, groves of whispering pine;
Scatter soft dews, waft pure sea-scent of brine;
In sweet repose man's pain, man's love resume!

Deep-bosomed night! Not here where down the marge
Marble with palaces those lamps of earth
Tremble on trembling blackness; nay, far hence,
There on the lake where space is lone and large,
And man's life lost in broad indifference,
Lift thou the soul to spheres that gave her birth!
John Addington Symonds [1840-1893]

NIGHT

NIGHT is the time for rest;
   How sweet, when labors close,
To gather round an aching breast
   The curtain of repose,
Stretch the tired limbs, and lay the head
Down on our own delightful bed!

Night is the time for dreams;
   The gay romance of life,
When truth that is, and truth that seems,
   Blend in fantastic strife;
Ah! visions, less beguiling far
Than waking dreams by daylight are!

Night is the time for toil;
   To plough the classic field,
Intent to find the buried spoil
   Its wealthy furrows yield;
Till all is ours that sages taught,
That poets sang, or heroes wrought.

Night is the time to weep;
   To wet with unseen tears
Those graves of Memory, where sleep
   The joys of other years;
Hopes, that were Angels at their birth,
But perished young, like things of earth.

Night is the time to watch;
   O'er ocean's dark expanse,
To hail the Pleiades, or catch
   The full moon's earliest glance,

That brings into the homesick mind
All we have loved and left behind.

Night is the time for care;
    Brooding on hours misspent,
To see the spectre of Despair
    Come to our lonely tent;
Like Brutus, 'midst his slumbering host,
Summoned to die by Cæsar's ghost.

Night is the time to think;
    When, from the eye, the soul
Takes flight; and, on the utmost brink,
    Of yonder starry pole
Descries beyond the abyss of night
The dawn of uncreated light.

Night is the time to pray;
    Our Saviour oft withdrew
To desert mountains far away;
    So will his followers do,—
Steal from the throng to haunts untrod,
And hold communion there with God.

Night is the time for Death;
    When all around is peace,
Calmly to yield the weary breath,
    From sin and suffering cease,
Think of heaven's bliss, and give the sign
To parting friends;—such death be mine!
                    James Montgomery [1771–1854]

HE MADE THE NIGHT

VAST Chaos, of eld, was God's dominion;
'Twas His belovèd child, His own first-born;
And He was agèd ere the thought of morn
Shook the sheer steeps of dim Oblivion.
Then all the works of darkness being done
Through countless æons hopelessly forlorn,
Out to the very utmost verge and bourne,
God at the last, reluctant, made the sun.

He loved His darkness still, for it was old;
He grieved to see His eldest child take flight;
And when His *Fiat Lux* the death-knell tolled,
As the doomed Darkness backward by Him rolled,
   He snatched a remnant flying into light
    And strewed it with the stars, and called it Night.
            Lloyd Mifflin [1846–1921]

HYMN TO THE NIGHT

I HEARD the trailing garments of the Night
   Sweep through her marble halls!
I saw her sable skirts all fringed with light
   From the celestial walls!

I felt her presence, by its spell of might,
   Stoop o'er me from above;
The calm, majestic presence of the Night,
   As of the one I love.

I heard the sounds of sorrow and delight,
   The manifold, soft chimes,
That fill the haunted chambers of the Night,
   Like some old poet's rhymes.

From the cool cisterns of the midnight air
   My spirit drank repose;
The fountain of perpetual peace flows there,—
   From those deep cisterns flows.

O holy Night! from thee I learn to bear
   What man has borne before!
Thou layest thy finger on the lips of Care,
   And they complain no more.

Peace! Peace! Orestes-like I breathe this prayer!
   Descend with broad-winged flight,
The welcome, the thrice-prayed for, the most fair,
   The best-belovèd Night!
        Henry Wadsworth Longfellow [1807–1882]

NIGHT'S MARDI GRAS

NIGHT is the true democracy.   When day
  Like some great monarch with his train has passed,
  In regal pomp and splendor to the last,
The stars troop forth along the Milky Way,
A jostling crowd, in radiant disarray,
  On heaven's broad boulevard in pageants vast.
  And things of earth, the hunted and outcast,
Come from their haunts and hiding-places; yea,
Even from the nooks and crannies of the mind
  Visions uncouth and vagrant fancies start,
    And specters of dead joy, that shun the light,
And impotent regrets and terrors blind,
    Each one, in form grotesque, playing its part
    In the fantastic Mardi Gras of Night.
                    Edward J. Wheeler [1859-1922]

DAWN AND DARK

GOD with His million cares
  Went to the left or right,
Leaving our world; and the day
    Grew night.

Back from a sphere He came
  Over a starry lawn,
Looked at our world; and the dark
    Grew dawn.
                    Norman Gale [1862–

DAWN

HIS radiant fingers so adorning
  Earth that in silent joy she thrills,
The ancient day stands every morning
  Above the flowing eastern hills.

This day the new-born world hath taken
  Within his mantling arms of white,

And sent her forth by fear unshaken
  To walk among the stars in light.

Risen with laughter unto leaping,
  His feet untired, undimmed his eyes,
The old, old day comes up from sleeping,
  Fresh as a flower, for new emprise.

The curtain of the night is parted
  That once again the dawn may tread,
In spotless garments, ways uncharted
  And death a million times is dead.

Slow speechless music robed in splendor
  The deep sky sings eternally,
With childlike wonderment to render
  Its own unwearied symphony.

Reborn between the great suns spinning
  Forever where men's prayers ascend,
God's day in love hath its beginning,
  And the beginning hath no end.

George B. Logan, Jr. [1892–

A WOOD SONG

Now one and all, you Roses,
  Wake up, you lie too long!
This very morning closes
  The Nightingale his song;

Each from its olive chamber
  His babies every one
This very morning clamber
  Into the shining sun.

You Slug-a-beds and Simples,
  Why will you so delay!
Dears, doff your olive wimples,
  And listen while you may.

Ralph Hodgson [1871–

THE CHANGING YEAR

A SONG FOR THE SEASONS

WHEN the merry lark doth gild
  With his song the summer hours,
And their nests the swallows build
  In the roofs and tops of towers,
And the golden broom-flower burns
  All about the waste,
And the maiden May returns
  With a pretty haste,—
    Then, how merry are the times!
    The Spring times! the Summer times!

Now, from off the ashy stone
  The chilly midnight cricket crieth,
And all merry birds are flown,
  And our dream of pleasure dieth;
Now the once blue, laughing sky
  Saddens into gray,
And the frozen rivers sigh,
  Pining all away!
    Now, how solemn are the times!
    The Winter times! the Night times!

Yet, be merry; all around
  Is through one vast change revolving;
Even Night, who lately frowned,
  Is in paler dawn dissolving;
Earth will burst her fetters strange,
  And in Spring grow free;
All things in the world will change,
  Save—my love for thee!
    Sing then, hopeful are all times!
    Winter, Spring, Summer times!
            Bryan Waller Procter [1787-1874]

A SONG OF THE SEASONS

SING a song of Spring-time,
  The world is going round,
Blown by the south wind:
  Listen to its sound.
"Gurgle" goes the mill-wheel,
  "Cluck" clucks the hen;
And it's O for a pretty girl
  To kiss in the glen.

Sing a song of Summer,
  The world is nearly still,
The mill-pond has gone to sleep,
  And so has the mill.
Shall we go a-sailing,
  Or shall we take a ride,
Or dream the afternoon away
  Here, side by side?

Sing a song of Autumn,
  The world is going back;
They glean in the corn-field,
  And stamp on the stack.
Our boy, Charlie,
  Tall, strong, and light:
He shoots all the day
  And dances all the night.

Sing a song of Winter,
  The world stops dead;
Under snowy coverlid
  Flowers lie abed.
There's hunting for the young ones
  And wine for the old,
And a sexton in the churchyard
  Digging in the cold.

Cosmo Monkhouse [1840–1901]

TURN O' THE YEAR

THIS is the time when bit by bit
The days begin to lengthen sweet
And every minute gained is joy—
And love stirs in the heart of a boy.

This is the time the sun, of late
Content to lie abed till eight,
Lifts up betimes his sleepy head—
And love stirs in the heart of a maid.

This is the time we dock the night
Of a whole hour of candlelight;
When song of linnet and thrush is heard—
And love stirs in the heart of a bird.

This is the time when sword-blades green,
With gold and purple damascene,
Pierce the brown crocus-bed a-row—
And love stirs in a heart I know.

Katherine Tynan Hinkson [1861–1931]

THE WAKING YEAR

A LADY red upon the hill
　Her annual secret keeps;
A lady white within the field
　In placid lily sleeps!

The tidy breezes with their brooms
　Sweep vale, and hill, and tree!
Prithee, my pretty housewives!
　Who may expected be?

The neighbors do not yet suspect!
　The woods exchange a smile,—
Orchard, and buttercup, and bird,
　In such a little while!

And yet how still the landscape stands,
　How nonchalant the wood,
As if the resurrection
　Were nothing very odd!
　　　　　　　　　Emily Dickinson [1830–1886]

SONG

From "Pippa Passes"

THE year's at the spring,
　And day's at the morn;
Morning's at seven;
　The hill-side's dew-pearled;
The lark's on the wing;
　The snail's on the thorn;
God's in His Heaven—
　All's right with the world!
　　　　　　　　　Robert Browning [1812–1889]

EARLY SPRING

ONCE more the Heavenly Power
　Makes all things new,
And domes the red-plowed hills
　With loving blue;
The blackbirds have their wills,
　The throstles too.

Opens a door in Heaven;
　From skies of glass
A Jacob's ladder falls
　On greening grass,
And o'er the mountain-walls
　Young angels pass.

Before them fleets the shower,
　And burst the buds,
And shine the level lands,
　And flash the floods;
The stars are from their hands
　Flung through the woods,

The woods with living airs
    How softly fanned,
Light airs from where the deep,
    All down the sand,
Is breathing in his sleep,
    Heard by the land.

O, follow, leaping blood,
    The season's lure!
O heart, look down and up,
    Serene, secure,
Warm as the crocus cup,
    Like snow-drops, pure!

Past, Future glimpse and fade
    Through some slight spell,
A gleam from yonder vale,
    Some far blue fell,
And sympathies, how frail,
    In sound and smell!

Till at thy chuckled note,
    Thou twinkling bird,
The fairy fancies range,
    And, lightly stirred,
Ring little bells of change
    From word to word.

For now the Heavenly Power
    Makes all things new,
And thaws the cold, and fills
    The flower with dew;
The blackbirds have their wills,
    The poets too.

           Alfred Tennyson [1809-1892]

LINES WRITTEN IN EARLY SPRING

I HEARD a thousand blended notes,
While in a grove I sat reclined,
In that sweet mood when pleasant thoughts
Bring sad thoughts to the mind.

To her fair works did Nature link
The human soul that through me ran;
And much it grieved my heart to think
What Man has made of Man.

Through primrose tufts, in that sweet bower,
The periwinkle trailed its wreaths;
And 'tis my faith that every flower
Enjoys the air it breathes.

The birds around me hopped and played,
Their thoughts I cannot measure,—
But the least motion which they made
It seemed a thrill of pleasure.

The budding twigs spread out their fan
To catch the breezy air;
And I must think, do all I can,
That there was pleasure there.

If this belief from heaven be sent,
If such be Nature's holy plan,
Have I not reason to lament
What Man has made of Man?

William Wordsworth [1770–1850]

IN EARLY SPRING

O SPRING, I know thee! Seek for sweet surprise
  In the young children's eyes.
But I have learnt the years, and know the yet
  Leaf-folded violet.
Mine ear, awake to silence, can foretell
  The cuckoo's fitful bell.
I wander in a gray time that encloses
  June and the wild hedge-roses.
A year's procession of the flowers doth pass
  My feet, along the grass.
And all you sweet birds silent yet, I know
  The notes that stir you so,

Your songs yet half devised in the dim dear
   Beginnings of the year.
In these young days you meditate your part;
   I have it all by heart.
I know the secrets of the seeds of flowers
   Hidden and warm with showers,
And how, in kindling Spring, the cuckoo shall
   Alter his interval.
But not a flower or song I ponder is
   My own, but memory's.
I shall be silent in those days desired
   Before a world inspired.
O dear brown birds, compose your old song-phrases,
   Earth, thy familiar daisies.

The poet mused upon the dusky height,
   Between two stars towards night,
His purpose in his heart. I watched, a space,
   The meaning of his face:
There was the secret, fled from earth and skies,
   Hid in his gray young eyes.
My heart and all the Summer wait his choice,
   And wonder for his voice.
Who shall foretell his songs, and who aspire
   But to divine his lyre?
Sweet earth, we know thy dimmest mysteries,
   But he is lord of his.

Alice Meynell [1850–1922]

SPRING

From "Summer's Last Will and Testament"

SPRING, the sweet Spring, is the year's pleasant king;
Then blooms each thing, then maids dance in a ring,
Cold doth not sting, the pretty birds do sing—
   Cuckoo, jug-jug, pu-we, to-witta-woo!

The palm and may make country houses gay,
Lambs frisk and play, the shepherds pipe all day,
And we hear aye birds tune this merry lay—
   Cuckoo, jug-jug, pu-we, to-witta-woo!

The fields breathe sweet, the daisies kiss our feet,
Young lovers meet, old wives a-sunning sit,
In every street these tunes our ears do greet—
    Cuckoo, jug-jug, pu-we, to-witta-too!
     Spring, the sweet Spring!

Thomas Nashe [1567–1601]

A STARLING'S SPRING RONDEL

I CLINK my castanet
  And beat my little drum;
  For spring at last has come,
And on my parapet
Of chestnut, gummy-wet,
  Where bees begin to hum,
I clink my castanet,
  And beat my little drum.

"Spring goes," you say, "suns set."
  So be it! Why be glum?
  Enough, the spring has come;
And without fear or fret
I clink my castanet,
  And beat my little drum.

James Cousins [1873–

"WHEN DAFFODILS BEGIN TO PEER"

From "The Winter's Tale"

WHEN daffodils begin to peer,
  With heigh! the doxy, over the dale,
Why, then comes in the sweet o' the year;
  For the red blood reigns in the winter's pale.

The white sheet bleaching on the hedge,
  With heigh! the sweet birds, O, how they sing!
Doth set my pugging tooth on edge;
  For a quart of ale is a dish for a king.

The lark, that tirra-lirra chants,
  With heigh! with heigh! the thrush and the jay,
Are summer songs for me and my aunts,
  While we lie tumbling in the hay.

William Shakespeare [1564–1616]

SPRING

From "In Memoriam"

LXXXIII

DIP down upon the northern shore,
  O sweet new-year, delaying long;
  Thou doest expectant Nature wrong,
Delaying long, delay no more.

What stays thee from the clouded noons,
  Thy sweetness from its proper place?
  Can trouble live with April days,
Or sadness in the summer moons?

Bring orchis, bring the fox-glove spire,
  The little speedwell's darling blue,
  Deep tulips dashed with fiery dew,
Laburnums, dropping-wells of fire.

O thou, new-year, delaying long,
  Delayest the sorrow in my blood,
  That longs to burst a frozen bud,
And flood a fresher throat with song.

CXV

Now fades the last long streak of snow,
  Now burgeons every maze of quick
  About the flowering squares, and thick
By ashen roots the violets blow.

Now rings the woodland loud and long,
  The distance takes a lovelier hue,
  And drowned in yonder living blue
The lark becomes a sightless song.

Now dance the lights on lawn and lea,
  The flocks are whiter down the vale,
  And milkier every milky sail,
On winding stream or distant sea;

Where now the seamew pipes, or dives
  In yonder greening gleam, and fly
  The happy birds, that change their sky
To build and brood, that live their lives

From land to land; and in my breast
  Spring wakens too: and my regret
  Become an April violet,
And buds and blossoms like the rest.

            Alfred Tennyson [1809–1892]

"THE SPRING RETURNS"

THE Spring returns! What matters then that War
On the horizon like a beacon burns,
That Death ascends, man's most desirèd star,
That Darkness is his hope? The Spring returns!
Triumphant through the wider-archèd cope
She comes, she comes, unto her tyranny,
And at her coronation are set ope
The prisons of the mind, and man is free!
The beggar-garbed or over-bent with snows,
Each mortal, long defeated, disallowed,
Feeling her touch, grows stronger limbed, and knows
The purple on his shoulders and is proud.
  The Spring returns! O madness beyond sense,
  Breed in our bones thine own omnipotence!

            Charles Leonard Moore [1854–

"WHEN THE HOUNDS OF SPRING"

Chorus from "Atalanta in Calydon"

WHEN the hounds of spring are on winter's traces,
  The mother of months in meadow or plain
Fills the shadows and windy places
  With lisp of leaves and ripple of rain;

And the brown bright nightingale amorous
Is half assuaged for Itylus,
For the Thracian ships and the foreign faces,
    The tongueless vigil, and all the pain.

Come with bows bent and with emptying of quivers,
    Maiden most perfect, lady of light,
With a noise of winds and many rivers,
    With a clamor of waters, and with might;
Bind on thy sandals, O thou most fleet,
Over the splendor and speed of thy feet;
For the faint east quickens, the wan west shivers,
    Round the feet of the day and the feet of the night.

Where shall we find her, how shall we sing to her,
    Fold our hands round her knees, and cling?
O that man's heart were as fire and could spring to her,
    Fire, or the strength of the streams that spring!
For the stars and the winds are unto her
As raiment, as songs of the harp-player;
For the risen stars and the fallen cling to her,
    And the southwest-wind and the west-wind sing.

For winter's rains and ruins are over,
    And all the season of snows and sins;
The days dividing lover and lover,
    The light that loses, the night that wins;
And time remembered is grief forgotten,
And frosts are slain and flowers begotten,
And in green underwood and cover
    Blossom by blossom the spring begins.

The full streams feed on flower of rushes,
    Ripe grasses trammel a travelling foot,
The faint fresh flame of the young year flushes
    From leaf to flower and flower to fruit;
And fruit and leaf are as gold and fire,
And the oat is heard above the lyre,
And the hoofèd heel of a satyr crushes
    The chestnut-husk at the chestnut-root.

And Pan by noon and Bacchus by night,
　Fleeter of foot than the fleet-foot kid,
Follows with dancing and fills with delight
　The Mænad and the Bassarid;
And soft as lips that laugh and hide
The laughing leaves of the trees divide,
And screen from seeing and leave in sight
　The god pursuing, the maiden hid.

The ivy falls with the Bacchanal's hair
　Over her eyebrows hiding her eyes;
The wild vine slipping down leaves bare
　Her bright breast shortening into sighs;
The wild vine slips with the weight of its leaves,
But the berried ivy catches and cleaves
To the limbs that glitter, the feet that scare
　The wolf that follows, the fawn that flies.
Algernon Charles Swinburne [1837-1909]

SONG

Again rejoicing Nature sees
　Her robe assume its vernal hues;
Her leafy locks wave in the breeze,
　All freshly steeped in morning dews.

In vain to me the cowslips blaw,
　In vain to me the violets spring;
In vain to me in glen or shaw,
　The mavis and the lintwhite sing.

The merry ploughboy cheers his team,
　Wi' joy the tentie seedsman stalks,
But life to me's a weary dream,
　A dream of ane that never wauks.

The wanton coot the water skims,
　Amang the reeds the ducklings cry,
The stately swan majestic swims,
　And everything is blest but I.

The shepherd steeks his faulding slap,
　And owre the moorland whistles shrill;
Wi' wild, unequal, wand'ring step
　I meet him on the dewy hill.

And when the lark, 'tween light and dark,
　Blithe waukens by the daisy's side,
And mounts and sings on flittering wings,
　A woe-worn ghaist I hameward glide.

Come, Winter, with thine angry howl,
　And raging bend the naked tree;
Thy gloom will soothe my cheerless soul,
　When Nature all is sad like me!
　　　　　　　　　　Robert Burns [1759–1796]

TO SPRING

O Thou with dewy locks, who lookest down
Through the clear windows of the morning, turn
Thine angel eyes upon our western isle,
Which in full choir hails thy approach, O Spring!

The hills tell one another, and the listening
Valleys hear; all our longing eyes are turned
Up to thy bright pavilions: issue forth
And let thy holy feet visit our clime!

Come o'er the eastern hills, and let our winds
Kiss thy perfumèd garments; let us taste
Thy morn and evening breath; scatter thy pearls
Upon our lovesick land that mourns for thee.

O deck her forth with thy fair fingers; pour
Thy soft kisses on her bosom; and put
Thy golden crown upon her languished head,
Whose modest tresses are bound up for thee!
　　　　　　　　　　William Blake [1757–1827]

AN ODE ON THE SPRING

Lo! where the rosy-bosomed Hours,
  Fair Venus' train, appear,
Disclose the long-expecting flowers,
  And wake the purple year!
The Attic warbler pours her throat
Responsive to the cuckoo's note,
  The untaught harmony of spring:
While, whispering pleasure as they fly,
Cool Zephyrs through the clear blue sky
  Their gathered fragrance fling.

Where'er the oak's thick branches stretch
  A broader browner shade,
Where'er the rude and moss-grown beech
  O'er-canopies the glade,
Beside some water's rushy brink
With me the Muse shall sit, and think
  (At ease reclined in rustic state)
How vain the ardor of the crowd,
How low, how little are the proud,
  How indigent the great!

Still is the toiling hand of Care:
  The panting herds repose:
Yet, hark, how through the peopled air
  The busy murmur glows!
The insect-youth are on the wing,
Eager to taste the honied spring
  And float amid the liquid noon;
Some lightly o'er the current skim,
Some show their gaily-gilded trim
  Quick-glancing to the sun.

To Contemplation's sober eye
  Such is the race of Man:
And they that creep, and they that fly,
  Shall end where they began.

Alike the Busy and the Gay
But flutter through life's little day,
   In Fortune's varying colors dressed:
Brushed by the hand of rough Mischance,
Or chilled by Age, their airy dance
   They leave, in dust to rest.

Methinks I hear, in accents low,
   The sportive kind reply:
Poor moralist! and what art thou?
   A solitary fly!
Thy joys no glittering female meets,
No hive hast thou of hoarded sweets,
   No painted plumage to display;
On hasty wings thy youth is flown;
Thy sun is set, thy spring is gone—
   We frolic, while 'tis May.

Thomas Gray [1716–1771]

SPRING

SPRING, with that nameless pathos in the air
Which dwells with all things fair,
Spring, with her golden suns and silver rain,
Is with us once again.

Out in the lonely woods the jasmine burns
Its fragrant lamps, and turns
Into a royal court with green festoons
The banks of dark lagoons.

In the deep heart of every forest tree
The blood is all aglee,
And there's a look about the leafless bowers
As if they dreamed of flowers.

Yet still on every side we trace the hand
Of Winter in the land,
Save where the maple reddens on the lawn,
Flushed by the season's dawn;

Or where, like those strange semblances we find
That age to childhood bind,
The elm puts on, as if in Nature's scorn,
The brown of Autumn corn.

As yet the turf is dark, although you know
That, not a span below,
A thousand germs are groping through the gloom,
And soon will burst their tomb.

Already, here and there, on frailest stems
Appear some azure gems,
Small as might deck, upon a gala day,
The forehead of a fay.

In gardens you may note amid the dearth,
The crocus breaking earth;
And near the snowdrop's tender white and green,
The violet in its screen.

But many gleams and shadows needs must pass
Along the budding grass,
And weeks go by, before the enamored South
Shall kiss the rose's mouth.

Still there's a sense of blossoms yet unborn
In the sweet airs of morn;
One almost looks to see the very street
Grow purple at his feet.

At times a fragrant breeze comes floating by,
And brings, you know not why,
A feeling as when eager crowds await
Before a palace gate

Some wondrous pageant; and you scarce would start,
If from a beech's heart
A blue-eyed Dryad, stepping forth, should say,
"Behold me! I am May!"

Henry Timrod [1829–1867]

THE MEADOWS IN SPRING

'Tis a dull sight
  To see the year dying,
When winter winds
  Set the yellow wood sighing:
    Sighing, oh! sighing.

When such a time cometh,
  I do retire
Into an old room
  Beside a bright fire:
    Oh, pile a bright fire!

And there I sit
  Reading old things,
Of knights and lorn damsels,
  While the wind sings—
    Oh, drearily sings!

I never look out
  Nor attend to the blast;
For all to be seen
  Is the leaves falling fast:
    Falling, falling!

But close at the hearth,
  Like a cricket, sit I,
Reading of summer
  And chivalry—
    Gallant chivalry!

Then with an old friend
  I talk of our youth!
How 'twas gladsome, but often
  Foolish, forsooth:
    But gladsome, gladsome!

Or to get merry
  We sing some old rhyme,
That made the wood ring again
  In summer time—
    Sweet summer time!

Then go we to smoking,
  Silent and snug:
Naught passes between us,
  Save a brown jug—
    Sometimes!

And sometimes a tear
  Will rise in each eye,
Seeing the two old friends
  So merrily—
    So merrily!

And ere to bed
  Go we, go we,
Down on the ashes
  We kneel on the knee,
    Praying together!

Thus, then, live I,
  Till, 'mid all the gloom,
By heaven! the bold sun
  Is with me in the room
    Shining, shining!

Then the clouds part,
  Swallows soaring between;
The spring is alive,
  And the meadows are green!

I jump up, like mad,
  Break the old pipe in twain,
And away to the meadows,
  The meadows again!
              Edward Fitzgerald [1809–1883]

THE SPRING

WHEN wintry weather's all a-done,
An' brooks do sparkle in the zun,
An' nâisy-builden rooks do vlee
Wi' sticks toward their elem tree;
When birds do zing, an' we can zee

Upon the boughs the buds o' spring,—
Then I'm as happy as a king,
    A-vield wi' health an' zunsheen.

Vor then the cowslip's hangèn flower
A-wetted in the zunny shower,
Do grow wi' vi'lets, sweet o' smell,
Bezide the wood-screened graegle's bell;
Where drushes' aggs, wi' sky-blue shell,
    Do lie in mossy nest among
        The thorns, while they do zing their zong
            At evenèn in the zunsheen.

An' God do meäke his win' to blow
An' raïn to vall vor high an' low,
An' bid his mornèn zun to rise
Vor all alike, an' groun' an' skies
Ha' colors vor the poor man's eyes:
    An' in our trials He is near,
        To hear our mwoan an' zee our tear,
            An' turn our clouds to zunsheen.

An' many times when I do vind
Things all goo wrong, an' v'ok unkind,
To zee the happy veedèn herds,
An' hear the zingèn o' the birds,
Do soothe my sorrow mwore than words;
    Vor I do zee that 'tis our sin
        Do meäke woone's soul so dark 'ithin,
            When God would gi'e woone zunsheen.
                    William Barnes [1801–1886]

"WHEN SPRING COMES BACK TO ENGLAND"

WHEN Spring comes back to England
    And crowns her brows with May,
Round the merry moonlit world
    She goes the greenwood way:
She throws a rose to Italy,
    A fleur-de-lys to France;
But round her regal morris-ring
    The seas of England dance.

When Spring comes back to England
  And dons her robe of green,
There's many a nation garlanded
  But England is the Queen;
She's Queen, she's Queen of all the world
  Beneath the laughing sky,
For the nations go a-Maying
  When they hear the New Year cry—

"Come over the water to England,
  My old love, my new love,
Come over the water to England,
  In showers of flowery rain;
Come over the water to England,
  April, my true love;
And tell the heart of England
  The Spring is here again!"

Alfred Noyes [1880—

NEW LIFE

SPRING comes laughing down the valley
All in white, from the snow
Where the winter's armies rally
  Loth to go.
Beauty white her garments shower
On the world where they pass,—
Hawthorn hedges, trees in flower,
Daisies in the grass.
Tremulous with longings dim,
Thickets by the river's rim
Have begun to dream of green.
Every tree is loud with birds.
Bourgeon, heart,—do thy part!
Raise a slender stalk of words
From a root unseen.

Amelia Josephine Burr [1878—

"OVER THE WINTRY THRESHOLD"

OVER the wintry threshold
  Who comes with joy today,
So frail, yet so enduring,
  To triumph o'er dismay?

Ah, quick her tears are springing,
    And quickly they are dried,
For sorrow walks before her,
    But gladness walks beside.

She comes with gusts of laughter,—
    The music as of rills;
With tenderness and sweetness,
    The wisdom of the hills.

Her hands are strong to comfort,
    Her heart is quick to heed;
She knows the signs of sadness,
    She knows the voice of need;

There is no living creature,
    However poor or small,
But she will know its trouble,
    And hearken to its call.

Oh, well they fare forever,
    By mighty dreams possessed,
Whose hearts have lain a moment
    On that eternal breast.

Bliss Carman [1861–1929]

MARCH

SLAYER of winter, art thou here again?
O welcome, thou that bring'st the summer nigh!
The bitter wind makes not thy victory vain,
Nor will we mock thee for thy faint blue sky.
Welcome, O March! whose kindly days and dry
Make April ready for the throstle's song,
Thou first redresser of the winter's wrong!

Yea, welcome, March! and though I die ere June,
Yet for the hope of life I give thee praise,
Striving to swell the burden of the tune
That even now I hear thy brown birds raise,
Unmindful of the past or coming days;
Who sing, "O joy! a new year is begun!
What happiness to look upon the sun!"

O, what begetteth all this storm of bliss,
But Death himself, who, crying solemnly,
Even from the heart of sweet Forgetfulness,
Bids us, "Rejoice! lest pleasureless ye die.
Within a little time must ye go by.
Stretch forth your open hands, and, while ye live,
Take all the gifts that Death and Life may give."

William Morris [1834–1896]

SONG IN MARCH

Now are the winds about us in their glee,
Tossing the slender tree;
Whirling the sands about his furious car,
March cometh from afar;
Breaks the sealed magic of old Winter's dreams,
And rends his glassy streams;
Chafing with potent airs, he fiercely takes
Their fetters from the lakes,
And, with a power by queenly Spring supplied,
Wakens the slumbering tide.

With a wild love he seeks young Summer's charms
And clasps her to his arms;
Lifting his shield between, he drives away
Old Winter from his prey;—
The ancient tyrant whom he boldly braves,
Goes howling to his caves;
And, to his northern realm compelled to fly,
Yields up the victory;
Melted are all his bands, o'erthrown his towers,
And March comes bringing flowers.

William Gilmore Simms [1806–1870]

MARCH

Blossom on the plum,
  Wild wind and merry;
  Leaves upon the cherry,
And one swallow come.

Red windy dawn,
  Swift rain and sunny;
  Wild bees seeking honey,
Crocus on the lawn;
  Blossom on the plum.

Grass begins to grow,
  Dandelions come;
Snowdrops haste to go
After last month's snow;
Rough winds beat and blow,
  Blossom on the plum.

Nora Hopper [1871–1906]

WRITTEN IN MARCH

THE Cock is crowing,
The stream is flowing,
The small birds twitter,
The lake doth glitter,
The green field sleeps in the sun;
  The oldest and youngest
  Are at work with the strongest;
  The cattle are grazing,
  Their heads never raising;
There are forty feeding like one!

  Like an army defeated
  The snow hath retreated,
  And now doth fare ill
  On the top of the bare hill;
The ploughboy is whooping—anon—anon
  There's joy in the mountains;
  There's life in the fountains;
  Small clouds are sailing,
  Blue sky prevailing;
The rain is over and gone!

William Wordsworth [1770–1850]

THE PASSING OF MARCH

THE braggart March stood in the season's door
  With his broad shoulders blocking up the way,
Shaking the snow-flakes from the cloak he wore,
  And from the fringes of his kirtle gray.
Near by him April stood with tearful face,
  With violets in her hands, and in her hair
Pale, wild anemones; the fragrant lace
  Half-parted from her breast, which seemed like fair,
Dawn-tinted mountain snow, smooth-drifted there.

She on the blusterer's arm laid one white hand,
  But he would none of her soft blandishment,
Yet did she plead with tears none might withstand,
  For even the fiercest hearts at last relent.
And he, at last, in ruffian tenderness,
  With one swift, crushing kiss her lips did greet.
Ah, poor starved heart!—for that one rude caress,
  She cast her violets underneath his feet.
                    Robert Burns Wilson [1850–1916]

HOME THOUGHTS, FROM ABROAD

OH, to be in England
Now that April's there,
And whoever wakes in England
Sees, some morning, unaware,
That the lowest boughs and the brushwood sheaf
Round the elm-tree bole are in tiny leaf,
While the chaffinch sings on the orchard bough
In England—now!

And after April, when May follows
And the white-throat builds, and all the swallows!
Hark, where my blossomed pear-tree in the hedge
Leans to the field and scatters on the clover
Blossoms and dewdrops—at the bent spray's edge—
That's the wise thrush: he sings each song twice over,

Lest you should think he never could recapture
The first fine careless rapture!
And though the fields look rough with hoary dew,
All will be gay when noontide wakes anew
The buttercups, the little children's dower
—Far brighter than this gaudy melon-flower!

Robert Browning [1812–1889]

SONG

APRIL, April,
Laugh thy girlish laughter;
Then, the moment after,
Weep thy girlish tears!
April, that mine ears
Like a lover greetest,
If I tell thee, sweetest,
All my hopes and fears,
April, April,
Laugh thy golden laughter,
But, the moment after,
Weep thy golden tears!

William Watson [1858–1935]

AN APRIL ADORATION

SANG the sunrise on an amber morn—
"Earth, be glad! An April day is born.

"Winter's done, and April's in the skies,
Earth, look up with laughter in your eyes!"

Putting off her dumb dismay of snow,
Earth bade all her unseen children grow.

Then the sound of growing in the air
Rose to God a liturgy of prayer;

And the thronged succession of the days
Uttered up to God a psalm of praise.

Laughed the running sap in every vein,
Laughed the running flurries of warm rain,

Laughed the life in every wandering root,
Laughed the tingling cells of bud and shoot.

God in all the concord of their mirth
Heard the adoration-song of Earth.

Charles G. D. Roberts [1860–

SWEET WILD APRIL

O SWEET wild April
  Came over the hills,
He skipped with the winds
  And he tripped with the rills;
His raiment was all
  Of the daffodils.
     Sing hi,
     Sing hey,
     Sing ho!

O sweet wild April
  Came down the lea,
Dancing along
  With his sisters three:
Carnation, and Rose,
  And tall Lily.
     Sing hi,
     Sing hey,
     Sing ho!

O sweet wild April,
  On pastoral quill
Came piping in moonlight
  By hollow and hill,
In starlight at midnight,
  By dingle and rill.
     Sing hi,
     Sing hey,
     Sing ho!

Where sweet wild April
    His melody played,
Trooped cowslip, and primrose,
    And iris, the maid,
And silver narcissus,
    A star in the shade.
        Sing hi,
        Sing hey,
        Sing ho!

When sweet wild April
    Dipped down the dale,
Pale cuckoopint brightened,
    And windflower frail,
And white-thorn, the wood-bride,
    In virginal veil.
        Sing hi,
        Sing hey,
        Sing ho!

When sweet wild April
    Through deep woods pressed,
Sang cuckoo above him,
    And lark on his crest,
And Philomel fluttered
    Close under his breast.
        Sing hi,
        Sing hey,
        Sing ho!

O sweet wild April,
    Wherever you went
The bondage of winter
    Was broken and rent,
Sank elfin ice-city
    And frost-goblin's tent.
        Sing hi,
        Sing hey,
        Sing ho!

Yet sweet wild April,
    The blithe, the brave,
Fell asleep in the fields
    By a windless wave
And Jack-in-the-Pulpit
    Preached over his grave.
        Sing hi,
        Sing hey,
        Sing ho!

O sweet wild April,
    Farewell to thee!
And a deep sweet sleep
    To thy sisters three,—
Carnation, and Rose,
    And tall Lily.
        Sing hi,
        Sing hey,
        Sing ho!
            William Force Stead [18 -

SPINNING IN APRIL

Moon in heaven's garden, among the clouds that wander,
Crescent moon so young to see, above the April ways,
Whiten, bloom not yet, not yet, within the twilight yonder;
All my spinning is not done, for all the loitering days.

Oh, my heart has two wild wings that ever would be flying!
Oh, my heart's a meadow-lark that ever would be free!
Well it is that I must spin until the light be dying;
Well it is the little wheel must turn all day for me!

All the hill-tops beckon, and beyond the western meadows
Something calls me ever, calls me ever, low and clear:
A little tree as young as I, the coming summer shadows,—
The voice of running waters that I ever thirst to hear.

Oftentime the plea of it has set my wings a-beating;
Oftentimes it coaxes, as I sit in weary-wise,

Till the wild life hastens out to wild things all entreating,
And leaves me at the spinning-wheel, with dark, unseeing
eyes.

Josephine Preston Peabody [1874–1922]

SONG: ON MAY MORNING

Now the bright morning-star, day's harbinger,
Comes dancing from the east, and leads with her
The flowery May, who from her green lap throws
The yellow cowslip and the pale primrose.
Hail, bounteous May, that dost inspire
Mirth and youth and warm desire!
Woods and groves are of thy dressing,
Hill and dale doth boast thy blessing.
Thus we salute thee with our early song,
And welcome thee, and wish thee long.

John Milton [1608–1674]

A MAY BURDEN

THROUGH meadow-ways as I did tread,
The corn grew in great lustihead,
And hey! the beeches burgeonèd.
      By Goddès fay, by Goddès fay!
    It is the month, the jolly month,
    It is the jolly month of May.

God ripe the wines and corn, I say,
And wenches for the marriage-day,
And boys to teach love's comely play.
      By Goddès fay, by Goddès fay!
    It is the month, the jolly month,
    It is the jolly month of May.

As I went down by lane and lea,
The daisies reddened so, pardie!
"Blushets!" I said, " I well do see,
      By Goddès fay, by Goddès fay!
    The thing ye think of in this month,
    Heigho! this jolly month of May."

As down I went by rye and oats,
The blossoms smelt of kisses; throats
    Of birds turned kisses into notes;
       By Goddès fay, by Goddès fay!
    The kiss it is a growing flower,
    I trow, this jolly month of May.

God send a mouth to every kiss,
Seeing the blossom of this bliss
    By gathering doth grow, certes!
       By Goddès fay, by Goddès fay!
    Thy brow-garland pushed all aslant
    Tells—but I tell not, wanton May!

Francis Thompson [1859?–1907]

CORINNA'S GOING A-MAYING

GET up, get up for shame, the blooming morn
Upon her wings presents the god unshorn.
    See how Aurora throws her fair
    Fresh-quilted colors through the air:
    Get up, sweet slug-a-bed, and see
    The dew bespangling herb and tree.
Each flower has wept, and bowed toward the east,
Above an hour since: yet you not dressed;
    Nay! not so much as out of bed;
    When all the birds have matins said
    And sung their thankful hymns: 'tis sin,
    Nay, profanation, to keep in,
When as a thousand virgins on this day
Spring, sooner than the lark, to fetch in May.

Rise and put on your foliage, and be seen
To come forth, like the spring-time, fresh and green,
    And sweet as Flora. Take no care
    For jewels for your gown or hair:
    Fear not; the leaves will strew
    Gems in abundance upon you:
Besides, the childhood of the day has kept,
Against you come, some orient pearls unwept;

Come, and receive them while the light
Hangs on the dew-locks of the night,
    And Titan on the eastern hill
    Retires himself, or else stands still
Till you come forth.   Wash, dress, be brief in praying:
Few beads are best, when once we go a-Maying.

Come, my Corinna, come; and, coming, mark
How each field turns a street, each street a park
    Made green and trimmed with trees; see how
    Devotion gives each house a bough
    Or branch: each porch, each door, ere this,
    An ark, a tabernacle is,
Made up of white-thorn, neatly interwove;
As if here were those cooler shades of love.
    Can such delights be in the street
    And open fields, and we not see't?
    Come, we'll abroad; and let's obey
    The proclamation made for May:
And sin no more, as we have done, by staying;
But, my Corinna, come, let's go a-Maying.

There's not a budding boy or girl, this day,
But is got up, and gone to bring in May.
    A deal of youth, ere this, is come
    Back, and with white-thorn laden home.
    Some have despatched their cakes and cream
    Before that we have left to dream:
And some have wept, and wooed and plighted troth,
And chose their priest, ere we can cast off sloth:
    Many a green gown has been given;
    Many a kiss, both odd and even:
    Many a glance, too, has been sent
    From out the eye, love's firmament;
Many a jest told of the keys betraying
This night, and locks picked, yet we're not a-Maying.

Come, let us go, while we are in our prime,
And take the harmless folly of the time.
    We shall grow old apace, and die
    Before we know our liberty.

Our life is short, and our days run
   As fast away as does the sun;
And, as a vapor or a drop of rain,
Once lost, can ne'er be found again:
   So when or you or I are made
   A fable, song, or fleeting shade,
   All love, all liking, all delight
   Lies drowned with us in endless night.
Then while time serves, and we are but decaying,
Come, my Corinna, come, let's go a-Maying.

                Robert Herrick [1591–1674]

"SISTER, AWAKE!"

SISTER, awake! close not your eyes!
   The day her light discloses,
And the bright morning doth arise
   Out of her bed of roses.

See the clear sun, the world's bright eye,
   In at our window peeping:
Lo, how he blusheth to espy
   Us idle wenches sleeping!

Therefore awake! make haste, I say,
   And let us, without staying,
All in our gowns of green so gay
   Into the Park a-maying!

                Unknown

MAY

   MAY! queen of blossoms,
     And fulfilling flowers,
  With what pretty music
     Shall we charm the hours?
  Wilt thou have pipe and reed,
  Blown in the open mead?
  Or to the lute give heed
     In the green bowers?

Thou hast no need of us,
  Or pipe or wire;
Thou hast the golden bee
  Ripened with fire;
And many thousand more
Songsters, that thee adore,
Filling earth's grassy floor
  With new desire.

Thou hast thy mighty herds,
  Tame and free-livers;
Doubt not, thy music too
  In the deep rivers;
And the whole plumy flight
Warbling the day and night—
Up at the gates of light,
  See, the lark quivers!

        Edward Hovell-Thurlow [1781–1829]

MAY

COME walk with me along this willowed lane,
  Where, like lost coinage from some miser's store,
  The golden dandelions more and more
Glow, as the warm sun kisses them again!
For this is May! who with a daisy chain
  Leads on the laughing Hours; for now is o'er
  Long winter's trance. No longer rise and roar
His forest-wrenching blasts. The hopeful swain,
Along the furrow, sings behind his team;
  Loud pipes the redbreast—troubadour of spring,
  And vocal all the morning copses ring;
More blue the skies in lucent lakelets gleam;
  And the glad earth, caressed by murmuring showers,
  Wakes like a bride, to deck herself with flowers!

        Henry Sylvester Cornwell [1831–1886]

A SPRING LILT

THROUGH the silver mist
Of the blossom-spray
Trill the orioles: list
To their joyous lay!
"What in all the world, in all the world," they say,
"Is half so sweet, so sweet, is half so sweet as May?"

"June! June! June!"
Low croon
The brown bees in the clover.
"Sweet! sweet! sweet!"
Repeat
The robins, nested over.

Unknown

SUMMER LONGINGS

Ah! my heart is weary waiting,
Waiting for the May,—
Waiting for the pleasant rambles
Where the fragrant hawthorn-brambles,
With the woodbine alternating,
Scent the dewy way.
Ah! my heart is weary waiting,
Waiting for the May.

Ah! my heart is sick with longing,
Longing for the May,—
Longing to escape from study
To the young face fair and ruddy,
And the thousand charms belonging
To the summer's day.
Ah! my heart is sick with longing,
Longing for the May.

Ah! my heart is sore with sighing,
Sighing for the May,—
Sighing for their sure returning,
When the summer beams are burning,

Hopes and flowers that, dead or dying,
    All the winter lay.
Ah! my heart is sore with sighing,
    Sighing for the May.

Ah! my heart is pained with throbbing,
    Throbbing for the May,—
Throbbing for the seaside billows,
Or the water-wooing willows;
    Where, in laughing and in sobbing,
      Glide the streams away.
    Ah! my heart, my heart is throbbing,
      Throbbing for the May.

Waiting sad, dejected, weary,
    Waiting for the May:
Spring goes by with wasted warnings,—
Moonlit evenings, sunbright mornings,—
    Summer comes, yet dark and dreary
      Life still ebbs away;
    Man is ever weary, weary,
      Waiting for the May!
         Denis Florence MacCarthy [1817–1882]

MIDSUMMER

AROUND this lovely valley rise
The purple hills of Paradise.

O, softly on yon banks of haze,
Her rosy face the Summer lays!

Becalmed along the azure sky,
The argosies of cloudland lie,
Whose shores, with many a shining rift,
Far off their pearl-white peaks uplift.

Through all the long midsummer-day
The meadow-sides are sweet with hay.
I seek the coolest sheltered seat,
Just where the field and forest meet,—

Where grow the pine-trees tall and bland,
The ancient oaks austere and grand,
And fringy roots and pebbles fret
The ripples of the rivulet.

I watch the mowers, as they go
Through the tall grass, a white-sleeved row.
With even stroke their scythes they swing,
In tune their merry whetstones ring.
Behind the nimble youngsters run,
And toss the thick swaths in the sun.
The cattle graze, while, warm and still,
Slopes the broad pasture, basks the hill,
And bright, where summer breezes break,
The green wheat crinkles like a lake.

The butterfly and humblebee
Come to the pleasant woods with me;
Quickly before me runs the quail,
Her chickens skulk behind the rail;
High up the lone wood-pigeon sits,
And the woodpecker pecks and flits.
Sweet woodland music sinks and swells,
The brooklet rings its tinkling bells,
The swarming insects drone and hum,
The partridge beats its throbbing drum.
The squirrel leaps among the boughs,
And chatters in his leafy house.
The oriole flashes by; and, look!
Into the mirror of the brook,
Where the vain bluebird trims his coat,
Two tiny feathers fall and float.

As silently, as tenderly,
The down of peace descends on me.
O, this is peace! I have no need
Of friend to talk, of book to read:
A dear Companion here abides;
Close to my thrilling heart He hides;

The holy silence is His Voice:
I lie and listen, and rejoice.
    John Townsend Trowbridge [1827–1916]

A MIDSUMMER SONG

O, FATHER'S gone to market-town, he was up before the
    day,
And Jamie's after robins, and the man is making hay,
And whistling down the hollow goes the boy that minds the
    mill,
While mother from the kitchen-door is calling with a will:
        "Polly!—Polly!—The cows are in the corn!
            O, where's Polly?"

From all the misty morning air there comes a summer
    sound—
A murmur as of waters from skies and trees and ground.
The birds they sing upon the wing, the pigeons bill and coo,
And over hill and hollow rings again the loud halloo:
        "Polly!—Polly!—The cows are in the corn!
            O, where's Polly?"

Above the trees the honey-bees swarm by with buzz and
    boom,
And in the field and garden a thousand blossoms bloom.
Within the farmer's meadow a brown-eyed daisy blows,
And down at the edge of the hollow a red and thorny rose.
        But Polly!—Polly!—The cows are in the corn!
            O, where's Polly?

How strange at such a time of day the mill should stop its
    clatter!
The farmer's wife is listening now and wonders what's the
    matter.
O, wild the birds are singing in the wood and on the hill,
While whistling up the hollow goes the boy that minds the
    mill.
        But Polly!—Polly!—The cows are in the corn!
            O, where's Polly?
            Richard Watson Gilder [1844–1909]

JUNE

From the Prelude to "The Vision of Sir Launfal"

OVER his keys the musing organist,
  Beginning doubtfully and far away,
First lets his fingers wander as they list,
  And builds a bridge from Dreamland for his lay:
Then, as the touch of his loved instrument
  Gives hope and fervor, nearer draws his theme,
First guessed by faint auroral flushes sent
  Along the wavering vista of his dream.

Not only around our infancy
  Doth heaven with all its splendors lie;
Daily, with souls that cringe and plot,
  We Sinais climb and know it not.

Over our manhood bend the skies;
  Against our fallen and traitor lives
The great winds utter prophecies;
  With our faint hearts the mountain strives;
Its arms outstretched, the druid wood
  Waits with its benedicite;
And to our age's drowsy blood
  Still shouts the inspiring sea.

Earth gets its price for what Earth gives us;
  The beggar is taxed for a corner to die in,
The priest hath his fee who comes and shrives us,
  We bargain for the graves we lie in;
At the devil's booth are all things sold,
Each ounce of dross costs its ounce of gold;
  For a cap and bells our lives we pay,
Bubbles we buy with a whole soul's tasking:
  'Tis heaven alone that is given away,
'Tis only God may be had for the asking;
No price is set on the lavish summer;
June may be had by the poorest comer.

And what is so rare as a day in June?
    Then, if ever, come perfect days;
Then Heaven tries earth if it be in tune,
    And over it softly her warm ear lays;
Whether we look, or whether we listen,
We hear life murmur, or see it glisten;
Every clod feels a stir of might,
    An instinct within it that reaches and towers,
And, groping blindly above it for light,
    Climbs to a soul in grass and flowers;
The flush of life may well be seen
    Thrilling back over hills and valleys;
The cowslip startles in meadows green,
    The buttercup catches the sun in its chalice,
And there's never a leaf nor a blade too mean
    To be some happy creature's palace;
The little bird sits at his door in the sun,
    Atilt like a blossom among the leaves,
And lets his illumined being o'errun
    With the deluge of summer it receives;
His mate feels the eggs beneath her wings,
And the heart in her dumb breast flutters and sings;
He sings to the wide world and she to her nest,—
In the nice ear of Nature which song is the best?

Now is the high-tide of the year,
    And whatever of life hath ebbed away
Comes flooding back with a ripply cheer,
    Into every bare inlet and creek and bay;
Now the heart is so full that a drop overfills it,
We are happy now because God wills it;
No matter how barren the past may have been,
'Tis enough for us now that the leaves are green;
We sit in the warm shade and feel right well
How the sap creeps up and the blossoms swell;
We may shut our eyes, but we cannot help knowing
That skies are clear and grass is growing;
The breeze comes whispering in our ear,
That dandelions are blossoming near,
That maize has sprouted, that streams are flowing,

That the river is bluer than the sky,
That the robin is plastering his house hard by;
And if the breeze kept the good news back,
For other couriers we should not lack;
  We could guess it all by yon heifer's lowing,
And hark! how clear bold chanticleer,
Warmed with the new wine of the year,
  Tells all in his lusty crowing!

         James Russell Lowell [1819–1891]

JUNE

WHEN the bubble moon is young,
  Down the sources of the breeze,
Like a yellow lantern hung
  In the tops of blackened trees,
There is promise she will grow
Into beauty unforetold,
Into all unthought-of gold.
     Heigh ho!

When the Spring has dipped her foot,
  Like a bather, in the air,
And the ripples warm the root
  Till the little flowers dare,
There is promise she will grow
Sweeter than the Springs of old,
Fairer than was ever told.
     Heigh ho!

But the moon of middle night,
  Risen, is the rounded moon;
And the Spring of budding light
  Eddies into just a June.
Ah, the promise—was it so?
Nay, the gift was fairy gold;
All the new is over-old.
     Heigh ho!

         Harrison Smith Morris [1856–

HARVEST

SWEET, sweet, sweet,
     Is the wind's song,
Astir in the rippled wheat
     All day long,
It hath the brook's wild gayety,
     The sorrowful cry of the sea.
          Oh, hush and hear!
          Sweet, sweet and clear,
          Above the locust's whirr
          And hum of bee
     Rises that soft, pathetic harmony.

In the meadow-grass
     The innocent white daisies blow,
The dandelion plume doth pass
     Vaguely to and fro,—
          The unquiet spirit of a flower
          That hath too brief an hour.

Now doth a little cloud all white,
     Or golden bright,
Drift down the warm, blue sky;
     And now on the horizon line,
Where dusky woodlands lie,
     A sunny mist doth shine,
     Like to a veil before a holy shrine,
     Concealing, half-revealing, things divine.

          Sweet, sweet, sweet,
               Is the wind's song,
          Astir in the rippled wheat
               All day long.
          That exquisite music calls
               The reaper everywhere—
               Life and death must share.
          The golden harvest falls.

So doth all end,—
    Honored Philosophy,
    Science and Art,
        The bloom of the heart;—
Master, Consoler, Friend,
    Make Thou the harvest of our days
    To fall within Thy ways.
        Ellen Mackay Hutchinson Cortissoz [?–1933]

SCYTHE SONG

MOWERS, weary and brown, and blithe,
    What is the word methinks ye know,
Endless over-word that the Scythe
    Sings to the blades of the grass below?
Scythes that swing in the grass and clover,
    Something, still, they say as they pass;
What is the word that, over and over,
    Sings the Scythe to the flowers and grass?

Hush, ah hush, the Scythes are saying,
    Hush, and heed not, and fall asleep;
Hush, they say to the grasses swaying,
    Hush, they sing to the clover deep!
Hush—'tis the lullaby Time is singing—
    Hush, and heed not, for all things pass,
Hush, ah hush! and the Scythes are swinging
    Over the clover, over the grass!
        Andrew Lang [1844–1912]

SEPTEMBER

SWEET is the voice that calls
    From babbling waterfalls
In meadows where the downy seeds are flying;
    And soft the breezes blow,
    And eddying come and go,
In faded gardens where the rose is dying.

Among the stubbled corn
The blithe quail pipes at morn,
The merry partridge drums in hidden places,
And glittering insects gleam
Above the reedy stream,
Where busy spiders spin their filmy laces.

At eve, cool shadows fall
Across the garden wall,
And on the clustered grapes to purple turning;
And pearly vapors lie
Along the eastern sky,
Where the broad harvest-moon is redly burning.

Ah, soon on field and hill
The winds shall whistle chill,
And patriarch swallows call their flocks together
To fly from frost and snow,
And seek for lands where blow
The fairer blossoms of a balmier weather.

The pollen-dusted bees
Search for the honey-lees
That linger in the last flowers of September,
While plaintive mourning doves
Coo sadly to their loves
Of the dead summer they so well remember.

The cricket chirps all day,
"O fairest summer, stay!"
The squirrel eyes askance the chestnuts browning;
The wild fowl fly afar
Above the foamy bar,
And hasten southward ere the skies are frowning.

Now comes a fragrant breeze
Through the dark cedar-trees,
And round about my temples fondly lingers,
In gentle playfulness,
Like to the soft caress
Bestowed in happier days by loving fingers.

Yet, though a sense of grief
　　Comes with the falling leaf,
And memory makes the summer doubly pleasant,
　　In all my autumn dreams
　　A future summer gleams,
Passing the fairest glories of the present!

George Arnold [1834-1865]

INDIAN SUMMER

These are the days when birds come back,
A very few, a bird or two,
To take a backward look.

These are the days when skies put on
The old, old sophistries of June,—
A blue and gold mistake.

Oh, fraud that cannot cheat the bee,
Almost thy plausibility
Induces my belief,

Till ranks of seeds their witness bear,
And softly through the altered air
Hurries a timid leaf!

Oh, sacrament of summer days,
Oh, last communion in the haze,
Permit a child to join,

Thy sacred emblems to partake,
Thy consecrated bread to break,
Taste thine immortal wine!

Emily Dickinson [1830-1886]

PREVISION

Oh, days of beauty standing veiled apart,
　With dreamy skies and tender, tremulous air,
In this rich Indian summer of the heart
　Well may the earth her jewelled halo wear.

The long brown fields—no longer drear and dull—
   Burn with the glow of these deep-hearted hours.
Until the dry weeds seem more beautiful,
   More spiritlike than even summer's flowers.

But yesterday the world was stricken bare,
   Left old and dead in gray, enshrouding gloom;
To-day what vivid wonder of the air
   Awakes the soul of vanished light and bloom?

Sharp with the clean, fine ecstasy of death,
   A mightier wind shall strike the shrinking earth,
An exhalation of creative breath
   Wake the white wonder of the winter's birth.

In her wide Pantheon—her temple place—
   Wrapped in strange beauty and new comforting,
We shall not miss the Summer's full-blown grace,
   Nor hunger for the swift, exquisite Spring.
              Ada Foster Murray [1857–1936]

A SONG OF EARLY AUTUMN

WHEN late in summer the streams run yellow,
   Burst the bridges and spread into bays;
When berries are black and peaches are mellow,
   And hills are hidden by rainy haze;

When the goldenrod is golden still,
   But the heart of the sunflower is darker and sadder;
When the corn is in stacks on the slope of the hill,
   And slides o'er the path the stripèd adder;

When butterflies flutter from clover to thicket,
   Or wave their wings on the drooping leaf;
When the breeze comes shrill with the call of the cricket,
   Grasshopper's rasp, and rustle of sheaf;

When high in the field the fern-leaves wrinkle,
   And brown is the grass where the mowers have mown;
When low in the meadow the cow-bells tinkle,
   And small brooks crinkle o'er stock and stone;

When heavy and hollow the robin's whistle
  And shadows are deep in the heat of noon;
When the air is white with the down o' the thistle,
  And the sky is red with the harvest moon;

O, then be chary, young Robert and Mary,
  No time let slip, not a moment wait!
    If the fiddle would play it must stop its tuning;
    And they who would wed must be done with their
      mooning;
So let the churn rattle, see well to the cattle,
  And pile the wood by the barn-yard gate!

          Richard Watson Gilder [1844–1909]

TO AUTUMN

Season of mists and mellow fruitfulness!
Close bosom-friend of the maturing sun;
Conspiring with him how to load and bless
With fruit the vines that round the thatch-eaves run;
To bend with apples the mossed cottage-trees,
And fill all fruit with ripeness to the core;
To swell the gourd, and plump the hazel shells
With a sweet kernel; to set budding more,
And still more, later flowers for the bees,
Until they think warm days will never cease,
For Summer has o'erbrimmed their clammy cells.

Who hath not seen thee oft amid thy store?
Sometimes whoever seeks abroad may find
Thee sitting careless on a granary floor,
Thy hair soft-lifted by the winnowing wind;
Or on a half-reaped furrow sound asleep,
Drowsed with the fume of poppies, while thy hook
Spares the next swath and all its twinèd flowers;
And sometimes like a gleaner thou dost keep
Steady thy laden head across a brook;
Or by a cider-press, with patient look,
Thou watchest the last oozings, hours by hours.

Where are the songs of Spring? Ay, where are they?
Think not of them, thou hast thy music too,
While barrèd clouds bloom the soft-dying day
And touch the stubble-plains with rosy hue;
Then in a wailful choir the small gnats mourn
Among the river shallows, borne aloft
Or sinking as the light wind lives or dies;
And full-grown lambs loud bleat from hilly bourn;
Hedge-crickets sing, and now with treble soft
The redbreast whistles from a garden-croft,
And gathering swallows twitter in the skies.

John Keats [1795–1821]

ODE TO AUTUMN

I SAW old Autumn in the misty morn
Stand shadowless like Silence, listening
To silence, for no lonely bird would sing
Into his hollow ear from woods forlorn,
Nor lowly hedge nor solitary thorn;—
Shaking his languid locks all dewy bright
With tangled gossamer that fell by night,
  Pearling his coronet of golden corn.

Where are the songs of Summer?—With the sun,
Oping the dusky eyelids of the South,
Till shade and silence waken up as one,
And Morning sings with a warm odorous mouth.
Where are the merry birds?—Away, away,
On panting wings through the inclement skies,
      Lest owls should prey
      Undazzled at noonday,
And tear with horny beak their lustrous eyes.

Where are the blooms of Summer?—In the West,
Blushing their last to the last sunny hours,
When the mild Eve by sudden Night is pressed
Like tearful Proserpine, snatched from her flowers,
      To a most gloomy breast.

Where is the pride of Summer,—the green prime,—
The many, many leaves all twinkling?—Three
On the mossed elm; three on the naked lime
Trembling,—and one upon the old oak-tree!
    Where is the Dryad's immortality?—
Gone into mournful cypress and dark yew,
Or wearing the long gloomy Winter through
    In the smooth holly's green eternity.

The squirrel gloats on his accomplished hoard,
The ants have brimmed their garners with ripe grain,
    And honey bees have stored
The sweets of Summer in their luscious cells;
The swallows all have winged across the main;
But here the Autumn melancholy dwells,
    And sighs her tearful spells
Amongst the sunless shadows of the plain.
        Alone, alone,
        Upon a mossy stone,
She sits and reckons up the dead and gone,
With the last leaves for a love-rosary,
Whilst all the withered world looks drearily,
Like a dim picture of the drownèd past
In the hushed mind's mysterious far away,
Doubtful what ghostly thing will steal the last
Into that distance, gray upon the gray.

O go and sit with her, and be o'ershaded
Under the languid downfall of her hair:
She wears a coronal of flowers faded
Upon her forehead, and a face of care;—
There is enough of withered everywhere
To make her bower,—and enough of gloom;
There is enough of sadness to invite,
If only for the rose that died, whose doom
Is Beauty's,—she that with the living bloom
Of conscious cheeks most beautifies the light:
There is enough of sorrowing, and quite
Enough of bitter fruits the earth doth bear,—
Enough of chilly droppings for her bowl;

Enough of fear and shadowy despair,
To frame her cloudy prison for the soul!

Thomas Hood [1799–1845]

ODE TO THE WEST WIND

I

O WILD West Wind, thou breath of Autumn's being,
    Thou from whose unseen presence the leaves dead
Are driven, like ghosts from an enchanter fleeing,

    Yellow, and black, and pale, and hectic red,
Pestilence-stricken multitudes! O thou
    Who chariotest to their dark wintry bed

The wingèd seeds, where they lie cold and low,
    Each like a corpse within its grave, until
Thine azure sister of the Spring shall blow

    Her clarion o'er the dreaming earth, and fill
(Driving sweet buds like flocks to feed in air)
    With living hues and odors plain and hill;

Wild Spirit, which art moving everywhere;
Destroyer and preserver; hear, O hear!

II

Thou on whose stream, 'mid the steep sky's commotion,
    Loose clouds like earth's decaying leaves are shed,
Shook from the tangled boughs of heaven and ocean,

    Angels of rain and lightning! there are spread
On the blue surface of thine airy surge,
    Like the bright hair uplifted from the head

Of some fierce Mænad, even from the dim verge
    Of the horizon to the zenith's height,
The locks of the approaching storm. Thou dirge

Of the dying year, to which this closing night
Will be the dome of a vast sepulchre,
  Vaulted with all thy congregated might

Of vapors, from whose solid atmosphere
Black rain, and fire, and hail will burst: O hear!

III

Thou who didst waken from his summer dreams
  The blue Mediterranean, where he lay,
Lulled by the coil of his crystàlline streams,

  Beside a pumice isle in Baiæ's bay,
And saw in sleep old palaces and towers
  Quivering within the wave's intenser day,

All overgrown with azure moss, and flowers
  So sweet, the sense faints picturing them! Thou
For whose path the Atlantic's level powers

  Cleave themselves into chasms, while far below
The sea-blooms and the oozy woods which wear
  The sapless foliage of the ocean, know

Thy voice, and suddenly grow gray with fear,
And tremble and despoil themselves: O hear!

IV

If I were a dead leaf thou mightest bear;
  If I were a swift cloud to fly with thee;
A wave to pant beneath thy power, and share

  The impulse of thy strength, only less free
Than thou, O uncontrollable! If even
  I were as in my boyhood, and could be

The comrade of thy wanderings over heaven,
  As then, when to outstrip thy skiey speed
Scarce seemed a vision—I would ne'er have striven

As thus with thee in prayer in my sore need.
O! lift me as a wave, a leaf, a cloud!
    I fall upon the thorns of life!   I bleed!

A heavy weight of hours has chained and bowed
One too like thee—tameless, and swift, and proud.

V

Make me thy lyre, even as the forest is:
    What if my leaves are falling like its own?
The tumult of thy mighty harmonies

    Will take from both a deep, autumnal tone,
Sweet though in sadness.   Be thou, Spirit fierce,
    My spirit!   Be thou me, impetuous one!

Drive my dead thoughts over the universe,
    Like withered leaves, to quicken a new birth;
And, by the incantation of this verse,

    Scatter, as from an unextinguished hearth
Ashes and sparks, my words among mankind!
    Be through my lips to unawakened earth

The trumpet of a prophecy!   O Wind,
If Winter comes, can Spring be far behind?
                    Percy Bysshe Shelley [1792–1822]

AUTUMN: A DIRGE

THE warm sun is failing; the bleak wind is wailing;
The bare boughs are sighing; the pale flowers are dying;
        And the Year
On the earth, her death-bed, in a shroud of leaves dead,
        Is lying.
    Come, months, come away,
    From November to May;
    In your saddest array
    Follow the bier
    Of the dead, cold Year,
And like dim shadows watch by her sepulchre.

The chill rain is falling; the nipped worm is crawling;
  The rivers are swelling; the thunder is knelling
      For the Year;
  The blithe swallows are flown, and the lizards each gone
          To his dwelling;
        Come, months, come away;
        Put on white, black, and gray;
        Let your light sisters play—
        Ye, follow the bier
        Of the dead, cold Year,
And make her grave green with tear on tear.

Percy Bysshe Shelley [1792–1822]

AUTUMN

      THE morns are meeker than they were,
      The nuts are getting brown;
      The berry's cheek is plumper,
      The rose is out of town.
      The maple wears a gayer scarf,
      The field a scarlet gown.
      Lest I should be old-fashioned,
      I'll put a trinket on.

Emily Dickinson [1830–1886]

"WHEN THE FROST IS ON THE PUNKIN"

WHEN the frost is on the punkin and the fodder's in the
    shock,
And you hear the kyouck and gobble of the struttin' turkey-
    cock,
And the clackin' of the guineys, and the cluckin' of the hens,
And the rooster's hallylooer as he tiptoes on the fence;
O, it's then's the times a feller is a-feelin' at his best,
With the risin' sun to greet him from a night of peaceful
    rest,
As he leaves the house, bareheaded, and goes out to feed
    the stock,
When the frost is on the punkin and the fodder's in the
    shock.

They's something kindo' harty-like about the atmusfere
When the heat of summer's over and the coolin' fall is here—
Of course we miss the flowers, and the blossoms on the trees,
And the mumble of the hummin'-birds and buzzin' of the
  bees;
But the air's so appetizin'; and the landscape through the
  haze
Of a crisp and sunny morning of the airly autumn days
Is a pictur' that no painter has the colorin' to mock—
When the frost is on the punkin and the fodder's in the
  shock.

The husky, rusty russel of the tossels of the corn,
And the raspin' of the tangled leaves, as golden as the morn;
The stubble in the furries—kindo' lonesome-like, but still
A-preachin' sermuns to us of the barns they growed to fill;
The strawstack in the medder, and the reaper in the shed;
The hosses in theyr stalls below—the clover overhead!—
O, it sets my hart a-clickin' like the tickin' of a clock,
When the frost is on the punkin and the fodder's in the
  shock.

Then your apples all is getherd, and the ones a feller keeps
Is poured around the celler-floor in red and yeller heaps;
And your cider-makin's over, and your wimmern-folks is
  through
With their mince and apple-butter, and theyr souse and
  saussage, too! . . .
I don't know how to tell it—but ef sich a thing could be
As the Angels wantin' boardin', and they'd call around on
  me—
I'd want to 'commodate 'em—all the whole-indurin' flock—
When the frost is on the punkin and the fodder's in the shock.

James Whitcomb Riley [1849–1916]

KORE

YEA, she hath passed hereby, and blessed the sheaves,
  And the great garths, and stacks, and quiet farms,
  And all the tawny, and the crimson leaves.
Yea, she hath passed with poppies in her arms,

Under the star of dusk, through stealing mist,
And blessed the earth, and gone, while no man wist.

With slow, reluctant feet, and weary eyes,
And eye-lids heavy with the coming sleep,
With small breasts lifted up in stress of sighs,
She passed, as shadows pass, among the sheep;
While the earth dreamed, and only I was ware
Of that faint fragrance blown from her soft hair.

The land lay steeped in peace of silent dreams;
There was no sound amid the sacred boughs.
Nor any mournful music in her streams:
Only I saw the shadow on her brows,
Only I knew her for the yearly slain,
And wept, and weep until she come again.

Frederic Manning [18

OLD OCTOBER

HAIL, old October, bright and chill,
First freedman from the summer sun!
Spice high the bowl, and drink your fill!
Thank heaven, at last the summer's done!

Come, friend, my fire is burning bright,
A fire's no longer out of place,
How clear it glows! (there's frost to-night,)
It looks white winter in the face.

You've been to "Richard." Ah! you've seen
A noble play: I'm glad you went;
But what on earth does Shakespeare mean
By *"winter* of our *discontent?"*

Be mine the tree that feeds the fire!
Be mine the sun knows when to set!
Be mine the months when friends desire
To turn in here from cold and wet!

The sentry sun, that glared so long
O'erhead, deserts his summer post;
Ay, you may brew it hot and strong:
"The joys of winter"—come, a toast!

Shine on the kangaroo, thou sun!
Make far New Zealand faint with fear!
Don't hurry back to spoil our fun,
Thank goodness, old October's here!

Thomas Constable [1812–1881]

NOVEMBER

WHEN thistle-blows do lightly float
About the pasture-height,
And shrills the hawk a parting note,
And creeps the frost at night,
Then hilly ho! though singing so,
And whistle as I may,
There comes again the old heart pain
Through all the livelong day.

In high wind creaks the leafless tree
And nods the fading fern;
The knolls are dun as snow-clouds be,
And cold the sun does burn.
Then ho, hollo! though calling so,
I cannot keep it down;
The tears arise unto my eyes,
And thoughts are chill and brown.

Far in the cedars' dusky stoles,
Where the sere ground-vine weaves,
The partridge drums funereal rolls
Above the fallen leaves.
And hip, hip, ho! though cheering so,
It stills no whit the pain;
For drip, drip, drip, from bare-branch tip,
I hear the year's last rain.

So drive the cold cows from the hill,
And call the wet sheep in;
And let their stamping clatter fill
The barn with warming din.
And ho, folk, ho! though it be so
That we no more may roam,
We still will find a cheerful mind
Around the fire at home!

C. L. Cleaveland [18 – ?]

NOVEMBER

HARK you such sound as quivers? Kings will hear,
  As kings have heard, and tremble on their thrones;
  The old will feel the weight of mossy stones;
  The young alone will laugh and scoff at fear.
It is the tread of armies marching near,
  From scarlet lands to lands forever pale;
  It is a bugle dying down the gale;
  It is the sudden gushing of a tear.
And it is hands that grope at ghostly doors;
  And romp of spirit-children on the pave;
  It is the tender sighing of the brave
Who fell, ah! long ago, in futile wars;
    It is such sound as death; and, after all,
    'Tis but the forest letting dead leaves fall.

Mahlon Leonard Fisher [1874–

STORM FEAR

WHEN the wind works against us in the dark,
And pelts with snow
The lower chamber window on the east,
And whispers with a sort of stifled bark,
The beast,
"Come out! Come out!"—
It costs no inward struggle not to go,
Ah, no!
I count our strength,
Two and a child,
Those of us not asleep subdued to mark
How the cold creeps as the fire dies at length,—
How drifts are piled,
Dooryard and road ungraded,
Till even the comforting barn grows far away
And my heart owns a doubt
Whether 'tis in us to arise with day
And save ourselves unaided.

Robert Frost [1875–

WINTER: A DIRGE

THE wintry west extends his blast,
    And hail and rain does blaw;
Or the stormy north sends driving forth
    The blinding sleet and snaw:
While, tumbling brown, the burn comes down,
    And roars frae bank to brae;
And bird and beast in covert rest,
    And pass the heartless day.

"The sweeping blast, the sky o'ercast,"
    The joyless winter day,
Let others fear,—to me more dear
    Than all the pride of May;
The tempest's howl, it soothes my soul,
    My griefs it seems to join;
The leafless trees my fancy please,
    Their fate resembles mine!

Thou Power Supreme, whose mighty scheme
    These woes of mine fulfil,
Here, firm, I rest,—they must be best,
    Because they are Thy will.
Then all I want (oh, do Thou grant
    This one request of mine!)
Since to enjoy Thou dost deny,
    Assist me to resign!

Robert Burns [1759–1796]

OLD WINTER

OLD Winter sad, in snow yclad,
    Is making a doleful din;
But let him howl till he crack his jowl,
    We will not let him in.

Ay, let him lift from the billowy drift
    His hoary, haggard form,
And scowling stand, with his wrinkled hand
    Outstretching to the storm.

And let his weird and sleety beard
  Stream loose upon the blast,
And, rustling, chime to the tinkling rime
  From his bald head falling fast.

Let his baleful breath shed blight and death
  On herb and flower and tree;
And brooks and ponds in crystal bonds
  Bind fast, but what care we?

Let him push at the door,—in the chimney roar,
  And rattle the window-pane;
Let him in at us spy with his icicle eye,
  But he shall not entrance gain.

Let him gnaw, forsooth, with his freezing tooth,
  On our roof-tiles, till he tire;
But we care not a whit, as we jovial sit
  Before our blazing fire.

Come, lads, let's sing, till the rafters ring;
  Come, push the can about;—
From our snug fire-side this Christmas-tide
  We'll keep old Winter out.

                    Thomas Noel [1799–1861]

THE FROST

THE Frost looked forth, one still, clear night,
And he said, "Now I shall be out of sight;
So through the valley and over the height
  In silence I'll take my way.
I will not go like that blustering train,
The wind and the snow, the hail and the rain,
Who make so much bustle and noise in vain,
  But I'll be as busy as they!"

Then he went to the mountain, and powdered its crest,
He climbed up the trees, and their boughs he dressed
With diamonds and pearls, and over the breast
  Of the quivering lake he spread

A coat of mail, that it need not fear
The downward point of many a spear
That he hung on its margin, far and near,
    Where a rock could rear its head.

He went to the windows of those who slept,
And over each pane like a fairy crept;
Wherever he breathed, wherever he stepped,
    By the light of the moon were seen
Most beautiful things.   There were flowers and trees,
There were bevies of birds and swarms of bees,
There were cities, thrones, temples, and towers, and these
    All pictured in silver sheen!

But he did one thing that was hardly fair,—
He peeped in the cupboard, and, finding there
That all had forgotten for him to prepare,—
    "Now, just to set them a-thinking,
I'll bite this basket of fruit," said he;
"This costly pitcher I'll burst in three,
And the glass of water they've left for me
    Shall 'tchick!' to tell them I'm drinking."
                    Hannah Flagg Gould [1789–1865]

THE FROSTED PANE

One night came Winter noiselessly and leaned
    Against my window-pane.
In the deep stillness of his heart convened
    The ghosts of all his slain.

Leaves, and ephemera, and stars of earth,
    And fugitives of grass,—
White spirits loosed from bonds of mortal birth,
    He drew them on the glass.
                    Charles G. D. Roberts [1860–

THE FROST SPIRIT

He comes,—he comes,—the Frost Spirit comes! You may
    trace his footsteps now
On the naked woods and the blasted fields and the brown
    hill's withered brow.

He has smitten the leaves of the gray old trees where their
    pleasant green came forth,
And the winds, which follow wherever he goes, have shaken
    them down to earth.

He comes,—he comes,—the Frost Spirit comes! from the
    frozen Labrador,
From the icy bridge of the Northern seas, which the white
    bear wanders o'er,
Where the fisherman's sail is stiff with ice and the luckless
    forms below
In the sunless cold of the lingering night into marble statues
    grow!

He comes,—he comes,—the Frost Spirit comes! on the rush-
    ing Northern blast,
And the dark Norwegian pines have bowed as his fearful
    breath went past.
With an unscorched wing he has hurried on, where the fires of
    Hecla glow
On the darkly beautiful sky above and the ancient ice below.

He comes,—he comes,—the Frost Spirit comes! and the
    quiet lake shall feel
The torpid touch of his glazing breath, and ring to the
    skater's heel;
And the streams which danced on the broken rocks, or sang
    to the leaning grass,
Shall bow again to their winter chain, and in mournful silence
    pass.

He comes,—he comes,—the Frost Spirit comes! Let us meet
    him as we may,
And turn with the light of the parlor-fire his evil power
    away;
And gather closer the circle round, when that firelight dances
    high,
And laugh at the shriek of the baffled Fiend as his sounding
    wing goes by!

                John Greenleaf Whittier [1807–1892]

SNOW

Lo, what wonders the day hath brought,
  Born of the soft and slumbrous snow!
Gradual, silent, slowly wrought;
Even as an artist, thought by thought,
  Writes expression on lip and brow.

Hanging garlands the eaves o'erbrim,
  Deep drifts smother the paths below;
The elms are shrouded, trunk and limb,
And all the air is dizzy and dim
  With a whirl of dancing, dazzling snow.

Dimly out of the baffled sight
  Houses and church-spires stretch away;
The trees, all spectral and still and white,
Stand up like ghosts in the failing light,
  And fade and faint with the blinded day.

Down from the roofs in gusts are hurled
  The eddying drifts to the waste below;
And still is the banner of storm unfurled,
Till all the drowned and desolate world
  Lies dumb and white in a trance of snow.

Slowly the shadows gather and fall,
  Still the whispering snow-flakes beat;
Night and darkness are over all:
Rest, pale city, beneath their pall!
  Sleep, white world, in thy winding-sheet!

Clouds may thicken, and storm-winds breathe:
  On my wall is a glimpse of Rome,—
Land of my longing!—and underneath
Swings and trembles my olive-wreath;
  Peace and I are at home, at home!
                    Elizabeth Akers [1832–1911]

TO A SNOW–FLAKE

WHAT heart could have thought you?—
Past our devisal
(O filigree petal!)
Fashioned so purely,
Fragilely, surely,
From what Paradisal
Imagineless metal,
Too costly for cost?
Who hammered you, wrought you,
From argentine vapor?—
"God was my shaper.
Passing surmisal,
He hammered, He wrought me,
From curled silver vapor,
To lust of His mind:—
Thou couldst not have thought me!
So purely, so palely,
Tinily, surely,
Mightily, frailly,
Insculped and embossed,
With His hammer of wind,
And His graver of frost."

Francis Thompson [1859?-1907]

THE SNOW–SHOWER

STAND here by my side and turn, I pray,
  On the lake below thy gentle eyes;
The clouds hang over it, heavy and gray,
  And dark and silent the water lies;
And out of that frozen mist the snow
In wavering flakes begins to flow;
        Flake after flake
They sink in the dark and silent lake.

See how in a living swarm they come
  From the chambers beyond that misty veil;
Some hover in air awhile, and some
  Rush prone from the sky like summer hail.

All, dropping swiftly, or settling slow,
Meet, and are still in the depths below;
                    Flake after flake
Dissolved in the dark and silent lake.

Here delicate snow-stars, out of the cloud,
    Come floating downward in airy play,
Like spangles dropped from the glistening crowd
    That whiten by night the Milky Way;
There broader and burlier masses fall;
The sullen water buries them all,—
                    Flake after flake,—
All drowned in the dark and silent lake.

And some, as on tender wings they glide
    From their chilly birth-cloud, dim and gray,
Are joined in their fall, and, side by side,
    Come clinging along their unsteady way;
As friend with friend, or husband with wife,
Makes hand in hand the passage of life;
                    Each mated flake
Soon sinks in the dark and silent lake.

Lo! while we are gazing, in swifter haste
    Stream down the snows, till the air is white,
As, myriads by myriads madly chased,
    They fling themselves from their shadowy height.
The fair, frail creatures of middle sky,
What speed they make, with their grave so nigh;
                    Flake after flake
To lie in the dark and silent lake.

I see in thy gentle eyes a tear;
    They turn to me in sorrowful thought;
Thou thinkest of friends, the good and dear,
    Who were for a time, and now are not;
Like these fair children of cloud and frost,
That glisten a moment and then are lost,—
                    Flake after flake,—
All lost in the dark and silent lake.

Yet look again, for the clouds divide;
  A gleam of blue on the water lies;
And far away, on the mountain-side,
  A sunbeam falls from the opening skies;
But the hurrying host that flew between
The cloud and the water no more is seen;
      Flake after flake,
At rest in the dark and silent lake.

         William Cullen Bryant [1794–1878]

MIDWINTER

THE speckled sky is dim with snow,
The light flakes falter and fall slow;
Athwart the hill-top, rapt and pale,
Silently drops a silvery veil;
And all the valley is shut in
By flickering curtains gray and thin.

But cheerily the chickadee
Singeth to me on fence and tree;
The snow sails round him as he sings,
White as the down of angels' wings.

I watch the slow flakes as they fall
On bank and brier and broken wall;
Over the orchard, waste and brown,
All noiselessly they settle down,
Tipping the apple-boughs, and each
Light quivering twig of plum and peach.

On turf and curb and bower-roof
The snow-storm spreads its ivory woof;
It paves with pearl the garden-walk;
And lovingly round tattered stalk
And shivering stem its magic weaves
A mantle fair as lily-leaves.

The hooded beehive, small and low,
Stands like a maiden in the snow;
And the old door-slab is half hid
Under an alabaster lid.

All day it snows: the sheeted post
Gleams in the dimness like a ghost;
All day the blasted oak has stood
A muffled wizard of the wood;
Garland and airy cap adorn
The sumach and the wayside thorn,
And clustering spangles lodge and shine
In the dark tresses of the pine.

The ragged bramble, dwarfed and old,
Shrinks like a beggar in the cold;
In surplice white the cedar stands,
And blesses him with priestly hands.

Still cheerily the chickadee
Singeth to me on fence and tree:
But in my inmost ear is heard
The music of a holier bird;
And heavenly thoughts, as soft and white
As snow-flakes, on my soul alight,
Clothing with love my lonely heart,
Healing with peace each bruisèd part,
Till all my being seems to be
Transfigured by their purity.

             John Townsend Trowbridge [1827–1916]

A GLEE FOR WINTER

HENCE, rude Winter! crabbed old fellow,
Never merry, never mellow!
Well-a-day! in rain and snow
What will keep one's heart aglow?
Groups of kinsmen, old and young,
Oldest they old friends among;
Groups of friends, so old and true
That they seem our kinsmen too;
These all merry all together
Charm away chill Winter weather.

What will kill this dull old fellow?
Ale that's bright, and wine that's mellow!

Dear old songs for ever new;
Some true love, and laughter too;
Pleasant wit, and harmless fun,
And a dance when day is done.
Music, friends so true and tried,
Whispered love by warm fireside,
Mirth at all times all together,
Make sweet May of Winter weather.

Alfred Domett [1811–1887]

THE DEATH OF THE OLD YEAR

FULL knee-deep lies the winter snow,
And the winter winds are wearily sighing:
Toll ye the church-bell sad and slow,
And tread softly and speak low,
For the old year lies a-dying.
  Old year, you must not die;
  You came to us so readily,
  You lived with us so steadily,
  Old year, you shall not die.

He lieth still, he doth not move;
He will not see the dawn of day.
He hath no other life above,
He gave me a friend, and a true true-love,
And the New-year will take 'em away.
  Old year, you must not go;
  So long as you have been with us,
  Such joy as you have seen with us,
  Old year, you shall not go.

He frothed his bumpers to the brim;
A jollier year we shall not see.
But though his eyes are waxing dim,
And though his foes speak ill of him,
He was a friend to me.
  Old year, you shall not die;
  We did so laugh and cry with you.
  I've half a mind to die with you,
  Old year, if you must die.

He was full of joke and jest,
But all his merry quips are o'er.
To see him die, across the waste
His son and heir doth ride post-haste,
But he'll be dead before.
   Every one for his own.
   The night is starry and cold, my friend,
   And the New-year, blithe and bold, my friend,
   Comes up to take his own.

How hard he breathes! over the snow
I heard just now the crowing cock.
The shadows flicker to and fro:
The cricket chirps; the light burns low;
'Tis nearly twelve o'clock.
   Shake hands before you die.
   Old year, we'll dearly rue for you.
   What is it we can do for you?
   Speak out before you die.

His face is growing sharp and thin.
Alack! our friend is gone.
Close up his eyes; tie up his chin;
Step from the corpse, and let him in
That standeth there alone,
   And waiteth at the door.
   There's a new foot on the floor, my friend,
   And a new face at the door, my friend,
   A new face at the door.

Alfred Tennyson [1809–1892]

DIRGE FOR THE YEAR

"Orphan Hours, the Year is dead:
   Come and sigh, come and weep."
"Merry Hours, smile instead,
   For the Year is but asleep.
See, it smiles as it is sleeping,
Mocking your untimely weeping."

"As an earthquake rocks a corse
   In its coffin in the clay,
So white Winter, that rough nurse,
   Rocks the death-cold Year to-day;
Solemn Hours! wail aloud
For your mother in her shroud."

"As the wild air stirs and sways
   The tree-swung cradle of a child,
So the breath of these rude days
   Rocks the Year:—be calm and mild,
Trembling Hours; she will arise
With new love within her eyes.

"January gray is here,
   Like a sexton by her grave;
February bears the bier;
   March with grief doth howl and rave,
And April weeps—but, O, ye Hours,
Follow with May's fairest flowers."

Percy Bysshe Shelley [1792–1822]

WOOD AND FIELD AND RUNNING BROOK

WALDEINSAMKEIT

I DO not count the hours I spend
  In wandering by the sea;
The forest is my loyal friend,
  Like God it useth me.

In plains that room for shadows make
  Of skirting hills to lie,
Bound in by streams which give and take
  Their colors from the sky;

Or on the mountain-crest sublime,
  Or down the oaken glade,
O what have I to do with time?
  For this the day was made,

Cities of mortals woe-begone
  Fantastic care derides,
But in the serious landscape lone
  Stern benefit abides.

Sheen will tarnish, honey cloy,
  And merry is only a mask of sad,
But, sober on a fund of joy,
  The woods at heart are glad.

There the great Planter plants
  Of fruitful worlds the grain,
And with a million spells enchants
  The souls that walk in pain.

Still on the seeds of all he made
  The rose of beauty burns;
Through times that wear and forms that fade,
  Immortal youth returns.

The black ducks mounting from the lake,
  The pigeon in the pines,
The bittern's boom, a desert make
  Which no false art refines.

Down in yon watery nook,
  Where bearded mists divide,
The gray old gods whom Chaos knew,
  The sires of Nature, hide.

Aloft, in secret veins of air,
  Blows the sweet breath of song,
O, few to scale those uplands dare,
  Though they to all belong!

See thou bring not to field or stone
  The fancies found in books;
Leave authors' eyes, and fetch your own,
  To brave the landscape's looks.

Oblivion here thy wisdom is,
  Thy thrift, the sleep of cares;
For a proud idleness like this
  Crowns all thy mean affairs.
                    Ralph Waldo Emerson [1803–1882]

"WHEN IN THE WOODS I WANDER ALL
ALONE"

WHEN in the woods I wander all alone,
The woods that are my solace and delight,
Which I more covet than a prince's throne,
My toil by day and canopy by night;
(Light heart, light foot, light food, and slumber light,
These lights shall light us to old age's gate,
While monarchs, whom rebellious dreams affright,
Heavy with fear, death's fearful summons wait;)

Whilst here I wander, pleased to be alone,
Weighing in thought the world's no-happiness,
I cannot choose but wonder at its moan,
Since so plain joys the woody life can bless:
Then live who may where honied words prevail,
I with the deer, and with the nightingale!

Edward Hovell-Thurlow [1781–1829]

OUT IN THE FIELDS

THE little cares that fretted me,
   I lost them yesterday
Among the fields above the sea,
   Among the winds at play,
Among the lowing of the herds,
   The rustling of the trees,
Among the singing of the birds,
   The humming of the bees.

The foolish fears of what might pass
   I cast them all away
Among the clover-scented grass,
   Among the new-mown hay,
Among the hushing of the corn,
   Where drowsy poppies nod,
Where ill thoughts die and good are born—
   Out in the fields of God.

Unknown
[Has been erroneously attributed to Elizabeth
Barrett Browning and Louise Imogen Guiney]

ASPECTS OF THE PINES

TALL, somber, grim, against the morning sky
   They rise, scarce touched by melancholy airs,
Which stir the fadeless foliage dreamfully,
   As if from realms of mystical despairs.

Tall, somber, grim, they stand with dusky gleams
   Brightening to gold within the woodland's core,
Beneath the gracious noontide's tranquil beams,—
   But the weird winds of morning sigh no more.

A stillness, strange, divine, ineffable,
   Broods round and o'er them in the wind's surcease,

And on each tinted copse and shimmering dell
  Rests the mute rapture of deep hearted peace.

Last, sunset comes—the solemn joy and might
  Borne from the West when cloudless day declines—
Low, flute-like breezes sweep the waves of light,
  And, lifting dark green tresses of the pines,

Till every lock is luminous, gently float,
  Fraught with hale odors up the heavens afar,
To faint when twilight on her virginal throat
  Wears for a gem the tremulous vesper star.

              Paul Hamilton Hayne [1830–1886]

UNDER THE LEAVES

Oft have I walked these woodland paths,
  Without the blessed foreknowing
That underneath the withered leaves
  The fairest buds were growing.

To-day the south-wind sweeps away
  The types of autumn's splendor,
And shows the sweet arbutus flowers,—
  Spring's children, pure and tender.

O prophet-flowers!—with lips of bloom,
  Outvying in your beauty
The pearly tints of ocean shells,—
  Ye teach me faith and duty!

Walk life's dark ways, ye seem to say,
  With love's divine foreknowing
That where man sees but withered leaves,
  God sees sweet flowers growing.

              Albert Laighton [1829–1887]

"ON WENLOCK EDGE"

On Wenlock Edge the wood's in trouble;
His forest fleece the Wrekin heaves;
The gale, it plies the saplings double,
And thick on Severn snow the leaves.

'Twould blow like this through holt and hanger
When Uricon the city stood:
'Tis the old wind in the old anger,
But then it threshed another wood.

Then, 'twas before my time, the Roman
At yonder heaving hill would stare:
The blood that warms an English yeoman,
The thoughts that hurt him, they were there.

There, like the wind through woods in riot,
Through him the gale of life blew high;
The tree of man was never quiet:
Then 'twas the Roman, now 'tis I.

The gale, it plies the saplings double,
It blows so hard, 'twill soon be gone:
To-day the Roman and his trouble
Are ashes under Uricon.

Alfred Edward Housman [1859-1936]

"WHAT DO WE PLANT?"

WHAT do we plant when we plant the tree?
We plant the ship, which will cross the sea.
We plant the mast to carry the sails;
We plant the planks to withstand the gales—
The keel, the keelson, the beam, the knee;
We plant the ship when we plant the tree.

What do we plant when we plant the tree?
We plant the houses for you and me.
We plant the rafters, the shingles, the floors,
We plant the studding, the lath, the doors,
The beams and siding, all parts that be;
We plant the house when we plant the tree.

What do we plant when we plant the tree?
A thousand things that we daily see;

We plant the spire that out-towers the crag,
We plant the staff for our country's flag,
We plant the shade, from the hot sun free;
We plant all these when we plant the tree.

Henry Abbey [1842–1911]

THE TREE

I LOVE thee when thy swelling buds appear,
And one by one their tender leaves unfold,
As if they knew that warmer suns were near,
Nor longer sought to hide from winter's cold;
And when with darker growth thy leaves are seen
To veil from view the early robin's nest,
I love to lie beneath thy waving screen,
With limbs by summer's heat and toil oppressed;
And when the autumn winds have stripped thee bare,
And round thee lies the smooth, untrodden snow,
When naught is thine that made thee once so fair,
I love to watch thy shadowy form below,
And through thy leafless arms to look above
On stars that brighter beam when most we need their love.

Jones Very [1813–1880]

THE·BRAVE OLD OAK

A SONG to the oak, the brave old oak,
    Who hath ruled in the greenwood long;
Here's health and renown to his broad green crown,
    And his fifty arms so strong.
There's fear in his frown when the sun goes down,
    And the fire in the west fades out;
And he showeth his might on a wild midnight,
    When the storms through his branches shout.

        Then here's to the oak, the brave old oak,
            Who stands in his pride alone;
        And still flourish he, a hale green tree,
            When a hundred years are gone!

In the days of old, when the spring with cold
　　Had brightened his branches gray,
Through the grass at his feet crept maidens sweet,
　　To gather the dew of May.
And on that day to the rebeck gay
　　They frolicked with lovesome swains;
They are gone, they are dead, in the churchyard laid,
　　But the tree it still remains.

He saw the rare times when the Christmas chimes
　　Were a merry sound to hear,
When the squire's wide hall and the cottage small
　　Were filled with good English cheer.
Now gold hath sway we all obey,
　　And a ruthless king is he;
But he never shall send our ancient friend
　　To be tossed on the stormy sea.

　　　　　　　Henry Fothergill Chorley [1808–1872]

"THE GIRT WOAK TREE THAT'S IN THE DELL "

THE girt woak tree that's in the dell!
There's noo tree I do love so well;
　Vor times an' times when I wer young,
　I there've a-climbed, an' there've a-zwung,
An' picked the eäcorns green, a-shed
In wrestlèn storms vrom his broad head.
An' down below's the cloty brook
Where I did vish with line an' hook,
　An' beät, in plaÿsome dips and zwims,
　The foamy stream, wi' white-skinned lim's.
An' there my mother nimbly shot
Her knittèn-needles, as she zot
At evenèn down below the wide
Woak's head, wi' father at her zide.
An' I've a-plaÿed wi' many a bwoy,
That's now a man an' gone awoy;
　　Zoo I do like noo tree so well
　　'S the girt woak tree that's in the dell.

An' there, in leäter years, I roved
Wi' thik poor maïd I fondly loved,—
The maïd too feäir to die so soon,—
When evenèn twilight, or the moon,
Cast light enough 'ithin the pleäce
To show the smiles upon her feäce,
Wi' eyes so clear's the glassy pool,
An' lips an' cheäks so soft as wool.
There han' in han', wi' bosoms warm,
Wi' love that burned but thought noo **harm,**
Below the wide-boughed tree we passed
The happy hours that went too vast;
An' though she'll never be my wife,
She's still my leaden stär o' life.
She's gone: an' she've a-left to me
Her mem'ry in the girt woak tree;
    Zoo I do love noo tree so well
    'S the girt woak tree that's in the dell.

An' oh! mid never ax nor hook
Be brought to spweil his steätely look;
Nor ever roun' his ribby zides
Mid cattle rub ther heäiry hides;
Nor pigs rout up his turf, but keep
His lwonesome sheäde vor harmless **sheep;**
An' let en grow, an' let en spread,
An' let en live when I be dead.
But oh! if men should come an' vell
The girt woak tree that's in the dell,
An' build his planks 'ithin the zide
O' zome girt ship to plough the tide,
Then, life or death! I'd goo to sea,
A sailèn wi' the girt woak tree:
An' I upon his planks would stand,
An' die a-fightèn vor the land,—
The land so dear,—the land so free,—
The land that bore the girt woak tree;
    Vor I do love noo tree so well
    'S the girt woak tree that's in the dell.
                    William Barnes [1801–1886]

TO THE WILLOW-TREE

THOU art to all lost love the best,
  The only true plant found,
Wherewith young men and maids distressed,
  And left of love, are crowned.

When once the lover's rose is dead,
  Or laid aside forlorn:
Then willow-garlands 'bout the head
  Bedewed with tears are worn.

When with neglect, the lovers' bane,
  Poor maids rewarded be
For their love lost, their only gain
  Is but a wreath from thee.

And underneath thy cooling shade,
  When weary of the light,
The love-spent youth and love-sick maid
  Come to weep out the night.

Robert Herrick [1591–1674]

ENCHANTMENT

THE deep seclusion of this forest path,—
O'er which the green boughs weave a canopy;
Along which bluet and anemone
Spread dim a carpet; where the Twilight hath
Her cool abode; and, sweet as aftermath,
Wood-fragrance roams,—has so enchanted me,
That yonder blossoming bramble seems to be
A Sylvan resting, rosy from her bath:
Has so enspelled me with tradition's dreams,
That every foam-white stream that, twinkling, flows,
And every bird that flutters wings of tan,
Or warbles hidden, to my fancy seems
A Naiad dancing to a Faun who blows
Wild woodland music on the pipes of Pan.

Madison Cawein [1865–1914]

TREES

I THINK that I shall never see
A poem lovely as a tree.

A tree whose hungry mouth is pressed
Against the earth's sweet flowing breast;

A tree that looks at God all day
And lifts her leafy arms to pray;

A tree that may in summer wear
A nest of robins in her hair;

Upon whose bosom snow has lain;
Who intimately lives with rain.

Poems are made by fools like me,
But only God can make a tree.

Joyce Kilmer [1886–1918]

THE HOLLY-TREE

O READER! hast thou ever stood to see
    The Holly-tree?
The eye that contemplates it well perceives
    Its glossy leaves
Ordered by an Intelligence so wise
As might confound the Atheist's sophistries.

Below, a circling fence, its leaves are seen,
    Wrinkled and keen;
No grazing cattle, through their prickly round,
    Can reach to wound;
But, as they grow where nothing is to fear,
Smooth and unarmed the pointless leaves appear.

I love to view these things with curious eyes,
    And moralize;

And in this wisdom of the Holly-tree
    Can emblem see
Wherewith, perchance, to make a pleasant rhyme,—
One which may profit in the after-time.

Thus, though abroad, perchance, I might appear
    Harsh and austere;
To those who on my leisure would intrude,
    Reserved and rude;
Gentle at home amid my friends I'd be,
Like the high leaves upon the Holly-tree.

And should my youth—as youth is apt, I know,—
    Some harshness show,
All vain asperities I, day by day,
    Would wear away,
Till the smooth temper of my age should be
Like the high leaves upon the Holly-tree.

And as, when all the summer trees are seen
    So bright and green,
The Holly-leaves their fadeless hues display
    Less bright than they;
But when the bare and wintry woods we see,
What then so cheerful as the Holly-tree?—

So, serious should my youth appear among
    The thoughtless throng;
So would I seem, amid the young and gay,
    More grave than they;
That in my age as cheerful I might be
As the green winter of the Holly-tree.

Robert Southey [1774–1843]

THE PINE

THE elm lets fall its leaves before the frost,
    The very oak grows shivering and sere,
The trees are barren when the summer's lost:
    But one tree keeps its goodness all the year.

Green pine, unchanging as the days go by,
Thou art thyself beneath whatever sky:
   My shelter from all winds, my own strong pine,
   'Tis spring, 'tis summer, still, while thou art mine.

                    Augusta Webster [1837–1894]

"WOODMAN, SPARE THAT TREE"

WOODMAN, spare that tree!
   Touch not a single bough!
In youth it sheltered me,
   And I'll protect it now.
'Twas my forefather's hand
   That placed it near his cot;
There, woodman, let it stand,
   Thy axe shall harm it not!

That old familiar tree,
   Whose glory and renown
Are spread o'er land and sea,—
   And wouldst thou hew it down?
Woodman, forbear thy stroke!
   Cut not its earth-bound ties;
O, spare that agèd oak,
   Now towering to the skies!

When but an idle boy
   I sought its grateful shade;
In all their gushing joy
   Here, too, my sisters played.
My mother kissed me here;
   My father pressed my hand—
Forgive this foolish tear,
   But let that old oak stand!

My heart-strings round thee cling,
   Close as thy bark, old friend!
Here shall the wild-bird sing,
   And still thy branches bend.

Old tree! the storm still brave!
And, woodman, leave the spot;
While I've a hand to save,
Thy axe shall harm it not.

George Pope Morris [1802–1864]

THE BEECH TREE'S PETITION

O LEAVE this barren spot to me!
Spare, woodman, spare the beechen tree!
Though bush or floweret never grow
My dark unwarming shade below;
Nor summer bud perfume the dew
Of rosy blush, or yellow hue;
Nor fruits of autumn, blossom-born,
My green and glossy leaves adorn;
Nor murmuring tribes from me derive
Th' ambrosial amber of the hive;
Yet leave this barren spot to me:
Spare, woodman, spare the beechen tree!

Thrice twenty summers I have seen
The sky grow bright, the forest green;
And many a wintry wind have stood
In bloomless, fruitless solitude,
Since childhood in my pleasant bower
First spent its sweet and sportive hour;
Since youthful lovers in my shade
Their vows of truth and rapture made,
And on my trunk's surviving frame
Carved many a long-forgotten name.
Oh! by the sighs of gentle sound,
First breathed upon this sacred ground;
By all that Love has whispered here,
Or Beauty heard with ravished ear;
As Love's own altar honor me:
Spare, woodman, spare the beechen tree!

Thomas Campbell [1777–1844]

THE POPLAR FIELD

The poplars are felled; farewell to the shade;
And the whispering sound of the cool colonnade;
The winds play no longer and sing in the leaves,
Nor Ouse on his bosom their image receives.

Twelve years have elapsed since I first took a view
Of my favorite field, and the bank where they grew;
And now in the grass behold they are laid,
And the tree is my seat that once lent me a shade.

The blackbird has fled to another retreat,
Where the hazels afford him a screen from the heat;
And the scene where his melody charmed me before
Resounds with his sweet-flowing ditty no more.

My fugitive years are all hasting away,
And I must ere long lie as lowly as they,
With a turf on my breast and a stone at my head,
Ere another such grove shall arise in its stead.

'Tis a sight to engage me, if anything can,
To muse on the perishing pleasures of man;
Though his life be a dream, his enjoyments, I see,
Have a being less durable even than he.

William Cowper [1731–1800]

THE PLANTING OF THE APPLE–TREE

Come, let us plant the apple-tree.
 Cleave the tough greensward with the spade;
Wide let its hollow bed be made;
There gently lay the roots, and there
Sift the dark mould with kindly care,
    And press it o'er them tenderly,
As, round the sleeping infant's feet,
We softly fold the cradle-sheet;
    So plant we the apple-tree.

What plant we in this apple-tree?
Buds, which the breath of summer days
Shall lengthen into leafy sprays;
Boughs where the thrush, with crimson breast,
Shall haunt, and sing, and hide her nest;
   We plant, upon the sunny lea,
A shadow for the noontide hour,
A shelter from the summer shower,
   When we plant the apple-tree.

What plant we in this apple-tree?
Sweets for a hundred flowery springs
To load the May-wind's restless wings,
When, from the orchard-row, he pours
Its fragrance through our open doors;
   A world of blossoms for the bee,
Flowers for the sick girl's silent room,
For the glad infant sprigs of bloom,
   We plant with the apple-tree.

What plant we in this apple-tree?
Fruits that shall swell in sunny June,
And redden in the August noon,
And drop, when gentle airs come by,
That fan the blue September sky,
   While children come, with cries of glee,
And seek them where the fragrant grass
Betrays their bed to those who pass,
   At the foot of the apple-tree.

And when, above this apple-tree,
The winter stars are quivering bright,
And winds go howling through the night,
Girls, whose young eyes o'erflow with mirth,
Shall peel its fruit by cottage-hearth,
   And guests in prouder homes shall see,
Heaped with the grape of Cintra's vine
And golden orange of the line,
   The fruit of the apple-tree.

The fruitage of this apple-tree
Winds and our flag of stripe and star
Shall bear to coasts that lie afar,
Where men shall wonder at the view,
And ask in what fair groves they grew;
    And sojourners beyond the sea
Shall think of childhood's careless day,
And long, long hours of summer play,
    In the shade of the apple-tree.

Each year shall give this apple-tree
A broader flush of roseate bloom,
A deeper maze of verdurous gloom,
And loosen, when the frost-clouds lower,
The crisp brown leaves in thicker shower.
    The years shall come and pass, but we
Shall hear no longer, where we lie,
The summer's songs, the autumn's sigh,
    In the boughs of the apple-tree.

And time shall waste this apple-tree.
Oh, when its agèd branches throw
Thin shadows on the ground below,
Shall fraud and force and iron will
Oppress the weak and helpless still?
    What shall the tasks of mercy be,
Amid the toils, the strifes, the tears
Of those who live when length of years
    Is wasting this little apple-tree?

"Who planted this old apple-tree?"
The children of that distant day
Thus to some agèd man shall say;
And, gazing on its mossy stem,
The gray-haired man shall answer them:
    "A poet of the land was he,
Born in the rude but good old times;
'Tis said he made some quaint old rhymes,
    On planting the apple-tree."

                    William Cullen Bryant [1794-1878]

OF AN ORCHARD

GOOD is an Orchard, the Saint saith,
To meditate on life and death,
With a cool well, a hive of bees,
A hermit's grot below the trees.

Good is an Orchard: very good,
Though one should wear no monkish hood.
Right good, when Spring awakes her flute,
And good in yellowing time of fruit.

Very good in the grass to lie
And see the network 'gainst the sky,
A living lace of blue and green,
And boughs that let the gold between.

The bees are types of souls that dwell
With honey in a quiet cell;
The ripe fruit figures goldenly
The soul's perfection in God's eye.

Prayer and praise in a country home,
Honey and fruit: a man might come,
Fed on such meats, to walk abroad,
And in his Orchard talk with God.

Katherine Tynan Hinkson [1861–1931]

AN ORCHARD AT AVIGNON

THE hills are white, but not with snow:
  They are as pale in summer time,
For herb or grass may never grow
  Upon their slopes of lime.

Within the circle of the hills
  A ring, all flowering in a round,
An orchard-ring of almond fills
  The plot of stony ground.

More fair than happier trees, I think,
  Grown in well-watered pasture land
These parched and stunted branches, pink
  Above the stones and sand.

O white, austere, ideal place,
  Where very few will care to come,
Where spring hath lost the waving grace
  She wears for us at home!

Fain would I sit and watch for hours
  The holy whiteness of thy hills,
Their wreath of pale auroral flowers,
  Their peace the silence fills.

A place of secret peace thou art,
  Such peace as in an hour of pain
One moment fills the amazèd heart,
  And never comes again.

                    A. Mary F. Robinson [1857–

THE TIDE RIVER

From " The Water Babies "

CLEAR and cool, clear and cool,
By laughing shallow and dreaming pool;
  Cool and clear, cool and clear,
By shining shingle and foaming weir;
Under the crag where the ouzel sings,
And the ivied wall where the church-bell rings,
        Undefiled, for the undefiled;
  Play by me, bathe in me, mother and child.

  Dank and foul, dank and foul,
By the smoky town in its murky cowl;
  Foul and dank, foul and dank,
By wharf and sewer and slimy bank;
Darker and darker the farther I go,
Baser and baser the richer I grow;
        Who dare sport with the sin-defiled?
  Shrink from me, turn from me, mother and child.

Strong and free, strong and free,
The flood-gates are open, away to the sea.
Free and strong, free and strong,
Cleansing my streams as I hurry along,
To the golden sands, and the leaping bar,
And the taintless tide that awaits me afar.
As I lose myself in the infinite main,
Like a soul that has sinned and is pardoned again,
Undefiled, for the undefiled;
Play by me, bathe in me, mother and child.

Charles Kingsley [1819–1875]

THE BROOK'S SONG

From " The Brook "

I COME from haunts of coot and hern,
I make a sudden sally,
And sparkle out among the fern,
To bicker down a valley.

By thirty hills I hurry down,
Or slip between the ridges,
By twenty thorps, a little town,
And half a hundred bridges.

Till last by Philip's farm I flow
To join the brimming river,
For men may come and men may go,
But I go on for ever.

I chatter over stony ways,
In little sharps and trebles,
I bubble into eddying bays,
I babble on the pebbles.

With many a curve my banks I fret
By many a field and fallow,
And many a fairy foreland set
With willow-weed and mallow.

I chatter, chatter, as I flow
　　To join the brimming river,
For men may come and men may go,
　　But I go on for ever.

I wind about, and in and out,
　　With here a blossom sailing,
And here and there a lusty trout,
　　And here and there a grayling,

And here and there a foamy flake
　　Upon me, as I travel
With many a silvery water-break
　　Above the golden gravel,

And draw them all along, and flow
　　To join the brimming river,
For men may come and men may go,
　　But I go on for ever.

· I steal by lawns and grassy plots,
　　I slide by hazel covers;
I move the sweet forget-me-nots
　　That grow for happy lovers.

I slip, I slide, I gloom, I glance,
　　Among my skimming swallows:
I make the netted sunbeam dance
　　Against my sandy shallows.

I murmur under moon and stars
　　In brambly wildernesses;
I linger by my shingly bars;
　　I loiter round my cresses;

And out again I curve and flow
　　To join the brimming river,
For men may come and men may go,
　　But I go on for ever

Alfred Tennyson [1809–1892]

ARETHUSA

ARETHUSA arose
From her couch of snows
In the Acroceraunian mountains,—
From cloud and from crag,
With many a jag,
Shepherding her bright fountains.
She leapt down the rocks
With her rainbow locks
Streaming among the streams;
Her steps paved with green
The downward ravine
Which slopes to the western gleams:
And gliding and springing,
She went, ever singing,
In murmurs as soft as sleep;
The Earth seemed to love her,
And Heaven smiled above her,
As she lingered towards the deep.

Then Alpheus bold,
On his glacier cold,
With his trident the mountains strook,
And opened a chasm
In the rocks;—with the spasm
All Erymanthus shook.
And the black south wind
It unsealed behind
The urns of the silent snow,
And earthquake and thunder
Did rend in sunder
The bars of the springs below:
And the beard and the hair
Of the River-god were
Seen through the torrent's sweep,
As he followed the light
Of the fleet nymph's flight
To the brink of the Dorian deep.

"Oh, save me! Oh, guide me!
And bid the deep hide me!
For he grasps me now by the hair!"
    The loud Ocean heard,
    To its blue depth stirred,
And divided at her prayer;
    And under the water
    The Earth's white daughter
Fled like a sunny beam;
    Behind her descended,
    Her billows, unblended
With the brackish Dorian stream.
    Like a gloomy stain
    On the emerald main,
Alpheus rushed behind,—
    As an eagle pursuing
    A dove to its ruin
Down the streams of the cloudy wind.

    Under the bowers
    Where the Ocean Powers
Sit on their pearlèd thrones;
    Through the coral woods
    Of the weltering floods,
Over heaps of unvalued stones;
    Through the dim beams
    Which amid the streams
Weave a network of colored light;
    And under the caves
    Where the shadowy waves
Are as green as the forest's night:—
    Outspeeding the shark,
    And the swordfish dark,—
Under the Ocean's foam,
    And up through the rifts
    Of the mountain clifts,
They passed to their Dorian home.

    And now from their fountains
    In Enna's mountains,

Down one vale where the morning basks,
   Like friends once parted
   Grown single-hearted,
They ply their watery tasks.
   At sunrise they leap
   From their cradles steep
In the cave of the shelving hill;
   At noontide they flow
   Through the woods below
And the meadows of asphodel;
   And at night they sleep
   In the rocking deep
Beneath the Ortygian shore;—
   Like spirits that lie
   In the azure sky.
When they love but live no more.

          Percy Bysshe Shelley [1792–1822]

THE CATARACT OF LODORE

   "How does the water
   Come down at Lodore?"
My little boy asked me
Thus, once, once on a time;
And moreover he tasked me
To tell him in rhyme.
   Anon, at the word,
There first came one daughter,
   And then came another,
   To second and third
The request of their brother,
And to hear how the water
   Comes down at Lodore,
   With its rush and its roar,
   As many a time
They had seen it before.
So I told them in rhyme,
For of rhymes I had store;
   And 'twas in my vocation
   For their recreation

That so I should sing;
Because I was Laureate
To them and the King.

From its sources which well
In the tarn on the fell;
From its fountains
In the mountains,
Its rills and its gills;
Through moss and through brake,
It runs and it creeps
For a while, till it sleeps
In its own little lake.
And thence at departing,
Awakening and starting,
It runs through the reeds,
And away it proceeds,
Through meadow and glade,
In sun and in shade,
And through the wood-shelter,
Among crags in its flurry,
Helter-skelter,
Hurry-skurry.
Here it comes sparkling,
And there it lies darkling;
Now smoking and frothing
Its tumult and wrath in,
Till, in this rapid race
On which it is bent,
It reaches the place
Of its steep descent.

The cataract strong
Then plunges along,
Striking and raging
As if a war raging
Its caverns and rocks among;
Rising and leaping,
Sinking and creeping,

Swelling and sweeping,
Showering and springing,
Flying and flinging,
Writhing and ringing,
Eddying and whisking,
Spouting and frisking,
Turning and twisting,
Around and around
With endless rebound:
Smiting and fighting,
A sight to delight in;
Confounding, astounding,
Dizzying and deafening the ear with its sound.

Collecting, projecting,
Receding and speeding,
And shocking and rocking,
And darting and parting,
And threading and spreading,
And whizzing and hissing,
And dripping and skipping,
And hitting and splitting,
And shining and twining,
And rattling and battling,
And shaking and quaking,
And pouring and roaring,
And waving and raving,
And tossing and crossing,
And flowing and going,
And running and stunning,
And foaming and roaming,
And dinning and spinning,
And dropping and hopping,
And working and jerking,
And guggling and struggling,
And heaving and cleaving,
And moaning and groaning;

And glittering and frittering,
And gathering and feathering,

And whitening and brightening,
And quivering and shivering,
And hurrying and skurrying,
And thundering and floundering;

Dividing and gliding and sliding,
And falling and brawling and sprawling,
And driving and riving and striving,
And sprinkling and twinkling and wrinkling,
And sounding and bounding and rounding,
And bubbling and troubling and doubling,
And grumbling and rumbling and tumbling,
And clattering and battering and shattering;

Retreating and beating and meeting and sheeting,
Delaying and straying and playing and spraying,
Advancing and prancing and glancing and dancing,
Recoiling, turmoiling and toiling and boiling,
And gleaming and streaming and steaming and beaming,
And rushing and flushing and brushing and gushing,
And flapping and rapping and clapping and slapping,
And curling and whirling and purling and twirling,
And thumping and plumping and bumping and jumping,
And dashing and flashing and splashing and clashing;
And so never ending, but always descending,
Sounds and motions for ever and ever are blending
All at once and all o'er, with a mighty uproar,—
And this way the water comes down at Lodore.
                    Robert Southey [1774–1843]

SONG OF THE CHATTAHOOCHEE

Out of the hills of Habersham,
  Down the valleys of Hall,
I hurry amain to reach the plain,
Run the rapid and leap the fall,
Split at the rock and together again,
Accept my bed, or narrow or wide,
And flee from folly on every side
With a lover's pain to attain the plain

Far from the hills of Habersham,
    Far from the valleys of Hall.

All down the hills of Habersham,
    All through the valleys of Hall,
The rushes cried *Abide, abide*,
The wilful waterweeds held me thrall,
The laving laurel turned my tide,
The ferns and the fondling grass said *Stay*,
The dewberry dipped for to work delay,
And the little reeds sighed *Abide, abide.*
    Here in the hills of Habersham,
    Here in the valleys of Hall.

High o'er the hills of Habersham,
    Veiling the valleys of Hall,
The hickory told me manifold
Fair tales of shade, the poplar tall
Wrought me her shadowy self to hold,
The chestnut, the oak, the walnut, the pine,
Overleaning, with flickering meaning and sign,
Said, *Pass not, so cold, these manifold*
    Deep shades of the hills of Habersham,
    These glades in the valleys of Hall.

And oft in the hills of Habersham,
    And oft in the valleys of Hall,
The white quartz shone, and the smooth brook-stone
Did bar me of passage with friendly brawl,
And many a luminous jewel lone
—Crystals clear or a-cloud with mist,
Ruby, garnet and amethyst—
Made lures with the lights of streaming stone
    In the clefts of the hills of Habersham,
    In the beds of the valleys of Hall.

But oh, not the hills of Habersham,
    And oh, not the valleys of Hall
Avail: I am fain for to water the plain.
Downward the voices of Duty call—

Downward, to toil and be mixed with the main.
The dry fields burn, and the mills are to turn,
And a myriad flowers mortally yearn,
And the lordly main from beyond the plain
    Calls o'er the hills of Habersham,
    Calls through the valleys of Hall.

Sidney Lanier [1842–1881]

"FLOW GENTLY, SWEET AFTON"

FLOW gently, sweet Afton, among thy green braes;
Flow gently, I'll sing thee a song in thy praise;
My Mary's asleep by thy murmuring stream,
Flow gently, sweet Afton, disturb not her dream.

Thou stock-dove whose echo resounds through the glen,
Ye wild whistling blackbirds in yon thorny den,
Thou green-crested lapwing, thy screaming forbear;
I charge you disturb not my slumbering fair.

How lofty, sweet Afton, thy neighboring hills,
Far marked with the courses of clear-winding rills;
There daily I wander as noon rises high,
My flocks and my Mary's sweet cot in my eye.

How pleasant thy banks and green valleys below,
Where wild in the woodlands the primroses blow;
There oft as mild evening weeps over the lea,
The sweet-scented birk shades my Mary and me.

Thy crystal stream, Afton, how lovely it glides,
And winds by the cot where my Mary resides;
How wanton thy waters her snowy feet lave,
As, gathering sweet flowerets, she stems thy clear wave.

Flow gently, sweet Afton, among thy green braes;
Flow gently, sweet river, the theme of my lays;
My Mary's asleep by thy murmuring stream,
Flow gently, sweet Afton, disturb not her dream.

Robert Burns [1759–1796]

CANADIAN BOAT-SONG

WRITTEN ON THE RIVER ST. LAWRENCE

FAINTLY as tolls the evening chime
Our voices keep tune and our oars keep time.
Soon as the woods on shore look dim,
We'll sing at St. Ann's our parting hymn.
Row, brothers, row, the stream runs fast,
The rapids are near and the daylight's past.

Why should we yet our sail unfurl?
There is not a breath the blue wave to curl,
But, when the wind blows off the shore,
Oh, sweetly we'll rest our weary oar.
Blow, breezes, blow, the stream runs fast,
The rapids are near and the daylight's past.

Utawas' tide! this trembling moon
Shall see us float over thy surges soon.
Saint of this green isle! hear our prayers,
Oh, grant us cool heavens and favoring airs.
Blow, breezes, blow, the stream runs fast,
The rapids are near and the daylight's past.

Thomas Moore [1779–1852]

THE MARSHES OF GLYNN

GLOOMS of the live-oaks, beautiful-braided and woven
With intricate shades of the vines that myriad-cloven
Clamber the forks of the multiform boughs,—
        Emerald twilights,—
        Virginal shy lights,
Wrought of the leaves to allure to the whisper of vows,
When lovers pace timidly down through the green colon-
    nades
Of the dim sweet woods, of the dear dark woods,
    Of the heavenly woods and glades,
That run to the radiant marginal sand-beach within
        The wide sea-marshes of Glynn;—

Beautiful glooms, soft dusks in the noonday fire,—
Wildwood privacies, closets of lone desire,
Chamber from chamber parted with wavering arras of
    leaves,—
Cells for the passionate pleasure of prayer to the soul that
    grieves,
Pure with a sense of the passing of saints through the wood,
Cool for the dutiful weighing of ill with good;—

O braided dusks of the oak and woven shades of the vine,
While the riotous noonday sun of the June-day long did shine
Ye held me fast in your heart and I held you fast in mine;
But now when the noon is no more, and riot is rest,
And the sun is a-wait at the ponderous gate of the West,
And the slant yellow beam down the wood-aisle doth seem
Like a lane into heaven that leads from a dream,—
Ay, now, when my soul all day hath drunken the soul of the
    oak,
And my heart is at ease from men, and the wearisome sound
    of the stroke
  Of the scythe of time and the trowel of trade is low,
  And belief overmasters doubt, and I know that I know,
  And my spirit is grown to a lordly great compass within,
That the length and the breadth and the sweep of the
    marshes of Glynn
Will work me no fear like the fear they have wrought me of
    yore
When length was fatigue, and when breadth was but bitter-
    ness sore,
And when terror and shrinking and dreary unnamable pain
Drew over me out of the merciless miles of the plain,—

Oh, now, unafraid, I am fain to face
  The vast sweet visage of space.
To the edge of the wood I am drawn, I am drawn,
Where the gray beach glimmering runs, as a belt of the dawn,
  For a mete and a mark
  To the forest-dark:—
             So:
Affable live-oak. leaning low,—

Thus—with your favor—soft, with a reverent hand,
(Not lightly touching your person, Lord of the land!)
Bending your beauty aside, with a step I stand
On the firm-packed sand,
                        Free
By a world of marsh that borders a world of sea.
   Sinuous southward and sinuous northward the shimmering
      band
   Of the sand-beach fastens the fringe of the marsh to the
      folds of the land.
Inward and outward to northward and southward the beach-
   lines linger and curl
As a silver-wrought garment that clings to and follows the
   firm sweet limbs of a girl.
Vanishing, swerving, evermore curving again into sight,
Softly the sand-beach wavers away to a dim gray looping of
   light.
And what if behind me to westward the wall of the woods
   stands high?
The world lies east: how ample, the marsh and the sea and
   the sky!
A league and a league of marsh-grass, waist-high, broad in
   the blade,
Green, and all of a height, and unflecked with a light or a
   shade,
Stretch leisurely off, in a pleasant plain,
To the terminal blue of the main.

Oh, what is abroad in the marsh and the terminal sea?
   Somehow my soul seems suddenly free
From the weighing of fate and the sad discussion of sin,
By the length and the breadth and the sweep of the marshes
   of Glynn.

Ye marshes, how candid and simple and nothing-withhold-
   ing and free
Ye publish yourselves to the sky and offer yourselves to the
   sea!
Tolerant plains, that suffer the sea and the rains and the sun,
Ye spread and span like the catholic man who hath mightily
   won

God out of knowledge and good out of infinite pain
And sight out of blindness and purity out of a stain.

As the marsh-hen secretly builds on the watery sod,
Behold I will build me a nest on the greatness of God:
I will fly in the greatness of God as the marsh-hen flies
In the freedom that fills all the space 'twixt the marsh and
    the skies:
By so many roots as the marsh-grass sends in the sod
I will heartily lay me a-hold on the greatness of God:
Oh, like to the greatness of God is the greatness within
The range of the marshes, the liberal marshes of Glynn.

And the sea lends large, as the marsh: lo, out of his plenty
    the sea
Pours fast: full soon the time of the flood-tide must be:
Look how the grace of the sea doth go
About and about through the intricate channels that flow
        Here and there,
            Everywhere,
Till his waters have flooded the uttermost creeks and the low-
    lying lanes,
And the marsh is meshed with a million veins,
That like as with rosy and silvery essences flow
  In the rose-and-silver evening glow.
        Farewell, my lord Sun!
The creeks overflow: a thousand rivulets run
'Twixt the roots of the sod; the blades of the marsh-grass
    stir;
Passeth a hurrying sound of wings that westward whirr;
Passeth, and all is still; and the currents cease to run;
And the sea and the marsh are one.

How still the plains of the waters be!
The tide is in his ecstasy;
The tide is at his highest height:
        And it is night.

And now from the Vast of the Lord will the waters of sleep
Roll in on the souls of men,

But who will reveal to our waking ken
The forms that swim and the shapes that creep
                Under the waters of sleep?
And I would I could know what swimmeth below when the
        tide comes in
On the length and the breadth of the marvelous marshes of
        Glynn.

                                        Sidney Lanier [1842–1881]

THE TROSACHS

THERE'S not a nook within this solemn Pass
    But were an apt confessional for one
    Taught by his summer spent, his autumn gone,
That Life is but a tale of morning grass
Withered at eve.   From scenes of art which chase
    That thought away, turn, and with watchful eyes
    Feed it 'mid Nature's old felicities,
Rocks, rivers, and smooth lakes more clear than glass
Untouched, unbreathed upon.   Thrice happy quest,
    If from a golden perch of aspen spray
    (October's workmanship to rival May)
The pensive warbler of the ruddy breast
    That moral sweeten by a heaven-taught lay,
Lulling the year, with all its cares, to rest!

                                William Wordsworth [1770–1850]

HYMN

BEFORE SUNRISE, IN THE VALE OF CHAMOUNI

HAST thou a charm to stay the morning-star
In his steep course?   So long he seems to pause
On thy bald, awful head, O sovereign Blanc!
The Arve and Arveiron at thy base
Rave ceaselessly; but thou, most awful Form,
Risest from forth thy silent sea of pines,
How silently!   Around thee and above
Deep is the air and dark, substantial, black,

An ebon mass: methinks thou piercest it,
As with a wedge!   But when I look again,
It is thine own calm home, thy crystal shrine,
Thy habitation from eternity!
O dread and silent Mount!   I gazed upon thee,
Till thou, still present to the bodily sense,
Didst vanish from my thought: entranced in prayer
I worshiped the Invisible alone.

Yet, like some sweet beguiling melody,
So sweet, we know not we are listening to it,
Thou, the meanwhile, wast blending with my thought,
Yea, with my Life and Life's own secret joy:
Till the dilating Soul, enrapt, transfused,
Into the mighty vision passing—there,
As in her natural form, swelled vast to Heaven!

Awake, my soul! not only passive praise
Thou owest! not alone these swelling tears,
Mute thanks and secret ecstasy!   Awake,
Voice of sweet song!   Awake, my Heart, awake!
Green vales and icy cliffs, all join my Hymn.

Thou first and chief, sole sovereign of the Vale!
O, struggling with the darkness all the night,
And visited all night by troops of stars,
Or when they climb the sky or when they sink:
Companion of the morning-star at dawn,
Thyself Earth's rosy star, and of the dawn
Co-herald: wake, O wake, and utter praise!
Who sank thy sunless pillars deep in Earth?
Who filled thy countenance with rosy light?
Who made thee parent of perpetual streams?

And you, ye five wild torrents fiercely glad!
Who called you forth from night and utter death,
From dark and icy caverns called you forth,
Down those precipitous, black, jagged rocks,
For ever shattered and the same for ever?
Who gave you your invulnerable life,

Your strength, your speed, your fury, and your joy,
Unceasing thunder and eternal foam?
And who commanded (and the silence came),
Here let the billows stiffen, and have rest?

  Ye ice-falls! ye that from the mountain's brow
Adown enormous ravines slope amain—
Torrents, methinks, that heard a mighty voice,
And stopped at once amid their maddest plunge!
Motionless torrents! silent cataracts!
Who made you glorious as the Gates of Heaven
Beneath the keen full moon? Who bade the sun
Clothe you with rainbows? Who, with living flowers
Of loveliest blue, spread garlands at your feet?—
God! let the torrents, like a shout of nations,
Answer! and let the ice-plains echo, God!
God! sing ye meadow-streams with gladsome voice!
Ye pine-groves, with your soft and soul-like sounds!
And they too have a voice, yon piles of snow,
And in their perilous fall shall thunder, God!

  Ye living flowers that skirt the eternal frost!
Ye wild goats sporting round the eagle's nest!
Ye eagles, playmates of the mountain-storm!
Ye lightnings, the dread arrows of the clouds!
Ye signs and wonders of the elements!
Utter forth God, and fill the hills with praise!

  Thou too, hoar Mount! with thy sky-pointing peaks,
Oft from whose feet the avalanche, unheard,
Shoots downward, glittering through the pure serene,
Into the depth of clouds that veil thy breast—
Thou too again, stupendous Mountain! thou
That as I raise my head, awhile bowed low
In adoration, upward from thy base
Slow traveling with dim eyes suffused with tears,
Solemnly seemest, like a vapory cloud,
To rise before me—Rise, O ever rise!
Rise like a cloud of incense, from the Earth!
Thou kingly Spirit throned among the hills,

Thou dread ambassador from Earth to Heaven,
Great Hierarch! tell thou the silent sky,
And tell the stars, and tell yon rising sun,
Earth, with her thousand voices, praises God.

Samuel Taylor Coleridge [1772–1834]

THE PEAKS

IN the night
Gray, heavy clouds muffled the valleys,
And the peaks looked toward God alone.
    "O Master, that movest the wind with a finger,
    Humble, idle, futile peaks are we.
    Grant that we may run swiftly across the world
    To huddle in worship at Thy feet."

In the morning
A noise of men at work came through the clear blue miles,
And the little black cities were apparent.
    "O Master, that knowest the meaning of raindrops,
    Humble, idle, futile peaks are we.
    Give voice to us, we pray, O Lord,
    That we may sing Thy goodness to the sun."

In the evening
The far valleys were sprinkled with tiny lights.
    "O Master,
    Thou that knowest the value of kings and birds,
    Thou hast made us humble, idle, futile peaks.
    Thou only needest eternal patience;
    We bow to Thy wisdom, O Lord—
    Humble, idle, futile peaks."

In the night
Gray, heavy clouds muffled the valleys,
And the peaks looked toward God alone.

Stephen Crane [1871–1900]

KINCHINJUNGA

NEXT TO EVEREST HIGHEST OF MOUNTAINS

O WHITE priest of Eternity, around
Whose lofty summit veiling clouds arise
Of the earth's immemorial sacrifice
To Brahma, in whose breath all lives and dies;
O hierarch enrobed in timeless snows,
First-born of Asia, whose maternal throes
Seem changed now to a million human woes,
Holy thou art and still!   Be so, nor sound
One sigh of all the mystery in thee found.

For in this world too much is overclear,
Immortal ministrant to many lands,
From whose ice altars flow, to fainting sands,
Rivers that each libation poured expands.
Too much is known, O Ganges-giving sire:
Thy people fathom life, and find it dire;
Thy people fathom death, and, in it, fire
To live again, though in Illusion's sphere,
Behold concealed as grief is in a tear.

Wherefore continue, still enshrined, thy rites,
Though dark Tibet, that dread ascetic, falls,
In strange austerity, whose trance appals,—
Before thee, and a suppliant on thee calls.
Continue still thy silence high and sure,
That something beyond fleeting may endure—
Something that shall forevermore allure
Imagination on to mystic flights
Wherein alone no wing of evil lights.

Yea, wrap thy awful gulfs and acolytes
Of lifted granite round with reachless snows.
Stand for eternity, while pilgrim rows
Of all the nations envy thy repose.
Ensheath thy swart sublimities, unscaled;
Be that alone on earth which has not failed;
Be that which never yet has yearned nor ailed,

But since primeval Power upreared thy heights
Has stood above all deaths and all delights.

And though thy loftier brother shall be king,
High-priest be thou to Brahma unrevealed,
While thy white sanctity forever sealed
In icy silence leaves desire congealed,
In ghostly ministrations to the sun,
And to the mendicant stars and the moon-nun,
Be holy still, till east to west has run,
And till no sacrificial suffering
On any shrine is left to tell life's sting.

           Cale Young Rice [1872–

THE HILLS

MUSSOORIE and Chakrata Hill
  The Jumna flows between
And from Chakrata's hills afar
  Mussoorie's vale is seen.
The mountains sing together
In cloud or sunny weather,
The Jumna, through their tether,
  Foams white or plunges green.

The mountains stand and laugh at Time,
  They pillar up the Earth,
They watch the ages pass, they bring
  New centuries to birth.
They feel the daybreak shiver,
They see Time passing ever,
As flows the Jumna River
  As breaks the white sea-surf.

They drink the sun in a golden cup
  And in blue mist the rain;
With a sudden brightening they meet the lightning
  Or ere it strikes the plain.
They seize the sullen thunder
And take it up for plunder
And cast it down and under,
  And up and back again. . . .

. . . Here, in the hills of ages
    I met thee face to face;
O mother Earth, O lover Earth,
    Look down on me with grace.
Give me thy passion burning,
And thy strong patience, turning
All wrath to power, all yearning
    To truth, thy dwelling-place.
        Julian Grenfell [1888–1915]

HEMLOCK MOUNTAIN

By orange grove and palm-tree, we walked the southern
    shore,
Each day more still and golden than was the day before.
That calm and languid sunshine! How faint it made us
    grow
To look on Hemlock Mountain when the storm hangs low!

To see its rocky pastures, its sparse but hardy corn,
The mist roll off its forehead before a harvest morn;
To hear the pine-trees crashing across its gulfs of snow
Upon a roaring midnight when the whirlwinds blow.

Tell not of lost Atlantis, or fabled Avalon;
The olive, or the vineyard, no winter breathes upon;
Away from Hemlock Mountain we could not well forego,
For all the summer islands where the gulf tides flow.
        Sarah N. Cleghorn [1876–

SUNRISE ON RYDAL WATER

Come down at dawn from windless hills
    Into the valley of the lake,
Where yet a larger quiet fills
    The hour, and mist and water make
With rocks and reeds and island boughs
    One silence and one element,
Where wonder goes surely as once
        It went
    By Galilean prows.

Moveless the water and the mist,
  Moveless the secret air above,
Hushed, as upon some happy tryst
  The poised expectancy of love;
What spirit is it that adores
  What mighty presence yet unseen?
What consummation works apace
  Between
    These rapt enchanted shores?

Never did virgin beauty wake
  Devouter to the bridal feast
Than moves this hour upon the lake
  In adoration to the east.
Here is the bride a god may know,
  The primal will, the young consent,
Till surely upon the appointed mood
  Intent
    The god shall leap—and, lo,

Over the lake's end strikes the sun—
  White, flameless fire; some purity
Thrilling the mist, a splendor won
  Out of the world's heart. Let there be
Thoughts, and atonements, and desires;
  Proud limbs, and undeliberate tongue;
Where now we move with mortal care
  Among
    Immortal dews and fires.

So the old mating goes apace,
  Wind with the sea, and blood with thought,
Lover with lover; and the grace
  Of understanding comes unsought
When stars into the twilight steer,
  Or thrushes build among the may,
Or wonder moves between the hills,
  And day
    Comes up on Rydal mere.

John Drinkwater [1882–1937]

THE DESERTED PASTURE

I LOVE the stony pasture
That no one else will have.
The old gray rocks so friendly seem,
So durable and brave.

In tranquil contemplation
It watches through the year,
Seeing the frosty stars arise,
The slender moons appear.

Its music is the rain-wind,
Its choristers the birds,
And there are secrets in its heart
Too wonderful for words.

It keeps the bright-eyed creatures
That play about its walls,
Though long ago its milking herds
Were banished from their stalls.

Only the children come there,
For buttercups in May,
Or nuts in autumn, where it lies
Dreaming the hours away.

Long since its strength was given
To making good increase,
And now its soul is turned again
To beauty and to peace.

There in the early springtime
The violets are blue,
And adder-tongues in coats of gold
Are garmented anew.

There bayberry and aster
Are crowded on its floors,

When marching summer halts to praise
The Lord of Out-of-doors.

And there October passes
In gorgeous livery,—
In purple ash, and crimson oak,
And golden tulip tree.

And when the winds of winter
Their bugle blasts begin,
The snowy hosts of heaven arrive
To pitch their tents therein.

Bliss Carman [1861–1929]

TO MEADOWS

YE have been fresh and green;
  Ye have been filled with flowers;
And ye the walks have been
  Where maids have spent their hours.

Ye have beheld how they
  With wicker arks did come
To kiss and bear away
  The richer cowslips home.

Ye've heard them sweetly sing,
  And seen them in a round,
Each virgin, like a Spring,
  With honeysuckles crowned.

But now we see none here
  Whose silvery feet did tread,
And with dishevelled hair
  Adorned this smoother mead.

Like unthrifts, having spent
  Your stock, and needy grown,
Ye're left here to lament
  Your poor estates, alone.

Robert Herrick [1591–1674]

THE CLOUD

I BRING fresh showers for the thirsting flowers
    From the seas and the streams;
I bear light shade for the leaves when laid
    In their noonday dreams.
From my wings are shaken the dews that waken
    The sweet buds every one,
When rocked to rest on their mother's breast,
    As she dances about the sun.
I wield the flail of the lashing hail,
    And whiten the green plains under;
And then again I dissolve it in rain,
    And laugh as I pass in thunder.

I sift the snow on the mountains below,
    And their great pines groan aghast;
And all the night 'tis my pillow white,
    While I sleep in the arms of the blast.
Sublime on the towers of my skiey bowers
    Lightning my pilot sits;
In a cavern under is fettered the thunder,
    It struggles and howls at fits.

Over earth and ocean, with gentle motion,
    This pilot is guiding me,
Lured by the love of the Genii that move
    In the depths of the purple sea;
Over the rills, and the crags, and the hills,
    Over the lakes and the plains,
Wherever he dream, under mountain or stream,
    The Spirit he loves remains;
And I all the while bask in heaven's blue smile,
    Whilst he is dissolving in rains.

The sanguine Sunrise, with his meteor eyes,
    And his burning plumes outspread,
Leaps on the back of my sailing rack,
    When the morning star shines dead,

As on the jag of a mountain-crag,
    Which an earthquake rocks and swings,
An eagle alit one moment may sit
    In the light of its golden wings.
And, when Sunset may breathe, from the lit sea beneath,
    Its ardors of rest and of love,
And the crimson pall of eve may fall
    From the depth of heaven above,
With wings folded I rest on mine airy nest,
    As still as a brooding dove.

That orbèd maiden with white fire laden,
    Whom mortals call the Moon,
Glides glimmering o'er my fleece-like floor,
    By the midnight breezes strewn;
And wherever the beat of her unseen feet,
    Which only the angels hear,
May have broken the woof of my tent's thin roof,
    The Stars peep behind her and peer.
And I laugh to see them whirl and flee
    Like a swarm of golden bees,
When I widen the rent in my wind-built tent,
    Till the calm rivers, lakes, and seas,
Like strips of the sky fallen through me on high,
    Are each paved with the moon and these.

I bind the Sun's throne with a burning zone,
    And the Moon's with a girdle of pearl;
The volcanoes are dim, and the Stars reel and swim,
    When the Whirlwinds my banner unfurl.
From cape to cape, with a bridge-like shape,
    Over a torrent sea,
Sunbeam-proof, I hang like a roof;
    The mountains its columns be.
The triumphal arch through which I march,
    With hurricane, fire, and snow,
When the Powers of the air are chained to my chair,
    Is the million-colored bow;
The Sphere-fire above its soft colors wove,
    While the moist Earth was laughing below.

I am the daughter of Earth and Water,
    And the nursling of the Sky:
I pass through the pores of the ocean and shores;
    I change, but I cannot die.
For after the rain, when with never a stain
    The pavilion of heaven is bare,
And the winds and sunbeams with their convex gleams
    Build up the blue dome of air,
I silently laugh at my own cenotaph,
    And out of the caverns of rain,
Like a child from the womb, like a ghost from the tomb,
    I arise, and unbuild it again.

                    Percy Bysshe Shelley [1792–1822]

APRIL RAIN

    It is not raining rain for me,
        It's raining daffodils;
    In every dimpled drop I see
        Wild flowers on the hills.

    The clouds of gray engulf the day
        And overwhelm the town;
    It is not raining rain to me,
        It's raining roses down.

    It is not raining rain to me,
        But fields of clover bloom,
    Where any buccaneering bee
        Can find a bed and room.

    A health unto the happy,
        A fig for him who frets!
    It is not raining rain to me,
        It's raining violets.

                    Robert Loveman [1864–1923]

SUMMER INVOCATION

O GENTLE, gentle summer rain,
  Let not the silver lily pine,
The drooping lily pine in vain
  To feel that dewy touch of thine,—
To drink thy freshness once again,
O gentle, gentle summer rain!

In heat the landscape quivering lies;
  The cattle pant beneath the tree;
Through parching air and purple skies
  The earth looks up, in vain, for thee;
For thee—for thee, it looks in vain
O gentle, gentle summer rain.

Come thou, and brim the meadow streams,
  And soften all the hills with mist,
O falling dew! from burning dreams
  By thee shall herb and flower be kissed,
And Earth shall bless thee yet again,
O gentle, gentle summer rain.

William Cox Bennett [1820-1895]

APRIL RAIN

THE April rain, the April rain,
Comes slanting down in fitful showers,
  Then from the furrow shoots the grain,
And banks are edged with nestling flowers;
And in gray shaw and woodland bowers
  The cuckoo through the April rain
    Calls once again.

The April sun, the April sun,
Glints through the rain in fitful splendor,
  And in gray shaw and woodland dun
The little leaves spring forth and tender
Their infant hands, yet weak and slender,
  For warmth towards the April sun,
    One after one.

And between shower and shine hath birth
The rainbow's evanescent glory;
    Heaven's light that breaks on mist of earth!
Frail symbol of our human story,
It flowers through showers where, looming hoary,
    The rain-clouds flash with April mirth,
        Like Life on earth.

Mathilde Blind [1841–1896]

TO THE RAINBOW

TRIUMPHAL arch, that fill'st the sky
    When storms prepare to part,
I ask not proud Philosophy
    To teach me what thou art;—

Still seem, as to my childhood's sight,
    A midway station given
For happy spirits to alight
    Betwixt the earth and heaven.

Can all that Optics teach unfold
    Thy form to please me so,
As when I dreamt of gems and gold
    Hid in thy radiant bow?

When Science from Creation's face
    Enchantment's veil withdraws,
What lovely visions yield their place
    To cold material laws!

And yet, fair bow, no fabling dreams,
    But words of the Most High,
Have told why first thy robe of beams
    Was woven in the sky.

When o'er the green, undeluged earth
    Heaven's covenant thou didst shine,
How came the world's gray fathers forth
    To watch thy sacred sign!

And when its yellow luster smiled
  O'er mountains yet untrod,
Each mother held aloft her child
  To bless the bow of God.

Methinks, thy jubilee to keep,
  The first-made anthem rang
On earth, delivered from the deep,
  And the first poet sang.

Nor ever shall the Muse's eye
  Unraptured greet thy beam;
Theme of primeval prophecy,
  Be still the prophet's theme!

The earth to thee her incense yields,
  The lark thy welcome sings,
When, glittering in the freshened fields,
  The snowy mushroom springs.

How glorious is thy girdle, cast
  O'er mountain, tower, and town,
Or mirrored in the ocean vast,
  A thousand fathoms down!

As fresh in yon horizon dark,
  As young thy beauties seem,
As when the eagle from the ark
  First sported in thy beam:

For, faithful to its sacred page,
  Heaven still rebuilds thy span;
Nor lets the type grow pale with age,
  That first spoke peace to man.
               Thomas Campbell [1777–1844]

GREEN THINGS GROWING

MY GARDEN

A GARDEN is a lovesome thing, God wot!
       Rose plot,
           Fringed pool,
       Ferned grot—
           The veriest school
           Of peace; and yet the fool
Contends that God is not—
Not God! in gardens! when the eve is cool?
           Nay, but I have a sign:
           'Tis very sure God walks in mine.
                    Thomas Edward Brown [1830-1897]

THE GARDEN

How vainly men themselves amaze
To win the palm, the oak, or bays,
And their incessant labors see
Crowned from some single herb or tree,
Whose short and narrow-vergèd shade
Does prudently their toils upbraid;
While all the flowers and trees do close
To weave the garlands of repose!

Fair Quiet, have I found thee here,
And Innocence, thy sister dear?
Mistaken long, I sought you then
In busy companies of men:
Your sacred plants, if here below,
Only among the plants will grow:
Society is all but rude
To this delicious solitude.

No white nor red was ever seen
So amorous as this lovely green.
Fond lovers, cruel as their flame,
Cut in these trees their mistress' name:
Little, alas! they know or heed
How far these beauties hers exceed!
Fair trees! where'er your barks I wound,
No name shall but your own be found.

When we have run our passions' heat,
Love hither makes his best retreat:
The gods, that mortal beauty chase,
Still in a tree did end their race;
Apollo hunted Daphne so
Only that she might laurel grow;
And Pan did after Syrinx speed,
Not as a nymph, but for a reed.

What wondrous life is this I lead!
Ripe apples drop about my head;
The luscious clusters of the vine
Upon my mouth do crush their wine;
The nectarine and curious peach
Into my hands themselves do reach;
Stumbling on melons, as I pass,
Ensnared with flowers, I fall on grass.

Meanwhile the mind, from pleasure less,
Withdraws into its happiness;
The mind, that ocean where each kind
Does straight its own resemblance find;
Yet it creates, transcending these,
Far other worlds, and other seas;
Annihilating all that's made
To a green thought in a green shade.

Here at the fountain's sliding foot,
Or at some fruit-tree's mossy root,
Casting the body's vest aside,
My soul into the boughs does glide;

There, like a bird, it sits and sings,
Then whets and combs its silver wings,
And, till prepared for longer flight,
Waves in its plumes the various light.

Such was that happy Garden-state
While man there walked without a mate:
After a place so pure and sweet,
What other help could yet be meet!
But 'twas beyond a mortal's share
To wander solitary there:
Two paradises 'twere in one,
To live in Paradise alone.

How well the skilful gardener drew
Of flowers and herbs this dial new!
Where, from above, the milder sun
Does through a fragrant zodiac run:
And, as it works, the industrious bee
Computes its time as well as we.
How could such sweet and wholesome hours
Be reckoned, but with herbs and flowers!

Andrew Marvell [1621–1678]

A GARDEN

WRITTEN AFTER THE CIVIL WARS

SEE how the flowers, as at parade,
Under their colors stand displayed:
Each regiment in order grows,
That of the tulip, pink, and rose.
But when the vigilant patrol
Of stars walks round about the pole,
Their leaves, that to the stalks are curled,
Seem to their staves the ensigns furled.
Then in some flower's belovèd hut
Each bee, as sentinel, is shut,
And sleeps so too; but if once stirred,
She runs you through, nor asks the word.

O thou, that dear and happy Isle,
The garden of the world erewhile,
Thou Paradise of the four seas
Which Heaven planted us to please,
But, to exclude the world, did guard
With watery if not flaming sword;
What luckless apple did we taste
To make us mortal and thee waste!
Unhappy! shall we never more
That sweet militia restore,
When gardens only had their towers,
And all the garrisons were flowers;
When roses only arms might bear,
And men did rosy garlands wear?

Andrew Marvell [1621–1678]

A GARDEN SONG

HERE, in this sequestered close
Bloom the hyacinth and rose;
Here beside the modest stock
Flaunts the flaring hollyhock;
Here, without a pang, one sees
Ranks, conditions, and degrees.

All the seasons run their race
In this quiet resting-place;
Peach, and apricot, and fig
Here will ripen, and grow big;
Here is store and overplus,—
More had not Alcinoüs!

Here, in alleys cool and green,
Far ahead the thrush is seen;
Here along the southern wall
Keeps the bee his festival;
All is quiet else—afar
Sounds of toil and turmoil are.

Here be shadows large and long;
Here be spaces meet for song;

Grant, O garden-god, that I,
Now that none profane is nigh,—
Now that mood and moment please,
Find the fair Pierides!

Austin Dobson [1840–1921]

"IN GREEN OLD GARDENS"

IN green old gardens, hidden away
  From sight of revel and sound of strife,
    Where the bird may sing out his soul ere he die,
Nor fears for the night, so he lives his day;
Where the high red walls, which are growing gray
    With their lichen and moss embroideries,
  Seem sadly and sternly to shut out life,
Because it is often as red as they;

Where even the bee has time to glide
  (Gathering gayly his honey's store)
    Right to the heart of the old-world flowers—
China-asters and purple stocks,
Dahlias and tall red hollyhocks,
    Laburnums raining their golden showers,
  Columbines prim of the folded core,
And lupins, and larkspurs, and "London pride";

Where the heron is waiting amongst the reeds,
  Grown tame in the silence that reigns around,
    Broken only, now and then,
By shy woodpecker or noisy jay,
By the far-off watch-dog's muffled bay;
    But where never the purposeless laughter of men,
  Or the seething city's murmurous sound
Will float up over the river-weeds.

Here may I live what life I please,
  Married and buried out of sight,—
    Married to pleasure, and buried to pain,—
Hidden away amongst scenes like these,
Under the fans of the chestnut trees;

Living my child-life over again,
  With the further hope of a fallen delight,
Blithe as the birds and wise as the bees.

In green old gardens, hidden away
  From sight of revel and sound of strife,--
    Here have I leisure to breathe and move,
And to do my work in a nobler way;
To sing my songs, and to say my say;
    To dream my dreams, and to love my love;
  To hold my faith, and to live my life,
Making the most of its shadowy day.

Violet Fane [1843–1905]

A BENEDICTINE GARDEN

THROUGH all the wind-blown aisles of May,
Faint bells of perfume swing and fall.
Within this apple-petalled wall
(A gray east, flecked with rosy day)
The pink laburnum lays her cheek
In married, matchless, lovely bliss,
Against her golden mate, to seek
His airy kiss.

Tulips, in faded splendor drest,
Brood o'er their beds, a slumbrous gloom.
Dame Peony, red and ripe with bloom,
Swells the silk housing of her breast.
The Lilac, drunk to ecstasy,
Breaks her full flagons on the air,
And drenches home the reeling bee
Who found her fair.

O cowlèd Legion of the Cross,
What solemn pleasantry is thine,
Vowing to seek the life divine
Through abnegation and through loss!

Men but make monuments of sin
Who walk the earth's ambitious round;
Thou hast the richer realm within
This garden ground.

No woman's voice takes sweeter note
Than chanting of this plumèd choir.
No jewel ever wore the fire
Hung on a dewdrop's quivering throat.
A ruddier pomp and pageantry
Than world's delight o'erfleets thy sod;
And choosing this, thou hast in fee
The peace of God.

                              Alice Brown [1857–

AN AUTUMN GARDEN

My tent stands in a garden
Of aster and golden-rod,
Tilled by the rain and the sunshine,
And sown by the hand of God,—
An old New England pasture
Abandoned to peace and time,
And by the magic of beauty
Reclaimed to the sublime.

About it are golden woodlands
Of tulip and hickory;
On the open ridge behind it
You may mount to a glimpse of sea,—
The far-off, blue, Homeric
Rim of the world's great shield,
A border of boundless glamor
For the soul's familiar field.

In purple and gray-wrought lichen
The boulders lie in the sun;
Along its grassy footpath,
The white-tailed rabbits run.

The crickets work and chirrup
Through the still afternoon;
And the owl calls at twilight
Under the frosty moon.

The odorous wild grape clambers
Over the tumbling wall,
And through the autumnal quiet
The chestnuts open and fall.
Sharing time's freshness and fragrance,
Part of the earth's great soul,
Here man's spirit may ripen
To wisdom serene and whole.

Shall we not grow with the asters?—
Never reluctant nor sad,
Not counting the cost of being,
Living to dare and be glad.
Shall we not lift with the crickets
A chorus of ready cheer,
Braving the frost of oblivion,
Quick to be happy here?

The deep red cones of the sumach
And the woodbine's crimson sprays
Have bannered the common roadside
For the pageant of passing days.
These are the oracles Nature
Fills with her holy breath,
Giving them glory of color,
Transcending the shadow of death.

Here in the sifted sunlight
A spirit seems to brood
On the beauty and worth of being,
In tranquil, instinctive mood;
And the heart, athrob with gladness
Such as the wise earth knows,
Wells with a full thanksgiving
For the gifts that life bestows:

For the ancient and virile nurture
Of the teeming primordial ground,
For the splendid gospel of color,
The rapt revelations of sound;
For the morning-blue above us
And the rusted gold of the fern,
For the chickadee's call to valor
Bidding the faint-heart turn;

For fire and running water,
Snowfall and summer rain;
For sunsets and quiet meadows,
The fruit and the standing grain;
For the solemn hour of moonrise
Over the crest of trees,
When the mellow lights are kindled
In the lamps of the centuries.

For those who wrought aforetime,
Led by the mystic strain
To strive for the larger freedom,
And live for the greater gain;
For plenty and peace and playtime,
The homely goods of earth,
And for rare immaterial treasures
Accounted of little worth;

For art and learning and friendship,
Where beneficent truth is supreme,
Those everlasting cities
Built on the hills of dream;
For all things growing and goodly
That foster this life, and breed
The immortal flower of wisdom
Out of the mortal seed.

But most of all for the spirit
That can not rest nor bide
In stale and sterile convenience,
Nor safety proven and tried,

But still inspired and driven,
Must seek what better may be,
And up from the loveliest garden
Must climb for a glimpse of sea.
Bliss Carman [1861–1929]

UNGUARDED

THE Mistress of the Roses
    Is haply far away,
And through her garden closes
    What strange intruders stray.

See on its rustic spindles
    The sundrop's amber fire!
And the goldenrod enkindles
    The embers on its spire.

The dodder's shining tangle
    From the meadow brook steals in,
Where in this shadowed angle
    The pale lace-makers spin.

Here's Black-Eyed Susan weeping
    Into exotic air,
And Bouncing Bet comes creeping
    Back to her old parterre.

Now in this pleasant weather—
    So sweetly reconciled—
They dwell and dream together,
    The kin of court and wild.
Ada Foster Murray [1857–1936]

THE DESERTED GARDEN

I MIND me in the days departed,
How often underneath the sun,
With childish bounds I used to run
    To a garden long deserted.

The beds and walks were vanished quite;
And wheresoe'er had struck the spade,
The greenest grasses Nature laid
    To sanctify her right.

I called the place my wilderness;
For no one entered there but I;
The sheep looked in, the grass to espy,
    And passed it ne'ertheless.

The trees were interwoven wild,
And spread their boughs enough about
To keep both sheep and shepherd out,
    But not a happy child.

Adventurous joy it was for me!
I crept beneath the boughs, and found
A circle smooth of mossy ground
    Beneath a poplar tree.

Old garden rose-trees hedged it in,
Bedropt with roses waxen-white,
Well satisfied with dew and light
    And careless to be seen.

Long years ago, it might befall,
When all the garden flowers were trim,
The grave old gardener prided him
    On these the most of all.

Some lady, stately overmuch,
Here moving with a silken noise,
Has blushed beside them at the voice
    That likened her to such.

Or these, to make a diadem,
She often may have plucked and twined,
Half-smiling as it came to mind,
    That few would look at *them*.

Oh, little thought that lady proud,
A child would watch her fair white rose,
When buried lay her whiter brows,
    And silk was changed for shroud!

Nor thought that gardener, (full of scorns
For men unlearned and simple phrase,)
A child would bring it all its praise
    By creeping through the thorns!

To me upon my low moss seat,
Though never a dream the roses sent
Of science or love's compliment,
    I ween they smelt as sweet.

It did not move my grief to see
The trace of human step departed:
Because the garden was deserted,
    The blither place for me!

Friends, blame me not! a narrow ken
Hath childhood 'twixt the sun and sward;
We draw the moral afterward,
    We feel the gladness then.

And gladdest hours for me did glide
In silence at the rose-tree wall:
A thrush made gladness musical
    Upon the other side.

Nor he nor I did e'er incline
To peck or pluck the blossoms white;
How should I know but roses might
    Lead lives as glad as mine?

To make my hermit-home complete,
I brought clear water from the spring
Praised in its own low murmuring,
    And cresses glossy wet.

And so, I thought, my likeness grew
(Without the melancholy tale)
To "gentle hermit of the dale,"
    And Angelina too.

For oft I read within my nook
Such minstrel stories; till the breeze
Made sounds poetic in the trees,
    And then I shut the book.

If I shut this wherein I write,
I hear no more the wind athwart
Those trees, nor feel that childish heart
    Delighting in delight.

My childhood from my life is parted,
My footstep from the moss which drew
Its fairy circle round: anew
    The garden is deserted.

Another thrush may there rehearse
The madrigals which sweetest are;
No more for me! myself afar
    Do sing a sadder verse.

Ah me, ah me! when erst I lay
In that child's-nest so greenly wrought,
I laughed unto myself and thought
    "The time will pass away."

And still I laughed, and did not fear
But that, whene'er was passed away
The childish time, some happier play
    My womanhood would cheer.

I knew the time would pass away,
And yet, beside the rose-tree wall,
Dear God, how seldom, if at all,
    Did I look up to pray!

The time *is* past; and now that grows
The cypress high among the trees,
And I behold white sepulchres
   As well as the white rose,—

When graver, meeker thoughts are given,
And I have learnt to lift my face,
Reminded how earth's greenest place
   The color draws from heaven,—

It something saith for earthly pain,
But more for Heavenly promise free,
That I who was, would shrink to be
   That happy child again.

Elizabeth Barrett Browning [1806–1861]

A FORSAKEN GARDEN

In a coign of the cliff between lowland and highland,
   At the sea-down's edge between windward and lee,
Walled round with rocks as an inland island,
   The ghost of a garden fronts the sea.
A girdle of brushwood and thorn encloses
   The steep, square slope of the blossomless bed
Where the weeds that grew green from the graves of its
      roses
         Now lie dead.

The fields fall southward, abrupt and broken,
   To the low last edge of the long lone land.
If a step should sound or a word be spoken,
   Would a ghost not rise at the strange guest's hand?
So long have the gray, bare walks lain guestless,
   Through branches and briers if a man make way,
He shall find no life but the sea-wind's, restless
      Night and day.

The dense, hard passage is blind and stifled
   That crawls by a track none turn to climb
To the strait waste place that the years have rifled
   Of all but the thorns that are touched not of Time.

The thorns he spares when the rose is taken;
    The rocks are left when he wastes the plain.
The wind that wanders, the weeds wind-shaken,
        These remain.

Not a flower to be pressed of the foot that falls not;
    As the heart of a dead man the seed-plots are dry;
From the thicket of thorns whence the nightingale calls not,
    Could she call, there were never a rose to reply.
Over the meadows that blossom and wither
    Rings but the note of a sea-bird's song;
Only the sun and the rain come hither
        All year long.

The sun burns sere and the rain dishevels
    One gaunt bleak blossom of scentless breath.
Only the wind here hovers and revels
    In a round where life seems barren as death.
Here there was laughing of old, there was weeping,
    Haply, of lovers none ever will know,
Whose eyes went seaward a hundred sleeping
        Years ago.

Heart handfast in heart as they stood, "Look thither,"
    Did he whisper? "Look forth from the flowers to the
        sea;
For the foam-flowers endure when the rose-blossoms wither,
    And men that love lightly may die—but we?"
And the same wind sang and the same waves whitened,
    And or ever the garden's last petals were shed,
In the lips that had whispered, the eyes that had lightened,
        Love was dead.

Or they loved their life through, and then went whither?
    And were one to the end—but what end who knows?
Love deep as the sea as a rose must wither,
    As the rose-red seaweed that mocks the rose.
Shall the dead take thought for the dead to love them?
    What love was ever as deep as a grave?
They are loveless now as the grass above them
        Or the wave.

All are at one now, roses and lovers,
  Not known of the cliffs and the fields and the sea.
Not a breath of the time that has been hovers
  In the air now soft with a summer to be.
Not a breath shall there sweeten the seasons hereafter
  Of the flowers or the lovers that laugh now or weep,
When, as they that are free now of weeping and laughter,
      We shall sleep.

Here death may deal not again forever;
  Here change may come not till all change end.
From the graves they have made they shall rise up never,
  Who have left naught living to ravage and rend.
Earth, stones, and thorns of the wild ground growing,
  While the sun and the rain live, these shall be;
Till a last wind's breath, upon all these blowing,
      Roll the sea.

Till the slow sea rise and the sheer cliff crumble,
  Till terrace and meadow the deep gulfs drink,
Till the strength of the waves of the high tides humble
  The fields that lessen, the rocks that shrink;
Here now in his triumph where all things falter,
  Stretched out on the spoils that his own hand spread,
As a god self-slain on his own strange altar,
      Death lies dead.

Algernon Charles Swinburne [1837–1909]

GREEN THINGS GROWING

O THE green things growing, the green things growing,
The faint sweet smell of the green things growing!
I should like to live, whether I smile or grieve,
Just to watch the happy life of my green things growing.

O the fluttering and the pattering of those green things
      growing!
How they talk each to each, when none of us are knowing;
In the wonderful white of the weird moonlight
Or the dim dreamy dawn when the cocks are crowing.

I love, I love them so—my green things growing!
And I think that they love me, without false showing;
For by many a tender touch, they comfort me so much,
With the soft mute comfort of green things growing.

And in the rich store of their blossoms glowing
Ten for one I take they're on me bestowing:
Oh, I should like to see, if God's will it may be,
Many, many a summer of my green things growing!

But if I must be gathered for the angel's sowing,
Sleep out of sight awhile, like the green things growing,
Though dust to dust return, I think I'll scarcely mourn,
If I may change into green things growing.
                    Dinah Maria Mulock Craik [1826–1887]

A CHANTED CALENDAR

From "Balder"

FIRST came the primrose,
On the bank high,
Like a maiden looking forth
From the window of a tower
When the battle rolls below,
So looked she,
And saw the storms go by.

Then came the wind-flower
In the valley left behind,
As a wounded maiden, pale
With purple streaks of woe,
When the battle has rolled by
Wanders to and fro,
So tottered she,
Dishevelled in the wind.

Then came the daisies,
On the first of May,
Like a bannered show's advance

While the crowd runs by the way,
With ten thousand flowers about them they came trooping
  through the fields.

      As a happy people come,
      So came they,
      As a happy people come
      When the war has rolled away,
      With dance and tabor, pipe and drum,
      And all make holiday.

      Then came the cowslip,
      Like a dancer in the fair,
      She spread her little mat of green,
      And on it danced she.
      With a fillet bound about her brow,
      A fillet round her happy brow,
      A golden fillet round her brow,
      And rubies in her hair.

                    Sydney Dobell [1824–1874]

FLOWERS

SPAKE full well, in language quaint and olden
    One who dwelleth by the castled Rhine,
When he called the flowers, so blue and golden,
    Stars, that in earth's firmament do shine.

Stars they are, wherein we read our history,
    As astrologers and seers of eld;
Yet not wrapped about with awful mystery,
    Like the burning stars, which they beheld.

Wondrous truths, and manifold as wondrous,
    God hath written in those stars above;
But not less in the bright flowerets under us
    Stands the revelation of his love.

Bright and glorious is that revelation,
    Writ all over this great world of ours;
Making evident our own creation,
    In these stars of earth, these golden flowers.

And the Poet, faithful and far-seeing,
　　Sees, alike in stars and flowers, a part
Of the self-same, universal being,
　　Which is throbbing in his brain and heart.

Gorgeous flowerets in the sunlight shining,
　　Blossoms flaunting in the eye of day,
Tremulous leaves, with soft and silver lining,
　　Buds that open only to decay;

Brilliant hopes, all woven in gorgeous tissues,
　　Flaunting gayly in the golden light;
Large desires, with most uncertain issues,
　　Tender wishes, blossoming at night!

These in flowers and men are more than seeming;
　　Workings are they of the self-same powers
Which the Poet, in no idle dreaming,
　　Seeth in himself and in the flowers.

Everywhere about us are they glowing,
　　Some like stars, to tell us Spring is born;
Others, their blue eyes with tears o'erflowing,
　　Stand like Ruth amid the golden corn;

Not alone in Spring's armorial bearing,
　　And in Summer's green-emblazoned field,
But in arms of brave old Autumn's wearing,
　　In the centre of his brazen shield;

Not alone in meadows and green alleys,
　　On the mountain-top, and by the brink
Of sequestered pools in woodland valleys,
　　Where the slaves of nature stoop to drink;

Not alone in her vast dome of glory,
　　Not on graves of bird and beast alone,
But in old cathedrals, high and hoary,
　　On the tombs of heroes, carved in stone;

In the cottage of the rudest peasant;
In ancestral homes, whose crumbling towers,
Speaking of the Past unto the Present,
Tell us of the ancient Games of Flowers;

In all places, then, and in all seasons,
Flowers expand their light and soul-like wings,
Teaching us, by most persuasive reasons,
How akin they are to human things.

And with childlike, credulous affection,
We behold their tender buds expand;
Emblems of our own great resurrection,
Emblems of the bright and better land.

Henry Wadsworth Longfellow [1807–1882]

FLOWERS

I WILL not have the mad Clytie,
Whose head is turned by the sun;
The tulip is a courtly quean,
Whom, therefore, I will shun:
The cowslip is a country wench,
The violet is a nun;—
But I will woo the dainty rose,
The queen of every one.

The pea is but a wanton witch,
In too much haste to wed,
And clasps her rings on every hand;
The wolfsbane I should dread;
Nor will I dreary rosemarye,
That always mourns the dead;
But I will woo the dainty rose,
With her cheeks of tender red.

The lily is all in white, like a saint,
And so is no mate for me;
And the daisy's cheek is tipped with a blush,
She is of such low degree;

Jasmine is sweet, and has many loves,
    And the broom's betrothed to the bee;—
But I will plight with the dainty rose,
    For fairest of all is she.

Thomas Hood [1799–1845]

A CONTEMPLATION UPON FLOWERS

BRAVE flowers—that I could gallant it like you,
    And be as little vain!
You come abroad, and make a harmless show,
    And to your beds of earth again.
You are not proud: you know your birth:
For your embroidered garments are from earth.

You do obey your months and times, but I
    Would have it ever Spring:
My fate would know no Winter, never die,
    Nor think of such a thing.
O that I could my bed of earth but view
And smile, and look as cheerfully as you!

O teach me to see Death and not to fear,
    But rather to take truce!
How often have I seen you at a bier,
    And there look fresh and spruce!
You fragrant flowers! then teach me, that my breath
Like yours may sweeten and perfume my death.

Henry King [1592–1669]
*(Attributed to King in
the Harleian MSS.)*

ALMOND BLOSSOM

BLOSSOM of the almond trees,
April's gift to April's bees,
Birthday ornament of Spring,
Flora's fairest daughterling;
Coming when no flowerets dare
Trust the cruel outer air;
When the royal kingcup bold
Dares not don his coat of gold;

And the sturdy black-thorn spray
Keeps his silver for the May;—
Coming when no flowerets would,
Save thy lowly sisterhood,
Early violets, blue and white,
Dying for their love of light;—
Almond blossom, sent to teach us
That the spring days soon will reach us,
Lest, with longing over-tried,
We die, as the violets died;—
Blossom, clouding all the tree
With thy crimson broidery,
Long before a leaf of green
On the bravest bough is seen;—
Ah! when winter winds are swinging
All thy red bells into ringing,
With a bee in every bell,
Almond bloom, we greet thee well.

Edwin Arnold [1832–1904]

WHITE AZALEAS

AZALEAS—whitest of white!
  White as the drifted snow
Fresh-fallen out of the night,
  Before the coming glow
Tinges the morning light;
  When the light is like the snow,
    White,
And the silence is like the light:
  Light, and silence, and snow,—
    All—white!

White! not a hint
Of the creamy tint
  A rose will hold,
  The whitest rose, in its inmost fold;
Not a possible blush;
White as an embodied hush;

A very rapture of white;
A wedlock of silence and light:
White, white as the wonder undefiled
Of Eve just wakened in Paradise;
Nay, white as the angel of a child
That looks into God's own eyes!

Harriet McEwen Kimball [1834–1917]

BUTTERCUPS

THERE must be fairy miners
    Just underneath the mould,
Such wondrous quaint designers
    Who live in caves of gold.

They take the shining metals,
    And beat them into shreds;
And mould them into petals,
    To make the flowers' heads.

Sometimes they melt the flowers
    To tiny seeds like pearls,
And store them up in bowers
    For little boys and girls.

And still a tiny fan turns
    Above a forge of gold,
To keep, with fairy lanterns,
    The world from growing old.

Wilfrid Thorley [1878–

THE BROOM FLOWER

OH the Broom, the yellow Broom,
    The ancient poet sung it,
And dear it is on summer days
    To lie at rest among it.

I know the realms where people say
    The flowers have not their fellow;
I know where they shine out like suns,
    The crimson and the yellow.

I know where ladies live enchained
    In luxury's silken fetters,
And flowers as bright as glittering gems
    Are used for written letters.

But ne'er was flower so fair as this,
    In modern days or olden;
It groweth on its nodding stem
    Like to a garland golden.

And all about my mother's door
    Shine out its glittering bushes,
And down the glen, where clear as light
    The mountain-water gushes.

Take all the rest; but give me this,
    And the bird that nestles in it;
I love it, for it loves the Broom—
    The green and yellow linnet.

Well call the rose the queen of flowers,
    And boast of that of Sharon,
Of lilies like to marble cups,
    And the golden rod of Aaron:

I care not how these flowers may be
    Beloved of man and woman;
The Broom it is the flower for me,
    That groweth on the common.

Oh the Broom, the yellow Broom,
    The ancient poet sung it,
And dear it is on summer days
    To lie at rest among it.
                  Mary Howitt [1799–1888]

THE SMALL CELANDINE

THERE is a Flower, the lesser Celandine,
That shrinks, like many more, from cold and rain;
And, the first moment that the sun may shine,
Bright as the sun himself, 'tis out again!

When hailstones have been falling, swarm on swarm,
Or blasts the green field and the trees distressed,
Oft have I seen it muffled up from harm,
In close self-shelter, like a thing at rest.

But lately, one rough day, this Flower I passed
And recognized it, though an altered form,
Now standing forth an offering to the blast,
And buffeted at will by rain and storm.

I stopped, and said with inly-muttered voice,
"It doth not love the shower, nor seek the cold:
This neither is its courage, nor its choice,
But its necessity in being old.

"The sunshine may not cheer it, nor the dew;
It cannot help itself in its decay;
Stiff in its members, withered, changed of hue."
And, in my spleen, I smiled that it was gray.

To be a Prodigal's Favorite—then, worse truth,
A Miser's Pensioner—behold our lot!
O Man, that from thy fair and shining youth
Age might but take the things Youth needed not!

William Wordsworth [1770–1850]

TO THE SMALL CELANDINE

PANSIES, lilies, kingcups, daisies,
Let them live upon their praises;
    Long as there's a sun that sets,
Primroses will have their glory;
    Long as there are violets,
They will have a place in story:
There's a flower that shall be mine,
'Tis the little Celandine.

Eyes of some men travel far
For the finding of a star;
    Up and down the heavens they go,
Men that keep a mighty rout!

I'm as great as them, I trow,
Since the day I found thee out.
Little Flower!—I'll make a stir,
Like a sage astronomer.

Modest, yet withal an Elf
Bold, and lavish of thyself;
    Since we needs must first have met,
I have seen thee, high and low,
    Thirty years or more, and yet
'Twas a face I did not know;
Thou hast now, go where I may,
Fifty greetings in a day.

Ere a leaf is on a bush,
In the time before the thrush
    Has a thought about her nest,
Thou wilt come with half a call,
    Spreading out thy glossy breast
Like a careless Prodigal;
Telling tales about the sun,
When we've little warmth, or none.

Poets, vain men in their mood!
Travel with the multitude:
    Never heed them; I aver
That they all are wanton wooers;
    But the thrifty cottager,
Who stirs little out of doors,
Joys to spy thee near her home;
Spring is coming, Thou art come!

Comfort have thou of thy merit,
Kindly, unassuming Spirit!
    Careless of thy neighborhood,
Thou dost show thy pleasant face
    On the moor, and in the wood,
In the lane;—there's not a place,
Howsoever mean it be,
But 'tis good enough for thee.

Ill befall the yellow flowers,
Children of the flaring hours!
    Buttercups, that will be seen,
Whether we will see or no;
    Others, too, of lofty mien;
They have done as worldings do,
Taken praise that should be thine,
Little, humble Celandine!

Prophet of delight and mirth,
Ill-requited upon earth;
    Herald of a mighty band,
Of a joyous train ensuing,
    Serving at my heart's command,
Tasks that are no tasks renewing,
I will sing, as dost behove,
Hymns in praise of what I love!

William Wordsworth [1770–1850]

FOUR-LEAF CLOVER

I KNOW a place where the sun is like gold,
    And the cherry blossoms burst with snow,
And down underneath is the loveliest nook,
    Where the four-leaf clovers grow.

One leaf is for hope, and one is for faith,
    And one is for love, you know,
And God put another in for luck,—
    If you search, you will find where they grow.

But you must have hope, and you must have faith,
    You must love and be strong—and so,
If you work, if you wait, you will find the place
    Where the four-leaf clovers grow.

Ella Higginson [1862–

SWEET CLOVER

WITHIN what weeks the melilot
    Gave forth its fragrance, I, a lad,
Or never knew or quite forgot,
    Save that 'twas while the year is glad.

Now know I that in bright July
   It blossoms; and the perfume fine
Brings back my boyhood, until I
   Am steeped in memory as with wine.

Now know I that the whole year long,
   Though Winter chills or Summer cheers,
It writes along the weeks its song,
    Even as my youth sings through my years.

Wallace Rice [1859–1939]

"I WANDERED LONELY AS A CLOUD"

I WANDERED lonely as a cloud
That floats on high o'er vales and hills,
When all at once I saw a crowd,
A host, of golden daffodils;
Beside the lake, beneath the trees,
Fluttering and dancing in the breeze.

Continuous as the stars that shine
And twinkle in the milky way,
They stretched in never-ending line
Along the margin of a bay:
Ten thousand saw I at a glance,
Tossing their heads in sprightly dance.

The waves beside them danced; but they
Out-did the sparkling waves in glee:
A poet could not but be gay,
In such a jocund company:
I gazed—and gazed—but little thought
What wealth the show to me had brought:

For oft, when on my couch I lie
In vacant or in pensive mood,
They flash upon that inward eye
Which is the bliss of solitude;
And then my heart with pleasure fills,
And dances with the daffodils.

William Wordsworth [1770–1850]

TO DAFFODILS

FAIR Daffodils, we weep to see
　　You haste away so soon;
As yet the early-rising sun
　　Has not attained his noon.
　　　　　　　Stay, stay,
　　Until the hasting day
　　　　　　　Has run
　　But to the even-song;
And, having prayed together, we
　　Will go with you along.

We have short time to stay as you,
　　We have as short a spring;
As quick a growth to meet decay,
　　As you, or any thing.
　　　　　　　We die
　　As your hours do, and dry
　　　　　　　Away,
　　Like to the summer's rain;
Or as the pearls of morning's dew,
　　Ne'er to be found again.

Robert Herrick [1591–1674]

TO A MOUNTAIN DAISY

ON TURNING ONE DOWN WITH THE PLOUGH, IN APRIL 1786

WEE, modest, crimson-tippèd flower,
Thou's met me in an evil hour;
For I maun crush amang the stoure
　　　　Thy slender stem:
To spare thee now is past my power,
　　　　Thou bonny gem.

Alas! it's no thy neibor sweet,
The bonny lark, companion meet,
Bending thee 'mang the dewy weet,
　　　　Wi' speckled breast,
When upward-springing, blithe, to greet
　　　　The purpling east!

Cauld blew the bitter-biting north
Upon thy early, humble birth;
Yet cheerfully thou glinted forth
                Amid the storm,
Scarce reared above the parent earth
                Thy tender form.

The flaunting flowers our gardens yield
High sheltering woods and wa's maun shield;
But thou, beneath the random bield
                O' clod, or stane,
Adorns the histie stibble-field,
                Unseen, alane.

There, in thy scanty mantle clad,
Thy snawie bosom sunward spread,
Thou lifts thy unassuming head
                In humble guise;
But now the share uptears thy bed,
                And low thou lies!

Such is the fate of artless maid,
Sweet flowcret of the rural shade!
By love's simplicity betrayed,
                And guileless trust,
Till she, like thee, all soiled, is laid
                Low i' the dust.

Such is the fate of simple bard,
On life's rough ocean luckless starred!
Unskillful he to note the card
                Of prudent lore,
Till billows rage, and gales blow hard,
                And whelm him o'er!

Such fate to suffering worth is given,
Who long with wants and woes has striven,
By human pride or cunning driven
                To misery's brink,
Till, wrenched of every stay but Heaven,
                He, ruined, sink!

Even thou who mourn'st the Daisy's fate,
That fate is thine—no distant date;
Stern Ruin's ploughshare drives, elate,
    Full on thy bloom,
Till crushed beneath the furrow's weight
    Shall be thy doom.

      Robert Burns [1759–1796]

A FIELD FLOWER

THERE is a flower, a little flower
  With silver crest and golden eye,
That welcomes every changing hour,
  And weathers every sky.

The prouder beauties of the field
  In gay but quick succession shine;
Race after race their honors yield,
  They flourish and decline.

But this small flower, to Nature dear,
  While moons and stars their courses run,
Wreathes the whole circle of the year,
  Companion of the Sun.

It smiles upon the lap of May,
  To sultry August spreads its charms,
Lights pale October on his way,
  And twines December's arms.

The purple heath and golden broom
  On moory mountains catch the gale;
O'er lawns the lily sheds perfume,
  The violet in the vale.

But this bold floweret climbs the hill,
  Hides in the forest, haunts the glen,
Plays on the margin of the rill,
  Peeps round the fox's den.

Within the garden's cultured round
 It shares the sweet carnation's bed;
And blooms on consecrated ground
 In honor of the dead.

The lambkin crops its crimson gem;
 The wild bee murmurs on its breast;
The blue-fly bends its pensile stem
 Light o'er the skylark's nest.

'Tis Flora's page,—in every place,
 In every season, fresh and fair;
It opens with perennial grace,
 And blossoms everywhere.

On waste and woodland, rock and plain,
 Its humble buds unheeded rise;
The Rose has but a summer reign;
 The Daisy never dies!

     James Montgomery [1771–1854]

TO DAISIES, NOT TO SHUT SO SOON

SHUT not so soon; the dull-eyed night
 Has not as yet begun
To make a seizure on the light,
 Or to seal up the sun.

No marigolds yet closèd are,
 No shadows great appear;
Nor doth the early shepherd's star
 Shine like a spangle here.

Stay but till my Julia close
 Her life-begetting eye,
And let the whole world then dispose
 Itself to live or die.

     Robert Herrick [1591-1674]

DAISIES

OVER the shoulders and slopes of the dune
I saw the white daisies go down to the sea,
A host in the sunshine, an army in June,
The people God sends us to set our heart free.

The bobolinks rallied them up from the dell,
The orioles whistled them out of the wood;
And all of their saying was, "Earth, it is well!"
And all of their dancing was, "Life, thou art good!"

Bliss Carman [1861–1929]

TO THE DAISY

WITH little here to do or see
Of things that in the great world be,
Daisy! again I talk to thee,
     For thou art worthy:
Thou unassuming common-place
Of Nature, with that homely face,
And yet with something of a grace,
     Which love makes for thee!

Oft on the dappled turf at ease,
I sit, and play with similies,
Loose types of things through all degrees,
     Thoughts of thy raising:
And many a fond and idle name
I give to thee, for praise or blame,
As is the humor of the game,
     While I am gazing.

A nun demure, of lowly port;
Or sprightly maiden of love's court,
In thy simplicity the sport
     Of all temptations;
A queen in crown of rubies dressed
A starveling in a scanty vest;
Are all, as seem to suit thee best,
     Thy appellations.

A little Cyclops, with one eye
Staring to threaten and defy—
That thought comes next—and instantly
    The freak is over.
The shape will vanish,—and behold!
A silver shield with boss of gold,
That spreads itself, some fairy bold
    In fight to cover.

I see thee glittering from afar;—
And then thou art a pretty star;
Not quite so fair as many are
    In heaven above thee!
Yet like a star, with glittering crest,
Self-poised in air, thou seem'st to rest;—
May peace come never to his nest
    Who shall reprove thee!

Bright Flower! for by that name at last,
When all my reveries are past,
I call thee, and to that cleave fast,
    Sweet silent creature!
That breath'st with me in sun and air,
Do thou, as thou art wont, repair
My heart with gladness, and a share
    Of thy meek nature!
              William Wordsworth [1770–1850]

TO DAISIES

Ah, drops of gold in whitening flame
Burning, we know your lovely name—
Daisies, that little children pull!
Like all weak things, over the strong
Ye do not know your power for wrong,
And much abuse your feebleness.
Daisies, that little children pull,
As ye are weak, be merciful!
O hide your eyes! they are to me
Beautiful insupportably.

Or be but conscious ye are fair,
And I your loveliness could bear,
But, being fair so without art,
Ye vex the silted memories of my heart!

As a pale ghost yearning strays
With sundered gaze,
'Mid corporal presences that are
To it impalpable—such a bar
Sets you more distant than the morning-star.
Such wonder is on you, and amaze,
I look and marvel if I be
Indeed the phantom, or are ye?
The light is on your innocence
Which fell from me.
The fields ye still inhabit whence
My world-acquainted treading strays,
The country where I did commence;
And though ye shine to me so near,
So close to gross and visible sense,—
Between us lies impassable year on year.

To other time and far-off place
Belongs your beauty: silent thus,
Though to other naught you tell,
To me your ranks are rumorous
Of an ancient miracle.
Vain does my touch your petals graze,
I touch you not; and though ye blossom here,
Your roots are fast in alienated days.
Ye there are anchored, while Time's stream
Has swept me past them: your white ways
And infantile delights do seem
To look in on me like a face,
Dead and sweet, come back through dream,
With tears, because for old embrace
It has no arms.

                    These hands did toy,
Children, with you, when I was child,

And in each other's eyes we smiled:
Not yours, not yours the grievous-fair
Apparelling
With which you wet mine eyes; you wear,
Ah me, the garment of the grace
I wove you when I was a boy;
O mine, and not the year's your stolen Spring!
And since ye wear it,
Hide your sweet selves! I cannot bear it.
For when ye break the cloven earth
With your young laughter and endearment,
No blossomy carillon 'tis of mirth
To me; I see my slaughtered joy
Bursting its cerement.

Francis Thompson [1859?–1907]

TO THE DANDELION

DEAR common flower, that grow'st beside the way,
Fringing the dusty road with harmless gold,
    First pledge of blithesome May,
Which children pluck, and, full of pride, uphold,
    High-hearted buccaneers, o'erjoyed that they
An Eldorado in the grass have found,
Which not the rich earth's ample round
    May match in wealth, thou art more dear to me
    Than all the prouder summer-blooms may be.

Gold such as thine ne'er drew the Spanish prow
Through the primeval hush of Indian seas,
    Nor wrinkled the lean brow
Of age, to rob the lover's heart of ease;
    'Tis the Spring's largess, which she scatters now
To rich and poor alike, with lavish hand,
Though most hearts never understand
    To take it at God's value, but pass by
    The offered wealth with unrewarded eye.

Thou art my tropics and mine Italy;
To look at thee unlocks a warmer clime;
   The eyes thou givest me
Are in the heart, and heed not space or time:
   Not in mid June the golden-cuirassed bee
Feels a more summer-like warm ravishment
In the white lily's breezy tent,
   His fragrant Sybaris, than I, when first
   From the dark green thy yellow circles burst.

Then think I of deep shadows on the grass,
Of meadows where in sun the cattle graze,
   Where, as the breezes pass,
The gleaming rushes lean a thousand ways,
   Of leaves that slumber in a cloudy mass,
Or whiten in the wind, of waters blue
That from the distance sparkle through
   Some woodland gap, and of a sky above,
   Where one white cloud like a stray lamb doth move.

My childhood's earliest thoughts are linked with thee;
The sight of thee calls back the robin's song,
   Who, from the dark old tree
Beside the door, sang clearly all day long,
   And I, secure in childish piety,
Listened as if I heard an angel sing
With news from heaven, which he could bring
   Fresh every day to my untainted ears
   When birds and flowers and I were happy peers.

How like a prodigal doth nature seem,
When thou, for all thy gold, so common art!
   Thou teachest me to deem
More sacredly of every human heart,
   Since each reflects in joy its scanty gleam
Of heaven, and could some wondrous secret show,
Did we but pay the love we owe,
   And with a child's undoubting wisdom look
   On all these living pages of God's book.
              James Russell Lowell [1819–1891]

DANDELION

At dawn, when England's childish tongue
Lisped happy truths, and men were young,
Her Chaucer, with a gay content
Hummed through the shining fields, scarce bent
By poet's foot, and, plucking, set,
All lusty, sunny, dewy-wet,
A dandelion in his verse,
Like the first gold in childhood's purse.

At noon, when harvest colors die
On the pale azure of the sky,
And dreams through dozing grasses creep
Of winds that are themselves asleep,
Rapt Shelley found the airy ghost
Of that bright flower the spring loves most,
And ere one silvery ray was blown
From its full disk made it his own.

Now from the stubble poets glean
Scant flowers of thought; the Muse would wean
Her myriad nurslings, feeding them
On petals plucked from a dry stem.
For one small plumule still adrift,
The wind-blown dandelion's gift,
The fields once blossomy we scour
Where the old poets plucked the flower.
Annie Rankin Annan [1848–1925]

THE DANDELIONS

Upon a showery night and still,
    Without a sound of warning,
A trooper band surprised the hill,
    And held it in the morning.

We were not waked by bugle-notes,
    No cheer our dreams invaded,
And yet, at dawn, their yellow coats
    On the green slopes paraded.

We careless folk the deed forgot;
　Till one day, idly walking,
We marked upon the self-same spot
　A crowd of veterans talking.

They shook their trembling heads and gray
　With pride and noiseless laughter;
When, well-a-day! they blew away,
　And ne'er were heard of after!
Helen Gray Cone [1859–1934]

TO THE FRINGED GENTIAN

Thou blossom bright with autumn dew,
And colored with the heaven's own blue,
That openest when the quiet light
Succeeds the keen and frosty night,

Thou comest not when violets lean
O'er wandering brooks and springs unseen,
Or columbines, in purple dressed,
Nod o'er the ground-bird's hidden nest.

Thou waitest late and com'st alone,
When woods are bare and birds are flown,
And frost and shortening days portend
The agèd year is near his end.

Then doth thy sweet and quiet eye
Look through its fringes to the sky,
Blue—blue—as if that sky let fall
A flower from its cerulean wall.

I would that thus, when I shall see
The hour of death draw near to me,
Hope, blossoming within my heart,
May look to heaven as I depart.
William Cullen Bryant [1794–1878]

GOLDENROD

Wʜᴇɴ the wayside tangles blaze
  In the low September sun,
When the flowers of Summer days
  Droop and wither, one by one,
Reaching up through bush and brier,
Sumptuous brow and heart of fire,
Flaunting high its wind-rocked plume,
Brave with wealth of native bloom,—
      Goldenrod!

When the meadow, lately shorn,
  Parched and languid, swoons with pain,
When her life-blood, night and morn,
  Shrinks in every throbbing vein,
Round her fallen, tarnished urn
Leaping watch-fires brighter burn;
Royal arch o'er Autumn's gate,
Bending low with lustrous weight,—
      Goldenrod!

In the pasture's rude embrace,
  All o'errun with tangled vines,
Where the thistle claims its place,
  And the straggling hedge confines,
Bearing still the sweet impress
Of unfettered loveliness,
In the field and by the wall,
Binding, clasping, crowning all,—
      Goldenrod!

Nature lies disheveled pale,
  With her feverish lips apart,—
Day by day the pulses fail,
  Nearer to her bounding heart;
Yet that slackened grasp doth hold
Store of pure and genuine gold;

Quick thou comest, strong and free,
Type of all the wealth to be,—
Goldenrod!
Elaine Goodale Eastman [1863-

LESSONS FROM THE GORSE

MOUNTAIN gorses, ever-golden,
Cankered not the whole year long!
Do ye teach us to be strong,
Howsoever pricked and holden,
Like your thorny blooms, and so
Trodden on by rain and snow,
Up the hill-side of this life, as bleak as where ye grow?

Mountain blossoms, shining blossoms,
Do ye teach us to be glad
When no summer can be had,
Blooming in our inward bosoms?
Ye whom God preserveth still,
Set as lights upon a hill,
Tokens to the wintry earth that Beauty liveth still!

Mountain gorses, do ye teach us
From that academic chair
Canopied with azure air,
That the wisest word man reaches
Is the humblest he can speak?
Ye, who live on mountain peak,
Yet live low along the ground, beside the grasses meek!

Mountain gorses, since Linnæus
Knelt beside you on the sod,
For your beauty thanking God,—
For your teaching, ye should see us
Bowing in prostration new!
Whence arisen,—if one or two
Drops be on our cheeks—O world, they are not tears but dew.
Elizabeth Barrett Browning [1806-1861]

THE VOICE OF THE GRASS

HERE I come creeping, creeping everywhere;
    By the dusty roadside,
    On the sunny hillside,
    Close by the noisy brook,
    In every shady nook,
I come creeping, creeping everywhere.

Here I come creeping, smiling everywhere;
    All round the open door,
    Where sit the agèd poor;
    Here where the children play,
    In the bright and merry May,
I come creeping, creeping everywhere.

Here I come creeping, creeping everywhere;
    In the noisy city street
    My pleasant face you'll meet,
    Cheering the sick at heart
    Toiling his busy part,—
Silently creeping, creeping everywhere.

Here I come creeping, creeping everywhere;
    You cannot see me coming,
    Nor hear my low sweet humming;
    For in the starry night,
    And the glad morning light,
I come quietly creeping everywhere.

Here I come creeping, creeping everywhere;
    More welcome than the flowers
    In summer's pleasant hours;
    The gentle cow is glad,
    And the merry bird not sad,
To see me creeping, creeping everywhere.

Here I come creeping, creeping everywhere;
    When you're numbered with the dead
    In your still and narrow bed,

In the happy spring I'll come
And deck your silent home,—
Creeping, silently creeping everywhere.

Here I come creeping, creeping everywhere;
My humble song of praise
Most joyfully I raise
To Him at whose command
I beautify the land,
Creeping, silently creeping everywhere.

Sarah Roberts Boyle [1812–1869]

A SONG THE GRASS SINGS

THE violet is much too shy,
The rose too little so;
I think I'll ask the buttercup
If I may be her beau.

When winds go by, I'll nod to her
And she will nod to me,
And I will kiss her on the cheek
As gently as may be.

And when the mower cuts us down,
Together we will pass,
I smiling at the buttercup,
She smiling at the grass.

Charles G. Blandȩn [1857–

THE WILD HONEYSUCKLE

FAIR flower, that dost so comely grow,
Hid in this silent, dull retreat,
Untouched thy honied blossoms blow,
Unseen thy little branches greet:
No roving foot shall crush thee here,
No busy hand provoke a tear.

By Nature's self in white arrayed,
  She bade thee shun the vulgar eye,
And planted here the guardian shade,
  And sent soft waters murmuring by;
    Thus quietly thy summer goes,
    Thy days declining to repose.

Smit with those charms, that must decay,
  I grieve to see your future doom;
They died—nor were those flowers more gay,
  The flowers that did in Eden bloom;
    Unpitying frosts and Autumn's power
    Shall leave no vestige of this flower.

From morning suns and evening dews
  At first thy little being came;
If nothing once, you nothing lose,
  For when you die you are the same;
    The space between is but an hour,
    The frail duration of a flower.

Philip Freneau [1752–1832]

THE IVY GREEN

Oh, a dainty plant is the Ivy green,
  That creepeth o'er ruins old!
Of right choice food are his meals I ween,
  In his cell so lone and cold.
The wall must be crumbled, the stone decayed,
  To pleasure his dainty whim;
And the mouldering dust that years have made
  Is a merry meal for him.
    Creeping where no life is seen,
    A rare old plant is the Ivy green.

Fast he stealeth on, though he wears no wings,
  And a staunch old heart has he.
How closely he twineth, how tight he clings
  To his friend the huge Oak Tree!

And slily he traileth along the ground,
   And his leaves he gently waves,
As he joyously hugs and crawleth round
   The rich mould of dead men's graves.
      Creeping where grim death has been,
      A rare old plant is the Ivy green.

Whole ages have fled and their works decayed,
   And nations have scattered been;
But the stout old Ivy shall never fade,
   From its hale and hearty green.
The brave old plant, in its lonely days,
   Shall fatten upon the past:
For the stateliest building man can raise
   Is the Ivy's food at last.
      Creeping on, where time has been,
      A rare old plant is the Ivy green.
             Charles Dickens [1812–1870]

YELLOW JESSAMINE

In tangled wreaths, in clustered gleaming stars,
   In floating, curling sprays,
The golden flower comes shining through the woods
   These February days;
Forth go all hearts, all hands, from out the town,
   To bring her gayly in,
This wild, sweet Princess of far Florida—
   The yellow jessamine.

The live-oaks smile to see her lovely face
   Peep from the thickets; shy,
She hides behind the leaves her golden buds
   Till, bolder grown, on high
She curls a tendril, throws a spray, then flings
   Herself aloft in glee,
And, bursting into thousand blossoms, swings
   In wreaths from tree to tree.

The dwarf-palmetto on his knees adores
 This Princess of the air;
The lone pine-barren broods afar and sighs,
 "Ah! come, lest I despair;"
The myrtle-thickets and ill-tempered thorns
 Quiver and thrill within,
As through their leaves they feel the dainty touch
 Of yellow jessamine.

The garden-roses wonder as they see
 The wreaths of golden bloom,
Brought in from the far woods with eager haste
 To deck the poorest room,
The rich man's house, alike; the loaded hands
 Give sprays to all they meet,
Till, gay with flowers, the people come and go,
 And all the air is sweet.

The Southern land, well weary of its green
 Which may not fall nor fade,
Bestirs itself to greet the lovely flower
 With leaves of fresher shade;
The pine has tassels, and the orange-trees
 Their fragrant work begin:
The spring has come—has come to Florida,
 With yellow jessamine.
    Constance Fenimore Woolson [1840–1894]

KNAPWEED

By copse and hedgerow, waste and wall,
 He thrusts his cushions red;
O'er burdock rank, o'er thistles tall,
 He rears his hardy head:
Within, without, the strong leaves press,
 He screens the mossy stone,
Lord of a narrow wilderness,
 Self-centred and alone.

He numbers no observant friends,
    He soothes no childish woes,
Yet nature nurtures him, and tends
    As duly as the rose;
He drinks the blessèd dew of heaven,
    The wind is in his ears,
To guard his growth the planets seven
    Swing in their airy spheres.

The spirits of the fields and woods
    Throb in his sturdy veins:
He drinks the secret, stealing floods,
    And swills the volleying rains:
And when the bird's note showers and breaks
    The wood's green heart within,
He stirs his plumy brow and wakes
    To draw the sunlight in.

Mute sheep that pull the grasses soft
    Crop close and pass him by,
Until he stands alone, aloft,
    In surly majesty.
No fly so keen, no bee so bold,
    To pierce that knotted zone;
He frowns as though he guarded gold,
    And yet he garners none.

And so when autumn winds blow late,
    And whirl the chilly wave,
He bows before the common fate,
    And drops beside his grave.
None ever owed him thanks or said
    "A gift of gracious heaven."
Down in the mire he droops his head;
    Forgotten, not forgiven.

Smile on, brave weed! let none inquire
    What made or bade thee rise:
Toss thy tough fingers high and higher
    To flout the drenching skies.

Let others toil for others' good,
    And miss or mar their own;
Thou hast brave health and fortitude
    To live and die alone!

          Arthur Christopher Benson [1862–1925]

MOLY

The root is hard to loose
From hold of earth by mortals; but God's power
Can all things do. 'Tis black, but bears a flower
As white as milk.

            —Chapman's *Homer*

TRAVELER, pluck a stem of moly,
If thou touch at Circe's isle,—
Hermes' moly, growing solely
To undo enchanter's wile!
When she proffers thee her chalice,—
Wine and spices mixed with malice,—
When she smites thee with her staff,
To transform thee, do thou laugh!
Safe thou art if thou but bear
The least leaf of moly rare.
Close it grows beside her portal,
Springing from a stock immortal,—
Yes! and often has the Witch
Sought to tear it from its niche;
But to thwart her cruel will
The wise God renews it still.
Though it grows in soil perverse,
Heaven hath been its jealous nurse,
And a flower of snowy mark
Springs from root and sheathing dark;
Kingly safeguard, only herb
That can brutish passion curb!
Some do think its name should be
Shield-Heart, White Integrity.
Traveler, pluck a stem of moly,
If thou touch at Circe's isle,—
Hermes' moly, growing solely
To undo enchanter's wile!

          Edith M. Thomas [1854–1925]

THE MORNING-GLORY

Was it worth while to paint so fair
 Thy every leaf—to vein with faultless art
Each petal, taking the boon light and air
 Of summer so to heart?

To bring thy beauty unto perfect flower,
 Then, like a passing fragrance or a smile,
Vanish away, beyond recovery's power—
 Was it, frail bloom, worth while?

Thy silence answers: "Life was mine!
 And I, who pass without regret or grief,
Have cared the more to make my moment fine,
 Because it was so brief.

"In its first radiance I have seen
 The sun!—why tarry then till comes the night?
I go my way, content that I have been
 Part of the morning light!"

Florence Earle Coates [1850–1927]

THE MOUNTAIN HEART'S-EASE

By scattered rocks and turbid waters shifting,
 By furrowed glade and dell,
To feverish men thy calm, sweet face uplifting,
 Thou stayest them to tell

The delicate thought that cannot find expression,
 For ruder speech too fair,
That, like thy petals, trembles in possession,
 And scatters on the air.

The miner pauses in his rugged labor,
 And, leaning on his spade,
Laughingly calls unto his comrade-neighbor
 To see thy charms displayed.

But in his eyes a mist unwonted rises,
    And for a moment clear
Some sweet home face his foolish thought surprises
    And passes in a tear,—

Some boyish vision of his Eastern village,
    Of uneventful toil,
Where golden harvests followed quiet tillage
    Above a peaceful soil.

One moment only, for the pick, uplifting,
    Through root and fibre cleaves,
And on the muddy current slowly drifting
    Are swept thy bruisèd leaves.

And yet, O poet, in thy homely fashion,
    Thy work thou dost fulfil,
For on the turbid current of his passion
    Thy face is shining still!

                    Bret Harte [1839–1902]

THE PRIMROSE

Ask me why I send you here
This sweet Infanta of the year?
Ask me why I send to you
This Primrose, thus bepearled with dew?
I will whisper to your ears:—
The sweets of love are mixed with tears.

Ask me why this flower does show
So yellow-green, and sickly too?
Ask me why the stalk is weak
And bending, yet it doth not break?
I will answer:—These discover
What fainting hopes are in a lover.

                    Robert Herrick [1591–1674]

TO PRIMROSES FILLED WITH MORNING DEW

WHY do ye weep, sweet babes? Can tears
      Speak grief in you,
      Who were but born
   Just as the modest morn
   Teemed her refreshing dew?
Alas, you have not known that shower
      That mars a flower,
      Nor felt the unkind
   Breath of a blasting wind,
   Nor are ye worn with years,
      Or warped, as we,
      Who think it strange to see
Such pretty flowers, like to orphans young,
To speak by tears, before ye have a tongue.

Speak, whimpering younglings, and make known
      The reason why
      Ye droop and weep;
   Is it for want of sleep,
   Or childish lullaby?
   Or that ye have not seen as yet
      The violet?
      Or brought a kiss
From that Sweet-heart, to this?
—No, no, this sorrow shown
      By your tears shed,
   Would have this lecture read,
That things of greatest, so of meanest worth,
Conceived with grief are, and with tears brought forth.
            Robert Herrick [1591–1674]

TO AN EARLY PRIMROSE

MILD offspring of a dark and sullen sire!
Whose modest form, so delicately fine,
      Was nursed in whirling storms
      And cradled in the winds;

Thee, when young Spring first questioned Winter's sway,
And dared the sturdy blusterer to the fight,
    Thee on this bank he threw
    To mark his victory.

In this low vale, the promise of the year,
Serene, thou openest to the nipping gale,
    Unnoticed and alone,
    Thy tender elegance.

So Virtue blooms, brought forth amid the storms
Of chill adversity; in some lone walk
    Of life she rears her head,
    Obscure and unobserved;

While every bleaching breeze that on her blows
Chastens her spotless purity of breast,
    And hardens her to bear
    Serene the ills of life.
          Henry Kirke White [1785–1806]

THE RHODORA

ON BEING ASKED WHENCE IS THE FLOWER

In May, when sea-winds pierced our solitudes,
I found the fresh Rhodora in the woods,
Spreading its leafless blooms in a damp nook,
To please the desert and the sluggish brook.
The purple petals, fallen in the pool,
Made the black water with their beauty gay;
Here might the red-bird come his plumes to cool,
And court the flower that cheapens his array.
Rhodora! if the sages ask thee why
This charm is wasted on the earth and sky,
Tell them, dear, that if eyes were made for seeing,
Then Beauty is its own excuse for being:
Why thou wert there, O rival of the rose!
I never thought to ask, I never knew:
But, in my simple ignorance, suppose
The self-same Power that brought me there brought you.
          Ralph Waldo Emerson [1803–1882]

THE ROSE

A ROSE, as fair as ever saw the North,
Grew in a little garden all alone;
A sweeter flower did Nature ne'er put forth,
Nor fairer garden yet was never known:
The maidens danced about it morn and noon,
And learnèd bards of it their ditties made;
The nimble fairies by the pale-faced moon
Watered the root and kissed her pretty shade.
But well-a-day!—the gardener careless grew;
The maids and fairies both were kept away,
And in a drought the caterpillars threw
Themselves upon the bud and every spray.
　　God shield the stock! If heaven send no supplies,
　　The fairest blossom of the garden dies.

　　　　　　　　　　　　　　William Browne [1591–1643]

WILD ROSES

On long, serene midsummer days
　　Of ripening fruit and yellow grain,
How sweetly, by dim woodland ways,
　　In tangled hedge or leafy lane,
Fair wild-rose thickets, you unfold
Those pale pink stars with hearts of gold!

Your sleek patrician sisters dwell
　　On lawns where gleams the shrub's trim bosk,
In terraced gardens, tended well,
　　Near pebbled walk and quaint kiosk.
In costliest u.ns their colors rest;
They beam on beauty's fragrant breast!

But you in lowly calm abide,
　　Scarce heeded save by breeze or bee;
You know what splendor, pomp and pride
　　Full oft your brilliant sisters see;
What sorrow too, and bitter fears;
What mad farewells and hopeless tears.

How some are kept in old, dear books,
   That once in bridal wreaths were worn;
How some are kissed, with tender looks,
   And later tossed aside with scorn;
How some their taintless petals lay
On icy foreheads, pale as they!

So, while these truths you vaguely guess,
   A-bloom in many a lonesome spot,
Shy roadside roses, may you bless
   The fate that rules your modest lot,
Like rustic maids that meekly stand
Below the ladies of their land!

                Edgar Fawcett [1847–1904]

THE ROSE OF MAY

Ah! there's the lily, marble pale,
The bonny broom, the cistus frail;
The rich sweet pea, the iris blue,
The larkspur with its peacock hue;
All these are fair, yet hold I will
That the Rose of May is fairer still.

'Tis grand 'neath palace walls to grow,
To blaze where lords and ladies go;
To hang o'er marble founts, and shine
In modern gardens, trim and fine;
But the Rose of May is only seen
Where the great of other days have been.

The house is mouldering stone by stone,
The garden-walks are overgrown;
The flowers are low, the weeds are high,
The fountain-stream is choked and dry,
The dial-stone with moss is green,
Where'er the Rose of May is seen.

The Rose of May its pride displayed
Along the old stone balustrade;
And ancient ladies, quaintly dight,
In its pink blossoms took delight;
And on the steps would make a stand
To scent its fragrance—fan in hand.

Long have been dead those ladies gay;
Their very heirs have passed away;
And their old portraits, prim and tall,
Are mouldering in the mouldering hall;
The terrace and the balustrade
Lie broken, weedy and decayed.

But blithe and tall the Rose of May
Shoots upward through the ruin gray;
With scented flower, and leaf pale green,
Such rose as it hath never been,
Left, like a noble deed, to grace
The memory of an ancient race.

Mary Howitt [1799–1888]

A ROSE

BLOWN in the morning, thou shalt fade ere noon.
What boots a life which in such haste forsakes thee?
Thou'rt wondrous frolic, being to die so soon,
And passing proud a little color makes thee.
If thee thy brittle beauty so deceives,
Know then the thing that swells thee is thy bane;
For the same beauty doth, in bloody leaves,
The sentence of thy early death contain.
Some clown's coarse lungs will poison thy sweet flower,
If by the careless plough thou shalt be torn;
And many Herods lie in wait each hour
To murder thee as soon as thou art born—
  Nay, force thy bud to blow—their tyrant breath
  Anticipating life, to hasten death!

Richard Fanshawe [1608–1666]

THE SHAMROCK

WHEN April rains make flowers bloom
    And Johnny-jump-ups come to light,
And clouds of color and perfume
    Float from the orchards pink and white,
I see my shamrock in the rain,
    An emerald spray with raindrops set,
Like jewels on Spring's coronet,
    So fair, and yet it breathes of pain.

The shamrock on an older shore
    Sprang from a rich and sacred soil
Where saint and hero lived of yore,
    And where their sons in sorrow toil;
And here, transplanted, it to me
    Seems weeping for the soil it left:
The diamonds that all others see
    Are tears drawn from its heart bereft.

When April rain makes flowers grow,
    And sparkles on their tiny buds
That in June nights will over-blow
    And fill the world with scented floods,
The lonely shamrock in our land—
    So fine among the clover leaves—
For the old springtime often grieves,—
    I feel its tears upon my hand.
                    Maurice Francis Egan [1852–1924]

TO VIOLETS

WELCOME, maids of honor,
        You do bring
        In the Spring,
    And wait upon her.

She has virgins many,
    Fresh and fair;
        Yet you are
More sweet than any.

You're the maiden posies,
    And, so graced,
        To be placed
'Fore damask roses.

Yet, though thus respected,
    By and by
        Ye do lie,
Poor girls, neglected.

                        Robert Herrick [1591–1674]

THE VIOLET

O FAINT, delicious, spring-time violet!
    Thine odor, like a key,
Turns noiselessly in memory's wards to let
    A thought of sorrow free.

The breath of distant fields upon my brow
    Blows through that open door
The sound of wind-borne bells, more sweet and low,
    And sadder than of yore.

It comes afar, from that belovèd place,
    And that belovèd hour,
When life hung ripening in love's golden grace,
    Like grapes above a bower.

A spring goes singing through its reedy grass;
    The lark sings o'er my head,
Drowned in the sky—O, pass, ye visions, pass!
    I would that I were dead!—

Why hast thou opened that forbidden door,
    From which I ever flee?
O vanished Joy! O Love, that art no more,
    Let my vexed spirit be!

O violet! thy odor through my brain
    Hath searched, and stung to grief
This sunny day, as if a curse did stain
    Thy velvet leaf.
        William Wetmore Story [1819–1895]

TO A WOOD–VIOLET

In this secluded shrine,
    O miracle of grace,
No mortal eye but mine
    Hath looked upon thy face.

No shadow but mine own
    Hath screened thee from the sight
Of Heaven, whose love alone
    Hath led me to thy light.

Whereof—as shade to shade
    Is wedded in the sun—
A moment's glance hath made
    Our souls forever one.
        John Banister Tabb [1845–1909]

THE VIOLET AND THE ROSE

The violet in the wood, that's sweet to-day,
    Is longer sweet than roses of red June;
Set me sweet violets along my way,
    And bid the red rose flower, but not too soon.
Ah violet, ah rose, why not the two?
Why bloom not all fair flowers the whole year through?
    Why not the two, young violet, ripe rose?
    Why dies one sweetness when another blows?
        Augusta Webster [1837–1894]

TO A WIND–FLOWER

Teach me the secret of thy loveliness,
    That, being made wise, I may aspire to be
As beautiful in thought, and so express
    Immortal truths to earth's mortality;

Though to my soul ability be less
    Than 'tis to thee, O sweet anemone.

Teach me the secret of thy innocence,
    That in simplicity I may grow wise,
Asking from Art no other recompense
    Than the approval of her own just eyes;
So may I rise to some fair eminence,
    Though less than thine, O cousin of the skies.

Teach me these things, through whose high knowledge, I,—
    When Death hath poured oblivion through my veins,
And brought me home, as all are brought, to lie
    In that vast house, common to serfs and thanes,—
I shall not die, I shall not utterly die,
    For beauty born of beauty—*that* remains.

                    Madison Cawein [1865–1914]

TO BLOSSOMS

FAIR pledges of a fruitful tree,
    Why do ye fall so fast?
    Your date is not so past
But you may stay yet here awhile
    To blush and gently smile,
        And go at last.

What! were ye born to be
    An hour or half's delight,
    And so to bid good-night?
'Twas pity Nature brought you forth
    Merely to show your worth
        And lose you quite.

But you are lovely leaves, where we
    May read how soon things have
    Their end, though ne'er so brave:
And after they have shown their pride
    Like you awhile, they glide
        Into the grave.

                    Robert Herrick [1591–1674]

"'TIS THE LAST ROSE OF SUMMER"

'TIS the last rose of summer,
   Left blooming alone;
All her lovely companions
   Are faded and gone;
No flower of her kindred,
   No rose-bud is nigh,
To reflect back her blushes,
   Or give sigh for sigh.

I'll not leave thee, thou lone one!
   To pine on the stem;
Since the lovely are sleeping,
   Go, sleep thou with them.
Thus kindly I scatter
   Thy leaves o'er the bed
Where thy mates of the garden
   Lie scentless and dead.

So soon may *I* follow,
   When friendships decay,
And from Love's shining circle
   The gems drop away.
When true hearts lie withered,
   And fond ones are flown,
O who would inhabit
   This bleak world alone?

Thomas Moore [1779–1852]

THE DEATH OF THE FLOWERS

THE melancholy days are come, the saddest of the year,
Of wailing winds, and naked woods, and meadows brown
   and sere.
Heaped in the hollows of the grove, the autumn leaves lie
   dead;
They rustle to the eddying gust, and to the rabbit's tread;
The robin and the wren are flown, and from the shrubs the jay,
And from the wood-top calls the crow through all the gloomy
   day.

Where are the flowers, the fair young flowers, that lately
    sprang and stood
In brighter light and softer airs, a beauteous sisterhood?
Alas! they all are in their graves, the gentle race of flowers
Are lying in their lowly beds, with the fair and good of ours.
The rain is falling where they lie, but the cold November
    rain
Calls not from out the gloomy earth the lovely ones again.

The wind-flower and the violet, they perished long ago,
And the brier-rose and the orchis died amid the summer
    glow;
But on the hill the golden-rod, and the aster in the wood,
And the yellow sun-flower by the brook, in autumn beauty
    stood,
Till fell the frost from the clear cold heaven, as falls the
    plague on men,
And the brightness of their smile was gone, from upland,
    glade, and glen.

And now, when comes the calm mild day, as still such days
    will come,
To call the squirrel and the bee from out their winter home;
When the sound of dropping nuts is heard, though all the
    trees are still,
And twinkle in the smoky light the waters of the rill,
The south wind searches for the flowers whose fragrance
    late he bore,
And sighs to find them in the wood and by the stream no
    more.

And then I think of one who in her youthful beauty died,
The fair meek blossom that grew up and faded by my side.
In the cold moist earth we laid her, when the forest cast the
    leaf,
And we wept that one so lovely should have a life so brief:
Yet not unmeet it was that one like that young friend of
    ours,
So gentle and so beautiful, should perish with the flowers.
                    William Cullen Bryant [1794-1878]

GOD'S CREATURES

ONCE ON A TIME

ONCE on a time I used to dream
Strange spirits moved about my way,
And I might catch a vagrant gleam,
A glint of pixy or of fay;
Their lives were mingled with my own,
So far they roamed, so near they drew;
And when I from a child had grown,
I woke—and found my dream was true.

For one is clad in coat of fur,
And one is decked with feathers gay;
Another, wiser, will prefer
A sober suit of Quaker gray:
This one's your servant from his birth,
And that a Princess you must please,
And this one loves to wake your mirth,
And that one likes to share your ease.

O gracious creatures, tiny souls!
You seem so near, so far away,
Yet while the cloudland round us rolls,
We love you better every day.
Margaret Benson [18 –

TO A MOUSE

ON TURNING UP HER NEST WITH THE PLOW, NOVEMBER, 1785

WEE, sleekit, cow'rin', tim'rous beastie,
O, what a panic's in thy breastie!
Thou need na start awa' sae hasty,
Wi' bickering brattle!
I wad be laith to rin an' chase thee,
Wi' murd'ring pattle!

I'm truly sorry man's dominion
Has broken Nature's social union,
An' justifies that ill opinion,
    Which makes thee startle
At me, thy poor, earth-born companion,
    An' fellow-mortal!

I doubt na, whiles, but thou may thieve;
What then? poor beastie, thou maun live!
A daimen icker in a thrave
    'S a sma' request;
I'll get a blessin' wi' the laive,
    And never miss't!

Thy wee bit housie, too, in ruin!
Its silly wa's the win's are strewin'!
An' naething, now, to big a new ane,
    O' foggage green!
An' bleak December's winds ensuin',
    Baith snell an' keen!

Thou saw the fields laid bare an' waste,
An' weary winter comin' fast,
An' cozie here, beneath the blast,
    Thou thought to dwell,—
Till, crash! the cruel coulter passed
    Out through thy cell.

That wee bit heap o' leaves an' stibble
Has cost thee mony a weary nibble!
Now thou's turned out, for a' thy trouble,
    But house or hald,
To thole the winter's sleety dribble,
    An' cranreuch cauld!

But, Mousie, thou art no thy lane,
In proving foresight may be vain:
The best-laid schemes o' mice an' men,
    Gang aft a-gley,
An' lea'e us naught but grief an' pain,
    For promised joy!

Still thou art blest, compared wi' me!
The present only toucheth thee:
But, och! I backward cast my e'e
        On prospects drear!
An' forward, though I canna see,
        I guess an' fear!

                    Robert Burns [1759–1796]

THE GRASSHOPPER

HAPPY insect, what can be
In happiness compared to thee?
Fed with nourishment divine,
The dewy morning's gentle wine!
Nature waits upon thee still,
And thy verdant cup does fill;
'Tis filled wherever thou dost tread,
Nature's self's thy Ganymede.
Thou dost drink, and dance, and sing,
Happier than the happiest king!
All the fields which thou dost see,
All the plants belong to thee;
All the summer hours produce,
Fertile made with early juice.
Man for thee does sow and plow,
Farmer he, and landlord thou!
Thou dost innocently enjoy;
Nor does thy luxury destroy.
The shepherd gladly heareth thee,
More harmonious than he.
Thee country hinds with gladness hear,
Prophet of the ripened year!
Thee Phoebus loves, and does inspire
Phoebus is himself thy sire.
To thee, of all things upon earth,
Life is no longer than thy mirth.
Happy insect! happy thou,
Dost neither age nor winter know;
But when thou'st drunk, and danced, and sung
Thy fill, the flowery leaves among.

(Voluptuous and wise withal,
  Epicurean animal!)
Sated with thy summer feast,
Thou retir'st to endless rest.
    After Anacreon, by Abraham Cowley [1618–1667]

ON THE GRASSHOPPER AND CRICKET

THE poetry of earth is never dead:
When all the birds are faint with the hot sun,
And hide in cooling trees, a voice will run
From hedge to hedge about the new-mown mead:
That is the Grasshopper's—he takes the lead
In summer luxury,—he has never done
With his delights, for when tired out with fun,
He rests at ease beneath some pleasant weed.
The poetry of earth is ceasing never:
On a lone winter evening, when the frost
Has wrought a silence, from the stove there shrills
The Cricket's song, in warmth increasing ever,
And seems to one in drowsiness half-lost,
The Grasshopper's among the grassy hills.
    John Keats [1795–1821]

TO THE GRASSHOPPER AND THE CRICKET

GREEN little vaulter in the sunny grass,
Catching your heart up at the feel of June;
Sole voice that's heard amidst the lazy noon,
When even the bees lag at the summoning brass;
And you, warm little housekeeper, who class
With those who think the candles come too soon,
Loving the fire, and with your tricksome tune
Nick the glad silent moments as they pass;
O sweet and tiny cousins, that belong
One to the fields, the other to the hearth,

Both have your sunshine; both, though small, are strong
At your clear hearts; and both seem given to earth
To sing in thoughtful ears their natural song—
In-doors and out, summer and winter, Mirth.

Leigh Hunt [1784–1859]

THE CRICKET

LITTLE inmate, full of mirth,
Chirping on my kitchen hearth,
Wheresoe'er be thine abode
Always harbinger of good,
Pay me for thy warm retreat
With a song more soft and sweet;
In return thou shalt receive
Such a strain as I can give.

Thus thy praise shall be expressed,
Inoffensive, welcome guest!
While the rat is on the scout,
And the mouse with curious snout,
With what vermin else infest
Every dish, and spoil the best;
Frisking thus before the fire,
Thou hast all thy heart's desire.

Though in voice and shape they be
Formed as if akin to thee,
Thou surpassest, happier far,
Happiest grasshoppers that are;
Theirs is but a summer's song,
Thine endures the winter long,
Unimpaired, and shrill, and clear,
Melody throughout the year.

Neither night nor dawn of day
Puts a period to thy play:
Sing then—and extend thy span
Far beyond the date of man;

Wretched man, whose years are spent
In repining discontent,
Lives not, agèd though he be,
Half a span, compared with thee.

From the Latin of Vincent Bourne,
by William Cowper [1731–1800]

TO A CRICKET

VOICE of summer, keen and shrill,
   Chirping round my winter fire,
   Of thy song I never tire,
Weary others as they will,
For thy song with summer's filled—
   Filled with sunshine, filled with June;
   Firelight echo of that noon
Heard in fields when all is stilled
   In the golden light of May,
   Bringing scents of new-mown hay,
   Bees, and birds, and flowers away,
Prithee, haunt my fireside still,
Voice of summer, keen and shrill.

William Cox Bennett [1820–1895]

TO AN INSECT

I LOVE to hear thine earnest voice,
   Wherever thou art hid,
Thou testy little dogmatist,
   Thou pretty Katydid!
Thou mindest me of gentlefolks,—
   Old gentlefolks are they,—
Thou say'st an undisputed thing
   In such a solemn way.

Thou art a female, Katydid!
   I know it by the trill
That quivers through thy piercing notes,
   So petulant and shrill;

I think there is a knot of you
  Beneath the hollow tree,—
A knot of spinster Katydids,—
  Do Katydids drink tea?

Oh, tell me where did Katy live,
  And what did Katy do?
And was she very fair and young,
  And yet so wicked, too?
Did Katy love a naughty man,
  Or kiss more cheeks than one?
I warrant Katy did no more
  Than many a Kate has done.

Dear me! I'll tell you all about
  My fuss with little Jane,
And Ann, with whom I used to walk
  So often down the lane,
And all that tore their locks of black,
  Or wet their eyes of blue,—
Pray tell me, sweetest Katydid,
  What did poor Katy do?

Ah no! the living oak shall crash,
  That stood for ages still,
The rock shall rend its mossy base
  And thunder down the hill,
Before the little Katydid
  Shall add one word, to tell
The mystic story of the maid
  Whose name she knows so well.

Peace to the ever-murmuring race!
  And when the latest one
Shall fold in death her feeble wings
  Beneath the autumn sun,
Then shall she raise her fainting voice,
  And lift her drooping lid,
And then the child of future years
  Shall hear what Katy did.
                    Oliver Wendell Holmes [1809–1894]

THE SNAIL

To grass, or leaf, or fruit, or wall,
The snail sticks close, nor fears to fall,
As if he grew there, house and all
         Together.

Within that house secure he hides,
When danger imminent betides,
Of storm, or other harm besides
         Of weather.

Give but his horns the slightest touch,
His self-collecting power is such,
He shrinks into his house with much
         Displeasure.

Where'er he dwells, he dwells alone,
Except himself, has chattels none,
Well satisfied to be his own
         Whole treasure.

Thus, hermit-like, his life he leads,
Nor partner of his banquet needs,
And if he meets one, only feeds
         The faster.

Who seeks him must be worse than blind
(He and his house are so combined),
If, finding it, he fails to find
         Its master.
         From the Latin of Vincent Bourne,
            by William Cowper [1731–1800]

THE HOUSEKEEPER

The frugal snail, with forecast of repose,
Carries his house with him where'er he goes;
Peeps out,—and if there comes a shower of rain,
Retreats to his small domicile amain.

Touch but a tip of him, a horn,—'tis well,—
He curls up in his sanctuary shell.
He's his own landlord, his own tenant; stay
Long as he will, he dreads no Quarter Day.
Himself he boards and lodges; both invites
And feasts himself; sleeps with himself o' nights.
He spares the upholsterer trouble to procure
Chattels; himself is his own furniture,
And his sole riches.   Whereso'er he roam,—
Knock when you will,—he's sure to be at home.

From the Latin of Vincent Bourne,
by Charles Lamb [1775–1834]

THE HUMBLE–BEE

BURLY, dozing humble-bee,
Where thou art is clime for me.
Let them sail for Porto Rique,
Far-off heats through seas to seek;
I will follow thee alone,
Thou animated torrid-zone!
Zigzag steerer, desert cheerer,
Let me chase thy waving lines;
Keep me nearer, me thy hearer,
Singing over shrubs and vines.

Insect lover of the sun,
Joy of thy dominion!
Sailor of the atmosphere;
Swimmer through the waves of air;
Voyager of light and noon;
Epicurean of June;
Wait, I prithee, till I come
Within earshot of thy hum,—
All without is martyrdom.

When the south wind, in May days,
With a net of shining haze
Silvers the horizon wall,
And with softness touching all,

Tints the human countenance
With a color of romance,
And infusing subtle heats,
Turns the sod to violets,
Thou, in sunny solitudes,
Rover of the underwoods,
The green silence dost displace
With thy mellow, breezy bass.

Hot midsummer's petted crone,
Sweet to me thy drowsy tone
Tells of countless sunny hours,
Long days, and solid banks of flowers;
Of gulfs of sweetness without bound
In Indian wildernesses found;
Of Syrian peace, immortal leisure,
Firmest cheer, and birdlike pleasure.

Aught unsavory or unclean
Hath my insect never seen;
But violets and bilberry bells,
Maple-sap and daffodels,
Grass with green flag half-mast high,
Succory to match the sky,
Columbine with horn of honey,
Scented fern, and agrimony,
Clover, catchfly, adder's tongue
And brier-roses, dwelt among;
All beside was unknown waste,
All was picture as he passed.

Wiser far than human seer,
Yellow-breeched philosopher!
Seeing only what is fair,
Sipping only what is sweet,
Thou dost mock at fate and care,
Leave the chaff, and take the wheat.
When the fierce northwestern blast
Cools sea and land so far and fast,
Thou already slumberest deep;
Woe and want thou canst outsleep;

Want and woe, which torture us,
Thy sleep makes ridiculous.
                Ralph Waldo Emerson [1803–1882]

TO A BUTTERFLY

I'VE watched you now a full half-hour,
Self-poised upon that yellow flower;
And, little Butterfly! indeed
I know not if you sleep or feed.
How motionless! not frozen seas
More motionless! and then
What joy awaits you, when the breeze
Has found you out among the trees,
And calls you forth again!

This plot of orchard-ground is ours;
My trees they are, my Sister's flowers;
Here rest your wings when they are weary;
Here lodge as in a sanctuary!
Come often to us, fear no wrong;
Sit near us on the bough!
We'll talk of sunshine and of song,
And summer days, when we are young;
Sweet childish days, that were as long
As twenty days are now.
                William Wordsworth [1770–1850]

ODE TO A BUTTERFLY

THOU spark of life that wavest wings of gold,
Thou songless wanderer mid the songful birds,
With Nature's secrets in thy tints unrolled
Through gorgeous cipher, past the reach of words,
    Yet dear to every child
    In glad pursuit beguiled,
Living his unspoiled days mid flowers and flocks and herds!

Thou wingèd blossom, liberated thing,
What secret tie binds thee to other flowers,
Still held within the garden's fostering?
Will they too soar with the completed hours,
  Take flight, and be like thee
  Irrevocably free,
Hovering at will o'er their parental bowers?

Or is thy luster drawn from heavenly hues,—
A sumptuous drifting fragment of the sky,
Caught when the sunset its last glance imbues
With sudden splendor, and the tree-tops high
  Grasp that swift blazonry,
  Then lend those tints to thee,
On thee to float a few short hours, and die?

Birds have their nests; they rear their eager young,
And flit on errands all the livelong day;
Each fieldmouse keeps the homestead whence it sprung;
But thou art Nature's freeman,—free to stray
  Unfettered through the wood,
  Seeking thine airy food,
The sweetness spiced on every blossomed spray.

The garden one wide banquet spreads for thee,
O daintiest reveller of the joyous earth!
One drop of honey gives satiety;
A second draught would drug thee past all mirth.
  Thy feast no orgy shows;
  Thy calm eyes never close,
Thou soberest sprite to which the sun gives birth.

And yet the soul of man upon thy wings
Forever soars in aspiration; thou
His emblem of the new career that springs
When death's arrest bids all his spirit bow.
  He seeks his hope in thee
  Of immortality.
Symbol of life, me with such faith endow!
    Thomas Wentworth Higginson [1823-1911]

THE BUTTERFLY

I HOLD you at last in my hand,
  Exquisite child of the air.
Can I ever understand
  How you grew to be so fair?

You came to my linden tree
  To taste its delicious sweet,
I sitting here in the shadow and shine
  Playing around its feet.

Now I hold you fast in my hand,
  You marvelous butterfly,
Till you help me to understand
  The eternal mystery.

From that creeping thing in the dust
  To this shining bliss in the blue!
God give me courage to trust
  I can break my chrysalis too!

                    Alice Freeman Palmer [1855-1902]

FIREFLIES

I SAW, one sultry night above a swamp,
The darkness throbbing with their golden pomp!
And long my dazzled sight did they entrance
With the weird chaos of their dizzy dance!
Quicker than yellow leaves, when gales despoil,
Quivered the brilliance of their mute turmoil,
Within whose light was intricately blent
Perpetual rise, perpetual descent.
As though their scintillant flickerings had met
In the vague meshes of some airy net!
And now mysteriously I seemed to guess,
While watching their tumultuous loveliness,
What fervor of deep passion strangely thrives
In the warm richness of these tropic lives,
Whose wings can never tremble but they show
These hearts of living fire that beat below!

                    Edgar Fawcett [1847-1904]

THE BLOOD HORSE

GAMARRA is a dainty steed,
Strong, black, and of a noble breed,
Full of fire, and full of bone,
With all his line of fathers known;
Fine his nose, his nostrils thin,
But blown abroad by the pride within!
His mane is like a river flowing,
And his eyes like embers glowing
In the darkness of the night,
And his pace as swift as light.

Look,—how 'round his straining throat
Grace and shifting beauty float!
Sinewy strength is in his reins,
And the red blood gallops through his veins;
Richer, redder, never ran
Through the boasting heart of man.
He can trace his lineage higher
Than the Bourbon dare aspire,—
Douglas, Guzman, or the Guelph,
Or O'Brien's blood itself!

He, who hath no peer, was born,
Here, upon a red March morn;
But his famous fathers dead
Were Arabs all, and Arab bred,
And the last of that great line
Trod like one of a race divine!
And yet,—he was but friend to one
Who fed him at the set of sun,
By some lone fountain fringed with green:
With him, a roving Bedouin,
He lived, (none else would he obey
Through all the hot Arabian day),
And died untamed upon the sands
Where Balkh amidst the desert stands.

Bryan Waller Procter [1787-1874]

BIRDS

SURE maybe ye've heard the storm-thrush
  Whistlin' bould in March,
Before there's a primrose peepin' out,
  Or a wee red cone on the larch;
Whistlin' the sun to come out o' the cloud,
  An' the wind to come over the sea,
But for all he can whistle so clear an' loud,
  He's never the bird for me.

Sure maybe ye've seen the song-thrush
  After an April rain
Slip from in-undher the drippin' leaves,
  Wishful to sing again;
An' low wi' love when he's near the nest,
  An' loud from the top o' the tree,
But for all he can flutter the heart in your breast,
  He's never the bird for me.

Sure maybe ye've heard the cushadoo
  Callin' his mate in May,
When one sweet thought is the whole of his life,
  An' he tells it the one sweet way.
But my heart is sore at the cushadoo
  Filled wid his own soft glee,
Over an' over his "me an' you!"
  He's never the bird for me.

Sure maybe ye've heard the red-breast
  Singin' his lone on a thorn,
Mindin' himself o' the dear days lost,
  Brave wid his heart forlorn.
The time is in dark November,
  An' no spring hopes has he:
"Remember," he sings, "remember!"
  Ay, *thon's* the wee bird for me.

                    Moira O'Neill [18

BIRDS

BIRDS are singing round my window,
  Tunes the sweetest ever heard,
And I hang my cage there daily,
  But I never catch a bird.

So with thoughts my brain is peopled,
  And they sing there all day long:
But they will not fold their pinions
  In the little cage of Song!
  Richard Henry Stoddard [1825–1903]

SEA–BIRDS

O LONESOME sea-gull, floating far
  Over the ocean's icy waste,
Aimless and wide thy wanderings are,
  Forever vainly seeking rest:—
  Where is thy mate, and where thy nest?

'Twixt wintry sea and wintry sky,
  Cleaving the keen air with thy breast,
Thou sailest slowly, solemnly;
  No fetter on thy wing is pressed:—
  Where is thy mate, and where thy nest?

O restless, homeless human soul,
  Following for aye thy nameless quest,
The gulls float, and the billows roll;
  Thou watchest still, and questionest:—
  Where is *thy* mate, and where thy nest?
  Elizabeth Akers [1832–1911]

THE LITTLE BEACH–BIRD

THOU little bird, thou dweller by the sea,
  Why takest thou its melancholy voice,
    And with that boding cry
    Why o'er the waves dost fly?
  O, rather, bird, with me
    Through the fair land rejoice!

Thy flitting form comes ghostly dim and pale,
    As driven by a beating storm at sea;
        Thy cry is weak and scared,
        As if thy mates had shared
The doom of us. Thy wail,—
    What doth it bring to me?

Thou call'st along the sand, and haunt'st the surge,
    Restless, and sad; as if, in strange accord
        With the motion and the roar
        Of waves that drive to shore,
One spirit did ye urge—
    The Mystery—the Word.

Of thousands, thou, both sepulchre and pall,
    Old Ocean! A requiem o'er the dead,
        From out thy gloomy cells,
        A tale of mourning tells,—
Tells of man's woe and fall,
    His sinless glory fled.

Then turn thee, little bird, and take thy flight
    Where the complaining sea shall sadness bring
        Thy spirit nevermore.
        Come, quit with me the shore,
For gladness and the light,
    Where birds of summer sing.
                    Richard Henry Dana [1787–1879]

THE BLACKBIRD

How sweet the harmonies of afternoon:
    The Blackbird sings along the sunny breeze
His ancient song of leaves, and summer boon;
    Rich breath of hayfields streams through whispering trees;
And birds of morning trim their bustling wings,
And listen fondly—while the Blackbird sings.

How soft the lovelight of the West reposes
    On this green valley's cheery solitude,
On the trim cottage with its screen of roses,
    On the gray belfry with its ivy hood,

And murmuring mill-race, and the wheel that flings
Its bubbling freshness—while the Blackbird sings.

The very dial on the village church
   Seems as 'twere dreaming in a dozy rest;
The scribbled benches underneath the porch
   Bask in the kindly welcome of the West;
But the broad casements of the old Three Kings
Blaze like a furnace—while the Blackbird sings.

And there beneath the immemorial elm
   Three rosy revellers round a table sit,
And through gray clouds give laws unto the realm,
   Curse good and great, but worship their own wit.
And roar of fights, and fairs, and junketings,
Corn, colts, and curs—the while the Blackbird sings.

Before her home, in her accustomed seat,
   The tidy Grandam spins beneath the shade
Of the old honeysuckle, at her feet
   The dreaming pug, and purring tabby laid;
To her low chair a little maiden clings,
And spells in silence—while the Blackbird sings.

Sometimes the shadow of a lazy cloud
   Breathes o'er the hamlet with its gardens green.
While the far fields with sunlight overflowed
   Like golden shores of Fairyland are seen;
Again, the sunshine on the shadow springs,
And fires the thicket where the Blackbird sings.

The woods, the lawn, the peakèd Manorhouse,
   With its peach-covered walls, and rookery loud,
The trim, quaint garden alleys, screened with boughs,
   The lion-headed gates, so grim and proud,
The mossy fountain with its murmurings,
Lie in warm sunshine—while the Blackbird sings.

The ring of silver voices, and the sheen
   Of festal garments—and my Lady streams
With her gay court across the garden green;
   Some laugh, and dance, some whisper their love-dreams;

And one calls for a little page; he strings
Her lute beside her—while the Blackbird sings.

A little while—and lo! the charm is heard,
   A youth, whose life has been all Summer, steals
Forth from the noisy guests around the board,
   Creeps by her softly; at her footstool kneels;
And, when she pauses, murmurs tender things
Into her fond ear—while the Blackbird sings.

The smoke-wreaths from the chimneys curl up higher,
   And dizzy things of eve begin to float
Upon the light; the breeze begins to tire;
   Half way to sunset with a drowsy note
The ancient clock from out the valley swings;
The Grandam nods—and still the Blackbird sings.

Far shouts and laughter from the farmstead peal,
   Where the great stack is piling in the sun;
Through narrow gates o'erladen wagons reel,
   And barking curs into the tumult run;
While the inconstant wind bears off, and brings
The merry tempest—and the Blackbird sings.

On the high wold the last look of the sun
   Burns, like a beacon, over dale and stream;
The shouts have ceased, the laughter and the fun;
   The Grandam sleeps, and peaceful be her dream;
Only a hammer on an anvil rings;
The day is dying—still the Blackbird sings.

Now the good Vicar passes from his gate
   Serene, with long white hair; and in his eye
Burns the clear spirit that hath conquered Fate,
   And felt the wings of immortality;
His heart is thronged with great imaginings,
And tender mercies—while the Blackbird sings.

Down by the brook he bends his steps, and through
   A lowly wicket; and at last he stands
Awful beside the bed of one who grew
   From boyhood with him—who, with lifted hands

And eyes, seems listening to far welcomings,
And sweeter music than the Blackbird sings.

Two golden stars, like tokens from the Blest,
    Strike on his dim orbs from the setting sun;
His sinking hands seem pointing to the West;
    He smiles as though he said—"Thy will be done":
His eyes, they see not those illuminings;
His ears, they hear not what the Blackbird sings.

Frederick Tennyson [1807–1898]

THE BLACKBIRD

WHEN smoke stood up from Ludlow
    And mist blew off from Teme,
And blithe afield to ploughing
    Against the morning beam
    I strode beside my team,

The blackbird in the coppice
    Looked out to see me stride,
And hearkened as I whistled
    The trampling team beside,
    And fluted and replied:

"Lie down, lie down, young yeoman;
    What use to rise and rise?
Rise man a thousand mornings
    Yet down at last he lies,
    And then the man is wise."

I heard the tune he sang me,
    And spied his yellow bill;
I picked a stone and aimed it
    And threw it with a will:
    Then the bird was still.

Then my soul within me
    Took up the blackbird's strain,
And still beside the horses
    Along the dewy lane
    It sang the song again:

"Lie down, lie down, young yeoman;
  The sun moves always west;
The road one treads to labor
  Will lead one home to rest,
    And that will be the best."

      Alfred Edward Housman [1859–1936]

THE BLACKBIRD

THE nightingale has a lyre of gold;
  The lark's is a clarion call,
And the blackbird plays but a box-wood flute,
  But I love him best of all.

For his song is all of the joy of life,
  And we in the mad, spring weather,
We too have listened till he sang
  Our hearts and lips together.

      William Ernest Henley [1849–1903]

THE BLACKBIRD

Ov all the birds upon the wing
Between the zunny showers o' spring,—
Vor all the lark, a-swingèn high,
Mid zing below a cloudless sky,
An' sparrows, clust'rèn roun' the bough,
Mid chatter to the men at plough,—
The blackbird, whisslèn in among
The boughs, do zing the gayest zong.

Vor we do hear the blackbird zing
His sweetest ditties in the spring,
When nippèn win's noo mwore do blow
Vrom northern skies, wi' sleet or snow,
But drēve light doust along between
The leäne-zide hedges, thick an' green;
An' zoo the blackbird in among
The boughs do zing the gaÿest zong.

'Tis blithe, wi' newly-opened eyes,
To zee the mornèn's ruddy skies;
Or, out a-haulèn frith or lops
Vrom new-plēshed hedge or new-velled copse,
To rest at noon in primrwose beds
Below the white-barked woak-trees' heads;
But there's noo time, the whole däy long,
Lik' evenèn wi' the blackbird's zong.

Vor when my work is all a-done
Avore the zettèn o' the zun,
Then blushèn Jeäne do walk along
The hedge to meet me in the drong,
An' stay till all is dim an' dark
Bezides the ashen tree's white bark;
An' all bezides the blackbird's shrill
An' runnèn evenèn-whissle's still.

An' there in bwoyhood I did rove
Wi' pryèn eyes along the drove
To vind the nest the blackbird meäde
O' grass-stalks in the high bough's sheäde;
Or climb aloft, wi' clingèn knees,
Vor crows' aggs up in swaÿèn trees,
While frightened blackbirds down below
Did chatter o' their little foe.
An' zoo there's noo pleäce lik' the drong,
Where I do hear the blackbird's zong.

William Barnes [1801–1886]

ROBERT OF LINCOLN

Merrily swinging on brier and weed,
　　Near to the nest of his little dame,
Over the mountain-side or mead,
　　Robert of Lincoln is telling his name:
　　　　Bob-o'-link, bob-o'-link,
　　　　　Spink, spank, spink;
Snug and safe is that nest of ours,
Hidden among the summer flowers.
　　　　　　　　Chee, chee, chee.

Robert of Lincoln is gayly dressed,
　Wearing a bright black wedding-coat;
White are his shoulders and white his crest.
　Hear him call in his merry note:
　　Bob-o'-link, bob-o'-link,
　　Spink, spank, spink;
Look, what a nice new coat is mine,
Sure there was never a bird so fine.
　　　　　　　　　Chee, chee, chee.

Robert of Lincoln's Quaker wife,
　Pretty and quiet, with plain brown wings,
Passing at home a patient life,
　Broods in the grass while her husband sings:
　　Bob-o'-link, bob-o'-link,
　　Spink, spank, spink;
Brood, kind creature; you need not fear
Thieves and robbers while I am here.
　　　　　　　　　Chee, chee, chee.

Modest and shy as a nun is she;
　One weak chirp is her only note.
Braggart and prince of braggarts is he,
　Pouring boasts from his little throat:
　　Bob-o'-link, bob-o'-link,
　　Spink, spank, spink;
Never was I afraid of man;
Catch me, cowardly knaves, if you can!
　　　　　　　　　Chee, chee, chee.

Six white eggs on a bed of hay,
　Flecked with purple, a pretty sight!
There as the mother sits all day,
　Robert is singing with all his might:
　　Bob-o'-link, bob-o'-link,
　　Spink, spank, spink;
Nice good wife, that never goes out,
Keeping house while I frolic about.
　　　　　　　　　Chee, chee, chee.

Soon as the little ones chip the shell,
Six wide mouths are open for food;
Robert of Lincoln bestirs him well,
Gathering seeds for the hungry brood.
Bob-o'-link, bob-o'-link,
Spink, spank, spink;
This new life is likely to be
Hard for a gay young fellow like me.
Chee, chee, chee.

Robert of Lincoln at length is made
Sober with work, and silent with care;
Off is his holiday garment laid,
Half forgotten that merry air:
Bob-o'-link, bob-o'-link,
Spink, spank, spink;
Nobody knows but my mate and I
Where our nest and our nestlings lie.
Chee, chee, chee.

Summer wanes; the children are grown;
Fun and frolic no more he knows;
Robert of Lincoln's a humdrum crone;
Off he flies, and we sing as he goes:
Bob-o'-link, bob-o'-link,
Spink, spank, spink;
When you can pipe that merry old strain,
Robert of Lincoln, come back again.
Chee, chee, chee.
William Cullen Bryant [1794–1878]

THE O'LINCON FAMILY

A FLOCK of merry singing-birds were sporting in the grove;
Some were warbling cheerily, and some were making love:
There were Bobolincon, Wadolincon, Winterseeble, Con-
quedle,—
A livelier set was never led by tabor, pipe, or fiddle,—
Crying, "Phew, shew, Wadolincon, see, see, Bobolincon,
Down among the tickletops, hiding in the buttercups!

I know a saucy chap, I see his shining cap
Bobbing in the clover there—see, see, see!"

Up flies Bobolincon, perching on an apple-tree,
Startled by his rival's song, quickened by his raillery,
Soon he spies the rogue afloat, curveting in the air,
And merrily he turns about, and warns him to beware!
" 'Tis you that would a-wooing go, down among the rushes
      O!
But wait a week, till flowers are cheery,—wait a week, and,
      ere you marry,
Be sure of a house wherein to tarry!
Wadolink, Whiskodink, Tom Denny, wait, wait, wait!"

Every one's a funny fellow; every one's a little mellow;
Follow, follow, follow, follow, o'er the hill and in the hollow!
Merrily, merrily, there they hie; now they rise and now they
      fly;
They cross and turn, and in and out, and down in the mid-
      dle and wheel about,—
With a "Phew, shew, Wadolincon! listen to me, Bobo-
      lincon!—
Happy's the wooing that's speedily doing, that's speedily
      doing,
That's merry and over with the bloom of the clover!
Bobolincon, Wadolincon, Winterseeble, follow, follow, fol-
      low me!"

                                   Wilson Flagg [1805–1884]

THE BOBOLINK

BOBOLINK! that in the meadow,
Or beneath the orchard's shadow,
Keepest up a constant rattle
Joyous as my children's prattle,
Welcome to the north again!
Welcome to mine ear thy strain,
Welcome to mine eye the sight
Of thy buff, thy black and white.

Brighter plumes may greet the sun
By the banks of Amazon;
Sweeter tones may weave the spell
Of enchanting Philomel;
But the tropic bird would fail,
And the English nightingale,
If we should compare their worth
With thine endless, gushing mirth.

When the ides of May are past,
June and Summer nearing fast,
While from depths of blue above
Comes the mighty breath of love,
Calling out each bud and flower
With resistless, secret power,
Waking hope and fond desire,
Kindling the erotic fire,
Filling youths' and maidens' dreams
With mysterious, pleasing themes;
Then, amid the sunlight clear
Floating in the fragrant air,
Thou dost fill each heart with pleasure
By thy glad ecstatic measure.

A single note, so sweet and low,
Like a full heart's overflow,
Forms the prelude; but the strain
Gives no such tone again,
For the wild and saucy song
Leaps and skips the notes among,
With such quick and sportive play,
Ne'er was madder, merrier lay.

Gayest songster of the Spring!
Thy melodies before me bring
Visions of some dream-built land,
Where, by constant zephyrs fanned,
I might walk the livelong day,
Embosomed in perpetual May.
Nor care nor fear thy bosom knows;
For thee a tempest never blows;

But when our northern Summer's o'er,
By Delaware's or Schuylkill's shore
The wild rice lifts its airy head,
And royal feasts for thee are spread.
And when the Winter threatens there,
Thy tireless wings yet own no fear.
But bear thee to more southern coasts,
Far beyond the reach of frosts.

Bobolink! still may thy gladness
Take from me all taint of sadness;
Fill my soul with trust unshaken
In that Being who has taken
Care for every living thing,
In Summer, Winter, Fall, and Spring.
              Thomas Hill [1818–1891]

MY CATBIRD

A CAPRICCIO

NIGHTINGALE I never heard,
Nor skylark, poet's bird;
But there is an æther-winger
So surpasses every singer,
(Though unknown to lyric fame,)
That at morning, or at nooning,
When I hear his pipe a-tuning,
Down I fling Keats, Shelley, Wordsworth,—
What are all their songs of birds worth?
All their soaring
Souls' outpouring?
When my Mimus Carolinensis,
(That's his Latin name,)
When my warbler wild commences
Song's hilarious rhapsody,
Just to please himself and me!
Primo Cantante!
Scherzo! Andante!
Piano, pianissimo!
Presto, prestissimo!

Hark! are there nine birds or ninety and nine?
And now a miraculous gurgling gushes
Like nectar from Hebe's Olympian bottle,
The laughter of tune from a rapturous throttle!
Such melody must be a hermit-thrush's!
But that other caroler, nearer,
Outrivaling rivalry with clearer
Sweetness incredibly fine!
Is it oriole, redbird, or bluebird,
Or some strange, un-Auduboned new bird?
All one, sir, both this bird and that bird,
The whole flight are all the same catbird!
The whole visible and invisible choir you see
On one lithe twig of yon green tree.
Flitting, feathery Blondel!
Listen to his rondel!
To his lay romantical!
To his sacred canticle!
Hear him lilting,
See him tilting,
His saucy head and **tail,** and fluttering
While uttering
All the difficult operas under the sun
Just for fun;
Or in tipsy revelry,
Or at love devilry,
Or, disdaining his divine gift and art,
Like an inimitable poet
Who captivates the world's heart
And don't know it.
Hear him lilt!
See him tilt!
Then suddenly he stops,
Peers about, flirts, hops,
As if looking where he might gather **up**
The wasted ecstasy just spilt
From the quivering cup
Of his bliss overrun.
Then, as in mockery of all
The tuneful spells that e'er did fall

From vocal pipe, or evermore shall rise,
He snarls, and mews, and flies.
William Henry Venable [1836–1920]

THE HERALD CRANE

OH! say you so, bold sailor
  In the sun-lit deeps of sky!
Dost thou so soon the seed-time tell
  In thy imperial cry,
As circling in yon shoreless sea
  Thine unseen form goes drifting by?

I cannot trace in the noon-day glare
  Thy regal flight, O crane!
From the leaping might of the fiery light
  Mine eyes recoil in pain,
But on mine ear, thine echoing cry
  Falls like a bugle strain.

The mellow soil glows beneath my feet,
  Where lies the buried grain;
The warm light floods the length and breadth
  Of the vast, dim, shimmering plain,
Throbbing with heat and the nameless thrill
  Of the birth-time's restless pain.

On weary wing, plebeian geese
  Push on their arrowy line
Straight into the north, or snowy brant
  In dazzling sunshine, gloom and shine;
But thou, O crane, save for thy sovereign cry,
  At thy majestic height
On proud, extended wings sweep'st on
  In lonely, easeful flight.

Then cry, thou martial-throated herald!
  Cry to the sun, and sweep
And swing along thy mateless, tireless course
  Above the clouds that sleep

Afloat on lazy air—cry on! Send down
    Thy trumpet note—it seems
The voice of hope and dauntless will,
    And breaks the spell of dreams.
                                    Hamlin Garland [1860–1940]

THE CROW

WITH rakish eye and plenished crop,
    Oblivious of the farmer's gun,
Upon the naked ash-tree top
    The Crow sits basking in the sun.

An old ungodly rogue, I wot!
    For, perched in black against the blue,
His feathers, torn with beak and shot,
    Let woeful glints of April through.

The year's new grass, and, golden-eyed,
    The daisies sparkle underneath,
And chestnut-trees on either side
    Have opened every ruddy sheath.

But doubtful still of frost and snow,
    The ash alone stands stark and bare,
And on its topmost twig the Crow
    Takes the glad morning's sun and air.
                                    William Canton [1845–

TO THE CUCKOO

HAIL, beauteous stranger of the grove!
    Thou messenger of Spring!
Now Heaven repairs thy rural seat,
    And woods thy welcome ring.

What time the daisy decks the green,
    Thy certain voice we hear:
Hast thou a star to guide thy path,
    Or mark the rolling year?

Delightful visitant! with thee
  I hail the time of flowers,
And hear the sound of music sweet
  From birds among the bowers.

The school-boy, wandering through the wood
  To pull the primrose gay,
Starts, the new voice of Spring to hear,
  And imitates thy lay.

What time the pea puts on the bloom,
  Thou fli'st thy vocal vale,
An annual guest in other lands,
  Another Spring to hail.

Sweet bird! thy bower is ever green,
  Thy sky is ever clear;
Thou hast no sorrow in thy song,
  No Winter in thy year!

O could I fly, I'd fly with thee!
  We'd make, with joyful wing,
Our annual visit o'er the globe,
  Companions of the Spring.
                John Logan [1748–1788]

THE CUCKOO

WE heard it calling, clear and low,
  That tender April morn; we stood
  And listened in the quiet wood,
We heard it, ay, long years ago.

It came, and with a strange, sweet cry,
  A friend, but from a far-off land;
  We stood and listened, hand in hand,
And heart to heart, my Love and I.

In dreamland then we found our joy,
  And so it seemed as 'twere the Bird
  That Helen in old times had heard
At noon beneath the oaks of Troy.

O time far off, and yet so near!
    It came to her in that hushed grove,
    It warbled while the wooing throve,
It sang the song she loved to hear.

And now I hear its voice again,
    And still its message is of peace,
    It sings of love that will not cease—
For me it never sings in vain.

            Frederick Locker-Lampson [1821–1895]

TO THE CUCKOO

O BLITHE New-comer! I have heard,
    I hear thee and rejoice.
O Cuckoo! shall I call thee Bird,
    Or but a wandering Voice?

While I am lying on the grass
    Thy twofold shout I hear;
From hill to hill it seems to pass,
    At once far off, and near.

Though babbling only to the Vale
    Of sunshine and of flowers,
Thou bringest unto me a tale
    Of visionary hours.

Thrice welcome, darling of the Spring!
    Even yet thou art to me
No bird, but an invisible thing,
    A voice, a mystery;

The same whom in my school-boy days
    I listened to; that Cry
Which made me look a thousand ways,
    In bush, and tree, and sky.

To seek thee did I often rove
    Through woods and on the green;
And thou wert still a hope, a love;
    Still longed for, never seen.

And I can listen to thee yet;
   Can lie upon the plain
And listen, till I do beget
   That golden time again.

O blessèd Bird! the earth we pace
   Again appears to be
An unsubstantial, faery place;
   That is fit home for Thee!
         William Wordsworth [1770–1850]

THE EAGLE

A FRAGMENT

HE clasps the crag with crooked hands;
Close to the sun in lonely lands,
Ringed with the azure world, he stands.

The wrinkled sea beneath him crawls;
He watches from his mountain walls,
And like a thunderbolt he falls.
         Alfred Tennyson [1809–1892]

THE HAWKBIT

How sweetly on the autumn scene,
When haws are red amid the green,
The hawkbit shines with face of cheer,
The favorite of the faltering year!

When days grow short and nights grow cold,
How fairly gleams its eye of gold
On pastured field and grassy hill,
Along the roadside and the rill!

It seems the spirit of a flower,
This offspring of the autumn hour,
Wandering back to earth to bring
Some kindly afterthought of spring.

A dandelion's ghost might so
Amid Elysian meadows blow,
Become more fragile and more fine
Breathing the atmosphere divine.
Charles G. D. Roberts [1860–

THE HERON

O MELANCHOLY Bird, a winter's day
Thou standest by the margin of the pool,
And, taught by God, dost thy whole being school
To Patience, which all evil can allay.
God has appointed thee the Fish thy prey;
And given thyself a lesson to the Fool
Unthrifty, to submit to moral rule,
And his unthinking course by thee to weigh.
There need not schools, nor the Professor's chair,
Though these be good, true wisdom to impart;
He, who has not enough for these to spare
Of time, or gold, may yet amend his heart,
And teach his soul, by brooks and rivers fair:
Nature is always wise in every part.
Edward Hovell-Thurlow [1781–1829]

THE JACKDAW

THERE is a bird, who by his coat,
And by the hoarseness of his note,
    Might be supposed a crow;
A great frequenter of the church,
Where bishop-like he finds a perch,
    And dormitory too.

Above the steeple shines a plate,
That turns and turns, to indicate
    From what point blows the weather;
Look up—your brains begin to swim,
'Tis in the clouds—that pleases him,
    He chooses it the rather.

Fond of the speculative height,
Thither he wings his airy flight,
    And thence securely sees
The bustle and the raree-show,
That occupy mankind below,
    Secure and at his ease.

You think, no doubt, he sits and muses
On future broken bones and bruises,
    If he should chance to fall.
No: not a single thought like that
Employs his philosophic pate,
    Or troubles it at all.

He sees that this great roundabout,
The world, with all its medley rout,
    Church, army, physic, law,
Its customs, and its businesses
Is no concern at all of his,
    And says—what says he?—"Caw."

Thrice happy bird! I too have seen
Much of the vanities of men;
    And, sick of having seen 'em,
Would cheerfully these limbs resign
For such a pair of wings as thine,
    And such a head between 'em.

From the Latin of Vincent Bourne,
by William Cowper [1731–1800]

THE GREEN LINNET

BENEATH these fruit-tree boughs that shed
Their snow-white blossoms on my head,
With brightest sunshine round me spread
    Of Spring's unclouded weather,
In this sequestered nook how sweet
To sit upon my orchard-seat!
And flowers and birds once more to greet,
    My last year's friends together.

One have I marked, the happiest guest
In all this covert of the blest:
Hail to Thee, far above the rest
   In joy of voice and pinion!
Thou, Linnet! in thy green array
Presiding Spirit here to-day
Dost lead the revels of the May,
   And this is thy dominion.

While birds, and butterflies, and flowers
Make all one band of paramours,
Thou, ranging up and down the bowers,
   Art sole in thy employment;
A Life, a Presence like the air,
Scattering thy gladness without care,
Too blest with any one to pair,
   Thyself thy own enjoyment.

Amid yon tuft of hazel trees,
That twinkle to the gusty breeze,
Behold him perched in ecstasies,
   Yet seeming still to hover;
There! where the flutter of his wings
Upon his back and body flings
Shadows and sunny glimmerings,
   That cover him all over.

My dazzled sight he oft deceives—
A Brother of the dancing leaves;
Then flits, and from the cottage-eaves
   Pours forth his song in gushes,
As if by that exulting strain
He mocked and treated with disdain
The voiceless Form he chose to feign
   While fluttering in the bushes.

          William Wordsworth [1770–1850]

TO THE MAN–OF–WAR–BIRD

Thou who hast slept all night upon the storm,
Waking renewed on thy prodigious pinions,

(Burst the wild storm? above it thou ascended'st,
And rested on the sky, thy slave that cradled thee,)
Now a blue point, far, far in heaven floating,
As to the light emerging here on deck I watch thee,
(Myself a speck, a point on the world's floating vast.)

Far, far at sea,
After the night's fierce drifts have strewn the shore with
    wrecks,
With re-appearing day as now so happy and serene,
The rosy and elastic dawn, the flashing sun,
The limpid spread of air cerulean,
Thou also re-appearest.

Thou born to match the gale, (thou art all wings,)
To cope with heaven and earth and sea and hurricane,
Thou ship of air that never furl'st thy sails,
Days, even weeks untired and onward, through spaces,
    realms gyrating,
At dusk that look'st on Senegal, at morn America,
That sport'st amid the lightning-flash and thunder-cloud,
In them, in thy experiences, hadst thou my soul,
What joys! what joys were thine!
             Walt Whitman [1819–1892]

THE MARYLAND YELLOW-THROAT

WHEN May bedecks the naked trees
With tassels and embroideries,
And many blue-eyed violets beam
Along the edges of the stream,
I hear a voice that seems to say,
Now near at hand, now far away,
    "*Witchery—witchery—witchery.*"

An incantation so serene,
So innocent, befits the scene:
There's magic in that small bird's note—
See, there he flits—the Yellow-throat;
A living sunbeam, tipped with wings,
A spark of light that shines and sings
    "*Witchery—witchery—witchery.*"

You prophet with a pleasant name,
If out of Mary-land you came,
You know the way that thither goes
Where Mary's lovely garden grows:
Fly swiftly back to her, I pray,
And try, to call her down this way,
 "Witchery—witchery—witchery!"

Tell her to leave her cockle-shells,
And all her little silver bells
That blossom into melody,
And all her maids less fair than she.
She does not need these pretty things,
For everywhere she comes, she brings
 "Witchery—witchery—witchery!"

The woods are greening overhead,
And flowers adorn each mossy bed;
The waters babble as they run—
One thing is lacking, only one:
If Mary were but here to-day,
I would believe your charming lay,
 "Witchery—witchery—witchery!"

Along the shady road I look—
Who's coming now across the brook?
A woodland maid, all robed in white—
The leaves dance round her with delight,
The stream laughs out beneath her feet—
Sing, merry bird, the charm's complete,
 "Witchery—witchery—witchery!"
      Henry Van Dyke [1852–1933]

LAMENT OF A MOCKING–BIRD

SILENCE instead of thy sweet song, my bird,
 Which through the darkness of my winter days
Warbling of summer sunshine still was heard;
 Mute is thy song, and vacant is thy place.

The spring comes back again, the fields rejoice,
  Carols of gladness ring from every tree;
But I shall hear thy wild triumphant voice
  No more: my summer song has died with thee.

What didst thou sing of, O my summer bird?
  The broad, bright, brimming river, whose swift sweep
And whirling eddies by the home are heard,
  Rushing, resistless, to the calling deep.

What didst thou sing of, thou melodious sprite?
  Pine forests, with smooth russet carpets spread,
Where e'en at noonday dimly falls the light,
  Through gloomy blue-green branches overhead.

What didst thou sing of, O thou jubilant soul?
  Ever-fresh flowers and never-leafless trees,
Bending great ivory cups to the control
  Of the soft swaying, orange scented breeze.

What didst thou sing of, thou embodied glee?
  The wide wild marshes with their clashing reeds
And topaz-tinted channels, where the sea
  Daily its tides of briny freshness leads.

What didst thou sing of, O thou wingèd voice?
  Dark, bronze-leaved oaks, with silver mosses crowned,
Where thy free kindred live, love, and rejoice,
  With wreaths of golden jasmine curtained round.

These didst thou sing of, spirit of delight!
  From thy own radiant sky, thou quivering spark!
These thy sweet southern dreams of warmth and light,
  Through the grim northern winter drear and dark.

Frances Anne Kemble [1809–1893]

"O NIGHTINGALE! THOU SURELY ART"

O NIGHTINGALE! thou surely art
A creature of a "fiery heart":—
These notes of thine—they pierce and pierce;
Tumultuous harmony and fierce!

Thou sing'st as if the God of wine
Had helped thee to a Valentine;
A song in mockery and despite
Of shades, and dews, and silent night;
And steady bliss, and all the loves
Now sleeping in these peaceful groves.

I heard a Stock-dove sing or say
His homely tale, this very day;
His voice was buried among trees,
Yet to be come at by the breeze:
He did not cease, but cooed—and cooed;
And somewhat pensively he wooed:
He sang of love, with quiet blending,
Slow to begin, and never ending;
Of serious faith, and inward glee;
That was the Song—the Song for me!

William Wordsworth [1770–1850]

PHILOMEL

As it fell upon a day
In the merry month of May,
Sitting in a pleasant shade
Which a grove of myrtles made,
Beasts did leap and birds did sing,
Trees did grow and plants did spring;
Everything did banish moan
Save the Nightingale alone:
She, poor bird, as all forlorn
Leaned her breast up-till a thorn,
And there sung the doleful'st ditty,
That to hear it was great pity.
Fie, fie, fie ! now would she cry;
Tereu, Tereu ! by and by;
That to hear her so complain
Scarce I could from tears refrain;
For her griefs so lively shown
Made me think upon mine own.

Ah! thought I, thou mourn'st in vain,
None takes pity on thy pain:
Senseless trees they cannot hear thee,
Ruthless beasts they will not cheer thee:
King Pandion he is dead,
All thy friends are lapped in lead;
All thy fellow birds do sing
Careless of thy sorrowing:
Even so, poor bird, like thee,
None alive will pity me.

Richard Barnfield [1574–1627]

PHILOMELA

Hark! ah, the nightingale—
The tawny-throated!
Hark, from that moonlit cedar what a burst!
What triumph! hark!—what pain!

O wanderer from a Grecian shore,
Still, after many years, in distant lands,
Still nourishing in thy bewildered brain
That wild, unquenched, deep-sunken, old-world pain—
Say, will it never heal?
And can this fragrant lawn
With its cool trees, and night,
And the sweet, tranquil Thames,
And moonshine, and the dew,
To thy racked heart and brain
Afford no balm?

Dost thou to-night behold,
Here, through the moonlight on this English grass,
The unfriendly palace in the Thracian wild?
Dost thou again peruse
With hot cheeks and seared eyes
The too clear web, and thy dumb sister's shame?
Dost thou once more assay
Thy flight, and feel come over thee,

Poor fugitive, the feathery change
Once more, and once more seem to make resound
With love and hate, triumph and agony,
Lone Daulis, and the high Cephissian vale?
Listen, Eugenia—
How thick the bursts come crowding through the leaves!
Again—thou hearest?
Eternal passion!
Eternal pain!

Matthew Arnold [1822–1888]

ON A NIGHTINGALE IN APRIL

THE yellow moon is a dancing phantom
    Down secret ways of the flowing shade;
And the waveless stream has a murmuring whisper
        Where the alders wave.

Not a breath, not a sigh, save the slow stream's whisper:
    Only the moon is a dancing blade
That leads a host of the Crescent warriors
        To a phantom raid.

Out of the Lands of Faerie a summons,
    A long, strange cry that thrills through the glade:—
The gray-green glooms of the elm are stirring,
        Newly afraid.

Last heard, white music, under the olives
    Where once Theocritus sang and played—
Thy Thracian song is the old new wonder,
        O moon-white maid!

William Sharp [1855–1905]

TO THE NIGHTINGALE

DEAR chorister, who from those shadows sends,
Ere that the blushing morn dare show her light,
Such sad lamenting strains, that night attends,
Become all ear, stars stay to hear thy plight:

If one whose grief even reach of thought transcends,
Who ne'er, not in a dream, did taste delight,
May thee importune who like care pretends,
And seems to joy in woe, in woe's despite;
Tell me (so may thou fortune milder try,
And long, long sing) for what thou thus complains,
Since, winter gone, the sun in dappled sky
Now smiles on meadows, mountains, woods, and plains?
  The bird, as if my questions did her move,
  With trembling wings sobbed forth, "I love! I love!"
                    William Drummond [1585–1649]

THE NIGHTINGALE

To-night retired, the queen of heaven
    With young Endymion stays;
And now to Hesper it is given
Awhile to rule the vacant sky,
Till she shall to her lamp supply
    A stream of brighter rays. . . .

Propitious send thy golden ray,
    Thou purest light above:
Let no false flame seduce to stray
Where gulf or steep lie hid for harm;
But lead where music's healing charm
    May soothe afflicted love.

To them, by many a grateful song
    In happier seasons vowed,
These lawns, Olympia's haunt, belong:
Oft by yon silver stream we walked,
Or fixed, while Philomela talked,
    Beneath yon copses stood.

Nor seldom, where the beechen boughs
    That roofless tower invade,
We came, while her enchanting Muse
The radiant moon above us held:
Till, by a clamorous owl compelled,
    She fled the solemn shade.

But hark!   I hear her liquid tone!
  Now, Hesper, guide my feet
Down the red marl with moss o'ergrown,
Through yon wild thicket next the plain,
Whose hawthorns choke the winding lane
  Which leads to her retreat.

See the green space: on either hand
  Enlarged it spreads around:
See, in the midst she takes her stand,
Where one old oak his awful shade
Extends o'er half the level mead,
  Enclosed in woods profound.

Hark! how through many a melting note
  She now prolongs her lays:
How sweetly down the void they float!
The breeze their magic path attends;
The stars shine out; the forest bends;
  The wakeful heifers gaze.

Whoe'er thou art whom chance may bring
  To this sequestered spot,
If then the plaintive Siren sing,
O softly tread beneath her bower
And think of Heaven's disposing power,
  Of man's uncertain lot.

O think, o'er all this mortal stage
  What mournful scenes arise:
What ruin waits on kingly rage;
How often virtue dwells with woe;
How many griefs from knowledge flow;
  How swiftly pleasure flies!

O sacred bird! let me at eve,
  Thus wandering all alone,
Thy tender counsel oft receive,
Bear witness to thy pensive airs,
And pity Nature's common cares,
  Till I forget my own.

                    Mark Akenside [1721–1770]

TO THE NIGHTINGALE

O NIGHTINGALE that on yon bloomy spray
  Warblest at eve, when all the woods are still,
  Thou with fresh hope the lover's heart dost fill,
While the jolly hours lead on propitious May.
Thy liquid notes that close the eye of day,
  First heard before the shallow cuckoo's bill,
  Portend success in love. O, if Jove's will
Have linked that amorous power to thy soft lay,
  Now timely sing, ere the rude bird of hate
Foretell my hopeless doom, in some grove nigh;
  As thou from year to year hast sung too late
For my relief, yet hadst no reason why.
  Whether the Muse or Love call thee his mate,
Both them I serve, and of their train am I.

John Milton [1608–1674]

PHILOMELA

THE Nightingale, as soon as April bringeth
  Unto her rested sense a perfect waking,
While late-bare Earth, proud of new clothing, springeth,
  Sings out her woes, a thorn her song-book making;
    And mournfully bewailing,
    Her throat in tunes expresseth
    What grief her breast oppresseth,
For Tereus' force on her chaste will prevailing.

O Philomela fair, O take some gladness
That here is juster cause of plaintful sadness !
  Thine earth now springs, mine fadeth;
  Thy thorn without, my thorn my heart invadeth.

Alas! she hath no other cause of anguish
  But Tereus' love, on her by strong hand wroken;
Wherein she suffering, all her spirits languish,
  Full womanlike, complains her will was broken,

But I, who, daily craving,
　　Cannot have to content me,
　　Have more cause to lament me,
Since wanting is more woe than too much having.

　　O Philomela fair, O take some gladness
　　That here is juster cause of plaintful sadness!
　　　Thine earth now springs, mine fadeth;
　　　Thy thorn without, my thorn my heart invadeth.
　　　　　　　　　　Philip Sidney [1554–1586]

ODE TO A NIGHTINGALE

MY heart aches, and a drowsy numbness pains
　　My sense, as though of hemlock I had drunk,
Or emptied some dull opiate to the drains
　　One minute past, and Lethe-wards had sunk:
'Tis not through envy of thy happy lot,
　　But being too happy in thy happiness,—
　　　That thou, light-wingèd Dryad of the trees,
　　　　In some melodious plot
　　Of beechen green, and shadows numberless,
　　　Singest of summer in full-throated ease.

O for a draught of vintage, that hath been
　　Cooled a long age in the deep-delvèd earth,
Tasting of Flora and the country green,
　　Dance, and Provençal song, and sunburnt mirth!
O for a beaker full of the warm South,
　　Full of the true, the blushful Hippocrene,
　　　With beaded bubbles winking at the brim,
　　　　And purple-stainèd mouth;
　　That I might drink, and leave the world unseen,
　　　And with thee fade away into the forest dim:

Fade far away, dissolve, and quite forget
　　What thou among the leaves hast never known,
The weariness, the fever, and the fret,
　　Here, where men sit and hear each other groan;

Where palsy shakes a few, sad, last gray hairs,
   Where youth grows pale, and specter-thin, and dies;
      Where but to think is to be full of sorrow
         And leaden-eyed despairs;
   Where Beauty cannot keep her lustrous eyes,
      Or new Love pine at them beyond to-morrow.

Away! away! for I will fly to thee,
   Not charioted by Bacchus and his pards,
But on the viewless wings of Poesy,
   Though the dull brain perplexes and retards:
Already with thee! tender is the night,
   And haply the Queen-Moon is on her throne,
      Clustered around by all her starry Fays;
         But here there is no light,
Save what from heaven is with the breezes blown
      Through verdurous glooms and winding mossy ways.

I cannot see what flowers are at my feet,
   Nor what soft incense hangs upon the boughs,
But, in embalmèd darkness, guess each sweet
   Wherewith the seasonable month endows
The grass, the thicket, and the fruit-tree wild;
   White hawthorn, and the pastoral eglantine;
      Fast-fading violets covered up in leaves;
         And mid-May's eldest child,
The coming musk-rose, full of dewy wine,
      The murmurous haunt of flies on summer eves.

Darkling I listen; and, for many a time
   I have been half in love with easeful Death,
Called him soft names in many a musèd rhyme,
   To take into the air my quiet breath;
Now more than ever seems it rich to die,
   To cease upon the midnight with no pain,
      While thou art pouring forth thy soul abroad
         In such an ecstasy!
   Still wouldst thou sing, and I have ears in vain—
      To thy high requiem become a sod.

Thou wast not born for death, immortal Bird!
No hungry generations tread thee down;
The voice I hear this passing night was heard
In ancient days by emperor and clown:
Perhaps the self-same song that found a path
   Through the sad heart of Ruth, when, sick for home,
     She stood in tears amid the alien corn;
       The same that oft-times hath
   Charmed magic casements, opening on the foam
   Of perilous seas, in faery lands forlorn.

Forlorn! the very word is like a bell
To toll me back from thee to my sole self!
Adieu! the fancy cannot cheat so well
   As she is famed to do, deceiving elf.
Adieu! adieu! thy plaintive anthem fades
   Past the near meadows, over the still stream,
     Up the hill-side; and now 'tis buried deep
       In the next valley-glades:
Was it a vision, or a waking dream?
Fled is that music:—Do I wake or sleep?

             John Keats [1795–1821]

SONG

'Tis sweet to hear the merry lark,
   That bids a blithe good-morrow;
But sweeter to hark, in the twinkling dark,
   To the soothing song of sorrow.
Oh nightingale!   What doth she ail?
   And is she sad or jolly?
For ne'er on earth was sound of mirth
   So like to melancholy.

The merry lark, he soars on high,
   No worldly thought o'ertakes him;
He sings aloud to the clear blue sky,
   And the daylight that awakes him.
As sweet a lay, as loud, as gay,
   The nightingale is trilling;
With feeling bliss, no less than his,
   Her little heart is thrilling.

Yet ever and anon, a sigh
  Peers through her lavish mirth;
For the lark's bold song is of the sky,
  And hers is of the earth.
By night and day, she tunes her lay,
  To drive away all sorrow;
For bliss, alas! to-night must pass,
  And woe may come to-morrow.

Hartley Coleridge [1796–1840]

BIRD SONG

THE robin sings of willow-buds,
  Of snowflakes on the green;
The bluebird sings of Mayflowers,
  The crackling leaves between;
The veery has a thousand tales
  To tell to girl and boy;
But the oriole, the oriole,
  Sings, "Joy! joy! joy!"

The pewee calls his little mate,
  Sweet Phœbe, gone astray,
The warbler sings, "What fun, what fun,
  To tilt upon the spray!"
The cuckoo has no song, but clucks,
  Like any wooden toy;
But the oriole, the oriole,
  Sings, "Joy! joy! joy!"

The grosbeak sings the rose's birth,
  And paints her on his breast;
The sparrow sings of speckled eggs,
  Soft brooded in the nest.
The wood-thrush sings of peace, "Sweet peace,
  Sweet peace," without alloy;
But the oriole, the oriole,
  Sings "Joy! joy! joy!"

Laura E. Richards [1850–

THE SONG THE ORIOLE SINGS

THERE is a bird that comes and sings
　　In a professor's garden-trees;
Upon the English oak he swings,
　　And tilts and tosses in the breeze.

I know his name, I know his note,
　　That so with rapture takes my soul;
Like flame the gold beneath his throat,
　　His glossy cope is black as coal.

O oriole, it is the song
　　You sang me from the cottonwood,
Too young to feel that I was young,
　　Too glad to guess if life were good.

And while I hark, before my door,
　　Adown the dusty Concord Road,
The blue Miami flows once more
　　As by the cottonwood it flowed.

And on the bank that rises steep,
　　And pours a thousand tiny rills,
From death and absence laugh and leap
　　My school-mates to their flutter-mills.

The blackbirds jangle in the tops
　　Of hoary-antlered sycamores;
The timorous killdee starts and stops
　　Among the drift-wood on the shores.

Below, the bridge—a noonday fear
　　Of dust and shadow shot with sun—
Stretches its gloom from pier to pier,
　　Far unto alien coasts unknown.

And on these alien coasts, above,
　　Where silver ripples break the stream's
Long blue, from some roof-sheltering grove
　　A hidden parrot scolds and screams.

Ah, nothing, nothing!   Commonest things:
  A touch, a glimpse, a sound, a breath—
It is a song the oriole sings—
  And all the rest belongs to death.

But oriole, my oriole,
  Were some bright seraph sent from bliss
With songs of heaven to win my soul
  From simple memories such as this,

What could he tell to tempt my ear
  From you?   What high thing could there be,
So tenderly and sweetly dear
  As my lost boyhood is to me?

William Dean Howells [1837–1920]

TO AN ORIOLE

How falls it, oriole, thou hast come to fly
In tropic splendor through our Northern sky?

At some glad moment was it nature's choice
To dower a scrap of sunset with a voice?

Or did some orange tulip, flaked with black,
In some forgotten garden, ages back,

Yearning toward Heaven until its wish was heard,
Desire unspeakably to be a bird?

Edgar Fawcett [1847–1904]

SONG: THE OWL

When cats run home and light is come,
  And dew is cold upon the ground,
And the far-off stream is dumb,
  And the whirring sail goes round,
  And the whirring sail goes round;

Alone and warming his five wits,
The white owl in the belfry sits.

When merry milkmaids click the latch,
   And rarely smells the new-mown hay,
And the cock hath sung beneath the thatch
   Twice or thrice his roundelay,
   Twice or thrice his roundelay;
Alone and warming his five wits,
The white owl in the belfry sits.

                Alfred Tennyson [1809–1892]

SWEET SUFFOLK OWL

SWEET Suffolk owl, so trimly dight
With feathers, like a lady bright;
Thou sing'st alone, sitting by night,
   "Te whit! Te whoo!"

Thy note that forth so freely rolls
With shrill command the mouse controls;
And sings a dirge for dying souls.
   "Te whit! Te whoo!"

                Thomas Vautor [fl. 1616]

THE PEWEE

THE listening Dryads hushed the woods;
   The boughs were thick, and thin and few
   The golden ribbons fluttering through;
Their sun-embroidered, leafy hoods
   The lindens lifted to the blue:
Only a little forest-brook
The farthest hem of silence shook:
When in the hollow shades I heard,—
Was it a spirit, or a bird?
Or, strayed from Eden, desolate,
Some Peri calling to her mate,
   Whom nevermore her mate would cheer?
     "Pe-ri! pe-ri! peer!"

Through rocky clefts the brooklet fell
  With plashy pour, that scarce was sound,
  But only quiet less profound,
A stillness fresh and audible:
  A yellow leaflet to the ground
Whirled noiselessly: with wing of gloss
A hovering sunbeam brushed the moss,
And, wavering brightly over it,
Sat like a butterfly alit:
The owlet in his open door
Stared roundly: while the breezes bore
  The plaint to far-off places drear,—
    "Pe-ree! pe-ree! peer!"

To trace it in its green retreat
  I sought among the boughs in vain;
  And followed still the wandering strain,
So melancholy and so sweet
  The dim-eyed violets yearned with pain.
'Twas now a sorrow in the air,
Some nymph's immortalized despair
Haunting the woods and waterfalls;
And now, at long, sad intervals,
Sitting unseen in dusky shade,
His plaintive pipe some fairy played,
  With long-drawn cadence thin and clear,—
    "Pe-wee! pe-wee! peer!"

Long-drawn and clear its closes were,—
  As if the hand of Music through
  The somber robe of Silence drew
A thread of golden gossamer:
  So pure a flute the fairy blew.
Like beggared princes of the wood,
In silver rags the birches stood;
The hemlocks, lordly counselors,
Were dumb; the sturdy servitors,
In beechen jackets patched and gray,
Seemed waiting spellbound all the day
  That low, entrancing note to hear,—
    "Pe-wee! pe-wee! peer!"

I quit the search, and sat me down
    Beside the brook, irresolute,
    And watched a little bird in suit
Of sober olive, soft and brown,
    Perched in the maple-branches, mute:
With greenish gold its vest was fringed,
Its tiny cap was ebon-tinged,
With ivory pale its wings were barred,
And its dark eyes were tender-starred.
"Dear bird," I said, "what is thy name?"
And thrice the mournful answer came,
    So faint and far, and yet so near,—
        "Pe-wee! pe-wee! peer!"

For so I found my forest bird,—
    The pewee of the loneliest woods,
    Sole singer in these solitudes,
Which never robin's whistle stirred,
    Where never bluebird's plume intrudes.
Quick darting through the dewy morn,
The redstart trilled his twittering horn,
And vanished in thick boughs: at even,
Like liquid pearls fresh showered from heaven,
The high notes of the lone wood-thrush
Fall on the forest's holy hush:
    But thou all day complainest here,—
        "Pe-wee! pe-wee! peer!"

Hast thou, too, in thy little breast,
    Strange longings for a happier lot,—
    For love, for life, thou know'st not what,—
A yearning, and a vague unrest,
    For something still which thou hast not?—
Thou soul of some benighted child
That perished, crying in the wild!
Or lost, forlorn, and wandering maid,
By love allured, by love betrayed,
Whose spirit with her latest sigh
Arose, a little wingèd cry,
    Above her chill and mossy bier!
        "Dear me! dear me! dear!"

Ah, no such piercing sorrow mars
  The pewee's life of cheerful ease!
  He sings, or leaves his song to seize
An insect sporting in the bars
  Of mild bright light that gild the trees.
  A very poet he! For him
All pleasant places still and dim:
His heart, a spark of heavenly fire,
Burns with undying, sweet desire:
And so he sings; and so his song,
Though heard not by the hurrying throng,
  Is solace to the pensive ear:
    "Pewee! pewee! peer!"
      John Townsend Trowbridge [1827–1916]

ROBIN REDBREAST

SWEET Robin, I have heard them say
That thou wert there upon the day
The Christ was crowned in cruel scorn
And bore away one bleeding thorn,—
That so the blush upon thy breast,
In shameful sorrow, was impressed;
And thence thy genial sympathy
With our redeemed humanity.

Sweet Robin, would that I might be
Bathed in my Saviour's blood, like thee;
Bear in my breast, whate'er the loss,
The bleeding blazon of the cross;
Live ever, with thy loving mind,
In fellowship with human-kind;
And take my pattern still from thee,
In gentleness and constancy.
      George Washington Doane [1799–1859]

ROBIN REDBREAST

GOOD-BY, good-by to Summer!
  For Summer's nearly done;
The garden smiling faintly,
  Cool breezes in the sun;

Our thrushes now are silent,
  Our swallows flown away,—
But Robin's here in coat of brown,
  And scarlet breast-knot gay.
    Robin, Robin Redbreast,
      O Robin dear!
    Robin sings so sweetly
      In the falling of the year.

Bright yellow, red, and orange,
  The leaves come down in hosts;
The trees are Indian princes,
  But soon they'll turn to ghosts;
The scanty pears and apples
  Hang russet on the bough;
It's Autumn, Autumn, Autumn late,
  'Twill soon be Winter now.
    Robin, Robin Redbreast,
      O Robin dear!
    And what will this poor Robin do?
      For pinching days are near.

The fireside for the cricket,
  The wheat-stack for the mouse,
When trembling night-winds whistle
  And moan all round the house.
The frosty ways like iron,
  The branches plumed with snow,—
Alas! in Winter dead and dark,
  Where can poor Robin go?
    Robin, Robin Redbreast,
      O Robin dear!
    And a crumb of bread for Robin,
      His little heart to cheer!
          William Allingham [1824–1889]

THE SANDPIPER

Across the narrow beach we flit,
  One little sandpiper and I,
And fast I gather, bit by bit,
  The scattered driftwood bleached and dry.

The wild waves reach their hands for it,
  The wild wind raves, the tide runs high,
As up and down the beach we flit,—
  One little sandpiper and I.

Above our heads the sullen clouds
  Scud black and swift across the sky;
Like silent ghosts in misty shrouds
  Stand out the white lighthouses high.
Almost as far as eye can reach
  I see the close-reefed vessels fly,
As fast we flit along the beach,—
  One little sandpiper and I.

I watch him as he skims along,
  Uttering his sweet and mournful cry.
He starts not at my fitful song,
  Or flash of fluttering drapery.
He has no thought of any wrong;
  He scans me with a fearless eye:
Staunch friends are we, well tried and strong,
  The little sandpiper and I.

Comrade, where wilt thou be to-night
  When the loosed storm breaks furiously?
My driftwood fire will burn so bright!
  To what warm shelter canst thou fly?
I do not fear for thee, though wroth
  The tempest rushes through the sky:
For are we not God's children both,
  Thou, little sandpiper, and I?

Celia Thaxter [1835–1894]

THE SEA–MEW

How joyously the young sea-mew
Lay dreaming on the waters blue,
Whereon our little bark had thrown
A little shade, the only one,—
But shadows ever man pursue.

Familiar with the waves and free
As if their own white foam were he,
His heart upon the heart of ocean
Lay learning all its mystic motion,
And throbbing to the throbbing sea.

And such a brightness in his eye,
As if the ocean and the sky
Within him had lit up and nursed
A soul God gave him not at first
To comprehend their majesty.

We were not cruel, yet did sunder
His white wing from the blue waves under,
And bound it, while his fearless eyes
Shone up to ours in calm surprise,
As deeming us some ocean wonder!

We bore our ocean bird unto
A grassy place, where he might view
The flowers that curtsey to the bees,
The waving of the tall green trees,
The falling of the silver dew.

But flowers of earth were pale to him
Who had seen the rainbow fishes swim;
And when earth's dew around him lay
He thought of ocean's wingèd spray,
And his eye waxèd sad and dim.

The green trees round him only made
A prison with their darksome shade;
And dropped his wing, and mournèd he
For his own boundless glittering sea—
Albeit he knew not they could fade.

Then One her gladsome face did bring,
Her gentle voice's murmuring,
In ocean's stead his heart to move
And teach him what was human love:
He thought it a strange, mournful thing.

He lay down in his grief to die
(First looking to the sea-like sky
That hath no waves!), because, alas!
Our human touch did on him pass,
And, with our touch, our agony.

Elizabeth Barrett Browning [1806–1861]

TO A SKYLARK

Up with me! up with me into the clouds!
  For thy song, Lark, is strong;
Up with me, up with me into the clouds!
  Singing, singing,
With clouds and sky about thee ringing,
  Lift me, guide me till I find
That spot which seems so to thy mind!

I have walked through wildernesses dreary
And to-day my heart is weary;
Had I now the wings of a Fairy,
Up to thee would I fly.
There is madness about thee, and joy divine
In that song of thine;
Lift me, guide me high and high
To thy banqueting-place in the sky.

    Joyous as morning
Thou art laughing and scorning;
Thou hast a nest for thy love and thy rest.
And, though little troubled with sloth,
Drunken Lark! thou would'st be loth
To be such a traveler as I.
Happy, happy Liver,
With a soul as strong as a mountain river
Pouring out praise to the Almighty Giver,
    Joy and jollity be with us both!

Alas! my journey, rugged and uneven,
Through prickly moors or dusty ways must wind;
But hearing thee, or others of thy kind,
As full of gladness and as free of heaven,

I, with my fate contented, will plod on,
And hope for higher raptures, when life's day is done.
William Wordsworth [1770–1850]

TO A SKYLARK

ETHEREAL minstrel! pilgrim of the sky!
Dost thou despise the earth where cares abound?
Or, while the wings aspire, are heart and eye
Both with thy nest upon the dewy ground?
Thy nest which thou canst drop into at will,
Those quivering wings composed, that music still!

To the last point of vision, and beyond,
Mount, daring warbler!—that love-prompted strain
—'Twixt thee and thine a never-failing bond—
Thrills not the less the bosom of the plain:
Yet might'st thou seem, proud privilege! to sing
All independent of the leafy spring.

Leave to the nightingale her shady wood;
A privacy of glorious light is thine,
Whence thou dost pour upon the world a flood
Of harmony, with instinct more divine:
Type of the wise, who soar, but never roam—
True to the kindred points of Heaven and Home!
William Wordsworth [1770–1850]

THE SKYLARK

BIRD of the wilderness,
Blithesome and cumberless,
Sweet be thy matin o'er moorland and lea!
Emblem of happiness,
Blest is thy dwelling-place—
O to abide in the desert with thee!

Wild is thy lay and loud,
Far in the downy cloud,

Love gives it energy, love gave it birth.
    Where, on thy dewy wing,
    Where art thou journeying?
Thy lay is in heaven, thy love is on earth.

    O'er fell and fountain sheen,
    O'er moor and mountain green,
O'er the red streamer that heralds the day,
    Over the cloudlet dim,
    Over the rainbow's rim,
Musical cherub, soar, singing, away!

    Then, when the gloaming comes,
    Low in the heather blooms
Sweet will thy welcome and bed of love be!
    Emblem of happiness,
    Blest is thy dwelling-place—
O to abide in the desert with thee!

James Hogg [1770–1835]

THE SKYLARK

How the blithe Lark runs up the golden stair
    That leans through cloudy gates from Heaven to Earth,
And all alone in the empyreal air
    Fills it with jubilant sweet songs of mirth;
      How far he seems, how far
        With the light upon his wings,
      Is it a bird, or star
        That shines, and sings?

What matter if the days be dark and frore,
    That sunbeam tells of other days to be,
And singing in the light that floods him o'er
    In joy he overtakes Futurity;
      Under cloud-arches vast
        He peeps, and sees behind
      Great Summer coming fast
        Adown the wind!

And now he dives into a rainbow's rivers,
  In streams of gold and purple he is drowned,
Shrilly the arrows of his song he shivers,
  As though the stormy drops were turned to sound;
    And now he issues through,
      He scales a cloudy tower,
    Faintly, like falling dew,
      His fast notes shower.

Let every wind be hushed, that I may hear
  The wondrous things he tells the World below,
Things that we dream of he is watching near,
  Hopes that we never dreamed he would bestow;
    Alas! the storm hath rolled
      Back the gold gates again,
    Or surely he had told
      All Heaven to men!

So the victorious Poet sings alone,
  And fills with light his solitary home,
And through that glory sees new worlds foreshown,
  And hears high songs, and triumphs yet to come;
    He waves the air of Time
      With thrills of golden chords,
    And makes the world to climb
      On linkèd words.

What if his hair be gray, his eyes be dim,
  If wealth forsake him, and if friends be cold,
Wonder unbars her thousand gates to him,
  Truth never fails, nor Beauty waxes old;
    More than he tells his eyes
      Behold, his spirit hears,
    Of grief, and joy, and sighs
      'Twixt joy and tears.

Blest is the man who with the sound of song
  Can charm away the heartache, and forget
The frost of Penury, and the stings of Wrong,
  And drown the fatal whisper of Regret!

Darker are the abodes
Of Kings, though his be poor,
While Fancies, like the Gods,
Pass through his door.

Singing thou scalest Heaven upon thy wings,
Thou liftest a glad heart into the skies;
He maketh his own sunrise, while he sings,
And turns the dusty Earth to Paradise;
I see thee sail along
Far up the sunny streams,
Unseen, I hear his song,
I see his dreams.

Frederick Tennyson [1807–1898]

TO A SKYLARK

HAIL to thee, blithe spirit!
Bird thou never wert,
That from heaven, or near it,
Pourest thy full heart
In profuse strains of unpremeditated art.

Higher still and higher,
From the earth thou springest
Like a cloud of fire;
The blue deep thou wingest,
And singing still dost soar, and soaring ever singest.

In the golden lightning
Of the sunken sun,
O'er which clouds are bright'ning,
Thou dost float and run;
Like an unbodied joy whose race is just begun.

The pale purple even
Melts around thy flight;
Like a star of heaven
In the broad daylight
Thou art unseen, but yet I hear thy shrill delight.

Keen as are the arrows
Of that silver sphere,
Whose intense lamp narrows
In the white dawn clear,
Until we hardly see, we feel that it is there.

All the earth and air
With thy voice is loud,
As, when night is bare,
From one lonely cloud
The moon rains out her beams, and heaven is overflowed.

What thou art we know not;
What is most like thee?
From rainbow clouds there flow not
Drops so bright to see
As from thy presence showers a rain of melody.

Like a poet hidden
In the light of thought,
Singing hymns unbidden
Till the world is wrought
To sympathy with hopes and fears it heeded not:

Like a high-born maiden
In a palace tower,
Soothing her love-laden
Soul in secret hour
With music sweet as love, which overflows her bower:

Like a glow-worm golden
In a dell of dew,
Scattering unbeholden
Its aerial hue
Among the flowers and grass, which screen it from the view:

Like a rose embowered
In its own green leaves,
By warm winds deflowered,
Till the scent it gives
Makes faint with too much sweet these heavy-winged
thieves:

Sound of vernal showers
   On the twinkling grass,
Rain-awakened flowers,
   All that ever was
Joyous, and clear, and fresh, thy music doth surpass.

Teach us, sprite or bird,
   What sweet thoughts are thine:
I have never heard
   Praise of love or wine
That panted forth a flood of rapture so divine.

Chorus hymeneal,
   Or triumphal chaunt,
Matched with thine would be all
   But an empty vaunt—
A thing wherein we feel there is some hidden want.

What objects are the fountains
   Of thy happy strain?
What fields, or waves, or mountains?
   What shapes of sky or plain?
What love of thine own kind? what ignorance of pain?

With thy clear keen joyance
   Languor cannot be:
Shadow of annoyance
   Never came near thee:
Thou lovest; but ne'er knew love's sad satiety.

Waking or asleep,
   Thou of death must deem
Things more true and deep
   Than we mortals dream,
Or how could thy notes flow in such a crystal stream?

We look before and after,
   And pine for what is not:
Our sincerest laughter
   With some pain is fraught;
Our sweetest songs are those that tell of saddest thought.

Yet if we could scorn
Hate, and pride, and fear;
If we were things born
Not to shed a tear,
I know not how thy joy we ever should come near.

Better than all measures
Of delightful sound,
Better than all treasures
That in books are found,
Thy skill to poet were, thou scorner of the ground!

Teach me half the gladness
That thy brain must know,
Such harmonious madness
From my lips would flow,
The world should listen then, as I am listening now.

Percy Bysshe Shelley [1792–1822]

THE STORMY PETREL

A THOUSAND miles from land are we,
Tossing about on the roaring sea,—
From billow to bounding billow cast,
Like fleecy snow on the stormy blast.
The sails are scattered abroad like weeds;
The strong masts shake like quivering reeds;
The mighty cables and iron chains,
The hull, which all earthly strength disdains,—
They strain and they crack; and hearts like stone
Their natural, hard, proud strength disown.

Up and down!—up and down!
From the base of the wave to the billow's crown,
And amidst the flashing and feathery foam
The stormy petrel finds a home,—
A home, if such a place may be
For her who lives on the wide, wide sea,
On the craggy ice, in the frozen air,
And only seeketh her rocky lair

To warm her young, and to teach them to spring
At once o'er the waves on their stormy wing!

O'er the deep!—o'er the deep!
Where the whale and the shark and the swordfish sleep,—
Outflying the blast and the driving rain,
The petrel telleth her tale—in vain;
For the mariner curseth the warning bird
Which bringeth him news of the storm unheard!
Ah! thus does the prophet, of good or ill,
Meet hate from the creatures he serveth still;
Yet he ne'er falters,—so, petrel, spring
Once more o'er the waves on thy stormy wing!

Bryan Waller Procter [1787–1874]

THE FIRST SWALLOW

THE gorse is yellow on the heath,
    The banks with speedwell flowers are gay,
The oaks are budding, and, beneath,
The hawthorn soon will bear the wreath,
    The silver wreath, of May.

The welcome guest of settled Spring,
    The swallow, too, has come at last;
Just at sunset, when thrushes sing,
I saw her dash with rapid wing,
    And hailed her as she passed.

Come, summer visitant, attach
    To my reed roof your nest of clay,
And let my ear your music catch,
Low twittering underneath the thatch
    At the gray dawn of day.

Charlotte Smith [1749–1806]

TO A SWALLOW BUILDING UNDER OUR EAVES

THOU too hast traveled, little fluttering thing,—
Hast seen the world, and now thy weary wing

Thou too must rest.
But much, my little bird, could'st thou but tell,
I'd give to know why here thou lik'st so well
To build thy nest.

For thou hast passed fair places in thy flight;
A world lay all beneath thee where to light;
And, strange thy taste,
Of all the varied scenes that met thine eye,
Of all the spots for building 'neath the sky,
To choose this waste!

Did fortune try thee?—was thy little purse
Perchance run low, and thou, afraid of worse,
Felt here secure?
Ah, no! thou need'st not gold, thou happy one!
Thou know'st it not. Of all God's creatures, man
Alone is poor.

What was it, then?—some mystic turn of thought,
Caught under German eaves, and hither brought,
Marring thine eye
For the world's loveliness, till thou art grown
A sober thing that dost but mope and moan,
Not knowing why?

Nay, if thy mind be sound, I need not ask,
Since here I see thee working at thy task
With wing and beak.
A well-laid scheme doth that small head contain,
At which thou work'st, brave bird, with might and main,
Nor more need'st seek.

In truth, I rather take it thou hast got
By instinct wise much sense about thy lot,
And hast small care
Whether an Eden or a desert be
Thy home, so thou remain'st alive, and free
To skim the air.

God speed thee, pretty bird! May thy small nest
With little ones all in good time be blest.

I love thee much;
For well thou managest that life of thine,
While I—oh, ask not what I do with mine!
Would I were such!
Jane Welsh Carlyle [1801–1866]

CHIMNEY SWALLOWS

I SLEPT in an old homestead by the sea:
  And in their chimney nest,
At night the swallows told home-lore to me,
  As to a friendly guest.

A liquid twitter, low, confiding, glad,
  From many glossy throats,
Was all the voice; and yet its accents had
  A poem's golden notes.

Quaint legends of the fireside and the shore,
  And sounds of festal cheer,
And tones of those whose tasks of love are o'er,
  Were breathed into mine ear;

And wondrous lyrics, felt but never sung,
  The heart's melodious bloom;
And histories, whose perfumes long have clung
  About each hallowed room.

I heard the dream of lovers, as they found
  At last their hour of bliss,
And fear and pain and long suspense were drowned
  In one heart-healing kiss.

I heard the lullaby of babes, that grew
  To sons and daughters fair;
And childhood's angels, singing as they flew,
  And sobs of secret prayer.

I heard the voyagers who seemed to sail
  Into the sapphire sky,
And sad, weird voices in the autumn gale,
  As the swift ships went by;

And sighs suppressed and converse soft and low
    About the sufferer's bed,
And what is uttered when the stricken know
    That the dear one is dead;

And steps of those who, in the Sabbath light,
    Muse with transfigured face;
And hot lips pressing, through the long, dark night,
    The pillow's empty place;

And fervent greetings of old friends, whose path
    In youth had gone apart,
But to each other brought life's aftermath,
    With uncorroded heart.

The music of the seasons touched the strain,
    Bird-joy and laugh of flowers,
The orchard's bounty and the yellow grain,
    Snow storm and sunny showers;

And secrets of the soul that doubts and yearns
    And gropes in regions dim,
Till, meeting Christ with raptured eye, discerns
    Its perfect life in Him.

So, thinking of the Master and his tears,
    And how the birds are kept,
I sank in arms that folded me from fears,
    And like an infant, slept.

Horatio Nelson Powers [1826–1890]

ITYLUS

SWALLOW, my sister, O sister swallow,
    How can thine heart be full of the spring?
      A thousand summers are over and dead.
What hast thou found in the spring to follow?
    What hast thou found in thine heart to sing?
      What wilt thou do when the summer is shed?

O swallow, sister, O fair swift swallow,
  Why wilt thou fly after spring to the south,
    The soft south whither thine heart is set?
Shall not the grief of the old time follow?
  Shall not the song thereof cleave to thy mouth?
    Hast thou forgotten ere I forget?

Sister, my sister, O fleet sweet swallow,
  Thy way is long to the sun and the south;
    But I, fulfilled of my heart's desire,
Shedding my song upon height, upon hollow,
  From tawny body and sweet small mouth
    Feed the heart of the night with fire.

I the nightingale all spring through,
  O swallow, sister, O changing swallow,
    All spring through till the spring be done,
Clothed with the light of the night on the dew,
  Sing, while the hours and the wild birds follow,
    Take flight and follow and find the sun.

Sister, my sister, O soft light swallow,
  Though all things feast in the spring's guest-chamber,
    How hast thou heart to be glad thereof yet?
For where thou fliest I shall not follow,
  Till life forget and death remember,
    Till thou remember and I forget.

Swallow, my sister, O singing swallow,
  I know not how thou hast heart to sing.
    Hast thou the heart? is it all passed over?
Thy lord the summer is good to follow,
  And fair the feet of thy lover the spring:
    But what wilt thou say to the spring thy lover?

O swallow, sister, O fleeting swallow,
  My heart in me is a molten ember
    And over my head the waves have met.
But thou wouldst tarry or I would follow
  Could I forget or thou remember,
    Couldst thou remember and I forget.

O sweet stray sister, O shifting swallow,
  The heart's division divideth us.
    Thy heart is light as a leaf of a tree;
But mine goes forth among sea-gulfs hollow
  To the place of the slaying of Itylus,
    The feast of Daulis, the Thracian sea.

O swallow, sister, O rapid swallow,
  I pray thee sing not a little space.
    Are not the roofs and the lintels wet?
The woven web that was plain to follow,
  The small slain body, the flower-like face,
    Can I remember if thou forget?

O sister, sister, thy first-begotten!
  The hands that cling and the feet that follow,
    The voice of the child's blood crying yet,
Who hath remembered me ? who hath forgotten ?
  Thou hast forgotten, O summer swallow,
    But the world shall end when I forget.

Algernon Charles Swinburne [1837–1909]

THE THROSTLE

"Summer is coming, summer is coming,
  I know it, I know it, I know it.
Light again, leaf again, life again, love again,"
  Yes, my wild little Poet.

Sing the new year in under the blue.
  Last year you sang it as gladly.
"New, new, new, new!" Is it then *so* new
  That you should carol so madly?

"Love again, song again, nest again, young again,"
  Never a prophet so crazy!
And hardly a daisy as yet, little friend,
  See, there is hardly a daisy.

"Here again, here, here, here, happy year!"
  O warble unchidden, unbidden!
Summer is coming, is coming, my dear,
  And all the winters are hidden.

Alfred Tennyson [1809–1892]

OVERFLOW

Hush!
With sudden gush
As from a fountain, sings in yonder bush
  The Hermit Thrush.

Hark!
Did ever Lark
With swifter scintillations fling the spark
  That fires the dark?

Again,
Like April rain
Of mist and sunshine mingled, moves the strain
  O'er hill and plain.

Strong
As love, O Song,
In flame or torrent sweep through Life along,
  O'er grief and wrong.

John Banister Tabb [1845–1909]

JOY-MONTH

Oh, hark to the brown thrush! hear how he sings!
  How he pours the dear pain of his gladness!
What a gush! and from out what golden springs!
  What a rage of how sweet madness!

And golden the buttercup blooms by the way,
  A song of the joyous ground;
While the melody rained from yonder spray
  Is a blossom in fields of sound.

How glisten the eyes of the happy leaves!
    How whispers each blade, "I am blest!"
Rosy Heaven his lips to flowered earth gives,
    With the costliest bliss of his breast.

Pour, pour of the wine of thy heart, O Nature!
    By cups of field and of sky,
By the brimming soul of every creature!—
    Joy-mad, dear Mother, am I.

Tongues, tongues for my joy, for my joy! more tongues!—
    Oh, thanks to the thrush on the tree,
To the sky, and to all earth's blooms and songs!
    They utter the heart in me.

                        David Atwood Wasson [1823–1887]

MY THRUSH

        ALL through the sultry hours of June,
        From morning blithe to golden noon,
            And till the star of evening climbs
        The gray-blue East, a world too soon,
            There sings a Thrush amid the limes.

        God's poet, hid in foliage green,
        Sings endless songs, himself unseen;
            Right seldom come his silent times.
        Linger, ye summer hours serene!
            Sing on, dear Thrush, amid the limes!

        Nor from these confines wander out,
        Where the old gun, bucolic lout,
            Commits all day his murderous crimes:
        Though cherries ripe are sweet, no doubt,
            Sweeter thy song amid the limes.

        May I not dream God sends thee there,
        Thou mellow angel of the air,
            Even to rebuke my earthlier rhymes
        With music's soul, all praise and prayer?
            Is that thy lesson in the limes?

Closer to God art thou than I:
His minstrel thou, whose brown wings fly
        Through silent ether's summer climes.
    Ah, never may thy music die!
        Sing on, dear Thrush, amid the limes!

                    Mortimer Collins [1827–1876]

"BLOW SOFTLY, THRUSH"

BLOW softly, thrush, upon the hush
That makes the least leaf loud,
Blow, wild of heart, remote, apart
From all the vocal crowd,
Apart, remote, a spirit note
That dances meltingly afloat,
Blow faintly, thrush!
And build the green-hid waterfall
I hated for its beauty, and all
The unloved vernal rapture and flush,
The old forgotten lonely time,
Delicate thrush!
Spring's at the prime, the world's in chime,
And my love is listening nearly;
O lightly blow the ancient woe,
Flute of the wood, blow clearly!
Blow, she is here, and the world all dear,
Melting flute of the hush,
Old sorrow estranged, enriched, sea-changed,
Breathe it, veery thrush!

                    Joseph Russell Taylor [1868–1933]

THE BLACK VULTURE

ALOOF within the day's enormous dome,
He holds unshared the silence of the sky.
Far down his bleak, relentless eyes descry
The eagle's empire and the falcon's home—
Far down, the galleons of sunset roam;
His hazards on the sea of morning lie;
Serene, he hears the broken tempest sigh
Where cold sierras gleam like scattered foam.
And least of all he holds the human swarm—
Unwitting now that envious men prepare
To make their dream and its fulfillment one

When, poised above the caldrons of the storm,
Their hearts, contemptuous of death, shall dare
His roads between the thunder and the sun.

George Sterling [1869–1926]

WILD GEESE

How oft against the sunset sky or moon
    I watched that moving zigzag of spread wings
In unforgotten Autumns gone too soon,
    In unforgotten Springs!
Creatures of desolation, far they fly
    Above all lands bound by the curling foam;
In misty fens, wild moors and trackless sky
    These wild things have their home.
They know the tundra of Siberian coasts.
    And tropic marshes by the Indian seas;
They know the clouds and night and starry hosts
    From Crux to Pleiades.
Dark flying rune against the western glow—
    It tells the sweep and loneliness of things,
Symbol of Autumns vanished long ago.
    Symbol of coming Springs!

Frederick Peterson [1859–1938]

TO A WATERFOWL

WHITHER, midst falling dew,
While glow the heavens with the last steps of day,
Far, through their rosy depths, dost thou pursue
    Thy solitary way?

    Vainly the fowler's eye
Might mark thy distant flight to do thee wrong,
As, darkly painted on the crimson sky,
    Thy figure floats along.

    Seek'st thou the plashy brink
Of weedy lake, or marge of river wide,
Or where the rocking billows rise and sink
    On the chafed ocean-side?

    There is a Power whose care
Teaches thy way along that pathless coast,—
The desert and illimitable air,—
    Lone wandering, but not lost.

All day thy wings have fanned
At that far height, the cold, thin atmosphere,
Yet stoop not, weary, to the welcome land,
    Though the dark night is near.

And soon that toil shall end;
Soon shalt thou find a summer home, and rest,
And scream among thy fellows; reeds shall bend.
    Soon, o'er thy sheltered nest.

Thou'rt gone, the abyss of heaven
Hath swallowed up thy form; yet, on my heart
Deeply hath sunk the lesson thou hast given,
    And shall not soon depart.

He who, from zone to zone,
Guides through the boundless sky thy certain flight,
In the long way that I must tread alone,
    Will lead my steps aright.

William Cullen Bryant [1794–1878]

THE WOOD–DOVE'S NOTE

MEADOWS with yellow cowslips all aglow,
    Glory of sunshine on the uplands bare,
And faint and far, with sweet elusive flow,
    The Wood-dove's plaintive call,
               "O where! where! where!"

Straight with old Omar in the almond grove
    From whitening boughs I breathe the odors rare
And hear the princess mourning for her love
    With sad unwearied plaint,
               "O where! where! where!"

New madrigals in each soft pulsing throat—
    New life upleaping to the brooding air—
Still the heart answers to that questing note,
    "Soul of the vanished years,
            O where! where! where!"

Emily Huntington Miller [1833–1913]

THE SEA

SONG FOR ALL SEAS, ALL SHIPS

I

To-day a rude brief recitative,
Of ships sailing the seas, each with its special flag or ship-
 signal,
Of unnamed heroes in the ships—of waves spreading and
 spreading far as the eye can reach,
Of dashing spray, and the winds piping and blowing,
And out of these a chant for the sailors of all nations,
Fitful, like a surge.

Of sea-captains young or old, and the mates, and of all in-
 trepid sailors,
Of the few, very choice, taciturn, whom fate can never
 surprise nor death dismay,
Picked sparingly without noise by thee, old ocean, chosen by
 thee,
Thou sea that pickest and cullest the race in time, and unit-
 est nations,
Suckled by thee, old husky nurse, embodying thee,
Indomitable, untamed as thee.

(Ever the heroes on water or on land, by ones or twos appearing,
Ever the stock preserved and never lost, though rare, enough
 for seed preserved.)

II

Flaunt out, O sea, your separate flags of nations!
Flaunt out visible as ever the various ship-signals!
But do you reserve especially for yourself and for the soul of
 man one flag above all the rest,
A spiritual woven signal for all nations, emblem of man elate
 above death,

Token of all brave captains and all intrepid sailors and mates,
And all that went down doing their duty,
Reminiscent of them, twined from all intrepid captains
    young or old,
A pennant universal, subtly waving all time, o'er all brave
    sailors,
All seas, all ships.

                            Walt Whitman [1819-1892]

STANZAS

From " The Triumph of Time "

I WILL go back to the great sweet mother,—
    Mother and lover of men, the Sea.
I will go down to her, I and none other,
    Close with her, kiss her, and mix her with me;
Cling to her, strive with her, hold her fast;
O fair white mother, in days long past
Born without sister, born without brother,
    Set free my soul as thy soul is free.

O fair green-girdled mother of mine,
    Sea, that art clothed with the sun and the rain,
Thy sweet hard kisses are strong like wine,
    Thy large embraces are keen like pain.
Save me and hide me with all thy waves,
Find me one grave of thy thousand graves,
Those pure cold populous graves of thine,
    Wrought without hand in a world without stain.

I shall sleep, and move with the moving ships,
    Change as the winds change, veer in the tide;
My lips will feast on the foam of thy lips,
    I shall rise with thy rising, with thee subside;
Sleep, and not know if she be, if she were,
Filled full with life to the eyes and hair,
As a rose is fulfilled to the rose-leaf tips
    With splendid summer and perfume and pride.

This woven raiment of nights and days,
    Were it once cast off and unwound from me,
Naked and glad would I walk in thy ways,
    Alive and aware of thy waves and thee;
Clear of the whole world, hidden at home,
Clothed with the green, and crowned with the foam,
A pulse of the life of thy straits and bays,
    A vein in the heart of the streams of the Sea.

Fair mother, fed with the lives of men,
    Thou art subtle and cruel of heart, men say;
Thou hast taken, and shalt not render again;
    Thou art full of thy dead, and cold as they.
But death is the worst that comes of thee;
Thou art fed with our dead, O Mother, O Sea,
But when hast thou fed on our hearts? or when
    Having given us love, hast thou taken away?

O tender-hearted, O perfect lover,
    Thy lips are bitter, and sweet thine heart.
The hopes that hurt and the dreams that hover,
    Shall they not vanish away and apart?
But thou, thou art sure, thou art older than earth;
Thou art strong for death and fruitful of birth;
Thy depths conceal and thy gulfs discover;
    From the first thou wert; in the end thou art.

                    Algernon Charles Swinburne [1837–1909]

THE SEA

From " Childe Harold's Pilgrimage "

THERE is a pleasure in the pathless woods,
There is a rapture on the lonely shore,
There is society where none intrudes
By the deep Sea, and music in its roar:
I love not Man the less, but Nature more,
From these our interviews, in which I steal
From all I may be, or have been before,
To mingle with the Universe, and feel
What I can ne'er express, yet can not all conceal.

Roll on, thou deep and dark blue Ocean, roll!
Ten thousand fleets sweep over thee in vain;
Man marks the earth with ruin, his control
Stops with the shore; upon the watery plain
The wrecks are all thy deed, nor doth remain
A shadow of man's ravage, save his own,
When, for a moment, like a drop of rain,
He sinks into thy depths with bubbling groan,
Without a grave, unknelled, uncoffined, and unknown.

His steps are not upon thy paths, thy fields
Are not a spoil for him,—thou dost arise
And shake him from thee; the vile strength he wields
For earth's destruction thou dost all despise,
Spurning him from thy bosom to the skies,
And send'st him, shivering in thy playful spray
And howling, to his Gods, where haply lies
His petty hope in some near port or bay,
And dashest him again to earth:—there let him lay.

The armaments which thunderstrike the walls
Of rock-built cities, bidding nations quake
And monarchs tremble in their capitals,
The oak leviathans, whose huge ribs make
Their clay creator the vain title take
Of lord of thee and arbiter of war,—
These are thy toys, and, as the snowy flake,
They melt into thy yeast of waves, which mar
Alike the Armada's pride or spoils of Trafalgar.

Thy shores are empires, changed in all save thee;—
Assyria, Greece, Rome, Carthage, what are they?
Thy waters washed them power while they were free,
And many a tyrant since; their shores obey
The stranger, slave, or savage; their decay
Has dried up realms to deserts:—not so thou;
Unchangeable save to thy wild waves' play,
Time writes no wrinkle on thine azure brow;
Such as creation's dawn beheld, thou rollest now.

Thou glorious mirror, where the Almighty's form
Glasses itself in tempests; in all time,
Calm or convulsed,—in breeze, or gale, or storm,
Icing the pole, or in the torrid clime
Dark-heaving;—boundless, endless, and sublime,—
The image of Eternity,—the throne
Of the Invisible; even from out thy slime
The monsters of the deep are made; each zone
Obeys thee; thou goest forth, dread, fathomless, alone.

And I have loved thee, Ocean! and my joy
Of youthful sports was on thy breast to be
Borne, like thy bubbles, onward. From a boy
I wantoned with thy breakers,—they to me
Were a delight; and if the freshening sea
Made them a terror, 'twas a pleasing fear;
For I was as it were a child of thee,
And trusted to thy billows far and near,
And laid my hand upon thy mane,—as I do here.

George Gordon Byron [1788–1824]

ON THE SEA

It keeps eternal whisperings around
    Desolate shores, and with its mighty swell
    Gluts twice ten thousand caverns, till the spell
Of Hecate leaves them their old shadowy sound.
Often 'tis in such gentle temper found,
    That scarcely will the very smallest shell
    Be moved for days from whence it sometime fell,
When last the winds of heaven were unbound.
Oh ye! who have your eye-balls vexed and tired,
    Feast them upon the wideness of the Sea;
        Oh ye! whose ears are dinned with uproar rude,
    Or fed too much with cloying melody,—
        Sit ye near some old cavern's mouth, and brood
Until ye start, as if the sea-nymphs quired!

John Keats [1795–1821]

"WITH SHIPS THE SEA WAS SPRINKLED"

WITH ships the sea was sprinkled far and nigh,
Like stars in heaven, and joyously it showed;
Some lying fast at anchor in the road,
Some veering up and down, one knew not why.
A goodly vessel did I then espy
Come like a giant from a haven broad;
And lustily along the bay she strode,
Her tackling rich, and of apparel high.
This ship was naught to me, nor I to her,
Yet I pursued her with a lover's look;
This ship to all the rest did I prefer:
When will she turn, and whither? She will brook
No tarrying; where she comes the winds must stir:
On went she,—and due north her journey took.

William Wordsworth [1770–1850]

A SONG OF DESIRE

THOU dreamer with the million moods,
    Of restless heart like me,
Lay thy white hands against my breast
    And cool its pain, O Sea!

O wanderer of the unseen paths,
    Restless of heart as I,
Blow hither, from thy caves of blue,
    Wind of the healing sky!

O treader of the fiery way,
    With passionate heart like mine,
Hold to my lips thy healthful cup
    Brimmed with its blood-red wine!

O countless watchers of the night,
    Of sleepless heart like me,
Pour your white beauty in my soul,
    Till I grow calm as ye!

O sea, O sun, O wind and stars,
(O hungry heart that longs!)
Feed my starved lips with life, with love,
And touch my tongue with songs!

Frederic Lawrence Knowles [1869–1905]

THE PINES AND THE SEA

BEYOND the low marsh-meadows and the beach,
Seen through the hoary trunks of windy pines,
The long blue level of the ocean shines.
The distant surf, with hoarse, complaining speech,
Out from its sandy barrier seems to reach;
And while the sun behind the woods declines,
The moaning sea with sighing boughs combines,
And waves and pines make answer, each to each.
O melancholy soul, whom far and near,
In life, faith, hope, the same sad undertone
Pursues from thought to thought! thou needs must hear
An old refrain, too much, too long thine own:
'Tis thy mortality infects thine ear;
The mournful strain was in thyself alone.

Christopher Pearse Cranch [1813–1892]

SEA FEVER

I MUST go down to the seas again, to the lonely sea and the
sky,
And all I ask is a tall ship and a star to steer her by;
And the wheel's kick and the wind's song and the white
sail's shaking,
And a gray mist on the sea's face, and a gray dawn breaking.

I must go down to the seas again, for the call of the running
tide
Is a wild call and a clear call that may not be denied;
And all I ask is a windy day with the white clouds flying,
And the flung spray and the blown spume, and the sea-
gulls crying.

I must go down to the seas again, to the vagrant gipsy life,
To the gull's way and the whale's way where the wind's
like a whetted knife;
And all I ask is a merry yarn from a laughing fellow-rover,
And quiet sleep and a sweet dream when the long trick's
over.

John Masefield [1878–

HASTINGS MILL

As I went down by Hastings Mill I lingered in my going
To smell the smell of piled-up deals and feel the salt wind
blowing,
To hear the cables fret and creak and the ropes stir and sigh
(Shipmate, my shipmate!) as in days gone by.

As I went down by Hastings Mill I saw a ship there lying,
About her tawny yards the little clouds of sunset flying;
And half I took her for the ghost of one I used to know
(Shipmate, my shipmate!) many years ago.

As I went down by Hastings Mill I saw while I stood dream-
ing
The flicker of her riding light along the ripples streaming,
The bollards where we made her fast and the berth where
she did lie
(Shipmate, my shipmate!) in the days gone by.

As I went down by Hastings Mill I heard a fellow singing,
Chipping off the deep sea rust above the tide a-swinging,
And well I knew the queer old tune and well the song he sung
(Shipmate, my shipmate!) when the world was young.

And past the rowdy Union Wharf, and by the still tide
sleeping,
To a randy dandy deep sea tune my heart in time was keep-
ing,
To the thin far sound of a shadowy watch a-hauling,
And the voice of one I knew across the high tide calling
(Shipmate, my shipmate!) and the late dusk falling!

Cecily Fox-Smith [1882–

"A WET SHEET AND A FLOWING SEA"

A WET sheet and a flowing sea,
  A wind that follows fast,
And fills the white and rustling sail,
  And bends the gallant mast;
And bends the gallant mast, my boys,
  While, like the eagle free,
Away the good ship flies, and leaves
  Old England on the lee.

O for a soft and gentle wind!
  I heard a fair one cry;
But give to me the snoring breeze
  And white waves heaving high;
And white waves heaving high, my boys,
  The good ship tight and free—
The world of waters is our home,
  And merry men are we.

There's tempest in yon hornèd moon,
  And lightning in yon cloud;
And hark the music, mariners!
  The wind is piping loud;
The wind is piping loud, my boys,
  The lightning flashes free—
While the hollow oak our palace is,
  Our heritage the sea.

             Allan Cunningham [1784–1842]

THE SEA

THE sea! the sea! the open sea!
The blue, the fresh, the ever free!
Without a mark, without a bound,
It runneth the earth's wide regions round;
It plays with the clouds; it mocks the skies;
Or like a cradled creature lies.

I'm on the sea! I'm on the sea!
I am where I would ever be;

With the blue above, and the blue below,
And silence wheresoe'er I go;
If a storm should come and awake the deep,
What matter? *I* shall ride and sleep.

I love, O, how I love to ride
On the fierce, foaming, bursting tide,
When every mad wave drowns the moon
Or whistles aloft his tempest tune,
And tells how goeth the world below,
And why the sou'west blasts do blow.

I never was on the dull, tame shore,
But I loved the great sea more and more,
And backwards flew to her billowy breast,
Like a bird that seeketh its mother's nest;
And a mother she was, and is, to me;
For I was born on the open sea!

The waves were white, and red the morn,
In the noisy hour when I was born;
And the whale it whistled, the porpoise rolled,
And the dolphins bared their backs of gold;
And never was heard such an outcry wild
As welcomed to life the ocean-child!

I've lived since then, in calm and strife,
Full fifty summers, a sailor's life,
With wealth to spend and a power to range,
But never have sought nor sighed for change;
And Death, whenever he comes to me,
Shall come on the wild, unbounded sea!

Bryan Waller Procter [1787–1874]

SAILOR'S SONG

From "Death's Jest-Book"

To sea, to sea! The calm is o'er;
    The wanton water leaps in sport,
And rattles down the pebbly shore;
    The dolphin wheels, the sea-cows snort,

And unseen mermaids' pearly song
Comes bubbling up, the weeds among.
  Fling broad the sail, dip deep the oar;
    To sea, to sea! the calm is o'er.

To sea, to sea! our wide-winged bark
  Shall billowy cleave its sunny way,
And with its shadow, fleet and dark,
  Break the caved Tritons' azure day,
Like mighty eagle soaring light
O'er antelopes on Alpine height.
    The anchor heaves, the ship swings free,
    The sails swell full.   To sea, to sea!

Thomas Lovell Beddoes [1803–1849]

"A LIFE ON THE OCEAN WAVE"

A LIFE on the ocean wave,
  A home on the rolling deep,
Where the scattered waters rave,
  And the winds their revels keep!
Like an eagle caged, I pine
  On this dull, unchanging shore:
Oh! give me the flashing brine,
  The spray and the tempest's roar!

Once more on the deck I stand
  Of my own swift-gliding craft:
Set sail! farewell to the land!
  The gale follows fair abaft.
We shoot through the sparkling foam
  Like an ocean-bird set free;—
Like the ocean-bird, our home
  We'll find far out on the sea.

The land is no longer in view,
  The clouds have begun to frown;
But with a stout vessel and crew,
  We'll say, Let the storm come down!

And the song of our hearts shall be,
    While the winds and the waters rave,
A home on the rolling sea!
    A life on the ocean wave!

Epes Sargent [1813–1880]

TACKING SHIP OFF SHORE

THE weather-leech of the topsail shivers,
    The bowlines strain, and the lee-shrouds slacken,
The braces are taut, the lithe boom quivers,
    And the waves with the coming squall-cloud blacken.

Open one point on the weather-bow,
    Is the lighthouse tall on Fire Island Head.
There's a shade of doubt on the captain's brow,
    And the pilot watches the heaving lead.

I stand at the wheel, and with eager eye
    To sea and to sky and to shore I gaze,
Till the muttered order of "Full and by!"
    Is suddenly changed for "Full for stays!"

The ship bends lower before the breeze,
    As her broadside fair to the blast she lays;
And she swifter springs to the rising seas,
    As the pilot calls, "Stand by for stays!"

It is silence all, as each in his place,
    With the gathered coil in his hardened hands,
By tack and bowline, by sheet and brace,
    Waiting the watchword impatient stands.

And the light on Fire Island Head draws near,
    As, trumpet-winged, the pilot's shout
From his post on the bowsprit's heel I hear,
    With the welcome call of "Ready! About!"

No time to spare!   It is touch and go;
    And the captain growls, "Down helm! hard down!"
As my weight on the whirling spokes I throw,
    While heaven grows black with the storm-cloud's frown.

High o'er the knight-heads flies the spray,
　　As we meet the shock of the plunging sea;
And my shoulder stiff to the wheel I lay,
　　As I answer, "Ay, ay, sir!　Ha-a-rd a-lee!"

With the swerving leap of a startled steed
　　The ship flies fast in the eye of the wind,
The dangerous shoals on the lee recede,
　　And the headland white we have left behind.

The topsails flutter, the jibs collapse,
　　And belly and tug at the groaning cleats;
The spanker slats, and the mainsail flaps;
　　And thunders the order, "Tacks and sheets!"

Mid the rattle of blocks and the tramp of the crew,
　　Hisses the rain of the rushing squall:
The sails are aback from clew to clew,
　　And now is the moment for "Mainsail, haul!"

And the heavy yards, like a baby's toy,
　　By fifty strong arms are swiftly swung:
She holds her way, and I look with joy
　　For the first white spray o'er the bulwarks flung.

"Let go, and haul!"　'Tis the last command,
　　And the head-sails fill to the blast once more:
Astern and to leeward lies the land,
　　With its breakers white on the shingly shore.

What matters the reef, or the rain, or the squall?
　　I steady the helm for the open sea;
The first mate clamors, "Belay, there, all!"
　　And the captain's breath once more comes free.

And so off shore let the good ship fly;
　　Little care I how the gusts may blow,
In my fo'castle bunk, in a jacket dry.
　　Eight bells have struck, and my watch is below.

Walter Mitchell [1826–1908]

IN OUR BOAT

STARS trembling o'er us and sunset before us,
　　Mountains in shadow and forests asleep;
Down the dim river we float on forever,
　　Speak not, ah, breathe not—there's peace on the deep.

Come not, pale sorrow, flee till to-morrow;
　　Rest softly falling o'er eyelids that weep;
While down the river we float on forever,
　　Speak not, ah, breathe not—there's peace on the deep.

As the waves cover the depths we glide over,
　　So let the past in forgetfulness sleep,
While down the river we float on forever,
　　Speak not, ah, breathe not—there's peace on the deep.

Heaven shine above us, bless all that love us;
　　All whom we love in thy tenderness keep!
While down the river we float on forever,
　　Speak not, ah, breathe not—there's peace on the deep.
　　　　　　Dinah Maria Mulock Craik [1826–1887]

POOR JACK

GO, patter to lubbers and swabs, do ye see,
　　'Bout danger, and fear, and the like;
A water-tight boat and good sea-room for me,
　　And it ain't to a little I'll strike.
Though the tempest topgallant-masts smack smooth should
　　　　smite,
　　And shiver each splinter of wood,—
Clear the deck, stow the yards, and house everything tight,
　　And under reefed foresail we'll scud:
Avast! nor don't think me a milksop so soft
　　To be taken for trifles aback;
For they say there's a Providence sits up aloft,
　　To keep watch for the life of poor Jack!

I heard our good chaplain palaver one day
    About souls, heaven, mercy, and such;
And, my timbers! what lingo he'd coil and belay;
    Why, 'twas just all as one as High Dutch;
For he said how a sparrow can't founder, d'ye see,
    Without orders that come down below;
And a many fine things that proved clearly to me
    That Providence takes us in tow:
"For," says he, "do you mind me, let storms e'er so oft
    Take the topsails of sailors aback,
There's a sweet little cherub that sits up aloft,
    To keep watch for the life of poor Jack!"

I said to our Poll,—for, d'ye see, she would cry,
    When last we weighed anchor for sea,—
"What argufies sniveling and piping your eye?
    Why, what a blamed fool you must be!
Can't you see, the world's wide, and there's room for us
      all,
    Both for seamen and lubbers ashore?
And if to old Davy I should go, friend Poll,
    You never will hear of me more.
What then? All's a hazard: come, don't be so soft:
    Perhaps I may laughing come back;
For, d'ye see, there's a cherub sits smiling aloft,
    To keep watch for the life of poor Jack!"

D'ye mind me, a sailor should be every inch
    All as one as a piece of the ship,
And with her brave the world, without offering to flinch
    From the moment the anchor's a-trip.
As for me, in all weathers, all times, sides, and ends,
    Naught's a trouble from duty that springs,
For my heart is my Poll's, and my rhino's my friend's,
    And as for my will, 'tis the king's.
Even when my time comes, ne'er believe me so soft
    As for grief to be taken aback;
For the same little cherub that sits up aloft
    Will look out a good berth for poor Jack!
               Charles Dibdin [1745–1814]

"ROCKED IN THE CRADLE OF THE DEEP"

ROCKED in the cradle of the deep
I lay me down in peace to sleep;
Secure I rest upon the wave,
For Thou, O Lord! hast power to save.
I know Thou wilt not slight my call,
For Thou dost mark the sparrow's fall;
And calm and peaceful shall I sleep,
Rocked in the cradle of the deep.

When in the dead of night I lie
And gaze upon the trackless sky,
The star-bespangled heavenly scroll,
The boundless waters as they roll,—
I feel Thy wondrous power to save
From perils of the stormy wave:
Rocked in the cradle of the deep,
I calmly rest and soundly sleep.

And such the trust that still were mine,
Though stormy winds swept o'er the brine,
Or though the tempest's fiery breath
Roused me from sleep to wreck and death.
In ocean cave, still safe with Thee
The germ of immortality!
And calm and peaceful shall I sleep,
Rocked in the cradle of the deep.

Emma Hart Willard [1787–1870]

OUTWARD

WHITHER away, O Sailor! say?
Under the night, under the day,
Yearning sail and flying spray
Out of the black into the blue,
Where are the great Winds bearing you?

Never port shall lift for me
Into the sky, out of the sea!

Into the blue or into the black,
Onward, outward, never back!
Something mighty and weird and dim
Calls me under the ocean rim!

Sailor under sun and moon,
'Tis the ocean's fatal rune.
Under yon far rim of sky
Twice ten thousand others lie.
Love is sweet and home is fair,
And your mother calls you there.

Onward, outward I must go
Where the mighty currents flow.
Home is anywhere for me
On this purple-tented sea.
Star and Wind and Sun my brothers,
Ocean one of many mothers.
Onward under sun and star
Where the weird adventures are!
Never port shall lift for me—
I am Wind and Sky and Sea!

John G. Neihardt [1881–

A PASSER-BY

WHITHER, O splendid ship, thy white sails crowding,
   Leaning across the bosom of the urgent West,
That fearest nor sea rising, nor sky clouding,
   Whither away, fair rover, and what thy quest?
   Ah! soon, when Winter has all our vales oppressed,
When skies are cold and misty, and hail is hurling,
   Wilt thou glide on the blue Pacific, or rest
In a summer haven asleep, thy white sails furling.

I there before thee, in the country that well thou knowest,
   Already arrived, am inhaling the odorous air:
I watch thee enter unerringly where thou goest,
   And anchor queen of the strange shipping there,

Thy sails for awnings spread, thy masts bare:
Nor is aught from the foaming reef to the snow-capped
    grandest
  Peak, that is over the feathery palms, more fair
Than thou, so upright, so stately and still thou standest.

And yet, O splendid ship, unhailed and nameless,
  I know not if, aiming a fancy, I rightly divine
That thou hast a purpose joyful, a courage blameless,
  Thy port assured in a happier land than mine.
  But for all I have given thee, beauty enough is thine,
As thou, aslant with trim tackle and shrouding,
  From the proud nostril curve of a prow's line
In the offing scatterest foam, thy white sails crowding.

Robert Bridges [1844-1930]

OFF RIVIÈRE DU LOUP

O SHIP incoming from the sea
  With all your cloudy tower of sail,
Dashing the water to the lee,
  And leaning grandly to the gale,

The sunset pageant in the west
  Has filled your canvas curves with rose,
And jeweled every toppling crest
  That crashes into silver snows!

You know the joy of coming home,
  After long leagues to France or Spain
You feel the clear Canadian foam
  And the gulf water heave again.

Between these somber purple hills
  That cool the sunset's molten bars,
You will go on as the wind wills,
  Beneath the river's roof of stars.

You will toss onward toward the lights
  That spangle over the lonely pier,
By hamlets glimmering on the heights,
  By level islands black and clear.

You will go on beyond the tide,
Through brimming plains of olive sedge,
Through paler shadows light and wide,
The rapids piled along the ledge.

At evening off some reedy bay
You will swing slowly on your chain,
And catch the scent of dewy hay,
Soft blowing from the pleasant plain.

Duncan Campbell Scott [1862–

CHRISTMAS AT SEA

THE sheets were frozen hard, and they cut the naked hand;
The decks were like a slide, where a seaman scarce could
　　stand;
The wind was a nor'-wester, blowing squally off the sea;
And cliffs and spouting breakers were the only things a-lee.

They heard the surf a-roaring before the break of day;
But 'twas only with the peep of light we saw how ill we lay.
We tumbled every hand on deck instanter, with a shout,
And we gave her the maintops'l, and stood by to go about.

All day we tacked and tacked between the South Head and
　　the North;
All day we hauled the frozen sheets, and got no further
　　forth;
All day as cold as charity, in bitter pain and dread,
For very life and nature we tacked from head to head.

We gave the South a wider berth, for there the tide-race
　　roared;
But every tack we made brought the North Head close
　　aboard;
So's we saw the cliffs and houses, and the breakers running
　　high,
And the coastguard in his garden, with his glass against
　　his eye.

The frost was on the village roofs as white as ocean foam;
The good red fires were burning bright in every 'longshore
    home;
The windows sparkled clear, and the chimneys volleyed out;
And I vow we sniffed the victuals as the vessel went about.

The bells upon the church were rung with a mighty jovial
    cheer;
For it's just that I should tell you how (of all days in the
    year)
This day of our adversity was blessèd Christmas morn,
And the house above the coastguard's was the house where
    I was born.

O well I saw the pleasant room, the pleasant faces there,
My mother's silver spectacles, my father's silver hair;
And well I saw the firelight, like a flight of homely elves,
Go dancing round the china-plates that stand upon the
    shelves.

And well I knew the talk they had, the talk that was of me,
Of the shadow on the household and the son that went to
    sea;
And O the wicked fool I seemed, in every kind of way,
To be here and hauling frozen ropes on blessèd Christmas
    Day.

They lit the high sea-light, and the dark began to fall.
"All hands to loose topgallant sails," I heard the captain
    call.
"By the Lord, she'll never stand it," our first mate, Jack-
    son, cried.
"It's the one way or the other, Mr. Jackson," he replied.

She staggered to her bearings, but the sails were new and
    good,
And the ship smelt up to windward, just as though she
    understood.
As the winter's day was ending, in the entry of the night,
We cleared the weary headland, and passed below the light.

And they heaved a mighty breath, every soul on board but
    me,
As they saw her nose again pointing handsome out to sea;
But all that I could think of, in the darkness and the cold,
Was just that I was leaving home and my folks were grow-
    ing old.

                Robert Louis Stevenson [1850–1894]

THE PORT O' HEART'S DESIRE

DOWN around the quay they lie, the ships that sail to
    sea,
On shore the brown-cheeked sailormen they pass the jest
    with me,
But soon their ships will sail away with winds that never
    tire,
And there's one that will be sailing to the Port o' Heart's
    Desire.

The Port o' Heart's Desire, and it's, oh, that port for me,
And that's the ship that I love best of all that sail the sea;
Its hold is filled with memories, its prow it points away
To the Port o' Heart's Desire, where I roamed a boy at
    play.

Ships that sail for gold there be, and ships that sail for
    fame,
And some were filled with jewels bright when from Cathay
    they came,
But give me still yon white sail in the sunset's mystic fire,
That the running tides will carry to the Port o' Heart's
    Desire.

It's you may have the gold and fame, and all the jewels,
    too,
And all the ships, if they were mine, I'd gladly give to you,
I'd give them all right gladly, with their gold and fame
    entire,
If you would set me down within the Port o' Heart's Desire.

Oh, speed you, white-winged ship of mine, oh, speed you to
    the sea,
Some other day, some other tide, come back again for me;
Come back with all the memories, the joys and e'en the
    pain,
And take me to the golden hills of boyhood once again.
            John S. McGroarty [1862–

ON THE QUAY

I'VE never traveled for more'n a day,
    I never was one to roam,
      But I likes to sit on the busy quay,
      Watchin' the ships that says to me—
"Always somebody goin' away,
    Somebody gettin' home."

I likes to think that the world's so wide—
    'Tis grand to be livin' there,
      Takin' a part in its goin's on. . . .
      Ah, now ye're laughin' at poor old John,
Talkin' o' works o' the world wi' pride
    As if he was doin' his share!

But laugh if ye will!   When ye're old as me
    Ye'll find 'tis a rare good plan
      To look at the world—an' love it too!—
      Though never a job are ye fit to do. . . .
Oh! 'tisn't all sorrow an' pain to see
    The work o' another man.

'Tis good when the heart grows big at last,
    Too big for trouble to fill—
      Wi' room for the things that was only stuff
      When workin' an' winnin' seemed more'n enough—
Room for the world, the world so vast,
    Wi' its peoples an' all their skill.

That's what I'm thinkin' on all the days
    I'm loafin' an' smokin' here,

An' the ships do make me think the most
  (Of readin' in books 'tis little I'd boast),—
But the ships, they carries me long, long ways,
  An' draws far places near.

I sees the things that a sailor brings,
  I hears the stories he tells. . . .
    'Tis surely a wonderful world, indeed!
    'Tis more'n the peoples can ever need!
An' I praises the Lord—to myself I sings—
  For the world in which I dwells.

An' I loves the ships more every day
  Though I never was one to roam.
    Oh! the ships is comfortin' sights to see,
      An' they means a lot when they says to me—
"Always somebody goin' away,
  Somebody gettin' home."

John Joy Bell [1871–1934]

THE FORGING OF THE ANCHOR

COME, see the Dolphin's anchor forged! 'tis at a white heat
  now—
The bellows ceased, the flames decreased; though, on the
  forge's brow,
The little flames still fitfully play through the sable mound,
And fitfully you still may see the grim smiths ranking round;
All clad in leathern panoply, their broad hands only bare,
Some rest upon their sledges here, some work the windlass
  there.

The windlass strains the tackle-chains—the black mold
  heaves below;
And red and deep, a hundred veins burst out at every throe.
It rises, roars, rends all outright—O Vulcan, what a glow!
'Tis blinding white, 'tis blasting bright—the high sun shines
  not so!
The high sun sees not, on the earth, such fiery fearful show!
The roof-ribs swarth, the candent hearth, the ruddy lurid
  row

Of smiths that stand, an ardent band, like men before the
foe!
As, quivering through his fleece of flame, the sailing monster
slow
Sinks on the anvil—all about, the faces fiery grow:
"Hurrah!" they shout, "leap out, leap out!" bang, bang!
the sledges go;
Hurrah! the jetted lightnings are hissing high and low;
A hailing fount of fire is struck at every squashing blow;
The leathern mail rebounds the hail; the rattling cinders
strow
The ground around; at every bound the sweltering fountains
flow;
And, thick and loud, the swinking crowd at every stroke
pant "ho!"

Leap out, leap out, my masters! leap out, and lay on load!
Let's forge a goodly anchor—a bower thick and broad;
For a heart of oak is hanging on every blow, I bode;
And I see the good ship riding, all in a perilous road,—
The low reef roaring on her lee; the roll of ocean poured
From stem to stern, sea after sea; the mainmast by the
board;
The bulwarks down; the rudder gone; the boats stove at the
chains;
But courage still, brave mariners—the bower yet remains!
And not an inch to flinch he deigns—save when ye pitch sky
high;
Then moves his head, as though he said, "Fear nothing—
here am I!"

Swing in your strokes in order; let foot and hand keep time;
Your blows make music sweeter far than any steeple's chime.
But while ye swing your sledges, sing, and let the burthen
be—
The anchor is the anvil king, and royal craftsmen we!
Strike in, strike in!—the sparks begin to dull their rustling
red;
Our hammers ring with sharper din—our work will soon be
sped;

Our anchor soon must change his bed of fiery rich array
For a hammock at the roaring bows, or an oozy couch of
　　clay;
Our anchor soon must change the lay of merry craftsmen
　　here
For the yeo-heave-o, and the heave-away, and the sighing
　　seamen's cheer—
When, weighing slow, at eve they go, far, far from love and
　　home;
And sobbing sweethearts, in a row, wail o'er the ocean-
　　foam.

In livid and obdurate gloom, he darkens down at last;
A shapely one he is, and strong, as e'er from cat was cast.
O trusted and trustworthy guard! if thou hadst life like me,
What pleasure would thy toils reward beneath the deep-
　　green sea!
O deep sea-diver, who might then behold such sights as
　　thou?—
The hoary monster's palaces!—Methinks what joy 'twere
　　now
To go plumb-plunging down, amid the assembly of the
　　whales,
And feel the churned sea round me boil beneath their scourg-
　　ing tails!
Then deep in tangle-woods to fight the fierce sea-unicorn,
And send him foiled and bellowing back, for all his ivory
　　horn;
To leave the subtle sworder-fish of bony blade forlorn;
And for the ghastly-grinning shark, to laugh his jaws to
　　scorn:
To leap down on the kraken's back, where 'mid Norwegian
　　isles
He lies, a lubber anchorage for sudden shallowed miles—
Till, snorting like an under-sea volcano, off he rolls;
Meanwhile to swing, a-buffeting the far astonished shoals
Of his back-browsing ocean-calves; or, haply, in a cove
Shell-strown, and consecrate of old to some Undine's love,
To find the long-haired mermaidens; or, hard by icy lands,
To wrestle with the sea-serpent, upon cerulean sands.

O broad-armed fisher of the deep! whose sports can equal
    thine?
The Dolphin weighs a thousand tons, that tugs thy cable-
    line;
And night by night 'tis thy delight, thy glory day by day,
Through sable sea and breaker white the giant game to play.
But, shamer of our little sports! forgive the name I gave:
A fisher's joy is to destroy—thine office is to save.
O lodger in the sea-kings' halls! couldst thou but understand
Whose be the white bones by thy side—or who that dripping
    band,
Slow swaying in the heaving wave, that round about thee
    bend,
With sounds like breakers in a dream blessing their ancient
    friend—
Oh, couldst thou know what heroes glide with larger steps
    round thee,
Thine iron side would swell with pride—thou'dst leap within
    the sea!

Give honor to their memories who left the pleasant strand
To shed their blood so freely for the love of fatherland—
Who left their chance of quiet age and grassy churchyard
    grave
So freely, for a restless bed amid the tossing wave!
Oh, though our anchor may not be all I have fondly sung,
Honor him for their memory whose bones he goes among!

               Samuel Ferguson [1810–1886]

DRIFTING

    My soul to-day
    Is far away,
Sailing the Vesuvian Bay;
    My wingèd boat,
    A bird afloat,
Swings round the purple peaks remote:—

    Round purple peaks
    It sails, and seeks

Blue inlets and their crystal creeks,
   Where high rocks throw,
   Through deeps below,
A duplicated golden glow.

   Far, vague, and dim,
   The mountains swim;
While on Vesuvius' misty brim,
   With outstretched hands,
   The gray smoke stands
O'erlooking the volcanic lands.

   Here Ischia smiles
   O'er liquid miles;
And yonder, bluest of the isles,
   Calm Capri waits,
   Her sapphire gates
Beguiling to her bright estates.

   I heed not, if
   My rippling skiff
Float swift or slow from cliff to cliff;
   With dreamful eyes
   My spirit lies
Under the walls of Paradise.

   Under the walls
   Where swells and falls
The Bay's deep breast at intervals,
   At peace I lie,
   Blown softly by,
A cloud upon this liquid sky.

   The day, so mild,
   Is Heaven's own child,
With Earth and Ocean reconciled;
   The airs I feel
   Around me steal
Are murmuring to the murmuring keel.

Over the rail
My hand I trail
Within the shadow of the sail,
A joy intense,
The cooling sense
Glides down my drowsy indolence.

With dreamful eyes
My spirit lies
Where Summer sings and never dies,—
O'erveiled with vines
She glows and shines
Among her future oil and wines.

Her children, hid
The cliffs amid,
Are gamboling with the gamboling kid;
Or down the walls,
With tipsy calls,
Laugh on the rocks like waterfalls.

The fisher's child,
With tresses wild,
Unto the smooth, bright sand beguiled,
With glowing lips
Sings as she skips,
Or gazes at the far-off ships.

Yon deep bark goes
Where traffic blows,
From lands of sun to lands of snows;—
This happier one,
Its course is run
From lands of snow to lands of sun.

O happy ship,
To rise and dip,
With the blue crystal at your lip!
O happy crew,
My heart with you
Sails, and sails, and sings anew!

No more, no more
The worldly shore
Upbraids me with its loud uproar!
With dreamful eyes
My spirit lies
Under the walls of Paradise!
Thomas Buchanan Read [1822–1872]

"HOW'S MY BOY?"

"Ho, sailor of the sea!
How's my boy—my boy?"
"What's your boy's name, good wife,
And in what good ship sailed he?"

"My boy John—
He that went to sea—
What care I for the ship, sailor?
My boy's my boy to me.

"You come back from sea
And not know my John?
I might as well have asked some landsman
Yonder down in the town.
There's not an ass in all the parish
But he knows my John.

"How's my boy—my boy?
And unless you let me know,
I'll swear you are no sailor,
Blue jacket or no,
Brass button or no, sailor,
Anchor and crown or no!
Sure his ship was the Jolly Briton."—
"Speak low, woman, speak low!"

"And why should I speak low, sailor,
About my own boy John?
If I was loud as I am proud
I'd sing him o'er the town!

Why should I speak low, sailor?"
"That good ship went down."

"How's my boy—my boy?
What care I for the ship, sailor,
I never was aboard her.
Be she afloat, or be she aground,
Sinking or swimming, I'll be bound,
Her owners can afford her!
I say, how's my John?"
"Every man on board went down,
Every man aboard her."

"How's my boy—my boy?
What care I for the men, sailor?
I'm not their mother—
How's my boy—my boy?
Tell me of him and no other!
How's my boy—my boy?"

Sydney Dobell [1824–1874]

THE LONG WHITE SEAM

As I came round the harbor buoy,
    The lights began to gleam,
No wave the land-locked water stirred,
    The crags were white as cream;
And I marked my love by candlelight
    Sewing her long white seam.
        It's aye sewing ashore, my dear,
            Watch and steer at sea,
        It's reef and furl, and haul the line,
            Set sail and think of thee.

I climbed to reach her cottage door;
    O sweetly my love sings!
Like a shaft of light her voice breaks forth,
    My soul to meet it springs
As the shining water leaped of old,
    When stirred by angel wings.

Aye longing to list anew,
    Awake and in my dream,
But never a song she sang like this,
    Sewing her long white seam.

Fair fall the lights, the harbor lights,
    That brought me in to thee,
And peace drop down on that low roof
    For the sight that I did see,
And the voice, my dear, that rang so clear
    All for the love of me.
        For O, for O, with brows bent low
            By the candle's flickering gleam,
        Her wedding-gown it was she wrought,
            Sewing the long white seam.
                    Jean Ingelow [1820–1897]

STORM SONG

THE clouds are scudding across the moon;
    A misty light is on the sea;
The wind in the shrouds has a wintry tune,
    And the foam is flying free.

Brothers, a night of terror and gloom
    Speaks in the cloud and gathering roar;
Thank God, He has given us broad sea-room,
    A thousand miles from shore.

Down with the hatches on those who sleep!
    The wild and whistling deck have we;
Good watch, my brothers, to-night we'll keep,
    While the tempest is on the sea!

Though the rigging shriek in his terrible grip,
    And the naked spars be snapped away,
Lashed to the helm, we'll drive our ship
    In the teeth of the whelming spray!

Hark! how the surges o'erleap the deck!
　Hark! how the pitiless tempest raves!
Ah, daylight will look upon many a wreck
　Drifting over the desert waves.

Yet, courage, brothers! we trust the wave,
　With God above us, our guiding chart.
So, whether to harbor or ocean-grave,
　Be it still with a cheery heart!
                        Bayard Taylor [1825–1878]

THE MARINER'S DREAM

In slumbers of midnight the sailor-boy lay;
　His hammock swung loose at the sport of the wind;
But watch-worn and weary, his cares flew away,
　And visions of happiness danced o'er his mind.

He dreamed of his home, of his dear native bowers,
　And pleasures that waited on life's merry morn;
While Memory stood sideways, half covered with flowers,
　And restored every rose, but secreted its thorn.

Then Fancy her magical pinions spread wide,
　And bade the young dreamer in ecstasy rise;
Now far, far behind him the green waters glide,
　And the cot of his forefathers blesses his eyes.

The jessamine clambers in flowers o'er the thatch,
　And the swallow sings sweet from her nest in the wall;
All trembling with transport he raises the latch,
　And the voices of loved ones reply to his call.

A father bends o'er him with looks of delight;
　His cheek is impearled with a mother's warm tear;
And the lips of the boy in a love-kiss unite
　With the lips of the maid whom his bosom holds dear.

The heart of the sleeper beats high in his breast;
　Joy quickens his pulses, his hardships seem o'er;
And a murmur of happiness steals through his rest,—
　"O God! thou hast blessed me,—I ask for no more."

Ah! whence is that flame which now bursts on his eye?
    Ah! what is that sound which now larums his ear?
'Tis the lightning's red glare, painting hell on the sky!
    'Tis the crash of the thunder, the groan of the sphere!

He springs from his hammock, he flies to the deck;
    Amazement confronts him with images dire;
Wild winds and mad waves drive the vessel a wreck;
    The masts fly in splinters; the shrouds are on fire.

Like mountains the billows tremendously swell;
    In vain the lost wretch calls on mercy to save;
Unseen hands of spirits are ringing his knell,
    And the death-angel flaps his broad wing o'er the wave!

O sailor-boy, woe to thy dream of delight!
    In darkness dissolves the gay frost-work of bliss.
Where now is the picture that Fancy touched bright,—
    Thy parents' fond pressure, and love's honeyed kiss?

O sailor-boy! sailor-boy! never again
    Shall home, love, or kindred thy wishes repay;
Unblessed and unhonored, down deep in the main,
    Full many a fathom, thy frame shall decay.

No tomb shall e'er plead to remembrance for thee,
    Or redeem form or fame from the merciless surge;
But the white foam of waves shall thy winding-sheet be,
    And winds, in the midnight of winter, thy dirge!

On a bed of green sea-flowers thy limbs shall be laid,—
    Around thy white bones the red coral shall grow;
Of thy fair yellow locks threads of amber be made,
    And every part suit to thy mansion below.

Days, months, years, and ages shall circle away,
    And still the vast waters above thee shall roll;
Earth loses thy pattern forever and aye,—
    O sailor-boy! sailor-boy! peace to thy soul!

William Dimond [1780?–1837?]

THE INCHCAPE ROCK

No stir in the air, no stir in the sea,
The ship was still as she could be;
Her sails from Heaven received no motion,
Her keel was steady in the ocean.

Without either sign or sound of their shock,
The waves flowed over the Inchcape Rock;
So little they rose, so little they fell,
They did not move the Inchcape Bell.

The holy Abbot of Aberbrothok
Had placed that bell on the Inchcape Rock;
On a buoy in the storm it floated and swung,
And over the waves its warning rung.

When the rock was hid by the surges' swell,
The mariners heard the warning bell;
And then they knew the perilous Rock,
And blessed the Abbot of Aberbrothok.

The Sun in heaven was shining gay,
All things were joyful on that day;
The sea-birds screamed as they wheeled around,
And there was joyance in their sound.

The buoy of the Inchcape Bell was seen,
A darker speck on the ocean green;
Sir Ralph, the Rover, walked his deck,
And he fixed his eye on the darker speck.

He felt the cheering power of spring,
It made him whistle, it made him sing;
His heart was mirthful to excess;
But the Rover's mirth was wickedness.

His eye was on the Inchcape float;
Quoth he, "My men, put out the boat;
And row me to the Inchcape Rock,
And I'll plague the Abbot of Aberbrothok."

The boat is lowered, the boatmen row,
And to the Inchcape Rock they go;
Sir Ralph bent over from the boat,
And cut the Bell from the Inchcape float.

Down sank the Bell with a gurgling sound;
The bubbles rose, and burst around.
Quoth Sir Ralph, "The next who comes to the Rock
Will not bless the Abbot of Aberbrothok."

Sir Ralph, the Rover, sailed away,
He scoured the seas for many a day;
And now, grown rich with plundered store,
He steers his course for Scotland's shore.

So thick a haze o'erspreads the sky
They cannot see the Sun on high;
The wind hath blown a gale all day;
At evening it hath died away.

On the deck the Rover takes his stand;
So dark it is they see no land.
Quoth Sir Ralph, "It will be lighter soon,
For there is the dawn of the rising Moon."

"Canst hear," said one, "the breakers roar?
For yonder, methinks, should be the shore."
"Now where we are I cannot tell,
But I wish we could hear the Inchcape Bell."

They hear no sound; the swell is strong;
Though the wind hath fallen, they drift along,
Till the vessel strikes with a shivering shock,—
"O Christ! it is the Inchcape Rock."

Sir Ralph, the Rover, tore his hair;
He cursed himself in his despair.
The waves rush in on every side;
The ship is sinking beneath the tide.

But, even in his dying fear,
One dreadful sound he seemed to hear,—
A sound as if, with the Inchcape Bell,
The Devil below was ringing his knell.

Robert Southey [1774–1843]

THE SEA

THROUGH the night, through the night,
    In the saddest unrest,
Wrapped in white, all in white,
    With her babe on her breast,
Walks the mother so pale,
Staring out on the gale,
        Through the night!

Through the night, through the night,
    Where the sea lifts the wreck,
Land in sight, close in sight,
    On the surf-flooded deck,
Stands the father so brave,
Driving on to his grave
        Through the night!

Richard Henry Stoddard [1825–1903]

THE SANDS OF DEE

"O MARY, go and call the cattle home,
    And call the cattle home,
    And call the cattle home
Across the sands of Dee!"
The western wind was wild and dank with foam,
    And all alone went she.

The western tide crept up along the sand,
    And o'er and o'er the sand,
    And round and round the sand,
As far as eye could see.
The rolling mist came down and hid the land:
    And never home came she.

"Oh! is it weed, or fish, or floating hair—
   A tress of golden hair,
   A drownèd maiden's hair
Above the nets at sea?
Was never salmon yet that shone so fair
   Among the stakes on Dee."

They rowed her in across the rolling foam,
   The cruel crawling foam,
   The cruel hungry foam,
To her grave beside the sea:
But still the boatmen hear her call the cattle home
   Across the sands of Dee!

Charles Kingsley [1819–1875]

THE THREE FISHERS

THREE fishers went sailing away to the West,
   Away to the West as the sun went down;
Each thought on the woman who loved him the best,
   And the children stood watching them out of the town;
For men must work, and women must weep,
And there's little to earn, and many to keep,
   Though the harbor bar be moaning.

Three wives sat up in the lighthouse tower
   And they trimmed the lamps as the sun went down;
They looked at the squall, and they looked at the shower,
   And the night-rack came rolling up ragged and brown.
But men must work, and women must weep,
Though storms be sudden, and waters deep,
   And the harbor bar be moaning.

Three corpses lay out on the shining sands
   In the morning gleam as the tide went down,
And the women are weeping and wringing their hands
   For those who will never come home to the town;
For men must work, and women must weep,
And the sooner it's over, the sooner to sleep;
   And good-by to the bar and its moaning.

Charles Kingsley [1819–1875]

BALLAD

In the summer even,
　While yet the dew was hoar,
I went plucking purple pansies,
　Till my love should come to shore.
The fishing-lights their dances
　Were keeping out at sea,
And come, I sung, my true love!
　Come hasten home to me!

But the sea, it fell a-moaning,
　And the white gulls rocked thereon;
And the young moon dropped from heaven,
　And the lights hid one by one.
All silently their glances
　Slipped down the cruel sea,
And wait! cried the night and wind and storm,--
　Wait, till I come to thee!
　　　　　Harriet Prescott Spofford [1835–1921]

THE NORTHERN STAR

A TYNEMOUTH SHIP

　　The Northern Star
　　Sailed over the bar
Bound to the Baltic Sea;
　　In the morning gray
　　She stretched away:—
'Twas a weary day to me!

　　For many an hour
　　In sleet and shower
By the lighthouse rock I stray;
　　And watch till dark
　　For the wingèd bark
Of him that is far away.

　　The castle's bound
　　I wander round,

Amidst the grassy graves:
    But all I hear
    Is the north wind drear,
And all I see are the waves.

    The Northern Star
    Is set afar!
Set in the Baltic Sea:
    And the waves have spread
    The sandy bed
That holds my Love from me.

Unknown

THE FISHER'S WIDOW

THE boats go out and the boats come in
Under the wintry sky;
And the rain and foam are white in the wind,
And the white gulls cry.

She sees the sea when the wind is wild
Swept by a windy rain;
And her heart's a-weary of sea and land
As the long days wane.

She sees the torn sails fly in the foam,
Broad on the sky-line gray;
And the boats go out and the boats come in,
But there's one away.

Arthur Symons [1865–

CALLER HERRIN'

Wha'll buy my caller herrin'?
They're bonny fish and halesome farin';
    Wha'll buy my caller herrin',
    New drawn frae the Forth?

When ye were sleepin' on your pillows,
Dreamed ye aught o' our puir fellows,

Darkling as they faced the billows,
A' to fill the woven willows?
 Buy my caller herrin',
 New drawn frae the Forth !

Wha'll buy my caller herrin'?
They're no brought here without brave darin';
Buy my caller herrin',
Hauled through wind and rain.
 Wha'll buy my caller herrin',
 New drawn frae the Forth ?

Wha'll buy my caller herrin'?
Oh, ye may ca' them vulgar farin';
Wives and mithers, maist despairin',
Ca' them lives o' men.
 Wha'll buy my caller herrin',
 New drawn frae the Forth ?

When the creel o' herrin' passes,
Ladies, clad in silks and laces,
Gather in their braw pelisses,
Cast their heads, and screw their faces.
 Wha'll buy my caller herrin',
 New drawn frae the Forth ?

Caller herrin's no got lightly:—
Ye can trip the spring fu' tightlie;
Spite o' tauntin', flauntin', flingin',
Gow has set you a' a-singin'
 "Wha'll buy my caller herrin',
 New drawn frae the Forth ?"

Neebor wives! now tent my tellin':
When the bonny fish ye're sellin',
At ae word be, in ye're dealin'!
Truth will stand, when a' thing's failin'!
 Wha'll buy my caller herrin',
 New drawn frae the Forth ?
     Carolina Nairne [1766-1845]

HANNAH BINDING SHOES

POOR lone Hannah,
Sitting at the window, binding shoes:
 Faded, wrinkled,
Sitting, stitching, in a mournful muse.
  Bright-eyed beauty once was she,
  When the bloom was on the tree;—
  Spring and winter,
Hannah's at the window, binding shoes.

 Not a neighbor
Passing, nod or answer will refuse
 To her whisper,
"Is there from the fishers any news?"
  Oh, her heart's adrift with one
  On an endless voyage gone;—
  Night and morning,
Hannah's at the window, binding shoes.

 Fair young Hannah,
Ben, the sunburnt fisher, gaily wooes;
 Hale and clever,
For a willing heart and hand he sues.
  May-day skies are all aglow,
  And the waves are laughing so!
  For her wedding
Hannah leaves her window and her shoes.

 May is passing;
'Mid the apple-boughs a pigeon cooes:
 Hannah shudders,
For the mild south-wester mischief brews.
  Round the rocks of Marblehead,
  Outward bound, a schooner sped;
  Silent, lonesome,
Hannah's at the window, binding shoes.

 'Tis November:
Now no tear her wasted cheek bedews,
 From Newfoundland
Not a sail returning will she lose,

Whispering hoarsely: "Fishermen,
Have you, have you heard of Ben?"
  Old with watching,
Hannah's at the window, binding shoes.

  Twenty winters
Bleak and drear the ragged shore she views.
  Twenty seasons:—
Never one has brought her any news.
    Still her dim eyes silently
    Chase the white sails o'er the sea;—
    Hopeless, faithful,
Hannah's at the window, binding shoes.

                    Lucy Larcom [1824–1893]

THE SAILOR

A ROMAIC BALLAD

THOU that hast a daughter
  For one to woo and wed,
Give her to a husband
  With snow upon his head;
Oh, give her to an old man,
  Though little joy it be,
Before the best young sailor
  That sails upon the sea!

How luckless is the sailor
  When sick and like to die;
He sees no tender mother,
  No sweetheart standing by.
Only the captain speaks to him,—
  Stand up, stand up, young man,
And steer the ship to haven,
  As none beside thee can.

Thou says't to me, "Stand, stand up";
  I say to thee, take hold,
Lift me a little from the deck,
  My hands and feet are cold.

And let my head, I pray thee,
  With handkerchiefs be bound;
There, take my love's gold handkerchief,
  And tie it tightly round.

Now bring the chart, the doleful chart;
  See, where these mountains meet—
The clouds are thick around their head,
  The mists around their feet:
Cast anchor here; 'tis deep and safe
  Within the rocky cleft;
The little anchor on the right,
  The great one on the left.

And now to thee, O captain,
  Most earnestly I pray,
That they may never bury me
  In church or cloister gray;—
But on the windy sea-beach,
  At the ending of the land,
All on the surfy sea-beach,
  Deep down into the sand.

For there will come the sailors,
  Their voices I shall hear,
And at casting of the anchor
  The yo-ho loud and clear;
And at hauling of the anchor
  The yo-ho and the cheer,—
Farewell, my love, for to thy bay
  I never more may steer!
                    William Allingham [1824–1889]

THE BURIAL OF THE DANE

BLUE gulf all around us,
  Blue sky overhead—
Muster all on the quarter,
  We must bury the dead!

The Burial of the Dane

It is but a Danish sailor,
　Rugged of front and form;
A common son of the forecastle,
　Grizzled with sun and storm.

His name, and the strand he hailed from
　We know, and there's nothing more!
But perhaps his mother is waiting
　In the lonely Island of Fohr.

Still, as he lay there dying,
　Reason drifting awreck,
" 'Tis my watch," he would mutter,
　"I must go upon deck!"

Aye, on deck, by the foremast!
　But watch and lookout are done;
The Union Jack laid o'er him,
　How quiet he lies in the sun!

Slow the ponderous engine,
　Stay the hurrying shaft;
Let the roll of the ocean
　Cradle our giant craft;
Gather around the grating,
　Carry your messmate aft!

Stand in order, and listen
　To the holiest page of prayer!
Let every foot be quiet,
　Every head be bare—
The soft trade-wind is lifting
　A hundred locks of hair.

Our captain reads the service,
　(A little spray on his cheeks)
The grand old words of burial,
　And the trust a true heart seeks:—
"We therefore commit his body
　To the deep"—and, as he speaks,

Launched from the weather railing,
    Swift as the eye can mark,
The ghastly, shotted hammock
    Plunges, away from the shark,
Down, a thousand fathoms,
    Down into the dark!

A thousand summers and winters
    The stormy Gulf shall roll
High o'er his canvas coffin;
    But, silence to doubt and dole:—
There's a quiet harbor somewhere
    For the poor aweary soul.

Free the fettered engine,
    Speed the tireless shaft,
Loose to'gallant and topsail,
    The breeze is fair abaft!

Blue sea all around us,
    Blue sky bright o'erhead—
Every man to his duty,
    We have buried our dead!
             Henry Howard Brownell [1820–1872]

TOM BOWLING

HERE, a sheer hulk, lies poor Tom Bowling,
    The darling of our crew;
No more he'll hear the tempest howling,
    For death has broached him to.
His form was of the manliest beauty,
    His heart was kind and soft;
Faithful, below, he did his duty;
    But now he's gone aloft.

Tom never from his word departed,
    His virtues were so rare;
His friends were many and true-hearted,
    His Poll was kind and fair:

And then he'd sing, so blithe and jolly,
  Ah, many's the time and oft!
But mirth is turned to melancholy,
  For Tom is gone aloft.

Yet shall poor Tom find pleasant weather,
  When He, who all commands,
Shall give, to call Life's crew together,
  The word to "pipe all hands."
Thus Death, who Kings and Tars despatches,
  In vain Tom's life has doffed;
For, though his body's under hatches,
  His soul is gone aloft.

Charles Dibdin [1745–1814]

MESSMATES

He gave us all a good-by cheerily
  At the first dawn of day;
We dropped him down the side full drearily
  When the light died away.
It's a dead dark watch that he's a-keeping there,
And a long, long night that lags a-creeping there,
Where the Trades and the tides roll over him
  And the great ships go by.

He's there alone with green seas rocking him
  For a thousand miles around;
He's there alone with dumb things mocking him,
  And we're homeward bound.
It's a long, lone watch that he's a-keeping there,
And a dead cold night that lags a-creeping there, '
While the months and the years roll over him
  And the great ships go by.

I wonder if the tramps come near enough,
  As they thrash to and fro,
And the battleships' bells ring clear enough
  To be heard down below;

If through all the lone watch that he's a-keeping there,
And the long, cold night that lags a-creeping there,
The voices of the sailor-men shall comfort him
   When the great ships go by.

Henry Newbolt [1862–1938]

THE LAST BUCCANEER

OH, England is a pleasant place for them that's rich and high,
But England is a cruel place for such poor folks as I;
And such a port for mariners I ne'er shall see again
As the pleasant Isle of Avès, beside the Spanish main.

There were forty craft in Avès that were both swift and stout,
All furnished well with small arms and cannons round about;
And a thousand men in Avès made laws so fair and free
To choose their valiant captains and obey them loyally.

Thence we sailed against the Spaniard with his hoards of
   plate and gold,
Which he wrung with cruel tortures from Indian folk of old;
Likewise the merchant captains, with hearts as hard as stone,
Who flog men and keelhaul them, and starve them to the
   bone.

Oh, the palms grew high in Avès, and fruits that shone like
   gold,
And the colibris and parrots they were gorgeous to behold;
And the negro maids to Avès from bondage fast did flee,
To welcome gallant sailors, a-sweeping in from sea.

Oh, sweet it was in Avès to hear the landward breeze,
A-swing with good tobacco in a net between the trees,
With a negro lass to fan you, while you listened to the roar
Of the breakers on the reef outside, that never touched the
   shore.

But Scripture saith, an ending to all fine things must be;
So the King's ships sailed on Avès, and quite put down were
   we.

All day we fought like bulldogs, but they burst the booms at
    night;
And I fled in a piragua, sore wounded, from the fight.

Nine days I floated starving, and a negro lass beside,
Till for all I tried to cheer her, the poor young thing she died;
But as I lay a-gasping, a Bristol sail came by,
And brought me home to England here, to beg until I die.

And now I'm old and going—I'm sure I can't tell where;
One comfort is, this world's so hard, I can't be worse off
    there:
If I might but be a sea-dove, I'd fly across the main,
To the pleasant Isle of Avès, to look at it once again.

Charles Kingsley [1819–1875]

THE LAST BUCCANEER

THE winds were yelling, the waves were swelling,
    The sky was black and drear,
When the crew with eyes of flame brought the ship without a
    name
    Alongside the last Buccaneer.

"Whence flies your sloop full sail before so fierce a gale,
    When all others drive bare on the seas?
Say, come ye from the shore of the holy Salvador,
    Or the gulf of the rich Caribbees?"

"From a shore no search hath found, from a gulf no line can
    sound,
    Without rudder or needle we steer;
Above, below our bark dies the sea-fowl and the shark,
    As we fly by the last Buccaneer.

"To-night there shall be heard on the rocks of Cape de Verde
    A loud crash and a louder roar;
And to-morrow shall the deep with a heavy moaning sweep
    The corpses and wreck to the shore."

The stately ship of Clyde securely now may ride
      In the breath of the citron shades;
And Severn's towering mast securely now hies fast,
      Through the seas of the balmy Trades.

From St. Jago's wealthy port, from Havannah's royal fort,
      The seaman goes forth without fear;
For since that stormy night not a mortal hath had sight
      Of the flag of the last Buccaneer.

                    Thomas Babington Macaulay [1800–1859]

THE LEADSMAN'S SONG

FOR England, when with favoring gale,
Our gallant ship up Channel steered,
And scudding, under easy sail,
The high blue western lands appeared,
To heave the lead the seaman sprang,
And to the pilot cheerly sang,
      "By the deep—Nine."

And bearing up to gain the port,
Some well-known object kept in view,
An abbey tower, a ruined fort,
A beacon to the vessel true;
While oft the lead the seaman flung,
And to the pilot cheerly sung,
      "By the mark—Seven."

And as the much-loved shore we near,
With transport we behold the roof
Where dwelt a friend or partner dear,
Of faith and love and matchless proof.
The lead once more the seaman flung,
And to the watchful pilot sung,
      "Quarter less—Five."

Now to her berth the ship draws nigh,
With slackened sail she feels the tide,
Stand clear the cable is the cry,
The anchor's gone, we safely ride.

The watch is set, and through the night,
We hear the seaman with delight
   Proclaim—"All's well."
               Charles Dibdin [1745-1814]

HOMEWARD BOUND

HEAD the ship for England!
   Shake out every sail!
Blithe leap the billows,
   Merry sings the gale.
Captain, work the reckoning;
   How many knots a day?—
Round the world and home again,
   That's the sailor's way!

We've traded with the Yankees,
   Brazilians and Chinese;
We've laughed with dusky beauties
   In shade of tall palm-trees;
Across the line and Gulf-Stream—
   Round by Table Bay—
Everywhere and home again,
   That's the sailor's way!

Nightly stands the North Star
   Higher on our bow;
Straight we run for England;
   Our thoughts are in it now.
Jolly times with friends ashore,
   When we've drawn our pay!—
All about and home again,
   That's the sailor's way!

Tom will to his parents,
   Jack will to his dear,
Joe to wife and children,
   Bob to pipes and beer;
Dicky to the dancing-room,
   To hear the fiddles play;—
Round the world and home again,
   That's the sailor's way!
            William Allingham [1824-1889]

THE SIMPLE LIFE

THE LAKE ISLE OF INNISFREE

I WILL arise and go now, and go to Innisfree,
  And a small cabin build there, of clay and wattles made;
Nine bean rows will I have there, a hive for the honey bee,
  And live alone in the bee-loud glade.

And I shall have some peace there, for peace comes dropping
    slow,
  Dropping from the veils of the morning to where the
    cricket sings;
There midnight's all a glimmer, and noon a purple glow,
  And evening full of the linnet's wings.

I will arise and go now, for always, night and day,
  I hear lake-water lapping with low sounds by the shore;
While I stand on the roadway, or on the pavements gray,
  I hear it in the deep heart's core.

                    William Butler Yeats [1865–1939]

A WISH

  ' MINE be a cot beside the hill;
    A bee-hive's hum shall soothe my ear;
  A willowy brook that turns a mill,
    With many a fall shall linger near.

  The swallow, oft, beneath my thatch
    Shall twitter from her clay-built nest;
  Oft shall the pilgrim lift the latch,
    And share my meal, a welcome guest.

  Around my ivied porch shall spring
    Each fragrant flower that drinks the dew;
  And Lucy, at her wheel, shall sing
    In russet-gown and apron blue.

1634

The village-church among the trees,
Where first our marriage-vows were given,
With merry peals shall swell the breeze
And point with taper spire to Heaven.

Samuel Rogers [1763–1855]

ODE ON SOLITUDE

HAPPY the man, whose wish and care
A few paternal acres bound,
Content to breathe his native air
        In his own ground.

Whose herds with milk, whose fields with bread,
Whose flocks supply him with attire;
Whose trees in summer yield him shade,
        In winter, fire.

Blest, who can unconcernedly find
Hours, days, and years, slide soft away
In health of body, peace of mind,
        Quiet by day;

Sound sleep by night; study and ease
Together mixed, sweet recreation,
And innocence, which most does please,
        With meditation.

Thus let me live, unseen, unknown;
Thus unlamented let me die;
Steal from the world, and not a stone
        Tell where I lie.

Alexander Pope [1688–1744]

"THRICE HAPPY HE"

THRICE happy he, who by some shady grove,
Far from the clamorous world, doth live his own;
Though solitary, who is not alone,
But doth converse with that eternal love.

O how more sweet is birds' harmonious moan,
Or the soft sobbings of the widowed dove,
Than those smooth whisperings near a prince's throne,
Which good make doubtful, do the evil approve!
Or how more sweet is Zephyr's wholesome breath,
And sighs perfumed which do the flowers unfold,
Than that applause vain honor doth bequeath!
How sweet are streams to poison drunk in gold!
The world is full of horrors, falsehoods, slights;
Woods' silent shades have only true delights.

William Drummond [1585–1649]

"UNDER THE GREENWOOD TREE"

From "As You Like It"

UNDER the greenwood tree,
Who loves to lie with me,
And turn his merry note
Unto the sweet bird's throat,
Come hither, come hither, come hither:
Here shall he see
No enemy
But winter and rough weather.

Who doth ambition shun,
And loves to live i' the sun,
Seeking the food he eats,
And pleased with what he gets,
Come hither, come hither, come hither:
Here shall he see
No enemy
But winter and rough weather.

William Shakespeare [1564–1616]

CORIDON'S SONG

In "The Complete Angler"

OH, the sweet contentment
The countryman doth find,
High trolollie lollie loe,
High trolollie lee,

That quiet contemplation
Possesseth all my mind:
　　Then care away,
　　And wend along with me.

For courts are full of flattery,
As hath too oft been tried;
　　High trolollie lollie loe,
　　High trolollie lee,
The city full of wantonness,
And both are full of pride:

But oh, the honest countryman
Speaks truly from his heart,
　　High trolollie lollie loe,
　　High trolollie lee,
His pride is in his tillage,
His horses and his cart:

Our clothing is good sheepskins,
Gray russet for our wives,
　　High trolollie lollie loe,
　　High trolollie lee,
Tis warmth and not gay clothing
That doth prolong our lives:

The plowman, though he labor hard
Yet on the holiday,
　　High trolollie lollie loe,
　　High trollolie lee,
No emperor so merrily
Does pass his time away:

To recompense our tillage
The heavens afford us showers;
　　High trolollie lollie loe,
　　High trolollie lee,
And for our sweet refreshments
The earth affords us bowers:

The cuckoo and the nightingale
Full merrily do sing,
   High trolollie lollie loe,
   High trolollie lee,
And with their pleasant roundelays
Bid welcome to the spring:

This is not half the happiness
The countryman enjoys;
   High trolollie lollie loe,
   High trolollie lee,
Though others think they have as much
Yet he that says so lies:
   Then come away, turn
   Countryman with me.

John Chalkhill [fl. 1648]

THE OLD SQUIRE

I LIKE the hunting of the hare
   Better than that of the fox;
I like the joyous morning air,
   And the crowing of the cocks.

I like the calm of the early fields,
   The ducks asleep by the lake,
The quiet hour which nature yields
   Before mankind is awake.

I like the pheasants and feeding things
   Of the unsuspicious morn;
I like the flap of the wood-pigeon's wings
   As she rises from the corn.

I like the blackbird's shriek, and his rush
   From the turnips as I pass by,
And the partridge hiding her head in a bush,
   For her young ones cannot fly.

I like these things, and I like to ride,
   When all the world is in bed,
To the top of the hill where the sky grows wide,
   And where the sun grows red.

The beagles at my horse-heels trot
   In silence after me;
There's Ruby, Roger, Diamond, Dot,
   Old Slut and Margery,—

A score of names well used, and dear,
   The names my childhood knew;
The horn with which I rouse their cheer,
   Is the horn my father blew.

I like the hunting of the hare
   Better than that of the fox;
The new world still is all less fair
   Than the old world it mocks.

I covet not a wider range
   Than these dear manors give;
I take my pleasures without change,
   And as I lived I live.

I leave my neighbors to their thought;
   My choice it is, and pride,
On my own lands to find my sport,
   In my own fields to ride.

The hare herself no better loves
   The field where she was bred,
Than I the habit of these groves,
   My own inherited.

I know my quarries every one,
   The meuse where she sits low;
The road she chose to-day was run
   A hundred years ago.

The lags, the gills, the forest ways,
   The hedgerows one and all,
These are the kingdoms of my chase,
   And bounded by my wall;

Nor has the world a better thing,
   Though one should search it round,
Than thus to live one's own sole king,
   Upon one's own sole ground.

I like the hunting of the hare;
   It brings me, day by day,
The memory of old days as fair,
   With dead men passed away.

To these, as homeward still I ply
   And pass the churchyard gate,
Where all are laid as I must lie
   I stop and raise my hat.

I like the hunting of the hare;
   New sports I hold in scorn.
I like to be as my fathers were,
   In the days ere I was born.

          Wilfrid Scawen Blunt [1840–1922]

INSCRIPTION IN A HERMITAGE

Beneath this stony roof reclined,
I soothe to peace my pensive mind;
And while, to shade my lowly cave,
Embowering elms their umbrage wave;
And while the maple dish is mine—
The beechen cup, unstained with wine—
I scorn the gay licentious crowd,
Nor heed the toys that deck the proud.

Within my limits, lone and still,
The blackbird pipes in artless trill;
Fast by my couch, congenial guest,
The wren has wove her mossy nest;
From busy scenes and brighter skies,
To lurk with innocence, she flies,
Here hopes in safe repose to dwell,
Nor aught suspects the sylvan cell.

At morn I take my customed round,
To mark how buds yon shrubby mound,
And every opening primrose count,
That trimly paints my blooming mount;
Or o'er the sculptures, quaint and rude,
That grace my gloomy solitude,
I teach in winding wreaths to stray
Fantastic ivy's gadding spray.

At eve, within yon studious nook,
I ope my brass-embossèd book,
Portrayed with many a holy deed
Of martyrs, crowned with heavenly meed;
Then, as my taper waxes dim,
Chant, ere I sleep, my measured hymn,
And at the close, the gleams behold
Of parting wings, be-dropt with gold.

While such pure joys my bliss create,
Who but would smile at guilty state?
Who but would wish his holy lot
In calm oblivion's humble grot?
Who but would cast his pomp away,
To take my staff, and amice gray;
And to the world's tumultuous stage
Prefer the blameless hermitage?

Thomas Warton [1728–1790]

THE RETIREMENT

FAREWELL, thou busy world, and may
    We never meet again;
Here I can eat and sleep and pray,
And do more good in one short day
    Than he who his whole age outwears
Upon the most conspicuous theaters,
Where naught but vanity and vice appears.

Good God! how sweet are all things here!
How beautiful the fields appear!

How cleanly do we feed and lie!
Lord! what good hours do we keep!
How quietly we sleep!
    What peace, what unanimity!
How innocent from the lewd fashion
Is all our business, all our recreation!

O, how happy here's our leisure!
O, how innocent our pleasure!
O ye valleys! O ye mountains!
O ye groves, and crystal fountains!
How I love, at liberty,
By turns to come and visit ye!
Dear solitude, the soul's best friend,
That man acquainted with himself dost make,
And all his Maker's wonders to attend,
    With thee I here converse at will,
    And would be glad to do so still,
For it is thou alone that keep'st the soul awake.

How calm and quiet a delight
    Is it, alone,
To read and meditate and write,
    By none offended, and offending none!
To walk, ride, sit, or sleep at one's own ease;
And, pleasing a man's self, none other to displease.

O my belovèd nymph, fair Dove,
Princess of rivers, how I love
    Upon thy flowery banks to lie,
And view thy silver stream,
When gilded by a Summer's beam!
    And in it all thy wanton fry
    Playing at liberty,
And, with my angle, upon them
    The all of treachery
    I ever learned industriously to try!

Such streams Rome's yellow Tiber cannot show,
The Iberian Tagus, or Ligurian Po;

The Maese, the Danube, and the Rhine,
Are puddle-water, all, compared with thine;
And Loire's pure streams yet too polluted are
With thine, much purer, to compare;
The rapid Garonne and the winding Seine
Are both too mean,
　　Belovèd Dove, with thee
　　To vie priority;
Nay, Tame and Isis, when conjoined, submit,
And lay their trophies at thy silver feet.

O my belovèd rocks, that rise
To awe the earth and brave the skies!
From some aspiring mountain's crown
　　How dearly do I love,
Giddy with pleasure to look down;
　　And from the vales to view the noble heights above;
O my belovèd caves! from dog-star's heat,
And all anxieties, my safe retreat;
What safety, privacy, what true delight,
In the artificial light
　　Your gloomy entrails make,
　　Have I taken, do I take!
How oft, when grief has made me fly,
To hide me from society
E'en of my dearest friends, have I,
　　In your recesses' friendly shade,
　　All my sorrows open laid,
And my most secret woes intrusted to your privacy!

Lord! would men let me alone,
What an over-happy one
　　Should I think myself to be—
Might I in this desert place,
(Which most men in discourse disgrace)
　　Live but undisturbed and free!
Here, in this despised recess,
　　Would I, maugre Winter's cold,
And the Summer's worst excess,
　　Try to live out to sixty full years old:

And, all the while,
    Without an envious eye
On any thriving under Fortune's smile,
    Contented live, and then contented die.

Charles Cotton [1630–1687]

THE COUNTRY FAITH

Here in the country's heart,
    Where the grass is green,
Life is the same sweet life
    As it e'er hath been.

Trust in a God still lives,
    And the bell at morn
Floats with a thought of God
    O'er the rising corn.

God comes down in the rain,
    And the crop grows tall—
This is the country faith
    And best of all!

Norman Gale [1862–

TRULY GREAT

My walls outside must have some flowers,
    My walls within must have some books;
A house that's small; a garden large,
    And in it leafy nooks:

A little gold that's sure each week;
    That comes not from my living kind,
But from a dead man in his grave,
    Who cannot change his mind:

A lovely wife, and gentle too;
    Contented that no eyes but mine
Can see her many charms, nor voice
    To call her beauty fine:

Where she would in that stone cage live,
    A self-made prisoner, with me;

While many a wild bird sang around,
    On gate, on bush, on tree.

And she sometimes to answer them,
    In her far sweeter voice than all;
Till birds, that loved to look on leaves,
    Will doat on a stone wall.

With this small house, this garden large,
    This little gold, this lovely mate,
With health in body, peace at heart—
    Show me a man more great.

William H. Davies [1870–1940]

EARLY MORNING AT BARGIS

CLEAR air and grassy lea,
    Stream-song and cattle-bell—
Dear man, what fools are we
    In prison-walls to dwell!

To live our days apart
    From green things and wide skies,
And let the wistful heart
    Be cut and crushed with lies!

Bright peaks!—And suddenly
    Light floods the placid dell,
The grass-tops brush my knee:
A good crop it will be,
    So all is well!
O man, what fools are we
    In prison-walls to dwell!

Hermann Hagedorn [1882–

THE CUP

THE cup I sing is a cup of gold
Many and many a century old,
Sculptured fair, and over-filled
With wine of a generous vintage, spilled

In crystal currents and foaming tides
All round its luminous, pictured sides.
Old Time enameled and embossed
This ancient cup at an infinite cost.
Its frame he wrought of metal that run
Red from the furnace of the sun.
Ages on ages slowly rolled
Before the glowing mass was cold,
And still he toiled at the antique mold,—
Turning it fast in his fashioning hand,
Tracing circle, layer, and band,
Carving figures quaint and strange,
Pursuing, through many a wondrous change,
The symmetry of a plan divine.
At last he poured the lustrous wine,
Crowned high the radiant wave with light,
And held aloft the goblet bright,
Half in shadow, and wreathed in mist
Of purple, amber, and amethyst.

This is the goblet from whose brink
All creatures that have life must drink:
Foemen and lovers, haughty lord,
And sallow beggar with lips abhorred.
The new-born infant, ere it gain
The mother's breast, this wine must drain.
The oak with its subtle juice is fed,
The rose drinks till her cheeks are red,
And the dimpled, dainty violet sips
The limpid stream with loving lips.
It holds the blood of sun and star,
And all pure essences that are:
No fruit so high on the heavenly vine,
Whose golden hanging clusters shine
On the far-off shadowy midnight hills,
But some sweet influence it distils
That slideth down the silvery rills.
Here Wisdom drowned her dangerous thought,
The early gods their secrets brought;

Beauty, in quivering lines of light,
Ripples before the ravished sight:
And the unseen mystic spheres combine
To charm the cup and drug the wine.

All day I drink of the wine, and deep
In its stainless waves my senses steep;
All night my peaceful soul lies drowned
In hollows of the cup profound;
Again each morn I clamber up
The emerald crater of the cup,
On massive knobs of jasper stand
And view the azure ring expand:
I watch the foam-wreaths toss and swim
In the wine that o'erruns the jeweled rim:—
Edges of chrysolite emerge,
Dawn-tinted, from the misty surge:
My thrilled, uncovered front I lave,
My eager senses kiss the wave,
And drain, with its viewless draught, the lore
That kindles the bosom's secret core,
And the fire that maddens the poet's brain
With wild sweet ardor and heavenly pain.

John Townsend Trowbridge [1827–1916]

A STRIP OF BLUE

I DO not own an inch of land,
    But all I see is mine,—
The orchards and the mowing-fields,
    The lawns and gardens fine.
The winds my tax-collectors are,
    They bring me tithes divine,—
Wild scents and subtle essences,
    A tribute rare and free;
And, more magnificent than all,
    My window keeps for me
A glimpse of blue immensity,—
    A little strip of sea.

Richer am I than he who owns
　　Great fleets and argosies;
I have a share in every ship
　　Won by the inland breeze
To loiter on yon airy road
　　Above the apple-trees.
I freight them with my untold dreams;
　　Each bears my own picked crew;
And nobler cargoes wait for them
　　Than ever India knew,—
My ships that sail into the East
　　Across that outlet blue.

Sometimes they seem like living shapes,
　　The people of the sky,—
Guests in white raiment coming down
　　From Heaven, which is close by;
I call them by familiar names,
　　As one by one draws nigh,
So white, so light, so spirit-like,
　　From violet mists they bloom!
The aching wastes of the unknown
　　Are half reclaimed from gloom,
Since on life's hospitable sea
　　All souls find sailing-room.

The ocean grows a weariness
　　With nothing else in sight;
Its east and west, its north and south,
　　Spread out from morn to night;
We miss the warm, caressing shore,
　　Its brooding shade and light.
A part is greater than the whole;
　　By hints are mysteries told.
The fringes of eternity,—
　　God's sweeping garment-fold,
In that bright shred of glittering sea,
　　I reach out for, and hold.

The sails, like flakes of roseate pearl,
　　Float in upon the mist;

The waves are broken precious stones,—
　Sapphire and amethyst,
Washed from celestial basement walls
　By suns unsetting kissed.
Out through the utmost gates of space,
　Past where the gray stars drift,
To the widening Infinite, my soul
　Glides on, a vessel swift;
Yet loses not her anchorage
　In yonder azure rift.

Here sit I, as a little child:
　The threshold of God's door
Is that clear band of chrysoprase;
　Now the vast temple floor,
The blinding glory of the dome
　I bow my head before:
Thy universe, O God, is home,
　In height or depth, to me;
Yet here upon thy footstool green
　Content am I to be;
Glad, when is opened unto my need
　Some sea-like glimpse of thee.

Lucy Larcom [1824–1893]

AN ODE TO MASTER ANTHONY STAFFORD

TO HASTEN HIM INTO THE COUNTRY

Come, spur away!
I have no patience for a longer stay,
　But must go down
And leave the chargeable noise of this great town:
　I will the country see,
　Where old simplicity,
　　Though hid in gray,
　　Doth look more gay
Than foppery in plush and scarlet clad.
　Farewell, you city wits, that are
　Almost at civil war—
'Tis time that I grow wise, when all the world grows mad.

More of my days
I will not spend to gain an idiot's praise;
Or to make sport
For some slight Puisne of the Inns of Court.
Then, worthy Stafford, say,
How shall we spend the day?
With what delights
Shorten the nights?
When from this tumult we are got secure,
Where mirth with all her freedom goes,
Yet shall no finger lose;
Where every word is thought, and every thought is pure?

There from the tree
We'll cherries pluck, and pick the strawberry;
And every day
Go see the wholesome country girls make hay,
Whose brown hath lovelier grace
Than any painted face
That I do know
Hyde Park can show:
Where I had rather gain a kiss than meet
(Though some of them in greater state
Might court my love with plate)
The beauties of the Cheap, and wives of Lombard Street.

But think upon
Some other pleasures: these to me are none.
Why do I prate
Of women, that are things against my fate!
I never mean to wed
That torture to my bed:
My Muse is she
My love shall be.
Let clowns get wealth and heirs: when I am gone
And that great bugbear, grisly Death,
Shall take this idle breath,
If I a poem leave, that poem is my son.

Of this no more!
We'll rather taste the bright Pomona's store.

No fruit shall 'scape
Our palates, from the damson to the grape.
Then, full, we'll seek a shade,
And hear what music's made;
How Philomel
Her tale doth tell,
And how the other birds do fill the choir;
The thrush and blackbird lend their throats,
Warbling melodious notes;
We will all sports enjoy which others but desire.

Ours is the sky,
Where at what fowl we please our hawk shall fly:
Nor will we spare
To hunt the crafty fox or timorous hare;
But let our hounds run loose
In any ground they'll choose;
The buck shall fall,
The stag, and all.
Our pleasures must from their own warrants be,
For to my Muse, if not to me,
I'm sure all game is free:
Heaven, earth, are all but parts of her great royalty.

And when we mean
To taste of Bacchus' blessings now and then,
And drink by stealth
A cup or two to noble Barkley's health,
I'll take my pipe and try
The Phrygian melody;
Which he that hears,
Lets through his ears
A madness to distemper all the brain:
Then I another pipe will take
And Doric music make,
To civilize with graver notes our wits again.

Thomas Randolph [1605–1635]

"THE MIDGES DANCE ABOON THE BURN"

THE midges dance aboon the burn;
  The dews begin to fa';
The paitricks doun the rushy holm
  Set up their e'ening ca'.
Now loud and clear the blackbird's sang
  Rings through the briery shaw,
While, flitting gay, the swallows play
  Around the castle wa'.

Beneath the golden gloamin' sky
  The mavis mends her lay;
The redbreast pours his sweetest strains
  To charm the lingering day;
While weary yeldrins seem to wail
  Their little nestlings torn,
The merry wren, frae den to den,
  Gaes jinking through the thorn.

The roses fauld their silken leaves,
  The foxglove shuts its bell;
The honeysuckle and the birk
  Spread fragrance through the dell.—
Let others crowd the giddy court
  Of mirth and revelry,
The simple joys that Nature yields
  Are dearer far to me.

Robert Tannahill [1774-1810]

THE PLOW

ABOVE yon somber swell of land
  Thou seest the dawn's grave orange hue,
With one pale streak like yellow sand,
  And over that a vein of blue.

The air is cold above the woods;
  All silent is the earth and sky,
Except with his own lonely moods
  The blackbird holds a colloquy.

Over the broad hill creeps a beam,
  Like hope that gilds a good man's brow;
And now ascends the nostril-steam
  Of stalwart horses come to plow.

Ye rigid plowmen, bear in mind
  Your labor is for future hours!
Advance—spare not—nor look behind—
  Plow deep and straight with all your powers.

Richard Hengist Horne [1803–1884]

THE USEFUL PLOW

A COUNTRY life is sweet!
In moderate cold and heat,
  To walk in the air how pleasant and fair!
In every field of wheat,
  The fairest of flowers adorning the bowers,
And every meadow's brow;
  So that I say, no courtier may
  Compare with them who clothe in gray,
And follow the useful plow.

They rise with the morning lark,
And labor till almost dark,
  Then, folding their sheep, they hasten to sleep
While every pleasant park
  Next morning is ringing with birds that are singing
On each green, tender bough.
  With what content and merriment
  Their days are spent, whose minds are bent
To follow the useful plow.

Unknown

"TO ONE WHO HAS BEEN LONG IN CITY PENT"

To one who has been long in city pent,
  'Tis very sweet to look into the fair
And open face of heaven,—to breathe a prayer
Full in the smile of the blue firmament.

Who is more happy, when, with heart's content,
Fatigued he sinks into some pleasant lair
Of wavy grass, and reads a debonair
And gentle tale of love and languishment?
Returning home at evening, with an ear
Catching the notes of Philomel,—and eye
Watching the sailing cloudlet's bright career,
He mourns that day so soon has glided by,
E'en like the passage of an angel's tear
That falls through the clear ether silently.

John Keats [1795–1821]

THE QUIET LIFE

WHAT pleasure have great princes
More dainty to their choice
Than herdsmen wild, who careless
In quiet life rejoice,
And fortune's fate not fearing
Sing sweet in summer morning?

Their dealings plain and rightful,
Are void of all deceit;
They never know how spiteful
It is to kneel and wait
On favorite, presumptuous,
Whose pride is vain and sumptuous.

All day their flocks each tendeth;
At night, they take their rest;
More quiet than who sendeth
His ship unto the East,
Where gold and pearl are plenty;
But getting, very dainty.

For lawyers and their pleading.
They 'steem it not a straw;
They think that honest meaning
Is of itself a law:
Whence conscience judgeth plainly,
They spend no money vainly.

O happy who thus liveth!
Not caring much for gold;
With clothing which sufficeth
To keep him from the cold.
Though poor and plain his diet
Yet merry it is, and quiet.

William Byrd [1538?–1623]

THE WISH

WELL then, I now do plainly see
This busy world and I shall ne'er agree;
The very honey of all earthly joy
Does, of all meats, the soonest cloy;
   And they, methinks, deserve my pity
Who for it can endure the stings,
The crowd, and buzz, and murmurings
   Of this great hive, the city!

Ah, yet, ere I descend to the grave,
May I a small house and large garden have;
And a few friends, and many books, both true,
Both wise, and both delightful too!
   And since Love ne'er will from me flee,—
A mistress moderately fair,
And good as guardian-angels are,
   Only beloved, and loving me!

O fountains! when in you shall I
Myself eased of unpeaceful thoughts espy?
O fields! O woods! when, when shall I be made
The happy tenant of your shade?
   Here's the spring-head of pleasure's flood!
Here's wealthy Nature's treasury,
Where all the riches lie, that she
   Has coined and stamped for good.

Pride and ambition here
Only in far-fetched metaphors appear;
Here naught but winds can hurtful murmurs scatter,
And naught but echo flatter.

The gods, when they descended, hither
From heaven did always choose their way;
And therefore we may boldly say
    That 'tis the way too thither.

How happy here should I
And one dear She live, and embracing die!
She who is all the world, and can exclude
In deserts solitude.
    I should have then this only fear:
Lest men, when they my pleasures see,
Should hither throng to live like me,
    And so make a city here.

                Abraham Cowley [1618-1667]

EXPOSTULATION AND REPLY

"WHY, William, on that old gray stone,
Thus for the length of half a day,
Why, William, sit you thus alone,
And dream your time away?

"Where are your books?—that light bequeathed
To beings else forlorn and blind!
Up! up! and drink the spirit breathed
From dead men to their kind.

"You look round on your Mother Earth,
As if she for no purpose bore you;
As if you were her first-born birth,
And none had lived before you!"

One morning thus, by Esthwaite lake,
When life was sweet, I knew not why,
To me my good friend Matthew spake,
And thus I made reply:

"The eye—it cannot choose but see;
We cannot bid the ear be still;
Our bodies feel, where'er they be,
Against or with our will.

"Nor less I dream that there are Powers
Which of themselves our minds impress;
That we can feed this mind of ours
In a wise passiveness.

"Think you, 'mid all this mighty sum
Of things forever speaking,
That nothing of itself will come,
But we must still be seeking?

"—Then ask not wherefore, here, alone,
Conversing as I may,
I sit upon this old gray stone,
And dream my time away."

William Wordsworth [1770–1850]

THE TABLES TURNED

AN EVENING SCENE ON THE SAME SUBJECT

Up! up! my friend, and quit your books;
Or surely you'll grow double:
Up! up! my friend, and clear your looks;
Why all this toil and trouble?

The sun, above the mountain's head,
A freshening luster mellow
Through all the long green fields has spread,
His first sweet evening yellow.

Books! 'tis a dull and endless strife:
Come, hear the woodland linnet,
How sweet his music! on my life
There's more of wisdom in it.

And hark! how blithe the throstle sings!
He, too, is no mean preacher:
Come forth into the light of things,
Let Nature be your teacher.

She has a world of ready wealth,
Our minds and hearts to bless—
Spontaneous wisdom breathed by health,
Truth breathed by cheerfulness.

One impulse from a vernal wood
May teach you more of man,
Of moral evil and of good,
Than all the sages can.

Sweet is the lore which Nature brings;
Our meddling intellect
Misshapes the beauteous forms of things:—
We murder to dissect.

Enough of Science and of Art;
Close up those barren leaves;
Come forth, and bring with you a heart
That watches and receives.

William Wordsworth [1770–1850]

SIMPLE NATURE

Be it not mine to steal the cultured flower
    From any garden of the rich and great,
Nor seek with care, through many a weary hour,
    Some novel form of wonder to create.
Enough for me the leafy woods to rove,
    And gather simple cups of morning dew,
Or, in the fields and meadows that I love,
    Find beauty in their bells of every hue.
Thus round my cottage floats a fragrant air,
    And though the rustic plot be humbly laid,
Yet, like the lilies gladly growing there,
    I have not toiled, but take what God has made.
        My Lord Ambition passed, and smiled in scorn;
        I plucked a rose, and, lo! it had no thorn.

George John Romanes [1848–1894]

"I FEAR NO POWER A WOMAN WIELDS"

I FEAR no power a woman wields
While I can have the woods and fields,
With comradeship alone of gun,
Gray marsh-wastes and the burning sun.

For aye the heart's most poignant pain
Will wear away 'neath hail and rain,
And rush of winds through branches bare
With something still to do and dare.—

The lonely watch beside the shore,
The wild-fowl's cry, the sweep of oar,
The paths of virgin sky to scan
Untrod, and so uncursed by man.

Gramercy, for thy haunting face,
Thy charm of voice and lissome grace,
I fear no power a woman wields
While I can have the woods and fields.

Ernest McGaffey [1861-

A RUNNABLE STAG

WHEN the pods went pop on the broom, green broom
    And apples began to be golden-skinned,
We harbored a stag in the Priory coomb,
    And we feathered his trail up-wind, up-wind,
    We feathered his trail up-wind—
        A stag of warrant, a stag, a stag,
        A runnable stag, a kingly crop,
        Brow, bay and tray and three on top,
        A stag, a runnable stag.

Then the huntsman's horn rang yap, yap, yap,
    And "Forwards" we heard the harborer shout;
But 'twas only a brocket that broke a gap
    In the beechen underwood, driven out,
    From the underwood antlered out

By warrant and might of the stag, the stag,
The runnable stag, whose lordly mind
Was bent on sleep, though beamed and tined
He stood, a runnable stag.

So we tufted the covert till afternoon
With Tinkerman's Pup and Bell-of-the-North;
And hunters were sulky and hounds out of tune
Before we tufted the right stag forth,
Before we tufted him forth,
The stag of warrant, the wily stag,
The runnable stag with his kingly crop,
Brow, bay and tray and three on top,
The royal and runnable stag.

It was Bell-of-the-North and Tinkerman's Pup
That stuck to the scent till the copse was drawn.
"Tally ho! tally ho!" and the hunt was up,
The tufters whipped and the pack laid on,
The resolute pack laid on,
And the stag of warrant away at last,
The runnable stag, the same, the same,
His hoofs on fire, his horns like flame,
A stag, a runnable stag.

"Let your gelding be: if you check or chide
He stumbles at once and you're out of the hunt;
For three hundred gentlemen, able to ride,
On hunters accustomed to bear the brunt,
Accustomed to bear the brunt,
Are after the runnable stag, the stag,
The runnable stag with his kingly crop,
Brow, bay and tray and three on top,
The right, the runnable stag."

By perilous paths in coomb and dell,
The heather, the rocks, and the river-bed,
The pace grew hot, for the scent lay well,
And a runnable stag goes right ahead,
The quarry went right ahead—
Ahead, ahead, and fast and far;
His antlered crest, his cloven hoof,

Brow, bay and tray and three aloof,
The stag, the runnable stag.

For a matter of twenty miles and more,
  By the densest hedge and the highest wall,
Through herds of bullocks he baffled the lore
  Of harborer, huntsman, hounds and all,
  Of harborer, hounds and all—
    The stag of warrant, the wily stag,
    For twenty miles, and five and five,
    He ran, and he never was caught alive,
    This stag, this runnable stag.

When he turned at bay in the leafy gloom,
  In the emerald gloom where the brook ran deep,
He heard in the distance the rollers boom,
  And he saw in a vision of peaceful sleep,
  In a wonderful vision of sleep,
    A stag of warrant, a stag, a stag,
    A runnable stag in a jewelled bed,
    Under the sheltering ocean dead,
    A stag, a runnable stag.

So a fateful hope lit up his eye,
  And he opened his nostrils wide again,
And he tossed his branching antlers high
  As he headed the hunt down the Charloch glen,
  As he raced down the echoing glen—
    For five miles more, the stag, the stag,
    For twenty miles, and five and five,
    Not to be caught now, dead or alive,
    The stag, the runnable stag.

Three hundred gentlemen, able to ride,
  Three hundred horses as gallant and free,
Beheld him escape on the evening tide,
  Far out till he sank in the Severn Sea,
  Till he sank in the depths of the sea—
    The stag, the buoyant stag, the stag
    That slept at last in a jewelled bed
    Under the sheltering ocean spread,
    The stag, the runnable stag.

                    John Davidson [1857–1909]

HUNTING–SONG

From " King Arthur "

OH, who would stay indoor, indoor,
When the horn is on the hill? (*Bugle:* Tarantara!
With the crisp air stinging, and the huntsmen singing,
And a ten-tined buck to kill!

Before the sun goes down, goes down,
We shall slay the buck of ten; (*Bugle:* Tarantara!
And the priest shall say benison, and we shall ha'e venison,
When we come home again.

Let him that loves his ease, his ease,
Keep close and house him fair; (*Bugle:* Tarantara!
He'll still be a stranger to the merry thrill of danger
And the joy of the open air.

But he that loves the hills, the hills,
Let him come out to-day! (*Bugle:* Tarantara!
For the horses are neighing, and the hounds are baying,
And the hunt's up, and away!

Richard Hovey [1864–1900]

" A–HUNTING WE WILL GO "

From " Don Quixote in England "

THE dusky night rides down the sky,
    And ushers in the morn;
The hounds all join in glorious cry,
    The huntsman winds his horn.
                And a-hunting we will go.

The wife around her husband throws
    Her arms to make him stay;
"My dear, it rains, it hails, it blows;
    You cannot hunt to-day."
                Yet a-hunting we will go.

Away they fly to 'scape the rout,
    Their steeds they soundly switch;
Some are thrown in, and some thrown out,
    And some thrown in the ditch.
                Yet a-hunting we will go.

Sly Reynard now like lightning flies,
    And sweeps across the vale;
And when the hounds too near he spies,
    He drops his bushy tail.
                Then a-hunting we will go.

Fond Echo seems to like the sport,
    And join the jovial cry;
The woods, the hills, the sound retort,
    And music fills the sky,
                When a-hunting we do go.

At last his strength to faintness worn,
    Poor Reynard ceases flight;
Then hungry, homeward we return,
    To feast away the night.
                And a-drinking we do go.

Ye jovial hunters, in the morn
    Prepare then for the chase;
Rise at the sounding of the horn
    And health with sport embrace,
                When a-hunting we do go.

                    Henry Fielding [1707-1754]

THE ANGLER'S INVITATION

COME when the leaf comes, angle with me,
Come when the bee hums over the lea,
        Come with the wild flowers—
        Come with the wild showers—
Come when the singing bird calleth for thee!

Then to the stream side, gladly we'll hie,
Where the gray trout glide silently by,
        Or in some still place
        Over the hill face
Hurrying onward, drop the light fly.

Then, when the dew falls, homeward we'll speed
To our own loved walls down on the mead,
    There, by the bright hearth,
    Holding our night mirth,
We'll drink to sweet friendship in need and in deed.
                   Thomas Tod Stoddart [1810–1880]

THE ANGLER'S WISH

From "The Complete Angler"

I IN these flowery meads would be,
These crystal streams should solace me;
To whose harmonious bubbling noise
I, with my angle, would rejoice,
    Sit here, and see the turtle-dove
    Court his chaste mate to acts of love;

Or, on that bank, feel the west-wind
Breathe health and plenty; please my mind,
To see sweet dewdrops kiss these flowers,
And then washed off by April showers;
    Here, hear my Kenna sing a song:
    There, see a blackbird feed her young,

Or a laverock build her nest;
Here, give my weary spirits rest,
And raise my low-pitched thoughts above
Earth, or what poor mortals love:
    Thus, free from lawsuits, and the noise
    Of princes' courts, I would rejoice;

Or, with my Bryan and a book,
Loiter long days near Shawford brook;
There sit by him, and eat my meat;
There see the sun both rise and set;
There bid good morning to next day;
There meditate my time away;
    And angle on; and beg to have
    A quiet passage to a welcome grave.
                   Izaac Walton [1593–1683]

THE ANGLER

In "The Complete Angler"

O THE gallant fisher's life,
  It is the best of any!
'Tis full of pleasure, void of strife,
  And 'tis beloved by many;
        Other joys
        Are but toys;
        Only this
        Lawful is;
        For our skill
        Breeds no ill,
  But content and pleasure.

In a morning, up we rise,
  Ere Aurora's peeping;
Drink a cup to wash our eyes,
  Leave the sluggard sleeping;
        Then we go
        To and fro,
        With our knacks
        At our backs,
        To such streams
        As the Thames,
  If we have the leisure.

When we please to walk abroad
  For our recreation,
In the fields is our abode,
  Full of delectation,
        Where, in a brook,
        With a hook,—
        Or a lake,—
        Fish we take;
        There we sit,
        For a bit,
  Till we fish entangle.

We have gentles in a horn,
  We have paste and worms too;
We can watch both night and morn,
  Suffer rain and storms too;
      None do here
      Use to swear:
      Oaths do fray
      Fish away;
      We sit still,
      Watch our quill:
Fishers must not wrangle.

If the sun's excessive heat
  Make our bodies swelter,
To an osier hedge we get,
  For a friendly shelter;
      Where, in a dike,
      Perch or pike,
      Roach or dace,
      We do chase,
      Bleak or gudgeon,
      Without grudging;
We are still contented.

Or we sometimes pass an hour
  Under a green willow,
That defends us from a shower,
  Making earth our pillow:
      Where we may
      Think and pray,
      Before death
      Stops our breath;
      Other joys
      Are but toys,
And to be lamented.

                    John Chalkhill [fl. 1648]

WANDERLUST

TO JANE: THE INVITATION

BEST and Brightest, come away!
Fairer far than this fair day,
Which, like thee, to those in sorrow,
Comes to bid a sweet good-morrow
To the rough year just awake
In its cradle on the brake.
The brightest hour of unborn Spring
Through the winter wandering,
Found, it seems, the halcyon morn
To hoar February born;
Bending from Heaven, in azure mirth,
It kissed the forehead of the earth,
And smiled upon the silent sea,
And bade the frozen streams be free,
And waked to music all their fountains,
And breathed upon the frozen mountains,
And like a prophetess of May
Strewed flowers upon the barren way,
Making the wintry world appear
Like one on whom thou smilest, Dear.

Away, away, from men and towns,
To the wild wood and the downs—
To the silent wilderness
Where the soul need not repress
Its music, lest it should not find
An echo in another's mind,
While the touch of Nature's art
Harmonizes heart to heart.

I leave this notice on my door
For each accustomed visitor:—

"I am gone into the fields
To take what this sweet hour yields;—
Reflection, you may come to-morrow,
Sit by the fireside with Sorrow.—
You with the unpaid bill, Despair,—
You tiresome verse-reciter, Care,—
I will pay you in the grave,—
Death will listen to your stave.
Expectation too, be off!
To-day is for itself enough;
Hope, in pity mock not Woe
With smiles, nor follow where I go;
Long having lived on thy sweet food,
At length I find one moment's good
After long pain—with all your love,
This you never told me of."

Radiant Sister of the Day
Awake! arise! and come away!
To the wild woods and the plains,
To the pools where winter rains
Image all their roof of leaves,
Where the pine its garland weaves
Of sapless green, and ivy dun,
Round stems that never kiss the sun.
Where the lawns and pastures be,
And the sandhills of the sea;—
Where the melting hoar-frost wets
The daisy-star that never sets,
And wind-flowers, and violets,
Which yet join not scent to hue,
Crown the pale year weak and new;
When the night is left behind
In the deep east, dun and blind,
And the blue noon is over us,
And the multitudinous
Billows murmur at our feet,
Where the earth and ocean meet,
And all things seem only one
In the universal sun.

Percy Bysshe Shelley [1792–1822]

"MY HEART'S IN THE HIGHLANDS"

My heart's in the Highlands, my heart is not here;
My heart's in the Highlands a-chasing the deer;
A-chasing the wild deer, and following the roe,—
My heart's in the Highlands wherever I go.

Farewell to the Highlands, farewell to the North,
The birthplace of valor, the country of worth;
Wherever I wander, wherever I rove,
The hills of the Highlands for ever I love.

Farewell to the mountains high covered with snow;
Farewell to the straths and green valleys below;
Farewell to the forests and wild-hanging woods;
Farewell to the torrents and loud-pouring floods.

My heart's in the Highlands, my heart is not here;
My heart's in the Highlands a-chasing the deer,
A-chasing the wild deer, and following the roe,—
My heart's in the Highlands wherever I go.

Robert Burns [1759–1796]

"AFAR IN THE DESERT"

Afar in the desert I love to ride,
With the silent Bush-boy alone by my side.
When the sorrows of life the soul o'ercast,
And, sick of the present, I cling to the past;
When the eye is suffused with regretful tears,
From the fond recollections of former years;
And shadows of things that have long since fled
Flit over the brain, like the ghosts of the dead:
Bright visions of glory that vanished too soon;
Day-dreams that departed ere manhood's noon;
Attachments by fate or falsehood reft;
Companions of early days lost or left—
And my native land—whose magical name
Thrills to the heart like electric flame;

The home of my childhood; the haunts of my prime;
All the passions and scenes of that rapturous time
When the feelings were young, and the world was new,
Like the fresh bowers of Eden unfolding to view;
All—all now forsaken—forgotten—foregone!
And I—a lone exile remembered of none—
My high aims abandoned,—my good acts undone—
Aweary of all that is under the sun—
With that sadness of heart which no stranger may scan,
I fly to the desert afar from man.

Afar in the desert I love to ride,
With the silent Bush-boy alone by my side,
When the wild turmoil of this wearisome life,
With its scenes of oppression, corruption, and strife—
The proud man's frown, and the base man's fear—
The scorner's laugh, and the sufferer's tear—
And malice, and meanness, and falsehood, and folly,
Dispose me to musing and dark melancholy;
When my bosom is full, and my thoughts are high,
And my soul is sick with the bondman's sigh—
Oh! then there is freedom, and joy, and pride,
Afar in the desert alone to ride!
There is rapture to vault on the champing steed,
And to bound away with the eagle's speed,
With the death-fraught firelock in my hand—
The only law of the Desert Land!

Afar in the desert I love to ride,
With the silent Bush-boy alone by my side.
Away—away from the dwellings of men,
By the wild deer's haunt, by the buffalo's glen;
By valleys remote where the oribi plays,
Where the gnu, the gazelle, and the hartebeest graze,
And the kudu and eland unhunted recline
By the skirts of gray forest o'erhung with wild vine:
Where the elephant browses at peace in his wood,
And the river-horse gambols unscared in the flood,
And the mighty rhinoceros wallows at will
In the fen where the wild ass is drinking his fill.

Afar in the desert I love to ride,
With the silent Bush-boy alone by my side.
O'er the brown karroo, where the bleating cry
Of the springbok's fawn sounds plaintively:
And the timorous quagga's shrill whistling neigh
Is heard by the fountain at twilight gray;
Where the zebra wantonly tosses his mane,
With wild hoof scouring the desolate plain;
And the fleet-footed ostrich over the waste
Speeds like a horseman who travels in haste,
Hieing away to the home of her rest,
Where she and her mate have scooped their nest,
Far hid from the pitiless plunderer's view
In the pathless depths of the parched karroo.

Afar in the desert I love to ride,
With the silent Bush-boy alone by my side.
Away—away—in the wilderness vast
Where the white man's foot hath never passed,
And the quivered Coranna or Bechuan
Hath rarely crossed with his roving clan:
A region of emptiness, howling and drear,
Which man hath abandoned from famine and fear;
Which the snake and the lizard inhabit alone,
With the twilight bat from the yawning stone;
Where grass, nor herb, nor shrub takes root,
Save poisonous thorns that pierce the foot;
And the bitter melon, for food and drink,
Is the pilgrim's fare by the salt-lake's brink;
A region of drought, where no river glides,
Nor rippling brook with osiered sides;
Where sedgy pool, nor bubbling fount,
Nor tree, nor cloud, nor misty mount,
Appears, to refresh the aching eye;
But the barren earth and the burning sky,
And the blank horizon, round and round,
Spread—void of living sight or sound.
And here, while the night-winds round me sigh,
And the stars burn bright in the midnight sky,

As I sit apart by the desert stone,
Like Elijah at Horeb's cave, alone,
"A still small voice" comes through the wild,
Like a father consoling his fretful child,
Which banishes bitterness, wrath, and fear.
Saying—Man is distant, but God is near!

Thomas Pringle [1789–1834]

SPRING SONG IN THE CITY

WHO remains in London,
  In the streets with me,
Now that Spring is blowing
  Warm winds from the sea;
Now that trees grow green and tall,
  Now the sun shines mellow,
And with moist primroses all
  English lanes are yellow?

Little barefoot maiden,
  Selling violets blue,
Hast thou ever pictured
  Where the sweetlings grew?
Oh, the warm wild woodland ways,
  Deep in dewy grasses,
Where the wind-blown shadow strays,
  Scented as it passes!

Peddler breathing deeply,
  Toiling into town,
With the dusty highway
  You are dusky brown;
Hast thou seen by daisied leas,
  And by rivers flowing,
Lilac-ringlets which the breeze
  Loosens lightly blowing?

Out of yonder wagon
  Pleasant hay-scents float,
He who drives it carries
  A daisy in his coat:

Oh, the English meadows, fair
  Far beyond all praises!
Freckled orchids everywhere
  Mid the snow of daisies!

Now in busy silence
  Broods the nightingale,
Choosing his love's dwelling
  In a dimpled dale;
Round the leafy bower they raise
  Rose-trees wild are springing;
Underneath, through the green haze,
  Bounds the brooklet singing.

And his love is silent
  As a bird can be,
For the red buds only
  Fill the red rose-tree;
Just as buds and blossoms blow
  He'll begin his tune,
When all is green and roses glow
  Underneath the moon.

Nowhere in the valleys
  Will the wind be still,
Everything is waving,
  Wagging at his will:
Blows the milkmaid's kirtle clean
  With her hand pressed on it;
Lightly o'er the hedge so green
  Blows the plowboy's bonnet.

Oh, to be a-roaming
  In an English dell!
Every nook is wealthy,
  All the world looks well,
Tinted soft the Heavens glow,
  Over Earth and Ocean,
Waters flow, breezes blow,
  All is light and motion!

Robert Buchanan [1841–1901]

IN CITY STREETS

YONDER in the heather there's a bed for sleeping,
　　Drink for one athirst, ripe blackberries to eat;
Yonder in the sun the merry hares go leaping,
　　And the pool is clear for travel-wearied feet.

Sorely throb my feet, a-tramping London highways,
　　(Ah! the springy moss upon a northern moor!)
Through the endless streets, the gloomy squares and by
　　　　ways,
　　Homeless in the City, poor among the poor!

London streets are gold—ah, give me leaves a-glinting
　　'Midst gray dykes and hedges in the autumn sun!
London water's wine, poured out for all unstinting—
　　God!　For the little brooks that tumble as they run!

Oh, my heart is fain to hear the soft wind blowing,
　　Soughing through the fir-tops up on northern fells!
Oh, my eye's an ache to see the brown burns flowing
　　Through the peaty soil and tinkling heather-bells.

　　　　　　　　　　　　Ada Smith [18　–

THE VAGABOND

(To an Air of Schubert)

GIVE to me the life I love,
　　Let the lave go by me,
Give the jolly heaven above
　　And the byway nigh me.
Bed in the bush with stars to see,
　　Bread I dip in the river—
There's the life for a man like me,
　　There's the life for ever.

Let the blow fall soon or late,
　　Let what will be o'er me;
Give the face of earth around
　　And the road before me.

Wealth I seek not, hope nor love,
    Nor a friend to know me;
All I seek, the heaven above
    And the road below me.

Or let autumn fall on me
    Where afield I linger,
Silencing the bird on tree,
    Biting the blue finger.
White as meal the frosty field—
    Warm the fireside haven—
Not to autumn will I yield,
    Not to winter even!

Let the blow fall soon or late,
    Let what will be o'er me;
Give the face of earth around,
    And the road before me.
Wealth I ask not, hope nor love,
    Nor a friend to know me;
All I ask, the heaven above
    And the road below me.
                Robert Louis Stevenson [1850–1894]

IN THE HIGHLANDS

In the highlands, in the country places,
Where the old plain men have rosy faces,
And the young fair maidens
    Quiet eyes;
Where essential silence cheers and blesses
And for ever in the hill-recesses
    Her more lovely music
Broods and dies.—

O to mount again where erst I haunted;
Where the old red hills are bird-enchanted,
And the low green meadows
    Bright with sward;

And when even dies, the million-tinted,
And the night has come, and planets glinted,
Lo, the valley hollow
Lamp-bestarred!

O to dream, O to awake and wander
There, and with delight to take and render,
Through the trance of silence,
Quiet breath!
Lo! for there, among the flowers and grasses,
Only the mightier movement sounds and passes;
Only winds and rivers,
Life and Death.

Robert Louis Stevenson [1850–1894]

THE SONG MY PADDLE SINGS

West wind, blow from your prairie nest,
Blow from the mountains, blow from the west.
The sail is idle, the sailor too;
O wind of the west, we wait for you!
Blow, blow!
I have wooed you so,
But never a favor you bestow.
You rock your cradle the hills between,
But scorn to notice my white lateen.

I stow the sail and unship the mast:
I wooed you long, but my wooing's past;
My paddle will lull you into rest:
O drowsy wind of the drowsy west,
Sleep, sleep!
By your mountains steep,
Or down where the prairie grasses sweep,
Now fold in slumber your laggard wings,
For soft is the song my paddle sings.

Be strong, O paddle! be brave, canoe!
The reckless waves you must plunge into.

Reel, reel,
On your trembling keel,
But never a fear my craft will feel.

We've raced the rapids; we're far ahead:
The river slips through its silent bed.
Sway, sway,
As the bubbles spray
And fall in tinkling tunes away.

And up on the hills against the sky,
A fir tree rocking its lullaby
Swings, swings,
Its emerald wings,
Swelling the song that my paddle sings.

                    E. Pauline Johnson [1862–1913]

THE GIPSY TRAIL

THE white moth to the closing vine,
    The bee to the opened clover,
And the gipsy blood to the gipsy blood
    Ever the wide world over.

Ever the wide world over, lass,
    Ever the trail held true,
Over the world and under the world,
    And back at the last to you.

Out of the dark of the gorgio camp,
    Out of the grime and the gray
(Morning waits at the end of the world),
    Gipsy, come away!

The wild boar to the sun-dried swamp,
    The red crane to her reed,
And the Romany lass to the Romany lad
    By the tie of a roving breed.

Morning waits at the end of the world
  Where winds unhaltered play,
Nipping the flanks of their plunging ranks,
  Till the white sea-horses neigh.

The pied snake to the rifted rock,
  The buck to the stony plain,
And the Romany lass to the Romany lad,
  And both to the road again.

Both to the road again, again!
  Out on a clean sea-track—
Follow the cross of the gipsy trail
  Over the world and back!

Follow the Romany patteran
  North where the blue bergs sail,
And the bows are gray with the frozen spray,
  And the masts are shod with mail.

Follow the Romany patteran
  Sheer to the Austral Light,
Where the besom of God is the wild south wind,
  Sweeping the sea-floors white.

Follow the Romany patteran
  West to the sinking sun,
Till the junk-sails lift through the houseless drift,
  And the east and the west are one.

Follow the Romany patteran
  East where the silence broods
By a purple wave on an opal beach
  In the hush of the Mahim woods.

The wild hawk to the wind-swept sky,
  The deer to the wholesome wold,
And the heart of a man to the heart of a maid,
  As it was in the days of old.

The heart of a man to the heart of a maid—
  Light of my tents, be fleet!
Morning waits at the end of the world,
  And the world is all at our feet!

          Rudyard Kipling [1865–1936]

WANDER-THIRST

BEYOND the East the sunrise, beyond the West the sea,
And East and West the wander-thirst that will not let me be;
It works in me like madness, dear, to bid me say good-by!
For the seas call and the stars call, and oh, the call of the sky!

I know not where the white road runs, nor what the blue
    hills are,
But man can have the sun for friend, and for his guide a star;
And there's no end of voyaging when once the voice is heard,
For the river calls and the road calls, and oh, the call of a
    bird!

Yonder the long horizon lies, and there by night and day
The old ships draw to home again, the young ships sail away;
And come I may, but go I must, and if men ask you why,
You may put the blame on the stars and the sun and the
    white road and the sky!

          Gerald Gould [1885–1936]

THE FOOTPATH WAY

THE winding road lies white and bare,
Heavy in dust that takes the glare;
The thirsty hedgerows and parched grass
Dream of a time when no road was.

Beyond, the fields are full in view,
Heavy in herbage and in dew;
The great-eyed kine browse thankfully;
Come, take the footpath way with me!

This stile, where country lovers tryst,
Where many a man and maid have kissed,
Invites us sweetly, and the wood
Beckons us to her solitude.

Leave men and lumbering wains behind,
And dusty roads, all blank and blind;
Come tread on velvet and on silk,
Damasked with daisies, white as milk.

Those dryads of the wood, that some
Call the wild hyacinths, now are come,
And hold their revels in a night
Of emerald flecked with candle-light.

The fountains of the meadows play,
This is the wild bee's holiday;
When summer-snows have sweetly dressed
The pasture like a wedding-guest,

By fields of beans that shall eclipse
The honey on the rose's lips,
With woodruff and the new hay's breath,
And wild thyme sweetest in her death,

Skirting the rich man's lawn and hall,
The footpath way is free to all;
For us his pinks and roses blow:
Fling him thanksgiving ere we go!

By orchards yet in rosy veils,
By hidden nests of nightingales,
Through lonesome valleys where all day
The rabbit people scurry and play,

The footpath sets her tender lure.
This is the country for the poor;
The high-road seeks the crowded sea;
Come, take the footpath way with me!
                    Katherine Tynan Hinkson [1861-1931]

A MAINE TRAIL

COME follow, heart upon your sleeve,
  The trail, a-teasing by,
Past tasseled corn and fresh-mown hay,
  Trim barns and farm-house shy,
Past hollyhocks and white well-sweep,
  Through pastures bare and wild,
Oh come, let's fare to the heart-o'-the-wood
  With the faith of a little child.

Strike in by the gnarled way through the swamp
  Where late the laurel shone,
An intimate close where you meet yourself
  And come unto your own,
By bouldered brook to the hidden spring
  Where breath of ferns blows sweet
And swift birds break the silence as
  Their shadows cross your feet.

Stout-hearted thrust through gold-green copse
  To garner the woodland glee,
To weave a garment of warm delight,
  Of sunspun ecstasy;
'Twill shield you all winter from frosty eyes,
  'Twill shield your heart from cold;
Such greens!—how the Lord Himself loves green!
  Such sun!—how He loves the gold!

Then on till flaming fireweed
  Is quenched in forest deep;
Tread soft! The sumptuous paven moss
  Is spread for Dryads' sleep;
And list ten thousand thousand spruce
  Lift up their voice to God—
We can a little understand,
  Born of the self-same sod.

Oh come, the welcoming trees lead on,
  Their guests are we to-day;
Shy violets smile, proud branches bow,
  Gay mushrooms mark the way;

The silence is a courtesy,
   The well-bred calm of kings;
Come haste! the hour sets its face
   Unto great Happenings.
       Gertrude Huntington McGiffert [18 -

AFOOT

COMES the lure of green things growing,
Comes the call of waters flowing—
   And the wayfarer desire
Moves and wakes and would be going.

Hark the migrant hosts of June
Marching nearer noon by noon!
   Hark the gossip of the grasses
Bivouacked beneath the moon!

Long the quest and far the ending
When my wayfarer is wending—
   When desire is once afoot,
Doom behind and dream attending!

In his ears the phantom chime
Of incommunicable rhyme,
   He shall chase the fleeting camp-fires
Of the Bedouins of Time.

Farer by uncharted ways,
Dumb as death to plaint or praise,
   Unreturning he shall journey,
Fellow to the nights and days;

Till upon the outer bar
Stilled the moaning currents are,
   Till the flame achieves the zenith,
Till the moth attains the star,

Till through laughter and through tears
Fair the final peace appears,
   And about the watered pastures
Sink to sleep the nomad years!
       Charles G. D. Roberts [1860–

FROM ROMANY TO ROME

UPON the road to Romany
    It's stay, friend, stay!
There's lots o' love and lots o' time
    To linger on the way;
Poppies for the twilight,
    Roses for the noon,
It's happy goes as lucky goes
    To Romany in June.

But on the road to Rome—oh,
    It's march, man, march!
The dust is on the chariot wheels,
    The sere is on the larch,
Helmets and javelins
    And bridles flecked with foam—
The flowers are dead, the world's ahead
    Upon the road to Rome.

But on the road to Rome—ah,
    It's fight, man, fight!
Footman and horseman
    Treading left and right,
Camp-fires and watch-fires
    Ruddying the gloam—
The fields are gray and worn away
    Along the road to Rome.

Upon the road to Romany
    It's sing, boys, sing!
Though rag and pack be on our back
    We'll whistle to the King.
Wine is in the sunshine,
    Madness in the moon,
And de'il may care the road we fare
    To Romany in June.

Along the road to Rome, alas!
    The glorious dust is whirled,
Strong hearts are fierce to see
    The City of the World;

Yet footfall or bugle-call
　　Or thunder as ye will,
Upon the road to Romany
　　The birds are calling still!
　　　　　　Wallace Irwin [1875–

THE TOIL OF THE TRAIL

WHAT have I gained by the toil of the trail?
I know and know well.
I have found once again the lore I had lost
In the loud city's hell.

I have broadened my hand to the cinch and the axe,
I have laid my flesh to the rain;
I was hunter and trailer and guide;
I have touched the most primitive wildness again.

I have threaded the wild with the stealth of the deer,
No eagle is freer than I;
No mountain can thwart me, no torrent appall,
I defy the stern sky.
So long as I live these joys will remain,
I have touched the most primitive wildness again.
　　　　　　Hamlin Garland [1860–1940]

DO YOU FEAR THE WIND?

Do you fear the force of the wind,
　　The slash of the rain?
Go face them and fight them,
　　Be savage again.
Go hungry and cold like the wolf,
　　　Go wade like the crane:
The palms of your hands will thicken,
　　The skin of your cheek will tan,
You'll grow ragged and weary and swarthy,
　　　But you'll walk like a man!
　　　　　　Hamlin Garland [1860–1940]

THE KING'S HIGHWAY

" El Camino Real "

ALL in the golden weather, forth let us ride to-day,
You and I together, on the King's Highway,
The blue skies above us, and below the shining sea;
There's many a road to travel, but it's this road for me.

It's a long road and sunny, and the fairest in the world—
There are peaks that rise above it in their snowy mantles
    curled,
And it leads from the mountains through a hedge of chap-
    arral,
Down to the waters where the sea gulls call.

It's a long road and sunny, it's a long road and old,
And the brown padres made it for the flocks of the fold;
They made it for the sandals of the sinner-folk that trod
From the fields in the open to the shelter-house of God.

They made it for the sandals of the sinner-folk of old;
Now the flocks they are scattered and death keeps the fold;
But you and I together we will take the road to-day,
With the breath in our nostrils, on the King's Highway.

We will take the road together through the morning's golden
    glow,
And we'll dream of those who trod it in the mellowed long
    ago;
We will stop at the Missions where the sleeping padres lay,
And we'll bend a knee above them for their souls' sake to
    pray.

We'll ride through the valleys where the blossom's on the
    tree,
Through the orchards and the meadows with the bird and
    the bee,
And we'll take the rising hills where the manzanitas grow,
Past the gray tails of waterfalls where blue violets blow.

Old Conquistadores, O brown priests and all,
Give us your ghosts for company when night begins to fall;
There's many a road to travel, but it's this road to-day,
With the breath of God about us on the King's Highway.

John S. McGroarty [1862–

THE FORBIDDEN LURE

"LEAVE all and follow—follow!"
    Lure of the sun at dawn,
Lure of a wind-paced hollow,
    Lure of the stars withdrawn;
Lure of the brave old singing
    Brave perished minstrels knew;
Of dreams like sea-fog clinging
    To boughs the night sifts through:

"Leave all and follow—follow!"
    The sun goes up the day;
Flickering wing of swallow,
    Blossoms that blow away,—
What would you, luring, luring,
    When I must bide at home?
My heart will break her mooring
    And die in reef-flung foam!

Oh, I must never listen,
    Call not outside my door.
Green leaves, you must not glisten
    Like water, any more.
Oh, Beauty, wandering Beauty,
    Pass by; speak not. For see,
By bed and board stands Duty
    To snatch my dreams from me!

Fannie Stearns Davis [1884–

THE WANDER–LOVERS

DOWN the world with Marna!
That's the life for me!
Wandering with the wandering wind,
Vagabond and unconfined!

Roving with the roving rain
Its unboundaried domain!
Kith and kin of wander-kind,
Children of the sea!

Petrels of the sea-drift!
Swallows of the lea!
Arabs of the whole wide girth
Of the wind-encircled earth!
In all climes we pitch our tents,
Cronies of the elements,
With the secret lords of birth
Intimate and free.

All the seaboard knows us
From Fundy to the Keys;
Every bend and every creek
Of abundant Chesapeake;
Ardise hills and Newport coves
And the far-off orange groves,
Where Floridian oceans break,
Tropic tiger seas.

Down the world with Marna,
Tarrying there and here!
Just as much at home in Spain
As in Tangier or Touraine!
Shakespeare's Avon knows us well,
And the crags of Neufchâtel;
And the ancient Nile is fain
Of our coming near.

Down the world with Marna,
Daughter of the air!
Marna of the subtle grace,
And the vision in her face!
Moving in the measures trod
By the angels before God!
With her sky-blue eyes amaze
And her sea-blue hair!

Marna with the trees' life
In her veins a-stir!
Marna of the aspen heart
Where the sudden quivers start!
Quick-responsive, subtle, wild!
Artless as an artless child,
Spite of all her reach of art!
Oh, to roam with her!

Marna with the wind's will,
Daughter of the sea!
Marna of the quick disdain,
Starting at the dream of stain!
At a smile with love aglow,
At a frown a statued woe,
Standing pinnacled in pain
Till a kiss sets free!

Down the world with Marna,
Daughter of the fire!
Marna of the deathless hope,
Still alert to win new scope
Where the wings of life may spread
For a flight unhazarded!
Dreaming of the speech to cope
With the heart's desire!

Marna of the far quest
After the divine!
Striving ever for some goal
Past the blunder-god's control!
Dreaming of potential years
When no day shall dawn in fears!
That's the Marna of my soul,
Wander-bride of mine!

Richard Hovey [1864–1900]

THE SEA GIPSY

I AM fevered with the sunset,
I am fretful with the bay,
For the wander-thirst is on me
And my soul is in Cathay.

There's a schooner in the offing,
With her topsails shot with fire,
And my heart has gone aboard her
For the Islands of Desire.

I must forth again to-morrow!
With the sunset I must be
Hull down on the trail of rapture
In the wonder of the Sea.

Richard Hovey [1864–1900]

A VAGABOND SONG

THERE is something in the autumn that is native to my
   blood—
Touch of manner, hint of mood;
And my heart is like a rhyme,
With the yellow and the purple and the crimson keeping
   time.

The scarlet of the maples can shake me like a cry
Of bugles going by.
And my lonely spirit thrills
To see the frosty asters like a smoke upon the hills.

There is something in October sets the gipsy blood astir;
We must rise and follow her,
When from every hill of flame
She calls and calls each vagabond by name.

Bliss Carman [1861–1929]

SPRING SONG

MAKE me over, Mother April,
When the sap beings to stir!
When thy flowery hand delivers
All the mountain-prisoned rivers,
And thy great heart beats and quivers
To revive the days that were,
Make me over, Mother April,
When the sap begins to stir!

Take my dust and all my dreaming,
Count my heart-beats one by one,
Send them where the winters perish;
Then some golden noon recherish
And restore them in the sun,
Flower and scent and dust and dreaming,
With their heart-beats every one!

Set me in the urge and tide-drift
Of the streaming hosts a-wing!
Breast of scarlet, throat of yellow,
Raucous challenge, wooings mellow—
Every migrant is my fellow,
Making northward with the spring.
Loose me in the urge and tide-drift
Of the streaming hosts a-wing!

Shrilling pipe or fluting whistle,
In the valleys come again;
Fife of frog and call of tree-toad,
All my brothers, five or three-toed,
With their revel no more vetoed,
Making music in the rain;
Shrilling pipe or fluting whistle,
In the valleys come again.

Make me of thy seed to-morrow,
When the sap begins to stir!
Tawny light-foot, sleepy bruin,
Bright-eyes in the orchard ruin,
Gnarl the good life goes askew in,
Whiskey-jack, or tanager,—
Make me anything to-morrow,
When the sap begins to stir!

Make me even (How do I know?)
Like my friend the gargoyle there;
It may be the heart within him
Swells that doltish hands should pin him
Fixed forever in mid-air.
Make me even sport for swallows,
Like the soaring gargoyle there!

Give me the old clue to follow,
Through the labyrinth of night!
Clod of clay with heart of fire,
Things that burrow and aspire,
With the vanishing desire,
For the perishing delight,—
Only the old clue to follow,
Through the labyrinth of night!

Make me over, Mother April,
When the sap begins to stir!
Fashion me from swamp or meadow,
Garden plot or ferny shadow,
Hyacinth or humble burr!
Make me over, Mother April,
When the sap begins to stir!

Let me hear the far, low summons,
When the silver winds return;
Rills that run and streams that stammer,
Goldenwing with his loud hammer,
Icy brooks that brawl and clamor,
Where the Indian willows burn;
Let me hearken to the calling,
When the silver winds return,

Till recurring and recurring,
Long since wandered and come back,
Like a whim of Grieg's or Gounod's,
This same self, bird, bud, or Bluenose,
Some day I may capture (Who knows?)
Just the one last joy I lack,
Waking to the far new summons,
When the old spring winds come back.

For I have no choice of being,
When the sap begins to climb,—
Strong insistence, sweet intrusion,
Vasts and verges of illusion,—
So I win, to time's confusion,
The one perfect pearl of time,

Joy and joy and joy forever,
Till the sap forgets to climb!

Make me over in the morning
From the rag-bag of the world!
Scraps of dream and duds of daring,
Home-brought stuff from far sea-faring,
Faded colors once so flaring,
Shreds of banners long since furled!
Hues of ash and glints of glory,
In the rag-bag of the world!

Let me taste the old immortal
Indolence of life once more;
Not recalling nor foreseeing,
Let the great slow joys of being
Well my heart through as of yore!
Let me taste the old immortal
Indolence of life once more!

Give me the old drink for rapture,
The delirium to drain,
All my fellows drank in plenty
At the Three Score Inns and Twenty
From the mountains to the main!
Give me the old drink for rapture,
The delirium to drain!

Only make me over, April,
When the sap begins to stir!
Make me man or make me woman,
Make me oaf or ape or human,
Cup of flower or cone of fir;
Make me anything but neuter
When the sap begins to stir!

Bliss Carman [1861-1929]

THE MENDICANTS

WE are as mendicants who wait
   Along the roadside in the sun.
Tatters of yesterday and shreds
   Of morrow clothe us every one.

And some are dotards, who believe
  And glory in the days of old;
While some are dreamers, harping still
  Upon an unknown age of gold.

Hopeless or witless! Not one heeds,
  As lavish Time comes down the way
And tosses in the suppliant hat
  One great new-minted gold To-day.

Ungrateful heart and grudging thanks,
  His beggar's wisdom only sees
Housing and bread and beer enough;
  He knows no other things than these.

O foolish ones, put by your care!
  Where wants are many, joys are few;
And at the wilding springs of peace,
  God keeps an open house for you.

But that some Fortunatus' gift
  Is lying there within his hand,
More costly than a pot of pearls,
  His dullness does not understand.

And so his creature heart is filled;
  His shrunken self goes starved away.
Let him wear brand-new garments still,
  Who has a threadbare soul, I say.

But there be others, happier few,
  The vagabondish sons of God,
Who know the by-ways and the flowers,
  And care not how the world may plod.

They idle down the traffic lands,
  And loiter through the woods with spring;
To them the glory of the earth
  Is but to hear a bluebird sing.

They too receive each one his Day;
　　But their wise heart knows many things
Beyond the sating of desire,
　　Above the dignity of kings.

One I remember kept his coin,
　　And laughing flipped it in the air;
But when two strolling pipe-players
　　Came by, he tossed it to the pair.

Spendthrift of joy, his childish heart
　　Danced to their wild outlandish bars;
Then supperless he laid him down
　　That night, and slept beneath the stars.
　　　　　　　　Bliss Carman [1861–1929]

THE JOYS OF THE ROAD

Now the joys of the road are chiefly these:
A crimson touch on the hard-wood trees;

A vagrant's morning wide and blue,
In early fall, when the wind walks, too;

A shadowy highway cool and brown
Alluring up and enticing down

From rippled water to dappled swamp,
From purple glory to scarlet pomp;

The outward eye, the quiet will,
And the striding heart from hill to hill;

The tempter apple over the fence;
The cobweb bloom on the yellow quince;

The palish asters along the wood,—
A lyric touch of the solitude;

An open hand, an easy shoe,
And a hope to make the day go through,—

Another to sleep with, and a third
To wake me up at the voice of a bird;

The resonant far-listening morn,
And the hoarse whisper of the corn;

The crickets mourning their comrades lost,
In the night's retreat from the gathering frost;

(Or is it their slogan, plaintive and shrill,
As they beat on their corselets, valiant still?)

A hunger fit for the kings of the sea,
And a loaf of bread for Dickon and me;

A thirst like that of the Thirsty Sword,
And a jug of cider on the board;

An idle noon, a bubbling spring,
The sea in the pine-tops murmuring;

A scrap of gossip at the ferry;
A comrade neither glum nor merry,

Asking nothing, revealing naught,
But minting his words from a fund of thought,

A keeper of silence eloquent,
Needy, yet royally well content,

Of the mettled breed, yet abhorring strife,
And full of the mellow juice of life,

A taster of wine, with an eye for a maid,
Never too bold, and never afraid,

Never heart-whole, never heart-sick,
(These are the things I worship in Dick)

No fidget and no reformer, just
A calm observer of ought and must,

A lover of books, but a reader of man,
No cynic and no charlatan,

Who never defers and never demands,
But, smiling, takes the world in his hands, —

Seeing it good as when God first saw
And gave it the weight of his will for law.

And O the joy that is never won,
But follows and follows the journeying sun,

By marsh and tide, by meadow and stream,
A will-o'-the-wind, a light-o'-dream,

Delusion afar, delight anear,
From morrow to morrow, from year to year,

A jack-o'-lantern, a fairy fire,
A dare, a bliss, and a desire!

The racy smell of the forest loam,
When the stealthy, sad-heart leaves go home;

(O leaves, O leaves, I am one with you,
Of the mould and the sun and the wind and the dew!)

The broad gold wake of the afternoon;
The silent fleck of the cold new moon;

The sound of the hollow sea's release
From stormy tumult to starry peace;

With only another league to wend;
And two brown arms at the journey's end!

These are the joys of the open road—
For him who travels without a load.

Bliss Carman [1861–1929]

THE SONG OF THE FOREST RANGER

Oh, to feel the fresh breeze blowing
   From lone ridges yet untrod!
Oh, to see the far peak growing
   Whiter as it climbs to God!

Where the silver streamlet rushes
  I would follow—follow on
Till I heard the happy thrushes
  Piping lyrics to the dawn.

I would hear the wild rejoicing
  Of the wind-blown cedar tree,
Hear the sturdy hemlock voicing
  Ancient epics of the sea.

Forest aisles would I be winding,
  Out beyond the gates of Care;
And, in dim cathedrals, finding
  Silence at the shrine of Prayer.

When the mystic night comes stealing
  Through my vast, green room afar,
Never king had richer ceiling—
  Bended bough and yellow star!

Ah, to list the sacred preaching
  Of the forest's faithful fir,
With his strong arms upward reaching—
  Mighty, trustful worshipper!

Come and learn the joy of living!
  Come and you will understand
How the sun his gold is giving
  With a great, impartial hand!

How the patient pine is climbing,
  Year by year to gain the sky;
How the rill makes sweetest rhyming,
  Where the deepest shadows lie.

I am nearer the great Giver,
  Where His handiwork is crude;
Friend am I of peak and river,
  Comrade of old Solitude.

Not for me the city's riot!
Not for me the towers of Trade!
I would seek the house of Quiet,
That the Master Workman made!

Herbert Bashford [1871–1928]

A DROVER

To Meath of the pastures,
From wet hills by the sea,
Through Leitrim and Longford,
Go my cattle and me.

I hear in the darkness
Their slipping and breathing—
I name them the bye-ways
They're to pass without heeding;

Then the wet, winding roads,
Brown bogs with black water;
And my thoughts on white ships
And the King o' Spain's daughter.

O! farmer, strong farmer!
You can spend at the fair;
But your face you must turn
To your crops and your care.

And soldiers—red soldiers!
You've seen many lands;
But you walk two by two,
And by captain's commands.

O! the smell of the beasts,
The wet wind in the morn;
And the proud and hard earth
Never broken for corn;

And the crowds at the fair,
The herds loosened and blind,
Loud words and dark faces
And the wild blood behind.

(O! strong men, with your best
I would strive breast to breast,
I could quiet your herds
With my words, with my words.)

I will bring you, my kine,
Where there's grass to the knee;
But you'll think of scant croppings
Harsh with salt of the sea.

Padriac Colum [1881–

BALLAD OF LOW–LIE–DOWN

JOHN-A-DREAMS and Harum-Scarum
  Came a-riding into town:
At the Sign o' the Jug-and-Jorum
  There they met with Low-lie-down.

Brave in shoes of Romany leather,
  Bodice blue and gypsy gown,
And a cap of fur and feather,
  In the inn sat Low-lie-down.

Harum-Scarum kissed her lightly;
  Smiled into her eyes of brown:
Clasped her waist and held her tightly,
  Laughing, "Love me, Low-lie-down!"

Then with many an oath and swagger,
  As a man of great renown,
On the board he clapped his dagger,
  Called for sack and sat him down.

So a while they laughed together;
  Then he rose and with a frown
Sighed, "While still 'tis pleasant weather,
  I must leave thee, Low-lie-down."

So away rode Harum-Scarum;
  With a song rode out of town;
At the Sign o' the Jug-and-Jorum
  Weeping tarried Low-lie-down.

Then this John-a-dreams, in tatters,
  In his pocket ne'er a crown,
Touched her, saying, "Wench, what matters!
  Dry your eyes and, come, sit down.

"Here's my hand: we'll roam together,
  Far away from thorp and town.
Here's my heart,—for any weather,—
  And my dreams, too, Low-lie-down.

"Some men call me dreamer, poet:
  Some men call me fool and clown—
What I am but you shall know it,
  Only you, sweet Low-lie-down."

For a little while she pondered:
  Smiled: then said, "Let care go drown!"
Up and kissed him. . . . Forth they wandered,
  John-a-dreams and Low-lie-down.

                    Madison Cawein [1865–1914]

THE GOOD INN

From "The Inn of the Silver Moon."

WHAT care if the day
Be turned to gray,
What care if the night come soon!
We may choose the pace
Who bow for grace
At the Inn of the Silver Moon.

Ah, hurrying Sirs,
Drive deep your spurs,
For it's far to the steepled town—
Where the wallet's weight
Shall fix your state
And buy for ye smile or frown.
Through our tiles of green
Do the stars between
Laugh down from the skies of June,
And there's naught to pay
For a couch of hay
At the Inn of the Silver Moon.

You laboring lout,
Pull out, pull out,
With a hand to the creaking tire,
For it's many a mile
By path and stile
To the old wife crouched by the fire.
But the door is wide
In the hedgerow side,
And we ask not bowl nor spoon
Whose draught of must
Makes soft the crust
At the Inn of the Silver Moon.

Then, here's to the Inn
Of the empty bin,
To the Host of the trackless dune!
And here's to the friend
Of the journey's end
At the Inn of the Silver Moon.

Herman Knickerbocker Vielé [1856–1908]

NIGHT FOR ADVENTURES

SOMETIMES when fragrant summer dusk comes in with
   scent of rose and musk
   And scatters from their sable husk the stars like yellow
      grain,
Oh, then the ancient longing comes that lures me like a
   roll of drums
   To follow where the cricket strums his banjo in the lane.

And when the August moon comes up and like a shallow,
   silver cup
   Pours out upon the fields and roads her amber-colored
      beams,
A leafy whisper mounts and calls from out the forest's moss-
   grown halls
   To leave the city's somber walls and take the road of
      dreams.

A call that bids me rise and strip, and, naked all from toe
   to lip,

To wander where the dewdrops drip from off the silent
trees,
And where the hairy spiders spin their nets of silver, fragile-
thin,
And out to where the fields begin, like down upon the
breeze.

Into a silver pool to plunge, and like a great trout wheel
and lunge
Among the lily-bonnets and the stars reflected there;
With face upturned to lie afloat, with moonbeams rippling
round my throat,
And from the slimy grasses plait a chaplet for my hair.

Then, leaping from my rustic bath, to take some winding
meadow-path:
Across the fields of aftermath to run with flying feet,
And feel the dewdrop-weighted grass that bends beneath
me as I pass,
Where solemn trees in shadowy mass beyond the highway meet.

And, plunging deep within the woods, among the leaf-hung
solitudes
Where scarce one timid star intrudes into the breathless
gloom,
Go leaping down some fern-hid way to scare the rabbits in
their play,
And see the owl, a fantom gray, drift by on silent plume.

To fling me down at length and rest upon some damp and
mossy nest,
And hear the choir of surpliced frogs strike up a bubbling
tune;
And watch, above the dreaming trees, Orion and the Hyades
And all the stars, like golden bees, around the lily-moon.

Then who can say if I have gone a-gipsying from dusk till
dawn
In company with fay and faun, where firefly-lanterns
gleam?

And have I danced on cobwebs thin to Master Locust's
    mandolin—
  Or I have spent the night in bed, and was it all a dream?
                                    Victor Starbuck [1887–

SONG

From " The Way of Perfect Love "

SOMETHING calls and whispers, along the city street,
Through shrill cries of children and soft stir of feet,
And makes my blood to quicken and makes my flesh to pine.
The mountains are calling; the winds wake the pine.

Past the quivering poplars that tell of water near
The long road is sleeping, the white road is clear.
Yet scent and touch can summon, afar from brook and tree,
The deep boom of surges, the gray waste of sea.

Sweet to dream and linger, in windless orchard close,
On bright brows of ladies to garland the rose,
But all the time are glowing, beyond this little world,
The still light of planets and the star-swarms whirled.
                        Georgiana Goddard King [1871–1939]

THE VOORTREKKER

THE gull shall whistle in his wake, the blind wave break in
    fire,
He shall fulfill God's utmost will unknowing His desire;
And he shall see old planets pass and alien stars arise,
And give the gale his seaworn sail in shadow of new skies.
Strong lust of gear shall drive him forth and hunger arm
    his hand
To win his food from the desert rude, his foothold from the
    sand.
His neighbors' smoke shall vex his eyes, their voices break
    his rest,
He shall go forth till South is North, sullen and dispossessed.
He shall desire loneliness, and his desire shall bring
Hard on his heels a thousand wheels, a People, and a King;
He shall come back in his own track, and by his scarce-
    cooled camp;

There shall he meet the roaring street, the derrick, and the
    stamp;
There he shall blaze a nation's ways with hatchet and with
    brand,
Till on his last-won wilderness an Empire's outposts stand!
                   Rudyard Kipling [1865–1936]

THE LONG TRAIL

THERE's a whisper down the field where the year has shot
    her yield,
    And the ricks stand gray to the sun,
Singing: "Over then, come over, for the bee has quit the
    clover,
        And your English summer's done."
        You have heard the beat of the off-shore wind,
        And the thresh of the deep-sea rain;
        You have heard the song—how long? how long?
        Pull out on the trail again!

Ha' done with the Tents of Shem, dear lass,
We've seen the seasons through,
And it's time to turn on the old trail, our own trail, the out
    trail,
Pull out, pull out, on the Long Trail—the trail that is always
    new!

It's North you may run to the rime-ringed sun,
    Or South to the blind Horn's hate;
Or East all the way into Mississippi Bay,
    Or West to the Golden Gate;
        Where the blindest bluffs hold good, dear lass,
        And the wildest tales are true,
        And the men bulk big on the old trail, our own trail,
        the out trail,
        And life runs large on the Long Trail—the trail that is
        always new.

The days are sick and cold, and the skies are gray and old,
    And the twice-breathed airs blow damp;
And I'd sell my tired soul for the bucking beam-sea roll
    Of a black Bilbao tramp;

With her load-line over her hatch, dear lass,
    And a drunken Dago crew,
    And her nose held down on the old trail, our own trail,
        the out trail,
    From Cadiz south on the Long Trail—the trail that is
        always new.

There be triple ways to take, of the eagle or the snake,
    Or the way of a man with a maid;
But the sweetest way to me is a ship's upon the sea
    In the heel of the North-East Trade.
    Can you hear the crash on her bows, dear lass,
        And the drum of the racing screw,
        As she ships it green on the old trail, our own trail, the
            out trail,
        As she lifts and 'scends on the Long Trail—the trail
            that is always new?

See the shaking funnels roar, with the Peter at the fore,
    And the fenders grind and heave,
And the derricks clack and grate, as the tackle hooks the
        crate,
    And the fall-rope whines through the sheave;
        It's "Gang-plank up and in," dear lass,
        It's "Hawsers warp her through!"
        And it's "All clear aft" on the old trail, our own trail,
            the out trail,
        We're backing down on the Long Trail—the trail that
            is always new.

O the mutter overside, when the port-fog holds us tied,
    And the sirens hoot their dread!
When foot by foot we creep o'er the hueless viewless deep
    To the sob of the questing lead!
        It's down by the Lower Hope, dear lass,
        With the Gunfleet Sands in view,
        Till the Mouse swings green on the old trail, our own
            trail, the out trail,
        And the Gull Light lifts on the Long Trail—the trail
            that is always new.

O the blazing tropic night, when the wake's a welt of light
  That holds the hot sky tame,
And the steady fore-foot snores through the planet-powdered
    floors
   Where the scared whale flukes in flame!
     Her plates are flaked by the sun, dear lass,
     And her ropes are taut with the dew,
      For we're booming down on the old trail, our own trail,
      the out trail,
      We're sagging south on the Long Trail—the trail that
      is always new.

Then home, get her home, where the drunken rollers comb,
  And the shouting seas drive by,
And the engines stamp and ring, and the wet bows reel and
    swing,
   And the Southern Cross rides high!
     Yes, the old lost stars wheel back, dear lass,
     That blaze in the velvet blue.
     They're all old friends on the old trail, our own trail,
     the out trail,
     They're God's own guides on the Long Trail—the
     trail that is always new.

Fly forward, O my heart, from the Foreland to the Start—
  We're steaming all too slow,
And it's twenty thousand mile to our little lazy isle
   Where the trumpet-orchids blow!
     You have heard the call of the off-shore wind
     And the voice of the deep-sea rain;
     You have heard the song—how long—how long?
     Pull out on the trail again!

     The Lord knows what we may find, dear lass,
     And the Deuce knows what we may do—
     But we're back once more on the old trail, our own trail,
     the out trail,
     We're down, hull down, on the Long Trail—the trail
     that is always new!
             Rudyard Kipling [1865–1936]

PART IV

FAMILIAR VERSE, AND POEMS HUMOROUS AND SATIRIC

BALLADE OF THE PRIMITIVE JEST

"What did the dark-haired Iberian laugh at before the tall blonde Aryan drove him into the corners of Europe?"—BRANDER MATTHEWS

I AM an ancient Jest!
Palæolithic man
In his arboreal nest
The sparks of fun would fan;
My outline did he plan,
And laughed like one possessed,
'Twas thus my course began,
I am a Merry Jest!

I am an early Jest!
Man delved, and built, and span;
Then wandered South and West
The peoples Aryan,
I journeyed in their van;
The Semites, too, confessed,—
From Beersheba to Dan,—
I am a Merry Jest!

I am an ancient Jest!
Through all the human clan,
Red, black, white, free, oppressed,
Hilarious I ran!
I'm found in Lucian,
In Poggio, and the rest,
I'm dear to Moll and Nan!
I am a Merry Jest!

ENVOY

Prince, you may storm and ban—
Joe Millers *are* a pest,
Suppress me if you can!
I am a Merry Jest!

Andrew Lang [1844–1912]

THE KINDLY MUSE

TIME TO BE WISE

YES; I write verses now and then,
But blunt and flaccid is my pen,
No longer talked of by young men
　　　As rather clever:
In the last quarter are my eyes,
You see it by their form and size;
Is it not time then to be wise?
　　　Or now or never.

Fairest that ever sprang from Eve!
While Time allows the short reprieve,
Just look at me! would you believe
　　　'Twas once a lover?
I cannot clear the five-bar gate;
But, trying first its timber's state,
Climb stiffly up, take breath, and wait
　　　To trundle over.

Through gallopade I cannot swing
The entangling blooms of Beauty's spring:
I cannot say the tender thing,
　　　Be't true or false,
And am beginning to opine
Those girls are only half-divine
Whose waists yon wicked boys entwine
　　　In giddy waltz.

I fear that arm above that shoulder;
I wish them wiser, graver, older,
Sedater, and no harm if colder,

And panting less.
Ah! people were not half so wild
In former days, when, starchly mild,
Upon her high-heeled Essex smiled
The brave Queen Bess.

Walter Savage Landor [1775–1864]

UNDER THE LINDENS

UNDER the lindens lately sat
A couple, and no more, in chat;
I wondered what they would be at
Under the lindens.

I saw four eyes and four lips meet,
I heard the words, "How sweet! how sweet!"
Had then the Fairies given a treat
Under the lindens?

I pondered long and could not tell
What dainty pleased them both so well:
Bees! bees! was it your hydromel
Under the lindens?

Walter Savage Landor [1775–1864]

ADVICE

To write as your sweet mother does
Is all you wish to do.
Play, sing, and smile for others, Rose!
Let others write for you.

Or mount again your Dartmoor gray,
And I will walk beside,
Until we reach that quiet bay
Which only hears the tide.

Then wave at me your pencil, then
At distance bid me stand,
Before the caverned cliff, again
The creature of your hand.

And bid me then go past the nook
    To sketch me less in size;
There are but few content to look
    So little in your eyes.

Delight us with the gifts you have,
    And wish for none beyond:
To some be gay, to some be grave,
    To one (blest youth!) be fond.

Pleasures there are how close to Pain
    And better unpossessed!
Let poetry's too throbbing vein
    Lie quiet in your breast.
            Walter Savage Landor [1775–1864]

TO FANNY

NEVER mind how the pedagogue proses,
    You want not antiquity's stamp;
The lip, that such fragrance discloses,
    Oh! never should smell of the lamp.

Old Chloe, whose withering kisses
    Have long set the Loves at defiance,
Now, done with the science of blisses,
    May fly to the blisses of science!

Young Sappho, for want of employments,
    Alone o'er her Ovid may melt,
Condemned but to read of enjoyments,
    Which wiser Corinna had felt.

But for *you* to be buried in books—
    Oh, Fanny! they're pitiful sages;
Who could not in *one* of your looks
    Read more than in millions of pages!

Astronomy finds in your eyes
    Better light than she studies above,
And Music must borrow your sighs
    As the melody fittest for Love.

In Ethics—'tis you that can check,
  In a minute, their doubts and their quarrels;
Oh! show but that mole on your neck,
  And 'twill soon put an end to their morals.

Your Arithmetic only can trip
  When to kiss and to count you endeavor;
But eloquence glows on your lip
  When you swear that you'll love me for ever.

Thus you see what a brilliant alliance
  Of arts is assembled in you,—
A course of more exquisite science
  Man never need wish to pursue.

And, oh!—if a Fellow like me
  May confer a diploma of hearts,
With my lip thus I seal your degree,
  My divine little Mistress of Arts!

Thomas Moore [1779–1852]

"I'D BE A BUTTERFLY"

I'D be a Butterfly born in a bower,
  Where roses and lilies and violets meet;
Roving for ever from flower to flower,
  And kissing all buds that are pretty and sweet!
I'd never languish for wealth, or for power,
  I'd never sigh to see slaves at my feet:
I'd be a Butterfly born in a bower,
  Kissing all buds that are pretty and sweet.

O could I pilfer the wand of a fairy,
  I'd have a pair of those beautiful wings;
Their summer days' ramble is sportive and airy,
  They sleep in a rose when the nightingale sings.
Those who have wealth must be watchful and wary;
  Power, alas! naught but misery brings!
I'd be a Butterfly, sportive and airy,
  Rocked in a rose when the nightingale sings!

What, though you tell me each gay little rover
  Shrinks from the breath of the first autumn day:
Surely 'tis better when summer is over
  To die when all fair things are fading away.
Some in life's winter may toil to discover
  Means of procuring a weary delay—
I'd be a butterfly; living, a rover,
  Dying when fair things are fading away!

          Thomas Haynes Bayly [1797–1839]

" I'M NOT A SINGLE MAN "

LINES WRITTEN IN A YOUNG LADY'S ALBUM

A PRETTY task, Miss S——, to ask
  A Benedictine pen,
That cannot quite at freedom write
  Like those of other men.
No lover's plaint my Muse must paint
  To fill this page's span,
But be correct and recollect
  I'm not a single man.

Pray only think, for pen and ink
  How hard to get along,
That may not turn on words that burn,
  Or Love, the life of song!
Nine Muses, if I chooses, I
  May woo all in a clan;
But one Miss S—— I daren't address—
  I'm not a single man.

Scribblers unwed, with little head,
  May eke it out with heart,
And in their lays it often plays
  A rare first-fiddle part.
They make a kiss to rhyme with bliss,
  But if *I* so began,
I have my fears about my ears—
  I'm not a single man.

Upon your cheek I may not speak,
    Nor on your lip be warm,
I must be wise about your eyes,
    And formal with your form;
Of all that sort of thing, in short,
    On T. H. Bayly's plan,
I must not twine a single line—
    I'm not a single man.

A watchman's part compels my heart
    To keep you off its beat,
And I might dare as soon to swear
    At *you*, as at your feet.
I can't expire in passion's fire
    As other poets can—
My life (she's by) won't let me die—
    I'm not a single man.

Shut out from love, denied a dove,
    Forbidden bow and dart;
Without a groan to call my own,
    With neither hand nor heart;
To Hymen vowed, and not allowed
    To flirt e'en with your fan,
Here end, as just a friend, I must—
    I'm not a single man.

Thomas Hood [1799–1845]

TO ——

We met but in one giddy dance,
    Good-night joined hands with greeting;
And twenty thousand things may chance
    Before our second meeting;
For oh! I have been often told
    That all the world grows older,
And hearts and hopes to-day so cold,
    To-morrow must be colder.

If I have never touched the string
    Beneath your chamber, dear one,
And never said one civil thing
    When you were by to hear one,—

If I have made no rhymes about
    Those looks which conquer Stoics,
And heard those angel tones, without
    One fit of fair heroics,—

Yet do not, though the world's cold school
    Some bitter truths has taught me,
Oh, do not deem me quite the fool
    Which wiser friends have thought me!
There is one charm I still could feel,
    If no one laughed at feeling;
One dream my lute could still reveal,—
    If it were worth revealing.

But Folly little cares what name
    Of friend or foe she handles,
When merriment directs the game,
    And midnight dims the candles;
I know that Folly's breath is weak
    And would not stir a feather;
But yet I would not have her speak
    Your name and mine together.

Oh no! this life is dark and bright,
    Half rapture and half sorrow;
My heart is very full to-night,
    My cup shall be to-morrow!
But they shall never know from me,
    On any one condition,
Whose health made bright my Burgundy,
    Whose beauty was my vision!
            Winthrop Mackworth Praed [1802–1839]

THE VICAR

Some years ago, ere Time and Taste
    Had turned our parish topsy-turvy,
When Darnel Park was Darnel Waste,
    And roads as little known as scurvy,

The man who lost his way between
   St. Mary's Hill and Sandy Thicket,
Was always shown across the Green,
   And guided to the Parson's wicket.

Back flew the bolt of lissom lath;
   Fair Margaret, in her tidy kirtle,
Led the lorn traveller up the path
   Through clean-clipt rows of box and myrtle;
And Don and Sancho, Tramp and Tray,
   Upon the parlor steps collected,
Wagged all their tails, and seemed to say,
   "Our master knows you; you're expected!"

Up rose the Reverend Doctor Brown,
   Up rose the Doctor's "winsome marrow";
The lady laid her knitting down,
   Her husband clasped his ponderous Barrow;
Whate'er the stranger's caste or creed,
   Pundit or papist, saint or sinner,
He found a stable for his steed,
   And welcome for himself, and dinner.

If, when he reached his journey's end,
   And warmed himself in court or college,
He had not gained an honest friend,
   And twenty curious scraps of knowledge;—
If he departed as he came,
   With no new light on love or liquor,—
Good sooth, the traveller was to blame,
   And not the Vicarage, nor the Vicar.

His talk was like a stream which runs
   With rapid change from rocks to roses;
It slipped from politics to puns;
   It passed from Mahomet to Moses;
Beginning with the laws which keep
   The planets in their radiant courses,
And ending with some precept deep
   For dressing eels or shoeing horses.

He was a shrewd and sound divine,
    Of loud Dissent the mortal terror;
And when, by dint of page and line,
    He 'stablished Truth, or startled Error,
The Baptist found him far too deep,
    The Deist sighed with saving sorrow,
And the lean Levite went to sleep
    And dreamed of tasting pork to-morrow.

His sermon never said or showed
    That Earth is foul, that Heaven is gracious,
Without refreshment on the road
    From Jerome, or from Athanasius;
And sure a righteous zeal inspired
    The hand and head that penned and planned them,
For all who understood, admired,
    And some who did not understand them.

He wrote, too, in a quiet way,
    Small treatises, and smaller verses,
And sage remarks on chalk and clay,
    And hints to noble lords and nurses;
True histories of last year's ghost;
    Lines to a ringlet or a turban;
And trifles to the Morning Post,
    And nothings for Sylvanus Urban.

He did not think all mischief fair,
    Although he had a knack of joking;
He did not make himself a bear,
    Although he had a taste for smoking;
And when religious sects ran mad,
    He held, in spite of all his learning,
That if a man's belief is bad,
    It will not be improved by burning.

And he was kind, and loved to sit
    In the low hut or garnished cottage,
And praise the farmer's homely wit,
    And share the widow's homelier pottage.

At his approach complaint grew mild,
    And when his hand unbarred the shutter,
The clammy lips of Fever smiled
    The welcome which they could not utter.

He always had a tale for me
    Of Julius Caesar or of Venus;
From him I learned the rule of three,
    Cat's-cradle, leap-frog, and *Quæ genus.*
I used to singe his powdered wig,
    To steal the staff he put such trust in,
And make the puppy dance a jig
    When he began to quote Augustine.

Alack, the change! In vain I look
    For haunts in which my boyhood trifled;
The level lawn, the trickling brook,
    The trees I climbed, the beds I rifled.
The church is larger than before,
    You reach it by a carriage entry:
It holds three hundred people more,
    And pews are fitted up for gentry.

Sit in the Vicar's seat; you'll hear
    The doctrine of a gentle Johnian,
Whose hand is white, whose voice is clear,
    Whose phrase is very Ciceronian.
Where is the old man laid? Look down,
    And construe on the slab before you:
"*Hic jacet Gulielmus Brown,*
    Vir nullâ non donandus lauru."
                    Winthrop Mackworth Praed [1802–1839]

THE BELLE OF THE BALL–ROOM

YEARS, years ago, ere yet my dreams
    Had been of being wise or witty;
Ere I had done with writing themes,
    Or yawned o'er this infernal Chitty;—

Years, years ago, while all my joy
   Were in my fowling-piece and filly;
In short, while I was yet a boy,
   I fell in love with Laura Lilly.

I saw her at the County Ball;
   There, when the sounds of flute and fiddle
Gave signal sweet in that old hall
   Of hands across and down the middle,
Hers was the subtlest spell by far
   Of all that sets young hearts romancing:
She was our queen, our rose, our star;
   And then she danced,—oh, heaven, her dancing!

Dark was her hair, her hand was white;
   Her voice was exquisitely tender;
Her eyes were full of liquid light;
   I never saw a waist so slender;
Her every look, her every smile,
   Shot right and left a score of arrows;
I thought 'twas Venus from her isle,
   And wondered where she'd left her sparrows.

She talked of politics or prayers,—
   Of Southey's prose, or Wordsworth's sonnets,
Of danglers or of dancing bears,
   Of battles, or the last new bonnets;
By candle-light, at twelve o'clock,
   To me it mattered not a tittle,
If those bright lips had quoted Locke,
   I might have thought they murmured Little.

Through sunny May, through sultry June,
   I loved her with a love eternal;
I spoke her praises to the moon,
   I wrote them to the Sunday Journal.
My mother laughed; I soon found out
   That ancient ladies have no feeling:
My father frowned; but how should gout
   See any happiness in kneeling?

She was the daughter of a dean,
  Rich, fat, and rather apoplectic;
She had one brother just thirteen,
  Whose color was extremely hectic;
Her grandmother, for many a year,
  Had fed the parish with her bounty;
Her second cousin was a peer,
  And lord-lieutenant of the county.

But titles and the three-per-cents,
  And mortgages, and great relations,
And India bonds, and tithes and rents,
  Oh, what are they to love's sensations?
Black eyes, fair forehead, clustering locks,—
  Such wealth, such honors, Cupid chooses;
He cares as little for the stocks,
  As Baron Rothschild for the Muses.

She sketched; the vale, the wood, the beach,
  Grew lovelier from her pencil's shading;
She botanized; I envied each
  Young blossom in her boudoir fading:
She warbled Handel; it was grand,—
  She made the Catilina jealous;
She touched the organ; I could stand
  For hours and hours to blow the bellows.

She kept an album, too, at home,
  Well filled with all an album's glories;
Paintings of butterflies and Rome,
  Patterns for trimmings, Persian stories,
Soft songs to Julia's cockatoo,
  Fierce odes to famine and to slaughter,
And autographs of Prince Lèboo,
  And recipes for elder-water.

And she was flattered, worshipped, bored;
  Her steps were watched, her dress was noted;
Her poodle-dog was quite adored;
  Her sayings were extremely quoted.

She laughed, and every heart was glad,
  As if the taxes were abolished;
She frowned, and every look was sad,
  As if the opera were demolished.

She smiled on many just for fun,—
  I knew that there was nothing in it;
I was the first, the only one
  Her heart had thought of for a minute.
I knew it, for she told me so,
  In phrase which was divinely moulded;
She wrote a charming hand, and oh,
  How sweetly all her notes were folded!

Our love was like most other loves,—
  A little glow, a little shiver,
A rosebud and a pair of gloves,
  And "Fly Not Yet," upon the river;
Some jealousy of some one's heir,
  Some hopes of dying broken-hearted;
A miniature, a lock of hair,
  The usual vows,—and then we parted.

We parted: months and years rolled by;
  We met again four summers after.
Our parting was all sob and sigh,—
  Our meeting was all mirth and laughter;
For, in my heart's most secret cell,
  There had been many other lodgers;
And she was not the ball-room's belle,
  But only Mrs.—Something—Rogers!
          Winthrop Mackworth Praed [1802–1839]

THE FINE OLD ENGLISH GENTLEMAN

I'LL sing you a good old song,
  Made by a good old pate,
Of a fine old English gentleman
  Who had an old estate,

And who kept up his old mansion
　　At a bountiful old rate;
With a good old porter to relieve
　　The old poor at his gate,
Like a fine old English gentleman
　　All of the olden time.

His hall so old was hung around
　　With pikes and guns and bows,
And swords, and good old bucklers,
　　That had stood some tough old blows;
'Twas there "his worship" held his state
　　In doublet and trunk hose,
And quaffed his cup of good old sack,
　　To warm his good old nose,
Like a fine old English gentleman
　　All of the olden time.

When winter's cold brought frost and snow,
　　He opened house to all;
And though threescore and ten his years,
　　He featly led the ball;
Nor was the houseless wanderer
　　E'er driven from his hall;
For while he feasted all the great,
　　He ne'er forgot the small;
Like a fine old English gentleman
　　All of the olden time.

But time, though old, is strong in flight,
　　And years rolled swiftly by;
And Autumn's falling leaves proclaimed
　　This good old man must die!
He laid him down right tranquilly,
　　Gave up life's latest sigh;
And mournful stillness reigned around,
　　And tears bedewed each eye,
For this fine old English gentleman
　　All of the olden time.

Now surely this is better far
   Than all the new parade
Of theaters and fancy balls,
   "At home" and masquerade:
And much more economical,
   For all his bills were paid,
Then leave your new vagaries quite,
   And take up the old trade
Of a fine old English gentleman,
   All of the olden time.

Unknown

A TERNARIE OF LITTLES, UPON A PIPKIN OF JELLY SENT TO A LADY

A LITTLE Saint best fits a little Shrine,
A little Prop best fits a little Vine,
As my small Cruse best fits my little Wine.

A little Seed best fits a little Soil,
A little Trade best fits a little Toil,
As my small Jar best fits my little Oil.

A little Bin best fits a little Bread,
A little Garland fits a little Head,
As my small Stuff best fits my little Shed.

A little Hearth best fits a little Fire,
A little Chapel fits a little Quire,
As my small Bell best fits my little Spire.

A little Stream best fits a little Boat,
A little Lead best fits a little Float,
As my small Pipe best fits my little Note.

A little Meat best fits a little Belly,
As sweetly, lady, give me leave to tell ye,
This little Pipkin fits this little Jelly.

Robert Herrick [1591–1674]

CHIVALRY AT A DISCOUNT

FAIR cousin mine! the golden days
  Of old romance are over;
And minstrels now care naught for bays,
  Nor damsels for a lover;
And hearts are cold, and lips are mute
  That kindled once with passion,
And now we've neither lance nor lute,
  And tilting's out of fashion.

Yet weeping Beauty mourns the time
  When Love found words in flowers;
When softest sighs were breathed in rhyme,
  And sweetest songs in bowers;
Now wedlock is a sober thing—
  No more of chains or forges!—
A plain young man—a plain gold ring—
  The curate—and St. George's.

Then every cross-bow had a string,
  And every heart a fetter;
And making love was quite the thing,
  And making verses better;
And maiden-aunts were never seen,
  And gallant beaux were plenty;
And lasses married at sixteen,
  And died at one-and-twenty.

Then hawking was a noble sport,
  And chess a pretty science;
And huntsmen learned to blow a *morte*,
  And heralds a defiance;
And knights and spearmen showed their might,
  And timid hinds took warning;
And hypocras was warmed at night,
  And coursers in the morning.

Then plumes and pennons were prepared,
  And patron-saints were lauded;
And noble deeds were bravely dared,
  And noble dames applauded·

And Beauty played the leech's part,
　And wounds were healed with syrup;
And warriors sometimes lost a heart,
　But never lost a stirrup.

Then there was no such thing as Fear,
　And no such word as Reason;
And Faith was like a pointed spear,
　And Fickleness was treason;
And hearts were soft, though blows were **hard**;
　But when the fight was over,
A brimming goblet cheered the board,
　His Lady's smile the lover.

Ay, those were golden days! The **moon**
　Had then her true adorers;
And there were lyres and lutes in tune,
　And no such thing as snorers;
And lovers swam, and held at naught
　Streams broader than the Mersey;
And fifty thousand would have fought
　For a smile from Lady Jersey.

Then people wore an iron vest,
　And had no use for tailors;
And the artizans who lived the best
　Were armorers and nailers;
And steel was measured by the ell,
　And trousers lined with leather;
And jesters wore a cap and bell,
　And knights a cap and feather.

Then single folks might live at ease,
　And married ones might sever;
Uncommon doctors had their fees,
　But Doctor's Commons never;
O! had we in those times been bred,
　Fair cousin, for thy glances,
Instead of breaking Priscian's head,
　I had been breaking lances!
Edward Fitzgerald [1809–1883]

THE BALLAD OF BOUILLABAISSE

A STREET there is in Paris famous,
  For which no rhyme our language yields,
Rue Neuve des Petits Champs its name is—
  The New Street of the Little Fields;
And there's an inn, not rich and splendid,
  But still in comfortable case—
The which in youth I oft attended,
  To eat a bowl of Bouillabaisse.

This Bouillabaisse a noble dish is—
  A sort of soup, or broth, or brew,
Or hotchpotch of all sorts of fishes,
  That Greenwich never could outdo;
Green herbs, red peppers, mussels, saffern,
  Soles, onions, garlic, roach, and dace:
All these you eat at Terré's tavern,
  In that one dish of Bouillabaisse.

Indeed, a rich and savory stew 'tis;
  And true philosophers, methinks,
Who love all sorts of natural beauties,
  Should love good victuals and good drinks.
And Cordelier or Benedictine
  Might gladly, sure, his lot embrace,
Nor find a fast-day too afflicting,
  Which served him up a Bouillabaisse.

I wonder if the house still there is?
  Yes, here the lamp is as before;
The smiling, red-cheeked écaillère is
  Still opening oysters at the door.
Is Terré still alive and able?
  I recollect his droll grimace;
He'd come and smile before your table
  And hope you liked your Bouillabaisse.

We enter; nothing's changed or older.
  "How's Monsieur Terré, waiter, pray?"
The waiter stares and shrugs his shoulder;—
  "Monsieur is dead this many a day."

"It is the lot of saint and sinner.
   So honest Terré's run his race!"
"What will Monsieur require for dinner?"
   "Say, do you still cook Bouillabaisse?"

"Oh, oui, Monsieur," 's the waiter's answer;
   "Quel vin Monsieur désire-t-il?"
"Tell me a good one." "That I can, Sir;
   The Chambertin with yellow seal."
"So Terré's gone," I say, and sink in
   My old accustomed corner-place;
"He's done with feasting and with drinking,
   With Burgundy and Bouillabaisse."

My old accustomed corner here is,—
   The table still is in the nook;
Ah! vanished many a busy year is,
   This well-known chair since last I took,
When first I saw ye, *cari luoghi*,
   I'd scarce a beard upon my face,
And now a grizzled, grim old fogy,
   I sit and wait for Bouillabaisse.

Where are you, old companions trusty
   Of early days here met to dine?
Come, waiter! quick, a flagon crusty—
   I'll pledge them in the good old wine.
The kind old voices and old faces
   My memory can quick retrace;
Around the board they take their places,
   And share the wine and Bouillabaisse.

There's Jack has made a wondrous marriage;
   There's laughing Tom is laughing yet;
There's brave Augustus drives his carriage;
   There's poor old Fred in the *Gazette*;
On James's head the grass is growing:
   Good Lord! the world has wagged apace
Since here we set the Claret flowing,
   And drank, and ate the Bouillabaisse.

Ah me! how quick the days are flitting!
  I mind me of a time that's gone,
When here I'd sit, as now I'm sitting,
  In this same place—but not alone.
A fair young form was nestled near me,
  A dear, dear face looked fondly up,
And sweetly spoke and smiled to cheer me.
  —There's no one now to share my cup. . . .

I drink it as the Fates ordain it.
  Come, fill it, and have done with rhymes;
Fill up the lonely glass, and drain it
  In memory of dear old times.
Welcome the wine, whate'er the seal is;
  And sit you down and say your grace
With thankful heart, whate'er the meal is.
—Here comes the smoking Bouillabaisse!

      William Makepeace Thackeray [1811–1863]

TO MY GRANDMOTHER

SUGGESTED BY A PICTURE BY MR. ROMNEY

Under the elm a rustic seat
Was merriest Susan's pet retreat
To merry-make

THIS Relative of mine
Was she seventy-and-nine
  When she died?
By the canvas may be seen
How she looked at seventeen,
  As a Bride.

Beneath a summer tree
Her maiden reverie
  Has a charm;
Her ringlets are in taste;
What an arm! and what a waist
  For an arm!

With her bridal-wreath, bouquet,
Lace farthingale, and gay

Falbala,—
If Romney's touch be true,
What a lucky dog were you,
  Grandpapa!

Her lips are sweet as love;
They are parting! Do they move?
  Are they dumb?
Her eyes are blue, and beam
Beseechingly, and seem
  To say, "Come!"

What funny fancy slips
From atween these cherry lips?
  Whisper me,
Fair Sorceress in paint,
What canon says I mayn't
  Marry thee?

That good-for-nothing Time
Has a confidence sublime!
  When I first
Saw this Lady, in my youth,
Her winters had, forsooth,
  Done their worst.

Her locks, as white as snow,
Once shamed the swarthy crow;
  By-and-by
That fowl's avenging sprite
Set his cruel foot for spite
  Near her eye.

Her rounded form was lean,
And her silk was bombazine:
  Well I wot
With her needles would she sit,
And for hours would she knit.—
  Would she not?

Ah perishable clay!
Her charms had dropped away
    One by one:
But if she heaved a sigh
With a burden, it was, "Thy
    Will be done."

In travail, as in tears,
With the fardel of her years
    Overpressed,
In mercy she was borne
Where the weary and the worn
    Are at rest.

Oh, if you now are there,
And sweet as once you were,
    Grandmamma,
This nether world agrees
You'll all the better please
    Grandpapa.

        Frederick Locker-Lampson [1821–1895]

MY MISTRESS'S BOOTS

She has dancing eyes and ruby lips,
Delightful boots—and away she skips

THEY nearly strike me dumb,—
I tremble when they come
        Pit-a-pat:
This palpitation means
These Boots are Geraldine's—
        Think of that!

O, where did hunter win
So delicate a skin
        For her feet?
You lucky little kid,
You perished, so you did,
        For my Sweet.

The fairy stitching gleams
On the sides, and in the seams,

And reveals
That the Pixies were the wags
Who tipped these funny tags,
And these heels.

What soles to charm an elf!—
Had Crusoe, sick of self,
Chanced to view
One printed near the tide,
O, how hard he would have tried
For the two!

For Gerry's debonair,
And innocent and fair
As a rose;
She's an Angel in a frock,—
She's an Angel with a clock
To her hose!

The simpletons who squeeze
Their pretty toes to please
Mandarins,
Would positively flinch
From venturing to pinch
Geraldine's.

Cinderella's *lefts and rights*
To Geraldine's were frights:
And I trow
The Damsel, deftly shod,
Has dutifully trod
Until now.

Come, Gerry, since it suits
Such a pretty Puss (in Boots)
These to don,
Set your dainty hand awhile
On my shoulder, Dear, and I'll
Put them on.
        Frederick Locker-Lampson [1821–1895]

A GARDEN LYRIC

GERALDINE AND I

*Dite, Damasippe, deæque
Verum ob consilium donent tonsore.*

We have loitered and laughed in the flowery croft,
     We have met under wintry skies;
Her voice is the dearest voice, and soft
     Is the light in her wistful eyes;
It is bliss in the silent woods, among
     Gay crowds, or in any place,
To mould her mind, to gaze in her young
          Confiding face.

For ever may roses divinely blow,
     And wine-dark pansies charm
By that prim box path where I felt the glow
     Of her dimpled, trusting arm,
And the sweep of her silk as she turned and smiled
     A smile as pure as her pearls;
The breeze was in love with the darling Child,
          And coaxed her curls.

She showed me her ferns and woodbine sprays,
     Foxglove and jasmine stars,
A mist of blue in the beds, a blaze
     Of red in the celadon jars:
And velvety bees in convolvulus bells,
     And roses of bountiful Spring.
But I said—"Though roses and bees have spells,
          They have thorn, and sting."

She showed me ripe peaches behind a net
     As fine as her veil, and fat
Goldfish a-gape, who lazily met
     For her crumbs—I grudged them that!
A squirrel, some rabbits with long lop ears,
     And guinea-pigs, tortoise-shell—wee;
And I told her that eloquent truth inheres
          In all we see.

I lifted her doe by its lops, quoth I,
  "Even here deep meaning lies,—
Why have squirrels these ample tails, and why
  Have rabbits these prominent eyes?"
She smiled and said, as she twirled her veil,
  "For some nice little cause, no doubt—
If you lift a guinea-pig up by the tail
  His eyes drop out!"

Frederick Locker-Lampson [1821–1895]

MRS. SMITH

Heigh-ho! they're wed. The cards are dealt,
  Our frolic games are o'er;
I've laughed, and fooled, and loved. I've felt—
  As I shall feel no more!
Yon little thatch is where she lives,
  Yon spire is where she met me;—
I think that if she quite forgives,
  She cannot quite forget me.

LAST year I trod these fields with Di,—
Fields fresh with clover and with rye;
    They now seem arid:
Then Di was fair and single; how
Unfair it seems on me, for now
    Di's fair,—and married!

A blissful swain,—I scorned the song
Which tells us though young Love is strong,
    The Fates are stronger:
Then breezes blew a boon to men,
Then buttercups were bright, and then
    The grass was longer.

That day I saw, and much esteemed,
Di's ankles, that the clover seemed
    Inclined to smother:
It twitched, and soon untied (for fun)
The ribbons of her shoes, first one,
    And then the other.

I'm told that virgins augur some
Misfortune if their shoe-strings come

To grief on *Friday:*
And so did Di,—and then her pride
Decreed that shoe-strings so untied,
    Are "so untidy!"

Of course I knelt; with fingers deft
I tied the right, and tied the left:
    Says Di, "This stubble
Is very stupid!—as I live
I'm quite ashamed!—I'm shocked to give
    You so much trouble!"

For answer I was fain to sink
To what we all would say and think
    Were Beauty present:
"Don't mention such a simple act—
A trouble? not the least! In fact
    It's rather pleasant!"

I trust that Love will never tease
Poor little Di, or prove that he's
    A graceless rover.
She's happy now as *Mrs. Smith*—
But less polite when walking with
    Her chosen lover!

Heigh-ho! Although no moral clings
To Di's blue eyes, and sandal strings,
    We had our quarrels.
I think that Smith is thought an ass,—
I know that when they walk in grass
    She wears *balmorals*.
                    Frederick Locker-Lampson [1821–1895]

THE SKELETON IN THE CUPBOARD

THE characters of great and small
    Come ready made, we can't bespeak one;
Their sides are many, too, and all
    (Except ourselves) have got a weak one.

Some sanguine people love for life,
   Some love their hobby till it flings them.
How many love a pretty wife
   For love of the *éclat* she brings them! . . .

A little to relieve my mind
   I've thrown off this disjointed chatter,
But more because I'm disinclined
   To enter on a painful matter:
Once I was bashful; I'll allow
   I've blushed for words untimely spoken;
I still am rather shy, and now . . .
   And now the ice is fairly broken.

We all have secrets: you have one
   Which may n't be quite your charming spouse's;
We all lock up a Skeleton
   In some grim chamber of our houses;
Familiars who exhaust their days
   And nights in probing where our smart is,
And who, for all their spiteful ways,
   Are "silent, unassuming *Parties*."

We hug this Phantom we detest,
   Rarely we let it cross our portals:
It is a most exacting guest,
   And we are much afflicted mortals.
Your neighbor Gay, that jovial wight,
   As *Dives* rich, and brave as Hector,
Poor Gay steals twenty times a night,
   On shaking knees, to see his Specter.

Old *Dives* fears a pauper fate,
   So hoarding is his ruling passion:—
Some gloomy souls anticipate
   A waistcoat, straiter than the fashion!
She childless pines, that lonely wife,
   And secret tears are bitter shedding;
Hector may tremble all his life,
   And die,—but not of that he's dreading. . . .

Ah me, the World! How fast it spins!
  The beldams dance, the caldron bubbles;
They shriek, they stir it for our sins,
  And we must drain it for our troubles.
We toil, we groan; the cry for love
  Mounts up from this poor seething city,
And yet I know we have above
  A FATHER, infinite in pity.

When Beauty smiles, when Sorrow weeps,
  Where sunbeams play, where shadows darken,
One inmate of our dwelling keeps
  Its ghastly carnival; but hearken!
How dry the rattle of the bones!
  That sound was not to make *you* start meant:
Stand by! Your humble servant owns
  The Tenant of this Dark Apartment.

                    Frederick Locker-Lampson [1821–1895]

A TERRIBLE INFANT

I RECOLLECT a nurse called Ann,
  Who carried me about the grass,
And one fine day a fine young man
  Came up, and kissed the pretty lass:
She did not make the least objection!
    Thinks I, "Aha!
    When I can talk, I'll tell Mamma."
—And that's my earliest recollection.

                    Frederick Locker-Lampson [1821–1895]

COMPANIONS

A TALE OF A GRANDFATHER

I KNOW not of what we pondered
  Or made pretty pretence to talk,
As, her hand within mine, we wandered
  Toward the pool by the lime-tree walk,
While the dew fell in showers from the passion flowers
  And the blush-rose bent on her stalk.

I cannot recall her figure:
  Was it regal as Juno's own?
Or only a trifle bigger
  Than the elves who surround the throne
Of the Fairy Queen, and are seen, I ween,
  By mortals in dreams alone?

What her eyes were like I know not:
  Perhaps they were blurred with tears;
And perhaps in yon skies there glow not
  (On the contrary) clearer spheres.
No! as to her eyes I am just as wise
  As you or the cat, my dears.

Her teeth, I presume, were "pearly":
  But which was she, brunette or blonde?
Her hair, was it quaintly curly,
  Or as straight as a beadle's wand?
That I failed to remark: it was rather dark
  And shadowy round the pond.

Then the hand that reposed so snugly
  In mine,—was it plump or spare?
Was the countenance fair or ugly?
  Nay, children, you have me there!
My eyes were p'haps blurred; and besides I'd heard
  That it's horribly rude to stare.

And I,—was I brusque and surly?
  Or oppressively bland and fond?
Was I partial to rising early?
  Or why did we twain abscond,
When nobody knew, from the public view
  To prowl by a misty pond?

What passed, what was felt or spoken,—
  Whether anything passed at all,—
And whether the heart was broken
  That beat under that sheltering shawl,—
(If shawl she had on, which I doubt),—has gone,
  Yes, gone from me past recall.

Was I haply the lady's suitor?
  Or her uncle? I can't make out;
Ask your governess, dears, or tutor.
  For myself, I'm in hopeless doubt
As to why we were there, who on earth we were,
  And what this is all about.

Charles Stuart Calverley [1831–1884]

DOROTHY Q

A FAMILY PORTRAIT

GRANDMOTHER's mother: her age, I guess,
Thirteen summers, or something less;
Girlish bust, but womanly air;
Smooth, square forehead with uprolled hair;
Lips that lover has never kissed;
Taper fingers and slender wrist;
Hanging sleeves of stiff brocade;
So they painted the little maid.

On her hand a parrot green
Sits unmoving and broods serene.
Hold up the canvas full in view,—
Look! there's a rent the light shines through,
Dark with a century's fringe of dust,—
That was a Red-Coat's rapier-thrust!
Such is the tale the lady old,
Dorothy's daughter's daughter, told.

Who the painter was none may tell,—
One whose best was not over well;
Hard and dry, it must be confessed,
Flat as a rose that has long been pressed;
Yet in her cheek the hues are bright,
Dainty colors of red and white,
And in her slender shape are seen
Hint and promise of stately mien.

Look not on her with eyes of scorn,—
Dorothy Q. was a lady born!

Ay! since the galloping Normans came,
England's annals have known her name;
And still to the three-hilled rebel town
Dear is that ancient name's renown,
For many a civic wreath they won,
The youthful sire and the gray-haired son.

O Damsel Dorothy! Dorothy Q.!
Strange is the gift that I owe to you;
Such a gift as never a king
Save to daughter or son might bring,—
All my tenure of heart and hand,
All my title to house and land;
Mother and sister and child and wife
And joy and sorrow and death and life!

What if a hundred years ago
Those close-shut lips had answered No,
When forth the tremulous question came
That cost the maiden her Norman name,
And under the folds that look so still
The bodice swelled with the bosom's thrill?
Should I be I, or would it be
One tenth another, to nine tenths me?

Soft is the breath of a maiden's YES:
Not the light gossamer stirs with less;
But never a cable that holds so fast
Through all the battles of wave and blast,
And never an echo of speech or song
That lives in the babbling air so long!
There were tones in the voice that whispered then
You may hear to-day in a hundred men.

O lady and lover, how faint and far
Your images hover,—and here we are
Solid and stirring in flesh and bone,—
Edward's and Dorothy's—all their own,—
A goodly record for Time to show
Of a syllable spoken so long ago!—

Shall I bless you, Dorothy, or forgive
For the tender whisper that bade me live?

It shall be a blessing, my little maid!
I will heal the stab of the Red-Coat's blade,
And freshen the gold of the tarnished frame,
And gild with a rhyme your household name;
So you shall smile on us brave and bright
As first you greeted the morning's light,
And live untroubled by woes and fears
Through a second youth of a hundred years.

Oliver Wendell Holmes [1809–1894]

MY AUNT

My aunt! my dear unmarried aunt!
　　Long years have o'er her flown;
Yet still she strains the aching clasp
　　That binds her virgin zone;
I know it hurts her,—though she looks
　　As cheerful as she can;
Her waist is ampler than her life,
　　For life is but a span.

My aunt! my poor deluded aunt!
　　Her hair is almost gray;
Why will she train that winter curl
　　In such a spring-like way?
How can she lay her glasses down,
　　And say she reads as well,
When, through a double convex lens,
　　She just makes out to spell?

Her father,—grandpapa! forgive
　　This erring lip its smiles,—
Vowed she should make the finest girl
　　Within a hundred miles;
He sent her to a stylish school;
　　'Twas in her thirteenth June;
And with her, as the rules required,
　　"Two towels and a spoon."

They braced my aunt against a board,
  To make her straight and tall;
They laced her up, they starved her down,
  To make her light and small;
They pinched her feet, they singed her hair,
  They screwed it up with pins;—
Oh, never mortal suffered more
  In penance for her sins.

So, when my precious aunt was done,
  My grandsire brought her back;
(By daylight, lest some rabid youth
  Might follow on the track;)
"Ah!" said my grandsire, as he shook
  Some powder in his pan,
"What could this lovely creature do
  Against a desperate man!"

Alas! nor chariot, nor barouche,
  Nor bandit cavalcade,
Tore from the trembling father's arms
  His all-accomplished maid.
For her how happy had it been!
  And Heaven had spared to me
To see one sad, ungathered rose
  On my ancestral tree.
               Oliver Wendell Holmes [1809–1894]

THE LAST LEAF

I saw him once before,
As he passed by the door,
      And again
The pavement stones resound,
As he totters o'er the ground
      With his cane.

They say that in his prime,
Ere the pruning-knife of Time

Cut him down,
Not a better man was found
By the Crier on his round
Through the town.

But now he walks the streets,
And he looks at all he meets
Sad and wan,
And he shakes his feeble head,
That it seems as if he said,
"They are gone."

The mossy marbles rest
On the lips that he has pressed
In their bloom,
And the names he loved to hear
Have been carved for many a year
On the tomb.

My grandmamma has said,—
Poor old lady, she is dead
Long ago,—
That he had a Roman nose,
And his cheek was like a rose
In the snow;

But now his nose is thin,
And it rests upon his chin
Like a staff,
And a crook is in his back,
And a melancholy crack
In his laugh.

I know it is a sin
For me to sit and grin
At him here;
But the old three-cornered hat,
And the breeches, and all that,
Are so queer!

And if I should live to be
'The last leaf upon the tree
   In the spring,
Let them smile, as I do now,
At the old forsaken bough
   Where I cling.
   Oliver Wendell Holmes [1809–1894]

CONTENTMENT

"Man wants but little here below"

LITTLE I ask; my wants are few;
 I only wish a hut of stone,
(A *very plain* brown stone will do,)
  That I may call my own;—
And close at hand is such a one,
In yonder street that fronts the sun.

Plain food is quite enough for me;
 Three courses are as good as ten;—
If Nature can subsist on three,
  Thank Heaven for three. Amen!
I always thought cold victual nice;—
My *choice* would be vanilla-ice.

I care not much for gold or land;—
 Give me a mortgage here and there,—
Some good bank-stock, some note of hand,
  Or trifling railroad share,—
I only ask that Fortune send
A *little* more than I shall spend.

Honors are silly toys, I know,
 And titles are but empty names;
I would, *perhaps*, be Plenipo,—
  But only near St. James;
I'm very sure I should not care
To fill our Gubernator's chair.

Jewels are baubles; 'tis a sin
  To care for such unfruitful things;—
One good-sized diamond in a pin,—
    Some, *not so large*, in rings,—
A ruby, and a pearl, or so,
Will do for me;—I laugh at show.

My dame should dress in cheap attire;
    (Good heavy silks are never dear;)—
I own perhaps I *might* desire
    Some shawls of true Cashmere,—
Some marrowy crapes of China silk,
Like wrinkled skins on scalded milk.

I would not have the horse I drive
    So fast that folks must stop and stare;
An easy gait—two forty-five—
    Suits me; I do not care;—
Perhaps, for just a *single spurt*,
Some seconds less would do no hurt.

Of pictures, I should like to own
    Titians and Raphaels three or four,—
I love so much their style and tone,—
    One Turner, and no more,
(A landscape,—foreground golden dirt,—
The sunshine painted with a squirt.)

Of books but few,—some fifty score
    For daily use, and bound for wear;
The rest upon an upper floor;—
    Some *little* luxury *there*
Of red morocco's gilded gleam,
And vellum rich as country cream.

Busts, cameos, gems,—such things as these,
    Which others often show for pride,
I value for their power to please,
    And selfish churls deride;—
One Stradivarius, I confess,
Two meerschaums, I would fain possess.

Wealth's wasteful tricks I will not learn,
   Nor ape the glittering upstart fool;—
Shall not carved tables serve my turn,
    But *all* must be of buhl?
Give grasping pomp its double share,—
I ask but *one* recumbent chair.

Thus humble let me live and die,
   Nor long for Midas' golden touch;
If Heaven more generous gifts deny,
    I shall not miss them *much*,—
Too grateful for the blessing lent
Of simple tastes and mind content!

           Oliver Wendell Holmes [1809–1894]

THE BOYS

Has there any old fellow got mixed with the boys?
If there has, take him out, without making a noise.
Hang the Almanac's cheat and the Catalogue's spite!
Old Time is a liar! We're twenty to-night!

We're twenty! We're twenty! Who says we are more?
He's tipsy,—young jackanapes!—show him the door!
"Gray temples at twenty?"—Yes! *white* if we please!
Where the snow-flakes fall thickest there's nothing can
    freeze!

Was it snowing I spoke of? Excuse the mistake!
Look close,—you will not see a sign of a flake!
We want some new garlands for those we have shed,—
And these are white roses in place of the red.

We've a trick, we young fellows, you may have been told,
Of talking (in public) as if we were old:—
That boy we call "Doctor," and this we call "Judge;"
It's a neat little fiction,—of course it's all fudge.

That fellow's the "Speaker,"—the one on the right;
"Mr. Mayor," my young one, how are you to-night?

That's our "Member of Congress," we say when we chaff;
There's the "Reverend" What's his name?—don't make me
    laugh.

That boy with the grave mathematical look
Made believe he had written a wonderful book,
And the ROYAL SOCIETY thought it was *true!*
So they chose him right in; a good joke it was, too!

There's a boy, we pretend, with a three-decker brain,
That could harness a team with a logical chain;
When he spoke for our manhood in syllabled fire,
We called him "The Justice," but now he's "The Squire."

And there's a nice youngster of excellent pith,—
Fate tried to conceal him by naming him Smith;
But he shouted a song for the brave and the free,—
Just read on his medal, "My country," "of thee!"

You hear that boy laughing?—You think he's all fun;
But the angels laugh, too, at the good he has done;
The children laugh loud as they troop to his call,
And the poor man that knows him laughs loudest of all!

Yes, we're boys,—always playing with tongue or with pen,—
And I sometimes have asked,—Shall we ever be men?
Shall we always be youthful, and laughing, and gay,
Till the last dear companion drops smiling away?

Then here's to our boyhood, its gold and its gray!
The stars of its winter, the dews of its May!
And when we have done with our life-lasting toys,
Dear Father, take care of thy children, THE BOYS!
                    Oliver Wendell Holmes [1809–1894]

THE JOLLY OLD PEDAGOGUE

'TWAS a jolly old pedagogue, long ago,
    Tall and slender, and sallow and dry;
His form was bent, and his gait was slow,
His long, thin hair was as white as snow,

But a wonderful twinkle shone in his eye;
And he sang every night as he went to bed,
   "Let us be happy down here below:
The living should live, though the dead be dead,"
   Said the jolly old pedagogue, long ago.

He taught his scholars the rule of three,
   Writing, and reading, and history, too;
He took the little ones up on his knee,
For a kind old heart in his breast had he,
   And the wants of the littlest child he knew:
"Learn while you're young," he often said,
   "There is much to enjoy, down here below;
Life for the living, and rest for the dead!"
   Said the jolly old pedagogue, long ago.

With the stupidest boys he was kind and cool,
   Speaking only in gentlest tones;
The rod was hardly known in his school . . .
Whipping, to him, was a barbarous rule,
   And too hard work for his poor old bones;
Besides, it was painful, he sometimes said:
   "We should make life pleasant, down here below,
The living need charity more than the dead,"
   Said the jolly old pedagogue, long ago.

He lived in the house by the hawthorn lane,
   With roses and woodbine over the door;
His rooms were quiet, and neat, and plain,
But a spirit of comfort there held reign,
   And made him forget he was old and poor;
"I need so little," he often said;
   "And my friends and relatives here below
Won't litigate over me when I am dead,"
   Said the jolly old pedagogue, long ago.

But the pleasantest times that he had, of all,
   Were the sociable hours he used to pass,
With his chair tipped back to a neighbor's wall,
Making an unceremonious call,
   Over a pipe and a friendly glass:

This was the finest picture, he said,
　Of the many he tasted, here below;
"Who has no cronies, had better be dead!"
　Said the jolly old pedagogue, long ago.

Then the jolly old pedagogue's wrinkled face
　Melted all over in sunshiny smiles;
He stirred his glass with an old-school grace,
Chuckled, and sipped, and prattled apace,
　Till the house grew merry, from cellar to tiles:
"I'm a pretty old man," he gently said,
　"I've lingered a long while, here below;
But my heart is fresh, if my youth is fled!"
　Said the jolly old pedagogue, long ago.

He smoked his pipe in the balmy air,
　Every night when the sun went down,
While the soft wind played in his silvery hair,
Leaving its tenderest kisses there,
　On the jolly old pedagogue's jolly old crown:
And, feeling the kisses, he smiled and said,
　'Twas a glorious world, down here below;
"Why wait for happiness till we are dead?"
　Said the jolly old pedagogue, long ago.

He sat at his door, one midsummer night,
　After the sun had sunk in the west,
And the lingering beams of golden light
Made his kindly old face look warm and bright,
　While the odorous night-wind whispered "Rest!"
Gently, gently, he bowed his head. . . .
　There were angels waiting for him, I know;
He was sure of happiness, living or dead,
　This jolly old pedagogue, long ago!
George Arnold [1834–1865]

ON AN INTAGLIO HEAD OF MINERVA

Beneath the warrior's helm, behold
　The flowing tresses of the woman!
Minerva, Pallas, what you will—
　A winsome creature, Greek or Roman.

Minerva?   No! 'tis some sly minx
   In cousin's helmet masquerading;
If not—then Wisdom was a dame
   For sonnets and for serenading!

I thought the goddess cold, austere,
   Not made for love's despairs and blisses:
Did Pallas wear her hair like that?
   Was Wisdom's mouth so shaped for kisses?

The Nightingale should be her bird,
   And not the Owl, big-eyed and solemn:
How very fresh she looks, and yet
   She's older far than Trajan's Column!

The magic hand that carved this face,
   And set this vine-work round it running,
Perhaps ere mighty Phidias wrought,
   Had lost its subtle skill and cunning.

Who was he?   Was he glad or sad,
   Who knew to carve in such a fashion?
Perchance he graved the dainty head
   For some brown girl that scorned his passion.

Perchance, in some still garden-place,
   Where neither fount nor tree to-day is,
He flung the jewel at the feet
   Of Phryne, or perhaps 'twas Laïs.

But he is dust; we may not know
   His happy or unhappy story:
Nameless, and dead these centuries,
   His work outlives him,—there's his glory!

Both man and jewel lay in earth
   Beneath a lava-buried city;
The countless summers came and went,
   With neither haste, nor hate, nor pity.

Years blotted out the man, but left
   The jewel fresh as any blossom,
Till some Visconti dug it up,—
   To rise and fall on Mabel's bosom!

O nameless brother! see how Time
　　Your gracious handiwork has guarded:
See how your loving, patient art
　　Has come, at last, to be rewarded.

Who would not suffer slights of men,
　　And pangs of hopeless passion also,
To have his carven agate-stone
　　On such a bosom rise and fall so!

Thomas Bailey Aldrich [1837–1907]

THALIA

A MIDDLE-AGED LYRICAL POET IS SUPPOSED TO BE TAKING
FINAL LEAVE OF THE MUSE OF COMEDY. SHE HAS BROUGHT
HIM HIS HAT AND GLOVES, AND IS ABSTRACTEDLY PICKING
A THREAD OF GOLD HAIR FROM HIS COAT SLEEVE AS HE
BEGINS TO SPEAK:

I SAY it under the rose—
　　oh, thanks!—yes, under the laurel,
We part lovers, not foes;
　　we are not going to quarrel.

We have too long been friends
　　on foot and in gilded coaches,
Now that the whole thing ends,
　　to spoil our kiss with reproaches.

I leave you; my soul is wrung;
　　I pause, look back from the portal—
Ah, I no more am young,
　　and you, child, you are immortal!

Mine is the glacier's way,
　　yours is the blossom's weather—
When were December and May
　　known to be happy together?

Before my kisses grow tame,
　　before my moodiness grieve you,
While yet my heart is flame,
　　and I all lover, I leave you.

So, in the coming time,
   when you count the rich years over,
Think of me in my prime,
   and not as a white-haired lover,

Fretful, pierced with regret,
   the wraith of a dead Desire
Thrumming a cracked spinet
   by a slowly dying fire.

When, at last, I am cold—
   years hence, if the gods so will it—
Say, "He was true as gold,"
   and wear a rose in your fillet!

Others, tender as I,
   will come and sue for caresses,
Woo you, win you, and die—
   mind you, a rose in your tresses!

Some Melpomene woo,
   some hold Clio the nearest;
You, sweet Comedy—you
   were ever sweetest and dearest!

Nay, it is time to go.
   When writing your tragic sister
Say to that child of woe
   how sorry I was I missed her.

Really, I cannot stay,
   though "parting is such sweet sorrow" . . .
Perhaps I will, on my way
   down-town, look in to-morrow!
        Thomas Bailey Aldrich [1837–1907]

PAN IN WALL STREET

A. D. 1867

JUST where the Treasury's marble front
   Looks over Wall Street's mingled nations;
Where Jews and Gentiles most are wont
   To throng for trade and last quotations;

Where, hour by hour, the rates of gold
   Outrival, in the ears of people,
The quarter-chimes, serenely tolled
   From Trinity's undaunted steeple,—

Even there I heard a strange, wild strain
   Sound high above the modern clamor,
Above the cries of greed and gain,
   The curbstone war, the auction's hammer;
And swift, on Music's misty ways,
   It led, from all this strife for millions,
To ancient, sweet-to-nothing days
   Among the kirtle-robed Sicilians.

And as it stilled the multitude,
   And yet more joyous rose, and shriller,
I saw the minstrel, where he stood
   At ease against a Doric pillar:
One hand a droning organ played,
   The other held a Pan's-pipe (fashioned
Like those of old) to lips that made
   The reeds give out that strain impassioned.

'Twas Pan himself had wandered here
   A-strolling through this sordid city,
And piping to the civic ear
   The prelude of some pastoral ditty!
The demigod had crossed the seas,—
   From haunts of shepherd, nymph, and satyr,
And Syracusan times,—to these
   Far shores and twenty centuries later.

A ragged cap was on his head;
   But—hidden thus—there was no doubting
That, all with crispy locks o'erspread,
   His gnarlèd horns were somewhere sprouting;
His club-feet, cased in rusty shoes,
   Were crossed, as on some frieze you see them,
And trousers, patched of divers hues,
   Concealed his crooked shanks beneath them.

He filled the quivering reeds with sound,
    And o'er his mouth their changes shifted,
And with his goat's-eyes looked around
    Where'er the passing current drifted;
And soon, as on Trinacrian hills
    The nymphs and herdsmen ran to hear him,
Even now the tradesmen from their tills,
    With clerks and porters, crowded near him.

The bulls and bears together drew
    From Jauncey Court and New Street Alley,
As erst, if pastorals be true,
    Came beasts from every wooded valley;
The random passers stayed to list,—
    A boxer Ægon, rough and merry,
A Broadway Daphnis, on his tryst
    With Nais at the Brooklyn Ferry.

A one-eyed Cyclops halted long
    In tattered cloak of army pattern,
And Galatea joined the throng,—
    A blowsy, apple-vending slattern;
While old Silenus staggered out
    From some new-fangled lunch-house handy,
And bade the piper, with a shout,
    To strike up Yankee Doodle Dandy!

A newsboy and a peanut-girl
    Like little Fauns began to caper:
His hair was all in tangled curl,
    Her tawny legs were bare and taper;
And still the gathering larger grew,
    And gave its pence and crowded nigher,
While aye the shepherd-minstrel blew
    His pipe, and struck the gamut higher.

O heart of Nature, beating still
    With throbs her vernal passion taught her,—
Even here, as on the vine-clad hill,
    Or by the Arethusan water!

New forms may fold the speech, new lands
    Arise within these ocean-portals,
But Music waves eternal wands,—
    Enchantress of the souls of mortals!

So thought I,—but among us trod
    A man in blue, with legal baton,
And scoffed the vagrant demigod,
    And pushed him from the step I sat on.
Doubting I mused upon the cry,
    "Great Pan is dead!"—and all the people
Went on their ways:—and clear and high
    The quarter sounded from the steeple.
                Edmund Clarence Stedman [1833–1908]

UPON LESBIA—ARGUING

My Lesbia, I will not deny,
    Bewitches me completely;
She has the usual beaming eye,
    And smiles upon me sweetly:
But she has an unseemly way
Of contradicting what I say.

And, though I am her closest friend,
    And find her fascinating,
I cannot cordially commend
    Her method of debating:
Her logic, though she is divine,
Is singularly feminine.

Her reasoning is full of tricks,
    And butterfly suggestions,
I know no point to which she sticks,
    She begs the simplest questions;
And, when her premises are strong,
She always draws her inference wrong.

Broad, liberal views on men and things
    She will not hear a word of;
To prove herself correct she brings
    Some instance she has heard of;

The argument *ad hominem*
Appears her favorite strategem.

Old Socrates, with sage replies
   To questions put to suit him,
Would not, I think, have looked so wise
   With Lesbia to confute him;
He would more probably have bade
Xantippe hasten to his aid.

Ah! well, my fair philosopher,
   With clear brown eyes that glisten
So sweetly, that I much prefer
   To look at them than listen,
Preach me your sermon: have your way,
The voice is yours, whate'er you say.
             Alfred Cochrane [1865–

TO ANTHEA, WHO MAY COMMAND HIM
ANYTHING

(NEW STYLE)

AM I sincere?   I say I dote
On everything that Browning wrote;
I know some bits by heart to quote·
   But then She reads him.
I say—and is it strictly true?—
How I admire her cockatoo;
Well! in a way of course I do:
   But then She feeds him.

And I become, at her command,
The sternest Tory in the land;
The Grand Old Man is far from grand;
   But then She states it.
Nay! worse than that, I am so tame,
I once admitted—to my shame—
That football was a brutal game:
   Because She hates it.

My taste in Art she hailed with groans,
And I, once charmed with bolder tones,
Now love the yellows of Burne-Jones:
    But then She likes them.
My tuneful soul no longer hoards
Stray jewels from the Empire boards;
I revel now in Dvorak's chords:
    But then She strikes them.

Our age distinctly cramps a knight;
Yet, though debarred from tilt and fight,
I can admit that black is white,
    If She asserts it.
Heroes of old were luckier men
Than I—I venture now and then
To hint—retracting meekly when
    She controverts it.

Alfred Cochrane [1865–

THE EIGHT–DAY CLOCK

THE days of Bute and Grafton's fame,
Of Chatham's waning prime,
First heard your sounding gong proclaim
Its chronicle of Time;
Old days when Dodd confessed his guilt,
When Goldsmith drave his quill,
And genial gossip Horace built
His house on Strawberry Hill.

Now with a grave unmeaning face
You still repeat the tale,
High-towering in your somber case,
Designed by Chippendale;
Without regret for what is gone,
You bid old customs change,
As year by year you travel on
To scenes and voices strange.

We might have mingled with the crowd
Of courtiers in this hall,
The fans that swayed, the wigs that bowed,
But you have spoiled it all;
We might have lingered in the train
Of nymphs that Reynolds drew,
Or stared spell-bound in Drury Lane
At Garrick—but for you.

We might in Leicester Fields have swelled
The throng of beaux and cits,
Or listened to the concourse held
Among the Kitcat wits;
Have strolled with Selwyn in Pall Mall,
Arrayed in gorgeous silks,
Or in Great George Street raised a yell
For Liberty and Wilkes.

This is the life which you have known,
Which you have ticked away,
In one unmoved unfaltering tone
That ceased not day by day,
While ever round your dial moved
Your hands from span to span,
Through drowsy hours and hours that proved
Big with the fate of man.

A steady tick for fatal creeds,
For youth on folly bent,
A steady tick for worthy deeds,
And moments wisely spent;
No warning note of emphasis,
No whisper of advice,
To ruined rake or flippant miss,
For coquetry or dice.

You might, I think, have hammered out
With meaning doubly clear,
The midnight of a Vauxhall rout
In Evelina's ear;

Or when the night was almost gone,
You might, the deals between,
Have startled those who looked upon
The cloth when it was green.

But no, in all the vanished years
Down which your wheels have run,
Your message borne to heedless ears
Is one and only one—
No wit of men, no power of kings,
Can stem the overthrow
Wrought by this pendulum that swings
Sedately to and fro.

Alfred Cochrane [1865–

A PORTRAIT

IN sunny girlhood's vernal life
    She caused no small sensation,
But now the modest English wife
    To others leaves flirtation.
She's young still, lovely, debonair,
    Although sometimes her features
Are clouded by a thought of care
    For those two tiny creatures.

Each tiny, toddling, mottled mite
    Asserts with voice emphatic,
In lisping accents, "Mite is right,"
    Their rule is autocratic:
The song becomes, that charmed mankind,
    Their musical narcotic,
And baby lips than Love, she'll find,
    Are even more despotic.

Soft lullaby when singing there,
    And castles ever building,
Their destiny she'll carve in air,
    Bright with maternal gilding:

Young Guy, a clever advocate,
   So eloquent and able!
A powdered wig upon his pate,
   A coronet for Mabel!

Joseph Ashby-Sterry [1838–1917]

"OLD BOOKS ARE BEST"

OLD Books are best! With what delight
Does "Faithorne fecit" greet our sight
      On frontispiece or title-page
      Of that old time, when on the stage
"Sweet Nell" set "Rowley's" heart alight!

And you, O Friend, to whom I write,
Must not deny, e'en though you might,
      Through fear of modern pirates' rage,
      Old Books are best.

What though the print be not so bright,
The paper dark, the binding slight?
      Our author, be he dull or sage,
      Returning from that distant age
So lives again, we say of right:
      Old Books are best.

Beverly Chew [1850–1924]

IMPRESSION

IN these restrained and careful times
Our knowledge petrifies our rhymes;
Ah! for that reckless fire men had
When it was witty to be mad;

When wild conceits were piled in scores,
And lit by flaming metaphors,
When all was crazed and out of tune,—
Yet throbbed with music of the moon.

If we could dare to write as ill
As some whose voices haunt us still,
Even we, perchance, might call our own
Their deep enchanting undertone.

We are too diffident and nice,
Too learnèd and too over-wise,
Too much afraid of faults to be
The flutes of bold sincerity.

For, as this sweet life passes by,
We blink and nod with critic eye;
We've no words rude enough to give
Its charm so frank and fugitive.

The green and scarlet of the Park,
The undulating streets at dark,
The brown smoke blown across the blue,
This colored city we walk through;—

The pallid faces full of pain,
The field-smell of the passing wain,
The laughter, longing, perfume, strife,
The daily spectacle of life;—

Ah! how shall this be given to rhyme,
By rhymesters of a knowing time?
Ah! for the age when verse was clad,
Being godlike, to be bad and mad.

Edmund Gosse [1849–1928]

"WITH STRAWBERRIES"

WITH strawberries we filled a tray,
And then we drove away, away
    Along the links beside the sea,
    Where wave and wind were light and free,
And August felt as fresh as May.

And where the springy turf was gay
With thyme and balm and many a spray
    Of wild roses, you tempted me
        With strawberries!

A shadowy sail, silent and gray,
Stole like a ghost across the bay;

But none could hear me ask my fee,
And none could know what came to be.
Can sweethearts *all* their thirst allay
      With strawberries?
         William Ernest Henley [1849–1903]

BALLADE OF LADIES' NAMES

BROWN's for Lalage, Jones for Lelia,
  Robinson's bosom for Beatrice glows,
Smith is a Hamlet before Ophelia.
    The glamor stays if the reason goes!
    Every lover the years disclose
Is of a beautiful name made free.
    One befriends, and all others are foes.
Anna's the name of names for me.

Sentiment hallows the vowels of Delia;
  Sweet simplicity breathes from Rose;
Courtly memories glitter in Celia;
    Rosalind savors of quips and hose,
    Araminta of wits and beaux,
Prue of puddings, and Coralie
    All of sawdust and spangled shows;
Anna's the name of names for me.

Fie upon Caroline, Madge, Amelia—
  These I reckon the essence of prose!—
Cavalier Katherine, cold Cornelia,
    Portia's masterful Roman nose,
    Maud's magnificence, Totty's toes,
Poll and Bet with their twang of the sea,
    Nell's impertinence, Pamela's woes!
Anna's the name of names for me.

ENVOY

Ruth like a gillyflower smells and blows,
  Sylvia prattles of Arcadee,
Sybil mystifies, Connie crows,
    Anna's the name of names for me!
         William Ernest Henley [1849–1903]

TO A PAIR OF EGYPTIAN SLIPPERS

TINY slippers of gold and green,
  Tied with a mouldering golden cord!
What pretty feet they must have been
  When Cæsar Augustus was Egypt's lord!
Somebody graceful and fair you were!
  Not many girls could dance in these!
When did your shoemaker make you, dear,
  Such a nice pair of Egyptian "threes"?

Where were you measured? In Saïs, or On,
  Memphis, or Thebes, or Pelusium?
Fitting them neatly your brown toes upon,
  Lacing them deftly with finger and thumb,
I seem to see you!—so long ago,
  Twenty-one centuries, less or more!
And here are your sandals: yet none of us know
  What name, or fortune, or face you bore.

Your lips would have laughed, with a rosy scorn,
  If the merchant, or slave-girl, had mockingly said,
"The feet will pass, but the shoes they have worn
  Two thousand years onward Time's road shall tread,
And still be footgear as good as new!"
  To think that calf-skin, gilded and stitched,
Should Rome and the Pharaohs outlive— and you
  Be gone, like a dream, from the world you bewitched!

Not that we mourn you! 'Twere too absurd!
  You have been such a very long while away!
Your dry spiced dust would not value one word
  Of the soft regrets that my verse could say.
Sorrow and Pleasure, and Love and Hate,
  If you ever felt them, have vaporized hence
To this odor—so subtle and delicate—
  Of myrrh, and cassia, and frankincense.

Of course they embalmed you! Yet not so sweet
  Were aloes and nard, as the youthful glow
Which Amenti stole when the small dark feet
  Wearied of treading our world below.

To a Pair of Egyptian Slippers 1763

Look! it was flood-time in valley of Nile,
    Or a very wet day in the Delta, dear!
When your slippers tripped lightly their latest mile—
    The mud on the soles renders that fact clear.

You knew Cleopatra, no doubt! You saw
    Antony's galleys from Actium come.
But there! if questions could answers draw
    From lips so many a long age dumb,
I would not tease you with history,
    Nor vex your heart for the men that were;
The one point to learn that would fascinate me
    Is, where and what are you to-day, my dear!

You died, believing in Horus and Pasht,
    Isis, Osiris, and priestly lore;
And found, of course, such theories smashed
    By actual fact on the heavenly shore.
What next did you do? Did you transmigrate?
    Have we seen you since, all modern and fresh?
Your charming soul—so I calculate—
    Mislaid its mummy, and sought new flesh.

Were you she whom I met at dinner last week,
    With eyes and hair of the Ptolemy black,
Who still of this find in Fayoum would speak,
    And to Pharaohs and scarabs still carry us back?
A scent of lotus about her hung,
    And she had such a far-away wistful air
As of somebody born when the Earth was young;
    And she wore of gilt slippers a lovely pair.

Perchance you were married? These might have been
    Part of your *trousseau*—the wedding shoes;
And you laid them aside with the garments green,
    And painted clay Gods which a bride would use;
And, may be, to-day, by Nile's bright waters
    Damsels of Egypt in gowns of blue—
Great-great-great—very great—grand-daughters
    Owe their shapely insteps to you!

But vainly I beat at the bars of the Past,
    Little green slippers with golden strings!

For all you can tell is that leather will last
   When loves, and delightings, and beautiful things
Have vanished, forgotten—No! not quite that!
   I catch some gleam of the grace you wore
When you finished with Life's daily pit-a-pat,
   And left your shoes at Death's bedroom door.

You were born in the Egypt which did not doubt;
   You were never sad with our new-fashioned sorrows:
You were sure, when your play-days on Earth ran out,
   Of play-times to come, as we of our morrows!
Oh, wise little Maid of the Delta! I lay
   Your shoes in your mummy-chest back again,
And wish that one game we might merrily play
   At "Hunt the Slippers"—to see it all plain.

        Edwin Arnold [1832–1904]

WITHOUT AND WITHIN

My coachman, in the moonlight there,
   Looks through the side-light of the door;
I hear him with his brethren swear,
   As I could do,—but only more.

Flattening his nose against the pane,
   He envies me my brilliant lot,
Breathes on his aching fists in vain,
   And dooms me to a place more hot.

He sees me in to supper go,
   A silken wonder by my side,
Bare arms, bare shoulders, and a row
   Of flounces, for the door too wide.

He thinks how happy is my arm
   'Neath its white-gloved and jewelled load;
And wishes me some dreadful harm,
   Hearing the merry corks explode.

Meanwhile I inly curse the bore
   Of hunting still the same old coon,
And envy him, outside the door,
   In golden quiets of the moon.

The winter wind is not so cold
  As the bright smile he sees me win,
Nor the host's oldest wine so old
  As our poor gabble sour and thin.

I envy him the ungyved prance
  With which his freezing feet he warms,
And drag my lady's-chains and dance
  The galley-slave of dreary forms.

Oh, could he have my share of din,
  And I his quiet!—past a doubt
'Twould still be one man bored within,
  And just another bored without.

Nay, when, once paid my mortal fee,
  Some idler on my headstone grim
Traces the moss-blurred name, will he
  Think me the happier, or I him?
                James Russell Lowell [1819–1891]

"SHE WAS A BEAUTY"

SHE was a beauty in the days
  When Madison was President,
And quite coquettish in her ways,—
  On conquests of the heart intent.

  Grandpapa, on his right knee bent,
Wooed her in stiff, old-fashioned phrase,—
She was a beauty in the days
  When Madison was President.

  And when your roses where hers went
Shall go, my Rose, who date from Hayes,
  I hope you'll wear her sweet content
Of whom tradition lightly says:
She was a beauty in the days
  When Madison was President.
                Henry Cuyler Bunner [1855–1896]

NELL GWYNNE'S LOOKING-GLASS

GLASS antique, 'twixt thee and Nell
Draw we here a parallel.
She, like thee, was forced to bear
All reflections, foul or fair.
    Thou art deep and bright within,
      Depths as bright belonged to Gwynne;
    Thou art very frail as well,
    Frail as flesh is,—so was Nell.

Thou, her glass, art silver-lined,
She too, had a silver mind:
Thine is fresh till this far day,
Hers till death ne'er wore away:
    Thou dost to thy surface win
    Wandering glances, so did Gwynne;
    Eyes on thee love long to dwell,
    So men's eyes would do on Nell.

Life-like forms in thee are sought,
Such the forms the actress wrought;
Truth unfailing rests in you,
Nell, whate'er she was, was true.
    Clear as virtue, dull as sin,
    Thou art oft, as oft was Gwynne;
    Breathe on thee, and drops will swell:
    Bright tears dimmed the eyes of Nell.

Thine's a frame to charm the sight,
Framed was she to give delight;
Waxen forms here truly show
Charles above and Nell below;
    But between them, chin with chin,
    Stuart stands as low as Gwynne,—
    Paired, yet parted,—meant to tell
    Charles was opposite to Nell.

Round the glass wherein her face
Smiled so soft, her "arms" we trace;
Thou, her mirror, hast the pair,
Lion here, and leopard there.

She had part in these,—akin
To the lion-heart was Gwynne;
And the leopard's beauty fell
With its spots to bounding Nell.

Oft inspected, ne'er seen through,
Thou art firm, if brittle too;
So her will, on good intent,
Might be broken, never bent.
  What the glass was, when therein
  Beamed the face of glad Nell Gwynne,
  Was that face by beauty's spell
  To the honest soul of Nell.
      Laman Blanchard [1804–1845]

MIMNERMUS IN CHURCH

YOU promise heavens free from strife,
 Pure truth, and perfect change of will;
But sweet, sweet is this human life,
 So sweet, I fain would breathe it still:
Your chilly stars I can forego,
This warm kind world is all I know.

You say there is no substance here,
 One great reality above:
Back from that void I shrink in fear,
 And child-like hide myself in love:
Show me what angels feel.   Till then
I cling, a mere weak man, to men.

You bid me lift my mean desires
 From faltering lips and fitful veins
To sexless souls, ideal choirs,
 Unwearied voices, wordless strains:
My mind with fonder welcome owns
One dear dead friend's remembered tones.

Forsooth the present we must give
 To that which cannot pass away;
All beauteous things for which we live
 By laws of time and space decay.

But oh, the very reason why
I clasp them, is because they die.
                William Johnson-Cory [1823–1892]

CLAY

"WE are but clay," the preacher saith;
    "The heart is clay, and clay the brain,
And soon or late there cometh death
    To mingle us with earth again."

Well, let the preacher have it so,
    And clay we are, and clay shall be;—
Why iterate?—for this I know,
    That clay does very well for me.

When clay has such red mouths to kiss,
    Firm hands to grasp, it is enough:
How can I take it aught amiss
    We are not made of rarer stuff?

And if one tempt you to believe
    His choice would be immortal gold,
Question him, Can you then conceive
    A warmer heart than clay can hold?

Or richer joys than clay can feel?
    And when perforce he falters nay,
Bid him renounce his wish and kneel
    In thanks for this same kindly clay.
                Edward Verrall Lucas [1868–

AUCASSIN AND NICOLETE

WHAT magic halo rings thy head,
Dream-maiden of a minstrel dead?
What charm of faerie round thee hovers,
That all who listen are thy lovers?

What power yet makes our pulses thrill
To see thee at thy window-sill,
And by that dangerous cord down-sliding,
And through the moonlit garden gliding?

True maiden art thou in thy dread;
True maiden in thy hardihead;
True maiden when, thy fears half-over,
Thou lingerest to try thy lover.

And ah! what heart of stone or steel
But doth some stir unwonted feel,
When to the day new brightness bringing
Thou standest at the stair-foot singing!

Thy slender limbs in boyish dress,
Thy tones half glee, half tenderness,
Thou singest, 'neath the light tale's cover,
Of thy true love to thy true lover.

O happy lover, happy maid,
Together in sweet story laid;
Forgive the hand that here is baring
Your old loves for new lovers' staring!

Yet, Nicolete, why fear'st thou fame?
No slander now can touch thy name,
Nor Scandal's self a fault discovers,
Though each new year thou hast new lovers.

Nor, Aucassin, need'st thou to fear
These lovers of too late a year,
Nor dread one jealous pang's revival;
No lover now can be thy rival.

What flower considers if its blooms
Light haunts of men, or forest glooms?
What care ye though the world discovers
Your flowers of love, O flower of lovers!
                    Francis William Bourdillon [1852–1921]

PROVENÇAL LOVERS

AUCASSIN AND NICOLETTE

WITHIN the garden of Beaucaire
He met her by a secret stair,—
The night was centuries ago.
Said Aucassin, "My love, my pet,

These old confessors vex me so!
They threaten all the pains of hell
Unless I give you up, *ma belle*";—
Said Aucassin to Nicolette.

"Now who should there in Heaven be
To fill your place, *ma très-douce mie?*
To reach that spot I little care!
There all the droning priests are met;
All the old cripples, too, are there
That unto shrines and altars cling
To filch the Peter-pence we bring";—
Said Aucassin to Nicolette.

"There are the barefoot monks and friars
With gowns well tattered by the briars,
The saints who lift their eyes and whine:
I like them not—a starveling set!
Who'd care with folk like these to dine?
The other road 'twere just as well
That you and I should take, *ma belle!*"—
Said Aucassin to Nicolette.

"To purgatory I would go
With pleasant comrades whom we know,
Fair scholars, minstrels, lusty knights
Whose deeds the land will not forget,
The captains of a hundred fights,
The men of valor and degree:
We'll join that gallant company,"—
Said Aucassin to Nicolette.

"There, too, are jousts and joyance rare,
And beauteous ladies debonair,
The pretty dames, the merry brides,
Who with their wedded lords coquette
And have a friend or two besides,—
And all in gold and trappings gay,
With furs, and crests in vair and gray,"—
Said Aucassin to Nicolette.

"Sweet players on the cithern strings,
And they who roam the world like kings,
Are gathered there, so blithe and free!
Pardie! I'd join them now, my pet,
If you went also, *ma douce mie!*
The joys of Heaven I'd forego
To have you with me there below,"—
Said Aucassin to Nicolette.

Edmund Clarence Stedman [1833–1908]

ON THE HURRY OF THIS TIME

With slower pen men used to write,
Of old, when "letters" were "polite";
    In Anna's or in George's days,
    They could afford to turn a phrase,
Or trim a struggling theme aright.

They knew not steam; electric light
Not yet had dazed their calmer sight;—
    They meted out both blame and praise
        With slower pen.

Too swiftly now the Hours take flight!
What's read at morn is dead at night:
    Scant space have we for Art's delays,
    Whose breathless thought so briefly stays,
We may not work—ah! would we might!—
        With slower pen.

Austin Dobson [1840–1921]

"GOOD–NIGHT, BABETTE!"

Si vieillesse pouvait!—

SCENE.—*A small neat Room. In a high Voltaire Chair
sits a white-haired old Gentleman.*

MONSIEUR VIEUXBOIS   BABETTE

M. VIEUXBOIS (*turning querulously*)
Day of my life! Where *can* she get!
Babette! I say! Babette!—Babette!

BABETTE (*entering hurriedly*)
Coming, M'sieu'! If M'sieu' speaks
So loud, he won't be well for weeks!

M. VIEUXBOIS

Where have you been?

BABETTE

Why M'sieu' knows:—
April! . . . Ville d'Avray! . . . Ma'am'selle Rose!

M. VIEUXBOIS

Ah! I am old,—and I forget.
Was the place growing green, Babette?

BABETTE

But of a greenness!—yes, M'sieu'!
And then the sky so blue!—so blue!
And when I dropped my *immortelle*,
How the birds sang!
                    (*Lifting her apron to her eyes*)
                                This poor Ma'am'selle!

M. VIEUXBOIS

You're a good girl, Babette, but she,—
She was an Angel, verily.
Sometimes I think I see her yet
Stand smiling by the cabinet;
And once, I know, she peeped and laughed
Betwixt the curtains . . .
                        Where's the draught?
            (*She gives him a cup*)
Now I shall sleep, I think, Babette;—
Sing me your Norman *chansonnette*.

BABETTE (*sings*)

"Once at the Angelus,
    (Ere I was dead),
Angels all glorious
    Came to my bed;
Angels in blue and white
    Crowned on the Head."

M. VIEUXBOIS (*drowsily*)

"She was an Angel" . . . "Once she laughed" . . .
What, was I dreaming?
                    Where's the draught?

BABETTE (*showing the empty cup*)

The draught, M'sieu'?

M. VIEUXBOIS

How I forget!
I am so old!   But sing, Babette!

BABETTE (*sings*)

"*One was the Friend I left*
  Stark in the Snow;
One was the Wife that died
  Long,—long ago;
One was the Love I lost . . .
  How could she know?"

M. VIEUXBOIS (*murmuring*)

Ah, Paul! . . . old Paul! . . . Eulalie too!
And Rose . . . And O! "the sky so blue!"

BABETTE (*sings*)

"*One had my Mother's eyes,*
  Wistful and mild;
One had my Father's face;
  One was a Child:
All of them bent to me,—
  Bent down and smiled!"

(He is asleep!)

M. VIEUXBOIS (*almost inaudibly*)

"How I forget!"
"I am so old!" . . . "Good-night, Babette!"

Austin Dobson [1840–1921]

A DIALOGUE FROM PLATO

Le temps le mieux employé est celui qu'on perd.—CLAUDE TILLIER

I'D "read" three hours.   Both notes and text
  Were fast a mist becoming;
In bounced a vagrant bee, perplexed,
  And filled the room with humming,

Then out. The casement's leafage sways,
   And, parted light, discloses
Miss Di., with hat and book,—a maze
   Of muslin mixed with roses.

"You're reading Greek?" "I am—and you?"
   "O, mine's a mere romancer!"
"So Plato is." "Then read him—do;
   And I'll read mine for answer."

I read: "My Plato (Plato, too—
   That wisdom thus should harden!)
Declares 'blue eyes look doubly blue
   Beneath a Dolly Varden.'"

She smiled. "My book in turn avers
   (No author's name is stated)
That sometimes those Philosophers
   Are sadly mistranslated."

"But hear,—the next's in stronger style:
   The Cynic School asserted
That two red lips which part and smile
   May not be controverted!"

She smiled once more. "My book, I find,
   Observes some modern doctors
Would make the Cynics out a kind
   Of album-verse concoctors."

Then I: "Why not? 'Ephesian law,
   No less than time's tradition,
Enjoined fair speech on all who saw
   Diana's apparition.'"

She blushed,—this time. "If Plato's page
   No wiser precept teaches,
Then I'd renounce that doubtful sage,
   And walk to Burnham Beeches."

"Agreed," I said. "For Socrates
   (I find he too is talking)
Thinks Learning can't remain at ease
   When Beauty goes a-walking."

She read no more. I leapt the sill:
  The sequel's scarce essential—
Nay, more than this, I hold it still
  Profoundly confidential.

Austin Dobson [1840–1921]

THE LADIES OF ST. JAMES'S

A PROPER NEW BALLAD OF THE COUNTRY AND THE TOWN

Phyllida amo ante alias.—VIRGIL

THE ladies of St. James's
  Go swinging to the play;
Their footmen run before them,
  With a "Stand by! Clear the way!"
But Phyllida, my Phyllida!
  She takes her buckled shoon,
When we go out a-courting
  Beneath the harvest moon.

The ladies of St. James's
  Wear satin on their backs;
They sit all night at *Ombre*,
  With candles all of wax:
But Phyllida, my Phyllida!
  She dons her russet gown,
And runs to gather May dew
  Before the world is down.

The ladies of St. James's!
  They are so fine and fair,
You'd think a box of essences
  Was broken in the air:
But Phyllida, my Phyllida!
  The breath of heath and furze
When breezes blow at morning,
  Is not so fresh as hers.

The ladies of St. James's!
  They're painted to the eyes;
Their white it stays for ever,
  Their red it never dies:

But Phyllida, my Phyllida!
  Her color comes and goes;
It trembles to a lily,—
  It wavers to a rose.

The ladies of St. James's!
  You scarce can understand
The half of all their speeches,
  Their phrases are so grand:
But Phyllida, my Phyllida!
  Her shy and simple words
Are clear as after rain-drops
  The music of the birds.

The ladies of St. James's!
  They have their fits and freaks;
They smile on you—for seconds,
  They frown on you—for weeks:
But Phyllida, my Phyllida!
  Come either storm or shine,
From Shrove-tide unto Shrove-tide,
  Is always true—and mine.

My Phyllida! my Phyllida!
  I care not though they heap
The hearts of all St. James's,
  And give me all to keep;
I care not whose the beauties
  Of all the world may be,
For Phyllida—for Phyllida
  Is all the world to me!

                          Austin Dobson [1840–1921]

THE CURÉ'S PROGRESS

MONSIEUR the Curé down the street
  Comes with his kind old face,—
With his coat worn bare, and his straggling hair,
  And his green umbrella-case.

You may see him pass by the little "*Grande Place*",
  And the tiny "*Hotel-de-Ville*";
He smiles, as he goes, to the *fleuriste* Rose,
  And the *pompier* Théophile.

He turns, as a rule, through the "*Marché*" cool,
  Where the noisy fish-wives call;
And his compliment pays to the " *Belle Thérèse* ",
  As she knits in her dusky stall.

There's a letter to drop at the locksmith's shop,
  And Toto, the locksmith's niece,
Has jubilant hopes, for the Curé gropes
  In his tails for a *pain d'épice*.

There's a little dispute with a merchant of fruit,
  Who is said to be heterodox,
That will ended be with a "*Ma foi, oui!*"
  And a pinch from the Curé's box.

There is also a word that no one heard
  To the furrier's daughter Lou.;
And a pale cheek fed with a flickering red,
  And a "*Bon Dieu garde M'sieu'!*"

But a grander way for the *Sous-Préfet*,
  And a bow for Ma'am'selle Anne;
And a mock "off-hat" to the Notary's cat,
  And a nod to the Sacristan:—

For ever through life the Curé goes
  With a smile on his kind old face—
With his coat worn bare, and his straggling hair,
  And his green umbrella-case.

                              Austin Dobson [1840–1921]

A GENTLEMAN OF THE OLD SCHOOL

HE lived in that past Georgian day,
When men were less inclined to say
That "Time is Gold," and overlay

With toil their pleasure;
He held some land, and dwelt thereon,—
Where, I forget,—the house is gone;
His Christian name, I think, was John,—
      His surname, Leisure.

Reynolds has painted him, —a face
Filled with a fine, old-fashioned grace,
Fresh-colored, frank, with ne'er a trace
      Of trouble shaded;
The eyes are blue, the hair is dressed
In plainest way,—one hand is pressed
Deep in a flapped canary vest,
      With buds brocaded.

He wears a brown old Brunswick coat,
With silver buttons,—round his throat,
A soft cravat;—in all you note
      An elder fashion,—
A strangeness, which, to us who shine
In shapely hats,—whose coats combine
All harmonies of hue and line,
      Inspires compassion.

He lived so long ago, you see!
Men were untravelled then, but we,
Like Ariel, post o'er land and sea
      With careless parting;
He found it quite enough for him
To smoke his pipe in "garden trim,"
And watch, about the fish tank's brim,
      The swallows darting.

He liked the well-wheel's creaking tongue,—
He liked the thrush that fed her young,—
He liked the drone of flies among
      His netted peaches;
He liked to watch the sunlight fall
Athwart his ivied orchard wall;
Or pause to catch the cuckoo's call
      Beyond the beeches.

His were the times of Paint and Patch,
And yet no Ranelagh could match
The sober doves that round his thatch
        Spread tails and sidled;
He liked their ruffling, puffed content;
For him their drowsy wheelings meant
More than a Mall of Beaux that bent,
        Or Belles that bridled.

Not that, in truth, when life began
He shunned the flutter of the fan;
He too had maybe "pinked his man"
        In Beauty's quarrel;
But now his "fervent youth" had flown
Where lost things go; and he was grown
As staid and slow-paced as his own
        Old hunter, Sorrel.

Yet still he loved the chase, and held
That no composer's score excelled
The merry horn, when Sweetlip swelled
        Its jovial riot;
But most his measured words of praise
Caressed the angler's easy ways,—
His idly meditative days,—
        His rustic diet.

Not that his "meditating" rose
Beyond a sunny summer doze;
He never troubled his repose
        With fruitless prying;
But held, as law for high and low,
What God withholds no man can know,
And smiled away enquiry so,
        Without replying.

We read—alas, how much we read!—
The jumbled strifes of creed and creed
With endless controversies feed

Our groaning tables;
His books—and they sufficed him—were
Cotton's *Montaigne*, *The Grave* of Blair,
A "Walton"—much the worse for wear,
      And *Æsop's Fables.*

One more—*The Bible.* Not that he
Had searched its page as deep as we;
No sophistries could make him see
      Its slender credit;
It may be that he could not count
The sires and sons to Jesse's fount,—
He liked the "Sermon on the Mount,"—
      And more, he read it.

Once he had loved, but failed to wed,
A red-cheeked lass who long was dead;
His ways were far too slow, he said,
      To quite forget her;
And still when time had turned him gray,
The earliest hawthorn buds in May
Would find his lingering feet astray,
      Where first he met her.

"*In Cœlo Quies*" heads the stone
On Leisure's grave,—now little known,
A tangle of wild-rose has grown
      So thick across it;
The "Benefactions" still declare
He left the clerk an elbow-chair,
And "12 Pence Yearly to Prepare
      A Christmas Posset."

Lie softly, Leisure! Doubtless you,
With too serene a conscience drew
Your easy breath, and slumbered through
      The gravest issue;
But we, to whom our age allows
Scarce space to wipe our weary brows,
Look down upon your narrow house,
      Old friend, and miss you!
                    Austin Dobson [1840–1921]

ON A FAN

THAT BELONGED TO THE MARQUISE DE POMPADOUR

CHICKEN-SKIN, delicate, white,
  Painted by Carlo Vanloo,
Loves in a riot of light,
  Roses and vaporous blue;
  Hark to the dainty *frou-frou!*
Picture above, if you can,
  Eyes that could melt as the dew,—
This was the Pompadour's fan!

See how they rise at the sight,
  Thronging the *Œil de Bœuf* through,
Courtiers as butterflies bright,
  Beauties that Fragonard drew,
  Talon-rouge, falbala, queue,
Cardinal, Duke,—to a man,
  Eager to sigh or to sue,—
This was the Pompadour's fan!

Ah, but things more than polite
  Hung on this toy, *voyez-vous!*
Matters of state and of might,
  Things that great ministers do;
  Things that, maybe, overthrew
Those in whose brains they began;
  Here was the sign and the cue,—
This was the Pompadour's fan!

ENVOY

Where are the secrets it knew?
  Weavings of plot and of plan?
—But where is the Pompadour, too?
  This was the Pompadour's *Fan!*
                Austin Dobson [1840–1921]

"WHEN I SAW YOU LAST, ROSE"

WHEN I saw you last, Rose,
You were only so high;—
How fast the time goes!

Like a bud ere it blows,
You just peeped at the sky,
When I saw you last, Rose!

Now your petals unclose,
Now your May-time is nigh;—
How fast the time goes!

And a life,—how it grows!
You were scarcely so shy,
When I saw you last, Rose!

In your bosom it shows
There's a guest on the sly;
(How fast the time goes!)

Is it Cupid? Who knows!
Yet you used not to sigh,
When I saw you last, Rose;—
How fast the time goes!

                    Austin Dobson [1840–1921]

URCEUS EXIT

I INTENDED an Ode,
    And it turned to a Sonnet.
It began *à la mode*,
I intended an Ode;
But Rose crossed the road
    In her latest new bonnet;
I intended an Ode;
    And it turned to a Sonnet.

                    Austin Dobson [1840–1921]

A CORSAGE BOUQUET

MYRTILLA, to-night,
  Wears Jacqueminot roses.
She's the loveliest sight!
Myrtilla to-night:—
Correspondingly light
  My pocket-book closes.
Myrtilla, to-night
  Wears Jacqueminot roses.

Charles Henry Lüders [1858–1891]

TWO TRIOLETS

What he said:—
  THIS kiss upon your fan I press—
    Ah! Sainte Nitouche, you don't refuse it!
  And may it from its soft recess—
  This kiss upon your fan I press—
  Be blown to you, a shy caress,
    By this white down, whene'er you use it.
  This kiss upon your fan I press,—
    Ah, Sainte Nitouche, you *don't* refuse it!

What she thought:—
  To kiss a fan!
    What a poky poet!
  The stupid man
  To kiss a fan
  When he knows—that—he—can—
    Or ought to know it—
  To kiss a fan!
    What a poky poet!

Harrison Robertson [1856–

THE BALLAD OF DEAD LADIES *

FROM THE FRENCH OF FRANÇOIS VILLON 1450

TELL me now in what hidden way is
  Lady Flora the lovely Roman?
Where's Hipparchia, and where is Thais,
  Neither of them the fairer woman?

* For the original of this poem see page 3837.

Where is Echo, beheld of no man,
Only heard on river and mere,—
   She whose beauty was more than human? . . .
But where are the snows of yester-year?

Where's Héloise, the learnèd nun,
   For whose sake Abeilard, I ween,
Lost manhood and put priesthood on?
   (From Love he won such dule and teen!)
   And where, I pray you, is the Queen
Who willed that Buridan should steer
   Sewed in a sack's mouth down the Seine? . . .
But where are the snows of yester-year?

White Queen Blanche, like a queen of lilies,
   With a voice like any mermaiden,—
Bertha Broadfoot, Beatrice, Alice,
   And Ermengarde the lady of Maine,—
   And that good Joan whom Englishmen
At Rouen doomed and burned her there,—
   Mother of God, where are they then? . . .
But where are the snows of yester-year?

Nay, never ask this week, fair lord,
   Where they are gone, nor yet this year,
Except with this for an overword,—
   But where are the snows of yester-year?
         Dante Gabriel Rossetti [1828–1882]

BALLADE OF DEAD LADIES

AFTER VILLON

NAY, tell me now in what strange air
The Roman Flora dwells to-day,
Where Archippiada hides, and where
Beautiful Thais has passed away?
Whence answers Echo, afield, astray,
By mere or stream,—around, below?
Lovelier she than a woman of clay;
Nay, but where is the last year's snow?

Where is wise Héloïse, that care
Brought on Abeilard, and dismay?
All for her love he found a snare,
A maimed poor monk in orders gray;
And where's the Queen who willed to slay
Buridan, that in a sack must go
Afloat down Seine,—a perilous way—
Nay, but where is the last year's snow?

Where's that White Queen, a lily rare,
With her sweet song, the Siren's lay?
Where's Bertha Broad-foot, Beatrice fair?
Alys and Ermengarde, where are they?
Good Joan, whom English did betray
In Rouen town, and burned her? No,
Maiden and Queen, no man may say;
Nay, but where is the last year's snow?

ENVOY

Prince, all this week thou needst not pray,
Nor yet this year the thing to know.
One burden answers, ever and aye,
"Nay, but where is the last year's snow?"
Andrew Lang [1844–1912]

A BALLAD OF DEAD LADIES

AFTER VILLON

From "If I Were King"

I WONDER in what Isle of Bliss
    Apollo's music fills the air;
In what green valley Artemis
    For young Endymion spreads the snare:
    Where Venus lingers debonair:
The Wind has blown them all away—
    And Pan lies piping in his lair—
Where are the Gods of Yesterday?

Say where the great Semiramis
    Sleeps in a rose-red tomb; and where
The precious dust of Caesar is,
    Or Cleopatra's yellow hair:
    Where Alexander Do-and-Dare;
The Wind has blown them all away—
    And Redbeard of the Iron Chair;
Where are the Dreams of Yesterday?

Where is the Queen of Herod's kiss,
    And Phryne in her beauty bare;
By what strange sea does Tomyris
    With Dido and Cassandra share
    Divine Proserpina's despair;
The Wind has blown them all away—
    For what poor ghost does Helen care?
Where are the Girls of Yesterday?

ENVOY

Alas for lovers! Pair by pair
    The Wind has blown them all away:
The young and yare, the fond and fair:
    Where are the Snows of Yesterday?
             Justin Huntly McCarthy [1860–1936]

IF I WERE KING

AFTER VILLON

From "If I Were King"

ALL French folk, whereso'er ye be,
    Who love your country, sail and sand,
From Paris to the Breton sea,
    And back again to Norman strand,
    Forsooth ye seem a silly band,
Sheep without shepherd, left to chance—
    Far otherwise our Fatherland,
If Villon were the King of France!

The figure on the throne you see
   Is nothing but a puppet, planned
To wear the regal bravery
   Of silken coat and gilded wand.
   Not so we Frenchmen understand
The Lord of lion's heart and glance,
   And such a one would take command
If Villon were the King of France!

His counsellors are rogues, Perdie!
   While men of honest mind are banned
To creak upon the Gallows Tree,
   Or squeal in prisons over-manned;
   We want a chief to bear the brand,
And bid the damned Burgundians dance.
   God! Where the Oriflamme should stand
If Villon were the King of France!

ENVOY

Louis the Little, play the grand;
   Buffet the foe with sword and lance;
'Tis what would happen, by this hand,
   If Villon were the King of France!
           Justin Huntly McCarthy [1860–1936]

A BALLADE OF SUICIDE

THE gallows in my garden, people say,
Is new and neat and adequately tall.
I tie the noose on in a knowing way
As one that knots his necktie for a ball;
But just as all the neighbors—on the wall—
Are drawing a long breath to shout "Hurray!"
The strangest whim has seized me. . . . After all
I think I will not hang myself to-day.

To-morrow is the time I get my pay—
My uncle's sword is hanging in the hall—
I see a little cloud all pink and gray—
Perhaps the rector's mother will *not* call—

I fancy that I heard from Mr. Gall
That mushrooms could be cooked another way—
I never read the works of Juvenal—
I think I will not hang myself to-day.

The world will have another washing day;
The decadents decay; the pedants pall;
And H. G. Wells has found that children play,
And Bernard Shaw discovered that they squall;
Rationalists are growing rational—
And through thick woods one finds a stream astray,
So secret that the very sky seems small—
I think I will not hang myself to-day.

ENVOI

Prince, I can hear the trumpet of Germinal,
The tumbrils toiling up the terrible way;
Even to-day your royal head may fall—
I think I will not hang myself to-day.

Gilbert Keith Chesterton [1874–1936]

CHIFFONS!

THROUGH this our city of delight,
    This Paris of our joy and play,
This Paris perfumed, jeweled, bright,
    Rouged, powdered, amorous,—*ennuyê:*
    Across our gilded *Quartier,*
So fair to see, so frail *au fond,*
    Echoes—*mon Dieu!*—the Ragman's bray:

    " Mar - chand d'ha - bits!   Chif - fons!"

Foul, hunched, a plague to dainty sight,
    He limps *infect* by park and *quai,*
Voicing (for those that hear aright)
    His hunger-world, the dark *Marais.*
    Sexton of all we waste and fray,
He bags at last *pour tout de bon*
    Our trappings rare, our braveries gay,

    " Mar - chand d'ha - bits!   Chif - fons!"

Their lot is ours! A grislier wight,
　　The Ragman Time, takes day by day
Our beauty's bloom, our manly might,
　　Our *joie de vivre*, our gods of clay;
　　Till torn and worn and soiled and gray
Hot life rejects us—*nom de nom!*—
　　Rags! and our only requiem lay,

"*Mar - chand d'ha - bits!　　Chif - fons!*"

ENVOY

Princes take heed!—for where are they,
　　Valois, Navarre and Orléans? . . .
Death drones the answer, far away,

William Samuel Johnson [1859–1937]

THE COURT HISTORIAN

LOWER EMPIRE.　*Circa* A. D. 700

THE Monk Arnulphus uncorked his ink
　　That shone with a blood-red light
Just now as the sun began to sink;
　　His vellum was pumiced a silvery white;
"The Basileus"—for so he began—
"Is a royal sagacious Mars of a man,
　　Than the very lion bolder;
He has married the stately widow of Thrace—"
　　"Hush!" cried a voice at his shoulder.

His palette gleamed with a burnished green,
　　Bright as a dragon-fly's skin:
His gold-leaf shone like the robe of a queen,
　　His azure glowed as a cloud worn thin,
Deep as the blue of the king-whale's lair:
"The Porphyrogenita Zoë the fair
　　Is about to wed with a Prince much older,
Of an unpropitious mien and look—"
　　"Hush!" cried a voice at his shoulder.

The red flowers trellised the parchment page,
  The birds leaped up on the spray,
The yellow fruit swayed and drooped and swung,
  It was Autumn mixed up with May.
(O, but his cheek was shrivelled and shrunk!)
"The child of the Basileus," wrote the Monk,
  "Is golden-haired—tender the Queen's arms fold her.
Her step-mother Zoë doth love her so—"
  "Hush!" cried a voice at his shoulder.

The Kings and Martyrs and Saints and Priests
  All gathered to guard the text:
There was Daniel snug in the lions' den
  Singing no whit perplexed—
Brazen Samson with spear and helm—
"The Queen," wrote the Monk, "rules firm this realm,
  For the King gets older and older.
The Norseman Thorkill is brave and fair—"
  "Hush!" cried a voice at his shoulder.

Walter Thornbury [1828–1876]

MISS LOU

WHEN thin-strewn memory I look through,
  I see most clearly poor Miss Loo,
Her tabby cat, her cage of birds,
Her nose, her hair—her muffled words,
And how she would open her green eyes,
As if in some immense surprise,
Whenever as we sat at tea,
She made some small remark to me.

'Tis always drowsy summer when
From out the past she comes again;
The westering sunshine in a pool
Floats in her parlor still and cool;
While the slim bird its lean wires shakes,
As into piercing song it breaks;
Till Peter's pale-green eyes ajar
Dream, wake; wake, dream, in one brief bar;
And I am sitting, dull and shy,
And she with gaze of vacancy,

And large hands folded on the tray,
Musing the afternoon away;
Her satin bosom heaving slow
With sighs that softly ebb and flow,
And her plain face in such dismay,
It seems unkind to look her way;
Until all cheerful back will come
Her gentle gleaming spirit home:
And one would think that poor Miss Loo
Asked nothing else, if she had you.

Walter De la Mare [1873–

THE POET AND THE WOOD-LOUSE

A PORTLY Wood-louse, full of cares,
Transacted eminent affairs
Along a parapet where pears
Unripened fell
And vines embellished the sweet airs
With muscatel.

Day after day beheld him run
His scales a-twinkle in the sun
About his business never done;
Night's slender span he
Spent in the home his wealth had won—
A red-brick cranny.

Thus, as his Sense of Right directed,
He lived both honored and respected,
Cherished his children and protected
His duteous wife,
And naught of diffidence deflected
His useful life.

One mid-day, hastening to his Club,
He spied beside a water-tub
The owner of each plant and shrub
A humble Bard
Who turned upon the conscious grub
A mild regard.

"Eh?" quoth the Wood-louse, "Can it be
A Higher Power looks down to see

My praiseworthy activity
And notes me plying
My Daily Task?—Nor strange, dear me,
But gratifying!"

To whom the Bard: "I still divest
My orchard of the Insect Pest,
That you are such is manifest,
Prepare to die.—
And yet, how sweetly does your crest
Reflect the sky!

"Go then forgiven, (for what ails
Your naughty life this fact avails
To pardon) mirror in your scales
Celestial blue,
Till the sun sets and the light fails
The skies and you."

.   .   .   .   °

May all we proud and bustling parties
Whose lot in forum, street and mart is
Stand in conspectu Deitatis
And save our face,
Reflecting where our scaly heart is
Some skyey grace.

                    Helen Parry Eden [18

STUDENTS

John Brown and Jeanne at Fontainebleau—
'Twas Toussaint, just a year ago;
Crimson and copper was the glow
Of all the woods at Fontainebleau.
They peered into that ancient well,
And watched the slow torch as it fell.
John gave the keeper two whole sous,
And Jeanne that smile with which she woos
John Brown to folly. So they lose
The Paris train. But never mind!—
All-Saints are rustling in the wind,
And there's an inn, a crackling fire—
(It's *deux-cinquante*, but Jeanne's desire);

There's dinner, candles, country wine,
Jeanne's lips—philosophy divine!
There was a bosquet at Saint Cloud
Wherein John's picture of her grew
To be a Salon masterpiece—
Till the rain fell that would not cease.
Through one long alley how they raced!—
'Twas gold and brown, and all a waste
Of matted leaves, moss-interlaced.
Shades of mad queens and hunter-kings
And thorn-sharp feet of dryad-things
Were company to their wanderings;
Then rain and darkness on them drew.
The rich folks' motors honked and flew.
They hailed an old cab, heaven for two;
The bright Champs-Elysées at last—
Though the cab crawled it sped too fast.

Paris, upspringing white and gold:
Flamboyant arch and high-enscrolled
War-sculpture, big, Napoleonic—
Fierce chargers, angels histrionic;
The royal sweep of gardened spaces,
The pomp and whirl of columned Places;
The *Rive Gauche*, age-old, gay and gray;
The *impasse* and the loved café;
The tempting tidy little shops;
The convent walls, the glimpsed tree-tops;
Book-stalls, old men like dwarfs in plays;
Talk, work, and Latin Quarter ways.

May—Robinson's, the chestnut trees—
Were ever crowds as gay as these?
The quick pale waiters on a run,
The round green tables, one by one,
Hidden away in amorous bowers—
Lilac, laburnum's golden showers.
Kiss, clink of glasses, laughter heard,
And nightingales quite undeterred.
And then that last extravagance—
O Jeanne, a single amber glance

Will pay him!—"Let's play millionaire
For just two hours—on princely fare,
At some hotel where lovers dine
A *deux* and pledge across the wine."
They find a damask breakfast-room,
Where stiff silk roses range their bloom.
The garçon has a splendid way
Of bearing in *grand déjeuner*.
Then to be left alone, alone,
High up above Rue Castiglione;
Curtained away from all the rude
Rumors, in silken solitude;
And, John, her head upon your knees—
Time waits for moments such as these.

Florence Wilkinson [18

"ONE, TWO, THREE!"

IT was an old, old, old, old lady,
  And a boy that was half-past three;
And the way that they played together
  Was beautiful to see.

She couldn't go running and jumping,
  And the boy, no more could he;
For he was a thin little fellow,
  With a thin little twisted knee.

They sat in the yellow sunlight,
  Out under the maple tree;
And the game that they played I'll tell you,
  Just as it was told to me.

It was Hide-and-Go-Seek they were playing,
  Though you'd never have known it to be—
With an old, old, old, old lady,
  And a boy with a twisted knee.

The boy would bend his face down
  On his one little sound right knee,
And he'd guess where she was hiding,
  In guesses One, Two, Three!

"You are in the china-closet!"
  He would cry, and laugh with glee—
It wasn't the china closet,
  But he still had Two and Three.

"You are up in papa's big bedroom,
  In the chest with the queer old key!"
And she said: "You are *warm* and *warmer;*
  But you're not quite right," said she.

"It can't be the little cupboard
  Where mamma's things used to be—
So it must be the clothes-press, Gran'ma!"
  And he found her with his Three.

Then she covered her face with her fingers,
  That were wrinkled and white and wee,
And she guessed where the boy was hiding,
  With a One and a Two and a Three.

And they never had stirred from their places,
  Right under the maple tree—
This old, old, old, old lady
  And the boy with the lame little knee—
This dear, dear, dear old lady,
  And the boy who was half-past three.

                    Henry Cuyler Bunner [1855–1896]

THE CHAPERON

I TAKE my chaperon to the play—
  She thinks she's taking me.
And the gilded youth who owns the box,
  A proud young man is he;
But how would his young heart be hurt
  If he could only know
    That not for his sweet sake I go
    Nor yet to see the trifling show;
  But to see my chaperon flirt.

Her eyes beneath her snowy hair
　　They sparkle young as mine;
There's scarce a wrinkle in her hand
　　So delicate and fine.
And when my chaperon is seen,
　　They come from everywhere—
　　The dear old boys with silvery hair,
　　With old-time grace and old-time air,
To greet their old-time queen.

They bow as my young Midas here
　　Will never learn to bow
(The dancing-masters do not teach
　　That gracious reverence now);
With voices quavering just a bit,
　　They play their old parts through,
　　They talk of folk who used to woo,
　　Of hearts that broke in 'fifty-two—
Now none the worse for it.

And as those aged crickets chirp,
　　I watch my chaperon's face,
And see the dear old features take
　　A new and tender grace;
And in her happy eyes I see
　　Her youth awakening bright,
　　With all its hope, desire, delight—
　　Ah, me! I wish that I were quite
As young—as young as she!

Henry Cuyler Bunner [1855–1896]

"A PITCHER OF MIGNONETTE"

A PITCHER of mignonette
　　In a tenement's highest casement,—
Queer sort of flower-pot—yet
That pitcher of mignonette
Is a garden in heaven set,
　　To the little sick child in the basement—
　　The pitcher of mignonette,
　　In the tenement's highest casement.

Henry Cuyler Bunner [1855–1896]

OLD KING COLE

In Tilbury Town did Old King Cole
    A wise old age anticipate,
Desiring, with his pipe and bowl,
    No Khan's extravagant estate.
No crown annoyed his honest head,
    No fiddlers three were called or needed;
For two disastrous heirs instead
    Made music more that ever three did.

Bereft of her with whom his life
    Was harmony without a flaw,
He took no other for a wife,
    Nor sighed for any that he saw;
And if he doubted his two sons,
    And heirs, Alexis and Evander,
He might have been as doubtful once
    Of Robert Burns and Alexander.

Alexis, in his early youth,
    Began to steal—from old and young.
Likewise Evander, and the truth
    Was like a bad taste on his tongue.
Born thieves and liars, their affair
    Seemed only to be tarred with evil—
The most insufferable pair
    Of scamps that ever cheered the devil.

The world went on, their fame went on,
    And they went on—from bad to worse;
Till, goaded hot with nothing done,
    And each accoutered with a curse,
The friends of Old King Cole, by twos,
    And fours, and sevens, and elevens,
Pronounced unalterable views
    Of doings that were not of Heaven's.

And having learned again whereby
    Their baleful zeal had come about,
King Cole met many a wrathful eye
    So kindly that its wrath went out—

Or partly out. Say what they would,
   He seemed the more to court their candor;
But never told what kind of good
   Was in Alexis and Evander.

And Old King Cole, with many a puff
   That haloed his urbanity,
Would smoke till he had smoked enough,
   And listen most attentively.
He beamed as with an inward light
   That had the Lord's assurance in it;
And once a man was there all night,
   Expecting something every minute.

But whether from too little thought,
   Or too much fealty to the bowl,
A dim reward was all he got
   For sitting up with Old King Cole.
"Though mine," the father mused aloud,
   "Are not the sons I would have chosen,
Shall I, less evilly endowed,
   By their infirmity be frozen?

"They'll have a bad end, I'll agree,
   But I was never born to groan;
For I can see what I can see,
   And I'm accordingly alone.
With open heart and open door,
   I love my friends, I like my neighbors;
But if I try to tell you more,
   Your doubts will overmatch my labors.

"This pipe would never make me calm,
   This bowl my grief would never drown.
For grief like mine there is no balm
   In Gilead, or in Tilbury Town.
And if I see what I can see,
   I know not any way to blind it;
Nor more if any way may be
   For you to grope or fly to find it.

"There may be room for ruin yet,
   And ashes for a wasted love;

Or, like One whom you may forget,
  I may have meat you know not of.
And if I'd rather live than weep
  Meanwhile, do you find that surprising?
Why, bless my soul, the man's asleep!
  That's good. The sun will soon be rising."
                    Edwin Arlington Robinson [1869–1935]

THE MASTER MARINER

My grandshire sailed three years from home,
  And slew unmoved the sounding whale:
Here on the windless beach I roam
  And watch far out the hardy sail.

The lions of the surf that cry
  Upon this lion-colored shore
On reefs of midnight met his eye:
  He knew their fangs as I their roar.

My grandsire sailed uncharted seas,
  And toll of all their leagues he took:
I scan the shallow bays at ease,
  And tell their colors in a book.

The anchor-chains his music made
  And wind in shrouds and running-gear:
The thrush at dawn beguiles my glade,
  And once, 'tis said, I woke to hear.

My grandsire in his ample fist
  The long harpoon upheld to men:
Behold obedient to my wrist
  A gray gull's-feather for my pen!

Upon my grandsire's leathern cheek
  Five zones their bitter bronze had set:
Some day their hazards I will seek,
  I promise me at times. Not yet.

I think my grandsire now would turn
  A mild but speculative eye
On me, my pen and its concern,
  Then gaze again to sea—and sigh.
                    George Sterling [1869–1926]

A ROSE TO THE LIVING

A ROSE to the living is more
    Than sumptuous wreaths to the dead:
In filling love's infinite store,
A rose to the living is more,—
If graciously given before
    The hungering spirit is fled,—
A rose to the living is more
    Than sumptuous wreaths to the dead.

                    Nixon Waterman [1859–

A KISS

ROSE kissed me to-day.
    Will she kiss me to-morrow?
Let it be as it may,
Rose kissed me to-day
But the pleasure gives way
    To a savor of sorrow;—
Rose kissed me to-day,—
    Will she kiss me to-morrow?

                    Austin Dobson [1840–1921]

BIFTEK AUX CHAMPIGNONS

MIMI, do you remember—
    Don't get behind your fan—
That morning in September
    On the cliffs of Grand Manan,
Where to the shock of Fundy
    The topmost harebells sway
(*Campanula rotundi-
    folia: cf.* Gray)?

On the pastures high and level,
    That overlook the sea,
Where I wondered what the devil
    Those little things could be

That Mimi stooped to gather,
  As she strolled across the down,
And held her dress skirt rather—
  Oh, now, you need n't frown.

For you know the dew was heavy,
  And your boots, *I* know, were thin;
So a little extra brevi-
  ty in skirts was, sure, no sin.
Besides, who minds a cousin?
  First, second, even third,—
I've kissed 'em by the dozen,
  And they never once demurred.

"If one's allowed to ask it,"
  Quoth I, " *ma belle cousine,*
What have you in your basket?"
  (Those baskets white and green
The brave Passamaquoddies
  Weave out of scented grass,
And sell to tourist bodies
  Who through Mt. Desert pass.)

You answered, slightly frowning,
  "Put down your stupid book—
That everlasting Browning!—
  And come and help me look.
Mushroom you spik him English,
  I call him *champignon:*
I'll teach you to distinguish
  The right kind from the wrong."

There was no fog on Fundy
  That blue September day;
The west wind, for that one day,
  Had swept it all away.
The lighthouse glasses twinkled,
  The white gulls screamed and flew,
The merry sheep-bells tinkled,
  The merry breezes blew.

The bayberry aromatic,
   The papery immortelle,
(That give our grandma's attic
   That sentimental smell,
Tied up in little brush-brooms)
   Were sweet as new-mown hay,
While we went hunting mushrooms
   That blue September day.

                Henry Augustin Beers [1847–1926]

EVOLUTION

WHEN you were a Tadpole and I was a Fish,
In the Paleozoic time,
And side by side on the ebbing tide,
We sprawled through the ooze and slime,
Or skittered with many a caudal flip
Through the depths of the Cambrian fen—
My heart was rife with the joy of life,
For I loved you even then.

Mindless we lived, mindless we loved,
And mindless at last we died;
And deep in the rift of a Caradoc drift
We slumbered side by side.
The world turned on in the lathe of time,
The hot sands heaved amain,
Till we caught our breath from the womb of death,
And crept into life again.

We were Amphibians, scaled and tailed,
And drab as a dead man's hand.
We coiled at ease 'neath the dripping trees
Or trailed through the mud and sand,
Croaking and blind, with our three-clawed feet,
Writing a language dumb,
With never a spark in the empty dark
To hint at a life to come.

Yet happy we lived, and happy we loved,
And happy we died once more.

Our forms were rolled in the clinging mold
Of a Neocomian shore.
The æons came and the æons fled,
And the sleep that wrapped us fast
Was riven away in a newer day,
And the night of death was past.

Then light and swift through the jungle trees
We swung in our airy flights,
Or breathed the balms of the fronded palms
In the hush of the moonless nights.
And oh, what beautiful years were these
When our hearts clung each to each;
When life was filled and our senses thrilled
In the first faint dawn of speech!

Thus life by life, and love by love,
We passed through the cycles strange,
And breath by breath, and death by death,
We followed the chain of change.
Till there came a time in the law of life
When over the nursing sod
The shadows broke, and the soul awoke
In a strange, dim dream of God.

I was thewed like an Aurocks bull
And tusked like the great Cave-Bear,
And you, my sweet, from head to feet,
Were gowned in your glorious hair.
Deep in the gloom of a fireless cave,
When the night fell o'er the plain,
And the moon hung red o'er the river bed,
We mumbled the bones of the slain.

I flaked a flint to a cutting edge,
And shaped it with brutish craft;
I broke a shank from the woodland dank,
And fitted it, head to haft.
Then I hid me close in the reedy tarn,
Where the Mammoth came to drink—

Through brawn and bone I drave the stone,
And slew him upon the brink.

Loud I howled through the moonlit wastes,
Loud answered our kith and kin;
From west and east to the crimson feast
The clan came trooping in.
O'er joint and gristle and padded hoof,
We fought and clawed and tore,
And cheek by jowl, with many a growl,
We talked the marvel o'er.

I carved that fight on a reindeer bone
With rude and hairy hand;
I pictured his fall on the cavern wall
That men might understand.
For we lived by blood and the right of might,
Ere human laws were drawn,
And the Age of Sin did not begin
Till our brutal tusks were gone.

And that was a million years ago,
In a time that no man knows;
Yet here to-night in the mellow light,
We sit at Delmonico's.
Your eyes are deep as the Devon springs,
Your hair is as dark as jet,
Your years are few, your life is new,
Your soul untried, and yet—

Our trail is on the Kimmeridge clay,
And the scarp of the Purbeck flags;
We have left our bones in the Bagshot stones,
And deep in the Coralline crags.
Our love is old, and our lives are old,
And death shall come amain.
Should it come to-day, what man may say
We shall not live again?

God wrought our souls from the Tremadoc beds
And furnished them wings to fly;

He sowed our spawn in the world's dim dawn,
And I know that it shall not die;
Though cities have sprung above the graves
Where the crook-boned men made war,
And the ox-wain creaks o'er the buried caves
Where the mummied mammoths are.

Then, as we linger at luncheon here,
O'er many a dainty dish,
Let us drink anew to the time when you
Were a Tadpole and I was a Fish.

Langdon Smith [1858–1908]

A REASONABLE AFFLICTION

On his death-bed poor Lubin lies:
　　His spouse is in despair;
With frequent cries, and mutual sighs,
　　They both express their care.

"A different cause," says Parson Sly,
　　"The same effect may give:
Poor Lubin fears that he may die;
　　His wife, that he may live."

Matthew Prior [1664–1721]

A MORAL IN SEVRES

Upon my mantel-piece they stand,
　　While all its length between them lies;
He throws a kiss with graceful hand,
　　She glances back with bashful eyes.

The china Shepherdess is fair,
　　The Shepherd's face denotes a heart
Burning with ardor and despair.
　　Alas, they stand so far apart!

And yet, perhaps, if they were moved,
　　And stood together day by day,
Their love had not so constant proved,
　　Nor would they still have smiled so gay.

His hand the Shepherd might have kissed
　　The match-box Angel's heart to win;
The Shepherdess, his love have missed,
　　And flirted with the Mandarin.

But on my mantel-piece they stand,
　　While all its length between them lies;
He throws a kiss with graceful hand,
　　She glances back with bashful eyes.

Mildred Howells [1872–　　]

ON THE FLY-LEAF OF A BOOK OF OLD PLAYS

At Cato's Head in Russell Street
　　These leaves she sat a-stitching;
I fancy she was trim and neat,
　　Blue-eyed and quite bewitching.

Before her on the street below,
　　All powder, ruffs, and laces,
There strutted idle London beaux
　　To ogle pretty faces;

While, filling many a Sedan chair
　　With monstrous hoop and feather,
In paint and powder London's fair
　　Went trooping past together.

Swift, Addison, and Pope, mayhap
　　They sauntered slowly past her,
Or printer's boy, with gown and cap,
　　For Steele, went trotting faster.

For beau nor wit had she a look;
　　Nor lord nor lady minding,
She bent her head above this book,
　　Attentive to her binding.

And one stray thread of golden hair,
　　Caught on her nimble fingers,
Was stitched within this volume, where
　　Until to-day it lingers.

Past and forgotten, beaux and fair,
  Wigs, powder, all outdated;
A queer antique, the Sedan chair,
  Pope, stiff and antiquated.

Yet as I turn these odd, old plays,
  This single stray lock finding,
I'm back in those forgotten days,
  And watch her at her binding.
                    Walter Learned [1847-1915]

THE TALENTED MAN

A LETTER FROM A LADY IN LONDON TO A LADY AT LAUSANNE

DEAR Alice! you'll laugh when you know it,—
  Last week, at the Duchess's ball,
I danced with the clever new poet,—
  You've heard of him,—Tully St. Paul.
Miss Jonquil was perfectly frantic;
  I wish you had seen Lady Anne!
It really was very romantic,
  He *is* such a talented man!

He came up from Brazen Nose College,
  Just caught, as they call it, this spring;
And his head, love, is stuffed full of knowledge
  Of every conceivable thing.
Of science and logic he chatters,
  As fine and as fast as he can;
Though I am no judge of such matters,
  I'm sure he's a talented man.

His stories and jests are delightful;—
  Not stories or jests, dear, for you;
The jests are exceedingly spiteful,
  The stories not always *quite* true.
Perhaps to be kind and veracious
  May do pretty well at Lausanne;
But it never would answer,—good gracious!
  Chez nous—in a talented man.

He sneers,—how my Alice would scold him!—
    At the bliss of a sigh or a tear;
He laughed—only think!—when I told him
    How we cried o'er Trevelyan last year;
I vow I was quite in a passion;
    I broke all the sticks of my fan;
But sentiment's quite out of fashion,
    It seems, in a talented man.

Lady Bab, who is terribly moral,
    Has told me that Tully is vain,
And apt—which is silly—to quarrel,
    And fond—which is sad—of champagne.
I listened, and doubted, dear Alice,
    For I saw, when my Lady began,
It was only the Dowager's malice;—
    She *does* hate a talented man!

He's hideous, I own it. But fame, love,
    Is all that these eyes can adore;
He's lame,—but Lord Byron was lame, love,
    And dumpy,—but so is Tom Moore.
Then his voice,—*such* a voice! my sweet creature,
    It's like your Aunt Lucy's toucan:
But oh! what's a tone or a feature,
    When once one's a talented man?

My mother, you know, all the season,
    Has talked of Sir Geoffrey's estate;
And truly, to do the fool reason,
    He *has* been less horrid of late.
But to-day, when we drive in the carriage,
    I'll tell her to lay down her plan;—
If ever I venture on marriage,
    It must be a talented man!

P. S.—I have found, on reflection,
    One fault in my friend,—*entre nous;*
Without it, he'd just be perfection;—
    Poor fellow, he has not a *soul!*

And so, when he comes in September
  To shoot with my uncle, Sir Dan,
I've promised mamma to remember
  He's *only* a talented man!
          Winthrop Mackworth Praed [1802–1839]

A LETTER OF ADVICE

FROM MISS MEDORA TREVILIAN, AT PADUA, TO MISS
ARAMINTA VAVASOUR, IN LONDON

"Enfin, Monsieur, un homme aimable;
Voilà pourquoi je ne saurais l'aimer."—SCRIBE

You tell me you're promised a lover,
  My own Araminta, next week;
Why cannot my fancy discover
  The hue of his coat, and his cheek?
Alas! if he look like another,
  A vicar, a banker, a beau,
Be deaf to your father and mother,
  My own Araminta, say "No!"

Miss Lane, at her Temple of Fashion,
  Taught us both how to sing and to speak,
And we loved one another with passion,
  Before we had been there a week:
You gave me a ring for a token;
  I wear it wherever I go;
I gave you a chain,—it is broken?
  My own Araminta, say "No!"

O think of our favorite cottage,
  And think of our dear Lalla Rookh!
How we shared with the milkmaids their pottage,
  And drank of the stream from the brook;
How fondly our loving lips faltered,
  "What further can grandeur bestow?"
My heart is the same;—is yours altered?
  My own Araminta, say "No!"

Remember the thrilling romances
    We read on the bank in the glen;
Remember the suitors our fancies
    Would picture for both of us then;
They wore the red cross on their shoulder,
    They had vanquished and pardoned their foe—
Sweet friend, are you wiser or colder?
    My own Araminta, say "No!"

You know, when Lord Rigmarole's carriage,
    Drove off with your cousin Justine,
You wept, dearest girl, at the marriage,
    And whispered "How base she has been!"
You said you were sure it would kill you,
    If ever your husband looked so;
And you will not apostatize,—will you?
    My own Araminta, say "No!"

When I heard I was going abroad, love,
    I thought I was going to die;
We walked arm in arm to the road, love,
    We looked arm in arm to the sky;
And I said, "When a foreign postilion
    Has hurried me off to the Po,
Forget not Medora Trevilian:—
    My own Araminta, say "No!"

We parted! but sympathy's fetters
    Reach far over valley and hill;
I muse o'er your exquisite letters,
    And feel that your heart is mine still;
And he who would share it with me, love,—
    The richest of treasures below,—
If he's not what Orlando should be, love,
    My own Araminta, say "No!"

If he wears a top-boot in his wooing,
    If he comes to you riding a cob,
If he talks of his baking or brewing,
    If he puts up his feet on the hob,

If he ever drinks port after dinner,
　　If his brow or his breeding is low,
If he calls himself "Thompson" or "Skinner,"
　　My own Araminta, say "No!"

If he studies the news in the papers
　　While you are preparing the tea,
If he talks of the damps or the vapors
　　While moonlight lies soft on the sea,
If he's sleepy while you are capricious,
　　If he has not a musical "Oh!"
If he does not call Werther delicious,—
　　My own Araminta, say "No!"

If he ever sets foot in the city
　　Among the stockbrokers and Jews,
If he has not a heart full of pity,
　　If he don't stand six feet in his shoes,
If his lips are not redder than roses,
　　If his hands are not whiter than snow,
If he has not the model of noses,—
　　My own Araminta, say "No!"

If he speaks of a tax or a duty.
　　If he does not look grand on his knees,
If he's blind to a landscape of beauty,
　　Hills, valleys, rocks, waters, and trees,
If he dotes not on desolate towers,
　　If he likes not to hear the blast blow,
If he knows not the language of flowers,—
　　My own Araminta, say "No!"

He must walk like a god of old story
　　Come down from the home of his rest;
He must smile like the sun in his glory
　　On the buds he loves ever the best;
And oh! from its ivory portal
　　Like music his soft speech must flow!—
If he speak, smile, or walk like a mortal,
　　My own Araminta, say "No!"

Don't listen to tales of his bounty,
   Don't hear what they say of his birth,
Don't look at his seat in the county,
   Don't calculate what he is worth;
But give him a theme to write verse on,
   And see if he turns out his toe;—
If he's only an excellent person,
   My own Araminta, say "No!"

              Winthrop Mackworth Praed [1802–1839]

A *NICE* CORRESPONDENT

"There are plenty of roses" (the patriarch speaks)
"Alas not for me, on your lips and your cheeks;
Fair maiden rose-laden enough and to spare,
Spare, spare me that rose that you wear in your hair."

THE glow and the glory are plighted
   To darkness, for evening is come;
The lamp in Glebe Cottage is lighted,
   The birds and the sheep-bells are dumb.
I'm alone, for the others have flitted
   To dine with a neighbor at Kew:
Alone, but I'm not to be pitied—
    I'm thinking of you!

I wish you were here! Were I duller
   Than dull, you'd be dearer than dear;
I am dressed in your favorite color—
   Dear Fred, how I wish you were here!
I am wearing my lazuli necklace,
   The necklace you fastened askew!
Was there ever so rude or so reckless
    A Darling as you?

I want you to come and pass sentence
   On two or three books with a plot;
Of course you know "Janet's Repentance"?
   I am reading Sir *Waverley* Scott.

That story of Edgar and Lucy,
  How thrilling, romantic, and true!
The Master (his bride *was* a goosey!)
    Reminds me of you.

They tell me Cockaigne has been crowning
  A Poet whose garland endures;—
It was you that first told me of Browning,—
  That stupid old Browning of yours!
His vogue and his verve are alarming,
  I'm anxious to give him his due;
But, Fred, he's not nearly so charming
    A Poet as you!

I heard how you shot at The Beeches,
  I saw how you rode *Chanticleer*,
I have read the report of your speeches,
  And echoed the echoing cheer.
There's a whisper of hearts you are breaking,
  Dear Fred, I believe it, I do!
Small marvel that Folly is making
    Her Idol of you!

Alas for the World, and its dearly
  Bought triumph,—its fugitive bliss;
Sometimes I half wish I were merely
  A plain or a penniless Miss;
But, perhaps, one is blest with "a measure
  Of pelf," and I'm not sorry, too,
That I'm pretty, because it's a pleasure,
    My Darling, to you!

Your whim is for frolic and fashion,
  Your taste is for letters and art;—
This rhyme is the commonplace passion
  That glows in a fond woman's heart:
Lay it by in some sacred deposit
  For relics—we all have a few!
Love, some day they'll print it, because it
    Was written to You.
                    Frederick Locker-Lampson [1821–1895]

HER LETTER

I'M sitting alone by the fire,
   Dressed just as I came from the dance,
In a robe even *you* would admire,—
   It cost a cool thousand in France;
I'm be-diamonded out of all reason,
   My hair is done up in a cue:
In short, sir, "the belle of the season"
   Is wasting an hour upon you.

A dozen engagements I've broken;
   I left in the midst of a set;
Likewise a proposal, half spoken,
   That waits—on the stairs—for me yet.
They say he'll be rich,—when he grows up,—
   And then he adores me indeed;
And you, sir, are turning your nose up,
   Three thousand miles off, as you read.

"And how do I like my position?"
   "And what do I think of New York?"
"And now, in my higher ambition,
   With whom do I waltz, flirt, or talk?"
"And isn't it nice to have riches,
   And diamonds and silks, and all that?"
"And aren't they a change to the ditches
   And tunnels of Poverty Flat?"

Well, yes,—if you saw us out driving
   Each day in the Park, four-in-hand,
If you saw poor dear mamma contriving
   To look supernaturally grand,—
If you saw papa's picture, as taken
   By Brady, and tinted at that,—
You'd never suspect he sold bacon
   And flour at Poverty Flat.

And yet, just this moment, when sitting
   In the glare of the grand chandelier,—
In the bustle and glitter befitting
   The "finest *soirée* of the year,"—

In the mists of a *gaze de Chambéry*,
    And the hum of the smallest of talk,—
Somehow, Joe, I thought of the "Ferry,"
    And the dance that we had on "The Fork;"

Of Harrison's bar, with its muster
    Of flags festooned over the wall;
Of the candles that shed their soft lustre
    And tallow on head-dress and shawl;
Of the steps that we took to one fiddle,
    Of the dress of my queer *vis-à-vis;*
And how I once went down the middle
    With the man that shot Sandy McGee.

Of the moon that was quietly sleeping
    On the hill, when the time came to go;
Of the few baby peaks that were peeping
    From under their bedclothes of snow;
Of that ride,—that to me was the rarest;
    Of—the something you said at the gate.
Ah! Joe, then I wasn't an heiress
    To "the best-paying lead in the State."

Well, well, it's all past; yet it's funny
    To think, as I stood in the glare
Of fashion and beauty and money,
    That I should be thinking, right there,
Of some one who breasted high water,
    And swam the North Fork, and all that,
Just to dance with old Folinsbee's daughter,
    The Lily of Poverty Flat.

But goodness! what nonsense I'm writing!
    (Mamma says my taste still is low),
Instead of my triumphs reciting,
    I'm spooning on Joseph,—heigh-ho!
And I'm to be "finished" by travel,—
    Whatever's the meaning of that.
Oh, why did papa strike pay gravel
    In drifting on Poverty Flat?

Good-night!—here's the end of my paper;
  Good-night!—if the longitude please,—
For maybe, while wasting my taper,
  Your sun's climbing over the trees.
But know, if you haven't got riches,
  And are poor, dearest Joe, and all that,
That my heart's somewhere there in the ditches,
  And you've struck it,—on Poverty Flat.

Bret Harte [1830–1902]

A DEAD LETTER

A cœur blessé—l'ombre et le silence.—BALZAC

I

I DREW it from its china tomb;—
  It came out feebly scented
With some thin ghost of past perfume
  That dust and days had lent it.

An old, old letter;—folded still!
  To read with due composure,
I sought the sun-lit window-sill,
  Above the gray enclosure,

That, glimmering in the sultry haze,
  Faint-flowered, dimly shaded,
Slumbered like Goldsmith's Madam Blaize,
  - Bedizened and brocaded.

A queer old place!   You'd surely say
  Some tea-board garden-maker
Had planned it in Dutch William's day
  To please some florist Quaker,

So trim it was.   The yew-trees still,
  With pious care perverted,
Grew in the same grim shapes; and still
  The lipless dolphin spurted;

Still in his wonted state abode
  The broken-nosed Apollo;
And still the cypress-arbor showed
  The same umbrageous hollow.

Only,—as fresh young Beauty gleams
  From coffee-colored laces,
So peeped from its old-fashioned dreams
  The fresher modern traces;

For idle mallet, hoop, and ball
  Upon the lawn were lying;
A magazine, a tumbled shawl,
  Round which the swifts were flying;

And, tossed beside the Guelder rose,
  A heap of rainbow knitting,
Where, blinking in her pleased repose,
  A Persian cat was sitting.

"A place to love in,—live,—for aye,
  If we too, like Tithonus,
Could find some God to stretch the gray
  Scant life the Fates have thrown us;

"But now by steam we run our race,
  With buttoned heart and pocket;
Our Love's a gilded, surplus grace,—
  Just like an empty locket!

"'The time is out of joint.' Who will,
  May strive to make it better;
For me, this warm old window-sill,
  And this old dusty letter."

II

"Dear *John* (the letter ran), it can't, can't be,
  For Father's gone to *Chorley Fair* with *Sam,*
And Mother's storing Apples,—*Prue* and *Me*
  Up to our Elbows making Damson Jam:
But we shall meet before a Week is gone,—
''Tis a long Lane that has no Turning,' *John!*

"Only till Sunday next, and then you'll wait
   Behind the White-Thorn, by the broken Stile—
We can go round and catch them at the Gate,
   All to Ourselves, for nearly one long Mile;
Dear *Prue* won't look, and Father he'll go on,
And *Sam's* two Eyes are all for *Cissy, John!*

"*John*, she's so smart,—with every Ribbon new,
   Flame-colored Sack, and Crimson Padesoy:
As proud as proud; and has the Vapors too,
   Just like My Lady;—calls poor *Sam* a Boy,
And vows no Sweet-heart's worth the Thinking-on
Till he's past Thirty . . . I know better, *John!*

"My Dear, I don't think that I thought of much
   Before we knew each other, I and you;
And now, why, *John*, your least, least Finger-touch,
   Gives me enough to think a Summer through.
See, for I send you Something! There, 'tis gone!
Look in this corner,—mind you find it, *John!*

III

This was the matter of the note,—
   A long-forgot deposit,
Dropped in an Indian dragon's throat
   Deep in a fragrant closet,

Piled with a dapper Dresden world,—
   Beaux, beauties, prayers, and poses,—
Bonzes with squat legs undercurled,
   And great jars filled with roses.

Ah, heart that wrote! Ah, lips that kissed!
   You had no thought or presage
Into what keeping you dismissed
   Your simple old-world message!

A reverent one. Though we to-day
   Distrust beliefs and powers,
The artless, ageless things you say
   Are fresh as May's own flowers. . . .

I need not search too much to find
    Whose lot it was to send it,
That feel upon me yet the kind,
    Soft hand of her who penned it;

And see, through two-score years of smoke,
    In by-gone, quaint apparel,
Shine from yon time-black Norway oak
    The face of Patience Caryl,—

The pale, smooth forehead, silver-tressed;
    The gray gown, primly flowered;
The spotless, stately coif whose crest
    Like Hector's horse-plume towered;

And still the sweet half-solemn look
    Where some past thought was clinging,
As when one shuts a serious book
    To hear the thrushes singing.

I kneel to you! Of those you were,
    Whose kind old hearts grow mellow,—
Whose fair old faces grow more fair,
    As Point and Flanders yellow;

Whom some old store of garnered grief,
    Their placid temples shading,
Crowns like a wreath of autumn leaf
    With tender tints of fading.

Peace to your soul!   You died unwed—
    Despite this loving letter.
And what of John?   The less that's said
    Of John, I think, the better.
                    Austin Dobson [1840–1921]

THE NYMPH COMPLAINING FOR THE DEATH
OF HER FAWN

THE wanton troopers riding by
Have shot my fawn, and it will die.
Ungentle men! They cannot thrive
Who killed thee. Thou ne'er didst, alive,

Them any harm; alas! nor could
Thy death to them do any good.
I'm sure I never wished them ill,
Nor do I for all this; nor will:
But, if my simple prayers may yet
Prevail with Heaven to forget
Thy murder, I will join my tears
Rather than fail. But O my fears!
It cannot die so. Heaven's King
Keeps register of everything,
And nothing may we use in vain;
Even beasts must be with justice slain;
Else men are made their deodands.
Though they should wash their guilty hands
In this warm life-blood, which doth part
From thine, and wound me to the heart,
Yet could they not be clean; their stain
Is dyed in such a purple grain,
There is not such another in
The world to offer for their sin.

Inconstant Sylvio, when yet
I had not found him counterfeit,
One morning, I remember well,
Tied in this silver chain and bell,
Gave it to me: nay, and I know
What he said then—I'm sure I do.
Said he, "Look how your huntsman here
Hath taught a fawn to hunt his deer!"
But Sylvio soon had me beguiled:
This waxèd tame, while he grew wild,
And, quite regardless of my smart,
Left me his fawn, but took his heart.

Thenceforth I set myself to play
My solitary time away
With this; and very well content
Could so mine idle life have spent;
For it was full of sport, and light
Of foot and heart, and did invite

Me to its game: it seemed to bless
Itself in me. How could I less
Than love it? Oh, I cannot be
Unkind to a beast that loveth me!

Had it lived long, I do not know
Whether it, too, might have done so
As Sylvio did; his gifts might be
Perhaps as false, or more, than he.
But I am sure, for aught that I
Could in so short a time espy,
Thy love was far more better than
The love of false and cruel man.

With sweetest milk and sugar first
I it at mine own fingers nursed;
And as it grew, so every day,
It waxed more white and sweet than they.
It had so sweet a breath! and oft
I blushed to see its foot more soft,
And white, shall I say? than my hand—
Nay, any lady's of the land!

It was a wondrous thing how fleet
'Twas on those little silver feet.
With what a pretty skipping grace
It oft would challenge me the race;
And when't had left me far away,
'Twould stay, and run again, and stay;
For it was nimbler much than hinds,
And trod as if on the four winds.

I have a garden of my own,
But so with roses overgrown,
And lilies, that you would it guess
To be a little wilderness;
And all the spring-time of the year
It lovèd only to be there.
Among the beds of lilies I
Have sought it oft, where it should lie,

Yet could not, till itself would rise,
Find it, although before mine eyes;
For in the flaxen lilies' shade,
It like a bank of lilies laid.
Upon the roses it would feed,
Until its lips e'en seemed to bleed;
And then to me 'twould boldly trip,
And print those roses on my lip.
But all its chief delight was still
On roses thus itself to fill;
And its pure virgin lips to fold
In whitest sheets of lilies cold.
Had it lived long, it would have been
Lilies without, roses within.

O help! O help! I see it faint
And die as calmly as a saint!
See how it weeps! the tears do come
Sad, slowly, dropping like a gum.
So weeps the wounded balsam; so
The holy frankincense doth flow;
The brotherless Heliades
Melt in such amber tears as these.

I in a golden vial will
Keep these two crystal tears, and fill
It, till it doth overflow, with mine,
Then place it in Diana's shrine.

Now my sweet fawn is vanished to
Whither the swans and turtles go;
In fair Elysium to endure
With milk-white lambs and ermines pure.
O, do not run too fast, for I
Will but bespeak thy grave, and die.

First my unhappy statue shall
Be cut in marble; and withal
Let it be weeping too; but there
The engraver sure his art may spare;

For I so truly thee bemoan
That I shall weep though I be stone,
Until my tears, still dropping, wear
My breast, themselves engraving there;
Then at my feet shalt thou be laid,
Of purest alabaster made;
For I would have thine image be
White as I can, though not as thee.

Andrew Marvell [1621-1678]

ON THE DEATH OF A FAVORITE CAT, DROWNED IN A TUB OF GOLD FISHES

'TWAS on a lofty vase's side,
Where China's gayest art had dyed
  The azure flowers that blow;
Demurest of the tabby kind,
The pensive Selima, reclined,
  Gazed on the lake below.

Her conscious tail her joy declared;
The fair round face, the snowy beard,
  The velvet of her paws,
Her coat, that with the tortoise vies,
Her ears of jet, and emerald eyes,
  She saw; and purred applause.

Still had she gazed, but 'midst the tide
Two angel forms were seen to glide,
  The Genii of the stream:
Their scaly armor's Tyrian hue
Through richest purple to the view
  Betrayed a golden gleam.

The hapless Nymph with wonder saw:
A whisker first and then a claw,
  With many an ardent wish,
She stretched, in vain, to reach the prize.
What female heart can gold despise?
  What Cat's averse to fish?

Presumptous Maid! with looks intent
Again she stretched, again she bent,
  Nor knew the gulf between.
(Malignant Fate sat by, and smiled.)
The slippery verge her feet beguiled,
  She tumbled headlong in.

Eight times emerging from the flood
She mewed to every watery god,
  Some speedy aid to send.
No Dolphin came, no Nereid stirred:
Nor cruel Tom nor Susan heard,—
  A Favorite has no friend!

From hence, ye Beauties, undeceived,
Know, one false step is ne'er retrieved,
  And be with caution bold.
Not all that tempts your wandering eyes
And heedless hearts, is lawful prize;
  Nor all that glisters, gold.

                    Thomas Gray [1716–1771]

VERSES ON A CAT

CLUBBY! thou surely art, I ween,
A Puss of most majestic mien,
  So stately all thy paces!
With such a philosophic air
Thou seek'st thy professorial chair,
  And so demure thy face is!

And as thou sit'st, thine eye seems fraught
With such intensity of thought
  That could we read it, knowledge
Would seem to breathe in every mew,
And learning yet undreamt by you
  Who dwell in Hall or College.

Epitaph on a Hare

Oh! when in solemn taciturnity
Thy brain seems wandering through eternity,
   What happiness were mine
Could I then catch the thoughts that flow,
Thoughts such as ne'er were hatched below,
   But in a head like thine.

Oh then, throughout the livelong day,
With thee I'd sit and purr away
   In ecstasy sublime;
And in thy face, as from a book,
I'd drink in science at each look,
   Nor fear the lapse of time.

Charles Daubeny [1745-1827]

EPITAPH ON A HARE

HERE lies, whom hound did ne'er pursue,
   Nor swifter greyhound follow,
Whose foot ne'er tainted morning dew,
   Nor ear heard huntsman's hallo;

Old Tiney, surliest of his kind,
   Who, nursed with tender care,
And to domestic bounds confined,
   Was still a wild Jack-hare.

Though duly from my hand he took
   His pittance every night,
He did it with a jealous look,
   And, when he could, would bite.

His diet was of wheaten bread,
   And milk, and oats, and straw;
Thistles, or lettuces instead,
   With sand to scour his maw.

On twigs of hawthorn he regaled,
   On pippins' russet peel;
And, when his juicy salads failed,
   Sliced carrot pleased him well.

A Turkey carpet was his lawn,
  Whereon he loved to bound,
To skip and gambol like a fawn,
  And swing his rump around.

His frisking was at evening hours,
  For then he lost his fear;
But most before approaching showers,
  Or when a storm drew near.

Eight years and five round-rolling moons
  He thus saw steal away,
Dozing out all his idle noons,
  And every night at play.

I kept him for his humor's sake,
  For he would oft beguile
My heart of thoughts that made it ache,
  And force me to a smile.

But now, beneath this walnut-shade
  He finds his long, last home,
And waits, in snug concealment laid,
  Till gentler Puss shall come.

He, still more agèd, feels the shocks
  From which no care can save,
And, partner once of Tiney's box,
  Must soon partake his grave.
                    William Cowper [1731–1800]

ON THE DEATH OF MRS. THROCKMORTON'S
BULLFINCH

Ye Nymphs! if e'er your eyes were red
With tears o'er hapless favorites shed,
    O share Maria's grief!
Her favorite, even in his cage,
(What will not hunger's cruel rage?)
    Assassined by a thief.

On the Death of a Bullfinch   1827

Where Rhenus strays his vines among,
The egg was laid from which he sprung,
   And though by nature mute,
Or only with a whistle blessed,
Well-taught, he all the sounds expressed
   Of flageolet or flute.

The honors of his ebon poll
Were brighter than the sleekest mole;
   His bosom of the hue
With which Aurora decks the skies,
When piping winds shall soon arise
   To sweep away the dew.

Above, below, in all the house,
Dire foe alike of bird and mouse,
   No cat had leave to dwell;
And Bully's cage supported stood,
On props of smoothest-shaven wood,
   Large-built and latticed well.

Well-latticed,—but the grate, alas!
Not rough with wire of steel or brass,
   For Bully's plumage sake,
But smooth with wands from Ouse's side,
With which, when neatly peeled and dried,
   The swains their baskets make.

Night veiled the pole—all seemed secure—
When, led by instinct sharp and sure,
   Subsistence to provide,
A beast forth sallied on the scout,
Long-backed, long-tailed, with whiskered snout,
   And badger-colored hide.

He, entering at the study-door,
Its ample area 'gan explore;
   And something in the wind
Conjectured, sniffing round and round,
Better than all the books he found,
   Food, chiefly, for the mind.

Just then, by adverse fate impressed
A dream disturbed poor Bully's rest;
    In sleep he seemed to view
A rat, fast-clinging to the cage,
And, screaming at the sad presage,
    Awoke and found it true.

For, aided both by ear and scent,
Right to his mark the monster went—
    Ah, Muse! forbear to speak
Minute the horror that ensued;
His teeth were strong, the cage was wood—
    He left poor Bully's beak.

O had he made that too his prey!
That beak, whence issued many a lay
    Of such mellifluous tone,
Might have repaid him well, I wote,
For silencing so sweet a throat,
    Fast stuck within his own.

Maria weeps,—the Muses mourn;—
So, when by Bacchanalians torn,
    On Thracian Hebrus' side
The tree-enchanter Orpheus fell,
His head alone remained to tell
    The cruel death he died.

                    William Cowper [1731–1800]

AN ELEGY ON A LAP-DOG

Shock's fate I mourn; poor Shock is now no more:
Ye Muses! mourn; ye Chambermaids! deplore.
Unhappy Shock! Yet more unhappy fair,
Doomed to survive thy joy and only care.
Thy wretched fingers now no more shall deck,
And tie the favorite ribbon round his neck;
No more thy hand shall smooth his glossy hair,
And comb the wavings of his pendent ear.
Let cease thy flowing grief, forsaken maid!
All mortal pleasures in a moment fade:

Our surest hope is in an hour destroyed,
And love, best gift of Heaven, not long enjoyed.
   Methinks I see her frantic with despair,
Her streaming eyes, wrung hands, and flowing hair;
Her Mechlin pinners, rent, the floor bestrow,
And her torn fan gives real signs of woe.
Hence, Superstition! that tormenting guest,
That haunts with fancied fears the coward breast;
No dread events upon this fate attend,
Stream eyes no more, no more thy tresses rend.
Though certain omens oft forewarn a state,
And dying lions show the monarch's fate,
Why should such fears bid Celia's sorrow rise?
For, when a lap-dog falls, no lover dies.
   Cease, Celia, cease; restrain thy flowing tears.
Some warmer passion will dispel thy cares.
In man you'll find a more substantial bliss,
More grateful toying and a sweeter kiss.
   He's dead.   Oh! lay him gently in the ground!
And may his tomb be by this verse renowned:
Here Shock, the pride of all his kind, is laid,
Who fawned like man, but ne'er like man betrayed.

John Gay [1685–1732]

MY LAST TERRIER

I MOURN "Patroclus," whilst I praise
  Young "Peter" sleek before the fire,
A proper dog, whose decent ways
  Renew the virtues of his sire;
"Patroclus" rests in grassy tomb,
And "Peter" grows into his room.

For though, when Time or Fates consign
  The terrier to his latest earth,
Vowing no wastrel of the line
  Shall dim the memory of his worth,
I meditate the silkier breeds,
Yet still an Amurath succeeds:

Succeeds to bind the heart again
   To watchful eye and strenuous paw,
To tail that gratulates amain
   Or deprecates offended Law;
To bind, and break, when failing eye
And palsied paw must say good-bye.

Ah, had the dog's appointed day
   But tallied with his master's span,
Nor one swift decade turned to gray
   The busy muzzle's black and tan,
To reprobate in idle men
Their threescore empty years and ten!

Sure, somewhere o'er the Stygian strait
   "Panurge" and "Bito," "Tramp" and "Mike,"
In couchant conclave watch the gate,
   Till comes the last successive tyke,
Acknowledged with the countersign:
"Your master was a friend of mine."

In dreams I see them spring to greet,
   With rapture more than tail can tell,
Their master of the silent feet
   Who whistles o'er the asphodel,
And through the dim Elysian bounds
Leads all his cry of little hounds.

                    John Halsham [18 –

GEIST'S GRAVE

FOUR years!—and didst thou stay above
The ground, which hides thee now, but four?
And all that life, and all that love,
Were crowded, Geist! into no more?

Only four years those winning ways,
Which make me for thy presence yearn,
Called us to pet thee or to praise,
Dear little friend! at every turn?

That loving heart, that patient soul,
Had they indeed no longer span,
To run their course, and reach their goal
And read their homily to man?

That liquid, melancholy eye,
From whose pathetic, soul-fed springs
Seemed surging the Virgilian cry,
The sense of tears in mortal things—

That steadfast, mournful strain, consoled
By spirits gloriously gay,
And temper of heroic mould—
What, was four years their whole short day?

Yes, only four!—and not the course
Of all the centuries yet to come,
And not the infinite resource
Of Nature, with her countless sum

Of figures, with her fulness vast
Of new creation evermore,
Can ever quite repeat the past,
Or just thy little self restore.

Stern law of every mortal lot!
Which man, proud man, finds hard to bear,
And builds himself I know not what
Of second life I know not where.

But thou, when struck thine hour to go,
On us, who stood despondent by,
A meek last glance of love didst throw,
And humbly lay thee down to die.

Yet would we keep thee in our heart—
Would fix our favorite on the scene,
Nor let thee utterly depart
And be as if thou ne'er hadst been.

And so there rise these lines of verse
On lips that rarely form them now;
While to each other we rehearse:
Such ways, such arts, such looks hadst thou!

We stroke thy broad brown paws again,
We bid thee to thy vacant chair,
We greet thee by the window-pane,
We hear thy scuffle on the stair;

We see the flaps of thy large ears
Quick raised to ask which way we go;
Crossing the frozen lake, appears
Thy small black figure on the snow!

Nor to us only art thou dear,
Who mourn thee in thine English home;
Thou hast thine absent master's tear,
Dropped by the far Australian foam.

Thy memory lasts both here and there,
And thou shalt live as long as we.
And after that—thou dost not care!
In us was all the world to thee.

Yet, fondly zealous for thy fame,
Even to a date beyond our own,
We strive to carry down thy name
By mounded turf and graven stone.

We lay thee, close within our reach,
Here, where the grass is smooth and warm,
Between the holly and the beech,
Where oft we watched thy couchant form,

Asleep, yet lending half an ear
To travelers on the Portsmouth road;—
There choose we thee, O guardian dear,
Marked with a stone, thy last abode!

Then some, who through this garden pass,
When we too, like thyself, are clay,
Shall see thy grave upon the grass,
And stop before the stone, and say:

People who lived here long ago
Did by this stone, it seems, intend
To name for future times to know
The dachs-hound, Geist, their little friend.

              Matthew Arnold [1822–1888]

"HOLD"

I KNOW, where Hampshire fronts the Wight,
    A little church, where "after strife"
Reposes Guy de Blanquely, Knight,
    By Alison his wife:
I know their features' graven lines
    In time-stained marble monotone,
While crouched before their feet reclines
    Their little dog of stone!

I look where Blanquely Castle still
    Frowns o'er the oak wood's summer state,
(The maker of a patent pill
    Has purchased it of late),
And then through Fancy's open door
    I backward turn to days of old,
And see Sir Guy—a bachelor
    Who owns a dog called "Hold"!

I see him take the tourney's chance,
    And urge his coal-black charger on
To an arbitrament by lance
    For lovely Alison;
I mark the onset, see him hurl
    From broidered saddle to the dirt
His rival, that ignoble Earl—
    Black-hearted Massingbert!

Then Alison, with down-dropped eyes,
    Where happy tears bedim the blue,
Bestows a valuable prize
    And adds her hand thereto;
My lord, his surcoat streaked with sand,
    Remounts, low muttering curses hot,
And with a base-born, hireling band
    He plans a dastard plot!

.   .   .   .

'Tis night—Sir Guy has sunk to sleep,
    The castle keep is hushed and still—
See, up the spiral stairway creep,
    To work his wicked will,
Lord Massingbert of odious fame,
    Soft followed by his cut-throat staff;
Ah, "Hold" has justified his name
    And pinned his lordship's calf!

A growl, an oath, then torches flare;
    Out rings a sentry's startled shout;
The guard are racing for the stair,
    Half-dressed, Sir Guy runs out;
On high his glittering blade he waves,
    He gives foul Massingbert the point,
He carves the hired assassin knaves
    Joint from plebeian joint!

.   .   .   .

The Knight is dead—his sword is rust,
    But in his day I'm certain "Hold"
Wore, as his master's badge of trust,
    A collarette of gold:
And still I like to fancy that,
    Somewhere beyond the Styx's bound,
Sir Guy's tall phantom stoops to pat
    His little phantom hound!

                        Patrick R. Chalmers [18-

THE BARB OF SATIRE

THE VICAR OF BRAY

In good King Charles's golden days,
  When loyalty no harm meant,
A zealous high-churchman was I,
  And so I got preferment.
To teach my flock I never missed:
  Kings were by God appointed,
And lost are those that dare resist
  Or touch the Lord's anointed.
    And this is law that I'll maintain
      Until my dying day, sir,
    That whatsoever king shall reign,
      Still I'll be the Vicar of Bray, sir.

When royal James possessed the crown,
  And popery grew in fashion,
The penal laws I hooted down,
  And read the Declaration;
The Church of Rome I found would fit
  Full well my constitution;
And I had been a Jesuit
  But for the Revolution.

When William was our king declared,
  To ease the nation's grievance,
With this new wind about I steered,
  And swore to him allegiance;
Old principles I did revoke,
  Set conscience at a distance;
Passive obedience was a joke,
  A jest was non-resistance.

1835

When royal Anne became our queen,
    The Church of England's glory,
Another face of things was seen,
    And I became a Tory;
Occasional conformists base,
    I blamed their moderation,
And thought the Church in danger was,
    By such prevarication.

When George in pudding-time came o'er,
    And moderate men looked big, sir,
My principles I changed once more,
    And so became a Whig, sir;
And thus preferment I procured
    From our new Faith's defender,
And almost every day abjured
    The Pope and the Pretender.

The illustrious house of Hanover,
    And Protestant succession,
To these I do allegiance swear—
    While they can keep possession:
For in my faith and loyalty
    I nevermore will falter,
And George my lawful king shall be—
    Until the times do alter.
        And this is law that I'll maintain
            Until my dying day, sir,
        That whatsoever king shall reign,
            Still I'll be the Vicar of Bray, sir.
                                    Unknown

THE LOST LEADER

[WILLIAM WORDSWORTH]

JUST for a handful of silver he left us,
    Just for a ribbon to stick in his coat—
Found the one gift of which fortune bereft us,
    Lost all the others she lets us devote;

They, with the gold to give, doled him out silver,
  So much was theirs who so little allowed:
How all our copper had gone for his service!
  Rags—were they purple, his heart had been proud—
We that had loved him so, followed him, honored him,
  Lived in his mild and magnificent eye,
Learned his great language, caught his clear accents,
  Made him our pattern to live and to die!
Shakespeare was of us, Milton was for us,
  Burns, Shelley, were with us,—they watch from their
    graves!
He alone breaks from the van and the freemen,
  —He alone sinks to the rear and the slaves!
We shall march prospering,—not through his presence;
  Songs may inspirit us,—not from his lyre;
Deeds will be done,—while he boasts his quiescence,
  Still bidding crouch whom the rest bade aspire:
Blot out his name, then, record one lost soul more,
  One task more declined, one more footpath untrod,
One more devil's-triumph and sorrow for angels,
  One wrong more to man, one more insult to God!
Life's night begins: let him never come back to us!
  There would be doubt, hesitation and pain,
Forced praise on our part—the glimmer of twilight,
  Never glad confident morning again!
Best fight on well, for we taught him—strike gallantly,
  Menace our heart ere we master his own;
Then let him receive the new knowledge and wait us,
  Pardoned in heaven, the first by the throne!

Robert Browning [1812–1889]

ICHABOD

[DANIEL WEBSTER]

So fallen! so lost! the light withdrawn
  Which once he wore!
The glory from his gray hairs gone
  Forevermore!

The Barb of Satire

Revile him not, the Tempter hath
    A snare for all;
And pitying tears, not scorn and wrath,
    Befit his fall!

Oh, dumb be passion's stormy rage,
    When he who might
Have lighted up and led his age,
    Falls back in night.

Scorn! would the angels laugh, to mark
    A bright soul driven,
Fiend-goaded, down the endless dark,
    From hope and heaven!

Let not the land once proud of him
    Insult him now,
Nor brand with deeper shame his dim,
    Dishonored brow.

But let its humbled sons, instead,
    From sea to lake,
A long lament, as for the dead,
    In sadness make.

Of all we loved and honored, naught
    Save power remains;
A fallen angel's pride of thought,
    Still strong in chains.

All else is gone; from those great eyes
    The soul has fled:
When faith is lost, when honor dies,
    The man is dead!

Then, pay the reverence of old days
    To his dead fame;
Walk backward, with averted gaze,
    And hide the shame!

            John Greenleaf Whittier [1807-1892]

WHAT MR. ROBINSON THINKS

GUVENER B. is a sensible man;
  He stays to his home an' looks arter his folks;
He draws his furrer ez straight ez he can,
  An' into nobody's tater-patch pokes;
        But John P.
        Robinson he
  Sez he wunt vote fer Guvener B.

My! aint it terrible? Wut shall we du?
  We can't never choose him o' course,—thet's flat;
Guess we shall hev to come round, (don't you?)
  An' go in fer thunder an' guns, an' all that;
        Fer John P.
        Robinson he
  Sez he wunt vote fer Guvener B.

Gineral C. is a dreffle smart man:
  He's ben on all sides that give places or pelf;
But consistency still wuz a part of his plan,—
  He's ben true to *one* party,—an' thet is himself;—
        So John P.
        Robinson he
  Sez he shall vote fer Gineral C.

Gineral C. he goes in fer the war;
  He don't vally princerple more'n an old cud;
Wut did God make us raytional creeturs fer,
  But glory an' gunpowder, plunder an' blood?
        So John P.
        Robinson he
  Sez he shall vote fer Gineral C.

We were gittin' on nicely up here to our village,
  With good old idees o' wut's right an' wut aint,
We kind o' thought Christ went agin war an' pillage,
  An' thet eppyletts worn't the best mark of a saint;
        But John P.
        Robinson he
  Sez this kind o' thing's an exploded idee.

The side of our country must ollers be took,
  An' Presidunt Polk, you know, *he* is our country,
An' the angel thet writes all our sins in a book
  Puts the *debit* to him, an' to us the *per contry;*
      An' John P.
      Robinson he
  Sez this is his view o' the thing to a T.

Parson Wilbur he calls all these argimunts lies;
  Sez they're nothin' on airth but jest *fee, faw, fum;*
An' thet all this big talk of our destinies
  Is half on it ign'ance, an' t'other half rum;
      But John P.
      Robinson he
  Sez it aint no sech thing; an', of course, so must we.

Parson Wilbur sez *he* never heerd in his life
  That th' Apostles rigged out in their swaller-tail coats,
An' marched round in front of a drum an' a fife,
  To git some on 'em office, an' some on 'em votes;
      But John P.
      Robinson he
  Sez they didn't know everythin' down in Judee.

Wal, it's a marcy we've gut folks to tell us
  The rights an' the wrongs o' these matters, I vow,—
God sends country lawyers, an' other wise fellers,
  To start the world's team wen it gits in a slough;
      Fer John P.
      Robinson he
  Sez the world'll go right, ef he hollers out Gee!
                    James Russell Lowell [1819–1891]

THE DEBATE IN THE SENNIT

SOT TO A NURSERY RHYME

"HERE we stan' on the Constitution, by thunder!
  It's a fact o' wich ther's bushils o' proofs;
Fer how could we trample on 't so, I wonder,
  Ef't worn't thet it's ollers under our hoofs?"

The Debate in the Sennit

Sez John C. Calhoun, sez he;
"Human rights haint no more
Right to come on this floor,
No more'n the man in the moon," sez he.

"The North haint no kind o' bisness with nothin',
An' you've no idee how much bother it saves;
We aint none riled by their frettin' an' frothin',
We're *used* to layin' the string on our slaves,"
Sez John C. Calhoun, sez he;—
Sez Mister Foote,
"I should like to shoot
The holl gang, by the gret horn spoon!" sez he.

"Freedom's Keystone is Slavery, thet ther's no doubt on,
It's sutthin' thet's—wha'd'ye call it?—divine,—
An' the slaves thet we ollers *make* the most out on
Air them north o' Mason an' Dixon's line,"
Sez John C. Calhoun, sez he;—
"Fer all thet," sez Mangum,
" 'T would be better to hang 'em
An' so git red on 'er1 soon," sez he.

"The mass ough' to labor an' we lay on soffies,
Thet's the reason I want to spread Freedom's aree;
It puts all the cunninest on us in office,
An' reelises our Maker's orig'nal idee,"
Sez John C. Calhoun, sez he;—
"Thet's ez plain," sez Cass,
"Ez thet some one's an ass,
It's ez clear ez the sun is at noon," sez he.

"Now don't go to say I'm the friend of oppression,
But keep all your spare breath fer coolin' your broth,
Fer I ollers hev strove (at least thet's my impression)
To make cussed free with the rights o' the North,"
Sez John C. Calhoun, sez he;—
"Yes," sez Davis o' Miss.,
"The perfection o' bliss
Is in skinnin' thet same old coon," sez he.

"Slavery's a thing thet depends on complexion,
    It's God's law thet fetters on black skins don't chafe;
Ef brains wuz to settle it (horrid reflection!)
    Wich of our onnable body'd be safe?"
        Sez John C. Calhoun, sez he;—
            Sez Mister Hannegan,
            Afore he began agin,
        "Thet exception is quite oppertoon," sez he.

"Gen'nle Cass, Sir, you needn't be twitchin' your collar,
    Your merit's quite clear by the dut on your knees;
At the North we don't make no distinctions o' color;
    You can all take a lick at our shoes wen you please,"
        Sez John C. Calhoun, sez he;—
            Sez Mister Jarnagin,
            "They wun't hev to larn agin,
        They all on 'em know the old toon," sez he.

"The slavery question aint no ways bewilderin',
    North an' South hev one int'rest, it's plain to a glance,
No'thern men, like us patriarchs, don't sell their childrin,
    But they *du* sell themselves, ef they git a good chance,"
        Sez John C. Calhoun, sez he;—
            Sez Atherton here,
            "This is gittin' severe,
        I wish I could dive like a loon," sez he.

"It'll break up the Union, this talk about freedom,
    An' your fact'ry gals (soon ez we split) 'll make head,
An' gittin' some Miss chief or other to lead 'em,
    'll go to work raisin' permiscoous Ned,"
        Sez John C. Calhoun, sez he;—
            "Yes, the North," sez Colquitt,
            "Ef we Southeners all quit,
        Would go down like a busted balloon," sez he.

"Jest look wut is doin', wut annyky's brewin'
    In the beautiful clime o' the olive an' vine,
All the wise aristoxy's atumblin' to ruin,
    An' the sankylot's drorin' an' drinkin' their wine,"

Sez John C. Calhoun, sez he;—
  "Yes," sez Johnson, "in France
    They're beginnin' to dance
Beëlzebub's own rigadoon," sez he.

"The South's safe enough, it don't feel a mite skeery,
  Our slaves in their darkness an' dut air tu blest
Not to welcome with proud hallylugers the ery
  Wen our eagle kicks yourn from the naytional nest,"
  Sez John C. Calhoun, sez he;—
    "Oh," sez Westcott o' Florida,
    "Wut treason is horrider
Than our priv'leges tryin' to proon?" sez he.

"It's 'coz they're so happy, thet, wen crazy sarpints
  Stick their nose in our bizness, we git so darned riled;
We think it's our dooty to give pooty sharp hints,
  Thet the last crumb of Edin on airth sha'n't be spiled,"
  Sez John C. Calhoun, sez he;—
    "Ah," sez Dixon H. Lewis,
    "It perfectly true is
Thet slavery's airth's grettest boon," sez he.

        James Russell Lowell [1819–1891]

THE MARQUIS OF CARABAS

A SONG WITH A STOLEN BURDEN

OFF with your hat! along the street
  His Lordship's carriage rolls;
Respect to greatness—when it shines
  To cheer our darkened souls.
Get off the step, you ragged boys!
  Policeman, where's your staff?
This is a sight to check with awe
  The most irreverent laugh.
    Chapeau bas!
    Chapeau bas!
  Gloire au Marquis de Carabas!

Stand further back! we'll see him well;
  Wait till they lift him out:
It takes some time; his Lordship's old,
  And suffers from the gout.
Now look! he owns a castled park
  For every finger thin;
He has more sterling pounds a day
  Than wrinkles in his skin.

The founder of his race was son
  To a king's cousin, rich;
(The mother was an oyster wench—
  She perished in a ditch).
His patriot worth embalmed has been
  In poets' loud applause:
He made twelve thousand pounds a year
  By aiding France's cause.

The second marquis, of the stole
  Was groom to the second James;
He all but caught that recreant king
  When flying o'er the Thames.
Devotion rare! by Orange Will
  With a Scotch county paid;
He gained one more—in Ireland—when
  Charles Edward he betrayed.

He lived to see his son grow up
  A general famed and bold,
Who fought his country's fights—and one,
  For half a million, sold.
His son (alas! the house's shame)
  Frittered the name away:
Diced, wenched and drank—at last got shot,
  Through cheating in his play!

Now, see, where, focused on one head,
  The race's glories shine:
The head gets narrow at the top,
  But mark the jaw—how fine!

Don't call it satyr-like; you'd wound
  Some scores, whose honest pates
The self-same type present, upon
  The Carabas estates!

Look at his skin—at four-score years
  How fresh it gleams and fair:
He never tasted ill-dressed food,
  Or breathed in tainted air.
The noble blood glows through his veins
  Still, with a healthful pink;
His brow scarce wrinkled!—Brows keep so
  That have not got to think.

His hand 's ungloved!—it shakes, 'tis true,
  But mark its tiny size,
(High birth's true sign) and shape, as on
  The lackey's arm it lies.
That hand ne'er penned a useful line,
  Ne'er worked a deed of fame,
Save slaying one, whose sister he—
  Its owner—brought to shame.

They've got him in—he's gone to vote
  Your rights and mine away;
Perchance our lives, should men be scarce,
  To fight his cause for pay.
We are his slaves! he owns our lands,
  Our woods, our seas, and skies;
He'd have us shot like vicious dogs,
  Should we in murmuring rise!
      Chapeau bas!
      Chapeau bas!
    Gloire au Marquis de Carabas!
        Robert Brough [1828–1860]

A MODEST WIT

A SUPERCILIOUS nabob of the East—
  Haughty, being great—purse-proud, being rich—
A governor, or general, at the least,
  I have forgotten which—

Had in his family a humble youth,
  Who went from England in his patron's suit,
An unassuming boy, in truth
  A lad of decent parts, and good repute.

This youth had sense and spirit;
  But yet with all his sense,
  Excessive diffidence
Obscured his merit.

One day, at table, flushed with pride and wine,
  His Honor, proudly free, severely merry,
Conceived it would be vastly fine
  To crack a joke upon his secretary.

"Young man," he said, "by what art, craft, or trade,
  Did your good father gain a livelihood?" —
"He was a saddler, sir," Modestus said,
  "And in his time was reckoned good."

"A saddler, eh! and taught you Greek,
  Instead of teaching you to sew!
Pray, why did not your father make
  A saddler, sir, of you?"

Each parasite, then, as in duty bound,
The joke applauded, and the laugh went round.
  At length Modestus, bowing low,
Said (craving pardon, if too free he made),
  "Sir, by your leave, I fain would know
Your father's trade!"

"My father's trade! by heaven, that's too bad!
My father's trade? Why, blockhead, are you mad?
My father, sir, did never stoop so low—
He was a gentleman, I'd have you know."

"Excuse the liberty I take,"
  Modestus said, with archness on his brow,
"Pray, why did not your father make
  A gentleman of you?"

Selleck Osborn [1783–1826]

JOLLY JACK

WHEN fierce political debate
  Throughout the isie was storming,
And Rads attacked the throne and state,
  And Tories the reforming,
To calm the furious rage of each,
  And right the land demented,
Heaven sent us Jolly Jack, to teach
  The way to be contented.

Jack's bed was straw, 'twas warm and soft,
  His chair, a three-legged stool;
His broken jug was emptied oft,
  Yet, somehow, always full.
His mistress' portrait decked the wall,
  His mirror had a crack;
Yet, gay and glad, though this was all
  His wealth, lived Jolly Jack.

To give advice to avarice,
  Teach pride its mean condition,
And preach good sense to dull pretence,
  Was honest Jack's high mission.
Our simple statesman found his rule
  Of moral in the flagon,
And held his philosophic school
  Beneath the "George and Dragon."

When village Solons cursed the Lords,
  And called the malt-tax sinful,
Jack heeded not their angry words,
  But smiled and drank his skinful.
And when men wasted health and life,
  In search of rank and riches,
Jack marched aloof the paltry strife,
  And wore his threadbare breeches.

"I enter not the Church," he said,
  "But I'll not seek to rob it;"
So worthy Jack Joe Miller read,
  While others studied Cobbett.

His talk it was of feast and fun;
    His guide the Almanack;
From youth to age thus gaily run
    The life of Jolly Jack.

And when Jack prayed, as oft he would,
    He humbly thanked his Maker;
"I am," said he, "O Father good!
    Nor Catholic nor Quaker:
Give each his creed, let each proclaim
    His catalogue of curses;
I trust in Thee, and not in them,
    In Thee, and in Thy mercies!

"Forgive me if, midst all Thy works,
    No hint I see of damning;
And think there's faith among the Turks,
    And hope for e'en the Brahmin.
Harmless my mind is, and my mirth,
    And kindly is my laughter;
I cannot see the smiling earth,
    And think there's hell hereafter."

Jack died; he left no legacy,
    Save that his story teaches:—
Content to peevish poverty;
    Humility to riches.
Ye scornful great, ye envious small,
    Come follow in his track;
We all were happier, if we all
    Would copy Jolly Jack.
            William Makepeace Thackeray [1811–1863]

THE KING OF BRENTFORD *

AFTER BÉRANGER

THERE was a King in Brentford,—of whom no legends tell,
But who, without his glory,—could eat and sleep right well.
His Polly's cotton nightcap,—it was his crown of state,
He slept of evenings early,—and rose of mornings late.

* For the original of this poem see page 3840.

All in a fine mud palace,—each day he took four meals,
And for a guard of honor,—a dog ran at his heels.
Sometimes to view his kingdoms,—rode forth this monarch
    good,
And then a prancing jackass—he royally bestrode.

There were no costly habits—with which this King was
    cursed,
Except (and where's the harm on't?)—a somewhat lively
    thirst;
But people must pay taxes,—and Kings must have their
    sport;
So out of every gallon—His Grace he took a quart.

He pleased the ladies round him,—with manners soft and
    bland;
With reason good, they named him,—the father of his land.
Each year his mighty armies—marched forth in gallant
    show;
Their enemies were targets,—their bullets they were tow.

He vexed no quiet neighbor,—no useless conquest made,
But by the laws of pleasure,—his peaceful realm he swayed.
And in the years he reignèd,—through all this country wide,
There was no cause for weeping,—save when the good man
    died.

The faithful men of Brentford,—do still their King deplore,
His portrait yet is swinging,—beside an alehouse door.
And topers, tender-hearted,—regard his honest phiz,
And envy times departed,—that knew a reign like his.

William Makepeace Thackeray [1811–1863]

KAISER & CO.

DER Kaiser auf der Vaterland
Und Gott on high, all dings gommand;
Ve two, ach. don'd you understandt?
        Meinself—und Gott.

He reigns in heafen, und always shall,
Und mein own embire don'd vas shmall;

Ein noble bair, I dink you call
    Meinself—und Gott.

Vile some mens sing der power divine,
Mein soldiers sing der "Wacht am Rhein,"
Und drink der healt in Rhenish wein
    Auf me—und Gott.

Dere's France dot swaggers all aroundt,
She's ausgespicldt—she's no aggoundt;
To mooch ve dinks she don'd amoundt,
    Meinself—und Gott.

She vill not dare to fight again,
But if she shouldt, I'll show her blain
Dot Elsass und (in French) Lorraine
    Are mein—und Gott's.

Dere's grandma dinks she's nicht shmall beer,
Mit Boers und dings she interfere;
She'll learn none runs dis hemisphere
    But me—und Gott.

She dinks, goot frau, some ships she's got,
Und soldiers mit der sgarlet goat;
Ach! ve could knock dem—pouf! like dot,
    Meinself—und Gott.

In dimes auf peace, brebared for wars,
I bear der helm und sbear auf Mars,
Und care nicht for den dousant czars,
    Meinself—und Gott.

In short, I humor efery whim,
Mit aspect dark und visage grim,
Gott pulls mit me und I mit Him—
    Meinself—und Gott.
           Alexander Macgregor Rose [1846–1898]

NONGTONGPAW

JOHN BULL for pastime took a prance,
Some time ago, to peep at France;
To talk of sciences and arts,
And knowledge gained in foreign parts.

Monsieur, obsequious, heard him speak,
And answered John in heathen Greek:
To all he asked, 'bout all he saw,
'Twas, "*Monsieur, je vous n'entends pas.*"

John, to the Palais-Royal come,
Its splendor almost struck him dumb.
"I say, whose house is that there here?"
"House! *Je vous n'entends pas, Monsieur.*"
"What, Nongtongpaw again!" cries John;
"This fellow is some mighty Don:
No doubt he's plenty for the maw,—
I'll breakfast with this Nongtongpaw."

John saw Versailles from Marli's height,
And cried, astonished at the sight,
"Whose fine estate is that there here?"
"State! *Je vous n'entends pas, Monsieur.*'
"His? what, the land and houses too?
The fellow's richer than a Jew:
On everything he lays his claw!
I should like to dine with Nongtongpaw."

Next tripping came a courtly fair,
John cried, enchanted with her air,
"What lovely wench is that there here?"
"Ventch! *Je vous n'entends pas, Monsieur.*"
"What, he again? Upon my life!
A palace, lands, and then a wife
Sir Joshua might delight to draw:
I should like to sup with Nongtongpaw.

"But hold! whose funeral's that?" cries John.
"*Je vous n'entends pas.*"—"What, is he gone?
Wealth, fame, and beauty could not save
Poor Nongtongpaw, then, from the grave!
His race is run, his game is up,—
I'd with him breakfast, dine, and sup;
But since he chooses to withdraw,
Good night t' ye, Mounseer Nongtongpaw!"

Charles Dibdin [1745–1814]

THE LION AND THE CUB

How fond are men of rule and place,
Who court it from the mean and base!
These cannot bear an equal nigh,
But from superior merit fly.
They love the cellar's vulgar joke,
And lose their hours in ale and smoke.
There o'er some petty club preside;
So poor, so paltry, is their pride!
Nay, even with fools whole nights will sit,
In hopes to be supreme in wit.
If these can read, to these I write,
To set their worth in truest light.

A Lion-cub, of sordid mind,
Avoided all the lion kind;
Fond of applause, he sought the feasts
Of vulgar and ignoble beasts;
With asses all his time he spent,
Their club's perpetual president.
He caught their manners, looks, and airs;
An ass in everything but ears!
If e'er his Highness meant a joke,
They grinned applause before he spoke;
But at each word what shouts of praise!
"Good gods! how natural he brays!"

Elate with flattery and conceit,
He seeks his royal sire's retreat;
Forward, and fond to show his parts,
His Highness brays; the Lion starts.
"Puppy! that cursed vociferation
Betrays thy life and conversation:
Coxcombs, an ever-noisy race,
Are trumpets of their own disgrace."

"Why so severe?" the Cub replies;
"Our senate always held me wise!"

"How weak is pride," returns the sire:
"All fools are vain when fools admire!

> But know, what stupid asses prize,
> Lions and noble beasts despise."
> *John Gay* [1685–1732]

THE HARE WITH MANY FRIENDS

FRIENDSHIP, like love, is but a name,
Unless to one you stint the flame.
The child, whom many fathers share,
Hath seldom known a father's care.
'Tis thus in friendship; who depend
On many, rarely find a friend.

A Hare, who, in a civil way,
Complied with everything, like Gay,
Was known by all the bestial train,
Who haunt the wood, or graze the plain;
Her care was never to offend,
And every creature was her friend.

As forth she went at early dawn,
To taste the dew-besprinkled lawn,
Behind she hears the hunter's cries,
And from the deep-mouthed thunder flies:
She starts, she stops, she pants for breath;
She hears the near advance of death;
She doubles, to mislead the hound,
And measures back her mazy round:
Till, fainting in the public way,
Half dead with fear she gasping lay.

What transport in her bosom grew,
When first the Horse appeared in view!
"Let me," says she, "your back ascend,
And owe my safety to a friend.
You know my feet betray my flight:
To friendship every burden's light."

The Horse replied: "Poor honest Puss,
It grieves my heart to see thee thus;
Be comforted; relief is near,
For all your friends are in the rear."

She next the stately Bull implored;
And thus replied the mighty lord:

"Since every beast alive can tell
That I sincerely wish you well,
I may, without offence, pretend,
To take the freedom of a friend.
Love calls me hence; a favorite cow
Expects me near yon barley-mow;
And when a lady's in the case,
You know, all other things give place.
To leave you thus might seem unkind;
But see, the Goat is just behind."

    The Goat remarked her pulse was high,
Her languid head, her heavy eye;
"My back," says he, "may do you harm;
The Sheep's at hand, and wool is warm."

    The Sheep was feeble, and complained
His sides a load of wool sustained:
Said he was slow, confessed his fears,
For hounds eat sheep as well as Hares.

    She now the trotting Calf addressed,
To save from death a friend distressed.
"Shall I," says he, "of tender age,
In this important care engage?
Older and abler passed you by;
How strong are those, how weak am I!
Should I presume to bear you hence,
Those friends of mine may take offence.
Excuse me, then.   You know my heart;
But dearest friends, alas! must part.
How shall we all lament!   Adieu!
For see, the hounds are just in view."

               John Gay [1685–1732]

THE SYCOPHANTIC FOX AND THE GULLIBLE RAVEN

A RAVEN sat upon a tree,
  And not a word he spoke, for
His beak contained a piece of Brie,
  Or, maybe, it was Roquefort?
    We'll make it any kind you please—
    At all events, it was a cheese.

Beneath the tree's umbrageous limb
   A hungry fox sat smiling;
He saw the raven watching him,
   And spoke in words beguiling:
      "*J'admire*," said he, "*ton beau plumage*,"
      (The which was simply persiflage).

Two things there are, no doubt you know,
   To which a fox is used,—
A rooster that is bound to crow,
   A crow that's bound to roost,
      And whichsoever he espies
      He tells the most unblushing lies.

"Sweet fowl," he said, "I understand
   You're more than merely natty:
I hear you sing to beat the band
   And Adelina Patti.
      Pray render with your liquid tongue
      A bit from 'Gotterdammerung.' "

This subtle speech was aimed to please
   The crow, and it succeeded:
He thought no bird in all the trees
   Could sing as well as he did.
      In flattery completely doused,
      He gave the "Jewel Song" from "Faust."

But gravitation's law, of course,
   As Isaac Newton showed it,
Exerted on the cheese its force,
   And elsewhere soon bestowed it.
      In fact, there is no need to tell
      What happened when to earth it fell.

I blush to add that when the bird
   Took in the situation,
He said one brief, emphatic word,
   Unfit for publication.
      The fox was greatly startled, but
      He only sighed and answered "Tut!"

THE MORAL is: A fox is bound
  To be a shameless sinner.
And also: When the cheese comes round
  You know it's after dinner.
    But (what is only known to few)
    The fox is after dinner, too.

Guy Wetmore Carryl [1873–1904]

THE FRIEND OF HUMANITY AND THE KNIFE-GRINDER

FRIEND OF HUMANITY

NEEDY knife-grinder! whither are you going?
Rough is the road; your wheel is out of order.—
Bleak blows the blast;—your hat has got a hole in't.
    So have your breeches!

Weary knife-grinder! little think the proud ones
Who in their coaches roll along the turnpike-
Road, what hard work 'tis crying all day,
      "Knives and
    Scissors to grind O!"

Tell me, knife-grinder, how you came to grind knives?
Did some rich man tyrannically use you?
Was it the squire? or parson of the parish?
    Or the attorney?

Was it the squire for killing of his game? or
Covetous parson, for his tithes destraining?
Or roguish lawyer made you lose your little
    All in a lawsuit?

(Have you not read the Rights of Man, by Tom Paine?)
Drops of compassion tremble on my eyelids,
Ready to fall, as soon as you have told your
    Pitiful story.

Villon's Straight Tip to All Cross Coves 1857

KNIFE-GRINDER

Story? God bless you! I have none to tell, sir;
Only, last night, a-drinking at the Chequers,
This poor old hat and breeches, as you see, were
          Torn in a scuffle

Constables came up for to take me into
Custody; they took me before the justice;
Justice Oldmixon put me in the parish
          Stocks for a vagrant.

I should be glad to drink your honor's health in
A pot of beer, if you will give me sixpence;
But for my part, I never love to meddle
          With politics, sir.

FRIEND OF HUMANITY

I give thee sixpence!   I will see thee damned first,—
Wretch! whom no sense of wrongs can rouse to vengeance!—
Sordid, unfeeling, reprobate, degraded,
          Spiritless outcast!

(Kicks the Knife-grinder, overturns his wheel, and exit in a transport of republican enthusiasm and universal philanthropy.)

                              George Canning [1770–1827]

VILLON'S STRAIGHT TIP TO ALL CROSS COVES

" Tout aux tavernes et aux fiells."

SUPPOSE you screeve? or go cheap-jack?
    Or fake the broads? or fig a nag?
Or thimble-rig? or knap a yack?
    Or pitch a snide? or smash a rag?
    Suppose you duff? or nose and lag?
Or get the straight, and land your pot?
    How do you melt the multy swag?
Booze and the blowens cop the lot.

Fiddle, or fence, or mace, or mack;
    Or moskeneer, or flash the drag;
Dead-lurk a crib, or do a crack;
    Pad with a slang, or chuck a fag;

Bonnet, or tout, or mump and gag;
Rattle the tats, or mark the spot;
    You can not bag a single stag;
Booze and the blowens cop the lot.

Suppose you try a different tack,
    And on the square you flash your flag?
At penny-a-lining make your whack,
    Or with the mummers mug and gag?
    For nix, for nix the dibbs you bag!
At any graft, no matter what,
    Your merry goblins soon stravag:
Booze and the blowens cop the lot.

THE MORAL

It's up the spout and Charley Wag
With wipes and tickers and what not,
    Until the squeezer nips your scrag,
Booze and the blowens cop the lot.

William Ernest Henley [1849–1903]

VILLON'S BALLADE

OF GOOD COUNSEL, TO HIS FRIENDS OF EVIL LIFE

NAY, be you pardoner or cheat,
    Or cogger keen, or mumper shy,
You'll burn your fingers at the feat,
    And howl like other folks that fry.
    All evil folks that love a lie!
And where goes gain that greed amasses,
    By wile, and guile, and thievery?
'Tis all to taverns and to lasses!

Rhyme, rail, dance, play the cymbals sweet,
With game, and shame, and jollity,
    Go jigging through the field and street,
With *myst'ry* and *morality;*
    Win gold at *gleek,*—and that will fly,
Where all your gain at *passage* passes,—
    And that's? You know as well as I,
'Tis all to taverns and to lasses!

Nay, forth from all such filth retreat,
Go delve and ditch, in wet or dry,
Turn groom, give horse and mule their meat,
If you've no clerkly skill to ply;
You'll gain enough, with husbandry,
But—sow hempseed and such wild grasses,
And where goes all you take thereby?—
'Tis all to taverns and to lasses!

ENVOY

Your clothes, your hose, your broidery,
Your linen that the snow surpasses,
Or ere they're worn, off, off they fly,
'Tis all to taverns and to lasses!

Andrew Lang [1844–1912]

A LITTLE BROTHER OF THE RICH

To put new shingles on old roofs;
    To give old women wadded skirts;
To treat premonitory coughs
    With seasonable flannel shirts;
To soothe the stings of poverty
    And keep the jackal from the door,—
These are the works that occupy
    The Little Sister of the Poor.

She carries, everywhere she goes,
    Kind words and chickens, jams and coals;
Poultices for corporeal woes,
    And sympathy for downcast souls:
Her currant jelly, her quinine,
    The lips of fever move to bless;
She makes the humble sick-room shine
    With unaccustomed tidiness.

A heart of hers the instant twin
    And vivid counterpart is mine;
I also serve my fellow-men,
    Though in a somewhat different line.

The Poor, and their concerns, she has
   Monopolized, because of which
It falls to me to labor as
   A Little Brother of the Rich.

For their sake at no sacrifice
   Does my devoted spirit quail;
I give their horses exercise;
   As ballast on their yachts I sail.
Upon their tallyhos I ride
   And brave the chances of a storm;
I even use my own inside
   To keep their wines and victuals warm.

Those whom we strive to benefit
   Dear to our hearts soon grow to be;
I love my Rich, and I admit
   That they are very good to me.
Succor the Poor, my sisters,—I,
   While heaven shall still vouchsafe me health,
Will strive to share and mollify
   The trials of abounding wealth.

Edward Sandford Martin [1856–1939]

THE WORLD'S WAY

At Haroun's court it chanced, upon a time,
An Arab poet made this pleasant rhyme:

"The new moon is a horseshoe, wrought of God,
Wherewith the Sultan's stallion shall be shod."

On hearing this, the Sultan smiled, and gave
The man a gold-piece. *Sing again, O slave!*

Above his lute the happy singer bent,
And turned another gracious compliment.

And, as before, the smiling Sultan gave
The man a sekkah. *Sing again, O slave!*

Again the verse came, fluent as a rill
That wanders, silver-footed, down a hill.

The Sultan, listening, nodded as before,
Still gave the gold, and still demanded more.

The nimble fancy that had climbed so high
Grew weary with its climbing by and by:

Strange discords rose; the sense went quite amiss;
The singer's rhymes refused to meet and kiss:

Invention flagged, the lute had got unstrung,
And twice he sang the song already sung.

The Sultan, furious, called a mute, and said,
O Musta, straightway whip me off his head!

Poets! not in Arabia alone
You get beheaded when your skill is gone.
                    Thomas Bailey Aldrich [1837–1907]

FOR MY OWN MONUMENT

As doctors give physic by way of prevention,
    Mat, alive and in health, of his tombstone took care;
For delays are unsafe, and his pious intention
    May haply be never fulfilled by his heir.

Then take Mat's word for it, the sculptor is paid;
    That the figure is fine, pray believe your own eye;
Yet credit but lightly what more may be said,
    For we flatter ourselves, and teach marble to lie.

Yet counting as far as to fifty his years,
    His virtues and vices were as other men's are;
High hopes he conceived, and he smothered great fears,
    In a life parti-colored, half pleasure, half care.

Nor to business a drudge, nor to faction a slave,
    He strove to make interest and freedom agree;
In public employments industrious and grave,
    And alone with his friends, lord! how merry was he!

Now in equipage stately, now humbly on foot,
　　Both fortunes he tried, but to neither would trust;
And whirled in the round, as the wheel turned about,
　　He found riches had wings, and knew man was but dust.

This verse, little polished, though mighty sincere,
　　Sets neither his titles nor merit to view;
It says that his relics collected lie here,
　　And no mortal yet knows too if this may be true.

Fierce robbers there are that infest the highway,
　　So Mat may be killed, and his bones never found;
False witness at court, and fierce tempests at sea,
　　So Mat may yet chance to be hanged or be drowned.

If his bones lie in earth, roll in sea, fly in air,
　　To Fate we must yield, and the thing is the same;
And if passing thou giv'st him a smile or a tear,
　　He cares not—yet, prithee, be kind to his fame.
　　　　　　　　　　　　Matthew Prior [1664–1721]

THE BISHOP ORDERS HIS TOMB AT SAINT PRAXED'S CHURCH

Vanity, saith the preacher, vanity!
Draw round my bed: is Anselm keeping back?
Nephews—sons mine . . ah God, I know not!　Well—
She, men would have to be your mother once,
Old Gandolf envied me, so fair she was!
What's done is done, and she is dead beside,
Dead long ago, and I am Bishop since,
And as she died so must we die ourselves,
And thence ye may perceive the world's a dream.
Life, how and what is it?　As here I lie
In this state-chamber, dying by degrees,
Hours and long hours in the dead night, I ask
"Do I live, am I dead?"　Peace, peace seems all.
Saint Praxed's ever was the church for peace;
And so, about this tomb of mine.　I fought
With tooth and nail to save my niche, ye know:

—Old Gandolf cozened me, despite my care;
Shrewd was that snatch from out the corner South
He graced his carrion with, God curse the same!
Yet still my niche is not so cramped, but thence
One sees the pulpit o' the epistle-side,
And somewhat of the choir, those silent seats,
And up into the aery dome where live
The angels, and a sunbeam's sure to lurk:
And I shall fill my slab of basalt there,
And 'neath my tabernacle take my rest,
With those nine columns round me, two and two,
The odd one at my feet where Anselm stands:
Peach-blossom marble all, the rare, the ripe
As fresh-poured red wine of a mighty pulse.
—Old Gandolf with his paltry onion-stone,
Put me where I may look at him! True peach,
Rosy and flawless: how I earned the prize!
Draw close: that conflagration of my church
—What then? So much was saved if aught were missed!
My sons, ye would not be my death?   Go dig
The white-grape vineyard where the oil-press stood,
Drop water gently till the surface sink,
And if ye find. . . Ah God, I know not, I! . . .
Bedded in store of rotten fig-leaves soft,
And corded up in a tight olive-frail,
Some lump, ah God, of lapis lazuli,
Big as a Jew's head cut off at the nape,
Blue as a vein o'er the Madonna's breast. . .
Sons, all have I bequeathed you, villas, all,
That brave Frascati villa with its bath,
So, let the blue lump poise between my knees,
Like God the Father's globe on both his hands
Ye worship in the Jesu Church so gay,
For Gandolf shall not choose but see and burst!
Swift as a weaver's shuttle fleet our years:
Man goeth to the grave, and where is he?
Did I say basalt for my slab, sons?   Black—
'T was ever antique-black I meant!   How else
Shall ye contrast my frieze to come beneath?
The bas-relief in bronze ye promised me,

Those Pans and Nymphs ye wot of, and perchance
Some tripod, thyrsus, with a vase or so,
The Saviour at his sermon on the mount,
Saint Praxed in a glory, and one Pan
Ready to twitch the Nymph's last garment off,
And Moses with the tables . . . but I know
Ye mark me not! What do they whisper thee,
Child of my bowels, Anselm? Ah, ye hope
To revel down my villas while I gasp
Bricked o'er with beggar's mouldy travertine
Which Gandolf from his tomb-top chuckles at!
Nay, boys, ye love me—all of jasper, then!
'T is jasper ye stand pledged to, lest I grieve
My bath must needs be left behind, alas!
One block, pure green as a pistachio-nut,
There's plenty jasper somewhere in the world—
And have I not Saint Praxed's ear to pray
Horses for ye, and brown Greek manuscripts,
And mistresses with great smooth marbly limbs?
—That's if ye carve my epitaph aright,
Choice Latin, picked phrase, Tully's every word,
No gaudy ware like Gandolf's second line—
Tully, my masters? Ulpian serves his need!
And then how I shall lie through centuries,
And hear the blessed mutter of the mass,
And see God made and eaten all day long,
And feel the steady candle-flame, and taste
Good strong thick stupefying incense-smoke!
For as I lie here, hours of the dead night,
Dying in state and by such slow degrees,
I fold my arms as if they clasped a crook,
And stretch my feet forth straight as stone can point,
And let the bedclothes, for a mortcloth, drop
Into great laps and folds of sculptor's-work:
And as yon tapers dwindle, and strange thoughts
Grow, with a certain humming in my ears,
About the life before I lived this life,
And this life too, popes, cardinals and priests,
Saint Praxed at his sermon on the mount,
Your tall pale mother with her talking eyes,

And new-found agate urns as fresh as day,
And marble's language, Latin pure, discreet,
—Aha, ELUCESCEBAT quoth our friend?
No Tully, said I, Ulpian at the best!
Evil and brief hath been my pilgrimage.
All lapis, all, sons! Else I give the Pope
My villas! Will ye ever eat my heart?
Ever your eyes were as a lizard's quick,
They glitter like your mother's for my soul,
Or ye would heighten my impoverished frieze,
Piece out its starved design, and fill my vase
With grapes, and add a visor and a Term,
And to the tripod ye would tie a lynx
That in his struggle throws the thyrsus down,
To comfort me on my entablature
Whereon I am to lie till I must ask
"Do I live, am I dead?" There, leave me, there!
For ye have stabbed me with ingratitude
To death—ye wish it—God, ye wish it! Stone—
Gritstone, a-crumble! Clammy squares which sweat
As if the corpse they keep were oozing through—
And no more lapis to delight the world!
Well, go! I bless ye. Fewer tapers there,
But in a row: and, going, turn your backs
—Ay, like departing altar-ministrants,
And leave me in my church, the church for peace,
That I may watch at leisure if he leers—
Old Gandolf—at me, from his onion-stone,
As still he envied me, so fair she was!

                              Robert Browning [1812–1889]

UP AT A VILLA—DOWN IN THE CITY

AS DISTINGUISHED BY AN ITALIAN PERSON OF QUALITY

HAD I but plenty of money, money enough and to spare,
The house for me, no doubt, were a house in the city-square.
Ah, such a life, such a life, as one leads at the window
    there!

Something to see, by Bacchus, something to hear, at least!
There, the whole day long, one's life is a perfect feast;
While up at a villa one lives, I maintain it, no more than a
    beast.

Well now, look at our villa! stuck like the horn of a bull
Just on a mountain-edge as bare as the creature's skull,
Save a mere shag of a bush with hardly a leaf to pull!
—I scratch my own, sometimes, to see if the hair's turned
    wool.

But the city, oh the city—the square with the houses! Why?
They are stone-faced, white as a curd, there's something to
    take the eye!
Houses in four straight lines, not a single front awry!
You watch who crosses and gossips, who saunters, who
    hurries by;
Green blinds, as a matter of course, to draw when the sun
    gets high;
And the shops with fanciful signs which are painted prop-
    erly.

What of a villa?   Though winter be over in March by
    rights,
'Tis May perhaps ere the snow shall have withered well off
    the heights:
You've the brown ploughed land before, where the oxen
    steam and wheeze,
And the hills over-smoked behind by the faint gray olive
    trees.

Is it better in May, I ask you?   You've summer all at once;
In a day he leaps complete with a few strong April suns.
'Mid the sharp short emerald wheat, scarce risen three
    fingers well,
The wild tulip, at end of its tube, blows out its great red
    bell,
Like a thin clear bubble of blood, for the children to pick
    and sell.

Is it ever hot in the square? There's a fountain to spout
and splash!
In the shade it sings and springs; in the shine such foam-
bows flash
On the horses with curling fish-tails, that prance and paddle
and pash
Round the lady atop in the conch—fifty gazers do not
abash,
Though all that she wears is some weeds round her waist in
a sort of sash.

All the year round at the villa, nothing's to see though you
linger,
Except yon cypress that points like Death's lean lifted fore-
finger.
Some think fireflies pretty, when they mix in the corn and
mingle,
Or thrid the stinking hemp till the stalks of it seem a-tingle.
Late August or early September, the stunning cicala is
shrill
And the bees keep their tiresome whine round the resinous
firs on the hill.
Enough of the seasons,—I spare you the months of the
fever and chill.

Ere you open your eyes in the city, the blessed church-bells
begin:
No sooner the bells leave off, than the diligence rattles in:
You get the pick of the news, and it costs you never a
pin.
By and by there's the travelling doctor gives pills, lets
blood, draws teeth;
Or the Pulcinello-trumpet breaks up the market beneath.
At the post-office such a scene-picture—the new play, piping
hot!
And a notice how, only this morning, three liberal thieves
were shot.
Above it, behold the Archbishop's most fatherly of rebukes,
And beneath, with his crown and his lion, some little new
law of the Duke's!

Or a sonnet with flowery marge, to the Reverend Don So-
    and-so,
Who is Dante, Boccaccio, Petrarca, St. Jerome, and Cicero,
"And moreover," (the sonnet goes rhyming), "the skirts of
    St. Paul has reached,
Having preached us those six Lent-lectures more unctuous
    than ever he preached."
Noon strikes,—here sweeps the procession! our Lady borne
    smiling and smart
With a pink gauze gown all spangles, and seven swords
    stuck in her heart!
Bang-whang-whang, goes the drum, *tootle-te-tootle* the fife;
No keeping one's haunches still: it's the greatest pleasure in
    life.

But bless you, it's dear—it's dear! fowls, wine, at double
    the rate.
They have clapped a new tax upon salt, and what oil pays
    passing the gate
It's a horror to think of.   And so, the villa for me, not the
    city!
Beggars can scarcely be choosers: but still—ah, the pity,
    the pity!
Look, two and two go the priests, then the monks with
    cowls and sandals,
And the penitents dressed in white skirts, a-holding the
    yellow candles;
One, he carries a flag up straight, and another a cross with
    handles,
And the Duke's guard brings up the rear, for the better
    prevention of scandals.
Bang-whang-whang, goes the drum, *tootle-te-tootle* the fife.
Oh, a day in the city-square, there is no such pleasure in life!

                         Robert Browning [1812–1889]

ALL SAINTS'

In a church which is furnished with mullion and gable,
    With altar and reredos, with gargoyle and groin,
The penitents' dresses are sealskin and sable,
    The odor of sanctity's eau-de-cologne.

An Address to the Unco Guid 1869

But only could Lucifer, flying from Hades,
  Gaze down on this crowd with its paniers and paints,
He would say, as he looked at the lords and the ladies,
  "Oh, where is All Sinners' if this is All Saints'?"

        Edmund Yates [1831–1894]

AN ADDRESS TO THE UNCO GUID, OR THE RIGIDLY RIGHTEOUS

My son, these maxims make a rule,
  And lump them aye thegither:
The Rigid Righteous is a fool
  The Rigid Wise anither:
The cleanest corn that e'er was dight
  May hae some pyles o' caff in;
Sae ne'er a fellow-creature slight
  For random fits o' daffin.

        SOLOMON—Eccles. vii, 16.

OH ye wha are sae guid yoursel',
  Sae pious and sae holy,
Ye've naught to do but mark and tell
  Your neebor's fauts and folly:—
Whase life is like a weel-gaun mill,
  Supplied wi' store o' water,
The heapèd happer's ebbing still,
  And still the clap plays clatter.

Hear me, ye venerable core,
  As counsel for poor mortals,
That frequent pass douce Wisdom's door,
  For glaikit Folly's portals!
I, for their thoughtless, careless sakes,
  Would here propone defences,
Their donsie tricks, their black mistakes,
  Their failings and mischances.

Ye see your state wi' theirs compared,
  And shudder at the niffer;
But cast a moment's fair regard,
  What maks the mighty differ?
Discount what scant occasion gave
  That purity ye pride in,
And (what's aft mair than a' the lave)
  Your better art o' hidin'.

Think, when your castigated pulse
    Gies now and then a wallop,
What ragings must his veins convulse,
    That still eternal gallop:
Wi' wind and tide fair i' your tail,
    Right on ye scud your sea-way;—
But in the teeth o' baith to sail,
    It makes an unco lee-way.

See Social Life and Glee sit down,
    All joyous and unthinking,
Till, quite transmugrified, they've grown
    Debauchery and Drinking:
Oh, would they stay to calculate
    The eternal consequences;
Or your more dreaded hell to state,
    Damnation of expenses!

Ye high, exalted, virtuous dames,
    Tied up in godly laces,
Before ye gie poor Frailty names,
    Suppose a change o' cases;
A dear-loved lad, convenience snug,
    A treacherous inclination,—
But, let me whisper i' your lug,
    Ye're aiblins nae temptation.

Then gently scan your brother man,
    Still gentler sister woman;
Though they may gang a kennin' wrang,
    To step aside is human:
One point must still be greatly dark,
    The moving why they do it;
And just as lamely can ye mark
    How far perhaps they rue it.

Who made the heart, 'tis He alone
    Decidedly can try us;
He knows each chord,—its various tone,
    Each spring,—its various bias:

Then at the balance let's be mute;
  We never can adjust it;
What's done we partly may compute,
  But know not what's resisted.

Robert Burns [1759–1796]

THE DEACON'S MASTERPIECE, OR THE WONDERFUL "ONE-HOSS SHAY"

A LOGICAL STORY

HAVE you heard of the wonderful one-hoss shay,
That was built in such a logical way
It ran a hundred years to a day,
And then, of a sudden, it—ah, but stay,
I'll tell you what happened without delay,
Scaring the parson into fits,
Frightening people out of their wits,—
Have you ever heard of that, I say?

Seventeen hundred and fifty-five.
Georgius Secundus was then alive,—
Snuffy old drone from the German hive.
That was the year when Lisbon-town
Saw the earth open and gulp her down,
And Braddock's army was done so brown,
Left without a scalp to its crown.
It was on the terrible Earthquake-day
That the Deacon finished the one-hoss shay.

Now in building of chaises, I tell you what,
There is always *somewhere* a weakest spot,—
In hub, tire, felloe, in spring or thill,
In panel, or crossbar, or floor, or sill,
In screw, bolt, thoroughbrace,—lurking still,
Find it somewhere you must and will,—
Above or below, or within or without,—
And that's the reason, beyond a doubt,
That a chaise *breaks down*, but doesn't *wear out.*

But the Deacon swore (as Deacons do,
With an "I dew vum," or an "I tell *yeou*,")

He would build one shay to beat the taown
'N' the keounty 'n' all the kentry raoun';
It should be so built that it *couldn'* break daown:
"Fur," said the Deacon, " 't's mighty plain
Thut the weakes' place mus' stan' the strain;
'N' the way t' fix it, uz I maintain,
            Is only jest
T' make that place uz strong uz the rest."

So the Deacon inquired of the village folk
Where he could find the strongest oak,
That couldn't be split nor bent nor broke,—
That was for spokes and floor and sills;
He sent for lancewood to make the thills;
The crossbars were ash, from the straightest trees,
The panels of white-wood, that cuts like cheese,
But lasts like iron for things like these;
The hubs of logs from the "Settler's ellum,"—
Last of its timber,—they couldn't sell 'em,
Never an axe had seen their chips,
And the wedges flew from between their lips,
Their blunt ends frizzled like celery-tips;
Step and prop-iron, bolt and screw,
Spring, tire, axle, and linchpin too,
Steel of the finest, bright and blue;
Thoroughbrace bison-skin, thick and wide;
Boot, top, dasher, from tough old hide
Found in the pit when the tanner died.
That was the way he "put her through."
"There!" said the Deacon, "naow she'll dew!"

Do! I tell you, I rather guess
She was a wonder, and nothing less!
Colts grew horses, beards turned gray,
Deacon and deaconess dropped away,
Children and grandchildren—where were they?
But there stood the stout old one-hoss shay
As fresh as on Lisbon-earthquake-day!

EIGHTEEN HUNDRED;—it came and found
The Deacon's masterpiece strong and sound.

Eighteen hundred increased by ten;
"Hahnsum kerridge" they called it then.
Eighteen hundred and twenty came;—
Running as usual; much the same.
Thirty and Forty at last arrive,
And then come Fifty, and FIFTY-FIVE.

Little of all we value here
Wakes on the morn of its hundredth year
Without both feeling and looking queer.
In fact, there's nothing that keeps its youth,
So far as I know, but a tree and truth.
(This is a moral that runs at large;
Take it.—You're welcome.—No extra charge.)

FIRST OF NOVEMBER,—the Earthquake-day,—
There are traces of age in the one-hoss shay.
A general flavor of mild decay,
But nothing local, as one may say.
There couldn't be,—for the Deacon's art
Had made it so like in every part
That there wasn't a chance for one to start.
For the wheels were just as strong as the thills,
And the floor was just as strong as the sills,
And the panels just as strong as the floor,
And the whipple-tree neither less nor more,
And the back-crossbar as strong as the fore,
And spring and axle and hub *encore*.
And yet, *as a whole*, it is past a doubt
In another hour it will be *worn out!*

First of November, Fifty-five!
This morning the parson takes a drive.
Now, small boys, get out of the way!
Here comes the wonderful one-hoss shay,
Drawn by a rat-railed, ewe-necked bay.
"Huddup!" said the parson.—Off went they.

The parson was working his Sunday's text,—
Had got to *fifthly*, and stopped perplexed
At what the—Moses—was coming next.

All at once the horse stood still,
Close by the meet'n'-house on the hill.
First a shiver, and then a thrill,
Then something decidedly like a spill,—
And the parson was sitting upon a rock,
At half past nine by the meet'n'-house clock,—
Just the hour of the Earthquake shock!
What do you think the parson found,
When he got up and stared around?
The poor old chaise in a heap or mound,
As if it had been to the mill and ground!
You see, of course, if you're not a dunce,
How it went to pieces all at once,—
All at once, and nothing first,—
Just as bubbles do when they burst.

End of the wonderful one-hoss shay.
Logic is logic.   That's all I say.

                    Oliver Wendell Holmes [1809–1894]

BALLADE OF A FRIAR *

AFTER CLÉMENT MAROT

SOME ten or twenty times a day,
To bustle to the town with speed,
To dabble in what dirt he may,—
Le Frère Lubin's the man you need!
But any sober life to lead
Upon an exemplary plan,
Requires a Christian indeed,—
Le Frère Lubin is *not* the man!

Another's wealth on his to lay,
With all the craft of guile and greed,
To leave you bare of pence or pay,—
Le Frère Lubin's the man you need!
But watch him with the closest heed,
And dun him with what force you can,—
He'll not refund, howe'er you plead,—
Le Frère Lubin is *not* the man—

* For the original of this poem see page 3838.

An honest girl to lead astray,
With subtle saw and promised meed,
Requires no cunning crone and gray,—
Le Frère Lubin's the man you need!
He preaches an ascetic creed,
But,—try him with the water can—
A dog will drink, whate'er his breed,—
Le Frère Lubin is *not* the man!

ENVOY

In good to fail, in ill succeed,
Le Frère Lubin's the man you need!
In honest works to lead the van,
Le Frère Lubin is *not* the man!

                                  Andrew Lang [1844–1912]

THE CHAMELEON

OFT has it been my lot to mark
A proud, conceited, talking spark,
With eyes, that hardly served at most
To guard their master 'gainst a post,
Yet round the world the blade has been
To see whatever could be seen,
Returning from his finished tour,
Grown ten times perter than before;
Whatever word you chance to drop,
The traveled fool your mouth will stop;
"Sir, if my judgment you'll allow,
I've seen—and sure I ought to know,"
So begs you'd pay a due submission,
And acquiesce in his decision.

Two travelers of such a cast,
As o'er Arabia's wilds they passed,
And on their way in friendly chat,
Now talked of this, and then of that,
Discoursed awhile, 'mongst other matter,
Of the chameleon's form and nature.

"A stranger animal," cries one,
"Sure never lived beneath the sun.
A lizard's body, lean and long,
A fish's head, a serpent's tongue,
Its foot with triple claw disjoined;
And what a length of tail behind!
How slow its pace; and then its hue—
Who ever saw so fine a blue?"

"Hold, there," the other quick replies,
" 'Tis *green*,—I saw it with these eyes,
As late with open mouth it lay,
And warmed it in the sunny ray:
Stretched at its ease, the beast I viewed
And saw it eat the air for food."
"I've seen it, sir, as well as you,
And must again affirm it blue;
At leisure I the beast surveyed,
Extended in the cooling shade."
" 'Tis green, 'tis green, sir, I assure ye!"
"Green!" cries the other in a fury—
"Why, sir!—d'ye think I've lost my eyes?"
" 'Twere no great loss," the friend replies,
"For, if they always serve you thus,
You'll find them of but little use."

So high at last the contest rose,
From words they almost came to blows:
When luckily came by a third—
To him the question they referred,
And begged he'd tell 'em, if he knew,
Whether the thing was green or blue.
"Sirs," cries the umpire, "cease your pother!
The creature's neither one or t'other.
I caught the animal last night,
And viewed it o'er by candlelight:
I marked it well—'t was black as jet—
You stare—but, sirs, I've got it yet,
And can produce it." "Pray, sir, do·
I'll lay my life the thing is blue."

"And I'll be sworn, that when you've seen
The reptile, you'll pronounce him green."

"Well, then, at once to ease the doubt,"
Replies the man, "I'll turn him out:
And when before your eyes I've set him,
If you don't find him black, I'll eat him."
He said: then full before their sight
Produced the beast, and lo!—'twas white.

Both stared, the man looked wondrous wise—
"My children," the chameleon cries,
(Then first the creature found a tongue),
"You all are right, and all are wrong:
When next you talk of what you view,
Think others see as well as you:
Nor wonder, if you find that none
Prefers your eyesight to his own."

After De La Motte, by James Merrick [1720–1769]

THE BLIND MEN AND THE ELEPHANT

A HINDOO FABLE

IT was six men of Indostan
    To learning much inclined,
Who went to see the Elephant
    (Though all of them were blind),
That each by observation
    Might satisfy his mind.

The *First* approached the Elephant,
    And happening to fall
Against his broad and sturdy side,
    At once began to bawl:
"God bless me! but the Elephant
    Is very like a wall!"

The *Second*, feeling of the tusk,
    Cried, "Ho! what have we here
So very round and smooth and sharp?
    To me 'tis mighty clear

This wonder of an Elephant
     Is very like a spear!"

The *Third* approached the animal,
     And happening to take
The squirming trunk within his hands,
     Thus boldly up and spake:
"I see," quoth he, "the Elephant
     Is very like a snake!"

The *Fourth* reached out an eager hand,
     And felt about the knee.
"What most this wondrous beast is like
     Is mighty plain," quoth he;
" 'Tis clear enough the Elephant
     Is very like a tree!"

The *Fifth* who chanced to touch the ear,
     Said: "E'en the blindest man
Can tell what this resembles most;
     Deny the fact who can,
This marvel of an Elephant
     Is very like a fan!"

The *Sixth* no sooner had begun
     About the beast to grope,
Than, seizing on the swinging tail
     That fell within his scope,
"I see," quoth he, "the Elephant
     Is very like a rope!"

And so these men of Indostan
     Disputed loud and long,
Each in his own opinion
     Exceeding stiff and strong,
Though each was partly in the right,
     And all were in the wrong!

MORAL

So oft in theologic wars,
     The disputants, I ween,
Rail on in utter ignorance
     Of what each other mean,

And prate about an Elephant
Not one of them has seen!
John Godfrey Saxe [1816–1887]

THE PHILOSOPHER'S SCALES

A MONK, when his rites sacerdotal were o'er,
In the depths of his cell with its stone-covered floor,
Resigning to thought his chimerical brain,
Once formed the contrivance we now shall explain;
But whether by magic's or alchemy's powers
We know not; indeed, 'tis no business of ours.

Perhaps it was only by patience and care,
At last, that he brought his invention to bear.
In youth 'twas projected, but years stole away,
And ere 'twas complete he was wrinkled and gray;
But success is secure, unless energy fails;
And at length he produced the Philosopher's Scales.

"What were they?" you ask.   You shall presently see;
These scales were not made to weigh sugar and tea.
Oh no; for such properties wondrous had they,
That qualities, feelings, and thoughts they could weigh,
Together with articles small or immense,
From mountains or planets to atoms of sense.

Naught was there so bulky but there it would lay,
And naught so ethereal but there it would stay,
And naught so reluctant but in it must go:
All which some examples more clearly will show.

The first thing he weighed was the head of Voltaire,
Which retained all the wit that had ever been there;
As a weight, he threw in the torn scrap of a leaf
Containing the prayer of the penitent thief;
When the skull rose aloft with so sudden a spell
That it bounced like a ball on the roof of the cell.

One time he put in Alexander the Great,
With the garment that Dorcas had made, for a weight;
And though clad in armor from sandals to crown,
The hero rose up and the garment went down.

A long row of almshouses, amply endowed
By a well-esteemed Pharisee, busy and proud,
Next loaded one scale; while the other was pressed
By those mites the poor widow dropped into the chest:
Up flew the endowment, not weighing an ounce,
And down, down the farthing-worth came with a bounce.

By further experiments (no matter how)
He found that ten chariots weighed less than one plough;
A sword with gilt trappings rose up in the scale,
Though balanced by only a ten-penny nail;
A shield and a helmet, a buckler and spear,
Weighed less than a widow's uncrystallized tear.

A lord and a lady went up at full sail,
When a bee chanced to light on the opposite scale;
Ten doctors, ten lawyers, two courtiers, one earl,
Ten counsellors' wigs, full of powder and curl,
All heaped in one balance and swinging from thence,
Weighed less than a few grains of candor and sense;
A first-water diamond, with brilliants begirt,
Than one good potato just washed from the dirt;
Yet not mountains of silver and gold could suffice
One pearl to outweigh,—'twas the Pearl of Great Price.

Last of all, the whole world was bowled in at the grate,
With the soul of a beggar to serve for a weight,
When the former sprang up with so strong a rebuff
That it made a vast rent and escaped at the roof!
When balanced in air, it ascended on high,
And sailed up aloft, a balloon in the sky;
While the scale with the soul in't so mightily fell
That it jerked the philosopher out of his cell.

Jane Taylor [1783–1824]

THE MAIDEN AND THE LILY

A LILY in my garden grew,
    Amid the thyme and clover;
No fairer lily ever blew,
    Search all the wide world over.

Its beauty passed into my heart:
  I know 'twas very silly,
But I was then a foolish maid,
  And it—a perfect lily.

One day a learnèd man came by,
  With years of knowledge laden,
And him I questioned with a sigh,
  Like any foolish maiden:—
"Wise sir, please tell me wherein lies—
  I know the question's silly—
The something that my art defies,
  And makes a perfect lily."

He smiled, then bending plucked the flower,
  Then tore it, leaf and petal,
And talked to me for full an hour,
  And thought the point to settle:—
"Therein it lies," at length he cries;
  And I—I know 'twas silly—
Could only weep and say, "But where—
  O doctor, where's my lily?"

                    John Fraser [1750–1811]

THE OWL–CRITIC

"WHO stuffed that white owl?" No one spoke in the shop:
The barber was busy, and he couldn't stop;
The customers, waiting their turns, were all reading
The *Daily*, the *Herald*, the *Post*, little heeding
The young man who blurted out such a blunt question;
Not one raised a head, or even made a suggestion;
          And the barber kept on shaving.

"Don't you see, Mister Brown,"
Cried the youth with a frown,
"How wrong the whole thing is,
How preposterous each wing is,
How flattened the head is, how jammed down the neck is—
In short, the whole owl, what an ignorant wreck 'tis!

I make no apology;
I've learned owl-eology.
I've passed days and nights in a hundred collections,
And cannot be blinded to any deflections
Arising from unskilful fingers that fail
To stuff a bird right, from his beak to his tail.
Mister Brown! Mister Brown!
Do take that bird down,
Or you'll soon be the laughing-stock all over town!"
     And the barber kept on shaving.

"I've *studied* owls
And other night fowls,
And I tell you
What I know to be true:
An owl cannot roost
With his limbs so unloosed;
No owl in this world
Ever had his claws curled,
Ever had his legs slanted,
Ever had his bill canted,
Ever had his neck screwed
Into that attitude.
He can't *do* it, because
'Tis against all bird-laws.
Anatomy teaches,
Ornithology preaches
An owl has a toe
That *can't* turn out so!
I've made the white owl my study for years,
And to see such a job almost moves me to tears!
Mister Brown, I'm amazed
You should be so gone crazed
As to put up a bird
In that posture absurd!
To *look* at that owl really brings on a dizziness;
The man who stuffed *him* don't half know his business!"
     And the barber kept on shaving.

"Examine those eyes.
I'm filled with surprise

Taxidermists should pass
Off on you such poor glass;
So unnatural they seem
They'd make Audubon scream,
And John Burroughs laugh
To encounter such chaff.
Do take that bird down;
Have him stuffed again, Brown!"
            And the barber kept on shaving.

"With some sawdust and bark
I could stuff in the dark
An owl better than that.
I could make an old hat
Look more like an owl
Than that horrid fowl,
Stuck up there so stiff like a side of coarse leather.
In fact, about *him* there's not one natural feather."

Just then, with a wink and a sly normal lurch,
The owl, very gravely, got down from his perch,
Walked round, and regarded his fault-finding critic
(Who thought he was stuffed) with a glance analytic
And then fairly hooted, as if he would say:
"Your learning's at fault *this* time, any way;
Don't waste it again on a live bird, I pray.
I'm an owl; you're another.   Sir Critic, good-day!"
            And the barber kept on shaving.
                James Thomas Fields [1816–1881]

THE BALLAD OF IMITATION

C'est imiter quelqu'un que de planter des choux.—ALFRED DE MUSSET

IF they hint, O Musician, the piece that you played
    Is naught but a copy of Chopin or Spohr;
That the ballad you sing is but merely "conveyed"
    From the stock of the Arnes and the Purcells of yore;
    That there's nothing, in short, in the words or the score,
That is not as out-worn as the "Wandering Jew";
    Make answer—Beethoven could scarcely do more—
That the man who plants cabbages imitates, too!

If they tell you, Sir Artist, your light and your shade
  Are simply "adapted" from other men's lore;
That—plainly to speak of a "spade" as a "spade"—
  You've "stolen" your grouping from three or from four;
  That (however the writer the truth may deplore),
'Twas Gainsborough painted *your* "Little Boy Blue";
  Smile only serenely—though cut to the core—
For the man who plants cabbages imitates, too!

And you too, my Poet, be never dismayed
  If they whisper your Epic—"Sir Eperon d'Or"—
Is nothing but Tennyson thinly arrayed
  In a tissue that's taken from Morris's store;
  That no one, in fact, but a child could ignore
That you "lift" or "accommodate" all that you do;
  Take heart—though your Pegasus' withers be sore—
For the man who plants cabbages imitates, too!

POSTCRIPTUM.—And you, whom we all so adore,
  Dear Critics, whose verdicts are always so new!—
One word in your ear.   There were Critics before. . . .
  And the man who plants cabbages imitates, too!
                              Austin Dobson [1840–1921]

THE CONUNDRUM OF THE WORKSHOPS

WHEN the flush of a new-born sun fell first on Eden's green
    and gold,
Our father Adam sat under the Tree and scratched with a
    stick in the mould;
And the first rude sketch that the world had seen was joy
    to his mighty heart,
Till the Devil whispered behind the leaves: "It's pretty,
    but is it Art?"

Wherefore he called to his wife, and fled to fashion his
    work anew—
The first of his race who cared a fig for the first, most dread
    review;

And he left his lore to the use of his sons—and that was a
glorious gain
When the Devil chuckled: "Is it Art?" in the ear of the
branded Cain.

They builded a tower to shiver the sky and wrench the
stars apart,
Till the Devil grunted behind the bricks: "It's striking,
but is it Art?"
The stone was dropped at the quarry-side and the idle derrick swung,
While each man talked of the aims of Art, and each in an
alien tongue.

They fought and they talked in the North and the South,
they talked and they fought in the West,
Till the waters rose on the pitiful land, and the poor Red
Clay had rest—
Had rest till that dank, blank-canvas dawn when the dove
was preened to start,
And the Devil bubbled below the keel: "It's human, but
is it Art?"

The tale is as old as the Eden Tree—and new as the new-
cut tooth—
For each man knows ere his lip-thatch grows he is master
of Art and Truth;
And each man hears as the twilight nears, to the beat of
his dying heart,
The Devil drum on the darkened pane: "You did it, but
was it Art?"

We have learned to whittle the Eden Tree to the shape of
a surplice-peg,
We have learned to bottle our parents twain in the yelk of
an addled egg,
We know that the tail must wag the dog, for the horse is
drawn by the cart;
But the Devil whoops, as he whooped of old: "It's clever,
but is it Art?"

When the flicker of London sun falls faint on the Club-
    room's green and gold,
The sons of Adam sit them down and scratch with their
    pens in the mould—
They scratch with their pens in the mould of their graves,
    and the ink and the anguish start,
For the Devil mutters behind the leaves: "It's pretty, but
    is it Art?"

Now, if we could win to the Eden Tree where the Four
    Great Rivers flow,
And the Wreath of Eve is red on the turf as she left it long
    ago,
And if we could come when the sentry slept, and softly
    scurry through,
By the favor of God we might know as much—as our
    father Adam knew.

Rudyard Kipling [1865–1936]

THE V–A–S–E

From the madding crowd they stand apart,
The maidens four and the Work of Art;

And none might tell from sight alone
In which had Culture ripest grown,—

The Gotham Million fair to see,
The Philadelphia Pedigree,

The Boston Mind of azure hue,
Or the soulful Soul from Kalamazoo,—

For all loved Art in a seemly way,
With an earnest soul and a capital A.

Long they worshipped; but no one broke
The sacred stillness, until up spoke

The Western one from the nameless place,
Who blushing said: "What a lovely vace!"

Over three faces a sad smile flew,
And they edged away from Kalamazoo.

But Gotham's haughty soul was stirred
To crush the stranger with one small word.

Deftly hiding reproof in praise,
She cries: " 'Tis, indeed, a lovely vaze!"

But brief her unworthy triumph when
The lofty one from the home of Penn,

With the consciousness of two grandpapas,
Exclaims: "It is quite a lovely vahs!"

And glances round with an anxious thrill,
Awaiting the word of Beacon Hill.

But the Boston maid smiles courteouslee,
And gently murmurs: "Oh pardon me!

"I did not catch your remark, because
I was so entranced with that charming vaws!"

> *Dies erit praegelida*
> *Sinistra quum Bostonia.*
> James Jeffrey Roche [1847–1908]

HEM AND HAW

Hem and Haw were the sons of sin,
Created to shally and shirk;
Hem lay 'round and Haw looked on
While God did all the work.

Hem was a fogy, and Haw was a prig,
For both had the dull, dull mind;
And whenever they found a thing to do,
They yammered and went it blind.

Hem was the father of bigots and bores;
As the sands of the sea were they.
And Haw was the father of all the tribe
Who criticise to-day.

But God was an artist from the first,
And knew what he was about;
While over his shoulder sneered these two,
And advised him to rub it out.

They prophesied ruin ere man was made:
"Such folly must surely fail!"
And when he was done, "Do you think, my Lord,
He's better without a tail?"

And still in the honest working world,
With posture and hint and smirk,
These sons of the devil are standing by
While Man does all the work.

They balk endeavor and baffle reform,
In the sacred name of law;
And over the quavering voice of Hem,
Is the droning voice of Haw.

Bliss Carman [1861–1929]

MINIVER CHEEVY

MINIVER CHEEVY, child of scorn,
　Grew lean while he assailed the seasons;
He wept that he was ever born,
　And he had reasons.

Miniver loved the days of old
　When swords were bright and steeds were prancing;
The vision of a warrior bold
　Would set him dancing.

Miniver sighed for what was not,
　And dreamed, and rested from his labors;
He dreamed of Thebes and Camelot,
　And Priam's neighbors.

Miniver mourned the ripe renown
    That made so many a name so fragrant;
He mourned Romance, now on the town,
    And Art, a vagrant.

Miniver loved the Medici,
    Albeit he had never seen one;
He would have sinned incessantly
    Could he have been one.

Miniver cursed the commonplace,
    And eyed a khaki suit with loathing;
He missed the medieval grace
    Of iron clothing.

Miniver scorned the gold he sought,
    But sore annoyed was he without it;
Miniver thought, and thought, and thought,
    And thought about it.

Miniver Cheevy, born too late,
    Scratched his head and kept on thinking;
Miniver coughed, and called it fate,
    And kept on drinking.
                    Edwin Arlington Robinson [1869–1935]

THEN AG'IN

JIM BOWKER, he said, ef he'd had a fair show,
And a big enough town for his talents to grow,
And the least bit assistance in hoein' his row,
            Jim Bowker, he said,
He'd filled the world full of the sound of his name,
An' clumb the top round in the ladder of fame;
            It may have been so;
            I dunno;
            Jest so it might been,
            Then ag'in—

But he had tarnal luck—everythin' went ag'in him,
The arrers er fortune they allus 'ud pin him;
So he didn't get no chance to show off what was in him.

Jim Bowker, he said,
Ef he'd had a fair show, you couldn't tell where he'd come,
An' the feats he'd a-done, an' the heights he'd a-clumb—
It may have been so;
I dunno;
Jest so it might been,
Then ag'in—

But we're all like Jim Bowker, thinks I, more or less—
Charge fate for our bad luck, ourselves for success,
An' give fortune the blame for all our distress,
As Jim Bowker, he said.
Ef it hadn' been for luck an' misfortune an' sich,
We might a-been famous, an' might a-been rich.
It might be jest so;
I dunno;
Jest so it might been,
Then ag'in—

Sam Walter Foss [1858–1911]

A CONSERVATIVE

THE garden beds I wandered by
One bright and cheerful morn,
When I found a new-fledged butterfly,
A-sitting on a thorn,
A black and crimson butterfly,
All doleful and forlorn.

I thought that life could have no sting
To infant butterflies,
So I gazed on this unhappy thing
With wonder and surprise,
While sadly with his waving wing
He wiped his weeping eyes.

Said I, "What can the matter be?
Why weepest thou so sore?
With garden fair and sunlight free
And flowers in goodly store:"—
But he only turned away from me
And burst into a roar.

Cried he, "My legs are thin and few
    Where once I had a swarm!
Soft fuzzy fur—a joy to view—
    Once kept my body warm,
Before these flapping wing-things grew,
    To hamper and deform!"

At that outrageous bug I shot
    The fury of mine eye;
Said I, in scorn all burning hot,
    In rage and anger high,
"You ignominious idiot!
    Those wings are made to fly!

"I do not want to fly," said he,
    "I only want to squirm!"
And he drooped his wings dejectedly,
    But still his voice was firm:
"I do not want to be a fly!
    I want to be a worm!"

O yesterday of unknown lack!
    To-day of unknown bliss!
I left my fool in red and black,
    The last I saw was this,—
The creature madly climbing back
    Into his chrysalis.

            Charlotte Perkins Stetson Gilman [1860–1935]

SIMILAR CASES

THERE was once a little animal,
    No bigger than a fox,
And on five toes he scampered
    Over Tertiary rocks.
They called him Eohippus,
    And they called him very small,
And they thought him of no value—
    When they thought of him at all;

For the lumpish old Dinoceras
   And Coryphodon so slow
Were the heavy aristocracy
   In days of long ago.

Said the little Eohippus,
   "I am going to be a horse!
And on my middle finger-nails
   To run my earthly course!
I'm going to have a flowing tail!
   I'm going to have a mane!
I'm going to stand fourteen hands high
   On the psychozoic plain!"

The Coryphodon was horrified,
   The Dinoceras was shocked;
And they chased young Eohippus,
   But he skipped away and mocked.
And they laughed enormous laughter,
   And they groaned enormous groans,
And they bade young Eohippus
   Go view his father's bones.
Said they, "You always were as small
   And mean as now we see,
And that's conclusive evidence
   That you're always going to be.
What! Be a great, tall, handsome beast,
   With hoofs to gallop on?
Why! You'd have to change your nature!"
   Said the Loxolophodon.
They considered him disposed of,
   And retired with gait serene;
That was the way they argued
   In "the early Eocene."

There was once an Anthropoidal Ape,
   Far smarter than the rest,
And everything that they could do
   He always did the best;

So they naturally disliked him,
  And they gave him shoulders cool,
And when they had to mention him
  They said he was a fool.

Cried this pretentious Ape one day,
  "I'm going to be a Man!
And stand upright, and hunt, and fight,
  And conquer all I can!
I'm going to cut down forest trees,
  To make my houses higher!
I'm going to kill the Mastodon!
  I'm going to make a fire!"

Loud screamed the Anthropoidal Apes
  With laughter wild and gay;
They tried to catch that boastful one,
  But he always got away.
So they yelled at him in chorus,
  Which he minded not a whit;
And they pelted him with cocoanuts,
  Which didn't seem to hit.
And then they gave him reasons
  Which they thought of much avail,
To prove how his preposterous
  Attempt was sure to fail.
Said the sages, "In the first place,
  The thing cannot be done!
And, second, if it could be,
  It would not be any fun!
And, third, and most conclusive,
  And admitting no reply,
You would have to change your nature!
  We should like to see you try!"
They chuckled then triumphantly,
  These lean and hairy shapes,
For these things passed as arguments
  With the Anthropoidal Apes.

There was once a Neolithic Man,
  An enterprising wight,

Who made his chopping implements
    Unusually bright.
Unusually clever he,
    Unusually brave,
And he drew delightful Mammoths
    On the borders of his cave.
To his Neolithic neighbors,
    Who were startled and surprised,
Said he, "My friends, in course of time,
    We shall be civilized!
We are going to live in cities!
    We are going to fight in wars!
We are going to eat three times a day
    Without the natural cause!
We are going to turn life upside down
    About a thing called gold!
We are going to want the earth, and take
    As much as we can hold!
We are going to wear great piles of stuff
    Outside our proper skins!
We are going to have diseases!
    And Accomplishments!!   And Sins!!!"

Then they all rose up in fury
    Against their boastful friend,
For prehistoric patience
    Cometh quickly to an end.
Said one, "This is chimerical!
    Utopian!   Absurd!"
Said another, "What a stupid life!
    Too dull, upon my word!"
Cried all, "Before such things can come,
    You idiotic child,
You must alter Human Nature!"
    And they all sat back and smiled.
Thought they, "An answer to that last
    It will be hard to find!"
It was a clinching argument
    To the Neolithic Mind!
        Charlotte Perkins Stetson Gilman [1860–1935]

MAN AND THE ASCIDIAN

A MORALITY

"THE Ancestor remote of Man,"
Says Darwin, "is the Ascidian,"
A scanty sort of water-beast
That, ninety million years at least
Before Gorillas came to be,
Went swimming up and down the sea.

Their ancestors the pious praise,
And like to imitate their ways;
How, then, does our first parent live,
What lesson has his life to give?

The Ascidian tadpole, young and gay,
Doth Life with one bright eye survey,
His consciousness has easy play.
He's sensitive to grief and pain,
Has tail, a spine, and bears a brain,
And everything that fits the state
Of creatures we call vertebrate.
But age comes on; with sudden shock
He sticks his head against a rock!
His tail drops off, his eye drops in,
His brain's absorbed into his skin;
He does not move, nor feel, nor know
The tidal water's ebb and flow,
But still abides, unstirred, alone,
A sucker sticking to a stone.

And we, his children, truly we
In youth are, like the Tadpole, free.
And where we would we blithely go,
Have brains and hearts, and feel and know.
Then Age comes on!   To Habit we
Affix ourselves and are not free;
The Ascidian's rooted to a rock,
And we are bond-slaves of the clock;

Our rocks are Medicine—Letters—Law,
From these our heads we cannot draw:
Our loves drop off, our hearts drop in,
And daily thicker grows our skin.

Ah, scarce we live, we scarcely know
The wide world's moving ebb and flow,
The clanging currents ring and shock,
But we are rooted to the rock.
And thus at ending of his span,
Blind, deaf, and indolent, does Man
Revert to the Ascidian.

Andrew Lang [1844–1912]

THE CALF–PATH

ONE day, through the primeval wood,
A calf walked home, as good calves should;
But made a trail all bent askew,
A crooked trail as all calves do.

Since then two hundred years have fled,
And, I infer, the calf is dead.
But still he left behind his trail,
And thereby hangs my moral tale.

The trail was taken up next day
By a lone dog that passed that way;
And then a wise bell-wether sheep
Pursued the trail o'er vale and steep,
And drew the flock behind him, too,
As good bell-wethers always do.

And from that day, o'er hill and glade,
Through those old woods a path was made;
And many men wound in and out,
And dodged, and turned, and bent about
And uttered words of righteous wrath
Because 'twas such a crooked path.

But still they followed—do not laugh—
The first migrations of that calf,
And through this winding wood-way stalked,
Because he wobbled when he walked.

This forest path became a lane,
That bent, and turned, and turned again;
This crooked lane became a road,
Where many a poor horse with his load
Toiled on beneath the burning sun,
And traveled some three miles in one.
And thus a century and a half
They trod the footsteps of that calf.

The years passed on in swiftness fleet,
The road became a village street;
And this, before men were aware,
A city's crowded thoroughfare;
And soon the central street was this
Of a renowned metropolis;
And men two centuries and a half
Trod in the footsteps of that calf.

Each day a hundred thousand rout
Followed the zigzag calf about;
And o'er his crooked journey went
The traffic of a continent.
A hundred thousand men were led
By one calf near three centuries dead.
They followed still his crooked way,
And lost one hundred years a day;
For thus such reverence is lent
To well-established precedent.

A moral lesson this might teach,
Were I ordained and called to preach;
For men are prone to go it blind
Along the calf-paths of the mind,
And work away from sun to sun
To do what other men have done.

They follow in the beaten track,
And out and in, and forth and back,
And still their devious course pursue,
To keep the path that others do.

But how the wise old wood-gods laugh,
Who saw the first primeval calf!
Ah! many things this tale might teach,—
But I am not ordained to preach.

Sam Walter Foss [1858–1911]

WEDDED BLISS

"O COME and be my mate!" said the Eagle to the Hen;
        "I love to soar, but then
        I want my mate to rest
        Forever in the nest!"
        Said the Hen, "I cannot fly,
        I have no wish to try,
But I joy to see my mate careering through the sky!"
They wed, and cried, "Ah, this is Love, my own!"
And the Hen sat, and the Eagle soared, alone.

"O come and be my mate!" said the Lion to the Sheep;
        "My love for you is deep!
        I slay,—a Lion should,—
        But you are mild and good!"
        Said the Sheep, "I do no ill—
        Could not, had I the will—
But I joy to see my mate pursue, devour and kill."
They wed, and cried, "Ah, this is Love, my own!"
And the Sheep browsed, the Lion prowled, alone.

"O come and be my mate!" said the Salmon to the Clam;
        "You are not wise, but I am.
        I know the sea and stream as well;
        You know nothing but your shell."
        Said the Clam, "I'm slow of motion,
        But my love is all devotion,
And I joy to have my mate traverse lake and stream and
        ocean!"

They wed, and cried, "Ah, this is Love, my own!"
And the Clam sucked, the Salmon swam, alone.

Charlotte Perkins Stetson Gilman [1860–1935]

PARADISE: A HINDOO LEGEND

A HINDOO died; a happy thing to do,
When fifty years united to a shrew.
Released, he hopefully for entrance cries
Before the gates of Brahma's paradise.
"Hast been through purgatory?" Brahma said.
"I have been married!" and he hung his head.
"Come in! come in! and welcome, too, my son!
Marriage and purgatory are as one."
In bliss extreme he entered heaven's door,
And knew the peace he ne'er had known before.

He scarce had entered in the gardens fair,
Another Hindoo asked admission there.
The self-same question Brahma asked again:
"Hast been through purgatory?" "No; what then?"
"Thou canst not enter!" did the god reply.
"He who went in was there no more than I."
"All that is true, but he has married been,
And so on earth has suffered for all his sin."
"Married? Tis well, for I've been married twice."
"Begone! We'll have no fools in paradise!"

George Birdseye [1844–1919]

AD CHLOEN, M. A.

(FRESH FROM HER CAMBRIDGE EXAMINATION)

LADY, very fair are you,
And your eyes are very blue,
And your hose;
And your brow is like the snow,
And the various things you know
Goodness knows.

And the rose-flush on your cheek,
And your algebra and Greek
  Perfect are;
And that loving lustrous eye
Recognizes in the sky
  Every star.

You have pouting piquant lips,
You can doubtless an eclipse
  Calculate;
But for your cerulean hue,
I had certainly from you
  Met my fate.

If by an arrangement dual
I were Adams mixed with Whewell,
  Then some day
I, as wooer, perhaps might come
To so sweet an Artium
  Magistra.

Mortimer Collins [1827–1876]

"AS LIKE THE WOMAN AS YOU CAN"

"As like the Woman as you can"—
 (*Thus the New Adam was beguiled*)—
"So shall you touch the Perfect Man"—
 (*God in the Garden heard and smiled*).
"Your father perished with his day:
 A clot of passions fierce and blind,
He fought, he hacked, he crushed his way:
 Your muscles, Child, must be of mind.

"The Brute that lurks and irks within,
 How, till you have him gagged and bound,
Escape the foulest form of Sin?"
 (*God in the Garden laughed and frowned*).
"So vile, so rank, the bestial mood
 In which the race is bid to be,
It wrecks the Rarer Womanhood:
 Live, therefore, you, for Purity!

" No Fault in Women "

"Take for your mate no gallant croup,
   No girl all grace and natural will:
To work her mission were to stoop,
   Maybe to lapse, from Well to Ill.
Choose one of whom your grosser make"—
   (*God in the Garden laughed outright*)—
"The true refining touch may take,
   Till both attain to Life's last height.

"There, equal, purged of soul and sense,
   Beneficent, high-thinking, just,
Beyond the appeal of Violence,
   Incapable of common Lust,
In mental Marriage still prevail"—
   (*God in the Garden hid His face*)—
"Till you achieve that Female-Male
   In which shall culminate the race."
                    William Ernest Henley [1849–1903]

"NO FAULT IN WOMEN"

No fault in women to refuse
The offer which they most would choose:
No fault in women to confess
How tedious they are in their dress:
No fault in women to lay on
The tincture of vermilion,
And there to give the cheek a dye
Of white, where Nature doth deny:
No fault in women to make show
Of largeness, when they're nothing so;
When, true it is, the outside swells
With inward buckram, little else:
No fault in women, though they be
But seldom from suspicion free:
No fault in womankind at all,
If they but slip, and never fall.
                    Robert Herrick [1591–1674]

"ARE WOMEN FAIR?"

"ARE women fair?" Ay! wondrous fair to see too.
"Are women sweet?" Yea, passing sweet they be too;
Most fair and sweet to them that only love them;
Chaste and discreet to all save those that prove them.

"Are women wise?" Not wise, but they be witty.
"Are women witty?" Yea, the more the pity;
They are so witty, and in wit so wily,
That be you ne'er so wise, they will beguile ye.

"Are women fools?" Not fools, but fondlings many.
"Can women found be faithful unto any?"
When snow-white swans do turn to color sable,
Then women fond will be both firm and stable.

"Are women saints?" No saints, nor yet no devils.
"Are women good?" Not good, but needful evils;
So Angel-like, that devils I do not doubt them;
So needful evils, that few can live without them.

"Are women proud?" Ay! passing proud, and praise them.
"Are women kind?" Ay! wondrous kind and please them,
Or so imperious, no man can endure them,
Or so kind-hearted, any may procure them.

Francis Davison (?) [fl. 1602]

A STRONG HAND

TENDER-HANDED stroke a nettle,
    And it stings you for your pains;
Grasp it like a lad of mettle,
    And it soft as silk remains:

So it is with these fair creatures,
    Use them kindly, they rebel;
But be rough as nutmeg graters,
    And the rogues obey you well.

Aaron Hill [1685–1750]

WOMEN'S LONGING

From "Women Pleased"

TELL me what is that only thing
   For which all women long;
Yet, having what they most desire,
   To have it does them wrong?

'Tis not to be chaste, nor fair,
(Such gifts malice may impair),
Richly trimmed, to walk or ride,
Or to wanton unespied,
To preserve an honest name
And so to give it up to fame—
These are toys. In good or ill
They desire to have their will:
Yet, when they have it, they abuse it,
For they know not how to use it.

John Fletcher [1579–1625]

TRIOLET

ALL women born are so perverse
No man need boast their love possessing.
If naught seem better, nothing's worse:
All women born are so perverse.
From Adam's wife, that proved a curse,
Though God had made her for a blessing,
All women born are so perverse
No man need boast their love possessing.

Robert Bridges [1844–1930]

THE FAIR CIRCASSIAN

FORTY Viziers saw I go
Up to the Seraglio,
Burning, each and every man,
For the fair Circassian.

Ere the morn had disappeared,
Every Vizier wore a beard;
Ere the afternoon was born,
Every Vizier came back shorn.

"Let the man that woos to win
Woo with an unhairy chin;"
Thus she said, and as she bid
Each devoted Vizier did.

From the beards a cord she made,
Looped it to the balustrade,
Glided down and went away
To her own Circassia.

When the Sultan heard, waxed he
Somewhat wroth, and presently
In the noose themselves did lend
Every Vizier did suspend.

Sages all, this rhyme who read,
Guard your beards with prudent heed,
And beware the wily plans
Of the fair Circassians.

Richard Garnett [1835–1906]

THE FEMALE PHAETON

Thus Kitty, beautiful and young,
   And wild as colt untamed,
Bespoke the fair from whence she sprung,
   With little rage inflamed:

Inflamed with rage at sad restraint,
   Which wise mamma ordained;
And sorely vexed to play the saint,
   Whilst wit and beauty reigned:

"Shall I thumb holy books, confined
   With Abigails, forsaken?
Kitty's for other things designed,
   Or I am much mistaken.

"Must Lady Jenny frisk about,
   And visit with her cousins?
At balls must she make all the rout,
   And bring home hearts by dozens?

"What has she better, pray, than I,
   What hidden charms to boast,
That all mankind for her should die,
   Whilst I am scarce a toast?

"Dearest mamma! for once let me,
   Unchained, my fortune try;
I'll have my earl as well as she,
   Or know the reason why.

"I'll soon with Jenny's pride quit score,
   Make all her lovers fall:
They'll grieve I was not loosed before;
   She, I was loosed at all."

Fondness prevailed, mamma gave way;
   Kitty, at heart's desire,
Obtained the chariot for a day,
   And set the world on fire.

                    Matthew Prior [1664–1721]

THE LURE

"WHAT bait do you use," said a Saint to the Devil,
   "When you fish where the souls of men abound?"
"Well, for special tastes," said the King of Evil,
   "Gold and Fame are the best I've found."

"But for general use?" asked the Saint. "Ah, then,"
Said the Demon, "I angle for Man, not men,
         And a thing I hate
         Is to change my bait,
So I fish with a woman the whole year round."

                    John Boyle O'Reilly [1844–1890]

THE FEMALE OF THE SPECIES

WHEN the Himalayan peasant meets the he-bear in his
    pride,
He shouts to scare the monster, who will often turn aside;
But the she-bear thus accosted rends the peasant tooth and
    nail,
For the female of the species is more deadly than the male.

When Nag, the wayside cobra, hears the careless foot of man,
He will sometimes wriggle sideways and avoid it if he can;
But his mate makes no such motion where she camps beside
    the trail,
For the female of the species is more deadly than the male.

When the early Jesuit fathers preached to Hurons and
    Choctaws,
They prayed to be delivered from the vengeance of the
    squaws.
'Twas the women, not the warr ors, turned those stark
    enthusiasts pale,
For the female of the species is more deadly than the male.

Man's timid heart is bursting with the things he must not say,
For the Woman that God gave him isn't his to give away;
But when hunter meets with husband, each confirms the
    other's tale—
The female of the species is more deadly than the male.

Man, a bear in most relations—worm and savage other-
    wise,—
Man propounds negotiations, Man accepts the compromise.
Very rarely will he squarely push the logic of a fact
To its ultimate conclusion in unmitigated act.

Fear, or foolishness, impels him, ere he lay the wicked low,
To concede some form of trial even to his fiercest foe.
Mirth obscene diverts his anger—Doubt and Pity oft perplex
Him in dealing with an issue—to the scandal of The Sex!

But the Woman that God gave him, every fibre of her
    frame
Proves her launched for one sole issue, armed and engined
    for the same;
And to serve that single issue, lest the generations fail,
The female of the species must be deadlier than the male.

The Female of The Species 1907

She who faces Death by torture for each life beneath her breast
May not deal in doubt or pity—must not swerve for fact or jest.
These be purely male diversions—not in these her honor dwells.
She, the Other Law we live by, is that Law and nothing else.

She can bring no more to living than the powers that make her great
As the Mother of the Infant and the Mistress of the Mate;
And when Babe and Man are lacking and she strides unclaimed to claim
Her right as femme (and baron), her equipment is the same.

She is wedded to convictions—in default of grosser ties;
Her contentions are her children, Heaven help him who denies!—
He will meet no cool discussion, but the instant, white-hot, wild,
Wakened female of the species warring as for spouse and child.

Unprovoked and awful charges—even so the she-bear fights;
Speech that drips, corrodes, and poisons—even so the cobra bites;
Scientific vivisection of one nerve till it is raw
And the victim writhes in anguish—like the Jesuit with the squaw!

So it comes that Man, the coward, when he gathers to confer
With his fellow-braves in council, dare not leave a place for her
Where, at war with Life and Conscience, he uplifts his erring hands
To some God of Abstract Justice—which no woman understands.

And Man knows it! Knows, moreover, that the Woman that God gave him
Must command but may not govern—shall enthral but not enslave him.
And *She* knows, because She warns him, and Her instincts never fail,
That the Female of Her Species is more deadly than the Male.   *Rudyard Kipling* [1865–1936]

THE WOMAN WITH THE SERPENT'S TONGUE

SHE is not old, she is not young,
The woman with the Serpent's Tongue,
The haggard cheek, the hungering eye,
The poisoned words that wildly fly,
The famished face, the fevered hand,—
Who slights the worthiest in the land,
Sneers at the just, contemns the brave,
And blackens goodness in its grave.

In truthful numbers be she sung,
The Woman with the Serpent's Tongue;
Concerning whom, Fame hints at things
Told but in shrugs and whisperings:
Ambitious from her natal hour,
And scheming all her life for power;
With little left of seemly pride;
With venomed fangs she cannot hide;
Who half makes love to you to-day,
To-morrow gives her guest away.
Burnt up within by that strange soul
She cannot slake, or yet control:
Malignant-lipped, unkind, unsweet;
Past all example indiscreet;
Hectic, and always overstrung,—
The Woman with the Serpent's Tongue.

To think that such as she can mar
Names that among the noblest are!
That hands like hers can touch the springs
That move who knows what men and things?
That on *her* will *their* fates have hung!—
The Woman with the Serpent's Tongue.

William Watson [1858–1935]

SUPPOSE

How sad if, by some strange new law,
    All kisses scarred!
For she who is most beautiful
    Would be most marred.

And we might be surprised to see
Some lovely wife
Smooth-visaged, while a seeming prude
Was marked for life.

Anne Reeve Aldrich [1866–1892]

TOO CANDID BY HALF

As Tom and his wife were discoursing one day
Of their several faults in a bantering way,
  Said she, "Though my wit you disparage,
I'm sure, my dear husband, our friends will attest
This much, at the least, that my judgment is best."
  Quoth Tom, "So they said at our marriage."

John Godfrey Saxe [1816–1887]

FABLE

THE mountain and the squirrel
Had a quarrel,
And the former called the latter "Little Prig;"
Bun replied,
"You are doubtless very big;
But all sorts of things and weather
Must be taken in together,
To make up a year
And a sphere.
And I think it no disgrace
To occupy my place.
If I'm not so large as you,
You are not so small as I,
And not half so spry.

I'll not deny you make
A very pretty squirrel track;
Talents differ; all is well and wisely put;
If I cannot carry forests on my back,
Neither can you crack a nut."

Ralph Waldo Emerson [1803–1882]

WOMAN'S WILL

THAT man's a fool who tries by art and skill
To stem the torrent of a woman's will:
For if she will, she will; you may depend on't—
And if she won't, she won't—and there's an end on't.

Unknown

WOMAN'S WILL

MEN, dying, make their wills, but wives
    Escape a task so sad;
Why should they make what all their lives
    The gentle dames have had?

John Godfrey Saxe [1816–1887]

PLAYS

ALAS, how soon the hours are over
Counted us out to play the lover!
And how much narrower is the stage
Allotted us to play the sage!

But when we play the fool, how wide
The theatre expands! beside,
How long the audience sits before us!
How many prompters! what a chorus!

Walter Savage Landor [1775–1864]

THE REMEDY WORSE THAN THE DISEASE

I SENT for Ratcliffe; was so ill,
    That other doctors gave me over:
He felt my pulse, prescribed his pill,
    And I was likely to recover.

But, when the wit began to wheeze,
    And wine had warmed the politician,
Cured yesterday of my disease,
    I died last night of my physician.

Matthew Prior [1664–1721]

THE NET OF LAW

THE net of law is spread so wide,
No sinner from its sweep may hide.

Its meshes are so fine and strong,
They take in every child of wrong.

O wondrous web of mystery!
Big fish alone escape from thee!
                    James Jeffrey Roche [1847–1908]

COLOGNE

IN Köln, a town of monks and bones,
And pavements fanged with murderous stones,
And rags, and hags, and hideous wenches;
I counted two and seventy stenches,
All well defined, and several stinks!
Ye Nymphs that reign o'er sewers and sinks,
The river Rhine, it is well known,
Doth wash your city of Cologne;
But tell me, Nymphs! what power divine
Shall henceforth wash the river Rhine?
                    Samuel Taylor Coleridge [1772–1834]

EPITAPH ON CHARLES II

HERE lies our Sovereign Lord the King,
    Whose word no man relies on,
Who never said a foolish thing,
    Nor ever did a wise one.
                    John Wilmot [1647–1680]

CERTAIN MAXIMS OF HAFIZ

I

IF It be pleasant to look on, stalled in the packed *serai*,
Does not the Young Man try Its temper and pace ere he
    buy?

If She be pleasant to look on, what does the Young Man
  say?
"Lo! She is pleasant to look on, give Her to me today!"

II

Yea, though a Kaffir die, to him is remitted Jehannum
If he borrowed in life from a native at sixty per cent per
  annum.

III

Blister we not for *bursati?* So when the heart is vexed,
The pain of one maiden's refusal is drowned in the pain of
  the next.

IV

The temper of chums, the love of your wife, and a new
  piano's tune—
Which of the three will you trust at the end of an Indian
  June?

V

Who are the rulers of Ind—to whom shall we bow the knee?
Make your peace with the women, and men will make you
  L. G.

VI

Does the woodpecker flit round the young *ferash?* Does
  the grass clothe a new-built wall?
Is she under thirty, the woman who holds a boy in her
  thrall?

VII

If She grow suddenly gracious—reflect. Is it all for thee?
The black-buck is stalked through the bullock, and Man
  through jealousy.

VIII

Seek not for favor of women. So shall you find it indeed.
Does not the boar break cover just when you're lighting a
  weed?

IX

If He play, being young and unskilful, for shekels of silver
  and gold,
Take His money, my son, praising Allah. The kid was
  ordained to be sold.

X

With a "weed" among men or horses verily this is the
  best,
That you work him in office or dog-cart lightly—but give
  him no rest.

XI

Pleasant the snaffle of Courtship, improving the manners
  and carriage;
But the colt who is wise will abstain from the terrible thorn-
  bit of Marriage.

XII

As the thriftless gold of the *babul*, so is the gold that we
  spend
On a Derby Sweep, or our neighbor's wife, or the horse that
  we buy from a friend.

XIII

The ways of a man with a maid be strange, yet simple and
  tame
To the ways of a man with a horse, when selling or racing
  that same.

XIV

In public Her face turneth to thee, and pleasant Her smile
  when ye meet.
It is ill. The cold rocks of El-Gidar smile thus on the
  waves at their feet.
In public Her face is averted, with anger She nameth thy
  name.
It is well. Was there ever a loser content with the loss of
  the game?

XV

If She have spoken a word, remember thy lips are sealed,
And the Brand of the Dog is upon him by whom is the
secret revealed.
If She have written a letter, delay not an instant, but burn
it.
Tear it in pieces, O Fool, and the wind to her mate shall
return it!
If there be trouble to Herward, and a lie of the blackest
can clear,
Lie, while thy lips can move or a man is alive to hear.

XVI

My Son, if a maiden deny thee and scufflingly bid thee
give o'er,
Yet lip meets with lip at the lastward—get out! She has
been there before.
They are pecked on the ear and the chin and the nose who
are lacking in lore.

XVII

If we fall in the race, though we win, the hoof-slide is scarred
on the course.
Though Allah and Earth pardon Sin, remaineth forever
Remorse.

XVIII

"By all I am misunderstood!" if the Matron shall say, or
the Maid:—
"Alas! I do not understand," my son, be thou nowise
afraid.
In vain in the sight of the Bird is the net of the Fowler
displayed.

XIX

My Son, if I, Hafiz, thy father, take hold of thy knees in
my pain,
Demanding thy name on stamped paper, one day or one
hour—refrain.
Are the links of thy fetters so light that thou cravest another man's chain?

Rudyard Kipling [1865–1936]

A BAKER'S DUZZEN UV WIZE SAWZ

THEM ez wants, must choose.
Them ez hez, must lose.
Them ez knows, won't blab.
Them ez guesses, will gab.
Them ez borrows, sorrows.
Them ez lends, spends.
Them ez gives, lives.
Them ez keeps dark, is deep.
Them ez kin earn, kin keep.
Them ez aims, hits.
Them ez hez, gits.
Them ez waits, win.
Them ez *will, kin.*

Edward Rowland Sill [1841–1887]

EPIGRAMS

WHAT is an epigram? a dwarfish whole,
Its body brevity, and wit its soul.

Samuel Taylor Coleridge [1772–1834]

———

As in smooth oil the razor best is whet,
So wit is by politeness sharpest set;
Their want of edge from their offence is seen,
Both pain the heart when exquisitely keen.

Unknown

———

"I HARDLY ever ope my lips," one cries;
  "Simonides, what think you of my rule?"
"If you're a fool, I think you're very wise;
  If you are wise, I think you are a fool."

Richard Garnett [1835–1906]

———

PHILOSOPHER, whom dost thou most affect,
Stoics austere, or Epicurus' sect?
Friend, 'tis my grave infrangible design
With those to study, and with these to dine.

Richard Garnett [1835–1906]

Joy is the blossom, sorrow is the fruit,
Of human life; and worms are at the root.
Walter Savage Landor [1775–1864]

No truer word, save God's, was ever spoken,
Than that the largest heart is soonest broken.
Walter Savage Landor [1775–1864]

THIS house, where once a lawyer dwelt,
  Is now a smith's. Alas!
How rapidly the iron age
  Succeeds the age of brass!
William Erskine [1769–1822]

"I WOULD," says Fox, "a tax devise
  That shall not fall on me."
"Then tax receipts," Lord North replies,
  "For those you never see."
Richard Brinsley Sheridan [1751–1816]

YOU beat your pate, and fancy wit will come.
Knock as you please,—there's nobody at home.
Alexander Pope [1688–1744]

IF a man who turnips cries
  Cry not when his father dies,
  'Tis a proof that he would rather
  Have a turnip than a father.
Samuel Johnson [1709–1784]

LIFE is a jest, and all things show it;
I said so once, and now I know it.
John Gay [1685–1732]

I AM his Highness' dog at Kew.
Pray, sir, tell me,—whose dog are you?
Alexander Pope [1688–1744]

SIR, I admit your general rule,
That every poet is a fool,
But you yourself may serve to show it,
That every fool is not a poet.

Samuel Taylor Coleridge [1772–1834]

DAMIS, an author cold and weak,
Thinks as a critic he's divine;
Likely enough; we often make
Good vinegar of sorry wine.

Unknown

SWANS sing before they die—'twere no bad thing
Did certain persons die before they sing.

Samuel Taylor Coleridge [1772–1834]

HE who in his pocket hath no money
Should, in his mouth, be never without honey.

Unknown

NOBLES and heralds, by your leave,
Here lies what once was Matthew Prior,
The son of Adam and of Eve;
Can Bourbon or Nassau claim higher?

Matthew Prior [1664–1721]

HERE lie I, Martin Elginbrodde;
Hae mercy o' my soul, Lord God,
As I wad do were I Lord God,
And ye were Martin Elginbrodde.

George Macdonald [1824–1905]

WHO killed Kildare? Who dared Kildare to kill?
Death killed Kildare—who dare kill whom he will.

Jonathan Swift [1667–1745]

WITH death doomed to grapple,
Beneath the cold slab he
Who lied in the chapel
Now lies in the abbey.

Byron's epitaph for Pitt

WHEN doctrines meet with general approbation,
It is not heresy, but reformation.
David Garrick [1717-1779]

———

TREASON doth never prosper; what's the reason?
Why, if it prosper, none dare call it treason.
John Harington [1561-1612]

———

GOD bless the King—I mean the faith's defender!
God bless (no harm in blessing!) the Pretender!
But who pretender is, or who is King—
God bless us all!—that's quite another thing.
John Byrom [1692-1763]

———

'TIS highly rational, we can't dispute,
The Love, being naked, should promote a suit:
But doth not oddity to him attach
Whose fire's so oft extinguished by a match?
Richard Garnett [1835-1906]

———

"COME, come," said Tom's father, "at your time of life,
There's no longer excuse for thus playing the rake.—
It is time you should think, boy, of taking a wife."—
"Why, so it is, father,—whose wife shall I take?"
Thomas Moore [1779-1852]

———

WHEN Eve upon the first of men
The apple pressed with specious cant,
O, what a thousand pities then
That Adam was not Adam-ant!
Thomas Moore [1779-1852]

———

WHILST Adam slept, Eve from his side arose:
Strange! his first sleep should be his last repose!
Unknown

———

"WHAT? rise again with *all* one's bones,"
Quoth Giles, "I hope you fib:
I trusted, when I went to Heaven,
To go without my rib."
Samuel Taylor Coleridge [1772-1834]

HERE lies my wife: here let her lie!
Now she's at rest, and so am I.

John Dryden [1631–1700]

AFTER such years of dissension and strife,
Some wonder that Peter should weep for his wife;
But his tears on her grave are nothing surprising,—
He's laying her dust, for fear of its rising.

Thomas Hood [1799–1845]

WRITTEN ON A LOOKING-GLASS

I CHANGE, and so do women too;
But I reflect, which women never do.

Unknown

AN EPITAPH

A LOVELY young lady I mourn in my rhymes:
She was pleasant, good-natured, and civil sometimes.
Her figure was good: she had very fine eyes,
And her talk was a mixture of foolish and wise.
Her adorers were many, and one of them said,
"She waltzed rather well! It's a pity she's dead!"

George John Cayley [?]

ON THE ARISTOCRACY OF HARVARD

HERE's to good old Boston,
    The home of the bean and the cod,
Where the Lowells talk only to Cabots,
    And the Cabots talk only to God.

John Collins Bossidy [1860–1928]

ON THE DEMOCRACY OF YALE

HERE's to the town of New Haven,
    The home of the Truth and the Light,
Where God talks to Jones in the very same tones
    That He uses with Hadley and Dwight!

Frederick Scheetz Jones [1862–

ALAS FOR THE SOUTH

ALAS for the South! Her books grow fewer—
She was never much given to literature.

J. Gordon Coogler [1865–1901]

A GENERAL SUMMARY

WE are very slightly changed
From the semi-apes who ranged
   India's prehistoric clay;
Whoso drew the longest bow,
Ran his brother down, you know,
   As we run men down to-day.
"Dowb," the first of all his race,
Met the Mammoth face to face
   On the lake or in the cave,
Stole the steadiest canoe,
Ate the quarry others slew,
   Died—and took the finest grave.

When they scratched the reindeer-bone,
Someone made the sketch his own,
   Filched it from the artist—then,
Even in those early days,
Won a simple Viceroy's praise
   Through the toil of other men.
Ere they hewed the Sphinx's visage,
Favoritism governed kissage,
Even as it does in this age.

Who shall doubt "the secret hid
Under Cheops' pyramid"
Was that the contractor did
   Cheops out of several millions?
Or that Joseph's sudden rise
To Comptroller of Supplies
Was a fraud of monstrous size
   On King Pharaoh's swart Civilians?

Thus, the artless songs I sing
Do not deal with anything
   New or never said before.
As it was in the beginning,
Is to-day official sinning,
   And shall be for evermore!

Rudyard Kipling [1865–1936]

THE MIMICS

AN OMAR FOR LADIES

I

ONE for her Club and her own Latch-key fights,
Another wastes in Study her good Nights.
    Ah, take the Clothes and let the Culture go,
Nor heed the grumble of the Women's Rights!

Look at the Shop-girl all about us—"Lo,
The Wages of a month," she says, "I blow
    Into a Hat, and when my hair is waved,
Doubtless my Friend will take me to the Show."

And she who saved her coin for Flannels red,
And she who caught Pneumonia instead,
    Will both be Underground in Fifty Years,
And Prudence pays no Premium to the dead.

Th' exclusive Style you set your heart upon
Gets to the Bargain counters—and anon,
    Like monograms on a Saleslady's tie,
Cheers but a moment—soon for you 'tis gone.

Think, in the sad Four Hundred's gilded halls,
Whose endless Leisure ev'n themselves appalls,
    How Ping-pong raged so high—then faded out
To those far Suburbs that still chase its Balls.

They say Sixth Avenue and the Bowery keep
The *dernier cri* that once was far from cheap;
    Green veils, one season chic—Department stores
Mark down in vain—no profit shall they reap.

1921

The Mimics

II

I sometimes think that never lasts so long
The Style as when it starts a bit too strong;
　　That all the Pompadours the parterre boasts
Some Chorus-girl began, with Dance and Song.

And this Revival of the Chignon low
That fills the most of us with helpless Woe,
　　Ah, criticise it Softly! for who knows
What long-necked Peeress had to wear it so!

Ah, my belovèd, try each Style you meet;
To-day brooks no loose ends, you must be neat.
　　Tomorrow! why tomorrow you may be
Wearing it down your back like Marguerite!

For some we once admired, the Very Best
That ever a French hand-boned Corset prest,
　　Wore what they used to call Prunella Boots,
And put on Nightcaps ere they went to rest.

And we that now make fun of Waterfalls
They wore, and whom their Crinoline appalls,
　　Ourselves shall from old dusty Fashion plates
Assist our Children in their Costume balls.

Ah, make the most of what we yet may wear,
Before we grow so old that we don't care!
　　Before we have our Hats made all alike,
Sans Plumes, sans Wings, sans Chiffon, and—sans Hair!

III

Alike to her who Dines both Loud and Long,
Or her who Banting shuns the Dinner-gong,
　　Some Doctor from his Office chair will shout,
"It makes no Difference—both of you are Wrong!"

Why, all the Health-Reformers who discussed
High Heels and Corsets learnedly are thrust
　　Square-toed and Waistless forth; their Duds are
　　　scorned,
And Venus might as well have been a Bust.

Myself when slim did eagerly frequent
Delsarte and Ling, and heard great Argument
    Of muscles trained to Hold me up, but still
Spent on my Modiste what I'd always spent!

With walking Clubs I did the best I could;
With my own Feet I tramped my Ten Miles, good;
    And this was All that I got out of it—
I ate much more for Dinner than I should.

    .   .   .   .   .

And fear not lest your Rheumatism seize
The Joy of Life from other people's Sprees;
    The Art will not have Perished—*au contraire,*
Posterity will practise it with Ease!

When you and I have ceased Champagne to Sup,
Be sure there will be More to Keep it Up;
    And while we pat Old Tabby by the fire,
Full many a Girl will lead her Brindled Pup.
                Josephine Daskam Bacon [1876–

"WHEN LOVELY WOMAN"

AFTER GOLDSMITH

WHEN lovely woman wants a favor,
  And finds, too late, that man won't bend,
What earthly circumstance can save her
  From disappointment in the end?

The only way to bring him over,
  The last experiment to try,
Whether a husband or a lover,
  If he have feeling is—to cry.
            Phoebe Cary [1824–1871]

FRAGMENT IN IMITATION OF WORDSWORTH

    THERE is a river clear and fair,
    'Tis neither broad nor narrow;
    It winds a little here and there—
    It winds about like any hare;

And then it holds as straight a course
As, on the turnpike road, a horse,
Or, through the air, an arrow.

The trees that grow upon the shore
Have grown a hundred years or more;
So long there is no knowing:
Old Daniel Dobson does not know
When first those trees began to grow;
But still they grew, and grew, and grew,
As if they'd nothing else to do,
But ever must be growing.

The impulses of air and sky
Have reared their stately heads so high,
And clothed their boughs with green;
Their leaves the dews of evening quaff,—
And when the wind blows loud and keen,
I've seen the jolly timbers laugh,
And shake their sides with merry glee—
Wagging their heads in mockery.

Fixed are their feet in solid earth
Where winds can never blow;
But visitings of deeper birth
Have reached their roots below.
For they have gained the river's brink
And of the living waters drink.

There's little Will, a five years' child—
He is my youngest boy;
To look on eyes so fair and wild,
It is a very joy.
He hath conversed with sun and shower,
And dwelt with every idle flower,
As fresh and gay as them.
He loiters with the briar-rose,—
The blue-bells are his playfellows,
That dance upon their slender stem.

And I have said, my little Will,
Why should he not continue still

A thing of Nature's rearing?
A thing beyond the world's control—
A living vegetable soul,—
No human sorrow fearing.

It were a blessèd sight to see
That child become a willow-tree,
His brother trees among.
He'd be four times as tall as me,
And live three times as long.

Catherine M. Fanshawe [1765–1834]

ONLY SEVEN

AFTER WORDSWORTH

I MARVELLED why a simple child,
   That lightly draws its breath,
Should utter groans so very wild,
   And look as pale as death.

Adopting a parental tone,
   I asked her why she cried;
The damsel answered with a groan,
   "I've got a pain inside!

"I thought it would have sent me mad
   Last night about eleven."
Said I, "What is it makes you bad?
How many apples have you had?"
   She answered, "Only seven!"

"And are you sure you took no more,
   My little maid?" quoth I;
"Oh, please, sir, mother gave me four,
   But *they* were in a pie!"

"If that's the case," I stammered out,
   "Of course you've had eleven."
The maiden answered with a pout,
   "I ain't had more nor seven!"

I wondered hugely what she meant,
　　And said, "I'm bad at riddles;
But I know where little girls are sent
　　For telling taradiddles.

"Now, if you don't reform," said I,
　　"You'll never go to heaven."
But all in vain; each time I try,
That little idiot makes reply,
　　"I ain't had more nor seven!"

POSTSCRIPT:

To borrow Wordsworth's name was wrong,
　　Or slightly misapplied;
And so I'd better call my song
　　"Lines after Ache-inside."
　　　　　　Henry Sambrooke Leigh [1837-1883]

LUCY LAKE

AFTER WORDSWORTH

POOR Lucy Lake was overgrown,
　　But somewhat underbrained.
She did not know enough, I own,
　　To go in when it rained.

Yet Lucy was constrained to go;
　　Green bedding,—you infer.
Few people knew she died, but oh,
　　The difference to her!
　　　　　　Newton Mackintosh [1858-

JANE SMITH

AFTER WORDSWORTH

I JOURNEYED, on a winter's day,
　　Across the lonely wold;
No bird did sing upon the spray,
　　And it was very cold.

I had a coach with horses four,
    Three white (though one was black),
And on they went the common o'er,
    Nor swiftness did they lack.

A little girl ran by my side,
    And she was pinched and thin.
"Oh, please, sir, do give me a ride!
    I'm fetching mother's gin."

"Enter my coach, sweet child," said I,
    "For you shall ride with me;
And I will get you your supply
    Of mother's eau-de-vie."

The publican was stern and cold,
    And said: "Her mother's score
Is writ, as you shall soon behold,
    Behind the bar-room door!'

I blotted out the score with tears,
    And paid the money down;
And took the maid of thirteen years
    Back to her mother's town.

And though the past with surges wild
    Fond memories may sever,
The vision of that happy child
    Will leave my spirits never!

                    Rudyard Kipling [1865–1936]

FATHER WILLIAM

From " Alice in Wonderland "

AFTER SOUTHEY

"You are old, Father William," the young man said,
    "And your hair has become very white;
And yet you incessantly stand on your head—
    Do you think, at your age, it is right?"

"In my youth," Father William replied to his son,
  "I feared it might injure the brain;
But, now that I'm perfectly sure I have none,
  Why, I do it again and again."

"You are old," said the youth, "as I mentioned before,
  And have grown most uncommonly fat;
Yet you turned a back-somersault in at the door—
  Pray, what is the reason of that?"

"In my youth," said the sage, as he shook his gray locks,
  "I kept all my limbs very supple
By the use of this ointment—one shilling the box—
  Allow me to sell you a couple?"

"You are old," said the youth, "and your jaws are too weak
  For anything tougher than suet;
Yet you finished the goose, with the bones and the beak—
  Pray, how did you manage to do it?"

"In my youth," said his father, "I took to the law,
  And argued each case with my wife;
And the muscular strength which it gave to my jaw,
  Has lasted the rest of my life."

"You are old," said the youth, "one would hardly suppose
  That your eye was as steady as ever;
Yet you balanced an eel on the end of your nose—
  What made you so awfully clever?"

"I have answered three questions and that is enough,"
  Said his father; "don't give yourself airs!
Do you think I can listen all day to such stuff?
  Be off, or I'll kick you downstairs!"

                       Lewis Carroll [1832–1898]

THE NEW ARRIVAL

AFTER CAMPBELL

THERE came to port last Sunday night
  The queerest little craft,
Without an inch of rigging on;
  I looked and looked—and laughed!

It seemed so curious that she
  Should cross the Unknown water,
And moor herself within my room—
  My daughter! O, my daughter!

Yet by these presents witness all
  She's welcome fifty times,
And comes consigned in hope and love—
  And common-metre rhymes.
She has no manifest but this;
  No flag floats o'er the water;
She's too new for the British Lloyds—
  My daughter! O, my daughter!

Ring out, wild bells— and tame ones too;
  Ring out the lover's moon.
Ring in the little worsted socks,
  Ring in the bib and spoon.
Ring out the muse, ring in the nurse,
  Ring in the milk and water.
Away with paper, pen, and ink—
  My daughter! O, my daughter!

George Washington Cable [1844–1925]

DISASTER

AFTER MOORE

'TWAS ever thus from childhood's hour
  My fondest hopes would not decay:
I never loved a tree or flower
  Which was the first to fade away!
The garden, where I used to delve
  Short-frocked, still yields me pinks in plenty;
The pear-tree that I climbed at twelve,
  I see still blossoming, at twenty.

I never nursed a dear gazelle.
  But I was given a paroquet—
How I did nurse him if unwell!
  He's imbecile, but lingers yet.

He's green, with an enchanting tuft;
    He melts me with his small black eye:
He'd look inimitable stuffed,
    And knows it—but he will not die!

I had a kitten—I was rich
    In pets—but all too soon my kitten
Became a full-sized cat, by which
    I've more than once been scratched and bitten;
And when for sleep her limbs she curled
    One day beside her untouched plateful,
And glided calmly from the world,
    I freely own that I was grateful.

And then I bought a dog—a queen!
    Ah, Tiny, dear departing pug!
She lives, but she is past sixteen,
    And scarce can crawl across the rug.
I loved her beautiful and kind;
    Delighted in her pert Bow-wow:
But now she snaps if you don't mind;
    'Twere lunacy to love her now.

I used to think, shculd e'er mishap
    Betide my crumple-visaged Ti,
In shape of prowling thief, or trap,
    Or coarse bull-terrier—I should die.
But ah! disasters have their use;
    And life might e'en be too sunshiny:
Nor would I make myself a goose,
    If some big dog should swallow Tiny.

        Charles Stuart Calverley [1831-1884]

'TWAS EVER THUS

AFTER MOORE

I NEVER reared a young gazelle,
    (Because, you see, I never tried);
But had it known and loved me well,
    No doubt the creature would have died.

A Grievance

My rich and agèd Uncle John
　　Has known me long and loves me well
But still persists in living on—
　　I would he were a young gazelle.

I never loved a tree or flower;
　　But, if I had, I beg to say
The blight, the wind, the sun, or shower
　　Would soon have withered it away.
I've dearly loved my Uncle John,
　　From childhood to the present hour,
And yet he will go living on—
　　I would he were a tree or flower!

Henry Sambrooke Leigh [1837–1883]

A GRIEVANCE

AFTER BYRON

DEAR Mr. Editor: I wish to say—
　　If you will not be angry at my writing it—
But I've been used, since childhood's happy day,
　　When I have thought of something, to inditing it;
I seldom think of things; and, by the way,
　　Although this meter may not be exciting, it
Enables one to be extremely terse,
Which is not what one always is in verse.

I used to know a man,—such things befall
　　The observant wayfarer through Fate's domain—
He was a man, take him for all in all,
　　We shall not look upon his like again;
I know that statement's not original;
　　What statement is, since Shakespeare? or, since Cain,
What murder? I believe 'twas Shakespeare said it, or
Perhaps it may have been your Fighting Editor.

Though why an Editor should fight, or why
　　A Fighter should abase himself to edit,
Are problems far too difficult and high
　　For me to solve with any sort of credit.

Some greatly more accomplished man than I
    Must tackle them: let's say then Shakespeare said it;
And, if he did not, Lewis Morris may
(Or even if he did).   Some other day,

When I have nothing pressing to impart,
    I should not mind dilating on this matter.
I feel its import both in head and heart,
    And always did,—especially the latter.
I could discuss it in the busy mart
    Or on the lonely housetop; hold! this chatter
Diverts me from my purpose.   To the point:
The time, as Hamlet said, is out of joint,

And perhaps I was born to set it right,—
    A fact I greet with perfect equanimity.
I do not put it down to "cursèd spite,"
    I don't see any cause for cursing in it.   I
Have always taken very great delight
    In such pursuits since first I read divinity.
Whoever will may write a nation's songs
As long as I'm allowed to right its wrongs.

What's Eton but a nursery of wrong-righters,
    A mighty mother of effective men;
A training ground for amateur reciters,
    A sharpener of the sword as of the pen;
A factory of orators and fighters,
    A forcing-house of genius?   Now and then
The world at large shrinks back, abashed and beaten,
Unable to endure the glare of Eton.

I think I said I knew a man: what then?
    I don't suppose such knowledge is forbid.
We nearly all do, more or less, know men,—
    Or think we do; nor will a man get rid
Of that delusion while he wields a pen.
    But who this man was, what, if aught, he did,
Nor why I mentioned him, I do not know,
Nor what I "wished to say" a while ago.
                                    James Kenneth Stephen [1859-1892]

"NOT A SOU HAD HE GOT"

AFTER CHARLES WOLFE

Not a sou had he got—not a guinea or note—
  And he looked confoundedly flurried,
As he bolted away without paying his shot,
  And the landlady after him hurried.

We saw him again at dead of night,
  When home from the club returning;
We twigged the doctor beneath the light
  Of the gas-lamp brilliantly burning.

All bare and exposed to the midnight dews,
  Reclined in a gutter we found him;
And he looked like a gentleman taking a snooze
  With his Marshall cloak around him.

"The doctor's as drunk as the devil," we said,
  And we managed a shutter to borrow;
We raised him; and sighed at the thought that his head
  Would consumedly ache on the morrow.

We bore him home, and we put him to bed,
  And we told his wife and his daughter
To give him next morning a couple of red-
  Herrings, with soda-water.

Loudly they talked of his money that's gone,
  And his lady began to upbraid him;
But little he recked, so they let him snore on
  'Neath the counterpane, just as we laid him.

We tucked him in, and had hardly done,
  When, beneath the window calling,
We heard the rough voice of a son of a gun
  Of a watchman "One o'clock!" bawling.

Slowly and sadly we all walked down
  From his room on the uppermost story;
A rushlight we placed on the cold hearth-stone,
  And we left him alone in his glory.

                    Richard Harris Barham [1788–1845]

THE WHITING AND THE SNAIL

From "Alice in Wonderland"

AFTER MARY HOWITT

" WILL you walk a little faster?" said a whiting to a snail,
"There's a porpoise close behind us, and he's treading on my
 tail,
See how eagerly the lobsters and the turtles all advance!
They are waiting on the shingle—will you come and join
  the dance?
  Will you, won't you, will you, won't you, will you join
  the dance?
  Will you, won't you, will you, won't you, won't you join
  the dance?

"You can really have no notion how delightful it will be
When they take us up and throw us, with the lobsters, out
 to sea!"
But the snail replied, "Too far, too far!" and gave a look
  askance—
Said he thanked the whiting kindly, but he would not join
  the dance.
  Would not, could not, would not, could not, would not
  join the dance.
  Would not, could not, would not, could not, could not
  join the dance.

"What matters it how far we go?" his scaly friend re-
  plied.
"There is another shore, you know, upon the other side.
The further off from England the nearer is to France—
Then turn not pale, belovèd snail, but come and join the
  dance.
  Will you, won't you, will you, won't you, will you join
  the dance?
  Will you, won't you, will you, won't you, won't you join
  the dance?"

Lewis Carroll [1832–1898]

THE RECOGNITION

AFTER TENNYSON

HOME they brought her sailor son,
  Grown a man across the sea,
Tall and broad and black of beard,
  And hoarse of voice as man may be.

Hand to shake and mouth to kiss,
  Both he offered ere he spoke;
But she said, "What man is this
  Comes to play a sorry joke?"

Then they praised him,—called him "smart,"
  "Tightest lad that ever stept;"
But her son she did not know,
  And she neither smiled nor wept.

Rose, a nurse of ninety years,
  Set a pigeon-pie in sight;
She saw him eat:—" 'Tis he! 'tis he!"
  She knew him—by his appetite!
              Frederick William Sawyer [1810–1875]

THE HIGHER PANTHEISM IN A NUTSHELL

AFTER TENNYSON

ONE, who is not, we see: but one, whom we see not, is;
Surely this is not that: but that is assuredly this.

What, and wherefore, and whence? for under is over and
    under;
If thunder could be without lightning, lightning could be
    without thunder.

Doubt is faith in the main: but faith, on the whole, is doubt;
We cannot believe by proof: but could we believe without?

Why, and whither, and how? for barley and rye are not
    clover;
Neither are straight lines curves: yet over is under and
    over.

Two and two may be four: but four and four are not eight;
Fate and God may be twain: but God is the same thing as
    fate.

Ask a man what he thinks, and get from a man what he
    feels;
God, once caught in the fact, shows you a fair pair of heels.

Body and spirit are twins: God only knows which is which;
The soul squats down in the flesh, like a tinker drunk in a
    ditch.

One and two are not one: but one and nothing is two;
Truth can hardly be false, if falsehood cannot be true.

Once the mastodon was: pterodactyls were common as
    cocks;
Then the mammoth was God; now is He a prize ox.

Parallels all things are: yet many of these are askew.
You are certainly I: but certainly I am not you.

Springs the rock from the plain, shoots the stream from the
    rock;
Cocks exist for the hen: but hens exist for the cock.

God, whom we see not, is: and God, who is not, we see;
Fiddle, we know, is diddle: and diddle, we take it, is dee.
           Algernon Charles Swinburne [1837–1909]

THE WILLOW-TREE
AFTER HOOD

Long by the willow-trees
  Vainly they sought her,
Wild rang the mother's screams

O'er the gray water:
"Where is my lovely one?
  Where is my daughter?

"Rouse thee, Sir Constable—
  Rouse thee and look;
Fisherman, bring your net,
  Boatman, your hook.
Beat in the lily-beds,
  Dive in the brook!"

Vainly the constable
  Shouted and called her;
Vainly the fisherman
  Beat the green alder;
Vainly he flung the net,
  Never it hauled her!

Mother beside the fire
  Sat, her nightcap in;
Father, in easy chair,
  Gloomily napping,
When at the window-sill
  Came a light tapping!

And a pale countenance
  Looked through the casement.
Loud beat the mother's heart,
  Sick with amazement,
And at the vision which
  Came to surprise her,
Shrieked in an agony—
  "Lor'! it's Elizar!"

Yes, 'twas Elizabeth—
  Yes, 'twas their girl;
Pale was her cheek, and her
  Hair out of curl.
"Mother," the loving one,
  Blushing exclaimed,
"Let not your innocent
  Lizzy be blamed.

The Mimics

"Yesterday, going to Aunt
  Jones's to tea,
Mother, dear mother, I
  Forgot the door-key!
And as the night was cold
  And the way steep,
Mrs. Jones kept me to
  Breakfast and sleep."

Whether her Pa and Ma
  Fully believed her,
That we shall never know,
  Stern they received her;
And for the work of that
  Cruel, though short, night
Sent her to bed without
  Tea for a fortnight.

MORAL

Hey diddle diddlety,
  Cat and the fiddlety,
Maidens of England, take caution by she!
  Let love and suicide
  Never tempt you aside,
And always remember to take the door-key.
            William Makepeace Thackeray [1811–1863]

POETS AND LINNETS

AFTER ROBERT BROWNING

WHERE'ER there's a thistle to feed a linnet
And linnets are plenty, thistles rife—
Or an acorn-cup to catch dew-drops in it
There's ample promise of further life.
Now, mark how we begin it.

For linnets will follow, if linnets are minded,
As blows the white-feather parachute;
And ships will reel by the tempest blinded—
Aye, ships and shiploads of men to boot!
How deep whole fleets you'll find hid.

And we blow the thistle-down hither and thither
Forgetful of linnets, and men, and God.
The dew! for its want an oak will wither—
By the dull hoof into the dust is trod,
And then who strikes the cither?

But thistles were only for donkeys intended,
And that donkeys are common enough is clear,
And that drop! what a vessel it might have befriended,
Does it add any flavor to Glugabib's beer?
Well, there's my musing ended.   *Tom Hood* [1835–1874]

THE JAM–POT

THE Jam-pot—tender thought!
  I grabbed it—so did you.
"What wonder while we fought
  Together that it flew
In shivers?" you retort.

You should have loosed your hold
  One moment—checked your fist.
But, as it was, too bold
  You grappled and you missed.
More plainly—you were sold.

"Well, neither of us shared
  The dainty."   That your plea?
"Well, neither of us cared,"
  I answer. . . .   "Let me see.
How have your trousers fared?"
                    Rudyard Kipling [1865–1936]

BALLAD

AFTER WILLIAM MORRIS

PART I

THE auld wife sat at her ivied door,
  (*Butter and eggs and a pound of cheese*)
A thing she had frequently done before;
  And her spectacles lay on her aproned knees.

The piper he piped on the hill-top high,
  (*Butter and eggs and a pound of cheese*)

Till the cow said "I die," and the goose asked "Why?"
  And the dog said nothing, but searched for fleas.

The farmer he strode through the square farmyard;
  (*Butter and eggs and a pound of cheese*)
His last brew of ale was a trifle hard—
  The connection of which with the plot one sees.

The farmer's daughter hath frank blue eyes;
  (*Butter and eggs and a pound of cheese*)
She hears the rooks caw in the windy skies,
  As she sits at her lattice and shells her peas.

The farmer's daughter hath ripe red lips;
  (*Butter and eggs and a pound of cheese*)
If you try to approach her, away she skips
  Over tables and chairs with apparent ease.

The farmer's daughter hath soft brown hair;
  (*Butter and eggs and a pound of cheese*)
And I met with a ballad, I can't say where,
  Which wholly consisted of lines like these.

PART II

She sat, with her hands 'neath her dimpled cheeks,
  (*Butter and eggs and a pound of cheese*)
And spake not a word. While a lady speaks
  There is hope, but she didn't even sneeze.

She sat, with her hands 'neath her crimson cheeks,
  (*Butter and eggs and a pound of cheese*)
She gave up mending her father's breeks,
  And let the cat roll in her new chemise.

She sat, with her hands 'neath her burning cheeks,
  (*Butter and eggs and a pound of cheese*)
And gazed at the piper for thirteen weeks;
  Then she followed him out o'er the misty leas.

Her sheep followed her, as their tails did them.
  (*Butter and eggs and a pound of cheese*)
And this song is considered a perfect gem,
  And as to the meaning, it's what you please.

Charles Stuart Calverley [1831-1884]

THE POSTER-GIRL

AFTER DANTE GABRIEL ROSSETTI

THE blessèd Poster-girl leaned out
    From a pinky-purple heaven;
One eye was red and one was green;
    Her bang was cut uneven;
She had three fingers on her hand,
    And the hairs on her head were seven.

Her robe, ungirt from clasp to hem,
    No sunflowers did adorn,
But a heavy Turkish portiere
    Was very neatly worn;
And the hat that lay along her back
    Was yellow like canned corn.

It was a kind of wobbly wave
    That she was standing on,
And high aloft she flung a scarf
    That must have weighed a ton;
And she was rather tall—at least
    She reached up to the sun.

She curved and writhed, and then she said,
    Less green of speech than blue:
"Perhaps I *am* absurd—perhaps
    I *don't* appeal to you;
But my artistic worth depends
    Upon the point of view."

I saw her smile, although her eyes
    Were only smudgy smears;
And then she swished her swirling arms,
    And wagged her gorgeous ears,
She sobbed a blue-and-green-checked sob,
    And wept some purple tears.
                    Carolyn Wells [186 —

AFTER DILETTANTE CONCETTI

AFTER DANTE GABRIEL ROSSETTI

"Why do you wear your hair like a man,
          Sister Helen?
This week is the third since you began."
"I'm writing a ballad; be still if you can,
          Little brother.
      (O Mother Carey, mother!
What chickens are these between sea and heaven?)"

"But why does your figure appear so lean,
          Sister Helen?
And why do you dress in sage, sage green?"
"Children should never be heard, if seen,
          Little brother!
      (O Mother Carey, mother!
What fowls are a-wing in the stormy heaven!)"

"But why is your face so yellowy white,
          Sister Helen?
And why are your skirts so funnily tight?"
"Be quiet, you torment, or how can I write,
          Little brother?
      (O Mother Carey, mother!
How gathers thy train to the sea from the heaven!)"

"And who's Mother Carey, and what is her train,
          Sister Helen?
And why do you call her again and again?"
"You troublesome boy, why that's the refrain,
          Little brother.
      (O Mother Carey, mother!
What work is toward in the startled heaven?)"

"And what's a refrain?   What a curious word,
          Sister Helen!
Is the ballad you're writing about a sea-bird?"
"Not at all; why should it be?   Don't be absurd,

Little brother.
(O Mother Carey, mother!
Thy brood flies lower as lowers the heaven.)"

(A big brother speaketh:)

"The refrain you've studied a meaning had,
             Sister Helen!
It gave strange force to a weird ballàd.
But refrains have become a ridiculous 'fad',
             Little brother.
      And *Mother Carey, mother,*
Has a bearing on nothing in earth or heaven.

"But the finical fashion has had its day,
             Sister Helen.
And let's try in the style of a different lay
To bid it adieu in poetical way,
             Little brother.
      So, Mother Carey, mother!
Collect your chickens and go to—heaven."

(A pause.   Then the big brother singeth, accompanying him-
self in a plaintive wise on the triangle:)

"Look in my face.   My name is Used-to-was,
   I am also called Played-out and Done-to-death,
   And It-will-wash-no-more.   Awakeneth
Slowly, but sure awakening it has,
The common-sense of man; and I, alas!
   The ballad-burden trick, now known too well,
   Am turned to scorn, and grown contemptible—
A too transparent artifice to pass.

"What a cheap dodge I am!   The cats who dart
   Tin-kettled through the streets in wild surprise
   Assail judicious ears not otherwise;
And yet no critics praise the urchin's 'art',
Who to the wretched creature's caudal part
   Its foolish empty-jingling 'burden' ties."

                    Henry Duff Traill [1842–1900]

IF

AFTER SWINBURNE

IF life were never bitter,
    And love were always sweet,
Then who would care to borrow
A moral from to-morrow—
If Thames would always glitter,
    And joy would ne'er retreat,
If life were never bitter,
    And love were always sweet!

If care were not the waiter
    Behind a fellow's chair,
When easy-going sinners
Sit down to Richmond dinners,
And life's swift stream flows straighter,
    By Jove, it would be rare,
If care were not the waiter
    Behind a fellow's chair.

If wit were always radiant,
    And wine were always iced,
And bores were kicked out straightway
Through a convenient gateway;
Then down the year's long gradient
    'Twere sad to be enticed,
If wit were always radiant,
    And wine were always iced.

                    Mortimer Collins [1827–1876]

NEPHELIDIA

AFTER SWINBURNE

FROM the depth of the dreamy decline of the dawn through
    a notable nimbus of nebulous noonshine,
Pallid and pink as the palm of the flag-flower that flickers
    with fear of the flies as they float,

Nephelidia

Are the looks of our lovers that lustrously lean from a marvel of mystic, miraculous moonshine,
These that we feel in the blood of our blushes that thicken
and threaten with throbs through the throat?
Thicken and thrill as a theatre thronged at appeal of an
actor's appalled agitation,
Fainter with fear of the fires of the future than pale with
the promise of pride in the past;
Flushed with the famishing fulness of fever that reddens
with radiance of rathe recreation,
Gaunt as the ghastliest of glimpses that gleam through
the gloom of the gloaming when ghosts go aghast?

Nay, for the nick of the tick of the time is a tremulous
touch on the temples of terror,
Strained as the sinews yet strenuous with strife of the
dead who is dumb as the dust-heaps of death;
Surely no soul is it, sweet as the spasm of erotic, emotional,
exquisite error,
Bathed in the balms of beatified bliss, beatific itself by
beatitude's breath.
Surely no spirit or sense of a soul that was soft to the spirit
and soul of our senses
Sweetens the stress of suspiring suspicion that sobs in
the semblance and sound of a sigh;
Only this oracle opens Olympian in mystical moods and
triangular tenses,—
"Life is the lust of a lamp for the light that is dark till
the dawn of the day when we die."

Mild is the mirk and monotonous music of memory, melo-
diously mute as it may be,
While the hope in the heart of a hero is bruised by the
breach of men's rapiers, resigned to the rod;
Made meek as a mother whose bosom-beats bound with
the bliss-bringing bulk of a balm-breathing baby,
As they grope through the graveyard of creeds under
skies growing green at a groan for the grimness of
God.

Blank is the book of his bounty beholden of old, and its
    binding is blacker than bluer:
Out of blue into black is the scheme of the skies, and their
    dews are the wine of the blood-shed of things;
Till the darkling desire of delight shall be free as a fawn
    that is freed from the fangs that pursue her,
Till the heart-beats of hell shall be hushed by a hymn
    from the hunt that has harried the kennel of kings.

Algernon Charles Swinburne [1837–1909]

COMMONPLACES

AFTER HEINE

RAIN on the face of the sea,
    Rain on the sodden land,
And the window-pane is blurred with rain
    As I watch it, pen in hand.

Mist on the face of the sea,
    Mist on the sodden land,
Filling the vales as daylight fails,
    And blotting the desolate sand.

Voices from out of the mist,
    Calling to one another:
"Hath love an end, thou more than friend,
    Thou dearer than ever brother?"

Voices from out of the mist,
    Calling and passing away;
But I cannot speak, for my voice is weak,
    And. . . . this is the end of my lay.

Rudyard Kipling [1865–1936]

THE PROMISSORY NOTE

AFTER POE

IN the lonesome latter years
    (Fatal years!)
To the dropping of my tears
Danced the mad and mystic spheres

In a rounded, reeling rune,
    'Neath the moon,
To the dripping and the dropping of my tears.
    Ah, my soul is swathed in gloom,
      (Ulalume!)
    In a dim Titanic tomb,
    For my gaunt and gloomy soul
    Ponders o'er the penal scroll,
    O'er the parchment (not a rhyme),
    Out of place,—out of time,—
    I am shredded, shorn, unshifty,
      (Oh, the fifty!)
    And the days have passed, the three,
      Over me!
And the debit and the credit are as one to him and me!

    'Twas the random runes I wrote
    At the bottom of the note,
      (Wrote and freely
      Gave to Greeley)
    In the middle of the night,
    In the mellow, moonless night,
    When the stars were out of sight,
    When my pulses, like a knell,
      (Israfel!)
    Danced with dim and dying fays,
    O'er the ruins of my days,
    O'er the dimeless, timeless days,
    When the fifty, drawn at thirty,
    Seeming thrifty, yet the dirty
Lucre of the market, was the most that I could raise!

    Fiends controlled it,
      (Let him hold it!)
Devils held me for the inkstand and the pen;
    Now the days of grace are o'er,
      (Ah, Lenore!)
    I am but as other men;
    What is time, time, time,

To my rare and runic rhyme,
To my random, reeling rhyme,
By the sands along the shore,
Where the tempest whispers, "Pay him!" and I answer,
"Nevermore!"

Bayard Taylor [1825–1878]

MRS. JUDGE JENKINS

BEING THE ONLY GENUINE SEQUEL TO "MAUD MULLER"

AFTER WHITTIER

MAUD MULLER all that summer day
Raked the meadow sweet with hay;

Yet, looking down the distant lane,
She hoped the Judge would come again.

But when he came, with smile and bow,
Maud only blushed, and stammered, "Ha-ow?"

And spoke of her "pa," and wondered whether
He'd give consent they should wed together.

Old Muller burst in tears, and then
Begged that the Judge would lend him "ten";

For trade was dull and wages low,
And the "craps," this year, were somewhat slow.

And ere the languid summer died,
Sweet Maud became the Judge's bride.

But on the day that they were mated,
Maud's brother Bob was intoxicated;

And Maud's relations, twelve in all,
Were very drunk at the Judge's hall;

And when the summer came again,
The young bride bore him babies twain;

And the Judge was blest, but thought it strange
That bearing children made such a change.

For Maud grew broad, and red, and stout,
And the waist that his arm once clasped about

Was more than he now could span; and he
Sighed as he pondered, ruefully,

How that which in Maud was native grace
In Mrs. Jenkins was out of place;

And thought of the twins, and wished that they
Looked less like the men who raked the hay

On Muller's farm, and dreamed with pain
Of the day he wandered down the lane.

And, looking down that dreary track,
He half regretted that he came back.

For, had he waited, he might have wed
Some maiden fair and thoroughbred;

For there be women as fair as she,
Whose verbs and nouns do more agree.

Alas for maiden! alas for judge!
And the sentimental,—that's one-half "fudge";

For Maud soon thought the Judge a bore,
With all his learning and all his lore;

And the Judge would have bartered Maud's fair face
For more refinement and social grace.

If, of all words of tongue and pen,
The saddest are, "It might have been,"

More sad are these we daily see:
"It is, but hadn't ought to be."

                                    Bret Harte [1839–1902]

THE MODERN HIAWATHA
From "The Song of Milkanwatha"

HE killed the noble Mudjokivis,
With the skin he made him mittens,
Made them with the fur side inside,
Made them with the skin side outside,
He, to get the warm side inside,
Put the inside skin side outside:
He, to get the cold side outside,
Put the warm side fur side inside:
That's why he put the fur side inside,
Why he put the skin side outside,
Why he turned them inside outside.

George A. Strong [1832–1912]

HOW OFTEN

AFTER LONGFELLOW

THEY stood on the bridge at midnight,
   In a park not far from the town;
They stood on the bridge at midnight,
   Because they didn't sit down.

The moon rose o'er the city,
   Behind the dark church spire;
The moon rose o'er the city,
   And kept on rising higher.

How often, oh! how often
   They whispered words so soft;
How often, oh! how often,
   How often, oh! how oft.

Ben King [1857–1894]

"IF I SHOULD DIE TO–NIGHT" *
AFTER ARABELLA EUGENIA SMITH

IF I should die to-night
And you should come to my cold corpse and say,
Weeping and heartsick o'er my lifeless clay—
   If I should die to-night,

   * For the original of this poem see page 3037

And you should come in deepest grief and woe—
And say: "Here's that ten dollars that I owe,"
  I might arise in my large white cravat
  And say, "What's that?"

  If I should die to-night
And you should come to my cold corpse and kneel,
Clasping my bier to show the grief you feel,
  I say, if I should die to-night
And you should come to me, and there and then
Just even hint at paying me that ten,
  I might arise the while,
  But I'd drop dead again.

Ben King [1857–1894]

SINCERE FLATTERY

OF W. W. (AMERICANUS)

THE clear cool note of the cuckoo which has ousted the
    legitimate nest-holder,
The whistle of the railway guard dispatching the train to
    the inevitable collision,
The maiden's monosyllabic reply to a polysyllabic proposal,
The fundamental note of the last trump, which is presum-
    ably D natural;
All of these are sounds to rejoice in, yea, to let your very
    ribs re-echo with:
But better than all of them is the absolutely last chord of
    the apparently inexhaustible pianoforte player.

James Kenneth Stephen [1859–1892]

CULTURE IN THE SLUMS

INSCRIBED TO AN INTENSE POET

I. RONDEAU

"O CRIKEY, Bill!" she ses to me, she ses.
  "Look sharp," ses she, "with them there sossiges.
Yea! sharp with them there bags of mysteree!
For lo!" she ses, "for lo! old pal," ses she,
  "I'm blooming peckish, neither more nor less."

Was it not prime—I leave you all to guess
How prime!—to have a Jude in love's distress
    Come spooning round, and murmuring balmilee,
            "O crikey, Bill!"

For in such rorty wise doth Love express
His blooming views, and asks for your address,
    And makes it right, and does the gay and free.
    I kissed her—I did so!   And her and me
Was pals.   And if that ain't good business,
            "O crikey, Bill!"

II. VILLANELLE

Now ain't they utterly too-too
        (She ses, my Missus mine, ses she),
Them flymy little bits of Blue.

Joe, just you kool 'em—nice and skew
        Upon our old meogginee,
Now ain't they utterly too-too?

They're better than a pot'n' a screw,
        They're equal to a Sunday spree,
Them flymy little bits of Blue!

Suppose I put 'em up the flue,
        And booze the profits, Joe?   Not me.
Now ain't they utterly too-too?

I do the 'Igh Art fake, I do.
        Joe, I'm consummate; and I *see*
Them flymy little bits of Blue.

Which, Joe, is why I ses ter you—
        Æsthetic-like, and limp, and free—
Now *ain't* they utterly too-too,
Them flymy little bits of Blue?
                            William Ernest Henley [1849–1903]

THE POETS AT TEA

I.—(MACAULAY)

POUR, varlet, pour the water,
　　The water steaming hot!
A spoonful for each man of us,
　　Another for the pot!
We shall not drink from amber,
　　No Capuan slave shall mix
For us the snows of Athos
　　With port at thirty-six;
Whiter than snow the crystals
　　Grown sweet 'neath tropic fires,
More rich the herb of China's field,
The pasture-lands more fragrance yield;
Forever let Britannia wield
　　The teapot of her sires!

II.—(TENNYSON)

I think that I am drawing to an end:
For on a sudden came a gasp for breath,
And stretching of the hands, and blinded eyes,
And a great darkness falling on my soul.
O Hallelujah! . . .   Kindly pass the milk.

III.—(SWINBURNE)

As the sin that was sweet in the sinning
　　Is foul in the ending thereof,
As the heat of the summer's beginning
　　Is past in the winter of love:
O purity, painful and pleading!
　　O coldness, ineffably gray!
O hear us, our handmaid unheeding,
　　And take it away!

IV.—(COWPER)

The cosy fire is bright and gay,
　　The merry kettle boils away

And hums a cheerful song.
I sing the saucer and the cup;
Pray, Mary, fill the teapot up,
And do not make it strong.

V.—(BROWNING)

Tut! Bah! We take as another case—
Pass the pills on the window-sill; notice the capsule
(A sick man's fancy, no doubt, but I place
Reliance on trade-marks, Sir)—so perhaps you'll
Excuse the digression—this cup which I hold
Light-poised—Bah, it's spilt in the bed!—well, let's on
go—
Hold Bohea and sugar, Sir; if you were told
The sugar was salt, would the Bohea be Congo?

VI.—(WORDSWORTH)

"Come, little cottage girl, you seem
To want my cup of tea;
And will you take a little cream?
Now tell the truth to me."

She had a rustic, woodland grin,
Her cheek was soft as silk,
And she replied, "Sir, please put in
A little drop of milk."

"Why, what put milk into your head?
'Tis cream my cows supply;"
And five times to the child I said,
"Why, pig-head, tell me, why?"

"You call me pig-head," she replied;
"My proper name is Ruth.
I called that milk"—she blushed with pride—
"You bade me speak the truth."

VII.—(POE)

Here's a mellow cup of tea—golden tea!
What a world of rapturous thought its fragrance brings to
    me!
       Oh, from out the silver cells
       How it wells!
       How it smells!
Keeping tune, tune, tune,
To the tintinnabulation of the spoon.
And the kettle on the fire
Boils its spout off with desire,
With a desperate desire
And a crystalline endeavor
Now, now to sit, or never,
On the top of the pale-faced moon,
But he always came home to tea, tea, tea, tea, tea,
       Tea to the n-th.

VIII.—(ROSSETTI)

The lilies lie in my lady's bower,
(O weary mother, drive the cows to roost),
They faintly droop for a little hour;
My lady's head droops like a flower.

She took the porcelain in her hand
(O weary mother, drive the cows to roost);
She poured; I drank at her command;
Drank deep, and now—you understand!
(O weary mother, drive the cows to roost).

IX.—(BURNS)

Weel, gin ye speir, I'm no inclined,
Whusky or tay—to state my mind
    Fore ane or ither;
For, gin I tak the first, I'm fou,
And gin the next, I'm dull as you:
    Mix a' thegither.

X.—(WALT WHITMAN)

One cup for my self-hood,
Many for you. Allons, camerados, we will drink together,
O hand-in-hand! That tea-spoon, please, when you've
    done with it.
What butter-colored hair you've got. I don't want to be
    personal.
All right, then, you needn't. You're a stale-cadaver.
Eighteen-pence if the bottles are returned.
Allons, from all bat-eyed formulas.

Barry Pain [1864–1928]

WORDSWORTH

Two voices are there: one is of the deep;
It learns the storm cloud's thunderous melody,
Now roars, now murmurs with the changing sea,
Now birdlike pipes, now closes soft in sleep;
And one is of an old half-witted sheep
Which bleats articulate monotony,
And indicates that two and one are three,
That grass is green, lakes damp, and mountains steep:
And, Wordsworth, both are thine: at certain times,
Forth from the heart of thy melodious rhymes
The form and pressure of high thoughts will burst;
At other times—good Lord! I'd rather be
Quite unacquainted with the A, B, C,
Than write such hopeless rubbish as thy worst.

James Kenneth Stephen [1859–1892]